GREENS FAMILY LAW STATUTES

GREENS FAMILY LAW STATUTES

1996

Divisions K and M of The Parliament House Book
(Family Law; Succession, Trusts, Liferents
and Judicial Factors)

W GREEN/Sweet & Maxwell Ltd
EDINBURGH
1996

ISBN 0 414 01158 9

A catalogue record for this book is available
from the British Library

Printed and Bound in Great Britain by
Antony Rowe Ltd, Chippenham, Wiltshire

The contents of this book are reproduced from the Parliament House Book which is published in looseleaf form and regularly updated by *W Green, the Scottish Law Publisher*. The Parliament House Book contains all relevant statutory information on key areas in Scots Law.

Material in the Parliament House Book is set out in sections called Divisions. The first page of every Division lists its contents under the Division heading. The Division letters used in this book are those used for the equivalent Division in the Parliament House Book itself.

DIVISION K

Family Law

Statutes

Acts of Sederunt and Other Statutory Instruments

Notes

[THE NEXT PAGE IS K 11]

Marriage Act 1939

(2 & 3 Geo. 6, c. 33)

An Act to facilitate marriages in cases where one party resides in Scotland and the other in England and to make further provision as respects notices of marriage between parties one of whom resides in Scotland or England. [13th July 1939]

1. [Repealed by the Marriage (Scotland) Act 1977, Sched. 3.]

Power to accept notice and issue certificates where one party is residing in England or Scotland

2.—(1) Where—

(*a*) a marriage is intended to be solemnised in England between parties of whom one is residing in England, and

(*b*) by virtue of any enactment to which this subsection applies, a certificate issued to the other party otherwise than by a superintendent registrar in England may be treated for the purpose of the marriage as if it had been issued by such a registrar,

the superintendent registrar of the district in which the first-mentioned party is residing shall have power, and shall be deemed always to have had power, to accept notice of the marriage given by that party, subject to and in accordance with the provisions of section 4 of the Marriage Act 1836, as amended by any subsequent enactment, as if both parties were residing in different districts in England, and the provisions of the Marriage Acts 1811 to 1934, relating to notices of marriage and the issue of certificates for marriage shall apply, and shall be deemed always to have applied, accordingly.

(2) [Repealed by the Marriage (Scotland) Act 1977, Sched. 3.]

[1] (3) The enactment to which subsection (1) of this section applies is paragraph (*a*) of subsection (1) of section 1 of the Marriage of British Subjects (Facilities) Act 1915, and the enactment to which subsection (2) of this section applies is the said paragraph (*a*) as that enactment applies to Scotland.

NOTE

[1] As amended by the Marriage Act 1949, Sched. 5, Pt. I.

3. [Repealed by the Marriage Act 1949, Sched. 5, Pt. I.]

Short title and citation

4.—(1) This Act may be cited as the Marriage Act 1939.

. . . . . .

[1] Maintenance Orders Act 1950

(14 Geo. 6, c. 37)

An Act to enable certain maintenance orders and other orders relating to married persons and children to be made and enforced throughout the United Kingdom. [26th October 1950]

NOTE
[1] Act extended by the Children and Young Persons Act 1963, s. 30(3): see also S.I. 1951 No. 552 and S.I. 1980 Nos. 1727 and 1732, *infra*.

Part I

Jurisdiction

. . . . . .

Jurisdiction of Scottish courts

Jurisdiction of the sheriff in certain actions of aliment

[1] **6.** [Repealed by the Civil Jurisdiction and Judgments Act 1982, Sched. 14.]

Jurisdiction of the sheriff to make orders for custody and maintenance of pupil children

7. [Repealed by the Family Law Act 1986, Sched. 2.]

Jurisdiction of the sheriff in certain actions of affiliation and aliment

8. [Repealed by the Civil Jurisdiction and Judgments Act 1982, Sched. 14.]

Contributions under Children and Young Persons (Scotland) Act 1937 and National Assistance Act 1948

[1] **9.**—(1) A court in Scotland shall have jurisdiction in proceedings against a person residing in England or Northern Ireland—

(*a*) [Repealed by the Civil Jurisdiction and Judgments Act 1982 (c. 27), Sched. 14.]

[2](*aa*) for a contribution order under section 80 of the Social Work (Scotland) Act 1968 (enforcement of duty to make contributions by parents in respect of their children while in the care of a local authority under Part II of that Act or under a supervision requirement);

(*b*) for an order under section 43 of the National Assistance Act 1948 (which provides for the recovery from spouses or parents of sums in respect of assistance given under that Act);

[3](*c*) for an order under section 18 of the Supplementary Benefits Act 1976 (which provides for the recovery of expenditure on supplementary benefits from persons liable for maintenance);

(*d*) for an order under section 24 of the Social Security Act 1986 (which provides for the recovery of expenditure on income support from such persons).

[4] (2) A court in Scotland by which an order has been made under the said section 91 or the said section 43 or the said section 80 or the said section 18 or the said section 24 shall have jurisdiction in proceedings against a person residing in England or Northern Ireland for the revocation or variation of that order.

NOTES

[1] As amended by the Social Security Act 1986 (c. 50), Sched. 10, para. 36. Extended by the Merchant Shipping Act 1970 (c. 36), s. 17(7).

[2] Added by the Social Work (Scotland) Act 1968 (c. 49), Sched. 8, para. 33.

[3] Added by the Supplementary Benefits Act 1976 (c. 71), Sched. 7, para. 10.

[4] As amended by the Social Work (Scotland) Act 1968 (c. 49), Sched. 8 and the Supplementary Benefits Act 1976 (c. 71), Sched. 7, para. 10.

Jurisdiction of Northern Ireland courts

. . . . . .

Supplemental

14. [Repealed by the Child Care Act 1980 (c. 5), Sched. 6.]

Service of process

[1] **15.**—[2] (1) Where—

(*a*) proceedings are begun in a court having jurisdiction under or by virtue of the following, namely—

(i) this Part of this Act; or

(ii) sections 24(1) and 30(3) of the Domestic Proceedings and Magistrates' Courts Act 1978; or

(iii) section 92 of and Schedule 11 to the Children Act 1989; or

(iv) section 93(2)(*g*) of that Act (including that provision as applied in relation to Northern Ireland by section 116(3) of the Courts and Legal Services Act 1990).

(v) Article 26(1) or 32(2) of the Domestic Proceedings (Northern Ireland) Order 1980; or

[3] (vi) Article 5(2) of Schedule 4 to the Civil Jurisdiction and Judgments Act 1982; or

[4] (*b*) an action which contains a conclusion for aliment not falling within the scope of paragraph (*a*)(i) above is commenced in a sheriff court in Scotland,

and the person against whom the action or other proceedings is or are brought resides in another part of the United Kingdom, any summons or initial writ addressed to him in the proceedings may, if endorsed in accordance with the provisions of this section in that part of the United Kingdom, be served within that part of the United Kingdom as if it had been issued or authorised to be served, as the case may be, by the endorsing authority.

(2) A summons or writ may be endorsed under this section, in England by a justice of the peace, in Scotland by a sheriff, and in Northern Ireland by a resident magistrate; and the endorsement shall be made in the form numbered 1 in Schedule 2 to this Act, or any form to the like effect.

(3) In any proceedings in which a summons or writ is served under this section, the service may be proved by means of a declaration made in the form numbered 2 in Schedule 2 to this Act, or any form to the like effect, before a justice of the peace, sheriff, or resident magistrate, as the case may be.

(4) Nothing in this section shall be construed as authorising the service of a summons or writ otherwise than personally.

(5) Section 4 of the Summary Jurisdiction (Process) Act 1881, shall not apply to any process which may be served under this section; and nothing in this section or in any other enactment shall be construed as authorising the execution in one part of the United Kingdom of a warrant for the arrest of a person who fails to appear in answer to any such process issued in another part of the United Kingdom.

NOTES

[1] As amended by the Guardianship of Minors Act 1971 (c. 3), Sched. 1, and the Maintenance Orders (Reciprocal Enforcement) Act 1972 (c. 18), s.41(3). Applied by the Attachment of Earnings Act 1971 (c. 32), s.20(2), and by the Civil Jurisdiction and Judgments Act 1982 (c. 27), s. 36(5).

[2] As amended by the Children Act 1975 (c. 72), Sched. 3, para. 10; the Administration of Justice Act 1977 (c. 38), Sched. 3, para. 11; the Domestic Proceedings and Magistrates' Courts Act 1978 (c. 22), Sched. 2, para. 12; the Child Care Act 1980 (c. 5), Sched. 5, para. 2 and S.I. 1980 No. 564; and the Courts and Legal Services Act 1990 (c. 41), Sched. 16, para. 34.

[3] Added by the Civil Jurisdiction and Judgments Act 1982 (c. 27), s.16(5).

[4] As amended by the Civil Jurisdiction and Judgments Act 1982 (c. 27), Sched. 12, Pt. II, para. 2.

[1] PART II

ENFORCEMENT

NOTE

[1] Excluded by the Maintenance Orders (Reciprocal Enforcement) Act 1972 (c. 18), s.33(6). See the Magistrates' Courts Act 1980 (c. 43), ss.62(2), (6) and 65(2)(*d*).

Application of Part II

[1] **16.**—(1) Any order to which this section applies (in this Part of this Act referred to as a maintenance order) made by a court in any part of the United Kingdom may, if registered in accordance with the provisions of this Part of this Act in a court in another part of the United Kingdom, be enforced in accordance with those provisions in that other part of the United Kingdom.

[2] (2) This section applies to the following orders that is to say—

(*a*) an order for alimony, maintenance or other payments made or deemed to be made by a court in England under any of the following enactments:—

[3] (i) sections 15 to 17, 19 to 22, 30, 34 and 35 of the Matrimonial Causes Act 1965 and sections 22, 23(1), (2) and (4) and 27 of the Matrimonial Causes Act 1973 and section 14 or 17 of the Matrimonial and Family Proceedings Act 1984;

[4] (ii) Part I of the Domestic Proceedings and Magistrates' Courts Act 1978;

[5] (iii) Schedule 1 to the Children Act 1989;

(iv) [Repealed by the Family Law Reform Act 1987 (c. 42), Sched. 2, para. 12(*b*) and Sched. 4.]

[6,7] (v) paragraph 23 of Schedule 2 to the Children Act 1989, or section 43 of the National Assistance Act 1948;

[8] (vi) section 18 of the Supplementary Benefits Act 1976;

(vi) [Inserted by the Children Act 1975, Sched. 3, para. 11, but repealed by the Family Law Reform Act 1987, Sched. 2, para. 12(*c*).]

(vii) [Repealed by the Courts and Legal Services Act 1990, Sched. 20.]

[18] (viii) section 106 of the Social Security Administration Act 1992;

(*b*) a decree for payment of aliment granted by a court in Scotland, including—

[9] (i) an order for the payment of an annual or periodical allowance or a capital sum under section 2 of the Divorce (Scotland) Act 1938, or an order for the payment of a periodical allowance under section 26 of the Succession (Scotland) Act 1964 or section 5 of the Divorce (Scotland) Act 1976 or section 29 of the Matrimonial and Family Proceedings Act 1984, or an order for financial provision in the form of a monetary payment under section 8 of the Family Law (Scotland) Act 1985;

(ii) an order for the payment of weekly or periodical sums under subsection (2) of section 3 or subsection (4) of section 5 of the Guardianship of Infants Act 1925;

(iii) an order for the payment of sums in respect of aliment under subsection (3) of section 1 of the Illegitimate Children (Scotland) Act 1930;

(iv) a decree for payment of aliment under section 44 of the National Assistance Act 1948, or under section 26 of the Children Act 1948; and

[9a] (v) an order under section 43 of the National Assistance Act 1948;

[10] (vi) a contribution order under section 80 of, or a decree or an order made under section 81 of, the Social Work (Scotland) Act 1968;

[11] (vii) an order for the payment of weekly or other periodical sums under subsection (3) of section 11 of the Guardianship Act 1973;

[12] (viii) an order made on an application under section 18 or 19(8) of the Supplementary Benefits Act 1976;

[18] (ix) an order made on an application under section 106 of the Social Security Administration Act 1992.

(*c*) an order for alimony, maintenance or other payments made by a court in Northern Ireland under or by virtue of any of the following enactments:—

(i) subsection (2) of section 17, subsections (2) to (7) of section 19, subsection (2) of section 20, section 22 or subsection (1) of section 28 of the Matrimonial Causes Act (Northern Ireland) 1939;

(ii) the Summary Jurisdiction (Separation and Maintenance) Act (Northern Ireland) 1945;

[13] (iii) section 1 of the Illegitimate Children (Affiliation Orders) Act (Northern Ireland) 1924, section 159 of the Children and Young Persons Act (Northern Ireland) 1968 or Article 102 of the Health and Personal Social Services (Northern Ireland) Order 1972;

[14] (iv) section 156 of the Children and Young Persons Act (Northern Ireland) 1968, or Article 101 of the Health and Personal Social Services (Northern Ireland) Order 1972;

[15] (v) any enactment of the Parliament of Northern Ireland containing provisions corresponding with section 22(1), 34 or 35 of the Matrimonial Causes Act 1965, with section 22, 23(1), (2) or (4) or 27 of the Matrimonial Causes Act 1973, or with section 12(2) of the Guardianship of Minors Act 1971;

[16] (vi) Article 23 or 24 of the Supplementary Benefits (Northern Ireland) Order 1977;

[17] (vii) the Domestic Proceedings (Northern Ireland) Order 1980;

[18] (viii) any enactment applying in Northern Ireland and corresponding to section 106 of the Social Security Administration Act 1992;

[19] (ix) Article 18 or 21 of the Matrimonial Proceedings (Northern Ireland) Order 1989.

(3) For the purposes of this section, any order made before the commencement of the Matrimonial Causes Act (Northern Ireland) 1939, being an order which, if that Act had been in force, could have been made under or by virtue of any provision of that Act, shall be deemed to be an order made by virtue of that provision.

NOTES

[1] The Matrimonial Causes Act 1965, s.38, provides:

"(1) Without prejudice to the operation of section 38(1) of the Interpretation Act 1889 (which provides for references to enactments which are repealed and re-enacted to be construed as references to those enactments as re-enacted), any order for maintenance or other payments made by virtue of this Part of this Act or any corresponding enactment of the Parliament of Northern Ireland shall be included among the orders to which section 16 of the Maintenance Orders Act 1950, applies (which section specifies the orders enforceable under Part II of that Act): and any order for maintenance or other payments made by virtue of this Part of this Act shall be a maintenance order within the meaning of the Maintenance Orders Act 1958.

(2) This section, so far as it affects Part II of the Maintenance Orders Act 1950, shall extend to Scotland and Northern Ireland."

See also the Matrimonial Proceedings (Children) Act 1958, s.17; the Ministry of Social Security Act 1966, ss.23(6), 24(10)(*d*); the Family Law Reform Act 1969, ss.4(5), 6(7): the Matrimonial Proceedings and Property Act 1970, s.12.

Extended by the Family Law Reform Act 1969, ss.4(5)(*a*) and 6(7).

[2] As amended by the Guardianship of Minors Act 1971, Sched. 1, the Social Security Act 1986, Sched. 10, para. 39 and the Social Security (Consequential Provisions) Act 1992, Sched. 2, para. 3(1) (effective 1st July 1992: s.7(2)).

[3] As substituted by the Matrimonial Causes Act 1973, Sched. 2, para. 3. Amended by the Matrimonial and Family Proceedings Act 1984, Sched. 1, para. 1(*a*) and the Family Law (Scotland) Act 1985, Sched. 1, para. 3.

[4] As substituted by the Domestic Proceedings and Magistrates' Courts Act 1978, Sched. 2, para. 13.

[5] As amended by the Courts and Legal Services Act 1990, Sched. 16, para. 35(*a*).

[6] As amended by the Child Care Act 1980, Sched. 5, para. 3.

[7] As amended by the Courts and Legal Services Act 1990, Sched. 16, para. 35(*b*).

[8] Added by the Supplementary Benefits Act 1976, Sched. 7, para. 13. As amended by the Family Law Reform Act 1987 (c. 42), Sched. 2, para. 12(*d*).

[9] As amended by the Succession (Scotland) Act 1964, s.26(6), the Divorce (Scotland) Act 1976, Sched. 1, para. 1, the Administration of Justice Act 1977, Sched. 3, para. 12, the Matrimonial and Family Proceedings Act 1984, Sched. 1, para. 1(*b*) and the Family Law (Scotland) Act 1985, Sched. 1, para. 3.

[9a] As amended by the Civil Jurisdiction and Judgments Act 1982, Sched. 14.

[10] Added by the Social Work (Scotland) Act 1968, Sched. 8, para. 34.

[11] Added by the Guardianship Act 1973, Sched. 5, para. 4.

[12] Added by the Supplementary Benefits Act 1976, Sched. 7, para. 13. As amended by the Social Security and Housing Benefits Act 1982, Sched. 4, para. 2.

[13] As amended by S.I. 1977 No. 2158.

[14] Substituted by S.I. 1977 No. 2158.

[15] As substituted by the Matrimonial Causes Act 1973, Sched. 2, para. 3.

[16] Added by the Supplementary Benefits Act 1976, Sched. 7, para. 13 and substituted by S.I. 1977 No. 2158.

[17] Inserted by S.I. 1980 No. 564.

[18] Added by the Social Security Act 1986, Sched. 10, para. 39. As amended by the Family Law Reform Act 1987 (c. 42), Sched. 2, para. 12(*e*).

[19] Inserted by S.I. 1989 No. 678.

[THE NEXT PAGE IS K 17]

Procedure for registration of maintenance orders

[1] **17.**—(1) An application for the registration of a maintenance order under this Part of this Act shall be made in the prescribed manner to the appropriate authority, that is to say—

(*a*) where the maintenance order was made by a court of summary jurisdiction in England, a justice or justices acting for the same place as the court which made the order;

(*b*) where the maintenance order was made by a court of summary jurisdiction in Northern Ireland, a resident magistrate acting for the same petty sessions district as the court which made the order;

(*c*) in any other case, the prescribed officer of the court which made the order.

(2) If upon application made as aforesaid by or on behalf of the person entitled to payments under a maintenance order it appears that the person liable to make those payments resides in another part of the United Kingdom, and that it is convenient that the order should be enforceable there, the appropriate authority shall cause a certified copy of the order to be sent to the prescribed officer of a court in that part of the United Kingdom in accordance with the provisions of the next following subsection.

(3) The court to whose officer the certified copy of a maintenance order is sent under this section shall be—

(*a*) where the maintenance order was made by a superior court, the Supreme Court of Judicature in England, the Court of Session or the Supreme Court of Judicature of Northern Ireland, as the case may be;

(*b*) in any other case, a court of summary jurisdiction acting for the place in England or Northern Ireland in which the defendant appears to be, or, as the case may be, the sheriff court in Scotland within the jurisdiction of which he appears to be.

(4) Where the prescribed officer of any court receives a certified copy of a maintenance order sent to him under this section, he shall cause the order to be registered in that court in the prescribed manner, and shall give notice of the registration in the prescribed manner to the prescribed officer of the court which made the order.

(5) The officer to whom any notice is given under the last foregoing subsection shall cause particulars of the notice to be registered in his court in the prescribed manner.

(6) Where the sums payable under a maintenance order, being an order made by a court of summary jurisdiction in England or Northern Ireland, are payable to or through an officer of any court, that officer shall, if the person entitled to the payments so requests, make an application on behalf of that person for the registration of the order under this Part of this Act; but the person at whose request the application is made shall have the same liability for costs properly incurred in or about the application as if the application had been made by him.

(7) An order which is for the time being registered under this Part of this Act in any court shall not be registered thereunder in any other court.

NOTE

[1] See S.I. 1951 No. 552, *infra*.

Enforcement of registered orders

[1] **18.**—(1) Subject to the provisions of this section, a maintenance order registered under this Part of this Act in a court in any part of the United Kingdom may be enforced in that part of the United Kingdom in all respects as if it had been made by that court and as if that court had had jurisdiction to make it; and proceedings for or with respect to the enforcement of any such order may be taken accordingly.

[2] (1A) A maintenance order registered under this Part of this Act in a court of summary jurisdiction in England or Northern Ireland shall not

carry interest; but where a maintenance order so registered is registered in the High Court under Part I of the Maintenance Orders Act 1958 or section 36 of the Civil Jurisdiction and Judgments Act 1982, this subsection shall not prevent any sum for whose payment the order provides from carrying interest in accordance with section 2A of the said Act of 1958 or section 11A of the Maintenance and Affiliation Orders Act (Northern Ireland) 1966.

[2] (1B) A maintenance order made in Scotland which is registered under this Part of this Act in the Supreme Court in England or Northern Ireland shall, if interest is by the law of Scotland recoverable under the order, carry the like interest in accordance with subsection (1) of this section.

[2a] (2) Every maintenance order registered under this Part of this Act in a magistrates' court in England and Wales shall be enforceable as a magistrates' court maintenance order within the meaning of section 150(1) of the Magistrates' Courts Act 1980.

[3] (2A) Any person under an obligation to make payments under a maintenance order registered under this Part of this Act in a court of summary jurisdiction in England shall give notice of any change of address to the clerk of the court; and any person who without reasonable excuse fails to give such a notice shall be liable on summary conviction to a fine not exceeding level 2 on the standard scale.

(3) Every maintenance order registered under this Part of this Act in a court of summary jurisdiction in Northern Ireland shall be enforceable as if it were an order made by that court under the Summary Jurisdiction (Separation and Maintenance) Act (Northern Ireland) 1945, and the provisions of section 6 of that Act shall apply accordingly.

[4] (3A) Notwithstanding subsection (1) above, no court in England in which a maintenance order is registered under this Part of this Act shall enforce that order to the extent that it is for the time being registered in another court in England under Part I of the Maintenance Orders Act 1958.

[5] (3B) Notwithstanding subsection (1) above, no court in Northern Ireland in which a maintenance order is registered under this Part of this Act shall enforce that order to the extent that it is for the time being registered in another court in Northern Ireland under section 36 of the Civil Jurisdiction and Judgments Act 1982.

(4), (5) [Repealed by the Ministry of Social Security Act 1966 (c. 20), Sched. 8.]

(6) Except as provided by this section, no proceedings shall be taken for or with respect to the enforcement of a maintenance order which is for the time being registered in any court under this Part of this Act.

NOTES

[1] As amended by the Ministry of Social Security Act 1966 (c. 20), Sched. 8.

[2] Added by the Civil Jurisdiction and Judgments Act 1982 (c. 27), Sched. 11, para. 5.

[2a] As substituted by the Family Law Reform Act 1987 (c. 42), Sched. 2, para. 13.

[3] Added by the Matrimonial and Family Proceedings Act 1984 (c. 42), Sched. 1, para. 2. As amended by the Statute Law (Repeals) Act 1993 (c. 50), Sched. 1, Pt. XIV (effective 5th November 1993).

[4] Added by the Administration of Justice Act 1977 (c. 38), Sched. 3, para. 6. As amended by the Civil Jurisdiction and Judgments Act 1982 (c. 27), Sched. 11, para. 1.

[5] Added by the Civil Jurisdiction and Judgments Act 1982 (c. 27), Sched. 12, Pt. III, para. 1.

Functions of collecting officer, etc.

[1] **19.**—(1) Where a maintenance order made in England or Northern Ireland by a court of summary jurisdiction is registered in any court under this Part of this Act, any provision of the order by virtue of which sums payable thereunder are required to be paid through or to any officer or person on behalf of the person entitled thereto shall be of no effect so long as the order is so registered.

(2) Where a maintenance order is registered under this Part of this Act in a court of summary jurisdiction in England or Northern Ireland, the court shall, unless it is satisfied that it is undesirable to do so, order that all

payments to be made under the maintenance order (including any arrears accrued before the date of the registration) shall be made through the collecting officer of the court or the collecting officer of some other court of summary jurisdiction in England or Northern Ireland, as the case may be.

(3) An order made by a court of summary jurisdiction under subsection (2) of this section may be varied or revoked by a subsequent order.

(4) Where by virtue of the provisions of this section or any order made thereunder payments under a maintenance order cease to be or become payable through or to any officer or person, the person liable to make the payments shall, until he is given the prescribed notice to that effect, be deemed to comply with the maintenance order if he makes payments in accordance with the maintenance order and any order under this section of which he has received such notice.

(5) In any case where, by virtue of an order made under this section by a court in Northern Ireland, payments under a maintenance order are required to be made through the collecting officer of any court—

(*a*) subsections (3) and (4) of section 8 of the Illegitimate Children (Affiliation Orders) Act (Northern Ireland) 1924 (which regulate the functions of collecting officers in relation to affiliation orders), shall apply as if the maintenance order were an affiliation order within the meaning of that section and as if the order under this section were made under that Act, and references in those subsections to the mother and the putative father shall be construed accordingly; and

[THE NEXT PAGE IS K 19]

(*b*) subsection (2) of section 7 of the Summary Jurisdiction (Separation and Maintenance) Act (Northern Ireland) 1945 (which relates to the remuneration of persons through whom weekly sums are paid under that Act), shall have effect as if money paid in accordance with the order under this section were paid in pursuance of an order made under that Act.

NOTE

[1] S. 19 applied (England and Wales) by the Maintenance Orders Act 1958 (c. 39), ss. 2(6) and 5(5).

Arrears under registered maintenance orders

[1] **20.**—(1) Where application is made for the registration of a maintenance order under this Part of this Act, the applicant may lodge with the appropriate authority—

(*a*) if the payments under the order are required to be made to or through an officer of any court, a certificate in the prescribed form, signed by that officer, as to the amount of any arrears due under the order;

(*b*) in any other case, a statutory declaration or affidavit as to the amount of those arrears;

and if a certified copy of the maintenance order is sent to the prescribed officer of any court in pursuance of the application, the certificate, declaration or affidavit shall also be sent to that officer.

(2) In any proceedings for or with respect to the enforcement of a maintenance order which is for the time being registered in any court under this Part of this Act, a certificate, declaration or affidavit sent under this section to the appropriate officer of that court shall be evidence, and in Scotland sufficient evidence, of the facts stated therein.

(3) Where a maintenance order made by a court in England or Northern Ireland is registered in a court in Scotland, a person shall not be entitled, except with the leave of the last-mentioned court, to enforce, whether by diligence or otherwise, the payment of any arrears accrued and due under the order before the commencement of this Act; and on any application for leave to enforce the payment of any such arrears, the court may refuse leave, or may grant leave subject to such restrictions and conditions (including conditions as to the allowing of time for payment or the making of payment by instalments) as the court thinks proper, or may remit the payment of such arrears or of any part thereof.

NOTE

[1] See S.I. 1951 No. 552, *infra*.

Discharge and variation of maintenance orders registered in superior courts

21.—(1) The registration of a maintenance order in a superior court under this Part of this Act shaall not confer on that court any power to vary or discharge the order, or affect any jurisdiction of the court in which the order was made to vary or discharge the order.

[1] (2) Where a maintenance order made in Scotland is for the time being

(*a*) registered under this Part of this Act in a superior court and not registered under Part I of the Maintenance Orders Act 1958 or under section 36 of the Civil Jurisdiction and Judgments Act 1982, or

(*b*) registered in a court in England under that Part of that Act of 1958 by virtue of section 1(2) of that Act of 1958,

(*c*) registered in a court in Northern Ireland under section 36 of the Civil Jurisdiction and Judgments Act 1982,

the person liable to make payments under the order may, upon application made to that court in the prescribed manner, adduce before that court any evidence upon which he would be entitled to rely in any proceedings brought before the court by which the order was made for the variation or discharge of the order.

(3) A court before which evidence is adduced in accordance with the foregoing subsection shall cause a transcript or summary of that evidence,

signed by the deponent, to be sent to the prescribed officer of the court by which the order was made; and in any proceedings before the last-mentioned court for the variation or discharge of the order, the transcript or summary shall be evidence of the facts stated therein.

NOTE

[1] As amended by the Administration of Justice Act 1977, Sched. 3, para. 7 and by the Civil Jurisdiction and Judgments Act 1982, Sched. 12, Pt. III, para. 1(3).

Discharge and variation of maintenance orders registered in summary or sheriff courts

[1] **22.**—[2] (1) Where a maintenance order is for the time being registered under this Part of this Act in a court of summary jurisdiction or sheriff court, that court may, upon application made in the prescribed manner by or on behalf of the person liable to make periodical payments under the order or the person entitled to those payments, by order make such variation as the court thinks fit in the rate of the payments under the maintenance order; but no such variation shall impose on the persons liable to make payments under the maintenance order a liability to make payments in excess of the maximum rate (if any) authorised by the law for the time being in force in the part of the United Kingdom in which the maintenance order was made.

(2) For the purposes of subsection (1) of this section, a court in any part of the United Kingdom may take notice of the law in force in any other part of the United Kingdom.

(3) Section 15 of this Act shall apply to the service of process for the purposes of this section as it applies to the service of process in proceedings begun in a court having jurisdiction by virtue of Part I of this Act.

(4) Except as provided by subsection (1) of this section, no variation shall be made in the rate of the payments under a maintenance order which is for the time being registered under this Part of this Act in a court of summary jurisdiction or sheriff court, but without prejudice to any power of the court which made the order to discharge it or vary it otherwise than in respect of the rate of the payments thereunder.

(5) Where a maintenance order is for the time being registered under this Part of this Act in a court of summary jurisdiction or sheriff court—

(*a*) the person entitled to payments under the order or the person liable to make payments under the order may, upon application made in the prescribed manner to the court by which the order was made, or in which the order is registered, as the case may be, adduce in the prescribed manner before the court in which the application is made any evidence on which he would be entitled to rely in proceedings for the variation or discharge of the order;

(*b*) the court in which the application is made shall cause a transcript or summary of that evidence, signed by the deponent, to be sent to the prescribed officer of the court in which the order is registered or of the court by which the order was made, as the case may be; and in any proceedings for the variation or discharge of the order the transcript or summary shall be evidence of the facts stated therein.

NOTES

[1] See S.I. 1951 No. 552, *infra*.

[2] As amended by the Domestic Proceedings and Magistrates' Courts Act 1978, Sched. 2, para. 14.

Notice of variation, etc.

[1] **23.**—(1) Where a maintenance order registered under this Part of this Act is discharged or varied by any court, the prescribed officer of that court shall give notice of the discharge or variation in the prescribed manner—

(*a*) to the prescribed officer of any court in which the order is registered; and

(*b*) if the order was made by another court, to the prescribed officer of that court.

(2) Any officer to whom a notice is given under this section shall cause particulars of the notice to be registered in his court in the prescribed manner.

NOTE

[1] Substituted by the Administration of Justice Act 1977, Sched. 3, para. 8. See S.I. 1951 No. 552.

Cancellation of registration

24.—(1) At any time while a maintenance order is registered under this Part of this Act in any court, an application for the cancellation of the registration may be made in the prescribed manner to the prescribed officer of that court by or on behalf of the person entitled to payments under the order; and upon any such application that officer shall (unless proceedings for the variation of the order are pending in that court), cancel the registration, and thereupon the order shall cease to be registered in that court.

[1] (2) Where, after a maintenance order has been registered under this Part of this Act in a court of summary jurisdiction in England or Northern Ireland or a sheriff court in Scotland, it appears to the appropriate authority (as defined by section 17 of this Act), upon application made in the prescribed manner by or on behalf of the person liable to make payments under the order, that that person has ceased to reside in England, Northern Ireland or Scotland, as the case may be, the appropriate authority may cause a notice to that effect to be sent to the prescribed officer of any court in which the order is registered; and where such a notice is sent the prescribed officer shall cancel the registration of the maintenance order, and thereupon the order shall cease to be registered in that court.

[1,2] (3) Where the prescribed officer of any court cancels the registration of a maintenance order under this section, he shall give notice of the cancellation in the prescribed manner

(*a*) to the prescribed officer of the court by which the order was made; and

(*b*) to the prescribed officer of any court in which it is registered under Part I of the Maintenance Orders Act 1958 or section 36 of the Civil Jurisdiction and Judgments Act 1982.

[3] (3A) On receipt of a notice under subsection (3) above:—

(*a*) any such officer as is mentioned in paragraph (*a*) of that subsection shall cause particulars of the notice to be registered in his court in the prescribed manner; and

(*b*) any such officer as is mentioned in paragraph (*b*) of that subsection shall cause particulars of the notice to be registered in his court in the prescribed manner and shall cancel the registration of the order.

(4) Except as provided by subsection (5) of this section, the cancellation of the registration of a maintenance order shall not affect anything done in relation to the maintenance order while it was registered.

(5) On the cancellation of the registration of a maintenance order, any order made in relation thereto under subsection (2) of section 19 of this Act shall cease to have effect; but until the person liable to make payments under the maintenance order receives the prescribed notice of the cancellation, he shall be deemed to comply with the maintenance order if he makes payments in accordance with any order under the said subsection (2) which was in force immediately before the cancellation.

(6) Where, by virtue of an order made under subsection (2) of section 19 of this Act, sums payable under a maintenance order registered in a court of summary jurisdiction in England or Northern Ireland are payable through the collecting officer of any court, that officer shall, if the person

entitled to the payments so requests, make an application on behalf of that person for the cancellation of the registration.

NOTES

[1] As amended by the Administration of Justice Act 1977, Sched. 3, para. 9.

[2] As amended by the Civil Jurisdiction and Judgments Act 1982, Sched. 12, Pt. III, para. 1(4).

[3] Added by the Administration of Justice Act 1977, Sched. 3, para. 9.

Rules as to procedure of courts of summary jurisdiction

[1] **25.**—(1) The power of the Lord Chancellor to make rules under section 144 of the Magistrates' Courts Act 1980, shall include power to make rules for regulating the practice to be followed in courts of summary jurisdiction in England under this Part of this Act.

[2] (2) Rules made under section 23 of the Magistrates' Courts Act (Northern Ireland) 1964 may regulate the practice to be followed in courts of summary jurisdiction in Northern Ireland under this Part of this Act.

[3] (3) Rules made for the purposes of this Part of this Act may require that any order or other matter required under this Part of this Act to be registered in a court of summary jurisdiction in England or Northern Ireland shall be registered—

(*a*) in England, by means of a memorandum entered and signed by the prescribed officer of the court in the register kept pursuant to section 22 of the Summary Jurisdiction Act 1879;

(*b*) in Northern Ireland, by means of an entry made and signed by the prescribed officer of the court in the order book kept pursuant to the Magistrates' courts rules made under section 23(4) of the Magistrates' Courts Act (Northern Ireland) 1964.

NOTES

[1] As amended by the Magistrates' Courts Act 1980, Sched. 7, para. 8.

[2] As amended by the Judicature (Northern Ireland) Act 1978, Sched. 5.

[3] As amended by S.I. 1977 No. 2158.

Part III

General

Proof of declarations, etc.

26.—(1) Any document purporting to be a declaration made under section 15 of this Act, or to be a certified copy, statutory declaration, affidavit, certificate, transcript or summary made for the purposes of this Act or of any rules made thereunder shall, unless the contrary is shown, be deemed without further proof to be the document which it purports to be, and to have been duly certified, made or signed by or before the person or persons by or before whom it purports to have been certified, made or signed.

(2) Paragraph 7 of Schedule 2 to the Emergency Laws (Miscellaneous Provisions) Act 1947 (which relates to the proof of affiliation orders and maintenance orders and of orders for the discharge or variation of such orders), shall apply to the registration of orders under Part II of this Act, and to the cancellation of such registration, as it applies to the variation of orders; and for the purposes of that paragraph—

(*a*) a maintenance order registered under the said Part II in a court of summary jurisdiction; and

(*b*) any proceeding under the said Part II relating to a maintenance order made by or registered in such a court, being a proceeding of which a memorandum is required to be entered in the register kept by the clerk of that court pursuant to section 22 of the Summary Jurisdiction Act 1879,

shall be deemed to be an order made by that court.

General provisions as to jurisdiction

27.—(1) Nothing in this Act shall be construed as derogating from any jurisdiction exercisable, apart from the provisions of this Act, by any court in any part of the United Kingdom.

(2) It is hereby declared that any jurisdiction conferred by Part I of this Act, or any enactment therein referred to, upon a court in any part of the United Kingdom is exercisable notwithstanding that any party to the proceedings is not domiciled in that part of the United Kingdom; and any jurisdiction so conferred in affiliation proceedings shall be exercisable notwithstanding that the child to whom the proceedings relate was not born in that part of the United Kingdom.

(3) For the avoidance of doubt it is hereby declared that in relation to proceedings in which the sheriff has jurisdiction by virtue of the provisions of this Act there are the same rights of appeal and of remit to the Court of Session as there are in relation to the like proceedings in which the sheriff has jurisdiction otherwise than by virtue of the said provisions.

Interpretation

[1] **28.**—(1) In this Act the following expressions have the meanings hereby assigned to them, that is to say—

"certified copy", in relation to an order of any court, means a copy certified by the proper officer of the court to be a true copy of the order or of the official record thereof;

"collecting officer", in relation to a court of summary jurisdiction in England, means the person authorised to act as such under section 21 of the Justices of the Peace Act 1949, and in relation to a court of summary jurisdiction in Northern Ireland, means the officer appointed under subsection (1) of section 8 of the Illegitimate Children (Affiliation Orders) Act (Northern Ireland) 1924;

"enactment" includes any order, rule or regulation made in pursuance of any Act;

"England" includes Wales;

"prescribed" means, in relation to a court of summary jurisdiction in England or Northern Ireland, prescribed by rules made under section 15 of the Justices of the Peace Act 1949, or by rules made under section 23 of the Magistrates' Courts Act (Northern Ireland) 1964, as the case may be, and in relation to any other court means prescribed by rules of court.

(2) References in this Act to parts of the United Kingdom are references to England, Scotland and Northern Ireland.

(3) Any reference in this Act to any enactment shall be construed as a reference to that enactment as amended by any subsequent enactment, including this Act.

NOTE

[1] As amended by the Northern Ireland Act 1962, Sched. 4 and the Judicature (Northern Ireland) Act 1978, Sched. 5. See S.I. 1951 No. 552.

29. [Repealed by the Law Reform (Miscellaneous Provisions) (Scotland) Act 1966, Sched., Part I.]

30. [Repealed by the Statute Law Revision Act 1953 and the Northern Ireland Act 1955.]

31.—(1) [Repealed by the Northern Ireland Constitution Act 1973, Sched. 6, Pt. I.]

(2) Any reference in this Act to an enactment of the Parliament of Northern Ireland, or to an enactment which that Parliament has power to

amend, shall be construed, in relation to Northern Ireland, as a reference to that enactment as amended by any Act of that Parliament, whether passed before or after this Act, and to any enactment of that Parliament passed after this Act and re-enacting the said enactment with or without modifications.

Short title and commencement

32.—(1) This Act may be cited as the Maintenance Orders Act 1950.

(2) This Act shall come into force on the 1st day of January, 1951.

SCHEDULES

FIRST SCHEDULE

[Repealedby the Child Care Act 1980, Sched. 6.]

SECOND SCHEDULE

FORMS

FORM NO. 1: ENDORSEMENTS OF SUMMONS

I, A.B., a justice of the peace [sheriff] [resident magistrate] for the [county] of , hereby authorise the service of this summons [writ] in England [Scotland] [Northern Ireland] under section 15 of the Maintenance Orders Act, 1950.

Given under my hand this day of 19

FORM NO. 2: DECLARATION AS TO SERVICE

I, C.D. of hereby declare that on the day of 19 , I served E.F. of with the summons [writ] now shown to me and marked "A" by delivering a true copy for him.

(*Signed*) C.D.

Declared before me this day of ,19

A.B.

Justice of the Peace [sheriff] [resident magistrate] for the [county] of

Marriage (Scotland) Act 1956

(4 & 5 Eliz. 2, c. 70

An Act to amend the law with regard to notice of marriages intended to be celebrated or contracted in Scotland.

[2nd August 1956]

Notice of marriage intended to be celebrated or contracted in Scotland where one party has a parent residing there

1.—[1] (1) Where one party to a marriage intended to be solemnised in Scotland is residing in England and the other is residing in Scotland, the party residing in England may give notice of the intended marriage to the superintendent registrar of the registration district in which he has resided for the period of seven days immediately before the giving of the notice.

[1] (2) Where both parties to a marriage intended to be solemnised in Scotland are residing in England, whether in the same registration district or in different registration districts, and one of the parties has a parent who has his usual residence in Scotland,—

(*a*) the other party may give notice of the intended marriage to the superintendent registrar of the registration district in which he has resided for the period of seven days immediately before the giving of the notice;

(*b*) if the parties live in different registration districts, it shall not be necessary for notice of the intended marriage to be given to the superintendent registrar of the other registration district;

[2] (2A) Section 28(1) of the Marriage Act 1949 (which relates to the declaration to accompany a notice of marriage), shall apply for the purposes of subsections (1) and (2) above as if paragraph (*b*) of the said section 28(1) required the declaration to state—

(i) that the person giving the notice has for the period of seven days immediately before the giving of the notice had his usual place of residence within the registration district in which the notice is given, and

(ii) that the marriage is intended to be solemnised in Scotland, and

(iii) that the other party to the intended marriage is resident in Scotland, or has a parent who has his usual residence in Scotland, as the case may be.

[3] (3) A notice of marriage and declaration given and made in accordance with the foregoing provisions of this section if in other respects they comply with the requirements of the Marriage Act 1949, shall be treated as a notice of marriage and declaration given and made in accordance with that Act, and the provisions of that Act relating to the issue of certificates for marriage shall apply accordingly as if the marriage were intended to be solemnised in England.

(4) [Repealed by the Marriage (Scotland) Act 1977 (c. 15), Sched. 3.]

(5) In this section any reference to a parent of a party to an intended marriage includes a reference to—

(*a*) [Repealed by the Children Act 1975 (c. 72), Sched. 4, Pt. I.]

[4] (*b*) any spouse, widow, or widower of a parent of that party.

NOTES

[1] Substituted by the Marriage (Scotland) Act 1977 (c. 15), Sched. 2, para. 5.

[2] Added by the Marriage (Scotland) Act 1977 (c. 15), Sched. 2, para. 5.

[3] As amended by the Marriage (Scotland) Act 1977 (c. 15), Sched. 2, para. 5.

[4] As amended by the Children Act 1975 (c. 72), Sched. 4, Pt. I.

2, 3. [Repealed by the Marriage (Scotland) Act 1977 (c. 15), Sched. 3.]

Short title and citation

[1] **4.** This Act may be cited as the Marriage (Scotland) Act 1956.

NOTE

[1] As amended by the Marriage (Scotland) Act 1977 (c. 15), Sched. 3.

Matrimonial Proceedings (Children) Act 1958

(6 & 7 Eliz. 2, c. 40)

An act to extend the powers of courts to make orders in respect of children in connection with proceedings between husband and wife and to require arrangements with respect to children to be made to the satisfaction of the court before the making of a decree in such proceedings. [7th July 1958]

PART I

JURISDICTION IN ENGLAND AND WALES

. . . .

[1] PART II

JURISDICTION IN SCOTLAND

NOTE

[1] Pt. II extended by the Law Reform (Miscellaneous Provisions) (Scotland) Act 1966 (c. 19), s. 8(1).

Extension of jurisdiction of the court to further classes of children

7. [Repealed by the Law Reform (Parent and Child) (Scotland) Act 1986 (c. 9), Sched. 2.]

Duty of court in actions of divorce, etc., to consider arrangements for children's welfare before granting decree

[1] **8.**—[2] (1) Subject to the provisions of this section, in any action for divorce, nullity of marriage or separation the court shall not grant decree of divorce, nullity of marriage or separation unless and until the court is satisfied as respects every child for whose custody the court has power to make provision in that action—

(*a*) that arrangements have been made for the care and upbringing of the child and that those arrangements are satisfactory or are the best which can be devised in the circumstances; or

(*b*) that it is impracticable for the party or parties appearing before the court to make any such arrangements.

In this subsection "child" does not include a child with respect to whom the court has made an order under section 13(6) or 14(2) of the Family Law Act 1986.

(2) The court may, if it thinks fit, proceed to grant decree of divorce, nullity of marriage or separation without observing the requirements of the foregoing subsection if it appears that there are circumstances making it desirable that decree should be granted without delay and if the court has obtained a satisfactory undertaking from either or both of the parties to bring the question of the arrangements for the children before the court within a specified time.

(3) This section shall not apply in relation to actions commenced before the commencement of this Part of this Act.

NOTES

[1] Prospectively repealed by the Children (Scotland) Act 1995 (c. 36), Sched. 5, *infra*.

[2] As amended by the Law Reform (Parent and Child) (Scotland) Act 1986 (c. 9), Sched. 2 and by the Family Law Act 1986 (c. 55), Sched. 1, para. 4.

Jurisdiction of court as respects children where action dismissed or in case of non-adherence

[1] **9.**—[2] (1) Where an action commenced after the commencement of this Part of this Act for divorce, nullity of marriage or separation is dismissed at any stage after proof on the merits of the action has been allowed or decree of absolvitor is granted therein, the court before which the action was brought, may, subject to section 13(2) of the Family Law Act 1986, make such provision relating to parental rights as could be made if the action were still before the court.

(2) [Repealed by the Law Reform (Husband and Wife) (Scotland) Act 1984 (c. 15), Sched. 2.]

NOTES

[1] Prospectively repealed by the Children (Scotland) Act 1995 (c. 36), Sched. 5, *infra*.

[2] As amended by the Family Law (Scotland) Act 1985 (c. 37), Sched. 2, the Law Reform (Parent and Child) (Scotland) Act 1986 (c. 9), Sched. 1, para. 6 and the Family Law Act 1986 (c. 55), Sched. 1, para. 5. Restricted by the Family Law Act 1986 (c. 55), s. 13(2).

Power of court in actions of divorce, etc., to commit care of child to local authority or an individual

[1] **10.**—[1a] (1) Where it appears to the court as respects any child for whose custody the court has power to make provision in connection with an action for divorce, nullity of marriage or separation brought before it that there are exceptional circumstances making it impracticable or undesirable for the child to be entrusted to either of the parties to the marriage, the court may, if it thinks fit, make an order committing the care of the child to any other individual or to a local authority.

[THE NEXT PAGE IS K 27]

[2] (2) Where the court commits the care of the child to a local authority the authority specified in the order shall be the council of the region or islands area in which the child was, in the opinion of the court, resident before the order was made; and the court shall before making the order hear any representations from the authority, including any representations as to the making of an order for payments for the maintenance and education of the child.

(3) While an order under this section committing the care of a child to a local authority is in force with respect to any child, the child shall continue in the care of the local authority notwithstanding any claim by a parent or other person.

[3] (4) On the making of an order under this section committing the care of a child to a local authority, Part II of the Social Work (Scotland) Act 1968 (which relates to the treatment of children in care of local authorities) shall, subject to the provisions of this section, apply as if the child had been received by the local authority into their care under section 15 of that Act, so however that—

(*a*) the exercise by the local authority of their powers under or by virtue of sections 5, 20 to 22, 59 and 60 of that Act shall be subject to any directions given by the court, and

(*b*) section 23 of that Act (which relates to arrangements for the emigration of a child under the care of a local authority) shall not apply.

(5) [Repealed by the Mental Health (Scotland) Act 1960 (c. 61), Sched. 5.]

[4] (6) It shall be the duty of any parent or guardian of a child committed to the care of a local authority under this section to secure that the local authority are informed of his address for the time being; and a person who knowingly fails to comply with this subsection shall be liable on summary conviction to a fine not exceeding level 1 on the standard scale.

NOTES

[1] See the Domicile and Matrimonial Proceedings Act 1973 (c. 45), s. 10(1), Sched. 2, paras. 5 and 10 and Sched. 3, para. 11(1). Prospectively repealed by the Children (Scotland) Act 1995 (c. 36), Sched. 5, *infra*.

[1a] As amended by the Law Reform (Parent and Child) (Scotland) Act 1986 (c. 9), Sched. 2 and the Family Law Act 1986 (c. 55), Sched. 1, para. 6.

[2] As amended by the Local Government (Scotland) Act 1973 (c. 65), Sched. 27, Pt. II, para. 136. Prospective amendment in the Local Government etc. (Scotland) Act 1994 (c. 39), Sched. 13, para. 50(2), *infra*.

[3] Substituted by the Social Work (Scotland) Act 1968 (c. 49), Sched. 8, para. 42.

[4] As amended by the Criminal Justice Act 1967 (c. 80), s. 92, Sched. 3, Pt. I, and by virtue of the Criminal Procedure (Scotland) Act 1975 (c. 21), ss. 289F and 289G.

Reports as to arrangements for future care and upbringing of children

[1] **11.**—[2] (1) For the purpose of satisfying itself as to the proposed arrangements for the care and upbringing of any child as to whose custody the court has power to make orders, the court may, without prejudice to its power to appoint any other person, not being an officer of the local authority for the purpose, appoint an appropriate local authority to investigate and report to the court on all the circumstances of the child and on the proposed arrangements for the care and upbringing of the child.

(1A) In this section "local authority" has the same meaning as in the Social Work (Scotland) Act 1968.

(2) and (3) [Repealed by the Social Work (Scotland) Act 1968 (c. 49), Sched. 9.]

(4) If on consideration of a report furnished in pursuance of subsection (1) of this section the court, either *ex proprio motu* or on the application of any person concerned, thinks it expedient to do so, it may require the person who furnished the report to appear and to be examined on oath regarding any matter dealt with in the report, and such person may be examined or cross-examined accordingly.

(5) Any expenses incurred in connection with the preparation of a report by a local authority or other person appointed under this section shall form part of the expenses of the action and be defrayed by such party to the action as the court may direct, and the court may certify the amount of the expenses so incurred.

NOTES

[1] As amended by the Social Work (Scotland) Act 1968 (c. 49), Sched. 8, para. 43.

[2] As amended by the Law Reform (Parent and Child) (Scotland) Act 1986 (c. 9), Sched. 2 and the Family Law Act 1986 (c. 55), Sched. 1, para. 7. Prospectively amended by the Children (Scotland) Act 1995 (c. 36), Sched. 4, para. 9.

Power of court to provide for supervision of child

[1] **12.**—(1) If it appears to the court as respects any child for whose custody it has power to make provision in connection with an action for divorce, nullity of marriage or separation that there are exceptional circumstances making it desirable that the child should be under the supervision of an independent person, the court may, as respects any period during which the child is committed to the custody of any person, make an order placing the child under the supervision of a local authority.

[2] (2) Where the court makes an order under this section for supervision by a local authority that authority shall be the council of a region or islands area selected by the court and specified in the order.

(3) [Repealed by the Social Work (Scotland) Act 1968, Sched. 9.]

(4) The court shall not have power to make an order under this section as respects a child who in pursuance of an order under section 10 of this Act is in the care of a local authority.

NOTES

[1] As amended by the Social Work (Scotland) Act 1968 (c. 49), Sched. 9. See the Domicile and Matrimonial Proceedings Act 1973 (c. 45), s. 10(1) and Sched. 2, para. 11. Prospectively repealed by the Children (Scotland) Act 1995 (c. 36), Sched. 5, *infra*.

[2] As amended by the Local Government (Scotland) Act 1973 (c. 65), Sched. 27, Pt. II, para. 137. Prospective amendment in the Local Government etc. (Scotland) Act 1994 (c. 39), Sched. 13, para. 50(3), *infra*.

Power to prohibit in certain cases removal of child furth of Scotland or out of control of person having custody of him

13. [Repealed by the Family Law Act 1986 (c. 55), Sched. 2.]

Provisions as to actions of nullity of marriage, as to custody and access, and as to orders

14. [Repealed by the Law Reform (Parent and Child) (Scotland) Act 1986 (c. 9), Sched. 2.]

Interpretation of Part II

[1] **15.** In this Part of this Act, the expression "the court" means the Court of Session or the sheriff, the expression "child" means a child under sixteen years of age.

NOTE

[1] As amended by the Local Government (Scotland) Act 1973 (c. 65), Sched. 27, Pt. II, para. 138.

Part III

General

Expenses

16. There shall be paid out of moneys provided by Parliament any increase attributable to this Act in the sums payable out of moneys so provided—

(*a*) under section 47 of the Children Act 1948, or

(*b*) under Part I of the Local Government Act 1948, or the Local Government (Financial Provisions) (Scotland) Act 1954, as amended by the Valuation and Rating (Scotland) Act 1956.

[THE NEXT PAGE IS K 31]

Application of enactments regulating the enforcement of maintenance orders

[1] **17.** Any order for maintenance or other payments made by virtue of this Act or any corresponding enactment of the Parliament of Northern Ireland shall be included among the orders to which section 16 of the Maintenance Orders Act 1950, applies (which section specifies the maintenance orders which are enforceable under Part II of that Act).

NOTE

[1] As amended by the Matrimonial Causes Act 1965 (c. 72), Sched. 2.

Short title, extent and commencement

[1] **18.**—(1) This Act may be cited as the Matrimonial Proceedings (Children) Act 1958.

(2) Any reference in this Act to any enactment shall be construed as a reference to that enactment as amended or extended by any other Act, including this Act.

(3) This Act (except so far as it affects Part II of the Maintenance Orders Act 1950) shall not extend to Northern Ireland.

NOTE

[1] As amended by the Matrimonial Causes Act 1965 (c. 72), Sched. 2.

Legitimation (Scotland) Act 1968

(1968 c. 22)

An Act to amend and codify the law of Scotland relating to the legitimation of illegitimate persons by the subsequent marriage of their parents; to make provision in relation to the recognition under the law of Scotland of legitimation effected under foreign law and to the effects of such recognition; and for connected purposes. [8th May 1968]

Requirements and effects of legitimation

1.—[1] (1) Where the parents of an illegitimate person marry each other after the commencement of this Act, then if—

(*a*) the father of the said person is domiciled in Scotland at the date of the marriage, and

(*b*) the said person is living at that date,

the marriage shall, subject to the provisions of this Act, render that person legitimate with effect from the date of the marriage and confer on him the rights, and impose on him the obligations, of a legitimate person with effect from that date.

[2] (2) Subsection (1) above shall apply in relation to an illegitimate person who has been adopted by one of his natural parents as sole adoptive parent, where the adopter thereafter marries the other natural parent, as it applies in relation to any illegitimate person, to the effect of rendering that person the legitimate child of both natural parents; and in this Act "illegitimate", "legitimated" and cognate expressions shall be construed accordingly.

NOTES

[1] As amended by the Children Act 1975 (c. 72), Sched. 2, para. 6.

[2] Added by the Children Act 1975 (c. 72), Sched. 2, para. 6.

Scope of rights and obligations arising on legitimation

2.—(1) Subject to the provisions of this section, the legitimation of a person shall not confer any status or right, or impose any obligation, on that or any other person in respect of any time previous to the date of the legitimation.

(2) A person shall not be entitled, by virtue of his legitimation or of the legitimation of any other person—

(*a*) to any right in the intestate estate of a person dying after the commencement of this Act and before the date of the legitimation, or

(*b*) to legitim out of the estate of a person dying as aforesaid.

(3) The legitimation of a person shall not affect any right under a deed coming into operation after the commencement of this Act if that right has become indefeasibly vested in any other person before the date of the legitimation.

(4) Subject to the provisions of subsection (3) above—

(*a*) a legitimated person shall be entitled to any right under a deed coming into operation after the commencement of this Act, being a right his entitlement to which depends on his legitimacy, and

(*b*) a person other than the legitimated person shall be entitled to any right under such a deed, being a right his entitlement to which depends on the legitimacy of the legitimated person.

(5) Without prejudice to the foregoing provisions of this section, any reference (however expressed) in any deed coming into operation after the commencement of this Act to a child, or to issue, of a marriage shall be construed as including a reference—

(*a*) in either case, to any child legitimated by that marriage, and

(*b*) where the reference is to issue, to the issue, being legitimated persons, of any child of that marriage (including such issue of any child legitimated by that marriage).

(6) Without prejudice to the provisions of sections 23 and 24 of the Succession (Scotland) Act 1964 and of section 6(2) below, where any right is conferred or any obligation is imposed, whether by operation of law or under any deed coming into operation after the commencement of this Act, by reference to the relative seniority of the members of a class of persons, and that right is conferred or that obligation is imposed in terms which indicate that the class is one consisting of legitimate persons only, then—

(*a*) any member of that class who is a legitimated person shall rank as if he had been born on the date of his legitimation, and

(*b*) if two or more members of that class are legitimated persons whose dates of legitimation are the same, they shall rank as between themselves in accordance with their respective times of birth.

(7) Subject to the foregoing provisions of this section, the legitimation of a person shall enure to the benefit of any other person claiming any right arising after the commencement of this Act, being a right his entitlement to which depends on the legitimacy of the legitimated person.

(8) Subsection (1) above shall apply only in relation to the legitimation of a person by or under this Act.

Rights and obligations arising where parents of deceased illegitimate person marry

3.—(1) Where—

(*a*) an illegitimate person has died or dies, whether before or after the commencement of this Act, and

(*b*) that person would, if he had not died, have been legitimated on any date before or after such commencement or (by virtue of section 4 below) at such commencement,

the provisions of this Act shall apply for the purpose of determining the rights and obligations of any person living at or after the relevant date as if the illegitimate person had been legitimated with effect from that date.

(2) In subsection (1) above, the expression "the relevant date" means—

[THE NEXT PAGE IS K 59]

(*a*) the date which would have been the date of the legitimation of the illegitimate person, if that date occurs after the commencement of this Act;

(*b*) in any other case, the date of such commencement.

Legitimation of certain persons who were not legitimated by the marriage of their parents, etc.

4. Where—

(*a*) the parents of an illegitimate person have married each other before the commencement of this Act, and

(*b*) the father of the said person was domiciled in Scotland at the date of the marriage and

(*c*) that person was living at the date of the marriage, but

(*d*) by reason of the existence at any time previous to the marriage of an impediment thereto, the marriage did not, according to the law in force immediately before the commencement of this Act, render that person legitimate,

then, subject to the provisions of this Act—

(i) if the illegitimate person is living at the commencement of this Act, the marriage shall render that person legitimate with effect from the date of such commencement and confer on him the rights, and impose on him the obligations, of a legitimate person with effect from that date;

(ii) if the illegitimate person is not living at the commencement of this Act, the provisions of this Act shall apply for the purpose of determining the rights and obligations of any person living at or after the date of such commencement as if the illegitimate person had been legitimated with effect from that date.

Provisions relating to recognition of foreign legitimation

5.—(1) In this Act, unless the context otherwise requires—

(*a*) references to the legitimation of a person shall (subject to paragraph (*b*) below) be construed as including references to the recognition under the law of Scotland, whether before or after the commencement of this Act, of a person as being legitimated under the law of a country or territory outside Scotland by the subsequent marriage of his parents;

(*b*) references to the legitimation of a person under this Act shall be construed as including references to the recognition, after the commencement of this Act, of a person as being legitimated as aforesaid;

(*c*) subject to the provisions of subsection (3) below, references to the date of the legitimation of a person shall, in relation to a person recognised as being legitimated as aforesaid, be construed as references to the date which his legitimation was or is recognised as having effect from;

and "legitimated" shall be construed accordingly.

(2) Where after the commencement of this Act any person is legitimated under the law of a country or territory outside Scotland, the fact that the father of that person was at any time previous to his marriage to the mother of that person domiciled in a country or territory in which legitimation by subsequent marriage was not permitted by law shall not prevent the recognition of that person as being legitimated.

(3) A person legitimated after the commencement of this Act under the law of a country or territory outside Scotland shall not be recognised as being legitimated with effect from a date earlier than that on which his legitimation occurs.

(4) For the purposes of this section a person legitimated under the law of a country or territory outside Scotland shall be deemed to be so legiti-

mated by the subsequent marriage of his parents in any case where, under the law of the country or territory in question, the marriage of his parents was a condition necessary to his legitimation.

Additional provisions where legitimated person had previously been adopted by one or both parents

6.—(1) Where any person who has been adopted by his father and mother before the commencement of this Act is legitimated by virtue of section 4 above, the court by which the adoption order was made may, on the application of any of the parties concerned, revoke that order.

[1] (2) The revocation (under this section or otherwise) of any adoption order within the meaning of section 38 of the Adoption (Scotland) Act 1978 in consequence of the marriage of the parents of the adopted person to each other shall not affect the operation of sections 23 and 24 of the Succession (Scotland) Act 1964, in relation to an intestacy which occurred, or a deed which came into operation, before the revocation.

[2] (3) This section shall be construed as one with section 46 of the Adoption Act (Scotland) 1978; and any reference in that Act to that section shall be construed as including a reference to subsection (1) of this section.

NOTES

[1] As amended by the Children Act 1975 (c. 72), Sched. 2, para. 6, and the Adoption (Scotland) Act 1978 (c. 28), Sched. 3, para. 6.

[2] As amended by the Children Act 1975 (c. 72), Sched. 4, Pt. III, and the Adoption (Scotland) Act 1978 (c. 28), Sched. 3, para. 7.

Savings

7.—(1) The operation of any deed shall be affected by this Act only in so far as, in the construction of the deed, no contrary intention appears.

(2) The legitimation of any person—

(*a*) by virtue of section 4 of this Act, or

(*b*) under this Act, if he would not have been legitimated had this Act not been passed,

shall not confer any right on that or any other person under a deed which came into operation before the commencement of this Act.

(3) Subject to the provisions of subsection (2) above, where any person has been or is legitimated, any question as to the entitlement of that or any other person to a right under a deed which came into operation before the commencement of this Act shall, in so far as such entitlement depends on the legitimacy of the legitimated person, be determined in accordance with the law in force immediately before such commencement.

Interpretation

8.—(1) In this Act, unless the context otherwise requires—

"deed" includes any disposition, contract, instrument or writing, whether *inter vivos* or *mortis causa*;

"intestate estate" means so much of the estate of a person who has died as is undisposed of by testamentary disposition;

"marriage" includes putative marriage and voidable marriage.

(2) In this Act, unless the context otherwise requires, references to the legitimation of a person shall be construed as references to the legitimation of a person (whether by or under this Act or before the commencement thereof) by the subsequent marriage of his parents, and "legitimated" shall be construed accordingly.

(3) For the purposes of this Act a deed made in the exercise of a special power of appointment shall be deemed to come into operation at the date on which the deed creating the power came into operation.

(4) The provisions of this Act shall have effect in relation to any question as to the succession to, or devolution of, any title, honour or dignity after

the commencement of this Act as if the right to succeed to that title, honour or dignity were a right under a deed coming into operation after such commencement and as if the title, honour or dignity devolved in accordance with such a deed.

(5) Any reference in this Act to any other enactment shall be construed as a reference to that enactment as amended by any subsequent enactment, including this Act.

Short title, extent and commencement

9.—(1) This Act may be cited as the Legitimation (Scotland) Act 1968.

(2) This Act shall extend to Scotland only.

(3) This Act shall come into operation on the expiration of the period of one month beginning with the date on which it is passed.

[1] Social Work (Scotland) Act 1968

(1968 c. 49)

An Act to make further provision for promoting social welfare in Scotland; to consolidate with amendments certain enactments relating to the care and protection of children; to amend the law relating to the supervision and care of persons put on probation or released from prison etc.; to restrict the prosecution of children for offences; to establish children's panels to provide children's hearings in the case of children requiring compulsory measures of care; and for purposes connected with the aforesaid matters. [26th July 1968]

NOTE

[1] Saved by the Chronically Sick and Disabled Persons (Scotland) Act 1972 (c. 51), s. 1(2). Excluded by the Local Government (Scotland) Act 1973 (c. 65), Sched. 7A, para. 5 (inserted by the Local Government (Access to Information) Act 1985 (c. 43), Sched. 1, Pt. II. Extended by the Armed Forces Act 1991 (c. 62), s. 21(4). Applied by the Criminal Procedure (Scotland) Act 1975 (c. 21), s. 413; the Sexual Offences (Scotland) Act 1976 (c. 67), ss. 2A–2D (added by the Incest and Related Offences (Scotland) Act 1986 (c. 36), s. 1); the Education (Scotland) Act 1980 (c. 44), ss. 36(3), 65(5) and 135(1); the Mental Health (Scotland) Act 1984 (c. 36), s. 125(1); and the Foster Children (Scotland) Act 1984 (c. 56), s. 2(3). Power to modify: Children (Scotland) Act 1995 (c. 36), s. 33(5)(*a*) (prospective).

PART I

ADMINISTRATION

Performance of their duties by local authorities

Local authorities for the administration of the Act

1.—[0] (1) It shall be the duty of a local authority to enforce and execute within their area the provisions of this Act with respect to which the duty is not expressly, or by necessary implication, imposed on some other authority.

[1] (2) The local authorities for the purposes of this Act shall be regional and islands councils.

(3) [Repealed by the Local Government (Scotland) Act 1973 (c. 65), Sched. 27, Pt. II, para. 183 and Sched. 29.]

[2] (4) The functions of local health authorities in respect of their areas under the following enactments—

(*a*) [Repealed by the Children Act 1989 (c. 41), Sched. 15.]

(*b*) the Mental Health (Scotland) Act 1984;

(c) [Repealed by the National Health Service and Community Care Act 1990 (c. 19), Sched. 10.]

are hereby transferred to the local authorities of those areas.

(5) On the date of the commencement of Part III of this Act the functions of education authorities in relation to the establishments which immediately before that date were approved schools and the children resident therein shall be transferred to the local authorities in whose areas the said children are ordinarily resident or, in the case of children who have no ordinary residence in Scotland, such local authorities as the Secretary of State may determine.

(6) [Repealed by the Local Government (Scotland) Act 1973 (c. 65), Sched. 27, Pt. II, para. 183 and Sched. 29.]

NOTES

[0] Prospectively amended by the Children (Scotland) Act 1995 (c. 36), Sched. 4, para. 15(2), *infra*.

[1] As amended by the Local Government (Scotland) Act 1973 (c. 65), Sched. 27, Pt. II, para. 183. Applied by the Criminal Procedure (Scotland) Act 1975 (c. 21), s. 462(1). Prospective amendment in the Local Government etc. (Scotland) Act 1994 (c. 39), Sched. 13, para. 76(2), *infra*.

[2] As amended by the National Health Service (Scotland) Act 1972 (c. 58), Sched. 7, Pt. II, and the Mental Health (Scotland) Act 1984 (c. 36), Sched. 3, para. 14. See also the National Health Service (Scotland) Act 1978 (c. 29), Sched. 15, para. 15.

The social work committee

[1] **2.**—(1) Every local authority shall establish a social work committee for the purposes of their functions under this Act.

(2) Except as otherwise expressly provided, all matters relating to the performance of their functions under the following enactments—

[1a](a) this Act as read with sections 1 and 2(1) of the Chronically Sick and Disabled Persons Act 1970 and the Disabled Persons (Services, Consultation and Representation) Act 1986,

(b) Part IV of the Children and Young Persons (Scotland) Act 1937.

[2](bb) the Disabled Persons (Employment) Act 1958,

[3](c) sections 10 to 12 of the Matrimonial Proceedings (Children) Act 1958 and sections 11 and 12 of the Guardianship Act 1973,

[3a](d) the Foster Children (Scotland) Act 1984,

(e) the Adoption Act 1958,

(f) section 101(1) of the Housing Act 1964, and

[4](ff) section 9(1)(b) of the Housing (Homeless Persons) Act 1977,

(g) the enactments mentioned in subsection (4) of the foregoing section,

[5](h) the Children Act 1975,

[6](j) the Adoption (Scotland) Act 1978,

[6a](k) section 19 and Part X of the Children Act 1989,

[7](l) sections 21 to 23 of the Health and Social Services and Social Security Adjudications Act 1983,

[7](m) the Access to Personal Files Act 1987,

shall stand referred to the social work committee, and before exercising any of the said functions the authority shall, unless the matter is urgent, consider a report of the social work committee with respect thereto.

(3) [Repealed by the Local Government (Scotland) Act 1973 (c. 65), Sched. 29.]

(4) . . .

NOTES

[1] Saved by the Local Government (Scotland) Act 1973 (c. 65), s. 56(9), and applied by the Local Government (Scotland) Act 1975 (c. 30), s. 23(2). Prospective repeal in the Local Government etc. (Scotland) Act 1994 (c. 39), Sched. 14.

[1a] As amended by the Disabled Persons (Services, Consultation and Representation) Act 1986 (c. 33), s. 12(2).

[2] Inserted by the Local Government (Scotland) Act 1973 (c. 65), Sched. 27, Pt. II, para. 184.

[3] As amended by the Guardianship Act 1973 (c. 29), Sched. 5, para. 7.
[3a] As amended by the Foster Children (Scotland) Act 1984 (c. 56), Sched. 2, para. 4.
[4] Inserted by the Housing (Homeless Persons) Act 1977 (c. 48), s. 20(3).
[5] Added by the Children Act 1975 (c. 72), Sched. 3, para. 48.
[6] Added by the Adoption (Scotland) Act 1978 (c. 28), Sched. 3, para. 8.
[6a] Inserted by the Children Act 1989 (c. 41), Sched. 13, para. 18.
[7] Inserted by the National Health Service and Community Care Act 1990 (c. 19), Sched. 9, para. 10(2).

The director of social work

[1] **3.**—(1) For the purposes of their functions under the enactments referred to in section 2(2) of this Act, a local authority shall, in accordance with the provisions of this section, appoint an officer, to be known as the director of social work.

(2) The qualifications of the director of social work shall be such as the Secretary of State may prescribe.

(3), (4) [Repealed by the Local Government (Miscellaneous Provisions) (Scotland) Act 1981 (c. 23), Sched. 2, para. 14 and Sched. 4.]

(5) The director of social work shall hold his office during the pleasure of the local authority, but he shall not be removed therefrom, or be required to resign as an alternative thereto, except by a resolution of that authority passed by not less than two-thirds of the members present at a meeting of the authority, notice of which specifies as an item of business the consideration of the removal from office of the director of social work or his being required to resign.

(6) The director of social work of a local authority shall not, except with the consent of the Secretary of State, be employed by that authority in any other capacity.

(7) A local authority shall secure the provision of adequate staff for assisting the director of social work in the performance of his functions.

(8) The provisions as to remuneration and tenure of office contained in sections 82 and 92 of the Local Government (Scotland) Act 1947, so far as these provisions are not inconsistent with any of the foregoing provisions of this section, shall apply to directors of social work and their staffs.

(9) [Repeals s. 41 of the Children Act 1948 (c 43).]

NOTE

[1] Saved by the Local Government (Scotland) Act 1973 (c. 65), s. 64(5). Prospective substitution in the Local Government etc. (Scotland) Act 1994 (c. 39), s. 45, *infra*.

Provisions relating to performance of functions by local authorities

[1] **4.** Where a function is assigned to a local authority under this Act or section 7 (functions of local authorities) or 8 (provision of after-care services) of the Mental Health (Scotland) Act 1984 and a voluntary organisation or other person, including another local authority, is able to assist in the performance of that function, the local authority may make arrangements with such an organisation or other person for the provision of such assistance as aforesaid.

NOTE

[1] As amended by the National Health Service and Community Care Act 1990 (c. 19), Sched. 9, para. 10(3). Prospectively amended by the Children (Scotland) Act 1995 (c. 36), Sched. 4, para. 15(3).

Central Authority

Powers of Secretary of State

[1] **5.**—(1) Local authorities shall perform their functions under this Act under the general guidance of the Secretary of State.

[2] (1A) Without prejudice to subsection (1) above, the Secretary of State may issue directions to local authorities, either individually or collectively, as to the manner in which they are to exercise any of their functions under

this Act or any of the enactments mentioned in section 2(2) of this Act; and a local authority shall comply with any direction made under this subsection.

[3] (2) The Secretary of State may make regulations in relation to—

(*a*) the performance of the functions assigned to local authorities by this Act;

(*b*) the activities of voluntary organisations in so far as those activities are concerned with the like purposes;

[4] (*c*) the performance of the functions referred to social work committees under section 2(2)(*b*) to (*e*), (*h*) to (*k*) of this Act;

(*d*) [Repealed by the Children Act 1989 (c. 41), Sched. 15.]

(3) Without prejudice to the generality of the foregoing subsection, regulations under this section may make provision for the boarding-out of persons by local authorities and voluntary organisations, whether under any enactment or otherwise, and may provide—

(*a*) for the recording by local authorities and voluntary organisations of information relating to persons with whom persons are boarded out as aforesaid, and to persons who are willing to have persons boarded out with them;

[5] (*b*) for securing that persons shall not be boarded out in any household unless that household is for the time being approved by such local authority or voluntary organisation as may be prescribed by the regulations;

(*c*) in the case of a child, for securing that, where possible, the person with whom any child is to be boarded out is either of the same religious persuasion as the child or gives an undertaking that the child shall be brought up in that religious persuasion;

(*d*) for securing that persons boarded out as aforesaid, and the places in which they are boarded out, shall be supervised and inspected by a local authority or voluntary organisation, as the case may be, and that those persons shall be removed from those places if their welfare appears to require it.

NOTES

[1] Prospectively amended by the Local Government etc. (Scotland) Act 1994 (c. 39), Sched. 13, para. 76(3), *infra*, and the Children (Scotland) Act 1995 (c. 36), Sched. 4, para. 15(4), *infra*.

[2] Inserted by the National Health Service and Community Care Act 1990 (c. 19), s. 51.

[3] Substituted by the Children Act 1975 (c. 72), Sched. 3, para. 49.

[4] As amended by the Adoption (Scotland) Act 1978 (c. 28), Sched. 3, para. 9, and the Children Act 1989 (c. 41), Sched. 13, para. 19.

[5] See the Children (Scotland) Act 1995 (c. 36), s. 38(1)(*a*) (prospective).

Local authority plans for community care services

[1] **5A.**—(1) Within such period after the day appointed for the coming into force of this section as the Secretary of State may direct, and in accordance with the provisions of this section, each local authority shall prepare and publish a plan for the provision of community care services in their area.

(2) Each local authority shall from time to time review any plan prepared by them under subsection (1) above, and shall, in the light of any such review, prepare and publish—

(*a*) any modifications to the plan under review; or

(*b*) if the case requires, a new plan.

[2] (3) In preparing any plan or carrying out any review under subsection (1) or, as the case may be, subsection (2) above the authority shall consult—

(*a*) any Health Board providing services under the National Health Service (Scotland) Act 1978 in the area of the authority;

(*b*) in so far as the plan or, as the case may be, the review may affect or be affected by the provision or availability of housing, every district council in the area of the authority;

(*c*) such voluntary organisations as appear to the authority to represent the interests of persons who use or are likely to use any community care services within the area of the authority or the interests of private carers who, within that area, provide care to persons for whom, in the exercise of their functions under this Act or any of the enactments mentioned in section 2(2) of this Act, the local authority have a power or a duty to provide, or to secure the provision of, a service;

(*d*) such voluntary housing agencies and other bodies as appear to the authority to provide housing or community care services in their area; and

(*e*) such other persons as the Secretary of State may direct.

(4) In this section—

"community care services" means services, other than services for children, which a local authority are under a duty or have a power to provide, or to secure the provision of, under Part II of this Act or section 7 (functions of local authorities), 8 (provision of after-care services) or 11 (training and occupation of the mentally handicapped) of the Mental Health (Scotland) Act 1984; and

"private carer" means a person who is not employed to provide the care in question by any body in the exercise of its functions under any enactment.

NOTES

[1] Inserted by the National Health Service and Community Care Act 1990 (c. 19), s. 52.

[2] Prospective amendment in the Local Government etc. (Scotland) Act 1994 (c. 39), Sched. 13, para. 76(4), *infra*, including repeal of s. 5A(3)(*b*).

Complaints procedure

[1] **5B.**—[2] (1) Subject to the provisions of this section, the Secretary of State may by order require local authorities to establish a procedure whereby a person, or anyone acting on his behalf, may make representations (including complaints) in relation to the authority's discharge of, or failure to discharge, any of their functions under this Act, or any of the enactments referred to in section 2(2) of this Act, in respect of that person.

(2) For the purposes of subsection (1) of this section, "person" means any person for whom the local authority have a power or a duty to provide, or to secure the provision of, a service, and whose need or possible need for such a service has (by whatever means) come to the attention of the authority.

(3) An order under subsection (1) of this section may be commenced at different times in respect of such different classes of person as may be specified in the order.

[3] (4) In relation to a child, representations may be made by virtue of subsection (1) above by the child, or on his behalf by—

(*a*) his parent;

(*b*) any person having parental rights in respect of him;

(*c*) any local authority foster parent; or

(*d*) any other person appearing to the authority to have a sufficient interest in the child's wellbeing to warrant his making representations on the child's behalf.

[3] (5) In this section—

"child" means a child under the age of 18 years; and

"parent" and "parental rights" have the same meaning as in section 8 (interpretation) of the Law Reform (Parent and Child) (Scotland) Act 1986.

(6) A local authority shall comply with any directions given by the Secretary of State as to the procedure to be adopted in considering representations made as mentioned in subsection (1) of this section and as to the taking of such action as may be necessary in consequence of such representations.

(7) Every local authority shall give such publicity to the procedure established under this section as they consider appropriate.

NOTES

[1] Inserted by the National Health Service and Community Care Act 1990 (c. 19), s. 52.

[2] See S.I. 1990 No. 1519. Prospective amendment in the Local Government etc. (Scotland) Act 1994 (c. 39), Sched. 13, para. 76(5), *infra*.

[3] Prospectively amended by the Children (Scotland) Act 1995 (c. 36), Sched. 4, para. 15(5), *infra*.

Supervision of establishments providing accommodation for persons and inspection of records etc.

[1] **6.**—[2] (1) Any person duly authorised by the Secretary of State may enter any of the following places for the purpose of making such examinations into the state and management of the place, the facilities and services provided therein and the condition and treatment of the persons in it, as he thinks necessary and for the purpose of inspecting any records or registers (in whatever form they are held) relating to the place or to any person for whom services have been or are provided there by virtue of this Act or section 7 (functions of local authorities) or 8 (provision of after-care services) of the Mental Health (Scotland) Act 1984, that is to say—

(*a*) any residential or other establishment provided by a local authority or a voluntary organisation or other person for the purposes of this Act or section 7 or 8 of the said Act of 1984;

[3] (*b*) any place where there is being maintained—

(i) a foster child within the meaning of the Foster Children (Scotland) Act 1984,

(ii) a protected child within the meaning of section 32 of the Adoption (Scotland) Act 1978;

(iii) a child who has been placed for adoption by an adoption agency (within the meaning of section 1 of the Adoption (Scotland) Act 1978);

(*c*) any place where any person is for the time being boarded out by a local authority or a voluntary organisation;

(*d*) [Repealed by the Local Government and Planning (Scotland) Act 1982 (c. 43), Sched. 4, Pt. II.]

[2] (2) Any such person as aforesaid may at all reasonable times enter the offices of a local authority or of a voluntary organisation for the purpose of inspecting any records or registers relating to any establishment or place mentioned in the foregoing subsection or relating to any persons to whom the authority or organisation has made available advice, guidance or assistance in pursuance of this Act or section 7 or 8 of the said Act of 1984, or who may require such advice, guidance or assistance, and may carry out that inspection.

(2A) Any such person may require the owner of, or any person employed in, the establishment or place in question to furnish him with such information as he may request.

(2B) In exercising the power to inspect records and registers under this section a person—

(*a*) shall be entitled at any reasonable time to have access to, and inspect and check the operation of, any computer and any associated apparatus or material which is or has been in use in connection with the records or register in question; and

(*b*) may require—

(i) the person by whom or on whose behalf the computer is or has been so used; or

(ii) any person having charge of or otherwise concerned with the operation of the computer, apparatus or material,

to give him such reasonable assistance as he may require.

(2C) In exercising the power to inspect places under this section a person—

(*a*) may interview any person residing there in private—

(i) for the purpose of investigating any complaint as to that place or the services provided there; or

(ii) if he has reason to believe that the services being provided there for that person are not satisfactory; and

(*b*) may examine any such person in private.

(2D) No person may—

(*a*) exercise the power to inspect records or registers under subsection (1) or (2) above so as to inspect medical records; or

(*b*) exercise the power conferred by subsection (2C) (*b*) above, unless he is a registered medical practitioner and, in the case of the power conferred by subsection (1) or (2) above, the records or register relate to medical treatment given at the place in question.

(3) The power conferred by subsection (1) of this section may be exercised in respect of any place which an authorised person has reasonable cause to believe to be used as an establishment in respect of which the person carrying on the establishment is registrable under Part IV of this Act

(4) A person who proposes to exercise any power of entry or inspection conferred by this section shall if so required, produce a duly authenticated document showing his authority to exercise the power.

[4] (5) Any person who obstructs the exercise of any such power as aforesaid shall be guilty of an offence and liable on summary conviction to a fine not exceeding level 4 on the standard scale.

NOTES

[1] As amended by the National Health Service and Community Care Act 1990 (c. 19), s. 53 and Sched. 9, para. 10(4).

[2] Prospectively amended by the Children (Scotland) Act 1995 (c. 36), Sched. 4, para. 15(6), *infra*.

[3] As amended by the Children Act 1975 (c. 72), Sched. 3, para. 50, the Adoption (Scotland) Act 1978 (c. 28), Sched. 3, para. 10, and the Foster Children (Scotland) Act 1984, Sched. 2, para. 5.

[4] As amended by virtue of the Criminal Procedure (Scotland) Act 1975 (c. 21), ss. 289C and 289G and Sched. 7C.

Inquiries

[1] **6A.**—[2] (1) The Secretary of State may cause an inquiry to be held into the functions of a local authority under this Act or any of the enactments mentioned in section 2(2) of this Act, except in so far as those functions relate to persons under the age of 18.

(2) The Secretary of State may, before an inquiry is commenced, direct that it shall be held in private, but where no such direction has been given the person holding the inquiry may if he thinks fit hold it or any part of it in private.

(3) Subsections (2) to (8) of section 210 of the Local Government (Scotland) Act 1973 (powers in relation to local inquiries) shall apply in relation to an inquiry under this section as they apply in relation to a local inquiry under that section.

NOTES

[1] Inserted by the National Health Service and Community Care Act 1990 (c. 19), s. 54.

[2] Prospective amendment in the Local Government etc. (Scotland) Act 1994 (c. 39), Sched. 13, para. 76(6), *infra*. Prospectively substituted by the Children (Scotland) Act 1995 (c. 36), Sched. 4, para. 15(7), *infra*.

Legal authority inquiries into matters affecting children

6B. [Prospectively inserted by the Children (Scotland) Act 1995 (c. 36), s. 100, *infra*.]

7. [Repealed by the Local Government (Miscellaneous Provisions) (Scotland) Act 1981 (c. 23), s. 29 and Sched. 4.]

Research, training courses and financial and other assistance

Research

8.—(1) The Secretary of State may conduct or assist other persons in conducting research into any matter connected with his function or the functions of local authorities in relation to social welfare, and with the activities of voluntary organisations connected with those functions.

(2) Any local authority may conduct or assist other persons in conducting research into any matter connected with their functions in relation to social welfare.

(3) The Secretary of State and any local authority may make financial assistance available in connection with any research which they may conduct or which they may assist other persons in conducting under the provisions of this section.

Training courses and grants for training in social work

9.—[1] (1) The Secretary of State may provide courses of training for persons with a view to, or in the course of, their employment or the use of their services for the purposes of this Act.

[1] (2) The Secretary of State may make grants of such amounts, and subject to such conditions, as he may with the consent of the Treasury determine towards any fees or expenses incurred by persons undergoing training for any of the purposes of this Act in circumstances such that it appears to the Secretary of State requisite that the grants should be made, and may defray or contribute towards the cost of maintenance of persons undergoing such training.

(3) The Secretary of State may make grants of such amounts, and subject to such conditions, as he may with the consent of the Treasury determine towards expenses incurred by any body of persons in providing training as aforesaid.

NOTE

[1] Prospectively amended by the Children (Scotland) Act 1995 (c. 36), Sched. 4, para. 15(8), *infra*.

Financial and other assistance to voluntary organisations etc., for social work

10.—[1] (1) The Secretary of State may make grants and loans of such amounts, and subject to such conditions, as he may with the consent of the Treasury determine towards expenses incurred by voluntary organisations or other persons engaged in any activity connected with

(*a*) his functions;

(*b*) the functions of local authorities,

under this Act or under the enactments specified in paragraph (*a*) of section 1(4) and paragraphs (*b*) to (*e*), (*h*) and (*j*) of section 2(2) of this Act, in circumstances where it appears to the Secretary of State that such grants or loans should be made.

(2) The conditions on which any grants are paid under the foregoing subsection may include conditions for securing the repayment in whole or in part of such grants.

(3) A local authority may make contributions by way of grant or loan to any voluntary organisation the sole or primary object of which is to promote social welfare.

[2] (3A) In subsection (3) above, "voluntary organisation the sole or primary object of which is to promote social welfare" includes an adoption society approved under Part I of the Adoption (Scotland) Act 1978.

(4) A local authority may also make available to such a voluntary organisation as aforesaid the use of premises belonging to the authority on such terms as may be agreed, and furniture, vehicles or equipment (whether by way of gift, loan or otherwise) and the services of any staff employed by the authority in connection with the premises or other things belonging to the local authority which the voluntary organisation is permitted to use.

[3] (5) On the commencement of this Act, the power of the Secretary of State to give financial assistance and of local authorities to give financial and other assistance under section 65 of the Health Services and Public Health Act 1968 and section 16B of the National Health Service (Scotland) Act 1978 shall cease in so far as any such assistance may be given under this section.

NOTES

[1] As amended by the Children Act 1975 (c. 72), Sched. 3, para. 51(*a*), and the Adoption (Scotland) Act 1978 (c. 28), Sched. 3, para. 11. Prospectively amended by the Local Government etc. (Scotland) Act 1994 (c. 39), Sched. 13, para. 76(7), *infra*, and the Children (Scotland) Act 1995 (c. 36), Sched. 4, para. 15(9), *infra*.

[2] Inserted by the Children Act 1975 (c. 72), Sched. 3, para. 51(*b*). As amended by the Adoption (Scotland) Act 1978 (c. 28), Sched. 3, para. 12.

[3] As amended by the Health and Social Services and Social Security Adjudications Act 1983 (c. 41), Sched. 9, para. 8.

Acquisition of land

Acquisition of land

11.—[1] (1) A local authority may be authorised by the Secretary of State to purchase compulsorily any land, whether situated in or outside their area for the purposes of any of their functions under this Act.

(2) The Acquisition of Land (Authorisation Procedure) (Scotland) Act 1947 shall apply in relation to the compulsory purchase of land under this section as if the last foregoing subsection had been in force immediately before the commencement of that Act.

NOTE

[1] Prospectively amended by the Children (Scotland) Act 1995 (c. 36), Sched. 4, para. 15(10), *infra*.

[1] Part II

Promotion of Social Welfare by Local Authorities

NOTE

[1] Extended (*mod.*) by the Guardianship Act 1973 (c. 29), s. 11(5). Excluded by the Child Care Act 1980 (c. 5), s. 2(5). See also the Family Law Act 1986 (c. 55), s. 1(1)(*b*)(vi).

General

General social welfare services of local authorities

[1] **12.**—[2] (1) It shall be the duty of every local authority to promote social welfare by making available advice, guidance and assistance on such a scale as may be appropriate for their area, and in that behalf to make arrangements and to provide or secure the provision of such facilities (including the provision or arranging for the provision of residential and other establishments) as they may consider suitable and adequate, and such assistance may be given to, or in respect of, the persons specified in the next following subsection in kind or in cash, subject to subsections (3) and (4) of this section.

[2] (2) The persons specified for the purposes of the foregoing subsection are—

(*a*) a person, being a child under the age of 18, requiring assistance in kind, or in exceptional circumstances in cash, where such assistance appears to the local authority likely to diminish the need—
  (i) to receive him into, or to keep him in, care under this Part of this Act, or
  (ii) of his being referred to a children's hearing under Part III of this Act;

(*b*) a person in need requiring assistance in kind or, in exceptional circumstances constituting an emergency, in cash, where the giving of assistance in either form would avoid the local authority being caused greater expense in the giving of assistance in another form, or where probable aggravation of the person's need would cause greater expense to the local authority on a later occasion.

(3) Before giving assistance to, or in respect of, a person in cash under subsection (1) of this section a local authority shall have regard to his eligibility for receiving assistance from any other statutory body and, if he is so eligible, to the availability to him of that assistance in his time of need.

(4) Assistance given in kind or in cash to, or in respect of, persons under this section may be given unconditionally or subject to such conditions as to the repayment of the assistance, or of its value, whether in whole or in part, as the local authority may consider reasonable having regard to the means of the person receiving the assistance and to the eligibility of the person for assistance from any other statutory body.

(5) Nothing in the provisions of this section shall affect the performance by a local authority of their functions under any other enactment.

[3] (6) For the purposes of subsection (2) of this section "person in need" includes a person who is in need of care and attention arising out of drug or alcohol dependency or release from prison or other form of detention.

NOTES

[1] Saved by the Children (Scotland) Act 1995 (c. 36), s. 30(1) (prospective).

[2] Prospectively amended by the Children (Scotland) Act 1995 (c. 36), Sched. 4, para. 15(11), *infra*.

[3] Inserted by the National Health Service and Community Care Act 1990 (c. 19), Sched. 9, para. 10(5).

Duty of local authority to assess needs

[1] **12A.**—(1) Subject to the provisions of this section, where it appears to a local authority that any person for whom they are under a duty or have a power to provide, or to secure the provision of, community care services may be in need of any such services, the authority—

(*a*) shall make an assessment of the needs of that person for those services; and

(*b*) having regard to the results of that assessment, shall then decide whether the needs of that person call for the provision of any such services.

(2) Before deciding, under subsection (1)(*b*) of this section, that the needs of any person call for the provision of nursing care, a local authority shall consult a medical practitioner.

(3) If, while they are carrying out their duty under subsection (1) of this section, it appears to a local authority that there may be a need for the provision to any person to whom that subsection applies—

(*a*) of any services under the National Health Service (Scotland) Act 1978 by the Health Board—

(i) in whose area he is ordinarily resident; or

(ii) in whose area the services to be supplied by the local authority are, or are likely, to be provided; or

(*b*) of any services which fall within the functions of a housing authority (within the meaning of section 130 (housing) of the Local Government (Scotland) Act 1973) which is not the local authority carrying out the assessment,

the local authority shall so notify that Health Board or housing authority, and shall request information from them as to what services are likely to be made available to that person by that Health Board or housing authority; and, thereafter, in carrying out their said duty, the local authority shall take into account any information received by them in response to that request.

(4) Where a local authority are making an assessment under this section and it appears to them that the person concerned is a disabled person, they shall—

(*a*) proceed to make such a decision as to the services he requires as is mentioned in section 4 of the Disabled Persons (Services, Consultation and Representation) Act 1986 without his requesting them to do so under that section; and

(*b*) inform him that they will be doing so and of his rights under that Act.

(5) Nothing in this section shall prevent a local authority from providing or arranging for the provision of community care services for any person without carrying out a prior assessment of his needs in accordance with the preceding provisions of this section if, in the opinion of the authority, the condition of that person is such that he requires those services as a matter of urgency.

(6) If, by virtue of subsection (5) of this section, community care services have been provided for any person as a matter of urgency, then, as soon as practicable thereafter, an assessment of his needs shall be made in accordance with the preceding provisions of this section.

(7) This section is without prejudice to section 3 of the said Act of 1986.

(8) In this section—

"community care services" has the same meaning as in section 5A of this Act;

"disabled person" has the same meaning as in the said Act of 1986; and

"medical practitioner" means a fully registered person within the meaning of section 55 (interpretation) of the Medical Act 1983.

NOTE

[1] Inserted by the National Health Service and Community Care Act 1990 (c. 19), s. 55.

Power of local authorities to assist persons in need in disposal of produce of their work

13. Where, by virtue of the last foregoing section, a local authority make arrangements or provide or secure the provision of facilities for the engagement of persons in need (whether under a contract of service or otherwise) in suitable work, that local authority may assist such persons in disposing of the produce of their work.

Residential accommodation with nursing

[1] **13A.**—(1) Without prejudice to section 12 of this Act, a local authority shall make such arrangements as they consider appropriate and adequate for the provision of suitable residential accommodation where nursing is provided for persons who appear to them to be in need of such accommodation by reason of infirmity, age, illness or mental disorder, dependency on drugs or alcohol or being substantially handicapped by any deformity or disability.

(2) The arrangements made by virtue of subsection (1) above shall be made with a voluntary or other organisation or other person, being an organisation or person managing premises which are—

(*a*) a nursing home within the meaning of section 10(2)(*a*) of the Nursing Homes Registration (Scotland) Act 1938 in respect of which that organisation or person is registered or exempt from registration under that Act; or

(*b*) a private hospital registered under section 12 of the Mental Health (Scotland) Act 1984,

for the provision of accommodation in those premises.

(3) The provisions of section 6 of this Act apply in relation to premises where accommodation is provided for the purposes of this section as they apply in relation to establishments provided for the purposes of this Act.

NOTE

[1] Inserted by the National Health Service and Community Care Act 1990 (c. 19), s. 56.

Provision of care and after-care

Provision of care and after-care

[1] **13B.**—(1) Subject to subsection (2) below, a local authority may with the approval of the Secretary of State, and shall, if and to the extent that the Secretary of State so directs, make arrangements for the purpose of the prevention of illness, the care of persons suffering from illness, and the after-care of such persons.

(2) The arrangements which may be made under subsection (1) above do not include arrangements in respect of medical, dental or nursing care, or health visiting.

NOTE

[1] Inserted by the National Health Service and Community Care Act 1990 (c. 19), s. 56.

Home help

Home help and laundry facilities

14.—[1] (1) It shall be the duty of every local authority to provide on such scale as is adequate for the needs of their area, or to arrange for the provision on such a scale as is so adequate of, domiciliary services for households where such services are required owing to the presence, or the proposed presence, of a person in need or a person who is an expectant mother or lying-in, and every such authority shall have power to provide or arrange for the provision of laundry facilities for households for which domiciliary services are being, or can be, provided under this subsection.

(2) [Repealed by the Health and Social Services and Social Security Adjudications Act 1983 (c. 41), Sched. 10, Pt. I.]

(3) [Repealed by the National Health Service (Scotland) Act 1972 (c. 58), Sched. 7, Pt. II.]

(4) On the coming into operation of the provisions of this and the last two foregoing sections, the provisions of sections 13, 44 and 45 of the Health Services and Public Health Act 1968 shall cease to have effect.

NOTE

[1] As amended by the National Health Service and Community Care Act 1990 (c. 19), Sched. 9, para. 10(6).

Special provisions as to the care of children in need

Duty of local authority to provide for orphans, deserted children, etc.

[1] **15.**—(1) Without prejudice to the generality of the foregoing provisions of this Part of this Act, where it appears to a local authority with respect to a child in their area appearing to them to be under the age of 17—

(*a*) that he has neither parent nor guardian or has been and remains abandoned by his parent or guardian or is lost; or

(*b*) that his parent or guardian is, for the time being or permanently, prevented by reason of illness or mental disorder or bodily disease or infirmity or other incapacity or any other circumstances from providing for his proper accommodation, maintenance and upbringing; and

(*c*) in either case, that the intervention of the local authority under this section is necessary in the interests of the welfare of the child,

it shall be the duty of the local authority to receive the child into their care under this section.

(2) Where a local authority have received a child into their care under this section, it shall, subject to the provisions of this Part of this Act, be their duty to keep the child in their care so long as the welfare of the child appears to them to require it and the child has not attained the age of 18.

(3) If, at the time when a child is received into the care of a local authority under this section, the whereabouts of any parent or guardian of his are unknown, it shall be the duty of the local authority to take all reason-

able steps to discover them; and nothing in this section shall authorise a local authority to keep a child in their care under this section if any parent or guardian desires to take over the care of the child, and the local authority shall, in all cases where it appears to them consistent with the welfare of the child so to do, endeavour to secure that the care of the child is taken over either—

(*a*) by a parent or guardian of his, or

(*b*) by a relative or friend of his, being, where possible, a person of the same religious persuasion as the child or who gives an undertaking that the child will be brought up in that religious persuasion.

[2] (3A) Subsection (8) (penalty for taking away a child in care etc.) of section 17 of this Act shall apply to a child in the care of a local authority under this section, whether or not a resolution is in force under section 16 of this Act with respect to the child, if he has been in the care of that local authority throughout the preceding six months; and for the purposes of the application of paragraph (*b*) of that subsection in such a case a parent or guardian of the child shall not be taken to have lawful authority to take him away:

Provided that that subsection shall not by virtue of this subsection apply in relation to an act done—

(*a*) with the consent of the local authority, or

(*b*) by a parent or guardian of the child in relation to whom no resolution under section 16 of this Act is in effect with respect to the child and who has given the local authority not less than 28 days' notice in writing of his intention to do it.

[2] (3B) The Secretary of State may by order, a draft of which has been approved by each House of Parliament, amend subsection (3A) of this section by substituting a different period for the period of 28 days or of six months mentioned in that subsection (or for the period which by a previous order under this subsection, was substituted for that period).

(4) Where a local authority receive a child into their care under this section who is then ordinarily resident in the area of another local authority, that other local authority may within three months after the determination (whether by agreement between the authorities or under section 86 of this Act) of the ordinary residence of the child, or with the concurrence of the first-mentioned authority at any subsequent time, take over the care of the child; and a local authority shall not exercise their right to take over the care of a child under this subsection unless they are satisfied that the taking-over will not be detrimental to his welfare.

(5) Where under the last foregoing subsection a local authority take over the care of a child from another local authority, that other authority shall where possible inform the parent of the child that the care of the child has been so taken over.

NOTES

[1] Extended by the Adoption (Scotland) Act 1978 (c. 28), s. 34(3). Prospectively repealed by the Children (Scotland) Act 1995 (c. 36), Sched. 5, *infra*.

[2] Added by the Children Act 1975 (c. 72), s. 73. As amended by the Health and Social Services and Social Security Adjudications Act 1983 (c. 41), Sched. 2, para. 4.

Resolution by local authority in respect of assumption and vesting of parental rights and powers

[1] **16.**—(1) Subject to the provisions of this part of this Act, a local authority may resolve—

(*a*) that there shall vest in them the relevant parental rights and powers with respect to any child who is in their care under section 15 of this Act; or

[THE NEXT PAGE IS K 63]

(*b*) that there shall vest in a voluntary organisation which is an incorporated body, or a trust within the meaning of section 2(*a*) of the Trusts (Scotland) Act 1921, the relevant parental rights and powers with respect to any child who is in the care of that organisation,

if it appears to the local authority—

(i) that the parents of the child are dead and that he has no guardian; or

(ii) that there exists in respect of a parent or guardian of the child (the said parent or guardian being hereafter in this Part of this Act referred to as the person on whose account the resolution was passed) any of the circumstances specified in subsection (2) of this section; or

(iii) that a resolution under this subsection is in force in terms of sub-paragraph (ii) above in relation to one parent of the child and that parent is, or is likely to become, a member of the household comprising the child and his other parent; or

(iv) that throughout the three years preceding the passing of the resolution the child has been in the care of a local authority under section 15 of this Act, or in the care of a voluntary organisation or partly the one and partly the other.

[2] (2) The circumstances referred to in sub-paragraph (ii) of subsection (1) of this section are that the person on whose account the resolution was passed—

(*a*) has abandoned the child; or

(*b*) suffers from some permanent disability rendering him incapable of caring for the child; or

(*c*) while not falling within paragraph (*b*) of this subsection, suffers from a mental disorder (within the meaning of the Mental Health (Scotland) Act 1984) which renders him unfit to have the care of the child; or

(*d*) is of such habits or mode of life as to be unfit to have the care of the child; or

(*e*) has so persistently failed without reasonable cause to discharge the obligations of a parent or guardian as to be unfit to have the care of the child.

(3) In this section "the relevant parental rights and powers" means all the rights and powers in relation to the child (other than the right to consent or refuse to consent to the making of an application under section 18 or 55 of the Adoption Act 1976 or under section 18 or 49 of the Adoption (Scotland) Act 1978 and the right to agree or refuse to agree to the making of an adoption order)—

(*a*) where the resolution was passed by virtue of circumstances specified in sub-paragraph (i) of subsection (1) of this section, which the deceased parents would have if they were still living;

(*b*) where the resolution was passed by virtue of circumstances specified in sub-paragraph (ii) of that subsection, of the person on whose account the resolution was passed;

(*c*) where the resolution was passed by virtue of circumstances specified in sub-paragraph (iii) of that subsection, of the parent other than the one on whose account the previous resolution was passed;

(*d*) where the resolution was passed by virtue of circumstances specified in sub-paragraph (iv) of that subsection, of the parents or guardian of the child.

(4) A local authority shall not pass a resolution under paragraph (*b*) of subsection (1) of this section unless—

(*a*) it is satisfied that the child is not in the care of any local authority under any enactment; and

(*b*) it is satisfied that it is necessary in the interests of the welfare of the child for the parental rights and powers to be vested in the voluntary organisation; and (*c*) the child is living in the area of the local authority either in a residential establishment or with foster parents with whom he has been boarded out by the voluntary organisation in whose care he is; and

(*d*) that organisation has requested the local authority to pass the resolution.

[3] (5) In the case of a resolution passed under subsection (1) of this section by virtue of circumstances specified in sub-paragraph (ii), (iii) or (iv) thereof, the local authority, if the whereabouts of the person whose parental rights and powers have under the resolution vested in the local authority or in the voluntary organisation as the case may be are known to them, shall forthwith after the passing of the resolution serve on him notice in writing of the passing thereof.

(6) Every notice served by a local authority under subsection (5) of this section shall inform the person on whom the notice is served of his right to object to the resolution and of the effect of any objection made by him.

(7) If, not later than one month after notice is served on a person under subsection (5) of this section, he serves a counter-notice in writing on the local authority objecting to the resolution, the resolution shall, subject to the provisions of subsection (8) of this section, lapse on the expiry of fourteen days from the service of the counter-notice.

[3a] (8) Where a counter-notice has been served on a local authority under subsection (7) of this section, the authority may, not later than fourteen days after the receipt by them of the counter-notice, make a summary application in respect thereto to the sheriff having jurisdiction in the area of the authority, and in that event the resolution shall not lapse until the determination of the application; and the sheriff may, on the hearing of the application, order that the resolution shall not lapse by reason of the service of the counter-notice:

Provided that the sheriff shall not so order unless satisfied—

(*a*) that it is in the interests of the child to do so; and

(*b*) that the grounds mentioned in subsection (1) of this section on which the local authority purported to pass the resolution were made out; and

(*c*) that at the time of the hearing there continued to be grounds on which a resolution under subsection (1) of this section could be founded.

(9) While a resolution passed under subsection (1) of this section by virtue of circumstances specified in sub-paragraph (ii), (iii) or (iv) thereof is in force with respect to a child, that part of subsection (3) of section 15 of this Act from the words "and nothing in this section shall authorise" onwards shall not apply in relation to the person who, but for the resolution, would have the relevant parental rights and powers in relation to the child.

(10) Any notice under this section (including a counter-notice) may be served by post, but a notice served by a local authority under subsection (5) of this section shall not be duly served by post unless it is sent by registered post or recorded delivery service.

(11) A resolution under this section shall cease to have effect if—

(*a*) the child becomes the subject of an adoption order within the meaning of section 38 of the Adoption (Scotland) Act 1978; or

(*b*) an order in respect of the child is made under section 18 or 55 of the Adoption Act 1976 or under section 18 or 49 of the Adoption (Scotland) Act 1978; or

[4] (*c*) a guardian to the child is appointed under the Law Reform (Parent and Child) (Scotland) Act 1986; or

(*d*) it is a resolution under paragraph (*b*) of subsection (1) of this section and a resolution is passed under subsection (1) of section 16A of this Act in respect of the child; or

[5] (*e*) an event mentioned in paragraph (*a*) or (*b*) of section 25(1) of the Child Abduction and Custody Act 1985 occurs with respect to the child.

(12) If the whereabouts of any parent or guardian of a child have remained unknown for twelve months, and throughout that period the child has been in the care of a local authority under section 15 of this Act, or in the care of a voluntary organisation, or partly the one and partly the other, then for the purposes of this section that parent or guardian shall be deemed to have abandoned the child.

(13) The Secretary of State may by order, a draft of which has been approved by each House of Parliament, amend sub-paragraph (iv) of subsection (1) of this section to substitute a different period for the period of three years mentioned in that sub-paragraph (or for the period which, by a previous order under this subsection, was substituted for that period).

NOTES

[1] Substituted by the Children Act 1975 (c. 72), s. 74. As amended by the Adoption Act 1976 (c. 36), Sched. 3, para. 34, and the Adoption (Scotland) Act 1978 (c. 28), Sched. 3, paras. 13 and 14. Subs. (8): see the Child Abduction and Custody Act 1985 (c. 60), ss. 9(*d*), 20(2)(*d*) and Sched. 3, para. 5(4). See the Foster Children (Scotland) Act 1984 (c. 56), s. 7(1)(*d*). Prospectively repealed by the Children (Scotland) Act 1995 (c. 36), Sched. 5, *infra*.

[2] As amended by the Mental Health (Scotland) Act 1984 (c. 36), Sched. 3, para. 15.

[3] As amended by the Health and Social Services and Social Security Adjudications Act 1983 (c. 41), s. 7(1).

[3a] See the Child Abduction and Custody Act 1985 (c. 60), ss. 9(*d*), 20(2)(*d*) and Sched. 3, para. 5(iv).

[4] As amended by the Law Reform (Parent and Child) (Scotland) Act 1986 (c. 9), Sched. 1, para. 9, and the Age of Legal Capacity (Scotland) Act 1991 (c. 50), Sched. 1, para. 31.

[5] Inserted by the Child Abduction and Custody Act 1985 (c. 60), s. 25(6).

Duty of local authority to assume parental rights and powers vested in a voluntary organisation

[1] **16A.**—(1) If it appears to a local authority, having regard to the interests of the welfare of a child living within their area, the parental rights and powers in respect of whom are by virtue of a resolution under section 16(1)(*b*) of this Act (hereafter in this section referred to as "the earlier resolution") vested in a voluntary organisation, that it is necessary that the said parental rights and powers should no longer be vested in the organisation, the local authority shall resolve that the said parental rights and powers shall vest in them; and the said parental rights and powers shall so vest from the date of the resolution under this subsection.

(2) The local authority shall, within seven days of passing a resolution under subsection (1) of this section, by notice in writing inform—

(*a*) the organisation who but for that resolution; and

(*b*) any person, in so far as that person's whereabouts are known to them, who, but for that resolution and the earlier resolution,

would have the parental rights and powers in respect of the child, of the passing thereof.

[2] (3) On a summary application being made for the determining of a resolution under subsection (1) of this section by a person who but for that resolution and the earlier resolution would have the parental rights and powers in respect of the child, the sheriff having jurisdiction where the applicant resides may order that—

(*a*) the resolution under subsection (1) of this section shall continue to have effect; or

(*b*) the resolution under subsection (1) of this section shall cease to have effect and that the earlier resolution shall again take effect; or

(*c*) the resolution under subsection (1) of this section shall cease to have effect and that the parental rights and powers in respect of the child shall again vest in the applicant; or

(*d*) the resolution under subsection (1) of this section shall continue to have effect, but that either for a fixed period or until the sheriff, or if the order so provides, the local authority, otherwise directs, the local authority shall allow the care of the child to be taken over by, and the child to be under the control of, the applicant.

(4) In hearing an application under subsection (3) of this section the sheriff may consider whether there was any ground for the making of the earlier resolution, and if he is satisfied that there was no ground for the making of that earlier resolution he shall make an order under subsection (3)(*c*) of this section.

(5) In this section "the parental rights and powers" means all the rights and powers in relation to the child which in accordance with the earlier resolution were vested in the voluntary organisation.

(6) While a resolution under subsection (1) of this section is in force with respect to a child, the child shall be deemed to have been received into and to be in the care of the local authority by virtue of section 15 of this Act, and subsections (2) to (5) of that section shall apply accordingly; except that where the earlier resolution was passed by virtue of circumstances specified in sub-paragraph (ii), (iii) or (iv) of subsection (1) of section 16 of this Act, that part of subsection (3) of section 15 of this Act from the words "and nothing in this section shall authorise" onwards shall not apply in relation to the person who but for the earlier resolution and the resolution under subsection (1) of this section, would have the parental rights and powers in relation to the child.

(7) Subsection (11)(*a*), (*b*) and (*c*) of section 16, subsections (3) and (4) to (9) of section 17 and subsections (1), (2), (4) and (4A) of section 18 of this Act shall apply to a resolution under this section as they apply to a resolution under section 16(1)(*a*) of this Act.

(8) A notice served by a local authority under subsection (2) of this section shall not be duly served by post unless it is sent by registered post or recorded delivery service.

NOTES

[1] Inserted by the Children Act 1975 (c. 72), s. 75. Prospectively repealed by the Children (Scotland) Act 1995 (c. 36), Sched. 5, *infra*.

[2] See the Child Abduction and Custody Act 1985 (c. 60), ss. 9(*d*), 20(2)(*d*) and Sched. 3, para. 5(iv).

Effect of assumption by local authority of parental rights

[0] **17.**—(1), (2) [Repealed by the Children Act 1975 (c. 72), Sched. 4, Pt. V.]

[1] (3) A resolution under section 16(1)(*a*) of this Act shall not prevent the local authority in whom are vested in accordance with the resolution the parental rights and powers in respect of a child, from allowing, either for a fixed period or until the local authority otherwise determine, the care of the child to be taken over by, and the child to be under the control of, a parent, guardian, relative or friend in any case where it appears to the authority to be for the benefit of the child.

[2] (3A) A resolution under section 16(1)(*b*) of this Act shall not prevent the voluntary organisation, in whom are vested in accordance with the resolution the parental rights and powers in respect of a child, from allowing, either for a fixed period or until the voluntary organisation otherwise determine, the care of the child to be taken over by, and the child to be under the control of, a parent, guardian, relative or friend in any case where it appears to the voluntary organisation to be for the benefit of the child.

[3] (4) Where a resolution under section 16(1)(*a*) of this Act is in force in respect of a child and the child has ceased to be in the care of the local authority by whom the resolution was passed, then (without prejudice to the provisions of section 15 of this Act if those provisions apply) the local authority by whom the resolution was passed shall have power to receive the child back into their care in any circumstances in which it appears to them that their intervention under this subsection is necessary in the interests of the welfare of the child.

(5) Where a local authority receive a child into their care under the last foregoing subsection, the provisions of this Act, except subsection (4) of

section 15 thereof, shall apply as if the child had been received into their care under the said section 15.

[4] (6) A resolution under section 16 of this Act shall not relieve any person from any liability to maintain, or contribute to the maintenance of the child.

[5] (7) A resolution under the said section 16 shall not authorise a local authority or a voluntary organisation to cause a child to be brought up in any religious persuasion other than that in which he would have been brought up but for the resolution.

[6] (8) Any person who—

(*a*) knowingly assists or induces or persistently attempts to induce a child, in respect of whom a resolution under section 16 of this Act is in effect, to run away, or

(*b*) without lawful authority takes away such a child, or

(*c*) knowingly harbours or conceals such a child who has run away or who has been taken away or prevents him from returning,

shall be liable on summary conviction to a fine not exceeding level 5 on the standard scale or to imprisonment for a term not exceeding six months or to both such fine and such imprisonment.

[7] (9) Where—

(*a*) a local authority have, in accordance with subsection (3) of this section; or

(*b*) a voluntary organisation have, in accordance with subsection (3A) of this section,

allowed any person to take over the care of a child with respect to whom a resolution under the said section 16 is in force and have by notice in writing required that person to return the child at a time specified in the notice (which, if that person has been allowed to take over the care of the child for a fixed period, shall not be earlier than the end of that period) any person who harbours or conceals the child after that time or prevents him from returning as required by the notice shall be liable on summary conviction to a fine not exceeding level 5 on the standard scale or to imprisonment for a term not exceeding six months or to both such fine and such imprisonment.

[8] (10) Where an offence under subsection (8) or (9) of this section has been or is believed to have been committed, a constable, or any person authorised by any court or by any justice of the peace, may take and return the child to the local authority or voluntary organisation in whom are vested the parental rights and powers relating to the child.

NOTES

[0] See the Mental Health Act 1983 (c. 20), s. 27 (England and Wales), and the Mental Health (Scotland) Act 1984 (c. 36), ss. 10 and 54. Prospectively repealed by the Children (Scotland) Act 1995 (c. 36), Sched. 5, *infra*.

[1] As amended by the Children Act 1975 (c. 72), Sched. 3, para. 52(*a*).

[2] Added by the Children Act 1975 (c. 72), Sched. 3, para. 52(*b*).

[3] As amended by the Children Act 1975 (c. 72), Sched. 3, para. 52(*c*).

[4] As amended by the Children Act 1975 (c. 72), Sched. 3, para. 52(*d*).

[5] As amended by the Children Act 1975 (c. 72), Sched. 3, para. 52(*e*).

[6] As amended by the Children Act 1975 (c. 72), Sched. 3, para. 52(*f*), and by virtue of the Criminal Procedure (Scotland) Act 1975 (c. 21), ss. 289F and 289G.

[7] As amended by the Children Act 1975 (c. 72), Sched. 3, para. 52(*g*), and by virtue of the Criminal Procedure (Scotland) Act 1975 (c. 21), ss. 289F and 289G.

[8] Added by the Children Act 1975 (c. 72), s. 76.

Termination of access to child subject to resolution under section 16

[1] **17A.**—(1) A local authority or voluntary organisation may not terminate arrangements for access to a child who is the subject of a resolution under section 16 of this Act by his parent or guardian or refuse to make such arrangements unless they have first given the parent or guardian notice of termination or refusal in a form prescribed by order made by the Secretary of State.

(2) A notice under this section shall contain a statement that the parent or guardian has a right to apply to the sheriff for an order under section 17B of this Act.

(3) A notice terminating access shall state that access will be terminated as from the date of service of the notice.

(4) A local authority or voluntary organisation are not to be taken to terminate arrangements for access for the purposes of this section in a case where they propose to substitute new arrangements for access for existing arrangements.

(5) A local authority or voluntary organisation are not to be taken to refuse to make arrangements for access for the purposes of this section in a case where they postpone access for such reasonable period as appears to them to be necessary to enable them to consider what arrangements for access (if any) are to be made.

(6) A notice under this section may be served on a parent or guardian either by delivering it to him or by leaving it at his proper address or by sending it by post.

(7) For the purposes of this section, and of section 7 of the Interpretation Act 1978 in its application to this section, the proper address of a person shall be his last known address.

NOTE

[1] Inserted by the Health and Social Services and Social Security Adjudications Act 1983 (c. 41), s. 7(2). Prospectively repealed by the Children (Scotland) Act 1995 (c. 36), Sched. 5, *infra*.

Access orders

[1] **17B.**—(1) A parent or guardian on whom a notice under section 17A of this Act is served may apply by way of summary application to the sheriff (in the case of a local authority, the sheriff having jurisdiction in their area) for an order under this section (hereinafter referred to as an "access order").

(2) An access order shall be an order requiring the authority or organisation to allow the child's parent or guardian access to the child subject to such conditions as the order may specify with regard to commencement, frequency, duration or place of access or to any other matter for which it appears to the sheriff that provision ought to be made in connection with the requirement to allow access.

(3) Where an access order has been made—

(*a*) the parent or guardian named in the order; or

(*b*) the local authority or voluntary organisation

may apply by way of summary application to the sheriff for the variation or discharge of the order.

NOTE

[1] Inserted by the Health and Social Services and Social Security Adjudications Act 1983 (c. 41), s. 7(2). Prospectively repealed by the Children (Scotland) Act 1995 (c. 36), Sched. 5, *infra*.

Emergency order

[1] **17C.**—(1) The sheriff may make an order under this subsection where he is satisfied that continued access to a child by his parent or guardian in accordance with the terms of an access order will put the child's welfare seriously at risk.

(2) Subject to subsection (3) below, an order under subsection (1) of this section shall be an order suspending the operation of the access order for seven days beginning with the date of the order under subsection (1) of this section, or for such shorter period beginning with that date as may be specified in that order.

(3) If during the period for which the operation of the access order is suspended the local authority or voluntary organisation make an application for its variation or discharge to the sheriff, its operation shall be suspended until the date on which the application to vary or discharge it is determined or abandoned.

NOTE

[1] Inserted by the Health and Social Services and Social Security Adjudications Act 1983 (c. 41), s. 7(2). Prospectively repealed by the Children (Scotland) Act 1995 (c. 36), Sched. 5, *infra*.

Safeguarding of interest of child

[1] **17D.**—A court to which an application for an access order or any other application under section 17B or 17C of this Act or any appeal relating thereto is made shall regard the welfare of the child as the first and paramount consideration in determining the matter.

NOTE

[1] Inserted by the Health and Social Services and Social Security Adjudications Act 1983 (c. 41), s. 7(2). Prospectively repealed by the Children (Scotland) Act 1995 (c. 36), Sched. 5, *infra*.

Code of practice

[1] **17E.**—(1) The Secretary of State shall prepare, and from time to time revise, a code of practice with regard to access to children who are in care or who are subject to a supervision requirement under section 44 of this Act.

(2) Before preparing the code or making any alteration in it the Secretary of State shall consult such bodies as appear to him to be concerned.

(3) The Secretary of State shall lay copies of the code and of any alteration in the code before Parliament; and if either House of Parliament passes a resolution requiring the code or any alteration in it to be withdrawn the Secretary of State shall withdraw the code or alteration and, where he withdraws the code, shall prepare a code in substitution for the one which is withdrawn.

(4) No resolution shall be passed by either House of Parliament under subsection (3) above in respect of a code or alteration after the expiration of the period of 40 days beginning with the day on which a copy of the code or alteration was laid before that House; but for the purposes of this subsection no account shall be taken of any time during which Parliament is dissolved or prorogued or during which both Houses are adjourned for more than four days.

(5) The Secretary of State shall publish the code as for the time being in force.

NOTE

[1] Inserted by the Health and Social Services and Social Security Adjudications Act 1983 (c. 41), s. 7(2). Prospectively repealed by the Children (Scotland) Act 1995 (c. 36), Sched. 5, *infra*.

Duration and rescission of resolutions under section 16

[0] **18.**—(1) Subject to the provisions of this Part of this Act, a resolution under section 16 of this Act shall continue in force until the child with respect to whom it was passed attains the age of 18.

[1] (2) A resolution under the said section 16(1)(*a*) may be rescinded by resolution of the local authority if it appears to them that the rescinding of the resolution will be for the benefit of the child.

[2] (3) On a summary application for the determining of a resolution being made—

(*a*) in case of a resolution passed by virtue of sub-paragraph (i) of subsection (1) of the said section 16, by a person claiming to be a parent or guardian of the child;

(*b*) in the case of a resolution passed by virtue of circumstances specified in sub-paragraph (ii), (iii), or (iv) of subsection (1) of the said section 16, by the person who, but for the resolution, would have the parental rights and powers in relation to the child,

the sheriff, having jurisdiction where the applicant resides, if satisfied that there was no ground for the making of the resolution or that the resolution should in the interests of the child be determined, may by order determine the resolution, and the resolution shall thereupon cease to have effect;

Provided that, if the sheriff thinks fit, he may, in lieu of determining the resolution, order that, either for a fixed period or until he, or, if the order so provides, the local authority, otherwise direct, the local authority, and any voluntary organisation having parental rights and powers with respect to the child, shall allow the care of the child to be taken over by, and the child to be under the control of, the applicant.

[3] (4) A court may entertain an application under the Law Reform (Parent and Child) (Scotland) Act 1986 to appoint a guardian of a child notwithstanding that, by virtue of a resolution under section 16 of this Act, a local authority or voluntary organisation have parental rights with respect to him.

[4] (4A) A court may entertain an application under—

(*a*) section 12 of the Adoption (Scotland) Act 1978 for an adoption order in respect of a child;

(*b*) section 18 of the said Act of 1978 for an order declaring a child free for adoption;

(*c*) section 49 of the said Act of 1978 for an order vesting the parental rights and duties relating to a child;

notwithstanding that, by virtue of a resolution under section 16 of this Act, a local authority or a voluntary organisation have parental rights with respect to him.

NOTES

[0] Prospectively repealed by the Children (Scotland) Act 1995 (c. 36), Sched. 5, *infra*.

[1] As amended by the Children Act 1975 (c. 72), Sched. 3, para. 53(*a*).

[2] As amended by the Children Act 1975 (c. 72), Sched. 3, para. 53(*b*). See the Child Abduction and Custody Act 1985 (c. 60), ss. 9(*d*), 20(2)(*d*) and Sched. 3, para. 5(iv).

[3] As amended by the Children Act 1975 (c. 72), Sched. 3, para. 53(*c*) and Sched. 4, Pt. V, the Law Reform (Parent and Child) (Scotland) Act 1986 (c. 9), Sched. 1, para. 9, and the Age of Legal Capacity (Scotland) Act 1991 (c. 50), Sched. 1, para. 32.

[4] Added by the Children Act 1975 (c. 72), s. 77: paras. (*b*) and (*c*). As amended by the Adoption (Scotland) Act 1978 (c. 28), Sched. 3, para. 15.

Safeguarding of interests of children in proceedings relating to the assumption of parental rights

[1] **18A.**—[2] (1) In any proceedings under section 16(8), 16A(3), 17B, 17C or 18 (3) of this Act, the sheriff—

(*a*) shall consider whether it is necessary to appoint a person for the purpose of safeguarding the interests of the child in the proceedings; and

(*b*) without prejudice to any existing power to appoint a person to represent the interests of the child, may, if he thinks fit, appoint a person to act for the purpose specified in paragraph (*a*) above.

[3] (2) The power to make rules under section 32 of the Sheriff Courts (Scotland) Act 1971 shall include power to make rules providing for—

(*a*) the procedure in relation to the disposal of matters arising under this section;

(*b*) appointment under subsection (1) of this section, the functions of a person so appointed and any rights of such a person to information relating to the proceedings in question.

NOTES

[1] Inserted by the Children Act 1975 (c. 72), s. 78. Prospectively repealed by the Children (Scotland) Act 1995 (c. 36), Sched. 5, *infra*.

[2] As amended by the Health and Social Services and Social Security Adjudications Act 1983 (c. 41), s. 7(3).

[3] See S.I. 1985 No. 780.

19. [Repealed by the Foster Children (Scotland) Act 1984 (c. 56), Sched. 3.]

Duty of local authority to further the best interests of a child in their care and to afford opportunity for his proper development

[1] **20.**—[2] (1) Where a child is in the care of a local authority under any enactment or of a voluntary organisation, they shall, in reaching any decision relating to the child, give first consideration to the need to safeguard and promote the welfare of the child throughout his childhood; and shall so far as practicable ascertain the wishes and feelings of the child regarding the decision and give due consideration to them, having regard to his age and understanding.

(2) In providing for a child in their care as aforesaid, they shall make such use of facilities and services available for children in the care of their own parents as appears to the local authority or voluntary organisation reasonable in his case.

(3) Where a local authority or voluntary organisation allow the care of a child to be taken over under sections 17(3), 17(3A) or 18(3) of this Act, their duties in respect of the child under this section shall not be affected by that take-over.

NOTES

[1] As amended by the Health and Social Services and Social Security Adjudications Act 1983 (c. 41), Sched. 2, para. 5. Prospectively repealed by the Children (Scotland) Act 1995 (c. 36), Sched. 5, *infra*.

[2] Substituted by the Children Act 1975 (c. 72), s. 79.

Review of children in care

[1] **20A.**—[2] (1) Without prejudice to their general duty under section 20(1) of this Act, it shall be the duty of a local authority who have at any time had a child in their care throughout the preceding six months and have not during that period held a review of his case, to review his case as soon as is practicable after the expiration of that period and, if a supervision requirement is in force with respect to him, the local authority shall consider in the course of the review whether to refer his case to their reporter for review of that requirement by a children's hearing.

(2) The Secretary of State may by regulations—

(*a*) amend subsection (1) of this section by—

(i) substituting a different period for the period of six months mentioned in that subsection (or for any period which, by previous regulations under this subsection, was substituted for that period);

(ii) specifying different periods in respect of the first review under that subsection occurring after a child has been taken into care, and in respect of subsequent such reviews;

(*b*) make provision as to the manner in which cases are to be reviewed under this section;

(*c*) make provision as to the considerations to which the local authority are to have regard in reviewing cases under this section.

NOTES

[1] Inserted by the Children Act 1975 (c. 72), s. 80. Prospectively repealed by the Children (Scotland) Act 1995 (c. 36), Sched. 5, *infra*.

[2] Prospective amendment in the Local Government etc. (Scotland) Act 1994 (c. 39), Sched. 13, para. 76(8), *infra*.

[THE NEXT PAGE IS K 69]

Mode of provision of accommodation and maintenance

[0] **21.**—(1) Subject to the provisions of this section, a local authority shall discharge their duty to provide accommodation and maintenance for a child in their care—

(*a*) by boarding him out on such terms as to payment by the authority and otherwise as the authority may, subject to the provisions of this Act and regulations thereunder, determine; or

(*b*) by maintaining the child in a residential establishment.

[1] (2) Nothing in the foregoing subsection shall be construed as preventing a local authority from making use, in the case of any child, of any such facilities and services as are referred to in subsection (2) of section 20 of this Act, and for that purpose arranging for his accommodation and maintenance in any suitable manner not specified in the last foregoing subsection.

[2] (3) Arrangements may be made by a local authority under this section for boarding out a child in England or Wales or for maintaining him in any accommodation in England or Wales which a local authority in those countries is authorised to use for that purpose by virtue of section 23 of the Children Act 1989.

NOTES

[0] Prospectively repealed by the Children (Scotland) Act 1995 (c. 36), Sched. 5, *infra*.

[1] As amended by the Law Reform (Miscellaneous Provisions) (Scotland) Act 1985 (c. 73), Sched. 2, para. 9.

[2] As amended by the Child Care Act 1980 (c. 5), Sched. 5, para. 21, and the Children Act 1989 (c. 41), Sched. 13, para. 20.

Removal of children in residential establishments

[1] **22.** Notwithstanding any agreement made in connection with the placing of a child in a residential establishment under this Part of this Act by a local authority, the authority may at any time, and shall if required so to do by the person responsible for the establishment, remove the child from the establishment.

NOTE

[1] As amended by the Local Government (Scotland) Act 1973 (c. 65), Sched. 25, para. 41, and Sched. 29. See s. 87, *infra*. Prospectively repealed by the Children (Scotland) Act 1995 (c. 36), Sched. 5, *infra*.

Power of local authorities and voluntary organisations to arrange for emigration of children

[1] **23.**—(1) A local authority or a voluntary organisation may, with the consent of the Secretary of State, arrange or assist in arranging the emigration of any child in their care.

[2] (2) The Secretary of State shall not give his consent under this section unless he is satisfied that emigration would benefit the child, and that suitable arrangements have been or will be made for the child's reception and welfare in the country to which he is going, that the parent of the child has been consulted or that it is not practicable to consult him, and that the child consents:

Provided that where a child is too young to form or express a proper opinion on the matter, the Secretary of State may consent to his emigration notwithstanding that the child is unable to consent thereto in any case where the child is to emigrate in company with a parent, relative or friend of his, or is to emigrate for the purpose of joining a parent, relative or friend.

NOTES

[1] Prospectively repealed by the Children (Scotland) Act 1995 (c. 36), s. 28.

[2] As amended by the Health and Social Services and Social Security Adjudications Act 1983 (c. 41), Sched. 2, para. 6.

Financial assistance towards expenses of maintenance, education or training of persons over school age

[1] **24.**—(1) Without prejudice to the provisions of section 12 of this Act a local authority may make contributions to the cost of the accommodation and maintenance of any person—

(*a*) who is over school age but has not attained the age of 21; and

(*b*) who is, or has at any time after ceasing to be of school age been, in the care of a local authority,

in any place near the place where he may be employed or seeking employment, or in receipt of education or training.

(2) A local authority may make grants to persons who are over school age, but have not attained the age of 21, and who at or after the time when they ceased to be of school age were in the care of a local authority, to enable them to meet expenses connected with their receiving suitable education or training.

(3) Where a person—

(*a*) is engaged in a course of education or training at the time when he attains the age of 21; or

(*b*) having previously been engaged in a course of education or training which has been interrupted by any circumstances, resumes the course as soon as practicable,

then if a local authority are at the said time, or were at the time when the course was interrupted, as the case may be, making any contributions or grants in respect of him under any of the foregoing provisions of this section, their powers under those provisions shall continue with respect to him until the completion of the course.

NOTE

[1] Prospectively repealed by the Children (Scotland) Act 1995 (c. 36), Sched. 5, *infra*.

Power of local authority to guarantee indentures and other deeds of apprenticeship etc., of persons in their care

[1] **25.** While a person is in the care of a local authority by virtue of any enactment, the local authority may undertake any obligation by way of guarantee under any indentures or other deed of apprenticeship or articles of clerkship entered into by that person; and where the local authority have undertaken any such obligation under any such deed or articles they may at any time (whether or not the person concerned is still in their care) undertake the like obligation under any such deed or articles supplemental thereto.

NOTE

[1] Prospectively repealed by the Children (Scotland) Act 1995 (c. 36), s. 30(4), *infra*.

Restriction on removal of child from care of voluntary organisation

[1] **25A.**—(1) Section 17(8) of this Act shall apply in relation to a child who is not in the care of a local authority under section 15 of this Act but who is in the care of a voluntary organisation, as it applies by virtue of subsection (3A) of the said section 15 to a child in the care of a local authority except that, in the case of a child who is not in the care of a local authority, references in subsection (3A) to a local authority shall be construed as references to the voluntary organisation in whose care the child is.

(2) For the purposes of this section, a child is in the care of a voluntary organisation if the voluntary organisation is providing accommodation for the child in a residential establishment or has boarded out the child.

NOTE

[1] Added by the Children Act 1975 (c. 72), s. 81. Prospectively repealed by the Children (Scotland) Act 1995 (c. 36), Sched. 5, *infra*.

After-care of children formerly in care of local authorities or voluntary organisations

[1] **26.**—(1) Where it comes to the knowledge of a local authority that there is in their area any child over school age who at the time when he ceased to be of that age or at any subsequent time was, but is no longer,—

(*a*) in the care of a local authority, or

(*b*) in the care of a voluntary organisation,

then, unless the authority are satisfied that the welfare of the child does not require it, they shall be under a duty so long as he has not attained the age of 18 to advise, guide or assist him:

Provided that where in a case falling within paragraph (*b*) of this subsection the local authority are satisfied that the voluntary organisation have the necessary facilities, the local authority may make arrangements whereby, while the arrangements continue in force, he shall be advised, guided or assisted by the voluntary organisation instead of by the local authority.

(2) Where a child over school age—

(*a*) ceases to be in the care of a local authority under section 15 of this Act and proposes to reside in the area of another local authority, or

(*b*) ceases to be in the care of a voluntary organisation,

the authority or organisation shall inform the local authority for the area in which the child proposes to reside.

(3) Where it comes to the knowledge of a local authority or a voluntary organisation that a child whom they have been advising, guiding or assisting in pursuance of this section proposes to transfer or has transferred his residence to the area of another local authority, the first-mentioned local authority or, as the case may be, the voluntary organisation shall inform the other local authority.

NOTE

[1] Prospectively repealed by the Children (Scotland) Act 1995 (c. 36), Sched. 5, *infra*.

Supervision and care of persons out on probation or released from prisons etc.

Supervision and care of persons put on probation or released from prisons etc.

[1] **27.**—[2] (1) It shall be a function of every local authority under this Part of this Act to provide a service for the following purposes, that is to say—

(*a*) making available to any court such social background reports and other reports relating to persons appearing before the court which the court may require for the disposal of a case;

(*aa*), (*ab*) [Prospectively inserted by the Criminal Justice (Scotland) Act 1995 (c. 20), s. 66(*a*), *supra*, Division **E**.]

(*b*) the supervision of, and the provision of advice, guidance and assistance for—

(i) persons in their area who are under supervision by order of a court made in the exercise of its criminal jurisdiction by virtue of any enactment, and

(ii) persons in their area who, following on release from prison or any other form of detention, are required to be under supervision under any enactment or by the terms of an order or licence of the Secretary of State or of a condition or requirement imposed in pursuance of any enactment, and

(iii) without prejudice to sub-paragraphs (i) and (ii) above, persons in the area subject to a community service order under the Community Service by Offenders (Scotland) Act 1978 or a probation order which includes a requirement that the offender shall perform unpaid work; and

(iv) without prejudice to paragraphs (i) to (iii) above, persons in their area who are subject to supervised attendance orders under section 62 of the Law Reform (Miscellaneous Provisions) (Scotland) Act 1990; and

(v)–(vii) [Prospectively inserted by the Criminal Justice (Scotland) Act 1995 (c. 20), s. 66(*b*), *supra*, Division **E.**]

(*c*) the provision of advice, guidance and assistance for persons in their area who, within 12 months of their release from prison or any other form of detention, request such advice, guidance or assistance.

(2) For the purposes of the foregoing subsection every local authority shall, after consultation with the sheriffs having jurisdiction in their area, prepare a scheme (hereinafter referred to as a probation, community service and supervised attendance scheme) and submit it by such date, as he may require, to the Secretary of State for his approval.

(3) A probation, community service and supervised attendance scheme shall make provision with regard to the following matters—

(*a*) the manner in which any report requested by the court from the local authority is to be prepared and submitted to the court;

(*aa*) the matters to be included in such a report;

(*b*) arrangements for the attendance of officers of the local authority at the court;

[3] (*c*) arrangements for the co-operation of the local authorities with the courts, and such arrangements may include the appointment of one or more sheriffs having jurisdiction in their areas to the social work committee and to any sub-committee thereof;

(*d*) arrangements for the keeping of adequate records and statistics regarding the performance of functions under this section; and

(*e*) such other matters as the local authority considers relevant to the service to be provided.

(4) The Secretary of State may approve a probation, community service and supervised attendance scheme with or without modifications.

(5) A local authority may apply to the Secretary of State for the revision of a probation, community service and supervised attendance scheme and, if the Secretary of State so requires, shall prepare and submit to the Secretary of State for his approval a revised scheme or a modification of an existing scheme.

(6) Any function required by any enactment to be performed by a probation officer shall, after the coming into operation of this Part of this Act, be performed by an officer of the appropriate local authority.

(7) . . .

NOTES

[1] As amended by the Community Service by Offenders (Scotland) Act 1978 (c. 49), Sched. 2, para. 1, and the Law Reform (Miscellaneous Provisions) (Scotland) Act 1990 (c. 40), s. 61(4) and Sched. 6, para. 8.

[2] See the Local Government (Access to Information) Act 1985 (c. 43), Sched. 1, Pt. I, para. 7.

[3] Prospective amendment in the Local Government etc. (Scotland) Act 1994 (c. 39), Sched. 13, para. 76(9), *infra*.

Grants in respect of community service facilities

[1,2] **27A.**—(1) The Secretary of State may make to a local authority grants of such amounts and subject to such conditions as he may with the consent of the Treasury determine in respect of expenditure incurred by the authority in providing a service:

(*a*) for the purposes mentioned in section 27(1) of this Act; and

(*b*) for such other similar purposes as the Secretary of State may prescribe.

(2) Before exercising his power under subsection (1)(*b*) above the Secretary of State shall consult local authorities and such other bodies as he considers appropriate.

NOTES

[1] Inserted by the Community Service by Offenders (Scotland) Act 1978 (c. 49), s. 9. As amended by the Law Reform (Miscellaneous Provisions) (Scotland) Act 1990 (c. 40), s. 61(5).

[2] S.I. 1993 No. 721 (effective 1st April 1993) provides:

"**3.** A service provided by a local authority for the following purposes is prescribed as a service with a purpose similar to those mentioned in section 27(1) of the Act, in relation to which grants may be made to a local authority under section 27A(1) of the Act in respect of expenditure incurred by the authority in providing the service—

(*a*) making available to any court or to the Lord Advocate such social background reports and other reports relating to persons who have been charged with an offence and are to appear before a court, which the court or the Lord Advocate may require for the disposal of an application for bail; and

(*b*) the supervision of, and the provision of advice, guidance and assistance for, persons in their area who have been charged with an offence and are on bail subject to a condition of supervision by the local authority to secure any of the purposes described in section 1(2) (purposes for which conditions may be imposed in granting bail) of the Bail etc. (Scotland) Act 1988."

Grants in respect of hostel accommodation for persons under supervision

[1] **27B.**—(1) The Secretary of State may make to a local authority grants of such amount and subject to such conditions as he may with the consent of the Treasury determine in respect of expenditure incurred by the authority under this Act in—

(*a*) providing; or

(*b*) contributing by way of grant under section 10(3) of this Act to the provision by a voluntary organisation of,

residential accommodation wholly or mainly for the persons mentioned in subsection (2) below.

(2) The persons referred to in subsection (1) above are—

(*a*) persons mentioned in section 27(1)(*b*)(i) and (ii) of this Act;

(*b*) persons who have been charged with an offence and are on bail;

(*c*) persons who have been released from prison or any other form of detention but do not fall within section 27(1)(*b*)(ii) of this Act; and

(*d*) such other classes of persons as the Secretary of State may prescribe.

(3) Before exercising his power under subsection (2)(*d*) above the Secretary of State shall consult local authorities and such other persons as he considers appropriate.

NOTE

[1] Inserted by the Criminal Justice (Scotland) Act 1980 (c. 62), s. 79. As amended by the Law Reform (Miscellaneous Provisions) (Scotland) Act 1990 (c. 40), s. 61(6).

Ancillary

Burial or cremation of the dead

28.—[1] (1) A local authority may cause to be buried or cremated the body of any deceased person who immediately before his death was in the care of, or receiving assistance from, the authority:

Provided that the authority shall not cause the body to be cremated where cremation is not in accordance with the practice of the person's religious persuasion.

[2] (2) An authority may recover from the estate of the deceased person or from any person who was liable to maintain the deceased person immediately before his death expenses incurred under subsection (1) of this section and not reimbursed.

(3) [Prospectively added by the Children (Scotland) Act 1995 (c. 36), Sched. 4, para. 15(2)(*b*), *infra*.]

NOTES

[1] Prospectively amended by the Children (Scotland) Act 1995 (c. 36), Sched. 4, para. 15(12)(*a*), *infra*.

[2] As amended by the Social Security (Consequential Provisions) Act 1975 (c. 18), Sched. 2, para. 35 and the Social Security Act 1986 (c. 50), Sched. 11.

Power of local authority to defray expenses of parent, etc., visiting persons or attending funerals

[1] **29.**—(1) A local authority may make payments to any parent, relative or other person connected with a person in their care, or receiving assistance from them, in respect of travelling, subsistence or other expenses incurred by the parent, relative or other person in visiting the person, if it appears to the authority that the parent, relative or other person would not otherwise be able to visit the person without undue hardship and that the circumstances warrant the making of the payments.

(2) A local authority may make the like payments and in the like circumstances to any parent, relative or other person connected with a person who was in their care, or was receiving assistance from them, for the purposes of that parent, relative or other person attending the funeral of the person.

NOTE

[1] Subss. (1) and (2) prospectively amended, and subs. (3) prospectively added, by the Children (Scotland) Act 1995 (c. 36), Sched. 4, para. 15(13), *infra*.

[1] PART III

CHILDREN IN NEED OF COMPULSORY MEASURES OF CARE

NOTE

[1] Extended by the Criminal Procedure (Scotland) Act 1975 (c. 21), s. 168; applied by *ibid.*, ss. 296(3) and 364. See the Education (Scotland) Act 1980 (c. 44), s. 44, the Child Abduction and Custody Act 1985 (c. 60), s. 20(5) and Sched. 3, para. 5(v), the Family Law Act 1986 (c. 55), s. 1(1)(*b*)(vi) and the Legal Aid (Scotland) Act 1986 (c. 47), s. 29. Prospectively repealed by the Children (Scotland) Act 1995 (c. 36), Sched. 4, para. 15(14), *infra*, with saving for s. 31(1) and (3).

[THE NEXT PAGE IS K 71]

Definition of child and parent for Part III

[1] **30.**—[2] (1) Except where otherwise expressly provided, a child for the purposes of this Part of this Act means—

(*a*) a child who has not attained the age of 16 years;

(*b*) a child over the age of 16 years who has not attained the age of 18 years and in respect of whom a supervision requirement of a children's hearing is in force under this Part of this Act;

(*c*) a child whose case has been referred to a children's hearing in pursuance of Part V of this Act;

and for the purposes of the application of this Part of this Act to a person who has failed to attend school regularly without reasonable excuse includes a person who is over the age of 16 years but who is not over school age.

(2) For the said purposes the expression "parent" includes a guardian.

[3] (3) Where a child attains the age of 16 years after the date on which a children's hearing first sit to consider his case, but before the date of the conclusion of the proceedings on his case, the provisions of this Part of this Act and of any statutory instrument made thereunder shall continue to apply to him in relation to that case as if he had not attained that age.

NOTES

[1] Extended by the Criminal Procedure (Scotland) Act 1975, ss.171(2), 368(2), 462(1).

[2] As amended by the Education (Scotland) Act 1969, Sched. 2, Pt. II, para. 5.

[3] Added by the Social Work (Scotland) Act 1972, s.1.

Restriction on prosecution of children for offences

[1] **31.**—[2] (1) No child under the age of 16 years shall be prosecuted for any offence except on the instructions of the Lord Advocate, or at his instance; and no court, other than the High Court of Justiciary and the sheriff court, shall have jurisdiction over a child under the age of 16 years for an offence.

(2) [Repealed by the Health and Social Services and Social Security Adjudications Act 1983, Sched. 10, Pt. I.]

(3) Part IV of the Children and Young Persons (Scotland) Act 1937 shall have effect subject to the amendments set out in Schedule 2 to this Act.

NOTES

[1] For procedure in proceedings in a court against a child, see S.I. 1971 No. 446, Div. E.

[2] As amended by the Health and Social Services and Social Security Adjudications Act 1983, Sched. 2, para. 7.

Children in need of compulsory measures of care

32.—(1) A child may be in need of compulsory measures of care within the meaning of this Part of this Act if any of the conditions mentioned in the next following subsection is satisfied with respect to him.

(2) The conditions referred to in subsection (1) of this section are that—

(*a*) he is beyond the control of his parent; or

[1] (*b*) he is falling into bad associations or is exposed to moral danger; or

[1] (*c*) lack of parental care is likely to cause him unnecessary suffering or seriously to impair his health or development; or

[2] (*d*) any of the offences mentioned in Schedule 1 to the Criminal Procedure (Scotland) Act 1975 has been committed in respect of him or in respect of a child who is a member of the same household; or

[3] (*dd*) the child is, or is likely to become, a member of the same household as a person who has committed any of the offences mentioned in Schedule 1 to the Criminal Procedure (Scotland) Act 1975; or

(*e*) the child, being a female, is a member of the same household as a female in respect of whom an offence which constitutes the crime of incest has been committed by a member of that household; or

(*f*) he has failed to attend school regularly without reasonable excuse; or

(*g*) he has committed an offence; or

[4] (*gg*) he has misused a volatile substance by deliberately inhaling, other than for medicinal purposes, that substance's vapour; or

(*h*) he is a child whose case has been referred to a children's hearing in pursuance of Part V of this Act;

[5] (*i*) he is in the care of a local authority and his behaviour is such that special measures are needed for his adequate care and control.

(3) For the purposes of this Part of this Act "care" includes protection, control, guidance and treatment.

NOTES

[1] Substituted by the Children Act 1975, Sched. 3, para. 54.

[2] As amended by the Children Act 1975, Sched. 3, para. 54.

[3] Added by the Children Act 1975, Sched. 3, para. 54.

[4] Inserted by the Solvent Abuse (Scotland) Act 1983, s.1.

[5] Added by the Health and Social Services and Social Security Adjudications Act 1983, s.8(1).

Formation of children's panels

33.—(1) A panel (to be called "the children's panel") shall be formed for every local authority area for the purposes of this Part of this Act.

(2) Schedule 3 to this Act shall have effect with respect to the number, qualifications, appointment and tenure of office of members of a children's panel.

(3) A local authority shall cause to be published a list of the names and addresses of members of the children's panel for their area, and that list shall be open for public inspection at all reasonable times at the offices of the director of social work of the local authority, and at any place where an electors list for the locality is exhibited.

Children's hearings

34.—[1] (1) Sittings of members of the children's panel, hereinafter referred to as children's hearings, shall be constituted from the panel in accordance with the provisions of this section to perform, in respect of children who may require compulsory measures of care, the functions assigned to those hearings by this Part of this Act.

(2) A children's hearing shall consist of a chairman and two other members and shall have both a man and a woman among the members.

(3) It shall be the duty of a local authority to provide suitable accommodation and facilities dissociated from criminal courts and police stations for children's hearings for their area, and such accommodation and facilities may be provided in the area of another local authority.

NOTE

[1] Applied: see the Criminal Procedure (Scotland) Act 1975, s.462(1).

Safeguarding of interests of children before children's hearings etc.

[1] **34A.**—(1) In any proceedings—

(*a*) before a children's hearing;

(*b*) before the sheriff on an application under section 42(2)(*c*) of this Act;

(*c*) before the sheriff on an appeal under section 49 or 51 of this Act,

the chairman (in the case of proceedings referred to in paragraph (*a*) above) or the sheriff (in any other case)—

(i) shall consider whether it is necessary for the purpose of safe-guarding the interests of the child in the proceedings, because there is or may be a conflict, on any matter relevant to the proceedings, between the interests of the child and those of his parent, to appoint a person to act for that purpose; and

(ii) without prejudice to any existing power to appoint a person to represent the interests of the child, may, if he thinks fit, appoint a person to act for the purpose specified in paragraph (i) above.

(2) The power to make rules under—

(*a*) section 35(4) of this Act,

(*b*) section 32 of the Sheriff Courts (Scotland) Act 1971,

shall include power to make rules providing for—

(i) the procedure in relation to the disposal of matters arising under this section;

(ii) appointment under subsection (1) of this section, the functions of a person so appointed and any right of such person to information relating to the proceedings in question.

(3) The expenses of a person appointed under subsection (1) of this section shall—

(*a*) in so far as reasonably incurred by him in safeguarding the interests of the child in the proceedings, and

(*b*) except in so far as otherwise defrayed in terms of regulations made under section 103(2) of the Children Act 1975,

be borne by the local authority for whose area the children's panel from which the relevant children's hearing has been constituted is formed.

(4) For the purposes of subsection (3) of this section, "relevant children's hearing" means—

(*a*) in the case of proceedings referred to in subsection (1)(*a*) of this section, the children's hearing;

(*b*) in the case of proceedings referred to in subsection (1)(*b*) of this section, the children's hearing who have directed the application;

(*c*) in the case of proceedings referred to in subsection (1)(*c*) of this section, the children's hearing whose decision is being appealed against.

NOTE

[1] Inserted with effect from 30th June 1985 by the Children Act 1975, s.66. By S.I. 1984 No. 1702, Sched. 2, para. 2:

"Where relevant proceedings before a children's hearing or the sheriff as the case may be have commenced before [30th June 1985] but the children's hearing have not disposed of the case, or the sheriff determined the application, by [that] date, they shall not dispose of the case or determine the application until they have considered whether it is necessary to appoint a person to safeguard the interests of the child in accordance with section 18A or 34A of the 1968 Act respectively."

Provisions as to time, place, privacy and notification of children's hearings

35.—(1) Any children's hearing shall be conducted in private, and, subject to the provisions of any rules made under this section, no person other than a person whose presence is necessary for the proper consideration of the case which is being heard, or whose presence is permitted by the chairman, shall be present.

(2) The chairman shall take all reasonable steps to ensure that the number of persons present at a children's hearing at any one time is kept to a minimum.

(3) Nothing in the foregoing provisions of this section, or in any rules made thereunder, shall operate to prevent a member of the Council on Tribunals, or of the Scottish Committee of that Council, attending any children's hearing, or shall authorise the exclusion of bona fide representatives of a newspaper or news agency.

[THE NEXT PAGE IS K 73]

[0] (4) The Secretary of State may make rules for the constituting and arranging of children's hearings and for regulating the procedure of those hearings.

[0] (5) Without prejudice to the generality of the last foregoing subsection, rules under that subsection may make provision with respect to—

[1] (*a*) notification of the time and place of a children's hearing to the child and his parent and to such other persons as may be prescribed;

(*b*) the statement of the grounds for the referral of the case to a children's hearing and the rights of the child and his parent to dispute the said grounds;

(*c*) the right to appeal to the sheriff against a decision of a children's hearing and the notification of the procedure before him;

(*d*) the right of the child and his parent to be represented at the children's hearing;

(*e*) the entitlement of the child and his parent to the refund of such expenses as may be prescribed in connection with the children's hearing and any proceedings arising therefrom;

(*f*) persons whose presence shall be permitted at a children's hearing;

(*g*) the continuation of a children's hearing for further investigation of a case before that hearing and the number and duration of such continuations.

NOTES

[0] See S.I. 1986 No. 2291, *infra*.

[1] As amended by the Children Act 1975, Sched. 3, para. 55.

The reporter and deputies

[1] **36.**—[2] (1) For the purpose of arranging children's hearings and for the performance of such other functions in relation to the children's panel or to children's hearings as may be assigned to him by this Part of this Act, a local authority shall appoint an officer, whole-time or part-time, to be known as the reporter, and such other officers as deputies of the reporter as may be required.

[3] (2) The qualifications of a reporter shall be such as the Secretary of State may prescribe.

(3) [Repealed by the Local Government (Scotland) Act 1973, Sched. 27, Pt. II, para. 185 and Sched. 29.]

(4) A reporter may not be removed from office by a local authority or be required to resign except with the consent of the Secretary of State.

(5) A reporter of a local authority shall not, except with the consent of the Secretary of State, be employed by that or any other local authority in any capacity other than that of a reporter.

(6) A local authority shall secure the provision of adequate staff for assisting the reporter in the performance of his functions.

(7) [Repealed by the Local Government (Scotland) Act 1973, Sched. 27, Pt. II, para. 185 and Sched. 29.]

[4] (8) The Secretary of State may make rules in relation to the duties of the reporter.

NOTES

[1] Saved by the Local Government (Scotland) Act 1973, s.64(5).

[2] As amended by the Local Government (Scotland) Act 1973, Sched. 27, Pt. II, para. 185 and Sched. 29.

[3] As substituted by the Local Government (Scotland) Act 1973, Sched. 27, Pt. II, para. 185(*b*).

[4] See S.I. 1986 No. 2291, *infra*.

Power of reporters to conduct proceedings before a sheriff

[1] **36A.** The Secretary of State and the Lord Advocate may, by regulations—

(*a*) empower officers or any officer or class of officers appointed under section 36 of this Act, whether or not they are advocates or solicitors, to conduct before a sheriff—

(i) any proceedings which, under this Act are heard by the sheriff in chambers;
(ii) any application under section 37 or 40 of this Act in relation to a warrant;

(*b*) prescribe such requirements as they think fit as to qualifications, training or experience necessary for any officer to be so empowered.

NOTE
[1] Added by the Children Act 1975, s.82.

Reports of cases of children who may require compulsory measures of care and the interim detention of such children in places of safety

37.—(1) Where any person has reasonable cause to believe that a child may be in need of compulsory measures of care he may give to the reporter such information about the child as he may have been able to discover.

[1] (1A) Where a local authority receive information suggesting that a child may be in need of compulsory measures of care, they shall—

(*a*) cause enquiries to be made into the case unless they are satisfied that such enquiries are unnecessary; and
(*b*) if it appears to them that the child may be in need of compulsory measures of care, give to the reporter such information about the child as they may have been able to discover.

[2] (2) A constable or any person authorised by any court or by any justice of the peace may take to a place of safety any child—

(*a*) in respect of whom any of the offences mentioned in Schedule 1 to the Criminal Procedure (Scotland) Act 1975 has been or is believed to have been committed; or
(*b*) who is a member of the same household as a child in respect of whom such an offence has been or is believed to have been committed; or
(*c*) who is, or is likely to become, a member of the same household as a person who has committed or is believed to have committed such an offence; or
(*d*) in respect of whom an offence under section 21(1) of the Children and Young Persons (Scotland) Act 1937 has been or is believed to have been committed; or
(*e*) who is likely to be caused unnecessary suffering or serious impairment of health because there is, or is believed to be, in respect of the child a lack of parental care,

and any child so taken to a place of safety or any child who has taken refuge in a place of safety may be detained there until arrangements can be made for him to be brought before a children's hearing under the following provisions of this Part of this Act; and, where a child is so detained, the constable or the person authorised as aforesaid or the occupier of the place of safety shall forthwith inform the reporter of the case.

(3) A child shall not continue to be detained under the last foregoing subsection—

(*a*) where the reporter considers the child does not require compulsory measures of care, or
(*b*) after the day on which a children's hearing first sit to consider his case in pursuance of the next following subsection, or
(*c*) for a period exceeding seven days.

[3] (4) Where a child has been detained in a place of safety under subsection (2) of this section or under section 14(1), 296(3) or 323(1) of the said Act of 1975, and the reporter considers that the child may be in need of compulsory measures of care, he shall, wherever practicable, arrange a children's hearing to sit not later than in the course of the first lawful day after the commencement of the child's detention to consider the case under this Part of this Act, and, if that hearing are unable to dispose of the case and are satisfied that his further detention is necessary in his own interest, or

have reason to believe that he will run away during the investigation of his case, they may issue a warrant requiring the child to be detained in any place of safety for such a period not exceeding 21 days as may be necessary.

[4] (5) On cause shown a warrant authorising detention under the last foregoing subsection may be renewed by a children's hearing, on one occasion only, for the period mentioned in that subsection on the application of the reporter.

[1] (5A) Where a warrant has been renewed under subsection (5) of this section but it appears to the reporter—

(*a*) that the children's hearing will not be able to dispose of the child's case before the expiry of the period of detention required by the warrant as renewed; and

(*b*) that further detention of the child is necessary in the child's own interest,

the reporter may apply to the sheriff for a warrant requiring the child to be detained in a place of safety for such a period not exceeding 21 days as may be necessary and the sheriff may issue such a warrant if he is satisfied that such detention is necessary in the child's own interest.

[1] (5B) On cause shown a warrant authorising detention under subsection (5A) of this section may be renewed by the sheriff on one occasion only, for the period mentioned in that subsection on the application of the reporter.

(6) In this section any reference to a justice of the peace includes a reference to a sheriff and to a magistrate.

NOTES

[1] Added by the Children Act 1975, s.83.

[2] Substituted by the Children Act 1975, s.83.

[3] As amended by the Criminal Procedure (Scotland) Act 1975, Sched. 9, para. 42. Applied: see the Criminal Procedure (Scotland) Act 1975, s.296(4).

[4] As amended by the Children Act 1975, s.83.

Initial investigation of cases by reporter

38.—(1) Where a reporter receives information from any source of a case which may require a children's hearing to be arranged he shall, after making such initial investigation as he may think necessary, proceed with the case in accordance with the provisions of the next following section.

(2) Paragraph (*b*) of section 17(1) of the Police (Scotland) Act 1967 shall, in relation to a child to whom this Part of this Act applies, have effect as if that paragraph imposed a requirement on constables of a police force to make the reports required thereby to the appropriate reporter in addition to the appropriate prosecutor.

Action on initial investigation by reporter

39.—(1) Where the reporter decides that no further action on the case is required, he shall, where he considers this to be the proper course, so inform the child and his parent and the person who brought the case to his notice, or any of those persons.

(2) Where the reporter considers it to be the proper course, he shall refer the case to the local authority with a view to their making arrangements for the advice, guidance and assistance of the child and his family in accordance with Part II of this Act.

(3) Where it appears to the reporter that the child is in need of compulsory measures of care, he shall arrange a children's hearing to whom the case shall stand referred for consideration and determination.

(4) Where the reporter has arranged a children's hearing in pursuance of the last foregoing subsection, he shall request from the local authority a report on the child and his social background and it shall be the duty of the

authority to supply the report which may contain information from any such person as the reporter or the local authority may think fit.

(5) Where the reporter has decided that no further action on the case is required, or has taken action in pursuance of subsection (2) of this section, he shall not thereafter take action under subsection (3) of this section in relation to the same facts.

Attendance of child at children's hearing

40.—(1) Where a child has been notified by virtue of section 35 of this Act that his case has been referred to a children's hearing, he shall be under an obligation to attend that hearing in accordance with the notification.

[0] (2) Without prejudice to the provisions of section 42(1) of this Act, where a children's hearing are satisfied in a case concerned with an offence mentioned in Schedule 1 to the Criminal Procedure (Scotland) Act 1975 that the attendance of a child is not necessary for the just hearing of that case, or in any case where they are satisfied that it would be detrimental to the interest of the child to be present at the hearing of his case, the case, in whole or in part, may be considered in the absence of the child.

(3) The reporter shall be responsible for securing the attendance of a child at the hearing of his case before a children's hearing and at any subsequent hearing to which the case is continued.

(4) For the purpose of the last foregoing subsection, or where a child fails to attend at any hearing of his case, a children's hearing may, at the instance of the reporter on cause shown, or, as the case may be, of their own motion, issue a warrant for the apprehension of the child if satisfied of the necessity for such a course, and any warrant so issued shall be authority for bringing him before a children's hearing and for his detention in a place of safety.

(5) A child shall not continue to be detained under the last foregoing subsection—

(*a*) after the day on which a children's hearing first sit to consider his case in pursuance of the next following subsection, or

(*b*) for a period exceeding seven days.

(6) Where a child is apprehended in pursuance of subsection (4) of this section, and he cannot immediately be brought before a children's hearing, the reporter shall, wherever practicable, arrange a children's hearing to sit not later than in the course of the first lawful day after the apprehension of the child.

[1] (7) Where a children's hearing before whom a child is brought are unable to dispose of his case and—

(*a*) have reason to believe that the child may not attend at any hearing of his case, or at any proceedings arising from the case or may fail to comply with a requirement under section 43(4) of this Act; or

(*b*) are satisfied that detention of the child is necessary in his own interest,

they may issue a warrant requiring the child to be detained in a place of safety for such a period not exceeding 21 days as may be necessary.

[1] (8) On cause shown a warrant authorising detention under subsection (7) of this section may be renewed by a children's hearing on one occasion only, for the period mentioned in that subsection, on the application of the reporter.

[2] (8A) Where a warrant has been renewed under subsection (8) of this section but it appears to the reporter—

(*a*) that the children's hearing will not be able to dispose of the child's case before the expiry of the period of detention required by the warrant as renewed; and

(*b*) that further detention of the child is necessary in the child's own interest, the reporter may apply to the sheriff for a warrant requiring the child to be detained in a place of safety for such a period not exceeding 21 days as may be necessary, and the sheriff may issue such a warrant if he is satisfied that such detention is necessary in the child's own interest.

[2] (8B) On cause shown, a warrant authorising detention under subsection (8A) of this section may be renewed by the sheriff on one occasion only, for the period mentioned in that subsection, on the application of the reporter.

(9) A warrant of apprehension issued under this Part of this Act may be executed in like manner as a warrant of apprehension of an accused person issued by a court of summary jurisdiction and any enactment relating to the execution of a warrant of apprehension issued by a court of summary jurisdiction shall, with any necessary modifications, apply in relation to the execution of a warrant of apprehension issued under this Part of this Act as it applies to a warrant of apprehension issued by a court of summary jurisdiction.

NOTES

[0] As amended by the Criminal Procedure (Scotland) Act 1975, s. 460 (1)(*b*).

[1] Substituted by the Children Act 1975, s. 84 (*a*) and (*b*).

[2] Added by the Children Act 1975, s. 84(*c*).

Attendance of parent at children's hearing

41.—(1) A parent of a child shall have a right to attend at all stages of a children's hearing who are considering the case of his child.

(2) When a child's case is being considered by a children's hearing his parent shall attend at all stages of the hearing unless the children's hearing are satisfied that it would be unreasonable to require his attendance or that his attendance would be unnecessary to the consideration of the case.

[1] (3) Any person who fails to comply with the provisions of the foregoing subsection shall be guilty of an offence and shall on summary conviction be liable to a fine not exceeding level 3 on the standard scale.

NOTE

[1] As amended by virtue of the Criminal Procedure (Scotland) Act 1975, ss. 289F and 289G.

Conduct of children's hearing and application to sheriff for findings

[1] **42.**—(1) Subject to the provisions of subsections (7) and (8) of this section, at the commencement of a children's hearing and before proceeding to the consideration of the case, it shall be the duty of the chairman to explain to the child and his parent the grounds stated by the reporter for the referral of the case for the purpose of ascertaining whether these grounds are accepted in whole or in part by the child and his parent.

(2) Thereafter—

(*a*) where the child and his parent accept the grounds stated by the reporter for the referral the hearing shall proceed;

(*b*) where the child and his parent accept those grounds in part and the children's hearing consider it proper so to do the hearing may proceed in respect of the grounds so accepted; and

(*c*) in any other case, unless they decide to discharge the referral, the children's hearing shall direct the reporter to make application to the sheriff for a finding as to whether such grounds for the referral, as are not accepted by the child or his parent, are established having regard to the provisions of section 32 of this Act.

[2] (2A) Where the ground for referral is that the child is in need of compulsory measures of care because he has committed an offence, the sheriff to whom an application under subsection (2)(*c*) above shall be made shall be the sheriff who would have jurisdiction if the child were being prosecuted for that offence.

[3] (3) It shall be the duty of the chairman of a children's hearing who have made a direction under the last foregoing subsection to explain to

the child and his parent the purpose for which the application to the sheriff is being made, and to inform the child that he is under an obligation to attend the hearing of the application, and where a child fails to attend at the hearing of the application the sheriff may issue a warrant for the apprehension of the child; and any warrant so issued shall be authority for bringing him before the sheriff and for his detention in a place of safety until the sheriff can hear the application, but a child shall not be detained under this subsection after whichever is the earlier of the following—

(*a*) the expiry of 14 days beginning with the day on which he was first detained;

(*b*) the disposal of the application by the sheriff.

(4) An application under subsection (2) of this section shall be heard by the sheriff in chambers within 28 days of the lodging of the application and, without prejudice to their right to legal representation, a child or his parent may be represented at any diet fixed by the sheriff for the hearing of the application.

(5) Where a sheriff decides that none of the grounds in respect of which the application has been made has been established for the referral of a case to a children's hearing, he shall dismiss the application and discharge the referral in respect of those grounds.

[3] (6) Subject to subsection (6A) of this section, where the sheriff is satisfied on the evidence before him that any of the grounds in respect of which the application has been made has been established.

(*a*) he shall remit the case to the reporter to make arrangements for a children's hearing for consideration and determination of the case, and;

(*b*) if he is satisfied that detention of the child is necessary in his own interest or has reason to believe that the child will run away before the children's hearing sit to consider the case, he may issue a warrant requiring the detention of the child until the children's hearing sit to consider the case, but a child shall not be detained under this subsection after whichever is the earlier of the following—

(i) the expiry of three days beginning with the day on which he was first detained;

(ii) the consideration of his case by the children's hearing,

and where a ground for the referral of the case is the condition referred to in section 32(2)(*g*) of this Act, the sheriff in hearing the application shall apply to the evidence relating to that ground the standard of proof required in criminal procedure.

(6A) Notwithstanding the provisions of subsection (2)(*c*) of this section, where, in the course of the proceedings before the sheriff, the child and his parent accept any of the grounds in respect of which the application has been made, the sheriff may dispense with the hearing of evidence relating to that ground unless he is satisfied that in all the circumstances such evidence should be heard, and deem that ground to have been established for the purposes of this section.

(7) Where a children's hearing are satisfied that the child for any reason is not capable of understanding the explanation of the grounds of referral required by subsection (1) of this section, or in the course of, or at the conclusion of that explanation, it appears not to be understood by the child, the hearing shall, unless they decide to discharge the referral, direct the reporter to make application to the sheriff for a finding as to whether any of the grounds for the referral have been established, and the provisions of this section relating to an application to the sheriff under subsection (2)(*c*) thereof shall apply as they apply to an application under that subsection except that where any of the grounds for the referral are accepted by the child's parent, whether or not accepted by the child, then, notwithstanding subsection (6A) of this section, the sheriff may dispense with the hearing of

evidence relating to that ground if he is satisfied that in all the circumstances it would be reasonable to do so.

(8) The acceptance by a parent of the grounds of referral shall not be a requirement to proceeding with a case under this section where the parent is not present.

NOTES

[1] Extended by the Rehabilitation of Offenders Act 1974, s. 3. As amended by the Health and Social Services and Social Security Adjudications Act 1983, Sched. 2, para. 8. See the Civil Evidence (Scotland) Act 1988, s. 9.

[2] Added by the Criminal Justice (Scotland) Act 1980, Sched. 7, para. 21.

[3] As amended by the Law Reform (Miscellaneous Provisions) (Scotland) Act 1985, s. 25.

Discharge of referral and power of children's hearing to order further investigation after consideration of the facts

43.—(1) When a children's hearing have considered the grounds for the referral of a case, accepted or established under the last foregoing section, the report obtained under section 39(4) of this Act and such other relevant information as may be available to them, they shall proceed in accordance with the subsequent provisions of this section to consider on what course they should decide in the best interests of the child.

(2) Where a children's hearing decide that no further action is required they shall discharge the referral.

(3) Where a children's hearing consider that further investigation in relation to a child and his history is necessary to complete their consideration of his case they may continue the case to a subsequent hearing.

(4) For the purpose of such an investigation as aforesaid, a children's hearing may require a child to attend or reside at any clinic, hospital or establishment during a period not exceeding 21 days.

[THE NEXT PAGE IS K 79]

(5) Where a child fails to fulfil a requirement made in pursuance of the last foregoing subsection it shall be the duty of the reporter to arrange a children's hearing to consider the issue of a warrant for his detention under section 40 of this Act.

Disposal of case by children's hearing other than by discharge of referral

[0] **44.**—[1] (1) Subject to the provisions of this Part of this Act a children's hearing, where, after the consideration of his case, they decide that a child is in need of compulsory measures of care, may make a requirement, in this Act referred to as a supervision requirement, requiring him—

(*a*) to submit to supervision in accordance with such conditions as they may impose; or

(*b*) to reside in a residential establishment named in the requirement and be subject to such conditions as they may impose;

and a condition imposed by virtue of head (*a*) of this subsection may be a condition as to the place where the child is to reside, being a place other than a residential establishment, and the place may be a place in England or Wales where arrangements have been made in that behalf.

[2] (1A) A supervision requirement imposing a condition as to the place where a child is to reside in England or Wales shall be a like authority as in Scotland for the person in charge of the place to restrict the child's liberty to such an extent as that person may consider appropriate having regard to the terms of the supervision requirement.

(2) In making a supervision requirement requiring a child to reside in a residential establishment a children's hearing shall have regard to the religious persuasion of the child.

(3) Without prejudice to the provisions of this Part of this Act relating to the review of supervision requirements, a children's hearing may, where they are satisfied that such a course is proper, postpone the operation of a supervision requirement, but otherwise a supervision requirement shall have effect as from the date it is made.

(4) Where it appears to a children's hearing that the functions of the education authority under section 63 of the Education (Scotland) Act 1962 (ascertainment of children suffering from disability) may require to be exercised, they shall, in addition to any other course which they may take under this section, send a report to that effect to the education authority concerned.

[3] (5) It shall be the duty of the local authority to give effect to a supervision requirement made by a children's hearing for their area, and a child who is subject to such a supervision requirement shall, for the purposes of sections 16 to 18, 20, 20A, 24 to 26, 28 and 29 of this Act and section 18 of the Adoption (Scotland) Act 1978 (which, amongst other things, provides that an application by an adoption agency to dispense with parental agreement to the freeing of a child for adoption is competent only where the child is in the care of the agency), be in their care:

Provided that where the performance of a function under any of the said sections in relation to the child requires, or would be facilitated by, the variation or discharge of the supervision requirement, the local authority shall recommend a review of the requirement under this Part of this Act.

(6) In any case of urgent necessity in the interests of the child, or of the other children in a place, a director of social work may direct that a child who is required to reside in that place under this section be transferred to another place.

(7) Any child transferred under the last foregoing subsection shall have his case reviewed by a children's hearing within seven days of his transfer, in accordance with the following provisions of this Act.

(8) A supervision requirement shall be in such form as the Secretary of State may prescribe.[4]

NOTES
[0] Excluded by the Adoption (Scotland) Act 1978, s.65(3), as amended (*infra*).
[1] Applied: see the Criminal Procedure (Scotland) Act 1975, s.462(1). See the Child Abduction and Custody Act 1985, Sched. 3, para. 6.
[2] Added by the Children and Young Persons Act 1969, Sched. 5.
[3] As amended by the Law Reform (Miscellaneous Provisions) (Scotland) Act 1985, s.28. Amended by the Children Act 1975, Sched. 3, para. 56.
[4] See S.I. 1986 No. 2291, *infra*.

Rules as respects transmission of information and conveyance of children to residential establishments etc.

45. The Secretary of State may make rules providing for the transmission of information regarding children who are the subject of supervision requirements to the persons who are to be in charge of them, for the temporary accommodation, where necessary, of such children, and for the conveyance of such children to residential establishments and to other places where they may be required to reside.

Children to whom Part IV of the Mental Health (Scotland) Act 1960 may apply

[1] **46.**—(1) Where a children's hearing are of the opinion, after considering the case of any child, that an application for admission to hospital or a guardianship application under Part V of the Mental Health (Scotland) Act 1984 should be made to the sheriff in respect of the child, they shall make a report to that effect to the mental health officer concerned.

(2) Nothing in the provisions of the foregoing subsection shall affect the saving for arrangements for the voluntary treatment of mental disorder contained in section 17(2) of the said Act of 1984.

NOTE
[1] As amended by the Mental Health (Scotland) Act 1984, Sched. 3, para. 16.

Duration of supervision requirements and their variation

[1] **47.**—(1) No child shall continue to be subject to a supervision requirement for any time longer than is necessary in his interest; and where they consider that such a requirement in respect of a child should cease to have effect or should be varied, the local authority shall refer his case to their reporter for review of that requirement by a children's hearing and, if the hearing think proper, they may terminate the requirement, or continue or vary the requirement, and in the last event they may make any such supervision requirement as may be made under section 44 of this Act.

(2) A supervision requirement shall cease to have effect in respect of a child when he attains the age of 18 years and accordingly, within a period of three months ending on the day on which such a requirement will cease to have effect under this subsection, the local authority concerned shall refer the case to the reporter so that a children's hearing may advise whether the child still requires supervision or guidance, and in the event of the hearing so advising, the local authority shall provide such supervision or guidance as he is prepared to accept.

(3) Unless the context otherwise requires, any reference in this section and in the following provisions of this Act to a supervision requirement shall be construed as a reference to a supervision requirement which is for the time being in force in respect of a child.

NOTE
[1] See the Child Abduction and Custody Act 1985, Sched. 3, para. 6.

Review of requirement of children's hearing

[1] **48.**—(1) A supervision requirement shall be subject to review by a

children's hearing in accordance with the following provisions of this section.

(2) A supervision requirement shall be reviewed by a children's hearing where a local authority so recommends.

(3) No supervision requirement shall remain in force without review for a period extending beyond one year, and where a supervision requirement is not reviewed within the period of one year from the making or continuing of the requirement it shall cease to have effect at the expiration of that period.

(4) At any time after the expiration of any of the following periods, that is to say—

(*a*) a period of three months from the date of the making of a supervision requirement; or

(*b*) a period of three months from the date of a review of a supervision requirement where such a review varies a previous requirement; or

(*c*) a period of six months from the date of a review of a supervision requirement which is continued by that review,

a child or his parent may require a review of the requirement.

[1] (4A) If a supervision requirement has not been reviewed under this section during the period of nine months following the date when it was made or last reviewed (whichever is the later), the reporter may arrange for it to be reviewed.

(5) It shall be the duty of the reporter to ensure that any review required by this section is duly made and to make any necessary arrangements arising therefrom.

(6) Section 44 of this Act shall apply in relation to the disposal of a case by a children's hearing under this section as it applies to the disposal of a case under that section.

NOTE

[1] As amended by the Law Reform (Miscellaneous Provisions) (Scotland) Act 1985, s.29. See the Child Abduction and Custody Act 1985, Sched. 3, para. 6 .

Appeal against decision of a children's hearing

49.—(1) A child or his parent or both may, within a period of three weeks beginning with the date of any decision of a children's hearing, appeal to the sheriff in chambers against that decision, and the child or his parent or both shall be heard by the sheriff as to the reasons for the appeal.

(2) In any such appeal it shall be the duty of the reporter to ensure that all reports and statements available to the hearing along with the reports of their proceedings and the reasons for their decision are lodged with the sheriff clerk.

[1] (3) The reporter, whether or not he is conducting the proceedings, may be examined by the sheriff; and the sheriff may examine the reporter and the authors or compilers of any reports or statements, and may call for any further report which he considers may assist him in deciding the appeal.

(4) Where the sheriff decides that an appeal under this section has failed, he shall confirm the decision of the children's hearing.

(5) Where the sheriff is satisfied that the decision of the children's hearing is not justified in all the circumstances of the case he shall allow the appeal, and—

(*a*) where the appeal is against the issue of a warrant for detention he shall recall the warrant, and

(*b*) in any other case, he may, as he thinks fit, remit the case with the reasons for his decision to the children's hearing for reconsideration of their decision or discharge the child from any further hearing or other proceedings in relation to the grounds for the referral of the case.

(6) Where the sheriff is satisfied that an appeal under this section against the decision of a children's hearing at a review is frivolous, he may order that no appeal against a decision to continue the supervision requirement, which was the subject of that appeal, made on a subsequent review shall lie until the expiration of a period of twelve months beginning with the date of the order.

(7) An appeal under this section in respect of the issue of a warrant by a children's hearing shall be disposed of within three days of the lodging of the appeal, and failing such disposal the warrant shall forthwith cease to have effect.

(8) Where a child or his parent appeals under this section against a decision of a children's hearing in relation to a supervision requirement, the child or his parent may make application to a children's hearing for the suspension of the requirement appealed against, and it shall be the duty of the reporter forthwith to arrange a children's hearing to consider the application, and thereafter the hearing may grant or refuse the application.

NOTE

[1] As amended by the Children Act 1975, Sched. 3, para. 57.

Appeal to Court of Session

50.—(1) Subject to the provisions of this section, an appeal shall lie to the Court of Session, by way of stated case on a point of law or in respect of any irregularity in the conduct of the case, at the instance of a child or his parent or both or of a reporter acting on behalf of a children's hearing, from any decision of the sheriff under this Part of this Act, and no other or further appeal shall be competent.

(2) An application to the sheriff to state a case for the purpose of the foregoing subsection shall be made within a period of twenty-eight days beginning with the date of his decision.

(3) On deciding the appeal the Court of Session shall remit the case to the sheriff for disposal in accordance with such directions as the Court may give.

(4) No appeal shall lie under this section in respect of a decision of a children's hearing imposing a supervision requirement where the sole ground of the objection to that requirement is that the treatment prescribed thereby is inappropriate for the child.

Reconsideration by hearing after appeal, and subsequent appeal

51.—(1) Where the sheriff, by virtue of either of the last two foregoing sections, has remitted a case to a children's hearing for reconsideration of their decision the reporter shall arrange a children's hearing for that purpose.

(2) A child or his parent may, within a period of seven days beginning with the date of the decision of a children's hearing on a case remitted as aforesaid, appeal against the decision, and the provisions of subsections (2) to (8) of section 49 of this Act shall apply to such an appeal as they apply to an appeal under subsection (1) of the said section.

Power of Secretary of State to terminate a supervision requirement

52. Where, having regard to all the circumstances of a case and the interests of a child, the Secretary of State is satisfied that a supervision requirement in force in respect of the child should be terminated, he may by order terminate the requirement.

53. [Repealed by the Legal Aid (Scotland) Act 1986, Sched. 5.]

Transfer of case to another children's hearing

54.—(1) Where a children's hearing are satisfied, in a case being heard before them, that the case could be better considered by a children's hearing for the area of another local authority they may at any time during the course of the hearing request the reporter to arrange with the reporter of the other local authority, should he so agree, for a children's hearing to dispose of the case.

(2) Where a case has been transferred in pursuance of the last foregoing subsection, the grounds of referral accepted or established for the case shall not require to be further accepted or established for the purpose of the children's hearing to which the case has been transferred.

Presumption and determination of age

55. Where a person is brought before a children's hearing they shall make inquiry as to his age, and, if it appears to the hearing that the person is a child, they shall proceed with the case, and no decision or requirement of the hearing shall be invalidated by any subsequent proof that the age of that person has not been correctly stated to the hearing, and the age presumed or declared by the hearing to be the age of the person so brought before them shall, for the purposes of this Part of this Act, be deemed to be the true age of that person, and, where it appears to the hearing that the person so brought before them has attained the age of sixteen years, that person shall, for the purposes of this Part of this Act, be deemed not to be a child except as the Act otherwise provides.

Reference and remit of children's cases by courts to children's hearings

56.—(1) to (4) [Repealed by the Criminal Procedure (Scotland) Act 1975, Sched. 10.]

[1] (5) Where a court has remitted a case of a child or person under section 173 or 372 or 373 of the Criminal Procedure (Scotland) Act 1975, a certificate signed by the clerk of the court stating that the child or person has pleaded guilty to, or has been found guilty of, the offence to which the remit relates shall be conclusive evidence for the purpose of the remit that that offence has been committed by the child or person.

(6) [Repealed by the Criminal Procedure (Scotland) Act 1975, Sched. 10.]

NOTE

[1] As amended by the Criminal Procedure (Scotland) Act 1975, Sched. 9, para. 43.

Reference and remit of cases of certain young persons by courts to children's hearings

57.—(1) [Repealed by the Criminal Procedure (Scotland) Act 1975, Sched. 10.]

[1] (2) Where a court has remitted a case under section 373 of the Criminal Procedure (Scotland) Act 1975 the provisions of this Part of this Act shall apply to that person as if he were a child.

NOTE

[1] As amended by the Criminal Procedure (Scotland) Act 1975, Sched. 9, para. 44.

Prohibition of publication of proceedings

58.—[0] (1) Subject to the provisions of this section, no report of any proceedings in any children's hearing, or of any proceedings before the sheriff under section 42 of this Act, or of any appeal under this Part of this Act, which is made in a newspaper or a sound or television programme included in a programme service (within the meaning of the Broadcasting Act 1990) shall—

(*a*) reveal the name, address or school; or

(*b*) include any particulars calculated to lead to the identification,

of any child in any way concerned in a hearing and no picture shall be published in any newspaper or television programme included in such a programme service as being or including a picture of a child concerned as aforesaid.

[1] (2) Any person guilty of any offence against this section shall on summary conviction be liable to a fine not exceeding £250 in respect of each offence.

(3) The Secretary of State may in any case, if satisfied that it is in the interests of justice to do so, by order dispense with the requirements of subsection (1) of this section to such extent as may be specified in the order.

(4) This section shall extend to England and Wales.

NOTES

[0] As amended by the Broadcasting Act 1990, Sched. 20, para. 12, with effect from 1st January 1991.

[1] As amended by virtue of the Criminal Procedure (Scotland) Act 1975, ss.289F and 289G, and by the Cable and Broadcasting Act 1984, Sched. 5, para. 20.

Residence in secure accommodation

[1] **58A.**—(1) A child who is made subject to a supervision requirement under this Act may not be placed or kept in secure accommodation, except under the provisions of this Act.

(2) In this Act, "secure accommodation" means accommodation provided in a residential establishment in accordance with regulations made under section 60(1) of this Act for the purpose of restricting the liberty of children.

(3) Where a children's hearing decide, in accordance with section 44 of this Act, that a child is in need of compulsory measures of care, and they are satisfied that either—

(*a*) he has a history of absconding, and—

(i) he is likely to abscond unless he is kept in secure accommodation; and

(ii) if he absconds, it is likely that his physical, mental or moral welfare will be at risk; or

(*b*) he is likely to injure himself or other persons unless he is kept in secure accommodation,

they may make it a condition of a supervision requirement under subsection (1)(*b*) of the said section 44 that the child shall be liable to be placed and kept in secure accommodation in the named residential establishment at such times as the person in charge of that establishment, with the agreement of the director of social work of the local authority required to give effect to the supervision requirement, considers it necessary that he do so.

(4) The Secretary of State shall have power by regulations to make provision with respect to the placing in secure accommodation of any child—

(*a*) who is subject to a supervision requirement imposed under section 44 of this Act but not subject to a condition imposed under subsection (3) of this section; or

(*b*) who is not subject to such a supervision requirement but who is being cared for by a local authority or voluntary organisation in pursuance of such enactments as may be specified in the regulations,

and such regulations shall specify the circumstances which require to pertain before a child may be so placed under regulations made under this subsection and may specify different circumstances for different cases or classes of case.

NOTE

[1] Inserted by the Health and Social Services and Social Security Adjudications Act 1983, s. 8(4). For regulations see S.I. 1983 No. 1912, as amended by S.I. 1988 No. 841.

Time limits on keeping without reference to children's hearing

[1] **58B.**—(1) The Secretary of State shall by regulations prescribe—

(*a*) the maximum period during which a child may be kept under this Act in secure accommodation without the authority of a children's hearing or of the sheriff;

(*b*) the period within which the case of a child placed under this Act in secure accommodation shall be referred to the reporter and different periods may be prescribed in respect of different cases or classes of case.

(2) The Secretary of State shall by regulations make provision to enable a child who has been placed in secure accommodation under section 58A(4) of this Act or his parent to require that the child's case be brought before a children's hearing within a shorter period than would otherwise apply under regulations made under subsection (1)(*a*) of this section.

[2] (3) Where, in any case, a children's hearing direct the reporter to make application to the sheriff for a finding under section 42(2)(*c*) of this Act (finding that grounds for referral are established), they shall have power, if they are satisfied with regard to the criteria specified in paragraph (*a*) or (*b*) of section 58A(3) of this Act, to order that, pending the determination of his case in accordance with section 42(5) or (6) of this Act, the child shall be liable to be placed and kept in secure accommodation in a named residential establishment at such times as the person in charge of that establishment with the agreement of the director of social work of the local authority for the area of the children's hearing, considers necessary.

NOTES

[1] Inserted by the Health and Social Services and Social Security Adjudications Act 1983, s. 8(4). For regulations see S.I. 1983 No. 1912, as amended by S.I. 1988 No. 841.

[2] As amended by the Law Reform (Miscellaneous Provisions) (Scotland) Act 1985, s. 26(*a*) and Sched. 2, para. 10.

Review of secure accommodation condition

[1] **58C.**—(1) A condition imposed under section 58A(3) of this Act, requiring a child to reside in secure accommodation, shall be subject to review by a children's hearing at such time as the local authority recommends and otherwise at such times and in accordance with such provisions as the Secretary of State shall by regulations prescribe.

(2) A condition to which this section applies shall be reviewed when the supervision requirement is being reviewed, and may be reviewed separately from that review.

(3) A condition to which this section applies shall cease to have effect at the expiry of the period of three months after it was made, unless it has been reviewed and the condition has been ordered to continue.

[2] (4) A condition which is continued on review shall cease to have effect at the expiry of the period of—

(*a*) three months after it is first reviewed;

(*b*) three months after the second or any subsequent review,

unless it has been reviewed and the condition has been ordered to continue.

(5) Sections 44 and 48(5) of this Act shall apply to the review of conditions made under section 58A(3) of this Act as they apply to the review of supervision requirements.

(6) The Secretary of State may from time to time make regulations to vary the periods specified in this section.

NOTES

[1] Inserted by the Health and Social Services and Social Security Adjudications Act 1983, s. 8(4). For regulations see S.I. 1983 No. 1912, as amended by S.I. 1988 No. 841.

[2] As amended by S.I. 1988 No. 841.

Sheriff's power to direct condition to cease to have effect

[1] **58D.** Where under section 49(5) of this Act (appeal against decision of children's hearing) the sheriff is satisfied in a case in which there is in force a condition under section 58A(3) of this Act that the decision of the children's hearing is not justified in all the circumstances of the case he shall direct that the condition shall cease to have effect.

NOTE

[1] Inserted by the Health and Social Services and Social Security Adjudications Act 1983, s. 8(4).

Warrants to detain in secure accommodation

[1] **58E.**—(1) Where the sheriff or a children's hearing issues a warrant under any of sections 37, 40 and 42 of this Act (detention in a place of safety), he or they may, if satisfied with regard to the criteria specified in paragraph (*a*) or (*b*) of section 58A(3) of this Act, order that the child shall be liable to be placed and kept in secure accommodation in a named residential establishment at such times as the person in charge of that establishment, with the agreement of the director of social work of the local authority, considers necessary. The local authority referred to in this subsection is, in the case of a warrant issued or renewed by the sheriff, the local authority for the area of the children's hearing which was dealing with the child in respect of whom the warrant was issued and, in the case of a warrant issued or renewed by a children's hearing, the local authority for the area of that children's hearing.

(2) For the purposes of this section, the Secretary of State may make regulations amending, varying or disapplying any of the criteria specified in the said paragraphs (*a*) and (*b*) of section 58A(3) of this Act except in relation to a warrant under section 37 of this Act.

NOTE

[1] Inserted by the Health and Social Services and Social Security Adjudications Act 1983, s. 8(4). As amended by the Law Reform (Miscellaneous Provisions) (Scotland) Act 1985, s. 26(*b*).

Procedures for placing in secure accommodation

[1] **58F.**—(1) The Secretary of State may by regulations make provision for the procedures to be applied in the placing of children in secure accommodation, and without prejudice to the foregoing generality may make provision for the referral of cases to a children's hearing for review.

(2) Regulations under this section may specify the duties of the reporter in relation to the placing of children in secure accommodation.

(3) Regulations under this section may make provision for the parent of a child being informed of the placing of the child in secure accommodation.

NOTE

[1] Inserted by the Health and Social Services and Social Security Adjudications Act 1983, s. 8(4). For regulations see S.I. 1983 No. 1912, as amended by S.I. 1988 No. 841.

Transitional provisions

[1] **58G.** Regulations made under sections 58A to 58F of this Act may include such transitional provisions as the Secretary of State may consider necessary, including provisions varying the application of any provision in those sections for a transitional period, either generally, or in relation to specified classes of cases.

NOTE

[1] Inserted by the Health and Social Services and Social Security Adjudications Act 1983, s. 8(4). For regulations see S.I. 1983 No. 1912, as amended by S.I. 1988 No. 841.

Part IV

Residential and other Establishments

Provision of residential and other establishments

Provision of residential and other establishments by local authorities, and maximum period for repayment of sums borrowed for such provision

59.—[1] (1) Subject to section 13A of this Act, it shall be the duty of a local authority to provide and maintain such residential and other establishments as may be required for their functions under this Act, or arrange for the provision of such establishments.

(2) For the purpose of discharging their duty under the foregoing subsection a local authority may—

(*a*) themselves provide such establishments as aforesaid; or

(*b*) join with another local authority in providing those establishments; or

(*c*) secure the provision of such establishments by voluntary organisations or other persons including other local authorities.

(3) The maximum period for the repayment of sums borrowed by a local authority for the purposes of this section shall be such period not exceeding 60 years as may be sanctioned by the Secretary of State; and accordingly in Schedule 6 to the Local Government (Scotland) Act 1947, at the end, there shall be added the following entry, that is to say—

Section 59 of the Social Work (Scotland) Act 1968	Such period not exceeding 60 years as may be sanctioned by the Secretary of State

NOTE

[1] As amended by the National Health Service and Community Care Act 1990 (c. 19), Sched. 9, para. 10. Prospectively amended by the Children (Scotland) Act 1995 (c. 36), Sched. 4, para. 15(15).

Grants in respect of secure accommodation for children

[1] **59A.**—[2] (1) The Secretary of State may make to a local authority grants of such amount and subject to such conditions as he may with the consent of the Treasury determine in respect of expenditure incurred by the authority in—

(*a*) providing;

(*b*) joining with another local authority in providing; or

(*c*) contributing by way of grant under section 10(3) of this Act to the provision by a voluntary organisation of,

secure accommodation.

(2) The conditions subject to which grants are made under subsection (1) of this section may include conditions for securing the repayment in whole or in part of such grants.

(3) [Repealed by the Health and Social Services and Social Security Adjudications Act 1983 (c. 41), s. 8(2) and Sched. 10, Pt. I.]

NOTES

[1] Inserted by the Children Act 1975 (c. 72), s. 72.

[2] As amended by the Health and Social Services and Social Security Adjudications Act 1983 (c. 41), Sched. 10, Pt. I.

Control of residential and other establishments

60.—[1] (1) The Secretary of State may make regulations as to the conduct of residential and other establishments and for securing the welfare of persons resident or accommodated in them, and, without prejudice to the generality of those regulations, they may provide—

(*a*) for the construction of, and the accommodation provided in, those establishments, and their equipment, maintenance and management;

(*b*) for the classification, treatment and control of persons resident therein or attending thereat;

(*bb*) for the granting of approval by the Secretary of State for the provision and use of accommodation in residential establishments as secure accommodation;

(*c*) for the inspection of those establishments and the visiting of persons from time to time by visitors appointed in accordance with the regulations;

(*d*) for notice to be given to the Secretary of State or the local authority with which the person carrying on any such establishment is registered under any enactment of any change of the person in charge of the establishment;

(*e*) for requirements, in the case of children, as to the facilities which are to be given for them to receive a religious upbringing appropriate to the persuasion to which they belong;

(*ee*) for prescribing the minimum age below which a child's liberty shall not be restricted in secure accommodation except with the Secretary of State's consent;

(*f*) for making available in any of those establishments any service authorised by the National Health Service (Scotland) Act 1978;

and may contain different provisions for different classes of establishments, different classes of accommodation in residential and other establishments and different categories of persons.

(2) In the foregoing subsection, the expression "treatment" includes training, education and occupation, but does not include medical treatment.

[2] (3) Where any regulation made in pursuance of this section provides that this subsection shall have effect in relation to the regulation, any person who contravenes or fails to comply with the regulation or any requirement or direction under it shall be liable on summary conviction to a fine not exceeding level 4 on the standard scale.

NOTES

[1] As amended by the National Health Service (Scotland) Act 1978 (c. 24), Sched. 16, para. 29(1), and the Health and Social Services and Social Security Adjudications Act 1983 (c. 41), s. 8(3). For regulations see S.I. 1983 No. 1912, as amended by S.I. 1988 No. 841.

[2] As amended by virtue of the Criminal Procedure (Scotland) Act 1975 (c. 21), ss. 289C and 289G and Sched. 7C.

Registration of certain residential and other establishments

Restriction on carrying on of establishments

61.—[1,2] (1) The following provisions of this Part of this Act apply to any residential or other establishment the whole or a substantial part of whose function is to provide persons with such personal care or support, whether or not combined with board, and whether for reward or not, as may be required for the purposes of this Act.

[1] (1A) For the purposes of subsection (1) above—

[3] "establishment" does not include

(*a*) any establishment controlled or managed by a Government department or by a local authority or, subject to sections 61A and 63B below, required to be registered, or in respect of which a person is required to be registered, with a Government department or a local authority under any other enactment; or

(*b*) any establishment providing residential accommodation with nursing falling within section 13A of this Act;

"personal care" includes the provision of appropriate help with physical and social needs; and

"support" means counselling or other help provided as part of a planned programme of care.

[4] (2) Subject to section 62(8) and (8A) below an establishment shall not be carried on by any person unless he is for the time being registered in respect of it in a register kept for the purposes of this section by a local authority or, as the case may be, by the Secretary of State.

[5] (3) Any person who carries on an establishment in contravention of the provisions of subsection (2) of this section shall be guilty of an offence and liable on summary conviction to imprisonment for a term not exceeding three months or to a fine not exceeding level 4 on the standard scale or to both such imprisonment and such fine.

NOTES

[1] Substituted for the former subs. (1) by the Registered Establishments (Scotland) Act 1987 (c. 40), s. 1(1). As amended by the National Health Service and Community Care Act 1990 (c. 19), Sched. 9, para. 10.

[2] Prospectively substituted by the Children (Scotland) Act 1995 (c. 36), s. 34(2)(*a*), *infra*.

[3] Prospectively amended by the Children (Scotland) Act 1995 (c. 36), s. 34(2)(*b*), *infra*.

[4] As amended by the Registered Establishments (Scotland) Act 1987 (c. 40), s. 1(2). Prospectively amended by the Children (Scotland) Act 1995 (c. 36), s. 34(2)(*c*), *infra*. See also s. 38(1)(*b*) of that Act.

[5] As amended by virtue of the Criminal Procedure (Scotland) Act 1975 (c. 21), ss. 289C and 289G and Sched. 7C.

Voluntary registration

[1] **61A.**—(1) Any grant-aided school or independent school within the meaning of section 135(1) of the Education (Scotland) Act 1980 (which defines terms used in that Act) which performs functions such as are described in section 61(1) above may, but shall not be required to, apply for registration under this Part of this Act in accordance with the provisions of this section.

(2) Where an application for registration of a grant-aided school or independent school is granted, the establishment shall be entered in the register kept for the purposes of section 61(2) above by the local authority or, as the case may be, the Secretary of State.

(3) Any certificate of registration granted in respect of an establishment to which this section applies shall relate to the whole of the establishment, excepting any part thereof which is used exclusively for educational purposes.

(4) The provisions of this Part of this Act shall apply to establishments to which this section applies subject to the following—

(*a*) section 61(2) and (3) shall not apply;
(*b*) section 62(8) and (8A) shall not apply;
(*c*) section 65 shall not apply;
(*d*) the provisions of section 67(1) shall apply only where the person carrying on the establishment has been registered; and
(*e*) section 67(2) shall not apply.

NOTE

[1] Inserted by the Registered Establishments (Scotland) Act 1987 (c. 40), s. 2(1). Prospectively substituted by the Children (Scotland) Act 1995 (c. 36), s. 34(3), *infra*.

Registration

[1] **62.**—(1) Subject to the next following section, an application for registration in respect of an establishment under this section shall be made by the person intending to carry on the establishment to the local authority in the area of which the establishment is situated.

(2) The application shall be in such form and shall include information about such matters as may be prescribed by the Secretary of State, and the

Secretary of State may prescribe different requirements for the applications for different classes of establishments.

(3) Subject to the provisions of this section, the local authority shall, on receipt of an application under subsection (1) of this section, register the applicant in respect of the establishment named in the application and issue to him a certificate of registration:

Provided that the local authority may refuse to register the applicant if they are satisfied—

(*a*) that he or any person employed or proposed to be employed by him in the management of the establishment or any part thereof is not a fit person, whether by reason of age or otherwise, to carry on or to be so employed at an establishment of such a description as the establishment named in the application; or

(*b*) that for reasons connected with situation, construction, state of repair, accommodation, staffing or equipment, the establishment or any premises used in connection therewith are not fit to be used for an establishment of such a description as aforesaid; or

(*c*) that the way in which it is proposed to conduct the establishment is such as not to provide services or facilities reasonably required by persons resorting to such an establishment.

(4) Without prejudice to subsection (2) of this section, where the person registered in respect of an establishment proposes to employ a manager, that is, a person engaged to run the establishment from day to day, he shall

(*a*) include in the application for registration a note of the proposed manager's name; and

(*b*) inform the authority, within 28 days in either case, of—

(i) the departure of the manager presently employed, or

(ii) the employment of a new manager.

(4A) Where any person registered in respect of an establishment employs a manager at the date when this enactment comes into force, he shall within 28 days of that date inform the local authority of the manager's name.

(4B) Where any person registered in respect of an establishment intends to cease to carry on the establishment, he shall give the local authority at least 28 days' notice of that fact.

(4C) The local authority may at any time cancel the registration of a person in respect of an establishment—

(*a*) on any ground which would entitle them to refuse an application for the registration of that person in respect of an establishment; or

(*b*) on the ground that that person—

(i) has failed to notify the authority of a change in manager under subsection (4) above, or

(ii) has been convicted of an offence against this section or against any regulations under this Part of this Act relating to the conduct of an establishment; or

(*c*) on the ground that any other person has been convicted of such an offence as is mentioned in subparagraph (*b*)(ii) above in respect of that establishment; or

(*d*) on the ground that the annual fee for the continuation of registration has not been paid on the due date.

(5) It shall be a condition of the registration of any person in respect of an establishment that he shall comply with such reasonable conditions with regard to the proper operation of the establishment as the local authority may impose, and such conditions shall include conditions as to—

(*a*) the maximum number of persons (excluding persons carrying on or employed in the establishment and their families) who may be accommodated at any one time in the establishment, and

(*b*) the categories of persons who may be admitted to the establishment.

(5A) The local authority may, at their own instance or at that of the person registered in respect of the establishment, at any time—

(*a*) impose any new condition with regard to the operation of the establishment; or

(*b*) vary any condition imposed under subsection (5) or paragraph (*a*) above.

[2] (6) If any condition, new condition or variation of a condition imposed by or under subsection (5) or (5A) above or section 63A(7) below is not complied with, the person carrying on the establishment shall be guilty of an offence and shall be liable on summary conviction to a fine not exceeding level 4 on the standard scale or to imprisonment for a term not exceeding three months, or to both such fine and such imprisonment, and without prejudice to the foregoing provision the power of the local authority to cancel registration under subsection (4) of this section shall include power to cancel the registration on the ground that any such condition has not been complied with.

(6A) The certificate of registration issued under this section in respect of any premises shall include the following information—

(*a*) the name of the person registered in respect of the establishment;

(*b*) the name of any manager appointed by the person mentioned in paragraph (*a*) above;

(*c*) the address of the premises at which the establishment is to be carried on;

(*d*) the maximum number of persons who may be accommodated in the establishment under subsection (5)(*a*) above;

(*e*) the categories of persons who may be admitted to the establishment under subsection (5)(*b*) above,

and where any material change occurs in any of the information mentioned in this subsection the local authority shall issue a new certificate.

(6B) Where an establishment to which the provisions of this Part of this Act apply is being carried on the date when this enactment comes into force the local authority shall, within 60 days of that date, issue to the person carrying on that establishment a new certificate including the information mentioned in subsection (6A) above.

[2] (7) The certificate of registration under this section issued in respect of any establishment shall be kept affixed in a conspicuous place in the establishment; and if default is made in complying with this subsection the person carrying on the establishment shall be liable on summary conviction to a fine not exceeding level 1 on the standard scale and to a further fine not exceeding £2 in respect of each day during which the offence continues after conviction.

[THE NEXT PAGE IS K 84/3]

[3] (8) Notwithstanding anything in subsection (1) of this section, where the person registered under this section in respect of an establishment dies, his executor or his widow or any other member of his family may for a period not exceeding four weeks from his death, or such longer period as the local authority may sanction, carry on the establishment without being registered in respect thereof.

[3] (8A) Notwithstanding anything in subsection (1) of this section, where for any reason the person registered in respect of an establishment ceases to be so registered, the local authority may allow another person to carry on the establishment for such period not exceeding 60 days as the authority may sanction, and subject to such conditions as the authority think appropriate.

(9) Where an offence against this or the last foregoing section or any regulations under this Part of this Act relating to establishments has been committed by a body corporate, every person who at the time of the commission of the offence was a director, general manager, secretary or other similar officer of the body corporate, or was purporting to act in any such capacity, shall be deemed to be guilty of that offence unless he proves that the offence was committed without his consent or connivance and that he exercised all such diligence to prevent the commission of the offence as he ought to have exercised having regard to the nature of his functions in that capacity and to all the circumstances.

(10) The registers kept for the purposes of this section shall be available for inspection at all reasonable times, and a person inspecting any such register shall be entitled to make copies of entries therein.

NOTES

[1] As amended by the Registered Establishments (Scotland) Act 1987 (c. 40), s. 3.

[2] As amended by virtue of the Criminal Procedure (Scotland) Act 1975 (c. 21), ss. 289C, 289F, 289G and Sched. 7C.

[3] Excluded by s. 61A(2), *supra* as substituted (prospectively).

Certificate of registration as respects grant-aided or independent school

62A. [Prospectively inserted by the Children (Scotland) Act 1995 (c. 36), s. 34(4), *infra*.]

Special provisions for registration by Secretary of State

63.—(1) The Secretary of State may direct that applications for registration in respect of any establishment or any class of establishment shall be made to him and accordingly the provisions of the last foregoing section shall apply in relation to any such registration and to an application therefor with the substitution for any reference to a local authority of a reference to the Secretary of State.

(2) Where in pursuance of this section the Secretary of State registers a person in respect of an establishment, or cancels such a registration, he shall notify the local authority in whose area the establishment is situated.

(3) The Secretary of State may direct that persons registered with him in respect of any establishment or class of establishment under this section shall cease to be so registered and shall be registered by the appropriate local authority under this Part of this Act.

Appeals against conditions imposed on registration or subsequently

[1] **63A.**—(1) Not less than 14 days before determining—

(*a*) the conditions intended to be imposed under section 62(5) above in respect of the registration of any person in respect of an establishment; or

(*b*) any new condition or variation of an existing condition intended to be imposed under section 62(5A) above,

the Secretary of State or, as the case may be, the local authority shall send by recorded delivery service to the applicant or the person registered, as the case may be, notice of their intention.

(2) Every notice under subsection (1) above shall contain an intimation that if within 14 days after the receipt of the notice the applicant or, as the case may be, the person registered informs the authority or the Secretary of State in writing of his desire—

(*a*) to show cause, in person or by a representative, why the proposed conditions, new conditions or variation of existing conditions should not be imposed;

(*b*) to make representations as to what conditions, new conditions or variation of conditions should be imposed in substitution for those proposed,

the authority or the Secretary of State shall, before carrying out their intention, afford him an opportunity so to do.

(3) The local authority or the Secretary of State, after giving the applicant or the person registered, as the case may be, an opportunity of being heard by them, shall send a notice to him by recorded delivery service informing him of what conditions, new conditions or variation of conditions they have decided to impose.

(4) A person aggrieved by a notice of a local authority or of the Secretary of State under subsection (3) above may appeal to an appeal tribunal established by Schedule 5 to this Act, and any such appeal shall be brought within 21 days of the date of that notice.

(5) Where an appeal under subsection (4) above relates to the imposition of conditions on the initial registration of a person in respect of an establishment, the registration shall not take effect until—

(*a*) the appeal has been determined; or

(*b*) the time for bringing an appeal has elapsed without—

(i) an appeal having been brought, or

(ii) an appeal which has been intimated having been proceeded with,

and in either of the cases mentioned in paragraph (*b*) above the registration shall be subject to the conditions proposed in the notice sent to the applicant under subsection (3) above.

(6) Where an appeal under subsection (4) above relates to the proposed imposition of new conditions or of a variation of existing conditions, the new conditions or variation shall not take effect until—

(*a*) the appeal has been determined; or

(*b*) the time for bringing an appeal has elapsed without—

(i) an appeal having been brought, or

(ii) an appeal which has been intimated having been proceeded with.

(7) On any appeal under subsection (4) above the tribunal may confirm or vary any condition, new condition or variation of a condition against which the appeal is brought.

NOTE

[1] Inserted by the Registered Establishments (Scotland) Act 1987 (c. 40), s. 4.

Special provisions for jointly registrable establishments

[1] **63B.**—(1) Subject to the provisions of this section, where a person registered or intending to be registered under section 1 of the Nursing Homes Registration (Scotland) Act 1938 (which relates to the registration of nursing homes) in respect of an establishment intends that that establishment should also carry out functions in respect of which registration is required under this Act, the provisions of this Part of this Act shall apply in relation to the registration of that person for the purpose of carrying out those functions in that establishment.

(2) In this Part of this Act "jointly registrable establishment" means an establishment required to be registered under both this Part of this Act and the said Act of 1938.

(3) Any certificate of registration issued by a local authority to such a

person as is described in subsection (1) above shall relate to the whole of the establishment, excepting any part thereof which is used exclusively for the purpose of carrying out functions under the said Act of 1938.

(4) Where a local authority cancel the registration of a jointly registrable establishment under section 62(4) above they shall inform the Health Board responsible under the 1938 Act for the registration of that establishment of the fact of and the reasons for the cancellation.

(5) Any person who, on the date when this enactment comes into force, is carrying on a jointly registrable establishment which is not registered under this Part of this Act shall within three months of that date apply for such registration.

(6) No fee shall be chargeable by a local authority under section 64A below in respect of any application made by virtue of subsection (5) above.

NOTE

[1] Inserted by the Registered Establishments (Scotland) Act 1987 (c. 40), s. 5(1).

Appeals against refusal or cancellation of registration

64.—(1) Not less than 14 days before refusing an application for registration or cancelling any registration under this Part of this Act, the local authority or, as the case may be, the Secretary of State shall send by recorded delivery service to the applicant or to the person registered, as the case may be, notice of their intention.

(2) Every such notice shall state the grounds on which the local authority or the Secretary of State intend to refuse or cancel the registration and shall contain an intimation that if within 14 days after the receipt of the notice the applicant or person registered, as the case may be, informs the authority or the Secretary of State in writing of his desire to show cause, in person or by a representative, why the registration should not be refused or cancelled, as the case may be, the authority or the Secretary of State shall, before carrying out their intention, afford him an opportunity so to do.

(3) If the local authority or the Secretary of State, after giving the applicant or person registered, as the case may be, an opportunity of being heard by them, decide to refuse the application for registration, or to cancel the registration, they shall send a notice to that effect by recorded delivery service to the applicant or person registered, as the case may be.

(4) A person aggrieved by a notice of a local authority or of the Secretary of State refusing an application for registration under this Part of this Act or cancelling any registration thereunder may appeal to an appeal tribunal established by Schedule 5 to this Act; and the cancellation of any registration shall not take effect until the expiration of the time within which an appeal may be brought under this subsection or, where such an appeal is brought, before the determination of the appeal.

(5) Any appeal under this section shall be brought within 21 days from the date of the notice to which the appeal relates.

Registration fees

[1] **64A.**—(1) Subject to the provisions of this section, a local authority shall impose fees in respect of—

(*a*) an application for registration made by any person in respect of the carrying on of any establishment to which this section applies;

(*b*) the annual continuation of any such registration;

(*c*) an application made by the person registered in respect of the establishment for a variation in any condition imposed under section 62(5) or (5A) of this Act; and

(*d*) the issuing of a new certificate following any change in the information mentioned in section 62(6A) above made at the instance of or resulting from an application by the person registered in respect of the establishment.

(2) This section applies to any establishment such as is mentioned in section 61(1) of this Act which is a residential establishment other than any establishment—

(*a*) the whole or a substantial part of whose function is to accommodate children for the purposes of this Act; or

(*b*) such as is mentioned in section 61A above.

(3) The Secretary of State may prescribe—

(*a*) the maximum fees which may be imposed by local authorities under this section; and

(*b*) the times at which fees may be charged.

(4) Subject to subsection (3)(*a*) above, a local authority shall have regard to their reasonable expenses in carrying out their functions under this Part of this Act in fixing fees under this section:

Provided that where it appears to the authority to be appropriate they may charge a nominal fee, or remit the fee altogether.

(5) Where an application for registration in respect of an establishment has been made to a local authority before the coming into force of this section no fee shall be payable in respect of that registration.

NOTE

[1] Inserted by the Registered Establishments (Scotland) Act 1987 (c. 40), s. 6(1).

Removal of persons from establishments

[1] **65.**—[2] (1) Where—

(*a*) an establishment is carried on in contravention of section 61 of this Act; or

(*b*) notice of intention to cancel the registration in respect of an establishment has been given in pursuance of the last foregoing section;

a local authority where the person carrying on the establishment is registered, or ought to be so registered, with them may notwithstanding that the time for any appeal under the last foregoing section has not expired or that such an appeal is pending, forthwith remove from the establishment all or any of the persons for whom accommodation is being provided therein; or, in the case of an establishment in respect of which the person carrying it on is registered with him or ought to be so registered, the Secretary of State may in the like circumstances require the local authority in whose area the establishment is situated so to act, and the local authority shall comply with that requirement.

(2) In any case of urgent necessity the Secretary of State may exercise the power conferred on him by the foregoing subsection in respect of any establishment.

(3) For the performance of the functions of a local authority under subsection (1) of this section, any person authorised in that behalf by the authority may, on producing, if so required, a duly authenticated document showing his authority to do so, enter any premises in which the establishment in question is being carried on.

[3] (4) Any person who—

(*a*) obstructs the exercise of a power conferred by the last foregoing subsection; or

(*b*) re-occupies the premises for the purpose of carrying on the establishment without any appeal under section 64 above having been decided in his favour,

shall be liable on summary conviction to a fine not exceeding level 4 on the standard scale.

NOTES

[1] Excluded by s. 61A(2), *supra*, as substituted (prospectively).

[2] Prospectively amended by the Children (Scotland) Act 1995 (c. 36), s. 34(5), *infra*.

[3] As amended by virtue of the Criminal Procedure (Scotland) Act 1975 (c. 21), ss. 289C, 289G and Sched. 7C, and by the Registered Establishments (Scotland) Act 1987 (c. 40), s. 7.

Duty to furnish particulars of establishments

66.—(1) Subject to the next following subsection, it shall be the duty of the person in charge of an establishment to send to the local authority or, as the case may be, the Secretary of State such particulars of the establishment and the persons accommodated or to be accommodated therein as the Secretary of State may from time to time prescribe, and the Secretary of State may prescribe different particulars for different classes of establishments.

(2) A person in charge of an establishment shall comply with the provisions of the foregoing subsection—

(*a*) within three months from the date on which the establishment was first carried on; and

(*b*) in every year (other than the year in which the establishment was first carried on) before such date as may be prescribed.

(3) Where the Secretary of State varies the prescribed particulars to be furnished under subsection (1) of this section as respects establishments, then—

(*a*) the person in charge of an establishment shall send the prescribed particulars to the local authority or, as the case may be, to the Secretary of State within three months from the date of the variation; and

(*b*) as respects an establishment which was first carried on before, but not more than three months before, the date of the variation, paragraph (*a*) of the foregoing subsection shall not apply; and

(*c*) paragraph (*b*) of the foregoing subsection shall not apply as respects the year in which the variation is made.

[THE NEXT PAGE IS K 84/5]

[1] (4) A person who fails to furnish particulars in accordance with the foregoing provisions of this section shall be liable on summary conviction to a fine not exceeding level 1 on the standard scale and to a further fine not exceeding £2 in respect of each day during which the failure continues after conviction.

NOTE

[1] As amended by virtue of the Criminal Procedure (Scotland) Act 1975 (c. 21), ss. 289F and 289G.

Inspection of establishments by local authorities

[1] **67.**—(1) Any person duly authorised by a local authority may in the area of that authority enter any establishment where the person carrying on the establishment is registrable under section 62 of this Act for the purpose of making such examinations into the state and management of the place, and the condition and treatment of the persons in it, as he thinks necessary, and for the purpose of inspecting any records or registers (in whatever form they are held) relating to the place or to any person for whom services have been or are provided there by virtue of this Act or section 7 (functions of local authorities) or 8 (provision of after-care services) of the Mental Health (Scotland) Act 1984, and the provisions of subsections (2) to (2D), (4) and (5) of section 6 of this Act shall apply in relation to a person acting in pursuance of this section as they apply in relation to a person authorised by the Secretary of State acting in pursuance of that section.

(2) Any such person as aforesaid may at all reasonable times exercise the like powers of entry and inspection conferred on him by the foregoing subsection in respect of any place in the area of the local authority which is used or which that person has reasonable cause to believe is being used as an establishment in respect of which the person carrying it on is registrable under section 62 of this Act.

NOTE

[1] As amended by the National Health Service and Community Care Act 1990 (c. 19), Sched. 9, para. 10(9) and (10). Prospectively substituted by the Children (Scotland) Act 1995 (c. 36), s. 34(6), *infra*.

Visiting of persons in establishments on behalf of local authorities

68.—(1) It shall be the duty of local authorities from time to time to cause persons in establishments in their area to be visited in the interests of the well-being of the persons, and any person authorised in that behalf by a local authority may on producing if so required a duly authenticated document showing his authority to do so, enter any establishment in the area of the authority for the purpose of visiting the persons in the establishment.

[1] (2) Any person authorised in that behalf by a local authority may, on producing, if so required, such a document as aforesaid, enter any establishment outside the area of the authority for the purpose of visiting children in the establishment who are in the care or under the supervision of the authority under Part II or Part III of this Act or persons who are receiving assistance from the authority under this Act.

[2] (3) Any person who obstructs the exercise of a power conferred by this section shall be liable on summary conviction to a fine not exceeding level 3 on the standard scale.

(4) [Prospectively added by the Children (Scotland) Act 1995 (c. 36), Sched. 4, para. 15(16)(*b*), *infra*.]

NOTES

[1] Prospectively amended by the Children (Scotland) Act 1995 (c. 36), Sched. 15, para. 16(*a*), *infra*.

[2] As amended by virtue of the Criminal Procedure (Scotland) Act 1975 (c. 21), ss. 289E, 289F and 289G.

[1] Part V

Return and Removal of Children within United Kingdom

NOTE
[1] Prospectively repealed by the Children (Scotland) Act 1995 (c. 36), Sched. 5, *infra*.

Absence without leave

Abscondment from a place of safety, or from the control of a person imposed by a supervision requirement

[1] **69.**—(1) If a child—

(*a*) absconds from a place of safety in which he has been detained by virtue of this Act, or

(*b*) absconds from the control of a person under which he has been placed by a supervision requirement or by virtue of rules made by the Secretary of State under section 45 of this Act,

he may be arrested without a warrant in any part of the United Kingdom or the Channel Islands; and a court, if satisfied that there are reasonable grounds for believing that the child is within any premises, may grant a search warrant authorising a constable to search those premises for the child.

(2) A child arrested in pursuance of this section shall be brought back—

(*a*) in a case falling within paragraph (*a*) of subsection (1), to the place of safety,

(*b*) in a case falling within paragraph (*b*) of that subsection, to the person under whose control he has been placed.

(3) If, in the case of a child required to be brought back in pursuance of the last foregoing subsection—

(*a*) the occupier of the place of safety, or

(*b*) the person under whose control he has been placed,

is unwilling or unable to receive him, the child shall be detained in a place of safety until the reporter has considered, in pursuance of section 37 of this Act, whether the child may be in need of compulsory measures of care, or as the case may be, until he can be brought before a children's hearing for the consideration of his case or for a review of the supervision requirement to which he is subject.

(4) A children's hearing arranged for the purposes of the last foregoing subsection shall meet within a period of seven days from the date of the commencement of the detention of the child, and no child shall be detained under that subsection after the hearing have met or beyond that period.

(5) In this and the next following section any reference—

(*a*) to a child absconding includes a reference to his being unlawfully taken away;

(*b*) to a child absconding from a place or from the control of a person includes a reference to his absconding while being taken to, or awaiting being taken to, that place or that person as the case may be.

NOTE
[1] As amended by the Children Act 1975 (c. 72), Sched. 3, para. 58.

Abscondment from residential establishments

[1] **70.** If a child who is required by a supervision requirement to reside in a residential establishment—

(*a*) absconds from the establishment in which he resides; or

(*b*) absconds from any hospital or other institution in which he is temporarily residing; or

(*c*) being absent on leave from the residential establishment, either runs away from the person in whose charge he is or fails to return to the establishment at the end of his leave;

he may be arrested without a warrant in any part of the United Kingdom or the Channel Islands and brought back—

(i) in a case falling within paragraph (*b*) to the place from which he absconded; or

(ii) where he has run away from the person mentioned in paragraph (*c*), to that person; or

(iii) in any case, to the residential establishment;

and a court, if satisfied that there are reasonable grounds for believing that the child is within any premises, may grant a search warrant authorising a constable to search those premises for the child.

NOTE

[1] As amended by the Children Act 1975, Sched. 3, para. 59.

Harbouring

[1] **71.** Any person who knowingly—

(*a*) assists or induces or persistently attempts to induce a child so to act as to be liable to be brought back in pursuance of either of the two last foregoing sections, or

(*b*) harbours or conceals a child so liable or prevents him from returning to a place or person mentioned in either of those sections,

shall be liable on summary conviction to a fine not exceeding level 5 on the standard scale or to imprisonment for a term not exceeding six months or to both such fine and such imprisonment.

NOTE

[1] As amended by virtue of the Children Act 1975, s.108 and Sched. 3, para. 60, and the Criminal Procedure (Scotland) Act 1975, ss.289F and 289G.

Transfer

Supervision of children moving to England or Wales or Northern Ireland

[1] **72.**—(1) Where a children's hearing are satisfied that a child in respect of whom a supervision requirement under section 44(1)(*a*) of this Act is in force proposes to reside or is residing in England or Wales or in Northern Ireland they may either—

(*a*) discharge the supervision requirement; or

[3] (*b*) send notification of the requirement

(i) in the case of residence in England and Wales, to a youth court acting for the petty sessions area (within the meaning of the Children and Young Persons Act 1969);

(ii) in the case of residence in Northern Ireland, to a juvenile court acting for the petty sessions district (within the meaning of Part III of the Magistrates' Courts (Northern Ireland) Order 1981)

in which the child proposes to reside or is residing.

[2,3] (1A) A youth court to which notification of a supervision requirement is sent under this section may make a supervision order in respect of the person to whom the notification relates but, notwithstanding anything in section 76(1) of this Act, shall not include in the order a requirement authorised by section 12, 12A, 12AA, 12B or 12C of the Children and Young Persons Act 1969 unless that person is before the court when the supervision order is made; and in relation to a supervision order made by virtue of this subsection—

(*b*) section 17 of that Act shall have effect as if in paragraph (*a*) the references to three years and the date on which the order was originally made were respectively references to one year and the date on which the said notification was sent and as if in paragraph (*b*) the words from "the order was" to "and" were omitted.

[2,3] (2) A juvenile court to which notification of a supervision requirement is sent under this section may make in respect of the child subject to that requirement a supervision order placing him under the supervision of a

probation officer for a period not exceeding one year beginning with the day on which the notification was sent; and the provisions of the Children and Young Persons Act (Northern Ireland) 1950 shall apply to any such order as those provisions apply to a supervision order within the meaning of section 63(1)(*d*) of the said Act of 1950.

[3] (3) Where a case is disposed of by a youth court or as the case may be a juvenile court in pursuance of this section in respect of a child subject to a supervision requirement, the requirement shall cease to have effect.

NOTES

[1] Applied by the Child Abduction and Custody Act 1985 (c. 60), Sched. 3, para. 6.

[2] As amended by the Children and Young Persons Act 1969 (c. 54), Sched. 5, para. 58 and Sched. 6.

[3] As amended by the Criminal Justice Act 1991 (c. 53), Sched. 3, para. 9 and Sched. 13 (effective 1st October 1992: S.I. 1992 No. 333).

Supervision of children moving to Scotland

[1] **73.**—[2] (1) Where a juvenile court in England or Wales or in Northern Ireland is satisfied that a child in respect of whom a probation order or a supervision order is in force proposes to reside or is residing in Scotland, the court may either—

(*a*) discharge the probation order or supervision order; or

(*b*) send notification of that order to the reporter of the local authority for the area in which the child proposes to reside or is residing;

and on the receipt of such a notification it shall be the duty of the reporter

(i) in the case of a supervision order made by virtue of section 7A(4) of the Criminal Justice (Scotland) Act 1949, to notify the appropriate court and to transmit to that court all documents and certified copies of documents relating to the case which the reporter has received by virtue of section 76 of this Act;

(ii) in any other case

to arrange a children's hearing for the consideration and determination of the case under Part III of this Act.

In this subsection "the appropriate court" means the sheriff having jurisdiction in the area in which the child proposes to reside or is residing or, where the original probation order was imposed by the High Court of Justiciary, that Court.

(1A) Where a court in England or Wales is satisfied that a child in respect of whom the court proposes to make a supervision order is residing or proposes to reside in Scotland, the court may make the order notwithstanding anything in subsection (1) of section 18 of the Children and Young Persons Act 1969 (which relates to residence of the supervised person in England or Wales); and where the court makes a supervision order by virtue of this subsection—

(*a*) the areas to be named in the order in pursuance of subsection (2)(*a*) of the said section 18 shall be those in which the court is sitting;

(*b*) the order may require the supervised person to comply with directions of the supervisor with respect to his departure to Scotland, and any such requirement shall, for the purposes of sections 15 and 16 of that Act (which relate to the variation and discharge of supervision orders), be deemed to be included in the order in pursuance of section 12(2) of that Act; and

(*c*) the court shall send notification of the order as mentioned in paragraph (*b*) of the foregoing subsection and the provisions of that subsection relating to the duty of the reporter shall apply accordingly.

(2) For the purposes of a children's hearing arranged in pursuance of the foregoing provisions of this section the notification by a court of a probation order or supervision order shall be conclusive evidence of the existence of that order in relation to the child.

(3) When a children's hearing have disposed of a case referred to them under this section the probation order or the supervision order in respect of the child shall cease to have effect.

NOTES

[1] As amended by the Children and Young Persons Act 1969, s. 73(4), Sched. 5, para. 59 and Sched. 6.

[2] Extended by the Criminal Procedure (Scotland) Act 1975, ss. 189(6), 390(6) and 463(1).

Parent of a child in a residential establishment under a supervision requirement moving to England or Wales or Northern Ireland

[1] **74.**—[2] (1) Where a children's hearing are satisfied that the parent of a child who is required to reside in a residential establishment under a supervision requirement made under section 44(1)(*b*) of this Act proposes to reside or is residing in England or Wales or in Northern Ireland they shall review the requirement, and on such review they may as they think proper—

(*a*) discharge the supervision requirement;

(*b*) continue the supervision requirement;

(*c*) vary the supervision requirement by making a supervision requirement under subsection (1)(*a*) of the said section 44 and send notification of that requirement in accordance with section 72(1)(*b*) of this Act; or

(*d*) make a report on the case to the Secretary of State with a recommendation for the transfer of the child in accordance with the following provisions of this section.

(2) If the Secretary of State is for any reason unable to accept a recommendation for the transfer of a child made under paragraph (*d*) of subsection (1) of this section, he may refer the matter back to the children's hearing for their reconsideration of the case, or himself discharge the supervision requirement.

[2] (3) Where such a recommendation is made and is not dealt with under subsection (2) of this section, the Secretary of State may make an order transferring the child to the care of the managers of a school in Northern Ireland, being a training school within the meaning of the Children and Young Persons Act (Northern Ireland) 1950 or committing him to the care of the local authority or, as the case may be, of the welfare authority in whose area the parent of the child proposes to reside or is residing.

(4) The provisions of the said Act of 1950 shall apply to any order under this section transferring a child to the care of the managers of a training school as if it were a training school order made by a court on the date on which the supervision requirement was originally made under section 44 of this Act in respect of the child:

Provided that—

(*a*) notwithstanding anything in section 75 of the said Act of 1950, the order under this section shall not be authority for his detention in a training school after he has attained the age of 18 years,

(*b*) the contributions to be made in respect of him under section 126 of the said Act of 1950 shall be made by such council as may be named in the order under this section, being the council within whose district his parent proposes to reside or is residing at the time of the order.

(5) The provisions of the said Act of 1950 shall apply to any order

under this section committing a child to the care of a welfare authority as if it were an order made by a court under that Act.

[3] (6) An order under this section committing a child to the care of a local authority shall have effect as if it were a care order under the Children Act 1989, but as if section 31(8) were omitted.

NOTES

[1] As amended by the Children and Young Persons Act 1969, s. 73(4), Sched. 5, para. 60 and Sched. 6.

[2] See the Child Abduction and Custody Act 1985, Sched. 3, paras. 6 and 7.

[3] As amended by the Children Act 1989, Sched. 13, para. 21.

Parent of a child subject to an approved school order or a committal order moving to Scotland

[1] **75.**—(1) Where the Minister of Home Affairs for Northern Ireland is satisfied that the parent of a child who is subject to a training school order or an order under section 74(3) of this Act relating to a training school proposes to reside or is residing in Scotland, he may refer the case to the reporter of the local authority of the area in which the parent of the child is proposing to reside or is residing and if the case is so referred the reporter shall arrange a children's hearing for the consideration and determination of the case under Part III of this Act.

[2] (2) Where a child has been committed to the care of a local authority in England or Wales by a care order (other than an interim order) within the meaning of the Children Act 1989 or an order under section 74(3) of this Act, or committed to the care of a welfare authority in Northern Ireland under Part III of the Children and Young Persons Act (Northern Ireland) 1950 or Part I of the Education Act (Northern Ireland) 1947 or the said section 74(3) and that authority are satisfied that the parent of the child proposes to reside or is residing in Scotland, the authority may make the like reference of the case as mentioned in the foregoing subsection and the foregoing subsection and the reporter shall arrange a children's hearing accordingly.

(3) Any reference under subsection (1) or subsection (2) of this section shall include particulars of the training school order or order under the said section 74(3) relating to a training school or, as the case may be, of the order committing the child to the care of the local or welfare authority; and for the purposes of any children's hearing arranged pursuant to the reference those particulars shall be conclusive evidence of the existence of that order in relation to the child.

(4) When a children's hearing have disposed of a case referred to them under this section the order under the said section 74(3) or of the court in England or Wales or in Northern Ireland in respect of the child shall cease to have effect.

NOTES

[1] As amended by the Children and Young Persons Act 1969, s. 73(4), Sched. 5, para. 61 and Sched. 6.

[2] As amended by the Children Act 1989, Sched. 13, para. 22.

Procedure

[1] **76.**—(1) A children's hearing or court, in exercising any jurisdiciton under this Part of this Act in respect of a child, may proceed in the absence of the child or his parent or both.

(2) It shall be the duty of the reporter at any children's hearing arranged for the purposes of section 72 of this Act and of the clerk to any court referring a case to a reporter for the purposes of section 73 of this Act to ensure that all documents relating to the case or certified copies thereof are transmitted to the court or, as the case may be, to the reporter to which the case stands referred.

(3) Where a child is to be transferred from a residential establishment

in Scotland to any place in England or Wales or in Northern Ireland under this Part of this Act, it shall be the duty of the local authority responsible for the child to ensure the transfer of the child to that place.

(4) Where a children's hearing is arranged under this Part of this Act in respect of a child subject to a training school order or order under section 74(3) of this Act relating to a training school or committed to the care of a local authority in England or Wales or of a welfare authority in Northern Ireland, it shall be the duty of the managers of the training school or, as the case may be, of that local or welfare authority to ensure the transfer of the child to the place notified to them by the reporter.

NOTES

[1] As amended by the Children and Young Persons Act 1969 (c. 54), s. 73(4), Sched. 5, para. 62 and Sched. 6.

[2] Prospective amendment in the Local Government etc. (Scotland) Act 1994 (c. 39), Sched. 13, para. 76(24), *infra*.

Meaning of child for the purposes of this Part of this Act

77.—(1) "Child" in this Part of this Act means—

(*a*) for the purpose of sections 69 to 71, a child within the meaning of Part III of this Act,

(*b*) [Repealed by the Children and Young Persons Act 1969 (c. 54), ss. 72(4), 73(4) and Sched. 6.]

(*c*) for any other purpose, a person under 18.

(2) "Parent" in this Part of this Act includes a guardian.

Part VI

Contributions in respect of Children in Care etc.

Duty to make contributions in respect of children in care etc.

[1] **78.**—[2] (1) Where a child has been received into care under Part II of this Act or a supervision requirement to which this Part of this Act applies has been made in respect of him, contributions in respect of the child (hereinafter in this Part of this Act referred to as the "maintainable child") shall be payable—

(*a*) while the maintainable child is under 16 years of age, by his father and mother;

(*b*) if he is over 16 years of age, by the maintainable child himself.

[2] (2) Supervision requirements to which this Part of this Act applies are requirements made under paragraph (*a*) of section 44(1) of this Act which impose a condition of residence on a child, other than a condition that he resides at his own home, and requirements made under paragraph (*b*) of the said section 44(1).

[3] (2A) No contributions shall be payable under subsection (1)(*a*) of this section by a contributor during a period when he is in receipt of income support or family credit.

(3) In this Part of this Act "contributor" means a person liable to make contributions by virtue of subsection (1) of this section in respect of a maintainable child.

NOTES

[1] As amended by the Health and Social Services and Social Security Adjudications Act 1983 (c. 41), s. 19(6) and Sched. 10, Pt. I. Excluded by the Adoption (Scotland) Act 1978 (c. 28), s. 31(3).

[2] Subs. (1) prospectively amended and subs. (2) prospectively substituted by the Children (Scotland) Act 1995 (c. 36), Sched. 4, para. 15(17), *infra*.

[3] As amended by the Social Security Act 1986 (c. 50), Sched. 10, para. 41(1).

Recovery of contributions

[1] **78A.**—(1) Section 87 of this Act (charges for services and accommodation) shall not apply to the provision of services (including accommodation) under this Act in respect of maintainable children, and the provisions of this section shall apply thereto.

(2) A local authority providing such services may recover from a contributor a contribution (if any) of such amount as is reasonable and, subject to that, may recover—

[2] (*a*) a standard contribution determined by them in respect of maintainable children who are in their care or under their supervision; or

(*b*) such other contribution as they consider reasonable in the circumstances.

NOTES

[1] Inserted by the Health and Social Services and Social Security Adjudications Act 1983 (c. 41), s. 19(7).

[2] Prospectively amended by the Children (Scotland) Act 1995 (c. 36), Sched. 4, para. 15(18), *infra*.

Recipients of contributions

[1] **79.**—(1) Subject to the provisions of the following subsection, contributions payable under the last foregoing section shall be payable to the local authority within whose area the contributor is residing, and shall, in the case of contributions paid in respect of a maintainable child in the care or under the supervision of a local authority, other than the authority to whom the contributions are payable as aforesaid, be paid over by the last-mentioned authority to that other authority, but subject to such deductions in respect of services rendered by the local authority to whom the contributions were payable as may be agreed between the authorities concerned or as, in the default of agreement, may be determined by the Secretary of State.

(2) Where a contributor is for the time being residing in England or Wales or Northern Ireland contributions payable by him under the last foregoing section shall be payable to the local authority having the care or supervision of the child.

NOTE

[1] Subss. (1) and (2) prospectively amended by the Children (Scotland) Act 1995 (c. 36), Sched. 4, para. 15(19), *infra*.

Enforcement of duty to make contributions

[1] **80.**—(1) Where a child becomes a maintainable child by virtue of being received into care by a local authority under Part II of this Act or by virtue of a supervision requirement, any court of summary jurisdiction, having jurisdiction in the place where the contributor is for the time being residing, may, on the application of the local authority, at any time make an order on any contributor, hereinafter in this Act referred to as a contribution order, for weekly contributions in respect of the child of such amount as the court thinks proper.

(2), (3) [Repealed by the Debtors (Scotland) Act 1987 (c. 18), Sched. 8.]

(4) Subject to the following provisions of this section, a contribution order in respect of a maintainable child shall remain in force—

(*a*) if the child is in the care of a local authority under Part II of this Act, so long as he remains in their care under that Part;

(*b*) if the child is a maintainable child by virtue of a supervision requirement, so long as that requirement is in force.

(5) No contribution shall be payable, by virtue of a contribution order by a contributor who is the maintainable child's father or mother, in respect of any period after the maintainable child becomes 16.

(6) A contribution order may be revoked or varied by any court of summary jurisdiction having jurisdiction in the place where the contributor is for the time being residing and shall be enforceable in like manner as a decree for aliment.

(7) Where a contributor resides in England or Wales or Northern Ireland this section shall have effect as if for any reference to a court of summary jurisdiction having jurisdiction in a place where the contributor is for the time being residing there were substituted a reference to a court of summary jurisdiction having jurisdiction in any place within the area of the local authority having the care or supervision of the child.

NOTE

[1] Subss. (1), (4), (5) and (7) prospectively amended by the Children (Scotland) Act 1995 (c. 36), Sched. 4, para. 15(20), *infra*.

Provisions as to decrees for aliment

81.—(1) [Repealed by the Law Reform (Parent and Child) (Scotland) Act 1986 (c. 9), Sched. 2.]

[1] (2) Where a decree for aliment of a maintainable child is in force, on the application of the local authority concerned, any court of summary jurisdiction having jurisdiction in the place where the person liable under the decree is for the time being residing may, at any time, order the payments under the decree to be paid to the local authority who are from time to time entitled under either of the last two foregoing sections to receive contributions in respect of the child.

[2] (3) Where an order made under this section in respect to a decree for aliment is in force any sums received under the decree for aliment shall be applied in like manner as if they were contributions received under a contribution order.

(4)(*a*) In this section the local authority concerned means the local authority which may make application for a contribution order in respect of a child under the last foregoing section;

[3] (*b*) where the person liable to pay aliment for a child under a decree is resident in England or Wales or Northern Ireland, subsection (2) of this section shall have effect as if for the reference to a court of summary jurisdiction having jurisdiction in the place where that person is for the time being residing, there were substituted a reference to a court of summary jurisdiction having jurisdiction in any place within the area of the local authority concerned.

NOTES

[1] As amended by the Law Reform (Parent and Child) (Scotland) Act 1986 (c. 9), Sched. 1, para. 9 and Sched. 2.

[2] As amended by the Law Reform (Parent and Child) (Scotland) Act 1986 (c. 9), Sched. 2.

[3] As amended by the Law Reform (Parent and Child) (Scotland) Act 1986 (c. 9), Sched. 1, para. 9.

Recovery of arrears of contributions

82.—[1] (1) Where, by virtue of an order or decree made under either of the last two foregoing sections, any sum is payable to a local authority, the local authority in whose area the person liable under the order or decree is for the time being residing, or, as the case may be, the local authority having the care or supervision of the child to whom the order or decree relates, shall be entitled to receive and give a discharge for, and, if necessary, enforce payment of, any arrears accrued due under the order or decree, notwithstanding that those arrears may have accrued at a time when he was not resident in that area or, as the case may be, when the authority were not entitled to sums payable under the order or decree.

(2) In any proceedings under either of the last two foregoing sections a certificate purporting to be signed by the clerk to a local authority for the time being entitled to receive contributions, or by some other officer of the authority duly authorised in that behalf, and stating that any sum due to the authority under an order or decree is overdue and unpaid, shall be sufficient evidence of the facts stated therein.

NOTE

[1] Prospectively amended by the Children (Scotland) Act 1995 (c. 36), Sched. 4, para. 15(21), *infra*.

Variation of trusts

83.—(1) Where a child is by virtue of a supervision requirement removed from the care of any person and that person is entitled under any trust to receive any sum of money in respect of the maintenance of the child, on the application of the local authority concerned any court of summary jurisdiction, having jurisdiction in the place where that person is for the time being residing, may at any time order the whole or any part of the sums so payable under the trust to be paid to the local authority, to be applied by the authority for the benefit of the child in such manner as, having regard to the terms of the trust, the court may direct.

[1] (2) Where the person in whose care a child has been residing is for the time being residing in England or Wales or Northern Ireland the foregoing subsection shall have effect as if for the reference to a court having jurisdiction in the place where that person is residing there were substituted a reference to a court of summary jurisdiction having jurisdiction in any place within the area of the local authority having the care or supervision of the child.

NOTE

[1] Prospectively amended by the Children (Scotland) Act 1995 (c. 36), Sched. 4, para. 15(22), *infra*.

References in this Part of this Act to child being looked after

83A. [Prospectively inserted by the Children (Scotland) Act 1995 (c. 36), Sched. 4, para. 15(23), *infra*.]

Part VII

Miscellaneous and General

General

Transfer of assets and liabilities

84. Where any functions are transferred to a local authority by virtue of this Act property, rights, liabilities and obligations relating to the performance of those functions which immediately before the date of transfer were the property rights, liabilities and obligations of the body or person from which the functions are transferred shall on that date be transferred to and vest in the local authority or, as the case may be, the local authorities to which the functions have been transferred, and the provisions of Schedule 6 to this Act shall have effect for the purposes of this section.

Transfer and compensation of officers

85. [Repealed by the Local Government and Planning (Scotland) Act 1982 (c. 43), Sched. 4, Pt. I.]

Adjustments between authority providing accommodation etc., and authority of area of residence

86.—[1] (1) Any expenditure which apart from this section would fall to be borne by a local authority—

(*a*) in the provision under this Act of accommodation for a person ordinarily resident in the area of another local authority, or

(*b*) in the provision under Part II of this Act of services and facilities for a person ordinarily so resident (including, in the case of a child, any expenses incurred after he has ceased to be a child, and in the event of his care being taken over by virtue of section 15(4) of this Act including also any travelling or other expenses incurred in connection with the taking over), or

(*c*) for the conveyance of a person ordinarily resident as aforesaid, or

(*d*) in administering a supervision requirement in respect of a person ordinarily resident as aforesaid, or

(*e*) in the provision of accommodation, services or facilities for persons ordinarily so resident under section 7 (functions of local authorities) or 8 (provision of after-care services) of the Mental Health (Scotland) Act 1984,

shall be recoverable from the other local authority, and in this subsection any reference to another local authority includes a reference to a local authority in England or Wales.

(2) Any question arising under this section as to the ordinary residence of a person shall be determined by the Secretary of State, and the Secretary of State may determine that a person has no ordinary residence.

[2] (3) In determining for the purposes of subsection (1) of this section the ordinary residence of any person or child, any period during which he was a patient in a hospital provided under Part II of the National Health Service Act 1946 or Part II of the National Health Service (Scotland) Act 1978 or in a hospital managed by a National Health Service trust established under Part I of the National Health Service and Community Care Act 1990 or section 12A of the National Health Service (Scotland) Act 1978 or, in the case of a child, any period during which he resided in any place as an inmate of a school or other institution, or in accordance with the requirements of a supervision requirement, supervision order or probation order or the conditions of a recognizance, or while boarded out under this Act or under the Children and Young Persons (Scotland) Act 1937 by a local authority or education authority or placed with local authority foster parents under the Children Act 1989 shall be disregarded.

NOTES

[1] As amended by the National Health Service and Community Care Act 1990 (c. 19), Sched. 9, para. 10(11).

[2] As amended by the National Health Service (Scotland) Act 1972 (c. 58), Sched. 7, Pt. II, the National Health Service (Scotland) Act 1978 (c. 29), Sched. 16, para. 29(2), the Child Care Act 1980 (c. 5), Sched. 5, para. 22, the National Health Service and Community Care Act 1990 (c. 19), Sched. 9, para. 10(12), and the Children Act 1989 (c. 41), Sched. 13, para. 23 and Sched. 15.

Exclusion of powers to provide accommodation in certain cases

[1] **86A.**—(1) Subject to subsection (3) below, no accommodation may be provided under this Act for any person who, immediately before the date on which this section comes into force, was ordinarily resident in relevant premises.

(2) In subsection (1) above "relevant premises" means—

(*a*) any establishment in respect of which a person is registered under section 62 of this Act;

(*b*) any nursing home within the meaning of the Nursing Homes Registration (Scotland) Act 1938 in respect of which a person is registered or exempt from registration under that Act;

(*c*) any private hospital registered under section 12 of the Mental Health (Scotland) Act 1984; and

(*d*) such other premises as the Secretary of State may by regulations prescribe.

(3) The Secretary of State may by regulations provide that in such cases and subject to such conditions as may be prescribed subsection (1) above shall not apply in relation to such classes of persons as may be prescribed in the regulations.

(4) The Secretary of State shall by regulations prescribe the circumstances in which persons are to be treated as being ordinarily resident in any premises for the purposes of subsection (1) above.

(5) This section does not affect the validity of any contract made before the date on which this section comes into force for the provision of accommodation on or after that date or anything done in pursuance of such a contract.

NOTE

[1] Inserted by the National Health Service and Community Care Act 1990 (c. 19), s. 57. Prospective application of s. 86A(2) in the Social Security Act 1990 (c. 27), s. 9 (adding s. 22(2B) to the Social Security Act 1986 (c. 50)).

Charges that may be made for services and accommodation

[1] **87.**—[2] (1) Subject to sections 78 and 78A of this Act (contributions in respect of maintainable children) and to the following provisions of this section, a local authority providing a service under this Act or section 7 (functions of local authorities) or 8 (provision of after-care services) of the Mental Health (Scotland) Act 1984 may recover such charge (if any) for it as they consider reasonable.

[2] (1A) If a person—

(*a*) avails himself of a service provided under this Act or section 7 or 8 of the said Act of 1984; and

(*b*) satisfies the authority providing the service that his means are insufficient for it to be reasonably practicable for him to pay for the service the amount which he would otherwise be obliged to pay for it,

the authority shall not require him to pay more for it than it appears to them that it is reasonably practicable for him to pay.

(2) Persons, other than maintainable children, for whom accommodation is provided under this Act or section 7 of the said Act of 1984, shall be required to pay for that accommodation in accordance with the subsequent provisions of this section.

[3] (3) Subject to the following provisions of this section, accommodation provided under this Act or section 7 of the said Act of 1984 shall be regarded as accommodation provided under Part III of the National Assistance Act 1948, and sections 22(2) to (8) and 26(2) to (4) (as amended by the Schedule to the Housing (Homeless Persons) Act 1977, paragraph 2(1) of Schedule 4 to the Social Security Act 1980, section 20 of the Health and Social Services and Social Security Adjudications Act 1983 and paragraph 32 of Schedule 10 to the Social Security Act 1986) (charges for accommodation and provision of accommodation in premises maintained by voluntary organisations) and sections 42 (as amended by paragraph 5 of Schedule 1 to the Law Reform (Parent and Child) (Scotland) Act 1986) and 43 of the said Act of 1948 (which make provision for the mutual maintenance of wives and husbands and the maintenance of their children by recovery of assistance from persons liable for maintenance and for affiliation orders, etc.) shall apply accordingly.

(4) In the application of the said section 22, for any reference to the Minister there shall be substituted a reference to the Secretary of State, and in the application of the said section 26, any references to arrangements under a scheme for the provision of accommodation shall be con-

strued as references to arrangements made by a local authority with a voluntary organisation or any other person or body for the provision of accommodation under this Act or section 7 of the said Act of 1984.

(5) The Secretary of State may, with the consent of the Treasury, make regulations for modifying or adjusting the rates at which payments under this section are made, where such a course appears to him to be justified, and any such regulations may provide for the waiving of any such payment in whole or in part in such circumstances as may be specified in the regulations.

(6) [Repealed by the Social Security Act 1980 (c. 30), Sched. 4, para. 5(2) and Sched. 5, Pt. II.]

NOTES

[1] As amended by the Health and Social Services and Social Security Adjudications Act 1983 (c. 41), ss. 18 and 20(2), and the National Health Service and Community Care Act 1990 (c. 19), Sched. 9, para. 10(13).

[2] Prospectively amended by the Children (Scotland) Act 1995 (c. 36), Sched. 4, para. 15(25), *infra*.

[3] As amended by the Social Security Act 1980 (c. 30), Sched. 4, para. 5(1) and the Social Security Act 1986 (c. 50), Sched. 10, para. 41(2)(*a*), (*b*) and (*c*).

Duty of parents to notify change of address

[0] **88.**—(1) Where—

(*a*) a child is received into the care of a local authority under Part II of this Act; or

(*b*) he is subject to a supervision requirement,

the parents of the child shall keep the local authority responsible for the supervision or care of the child informed of the parents' address.

[1] (2) The parent of a child to whom the foregoing subsection relates and who knowingly fails to comply with the requirements of that subsection shall be liable on summary conviction to a fine of level 1 on the standard scale; but in any proceedings under this section it shall be a defence that the accused was at the material time residing at the same address as the other parent and had reasonable cause to believe that the other parent kept the local authority responsible for the supervision or the care of the child informed of the address of both parents.

[2] (3) A person who is making any payment to a local authority by virtue of any order or decree under Part VI of this Act shall be regarded as a parent for the purposes of this section.

NOTES

[0] Prospectively repealed by the Children (Scotland) Act 1995 (c. 36), Sched. 4, para. 15(26), *infra*.

[1] As amended by virtue of the Criminal Procedure (Scotland) Act 1975 (c. 21), ss. 289F and 289G.

[2] As amended by the Law Reform (Parent and Child) (Scotland) Act 1986 (c. 9), Sched. 1, para. 9.

89. [Repealed by the Tribunals and Inquiries Act 1971 (c. 62), Sched. 4, Pt. I.]

Orders, regulations etc.

90.—[1] (1) Any power to make regulations or orders (other than orders under sections 52 and 58 and Part V of this Act), or to make rules conferred on the Secretary of State by this Act shall be exercisable by statutory instrument.

(2) Any statutory instrument made in the exercise of any power to make regulations conferred by this Act shall be subject to annulment in pursuance of a resolution of either House of Parliament.

(3) Any power conferred by this Act to make orders shall include a power, exercisable in the like manner and subject to the same conditions, to vary or revoke any such order.

NOTE
[1] As amended by the Children and Young Persons Act 1969 (c. 54), s. 73(4), Sched. 5, para. 63 and Sched. 6. Prospectively amended by the Children (Scotland) Act 1995 (c. 36), Sched. 4, para. 15(27), *infra*.

Expenses

91. There shall be defrayed out of moneys provided by Parliament—

(*a*) any sums required for the payment of grants under this Act or any other expenses of the Secretary of State under this Act, and

(*b*) any increase attributable to the provisions of this Act in the sums payable out of such money under any other Act.

Effect of Act on rate support grant

92.—(1) The Secretary of State shall have power, by an order made in the like manner and subject to the like provisions as a rate support grant order, to vary the provisions of any rate support grant order made before the commencement of this Act for a grant period ending after the commencement of this Act.

(2) Any order made by virtue of this section may be made for all or any of the years comprised in the said rate support grant period, as may be specified in the order, and in respect of the year or years so specified shall increase the annual aggregate amount of the rate support grants to such extent as may appear to the Secretary of State to be appropriate having regard to any additional expenditure incurred or likely to be incurred by councils of counties or of large burghs in consequence of the passing of this Act.

(3) The provisions of this section shall have effect without prejudice to the exercise of any power conferred by section 4 of the Local Government (Scotland) Act 1966 (which confers power to vary rate support grant orders in consequence of unforeseen increases in the level of prices, costs or remuneration).

(4) In this section the expressions "rate support grant order" and "grant period" have the meanings respectively assigned to them by subsection (1) and subsection (3) of section 3 of the Local Government (Scotland) Act 1966.

Power of the Secretary of State to make grants

[1] **92A.** The Secretary of State may, with the approval of the Treasury, make grants out of money provided by Parliament towards any expenses of local authorities in respect of their functions under—

(*a*) Part II of this Act; and

(*b*) sections 7 and 8 of the Mental Health (Scotland) Act 1984,

in relation to persons suffering from mental illness.

NOTE
[1] Inserted by the National Health Service and Community Care Act 1990 (c. 19), s. 58.

Supplementary

Transitional provisions

93. The transitional provisions set out in Schedule 7 to this Act shall have effect for the purposes of the transition to the provisions of this Act from the law in force before the commencement of this Act.

Interpretation

[1] **94.**—[2] (1) In this Act, except where otherwise expressly provided or the context otherwise requires, the following expressions have the meanings hereby respectively assigned to them—

"approved school" means a school approved by the Secretary of State under section 79 of the Children and Young Persons Act 1933, "approved school order" has the meaning assigned to it by section 107(1) of the Children and Young Persons Act 1933,

"children's panel" and "children's hearing" have the meanings respectively assigned to them by sections 33(1) and 34(1) of this Act,

"compulsory measures of care" means, in relation to a child, such measure of care as may be imposed upon him by a children's hearing,

"constable" means a constable of a police force within the meaning of the Police (Scotland) Act 1967,

"contributor" and "contribution order" have the meanings respectively assigned to them by sections 78 and 80 of this Act,

[2a] "domiciliary services" means any services, being services provided in the home, which appear to a local authority to be necessary for the purpose of enabling a person to maintain as independent an existence as is practicable in his home;

"establishment" means an establishment managed by a local authority, voluntary organisation or any other person, which provides non-residential accommodation for the purposes of this Act, whether for reward or not,

"functions" shall include powers and duties,

[2b] "guardian" means a person appointed by deed or will or by order of a court of competent jurisdiction to be the guardian of a child, or in relation to a child includes any person who, in the opinion of the court or children's hearing having cognizance of any case in relation to the child or in which the child is concerned, has for the time being the custody or charge of or control over the child,

"hospital" means—

[3] (*a*) any hospital vested in the Secretary of State under the National Health Service (Scotland) Act 1978,

[3a] (*aa*) any hospital managed by a National Health Service trust established under section 12A of the National Health Service (Scotland) Act 1978;

(*b*) any private hospital registered under the Mental Health (Scotland) Act 1984, and

(*c*) any State hospital, within the meaning of Part VIII of the said Act of 1984,

"local authority", in relation to Scotland, has the meaning assigned to it by section 1(2) of this Act,

"maintainable child" has the meaning assigned to it by section 78 of this Act,

"mental disorder" has the meaning assigned to it by section 1(2) of the Mental Health (Scotland) Act 1984,

"mental health officer" means an officer of a local authority appointed to act as a mental health officer for the purposes of the said Act of 1984,

"parent" means either or both parents, and—

(*a*) [Repealed by the Children Act 1975 (c. 72), Sched. 4, Pt. I.]

(*b*) in relation to a child who is illegitimate means his mother to the exclusion of his father,

"performance", in relation to functions, includes the exercise of powers as well as the performance of duties, and "perform" shall be construed accordingly,

[THE NEXT PAGE IS K 85]

"persons in need" means persons who,

(*a*) are in need of care and attention arising out of infirmity, youth or age; or

(*b*) suffer from illness or mental disorder or are substantially handicapped by any deformity or disability; or

(*c*) [Repealed by the Housing (Homeless Persons) Act 1977 (c. 48), Sched.]

(*d*) being persons prescribed by the Secretary of State who have asked for assistance, are, in the opinion of a local authority, persons to whom the authority may appropriately make available the services and facilities provided by them under this Act,

"place of safety" means any residential or other establishment provided by a local authority, a police station, or any hospital, surgery or other suitable place, the occupier of which is willing temporarily to receive a child,

[4] "prescribed" means—

(*a*) in sections 3 and 36, prescribed by regulations,

(*b*) in section 44, prescribed by rules, and

(*c*) in sections 27A, 27B, 62(2), 64A(3), 66(1) and (2), 94, paragraphs 2(2) and (3), 4(3) and (4) of Schedule 7, prescribed by order, and "prescribe" shall be construed accordingly.

[5] "probation order", in relation to an order imposed by a court in England or Wales, has the meaning assigned to it by section 2 of the Powers of Criminal Courts Act 1973 and in relation to such an order, imposed by a court in Northern Ireland, has the same meaning as in the Probation Act (Northern Ireland) 1950,

"residential establishment" means an establishment managed by a local authority, voluntary organisation or any other person, which provides residential accommodation for the purposes of this Act, whether for reward or not,

[6] "school age" shall be construed in accordance with section 31 of the Education (Scotland) Act 1980,

[7] "supervision order", in relation to an order imposed by a court in England or Wales, means a supervision order under the Children and Young Persons Act 1969 or the Children Act 1989, and in relation to an order imposed by a court in Northern Ireland has the meaning assigned to it by section 63(1)(*d*) of the Children and Young Persons Act (Northern Ireland) 1950,

"supervision requirement" has the meaning assigned to it by section 44(1) of this Act,

"training school" means a school approved by the Ministry of Home Affairs for Northern Ireland under section 106 of the Children and Young Persons Act (Northern Ireland) 1950,

"training school order" means an order made by a court in Northern Ireland sending a child or young person to a training school,

"voluntary organisation" means a body the activities of which are carried on otherwise than for profit, but does not include any public or local authority,

"welfare authority" means a welfare authority constituted under the Public Health and Local Government (Administrative Provisions) Act (Northern Ireland) 1946.

(2) Unless the context requires, any reference in this Act to any other enactment is a reference thereto as amended, and includes a reference thereto as extended or applied by or under any other enactment including this Act.

(3) Without prejudice to the last foregoing subsection, any reference in the Act to an enactment of the Parliament of Northern Ireland, or to an enactment which that Parliament has power to amend, shall be construed,

in relation to Northern Ireland, as a reference to that enactment as amended by any Act of that Parliament, whether passed before or after this Act, and to any enactment of that Parliament passed after this Act and re-enacting the said enactment with or without modifications.

NOTES

[1] As amended by the Children and Young Persons Act 1969 (c. 54), Sched. 5 and the Children Act 1975 (c. 72), Sched. 4, Pt. I.

[2] As amended by the Mental Health (Scotland) Act 1984 (c. 36), Sched. 3, para. 17. Applied: see the Criminal Procedure (Scotland) Act 1975 (c. 21), s. 462(1), and the Education (Scotland) Act 1980 (c. 44), ss. 44(1) and 135(1). See S.I. 1986 No. 2291. Prospective amendments in the Children (Scotland) Act 1995 (c. 36), Sched. 4, para. 15(28), *infra*.

[2a] Inserted by the National Health Service and Community Care Act 1990 (c. 19), Sched. 9, para. 10(14)(*a*).

[2b] As amended by the Law Reform (Parent and Child) (Scotland) Act 1986 (c. 9), Sched. 1, para. 9, and the Age of Legal Capacity (Scotland) Act 1991 (c. 50), Sched. 2.

[3] As amended by the National Health Service (Scotland) Act 1978 (c. 29), Sched. 16, para. 29(3).

[3a] Inserted by the National Health Service and Community Care Act 1990 (c. 19), Sched. 9, para. 10(14)(*b*).

[4] Definition added by the Children and Young Persons Act 1969 (c. 54), Sched. 5. As amended by the Local Government (Scotland) Act 1973 (c. 65), Sched. 27, Pt. II, para. 186, the Registered Establishments (Scotland) Act 1987 (c. 40), s. 6(2) and the Law Reform (Miscellaneous Provisions) (Scotland) Act 1990 (c. 40), s. 61(7).

[5] As amended by the Powers of Criminal Courts Act 1973 (c. 62), Sched. 5, para. 30.

[6] Substituted by the Education (Scotland) Act 1976 (c. 20), Sched. 1, para. 14. As amended by the Education (Scotland) Act 1980 (c. 44), Sched. 4, and para. 5.

[7] As amended by the Courts and Legal Services Act 1990 (c. 41), Sched. 16, para. 36.

Minor and consequential amendments, repeals and savings

95.—(1) The enactments described in Schedule 8 to this Act shall have effect subject to the amendments therein specified, being minor amendments and amendments consequential on the foregoing provisions of this Act.

(2) The enactments described in Schedule 9 to this Act are hereby repealed to the extent specified in that Schedule.

[1] (3) Subject to any expression in this Act to the contrary, in so far as any appointment, agreement or any provision in a regulation or order made or any notice, direction, consent, approval, warrant or certificate given under any enactment repealed by this Act or registration effected, or deemed to have been effected, proceedings instituted or other thing done under any such enactment could have been made, passed, given, granted, effected, instituted or done under corresponding provision of this Act, it shall not be invalidated by this repeal, but shall have effect as if it had been made, passed, given, granted, effected, instituted or done to that corresponding provision and may be amended, varied, revoked or enforced accordingly, and in the case of any legal proceedings, may be continued and appealed against as if this Act had not been passed.

NOTE

[1] For regulations see S.I. 1983 No. 1912, as amended by S.I. 1988 No. 841.

96. [Repealed by the Northern Ireland Constitution Act 1973 (c. 36), Sched. 6, Pt. I.]

Extension of certain provisions of Act to England and Wales, Northern Ireland and the Channel Islands

[1] **97.**—[2] (1) The following provisions of this Act shall extend to England and Wales, that is to say—

section 44(1) (except head (*b*) and (1A)
section 58
section 86 and 87
Part V
section 98(3)

Schedule 2, paragraphs 7 and 13
Schedule 8
Part II of Schedule 9.

[3] (2) The following provisions of this Act shall extend to Northern Ireland, that is to say—

Part V
Schedule 8.

[3] (3) The following provisions of this Act shall extend to the Channel Islands, that is to say sections 69 to 71.

(4) Save as aforesaid, and except in so far as it relates to the interpretation or commencement of the provisions, this Act shall extend only to Scotand.

NOTES

[1] As amended by the Children and Young Persons Act 1969 (c. 54), s. 73(4) and Sched. 5, para. 65, and the Northern Ireland Constitution Act 1973 (c. 36), Sched. 6, Pt. I.

[2] Prospective amendments in the Children (Scotland) Act 1995 (c. 36), Sched. 4, para. 15(29)(*a*), *infra*.

[3] Prospectively repealed by the Children (Scotland) Act 1995 (c. 36), Sched. 4, para. 15(29)(*b*), *infra*.

Commencement

[1] **98.**—(1) This Act (except this section) shall come into operation on such date as the Secretary of State may by order appoint.

(2) Different dates may be appointed by order under this section for different purposes of this Act; and any reference in any provision of this Act to the commencement of this Act shall, unless otherwise provided by any such order, be construed as a reference to the date on which that provision comes into operation.

[2] (3) An order under this section may make such transitional provisions as appear to the Secretary of State to be necessary or expedient in connection with the provisions thereby brought into force, including such adaptations of those provisions or of any provision of this Act then in force as appear to the Secretary of State necessary or expedient for the purposes or in consequence of the operation of any provision of this Act before the coming into force of any other provision of this Act or of the Children and Young Persons Act 1969.

NOTES

[1] See S.I. 1969 Nos. 430 and 1274; S.I. 1970 Nos. 196 and 846, and S.I. 1971 Nos. 184 and 556.

[2] Added by the Children and Young Persons Act 1969 (c. 54), Sched. 5, para. 66.

Short title

99. This Act may be cited as the Social Work (Scotland) Act 1968.

SCHEDULES

Section 19

SCHEDULE 1

AMENDMENT OF CHILDREN ACT 1958

[Repealed by the Foster Children (Scotland) Act 1984 (c. 56), Sched. 3.]

Section 31

SCHEDULE 2

AMENDMENT OF PART IV OF THE CHILDREN AND YOUNG PERSONS (SCOTLAND) ACT 1937

PART I

General Adaptations

[1] 1. Subject to the provisions of Part II of this Schedule any reference to a child or to a young person shall be construed as a reference to a child within the meaning of Part III of the Social Work (Scotland) Act 1968.

NOTE
[1] Prospectively substituted by the Children (Scotland) Act 1995 (c. 36), Sched. 2, para. 15(30), *infra*.

---

[1] 2. Any reference to a court of summary jurisdiction or to a juvenile court shall be construed as a reference to the sheriff sitting summarily.

NOTE
[1] As amended by the Criminal Procedure (Scotland) Act 1975 (c. 21), Sched. 10, Pt. I.

Part II

Specific Adaptations

3.—(1) In section 40(1) for the words "apparently under the age of seventeen years" there shall be substituted the words "who is apparently a child".

(2) In section 40(2) for the words "apparently under the age of seventeen years" there shall be substituted the words "who is apparently a child," and for the words "remand home" there shall be substituted the words "place of safety other than a police station".

(3) After subsection (2) there shall be inserted the following subsections—

"(3) Where a person who is apparently a child has been detained under this section and is not so liberated as aforesaid and it is decided not to proceed with the charge against him a constable shall so inform the reporter of the local authority for the area in which the child is detained, and the child may continue to be detained in a place of safety until the reporter has decided on the course that should be taken with regard to the child under the provisions of Part III of the Social Work (Scotland) Act 1968.

(4) A child shall not continue to be detained under this section—

(*a*) where the reporter considers the child does not require compulsory measures of care, or

(*b*) after the day on which a children's hearing first sit to consider his case in pursuance of section 37(4) of the Social Work (Scotland) Act 1968, or

(*c*) for a period exceeding seven days."

4.—(1) In section 41, for subsection (1) there shall be substituted the following subsection—

"(1) Any court, on remanding or committing for trial a child who is not liberated on bail shall, instead of committing him to prison, commit him to the local authority in whose area the court is situated to be detained in a place of safety chosen by the local authority for the period for which he is remanded or until he is liberated in due course of law:

Provided that in the case of a child over fourteen years of age it shall not be obligatory on the court so to commit him if the court certifies that he is of so unruly a character that he cannot safely be so committed, or that he is of so depraved a character that he is not a fit person to be so detained."

(2) In subsection (2), for the words "young person" where first occurring there shall be substituted the words "child over fourteen years of age", and where secondly occurring there shall be substituted the word "child".

5. For section 43 there shall be substituted the following section—

Notice to local authority of charges against children, and duty of local authority to furnish reports and information to courts

"**43.**—(1) Where a child is to be brought before a court notification of the day and hour when, and the nature of the charge on which, the child is to be so brought shall be sent by the chief constable of the area in which the offence is alleged to have been committed, to the local authority for the area in which the court will sit.

(2) Where a local authority have received a notification under the foregoing subsection they shall make such investigations and render available to the court a report which shall contain such information as to the home surroundings of the child as appear to them will assist the court in the disposal of his case, and the report shall contain information, which the appropriate education authority shall have a duty to supply, as to the school record, health and character of the child."

6. In section 44, after the word "child" where first occurring there shall be inserted the words "under fourteen years of age".

7. In section 46(1) for the words "child or young person", in both places where these words occur, there shall be substituted the words "a person under the age of seventeen years".

8.—(1) In section 47(1) the words "until he can be brought before a juvenile court" shall be omitted wherever occurring.

(2) After subsection (1) there shall be inserted the following subsection—

"(1A) A child shall not continue to be detained under the last foregoing subsection—

(*a*) where the reporter considers the child does not require compulsory measures of care, or

(*b*) after the day on which a children's hearing first sit to consider his case in pursuance of section 37(4) of the Social Work (Scotland) Act 1968, or

(*c*) for a period exceeding seven days".

9. In section 48, for the words "any child or young person" there shall be substituted the words "any person under the age of seventeen", and for the words "the child or young person" there shall be substituted the words "the person".

[1] 10. For section 50 there shall be substituted the following section—

Child charged jointly with person who is not a child

"**50.** When a child has been charged with an offence jointly with a person who is not a child the provisions of sections 52 to 54 of this Act shall not apply to summary proceedings before the sheriff in respect of the charges."

NOTE

[1] As amended by the Children and Young Persons Act 1969 (c. 54), Sched. 6.

11.—(1) In section 52(1), for the words from the beginning to the words "a juvenile court", second occurring, there shall be substituted the words—

"Where summary proceedings are brought in respect of an offence alleged to have been committed by a child the sheriff shall sit either in a different building or room from that in which he usually sits or on different days from those on which other courts in the building are engaged in criminal proceedings; and no person shall be present at any sitting to which this subsection applies".

(2) For subsection (2) there shall be substituted the following subsection—

"(2) The power to make rules conferred on the High Court of Justiciary under section 76(1) of the Summary Jurisdiction (Scotland) Act 1954 shall include power to make rules as respects the procedure in cases to which the foregoing subsection applies."

12. In section 53(5), for the words from the beginning to the words "juvenile court", there shall be substituted the words "Any direction in any enactment that a charge shall be brought before a juvenile court shall be construed as a direction that he shall be brought before the sheriff sitting as a court of summary jurisdiction, and no such direction".

13. In section 54(1), after the word "report" there shall be inserted the words "of any summary proceedings in the sheriff court in respect of an offence by a child or", and for the words "child or young person" in both places where these words occur there shall be substituted the words "a person under the age of seventeen years".

14. In section 57(2), for the words from the beginning to "harm" there shall be substituted the words "Where a child is convicted on indictment".

15. In section 58, the words from the beginning to "imprisonment or" shall be omitted and for the words from "he be committed" to the end of the section, there shall be substituted the words "the child be detained for such period, not exceeding one month, as may be specified in the order in a place chosen by the local authority in whose area the court is situated."

16. [Repealed by the Criminal Justice (Scotland) Act 1987 (c. 41), Sched. 2.]

17. In section 59(2), after the words "for his" there shall be inserted the words "co-operation in securing the child's".

18. In section 62, for the words "an approved school" there shall be substituted the words "a residential establishment", and in paragraph (*c*), for the word "school" there shall be substituted the words "residential establishment".

19. In section 63(3), for the words "juvenile offenders" there shall be substituted the word "children", and the words "under the Probation of Offenders Act 1907" shall be omitted.

20. For section 67 there shall be substituted the following section—

"67. Any court by or before which a person is convicted of having committed in respect of a child any of the offences mentioned in the First Schedule to this Act or any offence under section 21 of this Act, may refer the child to the reporter of the local authority in whose area the child resides and certify that the said offence shall be a ground established for the purposes of Part III of the Social Work (Scotland) Act 1968."

Section 33

[1] SCHEDULE 3

Children's Panels

NOTE

[1] Saved by the Local Government (Scotland) Act 1973 (c. 65), s. 161(9).

Appointment

1. The Secretary of State shall appoint such number of members of children's panels for each local authority area as he considers appropriate and from among these members he shall appoint a chairman and a deputy chairman.

2. A member of a children's panel shall hold office for such period as is specified by the Secretary of State, but may be removed from office by the Secretary of State at any time.

[THE NEXT PAGE IS K 87]

Children's Panel Advisory Committee

[1] 3. Each local authority shall form a Children's Panel Advisory Committee consisting of

(i) in the case of the committee for the Strathclyde region, four members nominated by the local authority and six members nominated by the Secretary of State;

(ii) in any other case, two members nominated by the local authority and three members nominated by the Secretary of State.

NOTE

[1] As amended by the Local Government (Scotland) Act 1973, Sched. 27, Pt. II, para. 187, and Sched. 29. Saved by *ibid.*, s. 56(9)(*d*). Extended by the Local Government (Scotland) Act 1975, s. 23(2).

[1] 3A. The Secretary of State may, at the request of the local authority provide for an increase in the membership of the Children's Panel Advisory Committee for the area of the authority by such number, not exceeding five, of additional members as the authority specify in relation to their request, the additional members to be nominated as follows—

(*a*) the first, second and fourth additional members, by the Secretary of State;

(*b*) the third and fifth additional members, by the local authority.

NOTE

[1] As amended by the Law Reform (Miscellaneous Provisions) (Scotland) Act 1985, s. 24.

4. The chairman of the Children's Panel Advisory Committee shall be appointed by the Secretary of State from among the members he has nominated, and shall be resident in the area of the local authority.

5. It shall be the duty of the Children's Panel Advisory Committee—

(*a*) to submit names of possible panel members to the Secretary of State;

(*b*) to advise the Secretary of State as required on the suitability of persons referred to him as possible members; and

(*c*) to advise the Secretary of State on such matters relating to the general administration of panels as he may refer to them.

[1] 5A. The Children's Panel Advisory Committee shall have power—

(*a*) to appoint sub-committees;

(*b*) to appoint to any such sub-committee persons who are not members of the Children's Panel Advisory Committee; and

(*c*) to refer all or any of the duties set out in paragraph 5 above to any such sub-committee for their advice;

and the provisions of paragraph 8 below shall apply to any persons appointed under sub-paragraph (*b*) above as they apply to members of the Children's Panel Advisory Committee.

NOTE

[1] Added by the Local Government (Scotland) Act 1973, Sched. 27, Pt. II, para. 187.

Recruitment and Training of Panel Members

6. The Secretary of State may make such arrangements as he considers appropriate to recruit and train members or possible members of children's panels.

7. Each local authority may make such arrangements as they consider appropriate—

(*a*) to enable the Children's Panel Advisory Committee to obtain names for submission to the Secretary of State as possible panel members, and

(*b*) to train panel members or possible panel members.

Expenses of Panel Members

[1] 8.—(1) A local authority may pay—

(*a*) to a member or possible member of the children's panel in respect of his attendance at a children's hearing or at training arranged under paragraph 6 or 7 of this Schedule;

(*b*) to a member of the Children's Panel Advisory Committee, who is not also a member of a body to which sections 45 and 46 of the Local Government (Scotland) Act 1973 apply, in respect of his attendance at a meeting of the Committee;

(*c*) to a member or possible member of the children's panel or to such a member of the Children's Panel Advisory Committee as aforesaid in respect of the doing by him of anything approved by the authority, or anything of a class so approved, for the purpose of, or in connection with, the discharge of the functions of the panel or Committee, as the case may be;

allowances, in the nature of those payable under sections 45(4) and 46(1) of the said Act of 1973, being payments of such reasonable amounts as they may determine in any particular case or class of case and not exceeding the amounts prescribed under the said section 45(4) and specified under the said section 46(1) for the corresponding allowances under those provisions.

(2) A local authority may pay to a member of the Children's Panel Advisory Committee who is also a member of a body to which sections 45 and 46 of the said Act of 1973 apply—

(*a*) in respect of his attendance at a meeting of the Committee;

(*b*) in respect of the doing by him of anything approved by the authority, or anything of a class so approved, for the purpose of, or in connection with, the discharge of the functions of the Committee;

allowances, in the nature of those payable under the said section 45 and subsection (1) of the said section 46, being payments of such reasonable amounts as they may determine in any particular case or class of case and not exceeding the amounts prescribed under the said section 45 and specified under subsection (1) of the said section 46 for the corresponding allowances under those provisions.

NOTE

[1] As substituted by the Local Government (Scotland) Act 1975 (c. 30), s. 33. Prospective substitution of para. 8 in the Local Government and Housing Act 1989 (c. 42), Sched. 11, para. 15:

"**8.** A local authority may pay—

(*a*) to a member or possible member of the children's panel,

(*b*) to a member of the Children's Panel Advisory Committee,

such allowances as may be determined by the Secretary of State; and he may determine differently in relation to different cases or classes of case."

Section 53

SCHEDULE 4

Amendment of Legal Aid (Scotland) Act 1967

[Repealed by the Legal Aid (Scotland) Act 1986, Sched. 5.]

Section 64

SCHEDULE 5

Appeal Tribunals

1. For the purpose of enabling appeal tribunals to be constituted as occasion may require, there shall be appointed by the Secretary of State a panel (hereafter referred to as "the panel") of persons to act when required as members of any such tribunal.

2. No officer of any Government department shall be qualified to be appointed to the panel.

3. Any person appointed to be a member of the panel shall hold office for such period and subject to such conditions as may be determined by the Secretary of State.

4. Where any appeal is required to be determined by a tribunal constituted in accordance with this Schedule, the tribunal shall consist of a sheriff (or, if he is unable to act, a person qualified for appointment as sheriff nominated by the Lord President of the Court of Session), who shall be chairman, and two other members being impartial persons who shall be appointed from the panel by the Secretary of State.

5. The Secretary of State may—
   (*a*) pay to members of tribunals constituted as aforesaid such fees and allowances as he may with the consent of the Treasury determine.
   (*b*) defray the expenses of such tribunals up to such amounts as he may with the like consent determine.

6.—(1) The Secretary of State may make rules—
   (*a*) as to the tenure of office of members of the panel.
   (*b*) as to the procedure of tribunals and the procedure in connection with the bringing of matters before a tribunal. and as to the time within which matters may be brought before tribunals,
   (*c*) as to the payment by the Secretary of State to persons attending proceedings before tribunals of travelling and other allowances (including compensation for loss of remunerative time).

(2) The power under this paragraph to make rules as to procedure includes power to make provision as to the representation of one person in any proceedings by another person.

7. In this Schedule the expression "sheriff" does not include a sheriff-substitute, and means the sheriff of the county in which the establishment to which the appeal relates is situated or is proposed to be established.

Section 84

SCHEDULE 6

Transfer of Assets and Liabilities

1. Every agreement to which the transferor was a party immediately before the date of transfer shall have effect as from that date in favour of or against the transferee as if the transferee had been a party to the agreement instead of the transferor.

2. Where the functions of the transferor are transferred to more than one transferee the property, rights, liabilities and obligations of the transferor shall be allocated in such a manner as relates to the allocation of the functions transferred to each of the transferees.

3. Any legal or other proceedings to which the transferor is a party which are pending on the date of the transfer may be continued on or after that date as if the transferee instead of the transferor had been that party.

4. The Secretary of State may make regulations for facilitating the transfer of any property, rights, liabilities or obligations in pursuance of this Act.

5. In this Schedule—
   (*a*) "transferor" means a body or person from whom a function has been transferred under this Act and from whom any property, right, liability or obligation has been so transferred, and
   (*b*) "transferee" means a local authority to whom a function or any property, right, liability or obligation has been so transferred,

and "transfer of function" includes the giving of a function to a local authority which was previously performed by another body including another local authority.

Section 93

SCHEDULE 7

Transitional Provisions

. . . .

Section 95(1)

SCHEDULE 8

Minor and Consequential Amendments

[Schedule 8 makes amendments to the following enactments:]

Paragraph of Sched. 8	Enactment amended	Subject-matter
	Criminal Appeal (Scotland) Act 1926 (c. 15) [See Division E *supra*]	
1	S. 9(4)(*d*).	Places of safety.
	Children and Young Persons Act 1933 (c. 12)	
2	S. 70(2).	Supervision requirements.
3	S. 76(1B).	Supervision requirements.

Paragraph of Sched. 8	Enactment amended	Subject-matter
4	S. 90(6).	Supervision requirements.
5	S. 107(1).	Definition of "supervision requirement".
	Children and Young Persons (Scotland) Act 1937 (c. 37)	
6	S. 38(3).	Residential establishments.
7(1)	S. 87(1).	Residential training.
7(2)	S. 87(2) to (4).	Approved schools.
7(3)	S. 87(3).	Residential training.
8	S. 101(2A) inserted.	Local authority expenses.
9(1)	S. 103(1).	Children charged with offences.
9(2)	S. 103(1A) inserted.	Definition of "child".
9(3)	S. 103(5) inserted.	Definition of "child".
10	S. 110(1).	Definitions.
	National Health Service (Scotland) Act 1947 (c. 27)	
11(1)	S. 15(1)(*g*) inserted.	Provision of services under 1968 Act.
11(2)	S. 15(4).	Social work services.
12	S. 27(4) inserted.	Functions previously performed by health authorities.
13	S. 63.	Local authorities.
	National Assistance Act 1948 (c. 29)	
14	S. 32(1).	References to "local authority".
15	S. 41(1A) inserted.	Blind, etc. and handicapped persons.
16	S. 65(*f*) inserted.	Accommodation provided under Part IV of 1968 Act.
	Children Act 1948 (c. 43)	
17(1)	S. 1(4).	References to "local authority".
17(2)	S. 1(5).	Supervision requirements.
18	S. 13(1).	Boarding and residential establishments.
19	S. 59(1).	Definition of "supervision requirement".
	Nurseries and Child-Minders Regulation Act 1948 (c. 53)	
20	[Para. 20 repealed by the *Children Act* 1989 (c. 41), Sched. 15 with effect from 11th October 1991: S.I. 1991 No. 828.]	
	Criminal Justice Act 1948 (c. 58)	
21	S. 9(9) inserted.	Probation orders.
	Criminal Justice (Scotland) Act 1949 (c. 94)	
22(1)	S. 2(2) substituted.	Probation orders.
22(2)	S. 2(4).	Officers of the local authority.
22(3)	S. 2(6).	Probation orders.
22(4)	S. 2(8).	Officers of the local authority.
23	S. 3(4) and (6).	Officers of the local authority.
24	S. 5(1).	Officers of the local authority.
25	S. 8(1) substituted.	Security for good behaviour.
26	S. 9(1).	Age of young offenders.
27	S. 10.	Officers of the local authority, etc.
28(1)	S. 28(1)(*a*), (*b*) substituted.	Disposal by courts of young persons under and over 16.
28(2)	S. 28(3) and (4) substituted.	Detention of young persons.
28(3)	S. 28(5) substituted.	Removal from detention to place of safety.
29	S. 30(1).	Place of safety.
30	S. 78(1).	Definitions of "local authority" and "place of safety".
31(1)	Sched. 2.	Scottish equivalents of probation officers etc.
31(2)	Sched. 2 para. 2(1).	Scottish equivalents of probation officers etc.
31(3)	Sched. 2 para. 2(4)(*a*).	Scottish equivalents of probation officers etc.

Paragraph of Sched. 8	Enactment amended	Subject-matter
	Maintenance Orders Act 1950 (c. 37) [See Division K, *supra*]	
32	S. 8(1).	Reference to s.81 of 1968 Act.
33(1)	S. 9(1)(*aa*) inserted.	Contribution orders.
33(2)	S. 9(2).	Contribution orders.
34	S. 16(2)(*b*)(vi) inserted.	Contribution orders.
	Children and Young Persons Act 1956 (c. 24)	
35	[Act repealed by the Social Work (Scotland) Act 1968 (c. 49) and the Children and Young Persons Act 1969 (c. 54)].	Omission of references to Children and Young Persons (Scotland) Act 1937.
	Valuation and Rating (Scotland) Act 1956 (c. 60) [See Division O, *infra*]	
36(1)	S. 8(1)(*b*).	Local authorities.
36(2)	S. 8(1)(*c*) substituted.	Structures provided for disabled etc.
	Adoption Act 1958 (c. 5)	
37	S. 4(3)(*d*) inserted.	Assumption by local authority of parental rights.
38	S. 15(4).	Assumption by local authority of parental rights.
39	S. 36(2)(*a*).	Contribution in respect of child in care.
40	S. 43(3).	Provision for orphans etc.
41	S. 57.	Place of safety.
	Matrimonial Proceedings (Children) Act 1958 (c. 40) [See Division K, *supra*]	
42	S. 10(4) substituted.	Application of Part II of 1968 Act to child committed to care.
43(1)	S. 11(1) and (1A).	Report on future care arrangements.
43(2)	S. 11(5).	Report on future care arrangements.
	Children Act 1958 (c.65)	
44(1)	S. 2(3)(*b*).	Residential establishments.
44(2)	S. 2(4).	Supervision requirements.
45(1)	S. 6(*b*).	Supervision requirements.
45(2)	S. 6(*d*).	Assumption of parental rights and powers.
45(3)	S. 6(*e*).	Local authorities.
46	S. 7(4).	Application of Part II of 1968 Act.
47(1)	S. 17.	Definition of "place of safety".
47(2)	S. 17.	Definitions of "residential establishment" and "supervision requirement".
	Mental Health Act 1959 (c. 72)	
48	S. 10(1)(*a*)(iv) inserted.	Assumption of parental rights and powers.
49	S. 50(*d*) inserted.	Assumption of parental rights and powers.
	Mental Health (Scotland) Act 1960 (c. 61)	
50	Whole Act.	Substitution of local authority for local health authority.
51(1)	S. 7(1).	Ascertainment of mental deficiency.
51(2)	S. 7(2).	Ascertainment of mental deficiency.
52	S. 10(1)(*a*)(iv) inserted.	Assumption of parental rights and powers.
53	S. 30(2).	Guardianship applications.
54	S. 46(*c*), (*d*) substituted.	Assumption of parental rights and powers.
55	S. 57(3)(*b*).	Children under 16.

Paragraph of Sched. 8	Enactment amended	Subject-matter
56	S. 59(1).	Residential establishments.
57	S. 66(7)(*a*) substituted.	Criminal detainees.
58	S. 72(1).	Definitions of "guardian", "place of safety" and "residential establishment".
59	S. 111.	Definition of "local authority".
	Health Visiting and Social Work (Training) Act 1962 (c. 33)	
60	S. 3(5).	Promotion of social welfare by local authorities.
	Education (Scotland) Act 1962 (c. 47)	
61	S. 36(3).	Reference of children to reporters.
62(1)	S. 44(1).	Reference of children to reporters.
62(2)	S. 44(2).	Reference of children to reporters.
63	S. 65(1), (3), (4) and (5).	Local authorities.
64	S. 66(1).	Local authorities.
65	S. 85(5)(*c*).	Management and teaching in residential establishments.
66	S. 141(2)(*d*) inserted.	Residential establishments providing education.
67	S. 145(41A) and (46A) inserted.	Definitions of "residential establishment" and "supervision requirement".
	Children and Young Persons Act 1963 (c. 37)	
68	S. 55.	Power to arrange for emigrations.
69(1)	S. 57(2).	Sheriff sitting summarily.
69(2)	S. 57(3).	Sheriff sitting summarily.
	Criminal Justice (Scotland) Act 1963 (c. 39)	
70	S. 1(4).	Age of young offenders.
71	S. 7(1).	Age of young offenders.
72	S. 29.	Persons detained under 1937 Act, ss.57 and 58A.
	Registration of Births, Deaths and Marriages (Scotland) Act 1965 (c. 49)	
73(1)	S. 15(1) and (3).	Information on finding of infant.
73(2)	S. 15(4).	Information on finding of infant.
	Family Allowances Act 1965 (c. 53)	
74(1)	S. 11(1).	Exclusion of children detained.
74(2)	S. 11(3).	Exclusion where parental rights and powers assumed.

Section 95(2)

SCHEDULE 9

ENACTMENTS REPEALED

PART I

Repeals Extending to Scotland Only

Session and Chapter	Short Title	Extent of Repeal
1 Edw. 8 & 1 Geo. 6 c. 37.	The Children and Young Persons (Scotland) Act 1937.	In section 21(2), the words from "may take" to the end of the subsection. In section 42(1), the words "or is for any other reason brought before a court" and in subsection (2), the words "or taken to a place of safety" and the words "or the person by whom he is taken to the place of safety, as the case may be". In section 47(1) the words "until he can be brought before a juvenile court", wherever occurring.

Session and Chapter	Short Title	Extent of Repeal
		In section 49(1), the words "either as being in need of care or protection or", the words "or otherwise", and the words "and for securing that proper provision is made for his education and training".
		Section 49(2).
		Section 51.
		Section 53(2) and (3).
		Section 59(1) and in subsection (4), the words "under this section, or".
		Sections 60 and 61.
		In section 63(3) the words "under the Probation of Offenders Act 1907".
		Sections 65 and 66.
		Sections 68 to 86.
		Sections 88 to 98.
		Section 101(5) and (6).
		Section 106.
		Section 107(1)(*a*) and (2).
		Section 109.
		In section 110(1)— the following definitions— "Approved school"; "Approved school order"; "Headmaster"; "In need of care or protection"; in the definition of "Justice" the words "(except in section 51 of this Act)"; and the definition of "Managers".
		In section 110, in subsection (3)(*a*)(ii) the words "and the juvenile court for any area" and subsection (3)(*a*)(iv).
		Section 111.
		Section 112.
		Schedule 2.
		Schedule 3.
11 & 12 Geo. 6 c. 29.	The National Assistance Act 1948.	Section 21.
		Section 22(1).
		Sections 23 and 24.
		Section 26(1) and (5).
		Section 27.
		Sections 29 and 30.
		Section 32.
		Sections 34 to 40.
		Sections 50(3).
		Section 58(1) and (4).
11 & 12 Geo. 6 c. 43.	The Children Act 1948.	The whole Act.
12, 13 & 14 Geo. 6 c. 94.	The Criminal Justice (Scotland) Act 1949.	Section 2(3) and (9).
		Section 4(2) and (3).
		Section 5(3).
		In section 7, in subsection (2), the words from "to omit" to "and", and in subsection (4), the words "to (3)".
		Sections 11 to 13.

Session and Chapter	Short Title	Extent of Repeal
		In section 28, subsection (2), and in subsection (3), the words "a remand home or" and the words "home or". Sections 50 and 51. Sections 69 to 73. In section 75, subsections (1)(*a*), (3)(*a*) to (*d*) and (4) to (6). In section 78, in subsection (1)— in the definition of "appropriate court" the words "or supervision"; and the words "or person under supervision"; and the following definitions— "Approved probation hostel" and "Approved probation home"; "Approved school"; "Remand home"; "Salaried probation officer"; in the definition of "sentence", the words from "an order for custody" to the end of the definition; the following definitions— "Supervision order"; "Voluntary probation officer"; "Whole-time probation officer"; and "Young person". Schedule 1. In Schedule 2, in paragraph 2, in sub-paragraph (3), the words "appointed by the appropriate court", in sub-paragraph (4)(*b*), the words "named therein", in paragraph 3(*b*) the words "an approved probation hostel or home or in" and the word "other" and paragraph 7. Schedule 3.
14 Geo. 6 c. 37.	The Maintenance Orders Act 1950.	Schedule 1, so far as relating to the modification of the Children and Young Persons (Scotland) Act 1937.
15 & 16 Geo. 6 & 1 Eliz. 2 c. 61.	The Prisons (Scotland) Act 1952.	Section 18(1) to (3A). In section 32, in subsection (3), the words "who is not less than seventeen years of age", and subsection (4).
4 & 5 Eliz. 2 c. 24.	The Children and Young Persons Act 1956.	The whole Act.
4 & 5 Eliz. 2 c. 50.	The Family Allowances and National Insurance Act 1956.	The whole Act.
5 & 6 Eliz. 2 c. 1.	The Police, Fire and Probation Officers Remuneration Act 1956.	In section 1(1)(*d*), the words from "or" to "1949".
6 & 7 Eliz. 2 c. 40.	The Matrimonial Proceedings (Children) Act 1958.	Section 11(2) and (3). In section 12(1), the words "of a probation officer or", and section 12(3).
6 & 7 Eliz. 2 c. 65.	The Children Act 1958.	Section 1. Section 2(6) and (7).
7 & 8 Eliz. 2 c. 5.	The Adoption Act 1958.	Section 4(3)(*b*). In section 11(1), the words "or juvenile court". In section 15(3), the words from "or the Children" to "1937".

Session and Chapter	Short Title	Extent of Repeal
		In section 37(3), the words "in an approved school or".
8 & 9 Eliz. 2 c. 61.	The Mental Health (Scotland) Act 1960.	Sections 8 and 9. In section 10, in subsection (1), in paragraph (*a*), head (i), and at the end of head (ii) the word "or". Section 12(2). Sections 19 to 21. Section 46(*a*). In section 55(10), the words from "including" to the word "school". Section 56. In section 57, in subsection (3)(*b*), the words "or young person"; and subsection (5). Section 69(1)(*b*). Section 71. In section 72, the definitions of "approved school" and "remand home" and in the definition of "place of safety" the words "or young person" first occurring. In section 111(1), the definition of "residential home for persons suffering from mental disorder;".
10 & 11 Eliz. 2 c. 47.	The Education (Scotland) Act 1962.	Section 36(4) and (5). Section 44(3) and (4). Section 80(1)(*e*). In section 104 the words "(including an approved school)".
1963 c. 37.	The Children and Young Persons Act 1963.	Section 1. Sections 45 to 52. Section 58.
1963 c. 39.	The Criminal Justice (Scotland) Act 1963.	In section 11, in subsection (2), the words from "if the offender" to the words "detention centre", and subsections (3) and (5). Section 15. Part II. Schedule 2.
1968 c. 46.	The Health Services and Public Health Act 1968.	Section 13. Section 44. Section 45.

PART II

Repeals Extending to England and Wales

Session and Chapter	Short Title	Extent of Repeal
23 & 24 Geo. 5 c. 12.	The Children and Young Persons Act 1933.	In section 78(2) and (4), the words from "(including" to "1937)". In section 82(1), the words from "or" to "1937", and in the proviso, the words from "or where" to "Wales". In section 83(1), (2) and (4), the words "Scotland or" wherever occurring, and in subsection (5) the words from "in relation to Scotland" to "Department, and".

Session and Chapter	Short Title	Extent of Repeal
		In section 85(1) and (2), the words "or under the Children and Young Persons (Scotland) Act 1937". In Schedule 4, in paragraph 9, in sub-paragraph (1), the words from "or with the consent" to "to that Act", paragraph 9(3), and in paragraph 13, the words "or of the Children and Young Persons (Scotland) Act 1937" in both places where they occur.
6 & 7 Eliz. 2 c. 65.	The Children Act 1958.	In section 2(4), the words from "or of" to "1937". In section 17, in the definition of "fit person order", the words "or" to "1937".
7 & 8 Eliz. 2 c. 72.	The Mental Health Act 1959.	In section 10(1), in sub-paragraph (*a*), head (ii). In section 50, sub-paragraph (*b*).
1963 c. 37.	The Children and Young Persons Act 1963.	In section 12, the words "Scotland or". In section 45(1), the words "the Children and Young Persons (Scotland) Acts 1937 and 1956". Sections 51 and 52. Section 53(1)(*b*).
1965 c. 53.	The Family Allowances Act 1965.	In section 11, subsection (1)(*a*)(ii), in subsection (1)(*c*), the words "or an order under section 73(2) of the said Act of 1937", and in subsection (2), the words "or the said Act of 1937".

Age of Majority (Scotland) Act 1969

(1969 c. 39)

An Act to amend the law of Scotland relating to the age of majority; and for connected purposes. [25th July 1969]

Reduction of age of majority to 18

1.—(1) As from the date on which this Act comes into force a person shall attain majority on attaining the age of eighteen instead of on attaining the age of twenty-one; and a person shall attain majority on that date if he has then already attained the age of eighteen but not the age of twenty-one.

(2) The foregoing subsection applies for the purposes of any rule of law, and, in the absence of a definition or of any indication of a contrary intention, for the construction of "major", "majority", "full age", "perfect age", "complete age", "lawful age", "minor", "minority", "under age", "less age" and similar expressions in—

(*a*) any statutory provision, whether passed or made before, on or after the date on which this Act comes into force; and

(*b*) any deed executed on or after that date other than a deed made in the exercise of a special power of appointment where the deed creating the power was executed before that date.

(3) In the statutory provisions specified in Schedule 1 to this Act, for any reference to the age of twenty-one years or twenty-five years there shall be substituted a reference to the age of eighteen years.

(4) This section does not affect the construction of any such expression

as is referred to in subsection (2) of this section in any of the statutory provisions described in Schedule 2 to this Act.

(5) The Secretary of State may, by order made by statutory instrument, amend any provision in any local enactment passed on or before the date on which this Act comes into force by substituting a reference to the age of eighteen years for any reference therein to the age of twenty-one years; and any statutory instrument containing an order under this subsection shall be subject to annulment in pursuance of a resolution of either House of Parliament.

(6) Notwithstanding any rule of law, a testamentary instrument or codicil executed before the date on which this Act comes into force shall not be treated for the purposes of this section as made on or after that date by reason only that the instrument or codicil is confirmed by a codicil executed on or after that date.

(7) This section shall not affect the construction of any statutory provision where it is incorporated in and has effect as part of any deed the construction of which is not affected by this section.

(8) This section shall not prevent the making of an adoption order or provisional adoption order under the Adoption Act 1958 in respect of a person who has attained the age of eighteen if the application for the order was made before this Act comes into force, and in relation to any such case that Act shall have effect as if this section had not been enacted.

(9) Section 4 of the Entail Amendment (Scotland) Act 1875 (consent to disentail may be given at 21) is hereby repealed.

(10) In this section—

"statutory provision" means any enactment and any order, rule, regulation, byelaw or other instrument made in the exercise of a power conferred by any enactment; and

"deed" includes any disposition, contract, instrument or writing (not being a statutory provision), whether *inter vivos* or *mortis causa*.

Short title, interpretation, commencement and extent

2.—(1) This Act may be cited as the Age of Majority (Scotland) Act 1969.

(2) Except where the context otherwise requires, any reference in this Act to any enactment shall be construed as a reference to that enactment as amended, extended or applied by or under any other enactment.

(3) This Act shall come into force on such date as the Secretary of State may appoint by order made by statutory instrument.

(4) This Act shall extend to Scotland only.

[THE NEXT PAGE IS K 95]

SCHEDULES

Section 1(3)

SCHEDULE 1

STATUTORY PROVISIONS AMENDED BY SUBSTITUTING 18 FOR 21 OR 25 YEARS

[1] PART I

ENACTMENTS

NOTE

[1] As amended by the Friendly Societies Act 1974 (c. 46), Sched. 11; the Prescription and Limitation (Scotland) Act 1973 (c. 52), Sched. 5, Pt. I, the Customs and Excise Management Act 1979 (c. 2), Sched. 6, the Mental Health (Scotland) Act 1984 (c. 36), Sched. 5, and the Statute Law (Repeals) Act 1993 (c. 50), Sched. 1, Pt. VIII (effective 5th November 1993).

	Short title
c.6.	The Diligence Act 1621.
c.4.	The Minority Act 1663.
c.36.	The Entail Amendment Act 1848. Sections 1, 2 and 3.
c.46.	The Hypnotism Act 1952. Section 3.
c.57.	The Trusts (Scotland) Act 1961. Section 1(2).
c.2.	The Betting, Gaming and Lotteries Act 1963. Section 22(1) and (3).
c.12.	The Industrial and Provident Societies Act 1965. Section 20.

PART II

REGULATIONS AND RULES

. . . . . .

Section 1(4)

SCHEDULE 2

STATUTORY PROVISIONS UNAFFECTED BY SECTION 1

1. The Regency Acts 1937 to 1953.

[1] 2. Section 50 of the Local Government (Scotland) Act 1947.

3. [Repealed by the Finance Act 1969 (c. 32), Sched. 21.]

NOTE

[1] As amended by the Representation of the People Act 1983 (c. 2), Sched. 9, Pt. I.

[THE NEXT PAGE IS K 99]

[1] Maintenance Orders (Reciprocal Enforcement) Act 1972

(1972 c. 18)

An Act to make new provision, applying throughout the United Kingdom, in place of the Maintenance Orders (Facilities for Enforcement) Act 1920; to make provision with a view to the accession by the United Kingdom to the United Nations Convention on the Recovery Abroad of Maintenance done at New York on 20th June 1956; to make other provision for facilitating the recovery of maintenance by or from persons in the United Kingdom from or by persons in other countries; to extend the jurisdiction of magistrates' courts to hear complaints by or against persons outside England and Wales; and for purposes connected with the matters aforesaid.

[23rd March 1972]

NOTE

[1] See S.I. 1974 No. 939, 1975 No. 475, 1980 Nos. 291, 1727 and 1732, all reprinted *infra*.

[1] Part I

Reciprocal Enforcement of Maintenance Orders made in United Kingdom or Reciprocating Country

NOTE

[1] See Magistrates' Courts Act 1980, s. 65(1)(*f*). Extended by S.I. 1979 No. 1317, Sched. 2.

Orders in Council designating reciprocating countries

[1] **1.**—(1) Her Majesty, if satisfied that, in the event of the benefits conferred by this Part of this Act being applied to, or to particular classes of, maintenance orders made by the courts of any country or territory outside the United Kingdom, similar benefits will in that country or territory be applied to, or to those classes of, maintenance orders made by the courts of the United Kingdom, may by Order in Council designate that country or territory as a reciprocating country for the purposes of this Part of this Act; and, subject to subsection (2) below, in this Part of this Act "reciprocating country" means a country or territory that is for the time being so designated.

(2) A country or territory may be designated under subsection (1) above as a reciprocating country either as regards maintenance orders generally, or as regards maintenance orders other than those of any specified class, or as regards maintenance orders of one or more specified classes only; and a country or territory which is for the time being so designated otherwise than as regards maintenance orders generally shall for the purposes of this Part of this Act be taken to be a reciprocating country only as regards maintenance orders of the class to which the designation extends.

NOTE

[1] See S.I. 1974 No. 556, 1975 No. 2187, 1979 No. 115 and 1983 No. 1125.

Orders made by courts in the United Kingdom

Transmission of maintenance order made in United Kingdom for enforcement in reciprocating country

2.—[1] (1) Subject to subsection (2) below, where the payer under a maintenance order made, whether before or after the commencement of this

Part of this Act, by a court in the United Kingdom is residing or has assets in a reciprocating country, the payee under the order may apply for the order to be sent to that country for enforcement.

(2) Subsection (1) above shall not have effect in relation to a provisional order or to an order made by virtue of a provision of Part II of this Act.

(3) Every application under this section shall be made in the prescribed manner to the prescribed officer of the court which made the maintenance order to which the application relates.

[1] (4) If, on an application duly made under this section to the prescribed officer of a court in the United Kingdom, that officer is satisfied that the payer under the maintenance order to which the application relates is residing or has assets in a reciprocating country, the following documents, that is to say—

(*a*) a certified copy of the maintenance order;
(*b*) a certificate signed by that officer certifying that the order is enforceable in the United Kingdom;
(*c*) a certificate of arrears so signed;
(*d*) a statement giving such information as the officer possesses as to the whereabouts of the payer and the nature and location of his assets in that country;
(*e*) a statement giving such information as the officer possesses for facilitating the identification of the payer; and
(*f*) where available, a photograph of the payer;

shall be sent by that officer to the Secretary of State with a view to their being transmitted by the Secretary of State to the responsible authority in the reciprocating country if he is satisfied that the statement relating to the whereabouts of the payer and the nature and location of his assets in that country gives sufficient information to justify that being done.

(5) Nothing in this section shall be taken as affecting any jurisdiction of a court in the United Kingdom with respect to a maintenance order to which this section applies, and any such order may be enforced, varied or revoked accordingly.

NOTE

[1] As amended by the Civil Jurisdiction and Judgments Act 1982, Sched. 11, para. 9.

Power of magistrates' court to make provisional maintenance order against person residing in reciprocating country

3.—(1)–(4) [England and Wales.]

[1] (5) Where a sheriff makes a maintenance order which is by virtue of this section a provisional order, the following documents, that is to say—

(*a*) a certified copy of the maintenance order;
(*b*) a document, authenticated in the prescribed manner, setting out or summarising the evidence given in the proceedings;
(*c*) a certificate signed by the prescribed officer of the court certifying that the grounds stated in the certificate are the grounds on which the making of the order might have been opposed by the payer under the order;
(*d*) a statement giving such information as was available to the court as to the whereabouts of the payer;
(*e*) a statement giving such information as the officer possesses for facilitating the identification of the payer; and
(*f*) where available, a photograph of the payer;

shall be sent by that officer to the Secretary of State with a view to their being transmitted by the Secretary of State to the responsible authority in the reciprocating country in which the payer is residing if he is satisfied that the statement relating to the whereabouts of the payer gives sufficient information to justify that being done.

[1] (6) A maintenance order made by virtue of this section which has been confirmed by a competent court in a reciprocating country shall be treated for all purposes as if the sheriff who made the order had made it in the form in which it was confirmed and as if the order had never been a provisional order, and subject to section 5 of this Act, any such order may be enforced, varied or revoked accordingly.

(7) [Northern Ireland.]

NOTE

[1] As applied by s. 4(6), *infra*.

Power of sheriff to make provisional maintenance order against person residing in reciprocating country

4.—[1] (1) In any action where the sheriff has jurisdiction by virtue of Rule 2(5) of Schedule 8 to the Civil Jurisdiction and Judgments Act 1982 and the defender resides in a reciprocating country, any maintenance order granted by the sheriff shall be a provisional order.

(2) [Repealed by the Civil Jurisdiction and Judgments Act 1982 (c. 27), Sched. 12, Pt. II, para. 3(1).]

[2] (3) Where in any action in which the payment of aliment in respect of a child is claimed, being an action referred to in subsection (1) above, the sheriff is satisfied—

(*a*) that there are grounds on which a maintenance order containing a provision requiring the payment of aliment in respect of that child may be made in that action, but

(*b*) that he has no power to make that order unless he also makes an order providing for the custody of the child,

then, for the purpose of enabling the sheriff to make the maintenance order, the pursuer shall be deemed to be a person to whom the custody of the child has been committed by a decree of the sheriff which is for the time being in force.

[2] (4) In any action referred to in subsection (1) above—

(*a*) it shall not be necessary for the pursuer to obtain a warrant for the citation of any person, and the action may commence and proceed without such citation;

(*b*) no decree shall be granted in favour of the pursuer unless the grounds of action have been substantiated by sufficient evidence, and section 36(3) of the Sheriff Courts (Scotland) Act 1971 shall not apply in relation to any such action which is a summary cause.

[2] (5) No enactment empowering the sheriff to remit an action to the Court of Session shall apply in relation to proceedings referred to in subsection (1) above.

(6) Section 3(5) and (6) of this Act shall apply for the purposes of this section as they apply for the purposes of that section, with the substitution, for references to a magistrates' court, of references to the sheriff.

NOTES

[1] Repealed and new subs. (1) inserted by the Civil Jurisdiction and Judgments Act 1982 (c. 27), Sched. 12, Pt. II, para. 3(1).

[2] As amended by the Civil Jurisdiction and Judgments Act 1982 (c. 27), Sched. 12, Pt. II, para. 3(2). Prospectively repealed by the Children (Scotland) Act 1995 (c. 36), Sched. 5, *infra*.

Variation and revocation of maintenance order made in United Kingdom

5.—(1) This section applies to a maintenance order a certified copy of which has been sent to a reciprocating country in pursuance of section 2 of this Act and to a maintenance order made by virtue of section 3 or 4 thereof which has been confirmed by a competent court in such a country.

(2) A court in the United Kingdom having power to vary a maintenance order to which this section applies shall have power to vary that order by a provisional order.

[1] (3) Where the payer under a maintenance order to which this section applies is for the time being residing in a reciprocating country, the court shall not, on an application made by the payee under the order for the variation of the order, vary the order by increasing the rate of the payments thereunder otherwise than by a provisional order.

[1] (3A) It shall not be necessary for the payee under a maintenance order to which this section applies to intimate to any person the making by him of an application for a provisional order varying the said maintenance order by increasing the rate of the payments thereunder.

(4) Where a court in the United Kingdom makes a provisional order varying a maintenance order to which this section applies, the prescribed officer of the court shall send in the prescribed manner to the court in a reciprocating country having power to confirm the provisional order a certified copy of the provisional order together with a document, authenticated in the prescribed manner, setting out or summarising the evidence given in the proceedings.

(5) Where a certified copy of a provisional order made by a court in a reciprocating country, being an order varying or revoking a maintenance order to which this section applies, together with a document, duly authenticated, setting out or summarising the evidence given in the proceedings in which the provisional order was made, is received by the court in the United Kingdom which made the maintenance order, that court may confirm or refuse to confirm the provisional order and, if that order is an order varying the maintenance order, confirm it either without alteration or with such alterations as it thinks reasonable.

[1] (6) Where a certified copy of a provisional order varying or revoking a maintenance order to which this section applies is received by a court as mentioned in subsection (5) above, the prescribed officer of that court shall intimate to the payee under the maintenance order, in the prescribed manner, that the provisional order has been received as aforesaid and that, unless the payee enters appearance within the prescribed period, the court will confirm the provisional order under this section.

(7) Where a maintenance order to which this section applies has been varied by an order (including a provisional order which has been confirmed) made by a court in the United Kingdom or by a competent court in a reciprocating country, the maintenance order shall, as from the date on which under the provisions of the order the variation is to take effect, have effect as varied by that order and, where that order was a provisional order, as if that order had been made in the form in which it was confirmed and as if it had never been a provisional order.

[2] (8) Where a maintenance order to which this section applies has been revoked by an order made by a court in the United Kingdom or by a competent court in a reciprocating country, including a provisional order made by the last-mentioned court which has been confirmed by a court in the United Kingdom, the maintenance order shall, as from the date on which under the provisions of the order the revocation is to take effect, be deemed to have ceased to have effect except as respects any arrears due under the maintenance order at that date.

(9) Where before a maintenance order made by virtue of section 3 or 4 of this Act is confirmed a document, duly authenticated, setting out or summarising evidence taken in a reciprocating country for the purpose of proceedings relating to the confirmation of the order is received by the court in the United Kingdom which made the order, or that court, in compliance with a request made to it by a court in such a country, takes the evidence of a person residing in the United Kingdom for the purpose of such proceedings, the court in the United Kingdom which made the order shall consider that evidence and if, having done so, it appears to it that the order ought not to have been made—

(*a*) it shall, in such manner as may be prescribed, give to the person on whose application the maintenance order was made an opportunity to consider that evidence, to make representations with respect to it and to adduce further evidence; and

(*b*) after considering all the evidence and any representations made by that person, it may revoke the maintenance order.

(10) [Scottish adaptation: incorporated *supra*.]

NOTES

[1] As applied to Scotland by s. 5(10).

[2] As amended by the Domestic Proceedings and Magistrates' Courts Act 1978 (c. 22), s. 54.

Orders made by courts in reciprocating countries

Registration in United Kingdom court of maintenance order made in reciprocating country

6.—(1) This section applies to a maintenance order made, whether before or after the commencement of this Part of this Act, by a court in a reciprocating country, including such an order made by such a court which has been confirmed by a court in another reciprocating country but excluding a provisional order which has not been confirmed.

[1] (2) Where a certified copy of an order to which this section applies is received by the Secretary of State from the responsible authority in a reciprocating country, and it appears to the Secretary of State that the payer under the order is residing or has assets in the United Kingdom, he shall send the copy of the order to the prescribed officer of the appropriate court.

(3) Where the prescribed officer of the appropriate court receives from the Secretary of State a certified copy of an order to which this section applies, he shall, subject to subsection (4) below, register the order in the prescribed manner in that court.

[1] (4) Before registering an order under this section an officer of a court shall take such steps as he thinks fit for the purpose of ascertaining whether the payer under the order is residing or has assets within the jurisdiction of the court, and if after taking those steps he is satisfied that the payer is not residing and has no assets within the jurisdiction of the court he shall return the certified copy of the order to the Secretary of State with a statement giving such information as he possesses as to the whereabouts of the payer and the nature and location of his assets.

NOTE

[1] As amended by the Civil Jurisdiction and Judgments Act 1982 (c. 27), Sched. 11, para. 10.

Confirmation by United Kingdom court of provisional maintenance order made in reciprocating country

[0] **7.**—(1) This section applies to a maintenance order made, whether before or after the commencement of this Part of this Act, by a court in a reciprocating country being a provisional order.

(2) Where a certified copy of an order to which this section applies together with—

(*a*) a document, duly authenticated, setting out or summarising the evidence given in the proceedings in which the order was made; and

(*b*) a statement of the grounds on which the making of the order might have been opposed by the payer under the order,

is received by the Secretary of State from the responsible authority in a reciprocating country, and it appears to the Secretary of State that the payer under the order is residing in the United Kingdom, he shall send the copy of the order and documents which accompanied it to the prescribed officer of the appropriate court, and that court shall—

(i) if the payer under the order establishes any grounds on which he might have opposed the making of the order in the proceedings in which the order was made, refuse to confirm the order; and

(ii) in any other case, confirm the order either without alteration or with such alterations as it thinks reasonable.

(3) In any proceedings for the confirmation under this section of a provisional order, the statement received from the court which made the order of the grounds on which the making of the order might have been opposed by the payer under the order shall be conclusive evidence that the payer might have opposed the making of an order on any of those grounds.

[1] (4) On receiving a certified copy of a provisional order sent to him in pursuance of subsection (2) above the prescribed officer of the appropriate court shall intimate to the payer under the order, in the prescribed manner, that the order has been received as aforesaid and that, unless the payer enters appearance within the prescribed period, the court will confirm the order under this section.

(5) The prescribed officer of a court having power under this section to confirm a provisional order shall, if the court confirms the order, register the order in the prescribed manner in that court, and shall, if the court refuses to confirm the order, return the certified copy of the order and the documents which accompanied it to the Secretary of State.

[2] (6) If such intimation as is mentioned in subsection (4) above cannot be given to the payer under a provisional order in pursuance of that subsection the officer by whom the certified copy of the order was received shall return that copy and the documents which accompanied it to the Secretary of State with a statement giving such information as he possesses as to the whereabouts of the payer.

(7) This section shall apply to Scotland subject to the following modifications:—

. . .

(*c*) in any proceedings for the confirmation under this section of a provisional order made by a court in a reciprocating country, the sheriff shall apply the law in force in that country with respect to the sufficiency of evidence.

NOTES

[0] As amended by the Maintenance Orders (Reciprocal Enforcement) Act 1992 (c. 56), Sched. 1, para. 8(2) and (3) (effective 5th April 1993: S.I. 1993 No. 618).

[1] As applied to Scotland by s. 7(7)(*a*).

[2] As applied to Scotland by s. 7(7)(*b*).

Enforcement of maintenance order registered in United Kingdom court

[1] **8.**—(1) . . . a registered order may be enforced in the United Kingdom as if it had been made by the registering court and as if that court had had jurisdiction to make it; and proceedings for or with respect to the enforcement of any such order may be taken accordingly.

(6) In any proceedings for or with respect to the enforcement of an order which is for the time being registered in any court under this Part of this Act a certificate of arrears sent to the prescribed officer of the court shall be sufficient evidence of the facts stated therein.

[2] (7) Subject to subsection (8) below, sums of money payable under a registered order shall be payable in accordance with the order as from the date on which they are required to be paid under the provisions of the order.

[2] (8) The court having power under section 7 of this Act to confirm a provisional order may, if it decides to confirm the order, direct that the sums of money payable under it shall be deemed to have been payable in accordance with the order as from the date on which they are required to

be paid under the provisions of the order or such later date, as it may specify; and subject to any such direction, a maintenance order registered under the said section 7 shall be treated as if it had been made in the form in which it was confirmed and as if it had never been a provisional order.

(9) [Scottish adaptation: incorporated *supra*.]

(10) [Northern Ireland.]

NOTES

[1] As applied to Scotland by subs. (9).

[2] As amended by the Domestic Proceedings and Magistrates' Courts Act 1978, s. 54.

Variation and revocation of maintenance order registered in United Kingdom court

9.—(1) Subject to the provisions of this section, the registering court—

(*a*) shall have the like power, on an application made by the payer or payee under a registered order, to vary or revoke the order as if it had been made by the registering court and as if that court had had jurisdiction to make it; and

(*b*) shall have power to vary or revoke a registered order by a provisional order.

[1] (1A) The powers conferred by subsection (1) above are not exercisable in relation to so much of a registered order as provides for the payment of a lump sum.

[2] (1B) The registering court shall not vary or revoke a registered order if neither the payer nor the payee under the order is resident in the United Kingdom.

(2) The registering court shall not vary a registered order otherwise than by a provisional order unless—

(*a*) both the payer and the payee under the registered order are for the time being residing in the United Kingdom; or

(*b*) the application is made by the payee under the registered order; or

(*c*) the variation consists of a reduction in the rate of the payments under the registered order and is made solely on the ground that there has been a change in the financial circumstances of the payer since the registered order was made or, in the case of an order registered under section 7 of this Act, since the registered order was confirmed, and the courts in the reciprocating country in which the maintenance order in question was made do not have power, according to the law in force in that country, to confirm provisional orders varying maintenance orders.

(3) The registering court shall not revoke a registered order otherwise than by a provisional order unless both the payer and the payee under the registered order are for the time being residing in the United Kingdom.

(4) On an application for the revocation of a registered order the registering court shall, unless both the payer and the payee under the registered order are for the time being residing in the United Kingdom, apply the law applied by the reciprocating country in which the registered order was made; but where by virtue of this subsection the registering court is required to apply that law, that court may make a provisional order if it has reason to believe that the ground on which the application is made is a ground on which the order could be revoked according to the law applied by the reciprocating country, notwithstanding that it has not been established that it is such a ground.

[3] (4A) It shall not be necessary for the payer under a registered order to intimate to any person the making by him of an application for a provisional order varying or revoking the registered order.

(5) Where the registering court makes a provisional order varying or revoking a registered order the prescribed officer of the court shall send in the prescribed manner to the court in the reciprocating country which made the registered order a certified copy of the provisional order together with a document, authenticated in the prescribed manner, setting out or summarising the evidence given in the proceedings.

(6) Where a certified copy or a provisional order made by a court in a reciprocating country, being an order varing a registered order, together with a document, duly authenticated, setting out or summarising the evidence given in the proceedings in which the provisional order was made, is received by the registering court, that court may confirm the order either without alteration or with such alterations as it thinks reasonable or refuse to confirm the order.

[3] (7) Where a certified copy of a provisional order varying a registered order is received by the registering court as mentioned in subsection (6) above, the prescribed officer of that court shall intimate to the payer under the registered order, in the prescribed manner, that the provisional order has been received as aforesaid and that, unless the payer enters appearance within the prescribed period, the court will confirm the provisional order under this section.

[4] (8) Where a registered order has been varied by an order (including a provisional order which has been confirmed) made by a court in the United Kingdom or by a competent court in a reciprocating country, the registered order shall, as from the date on which under the provisions of the order the variation is to take effect, have effect as varied by that order and, where that order was a provisional order, as if that order had been made in the form in which it was confirmed and as if it had never been a provisional order.

[4] (9) Where a registered order has been revoked by an order made by a court in the United Kingdom or by a competent court in a reciprocating country, including a provisional order made by the first-mentioned court which has been confirmed by a competent court in a reciprocating country, the registered order shall, as from the date on which under the provisions of the order the revocation is to take effect, be deemed to have ceased to have effect except as respects any arrears due under the registered order at that date.

(10) The prescribed officer of the registering court shall register in the prescribed manner any order varying a registered order other than a provisional order which is not confirmed.

(11) [Scottish adaption: incorporated *supra.*]

NOTES

[1] Added by the Civil Jurisdiction and Judgments Act 1982, Sched. 11, para. 4.

[2] Added by the Civil Jurisdiction and Judgments Act 1982, Sched. 11, para. 12.

[3] As applied to Scotland by s.9(11).

[4] As amended by the Domestic Proceedings and Magistrates' Courts Act 1978, s.54.

Cancellation of registration and transfer of order

10.—(1) Where—

(*a*) a registered order is revoked by an order made by the registering court; or

(*b*) a registered order is revoked by a provisional order made by that court which has been confirmed by a court in a reciprocating country and notice of the confirmation is received by the registering court; or

(*c*) a registered order is revoked by an order made by a court in such a country and notice of the revocation is received by the registering court,

the prescribed officer of the registering court shall cancel the registration; but any arrears due under the registered order at the date when its registration is cancelled by virtue of this subsection shall continue to be recoverable as if the registration had not been cancelled.

[1] (2) Where the prescribed officer of the registering court is of opinion that the payer under a registered order is not residing in Scotland and has no assets within that jurisdiction against which the order can be effectively enforced, he shall cancel the registration of the order and . . . shall send the certified copy of the order to the Secretary of State.

(3), (4) [Omitted for Scotland by s.10(8).]

[2] (5) Where the certified copy of an order is received by the Secretary of State under this section and it appears to him that the payer under the order is residing or has assets in the United Kingdom, he shall transfer the order to the appropriate court by sending the certified copy of the order

[THE NEXT PAGE IS K 107]

together with the related documents to the prescribed officer of the appropriate court and, subject to subsection (6) below, that officer shall register the order in the prescribed manner in that court.

[2] (6) Before registering an order in pursuance of subsection . . . (5) above an officer of a court shall take such steps as he thinks fit for the purpose of ascertaining whether the payer is residing or has assets within the jurisdiction of the court, and if after taking those steps he is satisfied that the payer is not residing and has no assets within the jurisdiction of the court he shall send the certified copy of the order to the Secretary of State.

(7) The officer of a court who is required by any of the foregoing provisions of this section to send to the Secretary of State or to the prescribed officer of another court the certified copy of an order shall send with that copy—

(*a*) a certificate of arrears signed by him;

[2] (*b*) a statement giving such information as he possesses as to the whereabouts of the payer and the nature and location of his assets; and

(*c*) any relevant documents in his possession relating to the case.

(8) [Scottish adaptation: incorporated *supra*.]

NOTES

[1] As applied to Scotland by s. 10(8).

[2] As amended by the Civil Jurisdiction and Judgments Act 1982, Sched. 11, para. 13.

Steps to be taken by Secretary of State where payer under certain orders is not residing in the United Kingdom

11.—[1] (1) If at any time it appears to the Secretary of State that the payer under a maintenance order, a certified copy of which has been received by him from a reciprocating country, is not residing and has no assets in the United Kingdom he shall send to the responsible authority in that country or, if having regard to all the circumstances he thinks it proper to do so, to the responsible authority in another reciprocating country—

(*a*) the certified copy of the order in question and a certified copy of any order varying that order;

(*b*) if the order has at any time been a registered order, a certificate of arrears signed by the prescribed officer;

(*c*) a statement giving such information as the Secretary of State possesses as to the whereabouts of the payer and the nature and location of his assets; and

(*d*) any other relevant documents in his possession relating to the case.

(2) Where the documents mentioned in subsection (1) above are sent to the responsible authority in a reciprocating country other than that in which the order in question was made, the Secretary of State shall inform the responsible authority in the reciprocating country in which that order was made of what he has done.

NOTE

[1] As amended by the Civil Jurisdiction and Judgments Act 1982, Sched. 11, para. 14.

Appeals

Appeals

12.—(1) No appeal shall lie from a provisional order made in pursuance of any provision of this Part of this Act by a court in the United Kingdom.

(2) Where in pursuance of any such provision any such court confirms or refuses to confirm a provisional order made by a court in a reciprocating country, whether a maintenance order or an order varying or revoking a maintenance order, the payer or payee under the maintenance order, shall have the like right of appeal (if any) from the confirmation of, or refusal to confirm, the provisional order as he would have if that order were not a provisional order and the court which confirmed or refused to confirm it had made or, as the case may be, refused to make it.

(3) Where in pursuance of any such provision any such court makes, or refuses to make, an order varying or revoking a maintenance order made by a court in a reciprocating country, then, subject to subsection (1) above, the payer or payee under the maintenance order shall have the like right of appeal (if any) from that order or from the refusal to make it as he would have if the maintenance order had been made by the first-mentioned court.

(4) Nothing in this section (except subsection (1)) shall be construed as affecting any right of appeal conferred by any other enactment.

Evidence

Admissibility of evidence given in reciprocating country

13.—(1) A statement contained in—

(*a*) a document, duly authenticated, which purports to set out or summarise evidence given in proceedings in a court in a reciprocating country; or

(*b*) a document, duly authenticated, which purports to set out or summarise evidence taken in such a country for the purpose of proceedings in a court in the United Kingdom under this Part of this Act, whether in response to a request made by such a court or otherwise; or

(*c*) a document, duly authenticated, which purports to have been received in evidence in proceedings in a court in such a country or to be a copy of a document so received,

shall in any proceedings in a court in the United Kingdom relating to a maintenance order to which this Part of this Act applies be admissible as evidence of any fact stated therein to the same extent as oral evidence of that fact is admissible in those proceedings.

(2) A document purporting to set out or summarise evidence given as mentioned in subsection (1)(*a*) above, or taken as mentioned in subsection (1)(*b*) above, shall be deemed to be duly authenticated for the purposes of that subsection if the document purports to be certified by the judge, magistrate or other person before whom the evidence was given, or, as the case may be, by whom it was taken, to be the original document containing or recording, or, as the case may be, summarising, that evidence or a true copy of that document.

(3) A document purporting to have been received in evidence as mentioned in subsection (1)(*c*) above, or to be a copy of a document so received, shall be deemed to be duly authenticated for the purposes of that subsection if the document purports to be certified by a judge, magistrate or officer of the court in question to have been, or to be a true copy of a document which has been, so received.

(4) It shall not be necessary in any such proceedings to prove the signature or official position of the person appearing to have given such a certificate.

(5) Nothing in this section shall prejudice the admission in evidence of any document which is admissible in evidence apart from this section.

Obtaining of evidence needed for purpose of certain proceedings

14.—(1) Where for the purpose of any proceedings in a court in a reciprocating country relating to a maintenance order to which this Part of this Act applies a request is made by or on behalf of that court for the taking in the United Kingdom of the evidence of a person residing therein relating to matters specified in the request, such court in the United Kingdom as may be prescribed shall have power to take that evidence and, after giving notice of the time and place at which the evidence is to be taken to such persons and in such manner as it thinks fit, shall take the evidence in such manner as may be prescribed.

Evidence taken in compliance with such a request shall be sent in the prescribed manner by the prescribed officer of the court to the court in the reciprocating country by or on behalf of which the request was made.

(2) Where any person, not being the payer or the payee under the maintenance order to which the proceedings in question relate, is required by virtue of this section to give evidence before a court in the United Kingdom, the court may order that there shall be paid—

(*a*) if the court is a court in England, Wales or Scotland, out of moneys provided by Parliament; and

[1] (*b*) if the court is a court in Northern Ireland, out of moneys provided by Parliament,

such sums as appear to the court reasonably sufficient to compensate that person for the expense, trouble or loss of time properly incurred in or incidental to his attendance.

(3) [England and Wales.]

(4) Paragraphs 71 and 73 of Schedule 1 to the Sheriff Courts (Scotland) Act 1907(which provide for the citation of witnesses etc.) shall apply in relation to a sheriff having power under subsection (1) above to take the evidence of any person as if the proceedings in the court in a reciprocating country for the purpose of which a request for the taking of the evidence has been made were proceedings in the sheriff court.

(5) A court in the United Kingdom may for the purpose of any proceedings in that court under this Part of this Act relating to a maintenance order to which this Part of this Act applies request a court in a reciprocating country to take or provide evidence relating to such matters as may be specified in the request and may remit the case to that court for that purpose.

(6) [Northern Ireland.]

NOTE

[1] As amended by S.I. 1973 No. 2163.

Order, etc. made abroad need not be proved

15. For the purposes of this Part of this Act, unless the contrary is shown—

(*a*) any order made by a court in a reciprocating country purporting to bear the seal of that court or to be signed by any person in his capacity as a judge, magistrate or officer of the court, shall be deemed without further proof to have been duly sealed or, as the case may be, to have been signed by that person;

(*b*) the person by whom the order was signed shall be deemed without further proof to have been a judge, magistrate or officer, as the case may be, of that court when he signed it and, in the case of an officer, to have been authorised to sign it; and

(*c*) a document purporting to be a certified copy of an order made by a court in a reciprocating country shall be deemed without further proof to be such a copy.

Supplemental

Payment of sums under orders made abroad: conversion of currency

16.—(1) [England and Wales and Northern Ireland].

(2) Where the sums required to be paid under a registered order are expressed in a currency other than the currency of the United Kingdom, then, as from the relevant date, the order shall be treated as if it were an order requiring the payment of such sums in the currency of the United Kingdom as, on the basis of the rate of exchange prevailing at that date, are equivalent to the sums so required to be paid.

(3) Where the sum specified in any statement, being a statement of the amount of any arrears due under a maintenance order made by a court in a reciprocating country, is expressed in a currency other than the currency of the United Kingdom, that sum shall be deemed to be such sum in the

currency of the United Kingdom as, on the basis of the rate of exchange prevailing at the relevant date, is equivalent to the sum so specified.

[1] (4) For the purposes of this section a written certificate purporting to be signed by an officer of any bank in the United Kingdom certifying that a specified rate of exchange prevailed between currencies at a specified date and that at such rate a specified sum in the currency of the United Kingdom is equivalent to a specified sum in another specified currency shall be sufficient evidence of the rate of exchange so prevailing on that date and of the equivalent sums in terms of the respective currencies.

(5) In this section "the relevant date" means—

(*a*) in relation to a registered order or to a statement of arrears due under a maintenance order made by a court in a reciprocating country, the date on which the order first becomes a registered order or (if earlier) the date on which it is confirmed by a court in the United Kingdom;

(*b*) in relation to a registered order which has been varied, the date on which the last order varying that order is registered in a court in the United Kingdom or (if earlier) the date on which the last order varying that order is confirmed by such a court.

(6) [Scottish adaptation: incorporated *supra*.]

NOTE

[1] As applied to Scotland by s.16(6).

17, 18. [England and Wales and Northern Ireland.]

Rules for sheriff court

[1] **19.** Without prejudice to the generality of the powers conferred on the Court of Session by section 32 of the Sheriff Courts (Scotland) Act 1971 to regulate by act of sederunt the procedure of the sheriff court, the said powers shall include power—

(*a*) to prescribe the decrees granted, or other things done, by the sheriff, or an officer of the sheriff court, under this Part of this Act, or by a court in a reciprocating country, notice of which is to be given to such persons as the act of sederunt may provide and the manner in which such notice shall be given;

(*b*) to provide that evidence needed for the purpose of proceedings in a court in a reciprocating country relating to a maintenance order to which this Part of this Act applies may, in such cases and manner as the act of sederunt may provide, be taken by a sheriff clerk or sheriff clerk depute;

(*c*) to prescribe the cases and manner in which courts in reciprocating countries are to be informed of decrees granted, or other things done, by the sheriff under this Part of this Act;

(*d*) to prescribe the circumstances and manner in which cases may be remitted by the sheriff to courts in reciprocating countries;

(*e*) to prescribe the circumstances and manner in which the sheriff may for the purposes of this Part of this Act communicate with courts in reciprocating countries.

NOTE

[1] See S.I. 1980 No. 291, *infra*.

Restriction on enforcement of arrears under maintenance order registered in Scotland

20. Where a maintenance order is for the time being registered in the sheriff court under this Part of this Act, a person shall not be entitled, except with the leave of the sheriff, to enforce, whether by diligence or otherwise, the payment of any arrears due under the order, if either—

(*a*) the sheriff has made a provisional order under section 9 of this Act revoking the said maintenance order and the arrears accrued after the making of the said provisional order, or (*b*) the arrears accrued before the commencement of this Part of this Act; and on any application for leave to enforce the payment of any such arrears, the sheriff may refuse leave, or may grant leave subject to such restrictions and conditions (including conditions as to the allowing of time for payment or the making of payment by instalments) as he thinks appropriate, or may remit the payment of such arrears or of any part thereof.

Interpretation of Part I

21.—[1] (1) In this Part of this Act—

"affiliation order" means an order (however described) adjudging, finding or declaring a person to be the father of a child, whether or not it also provides for the maintenance of the child;

[1a] "the appropriate court" in relation to a person residing or having assets in England and Wales or in Northern Ireland means a magistrates' court, and in relation to a person residing or having assets in Scotland means a sheriff court, within the jurisdiction of which that person is residing or has assets;

"certificate of arrears", in relation to a maintenance order, means a certificate certifying that the sum specified in the certificate is to the best of the information or belief of the officer giving the certificate the amount of the arrears due under the order at the date of the certificate or, as the case may be, that to the best of his information or belief there are no arrears due thereunder at that date;

"certified copy", in relation to an order of a court, means a copy of the order certified by the proper officer of the court to be a true copy;

"court" includes any tribunal or person having power to make, confirm, enforce, vary or revoke a maintenance order;

"maintenance order" means an order (however described) of any of the following descriptions, that is to say—

[1b](*a*) an order (including an affiliation order or order consequent upon an affiliation order) which provides for the payment of a lump sum or the making of periodical payments towards the maintenance of any person, being a person whom the person liable to make payments under the order is, according to the law applied in the place where the order was made, liable to maintain;

[2] (*aa*) an order which has been made in Scotland, on or after the granting of a decree of divorce, for the payment of a periodical allowance by one party to the marriage to the other party; and

(*b*) an affiliation order or order consequent upon an affiliation order, being an order which provides for the payment by a person adjudged, found or declared to be a child's father of expenses incidental to the child's birth, or, where the child has died, of his funeral expenses,

and, in the case of a maintenance order which has been varied, means that order as varied;

"order", as respects Scotland, includes any interlocutor, and any decree or provision contained in an interlocutor;

"payee", in relation to a maintenance order, means the person entitled to the payments for which the order provides;

"payer", in relation to a maintenance order, means the person liable to make payments under the order;

[3] "prescribed", in relation to a magistrates' court in England and Wales or in Northern Ireland, means prescribed by rules made under section 144 of the Magistrates' Courts Act 1980 or by rules made in accordance with section 23 of the Magistrates' Courts Act (Northern Ireland) 1964, as the case may be, and in relation to any other court means prescribed by rules of court;

"provisional order" means (according to the context)—

(*a*) an order made by a court in the United Kingdom which is provisional only and has no effect unless and until confirmed, with or without alteration, by a competent court in a reciprocating country; or

(*b*) an order made by a court in a reciprocating country which is provisional only and has no effect unless and until confirmed, with or without alteration, by a court in the United Kingdom having power under this Part of this Act to confirm it;

"reciprocating country" has the meaning assigned to it by section 1 of this Act;

"registered order" means a maintenance order which is for the time being registered in a court in the United Kingdom under this Part of this Act;

"registering court", in relation to a registered order, means the court in which that order is for the time being registered under this Part of this Act;

"the responsible authority", in relation to a reciprocating country, means any person who in that country has functions similar to those of the Secretary of State under this Part of this Act.

[1b] "revoke and "revocation" include discharge.

[1c,4] (2) For the purposes of this Part of this Act an order shall be taken to be a maintenance order so far (but only so far) as it relates to the payment of a lump sum or the making of periodical payments as mentioned in paragraph (*a*) of the definition of "maintenance order" in subsection (1) above, to the payment of a periodical allowance as mentioned in paragraph (*aa*) of that definition, or to the payment by a person adjudged, found or declared to be a child's father of any such expenses as are mentioned in paragraph (*b*) of that definition.

(3) Any reference in this Part of this Act to the payment of money for the maintenance of a child shall be construed as including a reference to the payment of money for the child's education.

NOTES

[1] As amended by the Domestic Proceedings and Magistrates' Courts Act 1978 (c. 22), s. 55.

[1a] As amended by the Civil Jurisdiction and Judgments Act 1982 (c. 27), Sched. 11, para. 14.

[1b] Added by the Maintenance Orders (Reciprocal Enforcement) Act 1992 (c. 56), Sched. 1, para. 12 (effective 5th April 1993: S.I. 1993 No. 618).

[1c] As amended by the Civil Jurisdiction and Judgments Act 1982 (c. 27), Sched. 11, para. 4(2).

[2] Added by the Domestic Proceedings and Magistrates' Courts Act 1978 (c. 22), s. 55(*a*).

[3] As amended by the Magistrates' Courts Act 1980, Sched. 7.

[4] As amended by the Domestic Proceedings and Magistrates' Courts Act 1978 (c. 22), s. 55(*b*).

Amendments, repeals and transitional provisions

Amendments and repeals

22.—(1) The enactments mentioned in the Schedule to this Act shall have effect subject to the minor and consequential amendments specified therein.

[1] (2) The following are hereby repealed—

(*a*) the Maintenance Orders (Facilities for Enforcement) Act 1920;

(*b*) in the Magistrates' Courts Act 1952, in section 56(1) paragraph (*c*) and the words from "or in an order" to the end;

(*c*) in the Maintenance Orders Act 1958, section 19 and, in section 23(2), the words "section 19";

(*d*) in the South Africa Act 1962, paragraph 2 of Schedule 2.

NOTE

[1] S. 22(2) is not in force.

23, 24. [England and Wales and Northern Ireland.]

[1] PART II

RECIPROCAL ENFORCEMENT OF CLAIMS FOR THE RECOVERY OF MAINTENANCE

NOTE

[1] Applied by S.I. 1979 No. 1314, as amended by S.I. 1981 No. 1606 and 1984 No. 1824.

Convention countries

Convention countries

[1] **25.**—(1) Her Majesty may by Order in Council declare that any country or territory specified in the Order, being a country or territory

[THE NEXT PAGE IS K 113]

outside the United Kingdom to which the Maintenance Convention extends, is a convention country for the purposes of this Part of this Act.

(2) In this section "the Maintenance Convention" means the United Nations Convention on the Recovery Abroad of Maintenance done at New York on 20th June 1956.

NOTE

[1] See S.I. 1975 No. 423 and S.I. 1979 No. 279 (as amended by S.I. 1978 No. 279 and S.I. 1982 No. 1423).

Application by persons in the United Kingdom for recovery, etc. of maintenance in convention country

Application by person in United Kingdom for recovery, etc. of maintenance in convention country

[1] **26.**—(1) Where a person in the United Kingdom ("the applicant") claims to be entitled to recover in a convention country maintenance from another person, and that other person is for the time being subject to the jurisdiction of that country, the applicant may apply to the Secretary of State, in accordance with the provisions of this section, to have his claim for the recovery of maintenance from that other person transmitted to that country.

(2) Where the applicant seeks to vary any provision, made in a convention country for the payment by any other person of maintenance to the applicant, and that other person is for the time being subject to the jurisdiction of that country, the applicant may apply to the Secretary of State, in accordance with the provisions of this section, to have his application for the variation of that provision transmitted to that country.

(3) An application to the Secretary of State under subsection (1) or (2) above shall be made through the appropriate officer, and that officer shall assist the applicant in completing an application which will comply with the requirements of the law applied by the convention country and shall send the application to the Secretary of State, together with such other documents, if any, as are required by that law.

(4) On receiving an application from the appropriate officer the Secretary of State shall transmit it, together with any accompanying documents, to the appropriate authority in the convention country, unless he is satisfied that the application is not made in good faith or that it does not comply with the requirements of the law applied by that country.

(5) The Secretary of State may request the appropriate officer to obtain from the court of which he is an officer such information relating to the application as may be specified in the request, and it shall be the duty of the court to furnish the Secretary of State with the information he requires.

(6) [England and Wales and Northern Ireland.]

(7) Where the applicant is residing in Scotland the appropriate officer for the purposes of this section is the sheriff clerk or sheriff clerk depute of the sheriff court within the jurisdiction of which the applicant is residing.

NOTE

[1] See S.I. 1993 No. 591, *infra* (modification of s. 26 in relation to specified American states).

Application by person in convention country for recovery of maintenance in England, Wales or Northern Ireland

[27–30.]

Application by person in convention country for recovery of maintenance in Scotland

Application by person in convention country for recovery of maintenance in Scotland

31.—[0] (1) Where the Secretary of State receives from the appropriate authority in a convention country an application by a person in that country for the recovery of maintenance from another person who is for the time being residing in Scotland, he shall send the application, together with any accompanying documents, to the secretary of the Law Society of Scotland who shall send the application and any accompanying documents to a solicitor practising in the sheriff court within the jurisdiction of which that other person resides or to such other solicitor practising in Scotland as appears to the Secretary to be appropriate, for the purposes of enabling the solicitor to take on behalf of the applicant such steps as appear to the solicitor appropriate in respect of the application.

[1] (1A) Proceedings arising out of an application under subsection (1) above shall be treated as an action for aliment within the meaning of the Family Law (Scotland) Act 1985 and, subject to subsections (1B) to (1D) below, the provisions of that Act relating to aliment shall apply in relation to claims for maintenance in such proceedings and decrees therein.

[1] (1B) Without prejudice to subsection (2) below, any proceedings mentioned in subsection (1A) above shall be brought in the sheriff court.

[1] (1C) In its application to proceedings mentioned in subsection (1A) above, section 5 of the said Act of 1985 (power to vary or recall decree of aliment) shall be subject to section 34(1) of this Act.

[1] (1D) Where an application under subsection (1) above is for the recovery of maintenance from a person who is a former spouse of the applicant—

(*a*) then, for the purposes of the said Act of 1985, there shall be assumed to be an obligation of aliment within the meaning of that Act owed by the former spouse to the applicant;

(*b*) section 2(7) and (8) of that Act shall not apply; and

(*c*) an order for payment of maintenance in proceedings arising out of the application—

(i) shall, if subsisting at the death of the party making the payment, continue to operate against that party's estate, but without prejudice to the power of the court to vary or recall the order; and

(ii) shall cease to have effect on the re-marriage or death of the party receiving payment, except in relation to any arrears due under it.

[2] (2) Where in any proceedings arising out of such an application as aforesaid the sheriff, or (on appeal or remit) the Court of Session makes an order containing a provision requiring the payment of maintenance, the order shall be registered forthwith in the prescribed manner in the appropriate sheriff court by the sheriff clerk or sheriff clerk depute of that sheriff court; and where an order of the Court of Session varies or revokes a registered order of the sheriff, the said sheriff clerk or sheriff clerk depute shall amend the register accordingly.

[3] (2A) In subsection (2) above "the appropriate sheriff court" means the sheriff court making the order or (where the order is an order of the Court of Session) from which the remit or appeal has come.

(3) Without prejudice to the generality of the powers conferred on the Court of Session by section 32 of the Sheriff Courts (Scotland) Act 1971 to regulate by act of sederunt the procedure of the sheriff court, the said powers shall include power to prescribe the decrees granted, or other things done, by the sheriff, or an officer of the sheriff court, under this Part of this Act, notice of which is to be given to such persons as the act of sederunt may provide and the manner in which such notice shall be given.

[3,4] (4) Where an application under subsection (1) above is for the recovery of maintenance from a person who is a former spouse of the applicant an order containing a provision requiring the payment of such maintenance for the benefit of the applicant shall not be made in respect of that application unless—

(i) the marriage between the applicant and the said former spouse has been dissolved by a divorce which has been obtained in a country or territory outside the United Kingdom and which is recognised as valid by the law of Scotland;

(ii) an order for the payment of maintenance for the benefit of the applicant as a divorced person has, in or by reason of, or subsequent to, the divorce proceedings, been made by a court in a convention country;

(ii*a*) in a case where the order mentioned in paragraph (ii) above was made by a court of a different country from that in which the divorce was obtained, either the applicant or the said former spouse was resident in that different country at the time the application for the order so mentioned was made; and

(iii) the court making the order under this section is satisfied that the former spouse of the applicant has failed to comply with the order mentioned in paragraph (ii) above.

[5] (4A) In subsection (4)(i) above the reference to the dissolution of a marriage by divorce shall be construed as including a reference to the annulment of a purported marriage and any reference to a marriage, a divorce, a divorced person, a former spouse or divorce proceedings shall be construed accordingly.

(5) [Repealed by the Family Law (Scotland) Act 1985, Sched. 2.]

[1] (6) Section 8 of the Law Reform (Miscellaneous Provisions) (Scotland) Act 1966 (which relates to the variation and recall by the sheriff of certain orders made by the Court of Session) shall not apply to an order of the Court of Session registered under subsection (2) above.

NOTES

[0] As amended by the Legal Aid (Scotland) Act 1986. Sched. 3, para. 1(1).

[1] Subs. (1A) was inserted by the Domestic Proceedings and Magistrates' Courts Act 1978, s. 60(1), and substituted by subss. (1A)–(1D) by the Family Law (Scotland) Act 1985, Sched. 1, para. 6.

[2] As amended by the Domestic Proceedings and Magistrates' Courts Act 1978, s. 60(1).

[3] Added by the Domestic Proceedings and Magistrates' Courts Act 1978, s. 60(1).

[4] As amended by the Matrimonial and Family Proceedings Act 1984, s. 31.

[5] Inserted by the Family Law (Scotland) Act 1985, Sched. 1, para. 6(*b*).

Transfer, enforcement, variation and revocation of registered orders

Transfer of orders

32.—[1] (1) Where the prescribed officer of the registering court is of opinion that the payer under a registered order has ceased to reside in Scotland then, unless he is of opinion that the payer has ceased to reside in the United Kingdom, he shall, subject to subsection (2) below, send a certified copy of the order and the related documents to the Secretary of State, and if he is of opinion that the payer has ceased to reside in the United Kingdom he shall send a notice to that effect to the Secretary of State.

(2) [Omitted for Scotland by s. 32(9).]

(3) Where a certified copy of an order is received by the Secretary of State under this section and it appears to him that the payer under the order is still residing in the United Kingdom, he shall transfer the order to the appropriate court by sending the copy of the order and the related documents to the prescribed officer of the appropriate court and, subject to subsection (4) below, that officer shall register the order in the prescribed manner in that court.

[1] (4) Before registering an order in pursuance of subsection . . . (3) above an officer of a court shall take such steps as he thinks fit for the purpose of ascertaining whether the payer under the order is residing within the jurisdiction of the court, and if after taking those steps he is satisfied that the payer is not so residing he shall return the certified copy of the order and the related documents to the Secretary of State together with a

statement giving such information as he possesses as to the whereabouts of the payer.

(5) Where a certified copy of an order is received by the Secretary of State under this section and it appears to him that the payer under the order has ceased to reside in the United Kingdom he shall return the copy of the order and the related documents to the registering court.

[1] (6) An officer of a court on registering an order in the court in pursuance of subsection . . . (3) above shall give notice of the registration in the prescribed manner to the prescribed officer of the court in which immediately before its registration under this section the order was registered, and to the Secretary of State.

(7) The officer to whom notice is given under subsection (6) above shall on receiving the notice cancel the registration of the order in that court.

[2] (7A) The Secretary of State on receiving notice under subsection (6) above shall send a copy of the registered order and of the related documents to the Secretary of the Law Society of Scotland who shall send the copy of the order and of the related documents to a solicitor practising in the registering court or to such other solicitor practising in Scotland as appears to the Secretary to be appropriate for the purpose of enabling the solicitor to take, on behalf of the person entitled to the payments for which the order provides, such steps as appear to the solicitor appropriate to enforce the order.

[2] (7B) Where an order is registered in the sheriff court by virtue of subsection (3) above, any provision of the order by virtue of which the payments for which the order provides are required to be made through or to any officer or person on behalf of the person entitled thereto shall be of no effect so long as the order is so registered.

(8) In this section—

"the appropriate court", in relation to a person residing in England and Wales or in Northern Ireland, means a magistrates' court within the jurisdiction of which that person is residing;

"certificate of arrears" and "certified copy" have the same meanings respectively as in Part I of this Act;

"payer", in relation to a registered order, means the person liable to make payments under the order; and

"related documents" means—

(*a*) the application on which the order was made;

(*b*) a certificate of arrears signed by the prescribed officer of the registering court;

(*c*) a statement giving such information as he possesses as to the whereabouts of the payer; and

(*d*) any relevant documents in his possession relating to the case.

(9) In the application of this section to Scotland—

(*a*)–(*e*) [adaptations incorporated *supra*];

(*f*) "appropriate court," in relation to a person residing in Scotland, means the sheriff court within the jurisdiction of which that person is residing.

NOTES

[1] As applied to Scotland by s. 32(9).

[2] Inserted in application of section to Scotland by s. 32(9) As amended by the Legal Aid (Scotland) Act 1986, Sched. 3, para. 1(2) and Sched. 5.

Enforcement of orders

33.—(1) . . . a registered order which is registered in a court other than the court by which the order was made may be enforced as if it had been made by the registering court and as if that court had had jurisdiction to make it; and proceedings for or with respect to the enforcement of any such order may be taken in accordance with this subsection but not otherwise.

(2)–(4) [Omitted for Scotland by s. 33(7).]

[1] (5) In any proceedings for or with respect to the enforcement of an order which is for the time being registered in any court under this Part of this Act a certificate of arrears sent under section 32 of this Act to the prescribed officer of the court shall be sufficient evidence of the facts stated therein.

(6) Part II of the Maintenance Orders Act 1950 (enforcement of certain orders throughout the United Kingdom) shall not apply to a registered order.

(7) [Scottish adaptation: incorporated *supra*.]

NOTE

[1] As applied to Scotland by s. 33(7).

Variation and revocation of orders

34.—(1) Where a registered order is registered in a court other than the court by which the order was made, the registering court shall have the like power to vary or revoke the order as if it had been made by the registering court and as if that court had had jurisdiction to make it;[1] and no court other than the registering court shall have power to vary or revoke a registered order.

(2) Where the registering court revokes a registered order it shall cancel the registration.

[2] (3) Where the Secretary of State receives from the appropriate authority in a convention country an application by a person in that country for the variation of a registered order, he shall, if the registering court is a sheriff court, send the application, together with any documents accompanying it, to the Secretary of the Law Society of Scotland who shall send the application and any accompanying documents to a solicitor practising in the registering court or to such other solicitor practising in Scotland as appears to the Secretary to be appropriate for the purpose of enabling the solicitor to take on behalf of the applicant such steps as appear to the solicitor appropriate in respect of the application.

(4) Where a court in a part of the United Kingdom makes, or refuses to make, an order varying or revoking a registered order made by a court in

[THE NEXT PAGE IS K 117]

another part thereof, any person shall have the like right of appeal (if any) against the order or refusal as he would have if the registered order had been made by the first-mentioned court.

(5) [Scottish adaptation: incorporated *supra.*]

NOTES

[1] Subject to any power of the Court of Session on appeal: see the Domestic Proceedings and Magistrates' Courts Act 1978 (c. 22), s. 60(2).

[2] As applied to Scotland by s. 34(5). As amended by the Legal Aid (Scotland) Act 1986 (c. 47), Sched. 3, para. 1(3).

35. [England and Wales and Northern Ireland.]

Supplemental

Admissibility of evidence given in convention country

36.—[1] (1) A statement contained in—

(*a*) a document, duly authenticated, which purports to set out or summarise evidence given in proceedings in a court in a convention country; or

(*b*) a document, duly authenticated, which purports to set out or summarise evidence taken in such a country for the purpose of proceedings in a court in the United Kingdom under this Part of this Act, whether in response to a request made on behalf of such a court or otherwise; or

(*c*) a document, duly authenticated, which purports to have been received in evidence in proceedings in a court in such a country, or to be a copy of a document so received,

shall, in any proceedings in a magistrates' court or in, or remitted from, a sheriff court arising out of an application received by the Secretary of State as mentioned in section . . . 31(1) of this Act or an application made by any person for the variation or revocation of a registered order or in proceedings on appeal from any such proceedings, be admissible as evidence of any fact stated therein to the same extent as oral evidence of that fact is admissible in those proceedings.

(2) A document purporting to set out or summarise evidence given as mentioned in subsection (1)(*a*) above, or taken as mentioned in subsection (1)(*b*) above, shall be deemed to be duly authenticated for the purposes of that subsection if the document purports to be certified by the judge, magistrate or other person before whom the evidence was given or, as the case may be, by whom it was taken to be the original document containing or recording, or, as the case may be, summarising, that evidence or a true copy of that document.

(3) A document purporting to have been received in evidence as mentioned in subsection (1)(*c*) above, or to be a copy of a document so received, shall be deemed to be duly authenticated for the purposes of that subsection if the document purports to be certified by a judge, magistrate or officer of the court in question to have been, or to be a true copy of a document which has been, so received.

(4) It shall not be necessary in any such proceedings to prove the signature or official position of the person appearing to have given such a certificate.

(5) Nothing in this section shall prejudice the admission in evidence of any document which is admissible in evidence apart from this section.

NOTE

[1] As amended by the Domestic Proceedings and Magistrates' Courts Act 1978 (c. 22), s. 60(3), and, so far as affecting the text printed, the Maintenance Orders (Reciprocal Enforcement) Act 1992 (c. 56), Sched. 1, para. 17 (effective 5th April 1993: S.I. 1993 No. 618).

Obtaining of evidence for purpose of proceedings in United Kingdom court

37.—(1) A court in the United Kingdom may for the purpose of any proceedings in that court under this Part of this Act arising out of an application received by the Secretary of State from a convention country request the Secretary of State to make to the appropriate authority or court in the convention country a request for the taking in that country of the evidence of a person residing therein relating to matters connected with the application.

(2) A request made by a court under this section shall—

(*a*) give details of the application in question;

(*b*) state the name and address of the person whose evidence is to be taken; and

(*c*) specify the matters relating to which the evidence of that person is required.

(3) If the Secretary of State is satisfied that a request made to him under this section contains sufficient information to enable the evidence of the person named in the request relating to the matters specified therein to be taken by a court or person in the convention country, he shall transmit the request to the appropriate authority or court in that country.

Taking of evidence at request of court in convention country

38.—(1) Where a request is made to the Secretary of State by or on behalf of a court in a convention country to obtain the evidence of a person residing in the United Kingdom relating to matters connected with an application to which section 26 of this Act applies, the Secretary of State shall request such court, or such officer of a court, as he may determine to take the evidence of that person relating to such matters connected with that application as may be specified in the request.

(2) The court by which or officer by whom a request under subsection (1) above is received from the Secretary of State shall have power to take the evidence and, after giving notice of the time and place at which the evidence is to be taken to such persons and in such manner as it or he thinks fit, shall take the evidence of the person named in the request relating to the matters specified therein in such manner as may be prescribed; and the evidence so taken shall be sent in the prescribed manner by the prescribed officer to the court in the convention country by or on behalf of which the request referred to in subsection (1) above was made.

(3) Where any person, not being the person by whom the application mentioned in subsection (1) above was made is required by virtue of this section to give evidence before a court in the United Kingdom, the court may order that there shall be paid—

(*a*) if the court is a court in England, Wales or Scotland, out of moneys provided by Parliament; and

[1] (*b*) if the court is a court in Northern Ireland, out of moneys provided by Parliament,

such sums as appear to the court reasonably sufficient to compensate that person for the expense, trouble or loss of time properly incurred in or incidental to his attendance.

(4) [England and Wales.]

(5) Paragraphs 71 and 73 of Schedule 1 to the Sheriff Courts (Scotland) Act 1907 (which provide for the citation of witnesses, etc.) shall apply in relation to a sheriff court to which a request under subsection (1) above is made as if the application to which the request relates were proceedings in that court.

(6) [Northern Ireland.]

NOTE

[1] As amended by S.I. 1973 No. 2163.

Interpretation of Part II

39. In this Part of this Act—

[1] "maintenance", as respects Scotland, includes aliment and any sums which are payable, following divorce, by one former spouse for the support of the other;

[2] "maintenance order" has the same meaning as in Part I of this Act;

"order," as respects Scotland, includes any interlocutor, and any decree or provision contained in an interlocutor;

"prescribed" has the same meaning as in Part I of this Act;

"registered order" means an order which is for the time being registered in a court in the United Kingdom under this Part of this Act;

"registering court", in relation to a registered order, means the court in which that order is for the time being registered under this Part of this Act;

[2] "revoke" and "revocation" include discharge.

NOTES

[1] As amended by the Domestic Proceedings and Magistrates' Courts Act 1978 (c. 22), s. 60(4) and the Family Law (Scotland) Act 1985 (c. 37), Sched. 1, para. 7.

[2] Inserted by the Maintenance Orders (Reciprocal Enforcement) Act 1992 (c. 56), Sched. 1, para. 19 (effective 1st April 1993: S.I. 1993 No. 618).

Part III

Miscellaneous and Supplemental

Further provisions relating to enforcement of maintenance orders and to applications for recovery of maintenance

Power to apply Act to maintenance orders and applications for recovery of maintenance made in certain countries

[1] **40.** Where Her Majesty is satisfied—

[2] (*a*) that arrangements have been or will be made in a country or territory outside the United Kingdom to ensure that maintenance orders made by courts in the United Kingdom can be enforced in that country or territory or that applications by persons in the United Kingdom for the recovery of maintenance from persons in that country or territory can be entertained by courts in that country or territory; and

[2] (*b*) that in the interest of reciprocity it is desirable to ensure that maintenance orders made by courts in that country or territory can be enforced in the United Kingdom or, as the case may be, that applications by persons in that country or territory for the recovery of maintenance from persons in the United Kingdom can be entertained by courts in the United Kingdom,

Her Majesty may by Order in Council make provisions for applying the provisions of this Act, with such exceptions, adaptations and modifications as may be specified in the Order, to such orders or applications as are referred to in paragraphs (*a*) and (*b*) above and to maintenance and other orders made in connection with such applications by courts in the United Kingdom or in that country or territory.

NOTES

[1] See S.I. 1979 No. 1314 (as amended by S.I. 1984 No. 1824), 1981 No. 606, and 1993 Nos. 593 (*infra*) and 594 (*infra*).

[2] As amended by the Civil Jurisdiction and Judgments Act 1982 (c. 27), Sched. 11, para. 17 and Sched. 14.

Provisions with respect to certain orders of magistrates' courts

Complaint for variation, etc. of certain orders by or against persons outside England and Wales

41. [Repealed by the Children Act 1989 (c. 41), Sched. 15 (effective 14th October 1991: S.I. 1991 No. 828).]

Provisional order for maintenance of party to marriage made by magistrates' court to cease to have effect on remarriage of party

42.—[1] (1) Where a magistrates' court has, by virtue of section 3 of this Act, made a provisional maintenance order consisting of, or including, a provision such as is mentioned in section 2(1)(*a*) of the Domestic Proceedings and Magistrates' Courts Act 1978 (making of periodical payments by husband or wife) or Article 4(1)(*a*) of the Domestic Proceedings (Northern Ireland) Order 1980 and the order has been confirmed by a competent court in a reciprocating country, then, if after the making of that order the marriage of the parties to the proceedings in which the order was made is dissolved or annulled but the order continues in force, that order or, as the case may be, that provision thereof shall cease to have effect on the remarriage of the party in whose favour it was made, except in relation to any arrears due under it on the date of such remarriage and shall not be capable of being revived.

(2) For the avoidance of doubt it is hereby declared that references in this section to remarriage include references to a marriage which is by law void or voidable.

(3) In section 30(2) of the Matrimonial Proceedings and Property Act 1970 (which makes, in relation to such an order as is referred to in subsection (1) above which was confirmed in accordance with section 3 of the Maintenance Orders (Facilities for Enforcement) Act 1920, provision to the like effect as that subsection) the words from "but with the modification" to the end are hereby repealed.

NOTE

[1] As amended by the Domestic Proceedings and Magistrates' Courts Act 1978 (c. 22), Sched. 2, para. 37 and S.I. 1980 No. 564.

Supplemental provisions

43. [England and Wales and Northern Ireland.]

Eligibility for Legal Aid in Scotland

[1] **43A.**—(1) In connection with proceedings under Part I of this Act in relation to a maintenance order made by a court in a reciprocating country, where there is produced a certificate from the responsible authority in that

country to the effect that the payee would in that country, be financially eligible for complete or partial—

(i) legal aid; or

(ii) exemption from costs or expenses,

in proceedings there in relation to that maintenance order, sections 15 and 17 of the Legal Aid (Scotland) Act 1986 shall not apply in respect of the payee and, subject to the other provisions of that Act, legal aid shall under that Act be available to the payee without inquiry into the payee's resources.

(2) In connection with proceedings under Part II of this Act—

(*a*) arising out of an application received from a convention country for the recovery of maintenance; or

(*b*) relating to an order made in respect of such an application,

where there is produced a certificate from the appropriate authority in that country to the effect that the applicant would, in that country, be financially eligible for complete or partial—

(i) legal aid; or

(ii) exemption from costs or expenses,

in proceedings there for the recovery of maintenance, sections 15 and 17 of the said Act of 1986 shall not apply in respect of the applicant and, subject to the other provisions of that Act, legal aid shall under that Act be available to the applicant without inquiry into the applicant's resources.

(3) Where, in connection with proceedings under Part I or II of this Act, a person has received legal aid by virtue of subsection (1) or (2) above, advice and assistance under the said Act of 1986, shall, notwithstanding any financial conditions or requirements to make contributions imposed by sections 8 and 11 of that Act, be available in Scotland for that person, without inquiry into his resources, in connection with any matter incidental to, or arising out of, those proceedings.

(4) In subsection (1) above "maintenance order", "reciprocating country", "responsible authority" and "payee" have the same meanings respectively as in Part I of this Act; and in subsection (2) above "convention country" means a country or territory specified in an Order in Council under section 25(1) of this Act, "maintenance" has the same meaning as in Part II of this Act, and "appropriate authority" means the authority from which the Secretary of State received the application.

NOTE

[1] Added by the Domestic Proceedings and Magistrates' Courts Act 1978 (c. 22), s.61, and amended by the Legal Aid (Scotland) Act 1986 (c. 47), Sched. 3, para. 2.

Exclusion of certain enactments relating to evidence

44.—(1) [England and Wales.]

[1] (2) The Evidence (Proceedings in Other Jurisdictions) Act 1975 shall not apply to the taking of evidence in the United Kingdom for the taking of which section 14 or section 38 of this Act provides.

NOTE

[1] As amended by the Evidence (Proceedings in Other Jurisdictions) Act 1975 (c. 34), Sched. 1.

Orders in Council

45.—(1) An Order in Council under section 1, section 25 or section 40 of this Act may be varied or revoked by a subsequent Order in Council thereunder, and an Order made by virtue of this section may contain such incidental, consequential and transitional provisions as Her Majesty considers expedient for the purposes of that section.

(2) An Order in Council made under the said section 1 or the said section 40 shall be subject to annulment in pursuance of a resolution of either House of Parliament.

Financial provision

46. There shall be paid out of moneys provided by Parliament—

(*a*) any sums ordered by a court under section 14(2) or 38(3) of this Act to be paid out of moneys so provided; and

(*b*) any increase attributable to the provisions of this Act in the sums payable under the Legal Aid and Advice Act 1949 or the Legal Aid (Scotland) Act 1967 out of moneys so provided.

Interpretation: general

47.—(1) In this Act—

"enactment" includes an enactment of the Parliament of Northern Ireland;

"magistrates' court", in relation to Northern Ireland, means a court of summary jurisdiction within the meaning of section 1(1) of the Magistrates' Court Act (Northern Ireland) 1964.

(2) [Repealed by the Northern Ireland Constitution Act 1973, Sched. 6, Pt. I.]

[1] (3) Any reference in this Act to the jurisdiction of a court, where the reference is to assets being located or to a person residing within the jurisdiction of a court, shall be construed in relation to a magistrates' court in England and Wales as a reference to the petty sessions area, and in relation to a magistrates' court in Northern Ireland as a reference to the petty sessions district, for which the court acts.

(4) Any reference in this Act to any other enactment is a reference thereto as amended, and includes a reference thereto as extended or applied, by or under any other enactment.

NOTE

[1] As amended by the Civil Jurisdiction and Judgments Act 1982 (c. 27), Sched. 11, para. 18 and Sched. 14.

48. [Northern Ireland.]

Short title and commencement

49.—(1) This Act may be cited as the Maintenance Orders (Reciprocal Enforcement) Act 1972.

(2) This Act shall come into force on such day as the Secretary of State may by order made by statutory instrument appoint, and different days may be so appointed for different provisions of this Act, or for different purposes.

SCHEDULE

Consequential and Minor Amendments

The Magistrates' Courts Act 1952 (c. 55)

1. [Repealed by the Domestic Proceedings and Magistrates' Courts Act 1978 (c. 22), Sched. 3.]

The Army Act 1955 (c. 18) and the Air Force Act 1955 (c. 19)

2. [Amends s. 150 of each Act (enforcement of maintenance, etc., orders by deduction from pay).]

The Naval Discipline Act 1957 (c. 53)

3. [Amends s. 101 (service of process in proceedings for maintenance, etc.).]

The Maintenance Orders Act 1958 (c. 39)

4. [Repealed by the Civil Jurisdiction and Judgments Act 1982 (c. 27). Sched. 14.]
5. [Northern Ireland.]

The Administration of Justice Act 1970 (c. 31)

6. [Amends Sched. 8 (maintenance orders to which Part I of the Maintenance Orders Act 1958 applies).]

The Attachment of Earnings Act 1971 (c. 32)

7. [Amends Sched. 1 (maintenance orders to which the Act applies).]

Matrimonial Proceedings (Polygamous Marriages) Act 1972

(1972 c. 38)

An Act to enable matrimonial relief to be granted, and declarations concerning the validity of a marriage to be made, notwithstanding that the marriage in question was entered into under a law which permits polygamy, and to make a consequential amendment in the Nullity of Marriage Act 1971.

[29th June 1972]

. . . . . .

Matrimonial relief and declarations as to validity in respect of polygamous marriages: Scotland

2.—(1) A court in Scotland shall not be precluded from entertaining

[THE NEXT PAGE IS K 123]

proceedings for, or granting, any such decree as is mentioned in subsection (2) below by reason only that the marriage to which the proceedings relate was entered into under a law which permits polygamy.

[1] (2) The decrees referred to in subsection (1) above are—

(*a*) a decree of divorce;
(*b*) a decree of nullity of marriage;
(*c*) [Repealed by the Statute Law (Repeals) Act 1986 (c. 12), Sched., Pt. I.]
(*d*) a decree of separation;
(*e*) a decree of aliment;
(*f*) a decree of declarator that a marriage is valid or invalid;
(*g*) any other decree involving a determination as to the validity of a marriage;

and the reference in subsection (1) above to granting such a decree as aforesaid includes a reference to making any ancillary or incidental order which the court has power to make in proceedings for such a decree.

(3) This section has effect whether or not either party to the marriage in question has for the time being any spouse additional to the other party; and provision may be made by rules of court—

(*a*) for requiring notice of proceedings brought by virtue of this section to be served on any such other spouse; and
(*b*) for conferring on any such other spouse the right to be heard in any such proceedings,

in such cases as may be specified in the rules.

NOTE

[1] As amended by the Divorce Jurisdiction, Court Fees and Legal Aid (Scotland) Act 1983 (c. 12), Sched. 1, para. 13, the Law Reform (Husband and Wife) (Scotland) Act 1984 (c. 15), Sched. 1, para. 6, and the Family Law (Scotland) Act 1985 (c. 37), Sched. 1, para. 8.

Short title, interpretation

5.—(1) This Act may be cited as the Matrimonial Proceedings (Polygamous Marriages) Act 1972.

(2) References in this Act to any enactment shall be construed as references to that enactment as amended, and as including references thereto as extended or applied, by any subsequent enactment.

[1] Guardianship Act 1973

(1973 c. 29)

An Act to amend the law of England and Wales as to the guardianship of minors so as to make the rights of a mother equal with those of a father, and so as to make further provision with respect to applications and orders under section 9 of the Guardianship of Minors Act 1971 and with respect to the powers of a guardian under that Act in relation to the minor's property, and to amend section 4(2) of the Matrimonial Proceedings (Magistrates' Courts) Act 1960; to make provision in relation to like matters for Scotland; and for purposes connected therewith. [5th July 1973]

NOTE

[1] Prospectively repealed by the Children (Scotland) Act 1995 (c. 36), Sched. 5, *infra*.

. . . . . .

Part II

Scotland

10. [Repealed by the Law Reform (Parent and Child) (Scotland) Act 1986 (c. 9), Sched. 2.]

Jurisdiction and orders relating to care and custody of children

11.—[1] (1) Where an application relating to the custody of a child, other than an application to which Part II of the Matrimonial Proceedings (Children) Act 1958 applies, is made to a court—

(*a*) if it appears to the court that there are exceptional circumstances making it impracticable or undesirable for the child to be entrusted to either of the parents or to any other individual, the court may commit the care of the child to a specified local authority;

(*b*) if by an order made on that application either parent or any other person (other than a local authority) is given the custody of the child, but it appears to the court that there are exceptional circumstances making it desirable that the child should be under the supervision of a local authority, the court may order that the child shall be under the supervision of a specified local authority, subject to any directions given by the court;

but any order made by virtue of the above paragraphs shall cease to have effect when the child attains the age of sixteen.

[2] (2) While an order made by virtue of this section committing the care of a child to a local authority is in force with respect to any child the child shall continue in the care of the local authority notwithstanding any claim by a parent or other person.

(3) Where the court makes an order by virtue of subsection (1)(*a*) above committing the care of a child to a local authority, the court may make a further order requiring the payment by either parent to that authority while it has the care of the child of such weekly or other periodical sum towards the maintenance of the child as the court thinks reasonable having regard to the means of that parent.

[2] (4) Before making an order by virtue of subsection (1)(*a*) above, the court shall hear any representations from the local authority, including any representations as to the making of an order under subsection (3) above for payments to the authority.

[2] (5) On the making of an order by virtue of this section committing the care of a child to a local authority Part II of the Social Work (Scotland) Act 1968 (which relates to the treatment of children in care of local authorities) shall, subject to the provisions of this section, apply as if the child had been received by the local authority into their care under section 15 of that Act, so however that—

(*a*) the exercise by the local authority of their powers under or by virtue of sections 20 to 22 of that Act shall be subject to any directions given by the court; and

(*b*) section 23 of that Act (which relates to arrangements for the emigration of a child under the care of a local authority) shall not apply.

(6) [Repealed by the Law Reform (Parent and Child) (Scotland) Act 1986 (c. 9), Sched. 2.]

NOTES

[1] As amended by the Children Act 1975 (c. 72), s. 48(3), with effect from 1st September 1984.

[2] Extended by the Children Act 1975 (c. 72), ss. 17(4) and 53(3) and by the Adoption (Scotland) Act 1978 (c. 28), s. 26(3).

Provisions supplementary to section 11

12.—(1) Any order made by virtue of section 11 above may from time to time be varied or may be discharged by a subsequent order on the application of—

(*a*) either parent, or

[0](*b*) (after the death of either parent) any guardian, or

(*c*) any other person having custody of the child, or

(*d*) the specified local authority having the care or supervision of the child.

(2) [1] (*a*) Where any application, other than one to which Part II of the Matrimonial Proceedings (Children) Act 1958 applies, is made to a court for custody of a child or for the variation or discharge of any order (including an order made by virtue of section 11 above) relating to the custody of a child, the court shall have power to appoint a specified local authority or an individual not being an officer of the local authority to investigate and report to the court on all the circumstances of the child and on the proposed arrangements for the care and upbringing of the child.

[2] (*b*) If on consideration of a report furnished in pursuance of this subsection the court, either *ex proprio motu* or on the application of any person concerned, thinks it expedient to do so, it may require the person who furnished the report to appear and be examined on oath regarding any matter dealt with in the report, and such person may be examined or cross-examined accordingly.

[2,3] (*c*) Any expenses incurred in connection with the preparation of a report by a local authority or other person appointed under this subsection shall form part of the expenses of the action and be defrayed by such party to the action as the court may direct, and the court may certify the amount of the expenses so incurred.

[4] (3) Each parent or guardian of a child for the time being in the care of a local authority by virtue of an order under section 11(1)(*a*) above shall give notice to the authority of any change of address of that parent or guardian and any person who without reasonable excuse fails to comply with this subsection shall be liable on summary conviction to a fine not exceeding level 1 on the standard scale.

NOTES

[0] As amended by the Law Reform (Parent and Child) (Scotland) Act 1986, Sched. 2.

[1] As amended by the Children Act 1975, s. 48(4).

[2] Extended by the Children Act 1975, s. 49(3).

[3] Extended by the Children Act 1975, s. 17(4).

[4] As amended by virtue of the Criminal Procedure (Scotland) Act 1975, ss. 289F and 289G.

Interpretation of Part II

13.—[1] (1) In this Part of this Act—

"child" means a child under sixteen years of age;

"specified local authority" means a local authority within the meaning of the Social Work (Scotland) Act 1968.

NOTE

[1] Definition of "guardian" added by the Law Reform (Parent and Child) (Scotland) Act 1986, Sched. 1, para. 12, but repealed by the Age of Legal Capacity (Scotland) Act 1991, Sched. 2.

Consequential amendments

14. The enactments specified in Schedule 5 to this Act shall have effect subject to the amendments set out in the Schedule, being amendments consequential on the foregoing provisions of this Part of this Act.

PART III

GENERAL

Short title, citation, extent and commencement

15.—(1) This Act may be cited as the Guardianship Act 1973; and—

(*a*) Part I of this Act and the Guardianship of Minors Act 1971 may be cited together as the Guardianship of Minors Acts 1971 and 1973; and

(*b*) [Repealed by the Law Reform (Parent and Child) (Scotland) Act 1986 (c. 9), Sched. 2.]

(2) Part I of this Act shall not extend to Scotland or to Northern Ireland, and Part II shall not extend to England and Wales or to Northern Ireland, except that each Part shall extend throughout the United Kingdom in so far as it amends section 16 of the Maintenance Orders Act 1950.

[1] (3) This Act shall come into force on such day as the Secretary of State may appoint by order made by statutory instrument, and different days may be appointed for the coming into force of different provisions.

NOTE

[1] 8th May 1974: see S.I. 1974 No. 836

. . . .

Section 14

[1] SCHEDULE 5

CONSEQUENTIAL AMENDMENTS RELATING TO SCOTLAND

NOTE

[1] The amendments specified in this Schedule, so far as relating to Acts in *The Parliament House Book*, are given effect to in the prints of those Acts.

Domicile and Matrimonial Proceedings Act 1973

(1973 c. 45)

An Act to amend the law relating to the domicile of married women and persons not of full age, to matters connected with domicile and to jurisdiction in matrimonial proceedings including actions for reduction of consistorial decrees; to make further provision about the recognition of divorces and legal separations; and for purposes connected therewith. [25th July 1973]

PART I

DOMICILE

Husband and wife

Abolition of wife's dependent domicile

1.—(1) Subject to subsection (2) below, the domicile of a married woman as at any time after the coming into force of this section shall, instead of being the same as her husband's by virtue only of marriage, be ascertained by reference to the same factors as in the case of any other individual capable of having an independent domicile.

(2) Where immediately before this section came into force a woman was married and then had her husband's domicile by dependence, she is to be treated as retaining that domicile (as a domicile of choice, if it is not also her domicile of origin) unless and until it is changed by acquisition or revival of another domicile either on or after the coming into force of this section.

(3) This section extends to England and Wales, Scotland and Northern Ireland.

2.—[Repealed by the Family Law Act 1986, Sched. 2.]

Dependent domicile of child not living with his father

4.—(1) Subsection (2) of this section shall have effect with respect to the dependent domicile of a child as at any time after the coming into force of this section when his father and mother are alive but living apart.

(2) The child's domicile as at that time shall be that of his mother if—

(*a*) he then has his home with her and has no home with his father; or

(*b*) he has at any time had her domicile by virtue of paragraph (*a*) above and has not since had a home with his father.

(3) As at any time after the coming into force of this section, the domicile of a child whose mother is dead shall be that which she last had before she died if at her death he had her domicile by virtue of subsection (2) above and he has not since had a home with his father.

(4) Nothing in this section prejudices any existing rule of law as to the cases in which a child's domicile is regarded as being, by dependence, that of his mother.

[1] (5) In this section, "child" means a person incapable of having an independent domicile.

(6) This section extends to England and Wales, Scotland and Northern Ireland.

NOTE

[1] As repealed in part by the Children Act 1975, Sched. 4, Pt. I.

. . . . . .

PART III

JURISDICTION IN CONSISTORIAL CAUSES (SCOTLAND)

Jurisdiction of Court of Session

7.—[1] (1) Subsections (2) to (8) below shall have effect, subject to section 12(6) of this Act, with respect to the jurisdiction of the Court of Session to entertain—

(*a*) an action for divorce, separation, declarator of nullity of marriage, declarator of marriage, declarator of freedom and putting to silence.

(2) The Court shall have jurisdiction to entertain an action for divorce, separation or declarator of freedom and putting to silence if (and only if) either of the parties to the marriage in question—

(*a*) is domiciled in Scotland on the date when the action is begun; or

(*b*) was habitually resident in Scotland throughout the period of one year ending with that date.

(3) The Court shall have jurisdiction to entertain an action for declarator of marriage or declarator of nullity of marriage if (and only if) either of the parties to the marriage—

(*a*) is domiciled in Scotland on the date when the action is begun; or

(*b*) was habitually resident in Scotland throughout the period of one year ending with that date; or

(*c*) died before that date and either—

(i) was at death domiciled in Scotland, or

(ii) had been habitually resident in Scotland throughout the period of one year ending with the date of death.

(4) [Repealed by the Presumption of Death (Scotland) Act 1977, Sched. 2.]

(5) The Court shall, at any time when proceedings are pending in respect of which it has jurisdiction by virtue of subsection (2) or (3) above (or of this subsection), also have jurisdiction to entertain other proceedings, in respect of the same marriage, for divorce, separation or declarator of marriage, declarator of nullity of marriage or declarator of freedom and putting to silence, notwithstanding that jurisdiction would not be exercisable under subsection (2) or (3).

(6) Nothing in this section affects the rules governing the jurisdiction of the Court of Session to entertain, in an action for divorce, an application for payment by a co-defender of damages or expenses.

(7) The foregoing provisions of this section are without prejudice to any rule of law whereby the Court of Session has jurisdiction in certain circumstances to entertain actions for separation as a matter of necessity and urgency.

(8) No action for divorce in respect of a marriage shall be entertained by the Court of Session by virtue of subsection (2) or (5) above while proceedings for divorce or nullity of marriage, begun before the commencement of this Act, are pending (in respect of the same marriage) in England and Wales, Northern Ireland, the Channel Islands or the Isle of Man; and provision may be made by rules of court as to when, for the purposes of this subsection, proceedings are to be treated as begun or pending in any of those places.

NOTE

[1] As repealed in part by the Presumption of Death (Scotland) Act 1977 (c. 27), Sched. 2.

Jurisdiction of sheriff court in respect of actions for separation

[1] **8.**—(1) Subsections (2) to (4) below shall have effect, subject to section 12(6) of this Act, with respect to the jurisdiction of the sheriff court to entertain an action for separation or divorce.

(2) The court shall have jurisdiction to entertain an action for separation or divorce if (and only if)—

(*a*) either party to the marriage in question—

(i) is domiciled in Scotland at the date when the action is begun, or

(ii) was habitually resident there throughout the period of one year ending with that date; and

(*b*) either party to the marriage—

(i) was resident in the sheriffdom for a period of 40 days ending with that date, or

(ii) had been resident in the sheriffdom for a period of not less than 40 days ending not more than 40 days before the said date, and has no known residence in Scotland at that date.

(3) In respect of any marriage, the court shall have jurisdiction to entertain an action for separation or divorce (notwithstanding that jurisdiction would not be exercisable under subsection (2) above) if it is begun at a time when an original action is pending in respect of the marriage; and for this purpose "original action" means an action in respect of which the court has jurisdiction by virtue of subsection (2), or of this subsection.

(4) The foregoing provisions of this section are without prejudice to any jurisdiction of a sheriff court to entertain an action of separation or divorce remitted to it in pursuance of any enactment or rule of court.

NOTE

[1] As amended by the Divorce Jurisdiction, Court Fees and Legal Aid (Scotland) Act 1983 (c. 12), Sched. 1, para. 18.

9. [Repealed by the Law Reform (Miscellaneous Provisions) (Scotland) Act 1980 (c. 55), Sched. 3.]

Ancillary and collateral orders

10.—[1] (1) Where after the commencement of this Act—

(*a*) an application is made to the Court of Session or to a sheriff court for—

(i) the making as respects any person or property of an order under any of the enactments or rules of law specified in Part I or Part II of Schedule 2 to this Act, or

(ii) the variation or recall as respects any person or property of an order made (whether before or after the commencement of this Act) under any of those enactments or rules of law; and (*b*) the application is competently made in connection with an action for any of the following remedies, namely, divorce, separation, declarator of marriage and declarator of nullity of marriage (whether the application is made in the same proceedings or in other proceedings and whether it is made before or after the pronouncement of a final decree in the action),

then, if the court has or, as the case may be, had by virtue of this Act or of any enactment or rule of law in force before the commencement of this Act jurisdiction to entertain the action, it shall have jurisdiction to entertain the application as respects the person or property in question whether or not it would have jurisdiction to do so apart from this subsection.

(1A) [Prospectively inserted by the Children (Scotland) Act 1995 (c. 36), Sched. 4, para. 20(2)(*b*), *infra*.]

(2) It is hereby declared that where—

(*a*) the Court of Session has jurisdiction by virtue of this section to entertain an application for the variation or recall as respects any person of an order made by it, and

(*b*) the order is one to which section 8 (variation and recall by the sheriff of certain orders made by the Court of Session) of the Law Reform (Miscellaneous Provisions)(Scotland) Act 1966 applies,

then, for the purposes of any application under the said section 8 for the variation or recall of the order in so far as it relates to that person, the sheriff, as defined in that section, has jurisdiction as respects that person to exercise the power conferred on him by that section.

NOTE

[1] Prospectively amended by the Children (Scotland) Act 1995 (c. 36), Sched. 4, para. 20(2)(*a*), *infra*.

Sisting of certain actions

11. The provisions of Schedule 3 to this Act shall have effect with respect to the sisting of actions for any of the following remedies, namely, divorce, separation, declarator of marriage or declarator of nullity of marriage and with respect to the other matters mentioned in that Schedule; but nothing in that Schedule—

(*a*) requires or authorises a sist of an action which is pending when this Act comes into force; or

(*b*) prejudices any power to sist an action which is exercisable by any court apart from the Schedule.

Supplementary

12.—(1) In relation to any action for any of the following three remedies, namely, declarator of marriage, declarator of nullity of marriage, and declarator of freedom and putting to silence, references in this Part of this Act to the marriage shall be construed as including references to the alleged, or, as the case may be, the purported, marriage.

(2) References in this Part of this Act to an action for a particular remedy shall be construed, in relation to a case where the remedy is sought along with other remedies in one action, as references to so much of the proceedings in the action as relates to the particular remedy.

(3) References in this Part of this Act to the remedy of separation shall be construed, in relation to an action in a sheriff court, as references to the remedy of separation and aliment.

(4) For the purposes of this Act the period during which an action in the Court of Session or a sheriff court is pending shall be regarded as including any period while the taking of an appeal is competent and the period while any proceedings on appeal are pending; and in this subsection references to an appeal include references to a reclaiming motion.

(5) In this Part of this Act any reference to an enactment shall, unless the contrary intention appears, be construed as a reference to that enact-

ment as amended or extended, and as including a reference thereto as applied, by or under any other enactment (including this Act).

(6) Nothing in this Part of this Act affects any court's jurisdiction to entertain any proceedings begun before the commencement of this Act.

(7) Subject to subsection (6) above, the enactments described in Schedule 4 to this Act shall have effect subject to the amendments therein specified, being amendments consequential on the provisions of this Part of this Act.

. . . .

PART V

MISCELLANEOUS AND GENERAL

15, 16. [Repealed by the Family Law Act 1986, Sched. 2.]

Citation, etc.

17.—(1) This Act may be cited as the Domicile and Matrimonial Proceedings Act 1973.

(2) Subject to sections 6(4), 12(6) and 14(3) of this Act, the enactments specified in Schedule 6 to this Act (including certain enactments of the Parliament of Northern Ireland) are hereby repealed to the extent specified in the third column of that Schedule.

(3) [Repealed by the Zimbabwe Act 1979, Sched. 3.]

(4) Part II of this Act extends to England and Wales only; Part III extends to Scotland only; Part IV extends to Northern Ireland only; and this Part extends to the whole of the United Kingdom.

(5) This Act shall come into force on 1st January 1974.

. . . .

SCHEDULES

Section 10

SCHEDULE 2

ANCILLARY AND COLLATERAL ORDERS (SCOTLAND)

PART I

Enactments and rules of law referred to in section 10(1) and in Schedule 3, paragraph 11(1)

1, 2. [Repealed by the Family Law (Scotland) Act 1985, Sched. 2.]

[1] 2A. Any enactment or rule of law empowering a court to make an order for payment of aliment (including interim aliment).

NOTE

[1] Inserted by the Family Law (Scotland) Act 1985, Sched. 1, para. 9.

---

[1] 3. Paragraph (2) of section 5 of the Sheriff Courts (Scotland) Act 1907 so far as relating to orders for aliment and paragraph (2C) of the said section 5.

NOTE

[1] As amended by the Law Reform (Parent and Child) (Scotland) Act 1986, Sched. 1, para. 13.

---

[1] 4. Section 9 (orders with respect to children) of the Conjugal Rights (Scotland) Amendment Act 1861.

NOTE

[1] As amended by the Law Reform (Parent and Child) (Scotland) Act 1986, Sched. 2.

---

5. Section 10 of the Matrimonial Proceedings (Children) Act 1958 so far as relating to orders committing the care of a child to an individual.

6. Section 13 (power to prohibit in certain cases removal of child furth of Scotland or out of control of person having custody of him) of the Matrimonial Proceedings (Children) Act 1958.

7. Any enactment or rule of law empowering a court to vary or recall an order the power to make which is conferred by any enactment mentioned in this Part of this Schedule or by any rule of law so mentioned.

PART II

Further enactments and rules of law referred to in section 10(1)

8. [Repealed by the Law Reform (Parent and Child) (Scotland) Act 1986, Sched. 2.]

[1] 9. Section 2 (effect of divorce on property rights) of the Divorce (Scotland) Act 1938, both as originally enacted and as substituted by section 7 of the Divorce (Scotland) Act 1964.

[1]10. Section 10 of the Matrimonial Proceedings (Children) Act 1958, so far as relating to orders committing the care of a child to a local authority.

[THE NEXT PAGE IS K 133]

11. Section 12 (power of court to provide for supervision of child) of the Matrimonial Proceedings (Children) Act 1958.

12. Section 26 (orders for financial provision on divorce) and section 27 (orders relating to settlements and other dealings) of the Succession (Scotland) Act 1964.

[1] 12A. Section 5 (orders for financial provision) and section 6 (orders relating to settlement and other dealings) of the Divorce (Scotland) Act 1976.

NOTE

[1] Added by the Divorce (Scotland) Act 1976, Sched. 1, para. 5.

---

[1] 12B. Section 8 (orders for financial provision on divorce), section 17(1) (financial provision on declarator of nullity of marriage) and section 18 (orders relating to avoidance transactions) of the Family Law (Scotland) Act 1985.

NOTE

[1] Inserted by the Family Law (Scotland) Act 1985, Sched. 1, para. 9.

---

13. Any rule of law empowering a court, in connection with an action for declarator of nullity of marriage, to make an order for restitution of property as between the parties to the marriage or for the payment of damages by either of those parties.

14. Any rule of law empowering a court to make an order for the payment of expenses of the action in question by either party to the marriage.

15. Any enactment or rule of law empowering a court to vary or recall an order the power to make which is conferred by any enactment mentioned in this Part of this Schedule or by any rule of law so mentioned.

Section 11

SCHEDULE 3

Sisting of Consistorial actions (Scotland)

Interpretation

1. The following six paragraphs have effect for the interpretation of this Schedule.

2. "Consistorial action" means any action so far as it is one or more of the following, namely, actions for—

divorce,
separation,
declarator of marriage,
declarator of nullity of marriage.

3.—(1) "Another jurisdiction" means any country outside Scotland.

(2) "Related jurisdiction" means any of the following countries, namely, England and Wales, Northern Ireland, Jersey, Guernsey and the Isle of Man (the reference to Guernsey being treated as including Alderney and Sark).

4. For the purposes of this Schedule—

(*a*) in any action in the Court of Session or a sheriff court neither the taking of evidence on commission nor a separate proof relating to any preliminary plea shall be regarded as part of the proof in the action; and

(*b*) any such action is continuing if it is pending and not sisted.

5. Any reference in this Schedule to proceedings in another jurisdiction is to proceedings in a court of that jurisdiction and to any other proceedings in that jurisdiction which are of a description prescribed for the purposes of this paragraph; and provision may be made by rules of court as to when proceedings of any description in another jurisdiction are continuing for the purposes of this Schedule.

6. "Prescribed" means prescribed by rules of court.

Duty to furnish particulars of concurrent proceedings in another jurisdiction

7. While any consistorial action is pending in the Court of Session or a sheriff court and proof in that action has not begun, it shall be the duty of the pursuer, and of any other person who has entered appearance in the action, to furnish, in such manner and to such

persons and on such occasions as may be prescribed, such particulars as may be so prescribed of any proceedings which—

(*a*) he knows to be continuing in another jurisdiction; and

(*b*) are in respect of that marriage or capable of affecting its validity.

Mandatory sists

[1] 8. Where before the beginning of the proof in any action for divorce which is continuing in the Court of Session or in the sheriff court it appears to the court on the application of a party to the marriage—

(*a*) that in respect of the same marriage proceedings for divorce or nullity of marriage are continuing in a related jurisdiction; and

(*b*) that the parties to the marriage have resided together after the marriage was contracted; and

(*c*) that the place where they resided together when the action in the court concerned was begun or, if they did not then reside together, where they last resided together before the date on which that action was begun is in that jurisdiction; and

(*d*) that either of the said parties was habitually resident in that jurisdiction throughout the year ending with the date on which they last resided together before the date on which that action was begun;

it shall be the duty of the court, subject to paragraph 10(2) below, to sist the action before it.

NOTE

[1] As amended by the Divorce Jurisdiction, Court Fees and Legal Aid (Scotland) Act 1983, Sched. 1, para. 19.

Discretionary sists

[1] 9.—(1) Where before the beginning of the proof in any consistorial action which is continuing in the Court of Session or in a sheriff court, it appears to the court concerned—

(*a*) that any other proceedings in respect of the marriage in question or capable of affecting its validity are continuing in another jurisdiction, and

(*b*) that the balance of fairness (including convenience) as between the parties to the marriage is such that it is appropriate for those other proceedings to be disposed of before further steps are taken in the action in the said court

the court may then if it thinks fit sist that action.

(2) In considering the balance of fairness and convenience for the purposes of sub-paragraph (1)(*b*) above, the court shall have regard to all factors appearing to be relevant, including the convenience of witnesses and any delay or expense which may result from the proceedings being sisted, or not being sisted.

(3) Sub-paragraph (1) above is without prejudice to the duty imposed by paragraph 8 above.

(4) If, at any time after the beginning of the proof in any consistorial action which is pending in the Court of Session or a sheriff court, the court concerned is satisfied that a person has failed to perform the duty imposed on him in respect of the action and any such other proceedings as aforesaid by paragraph 7 above, sub-paragraph (1) of this paragraph shall have effect in relation to that action and to the other proceedings as if the words "before the beginning of the proof" were omitted; but no action in respect of the failure of a person to perform such a duty shall be competent.

NOTE

[1] As amended by the Divorce Jurisdiction, Court Fees and Legal Aid (Scotland) Act 1983, Sched. 1, para. 20 and Sched. 2.

Supplementary

10.—(1) Where an action is sisted in pursuance of paragraph 8 or 9 above, the court may if it thinks fit, on the application of a party to the action, recall the sist if it appears to the court that the other proceedings by reference to which the action was sisted are sisted or concluded or that a party to those other proceedings has delayed unreasonably in prosecuting those other proceedings.

(2) Where an action has been sisted in pursuance of paragraph 8 above by reference to some other proceedings, and the court recalls the sist in pursuance of the preceding sub-paragraph, the court shall not again sist the action in pursuance of the said paragraph 8.

11.—(1) The provisions of sub-paragraphs (2) and (3) below shall apply where an action for any of the following remedies, namely, divorce, separation and declarator of nullity of marriage, is sisted by reference to proceedings in a related jurisdiction for any of those remedies; and in this paragraph—

"custody" includes access to the child in question;

"the other proceedings", in relation to any sisted action, means the proceedings in another jurisdiction by reference to which the action was sisted;

[1] "the relevant order" means an interim order made by virtue of any of the enactments or rules of law specified in Part I of Schedule 2 to this Act; and

"sisted" means sisted in pursuance of this Schedule.

(2) Where an action such as is mentioned in sub-paragraph (1) above is sisted, then, without prejudice to the effect of the sist apart from this paragraph—

(*a*) the court shall not have power to make a relevant order in connection with the sisted action except in pursuance of paragraph (*c*) below; and

(*b*) subject to the said paragraph (*c*), any relevant order made in connection with the sisted action shall (unless the sist or the relevant order has been previously recalled) cease to have effect on the expiration of the period of three months beginning with the date on which the sist comes into operation; but

(*c*) if the court considers that as a matter of necessity and urgency it is necessary during or after that period to make a relevant order in connection with the sisted action or to extend or further extend the duration of a relevant order made in connection with the sisted action, the court may do so, and the order shall not cease to have effect by virtue of paragraph (*b*) above.

[1] (3) Where any action such as is mentioned in sub-paragraph (1) above is sisted and at the time when the sist comes into operation, an order is in force, or at a subsequent time an order comes into force, being an order made in connection with the other proceedings and providing for any of the following four matters, namely periodical payments for a spouse of the marriage in question, periodical payments for a child, the custody of a child, and the education of a child, then, as from the time when the sist comes into operation (in a case where the order is in force at that time) or (in any other case) on the coming into force of the order—

(*a*) any relevant order made in connection with the sisted action shall cease to have effect in so far as it makes for a spouse or child any provision for any of the said matters as respects which the same or different provision for that spouse or child is made by the other order; and

(*b*) the court shall not have power in connection with the sisted action to make a relevant order containing for a spouse or child provision for any of the matters aforesaid as respects which any provision for that spouse or child is made by the other order.

(4) Nothing in this paragraph affects any power of a court—

(*a*) to vary or recall a relevant order in so far as the order is for the time being in force; or

(*b*) to enforce a relevant order as respects any period when it is or was in force; or

(*c*) to make a relevant order in connection with an action which was, but is no longer, sisted.

NOTE

[1] Prospectively amended by the Children (Scotland) Act 1995 (c. 36), Sched. 4, para. 20(3), *infra*.

. . . . . .

Children Act 1975

(1975 c. 72)

An Act to make further provision for children.

[12th November 1975.]

PART I

ADOPTION

[Repealed by the Adoption (Scotland) Act 1978 (c. 28), Sched. 4.]

PART II

CUSTODY

. . . . . .

Custody in Scotland

Granting of custody

[0] **47.**—(1) [Repealed by the Law Reform (Parent and Child) (Scotland) Act 1986 (c. 9), Sched. 2.]

[1] (2) Notwithstanding the generality of section 3(1) of the Law Reform (Parent and Child) (Scotland) Act 1986, custody of a child shall not be granted in any proceedings to a person other than a parent or guardian of the child unless that person—

(*a*) being a relative or step-parent of the child, has the consent of a parent or guardian of the child and has had care and possession of the child for the three months preceding the making of the application for custody;

(*b*) has the consent of a parent or guardian of the child and has had care and possession of the child for a period or periods, before such application, which amounted to at least twelve months and included the three months preceding such application; or

(*c*) has had care and possession of the child for a period or periods before such application which amounted to at least three years and included the three months preceding such application; or

[2] (*d*) while not falling within paragraph (*a*), (*b*) or (*c*), can show cause why an order should be made awarding him custody of the child.

(3) [Repealed by the Law Reform (Parent and Child) (Scotland) Act 1986 (c. 9), Sched. 2.]

(4) The Secretary of State may by order a draft of which has been approved by each House of Parliament amend subsection (2)(*c*) to substitute a different period for the period of three years mentioned in that paragraph (or the period which by a previous order under this subsection was substituted for that period).

[3] (5) In relation to a grant of custody to which this section applies,

(*a*) "guardian" has the same meaning as in the Adoption (Scotland) Act 1978;

(*b*), (*c*) [Repealed by the Law Reform (Parent and Child) (Scotland) Act 1986 (c. 9), Sched. 2.].

(6) The form and manner of any consent required in terms of subsection (2)(*a*) or (*b*) may be prescribed by act of sederunt.

NOTES

[0] Prospectively repealed by the Children (Scotland) Act 1995 (c. 36), Sched. 4, para. 26(2), *infra*.

[1] As amended by the Law Reform (Parent and Child) (Scotland) Act 1986 (c. 9), Sched. 1, para. 14, and the Age of Legal Capacity (Scotland) Act 1991 (c. 50), Sched. 2.

[2] As amended by the Law Reform (Parent and Child) (Scotland) Act 1986 (c. 9), Sched. 2.

[3] As amended by the Adoption (Scotland) Act 1978 (c. 28), Sched. 3, para. 16.

Miscellaneous provisions relative to custody

[1] **48.**—[2] (1) A person making an application relating to the custody of a child shall, so far as practicable and in such manner as may be prescribed by act of sederunt, give notice of that application to each known parent of the child.

(2) Any order made by virtue of this Part of this Act may be varied or discharged by a subsequent order, either by the court *ex proprio motu* or on the application of any person concerned.

(3) [Amendment to the Guardianship Act 1973 (c. 29), s. 11(1), is given effect in the print of that Act.]

[THE NEXT PAGE IS K 149]

(4) [Amendment to the Guardianship Act 1973 (c. 29), s. 12(2)(*a*), is given effect in the print of that Act.]

NOTES

[1] Prospectively repealed by the Children (Scotland) Act 1995 (c. 36), Sched. 4, para. 26(2), *infra*.

[2] As amended by the Law Reform (Parent and Child) (Scotland) Act 1986 (c. 9), Sched. 2.

Notice to local authority of certain custody applications

[1] **49.**—[2] (1) Where an applicant for custody of a child is not a parent of the child, an order awarding custody to that applicant shall not except on cause shown be made unless the applicant—

(*a*) in any case where at the time of the application he resided in Scotland, has, within the seven days following the making of the application, given notice thereof to the local authority within whose area he resided at that time;

(*b*) in any other case, has within such time as the court may direct given, to such local authority in Scotland as the court may specify, notice of the making of the application.

(2) On receipt of a notice under subsection (1) the local authority shall investigate and report to the court on all the circumstances of the child and on the proposed arrangements for the care and upbringing of the child.

(3) Paragraphs (*b*) and (*c*) of subsection (2) of section 12 of the Guardianship Act 1973 shall apply in relation to an investigation and report in terms of this section as they apply in relation to an investigation and report in terms of paragraph (*a*) of subsection (2) of that section.

NOTES

[1] Prospectively repealed by the Children (Scotland) Act 1995 (c. 36), Sched. 4, para. 26(2), *infra*.

[2] As amended by the Law Reform (Parent and Child) (Scotland) Act 1986 (c. 9), Sched. 1, para. 14.

Payments towards maintenance of children

[1] **50.** Without prejudice to any existing powers and duties to make payments in respect of the maintenance of children, where custody of a child has been awarded to a person other than a parent of the child any local authority may make to that person payments for or towards the maintenance of the child.

NOTE

[1] Prospectively amended by the Children (Scotland) Act 1995 (c. 36), Sched. 4, para. 20(3), *infra*.

Restriction on removal of child where applicant has provided home for three years

[1] **51.**—[2] (1) Where a person has applied for custody of a child, it shall be an offence, except with the authority of a court or under authority conferred by any enactment or on the arrest of the child, to remove the child from the care and possession of the applicant against the will of the applicant if—

(*a*) the child has been in the care and possession of that person for a period or periods before the making of the application which amount to at least three years; and

(*b*) the application is pending in any court.

[2] (2) In any case where subsection (1) applies, and

(*a*) the child was in the care of a local authority before he began to have his home with the applicant, and

(*b*) the child remains in the care of a local authority,

the authority in whose care the child is shall not remove the child from the applicant's care and possession except—

(i) with the applicant's consent;

(ii) with the leave of a court; or

(iii) with the authority, in terms of Part III of the Social Work (Scotland) Act 1968, of a justice of the peace or a children's hearing.

[3] (3) Any person who contravenes the provisions of subsection (1) commits an offence and shall be liable on summary conviction to imprisonment for a term not exceeding three months or a fine not exceeding level 5 on the standard scale or both.

(4) The Secretary of State may by order, a draft of which has been approved by each House of Parliament, amend subsection (1) to substitute a different period for the period mentioned in that subsection (or for the period which, by a previous order under this subsection, was substituted for that period).

(5) [Prospectively added by the Children (Scotland) Act 1995 (c. 36), Sched. 4, para. 26(4), *infra*.]

NOTES

[1] As amended by the Health and Social Services and Social Security Adjudications Act 1983 (c. 41), Sched. 2, para. 25.

[2] Prospectively amended by the Children (Scotland) Act 1995 (c. 36), Sched. 4, para. 26(4), *infra*.

[3] As amended by virtue of the Criminal Procedure (Scotland) Act 1975 (c. 21), ss. 289F and 289G.

Return of child taken away in breach of section 51

[1] **52.** A court in which an application for custody of a child is pending may—

(*a*) on the application of a person from whose care and possession the child has been removed in breach of section 51, order the person who has so removed the child to return the child to the applicant;

(*b*) on the application of a person who has reasonable grounds for believing that another person is intending to remove the child from the applicant's care and possession in breach of section 51, by order direct that other person not to remove the child from the applicant's care and possession in breach of that section.

NOTE

[1] As amended by the Health and Social Services and Social Security Adjudications Act 1983 (c. 41), Sched. 2, para. 26. Prospectively amended by the Children (Scotland) Act 1995 (c. 36), Sched. 4, para. 26(5), *infra*.

Custody order on application for adoption in Scotland

[1] **53.**—[2] (1) Without prejudice to the provisions of section 19 (power to make an interim order giving custody), where on an application for an adoption order in respect of a child the court is of opinion—

(*a*) in the case of an applicant who is a relative of the child or a husband or wife of the mother or father of the child (whether applying alone or jointly with his or her spouse)—

(i) that the child's welfare would not be better safeguarded and promoted by the making of an adoption order in favour of the applicant than it would be by the making of a custody order in his favour; and

(ii) that it would be appropriate to make a custody order in favour of the applicant; or

(*b*) in any other case, that the making of a custody order in favour of the applicant would be more appropriate than the making of an adoption order in his favour,

the court shall direct that the application is to be treated as if it had been made for custody of the child.

(2) In the application of this Part of this Act to any case where a direction under subsection (1) has been made—

(*a*) for references in section 47(2) to the making of an application for custody there shall be substituted references to the making of an application for an adoption order;

(*b*) for the references in section 49 and paragraph (*a*) of subsection (1) of section 51 to the making of an application there shall be substituted references to the making of a direction in terms of subsection (1) of this section;

(*c*) in section 51(1) for the words "for custody of" there shall be substituted the words "for an adoption order in respect of".

(3) For the purposes of section 11 of the Guardianship Act 1973, any application in respect of which a direction has been made under subsection (1) of this section, is an application for custody of a child.

NOTES

[1] Prospectively repealed by the Children (Scotland) Act 1995 (c. 36), Sched. 4, para. 20(6), *infra*.

[2] As amended by the Law Reform (Parent and Child) (Scotland) Act 1986 (c. 9), Sched. 2 and the Family Law Act 1986 (c. 55), Sched. 2.

Jurisdiction of Scottish courts in certain applications for custody

54. [Repealed by the Family Law Act 1986 (c. 55), Sched. 2.]

Interpretation and extent of sections 47 to 55

55.—[1] (1) In sections 47 to 54 "child" means a person under the age of sixteen and "relative" means a grand-parent, brother, sister, uncle or aunt, whether of the full blood or half blood or by affinity.

[1] (2) Sections 47 to 54 and this section apply to Scotland only and shall be construed in accordance with section 1(1) of the Law Reform (Parent and Child) (Scotland) Act 1986.

NOTE

[1] As amended by the Law Reform (Parent and Child) (Scotland) Act 1986 (c. 9), Sched. 1, para. 14. Prospectively amended by the Children (Scotland) Act 1995 (c. 36), Sched. 4, para. 20(7), *infra*.

Part III

Care

. . . .

Conflict of interest between parent and child

. . . .

66.—[See the Social Work (Scotland) Act 1968 (c. 49), s. 34.]

. . . .

70.—[See the Criminal Procedure (Scotland) Act 1975 (c. 21), ss. 23, 24, 297 and 329.]

. . . .

82–84.—[See the Social Work (Scotland) Act 1968 (c. 49), ss. 36, 37 and 40. Prospectively repealed by the Children (Scotland) Act 1995 (c. 36), Sched. 4, para. 20(8), *infra*.]

. . . .

PART V

MISCELLANEOUS AND SUPPLEMENTAL

. . . . . .

Inquiries

. . . . . .

Inquiries in Scotland

[1] **99.**—[2] (1) In Scotland the Secretary of State may cause an inquiry to be held into any matter relating to—

(*a*) the functions of a local authority under the Social Work (Scotland) Act 1968 in so far as the matter relates to children;

[3] (*b*) the functions of a local authority under the enactments specified in paragraphs (*b*) to (*e*) and (*h*) to (*k*) of section 2(2) of the Social Work (Scotland) Act 1968;

(*c*) the functions of an adoption society;

(*d*) the functions of a voluntary organisation in so far as those functions relate to establishments to which sections 61 to 68 of the Social Work (Scotland) Act 1968 apply and in so far as the matter relates to children; or

(*e*) the detention of a child under—

(i) section 57 or 58A of the Children and Young Persons (Scotland) Act 1937; or

(ii) section 206 or 413 of the Criminal Procedure (Scotland) Act 1975.

(2) The Secretary of State may, before an inquiry is commenced, direct that it shall be held in private, but where no such direction has been given, the person holding the inquiry may if he thinks fit hold it or any part of it in private.

(3) Subsections (2) to (8) of section 210 of the Local Government (Scotland) Act 1973 (powers in relation to local inquiries) shall apply in relation to an inquiry under this section as they apply in relation to a local inquiry under that section.

(4) In this section "functions" includes powers and duties exercisable otherwise than by virtue of any enactment.

NOTES

[1] Prospectively repealed by the Children (Scotland) Act 1995 (c. 36), Sched. 4, para. 26(8), *infra*.

[2] Prospective amendment in the Local Government etc. (Scotland) Act 1994 (c. 39), Sched. 13, para. 103, *infra*, including insertion of new subs. (1)(*f*).

[3] As amended by the National Health Service and Community Care Act 1990 (c. 19), Sched. 9, para. 16 and Sched. 10.

Supplemental

Courts

[1] **100.**—(1) In this Act "authorised court", as respects an application for an order relating to a child, shall be construed as follows.

. . . . . .

(3) If the child is in Scotland when the application is made, the following are authorised courts—

(*a*) the Court of Session;

(*b*) the sheriff court of the sheriffdom within which the child is.

(4), (5) [Repealed by the Adoption (Scotland) Act 1978 (c. 28), Sched. 4.]

. . . .

(9) [Repealed by the Adoption (Scotland) Act 1978 (c. 28), Sched. 4.]

NOTE

[1] Prospectively repealed by the Children (Scotland) Act 1995 (c. 36), Sched. 4, para. 26(8), *infra*.

. . . .

Evidence of agreement and consent

[1] **102.**—[2] (1) Any agreement or consent which is required by Part II to be given to the making of any order or application for an order may be given in writing, and, if the document signifying the agreement or consent is—

(*a*) in the case of an application to which Part II applies, witnessed in accordance with rules of court,

it shall be sufficient evidence without further proof of the signature of the person by whom it was executed.

(2) A document signifying such agreement or consent which purports to be witnessed in accordance with rules or, as the case may be, with act of sederunt shall be presumed to be so witnessed, and to have been executed and witnessed on the date and at the place specified in the document, unless the contrary is proved.

(3) In the application of this section to Scotland—

(*a*) for "made under Part II" there is substituted "to which Part II applies";

(*b*) for "admissible in evidence" there is substituted "sufficient evidence"; and

(*c*) for "rules of court" there is substituted "act of sederunt".

NOTES

[1] Prospectively repealed by the Children (Scotland) Act 1995 (c. 36), Sched. 4, para. 26(8), *infra*.

[2] As amended by the Adoption (Scotland) Act 1978 (c. 28), Sched. 4.

Panel for curators ad litem **and reporting officers**

[1] **103.**—(1) The Secretary of State may by regulations[2] make provision for the establishment of one or more panels of persons from whom—

(*a*) curators *ad litem* and reporting officers may in accordance with rules or rules of court be appointed for the purposes of—

[3] (i) section 58 of the Adoption (Scotland) Act 1978;

(ii) section 32B of the Children and Young Persons Act 1969;

[4] (iii) section 7 of the Child Care Act 1980;

(*b*) persons may be appointed for the purposes of section 18A or 34A of the Social Work (Scotland) Act 1968.

(2) Regulations under subsection (1) may provide—

(*a*) for the defrayment by local authorities of expenses incurred by members of a panel established by virtue of that subsection; and

(*b*) for the payment by local authorities of fees and allowances for members of such a panel.

(3) In relation to Scotland, the reference in subsection (1) to guardians *ad litem* shall be construed as a reference to curators *ad litem*.

NOTES

[1] As amended by the Health and Social Services and Social Security Adjudications Act 1983 (c. 41), Sched. 2, para. 28. Prospectively repealed by the Children (Scotland) Act 1995 (c. 36), Sched. 4, para. 26(8), *infra*.

[2] See S.I. 1984 No. 566.

[3] As amended by the Adoption (Scotland) Act 1978 (c. 28), Sched. 3, para. 17.

[4] Substituted by the Child Care Act 1980 (c. 5), Sched. 5, para. 37.

. . . .

Periodic review of Act

[1] **105.** The Secretary of State shall, within three years of the first of the dates appointed by order by the Secretary of State under section 108(2) and, thereafter, every five years lay before Parliament a report on the operation of those sections of the Act which are in force at that time (including such sections as have been repealed by and re-enacted in the Adoption (Scotland) Act 1978); and the Secretary of State shall institute such research as is necessary to provide the information for these reports.

NOTE

[1] As amended by the Adoption (Scotland) Act 1978 (c. 28), Sched. 3, para. 18. Prospectively repealed by the Children (Scotland) Act 1995 (c. 36), s. 102, *infra*.

Regulations and orders

106.—(1) Where a power to make regulations or orders is exercisable by the Secretary of State by virtue of this Act, regulations or orders made in the exercise of that power shall be made by statutory instrument and may—

(*a*) make different provision in relation to different cases or classes of case, and

(*b*) exclude certain cases or classes of case.

(2) A statutory instrument containing regulations made by the Secretary of State under section 103 shall be subject to annulment in pursuance of a resolution of either House of Parliament.

(3) Any power conferred on the Secretary of State by this Act to make orders includes a power to vary or revoke an order so made.

Interpretation

[1] **107.**—(1) In this Act, unless the context otherwise requires—

"adoption order" means an order under section 8(1);

"adoption society" has the same meaning as in the Adoption (Scotland) Act 1978;

. . . .

"authorised court" shall be construed in accordance with section 100;

"child", except where used to express a relationship, means a person who has not attained the age of eighteen;

"guardian" means—

(*a*) a person appointed by deed or will in accordance with the provisions of the Guardianship of Infants Acts 1886 and 1925 or the Guardianship of Minors Act 1971 or by a court of competent jurisdiction to be the guardian of the child, and

(*b*) [Repealed by the Adoption (Scotland) Act 1978 (c. 28), Sched. 4.]

"home" shall be construed in accordance with section 87(3);

. . . .

"notice" means a notice in writing;

"relative" has the same meaning as in the 1958 Act;

. . . .

"the 1958 Act" means the Adoption Act 1958;

"voluntary organisation" means a body, other than a public or local authority, the activities of which are not carried on for profit.

(2) In this Act, in relation to Scotland, unless the context otherwise requires—

"actual custody" means care and possession;

"legal custody" means custody;

"local authority" means a regional or islands council; and

"Rules" means rules made by act of sederunt.

(2A) [Added (*prosp.*) by the Adoption Act 1976 (c. 36), Sched. 3, para. 43, but repealed by the Adoption (Scotland) Act 1978 (c. 28), Sched. 4.]

(3) Except so far as the context otherwise requires, any reference in this Act to an enactment shall be construed as a reference to that enactment as amended by or under any other enactment, including this Act.

(4) In this Act, except where otherwise indicated—

(*a*) a reference to a numbered Part, section or Schedule is a reference to the Part or section of, or the Schedule to, this Act so numbered, and

(*b*) a reference in a section to a numbered subsection is a reference to the subsection of that section so numbered, and

(*c*) a reference in a section, subsection or Schedule to a numbered paragraph is a reference to the paragraph of that section, subsection or Schedule so numbered.

NOTE

[1] As amended by the Adoption (Scotland) Act 1978 (c. 28), Sched. 3, para. 19 and Sched. 4. Prospectively repealed, except for the definitions of "adoption society", "child", and "voluntary organisation", by the Children (Scotland) Act 1995 (c. 36), Sched. 4, para. 26(9), *infra*.

Amendments, repeals, commencement and transitory provisions

108.—(1) Subject to the following provisions of this section—

(*a*) the enactment specified in Schedule 3 shall have effect subject to the amendments specified in that Schedule (being minor

[THE NEXT PAGE IS K 155]

amendments or amendments consequential on the preceding provisions of this Act), and

(*b*) the enactments specified in Schedule 4 are repealed to the extent shown in column 3 of that Schedule.

(2) This Act, except the provisions specified in subsections (3) and (4), shall come into force on such date as the Secretary of State may by order[1] appoint and different dates may be appointed for, or for different purposes of, different provisions.

(3) Sections 71, 72 and 82, this section, section 109 and paragraph 57 of Schedule 3 shall come into force on the passing of this Act.

(4) The following provisions of this Act shall come into force on 1st January 1976—

(*a*) sections 3, 8(9) and (10), 13, 59, 83 to 91, 94, 98, 99, 100 and 103 to 107;

(*b*) Schedules 1 and 2;

(*c*) in Schedule 3, paragraphs 1, 2, 3, 4, 6, 8, 9, 13(6), 15, 17, 18, 19, 20, 21(1)(2) and (4), 22 to 25, 27(*b*), 29, 33, 34(*b*), 35, 36(*b*), 38, 39(*c*)(*d*) and (*e*), 40, 43, 48, 49, 51(*a*), 52(*f*)(ii) and (*g*)(ii), 54, 55, 58 to 63, 65 to 70, 75(3), 77, 78, 81 and 83;

(*d*) Parts I, II and III of Schedule 4.

(5), (6) [Repealed by the Adoption (Scotland) Act 1978, Sched. 4.]

(7) Until the date so appointed [under subsection (2)] for section 18, section 21A of the Children and Young Persons Act 1969 shall have effect as if for references to section 25 there were substituted references to section 53 of the 1958 Act.

(8) An order under subsection (2) may make such transitional provision as appears to the Secretary of State to be necessary or expedient in connection with the provisions thereby brought into force, including such adaptations of those provisions or any provision of this Act then in force or any provision of the 1958 Act as appear to him to be necessary or expedient in consequence of the partial operation of this Act.

NOTE

[1] At the date of going to press the following commencement orders had been made, bringing the provisions listed into force for Scotland on the dates shown:—

S.I. 1977 No. 227 (7th March 1977): ss. 8(1)–(8), 10(1)–(2), 11(1)–(3), 12, 17(1), (2), (4), 21(4), 22(4), (5), (6), 27, 28(c)(ii), 29–31, 73, 74 (part), 76, 77 (part), 79, 81, Sched. 3 (part), Sched. 4 (part).

S.I. 1978 No. 1440 (23rd October 1978): s. 24.

S.I. 1982 No. 33 (1st February 1982): ss. 4–7, 28 (part), 32, 74 (part), 75, Sched. 3 (part), Sched. 4 (part).

S.I. 1984 No. 554 (1st September 1984): ss. 9, 14–16, 18–20, 22(1)–(3), 23, 25, 48(3), (4), 77 (part), 80, 102, Sched. 3 (part), Sched. 4 (part). For transitional provisions see Sched. 2 of the commencement order.

S.I. 1984 No. 1702 (30th June 1985); ss. 66, 78.

S.I. 1985 No. 1557 (1st April 1986): ss. 47, 48(1), (2), 49–55.

Ss. 1 and 2 were consolidated as ss. 1 and 2 of the Adoption (Scotland) Act 1978, and were brought into force on 1st February 1985 by S.I. 1984 No. 1050.

Short title and extent

109.—(1) This Act may be cited as the Children Act 1975.

. . . .

SCHEDULES

. . . .

Section 8

SCHEDULE 2

Status Conferred in Scotland by Adoption

[Relevant provisions of this Schedule were repealed by the Adoption (Scotland) Act 1978, Sched. 4.]

SCHEDULES 3 and 4

NOTE

Most of the minor and consequential amendments and repeals in these Schedules do not apply to material contained in *The Parliament House Book*.

Where they do so apply, and have been brought into force, they have been given effect.

[THE NEXT PAGE IS K 161]

Divorce (Scotland) Act 1976

(1976 c.39)

An Act to amend the law of Scotland relating to divorce and separation; to facilitate reconciliation of the parties in consistorial causes; to amend the law as to the power of the court to make orders relating to financial provision arising out of divorce and to settlements and other dealings by a party to the marriage, and as to the power of the court to award aliment to spouses in actions for aliment; to abolish the oath of calumny; and for purposes connected with the matters aforesaid.

[22nd July 1976]

Divorce

Irretrievable breakdown of marriage to be sole ground of divorce

1.—(1) In an action for divorce the court may grant decree of divorce if, but only if, it is established in accordance with the following provisions of this Act that the marriage has broken down irretrievably.

References in this Act (other than in section 5(1) and 13 of this Act) to an action for divorce are to be contrued as references to such an action brought after the commencement of this Act.

(2) The irretrievable breakdown of a marriage shall, subject to the following provisions of this Act, be taken to be established in an action for divorce if—

(*a*) since the date of the marriage the defender has committed adultery; or

(*b*) since the date of the marriage the defender has at any time behaved (whether or not as a result of mental abnormality and whether such behaviour has been active or passive) in such a way that the pursuer cannot reasonably be expected to cohabit with the defender; or

(*c*) the defender has wilfully and without reasonable cause deserted the pursuer; and during a continuous period of two years immediately succeeding the defender's desertion—

(i) there has been no cohabitation between the parties, and

(ii) the pursuer has not refused a genuine and reasonable offer by the defender to adhere; or

(*d*) there has been no cohabitation between the parties at any time during a continuous period of two years after the date of the marriage and immediately preceding the bringing of the action and the defender consents to the granting of decree of divorce; or

(*e*) there has been no cohabitation between the parties at any time during a continuous period of five years after the date of the marriage and immediately preceding the bringing of the action.

(3) The irretrievable breakdown of a marriage shall not be taken to be established in an action for divorce by reason of subsection (2)(*a*) of this section if the adultery mentioned in the said subsection (2)(*a*) has been connived at in such a way as to raise the defence of *lenocinium* or has been condoned by the pursuer's cohabitation with the defender in the knowledge or belief that the defender has committed the adultery.

(4) Provision shall be made by act of sederunt—

(*a*) for the purpose of ensuring that, where in an action for divorce to which subsection (2)(*d*) of this section relates the defender consents to the granting of decree, he has been given such information as will enable him to understand—

(i) the consequences to him of his consenting as aforesaid; and

(ii) the steps which he must take to indicate his consent; and

(*b*) prescribing the manner in which the defender in such an action shall indicate his consent, and any withdrawal of such consent, to the granting of decree;

and where the defender has indicated (and not withdrawn) his consent in the prescribed manner, such indication shall be sufficient evidence of such consent.

(5) Notwithstanding that irretrievable breakdown of a marriage has been established in an action for divorce by reason of subsection (2)(*e*) of this section, the court shall not be bound to grant decree in that action if in the opinion of the court the grant of decree would result in grave financial hardship to the defender.

For the purposes of this subsection, hardship shall include the loss of the chance of acquiring any benefit.

(6) In an action for divorce the standard of proof required to establish the ground of the action shall be on balance of probability.

Encouragement of reconciliation

2.—(1) At any time before granting decree in an action for divorce, if it appears to the court that there is a reasonable prospect of a reconciliation between the parties, it shall continue, or further continue, the action for such period as it thinks proper to enable attempts to be made to effect such a reconciliation; and if during any such continuation the parties cohabit with one another, no account shall be taken of such cohabitation for the purposes of that action.

(2) Adultery shall not be held to have been condoned within the mean-

ing of section 1(3) of this Act by reason only of the fact that after the commission of the adultery the pursuer has continued or resumed cohabitation with the defender, provided that the pursuer has not cohabited with the defender at any time after the end of the period of three months from the date on which such cohabitation as is referred to in the said section 1(3) was continued or resumed as aforesaid.

(3) The irretrievable breakdown of a marriage shall not be taken to be established in an action for divorce by reason of section 1(2)(*c*) of this Act if, after the expiry of the period mentioned in the said section 1(2)(*c*), the pursuer has resumed cohabitation with the defender and has cohabited with the defender at any time after the end of the period of three months from the date on which the cohabitation was resumed as aforesaid.

(4) In considering whether any period mentioned in paragraph (*c*), (*d*), or (*e*) of section 1(2) of this Act has been continuous no account shall be taken of any period or periods not exceeding six months in all during which the parties cohabited with one another; but no such period or periods during which the parties cohabited with one another shall count as part of the period of non-cohabitation required by any of those paragraphs.

Action for divorce following on decree of separation

3.—(1) The court may grant decree in an action for divorce notwithstanding that decree of separation has previously been granted to the pursuer on the same, or substantially the same, facts as those averred in support of the action for divorce; and in any such action (other than an action for divorce by reason of section 1(2)(*a*) of this Act) the court may treat an extract decree of separation lodged in process as sufficient proof of the facts upon which such decree was granted.

(2) Nothing in this section shall entitle the court to grant decree of divorce without receiving evidence from the pursuer.

Actions for separation

Actions for separation

4.—(1) Sections 1, 2 and 11 of this Act shall apply to an action for separation or separation and aliment brought after the commencement of this Act and decree in such action as those sections apply to an action for divorce and decree therein subject to—

(*a*) the modification that any reference to irretrievable breakdown of a marriage shall be construed as a reference to grounds justifying decree of separation of the parties to a marriage; and

(*b*) all other necessary modifications.

(2) In an action for separation or separation and aliment brought after the commencement of this Act, decree of separation shall not be pronounced except in accordance with the provisions of this section.

Financial provision for spouses and children

Orders for financial provision

[0] **5.**—(1) In an action for divorce (whether brought before or after the commencement of this Act), either party to the marriage may, at any time prior to decree being granted, apply to the court for any one or more of the following orders—

(*a*) an order for the payment to him or for his benefit by the other party to the marriage of a periodical allowance;

(*b*) an order for the payment to him or for his benefit by the other party to the marriage of a capital sum;

(*c*) an order varying the terms of any settlement made in contemplation of or during the marriage so far as taking effect on or after the termination of the marriage:

Provided that any reference in this subsection to payment by the other party to the marriage shall include a reference to payment out of any estate belonging to that party or held for his benefit.

(2) Where an application under the foregoing subsection has been made in an action, the court, on granting decree in that action, shall make with respect to the application such order, if any, as it thinks fit, having regard to the respective means of the parties to the marriage and to all the circumstances of the case, including any settlement or other arrangements made for financial provision for any child of the marriage.

(3) Where an application for an order for the payment of a periodical allowance under subsection (1)(*a*) of this section has been withdrawn or refused, or where no such application has been made, either party to the marriage may apply to the court for such an order after the date of the granting of decree of divorce if since that date there has been a change in the circumstances of either of the parties to the marriage; and the court shall make with respect to that application such order, if any, as it thinks fit, having regard to the factors mentioned in subsection (2) of this section.

[1] (4) Any order made under this section relating to the payment of a periodical allowance may, on an application by or on behalf of either party to the marriage (or his executor) on a change of circumstances, be varied or recalled by a subsequent order.

(5) Any order made under this section relating to payment of a periodical allowance—

(*a*) shall, on the death of the person by whom the periodical allowance is payable, continue to operate against that person's estate, but without prejudice to the making of an order under the last foregoing subsection;

(*b*) shall cease to have effect on the remarriage or death of the person to whom or for whose benefit the periodical allowance is payable, except in relation to any arrears due under it on the date of such remarriage or death.

(6) Provision shall be made by act of sederunt to impose upon the pursuer in an action for divorce to which section 1(2)(*d*) or 1(2)(*e*) of this Act relates a duty to inform the defender of his right to apply for—

(*a*) financial provision under this Act,

(*b*) an order providing for the custody, maintenance and education of any child of the marriage under section 9 of the Conjugal Rights (Scotland) Amendment Act 1861,

in such form and manner as the act of sederunt may require, and, for the purposes of this subsection, where the pursuer alleges that the address of the defender is unknown to him, he shall satisfy the court that all reasonable steps have been taken to ascertain it.

(7) Any reference in this section to a settlement shall be construed as including a settlement by way of a policy of assurance to which section 2 of the Married Women's Policies of Assurance (Scotland) Act 1880 relates.

NOTES

[0] Repealed by the Family Law (Scotland) Act 1985, Sched. 2 (but see *ibid.*, s.28(3)).

[1] Saved by the Forfeiture Act 1982, s.3.

6–8. [Repealed by the Family Law (Scotland) Act 1985, Sched. 2.]

Supplemental

Abolition of oath of calumny

9. In a consistorial action (whether brought before or after the commencement of this Act) the oath of calumny shall not be administered to the pursuer, and accordingly that oath is hereby abolished, but nothing in this section shall affect any rule of law relating to collusion.

Right of husband to cite paramour as a co-defender and to sue for damages abolished

10.—(1) After the commencement of this Act the following rights of a husband shall be abolished, that is to say—

(*a*) the right to cite a paramour of his wife as a co-defender in an action for divorce, and

(*b*) the right to claim or to obtain damages (including solatium) from a paramour by way of reparation.

(2) Nothing in the provisions of the foregoing subsection shall preclude the court from awarding the expenses of the action for or against the paramour or alleged paramour in accordance with the practice of the court.

(3) Section 7 of the Conjugal Rights (Scotland) Amendment Act 1861 (citation of a co-defender in an action for divorce and decree for expenses against him) shall cease to have effect.

Curator ad litem **to be appointed in certain cases**

11. Provision shall be made by act of sederunt for the purpose of securing that, where in an action for divorce the defender is suffering from mental illness, the court shall appoint a curator *ad litem* to the defender.

Amendments, repeals and transitional provisions

12.—(1) The enactments described in Schedule 1 to this Act shall have effect subject to the amendments specified therein in relation to them respectively.

(2) The enactments specified in columns 1 and 2 of Schedule 2 to this Act are hereby repealed to the extent specified in relation to them respectively in column 3 of that Schedule.

(3) Subject to the following provisions of this section and without prejudice to the operation of section 38 of the Interpretation Act 1889 (effect of repeals), nothing in this section shall affect any proceedings brought, anything done, or the operation of any order made, under any enactment repealed by this section; nor shall anything in this Act be taken to revive any rule of law superseded by any enactment repealed by this section.

(4) Anything which, prior to the commencement of this Act, could have been done under section 2 of the Divorce (Scotland) Act 1938 or section 26 or 27 of the Succession (Scotland) Act 1964 may, after the commencement of this Act, be done under the corresponding provision of section 5 or 6 of this Act.

(5) An order under section 2 of the Divorce (Scotland) Act 1938 for the payment of an annual or periodical allowance to or for the behoof of a child of the marriage may, after the commencement of this Act, be varied or recalled by a subsequent order under subsection (2) of that section as if that section had not been repealed by this Act.

(6) Subsection (5) of section 5 of this Act shall apply in relation to an order for the payment of an annual or periodical allowance under section 2 of the Divorce (Scotland) Act 1938 or of a periodical allowance under section 26 of the Succession (Scotland) Act 1964 as it applies in relation to an order for the payment of a periodical allowance under the said section 5.

Interpretation

13.—[1] (1) In this Act, unless the context otherwise requires—

"action for divorce" has the meaning assigned to it by section 1(1) of this Act;

"the court" means, in relation to any action, the Court of Session or the sheriff court, as the case may require.

(2) For the purposes of this Act, the parties to a marrriage shall be held to cohabit with one another only when they are in fact living together as man and wife; and "cohabitation" shall be construed accordingly.

(3) References to this Act to any enactment are references to that enactment as amended, and include references thereto as applied, by any other enactment, including, except where the context otherwise requires, this Act.

NOTE

[1] As amended by the Divorce Jurisdiction, Court Fees and Legal Aid (Scotland) Act 1983, Sched. 1, para. 22.

Citation, commencement and extent

14.—(1) This Act may be cited as the Divorce (Scotland) Act 1976.

(2) This Act except section 8 shall come into operation on 1st January 1977.

(3) So much of section 12 of, and Schedule 1 to, this Act as affects the operation of section 16 of the Maintenance Orders Act 1950 shall extend to England and Wales and to Northern Ireland as well as Scotland, but save as aforesaid this Act shall extend to Scotland only.

SCHEDULES

[1] SCHEDULE 1

ENACTMENTS AMENDED

[1] SCHEDULE 2

ENACTMENTS REPEALED

NOTE

[1] The amendments and repeals made by these Schedules to Acts printed in *The Parliament House Book* are shown in the prints of those Acts.

[1] Marriage (Scotland) Act 1977

(1977 c. 15)

An Act to make new provision for Scotland as respects the law relating to the constitution of marriage, and for connected purposes. [26th May 1977]

NOTE

[1] As amended by the Marriage (Prohibited Degrees of Relationship) Act 1986, Sched. 2.

Minimum age for marriage

Minimum age for marriage

1.—(1) No person domiciled in Scotland may marry before he attains the age of 16.

(2) A marriage solemnised in Scotland between persons either of whom is under the age of 16 shall be void.

Forbidden degrees

Marriage of related persons

2.—[1] (1) Subject to subsections (1A) and (1B) below, a marriage between a man and any woman related to him in a degree specified in column 1 of Schedule 1 to this Act, or between a woman and any man related to her in a degree specified in column 2 of that Schedule shall be void if solemnised—

(*a*) in Scotland; or

(*b*) at a time when either party is domiciled in Scotland.

[2] (1A) Subsection (1) above does not apply to a marriage between a man and any woman related to him in a degree specified in column 1 of paragraph 2 of Schedule 1 to this Act, or between a woman and any man related to her in a degree specified in column 2 of that paragraph, if—

(*a*) both parties have attained the age of 21 at the time of the marriage; and

(*b*) the younger party has not at any time before attaining the age of 18 lived in the same household as the other party and been treated by the other party as a child of his family.

[2] (1B) Subsection (1) above does not apply to a marriage between a man and any woman related to him in a degree specified in column 1 of paragraph 2A of Schedule 1 to this Act, or between a woman and any man related to her in a degree specified in column 2 of that paragraph, if both parties to the marriage have attained the age of 21 and the marriage is solemnized—

(*a*) in the case of a man marrying the mother of a former wife of his, after the death of both the former wife and the former wife's father;

(*b*) in the case of a man marrying a former wife of his son, after the death of both his son and his son's mother;

(*c*) in the case of a woman marrying the father of a former husband of hers, after the death of both the former husband and the former husband's mother;

(*d*) in the case of a woman marrying a former husband of her daughter, after the death of both her daughter and her daughter's father.

(2) For the purposes of this section a degree of relationship exists—

(*a*) in the case of a degree specified in paragraph 1 of Schedule 1 to this Act, whether it is of the full blood or the half blood;

(*b*) [Repealed by the Law Reform (Parent and Child) (Scotland) Act 1986, Sched. 2.]

(3) Where a person is related to another person in a degree not specified in Schedule 1 to this Act that degree of relationship shall not, in Scots law, bar a valid marriage between them; but this subsection is without prejudice to—

(*a*) the effect which a degree of relationship not so specified may have under the provisions of a system of law other than Scots law in a case where such provisions apply as the law of the place of celebration of a marriage or as the law of a person's domicile; or

(*b*) any rule of law that a marriage may not be contracted between persons either of whom is married to a third person.

[3] (4) References in this section and in Schedule 1 to this Act to relationships and degrees of relationship shall be construed in accordance with section 1(1) of the Law Reform (Parent and Child) (Scotland) Act 1986.

[2] (5) Where the parties to an intended marriage are related in a degree specified in paragraph 2 of Schedule 1 to this Act, either party may (whether or not an objection to the marriage has been submitted in accordance with section 5(1) of this Act) apply to the Court of Session for a declarator that the conditions specified in paragraphs (*a*) and (*b*) of subsection (1A) above are fulfilled in relation to the intended marriage.

NOTES
[1] As amended by the Marriage (Prohibited Degrees of Relationship) Act 1986, Sched. 2, para. 2.
[2] Inserted by the Marriage (Prohibited Degrees of Relationship) Act 1986, Sched. 2, para. 2.
[3] Inserted by the Law Reform (Parent and Child) (Scotland) Act 1986, Sched. 1, para. 17.

Preliminaries to regular marriage

Notice of intention to marry

3.—(1) Subject to subsections (2) to (4) below, each of the parties to a marriage intended to be solemnised in Scotland shall submit to the district registrar a notice, in the prescribed form[0] of intention to marry (in this Act referred to as a "marriage notice") accompanied by the prescribed fee,[1] his birth certificate and—

(*a*) if he has previously been married and the marriage has been dissolved, a copy of the decree of divorce, dissolution or annulment;

(*b*) in the case of a widow or widower, the death certificate of the former spouse;

(*c*) in any case where a certificate is required under subsection (5) below, that certificate.

[1a](*d*) where he is related to the other party in a degree specified in paragraph 2 of Schedule 1 to this Act, a declaration in the prescribed form stating—

(i) the degree of relationship; and

(ii) that the younger party has not at any time before attaining the age of 18 lived in the same household as the other party and been treated by the other party as a child of his family.

(2) If a party is unable to submit his birth certificate or any document referred to in paragraph (*a*) or (*b*) of subsection (1) above, he may in lieu thereof make a declaration stating that for reasons specified in that declaration it is impracticable for him to submit that certificate or document; and he shall provide the district registrar with such—

(*a*) information in respect of the matters to which such certificate or document would have related; and

(*b*) documentary evidence in support of that information,

as the district registrar may require.

(3) If any document submitted under subsection (1) above is written in a language other than English, the party submitting it shall attach to that document a translation of it in English certified by the translator as a correct translation.

(4) Where a party to a marriage intended to be solemnised in Scotland is residing in another part of the United Kingdom, he may submit to the district registrar a valid certificate for marriage (in this Act referred to as an "approved certificate") issued in that other part; and where that party so submits an approved certificate, he need not, unless the Registrar General so directs, comply with the other provisions of this section.

(5) A party to a marriage intended to be solemnised in Scotland who is not domiciled in any part of the United Kingdom is required, if practicable, to submit under subsection (1)(*c*) above a certificate issued by a competent authority in the state in which the party is domiciled, to the effect that he is not known to be subject to any legal incapacity (in terms of the law of that state) which would prevent his marrying:

Provided that such a party—

(i) may, where under the law of the state in which he is domiciled his personal law is that of another foreign state, submit in lieu of the said certificate a like certificate issued by a competent authority in that other state;

[2] (ii) need not submit a certificate under paragraph (*c*) of subsection (1) above (*a*) if he has been resident in the United Kingdom for

a period of two or more years immediately before the date on which he submits a marriage notice under that subsection in respect of the said marriage or (*b*) if no such certificate has been issued only by reason of the fact that the validity of a divorce or annulment granted by a court of civil jurisdiction in Scotland or entitled to recognition in Scotland under section 44 or 45 of the Family Law Act 1986 is not recognised in the state in which the certificate would otherwise have been issued.

NOTES

[0] See S.I. 1986 No. 1954.

[1] See S.I. 1993 No. 3152—£10.

[1a] Inserted by the Marriage (Prohibited Degrees of Relationship) Act 1986 (c. 16), Sched. 2, para. 3.

[2] As amended by the Family Law Act 1986 (c. 55), Sched. 1, para. 21.

Marriage notice book and list of intended marriages

4.—(1) On receipt of a marriage notice or an approved certificate in respect of a party to an intended marriage, the district registrar shall forthwith enter such particulars, extracted from such notice or certificate, as may be prescribed, together with the date of receipt by him of such notice or certificate, in a book (in this Act referred to as "the marriage notice book") supplied to him for that purpose by the Registrar General.

(2) The district registrar shall, in relation to each intended marriage in respect of which he has received a marriage notice or an approved certificate, and as soon as practicable after such receipt, make an entry giving the names of the parties to, and the proposed date of, that marriage in a list which he shall display in a conspicuous place at the registration office; and such entry shall remain so displayed until the said date has elapsed.

(3) Any person claiming that he may have reason to submit an objection to an intended marriage, or to the issue of a certificate under section 7 of this Act to a party to such marriage, may, free of charge and at any time when the registration office is open for public business, inspect any entry relating to the marriage in the marriage notice book.

Objections to marriage

5.—(1) Any person may at any time before the solemnisation of a marriage in Scotland submit an objection in writing thereto to the district registrar:

Provided that where the objection is on the ground mentioned in subsection (4)(*d*) below, it shall be accompanied by a supporting certificate signed by a registered medical practitioner.

(2) Where the district registrar receives an objection in accordance with subsection (1) above he shall—

(*a*) in any case where he is satisfied that the objection relates to no more than a misdescription or inaccuracy in the marriage notice or approved certificate, notify the parties to the marriage of the nature of the objection and make such enquiries into the matter mentioned in it as he thinks fit; and thereafter he shall, subject to the approval of the Registrar General, make any necessary correction to any document relating to the marriage;

(*b*) in any other case—

(i) forthwith notify the Registrar General of the objection;

(ii) pending consideration of the objection by the Registrar General, suspend the completion or issue of the Marriage Schedule in respect of the marriage;

(iii) where, in the case of a marriage to be solemnised by an approved celebrant, the Marriage Schedule has already been issued to the parties, if possible notify that celebrant of the objection and advise him not to solemnise the marriage pending the said consideration.

[1] (3) Subject to subsection (3A) below if the Registrar General is satisfied, on consideration of an objection of which he has received notification under subsection (2)(*b*)(i) above, that—

(*a*) there is a legal impediment to the marriage, he shall direct the district registrar to take all reasonable steps to ensure that the marriage does not take place and shall notify, or direct the district registrar to notify the parties to the intended marriage accordingly;

(*b*) there is no legal impediment to the marriage, he shall inform the district registrar to that effect.

[2] (3A) Where—

(*a*) an objection of which the Registrar General has received notification under subsection (2)(*b*)(i) above is on the ground that—

(i) the parties are related in a degree specified in paragraph 2 of Schedule 1 to this Act; and

(ii) the conditions specified in paragraphs (*a*) and (*b*) of section 2(1A) of this Act are not satisfied, and

(*b*) an extract decree of declarator that those conditions are satisfied, granted on an application under section 2(5) of this Act, is produced to the Registrar General,

the Registrar General shall inform the district registrar that there is no legal impediment to the marriage on that ground.

[1] (4) For the purposes of this section and section 6 of this Act, there is a legal impediment to a marriage where—

(*a*) that marriage would be void by virtue of section 2(1) of this Act;

(*b*) one of the parties is, or both are, already married;

(*c*) one or both of the parties will be under the age of 16 on the date of solemnisation of the intended marriage;

(*d*) one or both of the parties is or are incapable of understanding the nature of a marriage ceremony or of consenting to marriage;

(*e*) both parties are of the same sex; or

(*f*) one or both of the parties is, or are, not domiciled in Scotland and, on a ground other than one mentioned in paragraphs (*a*) to (*e*) above, a marriage in Scotland between the parties would be void *ab initio* according to the law of the domicile of the party or parties as the case may be.

(5) A person who has submitted an objection in accordance with subsection (1) above may at any time withdraw it:

Provided that the Registrar General shall be entitled to have regard to that objection notwithstanding such withdrawal.

NOTES

[1] As amended by the Marriage (Prohibited Degrees of Relationship) Act 1986 (c. 16), Sched. 2, para. 4.

[2] Inserted by the Marriage (Prohibited Degrees of Relationship) Act 1986 (c. 16), Sched. 2, para. 4.

The Marriage Schedule

6.—[0] (1) Where the district registrar has received a marriage notice or approved certificate in respect of each of the parties to a marriage intended to be solemnised in Scotland and is satisfied that there is no legal impediment to the marriage or, as the case may be, is informed by the Registrar General under section 5(3)(*b*) or (3A) of this Act that there is no such legal impediment, he shall, subject to subsection (2) below, complete a Marriage Schedule in the prescribed form.

(2) If a period of more than three months has elapsed since the date of receipt (as entered by the district registrar in the marriage notice book) of a marriage notice or an approved certificate in respect of a party to the marriage, the Registrar General may direct that the district registrar shall not complete the Marriage Schedule unless that party submits a new marriage notice or approved certificate to the district registrar.

(3) Subject to subsection (4) below, in the case of a marriage to be solemnised by an approved celebrant, the Marriage Schedule completed in accordance with subsection (1) above shall be issued by the district registrar at the registration office to one or both of the parties to the intended marriage.

(4) The district registrar shall not issue a Marriage Schedule under subsection (3) above—

[THE NEXT PAGE IS K 171]

(*a*) within 14 days of the date of receipt (as entered by him in the marriage notice book) of a marriage notice in respect of the marriage to which the Marriage Schedule relates, except where—
(i) he has received a written request from one or both of the parties for the issue of the Marriage Schedule on a specified date within the said 14 days stating the reason for the request; and
(ii) he has been authorised to issue the Marriage Schedule on that specified date by the Registrar General;
(*b*) on a date earlier than seven days before the date of the intended marriage unless he has been authorised to issue the Marriage Schedule on that earlier date by the Registrar General.

[1] (5) Subject to subsections (6) and (7) below and section 23A of this Act, a religious marriage may be solemnised only on the date and at the place specified in the Marriage Schedule.

(6) Subject to subsection (7) below, if, for any reason, the marriage cannot be solemnised on the date or at the place so specified and a new date or place is fixed for the marriage, the district registrar shall—
(*a*) issue another Marriage Schedule under subsection (3) above, in lieu of that already issued, specifying that new date or place; or
(*b*) substitute, or direct the approved celebrant to substitute, that new date or place in the Marriage Schedule already issued.

(7) Subsection (6) above shall not apply in a case where the new date fixed for the marriage is more than three months after the date for the marriage as specified in the Marriage Schedule already issued or where the new place so fixed is in a different registration district, but in such a case the Registrar General may, according to the circumstances, direct—
(*a*) the district registrar for the district in which the marriage is to be solemnised to proceed as in paragraph (*a*) or (*b*) (whichever the Registrar General considers the more appropriate) of subsection (6) above; or
(*b*) each party to the marriage to submit to the said district registrar a new marriage notice or approved certificate.

NOTES

[0] As amended by the Marriage (Prohibited Degrees of Relationship) Act 1986, Sched. 2, para. 5.

[1] As amended by the Law Reform (Miscellaneous Provisions) (Scotland) Act 1980, s.22(1)(*a*).

Marriage outside Scotland where a party resides in Scotland

7—[1] (1) Where a person residing in Scotland is a party to a marriage intended to be solemnised in—
(*a*) England or Wales with a party residing in England or Wales and desires; or
(*b*) any country, territory or place outside Great Britain, and, for the purpose of complying with the law in force in that country, territory or place, is required to obtain from a competent authority in Scotland,

a certificate in respect of his legal capacity to marry, he may submit in the form and with the fee and documents specified in section 3(1)(*a*), (*b*) and (*d*) of this Act, notice of intention to marry to the district registrar for the district in which he resides (the said registrar being in this section referred to as the "appropriate registrar") as if it were intended that the marriage should be solemnised in that district, and sections 3(2) and (3) and 4 of this Act shall apply accordingly.

(2) The appropriate registrar shall, if satisfied (after consultation, if the appropriate registrar considers it necessary, with the Registrar General) that a person who has by virtue of subsection (1) above submitted a marriage notice to him is not subject to any legal incapacity (in terms of Scots

law) which would prevent his marrying, issue to that person a certificate in the prescribed form that he is not known to be subject to any such incapacity:

Provided that the certificate shall not be issued earlier than 14 days after the date of receipt (as entered by the appropriate registrar in the marriage notice book) of the marriage notice.

(3) Any person may, at any time before a certificate is issued under subsection (2) above, submit to the appropriate registrar an objection in writing to such issue; and the objection shall be taken into account by the appropriate registrar in deciding whether, in respect of the person to whom the certificate would be issued, he is satisfied as mentioned in the said subsection (2).

NOTE

[1] As amended by the Marriage (Prohibited Degrees of Relationship) Act 1986, Sched. 2, para. 6.

Persons who may solemnise marriage

Persons who may solemnise marriage

8.—[1] (1) Subject to section 23A of this Act a marriage may be solemnised by and only by—

(*a*) a person who is

(i) a minister of the Church of Scotland; or

(ii) a minister, clergyman, pastor, or priest of a religious body prescribed by regulations made by the Secretary of State, or who, not being one of the foregoing, is recognised by a religious body so prescribed as entitled to solemnise marriages on its behalf; or

(iii) registered under section 9 of this Act; or

(iv) temporarily authorised under section 12 of this Act; or

(*b*) a person who is a district registrar or assistant registrar appointed under section 17 of this Act.

(2) In this Act—

(*a*) any such person as is mentioned in subsection (1)(*a*) above is referred to as an "approved celebrant," and a marriage solemnised by an approved celebrant is referred to as a "religious marriage";

(*b*) any such person as is mentioned in subsection (1)(*b*) above is referred to as an "authorised registrar," and a marriage solemnised by an authorised registrar is referred to as a "civil marriage."

NOTE

[1] As amended by the Law Reform (Miscellaneous Provisions) (Scotland) Act 1980, s.22(1)(*b*).

Religious marriages

Registration of nominated persons as celebrants

9.—(1) A religious body, not being—

(*a*) the Church of Scotland; or

(*b*) prescribed by virtue of section 8(1)(*a*)(ii) of this Act,

may nominate to the Registrar General any of its members who it desires should be registered under this section as empowered to solemnise marriages:

Provided that any such nominee must, at the date of his nomination, be 21 years of age or over.

(2) The Registrar General shall reject a nomination made under subsection (1) above if in his opinion—

(*a*) the nominating body is not a religious body; or

(*b*) the marriage ceremony used by that body is not of an appropriate form; or

(*c*) the nominee is not a fit and proper person to solemnise a marriage; or

(*d*) there are already registered under this section sufficient members of the same religious body as the nominee to mmeet the needs of that body.

(3) For the purposes of subsection (2)(*b*) above, a marriage ceremony is of an appropriate form if it includes, and is in no way inconsistent with—

(*a*) a declaration by the parties, in the presence of each other, the celebrant and two witnesses, that they accept each other as husband and wife; and

(*b*) a declaration by the celebrant, after the declaration mentioned in paragraph (*a*) of this subsection, that the parties are then husband and wife,

and the Registrar General may, before deciding whether to accept or reject a

nomination, require the nominating body to produce to him in writing the form of words used at its marriage ceremonies.

(4) Where the Registrar General accepts a nomination made to him under subsection (1) above, he—

(*a*) shall determine the period during which the nominee shall be empowered to solemnise marriages, being a period of not more than three years; and

(*b*) may determine that the nominee shall be empowered to solemnise marriages only in such area as the Registrar General may specify,

and may make his acceptance subject to such other conditions as he thinks fit:

Provided that nothing in paragraph (*a*) above shall preclude the Registrar General from accepting a further nomination of that nominee, in accordance with this section, to take effect at any time after the end of the period determined by the Registrar General under the said paragraph (*a*).

(5) The Registrar General shall—

(*a*) where he accepts a nomination made to him under subsection (1) above—

(i) so inform the nominee and the nominating body, specifying the period during which the acceptance shall have effect and any condition to which the acceptance is subject;

(ii) enter the name of the nominee, the nominating body and such other particulars as he deems appropriate in a register which he shall establish and maintain and which shall be made available for public inspection at all reasonable times without charge;

(*b*) where he rejects the nomination, by notice in writing inform the nominating body of the reasons for that rejection.

(6) The nominating body may, if aggrieved by a rejection under this section, within 28 days of receiving notice of that rejection, appeal to the Secretary of State, and on any such appeal the Secretary of State may direct the Registrar General to accept the nomination or may confirm its rejection and shall inform the nominating body of his direction or confirmation, as the case may be, and the reason for it; and such direction or confirmation shall be final:

Provided that if a reason given for a confirmation of the rejection of a nomination is that the nominating body is not a religious body, that body may, within 42 days of receiving notice of the confirmation, appeal against the confirmation to the Court of Session and seek the determination of that court as to whether the body is a religious body; and if—

(*a*) the court determine that the nominating body is a religious body; and

(*b*) the said reason was the only reason given for the confirmation,

that determination shall be given effect to by the Registrar General as if it were a direction under this subsection to accept the nomination.

Removal of celebrant's name from register

10.—(1) Subject to the provisions of this section, the Registrar General may remove the name of a person registered under section 9 of this Act from the register on the ground that—

(*a*) that person has requested that his name should be so removed; or

(*b*) the body which nominated that person under section 9 (1) of this Act no longer desires that he should be so registered; or

(*c*) the marriage ceremony used by the said body is no longer of an appropriate form within the meaning of section 9 (3) of this Act; or

(*d*) that person—

(i) has, while registered as an approved celebrant, been convicted of an offence under this Act; or

(ii) has, for the purpose of profit or gain, been carrying on a business of solemnising marriages; or

(iii) is not a fit and proper person to solemnise marriages; or

(iv) for any other reason, should not be so registered.

(2) The Registrar General shall not remove the name of a person from the register on any ground mentioned in subsection 1 (*d*) above unless he has given to that person at least 21 days notice in writing of his intention to do so.

(3) The Registrar General shall—

(*a*) in the notice given under subsection (2) above, specify the ground of removal and call upon the said person to show cause, within the period specified in the notice, why his name should not be removed from the register; and

(*b*) consider any representations made to him within the said period by that person.

(4) Where a person's name has been removed from the register on any of the grounds mentioned in paragraphs (*c*) and (*d*) of subsection (1) above, that person or the body which nominated him under section 9 (1) of this Act may, if aggrieved by the removal, within twenty-eight days of receiving notice of the removal appeal to the Secretary of State, and on any such appeal the Secretary of State may give such direction as he thinks proper to the Registrar General as to the removal from, or restoration to, the register of that name; and such direction shall be final.

(5) Where a person has received a notice in pursuance of subsection (2) above, he shall not solemnise a marriage unless and until his name is restored to the register or, as the case may be, the Registrar General has decided not to remove his name from the register.

Alterations to register maintained under section 9

11. A body registered in pursuance of section 9 (5) (*a*) (ii) of this Act shall notify the Registrar General of any of the following events (if practicable, within 21 days of its occurrence)—

(*a*) any change in the name or the address of the body or any amalgamation with any other religious body, giving the name and address of any approved celebrant who is a member of the body so registered;

(*b*) the death of an approved celebrant who is a member of the body so registered;

(*c*) any change of name, address or designation of an approved celebrant who is a member of the body so registered;

(*d*) the cessation of an approved celebrant who is a member of the body so registered from exercising the functions of an approved celebrant, giving his name and address;

and the Registrar General shall, on receipt of any such notification, make whatever alteration to the register maintained by him under section 9 of this Act as he considers necessary or desirable.

Temporary authorisation of celebrants

12. The Registrar General may, in accordance with such terms and conditions as may be specified in the authorisation, grant to any person a temporary written authorisation to solemnise—

(*a*) a marriage or marriages specified in the authorisation; or

(*b*) marriages during such period as shall be specified in the authorisation:

Provided that the authorised person must at the date of the granting of the authorisation be 21 years of age or over.

Preliminaries to solemnisation of religious marriages

13.—(1) A marriage shall not be solemnised by an approved celebrant unless—

(*a*) the parties produce to him before the marriage ceremony a Marriage Schedule, in respect of the marriage issued in accordance with this Act;

(*b*) both parties to the marriage are present; and

(*c*) two persons professing to be 16 years of age or over are present as witnesses.

(2), (3) [Repealed by the Law Reform (Miscellaneous Provisions (Scotland) Act 1980, Sched. 3.]

Form of ceremony to be used by approved celebrant

14. An approved celebrant who is a person specified—

(*a*) in section 8 (1) (*a*) (i) or (ii) of this Act shall not solemnise a marriage except in accordance with a form of ceremony recognised by the religious body to which he belongs as sufficient for the solemnisation of marriages;

(*b*) in section 8 (1) (*a*) (iii) or (iv) of this Act shall not solemnise a marriage except in accordance with a form of ceremony which includes and is in no way inconsistent with the declarations specified in section 9 (3) of this Act.

Registration of religious marriages

15.—(1) Immediately after the solemnisation of the marriage the Marriage Schedule shall be signed by the parties contracting the marriage, by both witnesses present thereat and by the approved celebrant.

(2) The parties to the marriage shall, within three days thereafter, deliver the Marriage Schedule, or send it by post or arrange that it is delivered, to the district registrar.

(3) As soon as possible after receipt of the Marriage Schedule, the district registrar shall cause the particulars as set forth in that Schedule to be entered in the register of marriages kept by him; and subject to subsection (4) below, he shall not register a religious marriage unless and until he receives a duly signed Marriage Schedule in respect of that marriage.

(4) Where the Registrar General is satisfied that a marriage has been properly solemnised and that the Marriage Schedule in respect of the marriage has been duly signed but has been lost or destroyed, he may direct the district registrar to complete an exact copy of the original Marriage Schedule and, so far as practicable, to arrange for its signature by those persons who signed the original Schedule; and as soon as possible thereafter, the district registrar shall cause the particulars as set forth in that copy to be entered in the register of marriages kept by him.

Registrar's power to require delivery of Marriage Schedule

16.—(1) Where after the expiration of 21 days from the date of marriage as entered in the Marriage Schedule that Schedule has not been delivered to the district registrar, he may serve a notice in the prescribed form on either of the parties to the marriage requiring that party within eight days from the date of service of the notice to deliver the said Schedule, or send it by post, to the district registrar.

(2) If any party on whom a notice has been served in pursuance of subsection (1) above fails to comply with the notice, the district registrar may serve on that party a second notice in the prescribed form requiring that party to attend personally at the registration office of the district registrar, within eight days from the date of service of the second notice, for the purpose of delivering the Marriage Schedule to the district registrar to enable him to register the marriage.

Civil marriages

Appointment of authorised registrars

17. For the purpose of affording reasonable facilities for the solemnisation of civil marriages throughout Scotland, the Registrar General—

(*a*) shall appoint such number of district registrars as he thinks necessary; and

(*b*) may, in respect of any district for which he has appointed a district registrar under paragraph (*a*) above, appoint one or more assistant registrars,

as persons who may solemnise marriages:

Provided that any person appointed under this section must, at the date of his appointment, be 21 years of age or over.

Places at which civil marriages may be solemnised

18.—(1) Subject to the provisions of this section, an authorised registrar shall solemnise a civil marriage in his registration office.

(2) An authorised registrar may, with the approval of the Registrar General, solemnise a civil marriage in the registration office of another authorised registrar.

(3) If either of the parties to an intended civil marriage is unable to attend the registration office of an authorised registrar for the solemnisation of the marriage, an authorised registrar may, subject to the following provisions of this section and on reimbursement of any additional expenditure incurred by him by virtue of this subsection, solemnise the marriage—

(*a*) at any place in his registration district other than his registration office; or

(*b*) with the approval of the Registrar General, at any place in any registration district in respect of which there is no authorised registrar.

(4) The authorised registrar shall not solemnise a marriage at any such place as is described in subsection (3) (*a*) or (*b*) above unless—

(*a*) application has been made to him by either of the parties to the intended marriage requesting him to solemnise the marriage at such a place and stating the reason why one of the parties is unable to attend a registration office; and

(*b*) subject to subsection (5) below, he is satisfied on consideration of the application that the party is unable to attend a registration office by reason of serious illness or serious bodily injury and that there is good reason why the marriage cannot be delayed until the party is able to attend a registration office.

(5) If the authorised registrar is not satisfied as mentioned in subsection (4) (*b*) above, he shall consult the Registrar General who may direct him to solemnise the marriage in accordance with the application made under subsection (4) (*a*) above or to refuse so to solemnise it.

Marriage ceremony and registration of marriage

19.—(1) An authorised registrar shall not solemnise a marriage within 14 days of the date of receipt (as entered in the marriage notice book) of a marriage notice in respect of that marriage, unless—

(*a*) he has received a written request from one or both of the parties to solemnise the marriage on a specified earlier date stating the reason for the request, and

(*b*) he has been authorised to solemnise the marriage on that earlier date by the Registrar General.

(2) A marriage shall not be solemnised by an authorised registrar unless—

(*a*) he has available to him at the time of the ceremony a Marriage Schedule, in respect of the marriage, completed in accordance with this Act and the prescribed fee[1] for the marriage has been paid;

(*b*) both parties to the marriage are present; and

(*c*) two persons professing to be 16 years of age or over are present as witnesses.

(3) Immediately after the solemnisation of the marriage the Marriage Schedule shall be signed by the parties contracting the marriage, by both witnesses present thereat and by the authorised registrar who solemnised it.

(4) As soon as possible after the Marriage Schedule has been signed in accordance with subsection (3) above—

(*a*) in a case where the marriage has been solemnised in the registration office of the authorised registrar who solemnised it or in any such place as is mentioned in section 18(3) of this Act, that authorised registrar;

(*b*) in a case where the marriage has been solemnised in the registration office of another authorised registrar, that other authorised registrar,

shall cause the particulars as set forth in that Schedule to be entered in the register of marriages kept by him.

NOTE

[1] See S.I. 1993 No. 3152—£40 (1st April 1994).

Second marriage ceremony

20.—(1) Where two persons have gone through a marriage ceremony with each other outside the United Kingdom, whether before or after the commencement of this Act, but they are not, or are unable to prove that they are, validly married to each other in Scots law, an authorised registrar, on an application made to him by those persons, may, subject to the approval of the Registrar General and to subsection (2) below, solemnise their marriage as if they had not already gone through a marriage ceremony with each other.

(2) Sections 3 to 6 and 18 and 19 of this Act shall apply for the purpose of solemnising a marriage under this section except that—

(*a*) there shall be submitted to the authorised registrar a statutory declaration by both parties—

(i) stating that they have previously gone through a marriage ceremony with each other; and

(ii) specifying the date and place at which, and the circumstances in which, they went through that ceremony;

(*b*) section 5(4)(*b*) of this Act shall not apply in respect of the parties already being married to each other;

(*c*) the Marriage Schedule shall contain such modifications as the Registrar General may direct to indicate that the parties have previously gone through a marriage ceremony with each other; and

(*d*) after the Marriage Schedule has been signed in accordance with section 19(3) of this Act, the authorised registrar shall make an endorsement on it in the following terms—

"The ceremony of marriage between the parties mentioned in this Schedule was performed in pursuance of section 20 of the Marriage (Scotland) Act 1977, following a statutory declaration by them that they had gone through a ceremony of marriage with each other on the day of 19 , at

Dated the day of 19 ,

(Signature of authorised registrar).

Irregular marriages

Registration of irregular marriages

21. Where decree of declarator establishing—

(*a*) a marriage by cohabitation with habit and repute; or

(*b*) a marriage contracted before 1st July 1940 by declaration *de praesenti* or by promise *subsequente copula*,

has been granted in the Court of Session, the principal clerk of Session shall forthwith cause the decree, the names, designations and addresses of the parties, and the date, as determined by the Court, on which the marriage was constituted to be intimated to the Registrar General, and on receipt of such intimation the Registrar General shall cause the marriage to be registered.

General

Interpreters at marriage ceremony

22.—(1) Where the person by whom a marriage is to be solemnised under this Act considers that it is necessary or desirable, he may use the services of an interpreter (not being a party or a witness to the marriage) at the marriage ceremony.

(2) The interpreter shall—

(*a*) before the marriage ceremony, sign a written statement that he understands, and is able to converse in, any language in respect of which he is to act as interpreter at that ceremony; and

(*b*) immediately after the marriage ceremony, furnish the person solemnising the marriage with a certificate written in English and signed by the interpreter that he has faithfully acted as interpreter at that ceremony.

(3) Any fee for the services of the interpreter shall be paid by the parties to the marriage.

Cancellation of entry in register of marriages

23. If a marriage in respect of which an entry has been made in a register of marriages is found or declared to be void, the Registrar General shall direct the cancellation of the entry.

Validity of registered marriage

[1] 23A.—(1) Subject to sections 1 and 2 of, and without prejudice to section 24(1) of this Act, where the particulars of any marriage at the ceremony in respect of which both parties were present are entered in a register of marriages by or at the behest of an appropriate registrar, the validity of that marriage shall not be questioned, in any legal proceedings whatsoever, on the ground of failure to comply with a requirement or restriction imposed by, under or by virtue of this Act.

(2) In subsection (1) above, "appropriate registrar" means—

(*a*) in the case of a civil marriage, an authorised registrar; and

(*b*) in any other case, a district registrar.

NOTE

[1] Inserted by the Law Reform (Miscellaneous Provisions) (Scotland) Act 1980 (c. 55), s. 22(1)(*d*).

Offences

24.—(1) Any person who—

(*a*) falsifies or forges any Marriage Schedule, certificate or declaration issued or made, or purporting to be issued or made, under this Act;

(*b*) knowingly uses, or gives or sends to any person as genuine, any false or forged Marriage Schedule, certificate, declaration or other document issued or made, or purporting to be issued or made, or required, under this Act;

(*c*) being an approved celebrant, solemnises a marriage without a Marriage Schedule in respect of the marriage, completed in accordance with this Act, being available to him at the time of the marriage ceremony;

(*d*) not being an approved celebrant or an authorised registrar, conducts a marriage ceremony in such a way as to lead the parties to the marriage to believe that he is solemnising a valid marriage; or

(*e*) being an approved celebrant or an authorised registrar, solemnises a marriage without both parties to the marriage being present,

shall be guilty of an offence and shall be liable—

(i) on conviction on indictment, to a fine or to imprisonment for a term not exceeding two years or to both;

[1] (ii) on summary conviction, to a fine not exceeding level 3 on the standard scale or to imprisonment for a term not exceeding three months or to both.

[1] (2) Any person who—

(*a*) solemnises a marriage in an area in which by virtue of section 9(4)(*b*) of this Act he is not permitted to solemnise a marriage;

(*b*) solemnises a marriage in contravention of section 10(5) of this Act;

(*c*) being a person temporarily authorised under section 12(*a*) of this Act, solemnises a marriage not specified in that authorisation;

(*d*) solemnises a marriage in contravention of section 14 of this Act; or

(*e*) being a party to a marriage, fails to comply with a notice served under section 16(2) of this Act,

shall be guilty of an offence and shall be liable on summary conviction to a fine not exceeding level 3 on the standard scale.

(3) Summary proceedings for an offence under this Act or, in relation to information supplied under or for the purposes of this Act, section 53(1)(*a*) of the Registration of Births, Deaths and Marriages (Scotland) Act 1965, may be commenced at any time within the period of three months from the date on which evidence sufficient in the opinion of the Lord Advocate to justify the proceedings comes to his knowledge or within the period of 12 months from the commission of the offence, whichever period last expires; and subsection (3) of section 331 of the Criminal Procedure (Scotland) Act 1975 (date of commencement of summary proceedings) shall have effect for the purposes of this section as it has effect for the purposes of that section.

NOTE

[1] As amended by virtue of the Criminal Procedure (Scotland) Act 1975, ss.289F and 289G.

Regulations

25.—(1) Any power to make regulations conferred by this Act shall be exercisable by statutory instrument and no such regulations shall be made by the Registrar General except with the approval of the Secretary of State.

(2) Any statutory instrument containing regulations which prescribe fees for the purposes of this Act shall be subject to annulment in pursuance of a resolution of either House of Parliament.

(3) The Statutory Instruments Act 1946 shall apply to a statutory instrument containing regulations made for the purposes of this Act by the Registrar General as if the regulations had been made by a Minister of the Crown.

Interpretation

26.—(1) Except where the context otherwise requires and subject to subsection (2) below, expressions used in this Act and in the Registration of Births, Deaths and Marriages (Scotland) Act 1965 have the same meanings in this Act as in that Act.

[1] (2) In this Act, except where the context otherwise requires—

"annulment" includes any decree or declarator of nullity of marriage, however expressed;

"approved celebrant" has the meaning assigned to it by section 8(2)(*a*) of this Act;

"authorised registrar" has the meaning assigned to it by section 8(2)(*b*) of this Act;

"district registrar" means the registrar for the registration district in which the marriage is to be or has been solemnised;

"name" includes surname;

[2] "prescribed" means prescribed by regulations made by the Registrar General;

"religious body" means an organised group of people meeting regularly for common religious worship.

(3) Except where the context otherwise requires, any reference in this Act to any other enactment shall be construed as a reference to that enactment as amended by or under any other enactment, including this Act.

NOTES

[1] As amended by the Family Law Act 1986, Sched. 1, para. 22.

[2] See S.I. 1986 No. 1954.

Transitional and saving provisions

27.—(1) Where, before the commencement of this Act—

(*a*) proclamation of banns or publication of notice has been applied for by one or both of the parties to; or

(*b*) a licence has been granted by a sheriff in respect of,

an intended marriage in accordance with an enactment repealed by this Act, then the marriage shall proceed in accordance with the enactments repealed by this Act as if they had not been so repealed:

Provided that this subsection shall cease to have effect in respect of the marriage if—

(i) a certificate of proclamation of banns or publication of notice issued in respect of the said application; or

(ii) the said licence,

ceases to be valid in accordance with any enactment so repealed.

(2) Any form used, and any requirement as to the particulars to be entered in any form used, for the purposes of any enactment repealed by this Act shall continue in force as though prescribed under this Act until other forms or particulars are so prescribed.

(3) Nothing in this Act shall affect the validity of any marriage solemnised or contracted before 1st January 1978.

(4) Nothing in the foregoing provisions of this section shall be taken as prejudicing the operation of section 38 of the Interpretation Act 1889 (which relates to the effect of repeals).

Consequential amendments and repeals

28.—(1) The enactments set out in Schedule 2 to this Act shall have effect subject to the amendments respectively specified in that Schedule, being amendments consequential on the provisions of this Act.

(2) The enactments set out in Schedule 3 to this Act are hereby repealed to the extent specified in column 3 of that Schedule.

Short title, commencement and extent

29.—(1) This Act may be cited as the Marriage (Scotland) Act 1977.

(2) This Act, except this section, shall come into force on 1st January 1978.

(3) This Act, except this section and, in so far as relating to the Marriage with Foreigners Act 1906, the Marriage Act 1939, the Marriage Act 1949 and the Marriage (Scotland) Act 1956, section 28, shall extend to Scotland only.

[THE NEXT PAGE IS K 181]

SCHEDULES

SCHEDULE 1

Degrees of Relationship

Column 1	*Column 2*
1.—Relationship by consanguinity	
Mother;	Father;
Daughter;	Son;
Father's mother;	Father's father;
Mother's mother;	Mother's father;
Son's daughter;	Son's son;
Daughter's daughter;	Daughter's son;
Sister;	Brother;
Father's sister;	Father's brother;
Mother's sister;	Mother's brother;
Brother's daughter	Brother's son;
Sister's daughter;	Sister's son;
Father's father's mother;	Father's father's father;
Father's mother's mother;	Father's mother's father;
Mother's father's mother;	Mother's mother's father;
Mother's mother's mother;	Son's son's son;
Son's son's daughter;	Son's daughter's son;
Son's daughter's daughter;	Daughter's son's son;
Daughter's son's daughter;	Daughter's daughter's son.
Daughter's daughter's daughter;	
[1]*2—Relationships by affinity referred to in section 2(1A)*	
Daughter of former wife;	Son of former husband;
Former wife of father;	Former husband of mother;
Former wife of father's father;	Former husband of father's mother;
Former wife of mother's father;	Former husband of mother's mother;
Daughter of son of former wife;	Son of son of former husband;
Daughter of daughter of former wife;	Son of daughter of former husband.
[1]*2A.—Relationships by affinity referred to in section 2(1B)*	
Mother of former wife;	Father of former husband;
Former wife of son;	Former husband of daughter.

NOTE

[1] As substituted by the Marriage (Prohibited Degrees of Relationship) Act 1986 (c. 16), Sched. 2, para. 7.

3.—Relationships by adoption	
Adoptive mother or former adoptive mother;	Adoptive father or former adoptive father;
Adopted daughter or former adopted daughter;	Adopted son or former adopted son.

[1] SCHEDULES 2 AND 3

NOTE

[1] The amendments and repeals contained in these Schedules have been given effect to in so far as they affect material contained in *The Parliament House Book*.

[1] Adoption (Scotland) Act 1978

(1978 c. 28)

An Act to consolidate the enactments relating to adoption in Scotland with amendments to give effect to recommendations of the Scottish Law Commission. [20th July 1978]

NOTE

[1] Act applied (with modifications) in relation to parental orders by S.I. 1994 No. 2804, *infra*.

PART I

THE ADOPTION SERVICE

The Adoption Service

Establishment of Adoption Service

Establishment of Adoption Service

[1] **1.**—(1) It is the duty of every local authority to establish and maintain within their area a service designed to meet the needs, in relation to adoption, of—

(*a*) children who have been or may be adopted;
(*b*) parents and guardians of such children; and
(*c*) persons who have adopted or may adopt a child;

and for that purpose to provide the requisite facilities, or secure that they are provided by approved adoption societies.

[2] (2) The facilities to be provided as part of the service maintained under subsection (1) include—

(*a*) temporary board and lodging where needed by pregnant women, mothers or children;
(*b*) arrangements for assessing children and prospective adopters, and placing children for adoption;
(*c*) counselling for persons with problems relating to adoption.

(3) The facilities of the service maintained under subsection (1) shall be provided in conjunction with the local authority's other social services and with approved adoption societies in their area, so that help may be given in a co-ordinated manner without duplication, omission or avoidable delay.

(4) The services maintained by local authorities under subsection (1) may be collectively referred to as "the Scottish Adoption Service", and a local authority or approved adoption society may be referred to as an adoption agency.

NOTES

[1] See the Foster Children (Scotland) Act 1984 (c. 56), s. 2(5).

[2] Para. (*a*) repealed (prospectively) and para. (*c*) substituted (prospectively) by the Children (Scotland) Act 1995 (c. 36), Sched. 2, para. 2, *infra*.

Local authorities' social work

[0] **2.** The social services referred to in section 1(3) are the functions of a local authority which stand referred to the authority's social work committee, including, in particular but without prejudice to the generality of the foregoing, a local authority's functions relating to—

(*a*) the promotion of the welfare of children by diminishing the need to receive children into care or keep them in care, including (in exceptional circumstances) the giving of assistance in cash;
(*b*) the welfare of children in the care of a local authority;

[1] (*c*) the welfare of children who are foster children within the meaning of the Foster Children (Scotland) Act 1984;

[2] (*d*) children who are subject to supervision orders made in matrimonial or custody proceedings;

(*e*) the provision of residential accommodation for expectant mothers and young children and of day-care facilities;

(*f*) the regulation and inspection of nurseries and child minders;

(*g*) care and other treatment of children through court proceedings and children's hearings.

NOTES

[0] Prospective amendment in the Local Government etc. (Scotland) Act 1994 (c. 39), Sched. 13, para. 111(2), *infra*.

[1] As amended by the Foster Children (Scotland) Act 1984 (c. 56).

[2] Prospectively repealed by the Children (Scotland) Act 1995 (c. 36), Sched. 5, *infra*.

[THE NEXT PAGE IS K 183]

Adoption societies

Approval of adoption societies

3.—[1,2] (1) Subject to regulations under section 9(1), a body which is a voluntary organisation and desires to act as an adoption society or, if it is already an adoption society, desires to continue to act as such may, in the manner specified by regulations made by the Secretary of State, apply to the Secretary of State for his approval to its doing so.

[2] (2) On an application under subsection (1), the Secretary of State shall take into account the matters relating to the applicant specified in subsections (3) to (5) and any other relevant considerations, and if, but only if, he is satisfied that the applicant is likely to make, or, if the applicant is an approved adoption society, is making, an effective contribution to the Scottish Adoption Service, he shall by notice to the applicant give his approval, which shall be operative from a date specified in the notice or, in the case of a renewal of approval, from the date of the notice.

(3) In considering the application, the Secretary of State shall have regard, in relation to the period for which approval is sought, to the following—

[3] (*a*) the applicant's adoption programme, including, in particular, its ability to make provision for children who are free for adoption,

(*aa*) [Prospectively inserted by the Children (Scotland) Act 1995 (c. 36), Sched. 2, para. 3, *infra.*]

(*b*) the number and qualifications of its staff,

(*c*) its financial resources, and

(*d*) the organisation and control of its operations.

(4) Where it appears to the Secretary of State that the applicant is likely to operate extensively within the area of a particular local authority he shall ask the authority whether they support the application, and shall take account of any views about it put to him by the authority.

[3] (5) Where the applicant is already an approved adoption society or, whether before or after the passing of this Act, previously acted as an adoption society, the Secretary of State, in considering the application, shall also have regard to the record and reputation of the applicant in the adoption field, and the areas within which and the scale on which it is currently operating or has operated in the past.

[3] (6) If after considering the application the Secretary of State is not satisfied that the applicant is likely to make or, as the case may be, is making an effective contribution to the Scottish Adoption Service, the Secretary of State shall, subject to section 5(1) and (2), by notice inform the applicant that its application is refused.

[3] (7) If not withdrawn earlier under section 4, approval given under this section shall last for a period of three years from the date on which it becomes operative, and shall then expire or, in the case of an approved adoption society whose further application for approval is pending at that time, shall expire on the date that application is granted or, as the case may be, refused.

NOTES

[1] As amended by the Health and Social Services and Social Security Adjudications Act 1983 (c. 41), Sched. 2, para. 38.

[2] Prospectively substituted by the Children (Scotland) Act 1995 (c. 36), s. 94(1), *infra*.

[3] Prospectively amended by the Children (Scotland) Act 1995 (c. 36), s. 94(1), *infra*.

Withdrawal of approval

4.—[1] (1) If, while approval of a body under section 3 is operative, it appears to the Secretary of State that the body is not making an effective contribution to the Scottish Adoption Service he shall, subject to section 5(3) and (4), by notice to the body withdraw the approval from a date specified in the notice.

(2) If an approved adoption society fails to provide the Secretary of State with information required by him for the purposes of carrying out his functions under subsection (1), or fails to verify such information in the manner required by him, he may by notice to the society withdraw the approval from a day specified in the notice.

(3) Where approval is withdrawn under subsection (1) or (2) or expires the Secretary of State may direct the body concerned to make such arrangements as to children who are in its care and other transitional matters as seem to him expedient.

NOTE

[1] Prospectively amended by the Children (Scotland) Act 1995 (c. 36), s. 94(2), *infra*.

Procedure on refusal to approve, or withdrawal of approval from, adoption societies

5.—(1) Before notifying a body which has applied for approval that the application is refused in accordance with section 3(6) the Secretary of State shall serve on the applicant a notice—

(*a*) setting out the reasons why he proposes to refuse the application;
(*b*) informing the applicant that it may make representations in writing to the Secretary of State within 28 days of the date of service of the notice.

(2) If any representations are made by the applicant in accordance with subsection (1), the Secretary of State shall give further consideration to the application taking into account those representations.

(3) The Secretary of State shall, before withdrawing approval of an adoption society in accordance with section 4(1), serve on the society a notice—

(*a*) setting out the reasons why he proposes to withdraw the approval; and
(*b*) informing the society that it may make representations in writing to the Secretary of State within 28 days of the date of service of the notice.

(4) If any representations are made by the society in accordance with subsection (3), the Secretary of State shall give further consideration to the withdrawal of approval under section 4(1) taking into account those representations.

(5) This section does not apply where the Secretary of State, after having considered any representations made by the applicant in accordance with this section, proposes to refuse approval or, as the case may be, to withdraw approval for reasons which have already been communicated to the applicant in a notice under this section.

Welfare of children

Duty to promote welfare of child

[1] **6.** In reaching any decision relating to the adoption of a child, a court or adoption agency shall have regard to all the circumstances, first consideration being given to the need to safeguard and promote the welfare of the child throughout his childhood; and shall so far as practicable ascertain the wishes and feelings of the child regarding the decision and give due consideration to them, having regard to his age and understanding.

NOTE

[1] Applied (with modifications) in relation to parental orders by S.I. 1994 No. 2804, *infra*. Prospectively substituted by the Children (Scotland) Act 1995 (c. 36), s. 95, *infra*.

Duty to consider alternatives to adoption

6A. [Prospectively inserted by the Children (Scotland) Act 1995 (c. 36), s. 96, *infra*.]

Religious upbringing of adopted child

7. An adoption agency shall in placing a child for adoption have regard (so far as is practicable) to any wishes of the child's parents and guardians as to the religious upbringing of the child.

Supplemental

Inactive or defunct adoption societies

[1] **8.**—(1) If it appears to the Secretary of State that an approved adoption society, or one in relation to which approval has been withdrawn under section 4 or has expired, is inactive or defunct he may, in relation to any child who is or was in the care of the society, direct what appears to him to be the appropriate local authority to take any such action as might have been taken by the society or by the society jointly with the authority; and if apart from this section the authority would not be entitled to take that action, or would not be entitled to take it without joining the society in the action, it shall be entitled to do so.

(2) Before giving a direction under subsection (1) the Secretary of State shall, if practicable, consult both the society and the authority.

NOTE

[1] Prospectively repealed by the Children (Scotland) Act 1995 (c. 36), Sched. 2, para. 4, *infra*.

Regulation of adoption agencies

9.—(1) The Secretary of State may by regulations prohibit unincorporated bodies from applying for approval under section 3; and he shall not approve any unincorporated body whose application is contrary to regulations made under this subsection.

[1] (2) The Secretary of State may make regulations for any purpose relating to the exercise of its functions by an approved adoption society.

(3) The Secretary of State may make regulations with respect to the exercise by local authorities of their functions of making or participating in arrangements for the adoption of children.

(3A) [Prospectively inserted by the Children (Scotland) Act 1995 (c. 36), Sched. 2, para. 5(*b*), *infra*.]

[2] (4) Any person who contravenes or fails to comply with regulations made under subsection (2) shall be guilty of an offence and liable on summary conviction to a fine not exceeding level 5 on the standard scale.

(5) Regulations under this section may make different provisions in relation to different cases or classes of cases and may exclude certain cases or classes of cases.

NOTES

[1] Prospectively amended by the Children (Scotland) Act 1995 (c. 36), Sched. 2, para. 5(*a*), *infra*.

[2] As amended by virtue of the Criminal Procedure (Scotland) Act 1975 (c. 21), ss. 289F and 289G.

10. [Repealed by the Health and Social Services and Social Security Adjudications Act 1983 (c. 41), Sched. 2, para. 39 and Sched. 10.]

Restriction on arranging adoptions and placing of children

11.—(1) A person other than an adoption agency shall not make arrangements for the adoption of a child, or place a child for adoption, unless the proposed adopter is a relative of the child.

[1] (2) An adoption society which is—

(*a*) approved as respects England and Wales under section 3 of the Adoption Act 1976; or

(*b*) registered as respects Northern Ireland under Article 4 of the Adoption (Northern Ireland) Order 1987, but which is not approved under section 3 of this Act, shall not act as an adoption society in Scotland except to the extent that the society considers it necessary to do so in the interests of a person mentioned in section 1 of that Act or, as the case may be, Article 3 of that Order.

[2] (3) A person who—

(*a*) takes part in the management or control of a body of persons which exists wholly or partly for the purpose of making arrangements for the adoption of children and which is not an approved adoption society or a local authority; or

(*b*) contravenes subsection (1); or

[3] (*c*) receives a child placed with him in contravention of subsection (1),

shall be guilty of an offence and liable on summary conviction to imprisonment for a term not exceeding three months or to a fine not exceeding level 5 on the standard scale or to both.

(4) In any proceedings for an offence under paragraph (*a*) of subsection (3), proof of things done or of words written, spoken or published (whether or not in the presence of any party to the proceedings) by any person taking part in the management or control of a body of persons, or in making arrangements for the adoption of children on behalf of the body, shall be sufficient evidence of the purpose for which that body exists.

(5) Section 26 shall apply where a person is convicted of a contravention of subsection (1) as it applies where an application for an adoption order is refused.

NOTES

[1] As substituted by the Children Act 1989 (c. 41), Sched. 10, para. 32.

[2] As amended by virtue of the Criminal Procedure (Scotland) Act 1975 (c. 21), ss. 289F and 289G.

[3] Prospectively substituted by the Children (Scotland) Act 1995 (c. 36), Sched. 2, para. 6, *infra*.

[1] PART II

ADOPTION ORDERS

NOTE

[1] See the Children (Scotland) Act 1995 (c. 36), ss. 54(2)(*c*) and 86(3), *infra* (prospective).

The making of adoption orders

Adoption orders

[1] **12.**—[2,3] (1) An adoption order is an order vesting the parental rights and duties relating to a child in the adopters, made on their application by an authorised court.

[3] (2) The order does not affect the parental rights and duties so far as they relate to any period before the making of the order.

[3,4] (3) The making of an adoption order operates to extinguish—

(*a*) any parental right or duty relating to the child which immediately before the making of the order was vested in a person (not being one of the adopters) who was—

(i) a parent of the child, or

(ii) a guardian of the child appointed by a deed or by the order of a court;

(*b*) any duty owed to or by the child—

(i) to pay or provide aliment in respect of any period occurring after the making of the order;

(ii) to make any payment arising out of parental rights and duties in respect of such a period.

(4) Nothing in subsection (3) shall—

(*a*) extinguish any duty arising under a deed or agreement which constitutes a trust or which expressly provides that the duty is not to be extinguished by the making of an adoption order;

(*b*) of itself terminate the appointment or functions of any judicial factor loco tutoris or curator bonis appointed to administer the whole or any part of the child's estate.

(5) An adoption order may not be made in relation to a child who is or has been married.

(6) An adoption order may contain such terms and conditions as the court thinks fit.

(7) An adoption order may be made notwithstanding that the child is already an adopted child.

[5] (8) An adoption order shall not be made in relation to a child of or over the age of 12 years unless with the child's consent; except that, where the court is satisfied that the child is incapable of giving his consent to the making of the order, it may dispense with that consent.

(9) [Prospectively added by the Children (Scotland) Act 1995 (c. 36), Sched. 2, para. 7, *infra*.]

NOTES

[1] Applied (with modifications) in relation to parental orders by S.I. 1994 No. 2804, *infra*.

[2] See the Child Abduction and Custody Act 1985 (c. 60), Sched. 3, para. 5(ii). See also the Family Law Act 1986 (c. 55), s. 1(1)(*b*)(ii).

[3] Prospectively amended by the Children (Scotland) Act 1995 (c. 36), Sched. 2, para. 7, *infra*.

[4] As amended by the Age of Legal Capacity (Scotland) Act 1991 (c. 50), Sched. 2. Prospectively amended, and subs. (3A) inserted, by the Children (Scotland) Act 1995 (c. 36), s. 97(1), *infra*. Prospective repeal in Sched. 5.

[5] As substituted by the Age of Legal Capacity (Scotland) Act 1991 (c. 50), s. 2(3)(*a*).

Child to live with adopters before order made

13.—(1) Where the applicant, or one of the applicants, is a parent, step-parent or relative of the child, or the child was placed with the applicants by an adoption agency, an adoption order shall not be made unless the child is at least nineteen weeks old and at all times during the preceding thirteen weeks had his home with the applicants or one of them.

(2) Where subsection (1) does not apply, an adoption order shall not be made unless the child is at least twelve months old and at all times during the preceding twelve months had his home with the applicants or one of them.

(3) An adoption order shall not be made unless the court is satisfied that sufficient opportunities to see the child with the applicant, or in the case of an application by a married couple, both applicants together in the home environment have been afforded—

(*a*) where the child was placed with the applicant by an adoption agency, to that agency, or

(*b*) in any other case, to the local authority within whose area the home is.

Adoption by married couple

14.—[1,2] (1) Subject to section 53(1) of the Children Act 1975 (which provides for the making of a custody order instead of an adoption order in certain cases), an adoption order shall not be made on the application of more than one person except in the circumstances specified in subsections (1A) and (1B).

[1] (1A) An adoption order may be made on the application of a married couple where both the husband and the wife have attained the age of 21 years.

[1] (1B) An adoption order may be made on the application of a married couple where—

(*a*) the husband or the wife—

(i) is the father or mother of the child; and

(ii) has attained the age of 18 years; and

(*b*) his or her spouse has attained the age of 21 years.

[2] (2) An adoption order shall not be made on the application of a married couple unless—

(*a*) at least one of them is domiciled in a part of the United Kingdom, or in the Channel Islands or the Isle of Man, or

(*b*) the application is for a Convention adoption order and section 17 is complied with.

NOTES

[1] Substituted for former subs. (1) by the Children Act 1989 (c. 41), Sched. 10, para. 33.

[2] Prospectively amended by the Children (Scotland) Act 1995 (c. 36), Sched. 2, para. 8, *infra*.

Adoption by one person

15.—[1,2] (1) Subject to section 53(1) of the Children Act 1975 (which provides for the making of a custody order instead of an adoption order in certain cases) an adoption order may be made on the application of one person where he has attained the age of twenty-one years and—

(*a*) is not married, or

(*b*) is married and the court is satisfied that—

(i) his spouse cannot be found, or

(ii) the spouses have separated and are living apart, and the separation is likely to be permanent, or

(iii) his spouse is by reason of ill-health, whether physical or mental, incapable of making an application for an adoption order.

[2] (2) An adoption order shall not be made on the application of one person unless—

(*a*) he is domiciled in a part of the United Kingdom, or in the Channel Islands or the Isle of Man, or

(*b*) the application is for a Convention adoption order and section 17 is complied with.

[3] (3) An adoption order shall not be made on the application of the mother or father of the child alone unless the court is satisfied that—

(*a*) the other natural parent is dead or cannot be found or, by virtue of section 28 of the Human Fertilisation and Embryology Act 1990, there is no other parent, or

(*b*) there is some other reason justifying the exclusion of the other natural parent,

and where such an order is made the reason justifying the exclusion of the other natural parent shall be recorded by the court.

NOTES

[1] Para. (*aa*) prospectively inserted, and para. (*b*) prospectively amended, by the Children (Scotland) Act 1995 (c. 36), s. 97(2), *infra*.

[2] Prospectively amended by the Children (Scotland) Act 1995 (c. 36), Sched. 2, para. 9, *infra*.

[3] As amended by the Human Fertilisation and Embryology Act 1990 (c. 37), Sched. 4, para. 6. Prospectively amended by the Children (Scotland) Act 1995 (c. 36), Sched. 5, *infra*.

Parental agreement

16.—(1) An adoption order shall not be made unless—

[1] (*a*) the child is free for adoption by virtue of an order made

(i) in Scotland under section 18;

(ii) in England and Wales under section 18 of the Adoption Act 1976; or

(iii) in Northern Ireland under Article 17(1) or 18(1) of the Adoption (Northern Ireland) Order 1987,

and not revoked; or

(*b*) in the case of each parent or guardian of the child the court is satisfied that—

(i) he freely, and with full understanding of what is involved, agrees unconditionally to the making of an adoption order (whether or not he knows the identity of the applicants), or

(ii) his agreement to the making of the adoption order should be dispensed with on a ground specified in subsection (2).

[2] (2) The grounds mentioned in subsection (1)(*b*) (ii) are that the parent or guardian—

(*a*) cannot be found or is incapable of giving agreement;

(*b*) is withholding his agreement unreasonably;

(*c*) has persistently failed without reasonable cause to discharge the parental duties in relation to the child;

(*d*) has abandoned or neglected the child;

(*e*) has persistently ill-treated the child;

(*f*) has seriously ill-treated the child (subject to subsection (5)).

(3) Subsection (1) does not apply in any case where the child is not a United Kingdom national and the application for the adoption order is for a Convention adoption order.

(4) Agreement is ineffective for the purposes of subsection (1)(*b*)(i) if given by the mother less than six weeks after the child's birth.

[3] (5) Subsection (2)(*f*) does not apply unless (because of the ill-treatment or for other reasons) the rehabilitation of the child within the household of the parent or guardian is unlikely.

NOTES

[1] As amended by the Children Act 1989 (c. 41), Sched. 10, para. 34.

[2] Prospectively substituted by the Children (Scotland) Act 1995 (c. 36), Sched. 2, para. 10, *infra*.

[3] Prospectively repealed by the Children (Scotland) Act 1995 (c. 36), Sched. 2, para. 10, *infra*.

Convention adoption order

17.—(1) An adoption order shall be made as a Convention adoption order if the application is for a Convention adoption order and the following conditions are satisfied both at the time of the application and when the order is made.

(2) The child—

(*a*) must be a United Kingdom national or a national of a Convention country, and

(*b*) must habitually reside in British territory or a Convention country, and

(*c*) must not be, or have been, married.

(3) The applicant or applicants and the child must not all be United Kingdom nationals living in British territory.

(4) If the application is by a married couple, either—

(*a*) each must be a United Kingdom national or a national of a Convention country, and both must habitually reside in Great Britain, or

(*b*) both must be United Kingdom nationals, and each must habitually reside in British territory or a Convention country,

and if the applicants are nationals of the same Convention country the adoption must not be prohibited by a specified provision (as defined in subsection (8)) of the internal law of that country.

(5) If the application is by one person, either—

(*a*) he must be a United Kingdom national or a national of a Convention country, and must habitually reside in Great Britain, or

(*b*) he must be a United Kingdom national and must habitually reside in British territory or a Convention country,

and if he is a national of a Convention country the adoption must not be prohibited by a specified provision (as defined in subsection (8)) of the internal law of that country.

(6) If the child is not a United Kingdom national the order shall not be made—

(*a*) except in accordance with the provisions, if any, relating to consents and consultations of the internal law relating to adoption of the Convention country of which the child is a national, and

(*b*) unless the court is satisfied that each person who consents to the order in accordance with that internal law does so with full understanding of what is involved.

(7) The reference to consents and consultations in subsection (6) does not include a reference to consent by and consultation with the applicant and members of the applicant's family (including his or her spouse), and for the purposes of subsection (6) consents may be proved in the manner prescribed by act of sederunt and the court shall be treated as the authority by whom, under the law mentioned in subsection (6), consents may be dispensed with and the adoption in question may be effected; and where the provisions there mentioned require the attendance before that authority of any person who does not reside in Great Britain, that requirement shall be treated as satisfied for the purposes of subsection (6) if—

(*a*) that person has been given a reasonable opportunity of communicating his opinion on the adoption in question to the proper officer or clerk of the court, or to an appropriate authority of the country in question, for transmission to the court; and

(*b*) where he has availed himself of that opportunity, his opinion has been transmitted to the court.

(8) In subsections (4) and (5) "specified provision" means a provision specified in an order of the Secretary of State as one notified to the Government of the United Kingdom in pursuance of the provisions of the Convention which relate to prohibitions on an adoption contained in the national law of the Convention country in question.

Freeing for adoption

Freeing child for adoption

[0] **18.**—[1] (1) Where, on an application by an adoption agency, an authorised court is satisfied in the case of each parent or guardian of the child that—

(*a*) he freely, and with full understanding of what is involved, agrees generally and unconditionally to the making of an adoption order, or

(*b*) his agreement to the making of an adoption order should be dispensed with on a ground specified in section 16(2),

the court shall, subject to subsection (8), make an order declaring the child free for adoption.

(2) No application shall be made under subsection (1) unless—

(*a*) it is made with the consent of a parent or guardian of a child, or

(*b*) the adoption agency is applying for dispensation under subsection (1)(*b*) of the agreement of each parent or guardian of the child, and the child is in the care of the adoption agency.

(3) No agreement required under subsection (1)(*a*) shall be dispensed with under subsection (1)(*b*) unless the child is already placed for adoption or the court is satisfied that it is likely that the child will be placed for adoption.

(4) An agreement by the mother of the child is ineffective for the purposes of this section if given less than six weeks after the child's birth.

[2,3] (5) On the making of an order under this section the parental rights and duties relating to the child vest in the adoption agency, and subsections (2) to (4) of section 12 apply as if the order were an adoption order and the agency were the adopters.

[4] (6) Before making an order under this section, the court shall satisfy itself, in relation to each parent or guardian of the child who can be found, that he has been given an opportunity of making, if he so wishes, a declar-

ation that he prefers not to be involved in future questions concerning the adoption of the child; and any such declaration shall be recorded by the court.

[3,5] (7) Before making an order under this section in the case of a child whose father is not married to the mother and who does not have any parental right in relation to the child, the court shall satisfy itself in relation to any person claiming to be the father that either—

(*a*) he has no intention of applying for any parental right under section 3 of the Law Reform (Parent and Child) (Scotland) Act 1986, or

(*b*) if he did apply for any parental right under that section the application would be likely to be refused.

[6] (8) An order under this section shall not be made in relation to a child of or over the age of 12 years unless with the child's consent; except that where the court is satisfied that the child is incapable of giving his consent to the making of the order, it may dispense with that consent.

(9) [Prospectively added by the Children (Scotland) Act 1995 (c. 36), Sched. 2, para. 11, *infra*.]

NOTES

[0] See the Social Work (Scotland) Act 1968 (c. 49), s. 44(5), and the Children (Scotland) Act 1995 (c. 36), ss. 54(2)(*c*) and 86(3) (prospective).

[1] Prospectively amended by the Children (Scotland) Act 1995 (c. 36), Sched. 2, para. 11, *infra*.

[2] As amended by the Children Act 1989 (c. 41), Sched. 10, para. 35.

[3] Prospectively substituted by the Children (Scotland) Act 1995 (c. 36), Sched. 2, para. 11, *infra*.

[4] As amended by the Health and Social Services and Social Security Adjudications Act 1983 (c. 41), Sched. 2, para. 40.

[5] As amended by the Law Reform (Parent and Child) (Scotland) Act 1986 (c. 9), Sched. 1, para. 18.

[6] As substituted by the Age of Legal Capacity (Scotland) Act 1991 (c. 50), s. 2(3)(*b*).

Progress reports to former parent

[1] **19.**—(1) This section and section 20 apply to any person ("the former parent") who was required to be given an opportunity of making a declaration under section 18(6) but did not do so.

(2) Within the fourteen days following the date twelve months after the making of the order under section 18, the adoption agency in which the parental rights and duties were vested on the making of the order, unless it has previously by notice to the former parent informed him that an adoption order has been made in respect of the child, shall by notice to the former parent inform him—

(*a*) whether an adoption order has been made in respect of the child, and (if not)

(*b*) whether the child has his home with a person with whom he has been placed for adoption.

(3) If at the time when the former parent is given notice under subsection (2) an adoption order has not been made in respect of the child, it is thereafter the duty of the adoption agency to give notice to the former parent of the making of an adoption order (if and when made), and meanwhile to give the former parent notice whenever the child is placed for adoption or ceases to have his home with a person with whom he has been placed for adoption.

(4) If at any time the former parent by notice makes a declaration to the adoption agency that he prefers not to be involved in future questions concerning the adoption of the child—

(*a*) the agency shall secure that the declaration is recorded by the court which made the order under section 18, and

(*b*) the agency is released from the duty of complying further with subsection (3) as respects that former parent.

NOTE

[1] Subss. (1)–(4) prospectively amended by the Children (Scotland) Act 1995 (c. 36), Sched. 2, para. 12, *infra*.

Revocation of s. 18 order

[1] **20.**—(1) The former parent, at any time more than 12 months after the making of the order under section 18 when—

(*a*) no adoption order has been made in respect of the child, and

(*b*) the child does not have his home with a person with whom he has been placed for adoption,

may apply to the court which made the order for a further order revoking it on the ground that he wishes to resume the parental rights and duties.

(2) While the application is pending the adoption agency having the parental rights and duties shall not place the child for adoption without the leave of the court.

[THE NEXT PAGE IS K 191]

(3) Where an order freeing a child for adoption is revoked under this section—

(*a*) the parental rights and duties relating to the child are vested in the individual or, as the case may be, the individuals in whom they vested immediately before that order was made;

(*b*) if the parental rights and duties, or any of them, vested in a local authority or voluntary organisation immediately before the order freeing the child for adoption was made, those rights and duties are vested in the individual or, as the case may be, the individuals in whom they vested immediately before they were vested in the authority or organisation; and

[2] (*c*) any duty extinguished by virtue of section 12(3)(*b*) is forthwith revived,

but the revocation does not affect any right or duty so far as it relates to any period before the date of the revocation.

(4) Subject to subsection (5), if the application is dismissed on the ground that to allow it would contravene the principle embodied in section 6—

(*a*) the former parent who made the application shall not be entitled to make any further application under subsection (1) in respect of the child, and

(*b*) the adoption agency is released from the duty of complying further with section 19(3) as respects that parent.

(5) Subsection (4)(*a*) shall not apply where the court which dismissed the application gives leave to the former parent to make a further application under subsection (1), but such leave shall not be given unless it appears to the court that because of a change in circumstances or for any other reason it is proper to allow the application to be made.

NOTES

[1] Subss. (1)–(5) prospectively amended, and subs. (1A) prospectively inserted, by the Children (Scotland) Act 1995 (c. 36), Sched. 2, para. 13, *infra*.

[2] As amended by the Children Act 1989 (c. 41), Sched. 10, para. 36 and Sched. 15.

Variation of section 18 order so as to substitute one adoption agency for another

[1] **21.**—[2] (1) On an application to which this section applies an authorised court may vary an order under section 18 so as to transfer the parental rights and duties relating to the child from the adoption agency in which they are vested under the order ("the existing agency") to another adoption agency ("the substitute agency").

(2) This section applies to any application made jointly by the existing agency and the would-be substitute agency.

[2] (3) Where an order under section 18 is varied under this section, section 19 shall apply as if the parental rights and duties relating to the child had vested in the substitute agency on the making of the order.

NOTES

[1] As substituted by the Children Act 1989 (c. 41), Sched. 10, para. 37.

[2] Prospectively amended by the Children (Scotland) Act 1995 (c. 36), Sched. 2, para. 14, *infra*.

Supplemental

Notification to local authority of adoption application

22.—(1) An adoption order shall not be made in respect of a child who was not placed with the applicant by an adoption agency unless the applicant has, at least three months before the date of the order, given notice to the local authority within whose area he has his home of his intention to apply for the adoption order.

(2) On receipt of such a notice the local authority shall investigate the matter and submit to the court a report of their investigation.

(3) Under subsection (2), the local authority shall in particular investigate,—

(*a*) so far as is practicable, the suitability of the applicant, and any other matters relevant to the operation of section 6 in relation to the application; and

(*b*) whether the child was placed with the applicant in contravention of section 11.

[1] (4) A local authority which receive notice under subsection (1) in respect of a child whom the authority know to be in the care of another local authority shall, not more than seven days after the receipt of the notice, inform that other local authority in writing that they have received the notice.

NOTE

[1] As amended by the Children Act 1989 (c. 41), Sched. 10, para. 38.

Children subject to supervision requirements

22A. [Prospectively inserted by the Children (Scotland) Act 1995 (c. 36), Sched. 2, para. 15, *infra*.]

Reports where child placed by agency

23. Where an application for an adoption order relates to a child placed by an adoption agency, the agency shall submit to the court a report on the suitability of the applicants and any other matters relevant to the operation of section 6, and shall assist the court in any manner the court may direct.

Restrictions on making adoption orders

24.—[1] (1) The court shall not proceed to determine an application for an adoption order in relation to a child where a previous application for a British adoption order made in relation to the child by the same persons was refused by any court unless—

(*a*) in refusing the previous application the court directed that this subsection should not apply, or

(*b*) it appears to the court that because of a change in circumstances or for any other reason it is proper to proceed with the application.

[2] (2) The court shall not make an adoption order in relation to a child unless it is satisfied that the applicants have not, as respects the child, contravened section 51.

NOTES

[1] Applied (with modifications) in relation to parental orders by S.I. 1994 No. 2804, *infra*.

[2] As amended by the Health and Social Services and Social Security Adjudications Act 1983 (c. 41), Sched. 2, para. 41. Prospectively substituted by the Children (Scotland) Act 1995 (c. 36), Sched. 2, para. 16, *infra*.

Interim orders

25.—[1] (1) Where on an application for an adoption order the requirements of sections 16(1) and 22(1) are complied with, the court may postpone the determination of the application and make an order vesting the custody of the child in the applicants for a probationary period not exceeding two years upon such terms for the aliment of the child and otherwise as the court thinks fit.

(2) Where the probationary period specified in an order under subsection (1) is less than two years, the court may by a further order extend the period to a duration not exceeding two years in all.

NOTE

[1] Prospectively amended by the Children (Scotland) Act 1995 (c. 36), Sched. 2, para. 17, *infra*.

Timetable for resolving question as to whether agreement to adoption orders etc. should be dispensed with

25A. [Prospectively inserted by the Children (Scotland) Act 1995 (c. 36), Sched. 2, para. 18, *infra*.]

Care etc. of child on refusal of adoption order

[1] **26.**—(1) Where on an application for an adoption order in relation to a child under the age of sixteen years the court refuses to make the adoption order then—

(*a*) if it appears to the court that there are exceptional circumstances making it desirable that the child should be under the supervision of an independent person, the court may order that the child shall be under the supervision of a specified local authority;

(*b*) if it appears to the court that there are exceptional circumstances making it impracticable or undesirable for the child to be entrusted to either of the parents or to any other individual, the court may by order commit the child to the care of a specified local authority.

(2) Where the court makes an order under subsection (1)(*b*), the order may require the payment by either parent to the local authority, while it has the care of the child, of such weekly or other periodical sum towards the aliment of the child as the court thinks reasonable.

(3) Subsections (2), (4) and (5) of section 11 of the Guardianship Act 1973 (jurisdiction and orders relating to care and custody of children) apply in relation to an order under this section as they apply in relation to an order under that section.

NOTE

[1] Applied (with modifications) to parental orders by S.I. 1994 No. 2804, *infra*. Prospectively repealed by the Children (Scotland) Act 1995 (c. 36), Sched. 5, *infra*.

PART III

CARE AND PROTECTION OF CHILDREN AWAITING ADOPTION

Restrictions on removal of children

Restrictions on removal where adoption agreed or application made under s. 18

[1] **27.**—[2,3] (1) While an application for an adoption order is pending in a case where a parent or guardian of the child has agreed to the making of the adoption order (whether or not he knows the identity of the applicant), the parent or guardian is not entitled, against the will of the person with whom the child has his home, to remove the child from the care and possession of that person except with the leave of the court.

[3] (2) While an application is pending for an order freeing a child for adoption and—

(*a*) the child is in the care of the adoption agency making the application, and

(*b*) the application was not made with the consent of each parent or guardian of the child,

no parent or guardian of the child who did not consent to the application is entitled, against the will of the person with whom the child has his home, to remove the child from the care and possession of that person except with the leave of the court.

[4] (3) Any person who contravenes subsection (1) or (2) shall be guilty of an offence and liable on summary conviction to imprisonment for a term not exceeding three months or a fine not exceeding level 5 on the standard scale or both.

(4), (5) [Repealed by the Health and Social Services and Social Security Adjudications Act 1983 (c. 41), Sched. 2, para. 42, and Sched. 10.]

NOTES

[1] As amended by the Health and Social Services and Social Security Adjudications Act 1983 (c. 41), Sched. 2, para. 43.

[2] Applied (with modifications) in relation to parental orders by S.I. 1994 No. 2804, *infra*.

[3] Prospectively substituted by the Children (Scotland) Act 1995 (c. 36), Sched. 2, para. 19, *infra*.

[4] As amended by virtue of the Criminal Procedure (Scotland) Act 1975 (c. 21), ss. 289F and 289G. Prospectively amended by the Children (Scotland) Act 1995 (c. 36), Sched. 2, para. 19, *infra*.

Restrictions on removal where applicant has provided home for five years

[1] **28.**—(1) While an application for an adoption order in respect of a child made by the person with whom the child has had his home for the five years preceding the application is pending, no person is entitled, against the will of the applicant, to remove the child from the applicant's care and possession except with the leave of the court or under authority conferred by any enactment or on the arrest of the child.

(2) Where a person ("the prospective adopter") gives notice to the local authority within whose area he has his home that he intends to apply for an adoption order in respect of a child who for the preceding five years has had his home with the prospective adopter, no person is entitled, against the will of the prospective adopter, to remove the child from the prospective adopter's care and possession, except with the leave of the court or under authority conferred by any enactment or on the arrest of the child, before—

(*a*) the prospective adopter applies for the adoption order, or

(*b*) the period of three months from the receipt of the notice by the local authority expires,

whichever occurs first.

(3) In any case where subsection (1) or (2) applies and—

(*a*) the child was in the care of a local authority before he began to have his home with the applicant or, as the case may be, the prospective adopter, and

(*b*) the child remains in the care of a local authority,

the authority in whose care the child is shall not remove the child from the care and possession of the applicant or of the prospective adopter except in accordance with section 30 or 31 or with leave of a court.

[2] (4) Subsection (3) does not apply where the removal of the child is authorised, in terms of Part III of the Social Work (Scotland) Act 1968, by a justice of the peace or a children's hearing.

[2] (5) A local authority which receives such notice as is mentioned in subsection (2) in respect of a child whom the authority know to be in the care of another local authority or of a voluntary organisation, shall, not more than seven days after the receipt of the notice, inform that other authority or the organisation in writing that they have received the notice.

(6) Subsection (2) does not apply to any further notice served by the prospective adopter on any local authority in respect of the same child during the period referred to in paragraph (*b*) of that subsection or within 28 days after its expiry.

[3] (7) Any person who contravenes subsection (1) or (2) shall be guilty of an offence and liable on summary conviction to imprisonment for a term not exceeding three months or a fine not exceeding level 5 on the standard scale or both.

(8), (9) [Repealed by the Health and Social Services and Social Security Adjudications Act 1983 (c. 41), Sched. 2, para. 42, and Sched. 10.]

(10) The Secretary of State may by order amend subsection (1) or (2) to substitute a different period for the period of five years mentioned in that subsection (or the period which by a previous order under this subsection, was substituted for that period).

(11) In subsections (2) and (3) "a court" means a court having jurisdiction to make adoption orders.

NOTES

[1] As amended by the Health and Social Services and Social Security Adjudications Act 1983 (c. 41), Sched. 2, para. 43.

[2] Prospectively amended by the Children (Scotland) Act 1995 (c. 36), Sched. 2, para. 20, *infra*.
[3] As amended by virtue of the Criminal Procedure (Scotland) Act 1975 (c. 21), ss. 289F and 289G.

Return of child taken away in breach of s. 27 or 28

[1] **29.**—(1) An authorised court may on the application of a person from whose care and possession a child has been removed in breach of section 27 or 28, or section 27 or 28 of the Adoption Act 1976 or Article 28 or 29 of the Adoption (Northern Ireland) Order 1987 order the person who has so removed the child to return the child to the applicant.

(2) An authorised court may on the application of a person who has reasonable grounds for believing that another person is intending to remove the child from the applicant's care and possession in breach of section 27 or 28, or section 27 or 28 of the Adoption Act 1976 or Article 28 or 29 of the Adoption (Northern Ireland) Order 1987 by order direct that other person not to remove the child from the applicant's care and possession in breach of section 27 or 28, or section 27 or 28 of the Adoption Act 1976 or Article 28 or 29 of the Adoption (Northern Ireland) Order 1987.

NOTE

[1] As amended by the Health and Social Services and Social Security Adjudications Act 1983 (c. 41), Sched. 2, paras. 43 and 44, and the Children Act 1989 (c. 41), Sched. 10, para. 39. Applied (with modifications) in relation to parental orders by S.I. 1994 No. 2804, *infra*.

Return of children placed for adoption by adoption agencies

30.—(1) Subject to subsection (2), at any time after a child has been delivered into the care and possession of any person in pursuance of arrangements made by an approved adoption society or local authority for the adoption of the child by that person, and before an adoption order has been made on the application of that person in respect of the child—

(*a*) that person may give notice in writing to the society or authority of his intention not to retain the care and possession of the child; or

(*b*) the society or authority may cause notice in writing to be given to that person of their intention not to allow the child to remain in his care and possession.

(2) No notice under paragraph (*b*) of subsection (1) shall be given in respect of a child in relation to whom an application has been made for an adoption order except with the leave of the court to which the application has been made.

(3) Where a notice is given to an adoption society or local authority by any person, or by such a society or authority to any person, under subsection (1), or where an application for an adoption order made by any person in respect of a child placed in his care and possession by such a society or authority is refused by the court or withdrawn, that person shall, within seven days after the date on which notice was given or the application refused or withdrawn, as the case may be, cause the child to be returned to the society or authority, who shall receive the child.

[THE NEXT PAGE IS K 195]

(4) Where the period specified in an interim order made under section 25 (whether as originally made or as extended under subsection (2) of that section) expires without an adoption order having been made in respect of the child, subsection (3) shall apply as if the application for an adoption order upon which the interim order was made had been refused at the expiration of that period.

(5) It shall be sufficient compliance with the requirements of subsection (3) if the child is delivered to, and is received by, a suitable person nominated for the purpose by the adoption society or local authority.

(6) Where an application for an adoption order is refused the court may, if it thinks fit at any time before the expiry of the period of seven days mentioned in subsection (3), order that period to be extended to a duration, not exceeding six weeks, specified in the order.

[1] (7) Any person who contravenes the provisions of this section shall be guilty of an offence and liable on summary conviction to imprisonment for a term not exceeding three months or to a fine not exceeding level 5 on the standard scale or to both; and the court by which the offender is convicted may order the child in respect of whom the offence is committed to be returned to his parent or guardian or to the adoption society or local authority which made the arrangements referred to in subsection (1).

NOTE

[1] As amended by virtue of the Criminal Procedure (Scotland) Act 1975 (c. 21), ss. 289F and 289G.

Application of s. 30 where child not placed for adoption

31.—(1) Where a person gives notice in pursuance of section 22(1) to the local authority within whose area he has his home of his intention to apply for an adoption order in respect of a child who is for the time being in the care of a local authority, not being a child who was delivered into the care and possession of that person in pursuance of such arrangements as are mentioned in section 30(1), that section shall apply as if the child had been so delivered, except that where the application is refused by the court or withdrawn the child need not be returned to the local authority in whose care he is unless that authority so require.

(2) Where notice of intention is given as aforesaid in respect of any child who is for the time being in the care of a local authority then, until the application for an adoption order has been made and disposed of, any right of the local authority to require the child to be returned to them otherwise than in pursuance of section 30 shall be suspended.

(3) While the child remains in the care and possession of the person by whom the notice is given no contribution shall be payable (whether under a contribution order or otherwise) in respect of the child by any person liable under section 78 of the Social Work (Scotland) Act 1968 to make contributions in respect of him (but without prejudice to the recovery of any sum due at the time the notice is given), unless twelve weeks have elapsed since the giving of the notice without the application being made or the application has been refused by the court or withdrawn.

Protected children

Meaning of "protected child"

[1] **32.**—(1) Where a person gives notice in pursuance of section 22(1) to the local authority within whose area he lives of his intention to apply for an adoption order in respect of a child, the child is for the purposes of this Part a protected child while he has his home with that person.

[2] (2) A child shall be deemed to be a protected child for the purposes of this Part if he is a protected child within the meaning of section 32 of the Adoption Act 1976 or Article 33 of the Adoption (Northern Ireland) Order 1987.

[3] (3) A child is not a protected child by reason of any such notice as is mentioned in subsection (1) while—

(*a*) he is in the care of any person in any such school, home or institution as is mentioned in section 2(2) of the Foster Children (Scotland) Act 1984; or

(*b*) he is resident in a residential establishment provided for persons suffering from mental disorder under section 59 of the Social Work (Scotland) Act 1968; or

(*c*) he is liable to be detained or subject to guardianship under section 17 or 39 of the Mental Health (Scotland) Act 1984.

(4) A protected child ceases to be a protected child when—

(*a*) the application for an adoption order lapses or is withdrawn;

(*b*) the application for an adoption order is granted or otherwise determined;

(*c*) an order is made awarding custody of the child;

(*d*) an order is made appointing a guardian of the child; or

(*e*) the child attains the age of eighteen years.

NOTES

[1] Prospectively repealed by the Children (Scotland) Act 1995 (c. 36), Sched. 2, para. 21, *infra*.

[2] As amended by the Children Act 1989 (c. 41), Sched. 10, para. 40.

[3] As amended by the Mental Health (Scotland) Act 1984 (c. 36), Sched. 3, para. 38, and the Foster Children (Scotland) Act 1984 (c. 56), Sched. 2, para. 7. See *ibid*. s. 2(5).

Duty of local authorities to secure well-being of protected children

[1] **33.**—(1) It shall be the duty of every local authority to secure that protected children within their area are visited from time to time by officers of the authority, who shall satisfy themselves as to the well-being of the children and give such advice as to their care and maintenance as may appear to be needed.

(2) Any officer of a local authority authorised to visit protected children may, after producing, if asked to do so, some duly authenticated document showing that he is so authorised, inspect any premises in the area of the authority in which such children are to be or are being kept.

NOTE

[1] Prospectively repealed by the Children (Scotland) Act 1995 (c. 36), Sched. 2, para. 21, *infra*.

Removal of protected children from unsuitable surroundings

[1,2] **34.**—(1) If the sheriff is satisfied, on the complaint of a local authority, that a protected child is being kept or is about to be received by any person who is unfit to have his care or in any premises or any environment detrimental or likely to be detrimental to him, the sheriff may make an order for his removal to a place of safety until he can be restored to a parent, relative or guardian of his, or until other arrangements can be made with respect to him; and on proof that there is imminent danger to the health or well-being of the child the power to make an order under this section may be exercised by a justice of the peace acting on the application of a person authorised to visit protected children.

(2) An order under this section may be executed by any person authorised to visit protected children or by any constable and may be executed on a Sunday.

(3) A local authority may receive into their care under section 15 of the Social Work (Scotland) Act 1968 any child removed under this section, whether or not the circumstances of the child are such that they fall within paragraphs (*a*) to (*c*) of subsection (1) of that section and notwithstanding that he may appear to the local authority to be over the age of seventeen years.

(4) Where a child is removed under this section the local authority shall, if practicable, inform a parent or guardian of the child, or any person who acts as his guardian.

NOTES

[1] Prospectively repealed by the Children (Scotland) Act 1995 (c. 36), Sched. 2, para. 21, *infra.*
[2] See the Foster Children (Scotland) Act 1984 (c. 56), s. 7(1)(*f*).

Notices and information to be given to local authorities

[1] **35.**—(1) Where a person who has a protected child in his care and possession changes his permanent address he shall, not less than two weeks before the change, or, if the change is made in an emergency, not later than one week after the change, give notice specifying the new address to the local authority in whose area his permanent address is before the change, and if the new address is in the area of another local authority, the authority to whom the notice is given shall inform that other local authority and give them such of the following particulars as are known to them, that is to say—

(*a*) the name, sex and date and place of birth of the child;

(*b*) the name and address of every person who is a parent or guardian or acts as guardian of the child or from whom the child has been or is to be received.

(2) If a protected child dies, the person in whose care and possession he was at his death shall within forty-eight hours give notice of the child's death to the local authority.

NOTE

[1] Prospectively repealed by the Children (Scotland) Act 1995 (c. 36), Sched. 2, para. 21, *infra.*

Offences relating to protected children

[1] **36.**—(1) A person shall be guilty of an offence if—

(*a*) being required under section 35 to give any notice or information, he fails to give the notice within the time specified in that provision or fails to give the information within a reasonable time, or knowingly makes or causes or procures another person to make any false or misleading statement in the notice or information;

(*b*) he refuses to allow the visiting of a protected child by a duly authorised officer of a local authority or the inspection under the power conferred by section 33(2), of any premises;

(*c*) he refuses to comply with an order under section 34 for the removal of any child or obstructs any person in the execution of such an order.

[2] (2) A person guilty of an offence under this section shall be liable on summary conviction to imprisonment for a term not exceeding three months or a fine not exceeding level 5 on the standard scale or both.

NOTES

[1] Prospectively repealed by the Children (Scotland) Act 1995 (c. 36), Sched. 2, para. 21, *infra.*

[2] As amended by virtue of the Criminal Procedure (Scotland) Act 1975 (c. 21), ss. 289F and 289G.

Miscellaneous provisions relating to protected children

[1] **37.**—(1) For the purposes of sections 14 and 323 of the Criminal Procedure (Scotland) Act 1975 (under which a warrant authorising the search for and removal of a child may be issued on suspicion of unnecessary suffering caused to, or certain offences committed against, the child), any refusal to allow the visiting of a protected child or the inspection of any premises by a person authorised to do so under section 33 shall be treated as giving reasonable cause for such a suspicion.

(2) A person who maintains a protected child shall be deemed for the purposes of the Life Assurance Act 1774 to have no interest in the life of the child.

NOTE

[1] Prospectively repealed by the Children (Scotland) Act 1995 (c. 36), Sched. 2, para. 21, *infra.*

[1] PART IV

STATUS OF ADOPTED CHILDREN

NOTE

[1] Saved by the Children (Scotland) Act 1995 (c. 36), s. 15(1) (prospective).

Meaning of "adoption order" in Part IV

38.—(1) In this Part "adoption order" means—

(*a*) an adoption order within the meaning of section 65(1);

(*b*) an adoption order under the Children Act 1975, the Adoption Act 1958, the Adoption Act 1950 or any enactment repealed by the Adoption Act 1950;

(*c*) an order effecting an adoption made in England, Wales, Northern Ireland, the Isle of Man or any of the Channel Islands;

(*d*) an "overseas adoption" within the meaning of section 65(2); or

(*e*) any other adoption recognised by the law of Scotland;

and cognate expressions shall be construed accordingly.

(2) The definition of adoption order includes, where the context admits, an adoption order which took effect before the commencement of the Children Act 1975.

Status conferred by adoption

39.—[1,2] (1) A child who is the subject of an adoption order shall be treated in law—

(*a*) where the adopters are a married couple, as if he had been born as a legitimate child of the marriage (whether or not he was in fact born after the marriage was constituted);

(*b*) in any other case, as if he had been born as a legitimate child of the adopter (but not as a child of any actual marriage of the adopter);

and as if he were not the child of any person other than the adopters or adopter.

[1,3] (2) Where a child has been adopted by one of his natural parents as sole adoptive parent and the adopter thereafter marries the other natural parent, subsection (1) shall not affect any enactment or rule of law whereby, by virtue of the marriage, the child is rendered the legitimate child of both natural parents.

[1] (3) This section has effect—

(*a*) in the case of an adoption before 1st January 1976, from that date, and

(*b*) in the case of any other adoption, from the date of the adoption.

[4] (4) Subject to the provisions of this Part, this section—

(*a*) applies for the construction of enactments or instruments passed or made before or after the commencement of this Act so far as the context admits; and

(*b*) does not affect things done or events occurring before the adoption or, where the adoption took place before 1st January 1976, before that date.

(5) This section has effect subject to the provisions of section 44.

NOTES

[1] Applied (with modifications) in relation to parental orders by S.I. 1994 No. 2804, *infra*.

[2] Subs. (1) prospectively substituted by the Children (Scotland) Act 1995 (c. 36), s. 97(3), *infra*.

[3] As amended by the Law Reform (Parent and Child) (Scotland) Act 1986 (c. 9), Sched. 1, para. 18.

[4] Saved by the Insurance Companies Act 1982 (c. 50), s. 50(7).

40. [Repealed by the British Nationality Act 1981 (c. 61), Sched. 9.]

Miscellaneous enactments

[0] **41.**—[1] (1) Section 39 does not apply in determining the forbidden degrees of consanguinity and affinity in respect of the law relating to marriage or in respect of the crime of incest, except that, on the making of an adoption order, the adopter and the child shall be deemed, for all time coming, to be within the said forbidden degrees in respect of the law relating to marriage and incest.

[2] (2) Section 39 does not apply for the purposes of any provision of—

(*a*) the British Nationality Act 1981,

(*b*) the Immigration Act 1971,

(*c*) any instrument having effect under an enactment within paragraph (*a*) or (*b*), or

[3] (*d*) any other law for the time being in force which determines British citizenship, British Dependent Territories citizenship, the status of a British National (Overseas) or British Overseas citizenship.

(3), (4), (5) [Repealed by the Social Security Act 1988 (c. 7), Sched. 5.]

NOTES

[0] Applied (with modifications) in relation to parental orders by S.I. 1994 No. 2804, *infra*.

[1] As amended by the Incest and Related Offences (Scotland) Act 1986 (c. 36), Sched. 1, para. 5.

[2] As amended by the British Nationality Act 1981 (c. 61), Scheds. 7 and 9.

[3] As amended by S.I. 1986 No. 948, Sched.

Pensions

42. Section 39(1) does not affect entitlement to a pension which is payable to or for the benefit of a child and is in payment at the time of his adoption.

Insurance

43. Where a child is adopted whose natural parent has effected an insurance with a friendly society or a collecting society or an industrial insurance company for the payment on the death of the child of money for funeral expenses, the rights and liabilities under the policy shall by virtue of the adoption be transferred to the adoptive parents who shall for the purposes of the enactments relating to such societies and companies be treated as the person who took out the policy.

Effect of s. 39 on succession and inter vivos **deed**

44. Section 39 (status conferred by adoption) does not affect the existing law relating to adopted persons in respect of—

(*a*) the succession to a deceased person (whether testate or intestate), and

(*b*) the disposal of property by virtue of any *inter vivos* deed.

Part V

Registration and Revocation of Adoption Orders and Convention Adoptions

Adopted Children Register

[1] **45.**—(1) The Registrar General for Scotland shall maintain at the General Register Office a register, to be called the Adopted Children Register, in which shall be made such entries as may be directed to be made therein by adoption orders, but no other entries.

(2) An extract of any entry in the Adopted Children Register maintained under this section, if purporting to be sealed or stamped with the seal of the General Register Office, shall, without any further or other

proof of that entry, be received as evidence of the adoption to which it relates and, where the entry contains a record of the date of the birth or the country of the birth of the adopted person, shall also be received as aforesaid as evidence of that date or country.

(3) The Registrar General for Scotland shall cause an index of the Adopted Children Register maintained under this section to be made and kept in the General Register Office; and the Registrar General for Scotland shall—

(*a*) cause a search to be made of that index on behalf of any person or permit that person to search the index himself, and

(*b*) issue to any person an extract of any entry in that register which that person may require,

in all respects upon and subject to the same terms, conditions and regulations as to payment of fees and otherwise as are applicable under the Registration of Births, Deaths and Marriages (Scotland) Act 1965 in respect of searches in other indexes kept in the General Register Office and in respect of the supply from that office of extracts of entries in the registers of births, deaths and marriages.

(4) The Registrar General for Scotland shall, in addition to the Adopted Children Register and the index thereto, keep such other registers and books, and make such entries therein, as may be necessary to record and make traceable the connection between any entry in the register of births which has been marked "Adopted" pursuant to paragraph 1 of Schedule 1 or any enactment at the time in force and any corresponding entry in the Adopted Children Register maintained under this section.

[2] (5) The registers and books kept under subsection (4) shall not be, nor shall any index thereof be, open to public inspection or search, nor, except under an order of the Court of Session or a sheriff, shall the Registrar General for Scotland furnish any information contained in or any copy or extract from any such registers or books to any person other than an adopted person who has attained the age of 17 years and to whom that information, copy or extract relates or a local authority Board or adoption society falling within subsection (6) which is providing counselling for that adopted person.

(6) Where the Registrar General for Scotland furnishes an adopted person with information under subsection (5), he shall advise that person that counselling services are available—

(*a*) if the person is in Scotland—

(i) from the local authority in whose area he is living;

(ii) where the adoption order relating to him was made in Scotland, from the local authority in whose area the court which made the order sat; or

(iii) from any other local authority in Scotland;

(*b*) if the person is in England and Wales—

(i) from the local authority in whose area he is living;

(ii) where the adoption order relating to him was made in England and Wales, from the local authority in whose area the court which made the order sat; or

(iii) from any other local authority in England and Wales;

(*c*) if the person is in Northern Ireland—

(i) from the Board in whose area he is living;

(ii) where the adoption order relating to him was made in Northern Ireland, from the Board in whose area the court which made the order sat; or

(iii) from any other Board;

(*d*) if the person is in the United Kingdom and his adoption was arranged by an adoption society—

(i) approved under section 3;

(ii) approved under section 3 of the Adoption Act 1976; or

(iii) registered under Article 4 of the Adoption (Northern Ireland) Order 1987,

from that society.

(6A) Where an adopted person who is in Scotland—

(*a*) is furnished with information under subsection (5); or

(*b*) applies for information under—

(i) section 51(1) of the Adoption Act 1976; or

(ii) Article 54 of the Adoption (Northern Ireland) Order 1987,

any body mentioned in subsection (6B) to which the adopted person applies for counselling shall have a duty to provide counselling for him.

(6B) The bodies referred to in subsection (6A) are—

(*a*) any local authority falling within subsection (6)(*a*); and

(*b*) any adoption society falling within subsection (6)(*d*) so far as it is acting as an adoption society in Scotland.

(7) Where an adopted person has arranged to receive counselling from a local authority, Board or adoption society falling within subsection (6), the Registrar General for Scotland shall, on receipt of a request from the local authority, Board or adoption society, and on payment of the appropriate fee, send to the authority Board or society an extract of the entry relating to the adopted person in the register of births.

(8) The provisions of the Registration of Births, Deaths and Marriages (Scotland) Act 1965 with regard to the correction of errors in entries shall apply to the Adopted Children Register maintained by the Registrar General for Scotland and to registration therein in like manner as they apply to any register of births and to registration therein.

(9) Schedule 1 to this Act, which, among other things, provides for the registration of adoptions and the amendment of adoption orders, shall have effect.

(10) In this section—

"Board" means a Health and Social Services Board established under Article 16 of the Health and Personal Social Services (Northern Ireland) Order 1972; and

"local authority", in relation to England and Wales, means the council of a county (other than a metropolitan county), a metropolitan district, a London borough or the Common Council of the City of London.

NOTES

[1] As amended by the Children Act 1989 (c. 41), Sched. 10, para. 41. Applied (with modifications) in relation to parental orders by S.I. 1994 No. 2804, *infra*.

[2] Prospectively amended by the Children (Scotland) Act 1995 (c. 36), Sched. 2, para. 22, *infra*.

Revocation of adoptions on legitimation

46.—[1] (1) Where the natural parents of a child, one of whom has adopted him in Scotland, have subsequently married each other, the court by which the adoption order was made may, on the application of any of the parties concerned, revoke that order.

(2) Where a person adopted by his father or mother alone by virtue of a regulated adoption has subsequently become a legitimated person on the marriage of his father and mother, the Court of Session may, upon an application under this subsection by the parties concerned, by order revoke the adoption.

NOTE

[1] As amended by the Law Reform (Parent and Child) (Scotland) Act 1986 (c. 9), Sched. 1, para. 18.

Annulment etc. of overseas adoptions

47.—(1) The Court of Session may, upon an application under this subsection, by order annul a regulated adoption or an adoption effected by a Convention adoption order—

(*a*) on the ground that at the relevant time the adoption was prohibited by a notified provision, if under the internal law then in force in the country of which the adopter was then a national or the adopters were then nationals the adoption could have been impugned on that ground;

(*b*) on the ground that at the relevant time the adoption contravened provisions relating to consents of the internal law relating to adoption of the country of which the adopted person was then a national, if under that law the adoption could then have been impugned on that ground;

(*c*) on any other ground on which the adoption can be impugned under the law for the time being in force in the country in which the adoption was effected.

(2) The Court of Session may, upon an application under this subsection—

(*a*) order that an overseas adoption or a determination shall cease to be valid in Great Britain on the ground that the adoption or determination is contrary to public policy or that the authority which purported to authorise the adoption or make the determination was not competent to entertain the case;

(*b*) decide the extent, if any, to which a determination has been affected by a subsequent determination.

(3) Any court in Great Britain may, in any proceedings in that court, decide that an overseas adoption or a determination shall, for the purposes of those proceedings, be treated as invalid in Great Britain on either of the grounds mentioned in subsection (2).

(4) An order or decision of the High Court on an application under subsection (2) of section 53 of the Adoption Act 1976 shall be recognised and have effect as if it were an order or decision of the Court of Session on an application under subsection (2) of this section.

(5) Except as provided by this section and section 46(2) the validity of an overseas adoption or a determination shall not be impugned in Scotland in proceedings in any court.

Provisions supplementary to ss. 46(2) and 47

48.—(1) Any application for an order under section 46(2) or 47 or a decision under section 47(2)(*b*) shall be made in the prescribed manner and within such period, if any, as may be prescribed.

(2) No application shall be made under section 46(2) or 47(1) in respect of an adoption unless immediately before the application is made the person adopted or the adopter habitually resides in Scotland or, as the case may be, both adopters habitually reside there.

(3) In deciding in pursuance of section 47 whether such an authority as is mentioned in section 53 was competent to entertain a particular case, a court shall be bound by any finding of fact made by the authority and stated by the authority to be so made for the purpose of determining whether the authority was competent to entertain the case.

(4) In section 47—

"determination" means such a determination as is mentioned in section 53;

"notified provision" means a provision specified in an order of the Secretary of State as one in respect of which a notification to or by the Government of the United Kingdom was in force at the relevant time in pursuance of the provisions of the Convention relating to prohibitions contained in the national law of the adopter; and

"relevant time" means the time when the adoption in question purported to take effect under the law of the country in which it purports to have been effected.

PART VI

MISCELLANEOUS AND SUPPLEMENTAL

Adoption of child abroad

[1] **49.**—[2] (1) Where on an application made in relation to a child by a person who is not domiciled in England and Wales or Scotland or Northern Ireland an authorised court is satisfied that he intends to adopt the child under the law of or within the country in which the applicant is domiciled, the court may, subject to the following provisions of this section, make an order vesting in him the parental rights and duties relating to the child.

(2) The provisions of Part II relating to adoption orders, except sections 12(1), 14(2), 15(2), 17 to 21 and 25, shall apply in relation to orders under this section as they apply in relation to adoption orders subject to the modification that in section 13(1) for "nineteen" and "thirteen" there are substituted "thirty-two" and "twenty-six" respectively.

(3) Section 45 and paragraphs 1 and 2(1) and (3) of Schedule 1 shall apply in relation to an order under this section as they apply in relation to an adoption order except that any entry in the register of births or the Adopted Children Register which is required to be marked in consequence of the making of an order under this section shall, in lieu of being marked with the word "Adopted" or "Re-adopted" (with or without the addition of the words "(England)" or "(Northern Ireland)"), be marked with the words "Proposed foreign adoption" or "Proposed foreign re-adoption", as the case may require.

(4) [Repealed by the Children Act 1989 (c. 41), Sched. 15.]

NOTES

[1] As amended by the Children Act 1989 (c. 41), Sched. 10, para. 42.

[2] Prospectively amended by the Children (Scotland) Act 1995 (c. 36), Sched. 2, para. 23, *infra*.

Restriction on removal of children for adoption outside Great Britain

50.—[1] (1) Except under the authority of an order under section 49, or under section 55 of the Adoption Act 1976 or Article 57 of the Adoption (Northern Ireland) Order 1987, it shall not be lawful for any person to take or send a child who is a British subject or a citizen of the Republic of Ireland out of Great Britain to any place outside the United Kingdom, the Channel Islands and the Isle of Man with a view to the adoption of the child by any person not being a parent or guardian or relative of the child; and any person who takes or sends a child out of Great Britain to any place in contravention of this subsection, or makes or takes part in any arrangements for transferring the care and possession of a child to any person for that purpose, shall be guilty of an offence and liable on summary conviction to imprisonment for a term not exceeding three months or to a fine not exceeding level 5 on the standard scale or to both.

(2) In any proceedings under this section, a report by a British consular officer or a deposition made before a British consular officer and authenticated under the signature of that officer shall, upon proof that the officer or the deponent cannot be found in the United Kingdom, be sufficient

[THE NEXT PAGE IS K 203]

evidence of the matters stated therein, and it shall not be necessary to prove the signature or official character of the person who appears to have signed any such report or deposition.

(3) A person shall be deemed to take part in arrangements for transferring the care and possession of a child to a person for the purpose referred to in subsection (1) if—

(*a*) he facilitates the placing of the child in the care and possession of that person; or

(*b*) he initiates or takes part in any negotiations of which the purpose or effect is the conclusion of any agreement or the making of any arrangement therefor, or if he causes another person to do so.

NOTE

[1] As amended by virtue of the Criminal Procedure (Scotland) Act 1975 (c. 21), ss. 289F and 289G and by the Children Act 1989 (c. 41), Sched. 10, para. 43. See the Children (Scotland) Act 1995 (c. 36), s. 86(3), *infra* (prospective).

Prohibition on certain payments

51.—[1] (1) Subject to the provisions of this section, it shall not be lawful to make or give to any person any payment or reward for or in consideration of—

(*a*) the adoption by that person of a child;

(*b*) the grant by that person of any agreement or consent required in connection with the adoption of a child;

(*c*) the transfer by that person of the care and possession of a child with a view to the adoption of the child; or

(*d*) the making by that person of any arrangements for the adoption of a child.

[1,2] (2) Any person who makes or gives, or agrees or offers to make or give, any payment or reward prohibited by this section, or who receives or agrees to receive or attempts to obtain any such payment or reward, shall be guilty of an offence and liable on summary conviction to imprisonment for a term not exceeding three months or to a fine not exceeding level 5 on the standard scale or to both; and the court may order any child in respect of whom the offence was committed to be removed to a place of safety until he can be restored to his parents or guardian or until other arrangements can be made for him.

(3) This section does not apply to any payment made to an adoption agency by a parent or guardian of a child or by a person who adopts or proposes to adopt a child, being a payment in respect of expenses reasonably incurred by the agency in connection with the adoption of the child, or to any payment or reward authorised by the court to which an application for an adoption order in respect of a child is made.

(4) This section does not apply to—

(*a*) any payment made by an adoption agency to a person who has applied or proposes to apply to a court for an adoption order or an order under section 49, being a payment of or towards any legal or medical expenses incurred or to be incurred by that person in connection with the application; or

(*b*) any payment made by an adoption agency to another adoption agency in consideration of the placing of a child in the care and possession of any person with a view to the child's adoption; or

(*c*) any payment made by an adoption agency to a voluntary organisation for the time being approved for the purposes of this paragraph by the Secretary of State as a fee for the services of that organisation in putting that adoption agency into contact with another adoption agency with a view to the making of arrangements between the adoption agencies for the adoption of a child.

[1] (5) If an adoption agency submits to the Secretary of State a scheme for the payment by the agency of allowances to persons who have adopted or

intend to adopt a child where arrangements for the adoption were made, or are to be made, by that agency, and the Secretary of State approves the scheme, this section shall not apply to any payment made in accordance with the scheme.

(6) The Secretary of State, in the case of a scheme approved by him under subsection (5), may at any time—

[3] (*a*) make, or approve the making by the agency of, alterations to the scheme;

(*b*) revoke the scheme.

[3] (7) The Secretary of State shall, within seven years of the date on which section 32 of the Children Act 1975 came into force and, thereafter, every five years, publish a report on the operation of the schemes since that date or since the publication of the last report.

(8) [Repealed by S.I. 1989 No. 194.]

[3] (9) The Secretary of State may by order made by statutory instrument at any time before the said anniversary repeal subsection (8) of this section.

[3] (10) An order under subsection (9) of this section shall not be made unless a report has been published under subsection (7) of this section.

[3] (11) Notwithstanding the expiry of subsection (5) of this section or the revocation of a scheme approved under this section, subsection (1) of this section shall not apply in relation to any payment made, whether before or after the expiry of subsection (5) or the revocation of the scheme, in accordance with a scheme which was approved under this section to a person to whom such payments were made—

(*a*) where the scheme was not revoked, before the expiry of subsection (5), or

(*b*) if the scheme was revoked, before the date of its revocation.

NOTES

[1] Prospectively amended by the Children (Scotland) Act 1995 (c. 36), Sched. 2, para. 24, *infra*.

[2] As amended by virtue of the Criminal Procedure (Scotland) Act 1975 (c. 21), ss. 289F and 289G.

[3] Prospectively repealed by the Children (Scotland) Act 1995 (c. 36), Sched. 2, para. 24, *infra*.

Adoption allowances schemes

51A. [Prospectively inserted by the Children (Scotland) Act 1995 (c. 36), Sched. 2, para. 25, *infra*.]

Transitional provisions as respects adoption allowances

51B. [Prospectively inserted by the Children (Scotland) Act 1995 (c. 36), Sched. 2, para. 35, *infra*.]

Restriction on advertisements

52.—(1) It shall not be lawful for any advertisement to be published indicating—

(*a*) that the parent or guardian of a child desires to cause a child to be adopted; or

(*b*) that a person desires to adopt a child; or

(*c*) that any person (not being an adoption agency) is willing to make arrangements for the adoption of a child.

[1] (2) Any person who causes to be published or knowingly publishes an advertisement in contravention of the provisions of this section shall be guilty of an offence and liable on summary conviction to a fine not exceeding level 5 on the standard scale.

NOTE

[1] As amended by virtue of the Criminal Procedure (Scotland) Act 1975 (c. 21), ss. 289F and 289G.

Effect of determination and orders made in England and Wales and overseas in adoption proceedings

[1] **53.**—(1) Where an authority of a Convention country or any British territory other than the United Kingdom having power under the law of that country or territory—

(*a*) to authorise or review the authorisation of a regulated adoption or a specified order; or

(*b*) to give or review a decision revoking or annulling a regulated adoption, a specified order or a Convention adoption order,

makes a determination in the exercise of that power, then, subject to sections 46(2) and 47 and any subsequent determination having effect under this subsection, the determination shall have effect in Scotland for the purpose of effecting, confirming or terminating the adoption in question or confirming its termination, as the case may be.

(2) Subsections (2) to (4) of section 12 shall apply in relation to an order freeing a child for adoption (other than an order under section 18) as if it were an adoption order; and on the revocation in England and Wales or Northern Ireland of an order freeing a child for adoption subsection (3) of section 20 shall apply as if the order had been revoked under that section.

(3) Sections 12(3) and (4) and 43 apply in relation to a child who is the subject of an order which is similar to an order under section 49 and is made (whether before or after this Act has effect) in England or Wales, Northern Ireland, the Isle of Man or any of the Channel Islands, as they apply in relation to a child who is the subject of an adoption order.

NOTE

[1] As amended by the Children Act 1989 (c. 41), Sched. 10, para. 44.

Evidence of adoption in England, Wales and Northern Ireland

54. Any document which is receivable as evidence of any matter—

(*a*) in England and Wales under section 50(2) of the Adoption Act 1976; or

[1] (*b*) in Northern Ireland under Article 63(1) of the Adoption (Northern Ireland) Order 1987,

shall also be so receivable in Scotland.

NOTE

[1] As amended by the Children Act 1989 (c. 41), Sched. 10, para. 45.

Evidence of agreement and consent

[1] **55.**—(1) Any agreement or consent which is required by this Act to be given to the making of an order or application for an order (other than an order to which section 17(6) applies) may be given in writing, and, if the document signifying the agreement or consent is witnessed in accordance with rules, it shall be sufficient evidence without further proof of the signature of the person by whom it was executed.

(2) A document signifying such agreement or consent which purports to be witnessed in accordance with rules, shall be presumed to be so witnessed, and to have been executed and witnessed on the date and at the place specified in the document, unless the contrary is proved.

NOTE

[1] Applied (with modifications) in relation to parental orders by S.I. 1994 No. 2804, *infra*.

Courts

56.—[1] (1) In this Act, "authorised court", as respects an application for an order relating to a child, shall be construed as follows.

[1] (2) Subject to subsections (4) and (5), if the child is in Scotland when the application is made, the following are authorised courts—

(*a*) the Court of Session;

(*b*) the sheriff court of the sheriffdom within which the child is.

(3) If, in the case of an application for an adoption order or for an order freeing a child for adoption, the child is not in Great Britain when the application is made, the Court of Session is the authorised court.

(4) In the case of an application for a Convention adoption order, paragraph (*b*) of subsection (2) does not apply.

(5) Subsection (2) does not apply in the case of an application under section 29 but for the purposes of such an application the following are authorised courts—

(*a*) if there is pending in respect of the child an application for an adoption order or an order freeing him for adoption, the court in which that application is pending;

(*b*) in any other case—

(i) the Court of Session;

(ii) the sheriff court of the sheriffdom within which the applicant resides.

NOTE

[1] Applied (with modifications) in relation to parental orders by S.I. 1994 No. 2804, *infra*.

Proceedings to be in private

[1] **57.** All proceedings before the court under Part II, section 29 or section 49 shall be heard and determined in private unless the court otherwise directs.

NOTE

[1] Applied (with modifications) in relation to parental orders by S.I. 1994 No. 2804, *infra*.

Curators ad litem **and reporting officers**

[1] **58.**—(1) For the purpose of any application for an adoption order or an order freeing a child for adoption or an order under section 20 or 49, rules shall provide for the appointment, in such cases as are prescribed—

(*a*) of a person to act as curator *ad litem* of the child upon the hearing of the application, with the duty of safeguarding the interests of the child in the prescribed manner;

(*b*) of a person to act as reporting officer for the purpose of witnessing agreements to adoption and performing such other duties as the rules may prescribe.

(2) A person who is employed—

(*a*) in the case of an application for an adoption order, by the adoption agency by whom the child was placed; or

(*b*) in the case of an application for an order freeing a child for adoption, by the adoption agency by whom the application was made; or

[2] (*c*) in the case of an application under section 20, by the adoption agency with the parental rights and duties relating to the child,

shall not be appointed to act as curator *ad litem* or reporting officer for the purposes of the application but, subject to that, the same person may if the court thinks fit be both curator *ad litem* and reporting officer.

(3) Rules may provide for the reporting officer to be appointed before the application is made.

NOTES

[1] Applied (with modifications) in relation to parental orders by S.I. 1994 No. 2804, *infra*.

[2] Prospectively amended by the Children (Scotland) Act 1995 (c. 36), Sched. 2, para. 26, *infra*.

Rules of procedure

[1] **59.**—(1) Subject to subsection (4), provision shall be made by act of sederunt with regard to any matter to be prescribed under this Act and generally with regard to all matters of procedure and incidental matters arising out of this Act and for carrying this Act into effect.

(2) In the case of—

(*a*) an application for an adoption order in relation to a child who is not free for adoption;

(*b*) an application for an order freeing a child for adoption,

rules shall require every person who can be found and whose agreement or consent to the making of the order is required to be given or dispensed with under this Act to be notified of a date and place where he may be heard on the application and of the fact that, unless he wishes or the court requires, he need not attend.

(3) In the case of an application under section 49, rules shall require every person who can be found, and whose agreement to the making of the order would be required if the application were for an adoption order (other than a Convention adoption order), to be notified as aforesaid.

[2] (4) This section does not apply to sections 9, 10, 11 and 32 to 37.

NOTES

[1] Applied (with modifications) in relation to parental orders by S.I. 1994 No. 2804, *infra*.

[2] Prospectively amended by the Children (Scotland) Act 1995 (c. 36), Sched. 2, para. 27, *infra*.

Orders, rules and regulations

[1] **60.**—(1) Any power to make orders or regulations conferred by this Act on the Secretary of State or the Registrar General for Scotland shall be exercisable by statutory instrument.

(2) A statutory instrument containing regulations made under any provision of this Act, except section 3(1), shall be subject to annulment in pursuance of a resolution of either House of Parliament.

[2] (3) An order under section 28(10) or 51(9) shall not be made unless a draft of the order has been approved by resolution of each House of Parliament.

(4) An order made under any provision of this Act may be revoked or varied by a subsequent order under that provision.

(5) Any order, rule or regulation made under this Act may make different provision for different circumstances and may contain such incidental and transitional provisions as the authority making the order or regulation considers expedient.

(6) The Registrar General for Scotland shall not make regulations under paragraph 1(1) of Schedule 1 except with the approval of the Secretary of State.

(7) The Statutory Instruments Act 1946 shall apply to a statutory instrument containing regulations made for the purposes of this Act by the Registrar General for Scotland as if the regulations had been made by a Minister of the Crown.

NOTES

[1] Applied (with modifications) in relation to parental orders by S.I. 1994 No. 2804, *infra*.

[2] Prospectively amended by the Children (Scotland) Act 1995 (c. 36), Sched. 2, para. 28, *infra*.

Offences by bodies corporate

61. Where an offence under this Act committed by a body corporate is proved to have been committed with the consent or connivance of or to be attributable to any neglect on the part of, any director, manager, member of the committee, secretary or other officer of the body, he as well as the body shall be deemed to be guilty of that offence and shall be liable to be proceeded against and punished accordingly.

Service of notices etc.

62. Any notice or information required to be given under this Act may be given by post.

Nationality

63.—(1) If the Secretary of State by order declares that a description of persons specified in the order has, in pursuance of the Convention, been notified to the Government of the United Kingdom as the description of persons who are deemed to possess the nationality of a particular Convention country, persons of that description shall, subject to the following provisions of this section, be treated for the purposes of this Act as nationals of that country.

(2) Subject to section 48(3) and subsection (3) of this section, where it appears to the court in any proceedings under this Act, or to any court by which a decision in pursuance of section 47(3) falls to be given, that a person is or was at a particular time a national of two or more countries, then—

(*a*) if it appears to the said court that he is or was then a United Kingdom national, he shall be treated for the purposes of those proceedings or that decision as if he were or had then been a United Kingdom national only;

(*b*) if, in a case not falling within paragraph (*a*), it appears to the said court that one only of those countries is or was then a Convention country, he shall be treated for those purposes as if he were or had then been a national of that country only;

(*c*) if, in a case not falling within paragraph (*a*), it appears to the said court that two or more of those countries are or were then Convention countries, he shall be treated for those purposes as if he were or had then been a national of such one only of those Convention countries as the said court considers is the country with which he is or was then most closely connected;

(*d*) in any other case, he shall be treated for those purposes as if he were or had then been a national of such one only of those countries as the said court considers is the country with which he is or was then most closely connected.

(3) A court in which proceedings are brought in pursuance of section 17, 46(2) or 47 shall be entitled to disregard the provisions of subsection (2) in so far as it appears to that court appropriate to do so for the purposes of those proceedings; but nothing in this subsection shall be construed as prejudicing the provisions of section 48(3).

(4) Where, after such inquiries as the court in question considers appropriate, it appears to the court in any proceedings under this Act, or to any court by which such a decision as aforesaid falls to be given, that a person has no nationality or no ascertainable nationality, he shall be treated for the purposes of those proceedings or that decision as a national of the country in which he resides or, where that country is one of two or more countries having the same law of nationality, as a national of those countries.

Internal law of a country

64.—(1) In this Act "internal law" in relation to any country means the law applicable in a case where no question arises as to the law in force in any other country.

(2) In any case where the internal law of a country falls to be ascertained for the purposes of this Act by any court and there are in force in that country two or more systems of internal law, the relevant system shall be ascertained in accordance with any rule in force throughout that country indicating which of the systems is relevant in the case in question or, if there is no such rule, shall be the system appearing to that court to be most closely connected with the case.

Interpretation

[0] **65.**—[1] (1) In this Act, unless the context otherwise requires—

"adoption agency" in sections 11, 13, 18 to 23 and 27 includes an adoption agency within the meaning of section 1 of the Adoption Act

1976 (adoption agencies in England and Wales) and an adoption agency within the meaning of Article 3 of the Adoption (Northern Ireland) Order 1987 (adoption agencies in Northern Ireland);

"adoption order"—

(*a*) means an order under section 12(1); and

(*b*) in sections 12(3) and (4), 18 to 20, 27, 28 and 30 to 32 and in the definition of "British adoption order" in this subsection includes an order under section 12 of the Adoption Act 1976 and Article 12 of the Adoption (Northern Ireland) Order 1987 (adoption orders in England and Wales and Northern Ireland respectively); and

(*c*) in sections 27, 28 and 30 to 32 includes an order under section 49, section 55 of the Adoption Act 1976 and Article 57 of the Adoption (Northern Ireland) Order 1987 (orders in relation to children being adopted abroad);

[1a] "adoption society" means a body of persons whose functions consist of or include the making of arrangements for the adoption of children;

"approved adoption society" means an adoption society approved under Part I and, in sections 30 and 45, includes an adoption society approved under Part I of the Adoption Act 1976;

"authorised court" shall be construed in accordance with section 56;

"body of persons" means any body of persons, whether incorporated or unincorporated;

"British adoption order" means—

(*a*) an adoption order as defined in this subsection; and

(*b*) an order under any provision for the adoption of a child effected under the law of any British territory outside the United Kingdom;

"British territory" means, for the purposes of any provision of this Act, any of the following countries, that is to say, Great Britain, Northern Ireland, the Channel Islands, the Isle of Man and a colony, being a country designated for the purposes of that provision by order of the Secretary of State or, if no country is so designated, any of those countries;

"child", except where used to express a relationship, means a person who has not attained the age of eighteen years;

"the Convention" means the Convention relating to the adoption of children concluded at The Hague on 15th November 1965 and signed on behalf of the United Kingdom on that date;

"Convention adoption order" means an adoption order made in accordance with section 17(1);

"Convention country" means any country outside British territory, being a country for the time being designated by an order of the Secretary of State as a country in which, in his opinion, the Convention is in force;

"England" includes Wales;

"guardian" means—

[2] (*a*) a person appointed by deed or will or by a court of competent jurisdiction to be the guardian of the child, and

[3] (*b*) in the case of a child whose father is not married to the mother, includes the father where he has, in relation to the child, guardianship, custody, access or any other parental right by virtue of an order by a court of competent jurisdiction;

"internal law" has the meaning assigned by section 64;

[3a] "local authority" means a regional or islands council and, in sections 13, 22, 28, 30, 31, 35(1) and 45, includes the council of a county (other than a metropolitan county), a metropolitan district, a London borough or the Common Council of the City of London;

"notice" means a notice in writing;

"order freeing a child for adoption" means an order under section 18 and, in sections 27(2) and 53 includes an order under—

(*a*) section 18 of the Adoption Act 1976; and

(*b*) Article 17 or 18 of the Adoption (Northern Ireland) Order 1987;

"overseas adoption" has the meaning assigned by subsection (2);

"place of safety" means any residential or other establishment provided by a local authority, a police station, or any hospital, surgery or other suitable place the occupier of which is willing temporarily to receive a child;

"prescribed" means prescribed by act of sederunt;

"Registrar General for Scotland" means the Registrar General of Births, Deaths and Marriages for Scotland;

"regulated adoption" means an overseas adoption of a description designated by an order under subsection (2) as that of an adoption regulated by the Convention;

"relative" in relation to a child means a grandparent, brother, sister, uncle or aunt, whether of the full blood or half-blood or by affinity and includes, where the child is illegitimate, the father of the child and any person who would be a relative within the meaning of this definition if the child were the legitimate child of his mother and father;

"rules" means rules made by act of sederunt;

"specified order" means any provision for the adoption of a child effected under enactments similar to section 12(1) and 17 in force in Northern Ireland or any British territory outside the United Kingdom;

"United Kingdom national" means, for the purposes of any provision of this Act, a citizen of the United Kingdom and Colonies satisfying such conditions, if any, as the Secretary of State may by order specify for the purposes of that provision;

"voluntary organisation" means a body, other than a public or local authority, the activities of which are not carried on for profit.

[3b] (2) In this Act "overseas adoption" means an adoption of such a description as the Secretary of State may by order specify, being a description of adoptions of children appearing to him to be effected under the law of any country outside Great Britain; and an order under this subsection may contain provision as to the manner in which evidence of an overseas adoption may be given.

[4] (3) For the purposes of this Act, a person shall be deemed to make arrangements for the adoption of a child if he enters into or makes any agreement or arrangement for, or for facilitating the adoption of the child by any other person, whether the adoption is effected, or is intended to be effected, in Great Britain or elsewhere, or if he initiates or takes part in any negotiations of which the purpose or effect is the conclusion of any agreement or the making of any arrangement therefor, or if he causes another person to do so, but the making, under section 44 of the Social Work (Scotland) Act 1968, by a children's hearing of a supervision requirement which, in respect that it provides as to where he is to reside, facilitates his being placed for adoption by an adoption agency, shall not constitute the making of such arrangements.

(4) Except so far as the context otherwise requires, any reference in this Act to an enactment shall be construed as a reference to that enactment as amended by or under any other enactment, including this Act.

(5) In this Act, except where otherwise indicated—

(*a*) a reference to a numbered Part, section or Schedule is a reference to the Part or section of, or the Schedule to, this Act so numbered, and

(*b*) a reference in a section to a numbered subsection is a reference to the subsection of that section so numbered, and (*c*) a reference in a section, subsection or Schedule to a numbered paragraph is a reference to the paragraph of that section, subsection or Schedule so numbered.

(6) [Prospectively added by the Children (Scotland) Act 1995 (c. 36), Sched. 2, para. 29(*c*), *infra*.

NOTES

[0] Applied (with modifications) in relation to parental orders by S.I. 1994 No. 2804, *infra*.

[1] As amended by the Health and Social Services and Social Security Adjudications Act 1983 (c. 41), Sched. 2, para. 45, and the Children Act 1989 (c. 41), Sched. 10, para. 46 and Sched. 15. Prospectively amended by the Children (Scotland) Act 1995 (c. 36), Sched. 2, para. 29(*a*), *infra*.

[1a] Prospectively amended by the Children (Scotland) Act 1995 (c. 36), s. 94(3), *infra*.

[2] As amended by the Law Reform (Parent and Child) (Scotland) Act 1986 (c. 9), Sched. 2.

[3] As amended by the Law Reform (Parent and Child) (Scotland) Act 1986 (c. 9), Sched. 1, para. 18, and the Age of Legal Capacity (Scotland) Act 1991 (c. 50), Sched. 1, para. 36.

[3a] Prospective amendment in the Local Government etc. (Scotland) Act 1994 (c. 39), Sched. 13, para. 111(3), *infra*.

[3b] See S.I. 1995 No. 1614 (People's Republic of China) (S.), amending S.I. 1973 No. 19.

[4] As amended by the Law Reform (Miscellaneous Provisions) (Scotland) Act 1985 (c. 73), s. 27. Prospectively amended by the Children (Scotland) Act 1995 (c. 36), Sched. 2, para. 29(*b*), *infra*.

Transitional provisions, amendments and repeals

66.—(1) The transitional provisions contained in Schedule 2 shall have effect.

(2) The enactments specified in Schedule 3 shall have effect subject to the amendments specified in that Schedule, being amendments consequential upon the provisions of this Act.

(3) The enactments specified in Schedule 4 are hereby repealed to the extent specified in column 3 of that Schedule.

Short title, commencement and extent

67.—(1) This Act may be cited as the Adoption (Scotland) Act 1978.

(2) This Act shall come into force on such date as the Secretary of State may by order[1] appoint and different dates may be appointed for different provisions.

(3) Until the date appointed under subsection (2) for sections 3, 4, 5 and 8, in this Act and in the Adoption Act 1958 "adoption agency" means a local authority or a registered adoption society within the meaning of the said Act of 1958.

(4) This Act shall extend to Scotland only.

NOTE

[1] S.I. 1984 No. 1050 brought the whole Act except ss. 1 and 2 into force on 1st September 1984, and ss. 1 and 2 into force on 1st February 1985. See also the Health and Social Services and Social Security Adjudications Act 1983 (c. 41), Sched. 2, para. 1.

SCHEDULES

Section 45

[1] SCHEDULE 1

Registration of Adoptions

NOTE

[1] Applied (with modifications) in relation to parental orders by S.I. 1994 No. 2804, *infra*. For form of entry in the Parental Order Register see S.I. 1994 No. 3147.

Registration of adoption orders

1.—(1) Every adoption order shall contain a direction to the Registrar General for Scotland to make in the Adopted Children Register maintained by him an entry recording the adoption in such form as the Registrar General for Scotland may by regulations specify.

(2) The direction contained in a Convention adoption order in pursuance of this paragraph shall include an instruction that the entry made in that register in consequence of the order shall be marked with the words "Convention order".

(3) For the purposes of compliance with the requirements of subparagraph (1)—

(*a*) where the precise date of the child's birth is not proved to the satisfaction of the

[THE NEXT PAGE IS K 211]

court, the court shall determine the probable date of his birth and the date so determined shall be specified in the order as the date of his birth;

(*b*) where the country of birth of the child is not proved to the satisfaction of the court, then, if it appears probable that the child was born within the United Kingdom, the Channel Islands or the Isle of Man, he shall be treated as having been born in Scotland, and in any other case the particulars of the country of birth may be omitted from the order and from the entry in the Adopted Children Register;

and the names to be specified in the order as the name and surname of the child shall be the name or names and surname stated in that behalf in the application for the adoption order, or, if no name or surname is so stated, the original name or names of the child and the surname of the applicant.

(4) There shall be produced with every application for an adoption order in respect of a child whose birth has been registered under the Registration of Births, Deaths and Marriages (Scotland) Act 1965 or under any enactment repealed by that Act an extract of the entry of the birth.

(5) Where on an application to a court for an adoption order in respect of a child (not being a child who has previously been the subject of an adoption order made by a court in Scotland under this Act or any enactment at the time in force) there is proved to the satisfaction of the court the identity of the child with a child to whom an entry in the register of births relates, any adoption order made in pursuance of the application shall contain a direction to the Registrar General for Scotland to cause the entry in that register to be marked with the word " Adopted ".

(6) Where an adoption order is made in respect of a child who has previously been the subject of an adoption order made by a court in Scotland under this Act or any enactment at the time in force, the order shall contain a direction to the Registrar General for Scotland to cause the previous entry in the Adopted Children Register to be marked with the word " Re-adopted ".

(7) Where an adoption order is made, the clerk of the court which made the order shall cause the order to be communicated to the Registrar General for Scotland and upon receipt of the communication the Registrar General for Scotland shall cause compliance to be made with the directions contained in the order.

Registration of adoptions in England, Northern Ireland, the Isle of Man and the Channel Islands

2.—(1) Where the Registrar General for Scotland is notified by the Registrar General that an adoption order has been made by a court in England in respect of a child to whom an entry in the register of births or the Adopted Children Register relates, the Registrar General for Scotland shall cause the entry to be marked " Adopted (England) " or, as the case may be, " Re-adopted (England) ".

(2) Where the Registrar General for Scotland is notified by the authority maintaining a register of adoptions in Northern Ireland, the Isle of Man or any of the Channel Islands that an order has been made in that country authorising the adoption of a child to whom an entry in the register of births or the Adopted Children Register relates, he shall cause the entry to be marked " Adopted " or " Re-adopted ", as the case may be, followed by the name in brackets of the country in which the order was made.

(3) Where, after an entry has been marked under the foregoing provisions of this paragraph, the Registrar General for Scotland is notified as aforesaid that the order has been quashed, that an appeal against the order has been allowed or that the order has been revoked, he shall cause the marking to be cancelled; and an extract of an entry in any register, being an entry the marking of which is cancelled under this sub-paragraph, shall be deemed to be accurate if and only if both the marking and the cancellation are omitted therefrom.

(4) The foregoing provisions of this paragraph shall apply in relation to orders corresponding to orders under section 49 as they apply in relation to orders authorising the adoption of a child; but any marking of an entry required by virtue of this sub-paragraph shall consist of the words " proposed foreign adoption " or, as the case may require, " proposed foreign re-adoption " followed by the name in brackets of the country in which the order was made.

Registration of overseas adoptions

3. If the Registrar General for Scotland is satisfied that an entry in the register of births relates to a person adopted under an overseas adoption and that he has sufficient particulars relating to that person to enable an entry, in the form specified for the purposes of this paragraph in regulations made under paragraph 1 (1), to be made in the Adopted Children Register in respect of that person, he shall—

(*a*) make such an entry in the Adopted Children Register; and

(*b*) if there is a previous entry in respect of that person in that register, mark the entry (or if there is more than one such entry the last of them) with the word " Re-adopted " followed by the name in brackets of the country in which the adoption was effected; and

(c) unless the entry in the register of births is already marked with the word " Adopted " (whether or not followed by other words), mark the entry with that word followed by the name in brackets of the country aforesaid.

Amendment of orders and rectification of registers

4.—(1) The court by which an adoption order has been made may, on the application of the adopter or of the adopted person, amend the order by the correction of any error in the particulars contained therein, and may—

(a) if satisfied on the application of the adopter or the adopted person that within one year beginning with the date of the order any new name has been given to the adopted person (whether in baptism or otherwise), or taken by him, either in lieu of or in addition to a name specified in the particulars required to be entered in the Adopted Children Register in pursuance of the order, amend the order by substituting or adding that name in those particulars, as the case may require;

(b) if satisfied on the application of any person concerned that a direction for the marking of an entry in the register of births or the Adopted Children Register included in the order in pursuance of sub-paragraph (5) or (6) of paragraph 1 was wrongly so included, revoke that direction.

(2) Where an adoption order is amended or a direction revoked under subparagraph (1), the clerk of the court shall cause the amendment to be communicated in the prescribed manner to the Registrar General for Scotland who shall as the case may require—

(a) cause the entry in the Adopted Children Register to be amended accordingly; or

(b) cause the marking of the entry in the register of births or the Adopted Children Register to be cancelled.

(3) Where an adoption order is quashed or an appeal against an adoption order allowed by any court, the court shall give directions to the Registrar General for Scotland to cancel any entry in the Adopted Children Register, and any marking of an entry in that Register, or the register of births as the case may be, which was effected in pursuance of the order.

(4) If the Registrar General for Scotland is satisfied—

(a) that a Convention adoption order or an overseas adoption has ceased to have effect, whether on annulment or otherwise; or

(b) that any entry or mark was erroneously made in pursuance of paragraph 3 in any register mentioned in that paragraph,

he may cause such alterations to be made in any such register as he considers are required in consequence of the cesser or to correct the error; and where an entry in such a register is amended in pursuance of this sub-paragraph, an extract of the entry shall be deemed to be accurate if and only if it shows the entry as amended but without indicating that it has been amended.

Marking of entries on re-registration of birth

5. Without prejudice to any other provision of this Act where, after an entry in the register of births has been marked in accordance with paragraph 2 or 3, the birth is re-registered under section 20 (1) of the Registration of Births, Deaths and Marriages (Scotland) Act 1965 (re-registration of birth in certain cases), the entry made on re-registration shall be marked in the like manner.

Cancellations in registers on legitimation

6. Where an adoption order is revoked under section 46 (1) the clerk of the court shall cause the revocation to be communicated in the prescribed manner to the Registrar General for Scotland who shall cause to be cancelled—

(a) the entry in the Adopted Children Register relating to the adopted person; and

(b) the marking with the word " Adopted " (or, as the case may be, with that word and the word " (England) ") or any entry relating to him in the register of births;

and an extract of an entry in any register, being an entry the marking of which is cancelled under this paragraph shall be deemed to be accurate if and only if both the marking and the cancellation are omitted therefrom.

7. In this Schedule, " Registrar General " means the Registrar General for England and Wales.

Section 66

SCHEDULE 2

Transitional Provisions and Savings

General

1. In so far as anything done under an enactment repealed by this Act could have been done under a corresponding provision of this Act it shall not be invalidated by the repeal but shall have effect as if done under that provision.

2. Where any period of time specified in an enactment repealed by this Act is current at the commencement of this Act, this Act shall have effect as if the corresponding provision thereof had been in force when that period began to run.

3. Nothing in this Act shall affect the enactments repealed by this Act in their operation in relation to offences committed before the commencement of this Act.

4. Any reference in any enactment or document, whether express or implied, to an enactment repealed by this Act shall, unless the context otherwise requires, be construed as a reference to the corresponding enactment in this Act.

Existing adoption orders

5.—(1) Without prejudice to paragraph 1, an adoption order made under an enactment at any time before this Act comes into force shall not cease to have effect by virtue only of a repeal effected by this Act.

(2) Paragraph 4(1) and (2) of Schedule 1 shall apply in relation to an adoption order made before this Act came into force as if the order had been made under section 12, but as if, in sub-paragraph (1)(*b*) of the said paragraph 4, there were substituted for the reference to paragraph 1(5) and (6) a reference—

(*a*) in the case of an order under the Adoption Act 1950, to section 20(4) and (5) of that Act,

(*b*) in the case of an order under the Adoption Act 1958, to section 23(4) and (5) of that Act.

(3) The power of the court under the said paragraph 4(1) to amend an order includes power in relation to an order made before 1st April 1959, to make on the application of the adopter or adopted person any such amendment of the particulars contained in the order as appears to be required to bring the order into the form in which it would have been made if paragraph 1 of Schedule 1 had applied to the order.

(4) Section 46(1) and paragraph 6 of Schedule 1 shall apply in relation to an adoption order made under an enactment at any time before this Act came into force as they apply in relation to an adoption order made under this Act.

Payments relating to adoptions

6. Section 51(8), (9) and (10) shall not have effect if, immediately before section 51 comes into force, there is in force in Scotland an order under section 50(8) of the Adoption Act 1958.

Registers of adoptions

7. Any register or index to a register kept under the Adoption Act 1958, or any register or index deemed to be part of such a register, shall be deemed to be part of the register or index kept under section 45.

Commencement of Act

8. An order under section 67(2) may make such transitional provision as appears to the Secretary of State to be necessary or expedient in connection with the provisions thereby brought into force, including such adaptations of those provisions or any provision of this Act then in force or any provision of the Adoption Act 1958 or the Children Act 1975 as appear to him to be necessary or expedient in consequence of the partial operation of this Act.

Section 66

SCHEDULE 3

CONSEQUENTIAL AMENDMENTS

[Amendments to Acts printed in *The Parliament House Book* have been given effect in the prints of those Acts.]

Section 66

SCHEDULE 4

REPEALS

[Repeals affecting Acts printed or formerly printed in *The Parliament House Book* have been given effect.]

Divorce Jurisdiction, Court Fees and Legal Aid (Scotland) Act 1983

(1983 c.12)

An Act to extend the jurisdiction of sheriffs in Scotland in relation to actions for divorce; to make provision as regards the sufficiency of evidence in certain actions for divorce in Scotland; to make new provision in Scotland as to the fees and outlays of counsel and solicitors in relation both to legal aid, and to the giving of legal advice and assistance under the Legal Advice and Assistance Act 1972; to make new provision in relation to the regulation of fees payable in the Scottish courts; and for connected purposes. [11th April 1983]

PART I

Jurisdiction and Evidence in Divorce Actions

Sheriffs to have jurisdiction in respect of actions for divorce

1. In section 5 of the Sheriff Courts (Scotland) Act 1907 (which relates to the jurisdiction of sheriffs), after paragraph (2A) there shall be inserted—

"(2B) Actions for divorce".

Rule requiring corroboration not to apply in certain undefended actions for divorce

2. [Repealed by the Civil Evidence (Scotland) Act 1988, Sched.]

[THE NEXT PAGE IS K 217]

Part II

Fees and Outlays in Relation to Legal Aid

3. [New s.14A of the Legal Aid (Scotland) Act 1967 is shown in the print of that Act. Section 3 was repealed by the Legal Aid (Scotland) Act 1986, Sched. 5, with saving: see note on p. G2. See now s. 33 of the 1986 Act: Division G, *supra*.]

Part III

Court Fees

4. [Substituted s.2 of the Courts of Law Fees (Scotland) Act 1895 is shown in the print of that Act.]

Part IV

Supplemental

. . . .

Minor and consequential amendments and repeals

6.—(1) The enactments specified in Schedule 1 to this Act shall have effect subject to the amendments specified in that Schedule, being minor amendments and amendments consequential upon the provisions of this Act.

(2) The enactments specified in Schedule 2 to this Act are repealed to the extent specified in the third column of that Schedule.

Citation, commencement and extent

7.—(1) This Act may be cited as the Divorce Jurisdiction, Court Fees and Legal Aid (Scotland) Act 1983.

(2) The following provisions of this Act, that is to say, section 2, this section, and paragraph 2 of Schedule 1 (together with so much of section 6(1) above as relates to that paragraph) shall come into force at the end of the period of two months beginning with the day on which it is passed.

[1] (3) The remaining provisions of this Act shall come into force on such day as the Secretary of State may by order made by statutory instrument appoint and different days may be appointed for different provisions or for different purposes of the same provision.

(4) This Act shall extend to Scotland only.

NOTE

[1] S.I. 1984 No. 253 brought ss.3 (part), 4, 5, 6 (part), Scheds. 1 (part) and 2 (part) into force on 1st April 1984 and the remainder of the Act into force on 1st May 1984.

SCHEDULES

Section 6(1)

[1] SCHEDULE 1

Minor and Consequential Amendments

NOTE

[1] Amendments to Acts reprinted in *The Parliament House Book* are given effect in the prints of those Acts.

Section 9(2)

[1] SCHEDULE 2

Enactments Repealed

NOTE

[1] Repeals to Acts reprinted in *The Parliament House Book* are given effect in the prints of those Acts.

Law Reform (Husband and Wife) (Scotland) Act 1984

(1984 c. 15)

An Act to amend the law relating to husband and wife and breach of promise of marriage and for connected purposes.

[24th May 1984]

Abolition of actions of breach of promise of marriage, adherence and enticement

Promise of marriage not an enforceable obligation

1.—(1) No promise of marriage or agreement between two persons to marry one another shall have effect under the law of Scotland to create any rights or obligations; and no action for breach of any such promise or agreement may be brought in any court in Scotland, whatever the law applicable to the promise or agreement.

(2) This section shall have effect in relation to any promise made or agreement entered into before it comes into force, but shall not affect any action commenced before it comes into force.

Actions of adherence and enticement abolished

2.—(1) No spouse shall be entitled to apply for a decree from any court in Scotland ordaining the other spouse to adhere.

(2) No person shall be liable in delict to any person by reason only of having induced the spouse of that person to leave or remain apart from that person.

(3) This section shall not affect any action commenced before this Act comes into force.

Abolition of miscellaneous rules relating to husband and wife

Curatory after marriage

3.—(1) No marriage person shall, by reason only of minority, be subject to the curatory of his parent or of any person appointed by his parent.

[1] (2) No wife shall, by reason only of minority, be subject to the curatory of her husband.

(3) Section 2 of the Married Women's Property (Scotland) Act 1920 (husband to be curator to his wife during her minority) is repealed.

NOTE

[1] Prospectively repealed by the Children (Scotland) Act 1995 (c. 36), Sched. 5, *infra*.

Abolition of husband's right to choose matrimonial home

4. Any rule of law entitling the husband, as between husband and wife, to determine where the matrimonial home is to be, shall cease to have effect.

Abolition of certain rules relating to ante-nuptial marriage contracts

5.—(1) In relation to an ante-nuptial contract of marriage entered into after this Act comes into force—

(*a*) any rule of law enabling a woman to create an alimentary right in her own favour in respect of any property provided by her shall cease to have effect;

(*b*) any rule of law whereby the marriage is onerous consideration for any provision of the contract, shallcease to have effect.

(2) Nothing in paragraph (*b*) of subsection (1) above shall affect the operation of any enactment relating to gifts in consideration of marriage.

Abolition of husband's remaining liability for wife's debts incurred before marriage

6.—(1) A husband shall not be liable, by reason only of being her husband, for any debts incurred by his wife before marriage.

(2) Subsection (1) above shall have effect in relation to any such debts, whether incurred before or after this Act comes into force.

(3) Section 4 of the Married Women's Property (Scotland) Act 1877 (liability of husband for wife's ante-nuptial debts limited to amount of property received through her) is repealed.

Abolition of Praepositura

7.—(1) For the purpose of determining a husband's liability for any obligation incurred by his wife after this Act comes into force, a married woman shall not be presumed as a matter of law to have been placed by her husband in charge of his domestic affairs, and any rule of law to the contrary shall cease to have effect.

(2) No warrant of inhibition or inhibition in whatever form may be granted at the instance of a husband for the purpose of cancelling his wife's authority to incur any obligation on his behalf.

(3) No such inhibition granted before the date this Act comes into force shall be registered on or after that date, and any such inhibition registered before that date shall be treated as discharged on that date.

Abolition of husband's liability for wife's judicial expenses when neither a party nor dominus litis

8. Any rule of law whereby a husband—

(*a*) who is not a party to an action between his wife and a third party, and

(*b*) who is not, in relation to that action, *dominus litis*,

may nevertheless be found liable in the expense of that action, shall cease to have effect.

General

Consequential amendments and repeals

9.—(1) The enactments specified in Schedule 1 shall have effect subject to the amendments specified in that Schedule, being amendments consequential to the provisions of this Act.

(2) The enactments specified in Schedule 2 are repealed to the extent specified in the third column of that Schedule.

Citation etc.

10.—(1) This Act may be cited as the Law Reform (Husband and Wife) (Scotland) Act 1984.

(2) This Act shall come into force at the end of the period of two months beginning with the day on which it is passed.

(3) This Act extends to Scotland only.

SCHEDULES

Section 9(1)

[1] SCHEDULE 1

ENACTMENTS AMENDED

NOTE
[1] Amendments to Acts reprinted in *The Parliament House Book* are given effect in the prints of those Acts.

Section 9(2)

[1] SCHEDULE 2

ENACTMENTS REPEALED

NOTE
[1] Repeals to Acts reprinted in *The Parliament House Book* are given effect in the prints of those Acts.

Child Abduction Act 1984

(1984 c. 37)

An Act to amend the criminal law relating to the abduction of children. [12th July 1984]

. . . . . .

PART II

OFFENCE UNDER LAW OF SCOTLAND

Offence in Scotland of parent, etc. taking or sending child out of United Kingdom

6.—(1) Subject to subsections (4) and (5) below, a person connected with a child under the age of 16 years commits an offence if he takes or sends the child out of the United Kingdom—

(*a*) without the appropriate consent if there is in respect of the child—

[1] (i) an order of a court in the United Kingdom awarding custody of the child to any person; or

(ii) an order of a court in England, Wales or Northern Ireland making the child a ward of court;

(*b*) if there is in respect of the child an order of a court in the United Kingdom prohibiting the removal of the child from the United Kingdom or any part of it.

(2) A person is connected with a child for the purposes of this section if—

(*a*) he is a parent or guardian of the child; or

[1] (*b*) there is in force an order of a court in the United Kingdom awarding custody of the child to him (whether solely or jointly with any other person); or

[2] (*c*) in the case of a child whose parents are not and have never been married to one another, there are reasonable grounds for believing that he is the father of the child.

(3) In this section, the "appropriate consent" means—

(*a*) in relation to a child to whom subsection (1)(*a*)(i) above applies—

(i) the consent of each person

(*a*) who is a parent or guardian of the child; or

[1] (*b*) to whom custody of the child has been awarded (whether solely or jointly with any other person) by an order of a court in the United Kingdom; or

(ii) the leave of that court;

(*b*) in relation to a child to whom subsection (1)(*a*)(ii) above applies, the leave of the court which made the child a ward of court;

Provided that, in relation to a child to whom more than one order referred to in subsection (1)(*a*) above applies, the appropriate consent may be that of any court which has granted an order as referred to in the said subsection (1)(*a*); and where one of these orders is an order referred to in the said subsection (1)(*a*)(ii) no other person as referred to in paragraph (*a*)(i) above shall be entitled to give the appropriate consent.

(4) In relation to a child to whom subsection (1)(*a*)(i) above applies, a person does not commit an offence by doing anything without the appropriate consent if—

(*a*) he does it in the belief that each person referred to in subsection (3)(*a*)(i) above—

(i) has consented; or

(ii) would consent if he was aware of all the relevant circumstances; or

(*b*) he has taken all reasonable steps to communicate with such other person but has been unable to communicate with him.

(5) In proceedings against any person for an offence under this section it shall be a defence for that person to show that at the time of the alleged offence he had no reason to believe that there was in existence an order referred to in subsection (1) above.

(6) For the purposes of this section—

(*a*) a person shall be regarded as taking a child if he causes or induces the child to accompany him or any other person, or causes the child to be taken; and

(*b*) a person shall be regarded as sending a child if he causes the child to be sent.

[2] (7) In this section "guardian" means a person appointed by deed or will or by order of a court of competent jurisdiction to be the guardian of a child.

NOTES

[1] Prospectively amended by the Children (Scotland) Act 1995 (c. 36), Sched. 4, para. 34, *infra*.

[2] As amended by the Law Reform (Parent and Child) (Scotland) Act 1986 (c. 9), Sched. 1, para. 20 and the Age of Legal Capacity (Scotland) Act 1991 (c. 50), Sched. 2.

Power of arrest

7. A constable may arrest without warrant any person whom he reasonably suspects of committing or having committed an offence under this Part of this Act.

Penalties and prosecutions

8. A person guilty of an offence under this Part of this Act shall be liable—

[1] (*a*) on summary conviction, to imprisonment for a term not exceeding three months or to a fine not exceeding the statutory maximum, or both; or

(*b*) on conviction on indictment, to imprisonment for a term not exceeding two years or to a fine, or both.

NOTE

[1] As amended by the Statute Law (Repeals) Act 1993 (c. 50), Sched. 1, Pt. XIV.

Proof and admissibility of certain documents

9.—(1) For the purposes of this Part of this Act, a document duly authenticated which purports to be—

(*a*) an order or other document issued by a court of the United Kingdom (other than a Scottish court) shall be sufficient evidence of any matter to which it relates;

(*b*) a copy of such an order or other document shall be deemed without further proof to be a true copy unless the contrary is shown, and shall be sufficient evidence of any matter to which it relates.

[THE NEXT PAGE IS K 223]

(2) A document is duly authenticated for the purposes of—
(*a*) subsection (1)(*a*) above if it purports to bear the seal of that court;
(*b*) subsection (1)(*b*) above if it purports to be certified by any person in his capacity as a judge, magistrate or officer of that court to be a true copy.

Evidence

10. In any proceedings in relation to an offence under this Part of this Act it shall be presumed, unless the contrary is shown, that the child named in the order referred to in section 6(1) above, or in any copy thereof, is the child in relation to whom the proceedings have been taken.

Part III

Supplementary

. . . . . .

Short title, commencement and extent

13.—(1) This Act may be cited as the Child Abduction Act 1984.

(2) This Act shall come into force at the end of the period of three months beginning with the day on which it is passed.

(3) Part I of this Act extends to England and Wales only, Part II extends to Scotland only and in Part III section 11(1) and (5)(*a*) and section 12 do not extend to Scotland and section 11(1), (2) and (5)(*a*) and (*c*) does not extend to Northern Ireland.

. . . . . .

Matrimonial and Family Proceedings Act 1984

(1984 c.42)

An Act . . . to make provision for financial relief to be available where a marriage has been dissolved or annulled, or the parties to a marriage have been legally separated, in a country overseas; to make related amendments in the Maintenance Orders (Reciprocal Enforcement) Act 1972 . . . and for connected purposes. [12th July 1984]

. . . . . .

Part IV

Financial Provision in Scotland After Overseas Divorce Etc.

Circumstances in which a Scottish court may entertain application for financial provision

28.—(1) Where parties to a marriage have been divorced in an overseas country, then, subject to subsection (4) below, if the jurisdictional requirements and the conditions set out in subsections (2) and (3) below respectively are satisfied, the court may entertain an application by one of the parties for an order for financial provision.

(2) The jurisdictional requirements mentioned in subsection (1) above are that—

(*a*) the applicant was domiciled or habitually resident in Scotland on the date when the application was made; and

(*b*) the other party to the marriage—

(i) was domiciled or habitually resident in Scotland on the date when the application was made; or

(ii) was domiciled or habitually resident in Scotland when the parties last lived together as husband and wife; or

(iii) on the date when the application was made, was an owner or tenant of, or had a beneficial interest in, property in Scotland which had at some time been a matrimonial home of the parties; and

(*c*) where the court is the sheriff court, either—

(i) one of the parties was, on the date when the application was made, habitually resident in the sheriffdom; or

(ii) paragraph (*b*)(iii) above is satisfied in respect of property wholly or partially within the sheriffdom.

(3) The conditions mentioned in subsection (1) above are that—

(*a*) the divorce falls to be recognised in Scotland;

(*b*) the other party to the marriage initiated the proceedings for divorce;

(*c*) the application was made within five years after the date when the divorce took effect;

(*d*) a court in Scotland would have had jurisdiction to entertain an action for divorce between the parties if such an action had been brought in Scotland immediately before the foreign divorce took effect;

(*e*) the marriage had a substantial connection with Scotland; and

(*f*) both parties are living at the time of the application.

(4) Where the jurisdiction of the court to entertain proceedings under this Part of this Act would fall to be determined by reference to the jurisdictional requirements imposed by virtue of Part I of the Civil Jurisdiction and Judgments Act 1982 (implementation of certain European conventions) then—

(*a*) satisfaction of the requirements of subsection (2) above shall not obviate the need to satisfy the requirements imposed by virtue of Part I of that Act; and

(*b*) satisfaction of the requirements imposed by virtue of Part I of that Act shall obviate the need to satisfy the requirements of subsection (2) above;

and the court shall entertain or not entertain the proceedings accordingly.

Disposal of application in Scotland

29.—(1) Subject to subsections (2) to (5) below, Scots law shall apply, with any necessary modifications, in relation to an application under section 28 above as it would apply if the application were being made in an action for divorce in Scotland.

(2) In disposing of an application entertained by it under the said section 28, the court shall exercise its powers so as to place the parties, in so far as it is reasonable and practicable to do so, in the financial position in which they would have been if the application had been disposed of, in an action for divorce in Scotland, on the date on which the foreign divorce took effect.

(3) In determining what is reasonable and practicable for the purposes of subsection (2) above, the court shall have regard in particular to—

(*a*) the parties' resources, present and foreseeable at the date of disposal of the application;

(*b*) any order made by a foreign court in or in connection with the divorce proceedings for the making of financial provision in whatever form, or the transfer of property, by one of the parties to the other; and

(*c*) subsection (5) below.

(4) Except where subsection (5) below applies, the court may make an order for an interim award of a periodical allowance where—

(*a*) it appears from the applicant's averments that in the disposal of the application an order for financial provision is likely to be made; and

(*b*) the court considers that such an interim award is necessary to avoid hardship to the applicant.

(5) Where but for section 28(2)(*b*)(iii) above the court would not have jurisdiction to entertain the application, the court may make an order—

(*a*) relating to the former matrimonial home or its furniture and plenishings; or

(*b*) that the other party to the marriage shall pay to the applicant a capital sum not exceeding the value of that other party's interest in the former matrimonial home and its furniture and plenishings,

but shall not be entitled to make any other order for financial provision.

Application of Part IV to annulled marriages

[1] **29A.** This Part of this Act shall apply to an annulment, of whatever nature, of a purported marriage, as it applies to a divorce, and references to marriage and divorce shall be construed accordingly.

NOTE

[1] Inserted by the Family Law (Scotland) Act 1985 (c. 37), Sched. 1, para. 12.

Interpretation of Part IV

30.—[1] (1) In the foregoing provisions of this Part of this Act unless the context otherwise requires—

"the court" means the Court of Session or the sheriff court:

"furniture and plenishings" has the meaning assigned by section 22 of the Matrimonial Homes (Family Protection) (Scotland) Act 1981;

"matrimonial home" has the meaning assigned by the said section 22;

"order for financial provision" means any one or more of the orders specified in section 8(1) of the Family Law (Scotland) Act 1985 (financial provision) or an order under section 13 of the Matrimonial Homes (Family Protection) (Scotland) Act 1981 (transfer of tenancy of matrimonial home);

"overseas country" means a country or territory outside the British Islands; and

"tenant" has the meaning assigned by the said section 22.

(2) Any reference in the foregoing provisions of this Part of this Act to a party to a marriage shall include a reference to a party to a marriage which has been terminated.

NOTE

[1] As amended by the Family Law (Scotland) Act 1985 (c. 37), Sched. 1, para. 13.

31. [Amendments to the Maintenance Orders (Reciprocal Enforcement) Act 1972 (c. 18), s. 31(4), are included in the print of that Act, *supra.*]

. . . . . .

Commencement

47.—(1) The provisions of this Act other than this section and section 48 below shall come into force as follows—

. . .

(*d*) Part IV and paragraphs 1(*b*), 6, 7 and 28 of Schedule 1 shall come into force on such day as the Lord Advocate appoints; . . .

(2) The power to appoint days for the coming into force of provisions of this Act shall be exercised by order made by statutory instrument.

Short title and extent

48.—(1) This Act may be cited as the Matrimonial and Family Proceedings Act 1984.

(2) Parts I to III and V and Schedules 2 and 3 extend to England and Wales only, Part IV extends to Scotland only and section 45 above extends to Northern Ireland only.

(3) Where any enactment amended by Schedule 1 extends to any part of the United Kingdom, the amendment extends to that part.

SCHEDULES

Section 46(1)

SCHEDULE 1

MINOR AND CONSEQUENTIAL AMENDMENTS

[Amendments to Acts printed in *The Parliament House Book* have been given effect in the prints of those Acts.]

[1] **Foster Children (Scotland) Act 1984**

(1984 c. 56)

An Act to consolidate certain enactments relating to foster children as they have effect in Scotland. [31st October 1984]

NOTE

[1] Excluded by the Children (Scotland) Act 1995 (c. 36), s. 38(6) (child provided with refuge) (prospectively).

ARRANGEMENT OF SECTIONS

Foster children for the purposes of the Act

Foster children

[1] **1.** Subject to section 2, a child is a foster child for the purposes of this Act if—

(*a*) he is below the upper limit of the compulsory school age, and (*b*) his care is undertaken by a person who is not a relative or guardian of his.

NOTE

[1] As amended by the Children Act 1989 (c. 41), Sched. 12, para. 41 and Sched. 15.

Exceptions to section 1

2.—[1] (1) A child is not a foster child while he is in the care of a local authority or a voluntary organisation or is boarded out by an education authority.

(2) A child is not a foster child while he is in the care of any person—

(*a*) in premises in which any parent, adult relative or guardian of his is for the time being residing;.

(*b*) in any residential establishment;

(*c*) in any school within the meaning of the Education (Scotland) Act 1980;

(*d*) in any hospital or in any nursing home registered or exempted from registration under the Nursing Homes Registration (Scotland) Act 1938;

(*e*) in any home or institution not specified in this section but maintained by a public or local authority; or

[2] (*f*) if he has been in that person's care for a period of less than 28 days and that person does not intend to undertake his care for any longer period.

[1] (3) A child is not a foster child while he is in the care of any person in compliance with a supervision order within the meaning of the Children and Young Persons Act 1969 or a supervision requirement within the meaning of the Social Work (Scotland) Act 1968 or a probation order.

(4) A child is not a foster child while he is liable to be detained or subject to guardianship under the Mental Health (Scotland) Act 1984.

[1] (5) A child is not a foster child—

(*a*) while he is placed in the care and possession of a person who proposes to adopt him under arrangements made by an adoption agency within the meaning of section 1 of the Adoption Act 1976 or section 1 of the Adoption (Scotland) Act 1978; or

(*b*) while he is a protected child within the meaning of section 32 of the said Act of 1978.

(6) Prospectively added by the Children (Scotland) Act 1995 (c. 36), Sched. 4, para. 35(2), *infra.*

NOTES

[1] Prospectively amended by the Children (Scotland) Act 1995 (c. 36), Sched. 4, para. 35(2), *infra.*

[2] As substituted by the Children Act 1989 (c. 41), Sched. 12, para. 42.

Duties of local authorities

Local authorities to ensure well-being of and to visit foster children

3.—(1) It shall be the duty of every local authority to secure the welfare of children within their area who are foster children.

[1] (2) Every local authority shall cause such children to be visited by officers of the authority in accordance with regulations made under subsection (3), who shall give such advice as to the care and maintenance of the children as may appear to be necessary.

[1] (3) The Secretary of State may make regulations requiring foster children in a local authority's area to be visited by an officer of the local authority on specified occasions or within specified periods of time.

[2] (4) Subsections (1) and (2) are without prejudice to the provisions of the Social Work (Scotland) Act 1968.

NOTES

[1] For transitional provisions see Sched. 1, paras. 4 and 5.

[2] Prospectively amended by the Children (Scotland) Act 1995 (c. 36), Sched. 4, para. 35(3), *infra*.

Notification of fostering to local authorities

Notification by parents

4.—(1) The Secretary of State may by regulations make provision for requiring parents whose children are, or are going to be maintained as foster children to give to the local authority for the area where the children are or are going to be, living as foster children, such information about the fostering as may be specified in the regulations.

(2) Regulations under this section may include such incidental and supplementary provisions as the Secretary of State thinks fit.

Notification by persons maintaining or proposing to maintain foster children

5—(1) A person who proposes to maintain as a foster child a child not already in his care shall give written notice thereof to the local authority in whose area the premises in which the child is to be kept are situated, not less than two weeks before he receives the child, unless he receives him in an emergency.

(2) A person who maintains a foster child—

(*a*) whom he received in an emergency, or

(*b*) who became a foster child while in his care,

shall give written notice thereof to the local authority in whose area the premises in which the child is being kept are situated not later than one week after he receives the child or, as the case may be, after the child becomes a foster child.

(3) A notice under subsection (1) or (2) shall specify the premises in which the child is to be or is being kept.

(4) Where a person who is maintaining a foster child changes his permanent address or the premises in which the child is kept, he shall give written notice to the local authority—

(*a*) not less than two weeks before the change, or

(*b*) if the change is made in an emergency, not later than one week after the change,

specifying the new address or premises; and if the new premises are in the area of another local authority, or of a local authority in England or Wales, the authority to whom the notice is given shall inform that other authority and give them such of the particulars mentioned in subsection (5) as are known to them.

(5) At the request of the local authority, a person maintaining or proposing to maintain a foster child shall give them, so far as known to him, the following particulars—

(*a*) the name, sex and date and place of birth of the child; and

(*b*) the name and address of every person who is a parent or guardian or acts as a guardian of the child or from whom the child was or is to be received.

(6) A person maintaining or proposing to maintain a foster child need not give a notice under subsection (1) or (2) if the child has within the last three months been maintained by him as a foster child but ceased to be a foster child while in his care or on removal from his care.

(7) A local authority may exempt any person from the duty of giving notices under this section, and any such exemption may be granted as regards all or any such notices for a specified period, and may be revoked at any time by notice in writing served on that person.

Notification by persons ceasing to maintain foster children

6.—(1) If a foster child dies, the person who was maintaining him shall give, not later than 48 hours after the death, written notice of the death to the local authority and to the person from whom the child was received.

(2) Where a foster child is removed or removes himself from the care of the person maintaining him, that person shall give, not later than 48 hours after the removal, the local authority and the person from whom the child was received the name and address, if known, of the person (if any) into whose care the child has been removed.

(3) Where a foster child ceases to be a foster child on his removal from the care of the person maintaining him that person need not give notice under subsection (2) but shall at the request of the local authority give them the same particulars as would have been required to be stated in the notice.

(4) A local authority may exempt any person from the duty of giving notices under this section, and any such exemption may be granted as regards all or any such notices for a specified period, and may be revoked at any time by notice in writing served on that person.

Disqualification for fostering

Persons disqualified from keeping foster children

7.—[1] (1) A person shall not maintain a foster child if—

(*a*) an order removing a child from his care has been made against him under this Act or any Act repealed by this Act or under section 12 of the Foster Children Act 1980;

(*b*) an order has been made under the Children and Young Persons Act 1933, the Children and Young Persons Act 1969, or the Children and Young Persons (Scotland) Act 1937, or a supervision requirement has been made under the Social Work (Scotland) Act 1968 and by virtue of the order or requirement a child was removed from his care;

(*c*) he has been convicted of any offence specified in Schedule 1 to the said Act of 1933 or Schedule 1 to the Criminal Procedure (Scotland) Act 1975, or has been placed on probation or discharged absolutely or conditionally for any such offence;

(*d*) his rights and powers with respect to a child have been vested in a local authority under section 2 of the Children Act 1948 or under section 16 of the Social Work (Scotland) Act 1968 or in a local authority in England or Wales under the said section 2 or section 3 of the Child Care Act 1980;

(*e*) an order under section 1(3) or (4) of the Nurseries and Child-Minders Regulation Act 1948 has been made against him refusing, or an order has been made under section 5 of that Act cancelling, the registration of any premises occupied by him or his registration;

(*f*) an order has been made under section 43 of the Adoption Act 1958, section 34 of the Adoption Act 1976 or section 34 of the Adoption (Scotland) Act 1978 for the removal of a protected child who was being kept or was about to be received by him, or

(*g*) he is disqualified from fostering a child privately (within the meaning of the Children Act 1989) by regulations made under section 68 of that Act,

unless he has disclosed that fact to the local authority and obtained their written consent.

(2) Where subsection (1) applies to any person, otherwise than by virtue of this subsection, it shall apply also to any other person who lives in the same premises as he does or who lives in premises at which he is employed.

NOTE

[1] As amended by the Children Act 1989 (c. 41), Sched. 12, para. 43 and Sched. 15. Prospectively amended by the Children (Scotland) Act 1995 (c. 36), Sched. 4, para. 35(4), *infra*.

Control by local authorities of fostering

Power to inspect premises

8. Any officer of a local authority authorised to visit foster children may, after producing, if asked to do so, some duly authenticated document showing that he is so authorised, inspect any premises in the area of the authority in which foster children are to be or are being kept.

Power to impose requirements as to the keeping of foster children

9.—(1) Where a person is keeping or proposes to keep foster children in premises used (while foster children are kept in them) wholly or mainly for that purpose, the local authority may impose on him requirements as to—

(*a*) the number, age and sex of the foster children who may be kept at any one time in the premises or any part of them;

(*b*) the accommodation and equipment to be provided for the children;

(*c*) the medical arrangements to be made for protecting the health of the children;

(*d*) the giving of particulars of the person for the time being in charge of the children;

(*e*) the number, qualifications or experience of the persons employed in looking after the children;

(*f*) the keeping of records

(2) A requirement imposed under paragraphs (*b*) to (*f*) of subsection (1) may be limited by the authority so as to apply only when the number of foster children kept in the premises exceeds a specified number.

(3) A person shall, after such time as the local authority may specify, comply with any requirement imposed on him under this section whenever a foster child is kept in the premises in question.

(4) A requirement imposed under this section shall be imposed by notice in writing addressed to the person on whom it is imposed and informing him of his right under section 11(1) to appeal against the requirement and of the time within which he may do so.

Power to prohibit the keeping of foster children

10.—(1) Where a person proposes to keep a foster child in any premises and the local authority are of opinion that it would be detrimental to that child to be kept by him in those premises, the local authority may prohibit him from doing so; and if the premises are not for the time being used by him for the keeping of any foster child and the local authority are of opinion that it would be detrimental to any foster child to be kept by him in those premises, the local authority may prohibit his use of the premises or the keeping of any foster child.

(2) Where a local authority impose a requirement on any person under section 9 as respects any premises, they may prohibit him from keeping foster children in the premises after the time specified for compliance with the requirement unless the requirement is complied with.

(3) A prohibition imposed under this section shall be imposed by notice in writing addressed to the person on whom it is imposed and informing him of his right under section 11(1) to appeal against the prohibition and of the time within which he may do so.

Proceedings

Appeal to sheriff against requirement or prohibition imposed under section 9 or 10

11.—(1) A person aggrieved by a requirement imposed under section 9, or by a prohibition imposed under section 10, may appeal to the sheriff within 14 days from the date on which he is notified of the requirement or prohibition; and where the appeal is against a requirement imposed under section 9, the requirement shall not have effect while the appeal is pending.

(2) Where the sheriff allows an appeal under subsection (1), the sheriff, instead of cancelling the requirement or prohibition—

(*a*) may vary the requirement or allow more time for compliance with it; or

(*b*) if an absolute prohibition has been imposed, may substitute for it a prohibition on using the premises after such time as the sheriff may specify unless such specified requirements as the local authority had power to impose under section 9 are complied with.

(3) Any requirement or prohibition specified or substituted under this section by the sheriff shall be deemed for the purposes of this Act, other than this section, to have been imposed by the local authority under section 9 or, as the case may be, section 10.

Removal of foster children kept in unsuitable surroundings

12.—(1) If the sheriff is satisfied, on the complaint of a local authority, that a foster child is being kept or is about to be received—

(*a*) by any person who is unfit to have his care, or

(*b*) in contravention of section 7 or of any prohibition imposed by a local authority under section 10, or

(*c*) in any premises or environment detrimental or likely to be detrimental to him,

the sheriff may make an order for his removal to a place of safety until he can be restored to a parent, relative or guardian of his or until other arrangements can be made with respect to him.

(2) On proof that there is imminent danger to the health or well-being of the child, the power to make an order under this section may be exercised by a justice of the peace acting on the application of a person authorised to visit foster children.

(3) An order under this section made on the ground that a prohibition of a local authority under section 10 has been contravened may require the removal from the premises of all the foster children kept there.

(4) An order under this section may be executed by any person authorised to visit foster children or by any constable.

[1] (5) A local authority may receive into their care under section 15 of the Social Work (Scotland) Act 1968 (duty of local authority to provide for orphans, deserted children, etc.) any child removed under this section, whether or not the circumstances of the child are such that they fall within paragraphs (*a*) to (*c*) of subsection (1) of the said section 15 and notwithstanding that he may appear to the local authority to be over the age of 17.

(6) Where a child is removed under this section, the local authority shall, if practicable, inform a parent or guardian of the child, or any person who acts as his guardian.

NOTE

[1] Prospectively substituted by the Children (Scotland) Act 1995 (c. 36), Sched. 4, para. 35(5), *infra*.

Search warrants

[1] **13.** A refusal to allow the visiting of a foster child or the inspection of any premises by a person authorised to do so under this Act shall be treated, for the purposes of sections 14 and 323 of the Criminal Procedure (Scotland) Act 1975 (under which a warrant authorising the search for and removal of a child may be issued on suspicion of any unnecessary suffering caused to, or certain offences committed against the child), as giving reasonable cause for such suspicion.

NOTE

[1] Prospectively amended by the Children (Scotland) Act 1995 (c. 36), Sched. 4, para. 35(6), *infra*.

Advertisements

Prohibition of advertisements relating to the fostering of children

14.—(1) No advertisement indicating that a person will undertake, or will arrange for, the care and maintenance of a child shall be published, unless it truly states that person's name and address.

(2) The Secretary of State may by regulations prohibit the parent or guardian of any child from publishing or causing to be published any advertisement indicating that foster parents are sought for the child.

(3) The Secretary of State may by regulations prohibit—

(*a*) a member of a class of persons specified in the regulations, or

(*b*) a person other than a person specified in the regulations, or other than a member of a class of persons so specified,

from publishing or causing to be published any advertisement indicating that he is willing to undertake, or to arrange for, the care and maintenance of a child.

(4) Regulations made under this section—

(*a*) may make different provision for different cases or classes of cases, and

(*b*) may exclude certain cases or classes of cases.

Offences

Offences relating to foster chidren

15.—(1) A person shall be guilty of an offence if—

(*a*) being required under any provision of this Act or of regulations made under section 4, to give any notice or information, he—

(i) fails to give the notice within the time specified in that provision, or

(ii) fails to give the information within a reasonable time, or

(iii) knowingly makes, or causes or procures another person to make, any false or misleading statement in the notice or information;

(*b*) he refuses to allow—

(i) the visiting of any foster child by a duly authorised officer of a local authority, or

(ii) the inspection under section 8 of any premises;

(*c*) he maintains a foster child in contravention of section 7;

(*d*) he fails to comply with any requirement imposed by a local authority under this Act or keeps any foster child in any premises in contravention of a prohibition so imposed;

(*e*) he refuses to comply with an order under this Act for the removal of any child or obstructs any person in the execution of such an order; or

(*f*) he causes to be published or knowingly publishes an advertisement in contravention of section 14 or of regulations made under that section.

(2) Where subsection (1) of section 7 applies to any person by virtue only of subsection (2) of that section he shall not be guilty of an offence under subsection (1)(*c*) above if he proves that he did not know, and had no reasonable ground for believing, that a person living or employed in the premises in which he lives was a person to whom subsection (1) of that section applies.

(3) A person guilty of an offence under this section shall be liable on summary conviction to imprisonment for a term not exceeding six months or a fine not exceeding level 5 on the standard scale or both.

Extension of provisions of the Act to other children

Extension of Act to certain school children during holidays

16.—(1) Where a child below the upper limit of the compulsory school age resides during school holidays in a school to which this section applies, then, if he so resides for a period exceeding one month, the provisions of this Act shall apply in relation to him as if section 2(2)(*c*) were omitted, but subject to the modifications specified in subsection (2).

(2) Where this Act applies to a child by virtue of subsection (1)—

(*a*) subsections (1) to (4) of section 5, sections 6, 9 and 10 and section 17 shall not apply; but

(*b*) the person undertaking the care and maintenance of children in the school during the school holidays shall, not less than two weeks before this Act first applies to a child in that school during those holidays, give written notice to the local authority that children to whom this Act applies will reside in the school during those holidays, and any such notice shall state the estimated number of the children.

(3) A local authority may exempt any person from the duty of giving notice under this section; and any such exemption may be granted for a specified period or indefinitely, and may be revoked at any time by notice in writing given to that person.

(4) This section applies to any school within the meaning of the Education (Scotland) Act 1980 which is not a school maintained by an education authority.

Extension of Act to certain children above compulsory school age

17. Where a child is a foster child on attaining the upper limit of the compulsory school age, this Act shall apply in relation to him as it applies in relation to a foster child, until

(*a*) he would, apart from that limit have ceased to be a foster child, or

(*b*) he reaches the age of 18, or

(*c*) he lives elsewhere than with the person with whom he was living when he attained the said limit,

whichever first occurs.

Miscellaneous and supplementary

Avoidance of insurances on lives of foster children

18. A person who maintains a foster child for reward shall be deemed for the purposes of the Life Assurance Act 1774 to have no interest in the life of the child.

Service of notices by post

19. Any notice or information required to be given under this Act may be given by post.

Regulations

20. Any power to make regulations conferred on the Secretary of State by this Act shall be exercisable by statutory instrument, which shall be subject to annulment in pursuance of a resolution of either House of Parliament.

Interpretation

21.—(1) In this Act—

"child" means a person under the age of 18;

"compulsory school age" means school age within the meaning of the Education (Scotland) Act 1980;

[1] "local authority" means the council of a region or islands area;

"local authority in England or Wales" means the council of a non-metropolitan county, metropolitan district or London borough, or the Common Council of the City of London;

"place of safety" means any residential or other establishment provided by a local authority, a police station, or any hospital, surgery or other suitable place, the occupier of which is willing temporarily to receive a child;

"relative" in relation to a child, means a grandparent, brother, sister, uncle or aunt whether of the full blood or half blood or by affinity and includes, where the child is illegitimate, the father of the child and any person who would be a relative within the meaning of this definition if the child were the legitimate child of his father and mother;

[2] "residential establishment" means an establishment managed by a local authority, voluntary organisation or any other person which provides residential accommodation for the purposes of the Social Work (Scotland) Act 1968 whether for reward or not;

[2] "supervision requirement" means a requirement made by a children's hearing which has decided that a child is in need of compulsory measures of care requiring him—

(*a*) to submit to supervision in accordance with such conditions as they may impose; or

(*b*) to reside in a residential establishment named in the requirement and be subject to such conditions as they may impose;

"voluntary organisation" means a body the activities of which are carried on otherwise than for profit.

(2) In this Act, except insofar as the context otherwise requires,—

(*a*) any reference to a numbered section or Schedule is a reference to the section of, or the Schedule to, this Act so numbered;

(*b*) a reference in a section to a numbered subsection is a reference to the subsections of that section so numbered;

(*c*) a reference in a section, subsection or Schedule to a numbered or lettered paragraph is a reference to the paragraph of that section, subsection or Schedule so numbered or lettered.

NOTES

[1] Prospectively amended by the Local Government etc. (Scotland) Act 1994 (c. 39), Sched. 13, para. 136, *infra*.

[2] Prospectively amended by the Children (Scotland) Act 1995 (c. 36), Sched. 4, para. 35(7), *infra*.

Transitional provisions, consequential amendments and repeals

22.—(1) This Act shall have effect subject to the transitional provisions set out in Schedule 1 to this Act.

(2) The enactments mentioned in Schedule 2 to this Act shall have effect subject to the amendments specified in that Schedule, being amendments consequential on the provisions of this Act.

(3) The enactments specified in Schedule 3 to this Act are hereby repealed to the extent specified in the third column of that Schedule.

(4) The inclusion in this Act of any express saving or amendment shall not be taken as prejudicing the operation of section 16 or 17 of the Interpretation Act 1978 (which relate to the effect of repeals).

Citation, etc.

23.—(1) This Act may be cited as the Foster Children (Scotland) Act 1984.

(2) This Act shall come into force at the end of the period of three months beginning with the day on which it is passed.

(3) This Act (except paragraph 8 of Schedule 2) extends to Scotland only.

SCHEDULES

Section 22

SCHEDULE 1

Transitional Provisions

General

1. Insofar as—
   (*a*) any requirement, prohibition, determination, order or regulation made by virtue of an enactment repealed by this Act, or
   (*b*) any direction or notice given by virtue of such an enactment, or
   (*c*) any proceedings begun by virtue of such an enactment, or
   (*d*) anything done or having effect as if done,

could, if a corresponding enactment in this Act were in force at the relevant time, have been made, given, begun or done by virtue of the corresponding enactment, it shall, if effective immediately before the corresponding enactment comes into force, continue to have effect thereafter as if made, given, begun or done by virtue of that corresponding enactment.

2. Where any enactment passed before this Act, or any instrument or document refers either expressly or by implication to an enactment repealed by this Act, the reference shall (subject to its context) be construed as or as including a reference to the corresponding provision of this Act.

3. Where any period of time specified in any enactment repealed by this Act is current at the commencement of this Act, this Act has effect as if its corresponding provision had been in force when that period began to run.

Visits by local authority officers under section 3(2)

4. Until such time as the Secretary of State may by order made by statutory instrument appoint, subsection (2) of section 3 shall have effect with the substitution for the words "in accordance with regulations made under subsection (3)" of the words "from time to time where the local authority considers such a course to be necessary or expedient for the purposes of subsection (1)".

Notification under section 5

5.—(1) In this paragraph "the relevant date" means the date on which regulations made under section 3(3) come into force.

(2) Every person who is maintaining a foster child within the area of a local authority on the relevant date and who before that date has not given notice in respect of the child to the local authority under subsection (1) or (2) of section 5 shall within eight weeks of that date give written notice to the local authority that he is maintaining the child.

Children above compulsory school age

6. Where immediately before the commencement of this Act Part I of the Children Act 1958 applied in relation to a child by virtue only of section 13 of that Act, this Act shall apply in relation to him as it applies in relation to a foster child, until—
   (*a*) he would, apart from the upper limit of the compulsory school age, have ceased to be a foster child, or
   (*b*) he reaches the age of 18, or
   (*c*) he lives elsewhere than with the person with whom he was living when he reached the said limit,

whichever first occurs.

. . . . . .

Section 22

SCHEDULE 2

Consequential Amendments

[Amendments to Acts reprinted in *The Parliament House Book* are given effect in the prints of those Acts.]

Section 22

SCHEDULE 3

REPEALS

[Repeals of Acts reprinted in *The Parliament House Book* have been given effect.]

Family Law (Scotland) Act 1985

(1985 c. 37)

An Act to make fresh provision in the law of Scotland regarding aliment; regarding financial and other consequences of decrees of divorce and of declarator of nullity of marriage; regarding property rights and legal capacity of married persons; and for connected purposes. [16th July 1985]

ARRANGEMENT OF SECTIONS

Obligation of aliment

1.—(1) From the commencement of this Act, an obligation of aliment shall be owed by, and only by—

(*a*) a husband to his wife;

(*b*) a wife to her husband;

(*c*) a father or mother to his or her child;

(*d*) a person to a child (other than a child who has been boarded out with him by a local or other public authority or a voluntary organisation) who has been accepted by him as a child of his family.

(2) For the purposes of this Act, an obligation of aliment is an obligation to provide such support as is reasonable in the circumstances, having regard to the matters to which a court is required or entitled to have regard under section 4 of this Act in determining the amount of aliment to award in an action for aliment.

(3) Any obligation of aliment arising under a decree or by operation of law and subsisting immediately before the commencement of this Act shall, except insofar as consistent with this section, cease to have effect as from the commencement of this Act.

(4) Nothing in this section shall affect any arrears due under a decree at the date of termination or cessation of an obligation of aliment, nor any rule of law by which a person who is owed an obligation of aliment may claim aliment from the executor of a deceased person or from any person enriched by the succession to the estate of a deceased person.

(5) In subsection (1) above—

"child" means a person—

(*a*) under the age of 18 years; or

(*b*) over that age and under the age of 25 years who is reasonably and appropriately undergoing instruction at an educational establishment, or training for employment or for a trade, profession or vocation;

"husband" and "wife" include the parties to a valid polygamous marriage.

Actions for aliment

2.—(1) A claim for aliment only (whether or not expenses are also sought) may be made, against any person owing an obligation of aliment, in the Court of Session or the sheriff court.

(2) Unless the court considers it inappropriate in any particular case, a claim for aliment may also be made, against any person owing an obligation of aliment, in proceedings—

(*a*) for divorce, separation, declarator of marriage or declarator of nullity of marriage;

(*b*) relating to orders for financial provision;

[1] (*c*) concerning rights and obligations in relation to children;

(*d*) concerning parentage or legitimacy;

(*e*) of any other kind, where the court considers it appropriate to include a claim for aliment.

(3) In this Act "action for aliment" means a claim for aliment in proceedings referred to in subsection (1) or (2) above.

[2] (4) An action for aliment may be brought—

(*a*) by a person (including a child) to whom the obligation of aliment is owed;

(*b*) by the curator bonis of an incapax;

(*c*) on behalf of a child under the age of 18 years, by—

(i) the parent or guardian of the child;

[1] (iii) a person entitled to, seeking or having custody or care of a child.

(5) A woman (whether married or not) may bring an action for aliment on behalf of her unborn child as if the child had been born, but no such action shall be heard or disposed of prior to the birth of the child.

(6) It shall be competent to bring an action for aliment, notwithstanding that the person for or on behalf of whom aliment is being claimed is living in the same household as the defender.

(7) It shall be a defence to an action for aliment brought by virtue of subsection (6) above that the defender is fulfilling the obligation of aliment, and intends to continue doing so.

(8) It shall be a defence to an action for aliment by or on behalf of a person other than a child under the age of 16 years that the defender is making an offer, which it is reasonable to expect the person concerned to accept, to receive that person into his household and to fulfil the obligation of aliment.

(9) For the purposes of subsection (8) above, in considering whether it is reasonable to expect a person to accept an offer, the court shall have regard among other things to any conduct, decree or other circumstances which appear to the court to be relevant: but the fact that a husband and wife have agreed to live apart shall not of itself be regarded as making it unreasonable to expect a person to accept such an offer.

(10) A person bringing an action for aliment under subsection (4)(*c*) above may give a good receipt for aliment paid under the decree in the action.

NOTES

[1] Prospectively substituted by the Children (Scotland) Act 1995 (c. 36), Sched. 4, para. 36, *infra*.

[2] As amended by the Age of Legal Capacity (Scotland) Act 1991 (c. 50), Sched. 1, para. 40 and Sched. 2.

Powers of court in action for aliment

3.—(1) The court may, if it thinks fit, grant decree in an action for aliment, and in granting such decree shall have power—

(*a*) to order the making of periodical payments, whether for a definite or an indefinite period or until the happening of a specified event;

(*b*) to order the making of alimentary payments of an occasional or special nature, including payments in respect of inlying, funeral or educational expenses;

(*c*) to backdate an award of aliment under this Act—

(i) to the date of the bringing of the action or to such later date as the court thinks fit; or

(ii) on special cause shown, to a date prior to the bringing of the action;

(*d*) to award less than the amount claimed even if the claim is undisputed.

(2) Nothing in subsection (1) above shall empower the court to substitute a lump sum for a periodical payment.

Amount of aliment

4.—(1) In determining the amount of aliment to award in an action for aliment, the court shall, subject to subsection (3) below, have regard—

(*a*) to the needs and resources of the parties;

(*b*) to the earning capacities of the parties;

(*c*) generally to all the circumstances of the case.

(2) Where two or more parties owe an obligation of aliment to another person, there shall be no order of liability, but the court, in deciding how much, if any, aliment to award against any of those persons, shall have regard, among the other circumstances of the case, to the obligation of aliment owed by any other person.

(3) In having regard under subsection (1)(*c*) above generally to all the circumstances of the case, the court—

(*a*) may, if it thinks fit, take account of any support, financial or otherwise, given by the defender to any person whom he maintains as a dependant in his household, whether or not the defender owes an obligation of aliment to that person; and

(*b*) shall not take account of any conduct of a party unless it would be manifestly inequitable to leave it out of account.

[1] (4) Where a court makes an award of aliment in an action brought by or on behalf of a child under the age of 16 years, it may include in that award such provision as it considers to be in all the circumstances reasonable in respect of the expenses incurred wholly or partly by the person having care of the child for the purpose of caring for the child.

NOTE

[1] Added by the Child Support Act 1991 (c. 48), Sched. 5, para. 5 (effective 5th April 1993: S.I. 1992 No. 2644, *infra*, subject to transitional provisions therein).

Variation or recall of decree of aliment

5.—(1) A decree granted in an action for aliment brought before or after the commencement of this Act may, on an application by or on behalf of either party to the action, be varied or recalled by an order of the court if since the date of the decree there has been a material change of circumstances.

[1] (1A) Without prejudice to the generality of subsection (1) above, the making of a maintenance assessment with respect to a child for whom the decree of aliment was granted is a material change of circumstances for the purposes of that subsection.

(2) The provisions of this Act shall apply to applications and orders under subsection (1) above as they apply to actions for aliment and decrees in such actions, subject to any necessary modifications.

(3) On an application under subsection (1) above, the court may, pending determination of the application, make such interim order as it thinks fit.

(4) Where the court backdates an order under subsection (1) above, the court may order any sums paid under the decree to be repaid.

NOTE

[1] Inserted by S.I. 1993 No. 660 (effective 5th April 1993).

Interim aliment

6.—(1) A claim for interim aliment shall be competent—

(*a*) in an action for aliment, by the party who claims aliment against the other party;

(*b*) in an action for divorce, separation, declarator of marriage or declarator of nullity of marriage, by either party against the other party,

on behalf of the claimant and any person on whose behalf he is entitled to act under section 2(4) of this Act.

(2) Where a claim under subsection (1) above has been made, then, whether or not the claim is disputed, the court may award by way of interim aliment the sum claimed or any lesser sum or may refuse to make such an award.

(3) An award under subsection (2) above shall consist of an award of periodical payments payable only until the date of the disposal of the action in which the award was made or such earlier date as the court may specify.

(4) An award under subsection (2) above may be varied or recalled by an order of the court; and the provisions of this section shall apply to an award so varied and the claim therefor as they applied to the original award and the claim therefor.

Agreements on aliment

7.—(1) Any provision in an agreement which purports to exclude future liability for aliment or to restrict any right to bring an action for aliment shall have no effect unless the provision was fair and reasonable in all the circumstances of the agreement at the time it was entered into.

(2) Where a person who owes an obligation of aliment to another person has entered into an agreement to pay aliment to or for the benefit of the other person, on a material change of circumstances application may be made to the court by or on behalf of either person for variation of the amount payable under the agreement or for termination of the agreement.

[1] (2A) Without prejudice to the generality of subsection (2) above, the making of a maintenance assessment with respect to a child to whom or for whose benefit aliment is payable under such an agreement is a material change of circumstances for the purposes of that subsection.

(3) Subsections (8) and (9) of section 2 of this Act (which afford a defence to an action for aliment in certain circumstances) shall apply to an

[THE NEXT PAGE IS K 241]

action to enforce such an agreement as is referred to in subsection (2) above as they apply to an action for aliment.

(4) In subsection (2) above "the court" means the court which would have jurisdiction and competence to entertain an action for aliment between the parties to the agreement to which the application under that subsection relates.

(5) In this section "agreement" means an agreement entered into before or after the commencement of this Act and includes a unilateral voluntary obligation.

NOTE

[1] Inserted by S.I. 1993 No. 660 (effective 5th April 1993).

Financial provision on divorce, etc.

Orders for financial provision

8.—(1) In an action for divorce, either party to the marriage may apply to the court for one or more of the following orders—

[1] (*a*) an order for the payment of a capital sum to him by the other party to the marriage;

[2](*aa*) an order for the transfer of property to him by the other party to the marriage;

(*b*) an order for the making of a periodical allowance to him by the other party to the marriage;

(*c*) an incidental order within the meaning of section 14(2) of this Act.

(2) Subject to sections 12 to 15 of this Act, where an application has been made under subsection (1) above, the court shall make such order, if any, as is—

(*a*) justified by the principles set out in section 9 of this Act; and

(*b*) reasonable having regard to the resources of the parties.

(3) An order under subsection (2) above is in this Act referred to as an "order for financial provision".

NOTES

[1] As amended by the Law Reform (Miscellaneous Provisions) (Scotland) Act 1990 (c. 40), Sched. 8, para. 34 and Sched. 9, with effect from 1st January 1991.

[2] Inserted by the Law Reform (Miscellaneous Provisions) (Scotland) Act 1990 (c. 40), Sched. 8, para. 34, with effect from 1st January 1991.

Principles to be applied

9.—(1) The principles which the court shall apply in deciding what order for financial provision, if any, to make are that—

(*a*) the net value of the matrimonial property should be shared fairly between the parties to the marriage;

(*b*) fair account should be taken of any economic advantage derived by either party from contributions by the other, and of any economic disadvantage suffered by either party in the interests of the other party or of the family;

(*c*) any economic burden of caring, after divorce, for a child of the marriage under the age of 16 years should be shared fairly between the parties;

(*d*) a party who has been dependent to a substantial degree on the financial support of the other party should be awarded such financial provision as is reasonable to enable him to adjust, over a period of not more than three years from the date of the decree of divorce, to the loss of that support on divorce;

(*e*) a party who at the time of the divorce seems likely to suffer serious financial hardship as a result of the divorce should be awarded such financial provision as is reasonable to relieve him of hardship over a reasonable period.

(2) In subsection (1)(*b*) above and section 11(2) of this Act—

"economic advantage" means advantage gained whether before or during the marriage and includes gains in capital, in income and in earning capacity, and "economic disadvantage" shall be construed accordingly;

"contributions" means contributions made whether before or during the marriage; and includes indirect and non-financial contributions and, in particular, any such contribution made by looking after the family home or caring for the family.

Sharing of value of matrimonial property

10.—(1) In applying the principle set out in section 9(1)(*a*) of this Act, the net value of the matrimonial property shall be taken to be shared fairly between the parties to the marriage when it is shared equally or in such other proportions as are justified by special circumstances.

(2) The net value of the matrimonial property shall be the value of the property at the relevant date after deduction of any debts incurred by the parties or either of them—

(*a*) before the marriage so far as they relate to the matrimonial property, and

(*b*) during the marriage,

which are outstanding at that date.

(3) In this section "the relevant date" means whichever is the earlier of—

(*a*) subject to subsection (7) below, the date on which the parties ceased to cohabit;

(*b*) the date of service of the summons in the action for divorce.

(4) Subject to subsection (5) below, in this section and in section 11 of this Act "the matrimonial property" means all the property belonging to the parties or either of them at the relevant date which was acquired by them or him (otherwise than by way of gift or succession from a third party)—

(*a*) before the marriage for use by them as a family home or as furniture or plenishings for such home; or

(*b*) during the marriage but before the relevant date.

(5) The proportion of any rights or interests of either party under a life policy or occupational pension scheme or similar arrangement referable to the period to which subsection (4)(*b*) above refers shall be taken to form part of the matrimonial property.

(6) In subsection (1) above "special circumstances", without prejudice to the generality of the words, may include—

(*a*) the terms of any agreement between the parties on the ownership or division of any of the matrimonial property;

(*b*) the source of the funds or assets used to acquire any of the matrimonial property where those funds or assets were not derived from the income or efforts of the parties during the marriage;

(*c*) any destruction, dissipation or alienation of property by either party;

(*d*) the nature of the matrimonial property, the use made of it (including use for business purposes or as a matrimonial home) and the extent to which it is reasonable to expect it to be realised or divided or used as security;

(*e*) the actual or prospective liability for any expenses of valuation or transfer of property in connection with the divorce.

(7) For the purposes of subsection (3) above no account shall be taken of any cessation of cohabitation where the parties thereafter resumed cohabitation, except where the parties ceased to cohabit for a continuous period of 90 days or more before resuming cohabitation for a period or periods of less than 90 days in all.

Factors to be taken into account

11.—(1) In applying the principles set out in section 9 of this Act, the following provisions of this section shall have effect.

(2) For the purposes of section 9(1)(*b*) of this Act, the court shall have regard to the extent to which—

(*a*) the economic advantages or disadvantages sustained by either party have been balanced by the economic advantages or disadvantages sustained by the other party, and

(*b*) any resulting imbalance has been or will be corrected by a sharing of the value of the matrimonial property or otherwise.

(3) For the purposes of section 9(1)(*c*) of this Act, the court shall have regard to—

(*a*) any decree or arrangement for aliment for the child;

(*b*) any expenditure or loss of earning capacity caused by the need to care for the child;

(*c*) the need to provide suitable accommodation for the child;

(*d*) the age and health of the child;

(*e*) the educational, financial and other circumstances of the child;

(*f*) the availability and cost of suitable child-care facilities or services;

(*g*) the needs and resources of the parties; and

(*h*) all the other circumstances of the case.

(4) For the purposes of section 9(1)(*d*) of this Act, the court shall have regard to—

(*a*) the age, health and earning capacity of the party who is claiming the financial provision;

(*b*) the duration and extent of the dependence of that party prior to divorce;

(*c*) any intention of that party to undertake a course of education or training;

(*d*) the needs and resources of the parties; and

(*e*) all the other circumstances of the case.

(5) For the purposes of section 9(1)(*e*) of this Act, the court shall have regard to—

(*a*) the age, health and earning capacity of the party who is claiming the financial provision;

(*b*) the duration of the marriage;

(*c*) the standard of living of the parties during the marriage;

(*d*) the needs and resources of the parties; and

(*e*) all the other circumstances of the case.

(6) In having regard under subsections (3) to (5) above to all the other circumstances of the case, the court may, if it thinks fit, take account of any support, financial or otherwise, given by the party who is to make the financial provision to any person whom he maintains as a dependant in his household whether or not he owes an obligation of aliment to that person.

(7) In applying the principles set out in section 9 of this Act, the court shall not take account of the conduct of either party unless—

(*a*) the conduct has adversely affected the financial resources which are relevant to the decision of the court on a claim for financial provision; or

(*b*) in relation to section 9(1)(*d*) or (*e*), it would be manifestly inequitable to leave the conduct out of account.

Orders for payment of capital sum or transfer of property

12.—(1) An order under section 8(2) of this Act for payment of a capital sum or transfer of property may be made—

(*a*) on granting decree of divorce; or

(*b*) within such period as the court on granting decree of divorce may specify.

(2) The court, on making an order referred to in subsection (1) above,

may stipulate that it shall come into effect at a specified future date.

(3) The court, on making an order under section 8(2) of this Act for payment of a capital sum, may order that the capital sum shall be payable by instalments.

(4) Where an order referred to in subsection (1) above has been made, the court may, on an application by either party to the marriage on a material change of circumstances, vary the date or method of payment of the capital sum or the date of transfer of property.

Orders for periodical allowance

13.—(1) An order under section 8(2) of this Act for a periodical allowance may be made—

(*a*) on granting decree of divorce;

(*b*) within such period as the court on granting decree of divorce may specify; or

(*c*) after decree of divorce where—

(i) no such order has been made previously;

(ii) application for the order has been made after the date of decree; and

(iii) since the date of decree there has been a change of circumstances.

(2) The court shall not make an order for a periodical allowance under section 8(2) of this Act unless—

(*a*) the order is justified by a principle set out in paragraph (*c*), (*d*) or (*e*) of section 9(1) of this Act; and

(*b*) it is satisfied that an order for payment of a capital sum or for transfer of property under that section would be inappropriate or insufficient to satisfy the requirements of the said section 8(2).

(3) An order under section 8(2) of this Act for a periodical allowance may be for a definite or an indefinite period or until the happening of a specified event.

(4) Where an order for a periodical allowance has been made under section 8(2) of this Act, and since the date of the order there has been a material change of circumstances, the court shall, on an application by or on behalf of either party to the marriage or his executor, have power by subsequent order—

(*a*) to vary or recall the order for a periodical allowance;

(*b*) to backdate such variation or recall to the date of the application therefor or, on cause shown, to an earlier date;

(*c*) to convert the order into an order for payment of a capital sum or for a transfer of property.

[1] (4A) Without prejudice to the generality of subsection (4) above, the making of a maintenance assessment with respect to a child who has his home with a person to whom the periodical allowance is made (being a child to whom the person making the allowance has an obligation of aliment) is a material change of circumstances for the purposes of that subsection.

(5) The provisions of this Act shall apply to applications and orders under subsection (4) above as they apply to applications for periodical allowance and orders on such applications.

(6) Where the court backdates an order under subsection (4)(*b*) above, the court may order any sums paid by way of periodical allowance to be repaid.

(7) An order for a periodical allowance made under section 8(2) of this Act—

(*a*) shall, if subsisting at the death of the party making the payment, continue to operate against the party's estate, but without prejudice to the making of an order under subsection (4) above;

(*b*) shall cease to have effect on the remarriage or death of the party receiving payment, except in relation to any arrears due under it.

NOTE
[1] Inserted by S.I. 1993 No. 660 (effective 5th April 1993).

Incidental orders

14.—(1) Subject to subsection (3) below, an incidental order may be made under section 8(2) of this Act before, on or after the granting or refusal of decree of divorce.

(2) In this Act, "an incidental order" means one or more of the following orders—

(*a*) an order for the sale of property;
(*b*) an order for the valuation of property;
(*c*) an order determining any dispute between the parties to the marriage as to their respective property rights by means of a declarator thereof or otherwise;
(*d*) an order regulating the occupation of the matrimonial home or the use of furniture and plenishings therein or excluding either party to the marriage from such occupation;
(*e*) an order regulating liability, as between the parties, for outgoings in respect of the matrimonial home or furniture or plenishings therein;
(*f*) an order that security shall be given for any financial provision;
(*g*) an order that payments shall be made or property transferred to any curator bonis or trustee or other person for the benefit of the party to the marriage by whom or on whose behalf application has been made under section 8(1) of this Act for an incidental order;
(*h*) an order setting aside or varying any term in an antenuptial or postnuptial marriage settlement;
(*j*) an order as to the date from which any interest on any amount awarded shall run;
(*k*) any ancillary order which is expedient to give effect to the principles set out in section 9 of this Act or to any order made under section 8(2) of this Act.

(3) An incidental order referred to in subsection (2)(*d*) or (*e*) above may be made only on or after the granting of decree of divorce.

(4) An incidental order may be varied or recalled by subsequent order on cause shown.

(5) So long as an incidental order granting a party to a marriage the right to occupy a matrimonial home or the right to use furniture and plenishings therein remains in force then—

(*a*) section 2(1), (2), (5)(*a*) and (9) of the Matrimonial Homes (Family Protection) (Scotland) Act 1981 (which confer certain general powers of management on a spouse in relation to a matrimonial home), and
[1] (*b*) subject to section 15(3) of this Act, section 12 of the said Act of 1981 and section 41 of the Bankruptcy (Scotland) Act 1985 (which protect the occupancy rights of a spouse against arrangements intended to defeat them),

shall, except to the extent that the order otherwise provides, apply in relation to the order—

(i) as if that party were a non-entitled spouse and the other party were an entitled spouse within the meaning of section 1(1) or 6(2) of the said Act of 1981 as the case may require;
(ii) as if the right to occupy a matrimonial home under that order were "occupancy rights" within the meaning of the said Act of 1981; and
(iii) with any other necessary modifications; and

subject to section 15(3) of this Act, section 11 of the said Act of 1981 (protection of spouse in relation to furniture and plenishings) shall apply in relation to the order as if that party were a spouse within the meaning of the said section 11 and the order were an order under section 3(3) or (4) of the said Act of 1981.

(6) In subsection (2)(*h*) above, "settlement" includes a settlement by way of a policy of assurance to which section 2 of the Married Women's Policies of Assurance (Scotland) Act 1880 relates.

(7) Notwithstanding subsection (1) above, the Court of Session may by Act of Sederunt make rules restricting the categories of incidental order which may be made under section 8(2) of this Act before the granting of decree of divorce.

NOTE

[1] As amended by the Bankruptcy (Scotland) Act 1985 (c. 66), Sched. 7, para. 23.

Rights of third parties

15.—(1) The court shall not make an order under section 8(2) of this Act for the transfer of property if the consent of a third party which is necessary under any obligation, enactment or rule of law has not been obtained.

(2) The court shall not make an order under section 8(2) of this Act for the transfer of property subject to security without the consent of the creditor unless he has been given an opportunity of being heard by the court.

(3) Neither an incidental order, nor any rights conferred by such an order, shall prejudice any rights of any third party insofar as those rights existed immediately before the making of the order.

Agreements on financial provision

16.—(1) Where the parties to a marriage have entered into an agreement as to financial provision to be made on divorce, the court may make an order setting aside or varying—

(*a*) any term of the agreement relating to a periodical allowance where the agreement expressly provides for the subsequent setting aside or variation by the court of that term; or

(*b*) the agreement or any term of it where the agreement was not fair and reasonable at the time it was entered into.

(2) The court may make an order—

(*a*) under subsection (1)(*a*) above at any time after granting decree of divorce; and

(*b*) under subsection (1)(*b*) above on granting decree of divorce or within such time thereafter as the court may specify on granting decree of divorce.

[1] (3) Without prejudice to subsections (1) and (2) above, where the parties to a marriage have entered into an agreement as to financial provision to be made on divorce and—

(*a*) the estate of the party by whom any periodical allowance is payable under the agreement has, since the date when the agreement was entered into, been sequestrated, the award of sequestration has not been recalled and the party has not been discharged;

(*b*) an analogous remedy within the meaning of section 10(5) of the Bankruptcy (Scotland) Act 1985 has, since that date, come into force and remains in force in respect of that party's estate;

(*c*) that party's estate is being administered by a trustee acting under a voluntary trust deed granted since that date by the party for the benefit of his creditors generally or is subject to an analogous arrangement; or

(*d*) by virtue of the making of a maintenance assessment, child support maintenance has become payable by either party to the agreement with respect to a child to whom or for whose benefit periodical allowance is paid under that agreement,

the court may, on or at any time after granting decree of divorce, make an order setting aside or varying any term of the agreement relating to the periodical allowance.

(4) Any term of an agreement purporting to exclude the right to apply for an order under subsection (1)(*b*) or (3) above shall be void.

(5) In this section, "agreement" means an agreement entered into before or after the commencement of this Act.

NOTE

[1] As amended by S.I. 1993 No. 660 (effective 5th April 1993).

Financial provision on declarator of nullity of marriage

17.—(1) Subject to the following provisions of this section, the provisions of this Act shall apply to actions for declarator of nullity of marriage as they apply to actions for divorce; and in this Act, unless the context otherwise requires, "action for divorce" includes an action for declarator of nullity of marriage and, in relation to such an action, "decree" and "divorce" shall be construed accordingly.

(2) In an action for declarator of nullity of marriage, it shall be competent for either party to claim interim aliment under section 6(1) of this Act notwithstanding that he denies the existence of the marriage.

(3) Any rule of law by virtue of which either party to an action for declarator of nullity of marriage may require restitution of property upon the granting of such declarator shall cease to have effect.

Supplemental

Orders relating to avoidance transactions

18.—(1) Where a claim has been made (whether before or after the commencement of this Act), being—

(*a*) an action for aliment,
(*b*) a claim for an order for financial provision, or
(*c*) an application for variation or recall of a decree in such an action or of an order for financial provision,

[THE NEXT PAGE IS K 247]

the party making the claim may, not later than one year from the date of the disposal of the claim, apply to the court for an order—

(i) setting aside or varying any transfer of, or transaction involving, property effected by the other party not more than five years before the date of the making of the claim; or

(ii) interdicting the other party from effecting any such transfer or transaction.

(2) Subject to subsection (3) below, on an application under subsection (1) above for an order the court may, if it is satisfied that the transfer or transaction had the effect of, or is likely to have the effect of, defeating in whole or in part any claim referred to in subsection (1) above, make the order applied for or such other order as it thinks fit.

(3) An order under subsection (2) above shall not prejudice any rights of a third party in or to the property where that third party—

(*a*) has in good faith acquired the property or any of it or any rights in relation to it for value; or

(*b*) derives title to such property or rights from any person who has done so.

(4) Where the court makes an order under subsection (2) above, it may include in the order such terms and conditions as it thinks fit and may make any ancillary order which it considers expedient to ensure that the order is effective.

Inhibition and arrestment

19.—(1) Where a claim has been made, being—

(*a*) an action for aliment, or

(*b*) a claim for an order for financial provision,

the court shall have power, on cause shown, to grant warrant for inhibition or warrant for arrestment on the dependence of the action in which the claim is made and, if it thinks fit, to limit the inhibition to any particular property or to limit the arrestment to any particular property or to funds not exceeding a specified value.

(2) In subsection (1) above, "the court" means the Court of Session in relation to a warrant for inhibition and the Court of Session or the sheriff, as the case may require, in relation to a warrant for arrestment on the dependence.

(3) This section is without prejudice to section 1 of the Law Reform (Miscellaneous Provisions) (Scotland) Act 1966 (wages, pensions, etc., to be exempt from arrestment on the dependence of an action).

Provision of details of resources

20. In an action—

(*a*) for aliment;

(*b*) which includes a claim for an order for financial provision; or

(*c*) which includes a claim for interim aliment,

the court may order either party to provide details of his resources or those relating to a child or incapax on whose behalf he is acting.

Award of aliment or custody where divorce or separation refused

[1] **21.** A court which refuses a decree of divorce or separation shall not, by virtue of such refusal, be prevented from making an order for aliment or an order regulating custody or education of, or access to, a child or an incidental order determining any dispute between the parties as to their respective property rights.

NOTE

[1] Prospectively amended by the Children (Scotland) Act 1995 (c. 36), Sched. 5, *infra*.

Expenses of action

22. The expenses incurred by a party to a marriage in pursuing or defending—

(*a*) an action for aliment brought by either party to the marriage on his own behalf against the other party;
(*b*) an action for divorce, separation, declarator of marriage or declarator of nullity of marriage;
(*c*) an application made after the commencement of this Act for variation or recall of a decree of aliment or an order for financial provision in an action brought before or after the commencement of this Act,

shall not be regarded as necessaries for which the other party to the marriage is liable.

Actions for aliment of small amounts

23. [New s. 3 of the Sheriff Courts (Civil Jurisdiction and Procedure) (Scotland) Act 1963 is printed in that Act, *supra*, Division D.]

Matrimonial property, etc.

Marriage not to affect property rights or legal capacity

24.—(1) Subject to the provisions of any enactment (including this Act), marriage shall not of itself affect—
(*a*) the respective rights of the parties to the marriage in relation to their property;
(*b*) the legal capacity of the parties to the marriage.

(2) Nothing in subsection (1) above affects the law of succession.

Presumption of equal shares in household goods

25.—(1) If any question arises (whether during or after a marriage) as to the respective rights of ownership of the parties to a marriage in any household goods obtained in prospect of or during the marriage other than by gift or succession from a third party, it shall be presumed, unless the contrary is proved, that each has a right to an equal share in the goods in question.

(2) For the purposes of subsection (1) above, the contrary shall not be treated as proved by reason only that while the parties were married and living together the goods in question were purchased from a third party by either party alone or by both in unequal shares.

(3) In this section "household goods" means any goods (including decorative or ornamental goods) kept or used at any time during the marriage in any matrimonial home for the joint domestic purposes of the parties to the marriage, other than—
(*a*) money or securities;
(*b*) any motor car, caravan or other road vehicle;
(*c*) any domestic animal.

Presumption of equal shares in money and property derived from housekeeping allowance

26. If any question arises (whether during or after a marriage) as to the right of a party to a marriage to money derived from any allowance made by either party for their joint household expenses or for similar purposes, or to any property acquired out of such money, the money or property shall, in the absence of any agreement between them to the contrary, be treated as belonging to each party in equal shares.

General

Interpretation

27.—(1) In this Act, unless the context otherwise requires—
"action" means an action brought after the commencement of this Act;

"action for aliment" has the meaning assigned to it by section 2(3) of this Act;

"aliment" does not include aliment *pendente lite* or interim aliment under section 6 of this Act;

"caravan" means a caravan which is mobile or affixed to the land;

[0] "child" includes a child whether or not his parents have ever been married to one another, and any reference to the child of a marriage (whether or not subsisting) includes a child (other than a child who has been boarded out with the parties, or one of them, by a local or other public authority or a voluntary organisation) who has been accepted by the parties as a child of the family;

[1] "child support maintenance" has the meaning assigned to it by section 3(6) of the Child Support Act 1991;

"the court" means the Court of Session or the sheriff, as the case may require;

"decree" in an action for aliment includes an order of the court awarding aliment;

"family" includes a one-parent family;

"incidental order" has the meaning assigned to it by section 14(2) of this Act;

[1] "maintenance assessment" has the meaning assigned to it by section 54 of the Child Support Act 1991;

"marriage", in relation to an action for declarator of nullity of marriage, means purported marriage;

[2] "matrimonial home" has the meaning assigned to it by section 22 of the Matrimonial Homes (Family Protection) (Scotland) Act 1981 as amended by section 13(10) of the Law Reform (Miscellaneous Provisions) (Scotland) Act 1985;

"needs" means present and foreseeable needs;

"obligation of aliment" shall be construed in accordance with section 1(2) of this Act;

"order for financial provision" means an order under section 8(2) of this Act and, in sections 18(1) and 22(*c*) of this Act, also includes an order under section 5(2) of the Divorce (Scotland) Act 1976;

"party to a marriage" and "party to the marriage" include a party to a marriage which has been terminated or annulled;

"property" in sections 8, 12, 13 and 15 of this Act does not include a tenancy transferable under section 13 of the Matrimonial Homes (Family Protection) (Scotland) Act 1981;

"resources" means present and foreseeable resources;

"voluntary organisation" means a body, other than a local or other public authority, the activities of which are not carried on for profit.

(2) For the purposes of this Act, the parties to a marriage shall be held to cohabit with one another only when they are in fact living together as man and wife.

NOTES

[0] As amended by the Law Reform (Parent and Child) (Scotland) Act 1986 (c. 9), Sched. 1, para. 21.

[1] Inserted by S.I. 1993 No. 660 (effective 5th April 1993).

[2] As amended by the Law Reform (Miscellaneous Provisions) (Scotland) Act 1985 (c. 73), Sched. 2, para. 31.

Amendments, repeals and savings

28.—(1) The enactments specified in Schedule 1 to this Act shall have effect subject to the amendments set out therein.

(2) The enactments specified in columns 1 and 2 of Schedule 2 to this Act are repealed to the extent specified in column 3 of that Schedule.

(3) Nothing in subsection (2) above shall affect the operation of section 5 (orders for financial provision) of the Divorce (Scotland) Act 1976 in relation to an action for divorce brought before the commencement of this Act; but in the continued operation of that section the powers of the court—

(*a*) to make an order for payment of periodical allowance under subsection (2) thereof; and

(*b*) to vary such an order under subsection (4) thereof,

shall include power to make such an order for a definite or an indefinite period or until the happening of a specified event.

Citation, commencement and extent

29.—(1) This Act may be cited as the Family Law (Scotland) Act 1985.

[1] (2) This Act shall come into operation on such day as the Secretary of State may appoint by order made by statutory instrument, and different days may be appointed for different purposes.

(3) An order under subsection (2) above may contain such transitional provisions and savings as appear to the Secretary of State necessary or expedient in connection with the provisions brought into force (whether wholly or partly) by the order.

(4) So much of section 28 of, and Schedule 1 to, this Act as affects the operation of the Maintenance Orders Act 1950 and the Maintenance Orders (Reciprocal Enforcement) Act 1972 shall extend to England and Wales and to Northern Ireland as well as to Scotland, but save as aforesaid this Act shall extend to Scotland only.

NOTE

[1] S.I. 1986 No. 1237 brought the whole Act, except s. 25, into force on 1st September 1986. S.I. 1988 No. 1887 brought s. 25 into force on 30th November 1988.

SCHEDULES

Section 28(1)

SCHEDULE 1

MINOR AND CONSEQUENTIAL AMENDMENTS

[Amendments to Acts printed in *The Parliament House Book* have been given effect in the prints of those Acts.]

Section 28(2)

SCHEDULE 2

[Repeals affecting Acts printed or formerly printed in *The Parliament House Book* have been given effect.]

[1] Child Abduction and Custody Act 1985

(1985 c. 60)

An Act to enable the United Kingdom to ratify two international Conventions relating respectively to the civil aspects of international child abduction and to the recognition and enforcement of custody decisions. [25th July 1985]

NOTE

[1] See the Family Law Act 1986 (c. 55), s. 1(1)(*b*)(vii).

ARRANGEMENT OF SECTIONS

PART I

INTERNATIONAL CHILD ABDUCTION

Section

PART I

INTERNATIONAL CHILD ABDUCTION

The Hague Convention

1.—(1) In this Part of this Act "the Convention" means the Convention on the Civil Aspects of International Child Abduction which was signed at The Hague on 25th October 1980.

(2) Subject to the provisions of this Part of this Act, the provisions of that Convention set out in Schedule 1 to this Act shall have the force of law in the United Kingdom.

Contracting States

[1] **2.**—(1) For the purposes of the Convention as it has effect under this Part of this Act the Contracting States other than the United Kingdom shall be those for the time being specified by an Order in Council under this section.

(2) An Order in Council under this section shall specify the date of the coming into force of the Convention as between the United Kingdom and any State specified in the Order; and, except where the Order otherwise provides, the Convention shall apply as between the United Kingdom and any State specified in the Order; and, except where the Order otherwise provides, the Convention shall apply as between the United Kingdom and that State only in relation to wrongful removals or retentions occurring on or after that date.

(3) Where the Convention applies, or applies only, to a particular territory or particular territories specified in a declaration made by a Contracting State under Article 39 or 40 of the Convention references to that State in subsections (1) and (2) above shall be construed as references to that territory or those territories.

NOTE

[1] The following Contracting States have been specified by S.I. 1986 No. 1159, as amended by S.I. 1993 No. 1573 and as supplemented by S.I. 1993 No. 3144, itself as amended by S.I. 1995 No. 1031.

Contracting States to the Convention	Territories specified in Declarations under Article 39 or 40 of the Convention	Date of Coming into Force as between the United Kingdom and the State or Territory
Argentina	—	1st June 1991
Australia	Australian States and mainland Territories	1st January 1987
Austria	—	1st October 1988
The Bahamas	—	1st January 1994
Belize	—	1st October 1989
Bosnia and Herzegovina	—	7th April 1992
Burkina	—	1st August 1992
Canada	Ontario	1st August 1986
	New Brunswick	1st August 1986
	British Columbia	1st August 1986
	Manitoba	1st August 1986
	Nova Scotia	1st August 1986
	Newfoundland	1st August 1986
	Prince Edward Island	1st August 1986
	Quebec	1st August 1986
	Yukon Territory	1st August 1986
	Saskatchewan	1st November 1986
	Alberta	1st February 1987
	Northwest Territories	1st April 1988
Chile	—	1st May 1994
Croatia	—	1st December 1991
Cyprus	—	1st February 1995
Denmark	—	1st July 1991
Ecuador	—	1st April 1992
Finland	—	1st August 1994
France	—	1st August 1986
Germany	—	1st December 1990
Greece	—	1st June 1993
Honduras	—	1st March 1994
Hungary	—	1st September 1986
Republic of Ireland	—	1st October 1991
Israel	—	1st December 1991
Italy	—	1st May 1995
Luxembourg	—	1st January 1987
Macedonia	—	1st December 1991
Mexico	—	1st September 1991
Monaco	—	1st February 1993
Netherlands	—	1st September 1990
New Zealand	—	1st August 1991
Norway	—	1st April 1989
Panama	—	1st May 1994
Poland	—	1st November 1992
Portugal	—	1st August 1986
Romania	—	1st February 1993
Slovenia	—	1st June 1994
Spain	—	1st September 1987
St. Kitts and Nevis	—	1st August 1994
Sweden	—	1st June 1989
Switzerland	—	1st August 1986
United States	—	1st July 1988
Yugoslavia	—	1st December 1991

Central Authorities

3.—(1) Subject to subsection (2) below, the functions under the Convention of a Central Authority shall be discharged—

(*a*) in England and Wales and in Northern Ireland by the Lord Chancellor; and

(*b*) in Scotland by the Secretary of State.

[THE NEXT PAGE IS K 253]

(2) Any application made under the Convention by or on behalf of a person outside the United Kingdom may be addressed to the Lord Chancellor as the Central Authority in the United Kingdom.

(3) Where any such application relates to a function to be discharged under subsection (1) above by the Secretary of State it shall be transmitted by the Lord Chancellor to the Secretary of State and where such an application is addressed to the Secretary of State but relates to a function to be discharged under subsection (1) above by the Lord Chancellor the Secretary of State shall transmit it to the Lord Chancellor.

Judicial authorities

4. The courts having jurisdiction to entertain applications under the Convention shall be—

(*a*) in England and Wales or in Northern Ireland the High Court; and
(*b*) in Scotland the Court of Session.

Interim powers

5. Where an application has been made to a court in the United Kingdom under the Convention, the court may, at any time before the application is determined, give such interim directions as it thinks fit for the purpose of securing the welfare of the child concerned or of preventing changes in the circumstances relevant to the determination of the application.

Reports

6. Where the Lord Chancellor or the Secretary of State is requested to provide information relating to a child under Article 7(*d*) of the Convention he may—

(*a*) request a local authority or a probation officer to make a report to him in writing with respect to any matter which appears to him to be relevant;
(*b*) request the Department of Health and Social Services for Northern Ireland to arrange for a suitably qualified person to make such a report to him;
(*c*) request any court to which a written report relating to the child has been made to send him a copy of the report;

and such a request shall be duly complied with.

Proof of documents and evidence

7.—(1) For the purposes of Article 14 of the Convention a decision or determination of a judicial or administrative authority outside the United Kingdom may be proved by a duly authenticated copy of the decision or determination; and any document purporting to be such a copy shall be deemed to be a true copy unless the contrary is shown.

(2) For the purposes of subsection (1) above a copy is duly authenticated if it bears the seal, or is signed by a judge or officer, of the authority in question.

(3) For the purposes of Articles 14 and 30 of the Convention any such document as is mentioned in Article 8 of the Convention, or a certified copy of any such document, shall be sufficient evidence of anything stated in it.

Declarations by United Kingdom courts

8. The High Court or Court of Session may, on an application made for the purposes of Article 15 of the Convention by any person appearing to the court to have an interest in the matter, make a declaration or declarator that the removal of any child from, or his retention outside, the United Kingdom was wrongful within the meaning of Article 3 of the Convention.

Suspension of court's powers in cases of wrongful removal

[1] **9.** The reference in Article 16 of the Convention to deciding on the merits of rights of custody shall be construed as a reference to—

[2] (*a*) making, varying or revoking a custody order, or a supervision order under section 31 of the Children Act 1989 or section 95(1), 97(2), 143(6) or 144 of the Children and Young Persons Act (Northern Ireland) 1968 (not being a custody order);

(*aa*) enforcing under section 29 of the Family Law Act 1986 a custody order within the meaning of Chapter V of Part I of that Act;

(*b*) registering or enforcing a decision under Part II of this Act;

(*c*) [Repealed by the Children Act 1989 (c. 41), Sched. 15 (effective 14th October 1991.]

[3] (*d*) determining a summary application under section 16(8), 16A(3) or 18(3) of the Social Work (Scotland) Act 1968;

(*e*) making a parental rights order under section 104 of the Children and Young Persons Act (Northern Ireland) 1968 or discharging such an order, or giving directions in lieu of the discharge of such an order, under section 106(2) of that Act.

NOTES

[1] As amended by the Family Law Act 1986 (c. 55), Sched. 1, para. 28.

[2] As amended by the Children Act 1989 (c. 41), Sched. 13, para. 57.

[3] Prospectively substituted by the Children (Scotland) Act 1995 (c. 36), Sched. 4, para. 37(2), *infra*.

Rules of court

10.—(1) An authority having power to make rules of court may make such provision for giving effect to this Part of this Act as appears to that authority to be necessary or expedient.

[THE NEXT PAGE IS K 257]

(2) Without prejudice to the generality of subsection (1) above, rules of court may make provision—

(*a*) with respect to the procedure on applications for the return of a child and with respect to the documents and information to be furnished and the notices to be given in connection with any such application;

(*b*) for the transfer of any such application between the appropriate courts in the different parts of the United Kingdom;

(*c*) for the giving of notices by or to a court for the purposes of the provisions of Article 16 of the Convention and section 9 above and generally as respects proceedings to which those provisions apply;

(*d*) for enabling a person who wishes to make an application under the Convention in a Contracting State other than the United Kingdom to obtain from any court in the United Kingdom an authenticated copy of any decision of that court relating to the child to whom the application is to relate.

Cost of applications

[1] **11.** The United Kingdom having made such a reservation as is mentioned in the third paragraph of Article 26 of the Convention, the costs mentioned in that paragraph shall not be borne by any Minister or other authority in the United Kingdom except so far as they fall to be so borne by virtue of the grant of legal aid or legal advice and assistance under Part III or IV of the Legal Aid Act 1988, the Legal Aid (Scotland) Act 1967, Part I of the Legal Advice and Assistance Act 1972 or the Legal Aid Advice and Assistance (Northern Ireland) Order 1981.

NOTE

[1] As amended by the Legal Aid Act 1988 (c. 34), Sched. 5, para. 16.

Part II

Recognition and Enforcement of Custody Decisions

The European Convention

12.—(1) In this Part of this Act "the Convention" means the European Convention on Recognition and Enforcement of Decisions concerning Custody of Children and on the Restoration of Custody of Children which was signed in Luxembourg on 20th May 1980.

(2) Subject to the provisions of this Part of this Act, the provisions of that Convention set out in Schedule 2 to this Act (which include Articles 9 and 10 as they have effect in consequence of a reservation made by the United Kingdom under Article 17) shall have the force of law in the United Kingdom.

Contracting States

[1] **13.**—(1) For the purposes of the Convention as it has effect under this Part of this Act the Contracting States other than the United Kingdom shall be those for the time being specified by an Order in Council under this section.

(2) An Order in Council under this section shall specify the date of the coming into force of the Convention as between the United Kingdom and any State specified in the Order.

(3) Where the Convention applies, or applies only, to a particular territory or particular territories specified by a Contracting State under Article 24 or 25 of the Convention references to that State in subsections (1) and (2) above shall be construed as references to that territory or those territories.

NOTE

[1] S.I. 1986 No. 1159, as amended by S.I. 1995 No. 1295, specifies the following states:

Contracting States to the Convention	Territories specified in Declarations under Article 24 or 25 of the Convention	Date of Coming into Force of Convention as between the United Kingdom and the State or Territory
Austria	—	1st August 1986
Belgium	—	1st August 1986
Cyprus	—	1st October 1986
Denmark	—	1st August 1991
Finland	—	1st August 1994
France	—	1st August 1986
Germany	—	1st February 1991
Greece	—	1st July 1993
The Republic of Ireland	—	1st October 1991
Italy	—	1st June 1995
Luxembourg	—	1st August 1986
Netherlands	—	1st September 1990
Norway	—	1st May 1989
Portugal	—	1st August 1986
Spain	—	1st August 1986
Sweden	—	1st July 1989
Switzerland	—	1st August 1986

Central Authorities

14.—(1) Subject to subsection (2) below, the functions under the Convention of a Central Authority shall be discharged—

(*a*) in England and Wales and in Northern Ireland by the Lord Chancellor; and

(*b*) in Scotland by the Secretary of State.

(2) Any application made under the Convention by or on behalf of a person outside the United Kingdom may be addressed to the Lord Chancellor as the Central Authority in the United Kingdom.

(3) Where any such application relates to a function to be discharged under subsection (1) above by the Secretary of State it shall be transmitted by the Lord Chancellor to the Secretary of State and where such an application is addressed to the Secretary of State but relates to a function to be discharged under subsection (1) above by the Lord Chancellor the Secretary of State shall transmit it to the Lord Chancellor.

Recognition of decisions

15.—(1) Articles 7 and 12 of the Convention shall have effect in accordance with this section.

(2) A decision to which either of those Articles applies which was made in a Contracting State other than the United Kingdom shall be recognised in each part of the United Kingdom as if made by a court having jurisdiction to make it in that part but—

(*a*) the appropriate court in any part of the United Kingdom may, on the application of any person appearing to it to have an interest in the matter, declare on any of the grounds specified in Article 9 or 10 of the Convention that the decision is not to be recognised in any part of the United Kingdom; and

(*b*) the decision shall not be enforceable in any part of the United Kingdom unless registered in the appropriate court under section 16 below.

(3) The references in Article 9(1)(*c*) of the Convention to the removal of the child are to his improper removal within the meaning of the Convention.

Registration of decisions

16.—(1) A person on whom any rights are conferred by a decision relating to custody made by an authority in a Contracting State other than the United Kingdom may make an application for the registration of the decision in an appropriate court in the United Kingdom.

(2) The Central Authority in the United Kingdom shall assist such a person in making such an application if a request for such assistance is made by him or on his behalf by the Central Authority of the Contracting State in question.

[THE NEXT PAGE IS K 259]

(3) An application under subsection (1) above or a request under subsection (2) above shall be treated as a request for enforcement for the purposes of Articles 10 and 13 of the Convention.

(4) The High Court or Court of Session shall refuse to register a decision if—

(*a*) the court is of the opinion that on any of the grounds specified in Article 9 or 10 of the Convention the decision should not be recognised in any part of the United Kingdom;

(*b*) the court is of the opinion that the decision is not enforceable in the Contracting State where it was made and is not a decision to which Article 12 of the Convention applies; or

(*c*) an application in respect of the child under Part I of this Act is pending.

(5) Where the Lord Chancellor is requested to assist in making an application under this section to the Court of Session he shall transmit the request to the Secretary of State and the Secretary of State shall transmit to the Lord Chancellor any such request to assist in making an application to the High Court.

(6) In this section "decision relating to custody" has the same meaning as in the Convention.

Variation and revocation of registered decisions

17.—(1) Where a decision which has been registered under section 16 above is varied or revoked by an authority in the Contracting State in which it was made, the person on whose behalf the application for registration of the decision was made shall notify the court in which the decision is registered of the variation or revocation.

(2) Where a court is notified under subsection (1) above of the revocation of a decision, it shall—

(*a*) cancel the registration, and

(*b*) notify such persons as may be prescribed by rules of court of the cancellation.

(3) Where a court is notified under subsection (1) above of the variation of a decision, it shall—

(*a*) notify such persons as may be prescribed by rules of court of the variation; and

(*b*) subject to any conditions which may be so prescribed, vary the registration.

(4) The court in which a decision is registered under section 16 above may also, on the application of any person appearing to the court to have an interest in the matter, cancel or vary the registration if it is satisfied that the decision has been revoked or, as the case may be, varied by an authority in the Contracting State in which it was made.

Enforcement of decisions

18. Where a decision relating to custody has been registered under section 16 above, the court in which it is registered shall have the same powers for the purpose of enforcing the decision as if it had been made by that court; and proceedings for or with respect to enforcement may be taken accordingly.

Interim powers

19. Where an application has been made to a court for the registration of a decision under section 16 above or for the enforcement of such a decision, the court may, at any time before the application is determined, give such interim directions as it thinks fit for the purpose of securing the welfare of the child concerned or of preventing changes in the circumstances relevant to the determination of the application or, in the case of an application for registration, to the determination of any subsequent application for the enforcement of the decision.

Suspension of court's powers

[1] **20.**—(1) Where it appears to any court in which such proceedings as are mentioned in subsection (2) below are pending in respect of a child that—

(*a*) an application has been made for the registration of a decision in respect of the child under section 16 above (other than a decision mentioned in subsection (3) below) or that such a decision is registered; and

(*b*) the decision was made in proceedings commenced before the proceedings which are pending,

the powers of the court with respect to the child in those proceedings shall be restricted as mentioned in subsection (2) below unless, in the case of an application for registration, the application is refused.

(2) Where subsection (1) above applies the court shall not—

[1a] (*a*) in the case of custody proceedings, make, vary or revoke any custody order, or a supervision order under section 31 of the Children Act 1989 or section 95(1), 97(2), 143(6) or 144 of the Children and Young Persons Act (Northern Ireland) 1968 (not being a custody order);

(*aa*) in the case of proceedings under section 29 of the Family Law Act 1986 for the enforcement of a custody order within the meaning of Chapter V of Part I of that Act, enforce that order;

(*b*), (*c*) [Repealed by the Children Act 1989, Sched. 15.]

[1b](*d*) in the case of proceedings in respect of a summary application under section 16(8), 16A(3) or 18(3) of the Social Work (Scotland) Act 1968, determine that application; or

(*e*) in the case of proceedings on a complaint under section 104(1) of the Children and Young Persons Act (Northern Ireland) 1968 or on an application under section 106(2) of that Act, make a parental rights order under section 104 or, as the case may be, discharge or give directions in lieu of the discharge of such an order under section 106(2) of that Act.

[2] (2A) Where it appears to the Secretary of State—

(*a*) that an application has been made for the registration of a decision in respect of a child under section 16 above (other than a decision mentioned in subsection (3) below); or

(*b*) that such a decision is registered,

the Secretary of State shall not make, vary or revoke any custody order in respect of the child unless, in the case of an application for registration, the application is refused.

[3] (3) The decision referred to in subsection (1) or (2A) above is a decision which is only a decision relating to custody within the meaning of section 16 of this Act by virtue of being a decision relating to rights of access.

(4) Paragraph (*b*) of Article 10(2) of the Convention shall be construed as referring to custody proceedings within the meaning of this Act.

[4] (5) This section shall apply to a children's hearing within the meaning of Part III of the Social Work (Scotland) Act 1968 as it does to a court.

NOTES

[1] As amended by the Family Law Act 1986 (c. 55), Sched. 1, para. 29.

[1a] As amended by the Children Act 1989 (c. 41), Sched. 13, para. 57.

[1b] Prospectively substituted by the Children (Scotland) Act 1995 (c. 36), Sched. 4, para. 37(3)(*a*), *infra*.

[2] Inserted by the Family Law Act 1986 (c. 55), s. 67(2).

[3] As amended by the Family Law Act 1986 (c. 55), s. 67(3).

[4] Prospectively amended by the Children (Scotland) Act 1995 (c. 36), Sched. 4, para. 37(3)(*b*), *infra*.

Reports

21. Where the Lord Chancellor or the Secretary of State is requested to make enquiries about a child under Article 15(1)(*b*) of the Convention he may—

(*a*) request a local authority or a probation officer to make a report to him in writing with respect to any matter relating to the child concerned which appears to him to be relevant;

(*b*) request the Department of Health and Social Services for Northern Ireland to arrange for a suitably qualified person to make such a report to him;

(*c*) request any court to which a written report relating to the child has been made to send him a copy of the report;

and any such request shall be duly complied with.

Proof of documents and evidence

22.—(1) In any proceedings under this Part of this Act a decision of an authority outside the United Kingdom may be proved by a duly authenticated copy of the decision; and any document purporting to be such a copy shall be deemed to be a true copy unless the contrary is shown.

(2) For the purposes of subsection (1) above a copy is duly authenticated if it bears the seal, or is signed by a judge or officer, of the authority in question.

(3) In any proceedings under this Part of this Act any such document as is mentioned in Article 13 of the Convention, or a certified copy of any such document, shall be sufficient evidence of anything stated in it.

Decisions of United Kingdom courts

23.—(1) Where a person on whom any rights are conferred by a decision relating to custody made by a court in the United Kingdom makes an application to the Lord Chancellor or the Secretary of State under Article 4 of the Convention with a view to securing its recognition or enforcement in another Contracting State, the Lord Chancellor or the Secretary of State may require the court which made the decision to furnish him with all or any of the documents referred to in Article 13(1)(*b*), (*c*) and (*d*) of the Convention.

(2) Where in any custody proceedings a court in the United Kingdom makes a decision relating to a child who has been removed from the United Kingdom, the court may also, on an application made by any person for the purposes of Article 12 of the Convention, declare the removal to have been unlawful if it is satisfied that the applicant has an interest in the matter and that the child has been taken from or sent or kept out of the United Kingdom without the consent of the person (or, if more than one, all the persons) having the right to determine the child's place of residence under the law of the part of the United Kingdom in which the child was habitually resident.

(3) In this section "decision relating to custody" has the same meaning as in the Convention.

Rules of court

24.—(1) An authority having power to make rules of court may make such provision for giving effect to this Part of this Act as appears to that authority to be necessary or expedient.

(2) Without prejudice to the generality of subsection (1) above, rules of court may make provision—

(*a*) with respect to the procedure on applications to a court under any provision of this Part of this Act and with respect to the documents and information to be furnished and the notices to be given in connection with any such application;

(*b*) for the transfer of any such application between the appropriate courts in the different parts of the United Kingdom;

(*c*) for the giving of directions requiring the disclosure of information about any child who is the subject of proceedings under this Part of this Act and for safeguarding its welfare.

PART III

SUPPLEMENTARY

Power to order disclosure of child's whereabouts

[1] **24A.**—(1) Where—

(*a*) in proceedings for the return of a child under Part I of this Act; or

(*b*) on an application for the recognition, registration or enforcement of a decision in respect of a child under Part II of this Act,

there is not available to the court adequate information as to where the child is, the court may order any person who it has reason to believe may have relevant information to disclose it to the court.

(2) A person shall not be excused from complying with an order under subsection (1) above by reason that to do so may incriminate him or his spouse of an offence; but a statement or admission made in compliance with such an order shall not be admissible in evidence against either of them in proceedings for any offence other than perjury.

NOTE

[1] Inserted by the Family Law Act 1986 (c. 55), s. 67(4).

Termination of existing custody orders, etc.

25.—(1) Where—

(*a*) an order is made for the return of a child under Part I of this Act; or

(*b*) a decision with respect to a child (other than a decision mentioned in subsection (2) below) is registered under section 16 of this Act,

any custody order relating to him shall cease to have effect.

(2) The decision referred to in subsection (1)(*b*) above is a decision which is only a decision relating to custody within the meaning of section 16 of this Act by virtue of being a decision relating to rights of access.

. . .

[1] (6) In section 16 of the Social Work (Scotland) Act 1968 (assumption of parental rights and powers by local authority) in subsection (11) after paragraph (*d*) there shall be inserted the words "; or

(*e*) an event mentioned in paragraph (*a*) or (*b*) of section 25(1) of the Child Abduction and Custody Act 1985 occurs with respect to the child."

. . .

NOTE

[1] Prospectively repealed by the Children (Scotland) Act 1995 (c. 36), Sched. 4, para. 37(4), *infra*.

Expenses

26. There shall be paid out of money provided by Parliament—

(*a*) any expenses incurred by the Lord Chancellor or the Secretary of State by virtue of this Act; and

(*b*) any increase attributable to this Act in the sums so payable under any other Act.

Interpretation

27.—[1] (1) In this Act "custody order" means (unless the contrary intention appears) any such order or authorisation as is mentioned in Schedule 3 to this Act and "custody proceedings" means proceedings in which an order within paragraphs 1, 2, 5, 6, 8 or 9 of that Schedule may be made, varied or revoked.

(2) For the purposes of this Act "part of the United Kingdom" means England and Wales, Scotland or Northern Ireland and "the appropriate court", in relation to England and Wales or Northern Ireland means the High Court and, in relation to Scotland, the Court of Session.

(3) In this Act "local authority" means—

(*a*) in relation to England and Wales, the council of a non-metropolitan county, a metropolitan district, a London borough or the Common Council of the City of London; and

[1a](*b*) in relation to Scotland, a regional or islands council.

[2] (4) In this Act a decision relating to rights of access in England and Wales means a decision as to the contact which a child may, or may not, have with any person.

NOTES

[1] As amended by the Family Law Act 1986 (c. 55), s. 67(5) and Sched. 1, para. 30.

[1a] Prospective amendment in the Local Government etc. (Scotland) Act 1994 (c. 39), Sched. 13, para. 139, *infra*.

[2] Added by the Children Act 1989 (c. 41), Sched. 13, para. 57. Prospectively amended by the Children (Scotland) Act 1995 (c. 36), Sched. 4, para. 37(5), *infra*.

Application as respects British Islands and colonies

28.—(1) Her Majesty may by Order in Council direct that any of the provisions of this Act specified in the Order shall extend, subject to such modifications as may be specified in the Order, to—

(*a*) the Isle of Man,

(*b*) any of the Channel Islands, and

(*c*) any colony.

[1] (2) Her Majesty may by Order in Council direct that this Act shall have effect in the United Kingdom as if any reference in this Act, or in any amendment made by this Act, to any order which may be made, or any proceedings which may be brought or any other thing which may be done in, or in any part of, the United Kingdom included a reference to any corresponding order which may be made or, as the case may be, proceedings which may be brought or other thing which may be done in any of the territories mentioned in subsection (1) above.

(3) An Order in Council under this section may make such consequential, incidental and supplementary provision as Her Majesty considers appropriate.

(4) An Order in Council under this section shall be subject to annulment in pursuance of a resolution of either House of Parliament.

NOTE

[1] Direction made as respects the Isle of Man by S.I. 1994 No. 2799 (effective 6th December 1994).

Short title, commencement and extent

29.—(1) This Act may be cited as the Child Abduction and Custody Act 1985.

(2) This Act shall come into force on such day as may be appointed by an order made by statutory instrument by the Lord Chancellor and the Lord Advocate; and different days may be so appointed for different provisions.

(3) This Act extends to Northern Ireland.

[THE NEXT PAGE IS K 263]

SCHEDULES

Section 1(2)

SCHEDULE 1

Convention on the Civil Aspects of International Child Abduction

Chapter I—Scope of the Convention

Article 3

The removal or the retention of a child is to be considered wrongful where—

(*a*) it is in breach of rights of custody attributed to a person, an institution or any other body, either jointly or alone, under the law of the State in which the child was habitually resident immediately before the removal or retention; and

(*b*) at the time of removal or retention those rights were actually exercised, either jointly or alone, or would have been so exercised but for the removal or retention.

The rights of custody mentioned in sub-paragraph (*a*) above may arise in particular by operation of law or by reason of a judicial or administrative decision, or by reason of an agreement having legal effect under the law of that State.

Article 4

The Convention shall apply to any child who was habitually resident in a Contracting State immediately before any breach of custody or access rights. The Convention shall cease to apply when the child attains the age of 16 years.

Article 5

For the purposes of this Convention—

(*a*) "rights of custody" shall include rights relating to the care of the person of the child and, in particular, the right to determine the child's place of residence;

(*b*) "rights of access" shall include the right to take a child for a limited period of time to a place other than the child's habitual residence.

Chapter II—Central Authorities

Article 7

Central Authorities shall co-operate with each other and promote co-operation amongst the competent authorities in their respective States to secure the prompt return of children and to achieve the other objects of this Convention.

In particular, either directly or through any intermediary, they shall take all appropriate measures—

(*a*) to discover the whereabouts of a child who has been wrongfully removed or retained;

(*b*) to prevent further harm to the child or prejudice to interested parties by taking or causing to be taken provisional measures;

(*c*) to secure the voluntary return of the child or to bring about an amicable resolution of the issues;

(*d*) to exchange, where desirable, information relating to the social background of the child;

(*e*) to provide information of a general character as to the law of their State in connection with the application of the Convention;

(*f*) to initiate or facilitate the institution of judicial or administrative proceedings with a view to obtaining the return of the child and, in a proper case, to make arrangements for organizing or securing the effective exercise of rights of access;

(*g*) where the circumstances so require, to provide or facilitate the provision of legal aid and advice, including the participation of legal counsel and advisers;

(*h*) to provide such administrative arrangements as may be necessary and appropriate to secure the safe return of the child;

(*i*) to keep each other informed with respect to the operation of this Convention and, as far as possible, to eliminate any obstacles to its application.

Chapter III—Return of Children

Article 8

Any person, institution or other body claiming that a child has been removed or retained in breach of custody rights may apply either to the Central Authority of the child's habitual residence or to the Central Authority of any other Contracting State for assistance in securing the return of the child.

The application shall contain—

(*a*) information concerning the identity of the applicant, of the child and of the person alleged to have removed or retained the child;

(*b*) where available, the date of birth of the child;

(*c*) the grounds on which the applicant's claim for return of the child is based;

(*d*) all available information relating to the whereabouts of the child and the identity of the person with whom the child is presumed to be.

The application may be accompanied or supplemented by—

(*e*) an authenticated copy of any relevant decision or agreement;

(*f*) a certificate or an affidavit emanating from a Central Authority, or other competent authority of the State of the child's habitual residence, or from a qualified person, concerning the relevant law of that State;

(*g*) any other relevant document.

Article 9

If the Central Authority which receives an application referred to in Article 8 has reason to believe that the child is in another Contracting State, it shall directly and without delay transmit the application to the Central Authority of that Contracting State and inform the requesting Central Authority, or the applicant, as the case may be.

Article 10

The Central Authority of the State where the child is shall take or cause to be taken all appropriate measures in order to obtain the voluntary return of the child.

Article 11

The judicial or administrative authorities of Contracting States shall act expeditiously in proceedings for the return of children.

If the judicial or administrative authority concerned has not reached a decision within six weeks from the date of commencement of the proceedings, the applicant or the Central Authority of the requested State, on its own initiative or if asked by the Central Authority of the requesting State, shall have the right to request a statement of the reasons for the delay. If a reply is received by the Central Authority of the requested State, that Authority shall transmit the reply to the Central Authority of the requesting State, or to the applicant, as the case may be.

Article 12

Where a child has been wrongfully removed or retained in terms of Article 3 and, at the date of the commencement of the proceedings before the judicial or administrative authority of the Contracting State where the child is, a period of less than one year has elapsed from the date of the wrongful removal or retention, the authority concerned shall order the return of the child forthwith.

The judicial or administrative authority, even where the proceedings have been commenced after the expiration of the period of one year referred to in the preceding paragraph, shall also order the return of the child, unless it is demonstrated that the child is now settled in its new environment.

Where the judicial or administrative authority in the requested State has reason to believe that the child has been taken to another State, it may stay the proceedings or dismiss the application for the return of the child.

Article 13

Notwithstanding the provisions of the preceding Article, the judicial or administrative authority of the requested State is not bound to order the return of the child if the person, institution or other body which opposes its return establishes that—

(*a*) the person, institution or other body having the care of the person of the child was not actually exercising the custody rights at the time of removal or retention, or had consented to or subsequently acquiesced in the removal or retention; or

(*b*) there is a grave risk that his or her return would expose the child to physical or psychological harm or otherwise place the child in an intolerable situation.

The judicial or administrative authority may also refuse to order the return of the child if it finds that the child objects to being returned and has attained an age and degree of maturity at which it is appropriate to take account of its views.

In considering the circumstances referred to in this Article, the judicial and administrative authorities shall take into account the information relating to the social background of the child provided by the Central Authority or other competent authority of the child's habitual residence.

Article 14

In ascertaining whether there has been a wrongful removal or retention within the meaning of Article 3, the judicial or administrative authorities of the requested State may take notice directly of the law of, and of judicial or administrative decisions, formally recognised or not in the State of the habitual residence of the child, without recourse to the specific procedures for the proof of that law or for the recognition of foreign decisions which would otherwise be applicable.

Article 15

The judicial or administrative authorities of a Contracting State may, prior to the making of an order for the return of the child, request that the applicant obtain from the authorities of the State of the habitual residence of the child a decision or other determination that the removal or retention was wrongful within the meaning of Article 3 of the Convention, where such a decision or determination may be obtained in that State. The Central Authorities of the Contracting States shall so far as practicable assist applicants to obtain such a decision or determination.

Article 16

After receiving notice of a wrongful removal or retention of a child in the sense of Article 3, the judicial or administrative authorities of the Contracting State to which the child has been removed or in which it has been retained shall not decide on the merits of rights of custody until it has been determined that the child is not to be returned under this Convention or unless an application under this Convention is not lodged within a reasonable time following receipt of the notice.

Article 17

The sole fact that a decision relating to custody has been given in or is entitled to recognition in the requested State shall not be a ground for refusing to return a child under this Convention, but the judicial or administrative authorities of the requested State may take account of the reasons for that decision in applying this Convention.

Article 18

The provisions of this Chapter do not limit the power of a judicial or administrative authority to order the return of the child at any time.

Article 19

A decision under this Convention concerning the return of the child shall not be taken to be a determination on the merits of any custody issue.

CHAPTER IV—RIGHTS OF ACCESS

Article 21

An application to make arrangements for organising or securing the effective exercise of rights of access may be presented to the Central Authorities of the Contracting States in the same way as an application for the return of a child.

The Central Authorities are bound by the obligations of co-operation which are set forth in Article 7 to promote the peaceful enjoyment of access rights and the fulfilment of any conditions to which the exercise of those rights may be subject. The Central Authorities shall take steps to remove, as far as possible, all obstacles to the exercise of such rights. The Central Authorities, either directly or through intermediaries, may initiate or assist in the institution of proceedings with a view to organising or protecting these rights and securing respect for the conditions to which the exercise of these rights may be subject.

CHAPTER V—GENERAL PROVISIONS

Article 22

No security, bond or deposit, however described, shall be required to guarantee the payment of costs and expenses in the judicial or administrative proceedings falling within the scope of this Convention.

Article 24

Any application, communication or other document sent to the Central Authority of the requested State shall be in the original language, and shall be accompanied by a translation into the official language or one of the official languages of the requested State or, where that is not feasible, a translation into French or English.

Article 26

Each Central Authority shall bear its own costs in applying this Convention.

Central Authorities and other public services of Contracting States shall not impose any charges in relation to applications submitted under this Convention. In particular, they may not require any payment from the applicant towards the costs and expenses of the proceedings or, where applicable, those arising from the participation of legal counsel or advisers. However, they may require the payment of the expenses incurred or to be incurred in implementing the return of the child.

However, a Contracting State may, by making a reservation in accordance with Article 42, declare that it shall not be bound to assume any costs referred to in the preceding paragraph resulting from the participation of legal counsel or advisers or from court proceedings, except insofar as those costs may be covered by its system of legal aid and advice.

Upon ordering the return of a child or issuing an order concerning rights of access under this Convention, the judicial or administrative authorities may, where appropriate, direct the person who removed or retained the child, or who prevented the exercise of rights of access, to pay necessary expenses incurred by or on behalf of the applicant, including travel expenses, any costs incurred or payments made for locating the child, the costs of legal representation of the applicant, and those of returning the child.

Article 27

When it is manifest that the requirements of this Convention are not fulfilled or that the application is otherwise not well founded, a Central Authority is not bound to accept the application. In that case, the Central Authority shall forthwith inform the applicant or the Central Authority through which the application was submitted, as the case may be, of its reasons.

Article 28

A Central Authority may require that the application be accompanied by a written authorisation empowering it to act on behalf of the applicant, or to designate a representative so to act.

Article 29

This Convention shall not preclude any person, institution or body who claims that there has been a breach of custody or access rights within the meaning of Article 3 or 21 from applying directly to the judicial or administrative authorities of a Contracting State, whether or not under the provisions of this Convention.

Article 30

Any application submitted to the Central Authorities or directly to the judicial or administrative authorities of a Contracting State in accordance with the terms of this Convention, together with documents and any other information appended thereto or provided by a Central Authority, shall be admissible in the courts or administrative authorities of the Contracting States.

Article 31

In relation to a State which in matters of custody of children has two or more systems of law applicable in different territorial units—

(*a*) any reference to habitual residence in that State shall be construed as referring to habitual residence in a territorial unit of that State;

(*b*) any reference to the law of the State of habitual residence shall be construed as referring to the law of the territorial unit in that State where the child habitually resides.

Article 32

In relation to a State which in matters of custody of children has two or more systems of law applicable to different categories of persons, any reference to the law of that State shall be construed as referring to the legal system specified by the law of that State.

Section 12(2)

SCHEDULE 2

European Convention on Recognition and Enforcement of Decisions Concerning Custody of Children

Article 1

For the purposes of this Convention:

(*a*) "child" means a person of any nationality, so long as he is under 16 years of age and has not the right to decide on his own place of residence under the law of his habitual residence, the law of his nationality or the internal law of the State addressed;
(*b*) "authority" means a judicial or administrative authority;
(*c*) "decision relating to custody" means a decision of an authority in so far as it relates to the care of the person of the child, including the right to decide on the place of his residence, or to the right of access to him.
(*d*) "improper removal" means the removal of a child across an international frontier in breach of a decision relating to his custody which has been given in a Contracting State and which is enforceable in such a State; "improper removal" also includes:
  (i) the failure to return a child across an international frontier at the end of a period of the exercise of the right of access to this child or at the end of any other temporary stay in a territory other than that where the custody is exercised;
  (ii) a removal which is subsequently declared unlawful within the meaning of Article 12.

Article 4

(1) Any person who has obtained in a Contracting State a decision relating to the custody of a child and who wishes to have that decision recognised or enforced in another Contracting State may submit an application for this purpose to the Central Authority in any Contracting State.

(2) The application shall be accompanied by the documents mentioned in Article 13.

(3) The Central Authority receiving the application, if it is not the Central Authority in the State addressed, shall send the documents directly and without delay to that Central Authority.

(4) The Central Authority receiving the application may refuse to intervene where it is manifestly clear that the conditions laid down by this Convention are not satisfied.

(5) The Central Authority receiving the application shall keep the applicant informed without delay of the progress of his application.

Article 5

(1) The Central Authority in the State addressed shall take or cause to be taken without delay all steps which it considers to be appropriate, if necessary by instituting proceedings before its competent authorities, in order:
(*a*) to discover the whereabouts of the child;
(*b*) to avoid, in particular by any necessary provisional measures, prejudice to the interests of the child or of the applicant;
(*c*) to secure the recognition or enforcement of the decision;
(*d*) to secure the delivery of the child to the applicant where enforcement is granted;
(*e*) to inform the requesting authority of the measures taken and their results.

(2) Where the Central Authority in the State addressed has reason to believe that the child is in the territory of another Contracting State it shall send the documents directly and without delay to the Central Authority of that State.

(3) With the exception of the cost of repatriation, each Contracting State undertakes not to claim any payment from an applicant in respect of any measures taken under paragraph (1) of this Article by the Central Authority of that State on the applicant's behalf, including the costs of proceedings and, where applicable, the costs incurred by the assistance of a lawyer.

(4) If recognition or enforcement is refused, and if the Central Authority of the State addressed considers that it should comply with a request by the applicant to bring in that State proceedings concerning the substance of the case, that authority shall use its best endeavours to secure the representation of the applicant in the proceedings under conditions no less favourable than those available to a person who is resident in and a national of that State and for this purpose it may, in particular, institute proceedings before its competent authorities.

Article 7

A decision relating to custody given in a Contracting State shall be recognised and, where it is enforceable in the State of origin, made enforceable in every other Contracting State.

Article 9

(1) [*Recognition and enforcement may be refused*] if:
(*a*) in the case of a decision given in the absence of the defendant or his legal representative, the defendant was not duly served with the document which instituted the proceedings or an equivalent document in sufficient time to enable him to arrange his defence; but such a failure to effect service cannot constitute a ground for refusing recognition or enforcement where service was not effected because the defendant

had concealed his whereabouts from the person who instituted the proceedings in the State of origin;

(*b*) in the case of a decision given in the absence of the defendant or his legal representative, the competence of the authority giving the decision was not founded:

(i) on the habitual residence of the defendant; or

(ii) on the last common habitual residence of the child's parents, at least one parent being still habitually resident there, or

(iii) on the habitual residence of the child;

(*c*) the decision is incompatible with a decision relating to custody which became enforceable in the State addressed before the removal of the child, unless the child has had his habitual residence in the territory of the requesting State for one year before his removal.

(3) In no circumstances may the foreign decision be reviewed as to its substance.

Article 10

(1) [*Recognition and enforcement may also be refused*] on any of the following grounds:

(*a*) if it is found that the effects of the decision are manifestly incompatible with the fundamental principles of the law relating to the family and children in the State addressed;

(*b*) if it is found that by reason of a change in the circumstances including the passage of time but not including a mere change in the residence of the child after an improper removal, the effects of the original decision are manifestly no longer in accordance with the welfare of the child;

(*c*) if at the time when the proceedings were instituted in the State of origin:

(i) the child was a national of the State addressed or was habitually resident there and no such connection existed with the State of origin;

(ii) the child was a national both of the State of origin and of the State addressed and was habitually resident in the State addressed;

(*d*) if the decision is incompatible with a decision given in the State addressed or enforceable in that State after being given in a third State, pursuant to proceedings begun before the submission of the request for recognition or enforcement, and if the refusal is in accordance with the welfare of the child.

(2) Proceedings for recognition or enforcement may be adjourned on any of the following grounds:

(*a*) if an ordinary form of review of the original decision has been commenced;

(*b*) if proceedings relating to the custody of the child, commenced before the proceedings in the State of origin were instituted, are pending in the State addressed;

(*c*) if another decision concerning the custody of the child is the subject of proceedings for enforcement or of any other proceedings concerning the recognition of the decision.

Article 11

(1) Decisions on rights of access and provisions of decisions relating to custody which deal with the rights of access shall be recognised and enforced subject to the same conditions as other decisions relating to custody.

(2) However, the competent authority of the State addressed may fix the conditions for the implementation and exercise of the right of access taking into account, in particular, undertakings given by the parties on this matter.

(3) Where no decision on the right of access has been taken or where recognition or enforcement of the decision relating to custody is refused, the central authority of the State addressed may apply to its competent authorities for a decision on the right of access if the person claiming a right of access so requests.

Article 12

Where, at the time of the removal of a child across an international frontier, there is no enforceable decision given in a Contracting State relating to his custody, the provisions of this Convention shall apply to any subsequent decision, relating to the custody of that child and declaring the removal to be unlawful, given in a Contracting State at the request of any interested person.

Article 13

(1) A request for recognition or enforcement in another Contracting State of a decision relating to custody shall be accompanied by:

(*a*) a document authorising the central authority of the State addressed to act on behalf of the applicant or to designate another representative for that purpose;

(*b*) a copy of the decision which satisfies the necessary conditions of authenticity;
(*c*) in the case of a decision given in the absence of the defendant or his legal representative, a document which establishes that the defendant was duly served with the document which instituted the proceedings or an equivalent document;
(*d*) if applicable, any document which establishes that, in accordance with the law of the State of origin, the decision is enforceable;
(*e*) if possible, a statement indicating the whereabouts or likely whereabouts of the child in the State addressed;
(*f*) proposals as to how the custody of the child should be restored.

Article 15

(1) Before reaching a decision under paragraph (1)(*b*) of Article 10, the authority concerned in the State addressed:
(*a*) shall ascertain the child's views unless this is impracticable having regard in particular to his age and understanding; and
(*b*) may request that any appropriate enquiries be carried out.

(2) The cost of enquiries in any Contracting State shall be met by the authorities of the State where they are carried out.

Requests for enquiries and the results of enquiries may be sent to the authority concerned through the central authorities.

Article 26

(1) In relation to a State which has in matters of custody two or more systems of law of territorial application:
(*a*) reference to the law of a person's habitual residence or to the law of a person's nationality shall be construed as referring to the system of law determined by the rules in force in that State or, if there are no such rules, to the system of law with which the person concerned is most closely connected;
(*b*) reference to the State of origin or to the State addressed shall be construed as referring, as the case may be, to the territorial unit where the decision was given or to the territorial unit where recognition or enforcement of the decision or restoration of custody is requested.

(2) Paragraph (1)(*a*) of this Article also applies *mutatis mutandis* to States which have in matters of custody two or more systems of law of personal application.

Section 27(1)

SCHEDULE 3

CUSTODY ORDERS

PART I

ENGLAND AND WALES

[1] 1. The following are the orders referred to in section 27(1) of this Act—
(*a*) a care order under the Children Act 1989 (as defined by section 31(11) of that Act, read with section 105(1) and Schedule 14);
(*b*) a residence order (as defined by section 8 of the Act of 1989); and
(*c*) any order made by a court in England and Wales under any of the following enactments—
(i) section 9(1), 10(1)(*a*) or 11(*a*) of the Guardianship of Minors Act 1971;
(ii) section 42(1) or (2) or 43(1) of the Matrimonial Causes Act 1973;
(iii) section 2(2)(*b*), 4(*b*) or (5) of the Guardianship Act 1973 as applied by section 34(5) of the Children Act 1975;
(iv) section 8(2)(*a*), 10(1) or 19(1)(ii) of the Domestic Proceedings and Magistrates Courts Act 1978;
(v) section 26(1)(*b*) of the Adoption Act 1976.

NOTE

[1] Substituted by the Children Act 1989 (c. 41), Sched. 13, para. 57(3) and Sched. 15.

2. An order made by the High Court in the exercise of its jurisdiction relating to wardship so far as it gives the care and control of a child to any person.

3. An order made by the Secretary of State under section 25(1) of the Children and Young Persons Act 1969 (except where the order superseded was made under section 74(1)(*a*) or (*b*) or 78(1) of the Children and Young Persons Act (Northern Ireland) 1968 or was made under section 97(2)(*a*) of that Act on a complaint by a person under whose supervision the child had been placed by an order under section 74(1)(*c*) of that Act).

4. An authorisation given by the Secretary of State under section 26(2) of the Children and Young Persons Act 1969 (except where the relevant order, within the meaning of that section, was made by virtue of the court which made it being satisfied that the child was guilty of an offence).

Part II

Scotland

[1] 5. An order made by a court of civil jurisdiction in Scotland under any enactment or rule of law with respect to the custody, care or control of a child or access to a child, excluding—
- (i) an order placing a child under the supervision of a local authority;
- (ii) an adoption order under section 12(1) of the Adoption (Scotland) Act 1978;
- (ii*a*) an order freeing a child for adoption made under section 18 of the Adoption (Scotland) Act 1978;
- (iii) an order relating to the tutory or curatory of a child;
- (iv) an order made under section 16(8), 16A(3) or 18(3) of the Social Work (Scotland) Act 1968;
- (v) an order made in the exercise of any power under Part III of the Social Work (Scotland) Act 1968 to authorise any person to take a child to a place of safety, to issue, renew or recall a warrant for the apprehension or detention of a child, or to order the detention of a child in secure accommodation;
- (vi) an order made in proceedings under this Act.

NOTE

[1] As amended by the Family Law Act 1986 (c. 55), Sched. 1, para. 31. Prospectively amended by the Children (Scotland) Act 1995 (c. 36), Sched. 4, para. 37(6)(*a*), *infra*.

[1] 6. A supervision requirement or other order made by a children's hearing in Scotland under section 44(1), 47, 48, 72(1) or 74(1) of the Social Work (Scotland) Act 1968.

NOTE

[1] Prospectively substituted by the Children (Scotland) Act 1995 (c. 36), Sched. 4, para. 37(6)(*b*), *infra*.

[1] 7. An order made by the Secretary of State under section 74(3) of the said Act of 1968.

NOTE

[1] Prospectively repealed by the Children (Scotland) Act 1995 (c. 36), Sched. 4, para. 37(6)(*c*), *infra*.

PART III

NORTHERN IRELAND

8. An order made by a court in Northern Ireland under any of the following enactments—
   (*a*) section 5 of the Guardianship of Infants Act 1886 (except so far as it relates to costs);
   (*b*) section 49 of the Mental Health Act (Northern Ireland) 1961;
   (*c*) any of the following provisions of the Children and Young Persons Act (Northern Ireland) 1968—
      (i) section 95(1)(*a*) or (*b*);
      (ii) in the case of a child or young person with respect to whom a supervision order under section 95(1)(*d*) has been made, section 97(2)(*a*);
      (iii) section 108;
      (iv) in the case of a child or young person committed to the care of a fit person under Part V of that Act, section 143(6)(*a*) or (*b*) or 144 (being, in the case of an order under section 144, an order corresponding to an order under section 95(1)(*a*) or (*b*) of that Act);
   (*d*) paragraph 7 of Schedule 9 to the Education and Libraries (Northern Ireland) Order 1972 (being an order corresponding to an order under section 95(1)(*a*) or (*b*) of the said Act of 1968);
   (*e*) Article 45(1) or (2) or 46 of the Matrimonial Causes (Northern Ireland) Order 1978;
   (*f*) Article 10(2)(*a*), 12(1) or 20(1)(ii) of the Domestic Proceedings (Northern Ireland) Order 1980.

9. An order made by the High Court in the exercise of its jurisdiction relating to wardship so far as it gives the care and control of a child to any person.

10. An order made by the Secretary of State under section 25(2) of the Children and Young Persons Act 1969 superseding an order within paragraph 1(1)(*b*) or (*c*) of this Schedule.

[THE NEXT PAGE IS K 271]

Law Reform (Parent and Child) (Scotland) Act 1986

(1986 c. 9)

An Act to make fresh provision in the law of Scotland with respect to the consequences of birth out of wedlock, the rights and duties of parents, the determination of parentage and the taking of blood samples in relation to the determination of parentage; to amend the law as to guardianship; and for connected purposes. [26 March 1986]

ARRANGEMENT OF SECTIONS

Legal equality of children

[0] **1.**—(1) The fact that a person's parents are not or have not been married to one another shall be left out of account in establishing the legal relationship between the person and any other person; and accordingly any such relationship shall have effect as if the parents were or had been married to one another.

(2) Subject to subsection (4) below, any reference (however expressed) in any enactment or deed to any relative shall, unless the contrary intention appears in the enactment or deed, be construed in accordance with subsection (1) above.

[1] (3) Subsection (1) above is subject to the following provisions of this Act—

(*a*) subsection (4) below;
(*b*) section 2(1)(*b*); and
(*c*) section 9(1).

(4) Nothing in this section shall apply to the construction or effect of—

(*a*) any enactment passed or made before the commencement of this Act unless the enactment is amended by Schedule 1 to this Act and, as so amended, otherwise provides;
(*b*) any deed executed before such commencement;
(*c*) any reference (however expressed) in any deed executed after such commencement to a legitimate or illegitimate person or relationship.

NOTES

[0] Saved by the Armed Forces Act 1991 (c. 62), ss. 14(6), 15(7) and 23(3). Excluded by the Children (Scotland) Act 1995 (c. 36), s. 3(1) (prospective).

[1] Excluded by the Income and Corporation Taxes Act 1988 (c. 1), s. 831(4). Prospectively substituted by the Children (Scotland) Act 1995 (c. 36), Sched. 4, para. 38(2), *infra*.

Parental rights and their exercise

[1] **2.**—(1) Subject to sections 3 and 4 of this Act—

(*a*) a child's mother shall have parental rights whether or not she is or has been married to the child's father;

(*b*) a child's father shall have parental rights only if he is married to the child's mother or was married to her at the time of the child's conception or subsequently.

(2) For the purposes of subsection (1)(*b*) above, the father shall be regarded as having been married to the mother at any time when he was a party to a purported marriage with her which was—

(*a*) voidable, or

(*b*) void, but believed by him in good faith at that time to be valid, whether that belief was due to an error of fact or an error of law.

(3) Nothing in this section shall affect any enactment or rule of law by virtue of which a parent may be granted or deprived of parental rights.

(4) Where two or more persons have any parental right, each of them may exercise that right without the consent of the other person or, as the case may be, any of the other persons unless any decree or deed conferring the right otherwise provides.

NOTE

[1] Prospectively repealed by the Children (Scotland) Act 1995 (c. 36), Sched. 5, *infra*.

Orders as to parental rights

[1] **3.**—(1) Any person claiming interest may make an application to the court for an order relating to parental rights and the court may make such order relating to parental rights as it thinks fit.

(2) In any proceedings relating to parental rights the court shall regard the welfare of the child involved as the paramount consideration and shall not make any order relating to parental rights unless it is satisfied that to do so will be in the interests of the child.

(3) [Repealed by the Age of Legal Capacity (Scotland) Act 1991 (c. 50), Sched. 2.]

NOTE

[1] Prospectively repealed by the Children (Scotland) Act 1995 (c. 36), Sched. 5, *infra*.

Power of parent to appoint guardian

[1] **4.** The parent of a child may appoint any person to be guardian of the child after his death, but any such appointment shall be of no effect unless—

(*a*) the appointment is in writing and signed by the parent; and

(*b*) the parent at the time of his death was guardian of the child or would have been such guardian if he had survived until after the birth of the child.

NOTE

[1] As substituted by the Age of Legal Capacity (Scotland) Act 1991 (c. 50), Sched. 1, para. 41. Prospectively repealed by the Children (Scotland) Act 1995 (c. 36), Sched. 5, *infra*.

Presumptions

5.—(1) A man shall be presumed to be the father of a child—

(*a*) if he was married to the mother of the child at any time in the period beginning with the conception and ending with the birth of the child;

(*b*) where paragraph (*a*) above does not apply, if both he and the mother of the child have acknowledged that he is the father and he has been registered as such in any register kept under section 13 (register of births and still-births) or section 44 (register of corrections etc.) of the Registration of Births, Deaths and Marriages (Scotland) Act 1965 or in any corresponding register kept under statutory authority in any part of the United Kingdom other than Scotland.

(2) Subsection (1)(*a*) above shall apply in the case of a void, voidable or irregular marriage as it applies in the case of a valid and regular marriage.

(3) Without prejudice to the effect under any rule of law which a decree of declarator in an action to which section 7 of this Act applies may have in relation to the parties, a decree of declarator in such an action shall give rise to a presumption to the same effect as the decree; and any such presumption shall displace any contrary presumption howsoever arising.

(4) Any presumption under this section may be rebutted by proof on a balance of probabilities.

Determination of parentage by blood sample

[1] **6.**—(1) This section applies where, for the purpose of obtaining evidence relating to the determination of parentage in civil proceedings, a sample of blood or other body fluid or of body tissue is sought by a party to the proceedings or by a curator ad litem.

[2] (2) Where such a sample is sought from a child under the age of 16 years, consent to the taking of the sample may be given by his guardian or any person having custody or care and control of him.

(3) Where such a sample is sought from any person who is incapable of giving consent, the court may consent to the taking of the sample where—

(*a*) there is no person who is entitled to give such consent, or

(*b*) there is such a person, but it is not reasonably practicable to obtain his consent in the circumstances, or he is unwilling to accept the responsibility of giving or withholding consent.

(4) The court shall not consent under subsection (3) above to the taking of such a sample from any person unless the court is satisfied that the taking of the sample would not be detrimental to the person's health.

NOTES

[1] As amended by the Law Reform (Miscellaneous Provisions) (Scotland) Act 1990 (c. 40), s. 70(3). By s. 70(4) the amendments apply to any civil proceedings brought in the Court of Session or the sheriff court—

(*a*) on or after the date of the commencement of s. 70 (1st January 1991); or

(*b*) before that date in a case where the proof has not by that date begun.

[2] As amended by the Age of Legal Capacity (Scotland) Act 1991 (c. 50), Sched. 1, para. 42. Prospectively amended by the Children (Scotland) Act 1995 (c. 36), Sched. 4, para. 38(3), *infra*.

Actions for declarator

7.—(1) An action for declarator of parentage, non-parentage, legitimacy, legitimation or illegitimacy may be brought in the Court of Session or the sheriff court.

(2) Such an action may be brought in the Court of Session if and only if the child was born in Scotland or the alleged or presumed parent or the child—

(*a*) is domiciled in Scotland on the date when the action is brought;

(*b*) was habitually resident in Scotland for not less than one year immediately preceding that date; or

(*c*) died before that date and either—

(i) was at the date of death domiciled in Scotland; or

(ii) had been habitually resident in Scotland for not less than one year immediately preceding the date of death.

(3) Such an action may be brought in the sheriff court if and only if—

(*a*) the child was born in the sheriffdom, or

(*b*) an action could have been brought in the Court of Session under subsection (2) above and the alleged or presumed parent or the child was habitually resident in the sheriffdom on the date when the action is brought or on the date of his death.

(4) [Repealed by the Civil Evidence (Scotland) Act 1988 (c. 32), Sched.]

(5) Nothing in any rule of law or enactment shall prevent the court making in any proceedings an incidental finding as to parentage, non-parentage, legitimacy, legitimation or illegitimacy for the purposes of those proceedings.

(6) In this section "the alleged or presumed parent" includes a person who claims or is alleged to be or not to be the parent.

Interpretation

[1] **8.** In this Act, unless the context otherwise requires, the following expressions shall have the following meanings respectively assigned to them—

"action for declarator" includes an application for declarator contained in other proceedings;

[2] "child", except where used to express a relationship, means—

(*a*) in relation to guardianship custody or access, a child under the age of 16 years;

(*b*), (*c*) [Repealed by the Age of Legal Capacity (Scotland) Act 1991 (c. 50), Sched. 2.]

(*d*) in relation to parental rights other than guardianship, custody or access, a child under the age of 18 years;

"the court" means the Court of Session or the sheriff;

"deed" means any disposition, contract, instrument or writing whether inter vivos or mortis causa;

"non-parentage" means that a person is not or was not the parent, or is not or was not the child, of another person;

"parent" includes natural parent;

"parentage" means that a person is or was the parent, or is or was the child, of another person;

[2] "parental rights" means guardianship, custody or access, as the case may require, and any right or authority relating to the welfare or upbringing of a child conferred on a parent by any rule of law.

NOTES

[1] As amended by the Age of Legal Capacity (Scotland) Act 1991 (c. 50), Sched. 1, para. 43 and Sched. 2.

[2] Prospectively repealed by the Children (Scotland) Act 1995 (c. 36), Sched. 5, *infra*.

Savings and supplementary provisions

9.—(1) Nothing in this Act shall—

(*a*) affect any rule of law whereby a child born out of wedlock takes the domicile of his mother as a domicile of origin or dependence;

(*b*) except to the extent that Schedules 1 and 2 to this Act otherwise provide, affect the law relating to adoption of children;

(*c*) apply to any title coat of arms, honour or dignity transmissible on the death of the holder thereof or affect the succession thereto or the devolution thereof;

(*d*) affect the right of legitim out of, or the right of succession to, the estate of any person who died before the commencement of this Act.

(2) The court may at any time vary or recall any order made under section 3 of this Act or consent given by it under section 6 of this Act.

Transitional provisions, amendments and repeals

10.—(1) The enactments specified in Schedule 1 to this Act shall have effect subject to the amendments set out in that Schedule.

(2) The enactments specified in Schedule 2 to this Act are hereby repealed to the extent set out in the third column of that Schedule.

Citation, commencement and extent

11.—(1) This Act may be cited as the Law Reform (Parent and Child) (Scotland) Act 1986.

(2) This Act shall come into operation on such day as the Secretary of State may appoint by order made by statutory instrument.

[THE NEXT PAGE IS K 277]

(3) An order under subsection (2) above may contain such transitional provisions and savings as appear to the Secretary of State necessary or expedient in connection with the coming into operation of this Act.

(4) This Act shall extend to Scotland only.

SCHEDULES

Section 10(1)

SCHEDULE 1

MINOR AND CONSEQUENTIAL AMENDMENTS

[Amendments to Acts printed in *The Parliament House Book* have been given effect in the prints of those Acts.]

Family Law Act 1986

(1986 c. 55)

An Act to amend the law relating to the jurisdiction of courts in the United Kingdom to make orders with regard to the custody of children; to make provision as to the recognition and enforcement of such orders throughout the United Kingdom; to make further provision as to the imposition, effect and enforcement of restrictions on the removal of children from the United Kingdom or from any part of the United Kingdom; to amend the law relating to the jurisdiction of courts in Scotland as to tutory and curatory; to amend the law relating to the recognition of divorces, annulments and legal separations; to make further provision with respect to the effect of divorces and annulments on wills; to amend the law relating to the powers of courts to make declarations relating to the status of a person; to abolish the right to petition for jactitation of marriage; to repeal the Greek Marriages Act 1884; to make further provision with respect to family proceedings rules; to amend the Child Abduction Act 1984, the Child Abduction (Northern Ireland) Order 1985 and the Child Abduction and Custody Act 1985; and for connected purposes. [7th November 1986]

ARRANGEMENT OF SECTIONS

PART I

CHILD CUSTODY

CHAPTER I

PRELIMINARY

CHAPTER II

JURISDICTION OF COURTS IN ENGLAND AND WALES

[Not applicable to Scotland.]

CHAPTER III

JURISDICTION OF COURTS IN SCOTLAND

CHAPTER IV

JURISDICTION OF COURTS IN NORTHERN IRELAND

[Not applicable to Scotland.]

CHAPTER V

RECOGNITION AND ENFORCEMENT

CHAPTER VI

MISCELLANEOUS AND SUPPLEMENTAL

PART II

RECOGNITION OF DIVORCES, ANNULMENTS AND LEGAL SEPARATIONS

Divorces, annulments and judicial separations granted in the British Islands

Overseas divorces, annulments and legal separations

[1] PART I

CHILD CUSTODY

NOTE
[1] As amended by the Children Act 1989, Sched. 13, para. 62.

CHAPTER I

PRELIMINARY

Orders to which Part I applies

[1] **1.**—(1) Subject to the following provisions of this section, in this Part "Part I order" means—

(*a*) a section 8 order made by a court in England and Wales under the Children Act 1989, other than an order varying or discharging such an order;

[2] (*b*) an order made by a court of civil jurisdiction in Scotland under any enactment or rule of law with respect to the custody, care or control of a child, access to a child or the education or upbringing of a child, excluding—

(i) an order committing the care of a child to a local authority or placing a child under the supervision of a local authority;

(ii) an adoption order as defined in section 12(1) of the Adoption (Scotland) Act 1978;

(iii) an order freeing a child for adoption made under section 18 of the said Act of 1978;

(iv) an order for the custody of a child made in the course of proceedings for the adoption of the child (other than an order made following the making of a direction under section 53(1) of the Children Act 1975);

(v) an order made under the Education (Scotland) Act 1980;

(vi) an order made under Part II or III of the Social Work (Scotland) Act 1968;

(vii) an order made under the Child Abduction and Custody Act 1985;

(viii) an order for the delivery of a child or other order for the enforcement of a Part I;

[3] (ix) an order relating to the guardianship of a child;

(*c*) an order made by a court in Northern Ireland under any of the following enactments—

(i) section 5 of the Guardianship of Infants Act 1886 (except so far as it relates to costs);

(ii) Article 45(1) of the Matrimonial Causes (Northern Ireland) Order 1978;

(iii) Article 45(2) of the Matrimonial Causes (Northern Ireland) Order 1978;

(iv) Article 10(2) or 20(1)(ii) of the Domestic Proceedings (Northern Ireland) Order 1980;

(*d*) an order made by a court in England and Wales in the exercise of the inherent jurisdiction of the High Court with respect to children—

(i) so far as it gives care of a child to any person or provides for contact with, or the education of, a child; but

(ii) excluding an order varying or revoking such an order;

(*e*) an order made by the High Court in Northern Ireland in the exercise of its jurisdiction relating to wardship—

(i) so far as it gives care and control of a child to any person or provides for the education of or access to a child; but

(ii) excluding an order relating to a child of whom care or care and control is (immediately after the making of the order) vested in the Department of Health and Social Services or a Health and Social Services Board.

(2) In this Part "Part I order" does not include—

(*a*) an order within subsection (1)(*c*) above which varies or revokes a previous order made under the same enactment;

(*c*) an order within paragraph (*e*) of subsection (1) above which varies or revokes a previous order within that paragraph.

(3) In this Part, "Part I order"—

(*a*) includes any order which would have been a custody order by virtue of this section in any form in which it was in force at any time before its amendment by the Children Act 1989; and (*b*) (subject to sections 32 and 40 of this Act) excludes any order which would have been excluded from being a custody order by virtue of this section in any such form.

(6) Provision may be made by act of sederunt prescribing, in relation to orders within subsection (1)(*b*) above, what constitutes an application for the purposes of this Part.

NOTES

[1] As amended by the Children Act 1989 (c. 41), Sched. 13, para. 63 and Sched. 15.

[2] Prospectively amended by the Children (Scotland) Act 1995 (c. 36), Sched. 4, para. 41(2), *infra*.

[3] As amended by the Age of Legal Capacity (Scotland) Act 1991 (c. 50), Sched. 1, para. 44.

Chapter II

Jurisdiction of Courts in England and Wales

. . . . . .

2–7. [Not applicable to Scotland.]

Chapter III

Jurisdiction of Courts in Scotland

Jurisdiction in independent proceedings.

8. A court in Scotland may entertain an application for a Part I order otherwise than in matrimonial proceedings only if it has jurisdiction under section 9, 10, 12 or 15(2) of this Act.

Habitual residence

9. Subject to section 11 of this Act, an application for a Part I order otherwise than in matrimonial proceedings may be entertained by—

(*a*) the Court of Session if, on the date of the application, the child concerned is habitually resident in Scotland;

(*b*) the sheriff if, on the date of the application, the child concerned is habitually resident in the sheriffdom.

Presence of child

10. Subject to section 11 of this Act, an application for a Part I order otherwise than in matrimonial proceedings may be entertained by—

(*a*) the Court of Session if, on the date of the application, the child concerned—

(i) is present in Scotland; and

(ii) is not habitually resident in any part of the United Kingdom;

(*b*) the sheriff if, on the date of the application,—

(i) the child is present in Scotland;

(ii) the child is not habitually resident in any part of the United Kingdom; and

(iii) either the pursuer or the defender in the application is habitually resident in the sheriffdom.

Provisions supplementary to sections 9 and 10

11.—[1] (1) Subject to subsection (2) below, the jurisdiction of the court to entertain an application for a Part I order with respect to a child by virtue of section 9, 10 or 15(2) of this Act is excluded if, on the date of the application, matrimonial proceedings are continuing in a court in any part of the United Kingdom in respect of the marriage of the parents of the child.

(2) Subsection (1) above shall not apply in relation to an application for a Part I order if the court in which the matrimonial proceedings are continuing has made one of the following orders, that is to say—

[1] (*a*) an order under section 2A(4), 13(6) or 21(5) of this Act (not being an order made by virtue of section 13(6)(*a*)(ii)); or

(*b*) an order under section 5(2), 14(2) or 22(2) of this Act which is recorded as made for the purpose of enabling Part I proceedings with respect to the child concerned to be taken in Scotland or, as the case may be, in another court in Scotland,

and that order is in force.

NOTE

[1] As amended by the Children Act 1989 (c. 41), Sched. 13, para. 68(*a*).

Emergency jurisdiction

12. Notwithstanding that any other court, whether within or outside Scotland, has jurisdiction to entertain an application for a Part I order, the Court of Session or the sheriff shall have jurisdiction to entertain such an application if—

(*a*) the child concerned is present in Scotland or, as the case may be, in the sheriffdom on the date of the application; and

(*b*) the Court of Session or sheriff considers that, for the protection of the child, it is necessary to make such an order immediately.

Jurisdiction ancillary to matrimonial proceedings

13.—(1) The jurisdiction of a court in Scotland to entertain an application for a Part I order in matrimonial proceedings shall be modified by the following provisions of this section.

[1] (2) A court in Scotland shall not have jurisdiction, after the dismissal of matrimonial proceedings or after decree of absolvitor is granted therein, to entertain an application for a Part I order under section 9(1) of the Matrimonial Proceedings (Children) Act 1958 unless the application therefor was made on or before such dismissal or the granting of the decree of absolvitor.

(3) Where, after a decree of separation has been granted, an application is made in the separation process for a Part I order, a court in Scotland shall not have jurisdiction to entertain that application if, on the date of the application, proceedings for divorce or nullity of marriage in respect of the marriage concerned are continuing in another court in the United Kingdom.

[1] (4) A court in Scotland shall not have jurisdiction to entertain an application for the variation of a Part I order made under section 9(1) of the Matrimonial Proceedings (Children) Act 1958 if, on the date of the application, matrimonial proceedings in respect of the marriage concerned are continuing in another court in the United Kingdom.

(5) Subsections (3) and (4) above shall not apply if the court in which the other proceedings there referred to are continuing has made—

[2] (*a*) an order under section 2A(4) or 21(5) of this Act or under subsection (6) below (not being an order made by virtue of paragraph (*a*)(ii) of that subsection), or

(*b*) an order under section 5(2), 14(2) or 22(2) of this Act which is recorded as made for the purpose of enabling Part I proceedings with respect to the child concerned to be taken in Scotland or, as the case may be, in another court in Scotland,

and that order is in force.

(6) A court in Scotland which has jurisdiction in matrimonial proceedings to entertain an application for a Part I order with respect to a child may make an order declining such jurisdiction if—

(*a*) it appears to the court with respect to that child that—

(i) but for section 11(1) of this Act, another court in Scotland would have jurisdiction to entertain an application for a Part I order, or

(ii) but for section 3(2), 6(3), 20(2) or 23(3) of this Act, a court in another part of the United Kingdom would have jurisdiction to make a Part I order or an order varying a Part I order; and

(*b*) the court considers that it would be more appropriate for Part I matters relating to that child to be determined in that other court or part.

(7) The court may recall an order made under subsection (6) above.

NOTES

[1] Prospectively amended by the Children (Scotland) Act 1995 (c. 36), Sched. 4, para. 41(3), *infra*.

[2] As amended by the Children Act 1989 (c. 41), Sched. 13, para. 68(*b*).

Power of court to refuse application or sist proceedings

14.—(1) A court in Scotland which has jurisdiction to entertain an application for a Part I order may refuse the application in any case where the matter in question has already been determined in other proceedings.

(2) Where, at any stage of the proceedings on an application made to a court in Scotland for a Part I order, it appears to the court—

(*a*) that proceedings with respect to the matters to which the application relates are continuing outside Scotland or in another court in Scotland; or

(*b*) that it would be more appropriate for those matters to be determined in proceedings outside Scotland or in another court in Scotland and that such proceedings are likely to be taken there,

the court may sist the proceedings on that application.

Duration, variation and recall of orders

15.—(1) Where, after the making by a court in Scotland of a Part I order ("the existing order") with respect to a child,—

(*a*) a Part I order, or an order varying a Part I order, competently made by another court in any part of the United Kingdom with respect to that child; or

[1] (*b*) an order for the custody of that child which is made outside the United Kingdom and recognised in Scotland by virtue of section 26 of this Act,

comes into force, the existing order shall cease to have effect so far as it makes provision for any matter for which the same or different provision is made by the order of the other court in the United Kingdom or, as the case may be, the order so recognised.

(2) Subject to sections 11(1) and 13(3) and (4) of this Act, a court in Scotland which has made a Part I order ("the original order") may, notwithstanding that it would no longer have jurisdiction to make the original order, make an order varying or recalling the original order; but if the original order has by virtue of subsection (1) above ceased to have effect so far as it makes provision for any matter, the court shall not have power to vary that order under this subsection so as to make provision for that matter.

(3) In subsection (2) above, an order varying an original order means any Part I order made with respect to the same child as the original order was made.

[1,2] (4) Where any person who is entitled to the custody of a child under a Part I order made by a court in Scotland ceases to be so entitled by virtue of subsection (1) above, then, if there is in force an order made by a court in Scotland under section 12(1) of the Matrimonial Proceedings (Children) Act 1958 or section 11(1)(*b*) of the Guardianship Act 1973 providing for the supervision of that child by a local authority, that order shall cease to have effect.

NOTES

[1] Prospectively amended by the Children (Scotland) Act 1995 (c. 36), Sched. 4, para. 41(4), *infra*.

[2] Prospectively amended by the Children (Scotland) Act 1995 (c. 36), Sched. 5, *infra*.

Tutory and curatory

[1] **16.**—(1) Subject to subsections (2) and (3) below, an application made after the commencement of this Part for an order relating to the guardianship of a child may be entertained by—

(*a*) the Court of Session if, on the date of the application, the child is habitually resident in Scotland,

(*b*) the sheriff if, on the date of the application, the child is habitually resident in the sheriffdom.

(2) Subsection (1) above shall not apply to an application for the appointment or removal of a judicial factor or of a *curator bonis* or any application made by such factor or curator.

(3) Subsection (1) above is without prejudice to any other ground of jurisdiction on which the Court of Session or the sheriff may entertain an application mentioned therein.

(4) Provision may be made by act of sederunt prescribing, in relation to orders relating to the guardianship of a child, what constitutes an application for the purposes of this Chapter.

NOTE

[1] As amended by the Age of Legal Capacity (Scotland) Act 1991 (c. 50), Sched. 1, para. 45.

Orders for delivery of child

[1] **17.**—(1) Subject to subsection (2) below, an application by one parent of a child for an order for the delivery of the child from the other parent, where the order is not sought to implement a Part I order, may be entertained by the Court of Session or a sheriff if, but only if, the Court of Session or, as the case may be, the sheriff would have jurisdiction under this Chapter to make a Part I order with respect to the child concerned.

(2) Subsection (1) above is without prejudice to the grounds of jurisdiction on which the Court of Session or a sheriff may entertain an application by a parent who is entitled to the custody of a child for an order for the delivery of the child from a parent who is not so entitled.

(3) Subsection (1) above shall apply to an application by one party to a marriage for an order for the delivery of the child concerned from the other party where the child is the child of one of the parties and has been accepted as one of the family by the other party as it applies to an application by one parent of a child for an order for the delivery of the child from the other parent.

NOTE

[1] Prospectively amended by the Children (Scotland) Act 1995 (c. 36), Sched. 4, para. 41(5)(*a*) and Sched. 5, *infra*.

Interpretation of Chapter III

18.—(1) In this Chapter—

"child" means a person who has not attained the age of 16;

"matrimonial proceedings" means proceedings for divorce, nullity of marriage or judicial separation.

[1] (2) In this Chapter, "the date of the application" means, where two or more applications are pending, the date of the first of those applications; and, for the purposes of this subsection, an application is pending until a Part I order or, in the case of an application mentioned in section 16(1) of this Act, an order relating to the guardianship of a child, has been granted in pursuance of the application or the court has refused to grant such an order.

NOTE

[1] As amended by the Age of Legal Capacity (Scotland) Act 1991 (c. 50), Sched. 1, para. 46.

Chapter IV

Jurisdiction of Courts in Northern Ireland

19–24. [Not applicable to Scotland.]

Chapter V

Recognition and Enforcement

Recognition of Part I orders: general

25.—(1) Where a Part I order made by a court in any part of the United Kingdom is in force with respect to a child who has not attained the age of 16, then, subject to subsection (2) below, the order shall be recognised in any other part of the United Kingdom as having the same effect in that other part as if it had been made by the appropriate court in that other part and as if that court had had jurisdiction to make it.

(2) Where a Part I order includes provision as to the means by which rights conferred by the order are to be enforced, subsection (1) above shall not apply to that provision.

(3) A court in a part of the United Kingdom in which a Part I order is recognised in accordance with subsection (1) above shall not enforce the order unless it has been registered in that part of the United Kingdom under section 27 of this Act and proceedings for enforcement are taken in accordance with section 29 of this Act.

Recognition: special Scottish rule

[1] **26.** Any rule of law whereby an order for the custody of a child made outside the United Kingdom is recognised in Scotland shall continue to have effect, except that, after the commencement of this Part, the ground for such recognition shall be that the order was made in the country where the child was habitually resident and not where he was domiciled.

NOTE

[1] Prospectively substituted by the Children (Scotland) Act 1995 (c. 36), Sched. 4, para. 41(6), *infra*.

Registration

27.—(1) Any person on whom any rights are conferred by a Part I order may apply to the court which made it for the order to be registered in another part of the United Kingdom under this section.

(2) An application under this section shall be made in the prescribed manner and shall contain the prescribed information and be accompanied by such documents as may be prescribed.

(3) On receiving an application under this section the court which made the Part I order shall, unless it appears to the court that the order is no longer in force, cause the following documents to be sent to the appropriate court in the part of the United Kingdom specified in the application, namely—

(*a*) a certified copy of the order, and

(*b*) where the order has been varied, prescribed particulars of any variation which is in force, and

(*c*) a copy of the application and of any accompanying documents.

(4) Where the prescribed officer of the appropriate court receives a certified copy of a Part I order under subsection (3) above, he shall forthwith cause the order, together with particulars of any variation, to be registered in that court in the prescribed manner.

(5) An order shall not be registered under this section in respect of a child who has attained the age of 16, and the registration of an order in

respect of a child who has not attained the age of 16 shall cease to have effect on the attainment by the child of that age.

Cancellation and variation of registration

28.—(1) A court which revokes, recalls or varies an order registered under section 27 of this Act shall cause notice of the revocation, recall or variation to be given in the prescribed manner to the prescribed officer of the court in which it is registered and, on receiving the notice, the prescribed officer—

(*a*) in the case of the revocation or recall of the order, shall cancel the registration, and

(*b*) in the case of the variation of the order, shall cause particulars of the variation to be registered in the prescribed manner.

(2) Where—

(*a*) an order registered under section 27 of this Act ceases (in whole or in part) to have effect in the part of the United Kingdom in which it was made, otherwise than because of its revocation, recall or variation, or

(*b*) an order registered under section 27 of this Act in Scotland ceases (in whole or in part) to have effect there as a result of the making of an order in proceedings outside the United Kingdom,

the court in which the order is registered may, of its own motion or on the application of any person who appears to the court to have an interest in the matter, cancel the registration (or, if the order has ceased to have effect in part, cancel the registration so far as it relates to the provisions which have ceased to have effect).

Enforcement

29.—(1) Where a Part I order has been registered under section 27 of this Act, the court in which it is registered shall have the same powers for the purpose of enforcing the order as it would have if it had itself made the order and had jurisdiction to make it; and proceedings for or with respect to enforcement may be taken accordingly.

(2) Where an application has been made to any court for the enforcement of an order registered in that court under section 27 of this Act, the court may, at any time before the application is determined, give such interim directions as it thinks fit for the purpose of securing the welfare of the child concerned or of preventing changes in the circumstances relevant to the determination of the application.

(3) The references in subsection (1) above to a Part I order do not include references to any provision of the order as to the means by which rights conferred by the order are to be enforced.

Staying or sisting of enforcement proceedings

30.—(1) Where in accordance with section 29 of this Act proceedings are taken in any court for the enforcement of an order registered in that court, any person who appears to the court to have an interest in the matter may apply for the proceedings to be stayed or sisted on the ground that he has taken or intends to take other proceedings (in the United Kingdom or elsewhere) as a result of which the order may cease to have effect, or may have a different effect, in the part of the United Kingdom in which it is registered.

(2) If after considering an application under subsection (1) above the court considers that the proceedings for enforcement should be stayed or sisted in order that other proceedings may be taken or concluded, it shall stay or sist the proceedings for enforcement accordingly.

(3) The court may remove a stay or recall a sist granted in accordance with subsection (2) above if it appears to the court—

(*a*) that there has been unreasonable delay in the taking or prosecution of the other proceedings referred to in that subsection, or (*b*) that those other proceedings are concluded and that the registered order, or a relevant part of it, is still in force.

(4) Nothing in this section shall affect any power exercisable apart from this section to grant, remove or recall a stay or sist.

Dismissal of enforcement proceedings

31.—(1) Where in accordance with section 29 of this Act proceedings are taken in any court for the enforcement of an order registered in that court, any person who appears to the court to have an interest in the matter may apply for those proceedings to be dismissed on the ground that the order has (in whole or in part) ceased to have effect in the part of the United Kingdom in which it was made.

(2) Where in accordance with section 29 of this Act proceedings are taken in the Court of Session for the enforcement of an order registered in that court, any person who appears to the court to have an interest in the matter may apply for those proceedings to be dismissed on the ground that the order has (in whole or in part) ceased to have effect in Scotland as a result of the making of an order in proceedings outside the United Kingdom.

(3) If, after considering an application under subsection (1) or (2) above, the court is satisfied that the registered order has ceased to have effect, it shall dismiss the proceedings for enforcement (or, if it is satisfied that the order has ceased to have effect in part, it shall dismiss the proceedings so far as they relate to the enforcement of provisions which have ceased to have effect).

Interpretation of Chapter V

32.—(1) In this Chapter—

"the appropriate court", in relation to England and Wales or Northern Ireland, means the High Court and, in relation to Scotland, means the Court of Session;

"Part I order" includes (except where the context otherwise requires) any order within section 1(3) of this Act which, on the assumptions mentioned in subsection (3) below—

(*a*) could have been made notwithstanding the provisions of this Part;

(*b*) would have been a Part I order for the purposes of this Part; and

(*c*) would not have ceased to have effect by virtue of section 6, 15 or 23 of this Act.

(2) In the application of this Chapter to Scotland, "Part I order" also includes (except where the context otherwise requires) any order within section 1(3) of this Act which, on the assumptions mentioned in subsection (3) below—

(*a*) would have been a Part I order for the purposes of this Part; and

(*b*) would not have ceased to have effect by virtue of section 6 or 23 of this Act,

and which, but for the provisions of this Part, would be recognised in Scotland under any rule of law.

(3) The said assumptions are—

(*a*) that this Part had been in force at all material times; and

(*b*) that any reference in section 1 of this Act to any enactment included a reference to any corresponding enactment previously in force.

Chapter VI

Miscellaneous and Supplemental

Power to order disclosure of child's whereabouts

33.—(1) Where in proceedings for or relating to a Part I order in respect of a child there is not available to the court adequate information as to where the child is, the court may order any person who it has reason to believe may have relevant information to disclose it to the court.

(2) A person shall not be excused from complying with an order under subsection (1) above by reason that to do so may incriminate him or his spouse of an offence; but a statement or admission made in compliance with such an order shall not be admissible in evidence against either of them in proceedings for any offence other than perjury.

[1] (3) A court in Scotland before which proceedings are pending for the enforcement of an order for the custody of a child made outside the United Kingdom which is recognised in Scotland shall have the same powers as it would have under subsection (1) above if the order were its own.

NOTE

[1] Prospectively amended by the Children (Scotland) Act 1995 (c. 36), Sched. 4, para. 41(7), *infra*.

34. [Not applicable to Scotland.]

Powers to restrict removal of child from jurisdiction

35.—(1) [Repealed by the Children Act 1989 (c. 41), Sched. 15.]

(2) In Article 38(1) of the Domestic Proceedings (Northern Ireland) Order 1980 (which enables courts to restrict the removal of a child from Northern Ireland) for the words "Northern Ireland" there shall be substituted the words "the United Kingdom, or out of any part of the United Kingdom specified in the order,".

[1] (3) A court in Scotland—

(*a*) at any time after the commencement of proceedings in connection with which the court would have jurisdiction to make a Part I order, or

(*b*) in any proceedings in which it would be competent for the court to grant an interdict prohibiting the removal of a child from its jurisdiction,

may, on an application by any of the persons mentioned in subsection (4) below, grant interdict or interim interdict prohibiting the removal of the child from the United Kingdom or any part of the United Kingdom, or out of the control of the person in whose custody the child is.

(4) The said persons are—

(*a*) any party to the proceedings,

[2] (*b*) the guardian of the child concerned, and

(*c*) any other person who has or wishes to obtain the custody or care of the child.

(5) In subsection (3) above "the court" means the Court of Session or the sheriff; and for the purposes of subsection (3)(*a*) above, proceedings shall be held to commence—

(*a*) in the Court of Session, when a summons is signeted or a petition is presented;

(*b*) in the sheriff court, when the warrant of citation is signed.

NOTES

[1] Prospectively amended by the Children (Scotland) Act 1995 (c. 36), Sched. 4, para. 41(8), *infra*.

[2] As amended by the Age of Legal Capacity (Scotland) Act 1991 (c. 50), Sched. 1, para. 47.

Effect of orders restricting removal

36.—(1) This section applies to any order made by a court in the United Kingdom prohibiting the removal of a child from the United Kingdom or from any specified part of it.

(2) An order to which this section applies shall have effect in each part of the United Kingdom other than the part in which it was made—

(*a*) as if it had been made by the appropriate court in that other part, and (*b*) in the case of an order which has the effect of prohibiting the child's removal to that other part, as if it had included a prohibition on his further removal to any place except one to which he could be removed consistently with the order.

(3) The references in subsections (1) and (2) above to prohibitions on a child's removal include references to prohibitions subject to exceptions; and in a case where removal is prohibited except with the consent of the court, nothing in subsection (2) above shall be construed as affecting the identity of the court whose consent is required.

(4) In this section "child" means a person who has not attained the age of 16; and this section shall cease to apply to an order relating to a child when he attains the age of 16.

Surrender of passports

37.—(1) Where there is in force an order prohibiting or otherwise restricting the removal of a child from the United Kingdom or from any specified part of it, the court by which the order was in fact made, or by which it is treated under section 36 of this Act as having been made, may require any person to surrender any United Kingdom passport which has been issued to, or contains particulars of, the child.

(2) In this section "United Kingdom passport" means a current passport issued by the Government of the United Kingdom.

38. [Not applicable to Scotland.]

Duty to furnish particulars of other proceedings

39. Parties to proceedings for or relating to a Part I order shall, to such extent and in such manner as may be prescribed, give particulars of other proceedings known to them which relate to the child concerned (including proceedings instituted abroad and proceedings which are no longer continuing).

Interpretation of Chapter VI

40.—(1) In this Chapter—

"the appropriate court" has the same meaning as in Chapter V;

"Part I order" includes (except where the context otherwise requires) any such order as is mentioned in section 32(1) of this Act.

(2) In the application of this Chapter to Scotland, "Part I order" also includes (except where the context otherwise requires) any such order as is mentioned in section 32(2) of this Act.

Habitual residence after removal without consent, etc.

41.—(1) Where a child who—

(*a*) has not attained the age of 16, and

(*b*) is habitually resident in a part of the United Kingdom,

becomes habitually resident outside that part of the United Kingdom in consequence of circumstances of the kind specified in subsection (2) below, he shall be treated for the purposes of this Part as continuing to be habitually resident in that part of the United Kingdom for the period of one year beginning with the date on which those circumstances arise.

(2) The circumstances referred to in subsection (1) above exist where the child is removed from or retained outside, or himself leaves or remains outside, the part of the United Kingdom in which he was habitually resident before his change of residence—

(*a*) without the agreement of the person or all the persons having, under the law of that part of the United Kingdom, the right to determine where he is to reside, or

(*b*) in contravention of an order made by a court in any part of the United Kingdom.

(3) A child shall cease to be treated by virtue of subsection (1) above as habitually resident in a part of the United Kingdom if, during the period there mentioned—

(*a*) he attains the age of 16, or

(*b*) he becomes habitually resident outside that part of the United Kingdom with the agreement of the person or persons mentioned in subsection (2)(*a*) above and not in contravention of an order made by a court in any part of the United Kingdom.

General interpretation of Part I

42.—[0] (1) In this Part—

"certified copy", in relation to an order of any court, means a copy certified by the prescribed officer of the court to be a true copy of the order or of the official record of the order;

"part of the United Kingdom" means England and Wales, Scotland or Northern Ireland;

"prescribed" means prescribed by rules of court or act of sederunt.

(2) For the purposes of this Part proceedings in England and Wales or in Northern Ireland for divorce, nullity or judicial separation in respect of the marriage of the parents of a child shall, unless they have been dismissed, be treated as continuing until the child concerned attains the age of 18 (whether or not a decree has been granted and whether or not, in the case of a decree of divorce or nullity of marriage, but decree has been made absolute).

(3) For the purposes of this Part, matrimonial proceedings in a court in Scotland which has jurisdiction in those proceedings to make a Part I order with respect to a child shall, unless they have been dismissed or decree of absolvitor has been granted therein, be treated as continuing until the child concerned attains the age of 16.

(4) Any reference in this Part to proceedings in respect of the marriage of the parents of a child shall, in relation to a child who, although not a child of both parties to the marriage, is a child of the family of those parties, be construed as a reference to proceedings in respect of that marriage; and for this purpose "child of the family"—

[1] (*a*) if the proceedings are in England and Wales, means any child who has been treated by both parties as a child of their family, except a child who is placed with those parties as foster parents by a local authority or a voluntary organisation;

[0] (*b*) if the proceedings are in Scotland, means any child of one of the parties who has been accepted as one of the family by the other party;

(*c*) if the proceedings are in Northern Ireland, means any child who has been treated by both parties as a child of their family, except a child who has been boarded out with those parties by or on behalf of the Department of Health and Social Services or a voluntary organisation.

(5) References in this Part to Part I orders include (except where the context otherwise requires) references to Part I orders as varied.

[2] (6) For the purposes of this Part each of the following orders shall be treated as varying the Part I order to which it relates—

(*a*) an order which provides for a person to be allowed contact with or to be given access to a child who is the subject of a Part I order, or which makes provision for the education of such a child,

(*b*) an order under Article 45(6) of the Matrimonial Causes (Northern Ireland) Order 1978,

(*c*) an order under Article 45(7) of that Order, and

(*d*) an order under Article 20(6) of the Domestic Proceedings (Northern Ireland) Order 1980;

and for the purposes of Chapter V of this Part and this Chapter, this subsection shall have effect as if any reference to any enactment included a reference to any corresponding enactment previously in force.

[3] (7) In this Part—

(*a*) references to Part I proceedings in respect of a child are references to any proceedings for a Part I order or an order corresponding to a Part I order and include, in relation to proceedings outside the United Kingdom, references to proceedings before a tribunal or other authority having power under the law having effect there to determine Part I matters; and

(*b*) references to Part I matters are references to matters that might be determined by a Part I order or an order corresponding to a Part I order.

NOTES

[0] Prospectively amended by the Children (Scotland) Act 1995 (c. 36), Sched. 4, para. 41(9), *infra*.

[1] As amended by the Children Act 1989 (c. 41), Sched. 13, para. 71(1).

[2] As amended by the Children Act 1989 (c. 41), Sched. 13, para. 71(2) and Sched. 15.

[3] Substituted by the Children Act 1989 (c. 41), Sched. 13, para. 62(3).

Application of Part I to dependent territories

[1] **43.**—(1) Her Majesty may by Order in Council make provision corresponding to or applying any of the foregoing provisions of this Part, with such modifications as appear to Her Majesty to be appropriate, for the purpose of regulating—

(*a*) in any dependent territory;

(*b*) as between any dependent territory and any part of the United Kingdom; or

(*c*) as between any dependent territory and any other such territory,

the jurisdiction of courts to make Part I orders, or orders corresponding to Part I orders, and the recognition and enforcement of such orders.

(2) In subsection (1) above "dependent territory" means any of the following territories—

(*a*) the Isle of Man,

(*b*) any of the Channel Islands, and

(*c*) any colony.

(3) An Order in Council under subsection (1) above may contain such consequential, incidental and supplementary provisions as appear to Her Majesty to be necessary or expedient.

(4) An Order in Council under subsection (1)(*b*) above which makes provision affecting the law of any part of the United Kingdom shall be subject to annulment in pursuance of a resolution of either House of Parliament.

NOTE

[1] See S.I. 1991 No. 1723, *infra*.

PART II

RECOGNITION OF DIVORCES, ANNULMENTS AND LEGAL SEPARATIONS

Divorces, annulments and judicial separations granted in the British Islands

Recognition in United Kingdom of divorces, annulments and judicial separations granted in the British Islands

44.—(1) Subject to section 52(4) and (5)(*a*) of this Act, no divorce or annulment obtained in any part of the British Islands shall be regarded as effective in any part of the United Kingdom unless granted by a court of civil jurisdiction.

(2) Subject to section 51 of this Act, the validity of any divorce, annulment or judicial separation granted by a court of civil jurisdiction in any part of the British Islands shall be recognised throughout the United Kingdom.

Overseas divorces, annulments and legal separations

Recognition in the United Kingdom of overseas divorces, annulments and legal separations

45. Subject to sections 51 and 52 of this Act, the validity of a divorce, annulment or legal separation obtained in a country outside the British Islands (in this Part referred to as an overseas divorce, annulment or legal separation) shall be recognised in the United Kingdom if, and only if, it is entitled to recognition—

(*a*) by virtue of sections 46 to 49 of this Act, or
(*b*) by virtue of any enactment other than this Part.

Grounds for recognition

46.—(1) The validity of an overseas divorce, annulment or legal separation obtained by means of proceedings shall be recognised if—

(*a*) the divorce, annulment or legal separation is effective under the law of the country in which it was obtained; and
(*b*) at the relevant date either party to the marriage—
(i) was habitually resident in the country in which the divorce, annulment or legal separation was obtained; or
(ii) was domiciled in that country; or
(iii) was a national of that country.

(2) The validity of an overseas divorce, annulment or legal separation obtained otherwise than by means of proceedings shall be recognised if—

(*a*) the divorce, annulment or legal separation is effective under the law of the country in which it was obtained;
(*b*) at the relevant date—
(i) each party to the marriage was domiciled in that country; or
(ii) either party to the marriage was domiciled in that country and the other party was domiciled in a country under whose law the divorce, annulment or legal separation is recognised as valid; and
(*c*) neither party to the marriage was habitually resident in the United Kingdom throughout the period of one year immediately preceding that date.

(3) In this section "the relevant date" means—

(*a*) in the case of an overseas divorce, annulment or legal separation obtained by means of proceedings, the date of the commencement of the proceedings;
(*b*) in the case of an overseas divorce, annulment or legal separation obtained otherwise than by means of proceedings, the date on which it was obtained.

(4) Where in the case of an overseas annulment, the relevant date fell after the death of either party to the marriage, any reference in subsection (1) or (2) above to that date shall be construed in relation to that party as a reference to the date of death.

(5) For the purpose of this section, a party to a marriage shall be treated as domiciled in a country if he was domiciled in that country either according to the law of that country in family matters or according to the law of the part of the United Kingdom in which the question of recognition arises.

Cross-proceedings and divorces following legal separations

47.—(1) Where there have been cross-proceedings, the validity of an overseas divorce, annulment or legal separation obtained either in the original proceedings or in the cross-proceedings shall be recognised if—

(*a*) the requirements of section 46(1)(*b*)(i), (ii) or (iii) of this Act are satisfied in relation to the date of the commencement either of the original proceedings or of the cross-proceedings, and
(*b*) the validity of the divorce, annulment or legal separation is otherwise entitled to recognition by virtue of the provisions of this Part.

(2) Where a legal separation, the validity of which is entitled to recognition by virtue of the provisions of section 46 of this Act or of subsection (1) above is converted, in the country in which it was obtained, into a divorce which is effective under the law of that country, the validity of the divorce shall be recognised whether or not it would itself be entitled to recognition by virtue of those provisions.

Proof of facts relevant to recognition

48.—(1) For the purpose of deciding whether an overseas divorce, annulment or legal separation obtained by means of proceedings is entitled to recognition by virtue of section 46 and 47 of this Act, any finding of fact

[THE NEXT PAGE IS K 293]

made (whether expressly or by implication) in the proceedings and on the basis of which jurisdiction was assumed in the proceedings shall—

(*a*) if both parties to the marriage took part in the proceedings, be conclusive evidence of the fact found; and

(*b*) in any other case, be sufficient proof of that fact unless the contrary is shown.

(2) In this section "finding of fact" includes a finding that either party to the marriage—

(*a*) was habitually resident in the country in which the divorce, annulment or legal separation was obtained; or

(*b*) was under the law of that country domiciled there; or

(*c*) was a national of that country.

(3) For the purposes of subsection (1)(*a*) above, a party to the marriage who has appeared in judicial proceedings shall be treated as having taken part in them.

Supplemental

Modifications of Part II in relation to countries comprising territories having different systems of law

49.—(1) In relation to a country comprising territories in which different systems of law are in force in matters of divorce, annulment or legal separation, the provisions of this Part mentioned in subsections (2) to (5) below shall have effect subject to the modifications there specified.

(2) In the case of a divorce, annulment or legal separation the recognition of the validity of which depends on whether the requirements of subsection (1)(*b*)(i) or (ii) of section 46 of this Act are satisfied, that section and, in the case of a legal separation, section 47(2) of this Act shall have effect as if each territory were a separate country.

(3) In the case of a divorce, annulment or legal separation the recognition of the validity of which depends on whether the requirements of subsection (1)(*b*)(iii) of section 46 of this Act are satisfied—

(*a*) that section shall have effect as if for paragraph (*a*) of subsection (1) there were substituted the following paragraph—

"(*a*) the divorce, annulment or legal separation is effective throughout the country in which it was obtained;"; and

(*b*) in the case of a legal separation, section 47(2) of this Act shall have effect as if for the words "is effective under the law of that country" there were substituted the words "is effective throughout that country".

(4) In the case of a divorce, annulment or legal separation the recognition of the validity of which depends on whether the requirements of subsection (2)(*b*) of section 46 of this Act are satisfied, that section and section 52(3) and (4) of this Act and, in the case of a legal separation, section 47(2) of this Act shall have effect as if each territory were a separate country.

(5) Paragraphs (*a*) and (*b*) of section 48(2) of this Act shall each have effect as if each territory were a separate country.

Non-recognition of divorce or annulment in another jurisdiction no bar to remarriage

50. Where, in any part of the United Kingdom—

(*a*) a divorce or annulment has been granted by a court of civil jurisdiction, or

(*b*) the validity of a divorce or annulment is recognised by virtue of this Part,

the fact that the divorce or annulment would not be recognised elsewhere shall not preclude either party to the marriage from re-marrying in that part of the United Kingdom or cause the re-marriage of either party (wherever the re-marriage takes place) to be treated as invalid in that part.

Refusal of recognition

51.—(1) Subject to section 52 of this Act, recognition of the validity of—

(*a*) a divorce, annulment or judicial separation granted by a court of civil jurisdiction in any part of the British Islands, or

(*b*) an overseas divorce, annulment or legal separation,

may be refused in any part of the United Kingdom if the divorce, annulment or separation was granted or obtained at a time when it was irreconcilable with a decision determining the question of the subsistence or validity of the marriage of the parties previously given (whether before or after the commencement of this Part) by a court of civil jurisdiction in that part of the United Kingdom or by a court elsewhere and recognised or entitled to be recognised in that part of the United Kingdom.

(2) Subject to section 52 of this Act, recognition of the validity of—

(*a*) a divorce or judicial separation granted by a court of civil jurisdiction in any part of the British Islands, or

(*b*) an overseas divorce or legal separation,

may be refused in any part of the United Kingdom if the divorce or separation was granted or obtained at a time when, according to the law of that part of the United Kingdom (including its rules of private international law and the provisions of this Part), there was no subsisting marriage between the parties.

(3) Subject to section 52 of this Act, recognition by virtue of section 45 of this Act of the validity of an overseas divorce, annulment or legal separation may be refused if—

(*a*) in the case of a divorce, annulment or legal separation obtained by means of proceedings, it was obtained—

(i) without such steps having been taken for giving notice of the proceedings to a party to the marriage as, having regard to the nature of the proceedings and all the circumstances, should reasonably have been taken; or

(ii) without a party to the marriage having been given (for any reason other than lack of notice) such opportunity to take part in the proceedings as, having regard to those matters, he should reasonably have been given; or

(*b*) in the case of a divorce, annulment or legal separation obtained otherwise than by means of proceedings—

(i) there is no official document certifying that the divorce, annulment or legal separation is effective under the law of the country in which it was obtained; or

(ii) where either party to the marriage was domiciled in another country at the relevant date, there is no official document certifying that the divorce, annulment or legal separation is recognised as valid under the law of that other country; or

(*c*) in either case, recognition of the divorce, annulment or legal separation would be manifestly contrary to public policy.

(4) In this section—

"official", in relation to a document certifying that a divorce, annulment or legal separation is effective, or is recognised as valid, under the law of any country, means issued by a person or body appointed or recognised for the purpose under that law;

"the relevant date" has the same meaning as in section 46 of this Act;

and subsection (5) of that section shall apply for the purposes of this section as it applies for the purposes of that section.

(5) Nothing in this Part shall be construed as requiring the recognition of any finding of fault made in any proceedings for divorce, annulment or separation or of any maintenance, custody or other ancillary order made in any such proceedings.

Provisions as to divorces, annulments etc. obtained before commencement of Part II

52.—(1) The provisions of this Part shall apply—

(*a*) to a divorce, annulment or judicial separation granted by a court of civil jurisdiction in the British Islands before the date of the commencement of this Part, and

(*b*) to an overseas divorce, annulment or legal separation obtained before that date,

as well as to one granted or obtained on or after that date.

(2) In the case of such a divorce, annulment or separation as is mentioned in subsection (1)(*a*) or (*b*) above, the provisions of this Part shall require or, as the case may be, preclude the recognition of its validity in relation to any time before that date as well as in relation to any subsequent time, but those provisions shall not—

(*a*) affect any property to which any person became entitled before that date, or

(*b*) affect the recognition of the validity of the divorce, annulment or separation if that matter has been decided by any competent court in the British Islands before that date.

(3) Subsections (1) and (2) above shall apply in relation to any divorce or judicial separation granted by a court of civil jurisdiction in the British Islands before the date of the commencement of this Part whether granted before or after the commencement of section 1 of the Recognition of Divorces and Legal Separations Act 1971.

(4) The validity of any divorce, annulment or legal separation mentioned in subsection (5) below shall be recognised in the United Kingdom whether or not it is entitled to recognition by virtue of any of the foregoing provisions of this Part.

(5) The divorces, annulments and legal separations referred to in subsection (4) above are—

(*a*) a divorce which was obtained in the British Islands before 1st January 1974 and was recognised as valid under rules of law applicable before that date;

(*b*) an overseas divorce which was recognised as valid under the Recognition of Divorces and Legal Separations Act 1971 and was not affected by section 16(2) of the Domicile and Matrimonial Proceedings Act 1973 (proceedings otherwise than in a court of law where both parties resident in United Kingdom);

(*c*) a divorce of which the decree was registered under section 1 of the Indian and Colonial Divorce Jurisdiction Act 1926;

(*d*) a divorce or annulment which was recognised as valid under section 4 of the Matrimonial Causes (War Marriages) Act 1944; and

(*e*) an overseas legal separation which was recognised as valid under the Recognition of Divorces and Legal Separations Act 1971.

53. [Not applicable to Scotland.]

Interpretation of Part II

54.—(1) In this Part—

"annulment" includes any decree or declarator of nullity of marriage, however expressed;

"part of the United Kingdom" means England and Wales, Scotland or Northern Ireland;

"proceedings" means judicial or other proceedings.

(2) In this Part "country" includes a colony or other dependent territory of the United Kingdom but for the purposes of this Part a person shall be treated as a national of such a territory only if it has a law of citizenship or nationality separate from that of the United Kingdom and he is a citizen or national of that territory under that law.

Part III

Declarations of Status

55.–63. [Not applicable to Scotland.]

Part IV

Miscellaneous and General

64.–66. [Not applicable to Scotland.]

Amendments of Child Abduction and Custody Act 1985

67. [Amendments to ss.20 and 27 and the insertion of new s.24A in the Child Abduction and Custody Act 1985, are shown in the print of that Act.]

Minor and consequential amendments, repeals and savings

68.—(1) The enactments and orders mentioned in Schedule 1 to this Act shall have effect subject to the amendments specified in that Schedule, being minor amendments and amendments consequential on the provisions of this Act.

(2) The enactments mentioned in Schedule 2 to this Act (which include some that are spent or no longer of practical utility) are hereby repealed to the extent specified in the third column of that Schedule.

(3), (4) [Not applicable to Scotland.]

Short title, commencement and extent

69.—(1) This Act may be cited as the Family Law Act 1986.

(2) Sections 64 to 67 of this Act shall come into force at the end of the period of two months beginning with the day on which this Act is passed.

[1] (3) Subject to subsection (2) above, this Act shall come into force on such day as the relevant Minister or Ministers may by order made by statutory instrument appoint; and different days may be so appointed for different provisions or for different purposes.

(4) In subsection (3) above "the relevant Minister or Ministers" means—

(*a*) in the case of an order which appoints a day only for Part III of this Act and its associated amendments and repeals, the Lord Chancellor;

(*b*) in any other case, the Lord Chancellor and the Lord Advocate.

(5) The following provisions of this Act, namely—

Chapter II of Part I;
section 53;
Part III;
sections 64 and 65;
section 68(3); and
paragraphs 9 to 17, 19 and 23 to 27 of Schedule 1 and section 68(1) so far as relating to those paragraphs,

extend to England and Wales only.

(6) The following provisions of this Act, namely—

Chapter III of Part I;
section 26; and
paragraphs 1, 3 to 8, 18, 21 and 22 of Schedule 1 and section 68(1) so far as relating to those paragraphs,

extend to Scotland only; and sections 34 and 38 of this Act do not extend to Scotland.

(7) The following provisions of this Act, namely—

Chapter IV of Part I;
section 66;
section 68(4); and
paragraphs 2 and 32 to 34 of Schedule 1 and section 68(1) so far as relating to those paragraphs,

extend to Northern Ireland only; and paragraph 20 of Schedule 1 to this Act and section 68(1) of this Act so far as relating to that paragraph do not extend to Northern Ireland.

NOTE

[1] S.I. 1988 No. 375 brought the provisions applicable to Scotland into force on 1st April 1988.

SCHEDULES

Section 68(1)

SCHEDULE 1

MINOR AND CONSEQUENTIAL AMENDMENTS

The Conjugal Rights (Scotland) Amendment Act 1861 (c. 86)

1. In section 9 of the Conjugal Rights (Scotland) Amendment Act 1861 (interim orders respecting children)—

(*a*) after the words "decree make" there shall be inserted the words "an order making";

(*b*) at the end there shall be added the following subsection—

"(2) An order made by a court under subsection (1) above may, on the application of any person concerned, be varied, recalled or set aside by a subsequent order by that court made at any time before the child concerned attains the age of sixteen."

The Guardianship of Infants Act 1886 (c. 27)

2. [Not applicable to Scotland.]

The Sheriff Courts (Scotland) Act 1907 (c. 51)

3. [Amends s. 6 (jurisdiction of sheriff): amendment incorporated in that Act—Division D, *supra.*]

The Matrimonial Proceedings (Children) Act 1958 (c. 40)

4–7. [These paragraphs amend respectively s. 8(1) (children's welfare in divorce etc.), s. 9(1) (jurisdiction as respects children), s. 10(1) (committing care of child to local authority etc.) and s. 11(1) (reports as to arrangements for children) of the 1958 Act: amendments incorporated in that Act, *supra.*]

The Law Reform (Miscellaneous Provisions) (Scotland) Act 1966 (c. 19)

8. [Amends s. 8(6) (variation of Court of Session orders by sheriff): amendment incorporated in that Act—Division D, *supra.*]

9–20. [Not applicable to Scotland.]

The Marriage (Scotland) Act 1977 (c. 15)

21 and 22. [Amend s. 3(5) (certificate of capacity to marry) and s. 26(2) (interpretation): amendments incorporated in that Act, *supra.*]

23–27. [Not applicable to Scotland.]

The Child Abduction and Custody Act 1985 (c. 60)

28–31. [These paragraphs amend respectively s. 9 (court's powers on wrongful removal), s. 20(2) (suspension of court's powers), s. 27(1) (interpretation) and para. 5 of Schedule 3 (custody orders in Scotland): amendments incorporated in that Act, *supra.*]

32–34. [Not applicable to Scotland.]

Section 68(2) SCHEDULE 2

REPEALS

Chapter	Short title	Extent of repeal
31 & 32 Vict. c. 20.	The Legitimacy Declaration Act (Ireland) 1868.	Section 2.
47 & 48 Vict. c. 20.	The Greek Marriages Act 1884.	The whole Act.
49 & 50 Vict. c. 27.	The Guardianship of Infants Act 1886.	In section 9, the words from "court within" to "reside".
16 & 17 Geo. 5. c. 40.	Indian and Colonial Divorce Jurisdiction Act 1926.	The whole Act.
3 & 4 Geo. 6. c. 35.	Indian and Colonial Divorce Jurisdiction Act 1940.	The whole Act.
7 & 8 Geo. 6. c. 43.	Matrimonial Causes (War Marriages) Act 1944.	The whole Act.
10 & 11 Geo. 6. c. 30.	Indian Independence Act 1947.	Section 17.
11 & 12 Geo. 6. c. 3.	Burma Independence Act 1947.	Section 4(3).
11 & 12 Geo. 6. c. 7.	Ceylon Independence Act 1947.	Section 3. In Schedule 2, paragraph 9.
14 Geo. 6. c. 20.	Colonial and Other Territories (Divorce Jurisdiction) Act 1950.	The whole Act.
14 Geo. 6. c. 37.	The Maintenance Orders Act 1950.	Section 7.
6 & 7 Eliz. 2. c. 40.	The Matrimonial Proceedings (Children) Act 1958.	Section 13.

Chapter	Short title	Extent of repeal
8 & 9 Eliz. 2. c. 52.	Cyprus Act 1960.	In the Schedule, paragraph 14.
8 & 9 Eliz. 2. c. 55	Nigeria Independence Act 1960.	In Schedule 2, paragraph 14.
9 & 10 Eliz. 2. c. 16.	Sierra Leone Independence Act 1961.	In Schedule 3, paragraph 15.
10 & 11 Eliz. 2. c. 1.	Tanganyika Independence Act 1961.	In Schedule 2, paragraph 15.
10 & 11 Eliz. 2. c. 23.	South Africa Act 1962.	In Schedule 3, paragraph 9.
10 & 11 Eliz. 2. c. 40.	Jamaica Independence Act 1962.	In Schedule 2, paragraph 14.
10 & 11 Eliz. 2. c. 54.	Trinidad and Tobago Independence Act 1962.	In Schedule 2, paragraph 14.
10 & 11 Eliz. 2. c. 57.	Uganda Independence Act 1962.	In Schedule 3, paragraph 13.
1963 c. 54.	Kenya Independence Act 1963.	Section 7.
1964 c. 46.	Malawi Independence Act 1964.	Section 6.
1964 c. 65.	Zambia Independence Act 1964.	Section 7.
1966 c. 19.	The Law Reform (Miscellaneous Provisions) (Scotland) Act 1966.	In section 8(2), the words "made in a consistorial action".
1966 c. 29.	Singapore Act 1966.	Section 2.
1968 c. 63.	The Domestic and Appellate Proceedings (Restriction of Publicity) Act 1968.	Section 2(1)(*a*).
1969 c. 29.	Tanzania Act 1969.	Section 2. In section 4(3), the words "or the Divorce Jurisdiction Acts". Section 7(1).
1971 c. 3.	The Guardianship of Minors Act 1971.	Section 15 (3) to (6). Section 17(2).
1971 c. 53.	Recognition of Divorces and Legal Separations Act 1971.	The whole Act.
1973 c. 18.	The Matrimonial Causes Act 1973.	Section 45. In section 50(2), in paragraph (*b*), the words "proceedings in a county court under section 45 above or to" and, in paragraph (*c*), the words "or to any aspect of section 47 above which is excepted by paragraph (*b*) above".
1973 c. 29.	The Guardianship Act 1973.	In section 1(6), the words from "except that" to the end. In section 2(1), the words "15", "and section 15(3) to (6)" and "they are". Section 5(3). In Schedule 2, in Part I, paragraph 3, and in Part II, the text of section 15(3) to (6) of the Guardianship of Minors Act 1971.
1973 c. 45.	Domicile and Matrimonial Proceedings Act 1973.	Section 2. Sections 15 and 16.
1973 c. 48.	The Pakistan Act 1973.	In section 4(5), the words from the beginning to "1940, and".
1975 c. 72.	The Children Act 1975.	In section 33(1), the words from "if" to the end.

Chapter	Short title	Extent of repeal
		In section 53(1), the words from "but where" to the end. Section 54. In section 100(8), the words "or 42".
1981 c. 54.	The Supreme Court Act 1981.	In section 26(*b*), the words "or jactitation of marriage".
1984 c. 42.	The Matrimonial and Family Proceedings Act 1984.	In Schedule 1, paragraph 14.
1985 c. 73.	The Law Reform (Miscellaneous Provisions) (Scotland) Act 1985.	Section 16.

[THE NEXT PAGE IS K 303]

Registered Establishments (Scotland) Act 1987

(1987 c. 40)

An Act to make further provision as to the registration of establishments under the Social Work (Scotland) Act 1968 . . . ; and for connected purposes. [15th May 1987]

[The provisions of this Act which amend the Social Work (Scotland) Act 1968, ss. 61–65 and 94(1), have been given effect in the print of that Act, *supra*. The Act was brought into force on 17th October 1988 by ministerial order dated 26th September 1988.]

Human Fertilisation and Embryology Act 1990

(1990 c. 37)

An Act to make provision in connection with human embryos and any subsequent development of such embryos; to prohibit certain practices in connection with embryos and gametes; to establish a Human Fertilisation and Embryology Authority; to make provision about the persons who in certain circumstances are to be treated in law as the parents of a child; and to amend the Surrogacy Arrangements Act 1985. [1st November 1990]

ARRANGEMENT OF SECTIONS

Grant, revocation and suspension of licences

Directions and guidance

Status

Information

Surrogacy

Abortion

Conscientious objection

Enforcement

Offences

Miscellaneous and General

Principal terms used

Meaning of "embryo", "gamete" and associated expressions

1.—(1) In this Act, except where otherwise stated—

(*a*) embryo means a live human embryo where fertilisation is complete, and

(*b*) references to an embryo include an egg in the process of fertilisation,

and, for this purpose, fertilisation is not complete until the appearance of a two cell zygote.

(2) This Act, so far as it governs bringing about the creation of an embryo, applies only to bringing about the creation of an embryo outside the human body; and in this Act—

(*a*) references to embryos the creation of which was brought about *in vitro* (in their application to those where fertilisation is complete) are to those where fertilisation began outside the human body whether or not it was completed there, and

(*b*) references to embryos taken from a woman do not include embryos whose creation was brought about *in vitro*.

(3) This Act, so far as it governs the keeping or use of an embryo, applies only to keeping or using an embryo outside the human body.

(4) References in this Act to gametes, eggs or sperm, except where otherwise stated, are to live human gametes, eggs or sperm but references below in this Act to gametes or eggs do not include eggs in the process of fertilisation.

Other terms

2.—(1) In this Act—

"the Authority" means the Human Fertilisation and Embryology Authority established under section 5 of this Act,

"directions" means directions under section 23 of this Act,

"licence" means a licence under Schedule 2 to this Act and, in relation to a licence, "the person responsible" has the meaning given by section 17 of this Act, and

"treatment services" means medical, surgical or obstetric services provided to the public or a section of the public for the purpose of assisting women to carry children.

(2) References in this Act to keeping, in relation to embryos or gametes, include keeping while preserved, whether preserved by cryopreservation or in any other way; and embryos or gametes so kept are referred to in this Act as "stored" (and "store" and "storage" are to be interpreted accordingly).

(3) For the purposes of this Act, a woman is not to be treated as carrying a child until the embryo has become implanted.

Activities governed by the Act

Prohibitions in connection with embryos

3.—(1) No person shall—

(*a*) bring about the creation of an embryo, or

(*b*) keep or use an embryo,

except in pursuance of a licence.

(2) No person shall place in a woman—
(*a*) a live embryo other than a human embryo, or
(*b*) any live gametes other than human gametes.
(3) A licence cannot authorise—
(*a*) keeping or using an embryo after the appearance of the primitive streak,
(*b*) placing an embryo in any animal,
(*c*) keeping or using an embryo in any circumstances in which regulations prohibit its keeping or use, or
(*d*) replacing a nucleus of a cell of an embryo with a nucleus taken from a cell of any person, embryo or subsequent development of an embryo.

(4) For the purposes of subsection (3)(*a*) above, the primitive streak is to be taken to have appeared in an embryo not later than the end of the period of 14 days beginning with the day when the gametes are mixed, not counting any time during which the embryo is stored.

Prohibition in connection with germ cells

[1] **3A.**—(1) No person shall, for the purpose of providing fertility services for any woman, use female germ cells taken or derived from an embryo or a foetus or use embryos created by using such cells.

(2) In this section—

"female germ cells" means cells of the female germ line and includes such cells at any stage of maturity and accordingly includes eggs; and

"fertility services" means medical, surgical or obstetric services provided for the purpose of assisting women to carry children.

NOTE

[1] Inserted by the Criminal Justice and Public Order Act 1994 (c. 33), s. 56(2) (effective 10th April 1995: S.I. 1995 No. 721).

Prohibitions in connection with gametes

4.—(1) No person shall—
(*a*) store any gametes, or
(*b*) in the course of providing treatment services for any woman, use the sperm of any man unless the services are being provided for the woman and the man together or use the eggs of any other woman, or
(*c*) mix gametes with the live gametes of any animal,
except in pursuance of a licence.

(2) A licence cannot authorise storing or using gametes in any circumstances in which regulations prohibit their storage or use.

(3) No person shall place sperm and eggs in a woman in any circumstances specified in regulations except in pursuance of a licence.

(4) Regulations made by virtue of subsection (3) above may provide that, in relation to licences only to place sperm and eggs in a woman in such circumstances, sections 12 to 22 of this Act shall have effect with such modifications as may be specified in the regulations.

(5) Activities regulated by this section or section 3 of this Act are referred to in this Act as "activities governed by this Act".

The Human Fertilisation and Embryology Authority, its functions and procedure; Licences, Directions and Guidance

5–26. [Not printed.]

Status

Meaning of "mother"

[1] **27.**—(1) The woman who is carrying or has carried a child as a result of the placing in her of an embryo or of sperm and eggs, and no other woman, is to be treated as the mother of the child.

(2) Subsection (1) above does not apply to any child to the extent that the child is treated by virtue of adoption as not being the child of any person other than the adopter or adopters.

(3) Subsection (1) above applies whether the woman was in the United Kingdom or elsewhere at the time of the placing in her of the embryo or the sperm and eggs.

NOTE

[1] Saved by the Children (Scotland) Act 1995 (c. 36), s. 15(1) (prospective).

Meaning of "father"

[1] **28.**—(1) This section applies in the case of a child who is being or has been carried by a woman as the result of the placing in her of an embryo or of sperm and eggs or her artificial insemination.

[THE NEXT PAGE IS K 307]

(2) If—

(*a*) at the time of the placing in her of the embryo or the sperm and eggs or of her insemination, the woman was a party to a marriage, and

(*b*) the creation of the embryo carried by her was not brought about with the sperm of the other party to the marriage.

then, subject to subsection (5) below, the other party to the marriage shall be treated as the father of the child unless it is shown that he did not consent to the placing in her of the embryo or the sperm and eggs or to her insemination (as the case may be).

(3) If no man is treated, by virtue of subsection (2) above, as the father of the child but—

(*a*) the embryo or the sperm and eggs were placed in the woman, or she was artificially inseminated, in the course of treatment services provided for her and a man together by a person to whom a licence applies, and

(*b*) the creation of the embryo carried by her was not brought about with the sperm of that man,

then, subject to subsection (5) below, that man shall be treated as the father of the child.

(4) Where a person is treated as the father of the child by virtue of subsection (2) or (3) above, no other person is to be treated as the father of the child.

(5) Subsections (2) and (3) above do not apply—

(*a*) in relation to England and Wales and Northern Ireland, to any child who, by virtue of the rules of common law, is treated as the legitimate child of the parties to a marriage,

(*b*) in relation to Scotland, to any child who, by virtue of any enactment or other rule of law, is treated as the child of the parties to a marriage, or

(*c*) to any child to the extent that the child is treated by virtue of adoption as not being the child of any person other than the adopter or adopters.

(6) Where—

(*a*) the sperm of a man who had given such consent as is required by paragraph 5 of Schedule 3 to this Act was used for a purpose for which such consent was required, or

(*b*) the sperm of a man, or any embryo the creation of which was brought about with his sperm, was used after his death,

he is not to be treated as the father of the child.

(7) The references in subsection (2) above to the parties to a marriage at the time there referred to—

(*a*) are to the parties to a marriage subsisting at that time, unless a judicial separation was then in force, but

(*b*) include the parties to a void marriage if either or both of them reasonably believed at that time that the marriage was valid; and for the purposes of this subsection it shall be presumed, unless the contrary is shown, that one of them reasonably believed at that time that the marriage was valid.

(8) This section applies whether the woman was in the United Kingdom or elsewhere at the time of the placing in her of the embryo or the sperm and eggs or her artificial insemination.

(9) In subsection (7)(*a*) above, "judicial separation" includes a legal separation obtained in a country outside the British Islands and recognised in the United Kingdom.

NOTE

[1] Saved by the Children (Scotland) Act 1995 (c. 36), s. 15(1) (prospective).

Effect of sections 27 and 28

[1] **29.**—(1) Where by virtue of section 27 or 28 of this Act a person is to be treated as the mother or father of a child, that person is to be treated in law as the mother or, as the case may be, father of the child for all purposes.

(2) Where by virtue of section 27 or 28 of this Act a person is not to be treated as the mother or father of a child, that person is to be treated in law as not being the mother or, as the case may be, father of the child for any purpose.

(3) Where subsection (1) or (2) above has effect, references to any relationship between two people in any enactment, deed or other instrument or document (whenever passed or made) are to be read accordingly.

(4) In relation to England and Wales and Northern Ireland, nothing in the provisions of section 27(1) or 28(2) to (4), read with this section, affects—

(*a*) the succession to any dignity or title of honour or renders any person capable of succeeding to or transmitting a right to succeed to any such dignity or title, or

(*b*) the devolution of any property limited (expressly or not) to devolve (as nearly as the law permits) along with any dignity or title of honour.

(5) In relation to Scotland—

(*a*) those provisions do not apply to any title, coat of arms, honour or dignity transmissible on the death of the holder thereof or affect the succession thereto or the devolution thereof, and

(*b*) where the terms of any deed provide that any property or interest in property shall devolve along with a title, coat of arms, honour or dignity, nothing in those provisions shall prevent that property or interest from so devolving.

NOTE

[1] Saved by the Children (Scotland) Act 1995 (c. 36), s. 15(1) (prospective).

Parental orders in favour of gamete donors

[1] **30.**—(1) The court may make an order providing for a child to be treated in law as the child of the parties to a marriage (referred to in this section as "the husband" and "the wife") if—

(*a*) the child has been carried by a woman other than the wife as the result of the placing in her of an embryo or sperm and eggs or her artificial insemination,

(*b*) the gametes of the husband or the wife, or both, were used to bring about the creation of the embryo, and

(*c*) the conditions in subsections (2) to (7) below are satisfied.

(2) The husband and the wife must apply for the order within six months of the birth of the child or, in the case of a child born before the coming into force of this Act, within six months of such coming into force.

(3) At the time of the application and of the making of the order—

(*a*) the child's home must be with the husband and the wife, and

(*b*) the husband or the wife, or both of them, must be domiciled in a part of the United Kingdom or in the Channel Islands or the Isle of Man.

(4) At the time of the making of the order both the husband and the wife must have attained the age of eighteen.

(5) The court must be satisfied that both the father of the child (including a person who is the father by virtue of section 28 of this Act), where he is not the husband, and the woman who carried the child have freely, and with full understanding of what is involved, agreed unconditionally to the making of the order.

(6) Subsection (5) above does not require the agreement of a person who cannot be found or is incapable of giving agreement and the agreement of

the woman who carried the child is ineffective for the purposes of that subsection if given by her less than six weeks after the child's birth.

(7) The court must be satisfied that no money or other benefit (other than for expenses reasonably incurred) has been given or received by the husband or the wife for or in consideration of—

(*a*) the making of the order,

(*b*) any agreement required by subsection (5) above,

(*c*) the handing over of the child to the husband and the wife, or

(*d*) the making of any arrangements with a view to the making of the order,

unless authorised by the court.

(8) For the purposes of an application under this section—

(*a*) in relation to England and Wales, section 92(7) to (10) of, and Part I of Schedule 11 to, the Children Act 1989 (jurisdiction of courts) shall apply for the purposes of this section to determine the meaning of "the court" as they apply for the purposes of that Act and proceedings on the application shall be "family proceedings" for the purposes of that Act,

(*b*) in relation to Scotland, "the court" means the Court of Session or the sheriff court of the sheriffdom within which the child is, and

(*c*) in relation to Northern Ireland, "the court" means the High Court or any county court within whose division the child is.

(9) Regulations may provide—

(*a*) for any provision of the enactments about adoption to have effect, with such modifications (if any) as may be specified in the regulations, in relation to orders under this section, and applications for such orders, as it has effect in relation to adoption, and applications for adoption orders, and

(*b*) for references in any enactment to adoption, an adopted child or an adoptive relationship to be read (respectively) as references to the effect of an order under this section, a child to whom such an order applies and a relationship arising by virtue of the enactments about adoption, as applied by the regulations, and for similar expressions in connection with adoption to be read accordingly,

and the regulations may include such incidental or supplemental provision as appears to the Secretary of State necessary or desirable in consequence of any provision made by virtue of paragraph (*a*) or (*b*) above.

(10) In this section "the enactments about adoption" means the Adoption Act 1976, the Adoption (Scotland) Act 1978 and the Adoption (Northern Ireland) Order 1987.

(11) Subsection (1)(*a*) above applies whether the woman was in the United Kingdom or elsewhere at the time of the placing in her of the embryo or the sperm and eggs or her artificial insemination.

NOTE

[1] Saved by the Children (Scotland) Act 1995 (c. 36), s. 15(1) (prospective).

Information

The Authority's register of information

31.—(1) The Authority shall keep a register which shall contain any information obtained by the Authority which falls within subsection (2) below.

(2) Information falls within this subsection if it relates to—

(*a*) the provision of treatment services for any identifiable individual, or

(*b*) the keeping or use of the gametes of any identifiable individual or of an embryo taken from any identifiable woman,

or if it shows that any identifiable individual was, or may have been, born in consequence of treatment services.

(3) A person who has attained the age of eighteen ("the applicant") may by notice to the Authority require the Authority to comply with a request under subsection (4) below, and the Authority shall do so if—

(*a*) the information contained in the register shows that the applicant was, or may have been, born in consequence of treatment services, and

(*b*) the applicant has been given a suitable opportunity to receive proper counselling about the implications of compliance with the request.

(4) The applicant may request the Authority to give the applicant notice stating whether or not the information contained in the register shows that a person other than a parent of the applicant would or might, but for sections 27 to 29 of this Act, be a parent of the applicant and, if it does show that—

(*a*) giving the applicant so much of that information as relates to the person concerned as the Authority is required by regulations to give (but no other information), or

(*b*) stating whether or not that information shows that, but for sections 27 to 29 of this Act, the applicant, and a person specified in the request as a person whom the applicant proposes to marry, would or might be related.

(5) Regulations cannot require the Authority to give any information as to the identity of a person whose gametes have been used or from whom an embryo has been taken if a person to whom a licence applied was provided with the information at a time when the Authority could not have been required to give information of the kind in question.

(6) A person who has not attained the age of eighteen ("the minor") may by notice to the Authority specifying another person ("the intended spouse") as a person whom the minor proposes to marry require the Authority to comply with a request under subsection (7) below, and the Authority shall do so if—

(*a*) the information contained in the register shows that the minor was, or may have been, born in consequence of treatment services, and

(*b*) the minor has been given a suitable opportunity to receive proper counselling about the implications of compliance with the request.

(7) The minor may request the Authority to give the minor notice stating whether or not the information contained in the register shows that, but for sections 27 to 29 of this Act, the minor and the intended spouse would or might be related.

Information to be provided to Registrar General

32.—(1) This section applies where a claim is made before the Registrar General that a man is or is not the father of a child and it is necessary or desirable for the purpose of any function of the Registrar General to determine whether the claim is or may be well-founded.

(2) The Authority shall comply with any request made by the Registrar General by notice to the Authority to disclose whether any information on the register kept in pursuance of section 31 of this Act tends to show that the man may be the father of the child by virtue of section 28 of this Act and, if it does, disclose that information.

(3) In this section and section 33 of this Act, "the Registrar General" means the Registrar General for England and Wales, the Registrar General of Births, Deaths and Marriages for Scotland or the Registrar General for Northern Ireland, as the case may be.

Restrictions on disclosure of information

33.—(1) No person who is or has been a member or employee of the Authority shall disclose any information mentioned in subsection (2) below which he holds or has held as such a member or employee.

(2) The information referred to in subsection (1) above is—

(*a*) any information contained or required to be contained in the register kept in pursuance of section 31 of this Act, and

(*b*) any other information obtained by any member or employee of the Authority on terms or in circumstances requiring it to be held in confidence.

[THE NEXT PAGE IS K 310/1]

(3) Subsection (1) above does not apply to any disclosure of information mentioned in subsection (2)(*a*) above made—

(*a*) to a person as a member or employee of the Authority,

(*b*) to a person to whom a licence applies for the purposes of his functions as such,

(*c*) so that no individual to whom the information relates can be identified,

(*d*) in pursuance of an order of a court under section 34 or 35 of this Act,

(*e*) to the Registrar General in pursuance of a request under section 32 of this Act, or

(*f*) in accordance with section 31 of this Act.

(4) Subsection (1) above does not apply to any disclosure of information mentioned in subsection (2)(*b*) above—

(*a*) made to a person as a member or employee of the Authority,

(*b*) made with the consent of the person or persons whose confidence would otherwise be protected, or

(*c*) which has been lawfully made available to the public before the disclosure is made.

(5) No person who is or has been a person to whom a licence applies and no person to whom directions have been given shall disclose any information falling within section 31(2) of this Act which he holds or has held as such a person.

(6) Subsection (5) above does not apply to any disclosure of information made—

(*a*) to a person as a member or employee of the Authority,

(*b*) to a person to whom a licence applies for the purposes of his functions as such,

(*c*) so far as it identifies a person who, but for sections 27 to 29 of this Act, would or might be a parent of a person who instituted proceedings under section 1A of the Congenital Disabilities (Civil Liability) Act 1976, but only for the purpose of defending such proceedings, or instituting connected proceedings for compensation against that parent,

(*d*) so that no individual to whom the information relates can be identified,

(*e*) in pursuance of directions given by virtue of section 24(5) or (6) of this Act,

[1] (*f*) necessarily—

(i) for any purpose preliminary to proceedings, or

(ii) for the purposes of, or in connection with, any proceedings,

[1] (*g*) for the purpose of establishing, in any proceedings relating to an application for an order under subsection (1) of section 30 of this Act, whether the condition specified in paragraph (*a*) or (*b*) of that subsection is met, or

[1] (*h*) under section 3 of the Access to Health Records Act 1990 (right of access to health records).

[2] (6A) Paragraph (*f*) of subsection (6) above, so far as relating to disclosure for the purposes of, or in connection with, any proceedings, does not apply—

(*a*) to disclosure of information enabling a person to be identified as a person whose gametes were used, in accordance with consent given under paragraph 5 of Schedule 3 to this Act, for the purposes of treatment services in consequence of which an identifiable individual was, or may have been, born, or

(*b*) to disclosure, in circumstances in which subsection (1) of section 34 of this Act applies, of information relevant to the determination of the question mentioned in that subsection.

[2] (6B) In the case of information relating to the provision of treatment services for any identifiable individual—

(*a*) where one individual is identifiable, subsection (5) above does not apply to disclosure with the consent of that individual;

(*b*) where both a woman and a man treated together with her are identifiable, subsection (5) above does not apply—

(i) to disclosure with the consent of them both, or

(ii) if disclosure is made for the purpose of disclosing information about the provision of treatment services for one of them, to disclosure with the consent of that individual.

[2] (6C) For the purposes of subsection (6B) above, consent must be to disclosure to a specific person, except where disclosure is to a person who needs to know—

(*a*) in connection with the provision of treatment services, or any other description of medical, surgical or obstetric services, for the individual giving the consent,

(*b*) in connection with the carrying out of an audit of clinical practice, or

(*c*) in connection with the auditing of accounts.

[2] (6D) For the purposes of subsection (6B) above, consent to disclosure given at the request of another shall be disregarded unless, before it is given, the person requesting it takes reasonable steps to explain to the individual from whom it is requested the implications of compliance with the request.

[2] (6E) In the case of information which relates to the provision of treatment services for any identifiable individual, subsection (5) above does not apply to disclosure in an emergency, that is to say, to disclosure made—

(*a*) by a person who is satisfied that it is necessary to make the disclosure to avert an imminent danger to the health of an individual with whose consent the information could be disclosed under subsection (6B) above, and

(*b*) in circumstances where it is not reasonably practicable to obtain that individual's consent.

[2] (6F) In the case of information which shows that any identifiable individual was, or may have been, born in consequence of treatment services, subsection (5) above does not apply to any disclosure which is necessarily incidental to disclosure under subsection (6B) or (6E) above.

[2] (6G) Regulations may provide for additional exceptions from subsection (5) above, but no exception may be made under this subsection—

(*a*) for disclosure of a kind mentioned in paragraph (*a*) or (*b*) of subsection (6A) above, or

(*b*) for disclosure, in circumstances in which section 32 of this Act applies, of information having the tendency mentioned in subsection (2) of that section.

(7) This section does not apply to the disclosure to any individual of information which—

(*a*) falls within section 31(2) of this Act by virtue of paragraph (*a*) or (*b*) of that subsection, and

(*b*) relates only to that individual or, in the case of an individual treated together with another, only to that individual and that other.

(8) At the end of Part IV of the Data Protection Act 1984 (Exemptions) there is inserted—

"**Information about human embryos, etc.**

35A. Personal data consisting of information showing that an identifiable individual was, or may have been, born in consequence of treatment services (within the meaning of the Human Fertilisation and Embryology Act 1990) are exempt from the subject access provisions except so far as their disclosure under those provisions is made in accordance with section 31 of that Act (the Authority's register of information)."

[3] (9) In subsection (6)(*f*) above, references to proceedings include any formal procedure for dealing with a complaint.

NOTE

[1] Inserted by the Human Fertilisation and Embryology (Disclosure of Information) Act 1992 (c. 54), s. 1(2), in relation to information obtained before, as well as after, the passing of the Act (16th July 1992): s. 1(5).

[2] Inserted by the Human Fertilisation and Embryology (Disclosure of Information) Act 1992 (c. 54), s. 1(3), in relation to information obtained before, as well as after, the passing of the Act (16th July 1992): s. 1(5).

[3] Inserted by the Human Fertilisation and Embryology (Disclosure of Information) Act 1992 (c. 54), s. 1(4), in relation to information obtained before, as well as after, the passing of the Act (16th July 1992): s. 1(5).

Disclosure in interests of justice

34.—(1) Where in any proceedings before a court the question whether a person is or is not the parent of a child by virtue of sections 27 to 29 of this Act falls to be determined, the court may on the application of any party to the proceedings make an order requiring the Authority—

(*a*) to disclose whether or not any information relevant to that question is contained in the register kept in pursuance of section 31 of this Act, and

(*b*) if it is, to disclose so much of it as is specified in the order,

but such an order may not require the Authority to disclose any information falling within section 31(2)(*b*) of this Act.

(2) The court must not make an order under subsection (1) above unless it is satisfied that the interests of justice require it to do so, taking into account—

(*a*) any representations made by any individual who may be affected by the disclosure, and

(*b*) the welfare of the child, if under 18 years old, and of any other person under that age who may be affected by the disclosure.

(3) If the proceedings before the court are civil proceedings, it—

(*a*) may direct that the whole or any part of the proceedings on the application for an order under subsection (2) above shall be heard in camera, and

(*b*) if it makes such an order, may then or later direct that the whole or any part of any later stage of the proceedings shall be heard in camera.

(4) An application for a direction under subsection (3) above shall be heard in camera unless the court otherwise directs.

Disclosure in interests of justice: congenital disabilities etc.

35.—(1) [England and Wales and Northern Ireland.]

(2) Where, for the purposes of any action for damages in Scotland (including any such action which is likely to be brought) in which the damages claimed consist of or include damages or solatium in respect of personal injury (including any disease and any impairment of physical or mental condition), it is necessary to identify a person who would or might be the parent of a child but for sections 27 to 29 of this Act, the court may, on the application of any party to the action or, if the proceedings have not been commenced, the prospective pursuer, make an order requiring the Authority to disclose any information contained in the register kept in pursuance of section 31 of this Act identifying that person.

(3) Subsections (2) to (4) of section 34 of this Act apply for the purposes of this section as they apply for the purposes of that.

(4) [England and Wales and Northern Ireland.]

Surrogacy

Amendment of Surrogacy Arrangements Act 1985

36.—(1) After section 1 of the Surrogacy Arrangements Act 1985 there is inserted—

"**Surrogacy arrangements unenforceable**

1A. No surrogacy arrangement is enforceable by or against any of the persons making it."

(2) In section 1 of that Act (meaning of "surrogate mother", etc.)—

(*a*) in subsection (6), for "or, as the case may be, embryo insertion" there is substituted "or of the placing in her of an embryo, of an egg in the process of fertilisation or of sperm and eggs, as the case may be,", and

(*b*) in subsection (9), the words from "and whether" to the end are repealed.

Abortion

37. [Not printed.]

Conscientious objection

Conscientious objection

38.—(1) No person who has a conscientious objection to participating in any activity governed by this Act shall be under any duty, however arising, to do so.

(2) In any legal proceedings the burden of proof of conscientious objection shall rest on the person claiming to rely on it.

(3) In any proceedings before a court in Scotland, a statement on oath by any person to the effect that he has a conscientious objection to participating in a particular activity governed by this Act shall be sufficient evidence of that fact for the purpose of discharging the burden of proof imposed by subsection (2) above.

Enforcemenmt; Offences

39–42. [Not printed.]

Miscellaneous and General

43–46. [Not printed.]

Index

47. The expressions listed in the left-hand column below are respectively defined or (as the case may be) are to be interpreted in accordance with the provisions of this Act listed in the right-hand column in relation to those expressions.

Expression	*Relevant provision*
Activities governed by this Act	Section 4(5)
Authority	Section 2(1)
Carry, in relation to a child	Section 2(3)
Directions	Section 2(1)
Embryo	Section 1
Gametes, eggs or sperm	Section 1
Keeping, in relation to embryos or gametes	Section 2(2)

Expression	*Relevant provision*
Licence	Section 2(1)
Licence committee	Section 9(1)
Nominal licensee	Section 17(3)
Person responsible	Section 17(1)
Person to whom a licence applies	Section 17(2)
Statutory storage period	Section 14(3) to (5)
Store, and similar expressions, in relation to embryos or gametes	Section 2(2)
Treatment services	Section 2(1)

48. [Northern Ireland.]

Short title, commencement, etc.

49.—(1) This Act may be cited as the Human Fertilisation and Embryology Act 1990.

[1] (2) This Act shall come into force on such day as the Secretary of State may by order made by statutory instrument appoint and different days may be appointed for different provisions and for different purposes.

(3) Sections 27 to 29 of this Act shall have effect only in relation to children carried by women as a result of the placing in them of embryos or of sperm and eggs, or of their artificial insemination (as the case may be), after the commencement of those sections.

(4) [England and Wales.]

(5) Schedule 4 to this Act (which makes minor and consequential amendments) shall have effect.

(6) [Transitional.]

(7) [Channel Islands.]

NOTE

[1] Of the provisions reprinted, all were fully in force by 1st August 1991 (S.I. 1990 No. 2165 and 1991 No. 1400), except s. 30, of which subss. (9) and (10) came into force on 5th July 1994, and the remainder on 1st November 1994, by S.I. 1994 No. 1776.

Section 5

SCHEDULES

SCHEDULE 1

THE AUTHORITY: SUPPLEMENTARY PROVISIONS

. . . . . .

Section 11

SCHEDULE 2

ACTIVITIES FOR WHICH LICENCES MAY BE GRANTED

. . . . . .

Section 12

SCHEDULE 3

CONSENTS TO USE OF GAMETES OR EMBRYOS

. . . . . .

Section 49

SCHEDULE 4

MINOR AND CONSEQUENTIAL AMENDMENTS

1. [England and Wales.]

Social Security Act 1975 (c. 14)

2. [Amends s. 25(1) of the Social Security Act 1975, consolidated as s. 37(1)(*c*) of the Social Security Contributions and Benefits Act 1992 (c. 4).]
3. [Northern Ireland.]
4. [England and Wales.]
5. [Northern Ireland.]

Adoption (Scotland) Act 1978 (c. 28)

6. [Amends s. 15(3)(*a*) (conditions for making an adoption order on application of one parent): amendment incorporated in that Act, *supra*.]
7. [Northern Ireland.]

Human Organ Transplants Act 1989 (c. 31)

8. Sections 27 to 29 of this Act do not apply for the purposes of section 2 of the Human Organ Transplants Act 1989 (restrictions on transplants between persons not genetically related).
9. [Northern Ireland.]

Child Support Act 1991

(1991 c. 48)

ARRANGEMENT OF SECTIONS

The basic principles

An Act to make provision for the assessment, collection and enforcement of periodical maintenance payable by certain parents with respect to children of theirs who are not in their care; for the collection and enforcement of certain other kinds of maintenance; and for connected purposes. [25th July 1991]

The basic principles

The duty to maintain

1.—(1) For the purposes of this Act, each parent of a qualifying child is responsible for maintaining him.

(2) For the purposes of this Act, an absent parent shall be taken to have met his responsibility to maintain any qualifying child of his by making periodical payments of maintenance with respect to the child of such amount, and at such intervals, as may be determined in accordance with the provisions of this Act.

(3) Where a maintenance assessment made under this Act requires the making of periodical payments, it shall be the duty of the absent parent with respect to whom the assessment was made to make those payments.

Welfare of children: the general principle

2. Where, in any case which falls to be dealt with under this Act, the Secretary of State or any child support officer is considering the exercise of any discretionary power conferred by this Act, he shall have regard to the welfare of any child likely to be affected by his decision.

Meaning of certain terms used in this Act

3.—(1) A child is a "qualifying child" if—

(*a*) one of his parents is, in relation to him, an absent parent; or

(*b*) both of his parents are, in relation to him, absent parents.

(2) The parent of any child is an "absent parent", in relation to him, if—

(*a*) that parent is not living in the same household with the child; and

[THE NEXT PAGE IS K 311]

(*b*) the child has his home with a person who is, in relation to him, a person with care.

(3) A person is a "person with care", in relation to any child, if he is a person—

(*a*) with whom the child has his home;

(*b*) who usually provides day to day care for the child (whether exclusively or in conjunction with any other person); and

[1] (*c*) who does not fall within a prescribed category of person.

(4) The Secretary of State shall not, under subsection (3)(*c*), prescribe as a category—

(*a*) parents;

(*b*) guardians;

(*c*) persons in whose favour residence orders under section 8 of the Children Act 1989 are in force;

[2] (*d*) in Scotland, persons having the right to custody of a child.

(5) For the purposes of this Act there may be more than one person with care in relation to the same qualifying child.

(6) Periodical payments which are required to be paid in accordance with a maintenance assessment are referred to in this Act as "child support maintenance".

(7) Expressions are defined in this section only for the purposes of this Act.

NOTES

[1] See S.I. 1992 No. 1813, as amended by S.I. 1993 No. 913, 1994 No. 227 and 1995 Nos. 123 and 1045.

[2] Prospectively amended by the Children (Scotland) Act 1995 (c. 36), Sched. 4, para. 52(2), *infra*.

Child support maintenance

4.—(1) A person who is, in relation to any qualifying child or any qualifying children, either the person with care or the absent parent may apply to the Secretary of State for a maintenance assessment to be made under this Act with respect to that child, or any of those children.

(2) Where a maintenance assessment has been made in response to an application under this section the Secretary of State may, if the person with care or absent parent with respect to whom the assessment was made applies to him under this subsection, arrange for—

(*a*) the collection of the child support maintenance payable in accordance with the assessment;

(*b*) the enforcement of the obligation to pay child support maintenance in accordance with the assessment.

(3) Where an application under subsection (2) for the enforcement of the obligation mentioned in subsection (2)(*b*) authorises the Secretary of State to take steps to enforce that obligation whenever he considers it necessary to do so, the Secretary of State may act accordingly.

[1] (4) A person who applies to the Secretary of State under this section shall, so far as that person reasonably can, comply with such regulations as may be made by the Secretary of State with a view to the Secretary of State or the child support officer being provided with the information which is required to enable—

(*a*) the absent parent to be traced (where that is necessary);

(*b*) the amount of child support maintenance payable by the absent parent to be assessed; and

(*c*) that amount to be recovered from the absent parent.

(5) Any person who has applied to the Secretary of State under this section may at any time request him to cease acting under this section.

(6) It shall be the duty of the Secretary of State to comply with any request made under subsection (5) (but subject to any regulations made under subsection (8)).

(7) The obligation to provide information which is imposed by subsection (4)—

(*a*) shall not apply in such circumstances as may be prescribed; and

(*b*) may, in such circumstances as may be prescribed, be waived by the Secretary of State.

(8) The Secretary of State may by regulations make such incidental, supplemental or transitional provision as he thinks appropriate with respect to cases in which he is requested to cease to act under this section.

(9) No application may be made under this section if there is in force with respect to the person with care and absent parent in question a maintenance assessment made in response to an application under section 6.

NOTE

[1] See S.I. 1992 No. 1812, as amended by S.I. 1995 Nos. 123 and 1045.

Child support maintenance: supplemental provisions

5.—(1) Where—

(*a*) there is more than one person with care of a qualifying child; and

(*b*) one or more, but not all, of them have parental responsibility for (or, in Scotland, parental rights over) the child;

no application may be made for a maintenance assessment with respect to the child by any of those persons who do not have parental responsibility for (or, in Scotland, parental rights over) the child.

(2) Where more than one application for a maintenance assessment is made with respect to the child concerned, only one of them may be proceeded with.

[1] (3) The Secretary of State may by regulations make provisions as to which of two or more applications for a maintenance assessment with respect to the same child is to be proceeded with.

NOTE

[1] See S.I. 1992 No. 1813, as amended by S.I. 1993 No. 913, 1994 No. 227 and 1995 Nos. 123 and 1045.

Applications by those receiving benefit

6.—[1] (1) Where income support, family credit or any other benefit of a prescribed kind is claimed by or in respect of, or paid to or in respect of, the parent of a qualifying child she shall, if—

(*a*) she is a person with care of the child; and

(*b*) she is required to do so by the Secretary of State,

authorise the Secretary of State to take action under this Act to recover child support maintenance from the absent parent.

(2) The Secretary of State shall not require a person ("the parent") to give him the authorisation mentioned in subsection (1) if he considers that there are reasonable grounds for believing that—

(*a*) if the parent were to be required to give that authorisation; or

(*b*) if she were to give it,

there would be a risk of her, or of any child living with her, suffering harm or undue distress as a result.

(3) Subsection (2) shall not apply if the parent requests the Secretary of State to disregard it.

(4) The authorisation mentioned in subsection (1) shall extend to all children of the absent parent in relation to whom the parent first mentioned in subsection (1) is a person with care.

(5) That authorisation shall be given, without unreasonable delay, by completing and returning to the Secretary of State an application—

(*a*) for the making of a maintenance assessment with respect to the qualifying child or qualifying children; and

(*b*) for the Secretary of State to take action under this Act to recover, on her behalf, the amount of child support maintenance so assessed.

(6) Such an application shall be made on a form ("a maintenance application form") provided by the Secretary of State.

(7) A maintenance application form shall indicate in general terms the effect of completing and returning it.

(8) Subsection (1) has effect regardless of whether any of the benefits mentioned there is payable with respect to any qualifying child.

[2] (9) A person who is under the duty imposed by subsection (1) shall, so far as she reasonably can, comply with such regulations as may be made by the Secretary of State with a view to the Secretary of State or the child support officer being provided with the information which is required to enable—

(*a*) the absent parent to be traced;

(*b*) the amount of child support maintenance payable by the absent parent to be assessed; and

(*c*) that amount to be recovered from the absent parent.

(10) The obligation to provide information which is imposed by subsection (9)—

(*a*) shall not apply in such circumstances as may be prescribed; and

(*b*) may, in such circumstances as may be prescribed, be waived by the Secretary of State.

(11) A person with care who has authorised the Secretary of State under subsection (1) but who subsequently ceases to fall within that subsection may request the Secretary of State to cease acting under this section.

(12) It shall be the duty of the Secretary of State to comply with any request made under subsection (11) (but subject to any regulations made under subsection (13)).

(13) The Secretary of State may by regulations make such incidental or transitional provision as he thinks appropriate with respect to cases in which he is requested under subsection (11) to cease to act under this section.

(14) The fact that a maintenance assessment is in force with respect to a person with care shall not prevent the making of a new maintenance assessment with respect to her in response to an application under this section.

NOTES

[1] See S.I. 1992 No. 1813, as amended by S.I. 1993 No. 913, 1994 No. 227 and 1995 Nos. 123 and 1045.

[2] See S.I. 1992 No. 1812, as amended by S.I. 1995 Nos. 123 and 1045.

Right of child in Scotland to apply for assessment

7.—(1) A qualifying child who has attained the age of 12 years and who is habitually resident in Scotland may apply to the Secretary of State for a maintenance assessment to be made with respect to him if—

(*a*) no such application has been made by a person who is, with respect to that child, a person with care or an absent parent; or

(*b*) the Secretary of State has not been authorised under section 6 to take action under this Act to recover child support maintenance from the absent parent (other than in a case where he has waived any requirement that he should be so authorised).

(2) An application made under subsection (1) shall authorise the Secretary of State to make a maintenance assessment with respect to any other children of the absent parent who are qualifying children in the care of the same person as the child making the application.

(3) Where a maintenance assessment has been made in response to an application under this section the Secretary of State may, if the person with care, the absent parent with respect to whom the assessment was made or the child concerned applies to him under this subsection, arrange for—

(*a*) the collection of the child support maintenance payable in accordance with the assessment;

(*b*) the enforcement of the obligation to pay child support maintenance in accordance with the assessment.

(4) Where an application under subsection (3) for the enforcement of the obligation mentioned in subsection (3)(*b*) authorises the Secretary of State to take steps to enforce that obligation whenever he considers it necessary to do so, the Secretary of State may act accordingly.

[1] (5) Where a child has asked the Secretary of State to proceed under this section, the person with care of the child, the absent parent and the child concerned shall, so far as they reasonably can, comply with such regulations as may be made by the Secretary of State with a view to the Secretary of State or the child support officer being provided with the information which is required to enable—

(*a*) the absent parent to be traced (where that is necessary);

(*b*) the amount of child support maintenance payable by the absent parent to be assessed; and

(*c*) that amount to be recovered from the absent parent.

(6) The child who has made the application (but not the person having care of him) may at any time request the Secretary of State to cease acting under this section.

(7) It shall be the duty of the Secretary of State to comply with any request made under subsection (6) (but subject to any regulations made under subsection (9)).

(8) The obligation to provide information which is imposed by subsection (5)—

(*a*) shall not apply in such circumstances as may be prescribed by the Secretary of State; and

(*b*) may, in such circumstances as may be so prescribed, be waived by the Secretary of State.

(9) The Secretary of State may by regulations make such incidental, supplemental or transitional provision as he thinks appropriate with respect to cases in which he is requested to cease to act under this section.

NOTE

[1] See S.I. 1992 No. 1812, as amended by S.I. 1995 Nos. 123 and 1045.

Role of the courts with respect to maintenance for children

8.—(1) This subsection applies in any case where a child support officer would have jurisdiction to make a maintenance assessment with respect to a qualifying child and an absent parent of his on an application duly made by a person entitled to apply for such an assessment with respect to that child.

(2) Subsection (1) applies even though the circumstances of the case are such that a child support officer would not make an assessment if it were applied for.

(3) In any case where subsection (1) applies, no court shall exercise any power which it would otherwise have to make, vary or revive any maintenance order in relation to the child and absent parent concerned.

(4) Subsection (3) does not prevent a court from revoking a maintenance order.

(5) The Lord Chancellor or in relation to Scotland the Lord Advocate may by order provide that, in such circumstances as may be specified by the order, this section shall not prevent a court from exercising any power which it has to make a maintenance order in relation to a child if—

(*a*) a written agreement (whether or not enforceable) provides for the making, or securing, by an absent parent of the child of periodical payments to or for the benefit of the child; and

(*b*) the maintenance order which the court makes is, in all material respects, in the same terms as that agreement.

(6) This section shall not prevent a court from exercising any power which

it has to make a maintenance order in relation to a child if—

(*a*) a maintenance assessment is in force with respect to the child;

(*b*) the amount of the child support maintenance payable in accordance with the assessment was determined by reference to the alternative formula mentioned in paragraph 4(3) of Schedule 1; and

(*c*) the court is satisfied that the circumstances of the case make it appropriate for the absent parent to make or secure the making of periodical payments under a maintenance order in addition to the child support maintenance payable by him in accordance with the maintenance assessment.

(7) This section shall not prevent a court from exercising any power which it has to make a maintenance order in relation to a child if—

(*a*) the child is, will be or (if the order were to be made) would be receiving instruction at an educational establishment or undergoing training for a trade, profession or vocation (whether or not while in gainful employment); and

(*b*) the order is made solely for the purposes of requiring the person making or securing the making of periodical payments fixed by the order to meet some or all of the expenses incurred in connection with the provision of the instruction or training.

(8) This section shall not prevent a court from exercising any power which it has to make a maintenance order in relation to a child if—

(*a*) a disability living allowance is paid to or in respect of him; or

(*b*) no such allowance is paid but he is disabled,

and the order is made solely for the purpose of requiring the person making or securing the making of periodical payments fixed by the order to meet some or all of any expenses attributable to the child's disability.

(9) For the purposes of subsection (8), a child is disabled if he is blind, deaf or dumb or is substantially and permanently handicapped by illness, injury, mental disorder or congenital deformity or such other disability as may be prescribed.

(10) This section shall not prevent a court from exercising any power which it has to make a maintenance order in relation to a child if the order is made against a person with care of the child.

(11) In this Act "maintenance order", in relation to any child, means an order which requires the making or securing of periodical payments to or for the benefit of the child and which is made under—

(*a*) Part II of the Matrimonial Causes Act 1973;

(*b*) the Domestic Proceedings and Magistrates' Courts Act 1978;

(*c*) Part III of the Matrimonial and Family Proceedings Act 1984;

(*d*) the Family Law (Scotland) Act 1985;

(*e*) Schedule 1 to the Children Act 1989; or

(*f*) any other prescribed enactment,

and includes any order varying or reviving such an order.

Agreements about maintenance

9.—(1) In this section "maintenance agreement" means any agreement for the making, or for securing the making, of periodical payments by way of maintenance, or in Scotland aliment, to or for the benefit of any child.

(2) Nothing in this Act shall be taken to prevent any person from entering into a maintenance agreement.

(3) The existence of a maintenance agreement shall not prevent any party to the agreement, or any other person, from applying for a maintenance assessment with respect to any child to or for whose benefit periodical payments are to be made or secured under the agreement.

(4) Where any agreement contains a provision which purports to restrict the right of any person to apply for a maintenance assessment, that provision shall be void.

(5) Where section 8 would prevent any court from making a mainten-

ance order in relation to a child and an absent parent of his, no court shall exercise any power that it has to vary any agreement so as—

(*a*) to insert a provision requiring that absent parent to make or secure the making of periodical payments by way of maintenance, or in Scotland aliment, to or for the benefit of that child; or

(*b*) to increase the amount payable under such a provision.

Relationship between maintenance assessments and certain court orders and related matters

10.—(1) Where an order of a kind prescribed for the purposes of this subsection is in force with respect to any qualifying child with respect to whom a maintenance assessment is made, the order—

(*a*) shall, so far as it relates to the making or securing of periodical payments, cease to have effect to such extent as may be determined in accordance with regulations made by the Secretary of State; or

(*b*) where the regulations so provide, shall, so far as it relates, have effect subject to such modifications as may be so determined.

(2) Where an agreement of a kind prescribed for the purposes of this subsection is in force with respect to any qualifying child with respect to whom a maintenance assessment is made, the agreement—

(*a*) shall, so far as it relates to the making or securing of periodical payments, be unenforceable to such extent as may be determined in accordance with regulations made by the Secretary of State; or

(*b*) where the regulations so provide, shall, so far as it so relates, have effect subject to such modifications as may be so determined.

(3) Any regulations under this section may, in particular, make such provision with respect to—

(*a*) any case where any person with respect to whom an order or agreement of a kind prescribed for the purposes of subsection (1) or (2) has effect applies to the prescribed court, before the end of the prescribed period, for the order or agreement to be varied in the light of the maintenance assessment and of the provisions of this Act;

(*b*) the recovery of any arrears under the order or agreement which fell due before the coming into force of the maintenance assessment,

as the Secretary of State considers appropriate and may provide that, in prescribed circumstances, an application to any court which is made with respect to an order of a prescribed kind relating to the making or securing of periodical payments to or for the benefit of a child shall be treated by the court as an application for the order to be revoked.

(4) The Secretary of State may by regulations make provision for—

(*a*) notification to be given by the child support officer concerned to the prescribed person in any case where that officer considers that the making of a maintenance assessment has affected, or is likely to affect, any order of a kind prescribed for the purposes of this subsection;

(*b*) notification to be given by the prescribed person to the Secretary of State in any case where a court makes an order which it considers has affected, or is likely to affect, a maintenance assessment.

(5) Rules may be made under section 144 of the Magistrates' Courts Act 1980 (rules of procedure) requiring any person who, in prescribed circumstances, makes an application to a magistrates' court for a maintenance order to furnish the court with a statement in a prescribed form, and signed by a child support officer, as to whether or not, at the time when the statement is made, there is a maintenance assessment in force with respect to that person or the child concerned.

In this subsection—

"maintenance order" means an order of a prescribed kind for the making or securing of periodical payments to or for the benefit of a child; and

"prescribed" means prescribed by the rules.

. . . . . .

Special cases

Special cases

[1] **42.**—(1) The Secretary of State may by regulations provide that in prescribed circumstances a case is to be treated as a special case for the purposes of this Act.

(2) Those regulations may, for example, provide for the following to be special cases—

(*a*) each parent of a child is an absent parent in relation to the child;

(*b*) there is more than one person who is a person with care in relation to the same child;

(*c*) there is more than one qualifying child in relation to the same absent parent but the person who is the person with care in relation to one of those children is not the person who is the person with care in relation to all of them;

(*d*) a person is an absent parent in relation to more than one child and the other parent of each of those children is not the same person;

(*e*) the person with care has care of more than one qualifying child and there is more than one absent parent in relation to those children;

(*f*) a qualifying child has his home in two or more separate households.

[2] (3) The Secretary of State may by regulations make provisions with respect to special cases.

(4) Regulations made under subsection (3) may, in particular—

(*a*) modify any provision made by or under this Act, in its application to any special case or any special case falling within a prescribed category;

(*b*) make new provision for any such case; or

(*c*) provide for any prescribed provision made by or under this Act not to apply to any such case.

NOTES

[1] See S.I. 1992 No. 1815, as amended by S.I. 1993 No. 913, 1994 No. 227 and 1995 Nos. 123 and 1045.

[2] See S.I. 1992 No. 1813, as amended by S.I. 1993 No. 913, 1994 No. 227 and 1995 Nos. 123 and 1045.

. . . . . .

Jurisdiction

Jurisdiction

44.—(1) A child support officer shall have jurisdiction to make a maintenance assessment with respect to a person who is—

(*a*) a person with care;

(*b*) an absent parent; or

(*c*) a qualifying child,

only if that person is habitually resident in the United Kingdom.

(2) Where the person with care is not an individual, subsection (1) shall have effect as if paragraph (*a*) were omitted.

(3) The Secretary of State may by regulations make provision for the cancellation of any maintenance assessment where—

(*a*) the person with care, absent parent or qualifying child with respect to whom it was made ceases to be habitually resident in the United Kingdom;

(*b*) in a case falling within subsection (2), the absent parent or qualifying child with respect to whom it was made ceases to be habitually resident in the United Kingdom; or

(*c*) in such circumstances as may be prescribed, a maintenance order of a prescribed kind is made with respect to any qualifying child with respect to whom the maintenance assessment was made.

. . . . . .

Miscellaneous and supplemental

. . . .

Fees

47.—(1) The Secretary of State may by regulations provide for the payment, by the absent parent or the person with care (or by both), of such fees as may be prescribed in cases where the Secretary of State takes any action under section 4 or 6.

(2) The Secretary of State may by regulations provide for the payment, by the absent parent, the person with care or the child concerned (or by any or all of them), of such fees as may be prescribed in cases where the Secretary of State takes any action under section 7.

(3) Regulations made under this section—

(*a*) may require any information which is needed for the purpose of determining the amount of any such fee to be furnished, in accordance with the regulations, by such person as may be prescribed;

(*b*) shall provide that no such fees shall be payable by any person to or in respect of whom income support, family credit or any other benefit of a prescribed kind is paid; and

(*c*) may, in particular, make provision with respect to the recovery by the Secretary of State of any fees payable under the regulations.

. . . .

Right of audience: Scotland

49. In relation to any proceedings before the sheriff under any provision of this Act, the power conferred on the Court of Session by section 32 of the Sheriff Courts (Scotland) Act 1971 (power of Court of Session to regulate civil procedure in sheriff court) shall extend to the making of rules permitting a party to such proceedings, in such circumstances as may be specified in the rules, to be represented by a person who is neither an advocate nor a solicitor.

. . . .

Financial provisions

53. Any expenses of the Lord Chancellor or the Secretary of State under this Act shall be payable out of money provided by Parliament.

Interpretation

54. In this Act—

"absent parent", has the meaning given in section 3(2);

"adjudication officer" has the same meaning as in the benefit Acts; . . .

"benefit Acts" means the Social Security Acts 1975 to 1991; . . .

"child support maintenance" has the meaning given in section 3(6);

"child support officer" has the meaning given in section 13; . . .

"interim maintenance assessment" has the meaning given in section 12;

"liability order" has the meaning given in section 33(2);

"maintenance agreement" has the meaning given in section 9(1);

"maintenance assessment" means an assessment of maintenance made under this Act and, except in prescribed circumstances, includes an interim maintenance assessment;

"maintenance order" has the meaning given in section 8(11);

"maintenance requirement" means the amount calculated in accordance with paragraph 1 of Schedule 1;

"parent", in relation to any child, means any person who is in law the mother or father of the child;

[1] "parental responsibility" has the same meaning as in the Children Act 1989;

[2] "parental rights" has the same meaning as in the Law Reform (Parent and Child) (Scotland) Act 1986;

"person with care" has the meaning given in section 3(3);

"prescribed" means prescribed by regulations made by the Secretary of State;

"qualifying child" has the meaning given in section 3(1);

NOTES

[1] Prospectively substituted by the Children (Scotland) Act 1995 (c. 36), Sched. 4, para. 52(4)(*a*), *infra*.

[2] Prospectively repealed by the Children (Scotland) Act 1995 (c. 36), Sched. 4, para. 52(4)(*b*), *infra*.

Meaning of "child"

[1] **55.**—(1) For the purposes of this Act a person is a child if—

(*a*) he is under the age of 16;

(*b*) he is under the age of 19 and receiving full-time education (which is not advanced education)—

(i) by attendance at a recognised educational establishment; or

(ii) elsewhere, if the education is recognised by the Secretary of State; or

(*c*) he does not fall within paragraph (*a*) or (*b*) but—

(i) he is under the age of 18, and

(ii) prescribed conditions are satisfied with respect to him.

(2) A person is not a child for the purposes of this Act if he—

(*a*) is or has been married;

(*b*) has celebrated a marriage which is void; or

(*c*) has celebrated a marriage in respect of which a decree of nullity has been granted.

(3) In this section—

"advanced education" means education of a prescribed description; and

"recognised educational establishment" means an establishment recognised by the Secretary of State for the purposes of this section as being, or as comparable to, a university, college or school.

(4) Where a person has reached the age of 16, the Secretary of State may recognise education provided for him otherwise than at a recognised educational establishment only if the Secretary of State is satisfied that education was being so provided for him immediately before he reached the age of 16.

(5) The Secretary of State may provide that in prescribed circumstances education is or is not to be treated for the purposes of this section as being full-time.

(6) In determining whether a person falls within subsection (1)(*b*), no account shall be taken of such interruptions in his education as may be prescribed.

(7) The Secretary of State may by regulations provide that a person who ceases to fall within subsection (1) shall be treated as continuing to fall within that subsection for a prescribed period.

(8) No person shall be treated as continuing to fall within subsection (1) by virtue of regulations made under subsection (7) after the end of the week in which he reaches the age of 19.

NOTE

[1] See S.I. 1992 No. 1813, as amended by S.I. 1993 No. 913, 1994 No. 227 and 1995 Nos. 123 and 1045.

. . . . . .

Short title, commencement and extent, etc.

58.—(1) This Act may be cited as the Child Support Act 1991.

[1] (2) Section 56(1) and subsections (1) and (11) and (14) of this section shall come into force on the passing of this Act but otherwise this Act shall come into force on such date as may be appointed by order made by the Lord Chancellor, the Secretary of State or Lord Advocate, or by any of them acting jointly.

(3) Different dates may be appointed for different provisions of this Act and for different purposes (including, in particular, for different cases or categories of case).

(4) An order under subsection (2) may make such supplemental, incidental or transitional provision as appears to the person making the order to be necessary or expedient in connection with the provisions brought into force by the order, including such adaptations or modifications of—

(*a*) the provisions so brought into force;
(*b*) any provisions of this Act then in force; or
(*c*) any provision of any other enactment,

as appear to him to be necessary or expedient.

(5) Different provision may be made by virtue of subsection (4) with respect to different periods.

(6) Any provision made by virtue of subsection (4) may, in particular, include provision for—

(*a*) the enforcement of a maintenance assessment (including the collection of sums payable under the assessment) as if the assessment were a court order of a prescribed kind;
(*b*) the registration of maintenance assessments with the appropriate court in connection with any provision of a kind mentioned in paragraph (*a*);
(*c*) the variation, on application made to a court, of the provisions of a maintenance assessment relating to the method of making payments fixed by the assessment or the intervals at which such payments are to be made;
(*d*) a maintenance assessment, or an order of a prescribed kind relating to one or more children, to be deemed, in prescribed circumstances, to have been validly made for all purposes or for such purposes as may be prescribed.

In paragraph (*c*) "court" includes a single justice.

(7) The Lord Chancellor, the Secretary of State or the Lord Advocate may by order make such amendments or repeals in, or such modifications of, such enactments as may be specified in the order, as appear to him to be necessary or expedient in consequence of any provision made by or under this Act (including any provision made by virtue of subsection (4)).

(8) This Act shall, in its application to the Isles of Scilly, have effect subject to such exceptions, adaptations and modifications as the Secretary of State may by order prescribe.

(9) Sections 27, 35 and 48 and paragraph 7 of Schedule 5 do not extend to Scotland.

(10) Sections 7, 28 and 49 extend only to Scotland.

(11) With the exception of sections 23 and 56(1), subsections (1) to (3) of this section and Schedules 2 and 4, and (in so far as it amends any enactment extending to Northern Ireland) Schedule 5, this Act does not extend to Northern Ireland.

NOTE

[1] See S.I. 1992 No. 2644, *infra*.

. . . . . .

[1] Age of Legal Capacity (Scotland) Act 1991

(1991 c. 50)

An Act to make provision in the law of Scotland as to the legal capacity of persons under the age of 18 years to enter into transactions, as to the setting aside and ratification by the court of transactions entered into by such persons and as to guardians of persons under the age of 16 years; to make provision in the law of Scotland relating to the time and date at which a person shall be taken to attain a particular age; and for connected purposes. [25th July 1991]

NOTE

[1] See the Children (Scotland) Act 1995 (c. 36), s. 99 (registration of births by persons themselves children), *infra* (prospective).

ARRANGEMENT OF SECTIONS

Section

Age of legal capacity

1.—(1) As from the commencement of this Act—

(*a*) a person under the age of 16 years shall, subject to section 2 below, have no legal capacity to enter into any transaction;

(*b*) a person of or over the age of 16 years shall have legal capacity to enter into any transaction.

(2) Subject to section 8 below, any reference in any enactment to a pupil (other than in the context of education or training) or to a person under legal disability or incapacity by reason of nonage shall, insofar as it relates to any time after the commencement of this Act, be construed as a reference to a person under the age of 16 years.

(3) Nothing in this Act shall—

(*a*) apply to any transaction entered into before the commencement of this Act;

(*b*) confer any legal capacity on any person who is under legal disability or incapacity other than by reason of nonage;

(*c*) affect the delictual or criminal responsibility of any person;

(*d*) affect any enactment which lays down an age limit expressed in years for any particular purpose;

(*e*) prevent any person under the age of 16 years from receiving or holding any right, title or interest;

(*f*) affect any existing rule of law or practice whereby—

[1] (i) any civil proceedings may be brought or defended, or any step in civil proceedings may be taken, in the name of a person

under the age of 16 years who has no guardian or whose guardian is unable (whether by reason of conflict of interest or otherwise) or refuses to bring or defend such proceedings or take such step;

(ii) the court may, in any civil proceedings, appoint a curator *ad litem* to a person under the age of 16 years;

(iii) the court may, in relation to the approval of an arrangement under section 1 of the Trusts (Scotland) Act 1961, appoint a curator *ad litem* to a person of or over the age of 16 years but under the age of 18 years;

(iv) the court may appoint a curator bonis to any person;

[1] (*g*) prevent any person under the age of 16 years from—

(i) being appointed as guardian to any child of his, or

(ii) exercising parental rights in relation to any child of his.

(4) Any existing rule of law relating to the legal capacity of minors and pupils which is inconsistent with the provisions of this Act shall cease to have effect.

(5) Any existing rule of law relating to reduction of a transaction on the ground of minority and lesion shall cease to have effect.

NOTE

[1] Prospectively amended by the Children (Scotland) Act 1995 (c. 36), Sched. 4, para. 53(2), *infra*.

Exceptions to general rule

2.—(1) A person under the age of 16 years shall have legal capacity to enter into a transaction—

(*a*) of a kind commonly entered into by persons of his age and circumstances, and

(*b*) on terms which are not unreasonable.

(2) A person of or over the age of 12 years shall have testamentary capacity, including legal capacity to exercise by testamentary writing any power of appointment.

(3) A person of or over the age of 12 years shall have legal capacity to consent to the making of an adoption order in relation to him; and accordingly—

(*a*)–(*b*) [Substituted ss. 12(8) and 18(8) of the Adoption (Scotland) Act 1978 have been incorporated in the print of that Act, *supra*.]

[1] (4) A person under the age of 16 years shall have legal capacity to consent on his own behalf to any surgical, medical or dental procedure or treatment where, in the opinion of a qualified medical practitioner attending him, he is capable of understanding the nature and possible consequences of the procedure or treatment.

(4A)–(4C) [Prospectively inserted by the Children (Scotland) Act 1995 (c. 36), Sched. 4, para. 53(3), *infra*.]

(5)Any transaction—

(*a*) which a person under the age of 16 years purports to enter into after the commencement of this Act, and

(*b*) in relation to which that person does not have legal capacity by virtue of this section,

shall be void.

NOTE

[1] Saved by the Children (Scotland) Act 1995 (c. 36), s. 90, *infra* (prospective).

Setting aside of transactions

3.—(1) A person under the age of 21 years ("the applicant") may make application to the court to set aside a transaction which he entered into while he was of or over the age of 16 years but under the age of 18 years and which is a prejudicial transaction.

(2) In this section "prejudicial transaction" means a transaction which—

(*a*) an adult, exercising prudence, would not have entered into in the circumstances of the applicant at the time of entering into the transaction, and

(*b*) has caused or is likely to cause substantial prejudice to the applicant.

(3) Subsection (1) above shall not apply to—

(*a*) the exercise of testamentary capacity;

(*b*) the exercise by testamentary writing of any power of appointment;

(*c*) the giving of consent to the making of an adoption order;

(*d*) the bringing or defending of, or the taking of any step in, civil proceedings;

(*e*) the giving of consent to any surgical, medical or dental procedure or treatment;

(*f*) a transaction in the course of the applicant's trade, business or profession;

(*g*) a transaction into which any other party was induced to enter by virtue of any fraudulent misrepresentation by the applicant as to age or other material fact;

(*h*) a transaction ratified by the applicant after he attained the age of 18 years and in the knowledge that it could be the subject of an application to the court under this section to set it aside; or

(*j*) a transaction ratified by the court under section 4 below.

(4) Where an application to set aside a transaction can be made or could have been made under this section by the person referred to in subsection (1) above, such application may instead be made by that person's executor, trustee in bankruptcy, trustee acting under a trust deed for creditors or curator bonis at any time prior to the date on which that person attains or would have attained the age of 21 years.

(5) An application under this section to set aside a transaction may be made—

(*a*) by an action in the Court of Session or the sheriff court, or

(*b*) by an incidental application in other proceedings in such court,

and the court may make an order setting aside the transaction and such further order, if any, as seems appropriate to the court in order to give effect to the rights of the parties.

Ratification by court of proposed transaction

4.—(1) Where a person of or over the age of 16 years but under the age of 18 years proposes to enter into a transaction which, if completed, could be the subject of an application to the court under section 3 above to set aside, all parties to the proposed transaction may make a joint application to have it ratified by the court.

(2) The court shall not grant an application under this section if it appears to the court that an adult, exercising reasonable prudence and in the circumstances of the person referred to in subsection (1) above, would not enter into the transaction.

(3) An application under this section shall be made by means of a summary application—

(*a*) to the sheriff of the sheriffdom in which any of the parties to the proposed transaction resides, or

(*b*) where none of the said parties resides in Scotland, to the sheriff at Edinburgh,

and the decision of the sheriff on such application shall be final.

Guardians of persons under 16

5.—[1] (1) Except insofar as otherwise provided in Schedule 1 to this Act, as from the commencement of this Act any reference in any rule of law, enactment or document to the tutor or tutory of a pupil child shall be construed as a reference to the guardian or, as the case may be, guardianship of a person under the age of 16 years; and accordingly the guardian of such a person shall have in relation to him and his estate the powers and duties which, immediately before such commencement, a tutor had in relation to his pupil.

[2] (2) Subject to section 1(3)(*f*) above, as from the commencement of this Act no guardian of a person under the age of 16 years shall be appointed as such except under section 3 (orders as to parental rights) or section 4 (power of parent to appoint guardian) of the Law Reform (Parent and Child) (Scotland) Act 1986.

(3) As from the commencement of this Act, no person shall, by reason of age alone, be subject to the curatory of another person.

(4) As from the commencement of this Act, no person shall be appointed as factor *loco tutoris*.

NOTES

[1] Prospectively amended by the Children (Scotland) Act 1995 (c. 36), Sched. 4, para. 53(4), *infra*.

[2] Prospectively amended by the Children (Scotland) Act 1995 (c. 36), Sched. 4, para. 53(5), *infra*.

Attainment of age

6.—(1) The time at which a person attains a particular age expressed in years shall be taken to be the beginning of the relevant anniversary of the date of his birth.

(2) Where a person has been born on 29th February in a leap year, the relevant anniversary in any year other than a leap year shall be taken to be 1st March.

(3) The provisions of this section shall apply only to a relevant anniversary which occurs after the commencement of this Act.

Acquisition of domicile

7. The time at which a person first becomes capable of having an independent domicile shall be the date at which he attains the age of 16 years.

Transitional provision

8. Where any person referred to in section 6(4)(*b*), 17(3), 18(3) or 18A(2) of the Prescription and Limitation (Scotland) Act 1973 as having been under legal disability by reason of nonage was of or over the age of 16 years but under the age of 18 years immediately before the commencement of this Act, any period prior to such commencement shall not be reckoned as, or as part of, the period of five years, or (as the case may be) three years, specified respectively in section 6, 17, 18 or 18A of that Act.

Interpretation

9. In this Act, unless the context otherwise requires—

"existing" means existing immediately before the commencement of this Act;

[1] "parental rights" has the same meaning as in section 8 (interpretation) of the Law Reform (Parent and Child) (Scotland) Act 1986;

[2] "transaction" means a transaction having legal effect, and includes—

(*a*) any unilateral transaction;
(*b*) the exercise of testamentary capacity;
(*c*) the exercise of any power of appointment;
(*d*) the giving by a person of any consent having legal effect;
(*e*) the bringing or defending of, or the taking of any step in, civil proceedings;
(*f*) acting as arbiter or trustee;
(*g*) acting as an instrumentary witness.

NOTES

[1] Prospectively repealed by the Children (Scotland) Act 1995 (c. 36), Sched. 5, *infra*.

[2] Applied with modification by the Children (Scotland) Act 1995 (c. 36), s. 15(1) (prospective).

Amendments and repeals

10.—(1) The enactments mentioned in Schedule 1 to this Act shall have effect subject to the amendments therein specified.

(2) The enactments specified in Schedule 2 to this Act are repealed to the extent specified in the third column of that Schedule.

Short title, commencement and extent

11.—(1) This Act may be cited as the Age of Legal Capacity (Scotland) Act 1991.

(2) This Act shall come into force at the end of the period of two months beginning with the date on which it is passed.

(3) This Act shall extend to Scotland only.

SCHEDULES

SCHEDULE 1

AMENDMENT OF ENACTMENTS

[Amendments to Acts reprinted in *The Parliament House Book* have been given effect.]

SCHEDULE 2

REPEALS

[Repeals affecting Acts reprinted in *The Parliament House Book* have been given effect.]

Local Government etc. (Scotland) Act 1994

(1994 c. 39)

An Act . . . to create an office of Principal Reporter and transfer to him the functions of reporters to children's hearings; to establish a body to facilitate the performance by the Principal Reporter of his functions; to amend the Social Work (Scotland) Act 1968 in relation to children's hearings; . . . and for connected purposes.

[3rd November 1994]

ARRANGEMENT OF SECTIONS

PART I

. . . . . .

Social work

. . . . . .

PART III

THE PRINCIPAL REPORTER AND THE SCOTTISH CHILDREN'S REPORTER ADMINISTRATION

The Principal Reporter

PART I

. . . . . .

Social work

Chief social work officer

45. For section 3 of the Social Work (Scotland) Act 1968 (director of social work), there shall be substituted the following section—

Chief social work officer

3.—(1) For the purposes of their functions under this Act and the enactments mentioned in section 5(1B) of this Act, a local authority shall appoint an officer to be known as the chief social work officer.

(2) The qualifications of the chief social work officer shall be such as may be prescribed by the Secretary of State.

. . . . . .

PART III

THE PRINCIPAL REPORTER AND THE SCOTTISH CHILDREN'S REPORTER ADMINISTRATION

The Principal Reporter

The Principal Reporter

127.—(1) There shall be an officer, to be known as the "Principal Reporter", to whom there are hereby transferred the functions under the Social Work (Scotland) Act 1968 (hereafter referred to in this Part of this Act as "the 1968 Act") and the Criminal Procedure (Scotland) Act 1975 of reporters appointed under subsection (1) of section 36 of the 1968 Act, which subsection shall cease to have effect.

(2) The first appointment to the office of Principal Reporter shall be made by the Secretary of State on such terms and conditions as he may, with the approval of the Treasury, determine.

The Scottish Children's Reporter Administration

The Scottish Children's Reporter Administration

128.—(1) There shall be a body, to be known as the "Scottish Children's Reporter Administration" (hereinafter in this Act referred to as the "Administration").

(2) The Principal Reporter shall be the chief officer of the Administration.

[1] (3) The general purpose of the Administration shall be to facilitate the performance by the Principal Reporter of his functions under the 1968 Act and the Criminal Procedure (Scotland) Act 1975.

(4) Appointments to the office of Principal Reporter subsequent to the first such appointment shall be made by the Administration with the consent of the Secretary of State on such terms and conditions as it may, with the approval of the Secretary of State given with the consent of the Treasury, determine.

(5) The Administration shall have such other officers as are necessary in order to assist the Principal Reporter; they shall, subject to section 137 of this Act, be appointed by the Administration on such terms as it may, with the approval of the Secretary of State given with the consent of the Treasury, determine.

(6) Schedule 12 to this Act (which provides as to the status, constitution and proceedings of the Administration and other matters relating to it) shall have effect.

(7) The Administration shall be responsible for the management of its officers, including their discipline and removal from office and their deployment throughout Scotland for the purposes of performing their duties.

[1] (8) Nothing in this section or any other provision of this Act shall be taken as authorising the Administration to direct or guide the Principal Reporter in the performance of his functions under the 1968 Act and the Criminal Procedure (Scotland) Act 1975.

NOTE

[1] Prospectively amended by the Children (Scotland) Act 1995 (c. 36), Sched. 4, para. 57(2), *infra*.

Appeal against dismissal of Principal Reporter and other officers

129.—(1) If dismissed by the Administration, the Principal Reporter or any prescribed officer of the Administration may appeal to the Secretary of State against the dismissal.

(2) An officer may be prescribed for the purposes of this section by reference to a class thereof so prescribed.

(3) In an appeal under this section the Administration shall be the respondent.

(4) The—

(*a*) procedure in relation to an appeal under this section;

(*b*) effect of the making of such an appeal;

(*c*) powers of the Secretary of State to dispose of such an appeal (including powers to make directions as to liability for expenses); and

(*d*) effect of the exercise of such powers

shall be as prescribed.

(5) In this section, "prescribed" means prescribed by regulations made by the Secretary of State.

(6) Regulations under this section shall be made by statutory instrument subject to annulment in pursuance of a resolution of either House of Parliament.

Additional functions of the Principal Reporter

Annual report of Principal Reporter

130.—(1) The Principal Reporter shall—

(*a*) as soon as possible after the 31st March following upon the coming into force of this section make a report to the Administration on the exercise and performance to that date of—

[1] (i) his functions under the 1968 Act and the Criminal Procedure (Scotland) Act 1975; and

(ii) such functions as it has delegated to him under this Act; and

(*b*) make similar reports as to each subsequent period of twelve months ending on 31st March as soon as possible after the end of that period.

(2) If the date on which this section comes into force falls on a day after 30th September and before 31st March, the first report by the Principal Reporter under this section shall be for the period ending with the next succeeding 31st March.

NOTE

[1] Prospectively amended by the Children (Scotland) Act 1995 (c. 36), Sched. 4, para. 57(3), *infra*.

Delegation of Principal Reporter's functions

131.—(1) The Principal Reporter may delegate functions (other than that of making reports under section 130 of this Act) to other officers of the Administration.

(2) In performing any function delegated to him under subsection (1) above, an officer shall comply with any instructions or guidance given by the Principal Reporter.

(3) Any delegation made under subsection (1) above or instruction or guidance given for the purposes of subsection (2) above may be—

(*a*) to all officers, or to a class or classes of officer specified in the delegation, instruction or, as the case may be, guidance or to an individual officer so specified;

(*b*) of a general or specific character,

and may be varied or revoked by a subsequent delegation so made or a subsequent instruction or, as the case may be, subsequent guidance so given.

Functions of the Administration

Duty of Administration to provide accommodation etc. for children's hearings

132.—[1] (1) The Administration shall provide suitable accommodation and facilities for children's hearings under section 34 of the 1968 Act.

(2) Accommodation and facilities provided under subsection (1) above shall be provided for each local government area (but may be sited in another) and shall be dissociated from criminal courts and police stations.

NOTE

[1] Prospectively amended by the Children (Scotland) Act 1995 (c. 36), Sched. 4, para. 57(4), *infra*.

Ancillary powers of Administration

133. The Administration shall have power to do all such things as are incidental or conducive to the achievement of its general purpose and the performance of its functions, including power to acquire, hold and dispose of land or any interest in or right over land.

Directions by the Secretary of State

134.—(1) The Secretary of State may give the Administration directions of a general or specific character with regard to the achievement of its general purpose and discharge of its functions, and the Administration shall comply with any such directions.

(2) A direction given under this section may be varied or revoked by a subsequent direction so given.

Finance of the Administration

Government grants to the Administration

135.—(1) The Secretary of State may, with the approval of the Treasury, make to the Administration grants of such amounts as he thinks fit.

(2) A grant under this section may be made subject to such conditions as the Secretary of State may, with the approval of the Treasury, determine.

Reports, accounts etc. of the Administration

Reports, accounts etc. of the Administration

136.—(1) The Administration shall—

(*a*) furnish the Secretary of State with such returns, accounts and other information with respect to its property, and activities or proposed activities as he may, from time to time, require;

(*b*) afford him facilities for the verification of information so furnished; and

(*c*) for the purpose of such verification, permit any person authorised in that behalf by the Secretary of State to inspect and make copies of the accounts, books, documents or papers of the Administration and to give that person such explanation of anything he is entitled to inspect as he may reasonably require.

(2) The Administration shall—

(*a*) as soon as possible after the 31st March following upon the coming into force of section 128 of this Act make a report to the Secretary of State on the exercise and performance of its functions to that date incorporating in that report a copy of so much of the report made to it by the Principal Reporter as to that period as was made under section 130(1)(*a*)(i) of this Act; and

(*b*) make a similar report to him as to each subsequent period of twelve months ending on 31st March as soon as possible after the end of such period,

and a copy of every such report shall be laid before each House of Parliament by the Secretary of State:

Provided that if the date upon which the said section 128 comes into force falls on a day after 30th September and before 31st March, the first report of the Administration under this section shall be for the period ending with the next succeeding 31st March.

(3) The Administration shall keep proper accounts and other records, and shall prepare for each financial year a statement of account in such form as the Secretary of State with the approval of the Treasury may direct and shall submit those statements of account to the Secretary of State at such time as he may with the approval of the Treasury direct.

(4) The Secretary of State shall, on or before the 30th November in any year, transmit to the Comptroller and Auditor General the statement of account of the Administration for the financial year last ended.

(5) The Comptroller and Auditor General shall examine and certify the statements of account transmitted to him under subsection (4) above, and shall lay copies of them together with his report thereon before each House of Parliament.

(6) In this section "financial year" means the period beginning with the date upon which section 128 of this Act comes into force and ending with the 31st March following that date and èach period of twelve months thereafter:

Provided that if the date upon which the said section 128 comes into force falls on a day after 30th September and before 31st March, the first financial year of the Administration shall end with the next succeeding 31st March.

General and supplemental

Staff: application of Chapter 2 of Part I

137.—(1) Sections 8 (except subsections (3) and (4)), 9 and 12 of this Act shall apply also in relation to the transfer to the Administration of officers appointed under subsection (1) of section 36 of the 1968 Act and staff provided in pursuance of subsection (6) of that section with the following modifications—

(*a*) references to an existing local authority shall include references to an islands council and references to a new authority shall be construed as references to the Administration; and

(*b*) the reference in section 12(2)(*a*) to authorities which cease to exist by virtue of Chapter 1 of Part I of this Act shall include a reference to authorities which cease to have functions under section 36(1) and (6) of the 1968 Act.

(2) Section 10 of this Act shall, with the modification specified in subsection (3) below, apply in relation to persons ceasing to be officers appointed or staff provided as mentioned in subsection (1) above and being subsequently employed by the Administration as it applies in relation to persons ceasing to be employed by an existing local authority and being subsequently employed by another person.

(3) The modification referred to in subsection (2) above is that references in section 10 of this Act to an existing local authority shall include references to an islands council.

(4) Section 11 of this Act shall apply also in relation to the remuneration of officers appointed and staff provided as mentioned in subsection (1) above with the following modifications—

(*a*) references to an authority shall be construed as references only to an existing local authority and references to an existing local authority shall include references to an islands council;

(*b*) the reference in subsection (5) to the Secretary of State consulting associations of local authorities and employees of local authorities shall include a reference to the Secretary of State consulting the Administration; and

(*c*) the reference in subsection (7) to an authority not having ceased to exist shall include a reference to an authority not having ceased to have functions under section 36(1) and (6) of the 1968 Act.

(5) Section 13 of this Act shall apply in relation to officers appointed or staff provided as mentioned in subsection (1) above with the modification

that references in that section to an existing local authority shall include references to an islands council.

Property etc.: application of Chapter 3 of Part I

138.—(1) Chapter 3 of Part I of this Act shall, with the modifications specified in subsection (2) below, apply in relation to the transfer to the Principal Reporter or the Administration of the property, rights, liabilities and obligations of reporters appointed under section 36(1) of the 1968 Act and such property, rights, liabilities and obligations as a local authority for the purpose of that Act has for the purposes of—

(*a*) their functions under section 34(3) of that Act (duty to provide suitable accommodation and facilities for children's hearings); or

(*b*) providing accommodation and facilities for, or otherwise facilitating or supporting the performance of the functions of, reporters appointed under subsection (1) of section 36 of the 1968 Act or staff provided in pursuance of subsection (6) of that section.

(2) The modifications referred to in subsection (1) above are as follows—

(*a*) references in Chapter 3 of Part I of this Act to existing local authorities shall include references to reporters appointed under section 36(1) of the 1968 Act and to islands councils; and

(*b*) references in that Chapter to new local authorities shall include references to the Principal Reporter and to the Administration.

Part IV

Miscellaneous

Social work

Report by local authority for purpose of investigation preliminary to children's hearing

[1] **139.**—(1) In section 38 of the Social Work (Scotland) Act 1968 (initial investigation of cases by the reporter), after subsection (1), there shall be inserted—

"(1A) For the purposes of making any initial investigation under subsection (1) above, the Principal Reporter may request from the local authority a report on the child and his social background and it shall be the duty of the authority to supply the report which may contain information from any such person as the Principal Reporter or the local authority may think fit.

(1B) A report requested under subsection (1A) above may contain information additional to that given by the local authority under section 37(1A)(*b*) of this Act.".

(2) In section 39 of that Act (action on initial investigation), after subsection (4), there shall be inserted the following subsection—

"(4A) A report requested under subsection (4) above may contain information additional to that given in a report under section 38(1A) of this Act.".

NOTE

[1] Prospectively repealed by the Children (Scotland) Act 1995 (c. 36), Sched. 5, *infra*.

. . . . . .

SCHEDULE 13

Minor and Consequential Amendments

. . . . . .

The Matrimonial Proceedings (Children) Act 1958 (c. 40)

50.—(1) The Matrimonial Proceedings (Children) Act 1958 shall be amended in accordance with this paragraph.

(2) In section 10(2) (committal of child to local authority), for the words from "of the region" to "which" substitute "(constituted under section 2 of the Local Government etc. (Scotland) Act 1994) in whose area".

(3) In section 12(2) (supervision of child by local authority), for "the council of a region or islands area" substitute "a council constituted under section 2 of the Local Government etc. (Scotland) Act 1994".

. . . .

The Social Work (Scotland) Act 1968 (c. 49)

76.—(1) The Social Work (Scotland) Act 1968 shall be amended in accordance with this paragraph.

(2) In section 1(2) (local authorities for the administration of the Act), for the words "regional and islands councils" substitute the words "councils constituted under section 2 of the Local Government etc. (Scotland) Act 1994".

(3) In section 5 (powers of Secretary of State)—

(*a*) in subsection (1A) for the words "section 2(2) of this Act" there shall be substituted the words "subsection (1B) below"; and

(*b*) after subsection (1A) there shall be added—

"(1B) The enactments referred to in subsection (1A) above are—

(*a*) this Act as read with sections 1 and 2(1) of the Chronically Sick and Disabled Persons Act 1970 and the Disabled Persons (Services, Consultation and Representation) Act 1986;

(*b*) Part IV of the Children and Young Persons (Scotland) Act 1937;

(*c*) section 22(2) to (5A), (7) and (8), section 26(2) to (4) and sections 43, 45, 47 and 48 of the National Assistance Act 1948;

(*d*) The Disabled Persons (Employment) Act 1958;

(*e*) sections 10 to 12 of the Matrimonial Proceedings (Children) Act 1958, and sections 11 and 12 of the Guardianship Act 1973;

(*f*) sections 23, 24, 297 and 329 of the Criminal Procedure (Scotland) Act 1975;

(*g*) the Children Act 1975;

(*h*) the Adoption Act 1976;

(*i*) the Adoption (Scotland) Act 1978;

(*j*) sections 21 to 23 of the Health and Social Services and Social Security Adjudications Act 1983;

(*k*) the Mental Health (Scotland) Act 1984;

(*l*) the Foster Children (Scotland) Act 1984;

(*m*) sections 38(*b*) and 235 of the Housing (Scotland) Act 1987;

(*n*) the Access to Personal Files Act 1987; and

(*o*) section 19 and Part X of the Children Act 1989."; and

(*c*) in subsection (2), for paragraph (*c*) there shall be substituted—

"(*c*) the performance of the functions of local authorities under any of the enactments mentioned in paragraphs (*b*), (*d*), (*e*), (*g*), (*h*), (*i*), (*l*) and (*o*) of subsection (1B) above".

(4) In section 5A(3) (local authority plans for community care services)—

(*a*) paragraph (*b*) shall cease to have effect; and

(*b*) in paragraph (*c*), for "section 2(2)" substitute "5(1B)".

(5) In section 5B(1) (complaints procedure), for "referred to in section 2(2)" substitute "mentioned in section 5(1B)".

[1] (6) In section 6A (inquiries), for "section 2(2)" substitute "section 5(1B)".

(7) In section 10(1) (making of grants and loans for social work), for the words from "enactments" to "of this Act" substitute "mentioned in paragraphs (*b*), (*d*), (*e*), (*g*), (*h*), (*i*) and (*l*) of section 5(1B) of this Act".

(8) In section 20A(1) (powers of local authority in course of review of child in care) for "their reporter" substitute "the Principal Reporter".

(9) In section 27(3)(*c*) (content of probation, community service and supervised attendance scheme etc.), for the words from "the social" to the end substitute "a committee or subcommittee of such authorities".

[1] (10) In section 33(3) (publication of list of members of children's panels), for "offices of the director of social work" substitute "principal offices".

[1] (11) In section 34, subsection (3) (duty of local authority to provide suitable accommodation and facilities for children's hearings) shall cease to have effect.

[1] (12) In section 36 (the reporter)—

(*a*) subsection (4) shall cease to have effect;

(*b*) for subsection (5) substitute—

"(5) A reporter shall not, except with the consent of the Scottish Children's Reporter Administration, be employed by a local authority.";

(*c*) after subsection (5) insert—

"(5A) In subsections (2) and (5) above, "reporter" means the Principal Reporter or any officer of the Scottish Children's Reporter Administration to whom there is delegated, under section 131(1) of the Local Government etc. (Scotland) Act 1994 any function of the Principal Reporter under this Part of this Act or under the Criminal Procedure (Scotland) Act 1975.";

(*d*) subsection (6) shall cease to have effect; and

(*e*) in subsection (8), for "duties of the reporter" substitute "functions of the Principal Reporter under this Act and under the Criminal Procedure (Scotland) Act 1975".

[1] (13) In section 36A (power of reporters to conduct proceedings before sheriff)—

(*a*) in paragraph (*a*), for the words from "officers", where first occurring, to "solicitors" substitute the words "the reporter, whether or not he is an advocate or solicitor";

(*b*) in paragraph (*b*), for "officer" substitute "reporter"; and

(*c*) at the end add the following—

"In this section, "reporter" has the same meaning as it has in subsections (2) and (5) of section 36 of this Act.".

[1] (14) In section 38 (initial investigation of cases)—

(*a*) in subsection (1) for "a reporter"; and

(*b*) in subsection (2) for "the appropriate reporter",

substitute "the Principal Reporter".

[1] (15) In section 44(6) (direction as to transfer of child where disposal other than by discharge of referral), for "a director of social work" substitute "the chief social work officer".

[1] (16) In section 47(1) (duration and variation of supervision requirements) for "their reporter" substitute "the Principal Reporter".

[1] (17) In section 50(1) (appeal from sheriff to Court of Session) for "a reporter" substitute "the Principal Reporter".

[1] (18) In section 54 (transfer of case to another children's hearing), in subsection (1), for the words from "with" to "for a" substitute the words "for the other".

[1] (19) In section 58A(3) (residence in secure accommodation) for "director of social work" substitute "chief social work officer".

[1] (20) In section 58B(3) (order placing child in secure accommodation) for "director of social work" substitute "chief social work officer".

[1] (21) In section 58E(1) (warrants to detain in secure accommodation) for "director of social work" substitute "chief social work officer".

[1] (22) In section 73 (supervision of children moving to Scotland from England and Wales or Northern Ireland), in subsection (1), in paragraph (*b*), for the words from "reporter" to the end, substitute "Principal Reporter".

[1] (23) In section 75(1) (duties of reporter where parent of child subject to certain orders moves to Scotland), for the words from "reporter of the local authority" to "residing" substitute "Principal Reporter".

[1] (24) In section 76(2) (procedure in children's hearing and courts)—

(*a*) for "a reporter" substitute "the Principal Reporter"; and

(*b*) the words "to which the case stands referred" shall cease to have effect.

[1] (25) In Schedule 3 (children's panels)—

(*a*) in paragraph 3—

(i) at the beginning insert "Subject to paragraph 5B below,"; and

(ii) sub-paragraph (i) and, in sub-paragraph (ii), the words "in any other case," shall cease to have effect;

(*b*) after paragraph 5A insert—

"5B.—(1) Two or more local authorities may, for the purpose of discharging the function imposed on them by paragraph 3 above, make arrangements to form a Children's Panel Advisory Committee for their areas (hereafter referred to as a "joint advisory committee").

(2) A joint advisory committee shall not be formed in pursuance of arrangements made under sub-paragraph (1) above unless the authorities concerned have obtained the consent in writing of the Secretary of State.

(3) The Secretary of State may give a direction, in any case where a joint advisory

committee has not been formed, to two or more local authorities requiring them to form a joint advisory committee; and the local authorities shall comply with any such direction.

(4) The provisions of this Schedule shall apply, subject to any necessary modifications, to a joint advisory committee as they apply to a Children's Panel Advisory Committee formed under the said paragraph 3."; and

(*c*) in paragraph 7, for "may" substitute "shall".

(26) For "reporter", wherever occurring, substitute "Principal Reporter".

(27) Sub-paragraph (26) above does not affect any of the particular amendments made by this paragraph.

NOTE

[1] Prospectively repealed by the Children (Scotland) Act 1995 (c. 36), Sched. 5, *infra*.

. . . . . .

The Children Act 1975 (c. 72)

[1] 103. In section 99(1) of the Children Act 1975 (inquiries in Scotland)—

(*a*) in paragraph (*b*), for the words from "paragraphs" to "2(2)" substitute "paragraphs (*b*), (*e*), (*g*), (*h*), (*i*), (*l*) and (*o*) of section 5(1B)";

(*b*) the word "or" immediately preceding paragraph (*e*) shall cease to have effect; and

(*c*) after paragraph (*e*) insert "; or

(*f*) the functions of the Principal Reporter under Part III of the Local Government etc. (Scotland) Act 1994.".

NOTE

[1] Prospectively repealed by the Children (Scotland) Act 1995 (c. 36), Sched. 5, *infra*.

. . . . . .

The Adoption (Scotland) Act 1978 (c. 28)

111.—(1) The Adoption (Scotland) Act 1978 shall be amended in accordance with this paragraph.

(2) In section 2 (local authorities' social work), for the words from "which stand" to "committee" substitute the words "under any of the enactments mentioned in subsection (1B) of section 5 of the Social Work (Scotland) Act 1968 (power of Secretary of State to issue directions to local authorities in respect of their functions under certain enactments)".

(3) In section 65(1) (interpretation), in the definition of "local authority", for "regional or islands council" substitute "council constituted under section 2 of the Local Government etc. (Scotland) Act 1994".

. . . . . .

The Foster Children (Scotland) Act 1984 (c. 56)

136. In section 21(1) of the Foster Children (Scotland) Act 1984 (interpretation), in the definition of "local authority", for the words from "the" to "area" substitute "a council constituted under section 2 of the Local Government etc. (Scotland) Act 1994".

. . . . . .

The Child Abduction and Custody Act 1985 (c. 60)

139. In section 27(3)(*b*) of the Child Abduction and Custody Act 1985 (interpretation), for "regional or islands council" substitute "council constituted under section 2 of the Local Government etc. (Scotland) Act 1994".

Civil Evidence (Family Mediation) (Scotland) Act 1995

(1995 c. 6)

An Act to make provision for the inadmissibility as evidence in civil proceedings in Scotland of information as to what occurred during family mediation. [1st May 1995]

ARRANGEMENT OF SECTIONS

Section

Inadmissibility in civil proceedings of information as to what occurred during family mediation

1.—(1) Subject to section 2 of this Act, no information as to what occurred during family mediation to which this Act applies shall be admissible as evidence in any civil proceedings.

(2) This Act applies to family mediation—

(*a*) between two or more individuals relating to—

(i) the residence of a child;

(ii) the regulation of personal relations and direct contact between a child and any other person;

(iii) the control, direction or guidance of a child's upbringing;

(iv) the guardianship or legal representation of a child; or

(v) any other matter relating to a child's welfare;

(*b*) between spouses or former spouses concerning matters arising out of the breakdown or termination of their marriage;

(*c*) between parties to a purported marriage concerning matters arising out of the breakdown or annulment of their purported marriage;

(*d*) between co-habitants or former co-habitants concerning matters arising out of the breakdown or termination of their relationship; or

(*e*) of such other description as the Secretary of State may prescribe,

which is conducted by a person accredited as a mediator in family mediation to an organisation which is concerned with such mediation and which is approved for the purposes of this Act by the Lord President of the Court of Session.

(3) The Lord President of the Court of Session may—

(*a*) in approving an organisation under subsection (2) above, specify the period for which the approval is granted;

(*b*) if he thinks fit, withdraw the approval at any time.

(4) A certificate by the Lord President approving an organisation under subsection (2) above shall be—

(*a*) in such form as may be prescribed by Act of Sederunt; and

(*b*) admissible as evidence in any civil proceedings and sufficient evidence of the matters contained therein.

(5) A document purporting to be a certificate by the Lord President for the purposes of this Act shall be accepted by the court as such unless the contrary is proved.

(6) The Lord President may, in connection with the performance of any of his functions under this Act, require an organisation which is seeking, or has been granted, approval under subsection (2) above to provide him with such information as he thinks fit.

(7) For the purposes of subsection (2)(*d*) above, "co-habitants" means a man and a woman who are not married to each other but who are living together as if they were husband and wife.

(8) In this Act, "civil proceedings" does not include an arbitration or proceedings before a tribunal or inquiry.

(9) In this section and section 2 of this Act, any reference to what occurred during family mediation shall include a reference to what was said, written or observed during such mediation.

Exceptions to general rule of inadmissibility

2.—(1) Nothing in section 1 of this Act shall prevent the admissibility as evidence in civil proceedings—

(*a*) of information as to any contract entered into during family mediation or of the fact that no contract was entered into during such mediation;

(*b*) where any contract entered into as a result of family mediation is challenged in those civil proceedings, of information as to what occurred during family mediation which relates to the subject matter of that challenge;

(*c*) of information as to what occurred during family mediation if every participant (other than the mediator) in that mediation agrees that the information should be admitted as evidence; or

(*d*) of information as to what occurred during family mediation if those civil proceedings are proceedings—

(i) (whether under any enactment or otherwise) relating to a child's care or protection to which a local authority or a voluntary organisation is a party;

[1] (ii) under Part III of the Social Work (Scotland) Act 1968 before, or relating to, a children's hearing;

(iii) for an adoption order under section 12 of the Adoption (Scotland) Act 1978;

(iv) for an order under section 18 of the said Act of 1978 declaring a child free for adoption;

(v) against one of the participants, or the mediator, in a family mediation in respect of damage to property, or personal injury, alleged to have been caused by that participant or, as the case may be, mediator during family mediation; or

(vi) arising from the family mediation and to which the mediator is a party.

(2) For the purposes of this section—

(*a*) an individual, spouse, former spouse, party to a purported marriage, or co-habitant referred to in section 1(2) of this Act; and

(*b*) insofar as the family mediation includes any of the matters mentioned in section 1(2)(*a*) of this Act, a child who—

(i) is the subject of such a family mediation; and

(ii) at the time the family mediation took place was capable of understanding the nature and significance of the matters to which the information which is sought to be admitted as evidence relates,

shall be regarded as a participant in the family mediation.

(3) Notwithstanding anything in the Age of Legal Capacity (Scotland) Act 1991, any child who is regarded as a participant in family mediation by virtue of subsection (2) above shall have legal capacity to agree that information should be admitted as evidence.

(4) The Secretary of State may prescribe other persons or classes of person who shall be regarded for the purposes of this section as participants in a family mediation.

NOTE

[1] Prospectively amended by the Children (Scotland) Act 1995 (c. 36), Sched. 4, para. 59, *infra*.

Short title, construction, commencement and extent

3.—(1) This Act may be cited as the Civil Evidence (Family Mediation) (Scotland) Act 1995.

(2) In this Act, "prescribe", except in relation to an Act of Sederunt, means prescribe by regulations made by statutory instrument subject to annulment in pursuance of a resolution of either House of Parliament.

(3) This Act shall come into force on such day as the Lord Advocate may by order made by statutory instrument appoint; and such order may include such transitional or incidental provisions as appear to him to be necessary or expedient.

(4) This Act extends to Scotland only.

Children (Scotland) Act 1995

(1995 c. 36)

An Act to reform the law of Scotland relating to children, to the adoption of children and to young persons who as children have been looked after by a local authority; to make new provision as respects the relationship between parent and child and guardian and child in the law of Scotland; to make provision as respects residential establishments for children and certain other residential establishments; and for connected purposes.

[19th July 1995]

ARRANGEMENT OF SECTIONS

PART I

PARENTS, CHILDREN AND GUARDIANS

Parental responsibilities and parental rights

Guardianship

Administration of child's property

Court Orders

Jurisdiction and choice of law

Interpretation

PART II

PROMOTION OF CHILDREN'S WELFARE BY LOCAL AUTHORITIES AND BY CHILDREN'S HEARINGS ETC.

CHAPTER 1

SUPPORT FOR CHILDREN AND THEIR FAMILIES

Introductory

Provision of services

Advice and assistance for young persons formerly looked after by local authorities

Miscellaneous and General

CHAPTER 2

CHILDREN'S HEARINGS

Constitution of children's hearings

PART IV

GENERAL AND SUPPLEMENTAL

[1] PART I

PARENTS, CHILDREN AND GUARDIANS

NOTE
[1] See s. 54(2)(*b*) (reference by court to Principal Reporter).

Parental responsibilities and parental rights

Parental responsibilities

1.—(1) Subject to section 3(1)(*b*) and (3) of this Act, a parent has in relation to his child the responsibility—
(*a*) to safeguard and promote the child's health, development and welfare;
(*b*) to provide, in a manner appropriate to the stage of development of the child—
(i) direction;
(ii) guidance,
to the child;
(*c*) if the child is not living with the parent, to maintain personal relations and direct contact with the child on a regular basis; and
(*d*) to act as the child's legal representative,
but only in so far as compliance with this section is practicable and in the interests of the child.

(2) "Child" means for the purposes of—
(*a*) paragraphs (*a*), (*b*)(i), (*c*) and (*d*) of subsection (1) above, a person under the age of sixteen years;
(*b*) paragraph (*b*)(ii) of that subsection, a person under the age of eighteen years.

(3) The responsibilities mentioned in paragraphs (*a*) to (*d*) of subsection (1) above are in this Act referred to as "parental responsibilities"; and the child, or any person acting on his behalf, shall have title to sue, or to defend, in any proceedings as respects those responsibilities.

(4) The parental responsibilities supersede any analogous duties imposed on a parent at common law; but this section is without prejudice to any other duty so imposed on him or to any duty imposed on him by, under or by virtue of any other provision of this Act or of any other enactment.

Parental rights

2.—(1) Subject to section 3(1)(*b*) and (3) of this Act, a parent, in order to enable him to fulfil his parental responsibilities in relation to his child, has the right—

(*a*) to have the child living with him or otherwise to regulate the child's residence;

(*b*) to control, direct or guide, in a manner appropriate to the stage of development of the child, the child's upbringing;

(*c*) if the child is not living with him, to maintain personal relations and direct contact with the child on a regular basis; and

(*d*) to act as the child's legal representative.

(2) Subject to subsection (3) below, where two or more persons have a parental right as respects a child, each of them may exercise that right without the consent of the other or, as the case may be, of any of the others, unless any decree or deed conferring the right, or regulating its exercise, otherwise provides.

(3) Without prejudice to any court order, no person shall be entitled to remove a child habitually resident in Scotland from, or to retain any such child outwith, the United Kingdom without the consent of a person described in subsection (6) below.

(4) The rights mentioned in paragraphs (*a*) to (*d*) of subsection (1) above are in this Act referred to as "parental rights"; and a parent, or any person acting on his behalf, shall have title to sue, or to defend, in any proceedings as respects those rights.

(5) The parental rights supersede any analogous rights enjoyed by a parent at common law; but this section is without prejudice to any other right so enjoyed by him or to any right enjoyed by him by, under or by virtue of any other provision of this Act or of any other enactment.

(6) The description of a person referred to in subsection (3) above is a person (whether or not a parent of the child) who for the time being has and is exercising in relation to him a right mentioned in paragraph (*a*) or (*c*) of subsection (1) above; except that, where both the child's parents are persons so described, the consent required for his removal or retention shall be that of them both.

(7) In this section, "child" means a person under the age of sixteen years.

Provisions relating both to parental responsibilities and to parental rights

3.—(1) Notwithstanding section 1(1) of the Law Reform (Parent and Child) (Scotland) Act 1986 (provision for disregarding whether a person's parents are not, or have not been, married to one another in establishing the legal relationship between him and any other person)—

(*a*) a child's mother has parental responsibilities and parental rights in relation to him whether or not she is or has been married to his father; and

(*b*) without prejudice to any arrangements which may be made under subsection (5) below and subject to any agreement which may be made under section 4 of this Act, his father has such responsibilities and rights in relation to him only if married to the mother at the time of the child's conception or subsequently.

(2) For the purposes of subsection (1)(*b*) above, the father shall be regarded as having been married to the mother at any time when he was a party to a purported marriage with her which was—

(*a*) voidable; or

(*b*) void but believed by them (whether by error of fact or of law) in good faith at that time to be valid.

(3) Subsection (1) above is without prejudice to any order made under section 11 of this Act or section 3(1) of the said Act of 1986 (provision analogous to the said section 11 but repealed by this Act) or to any other order, disposal or resolution affecting parental responsibilities or parental rights; and nothing in subsection (1) above or in this Part of this Act shall affect any other—

(*a*) enactment (including any other provision of this Act or of that Act); or

(*b*) rule of law,

by, under or by virtue of which a person may have imposed on him (or be relieved of) parental responsibilities or may be granted (or be deprived of) parental rights.

(4) The fact that a person has parental responsibilities or parental rights in relation to a child shall not entitle that person to act in any way which would be incompatible with any court order relating to the child or the child's property, or with any supervision requirement made under section 70 of this Act.

(5) Without prejudice to section 4(1) of this Act, a person who has parental responsibilities or parental rights in relation to a child shall not abdicate those responsibilities or rights to anyone else but may arrange for some or all of them to be fulfilled or exercised on his behalf; and without prejudice to that generality any such arrangement may be made with a person who already has parental responsibilities or parental rights in relation to the child concerned.

(6) The making of an arrangement under subsection (5) above shall not affect any liability arising from a failure to fulfil parental responsibilities; and where any arrangements so made are such that the child is a foster child for the purposes of the Foster Children (Scotland) Act 1984, those arrangements are subject to the provisions of that Act.

Acquisition of parental rights and responsibilities by natural father

4.—(1) Where a child's mother has not been deprived of some or all of the parental responsibilities and parental rights in relation to him and, by virtue of subsection (1)(*b*) of section 3 of this Act, his father has no parental responsibilities or parental rights in relation to him, the father and mother, whatever age they may be, may by agreement provide that, as from the appropriate date, the father shall have the parental responsibilities and parental rights which (in the absence of any order under section 11 of this Act affecting those responsibilities and rights) he would have if married to the mother.

(2) No agreement under subsection (1) above shall have effect unless—

(*a*) in a form prescribed by the Secretary of State; and

(*b*) registered in the Books of Council and Session while the mother still has the parental responsibilities and parental rights which she had when the agreement was made.

(3) The date on which such registration as is mentioned in subsection (2)(*b*) above takes place shall be the "appropriate date" for the purposes of subsection (1) above.

(4) An agreement which has effect by virtue of subsection (2) above shall, subject only to section 11(11) of this Act, be irrevocable.

Care or control of child by person without parental responsibilities or parental rights

5.—(1) Subject to subsection (2) below, it shall be the responsibility of a person who has attained the age of sixteen years and who has care or control of a child under that age, but in relation to him either has no parental responsibilities or parental rights or does not have the parental responsibility mentioned in section 1(1)(*a*) of this Act, to do what is reasonable in all the circumstances to safeguard the child's health, development and welfare; and in fulfilling his responsibility under this section the person may in particular, even though he does not have the parental right mentioned in section 2(1)(*d*) of this Act, give consent to any surgical, medical or dental treatment or procedure where—

(*a*) the child is not able to give such consent on his own behalf; and

(*b*) it is not within the knowledge of the person that a parent of the child would refuse to give the consent in question.

(2) Nothing in this section shall apply to a person in so far as he has care or control of a child in a school ("school" having the meaning given by section 135(1) of the Education (Scotland) Act 1980).

Views of children

6.—(1) A person shall, in reaching any major decision which involves—

(*a*) his fulfilling a parental responsibility or the responsibility mentioned in section 5(1) of this Act; or

(*b*) his exercising a parental right or giving consent by virtue of that section,

have regard so far as practicable to the views (if he wishes to express them) of the child concerned, taking account of the child's age and maturity, and to those of any other person who has parental responsibilities or parental rights in relation to the child (and wishes to express those views); and without prejudice to the generality of this subsection a child twelve years of age or more shall be presumed to be of sufficient age and maturity to form a view.

(2) A transaction entered into in good faith by a third party and a person acting as legal representative of a child shall not be challengeable on the ground only that the child, or a person with parental responsibilities or parental rights in relation to the child, was not consulted or that due regard was not given to his views before the transaction was entered into.

Guardianship

Appointment of guardians

7.—(1) A child's parent may appoint a person to be guardian of the child in the event of the parent's death; but—

(*a*) such appointment shall be of no effect unless—

(i) in writing and signed by the parent; and

(ii) the parent, at the time of death, was entitled to act as legal representative of the child (or would have been so entitled if he had survived until after the birth of the child); and

(*b*) any parental responsibilities or parental rights (or the right to appoint a further guardian under this section) which a surviving parent has in relation to the child shall subsist with those which, by, under or by virtue of this Part of this Act, the appointee so has.

(2) A guardian of a child may appoint a person to take his place as guardian in the event of the guardian's death; but such appointment shall be of no effect unless in writing and signed by the person making it.

(3) An appointment as guardian shall not take effect until accepted, either expressly or impliedly by acts which are not consistent with any other intention.

(4) If two or more persons are appointed as guardians, any one or more of them shall, unless the appointment expressly provides otherwise, be entitled to accept office even if both or all of them do not accept office.

(5) Subject to any order under section 11 or 86 of this Act, a person appointed as a child's guardian under this section shall have, in respect of the child, the responsibilities imposed, and the rights conferred, on a parent by sections 1 and 2 of this Act respectively; and sections 1 and 2 of this Act shall apply in relation to a guardian as they apply in relation to a parent.

(6) Without prejudice to the generality of subsection (1) of section 6 of this Act, a decision as to the appointment of a guardian under subsection (1) or (2) above shall be regarded for the purposes of that section (or of that section as applied by subsection (5) above) as a major decision which involves exercising a parental right.

Revocation and other termination of appointment

8.—(1) An appointment made under section 7(1) or (2) of this Act revokes an earlier such appointment (including one made in an unrevoked will or codicil) made by the same person in respect of the same child, unless it is clear (whether as a result of an express provision in the later appointment or by any necessary implication) that the purpose of the later appointment is to appoint an additional guardian.

(2) Subject to subsections (3) and (4) below, the revocation of an appointment made under section 7(1) or (2) of this Act (including one made in an unrevoked will or codicil) shall not take effect unless the revocation is in writing and is signed by the person making the revocation.

(3) An appointment under section 7(1) or (2) of this Act (other than one made in a will or codicil) is revoked if, with the intention of revoking the appointment, the person who made it—

(*a*) destroys the document by which it was made; or

(*b*) has some other person destroy that document in his presence.

(4) For the avoidance of doubt, an appointment made under section 7(1) or (2) of this Act in a will or codicil is revoked if the will or codicil is revoked.

(5) Once an appointment of a guardian has taken effect under section 7 of this Act, then, unless the terms of the appointment provide for earlier termination, it shall terminate only by virtue of—

(*a*) the child concerned attaining the age of eighteen years;

(*b*) the death of the child or the guardian; or

(*c*) the termination of the appointment by a court order under section 11 of this Act.

Administration of child's property

Safeguarding of child's property

9.—(1) Subject to section 13 of this Act, this section applies where—

(*a*) property is owned by or due to a child;

(*b*) the property is held by a person other than a parent or guardian of the child; and

(*c*) but for this section, the property would be required to be transferred to a parent having parental responsibilities in relation to the child or to a guardian for administration by that parent or guardian on behalf of the child.

(2) Subject to subsection (4) below, where this section applies and the person holding the property is an executor or trustee, then—

(*a*) if the value of the property exceeds £20,000, he shall; or

(*b*) if that value is not less than £5,000 and does not exceed £20,000, he may, apply to the Accountant of Court for a direction as to the administration of the property.

(3) Subject to subsection (4) below, where this section applies and the person holding the property is a person other than an executor or trustee, then, if the value of the property is not less than £5,000, that person may apply to the Accountant of Court for a direction as to the administration of the property.

(4) Where the parent or guardian mentioned in subsection (1)(*c*) above has been appointed a trustee under a trust deed to administer the property concerned, subsections (2) and (3) above shall not apply, and the person holding the property shall transfer it to the parent or guardian.

(5) On receipt of an application under subsection (2) or (3) above, the Accountant of Court may do one, or (in so far as the context admits) more than one, of the following—

(*a*) apply to the court for the appointment of a judicial factor (whether or not the parent or guardian mentioned in subsection (1)(*c*) above) to administer all or part of the property concerned and in the event of the court making such an appointment shall direct that the property, or as the case may be part, concerned be transferred to the factor;

(*b*) direct that all or part of the property concerned be transferred to himself;

(*c*) direct that all or, in a case where the parent or guardian so mentioned has not been appointed by virtue of paragraph (*a*) above, part of the property concerned be transferred to the parent or guardian, to be administered on behalf of the child.

(6) A direction under subsection (5)(*c*) above may include such conditions as the Accountant of Court considers appropriate, including in particular a condition—

(*a*) that in relation to the property concerned no capital expenditure shall be incurred without his approval; or

(*b*) that there shall be exhibited annually to him the securities and bank books which represent the capital of the estate.

(7) A person who has applied under subsection (2) or (3) above for a direction shall not thereafter transfer the property concerned except in accordance with a direction under subsection (5) above.

(8) The Secretary of State may from time to time prescribe a variation in any sum referred to in subsections (2) and (3) above.

(9) In this section "child" means a person under the age of sixteen years who is habitually resident in Scotland.

Obligations and rights of person administering child's property

10.—(1) A person acting as a child's legal representative in relation to the administration of the child's property—

(*a*) shall be required to act as a reasonable and prudent person would act on his own behalf; and

(*b*) subject to any order made under section 11 of this Act, shall be entitled to do anything which the child, if of full age and capacity, could do in relation to that property;

and subject to subsection (2) below, on ceasing to act as legal representative, shall be liable to account to the child for his intromissions with the child's property.

(2) No liability shall be incurred by virtue of subsection (1) above in respect of funds which have been used in the proper discharge of the person's responsibility to safeguard and promote the child's health, development and welfare.

Court orders

Court orders relating to parental responsibilities etc.

11.—(1) In the relevant circumstances in proceedings in the Court of Session or sheriff court, whether those proceedings are or are not independent of any other action, an order may be made under this subsection in relation to—

(*a*) parental responsibilities;

(*b*) parental rights;

(*c*) guardianship; or

(*d*) subject to section 14(1) and (2) of this Act, the administration of a child's property.

(2) The court may make such order under subsection (1) above as it thinks fit; and without prejudice to the generality of that subsection may in particular so make any of the following orders—

(*a*) an order depriving a person of some or all of his parental responsibilities or parental rights in relation to a child;

(*b*) an order—

(i) imposing upon a person (provided he is at least sixteen years of age or is a parent of the child) such responsibilities; and

(ii) giving that person such rights;

(*c*) an order regulating the arrangements as to—

(i) with whom; or

(ii) if with different persons alternately or periodically, with whom during what periods, a child under the age of sixteen years is to live (any such order being known as a "residence order");

(*d*) an order regulating the arrangements for maintaining personal relations and direct contact between a child under that age and a person with whom the child is not, or will not be, living (any such order being known as a "contact order");

(*e*) an order regulating any specific question which has arisen, or may arise, in connection with any of the matters mentioned in paragraphs (*a*) to (*d*) of subsection (1) of this section (any such order being known as a "specific issue order");

(*f*) an interdict prohibiting the taking of any step of a kind specified in the interdict in the fulfilment of parental responsibilities or the exercise of parental rights relating to a child or in the administration of a child's property;

(*g*) an order appointing a judicial factor to manage a child's property or remitting the matter to the Accountant of Court to report on suitable arrangements for the future management of the property; or

(*h*) an order appointing or removing a person as guardian of the child.

(3) The relevant circumstances mentioned in subsection (1) above are—

(*a*) that application for an order under that subsection is made by a person who—

(i) not having, and never having had, parental responsibilities or parental rights in relation to the child, claims an interest;

(ii) has parental responsibilities or parental rights in relation to the child;

(iii) has had, but for a reason other than is mentioned in subsection (4) below no longer has, parental responsibilities or parental rights in relation to the child; or

(*b*) that although no such application has been made, the court (even if it declines to make any other order) considers it should make such an order.

(4) The reasons referred to in subsection (3)(*a*)(iii) above are that the parental responsibilities or parental rights have been–

(*a*) extinguished on the making of an adoption order;

(*b*) transferred to an adoption agency on the making of an order declaring the child free for adoption;

(*c*) extinguished by virtue of subsection (9) of section 30 of the Human Fertilisation and Embryology Act 1990 (provision for enactments about adoption to have effect with modifications) on the making of a parental order under subsection (1) of that section; or

(*d*) transferred to a local authority by a parental responsibilities order.

(5) In subsection (3)(*a*) above "person" includes (without prejudice to the generality of that subsection) the child concerned; but it does not include a local authority.

(6) In subsection (4) above—

"adoption agency" and "adoption order" have the same meanings as they are given, in section 18 of the Adoption (Scotland) Act 1978, by section 65(1) of that Act; and

"parental responsibilities order" has the meaning given by section 86(1) of this Act.

(7) Subject to subsection (8) below, in considering whether or not to make an order under subsection (1) above and what order to make, the court—

(*a*) shall regard the welfare of the child concerned as its paramount consideration and shall not make any such order unless it considers that it would be better for the child that the order be made than that none should be made at all; and

(*b*) taking account of the child's age and maturity, shall so far as practicable—

(i) give him an opportunity to indicate whether he wishes to express his views;
(ii) if he does so wish, give him an opportunity to express them; and
(iii) have regard to such views as he may express.

(8) The court shall, notwithstanding subsection (7) above, endeavour to ensure that any order which it makes, or any determination by it not to make an order, does not adversely affect the position of a person who has, in good faith and for value, acquired any property of the child concerned, or any right or interest in such property.

(9) Nothing in paragraph (*b*) of subsection (7) above requires a child to be legally represented, if he does not wish to be, in proceedings in the course of which the court implements that paragraph.

(10) Without prejudice to the generality of paragraph (*b*) of subsection (7) above, a child twelve years of age or more shall be presumed to be of sufficient age and maturity to form a view for the purposes both of that paragraph and of subsection (9) above.

(11) An order under subsection (1) above shall have the effect of depriving a person of a parental responsibility or parental right only in so far as the order expressly so provides and only to the extent necessary to give effect to the order; but in making any such order as is mentioned in paragraph (*a*) or (*b*) of subsection (2) above the court may revoke any agreement which, in relation to the child concerned, has effect by virtue of section 4(2) of this Act.

(12) Where the court makes a residence order which requires that a child live with a person who, immediately before the order is made does not have in relation to the child all the parental responsibilities mentioned in paragraphs (*a*), (*b*) and (*d*) of section 1(1), and the parental rights mentioned in paragraphs (*b*) and (*d*) of section 2(1), of this Act (those which he does not so have being in this subsection referred to as the "relevant responsibilities and rights") that person shall, subject to the provisions of the order or of any other order made under subsection (1) above, have the relevant responsibilities and rights while the residence order remains in force.

(13) Any reference in this section to an order includes a reference to an interim order or to an order varying or discharging an order.

Restrictions on decrees for divorce, separation or annulment affecting children

12.—(1) In any action for divorce, judicial separation or declarator of nullity of marriage, the court shall, where this section applies, consider (in the light of such information as is before the court as to the arrangements which have been, or are proposed to be, made for the upbringing of each child by virtue of which it applies) whether to exercise with respect to him the powers conferred by section 11 or 54 of this Act.

(2) Where, in any case to which this section applies, the court is of the opinion that—

(*a*) the circumstances of the case require, or are likely to require, it to exercise any power under section 11 or 54 of this Act with respect to the child concerned;
(*b*) it is not in a position to exercise that power without giving further consideration to the case; and
(*c*) there are exceptional circumstances which make it desirable in the interests of that child that it should not grant decree in the action until it is in a position to exercise such a power,

it shall postpone its decision on the granting of decree in the action until it is in such a position.

(3) This section applies where a child of the family has not reached the age of sixteen years at the date when the question first arises as to whether the court should give such consideration as is mentioned in subsection (1) above.

(4) In this section "child of the family", in relation to the parties to a marriage, means—

(*a*) a child of both of them; or

(*b*) any other child, not being a child who is placed with them as foster parents by a local authority or voluntary organisation, who has been treated by both of them as a child of their family.

Awards of damages to children

13.—(1) Where in any court proceedings a sum of money becomes payable to, or for the benefit of, a child under the age of sixteen years, the court may make such order relating to the payment and management of the sum for the benefit of the child as it thinks fit.

(2) Without prejudice to the generality of subsection (1) above, the court may in an order under this section—

(*a*) appoint a judicial factor to invest, apply or otherwise deal with the money for the benefit of the child concerned;

(*b*) order the money to be paid—

(i) to the sheriff clerk or the Accountant of Court; or

(ii) to a parent or guardian of that child,

to be invested, applied or otherwise dealt with, under directions of the court, for the benefit of that child; or

(*c*) order the money to be paid directly to that child.

(3) Where payment is made to a person in accordance with an order under this section, a receipt given by him shall be a sufficient discharge of the obligation to make the payment.

Jurisdiction and choice of law

Jurisdiction and choice of law in relation to certain matters

14.—(1) The Court of Session shall have jurisdiction to entertain an application for an order relating to the administration of a child's property if the child is habitually resident in, or the property is situated in, Scotland.

(2) A sheriff shall have jurisdiction to entertain such an application if the child is habitually resident in, or the property is situated in, the sheriffdom.

(3) Subject to subsection (4) below, any question arising under this Part of this Act—

(*a*) concerning—

(i) parental responsibilities or parental rights; or

(ii) the responsibilities or rights of a guardian,

in relation to a child shall, in so far as it is not also a question such as is mentioned in paragraph (*b*) below, be determined by the law of the place of the child's habitual residence at the time when the question arises;

(*b*) concerning the immediate protection of a child shall be determined by the law of the place where the child is when the question arises; and

(*c*) as to whether a person is validly appointed or constituted guardian of a child shall be determined by the law of the place of the child's habitual residence on the date when the appointment was made (the date of death of the testator being taken to be the date of appointment where an appointment was made by will), or the event constituting the guardianship occurred.

(4) Nothing in any provision of law in accordance with which, under subsection (3) above, a question which arises in relation to an application for, or the making of, an order under subsection (1) of section 11 of this Act falls to be determined, shall affect the application of subsection (7) of that section.

Interpretation

Interpretation of Part I

15.—(1) In this Part of this Act—

"child" means, where the expression is not otherwise defined, a person under the age of eighteen years;

"contact order" has the meaning given by section 11(2)(*d*) of this Act;

"parent", in relation to any person, means, subject to Part IV of the Adoption (Scotland) Act 1978 and sections 27 to 30 of the Human Fertilisation and Embryology Act 1990 and any regulations made under subsection (9) of the said section 30, someone, of whatever age, who is that person's genetic father or mother;

"parental responsibilities" has the meaning given by section 1(3) of this Act;

"parental rights" has the meaning given by section 2(4) of this Act;

"residence order" has the meaning given by section 11(2)(*c*) of this Act;

"specific issue order" has the meaning given by section 11(2)(*e*) of this Act; and

"transaction" has the meaning given by section 9 of the Age of Legal Capacity (Scotland) Act 1991 (except that, for the purposes of subsection (5)(*b*) below, paragraph (*d*) of the definition in question shall be disregarded).

(2) No provision in this Part of this Act shall affect any legal proceedings commenced, or any application made to a court, before that provision comes into effect; except that where, before section 11 of this Act comes into force, there has been final decree in a cause in which, as respects a child, an order for custody or access, or an order which is analogous to any such order as is mentioned in subsection (2) of that section, has been made, any application on or after the date on which the section does come into force for variation or recall of the order shall proceed as if the order had been made under that section.

(3) In subsection (2) above, the reference to final decree is to a decree or interlocutor which, taken by itself or along with previous interlocutors, disposes of the whole subject matter of the cause.

(4) Any reference in this Part of this Act to a person—

(*a*) having parental rights or responsibilities;

(*b*) acting as a legal representative; or

(*c*) being appointed a guardian,

is to a natural person only.

(5) Any reference in this Part of this Act to a person acting as the legal representative of a child is a reference to that person, in the interests of the child—

(*a*) administering any property belonging to the child; and

(*b*) acting in, or giving consent to, any transaction where the child is incapable of so acting or consenting on his own behalf.

(6) Where a child has legal capacity to sue, or to defend, in any civil proceedings, he may nevertheless consent to be represented in those proceedings by any person who, had the child lacked that capacity, would have had the responsibility to act as his legal representative.

Part II

Promotion of Children's Welfare by Local Authorities and by Children's Hearings etc.

Chapter 1

Support for Children and Their Families

Introductory

Welfare of child and consideration of his views

16.—(1) Where under or by virtue of this Part of this Act, a children's hearing decide, or a court determines, any matter with respect to a child the welfare of that child throughout his childhood shall be their or its paramount consideration.

(2) In the circumstances mentioned in subsection (4) below, a children's hearing or as the case may be the sheriff, taking account of the age and maturity of the child concerned, shall so far as practicable—

(*a*) give him an opportunity to indicate whether he wishes to express his views;

(*b*) if he does so wish, give him an opportunity to express them; and

(*c*) have regard to such views as he may express;

and without prejudice to the generality of this subsection a child twelve years of age or more shall be presumed to be of sufficient age and maturity to form a view.

(3) In the circumstances mentioned in subsection (4)(*a*)(i) or (ii) or (*b*) of this section, no requirement or order so mentioned shall be made with respect to the child concerned unless the children's hearing consider, or as the case may be the sheriff considers, that it would be better for the child that the requirement or order be made than that none should be made at all.

(4) The circumstances to which subsection (2) above refers are that—

(*a*) the children's hearing—

(i) are considering whether to make, or are reviewing, a supervision requirement;

(ii) are considering whether to grant a warrant under subsection (1) of section 66, or subsection (4) or (7) of section 69, of this Act or to provide under subsection (5) of the said section 66 for the continuation of a warrant;

(iii) are engaged in providing advice under section 60(10) of this Act; or

(iv) are drawing up a report under section 73(13) of this Act;

(*b*) the sheriff is considering—

(i) whether to make, vary or discharge a parental responsibilities order, a child assessment order or an exclusion order;

(ii) whether to vary or discharge a child protection order;

(iii) whether to grant a warrant under section 67 of this Act; or

(iv) on appeal, whether to make such substitution as is mentioned in section 51(5)(*c*)(iii) of this Act; or

(*c*) the sheriff is otherwise disposing of an appeal against a decision of a children's hearing.

(5) If, for the purpose of protecting members of the public from serious harm (whether or not physical harm)—

(*a*) a children's hearing consider it necessary to make a decision under or by virtue of this Part of this Act which (but for this paragraph) would not be consistent with their affording paramountcy to the consideration mentioned in subsection (1) above, they may make that decision; or (*b*) a court considers it necessary to make a determination under or by virtue of Chapters 1 to 3 of this Part of this Act which (but for this paragraph) would not be consistent with its affording such paramountcy, it may make that determination.

Duty of local authority to child looked after by them

17.—(1) Where a child is looked after by a local authority they shall, in such manner as the Secretary of State may prescribe—

[1] (*a*) safeguard and promote his welfare (which shall, in the exercise of their duty to him be their paramount concern);

(*b*) make such use of services available for children cared for by their own parents as appear to the authority reasonable in his case; and

(*c*) take such steps to promote, on a regular basis, personal relations and direct contact between the child and any person with parental responsibilities in relation to him as appear to them to be, having regard to their duty to him under paragraph (*a*) above, both practicable and appropriate.

(2) The duty under paragraph (*a*) of subsection (1) above includes, without prejudice to that paragraph's generality, the duty of providing advice and assistance with a view to preparing the child for when he is no longer looked after by a local authority.

(3) Before making any decision with respect to a child whom they are looking after, or proposing to look after, a local authority shall, so far as is reasonably practicable, ascertain the views of—

(*a*) the child;

(*b*) his parents;

(*c*) any person who is not a parent of his but who has parental rights in relation to him; and

(*d*) any other person whose views the authority consider to be relevant,

regarding the matter to be decided.

(4) In making any such decision a local authority shall have regard so far as practicable—

(*a*) to the views (if he wishes to express them) of the child concerned, taking account of his age and maturity;

(*b*) to such views of any person mentioned in subsection (3)(*b*) to (*d*) above as they have been able to ascertain; and

(*c*) to the child's religious persuasion, racial origin and cultural and linguistic background.

(5) If, for the purpose of protecting members of the public from serious harm (whether or not physical harm) a local authority consider it necessary to exercise, in a manner which (but for this paragraph) would not be consistent with their duties under this section, their powers with respect to a child whom they are looking after, they may do so.

(6) Any reference in this Chapter of this Part to a child who is "looked after" by a local authority, is to a child—

(*a*) for whom they are providing accommodation under section 25 of this Act;

(*b*) who is subject to a supervision requirement and in respect of whom they are the relevant local authority;

(*c*) who is subject to an order made, or authorisation or warrant granted, by virtue of Chapter 2, 3 or 4 of this Part of this Act, being an order, authorisation or warrant in accordance with which they have responsibilities as respects the child; or

(*d*) who is subject to an order in accordance with which, by virtue of regulations made under section 33(1) of this Act, they have such responsibilities.

(7) Regulations made by the Secretary of State under subsection (1) above may, without prejudice to the generality of that subsection, include—

(*a*) provision as to the circumstances in which the child may be cared for by the child's own parents; and
(*b*) procedures which shall be followed in the event of the child's death.

NOTE
[1] Saved: see s. 31(1) (review of case at prescribed intervals).

Duty of persons with parental responsibilities to notify change of address to local authority looking after child

18.—(1) Where a child is being looked after by a local authority, each natural person who has parental responsibilities in relation to the child shall, without unreasonable delay, inform that authority whenever the person changes his address.

(2) A person who knowingly fails to comply with the requirement imposed by subsection (1) above shall be liable on summary conviction to a fine of level 1 on the standard scale; but in any proceedings under this section it shall be a defence that—
(*a*) the change was to the same address as that to which another person who at that time had parental responsibilities in relation to the child was changing; and
(*b*) the accused had reasonable cause to believe that the other person had informed the authority of the change of address of them both.

Provision of services

Local authority plans for services for children

19.—(1) Within such period after the coming into force of this section as the Secretary of State may direct, each local authority shall prepare and publish a plan for the provision of relevant services for or in respect of children in their area.

(2) References to "relevant services" in this section are to services provided by a local authority under or by virtue of—
(*a*) this Part of this Act; or
(*b*) any of the enactments mentioned in section 5(1B)(*a*) to (o) of the Social Work (Scotland) Act 1968 (enactments in respect of which Secretary of State may issue directions to local authorities as to the exercise of their functions).

(3) A local authority shall from time to time review the plan prepared by them under subsection (1) above (as modified, or last substituted, under this subsection) and may, having regard to that review, prepare and publish—
(*a*) modifications (or as the case may be further modifications) to the plan reviewed; or
(*b*) a plan in substitution for that plan.

(4) The Secretary of State may, subject to subsection (5) below, issue directions as to the carrying out by a local authority of their functions under subsection (3) above.

(5) In preparing any plan, or carrying out any review, under this section a local authority shall consult—
(*a*) every Health Board and National Health Service trust providing services under the National Health Service (Scotland) Act 1978 in the area of the authority;
(*b*) such voluntary organisations as appear to the authority—
(i) to represent the interests of persons who use or are likely to use relevant services in that area; or
(ii) to provide services in that area which, were they to be provided by the authority, might be categorised as relevant services;
(*c*) the Principal Reporter appointed under section 127 of the Local Government etc. (Scotland) Act 1994;
(*d*) the chairman of the children's panel for that area;

(*e*) such housing associations, voluntary housing agencies and other bodies as appear to the authority to provide housing in that area; and

(*f*) such other persons as the Secretary of State may direct.

Publication of information about services for children

20.—(1) A local authority shall, within such period after the coming into force of this section as the Secretary of State may direct, and thereafter from time to time, prepare and publish information—

(*a*) about relevant services which are provided by them for or in respect of children (including, without prejudice to that generality, services for or in respect of disabled children or children otherwise affected by disability) in their area or by any other local authority for those children; and

(*b*) where they consider it appropriate, about services which are provided by voluntary organisations and by other persons for those children, being services which the authority have power to provide and which, were they to do so, they would provide as relevant services.

(2) In subsection (1) above, "relevant services" has the same meaning as in section 19 of this Act.

Co-operation between authorities

21.—(1) Where it appears to a local authority that an appropriate person could, by doing certain things, help in the exercise of any of their functions under this Part of this Act, they may, specifying what those things are, request the help of that person.

(2) For the purposes of subsection (1) above, persons who are appropriate are—

(*a*) any other local authority;

(*b*) a health board constituted under section 2 of the National Health Service (Scotland) Act 1978;

(*c*) a national health service trust established under section 12A of that Act; and

(*d*) any person authorised by the Secretary of State for the purposes of this section;

and an appropriate person receiving such a request shall comply with it provided that it is compatible with their own statutory or other duties and obligations and (in the case of a person not a natural person) does not unduly prejudice the discharge of any of their functions.

Promotion of welfare of children in need

22.—(1) A local authority shall—

(*a*) safeguard and promote the welfare of children in their area who are in need; and

(*b*) so far as is consistent with that duty, promote the upbringing of such children by their families,

by providing a range and level of services appropriate to the children's needs.

(2) In providing services under subsection (1) above, a local authority shall have regard so far as practicable to each child's religious persuasion, racial origin and cultural and linguistic background.

(3) Without prejudice to the generality of subsection (1) above—

(*a*) a service may be provided under that subsection—

(i) for a particular child;

(ii) if provided with a view to safeguarding or promoting his welfare, for his family; or

(iii) if provided with such a view, for any other member of his family; and (*b*) the services mentioned in that subsection may include giving assistance in kind or, in exceptional circumstances, in cash.

(4) Assistance such as is mentioned in subsection (3)(*b*) above may be given unconditionally or subject to conditions as to the repayment, in whole or in part, of it or of its value; but before giving it, or imposing such conditions, the local authority shall have regard to the means of the child concerned and of his parents and no condition shall require repayment by a person at any time when in receipt of—

(*a*) income support or family credit payable under the Social Security Contributions and Benefits Act 1992; or

(*b*) an income-based jobseeker's allowance payable under the Jobseekers Act 1995.

Children affected by disability

23.—(1) Without prejudice to the generality of subsection (1) of section 22 of this Act, services provided by a local authority under that subsection shall be designed—

(*a*) to minimise the effect on any—

(i) disabled child who is within the authority's area, of his disability; and

(ii) child who is within that area and is affected adversely by the disability of any other person in his family, of that other person's disability; and

(*b*) to give those children the opportunity to lead lives which are as normal as possible.

(2) For the purposes of this Chapter of this Part a person is disabled if he is chronically sick or disabled or suffers from mental disorder (within the meaning of the Mental Health (Scotland) Act 1984).

(3) Where requested to do so by a child's parent or guardian a local authority shall, for the purpose of facilitating the discharge of such duties as the authority may have under section 22(1) of this Act (whether or not by virtue of subsection (1) above) as respects the child, carry out an assessment of the child, or of any other person in the child's family, to determine the needs of the child in so far as attributable to his disability or to that of the other person.

Assessment of ability of carers to provide care for disabled children

24.—(1) Subject to subsection (2) below, in any case where—

(*a*) a local authority carry out under section 23(3) of this Act an assessment to determine the needs of a disabled child, and

(*b*) a person (in this section referred to as the "carer") provides or intends to provide a substantial amount of care on a regular basis for that child,

the carer may request the local authority, before they make a decision as to the discharge of any duty they may have under section 2(1) of the Chronically Sick and Disabled Persons Act 1970 or under section 22(1) of this Act as respects the child, to carry out an assessment of the carer's ability to continue to provide, or as the case may be to provide, care for that child; and if the carer makes such a request, the local authority shall carry out such an assessment and shall have regard to the results of it in making any such decision.

(2) No request may be made under subsection (1) above by a person who provides or will provide the care in question—

(*a*) under or by virtue of a contract of employment or other contract; or

(*b*) as a volunteer for a voluntary organisation.

(3) Where an assessment of a carer's ability to continue to provide, or as the case may be to provide, care for a child is carried out under subsection (1) above, there shall, as respects the child, be no requirement under section 8 of the Disabled Persons (Services, Consultation and Representation)

Act 1986 (carer's ability to continue to provide care to be considered in any decision as respects provision of certain services for disabled persons) to have regard to that ability.

(4) In this section "person" means a natural person.

Provision of accommodation for children, etc.

25.—(1) A local authority shall provide accommodation for any child who, residing or having been found within their area, appears to them to require such provision because—

(*a*) no-one has parental responsibility for him;

(*b*) he is lost or abandoned; or

(*c*) the person who has been caring for him is prevented, whether or not permanently and for whatever reason, from providing him with suitable accommodation or care.

(2) Without prejudice to subsection (1) above, a local authority may provide accommodation for any child within their area if they consider that to do so would safeguard or promote his welfare.

(3) A local authority may provide accommodation for any person within their area who is at least eighteen years of age but not yet twenty-one, if they consider that to do so would safeguard or promote his welfare.

(4) A local authority providing accommodation under subsection (1) above for a child who is ordinarily resident in the area of another local authority shall notify the other authority, in writing, that such provision is being made; and the other authority may at any time take over the provision of accommodation for the child.

(5) Before providing a child with accommodation under this section, a local authority shall have regard, so far as practicable, to his views (if he wishes to express them), taking account of his age and maturity; and without prejudice to the generality of this subsection a child twelve years of age or more shall be presumed to be of sufficient age and maturity to form a view.

(6) Subject to subsection (7) below—

(*a*) a local authority shall not provide accommodation under this section for a child if any person who—

(i) has parental responsibilities in relation to him and the parental rights mentioned in section 2(1)(*a*) and (*b*) of this Act; and

(ii) is willing and able either to provide, or to arrange to have provided, accommodation for him,

objects; and

(*b*) any such person may at any time remove the child from accommodation which has been provided by the local authority under this section.

(7) Paragraph (*a*) of subsection (6) above does not apply—

(*a*) as respects any child who, being at least sixteen years of age, agrees to be provided with accommodation under this section; or

(*b*) where a residence order has been made in favour of one or more persons and that person has, or as the case may be those persons have, agreed that the child should be looked after in accommodation provided by, or on behalf of, the local authority;

and paragraph (*b*) of that subsection does not apply where accommodation has been provided for a continuous period of at least six months (whether by a single local authority or, by virtue of subsection (4) above, by more than one local authority), unless the person removing the child has given the local authority for the time being making such provision at least fourteen days' notice in writing of his intention to remove the child.

(8) In this Part of this Act, accommodation means, except where the context otherwise requires, accommodation provided for a continuous period of more than twenty-four hours.

Manner of provision of accommodation to child looked after by local authority

26.—(1) A local authority may provide accommodation for a child looked after by them by—

(*a*) placing him with—

(i) a family (other than such family as is mentioned in paragraph (*a*) or (*b*) of the definition of that expression in section 93(1) of this Act);

(ii) a relative of his; or

(iii) any other suitable person,

on such terms as to payment, by the authority or otherwise, as the authority may determine;

(*b*) maintaining him in a residential establishment; or

(*c*) making such other arrangements as appear to them to be appropriate, including (without prejudice to the generality of this paragraph) making use of such services as are referred to in section 17(1)(*b*) of this Act.

(2) A local authority may arrange for a child whom they are looking after—

(*a*) to be placed, under subsection (1)(*a*) above, with a person in England and Wales or in Northern Ireland; or

(*b*) to be maintained in any accommodation in which—

(i) a local authority in England and Wales could maintain him by virtue of section 23(2)(*b*) to (*e*) of the Children Act 1989; or

(ii) an authority within the meaning of the Children (Northern Ireland) Order 1995 could maintain him by virtue of Article 27(2)(*b*) to (*e*) of that Order.

Day care for pre-school and other children

27.—(1) Each local authority shall provide such day care for children in need within their area who—

(*a*) are aged five or under; and

(*b*) have not yet commenced attendance at a school,

as is appropriate; and they may provide such day care for children within their area who satisfy the conditions mentioned in paragraphs (*a*) and (*b*) but are not in need.

(2) A local authority may provide facilities (including training, advice, guidance and counselling) for those—

(*a*) caring for children in day care; or

(*b*) who at any time accompany such children while they are in day care.

(3) Each local authority shall provide for children in need within their area who are in attendance at a school such care—

(*a*) outside school hours; or

(*b*) during school holidays,

as is appropriate; and they may provide such care for children within their area who are in such attendance but are not in need.

(4) In this section—

"day care" means any form of care provided for children during the day, whether or not it is provided on a regular basis; and

"school" has the meaning given by section 135(1) of the Education (Scotland) Act 1980.

Removal of power to arrange for emigration of children

28. Section 23 of the Social Work (Scotland) Act 1968 (which provides a power for local authorities and voluntary associations, with the consent of the Secretary of State, to make arrangements for the emigration of children in their care) shall cease to have effect.

Advice and assistance for young persons formerly looked after by local authorities

After-care

29.—(1) A local authority shall, unless they are satisfied that his welfare does not require it, advise, guide and assist any person in their area over school age but not yet nineteen years of age who, at the time when he ceased to be of school age or at any subsequent time was, but who is no longer, looked after by a local authority.

(2) If a person within the area of a local authority is at least nineteen, but is less than twenty-one years of age and is otherwise a person such as is described in subsection (1) above, he may by application to the authority request that they provide him with advice, guidance and assistance; and they may, unless they are satisfied that his welfare does not require it, grant that application.

(3) Assistance given under subsection (1) or (2) above may include assistance in kind or in cash.

(4) Where a person—

(*a*) over school age ceases to be looked after by a local authority; or

(*b*) described in subsection (1) above is being provided with advice, guidance or assistance by a local authority,

they shall, if he proposes to reside in the area of another local authority, inform that other local authority accordingly provided that he consents to their doing so.

Financial assistance towards expenses of education or training and removal of power to guarantee indentures etc.

30.—(1) Without prejudice to section 12 of the Social Work (Scotland) Act 1968 (general social welfare services of local authorities), a local authority may make—

(*a*) grants to any relevant person in their area to enable him to meet expenses connected with his receiving education or training; and

(*b*) contributions to the accommodation and maintenance of any such person in any place near where he may be—

(i) employed, or seeking employment; or

(ii) receiving education or training.

(2) Subject to subsection (3) below, a person is a relevant person for the purposes of subsection (1) above if—

(*a*) he is over school age but not yet twenty-one years of age; and

(*b*) at the time when he ceased to be of school age or at any subsequent time he was, but he is no longer, looked after by a local authority.

(3) A local authority making grants under paragraph (*a*), or contributions under paragraph (*b*)(ii), of subsection (1) above to a person may continue to make them, though he has in the meantime attained the age of twenty-one years, until he completes the course of education or training in question; but if, after he has attained that age, the course is interrupted by any circumstances they may only so continue if he resumes the course as soon as is practicable.

(4) Section 25 of the Social Work (Scotland) Act 1968 (which empowers a local authority to undertake obligations by way of guarantee under any indentures or other deed of apprenticeship or articles of clerkship entered into by a person in their care or under supplemental deeds or articles) shall cease to have effect.

Miscellaneous and General

Review of case of child looked after by local authority

31.—(1) Without prejudice to their duty under section 17(1)(*a*) of this Act, it shall be the duty of a local authority who are looking after a child to review his case at such intervals as may be prescribed by the Secretary of State.

(2) The Secretary of State may prescribe—

(*a*) different intervals in respect of the first such review and in respect of subsequent reviews;

(*b*) the manner in which cases are to be reviewed under this section;

(*c*) the considerations to which the local authority are to have regard in reviewing cases under this section.

Removal of child from residential establishment

32. A local authority, notwithstanding any agreement made in connection with the placing of a child in a residential establishment under this Chapter, or Chapter 4, of this Part of this Act by them—

(*a*) may, at any time; and

(*b*) shall, if requested to do so by the person responsible for the establishment,

remove a child so placed.

Effect of orders etc. made in different parts of the United Kingdom

33.—(1) The Secretary of State may make regulations providing for a prescribed order which is made by a court in England and Wales or in Northern Ireland, if that order appears to him to correspond generally to an order of a kind which may be made under this Part of this Act or to a supervision requirement, to have effect in prescribed circumstances and for prescribed purposes of the law of Scotland as if it were an order of that kind or, as the case may be, as if it were a supervision requirement.

(2) The Secretary of State may make regulations providing—

(*a*) for a prescribed order made under this Part of this Act by a court in Scotland; or

(*b*) for a supervision requirement,

if that order or requirement appears to him to correspond generally to an order of a kind which may be made under any provision of law in force in England and Wales or in Northern Ireland, to have effect in prescribed circumstances and for prescribed purposes of the law of England and Wales, or as the case may be of Northern Ireland, as if it were an order of that kind.

(3) Regulations under subsection (1) or (2)(*a*) above may provide for the order given effect for prescribed purposes to cease to have effect for those purposes, or for the purposes of the law of the place where the order was made, if prescribed conditions are satisfied.

(4) Where a child who is subject to a supervision requirement is lawfully taken to live in England and Wales or in Northern Ireland, the requirement shall cease to have effect if prescribed conditions are satisfied.

(5) Regulations under this section may modify any provision of—

(*a*) the Social Work (Scotland) Act 1968 or this Act in any application which the Acts may respectively have, by virtue of the regulations, in relation to an order made otherwise than in Scotland;

(*b*) the Children Act 1989 or the Children and Young Persons Act 1969 in any application which those Acts may respectively have, by virtue of the regulations, in relation to an order prescribed under subsection (2)(*a*) above or to a supervision requirement; or

(*c*) the Children (Northern Ireland) Order 1995 or the Children and Young Persons Act (Northern Ireland) 1968 in any application which they may respectively have, by virtue of the regulations, in relation to an order so prescribed or to a supervision requirement.

Registration and inspection of certain residential grant-aided and independent schools etc.

34.—(1) Part IV of the Social Work (Scotland) Act 1968 (which makes provision as regards residential and other establishments) shall be amended in accordance with this section.

(2) In section 61 (restriction on carrying on of establishments)—

(*a*) for subsection (1) there shall be substituted—

"(1) In so far as the context admits, the following provisions of this Part of this Act apply—

(*a*) except in the case mentioned in paragraph (*b*) below, to any residential or other establishment the whole or a substantial part of whose functions is to provide persons with such personal care or support, whether or not combined with board and whether for reward or not, as may be required for the purposes of this Act or of the Children (Scotland) Act 1995;

(*b*) in the case of a residential establishment which is a grant-aided or independent school (as respectively defined in section 135(1) of the Education (Scotland) Act 1980), to that establishment if any part of its functions are as described in paragraph (*a*) above.";

(*b*) in subsection (1A)—

(i) in paragraph (*a*) of the definition of "establishment", for the words "sections 61A and" there shall be substituted "section"; and

(ii) at the end of that definition there shall be added "but an establishment is not excluded for those purposes by paragraph (*a*) above by reason only of its being registrable by the Registrar of Independent Schools in Scotland;"; and

(*c*) in subsection (2), for the words "section 62(8) and (8A) below" there shall be substituted "sections 61A(1) and 62(8) and (8A) of this Act".

(3) For section 61A there shall be substituted—

"**Voluntary registration**

61A.—(1) A grant-aided or independent school, provided it is not a residential establishment the whole or a substantial part of whose functions is as described in subsection (1)(*a*) of section 61 of this Act, may be carried on by a person without his being registered in respect of it as mentioned in subsection (2) of that section; but he may if he wishes apply in accordance with section 62, or as the case may be 63, of this Act for such registration.

(2) Sections 62(8) and (8A) and 65 of this Act shall not apply in relation to establishments as respects which registration has been by virtue of subsection (1) above.".

(4) After section 62 there shall be inserted—

"**Certificate of registration as respects grant-aided or independent school**

62A. A certificate of registration granted under section 62 of this Act as respects an establishment which is a grant-aided, or independent, school shall relate to the whole of the establishment except so much as is used exclusively for educational purposes.".

(5) In section 65(1) (removal of persons from establishment), after the word "ought"—

(*a*) where it first occurs, there shall be inserted "(by virtue of subsections (2) and (3)) of section 61 of this Act)"; and

(*b*) where it occurs for the second time, there shall be inserted "(by virtue of the said subsections (2) and (3))".

(6) For section 67 there shall be substituted—

"**Entry to examine state and management of establishments etc.**

67.—(1) A person duly authorised by a local authority may in the area of that authority, at all reasonable times, enter, for a relevant purpose—

(*a*) any establishment as regards which a person is registered, or ought (by virtue of subsections (2) and (3) of section 61 of this Act) to be registered, under section 62 of this Act; or (*b*) any place which the person so authorised has reasonable cause to believe is being used as such an establishment,

and subsections (2A) to (2D), (4) and (5) of section 6 of this Act shall apply in respect of a person so authorised as they apply in respect of a person duly authorised under subsection (1) of that section.

(2) "Relevant purpose" in subsection (1) above means—

(*a*) the purpose of making such examinations into the state and management of the establishment or place, and the condition and treatment of the persons in it, as the person so authorised thinks necessary; or

(*b*) the purpose of inspecting any records, or registers (in whatever form they are held) relating to the place, or to any person for whom, under or by virtue of this Act, section 7 (functions of local authorities) or 8 (provision of after-care services) of the Mental Health (Scotland) Act 1984, or Part II of the Children (Scotland) Act 1995, services are being or have been provided in the place.".

Welfare of children in accommodation provided for purposes of school attendance

35. After section 125 of the Education (Scotland) Act 1980 there shall be inserted—

"*Children and young persons in accommodation*

Welfare of children and young persons in accommodation provided for purposes of school attendance

125A. Where, for the purposes of his being in attendance at a school, a child or young person is provided with residential accommodation, in a place in or outwith that school, by—

(*a*) an education authority, the board of management of a self-governing school or the managers of a grant-aided or independent school; or

(*b*) by any other person in pursuance of arrangements made by any such authority, board of management or managers,

the authority, board of management or managers in question shall have the duty to safeguard and promote the welfare of the child or young person while he is so accommodated; and the powers of inspection exercisable by virtue of section 66(1) of this Act shall include the power to inspect the place to determine whether his welfare is adequately safeguarded and promoted there.".

Welfare of certain children in hospitals and nursing homes etc.

36.—(1) Where a child is provided with residential accommodation by a person mentioned in subsection (3) below and it appears to the person that the child either—

(*a*) has had no parental contact for a continuous period of three months or more; or

(*b*) is likely to have no parental contact for a period which, taken with any immediately preceding period in which the child has had no such contact, will constitute a continuous period of three months or more,

the person shall (whether or not the child has been, or will be, so accommodated throughout the continuous period) so notify the local authority in whose area the accommodation is provided.

(2) A local authority receiving notification under subsection (1) above shall—

(*a*) take such steps as are reasonably practicable to enable them to determine whether the child's welfare is adequately safeguarded and promoted while he is so accommodated; and

(*b*) consider the extent to which (if at all) they should exercise any of their functions under this Act with respect to the child.

(3) The persons are—

(*a*) any health board constituted under section 2 of the National Health Service (Scotland) Act 1978;

(*b*) any national health service trust established under section 12A of that Act;

(*c*) any person carrying on—

(i) a private hospital registered under Part IV of the Mental Health (Scotland) Act 1984; or

(ii) a nursing home in respect of which either he is registered under section 1(3) of the Nursing Homes Registration (Scotland) Act 1938 or exemption has been granted under section 6 or 7 of that Act.

(4) For the purposes of subsection (1) above, a child has parental contact only when in the presence of a person having parental responsibilities in relation to him.

(5) A person duly authorised by a local authority may in the area of that authority, at all reasonable times, enter for the purposes of subsection (2) above or of determining whether there has been compliance with subsection (1) above any such place as is mentioned in sub-paragraph (i) or (ii) of subsection (3)(*c*) above and may for those purposes inspect any records or registers relating to that place; and subsections (2A) to (2D) and (4) of section 6 of the Social Work (Scotland) Act 1968 (exercise of powers of entry and inspection) shall apply in respect of a person so authorised as they apply in respect of a person duly authorised under subsection (1) of that section.

Modification of provisions of Children Act 1989 regarding disqualification from registration as child minder etc.

37. In paragraph 2 of Schedule 9 to the Children Act 1989 (which provides for regulations disqualifying certain persons from registration as a child minder or as a provider of day care for young children), at the end of sub-paragraph (1) there shall be added "unless he has—

(*a*) disclosed the fact to the appropriate local authority; and

(*b*) obtained their written consent.".

Short-term refuges for children at risk of harm

38.—(1) Where a child appears—

(*a*) to a local authority to be at risk of harm, they may at the child's request—

(i) provide him with refuge in a residential establishment both controlled or managed by them and designated by them for the purposes of this paragraph; or

(ii) arrange for a person whose household is approved by virtue of section 5(3)(*b*) of the Social Work (Scotland) Act 1968 (provision for securing that persons are not placed in any household unless the household has prescribed approval) and is designated by them for the purposes of this paragraph to provide him with refuge in that household,

for a period which does not exceed the relevant period;

(*b*) to a person who carries on a residential establishment in respect of which the person is for the time being registered (as mentioned in section 61(2) of that Act), or to any person for the time being employed in the management of that establishment, to be at risk of harm, the person to whom the child so appears may at the child's request provide him with refuge, for a period which does not exceed the relevant period, in the establishment but shall do so only if and to the extent that the local authority within whose area the establishment is situated have given their approval to the use of the establishment (or a part of the establishment) for the purposes of this paragraph.

(2) The Secretary of State may by regulations make provision as to—
(*a*) designation, for the purposes of paragraph (*a*) of subsection (1) above, of establishments and households;
(*b*) application for, the giving of and the withdrawal of, approval under paragraph (*b*) of subsection (1) above;
(*c*) requirements (if any) which must be complied with while any such approval remains in force;
(*d*) the performance by a person mentioned in the said paragraph (*b*) of anything to be done by him under that paragraph;
(*e*) the performance by a local authority of their functions under this section; and
(*f*) the giving, to such persons or classes of person as may be specified in the regulations, of notice as to the whereabouts of a child provided with refuge under this section,

and regulations made under this subsection may include such incidental and supplementary provisions as he thinks fit.

(3) While a child is being provided with refuge under, and in accordance with regulations made under, this section, none of the enactments mentioned in subsection (4) below shall apply in relation to him unless the commencement of the period of refuge has followed within two days of the termination of a prior period of refuge so provided to him by any person.

(4) The enactments are—
(*a*) section 89 of this Act and, so far as it applies in relation to anything done in Scotland, section 83 of this Act; and
(*b*) section 32(3) of the Children and Young Persons Act 1969 (compelling, persuading, inciting or assisting any person to be absent from detention etc.), so far as it applies in relation to anything done in Scotland.

(5) References in this section to the relevant period shall be construed as references either to a period which does not exceed seven days or, in such exceptional circumstances as the Secretary of State may prescribe, to a period which does not exceed fourteen days.

(6) A child who is provided with refuge for a period by virtue of such arrangements as are mentioned in subsection (1)(*a*) above shall not be regarded as a foster child for the purposes of the Foster Children (Scotland) Act 1984 by reason only of such provision.

Chapter 2

Children's Hearings

Constitution of children's hearings

Formation of children's panel and children's hearings

39.—(1) For every local government area there shall be a children's panel for the purposes of this Act, and any other enactment conferring powers on a children's hearing (or on such a panel).

(2) Schedule 1 to this Act shall have effect with respect to the recruitment, appointment, training and expenses of members of a children's panel and the establishment of Children's Panel Advisory Committees and joint advisory committees.

(3) Sittings of members of the children's panel (to be known as "children's hearings") shall be constituted from the panel in accordance with subsection (5) below.

(4) A children's hearing shall be constituted for the performance of the functions given to such a hearing by or by virtue of—
(*a*) this Act; or
(*b*) any other enactment conferring powers on a children's hearing.

(5) A children's hearing shall consist of three members, one of whom shall act as chairman; and shall not consist solely of male, or solely of female, members.

Qualifications, employment and duties of reporters

Qualification and employment of reporters

40.—(1) The qualifications of a reporter shall be such as the Secretary of State may prescribe.

(2) A reporter shall not, without the consent of the Scottish Children's Reporter Administration, be employed by a local authority.

(3) The Secretary of State may make regulations in relation to the functions of any reporter under this Act and the Criminal Procedure (Scotland) Act 1975.

(4) The Secretary of State and the Lord Advocate may—

(*a*) by regulations empower a reporter, whether or not he is an advocate or solicitor, to conduct before a sheriff any proceedings which under this Chapter or Chapter 3 of this Part of this Act are heard by the sheriff;

(*b*) prescribe such requirements as they think fit as to qualifications, training or experience necessary for a reporter to be so empowered.

(5) In this section, "reporter" means—

(*a*) the Principal Reporter; or

(*b*) any officer of the Scottish Children's Reporter Administration to whom there is delegated, under section 131(1) of the Local Government etc. (Scotland) Act 1994, any of the functions which the Principal Reporter has under this or any other enactment.

Safeguards for children

Safeguarding child's interests in proceedings

41.—(1) Subject to subsection (2) below, in any proceedings under this Chapter or Chapter 3 of this Part of this Act either at a children's hearing or before the sheriff, the hearing or, as the case may be, the sheriff—

(*a*) shall consider if it is necessary to appoint a person to safeguard the interests of the child in the proceedings; and

(*b*) if they, or he, so consider, shall make such an appointment, on such terms and conditions as appear appropriate.

(2) Subsection (1) above shall not apply in relation to proceedings under section 57 of this Act.

(3) Where a children's hearing make an appointment under subsection (1)(*b*) above, they shall state the reasons for their decision to make that appointment.

(4) The expenses of a person appointed under subsection (1) above shall—

(*a*) in so far as reasonably incurred by him in safeguarding the interests of the child in the proceedings, and

(*b*) except in so far as otherwise defrayed in terms of regulations made under section 101 of this Act,

be borne by the local authority—

(i) for whose area the children's panel from which the relevant children's hearing has been constituted is formed;

(ii) where there is no relevant children's hearing, within whose area the child resides.

(5) For the purposes of subsection (4) above, "relevant children's hearing" means, in the case of proceedings—

(*a*) at a children's hearing, that hearing;

(*b*) under section 68 of this Act, the children's hearing who have directed the application;

(*c*) on an appeal under section 51 of this Act, the children's hearing whose decision is being appealed against.

Conduct of proceedings at and in connection with children's hearing

Power of Secretary of State to make rules governing procedure at children's hearing etc.

42.—(1) Subject to the following provisions of this Act, the Secretary of State may make rules for constituting and arranging children's hearings and other meetings of members of the children's panel and for regulating their procedure.

(2) Without prejudice to the generality of subsection (1) above, rules under that subsection may make provision with respect to—

(*a*) the conduct of, and matters which shall or may be determined by, a business meeting arranged under section 64 of this Act;

(*b*) notification of the time and place of a children's hearing to the child and any relevant person in relation to the child and to such other persons as may be prescribed;

(*c*) how the grounds for referring the case to a children's hearing under section 65(1) of this Act are to be stated, and the right of the child and any such relevant person to dispute those grounds;

(*d*) the making available by the Principal Reporter, subject to such conditions as may be specified in the rules, of reports or information received by him to—

(i) members of the children's hearing;

(ii) the child concerned;

(iii) any relevant person; and

(iv) any other person or class of persons so specified;

(*e*) the procedure in relation to the disposal of matters arising under section 41(1) of this Act;

(*f*) the functions of any person appointed by a children's hearing under section 41(1) of this Act and any right of that person to information relating to the proceedings in question;

(*g*) the recording in writing of any statement given under section 41(3) of this Act;

(*h*) the right to appeal to the sheriff under section 51(1)(*a*) of this Act against a decision of the children's hearing and notification to such persons as may be prescribed of the proceedings before him;

(*i*) the right of the child and of any such relevant person to be represented at a children's hearing;

(*j*) the entitlement of the child, of any such relevant person and of any person who acts as the representative of the child or of any such relevant person to the refund of such expenses, incurred by the child or as the case may be the person or representative, as may be prescribed in connection with a children's hearing and with any proceedings arising from the hearing;

(*k*) persons whose presence shall be permitted at a children's hearing.

Privacy of proceedings at and right to attend children's hearing

43.—(1) Subject to subsection (3) below, a children's hearing shall be conducted in private, and, subject to any rules made under section 42 of this Act, no person other than a person whose presence is necessary for the proper consideration of the case which is being heard, or whose presence is permitted by the chairman, shall be present.

(2) The chairman shall take all reasonable steps to ensure that the number of persons present at a children's hearing at any one time is kept to a minimum.

(3) The following persons have the right to attend a children's hearing—

(*a*) a member of the Council on Tribunals, or of the Scottish Committee of that Council, in his capacity as such; and (*b*) subject to subsection (4) below, a bona fide representative of a newspaper or news agency.

(4) A children's hearing may exclude a person described in subsection (3)(*b*) above from any part or parts of the hearing where, and for so long as, they are satisfied that—

(*a*) it is necessary to do so, in the interests of the child, in order to obtain the child's views in relation to the case before the hearing; or

(*b*) the presence of that person is causing, or is likely to cause, significant distress to the child.

(5) Where a children's hearing have exercised the power conferred by subsection (4) above to exclude a person, the chairman may, after that exclusion has ended, explain to the person the substance of what has taken place in his absence.

Prohibition of publication of proceedings at children's hearing

44.—(1) No person shall publish any matter in respect of proceedings at a children's hearing, or before a sheriff on an application under section 57, section 60(7), section 65(7) or (9), section 76(1) or section 85(1) of this Act, or on any appeal under this Part of this Act, which is intended to, or is likely to, identify—

(*a*) any child concerned in the proceedings or appeal; or

(*b*) an address or school as being that of any such child.

(2) Any person who contravenes subsection (1) above shall be guilty of an offence and shall be liable on summary conviction to a fine not exceeding level 4 on the standard scale in respect of each such contravention.

(3) It shall be a defence in proceedings for an offence under this section for the accused to prove that he did not know, and had no reason to suspect, that the published matter was intended, or was likely, to identify the child or, as the case may be, the address or school.

(4) In this section "to publish" includes, without prejudice to the generality of that expression,—

(*a*) to publish matter in a programme service, as defined by section 201 of the Broadcasting Act 1990 (definition of programme service); and

(*b*) to cause matter to be published.

(5) The requirements of subsection (1) above may, in the interests of justice, be dispensed with by—

(*a*) the sheriff in any proceedings before him;

(*b*) the Court of Session in any appeal under section 51(11) of this Act; or

(*c*) the Secretary of State in relation to any proceedings at a children's hearing,

to such extent as the sheriff, the Court or the Secretary of State as the case may be considers appropriate.

Attendance of child and relevant person at children's hearing

45.—(1) Where a child has been notified in accordance with rules made under subsection (1) of section 42 of this Act by virtue of subsection (2)(*b*) of that section that his case has been referred to a children's hearing, he shall—

(*a*) have the right to attend at all stages of the hearing; and

(*b*) subject to subsection (2) below, be under an obligation to attend those stages in accordance with the notice.

(2) Without prejudice to subsection (1)(*a*) above and section 65(4) of this Act, where a children's hearing are satisfied—

(*a*) in a case concerned with an offence mentioned in Schedule 1 to the Criminal Procedure (Scotland) Act 1975, that the attendance of the child is not necessary for the just hearing of that case; or

(*b*) in any case, that it would be detrimental to the interests of the child for him to be present at the hearing of his case, they may release the child from the obligation imposed by subsection (1)(*b*) above.

(3) Subject to subsection (2) above, the Principal Reporter shall be responsible for securing the attendance of the child at the hearing of his case by a children's hearing (and at any subsequent hearing to which the case is continued under section 69(1)(*a*) of this Act).

(4) On the application of the Principal Reporter, a children's hearing, if satisfied on cause shown that it is necessary for them to do so, may issue, for the purposes of subsection (3) above, a warrant under this subsection to find the child, to keep him in a place of safety and to bring him before a children's hearing.

(5) Where a child has failed to attend a children's hearing in accordance with such notice as is mentioned in subsection (1) above, they may, either on the application of the Principal Reporter or of their own motion, issue a warrant under this subsection, which shall have the same effect as a warrant under subsection (4) above.

(6) A child who has been taken to a place of safety under a warrant granted under this section shall not be kept there after whichever is the earlier of—

(*a*) the expiry of seven days beginning on the day he was first so taken there; or

(*b*) the day on which a children's hearing first sit to consider his case in accordance with subsection (7) below.

(7) Where a child has been found in pursuance of a warrant under this section and he cannot immediately be brought before a children's hearing, the Principal Reporter shall, wherever practicable, arrange a children's hearing to sit on the first working day after the child was so found.

(8) Subject to section 46 of this Act, a person who is a relevant person as respects a child shall, where a children's hearing are considering the case of the child—

(*a*) have the right to attend at all stages of the hearing; and

(*b*) be obliged to attend at all stages of the hearing unless the hearing are satisfied that it would be unreasonable to require his attendance or that his attendance is unnecessary for the proper consideration of the case.

(9) Any person who fails to attend a hearing which, under subsection (8)(*b*) above, he is obliged to attend shall be guilty of an offence and shall be liable on summary conviction to a fine not exceeding level 3 on the standard scale.

Power to exclude relevant person from children's hearing

46.—(1) Where a children's hearing are considering the case of a child in respect of whom a person is a relevant person, they may exclude that person, or that person and any representative of his, or any such representative, from any part or parts of the hearing for so long as is necessary in the interests of the child, where they are satisfied that—

(*a*) they must do so in order to obtain the views of the child in relation to the case before the hearing; or

(*b*) the presence of the person or persons in question is causing, or is likely to cause, significant distress to the child.

(2) Where a children's hearing exercise the power conferred by subsection (1) above, the chairman of the hearing shall, after that exclusion has ended, explain to any person who was so excluded the substance of what has taken place in his absence.

Presumption and determination of age

47.—(1) Where a children's hearing has been arranged in respect of any person, the hearing—

(*a*) shall, at the commencement of the proceedings, make inquiry as to his age and shall proceed with the hearing only if he declares that he is a child or they so determine; and

(*b*) may, at any time before the conclusion of the proceedings, accept a declaration by the child, or make a fresh determination, as to his age.

(2) The age declared to, or determined by, a children's hearing to be the age of a person brought before them shall, for the purposes of this Part of this Act, be deemed to be the true age of that person.

(3) No decision reached, order continued, warrant granted or requirement imposed by a children's hearing shall be invalidated by any subsequent proof that the age of a person brought before them had not been correctly declared to the hearing or determined by them.

Transfer etc. of cases

Transfer of case to another children's hearing

48.—(1) Where a children's hearing are satisfied, in relation to a case which they are hearing, that it could be better considered by a children's hearing constituted from a children's panel for a different local government area, they may at any time during the course of the hearing request the Principal Reporter to arrange for such other children's hearing to dispose of the case.

(2) Where a case has been transferred in pursuance of subsection (1) above, the grounds of referral accepted or established for the case shall not require to be further accepted or established for the purposes of the children's hearing to which the case has been transferred.

Referral or remission to children's hearing where child guilty of an offence

49.—(1) In section 173 of the Criminal Procedure (Scotland) Act 1975 (reference or remission to children's hearing where child guilty of an offence: solemn proceedings), for subsections (1) to (3) there shall be substituted—

"(1) Where a person who is charged with an offence and pleads guilty to, or is found guilty of, that offence is a child who is not subject to a supervision requirement, the court on that plea or finding may—

(*a*) instead of making an order, remit the case to the Principal Reporter to arrange a children's hearing to dispose of the case; or

(*b*) request the Principal Reporter to arrange a children's hearing for the purpose of obtaining their advice as to the treatment of the child.

(2) Where a person, who is charged with an offence and pleads guilty to, or is found guilty of, that offence, is aged sixteen years or over and is subject to a supervision requirement, the court if it is—

(*a*) the High Court, may; and

(*b*) the sheriff court shall,

proceed in accordance with either paragraph (*a*) or (*b*) of subsection (1) above.

(3) Where a child who is charged with an offence and pleads guilty to, or is found guilty of, that offence—

(*a*) is aged under sixteen years; and

(*b*) is subject to a supervision requirement,

the court dealing with the case if it is—

(i) the High Court, may; and

(ii) the sheriff court, shall,

request the Principal Reporter to arrange a children's hearing for the purpose of obtaining their advice as to the treatment of the child.

(3A) Where a court has obtained the advice of a children's hearing in pursuance—

(*a*) of paragraph (*b*) of subsection (1) above; or

(*b*) of subsection (3) above,

the court, after consideration of the advice received from the children's hearing may, as it thinks proper, itself dispose of the case or remit the case as mentioned in paragraph (*a*) of the said subsection (1).".

(2) In section 372 of that Act (reference or remission to children's hearing where child guilty of an offence: summary proceedings), for subsections (1) to (3) there shall be substituted—

"(1) Where a person who is charged with an offence and pleads guilty to, or is found guilty of, that offence is a child who is not subject to a supervision requirement, the court on that plea or finding may—

(*a*) instead of making an order, remit the case to the Principal Reporter to arrange a children's hearing to dispose of the case; or

(*b*) request the Principal Reporter to arrange a children's hearing for the purpose of obtaining their advice as to the treatment of the child.

(2) Where a person, who is charged with an offence and pleads guilty to, or is found guilty of, that offence, is aged sixteen years or over and is subject to a supervision requirement, the court shall proceed in accordance with either paragraph (*a*) or (*b*) of subsection (1) above.

(3) Where a child who is charged with an offence and pleads guilty to, or is found guilty of, that offence—

(*a*) is aged under sixteen years; and

(*b*) is subject to a supervision requirement,

the court dealing with the case shall request the Principal Reporter to arrange a children's hearing for the purpose of obtaining their advice as to the treatment of the child.

(3A) Where a court has obtained the advice of a children's hearing in pursuance—

(*a*) of paragraph (*b*) of subsection (1) above; or

(*b*) of subsection (3) above,

the court, after consideration of the advice received from the children's hearing may, as it thinks proper, itself dispose of the case or remit the case as mentioned in paragraph (*a*) of the said subsection (1).".

Treatment of child's case on remission by court

50.—(1) Where a court has, under section 173, 372 or 373 of the Criminal Procedure (Scotland) Act 1975, remitted a case to a children's hearing for disposal, a certificate signed by the clerk of the court stating that the child or person concerned has pled guilty to, or has been found guilty of, the offence to which the remit relates shall be conclusive evidence for the purposes of the remit that the offence has been committed by the child or person.

(2) Where a court has under the said section 373 remitted a case to a children's hearing for disposal, the provisions of this Act shall apply to the person concerned as if he were a child.

Appeals

Appeal against decision of children's hearing or sheriff

51.—(1) Subject to subsection (15) below, a child or a relevant person (or relevant persons) or both (or all)—

(*a*) may, within a period of three weeks beginning with the date of any decision of a children's hearing, appeal to the sheriff against that decision; and (*b*) where such an appeal is made, shall be heard by the sheriff.

(2) The Principal Reporter shall, in respect of any appeal under subsection (1) above, ensure that all reports and statements available to the hearing, along with the reports of their proceedings and the reasons for the decision, are lodged with the sheriff clerk.

(3) The sheriff may, on appeal under subsection (1) above, hear evidence from, or on behalf of, the parties in relation to the decision; and, without prejudice to that generality, the sheriff may—

(*a*) examine the Principal Reporter;

(*b*) examine the authors or compilers of any reports or statements; and

(*c*) call for any further report which he considers may assist him in deciding the appeal.

(4) Where the sheriff decides that an appeal under this section has failed, he shall confirm the decision of the children's hearing.

(5) Where the sheriff is satisfied that the decision of the children's hearing is not justified in all the circumstances of the case he shall allow the appeal, and—

(*a*) where the appeal is against a warrant to find and keep or, as the case may be, to keep a child in a place of safety, he shall recall the warrant;

(*b*) where the child is subject to a supervision requirement containing a condition imposed under section 70(9) of this Act, he shall direct that the condition shall cease to have effect; and

(*c*) in any case, he may, as he thinks fit—

(i) remit the case with reasons for his decision to the children's hearing for reconsideration of their decision; or

(ii) discharge the child from any further hearing or other proceedings in relation to the grounds for the referral of the case; or

(iii) substitute for the disposal by the children's hearing any requirement which could be imposed by them under section 70 of this Act.

(6) Where a sheriff imposes a requirement under subsection (5)(*c*)(iii) above, that requirement shall for the purposes of this Act, except of this section, be treated as a disposal by the children's hearing.

(7) Where the sheriff is satisfied that an appeal under subsection (1) above against the decision of a children's hearing arranged under section 73(8) of this Act is frivolous, he may order that no subsequent appeal against a decision to continue (whether with or without any variation) the supervision requirement in question shall lie until the expiration of twelve months beginning with the date of the order.

(8) An appeal under subsection (1) above in respect of the issue of a warrant by a children's hearing shall be disposed of within three days of the lodging of the appeal; and failing such disposal the warrant shall cease to have effect at the end of that period.

(9) Where a child or a relevant person appeals under subsection (1) above against a decision of a children's hearing in relation to a supervision requirement, the child or the relevant person may make application to a children's hearing for the suspension of the requirement appealed against.

(10) It shall be the duty of the Principal Reporter forthwith to arrange a children's hearing to consider the application under subsection (9) above, and that hearing may grant or refuse the application.

(11) Subject to subsections (13) and (15) below, an appeal shall lie by way of stated case either on a point of law or in respect of any irregularity in the conduct of the case—

(*a*) to the sheriff principal from any decision of the sheriff—

(i) on an appeal under subsection (1) of this section;

(ii) on an application made under section 65(7) or (9) of this Act; or

(iii) on an application made under section 85(1) of this Act; and (*b*) to the Court of Session from any decision of the sheriff such as is mentioned in sub-paragraphs (i) to (iii) of paragraph (*a*) above and, with leave of the sheriff principal, from any decision of the sheriff principal on an appeal under that paragraph; and the decision of the Court of Session in the matter shall be final.

(12) An appeal under subsection (11) above may be made at the instance of—

(*a*) the child or any relevant person, either alone or together; or

(*b*) the Principal Reporter on behalf of the children's hearing.

(13) An application to the sheriff, or as the case may be the sheriff principal, to state a case for the purposes of an appeal under subsection (11)(*a*) or (*b*) above shall be made within a period of twenty-eight days beginning with the date of the decision appealed against.

(14) On deciding an appeal under subsection (11) above the sheriff principal or as the case may be the Court of Session shall remit the case to the sheriff for disposal in accordance with such directions as the court may give.

(15) No appeal shall lie under this section in respect of—

(*a*) a decision of the sheriff on an application under section 57 of this Act; or

(*b*) a decision of a children's hearing continuing a child protection order under section 59(4) of this Act.

Chapter 3

Protection and supervision of Children

Children requiring compulsory measures of supervision

Children requiring compulsory measures of supervision

52.—(1) The question of whether compulsory measures of supervision are necessary in respect of a child arises if at least one of the conditions mentioned in subsection (2) below is satisfied with respect to him.

(2) The conditions referred to in subsection (1) above are that the child—

(*a*) is beyond the control of any relevant person;

(*b*) is falling into bad associations or is exposed to moral danger;

(*c*) is likely—

(i) to suffer unnecessarily; or

(ii) be impaired seriously in his health or development,

due to a lack of parental care;

(*d*) is a child in respect of whom any of the offences mentioned in Schedule 1 to the Criminal Procedure (Scotland) Act 1975 (offences against children to which special provisions apply) has been committed;

(*e*) is, or is likely to become, a member of the same household as a child in respect of whom any of the offences referred to in paragraph (*d*) above has been committed;

(*f*) is, or is likely to become, a member of the same household as a person who has committed any of the offences referred in paragraph (*d*) above;

(*g*) is, or is likely to become, a member of the same household as a person in respect of whom an offence under sections 2A to 2C of the Sexual Offences (Scotland) Act 1976 (incest and intercourse with a child by step-parent or person in position of trust) has been committed by a member of that household;

(*h*) has failed to attend school regularly without reasonable excuse;

(*i*) has committed an offence;

(*j*) has misused alcohol or any drug, whether or not a controlled drug within the meaning of the Misuse of Drugs Act 1971;

(*k*) has misused a volatile substance by deliberately inhaling its vapour, other than for medicinal purposes;

(*l*) is being provided with accommodation by a local authority under section 25, or is the subject of a parental responsibilities order obtained under section 86, of this Act and, in either case, his behaviour is such that special measures are necessary for his adequate supervision in his interest or the interest of others.

(3) In this Part of this Act, "supervision" in relation to compulsory measures of supervision may include measures taken for the protection, guidance, treatment or control of the child.

Preliminary and investigatory measures

Provision of information to the Principal Reporter

53.—(1) Where information is received by a local authority which suggests that compulsory measures of supervision may be necessary in respect of a child, they shall—

(*a*) cause inquiries to be made into the case unless they are satisfied that such inquiries are unnecessary; and

(*b*) if it appears to them after such inquiries, or after being satisfied that such inquiries are unnecessary, that such measures may be required in respect of the child, give to the Principal Reporter such information about the child as they have been able to discover.

(2) A person, other than a local authority, who has reasonable cause to believe that compulsory measures of supervision may be necessary in respect of a child—

(*a*) shall, if he is a constable, give to the Principal Reporter such information about the child as he has been able to discover;

(*b*) in any other case, may give the Principal Reporter that information.

(3) A constable shall make any report required to be made under paragraph (*b*) of section 17(1) of the Police (Scotland) Act 1967 (duty to make reports in relation to commission of offences) in relation to a child to the Principal Reporter as well as to the appropriate prosecutor.

(4) Where an application has been made to the sheriff—

(*a*) by the Principal Reporter in accordance with a direction given by a children's hearing under section 65(7) or (9) of this Act; or

(*b*) by any person entitled to make an application under section 85 of this Act,

the Principal Reporter may request any prosecutor to supply him with any evidence lawfully obtained in the course of, and held by the prosecutor in connection with, the investigation of a crime or suspected crime, being evidence which may assist the sheriff in determining the application; and, subject to subsection (5) below, it shall be the duty of the prosecutor to comply with such a request.

(5) A prosecutor may refuse to comply with a request issued under subsection (4) above where he reasonably believes that it is necessary to retain the evidence for the purposes of any proceedings in respect of a crime, whether the proceedings have been commenced or are to be commenced by him.

(6) The Lord Advocate may direct that in any specified case or class of cases any evidence lawfully obtained in the course of an investigation of a crime or suspected crime shall be supplied, without the need for a request under subsection (4) above, to the Principal Reporter.

(7) In subsections (3), (4) and (5) above "crime" and "prosecutor" have the same meanings respectively given by section 462 of the Criminal Procedure (Scotland) Act 1975.

Reference to the Principal Reporter by court

54.—(1) Where in any relevant proceedings it appears to the court that any of the conditions in section 52(2)(*a*) to (*h*), (*j*), (*k*) or (*l*) of this Act is satisfied with respect to a child, it may refer the matter to the Principal Reporter, specifying the condition.

(2) In this section "relevant proceedings" means—

(*a*) an action for divorce or judicial separation or for declarator of marriage, nullity of marriage, parentage or non-parentage;

(*b*) proceedings relating to parental responsibilities or parental rights within the meaning of Part I of this Act;

(*c*) proceedings for an adoption order under the Adoption (Scotland) Act 1978 or for an order under section 18 of that Act declaring a child free for adoption; and

(*d*) proceedings for an offence against section 35 (failure by parent to secure regular attendance by his child at a public school), 41 (failure to comply with attendance order) or 42(3) (failure to permit examination of child) of the Education (Scotland) Act 1980.

(3) Where the court has referred a matter to the Principal Reporter under subsection (1) above, he shall—

(*a*) make such investigation as he thinks appropriate; and

(*b*) if he considers that compulsory measures of supervision are necessary,

arrange a children's hearing to consider the case of the child under section 69 of this Act; and subsection (1) of that section shall apply as if the condition specified by the court under subsection (1) above were a ground of referral established in accordance with section 68 of this Act.

Child assessment orders

55.—(1) A sheriff may grant an order under this section for an assessment of the state of a child's health or development, or of the way in which he has been treated (to be known as a "child assessment order"), on the application of a local authority if he is satisfied that—

(*a*) the local authority have reasonable cause to suspect that the child in respect of whom the order is sought is being so treated (or neglected) that he is suffering, or is likely to suffer, significant harm;

(*b*) such assessment of the child is required in order to establish whether or not there is reasonable cause to believe that the child is so treated (or neglected); and

(*c*) such assessment is unlikely to be carried out, or be carried out satisfactorily, unless the order is granted.

(2) Where—

(*a*) an application has been made under subsection (1) above; and

(*b*) the sheriff considers that the conditions for making a child protection order under section 57 of this Act are satisfied,

he shall make such an order under that section as if the application had been duly made by the local authority under that section rather than this section.

(3) A child assessment order shall—

(*a*) specify the date on which the assessment is to begin;

(*b*) have effect for such period as is specified in the order, not exceeding seven days beginning with the date specified by virtue of paragraph (*a*) above;

(*c*) require any person in a position to produce the child to—

(i) produce him to any authorised person;

(ii) permit that person or any other authorised person to carry out an assessment in accordance with the order; and

(iii) comply with any other conditions of the order; and

(*d*) be carried out by an authorised person in accordance with the terms of the order.

(4) A child assessment order may—

(*a*) where necessary, permit the taking of the child concerned to any place for the purposes of the assessment; and

(*b*) authorise the child to be kept at that place, or any other place, for such period of time as may be specified in the order.

(5) Where a child assessment order makes provision under subsection (4) above, it shall contain such directions as the sheriff considers appropriate as to the contact which the child shall be allowed to have with any other person while the child is in any place to which he has been taken or in which he is being kept under a child assessment order.

(6) In this section "authorised person" means any officer of the local authority, and any person authorised by the local authority to perform the assessment, or perform any part of it.

Initial investigation by the Principal Reporter

56.—(1) Where the Principal Reporter receives information from any source about a case which may require a children's hearing to be arranged he shall, after making such initial investigation as he thinks necessary, proceed with the case in accordance with subsection (4) or (6) below.

(2) For the purposes of making any initial investigation under subsection (1) above, the Principal Reporter may request from the local authority a report on the child and on such circumstances concerning the child as appear to him to be relevant; and the local authority shall supply the report which may contain such information, from any person whomsoever, as the Principal Reporter thinks, or the local authority think, fit.

(3) A report requested under subsection (2) above may contain information additional to that given by the local authority under section 53 of this Act.

(4) The Principal Reporter may decide, after an initial investigation under subsection (1) above, that a children's hearing does not require to be arranged; and where he so decides—

(*a*) he shall inform the child, any relevant person and the person who brought the case to his notice, or any of those persons, that he has so decided; and

(*b*) he may, if he considers it appropriate, refer the case to a local authority with a view to their making arrangements for the advice, guidance and assistance of the child and his family in accordance with Chapter 1 of this Part of this Act.

(5) Where the Principal Reporter has decided under subsection (4) above that a children's hearing does not require to be arranged, he shall not at any other time, on the basis solely of the information obtained during the initial investigation referred to in that subsection, arrange a children's hearing under subsection (6) below.

(6) Where it appears to the Principal Reporter that compulsory measures of supervision are necessary in respect of the child, he shall arrange a children's hearing to which he shall refer the case for consideration and determination.

(7) Where the Principal Reporter has arranged a children's hearing in accordance with subsection (6) above, he—

(*a*) shall, where he has not previously done so, request a report under subsection (2) above;

(*b*) may request from the local authority such information, supplementary or additional to a report requested under subsection (2) above, as he thinks fit;

and the local authority shall supply that report, or as the case may be information, and any other information which they consider to be relevant.

Measures for the emergency protection of children

Child protection orders

[1] **57.**—(1) Where the sheriff, on an application by any person, is satisfied that—

(*a*) there are reasonable grounds to believe that a child—

(i) is being so treated (or neglected) that he is suffering significant harm; or

(ii) will suffer such harm if he is not removed to and kept in a place of safety, or if he does not remain in the place where he is then being accommodated (whether or not he is resident there); and

(*b*) an order under this section is necessary to protect that child from such harm (or such further harm),

he may make an order under this section (to be known as a "child protection order").

(2) Without prejudice to subsection (1) above, where the sheriff on an application by a local authority is satisfied—

(*a*) that they have reasonable grounds to suspect that a child is being or will be so treated (or neglected) that he is suffering or will suffer significant harm;

(*b*) that they are making or causing to be made enquiries to allow them to decide whether they should take any action to safeguard the welfare of the child; and

(*c*) that those enquiries are being frustrated by access to the child being unreasonably denied, the authority having reasonable cause to believe that such access is required as a matter of urgency,

he may make a child protection order.

(3) Without prejudice to any additional requirement imposed by rules made by virtue of section 91 of this Act, an application for a child protection order shall—

(*a*) identify—

(i) the applicant; and

(ii) in so far as practicable, the child in respect of whom the order is sought;

(*b*) state the grounds on which the application is made; and

(*c*) be accompanied by such supporting evidence, whether in documentary form or otherwise, as will enable the sheriff to determine the application.

(4) A child protection order may, subject to such terms and conditions as the sheriff considers appropriate, do any one or more of the following—

(*a*) require any person in a position to do so to produce the child to the applicant;

(*b*) authorise the removal of the child by the applicant to a place of safety, and the keeping of the child at that place;

(*c*) authorise the prevention of the removal of the child from any place where he is being accommodated;

(*d*) provide that the location of any place of safety in which the child is being kept should not be disclosed to any person or class of person specified in the order.

(5) Notice of the making of a child protection order shall be given forthwith by the applicant to the local authority in whose area the child resides (where that authority is not the applicant) and to the Principal Reporter.

(6) In taking any action required or permitted by a child protection order or by a direction under section 58 of this Act the applicant shall only act where he reasonably believes that to do so is necessary to safeguard or promote the welfare of the child.

(7) Where by virtue of a child protection order a child is removed to a place of safety provided by a local authority, they shall, subject to the terms and conditions of that order and of any direction given under section

58 of this Act, have the like duties in respect of the child as they have under section 17 of this Act in respect of a child looked after by them.

NOTE
[1] See s. 51(15) (exclusion of appeal).

Directions in relation to contact and exercise of parental responsibilities and parental rights

58.—(1) When the sheriff makes a child protection order, he shall at that time consider whether it is necessary to give a direction to the applicant for the order as to contact with the child for—

(*a*) any parent of the child;
(*b*) any person with parental responsibilities in relation to the child; and
(*c*) any other specified person or class of persons;

and if he determines that there is such a necessity he may give such a direction.

(2) Without prejudice to the generality of subsection (1) above, a direction under that subsection may—

(*a*) prohibit contact with the child for any person mentioned in paragraphs (*a*) to (*c*) of that subsection;
(*b*) make contact with the child for any person subject to such conditions as the sheriff considers appropriate to safeguard and promote the welfare of the child.

(3) A direction under subsection (1) above may make different provision in relation to different persons or classes of person.

(4) A person applying for a child protection order under section 57(1) or (2) of this Act may at the same time apply to the sheriff for a direction in relation to the exercise or fulfilment of any parental responsibilities or parental rights in respect of the child concerned, if the person considers such a direction necessary to safeguard or promote the welfare of the child.

(5) Without prejudice to the generality of subsection (4) above, a direction under that subsection may be sought in relation to—

(*a*) any examination as to the physical or mental state of the child;
(*b*) any other assessment or interview of the child; or
(*c*) any treatment of the child arising out of such an examination or assessment,

which is to be carried out by any person.

(6) The sheriff may give a direction sought under subsection (4) above where he considers there is a necessity such as is mentioned in that subsection; and such a direction may be granted subject to such conditions, if any, as the sheriff (having regard in particular to the duration of the child protection order to which it relates) considers appropriate.

(7) A direction under this section shall cease to have effect when—

(*a*) the sheriff, on an application under section 60(7) of this Act, directs that it is cancelled; or
(*b*) the child protection order to which it is related ceases to have effect.

Initial hearing of case of child subject to child protection order

59.—(1) This section applies where—

(*a*) a child in respect of whom a child protection order has been made—
  (i) has been taken to a place of safety by virtue of section 57(4)(*b*) of this Act; or
  (ii) is prevented from being removed from any place by virtue of section 57(4)(*c*) of this Act;
(*b*) the Principal Reporter has not exercised his powers under section 60(3) of this Act to discharge the child from the place of safety; and
(*c*) the Principal Reporter has not received notice, in accordance with section 60(9) of this Act, of an application under subsection (7) of that section.

(2) Where this section applies, the Principal Reporter shall arrange a children's hearing to conduct an initial hearing of the child's case in order

to determine whether they should, in the interests of the child, continue the child protection order under subsection (4) below.

(3) A children's hearing arranged under subsection (2) above shall take place on the second working day after that order is implemented.

[1] (4) Where a children's hearing arranged under subsection (2) above are satisfied that the conditions for the making of a child protection order under section 57 of this Act are established, they may continue the child protection order and any direction given under section 58 of this Act (whether with or without variation of the order or, as the case may be, the direction) until the commencement of a children's hearing in relation to the child arranged in accordance with section 65(2) of this Act.

(5) In subsection (3) above, section 60 and section 65(2) of this Act any reference, in relation to the calculation of any period, to the time at which a child protection order is implemented shall be construed as a reference—

(*a*) in relation to such an order made under paragraph (*b*) of subsection (4) of section 57 of this Act, to the day on which the child was removed to a place of safety in accordance with the order; and

(*b*) in relation to such an order made under paragraph (*c*) of that subsection, to the day on which the order was made,

and "implement" shall be construed accordingly.

NOTE

[1] See s. 51(15) (exclusion of appeal).

Duration, recall or variation of child protection order

60.—(1) Where, by the end of twenty-four hours of a child protection order being made (other than by virtue of section 57(4)(*c*) of this Act), the applicant has made no attempt to implement the order it shall cease to have effect.

(2) Where an application made under subsection (7) below has not been determined timeously in accordance with subsection (8) below, the order to which the application relates shall cease to have effect.

(3) A child shall not be—

(*a*) kept in a place of safety under a child protection order;

(*b*) prevented from being removed from any place by such an order; or

(*c*) subject to any term or condition contained in such an order or a direction given under section 58 of this Act,

where the Principal Reporter, having regard to the welfare of the child, considers that, whether as a result of a change in the circumstances of the case or of further information relating to the case having been received by the Principal Reporter, the conditions for the making of a child protection order in respect of the child are no longer satisfied or that the term, condition or direction is no longer appropriate and notifies the person who implemented the order that he so considers.

(4) The Principal Reporter shall not give notice under subsection (3) above where—

(*a*) proceedings before a children's hearing arranged under section 59(2) of this Act in relation to the child who is subject to the child protection order have commenced; or

(*b*) the hearing of an application made under subsection (7) of this section has begun.

(5) Where the Principal Reporter has given notice under subsection (3) above, he shall also, in such manner as may be prescribed, notify the sheriff who made the order.

(6) A child protection order shall cease to have effect—

(*a*) where an initial hearing arranged under section 59(2) of this Act does not continue the order under subsection (4) of that section;

(*b*) where an application is made to the sheriff under subsection (7) below, on the sheriff recalling such order under subsection (13) below;

(*c*) on the person who implemented the order receiving notice from the Principal Reporter that he has decided not to refer the case of a child who is subject to the order to a children's hearing arranged in accordance with section 65(2) of this Act;

(*d*) on the Principal Reporter giving notice in accordance with subsection (3) above in relation to the order that he considers that the conditions for the making of it are no longer satisfied; or

(*e*) where such order is continued under section 59(4) of this Act or subsection (12)(*d*) below, on the commencement of a children's hearing arranged under section 65(2) of this Act.

(7) An application to the sheriff to set aside or vary a child protection order made under section 57 of this Act or a direction given under section 58 of this Act or such an order or direction continued (whether with or without variation) under section 59(4) of this Act, may be made by or on behalf of—

(*a*) the child to whom the order or direction relates;

(*b*) a person having parental rights over the child;

(*c*) a relevant person;

(*d*) any person to whom notice of the application for the order was given by virtue of rules; or

(*e*) the applicant for the order made under section 57 of this Act.

(8) An application under subsection (7) above shall be made—

(*a*) in relation to a child protection order made under section 57, or a direction given under section 58, of this Act, before the commencement of a children's hearing arranged in accordance with section 59(2) of this Act; and

(*b*) in relation to such an order or direction continued (whether with or without variation) by virtue of subsection (4) of the said section 59, within two working days of such continuation,

and any such application shall be determined within three working days of being made.

(9) Where an application has been made under subsection (7) above, the applicant shall forthwith give notice, in a manner and form prescribed by rules, to the Principal Reporter.

(10) At any time which is—

(*a*) after the giving of the notice required by subsection (9) above; but

(*b*) before the sheriff has determined the application in accordance with subsection (11) below,

the Principal Reporter may arrange a children's hearing the purpose of which shall be to provide any advice they consider appropriate to assist the sheriff in his determination of the application.

(11) The sheriff shall, after hearing the parties to the application and, if he wishes to make representations, the Principal Reporter, determine whether—

(*a*) the conditions for the making of a child protection order under section 57 of this Act are satisfied; or

(*b*) where the application relates only to a direction under section 58 of this Act, the direction should be varied or cancelled.

(12) Where the sheriff determines that the conditions referred to in subsection (11)(*a*) above are satisfied, he may—

(*a*) confirm or vary the order, or any term or condition on which it was granted;

(*b*) confirm or vary any direction given, in relation to the order, under section 58 of this Act;

(*c*) give a new direction under that section; or

(*d*) continue in force the order and any such direction until the commencement of a children's hearing arranged in accordance with section 65(2) of this Act.

(13) Where the sheriff determines that the conditions referred to in subsection (11)(*a*) above are not satisfied he shall recall the order and cancel any direction given under section 58 of this Act.

Emergency protection of children where child protection order not available

61.—(1) Where, on the application of any person, a justice of the peace is satisfied—

(*a*) both that the conditions laid down for the making of a child protection order in section 57(1) of this Act are satisfied and that it is probable that any such order, if made, would contain an authorisation in terms of paragraph (*b*) or (*c*) of subsection (4) of that section; but

(*b*) that it is not practicable in the circumstances for an application for such an order to be made to the sheriff or for the sheriff to consider such an application,

he may grant to the applicant an authorisation under this section.

(2) Where on the application of a local authority a justice of the peace is satisfied—

(*a*) both that the conditions laid down for the making of a child protection order in section 57(2) of this Act are satisfied and that it is probable that any such order, if made, would contain an authorisation in terms of paragraph (*b*) or (*c*) of subsection (4) of that section; but

(*b*) that it is not practicable in the circumstances for an application for such an order to be made to the sheriff or for the sheriff to consider such an application,

he may grant an authorisation under this section.

(3) An authorisation under this section may—

(*a*) require any person in a position to do so to produce the child to the applicant;

(*b*) prevent any person from removing a child from a place where he is then being accommodated;

(*c*) authorise the applicant to remove the child to a place of safety and to keep him there until the expiration of the authorisation.

(4) An authorisation under this section shall cease to have effect—

(*a*) twelve hours after being made, if within that time—

(i) arrangements have not been made to prevent the child's removal from any place specified in the authorisation; or

(ii) he has not been, or is not being, taken to a place of safety; or

(*b*) where such arrangements have been made or he has been so taken when—

(i) twenty-four hours have expired since it was so given; or

(ii) an application for a child protection order in respect of the child is disposed of,

whichever is the earlier.

(5) Where a constable has reasonable cause to believe that—

(*a*) the conditions for the making of a child protection order laid down in section 57(1) are satisfied;

(*b*) that it is not practicable in the circumstances for him to make an application for such an order to the sheriff or for the sheriff to consider such an application; and

(*c*) that, in order to protect the child from significant harm (or further such harm), it is necessary for him to remove the child to a place of safety,

he may remove the child to such a place and keep him there.

(6) The power conferred by subsection (5) above shall not authorise the keeping of a child in a place of safety for more than twenty-four hours from the time when the child is so removed.

(7) The authority to keep a child in a place of safety conferred by subsection (5) above shall cease on the disposal of an application in relation to the child for a child protection order.

(8) A child shall not be—

(*a*) kept in a place of safety; or

(*b*) prevented from being removed from any place,

under this section where the Principal Reporter considers that the conditions for the grant of an authorisation under subsection (1) or (2) above or the exercise of the power conferred by subsection (5) above are not satisfied, or that it is no longer in the best interests of the child that he should be so kept.

Regulations in respect of emergency child protection measures

62.—(1) The Secretary of State may make regulations concerning the duties in respect of a child of any person removing him to, and keeping him in, a place of safety under section 61 above.

(2) Regulations under this section may make provision requiring—

(*a*) notification of the removal of a child to be given to a person specified in the regulations;

(*b*) intimation to be given to any person of the place of safety at which a child is being kept;

(*c*) notification to be given to any person of the ceasing to have effect, under section 61(4)(*a*) of this Act, of an authorisation.

Children arrested by the police

Review of case of child arrested by police

63.—(1) Where the Principal Reporter has been informed by a constable, in accordance with section 296(3) of the Criminal Procedure (Scotland) Act 1975, that charges are not to be proceeded with against a child who has been detained in a place of safety in accordance with that section, the Principal Reporter shall, unless he considers that compulsory measures of supervision are not required in relation to the child, arrange a children's hearing to which he shall refer the case.

(2) A children's hearing arranged under subsection (1) above shall begin not later than the third day after the Principal Reporter received the information mentioned in that subsection.

(3) Where the Principal Reporter considers that a child of whose detention he has been informed does not require compulsory measures of supervision, he shall direct that the child shall no longer be kept in the place of safety.

(4) Subject to subsection (3) above, a child who has been detained in a place of safety may continue to be kept at that place until the commencement of a children's hearing arranged under subsection (1) above.

(5) Subject to subsection (6) below, a children's hearing arranged under subsection (1) above may—

(*a*) if they are satisfied that the conditions mentioned in subsection (2) of section 66 of this Act are satisfied, grant a warrant to keep the child in a place of safety; and

(*b*) direct the Principal Reporter to arrange a children's hearing for the purposes of section 65(1) of this Act,

and subsections (3) to (8) of the said section 66 shall apply to a warrant granted under this subsection as they apply to a warrant granted under subsection (1) of the said section 66.

(6) A child shall not be kept in a place of safety in accordance with a warrant granted under subsection (5) above where the Principal Reporter, having regard to the welfare of the child, considers that, whether as a result of a change in the circumstances of the case or of further information relating to the case having been received by the Principal Reporter—

(*a*) the conditions mentioned in section 66(2) of this Act are no longer satisfied in relation to the child; or

(*b*) the child is not in need of compulsory measures of supervision,

and where he does so consider he shall give notice to that effect to the person who is keeping the child in that place in accordance with the warrant.

Business meeting preparatory to children's hearing

Business meeting preparatory to children's hearing

64.—(1) At any time prior to the commencement of proceedings at the children's hearing, the Principal Reporter may arrange a meeting with members of the children's panel from which the children's hearing is to be constituted under section 39(4) of this Act for those proceedings (any such meeting being, in this Part of this Act referred to as a "business meeting").

(2) Where a business meeting is arranged under subsection (1) above, the Principal Reporter shall give notice to the child in respect of whom the proceedings are to be commenced and any relevant person in relation to the child—

(*a*) of the arrangement of the meeting and of the matters which may be considered and determined by the meeting;

(*b*) of their right to make their views on those matters known to the Principal Reporter; and

(*c*) of the duty of the Principal Reporter to present those views to the meeting.

(3) A business meeting, subject to subsection (4) below—

(*a*) shall determine such procedural and other matters as may be prescribed by rules under subsection (1) of section 42 of this Act by virtue of subsection (2)(*a*) of that section; and

(*b*) may give such direction or guidance to the Principal Reporter in relation to the performance of his functions in relation to the proceedings as they think appropriate.

(4) Before a business meeting makes such a determination or gives such direction or guidance to the Principal Reporter, the Principal Reporter shall present, and they shall consider, any views expressed to him by virtue of subsection (2)(*b*) above.

(5) Subject to any rules made under section 42(1) of this Act by virtue of subsection (2)(*a*) of that section and with the exception of sections 44 and, as regards any determination made by the business meeting under subsection (3)(*a*) above, 51, the provisions of this Act which relate to a children's hearing shall not apply to a business meeting.

Referral to, and disposal of case by, children's hearing

Referral to, and proceedings at, children's hearing

65.—(1) The Principal Reporter shall refer to the children's hearing, for consideration and determination on the merits, the case of any child in respect of whom he is satisfied that—

(*a*) compulsory measures of supervision are necessary, and

(*b*) at least one of the grounds specified in section 52(2) of this Act is established;

and he shall state such grounds in accordance with rules made under section 42(1) of this Act by virtue of subsection (2)(*c*) of that section.

(2) Where a referral is made in respect of a child who is subject to a child protection order made under section 57, and that order is continued under section 59(4) or 60(12)(*d*), of this Act, the Principal Reporter shall arrange for the children's hearing under subsection (1) above to take place on the eighth working day after the order was implemented.

(3) Where a referral is made in respect of a child who is subject to a supervision requirement, the children's hearing shall, before disposing of the referral in accordance with section 69(1)(*b*) or (*c*) of this Act, review that requirement in accordance with subsections (9) to (12) of section 73 of this Act.

(4) Subject to subsections (9) and (10) below, it shall be the duty of the chairman of the children's hearing to whom a child's case has been referred under subsection (1) above to explain to the child and the relevant person,

at the opening of proceedings on the referral, the grounds stated by the Principal Reporter for the referral in order to ascertain whether these grounds are accepted in whole or in part by them.

(5) Where the chairman has given the explanation required by subsection (4) above and the child and the relevant person accept the grounds for the referral, the children's hearing shall proceed in accordance with section 69 of this Act.

(6) Where the chairman has given the explanation required by subsection (4) above and the child and the relevant person accept the grounds in part, the children's hearing may, if they consider it appropriate to do so, proceed in accordance with section 69 of this Act with respect to those grounds which are accepted.

(7) Where the chairman has given the explanation required under subsection (4) above and either or both of the child and the relevant person—

(*a*) do not accept the grounds for the referral; or

(*b*) accept the grounds in part, but the children's hearing do not consider it appropriate to proceed with the case under subsection (6) above,

the hearing shall either direct the Principal Reporter to make an application to the sheriff for a finding as to whether such grounds for the referral as are not accepted by the child and the relevant person are established or shall discharge the referral.

(8) Subject to subsection (10) below, it shall be the duty of the chairman to explain to the child and to the relevant person the purpose for which the application to the sheriff is being made and to inform the child that he is under an obligation to attend the hearing before the sheriff.

(9) Where a children's hearing are satisfied that the child—

(*a*) for any reason will not be capable of understanding the explanation of the grounds for the referral required under subsection (4) above; or

(*b*) has not understood an explanation given under that subsection,

they shall either direct the Principal Reporter to make an application to the sheriff for a finding as to whether any of the grounds of the referral are established or discharge the referral.

(10) The acceptance by the relevant person of the grounds of the referral shall not be a requirement for a children's hearing proceeding under this section to consider a case where that person is not present.

Warrant to keep child where children's hearing unable to dispose of case

66.—(1) Without prejudice to any other power enjoyed by them under this Part of this Act and subject to subsection (5) below, a children's hearing—

(*a*) arranged to consider a child's case under this Part of this Act; and

(*b*) unable to dispose of the case,

may, if they are satisfied that one of the conditions mentioned in subsection (2) below is met, grant a warrant under this subsection.

(2) The conditions referred to in subsection (1) above are—

(*a*) that there is reason to believe that the child may—

(i) not attend at any hearing of his case; or

(ii) fail to comply with a requirement under section 69(3) of this Act; or

(*b*) that it is necessary that the child should be kept in a place of safety in order to safeguard or promote his welfare.

(3) A warrant under subsection (1) above may require any person named in the warrant—

(*a*) to find and to keep or, as the case may be, to keep the child in a place of safety for a period not exceeding twenty-two days after the warrant is granted;

(*b*) to bring the child before a children's hearing at such times as may be specified in the warrant.

(4) A warrant under subsection (1) above may contain such conditions as appear to the children's hearing to be necessary or expedient, and without prejudice to that generality may—

(*a*) subject to section 90 of this Act, require the child to submit to any medical or other examination or treatment; and

(*b*) regulate the contact with the child of any specified person or class of persons.

(5) Subject to subsection (8) below, at any time prior to its expiry, a warrant granted under this section may, on an application to the children's hearing, on cause shown by the Principal Reporter, be continued in force, whether with or without variation of any condition imposed by virtue of subsection (4) above, by the children's hearing for such further period, not exceeding twenty-two days, as appears to them to be necessary.

(6) Where a children's hearing are satisfied that either of the criteria specified in section 70(10) of this Act are satisfied, they may order that, pending the disposal of his case, the child shall be liable to be placed and kept in secure accommodation within a residential establishment at such times as the person in charge of that establishment, with the agreement of the chief social work officer of the relevant local authority, considers necessary.

(7) Where a children's hearing grant a warrant under subsection (1) above or continue such a warrant under subsection (5) above, they may order that the place of safety at which the child is to be kept shall not be disclosed to any person or class of persons specified in the order.

(8) A child shall not be kept in a place of safety or secure accommodation by virtue of this section for a period exceeding sixty-six days from the day when he was first taken to a place of safety under a warrant granted under subsection (1) above.

Warrant for further detention of child

67.—(1) Where a child is being kept in a place of safety by virtue of a warrant granted under section 66 of this Act or under this subsection, the Principal Reporter at any time prior to the expiry of that warrant may apply to the sheriff for a warrant to keep the child in that place after the warrant granted under the said section 66 or, as the case may be, this subsection has expired.

(2) A warrant under subsection (1) above shall only be granted on cause shown and—

(*a*) shall specify the date on which it will expire; and

(*b*) may contain any such requirement or condition as may be contained in a warrant granted under the said section 66.

(3) Where the sheriff grants a warrant under subsection (1) above, he may also make an order under this subsection in such terms as are mentioned in subsection (6) or (7) of the said section 66; and any order under this subsection shall cease to have effect when the warrant expires.

(4) An application under subsection (1) above may be made at the same time as, or during the hearing of, an application which the Principal Reporter has been directed by a children's hearing to make under section 65(7) or (9) of this Act.

Application to sheriff to establish grounds of referral

68.—(1) This section applies to applications under subsections (7) and (9) of section 65 of this Act and a reference in this section (except in subsection (8)) to "an application" is a reference to an application under either of those subsections.

(2) An application shall be heard by the sheriff within twenty-eight days of its being lodged.

(3) Where one of the grounds for the referral to which an application relates is the condition referred to in section 52(2)(*i*)—

(*a*) the application shall be made to the sheriff who would have jurisdiction if the child were being prosecuted for that offence; and

(*b*) in hearing the application in relation to that ground, the standard of proof required in criminal proceedings shall apply.

(4) A child shall—

(*a*) have the right to attend the hearing of an application; and

(*b*) subject to subsection (5) below, be under an obligation to attend such hearing;

and without prejudice to the right of each of them to be legally represented, the child and the relevant person may be represented by a person other than a legally qualified person at any diet fixed by the sheriff for the hearing of the application.

(5) Without prejudice to subsection (4)(*a*) above, the sheriff may dispense with the obligation imposed by subsection (4)(*b*) above where he is satisfied—

(*a*) in an application in which the ground of referral to be established is a condition mentioned in section 52(2)(*d*), (*e*), (*f*) or (*g*) of this Act, that the obligation to attend of the child is not necessary for the just hearing of that application; and

(*b*) in any application, that it would be detrimental to the interests of the child for him to be present at the hearing of the application.

(6) Where the child fails to attend the hearing of an application at which his attendance has not been dispensed with under subsection (5) above, the sheriff may grant an order to find and keep the child; and any order under this subsection shall be authority for bringing the child before the sheriff and, subject to subsection (7) below, for keeping him in a place of safety until the sheriff can hear the application.

(7) The child shall not be kept in a place of safety by virtue of subsection (6) above after whichever is the earlier of—

(*a*) the expiry of fourteen days beginning with the day on which the child is found; or

(*b*) the disposal of the application by the sheriff.

(8) Where in the course of the hearing of an application—

(*a*) under section 65(7) of this Act, the child and the relevant person accept any of the grounds for referral to which the application relates, the sheriff shall; or

(*b*) under section 65(9) of this Act, the relevant person accepts any of the grounds for referral to which the application relates, the sheriff may, if it appears to him reasonable to do so,

dispense with the hearing of evidence relating to that ground and deem the ground to be established for the purposes of the application, unless he is satisfied that, in all the circumstances of the case, the evidence should be heard.

(9) Where a sheriff decides that none of the grounds for referral in respect of which an application has been made are established, he shall dismiss the application, discharge the referral to the children's hearing in respect of those grounds and recall, discharge or cancel any order, warrant, or direction under this Chapter of this Act which relates to the child in respect of those grounds.

(10) Where the sheriff, after the hearing of any evidence or on acceptance in accordance with subsection (8) above, finds that any of the grounds for the referral to which the application relates is, or should be deemed to be, established—

(*a*) he shall remit the case to the Principal Reporter to make arrangements for a children's hearing to consider and determine the case; and

(*b*) he may if he is satisfied that—

(i) keeping the child in a place of safety is necessary in the child's best interests; or

(ii) there is reason to believe that the child will run away before the children's hearing sit to consider the case,

issue an order requiring, subject to subsection (12) below, that the child be kept in a place of safety until the children's hearing so sit.

(11) An order issued under subsection (10) above may, if the sheriff is satisfied that either of the criteria mentioned in section 70(10) of this Act is fulfilled, provide that the child shall be liable to be placed and kept in secure accommodation within a residential establishment at such times as the person in charge of the establishment, with the agreement of the chief social work officer of the relevant local authority, considers necessary.

(12) A child shall not be kept in a place of safety by virtue of subsection (10)(*b*) above after whichever is the earlier of the following—

(*a*) the expiry of three days beginning with the day on which he is first so kept; or

(*b*) the consideration of his case by the children's hearing arranged under subsection (10)(*a*) above.

Continuation or disposal of referral by children's hearing

69.—(1) Where the grounds of referral of the child's case stated by the Principal Reporter are accepted or are established in accordance with section 68 or section 85 of this Act, the children's hearing shall consider those grounds, any report obtained under section 56(7) of this Act and any other relevant information available to them and shall—

(*a*) continue the case to a subsequent hearing in accordance with subsection (2) below;

(*b*) discharge the referral of the case in accordance with subsection (12) below; or

(*c*) make a supervision requirement under section 70 of this Act.

(2) The children's hearing may continue the case to a subsequent hearing under this subsection where they are satisfied that, in order to complete their consideration of the case, it is necessary to have a further investigation of the case.

(3) Where a children's hearing continue the case under subsection (2) above, they may, for the purposes of the investigation mentioned by that subsection, require the child to attend, or reside at, any clinic, hospital or other establishment during a period not exceeding twenty-two days.

(4) Where a child fails to fulfil a requirement made under subsection (3) above, the children's hearing may, either on an application by the Principal Reporter or of their own motion, grant a warrant under this subsection.

(5) A warrant under subsection (4) above shall be authority—

(*a*) to find the child;

(*b*) to remove the child to a place of safety and keep him there; and

(*c*) where the place of safety is not the clinic, hospital or other establishment referred to in the requirement made under subsection (3) above, to take the child from the place of safety to such clinic, hospital or other establishment for the purposes of the investigation mentioned in subsection (2) above.

(6) A warrant under subsection (4) above shall be granted for such period as appears to the children's hearing to be appropriate, provided that no warrant shall permit the keeping of a child in a place of safety after whichever is the earlier of—

(*a*) the expiry of twenty-two days after the warrant is granted; or

(*b*) the day on which the subsequent hearing of the child's case by a children's hearing begins.

(7) Where a child's case has been continued under subsection (2) above and the children's hearing are satisfied that—

(*a*) keeping the child in a place of safety is necessary in the interests of safeguarding or promoting the welfare of the child; or (*b*) there is reason to believe that the child may not attend the subsequent hearing of his case,

they may grant a warrant requiring that the child be taken to and kept in a place of safety.

(8) A warrant under subsection (7) above shall cease to have effect on whichever is the earlier of—

(*a*) the expiry of twenty-two days after the warrant is granted; or

(*b*) the day on which the subsequent hearing of the child's case by a children's hearing begins.

(9) A warrant under subsection (4) or (7) above may contain such conditions as appear to the children's hearing to be necessary or expedient, and without prejudice to that generality may—

(*a*) subject to section 90 of this Act, require the child to submit to any medical or other examination or treatment;

(*b*) regulate the contact with the child of any specified person or class of persons.

(10) Where a child is to be kept at a place of safety under a warrant granted under this section or is to attend, or reside at, any place in accordance with a requirement made under subsection (3) above, the children's hearing may order that such place shall not be disclosed to any person or class of persons specified in the order.

(11) Where a child is to reside in a residential establishment by virtue of a requirement made or warrant granted under this section, the children's hearing may, if satisfied that either of the criteria mentioned in section 70(10) of this Act is fulfilled, order that while the requirement or warrant remains in effect he shall be liable to be placed in secure accommodation within that establishment at such times as the person in charge of the establishment, with the agreement of the chief social work officer of the relevant local authority, considers necessary.

(12) Where a children's hearing decide not to make a supervision requirement under section 70 of this Act they shall discharge the referral.

(13) On the discharge of the referral of the child's case any order, direction, or warrant under Chapter 2, or this Chapter, of this Act in respect of the child's case shall cease to have effect.

Disposal of referral by children's hearing: supervision requirements, including residence in secure accommodation

70.—(1) Where the children's hearing to whom a child's case has been referred under section 65(1) of this Act are satisfied that compulsory measures of supervision are necessary in respect of the child they may make a requirement under this section (to be known as a "supervision requirement").

(2) A children's hearing, where they decide to make such a requirement, shall consider whether to impose any condition such as is described in subsection (5)(*b*) below.

(3) A supervision requirement may require the child—

(*a*) to reside at any place or places specified in the requirement; and

(*b*) to comply with any condition contained in the requirement.

(4) The place or, as the case may be, places specified in a requirement under subsection (3)(*a*) above may, without prejudice to the generality of that subsection, be a place or places in England or Wales; and a supervision requirement shall be authority for the person in charge of such a place to restrict the child's liberty to such extent as that person may consider appropriate, having regard to the terms of the requirement.

(5) A condition imposed under subsection (3)(*b*) above may, without prejudice to the generality of that subsection—

(*a*) subject to section 90 of this Act, require the child to submit to any medical or other examination or treatment;

(*b*) regulate the contact with the child of any specified person or class of persons.

(6) A children's hearing may require, when making a supervision requirement, that any place where the child is to reside in accordance with the supervision requirement shall not be disclosed to any person specified in the requirement under this subsection or class of persons so specified.

(7) A children's hearing who make a supervision requirement may determine that the requirement shall be reviewed at such time during the duration of the requirement as they determine.

(8) A supervision requirement shall be in such form as the Secretary of State may prescribe by rules.

(9) Where a children's hearing are satisfied—

(*a*) that it is necessary to make a supervision requirement which includes a requirement under subsection (3)(*a*) above that the child reside in a named residential establishment; and

(*b*) that any of the criteria specified in subsection (10) below are satisfied,

they may specify in the requirement that the child shall be liable to be placed and kept in secure accommodation in that establishment during such period as the person in charge of that establishment, with the agreement of the chief social work officer of the relevant local authority, considers necessary.

(10) The criteria referred to in subsection (9) above are that the child—

(*a*) having previously absconded, is likely to abscond unless kept in secure accommodation, and, if he absconds, it is likely that his physical, mental or moral welfare will be at risk; or

(*b*) is likely to injure himself or some other person unless he is kept in such accommodation.

Duties of local authority with respect to supervision requirements

71.—(1) The relevant local authority shall, as respects a child subject to a supervision requirement, give effect to the requirement.

(2) Where a supervision requirement provides that the child shall reside—

(*a*) in relevant accommodation; or

(*b*) in any other accommodation not provided by a local authority,

the relevant local authority shall from time to time investigate whether, while the child is so resident, any conditions imposed by the supervision requirement are being fulfilled; and may take such steps as they consider reasonable if they find that such conditions are not being fulfilled.

(3) In this section, "relevant accommodation" means accommodation provided by the parents or relatives of the child or by any person associated with them or with the child.

Transfer of child subject to supervision requirement in case of necessity

72.—(1) In any case of urgent necessity, where it is in the interests of—

(*a*) a child who is required by a supervision requirement imposed under section 70(3)(*a*) of this Act to reside in a specific residential establishment or specific other accommodation; or

(*b*) other children in that establishment or accommodation,

the chief social work officer of the relevant local authority may direct that, notwithstanding that requirement, the child be transferred to another place.

(2) Any child transferred under subsection (1) above shall have his case reviewed, in accordance with section 73(8) of this Act, by a children's hearing within seven days of his transfer.

Duration and review of supervision requirement

73.—(1) No child shall continue to be subject to a supervision requirement for any period longer than is necessary in the interests of promoting or safeguarding his welfare.

(2) Subject to any variation or continuation of a supervision requirement under subsection (9) below, no supervision requirement shall remain in force for a period longer than one year.

(3) A supervision requirement shall cease to have effect in respect of a child not later than on his attaining the age of eighteen years.

(4) A relevant local authority shall refer the case of a child who is subject to a supervision requirement to the Principal Reporter where they are satisfied that—

(*a*) the requirement in respect of the child ought to cease to have effect or be varied;

(*b*) a condition contained in the requirement is not being complied with; or

(*c*) the best interests of the child would be served by their—

(i) applying under section 86 of this Act for a parental responsibilities order;

(ii) applying under section 18 of the Adoption (Scotland) Act 1978 for an order freeing the child for adoption; or

(iii) placing the child for adoption,

and they intend to apply for such an order or so place the child.

(5) Where the relevant local authority are aware that an application has been made and is pending, or is about to be made, under section 12 of the said Act of 1978 for an adoption order in respect of a child who is subject to a supervision requirement, they shall forthwith refer his case to the Principal Reporter.

(6) A child or any relevant person may require a review of a supervision requirement in respect of the child at any time at least three months after—

(*a*) the date on which the requirement is made; or

(*b*) the date of the most recent continuation, or variation, by virtue of this section of the requirement.

(7) Where a child is subject to a supervision requirement and, otherwise than in accordance with that requirement or with an order under section 11 of this Act, a relevant person proposes to take the child to live outwith Scotland, the person shall, not later than twenty-eight days before so taking the child, give notice of that proposal in writing to the Principal Reporter and to the relevant local authority.

(8) The Principal Reporter shall—

(*a*) arrange for a children's hearing to review any supervision requirement in respect of a child where—

(i) the case has been referred to him under subsection (4) or (5) above;

(ii) the review has been required under subsection (6) above;

(iii) the review is required by virtue of section 70(7) or section 72(2) of this Act;

(iv) he has received in respect of the child such notice as is mentioned in subsection (7) above; or

(v) in any other case, the supervision requirement will expire within three months; and

(*b*) make any arrangements incidental to that review.

(9) Where a supervision requirement is reviewed by a children's hearing arranged under subsection (8) above, they may—

(*a*) where they are satisfied that in order to complete the review of the supervision requirement it is necessary to have a further investigation of the child's case, continue the review to a subsequent hearing;

(*b*) terminate the requirement;

(*c*) vary the requirement;

(*d*) insert in the requirement any requirement which could have been imposed by them under section 70(3) of this Act; or

(*e*) continue the requirement, with or without such variation or insertion.

(10) Subsections (3) to (10) of section 69 of this Act shall apply to a continuation under paragraph (*a*) of subsection (9) above of a review of a supervision requirement as they apply to the continuation of a case under subsection (1)(*a*) of that section.

(11) Where a children's hearing vary or impose a requirement under subsection (9) above which requires the child to reside in any specified place or places, they may order that such place or places shall not be disclosed to any person or class of persons specified in the requirement.

(12) Where a children's hearing is arranged under subsection (8)(*a*)(v) above, they shall consider whether, if the supervision requirement is not continued, the child still requires supervision or guidance; and where a children's hearing consider such supervision or guidance is necessary, it shall be the duty of the local authority to provide such supervision or guidance as the child is willing to accept.

(13) Where a children's hearing is arranged by virtue of subsection (4)(*c*) or (5) above, then irrespective of what the hearing do under subsection (9) above they shall draw up a report which shall provide advice in respect of, as the case may be, the proposed application under section 86 of this Act or under section 18 of the said Act of 1978, or the proposed placing for adoption or the application, or prospective application, under section 12 of that Act, for any court which may subsequently require to come to a decision, in relation to the child concerned, such as is mentioned in subsection (14) below.

(14) A court which is considering whether, in relation to a child, to grant an application under section 86 of this Act or under section 18 or 12 of the said Act of 1978 and which, by virtue of subsection (13) above, receives a report as respects that child, shall consider the report before coming to a decision in the matter.

Further provision as respects children subject to supervision requirements

74. The Secretary of State may by regulations provide—

(*a*) for the transmission of information regarding a child who is subject to a supervision requirement to any person who, by virtue of that requirement, has, or is to have, control over the child;

(*b*) for the temporary accommodation, where necessary, of a child so subject; and

(*c*) for the conveyance of a child so subject—

(i) to any place in which, under the supervision requirement, he is to reside;

(ii) to any place to which he falls to be taken under subsection (1) or (5) of section 82 of this Act; or

(iii) to any person to whom he falls to be returned under subsection (3) of that section.

Powers of Secretary of State with respect to secure accommodation

75.—(1) The Secretary of State may by regulations make provision with respect to the placing in secure accommodation of any child—

(*a*) who is subject to a requirement imposed under section 70(3)(*a*) of this Act but not subject to a requirement under subsection (9) of that section; or

(*b*) who is not subject to a supervision requirement but who is being looked after by a local authority in pursuance of such enactments as may be specified in the regulations.

(2) Regulations under subsection (1) above may—

(*a*) specify the circumstances in which a child may be so placed under the regulations;

(*b*) make provision to enable a child who has been so placed or any relevant person to require that the child's case be brought before a children's hearing within a shorter period than would apply under regulations made under subsection (3) below; and (*c*) specify different circumstances for different cases or classes of case.

(3) Subject to subsection (4) below and without prejudice to subsection (2)(*b*) above, the Secretary of State may prescribe—

(*a*) the maximum period during which a child may be kept under this Act in secure accommodation without the authority of a children's hearing or of the sheriff;

(*b*) the period within which a children's hearing shall be arranged to consider the case of a child placed in secure accommodation by virtue of regulations made under this section (and different periods may be so prescribed in respect of different cases or classes of case).

(4) Subsection (8) of section 66 of this Act shall apply in respect of a child placed in secure accommodation under regulations made under this section as if such placing took place by virtue of that section.

(5) The Secretary of State may by regulations vary the period within which a review of a condition imposed under section 70(9) of this Act shall be reviewed under section 73 of this Act.

(6) The Secretary of State may by regulations make provision for the procedures to be applied in placing children in secure accommodation; and without prejudice to the generality of this subsection, such regulations may—

(*a*) specify the duties of the Principal Reporter in relation to the placing of children in secure accommodation;

(*b*) make provision for the referral of cases to a children's hearing for review; and

(*c*) make provision for any person with parental responsibilities in relation to the child to be informed of the placing of the child in secure accommodation.

Exclusion orders

Exclusion orders

76.—(1) Subject to subsections (3) to (9) below, where on the application of a local authority the sheriff is satisfied, in relation to a child, that the conditions mentioned in subsection (2) below are met, he may grant an order under this section (to be known as "an exclusion order") excluding from the child's family home any person named in the order (in this Part of this Act referred to as the "named person").

(2) The conditions are—

(*a*) that the child has suffered, is suffering, or is likely to suffer, significant harm as a result of any conduct, or any threatened or reasonably apprehended conduct, of the named person;

(*b*) that the making of an exclusion order against the named person—

(i) is necessary for the protection of the child, irrespective of whether the child is for the time being residing in the family home; and

(ii) would better safeguard the child's welfare than the removal of the child from the family home; and

(*c*) that, if an order is made, there will be a person specified in the application who is capable of taking responsibility for the provision of appropriate care for the child and any other member of the family who requires such care and who is, or will be, residing in the family home (in this section, sections 77 to 79 and section 91(3)(*f*) of this Act referred to as an "appropriate person").

(3) No application under subsection (1) above for an exclusion order shall be finally determined under this section unless—

(*a*) the named person has been afforded an opportunity of being heard by, or represented before, the sheriff; and

(*b*) the sheriff has considered any views expressed by any person on whom notice of the application has been served in accordance with rules making such provision as is mentioned in section 91(3)(*d*) of this Act.

(4) Where, on an application under subsection (1) above, the sheriff—

(*a*) is satisfied as mentioned in that subsection; but

(*b*) the conditions mentioned in paragraphs (*a*) and (*b*) of subsection (3) above for the final determination of the application are not fulfilled,

he may grant an interim order, which shall have effect as an exclusion order pending a hearing by the sheriff under subsection (5) below held within such period as may be specified in rules made by virtue of section 91(3)(*e*) of this Act.

(5) The sheriff shall conduct a hearing under this subsection within such period as may be specified in rules made by virtue of section 91(3)(*e*) of this Act, and, if satisfied at that hearing as mentioned in subsection (1) above, he may, before finally determining the application, confirm or vary the interim order, or any term or condition on which it was granted, or may recall such order.

(6) Where the conditions mentioned in paragraphs (*a*) and (*b*) of subsection (3) above have been fulfilled, the sheriff may, at any point prior to the final determination of the application, grant an interim order.

(7) An order under subsection (5) or (6) above shall have effect as an exclusion order pending the final determination of the application.

(8) Where—

(*a*) an application is made under subsection (1) above; and

(*b*) the sheriff considers that the conditions for making a child protection order under section 57 of this Act are satisfied,

he may make an order under that section as if the application had been duly made by the local authority under that rather than under this section.

(9) The sheriff shall not make an exclusion order if it appears to him that to do so would be unjustifiable or unreasonable, having regard to—

(*a*) all the circumstances of the case, including without prejudice to the generality of this subsection the matters specified in subsection (10) below; and

(*b*) any requirement such as is specified in subsection (11) below and the likely consequences in the light of that requirement of the exclusion of the named person from the family home.

(10) The matters referred to in subsection (9)(*a*) above are—

(*a*) the conduct of the members of the child's family (whether in relation to each other or otherwise);

(*b*) the respective needs and financial resources of the members of that family;

(*c*) the extent (if any) to which—

(i) the family home; and

(ii) any relevant item in that home,

is used in connection with a trade, business or profession by any member of the family.

(11) The requirement referred to in subsection (9)(*b*) above is a requirement that the named person (whether alone or with any other person) must reside in the family home, where that home—

(*a*) is or is part of an agricultural holding within the meaning of the Agricultural Holdings (Scotland) Act 1991; or

(*b*) is let, or is a home in respect of which possession is given, to the named person (whether alone or with any other person) by an employer as an incident of employment.

(12) In this Part of this Act—

"caravan" has the meaning given to it by section 29(1) of the Caravan Sites and Control of Development Act 1960;

"exclusion order", includes an interim order granted under subsection (4) above and such an order confirmed or varied under subsection (5) above and an interim order granted under subsection (6) above; except that in subsection (3) above and in section 79 of this Act, it does not include an interim order granted under subsection (4) above;

"family" has the meaning given in section 93(1) of this Act;

"family home" means any house, caravan, houseboat or other structure which is used as a family residence and in which the child ordinarily resides with any person described in subsection (13) below and the expression includes any garden or other ground or building attached to and usually occupied with, or otherwise required for the amenity or convenience of, the house, caravan, houseboat or other structure.

(13) The description of person referred to in the definition of "family home" in subsection (12) above, is a person who has parental responsibilities in relation to the child, or who ordinarily (and other than by reason only of his employment) has charge of, or control over him.

Effect of, and orders etc. ancillary to, exclusion order

77.—(1) An exclusion order shall, in respect of the home to which it relates, have the effect of suspending the named person's rights of occupancy (if any) and shall prevent him from entering the home, except with the express permission of the local authority which applied for the order.

(2) The sheriff, on the application of the local authority, may, if and in so far as he thinks fit, when making an exclusion order do any of the things mentioned in subsection (3) below.

(3) The things referred to in subsection (2) above are—

(*a*) grant a warrant for the summary ejection of the named person from the home;

(*b*) grant an interdict prohibiting the named person from entering the home without the express permission of the local authority;

(*c*) grant an interdict prohibiting the removal by the named person of any relevant item specified in the interdict from the home, except either—

(i) with the written consent of the local authority, or of an appropriate person; or

(ii) by virtue of a subsequent order of the sheriff;

(*d*) grant an interdict prohibiting the named person from entering or remaining in a specified area in the vicinity of the home;

(*e*) grant an interdict prohibiting the taking by the named person of any step of a kind specified in the interdict in relation to the child;

(*f*) make an order regulating the contact between the child and the named person,

and the sheriff may make any other order which he considers is necessary for the proper enforcement of a remedy granted by virtue of paragraph (*a*), (*b*) or (*c*) of this subsection.

(4) No warrant, interdict or order (except an interdict granted by virtue of paragraph (*b*) of subsection (3) above) shall be granted or made under subsection (2) above if the named person satisfies the sheriff that it is unnecessary to do so.

(5) Where the sheriff grants a warrant of summary ejection under subsection (2) above in the absence of the named person, he may give directions as to the preservation of any of that person's goods and effects which remain in the family home.

(6) The sheriff may make an order of the kind specified in subsection (3)(*f*) above irrespective of whether there has been an application for such an order.

(7) On the application of either the named person or the local authority, the sheriff may make the exclusion order, or any remedy granted under subsection (2) above, subject to such terms and conditions as he considers appropriate.

(8) In this Part of this Act references to a "relevant item" are references to any item within the home which both—

(*a*) is owned or hired by any member of the family concerned or an appropriate person or is being acquired by any such member or person under a hire purchase agreement or conditional sale agreement; and

(*b*) is reasonably necessary to enable the home to be used as a family residence,

but does not include any such vehicle, caravan or houseboat or such other structure so used as is mentioned in the definition of "family home" in section 76(12) of this Act.

Powers of arrest etc. in relation to exclusion order

78.—(1) The sheriff may, whether or not on an application such as is mentioned in subsection (2) below, attach a power of arrest to any interdict granted under section 77(2) of this Act by virtue of subsection (3) of that section.

(2) A local authority may at any time while an exclusion order has effect apply for such attachment of a power of arrest as is mentioned in subsection (1) above.

(3) A power of arrest attached to an interdict by virtue of subsection (1) above shall not have effect until such interdict, together with the attached power of arrest, is served on the named person.

(4) If, by virtue of subsection (1) above, a power of arrest is attached to an interdict, the local authority shall, as soon as possible after the interdict, together with the attached power of arrest, is served on the named person, ensure that there is delivered—

(*a*) to the chief constable of the police area in which the family home is situated; and

(*b*) where the interdict was granted by virtue of section 77(3)(*e*) of this Act, to the chief constable of the area in which the step or conduct which is prevented by the interdict may take place,

a copy of the application for the interdict and of the interlocutor granting the interdict together with a certificate of service of the interdict and, where the application to attach the power of arrest was made after the interdict was granted, a copy of that application and of the interlocutor above granting it and a certificate of service of the interdict together with the attached power of arrest.

(5) Where any interdict to which a power of arrest is attached by virtue of subsection (1) above is varied or recalled, the person who applied for the variation or recall shall ensure that there is delivered to each chief constable specified in subsection (4) above a copy of the application for such variation or recall and of the interlocutor granting the variation or recall.

(6) A constable may arrest without warrant the named person if he has reasonable cause for suspecting that person to be in breach of an interdict to which a power of arrest has been attached by virtue of subsection (1) above.

(7) Where a person has been arrested under subsection (6) above, the constable in charge of a police station may—

(*a*) if satisfied there is no likelihood of that person further breaching the interdict to which the power of arrest was attached under subsection (1) above, liberate him unconditionally; or

(*b*) refuse to liberate that person.

(8) Such a refusal to liberate an arrested person as is mentioned in subsection (7)(*b*) above, and the detention of that person until his appearance in court by virtue of either subsection (11) below, or any provision of the Criminal Procedure (Scotland) Act 1975, shall not subject that constable to any claim whatsoever.

(9) Where a person has been liberated under subsection (7)(*a*) above,

the facts and circumstances which gave rise to the arrest shall be reported to the procurator fiscal forthwith.

(10) Subsections (11) to (13) below apply only where—

(*a*) the arrested person has not been released under subsection (7)(*a*) above; and

(*b*) the procurator fiscal decides that no criminal proceedings are to be taken in respect of the facts and circumstances which gave rise to the arrest.

(11) A person arrested under subsection (6) above shall, wherever practicable, be brought before the sheriff sitting as a court of summary criminal jurisdiction for the district in which he was arrested not later than in the course of the first day after the arrest, such day not being a Saturday, a Sunday or a court holiday prescribed for that court under section 10 of the Bail etc. (Scotland) Act 1980, on which the sheriff is not sitting for the disposal of criminal business.

(12) Subsections (1) and (3) of section 3 of the Criminal Justice (Scotland) Act 1980 (intimation to a person named by the person arrested) shall apply to a person arrested under subsection (6) above as they apply to a person who has been arrested in respect of an offence.

(13) Where a person is brought before the sheriff under subsection (11) above—

(*a*) the procurator fiscal shall present to the court a petition containing—

(i) a statement of the particulars of the person arrested under subsection (6) above;

(ii) a statement of the facts and circumstances which gave rise to that arrest; and

(iii) a request that the person be detained for a further period not exceeding two days;

(*b*) the sheriff, if it appears to him that—

(i) the statement referred to in paragraph (*a*)(ii) above discloses a *prima facie* breach of interdict by the arrested person;

(ii) proceedings for breach of interdict will be taken; and

(iii) there is a substantial risk of violence by the arrested person against any member of the family, or an appropriate person, resident in the family home,

may order the arrested person to be detained for a period not exceeding two days; and

(*c*) the sheriff shall, in any case in which paragraph (*b*) above does not apply, order the release of the arrested person from custody (unless that person is in custody in respect of some other matter);

and in computing the period of two days referred to in paragraphs (*a*) and (*b*) above, no account shall be taken of a Saturday, a Sunday or any holiday in the court in which proceedings for breach of interdict will require to be raised.

(14) Where a person—

(*a*) is liberated under subsection (7)(*a*) above; or

(*b*) is to be brought before the sheriff under subsection (11) above,

the procurator fiscal shall at the earliest opportunity, and, in the case of a person to whom paragraph (*b*) above applies, before that person is brought before the sheriff, take all reasonable steps to intimate to—

(i) the local authority which made the application for the interdict;

(ii) an appropriate person who will reside in, or who remains in residence in, the family home mentioned in the order; and

(iii) any solicitor who acted for the appropriate person when the interdict was granted or to any other solicitor who the procurator fiscal has reason to believe acts for the time being for that person,

that he has decided that no criminal proceedings should be taken in respect of the facts and circumstances which gave rise to the arrest of the named person.

Duration, variation and recall of exclusion order

79.—(1) Subject to subsection (2) below, an exclusion order shall cease to have effect on a date six months after being made.

(2) An exclusion order shall cease to have effect on a date prior to the date mentioned in subsection (1) above where—

(*a*) the order contains a direction by the sheriff that it shall cease to have effect on that prior date;

(*b*) the sheriff, on an application under subsection (3) below, recalls the order before the date so mentioned; or

(*c*) any permission given by a third party to the spouse or partner of the named person, or to an appropriate person, to occupy the home to which the order relates is withdrawn.

(3) The sheriff may, on the application of the local authority, the named person, an appropriate person or the spouse or partner of the named person, if that spouse or partner is not excluded from the family home and is not an appropriate person, vary or recall an exclusion order and any warrant, interdict, order or direction granted or made under section 77 of this Act.

(4) For the purposes of this section, partners are persons who live together in a family home as if they were husband and wife.

Exclusion orders: supplementary provisions

80.—(1) The Secretary of State may make regulations with respect to the powers, duties and functions of local authorities in relation to exclusion orders.

(2) An application for an exclusion order, or under section 79(3) of this Act for the variation or recall of such an order or of any thing done under section 77(2) of this Act, shall be made to the sheriff for the sheriffdom within which the family home is situated.

Offences in connection with orders etc. for protection of children

Offences in connection with orders etc. for protection of children

81. A person who intentionally obstructs—

(*a*) any person acting under a child protection order;

(*b*) any person acting under an authorisation granted under section 61(1) or (2) of this Act; or

(*c*) a constable acting under section 61(5) of this Act,

shall, subject to section 38(3) and (4) of this Act, be guilty of an offence and shall be liable on summary conviction to a fine not exceeding level 3 on the standard scale.

Fugitive children and harbouring

Recovery of certain fugitive children

82.—(1) A child who absconds—

(*a*) from a place of safety in which he is being kept under or by virtue of this Part of this Act;

(*b*) from a place (in this section referred to as a "relevant place") which, though not a place of safety such as is mentioned in paragraph (*a*) above, is a residential establishment in which he is required to reside by virtue of section 70(3)(*a*) of this Act or a hospital or other institution in which he is temporarily residing while subject to such a requirement; or

(*c*) from a person who, by virtue of a supervision requirement or of section 74 of this Act, has control over him while he is being taken to, is awaiting being taken to, or (whether or not by reason of being on leave) is temporarily away from, such place of safety or relevant place, may be arrested without warrant in any part of the United Kingdom and taken to the place of safety or as the case may be the relevant place; and a court which is satisfied that there are reasonable grounds for believing that the child is within any premises may, where there is such power of arrest, grant a warrant authorising a constable to enter those premises and search for the child using reasonable force if necessary.

(2) Without prejudice to the generality of subsection (1) above, a child who at the end of a period of leave from a place of safety or relevant place fails to return there shall, for the purposes of this section, be taken to have absconded.

(3) A child who absconds from a person who, not being a person mentioned in paragraph (*c*) of subsection (1) above, is a person who has control over him by virtue of a supervision requirement may, subject to the same provisions as those to which an arrest under that subsection is subject, be arrested as is mentioned in that subsection and returned to that person; and the provision in that subsection for a warrant to be granted shall apply as respects such a child as it applies as respects a child mentioned in that subsection.

(4) If a child—

(*a*) is taken under subsection (1) above to a place of safety or relevant place; or

(*b*) is returned under subsection (3) above to a person,

but the occupier of that place of safety or of that relevant place, or as the case may be that person, is unwilling or unable to receive him, that circumstance shall be intimated forthwith to the Principal Reporter.

(5) Where intimation is required by subsection (4) above as respects a child, he shall be kept in a place of safety until—

(*a*) in a case where he is subject to a supervision requirement, he can be brought before a children's hearing for that requirement to be reviewed; or

(*b*) in any other case, the Principal Reporter has, in accordance with section 56(6) of this Act, considered whether compulsory measures of supervision are required in respect of him.

Harbouring

[1] **83.** A person who—

(*a*) knowingly assists or induces a child to abscond in circumstances which render the child liable to arrest under subsection (1) or (3) of section 82 of this Act;

(*b*) knowingly and persistently attempts to induce a child so to abscond;

(*c*) knowingly harbours or conceals a child who has so absconded; or

(*d*) knowingly prevents a child from returning—

(i) to a place mentioned in paragraph (*a*) or (*b*) of the said subsection (1);

(ii) to a person mentioned in paragraph (*c*) of that subsection, or in the said subsection (3),

shall, subject to section 38(3) and (4) of this Act, to section 51(5) and (6) of the Children Act 1989 and to Article 70(5) and (6) of the Children (Northern Ireland) Order 1995 (analogous provision for England and Wales and for Northern Ireland), be guilty of an offence and liable on summary conviction to a fine not exceeding level 5 on the standard scale or to imprisonment for a term not exceeding six months or to both such fine and such imprisonment.

NOTE

[1] Excluded, with saving: see s. 38(3) and (4) (child provided with refuge under that section).

Implementation of authorisations etc.

Implementation of authorisations etc.

84. Where an order, authorisation or warrant under this Chapter or Chapter 2 of this Part of this Act grants power to find a child and to keep him in a place of safety, such order, authorisation or warrant may be implemented as if it were a warrant for the apprehension of an accused person issued by a court of summary jurisdiction; and any enactment or rule of law applying to such a warrant shall, subject to the provisions of this Act, apply in like manner to the order, authorisation or warrant.

New evidence: review of establishment of grounds of referral

Application for review of establishment of grounds of referral

85.—(1) Subject to subsections (3) and (4) below, where subsection (2) below applies an application may be made to the sheriff for a review of a finding such as is mentioned in section 68(10) of this Act.

(2) This subsection applies where the sheriff, on an application made by virtue of subsection (7) or (9) of section 65 of this Act (in this section referred to as the "original application"), finds that any of the grounds of referral is established.

(3) An application under subsection (1) above may only be made where the applicant claims—

(*a*) to have evidence which was not considered by the sheriff on the original application, being evidence the existence or significance of which might materially have affected the determination of the original application;

(*b*) that such evidence—

(i) is likely to be credible and reliable; and

(ii) would have been admissible in relation to the ground of referral which was found to be established on the original application; and

(*c*) that there is a reasonable explanation for the failure to lead such evidence on the original application.

(4) An application under subsection (1) above may only be made by—

(*a*) the child in respect of whom the ground of referral was found to be established; or

(*b*) any person who is a relevant person in relation to that child.

(5) Where the sheriff on an application under subsection (1) above is not satisfied that any of the claims made in the application are established he shall dismiss the application.

(6) Where the sheriff is satisfied on an application under subsection (1) above that the claims made in the application are established, he shall consider the evidence and if, having considered it, he is satisfied that—

(*a*) none of the grounds of referral in the original application to which the application relates is established, he shall allow the application, discharge the referral to the children's hearing in respect of those grounds and proceed in accordance with subsection (7) below in relation to any supervision requirement made in respect of the child (whether or not varied under section 73 of this Act) in so far as it relates to any such ground; or

(*b*) any ground of referral in the original application to which the application relates is established, he may proceed in accordance with section 68(10) of this Act.

(7) Where the sheriff is satisfied as is mentioned in subsection (6)(*a*) above, he may—

(*a*) order that any supervision requirement so mentioned shall terminate—

(i) immediately; or

(ii) on such date as he may specify; or

(*b*) if he is satisfied that there is evidence sufficient to establish any ground of referral, being a ground which was not stated in the original application, find such ground established and proceed in accordance with section 68(10) of this Act in relation to that ground.

(8) Where the sheriff specifies a date for the termination of a supervision requirement in accordance with subsection (7)(*a*)(ii) above, he may, before such termination, order a variation of that requirement, of any requirement imposed under subsection (6) of section 70 of this Act, or of any determination made under subsection (7) of that section; and such variation may take effect—

(*a*) immediately; or

(*b*) on such date as he may specify.

(9) Where the sheriff orders the termination of a supervision requirement in accordance with subsection (7)(*a*) above, he shall consider whether, after such termination, the child concerned will still require supervision or guidance; and where he considers that such supervision or guidance will be necessary he shall direct a local authority to provide it in accordance with subsection (10) below.

(10) Where a sheriff has given a direction under subsection (9) above, it shall be the duty of the local authority to comply with that direction; but that duty shall be regarded as discharged where they offer such supervision or guidance to the child and he, being a child of sufficient age and maturity to understand what is being offered, is unwilling to accept it.

CHAPTER 4

PARENTAL RESPONSIBILITIES ORDERS, ETC.

Parental responsibilities orders

Parental responsibilities order: general

86.—(1) On the application of a local authority the sheriff may make an order transferring (but only during such period as the order remains in force) the appropriate parental rights and responsibilities relating to a child to them; and any such order shall be known as a "parental responsibilities order".

(2) A parental responsibilities order shall not be made unless the sheriff is satisfied that each relevant person either—

(*a*) freely, and with full understanding of what is involved, agrees unconditionally that the order be made; or

(*b*) is a person who—

(i) is not known, cannot be found or is incapable of giving agreement;

(ii) is withholding such agreement unreasonably;

(iii) has persistently failed, without reasonable cause, to fulfil one or other of the following parental responsibilities in relation to the child, that is to say the responsibility to safeguard and promote the child's health, development and welfare or, if the child is not living with him, the responsibility to maintain personal relations and direct contact with the child on a regular basis; or

(iv) has seriously ill-treated the child, whose reintegration into the same household as that person is, because of the serious ill-treatment or for other reasons, unlikely.

(3) The reference in subsection (1) above to the appropriate parental rights and responsibilities relating to the child is to all parental rights and responsibilities except any right to agree, or decline to agree—

(*a*) to the making of an application in relation to the child under section 18 (freeing for adoption) or 55 (adoption abroad) of the Adoption Act 1976, under section 18 or 49 of the Adoption (Scotland) Act 1978 or under Article 17, 18 or 57 of the Adoption (Northern Ireland) Order 1987 (corresponding provision for Scotland and Northern Ireland); or (*b*) to the making of an adoption order.

(4) A person is a relevant person for the purposes of this section if he is a parent of the child or a person who for the time being has parental rights in relation to the child.

(5) The sheriff may, in an order under this section, impose such conditions as he considers appropriate; and he may vary or discharge such an order on the application of the local authority, of the child, of any person who immediately before the making of the order is a relevant person or of any other person claiming an interest.

(6) An order under this section shall, if not first discharged by the sheriff, terminate on the occurrence of any of the following—

(*a*) the child attains the age of eighteen years;

(*b*) he becomes the subject—

(i) of an adoption order within the meaning of the Adoption (Scotland) Act 1978; or

(ii) of an order under section 18 (freeing for adoption) or 55 (adoption abroad) of the Adoption Act 1976, under section 18 or 49 of the said Act of 1978 or under Article 17, 18 or 57 of the Adoption (Northern Ireland) Order 1987 (corresponding provision for Scotland and Northern Ireland);

(*c*) an order is made for his return under Part I of the Child Abduction and Custody Act 1985; or

(*d*) a decision, other than a decision mentioned in section 25(2) of the said Act of 1985 (decisions relating to rights of access), is registered with respect to him under section 16 of that Act.

Further provision as respects parental responsibilities orders

87.—(1) Subject to subsections (2) and (3) below, where a parental responsibilities order is made as respects a child it shall be the duty of the local authority which applied for it (in this section and in section 88 of this Act referred to as the "appropriate authority") to fulfil the transferred responsibilities while the order remains in force.

(2) Notwithstanding that a parental responsibilities order has been made as respects a child, the appropriate authority may allow, either for a fixed period or until the authority otherwise determine, the child to reside with a parent, guardian, relative or friend of his in any case where it appears to the authority that so to allow would be for the benefit of the child.

(3) Without prejudice to any other provision of this Part of this Act, where by virtue of subsection (2) above a child is residing with a person, the appropriate authority may by notice in writing to the person require him to return the child to them by a time specified in the notice; and service of such notice shall be effected either by the authority leaving it in the person's hands or by their sending it to him, at his and the child's most recent known address, by recorded delivery service.

(4) For the purposes of any application for a parental responsibilities order, rules shall provide for the appointment, in such cases as are prescribed by such rules—

(*a*) of a person to act as curator *ad litem* to the child in question at the hearing of the application, safeguarding the interests of the child in such manner as may be so prescribed; and

(*b*) of a person (to be known as a "reporting officer") to witness agreements to parental responsibilities orders and to perform such other duties as may be so prescribed,

but one person may, as respects the child, be appointed both under paragraph (*a*) and under paragraph (*b*) above; so however that, where the applicant is a local authority, no employee of theirs shall be appointed under either or both of those paragraphs.

(5) Rules may provide for a person to be appointed reporting officer before the application in question is made.

Parental contact

88.—(1) This section applies where a parental responsibilities order is being made, or as the case may be is in force, as respects a child.

(2) The child shall, subject to subsection (3) below, be allowed reasonable contact by the appropriate authority with—

(*a*) each person who, immediately before the making of the parental responsibilities order, is a relevant person for the purposes of section 86 of this Act as respects the child; and

(*b*) where, immediately before that order was made—

(i) a residence order or contact order was in force with respect to the child, the person in whose favour the residence order or contact order was made;

(ii) a person was entitled to have the child residing with him under an order by a court of competent jurisdiction, that person.

(3) Without prejudice to subsection (4) below, on an application made to him by the child, by the appropriate authority or by any person with an interest, the sheriff may make such order as he considers appropriate as to the contact, if any, which is to be allowed between the child and any person specified in the order (whether or not a person described in paragraphs (*a*) and (*b*) of subsection (2) above).

(4) A sheriff, on making a parental responsibilities order, or at any time while such an order remains in force as respects a child, may make an order under subsection (3) above as respects the child even where no application has been made to him in that regard.

(5) An order under this section may impose such conditions as the sheriff considers appropriate; and he may vary or discharge such an order on the application of the child, the appropriate authority or any person with an interest.

(6) An order under this section shall, if not first discharged by the sheriff, terminate when the parental responsibilities order to which it is referable does.

Offences in relation to parental responsibilities orders

[1] **89.** Any person who, knowingly and without lawful authority or reasonable excuse—

(*a*) fails to comply with a notice under section 87(3) of this Act;

(*b*) harbours or conceals a child—

(i) as respects whom a parental responsibilities order has been made; and

(ii) who has run away, or been taken away or whose return is required by such a notice; or

(*c*) induces, assists or incites a child as respects whom any such order has been made to run away, or stay away, from a place where he is looked after or who takes away such a child from that place,

shall be guilty of an offence and liable, on summary conviction, to a fine not exceeding level 5 on the standard scale or to imprisonment for a term not exceeding six months or to both such fine and such imprisonment.

NOTE

[1] Excluded, with saving: see s. 38(3) and (4) (child provided with refuge under that section).

Miscellaneous

Consent of child to certain procedures

90. Nothing in this Part of this Act shall prejudice any capacity of a child enjoyed by virtue of section 2(4) of the Age of Legal Capacity (Scotland) Act 1991 (capacity of child with sufficient understanding to consent to surgical, medical or dental procedure or treatment); and without prejudice to that generality, where a condition contained, by virtue of—

(*a*) section 66(4)(*a*), section 67(2) or section 69(9)(*a*) of this Act, in a warrant; or

(*b*) section 70(5)(*a*) of this Act, in a supervision requirement,

requires a child to submit to any examination or treatment but the child has the capacity mentioned in the said section 2(4), the examination or treatment shall only be carried out if the child consents.

Procedural rules in relation to certain applications etc.

[1] **91.**—(1) All proceedings to which this section applies are civil proceedings for the purposes of section 32 of the Sheriff Courts (Scotland) Act 1971 (power of Court of Session to regulate civil procedure in the sheriff court).

(2) Any reference in this Part of this Act to regulation or prescription by rules in relation to any proceedings to which this section applies shall be construed, unless the context otherwise requires, as a reference to regulation or prescription by rules made under the said section 32.

(3) Without prejudice to the generality of the said section 32, rules may make provision as to—

(*a*) the functions of a person appointed by the sheriff under section 41(1) of this Act and any right of that person to information relating to the proceedings;

(*b*) the circumstances in which any person who has been given notice in accordance with such rules of an application for a child assessment order, or any other person specified in the rules, may apply to the court to have that order varied or discharged;

(*c*) the persons to whom notice of the making of a child protection order shall be given by the applicant for that order, and without prejudice to that generality may in making such provision require such notice to be given to either or both of the child and any relevant person in relation to that child;

(*d*) the persons to whom notice of an application for an exclusion order or, under section 79(3) of this Act, for the recall or variation of such an order or of anything done under section 77(2) of this Act shall be given;

(*e*) the period within which a hearing shall be held under subsection (5) of section 76 of this Act after the granting of an order under subsection (4) of that section;

(*f*) the service of any exclusion order on the named person and the appropriate person within such period as may be specified in the rules.

(4) In relation to any proceedings to which this section applies, rules may permit a party to such proceedings, in such circumstances as may be specified in the rules, to be represented by a person who is neither an advocate nor a solicitor.

(5) This section applies to any application made to the sheriff, and any other proceeding before the sheriff (whether on appeal or otherwise), under any provision of this Part of this Act.

NOTE

[1] Saved: see s. 57(3) (applications for child protection orders).

Legal aid in respect of certain proceedings

92. For section 29 of the Legal Aid (Scotland) Act 1986 substitute the following section—

"**Legal aid in respect of certain proceedings relating to children**

29.—(1) This section applies to legal aid in connection with—

(*a*) proceedings before the sheriff (including, without prejudice to that generality, proceedings on an appeal to the sheriff principal from a decision of the sheriff) in respect of any matter arising under Chapter 2 or 3 of Part II of the Children (Scotland) Act 1995 (in this section referred to as "the 1995 Act"); or

(*b*) an appeal to the Court of Session in connection with such proceedings.

(2) Subject to subsections (3) to (5) below, legal aid to which this section applies shall be available to a child and any relevant person in relation to him in connection with—

(*a*) proceedings before the sheriff on an application for a child protection order or child assessment order, or for the variation or recall of such an order;

(*b*) an appeal to the sheriff under section 51 of the 1995 Act against—

(i) a decision of a children's hearing to grant a warrant such as is mentioned in subsection (5)(*a*) of that subsection; or

(ii) any other decision of a children's hearing;

(*c*) an application—

(i) by virtue of section 65(7) or (9) of the 1995 Act for a finding as to whether the grounds for a referral are established; or

(ii) under section 85 of the 1995 Act for a review of such a finding;

(*d*) an appeal to the sheriff principal or to the Court of Session under section 51 of the 1995 Act.

(3) Legal aid shall be available under subsection (2)(*b*)(i) above on an application made to the sheriff without inquiry into the resources of the child or the relevant person.

(4) Legal aid shall be available under subsection (2)(*a*), (*b*)(ii) or (*c*) above on an application made to the sheriff if the sheriff is satisfied—

(*a*) that it is in the interests of the child that legal aid be made available; and

(*b*) after consideration of the financial circumstances of the child and any relevant person in relation to him that the expenses of the case cannot be met without undue hardship to the child or to any relevant person in relation to him or the dependants of any of them.

(5) Legal aid shall be available under subsection (2)(*d*) above on an application made to the Board if it is satisfied—

(*a*) after consideration of the financial circumstances of the child and any relevant person in relation to him that the expenses of the appeal cannot be met without undue hardship to the child or to any relevant person in relation to him or the dependants of any of them; and

(*b*) that the child, or as the case may be the relevant person, has substantial grounds for making or responding to the appeal and it is reasonable, in the particular circumstances of the case, that legal aid should be made available accordingly.

(6) The Board may require a person receiving legal aid under subsection (2)(*d*) above or subsection (9) below to comply with such conditions as it considers expedient to enable it to satisfy itself from time to time that it is reasonable for him to continue to receive such legal aid.

(7) Subject to subsection (8) below, legal aid to which this section applies shall be available in connection with proceedings before the sheriff on an application for an exclusion order (or for the variation or recall of such an order) to—

(*a*) a child;

(*b*) a relevant person in relation to a child;

(*c*) a person who is a named person, or will be such a person if the application is granted;

(*d*) a spouse or partner of a person mentioned in paragraph (*c*) above; and

(*e*) a person who is an appropriate person, or will be such a person if the application is granted.

(8) Legal aid shall be available under subsection (7) above on an application to the sheriff if the sheriff is satisfied after consideration of the financial circumstances of the applicant and, where the applicant is a child, of any relevant person or appropriate person in relation to him that the expenses of the case cannot be met without undue hardship to the applicant or any dependant of the applicant.

(9) Legal aid shall be available in connection with any appeal from a decision of the sheriff on an application for an exclusion order or for the variation or recall of such an order to any of the persons mentioned in paragraphs (*a*) to (*e*) of subsection (7) above on an application to the Board if it is satisfied—

(*a*) after consideration of the financial circumstances of the applicant and, where the applicant is a child, of any relevant person or appropriate person in relation to him, that the expenses of the appeal cannot be met without undue hardship to the applicant or any dependant of the applicant; and

(*b*) that the applicant has substantial grounds for making or responding to the appeal and that it is reasonable, in the particular circumstances of the case, that legal aid should be made available accordingly.

(10) Where in connection with any proceedings—

(*a*) the sheriff has been satisfied as is mentioned in subsection (4)(*b*) or subsection (8) above; or

(*b*) the Board has been satisfied as is mentioned in subsection (5)(*a*) or subsection (9)(*a*) above,

and has made legal aid available to any person, it shall not be necessary for the sheriff or, as the case may be, the Board to be so satisfied in respect of an application for legal aid by such a person in connection with any subsequent proceedings arising from such proceedings.

(11) Legal aid to which this section applies shall consist of representation by a solicitor and, where appropriate, by counsel in any proceedings (including any appeal) mentioned in subsection (1) above and shall include all such assistance as is usually given by solicitor or counsel in the steps preliminary or incidental to such proceedings.

(12) In this section—

(*a*) "child" and "relevant person" have the meanings given by section 93(2)(*b*) of the 1995 Act;

(*b*) "child protection order", "child assessment order" and "exclusion order" have the meanings given by section 93(1) of that Act;

(*c*) "named person" and "appropriate person" have the meanings given by section 76 of that Act; and

(*d*) "partner" shall be construed in accordance with section 79(4) of that Act.".

Interpretation of Part II

Interpretation of Part II

93.—(1) In this Part of this Act, unless the context otherwise requires,—

"accommodation" shall be construed in accordance with section 25(8) of this Act;

"chief social work officer" means an officer appointed under section 3 of the Social Work (Scotland) Act 1968;

"child assessment order" has the meaning given by section 55(1) of this Act;

"child protection order" has the meaning given by section 57(1) of this Act;

"children's hearing" shall be construed in accordance with section 39(3), but does not include a business meeting arranged under section 64, of this Act;

"compulsory measures of supervision" means, in respect of a child, such measures of supervision as may be imposed upon him by a children's hearing;

"constable" means a constable of a police force within the meaning of the Police (Scotland) Act 1967;

"contact order" has the meaning given by section 11(2)(*d*) of this Act;

"disabled" has the meaning given by section 23(2) of this Act;

"exclusion order" has the meaning given by section 76(12) of this Act;

"family", in relation to a child, includes—

(*a*) any person who has parental responsibility for the child; and

(*b*) any other person with whom the child has been living;

"local authority" means a council constituted under section 2 of the Local Government etc. (Scotland) Act 1994;

"local government area" shall be construed in accordance with section 1 of the said Act of 1994;

"parental responsibilities" has the meaning given by section 1(3) of this Act;

"parental responsibilities order" has the meaning given by section 86(1) of this Act;

"parental rights" has the meaning given by section 2(4) of this Act;

"place of safety", in relation to a child, means—

(*a*) a residential or other establishment provided by a local authority;

(*b*) a community home within the meaning of section 53 of the Children Act 1989;

(*c*) a police station; or

(*d*) a hospital, surgery or other suitable place, the occupier of which is willing temporarily to receive the child;

"the Principal Reporter" means the Principal Reporter appointed under section 127 of the said Act of 1994 or any officer of the Scottish Children's Reporter Administration to whom there is delegated, under section 131(1) of that Act, any function of the Principal Reporter under this Act;

"relevant local authority", in relation to a child who is subject to a warrant granted under this Part of this Act or to a supervision requirement, means the local authority for whose area the children's panel from which the children's hearing which granted the warrant or imposed the supervision requirement was formed;

"residence order" has the meaning given by section 11(2)(*c*) of this Act;

"residential establishment"—

(*a*) in relation to a place in Scotland, means an establishment (whether managed by a local authority, by a voluntary organisation or by any other person) which provides residential accommodation for children for the purposes of this Act or the Social Work (Scotland) Act 1968;

(*b*) in relation to a place in England and Wales, means a community home, voluntary home or registered children's home (within the meaning of the Children Act 1989); and

(*c*) in relation to a place in Northern Ireland, means a home provided under Part VIII of the Children (Northern Ireland) Order 1995, or a voluntary home, or a registered children's home (which have respectively the meanings given by that Order);

"school age" shall be construed in accordance with section 31 of the Education (Scotland) Act 1980;

"secure accommodation" means accommodation provided in a residential establishment, approved by the Secretary of State in accordance with regulations made under section 60(1)(*bb*) of the Social Work (Scotland) Act 1968 or under paragraph 4(2)(i) of Schedule 4 to the Children Act 1989, for the purpose of restricting the liberty of children;

"supervision requirement" has the meaning given by section 70(1) of this Act, and includes any condition contained in such a requirement or related to it;

"voluntary organisation" means a body (other than a public or local authority) whose activities are not carried on for profit; and

"working day" means every day except—

(*a*) Saturday and Sunday;

(*b*) December 25th and 26th; and

(*c*) January 1st and 2nd.

(2) For the purposes of—

(*a*) Chapter 1 and this Chapter (except this section) of this Part, "child" means a person under the age of eighteen years; and

(*b*) Chapters 2 and 3 of this Part—

"child" means—

(i) a child who has not attained the age of sixteen years;

(ii) a child over the age of sixteen years who has not attained the age of eighteen years and in respect of whom a supervision requirement is in force; or

(iii) a child whose case has been referred to a children's hearing by virtue of section 33 of this Act;

and for the purposes of the application of those Chapters to a person who has failed to attend school regularly without reasonable excuse includes a person who is over sixteen years of age but is not over school age; and

"relevant person" in relation to a child means—

(*a*) any parent enjoying parental responsibilities or parental rights under Part I of this Act;

(*b*) any person in whom parental responsibilities or rights are vested by, under or by virtue of this Act; and

(*c*) any person who appears to be a person who ordinarily (and other than by reason only of his employment) has charge of, or control over, the child.

(3) Where, in the course of any proceedings under Chapter 2 or 3 of this Part, a child ceases to be a child within the meaning of subsection (2) above, the provisions of those Chapters of this Part and of any statutory instrument made under those provisions shall continue to apply to him as if he had not so ceased to be a child.

(4) Any reference in this Part of this Act to a child—

(*a*) being "in need", is to his being in need of care and attention because—

(i) he is unlikely to achieve or maintain, or to have the opportunity of achieving or maintaining, a reasonable standard of health or development unless there are provided for him, under or by virtue of this Part, services by a local authority;

(ii) his health or development is likely significantly to be impaired, or further impaired, unless such services are so provided;

(iii) he is disabled; or

(iv) he is affected adversely by the disability of any other person in his family;

(*b*) who is "looked after" by a local authority, shall be construed in accordance with section 17(6) of this Act.

(5) Any reference to any proceedings under this Part of this Act, whether on an application or on appeal, being heard by the sheriff, shall be construed as a reference to such proceedings being heard by the sheriff in chambers.

Part III

Adoption

Approval of adoption society for specific services

94.—(1) In section 3 of the 1978 Act (approval of adoption societies)—

(*a*) for subsections (1) and (2) substitute—

"(1) Subject to any regulations made under section 9(1), a body which is a voluntary organisation may apply to the Secretary of State for his approval to its acting, or as the case may be continuing to act, as an adoption society, whether functioning generally or in relation to some service maintained, or to be maintained, as part of the Scottish Adoption Service and specified in the application (the service so specified being in this section and in section 4 referred to as the body's "specified service").

(1A) Application under subsection (1) shall be in such manner as may be specified in regulations made by the Secretary of State under this section.

(2) In considering an application under subsection (1), the Secretary of State shall take into account the matters relating to the applicant specified in subsections (3) to (5) and any other matters which appear to him to be relevant; and if, but only if, he is satisfied that, as the case may be, the applicant is likely to make, or is making, an effective contribution to the Scottish Adoption Service or to the applicant's specified service, he shall by notice to the applicant give the approval sought.

(2A) Approval under subsection (2) shall operate from such date as may be specified in the notice or, in the case of a renewal of approval, from the date of the notice.";

(*b*) in subsection (3)(*a*), the words ", including in particular its ability to make provision for children who are free for adoption" shall cease to have effect;

(*c*) in subsection (5), for the words "areas within which" substitute "geographical areas within which, the services as respects which";

(*d*) in subsection (6), after the word "Service" insert ", or as the case may be to the applicant's specified service"; and

(*e*) in subsection (7)—

(i) for the words "a period of" substitute "such period not exceeding"; and

(ii) after the word "operative" insert "as the Secretary of State may specify in the approval.".

(2) In section 4 of that Act (withdrawal of approval), after the word "Service" insert ", or as the case may be to the body's specified service,".

(3) In section 65(1) of that Act (interpretation), in the definition of "adoption society", after the word "for" insert ", or in connection with,".

Welfare of child paramount consideration

95. For section 6 of the 1978 Act substitute—

"**Duty to promote welfare of child**

6.—(1) Without prejudice to sections 12(8) and 18(8), in reaching any decision relating to the adoption of a child, a court or adoption agency shall have regard to all the circumstances but—

(*a*) shall regard the need to safeguard and promote the welfare of the child concerned throughout his life as the paramount consideration; and

(*b*) shall have regard so far as practicable—

(i) to his views (if he wishes to express them) taking account of his age and maturity; and

(ii) to his religious persuasion, racial origin and cultural and linguistic background.

(2) Without prejudice to the generality of paragraph (*b*) of subsection (1), a child twelve years of age or more shall be presumed to be of sufficient age and maturity to form a view for the purposes of that paragraph.".

Duty of adoption agency to consider alternatives to adoption

96. After section 6 of the 1978 Act there shall be inserted—

"**Duty to consider alternatives to adoption**

6A. In complying with its duties under section 6 of this Act, an adoption agency shall, before making any arrangements for the adoption of a child, consider whether adoption is likely best to meet the needs of that child or whether for him there is some better, practicable, alternative; and if it concludes that there is such an alternative it shall not proceed to make those arrangements.".

Adoption by person married to natural parent

97.—(1) In section 12 of the 1978 Act (making of adoption orders)—

(*a*) in subsection (3), at the beginning, insert "Subject to subsection (3A)"; and

(*b*) after subsection (3) insert—

"(3A) Where the adoption order is made by virtue of section 15(1)(*aa*), its making shall not operate to extinguish the parental responsibilities and parental rights which immediately before the making of the order were vested in the natural parent to whom the adopter is married.".

(2) In section 15(1) of that Act (adoption by one person)—

(*a*) after paragraph (*a*) insert—

"(*aa*) not being a person who may make application by virtue of paragraph (*b*) below, is married to a person—

(i) who is the natural parent of the child concerned; and

(ii) in whom are vested parental responsibilities and parental rights in relation to the child,"; and

(*b*) in paragraph (*b*), at the beginning insert—

"not being a person who may make application by virtue of paragraph (*aa*) above,".

(3) In section 39 of that Act (status conferred by adoption), for subsection (1) substitute—

"(1) A child who is the subject of an adoption order shall be treated in law—

(*a*) where the adopters are a married couple, as if—

(i) he had been born as a legitimate child of the marriage (whether or not he was in fact born after the marriage was constituted); and

(ii) he were not the child of any person other than the adopters;

(*b*) where the adoption order is made by virtue of section 15(1)(*aa*) as if—

(i) he had been born as a legitimate child of the marriage between the adopter and the natural parent to whom the adopter is married (whether or not he was in fact born after the marriage was constituted); and

(ii) he were not the child of any person other than the adopter and that natural parent; and

(*c*) in any other case, as if—

(i) he had been born as a legitimate child of the adopter; and

(ii) he were not the child of any person other than the adopter.".

Further amendments of the 1978 Act; and interpretation of Part III

98.—(1) Schedule 2 to this Act, which contains further amendments of the 1978 Act, shall have effect.

(2) In this Part of this Act, "the 1978 Act" means the Adoption (Scotland) Act 1978.

PART IV

GENERAL AND SUPPLEMENTAL

Registration of births by persons who are themselves children

99.—(1) In paragraph (*a*) of section 14(1) of the Registration of Births, Deaths and Marriages (Scotland) Act 1965 (duty of father and mother to give information of particulars of birth), for the words "father or mother of the child" substitute "child's father or mother (whether or not they have attained the age of sixteen years)".

(2) Where, at any time after the coming into force of the Age of Legal Capacity (Scotland) Act 1991 but before the coming into force of subsection (1) above, a person mentioned in the said paragraph (*a*) who had not at that time attained the age of sixteen years purported to fulfil the duty mentioned in the said section 14(1), he shall be presumed to have had legal capacity to fulfil that duty.

(3) In section 18 of the said Act of 1965 (registration of birth of child born out of wedlock), after subsection (2) add—

"(3) A person under the age of sixteen years has legal capacity—

(*a*) to make a request, declaration or statutory declaration under subsection (1) or (2)(*b*) above if, in the opinion of the registrar; or

(*b*) to make an application under subsection (2)(*c*) above if, in the opinion of the sheriff,

that person understands the nature of the request or, as the case may be, of the declaration, statutory declaration or application; and without prejudice to the generality of this subsection a person twelve years of age or more shall be presumed to be of sufficient age and maturity to have such understanding.".

(4) Where, at any time after the coming into force of the Age of Legal Capacity (Scotland) Act 1991 but before the coming into force of subsection (3) above, a person who had not at that time attained the age of sixteen years made a request, declaration, statutory declaration or application mentioned in subsection (1) or (2) of the said section 18 in relation to a child in respect of whose birth an entry was consequently made under the said subsection (1) in a register of births, or as the case may be under the said subsection (2) in the Register of Corrections etc., the person shall be presumed to have had legal capacity to make the request, declaration, statutory declaration, or application in question.

Inquiries into matters affecting children

100. After section 6A of the Social Work (Scotland) Act 1968 there shall be inserted—

"**Legal authority inquiries into matters affecting children**

6B.—(1) Without prejudice to section 6A(1) of this Act, a local authority may cause an inquiry to be held into their functions under this Act, or any of the enactments mentioned in section 5(1B) of this Act, in so far as those functions relate to children.

(2) The local authority may, before an inquiry under this section is commenced, direct that it be held in private; but where no such direction is given, the person holding the inquiry may if he thinks fit hold it, or any part of it, in private.

(3) Subsections (2) to (6) of section 210 of the Local Government (Scotland) Act 1973 (powers in relation to local inquiries) shall apply in relation to an inquiry under this section as they apply in relation to a local inquiry under that section, so however that, for the purposes of the application, any reference in those subsections to a Minister shall be construed as a reference to the local authority and any reference to an officer of his Department as a reference to an officer of that authority.

(4) The expenses incurred by a local authority in relation to an inquiry under this section (including such reasonable sum as the authority may determine for the services of any of their officers engaged in the inquiry) shall, unless the authority are of the opinion that those expenses should be defrayed in whole or in part by them, be paid by such party to the inquiry as they may direct; and the authority may certify the amount of the expenses so incurred;

(5) Any sum certified under subsection (4) above and to be defrayed in accordance with a direction under that subsection shall be a debt due by the party directed and shall be recoverable accordingly.

(6) The local authority may make an award as to the expenses of the parties at the inquiry and as to the parties by whom such expenses shall be paid.".

Panel for curators *ad litem*, reporting officers and safeguarders

101.—(1) The Secretary of State may by regulations make provision for the establishment of a panel of persons from whom—

(*a*) curators *ad litem* may be appointed under section 58 of the Adoption (Scotland) Act 1978 or under section 87(4) of this Act;

(*b*) reporting officers may be appointed under those sections; and

(*c*) persons may be appointed under section 41(1) of this Act.

(2) Regulations under subsection (1) above may provide, without prejudice to the generality of that subsection—

(*a*) for the appointment, qualifications and training of persons who may be appointed to that panel; and

(*b*) for the management and organisation of persons available for appointment from that panel.

(3) Regulations under subsection (1) above may provide for the expenses incurred by persons appointed from the panel to be defrayed by a local authority.

Removal of duty to report on operation of Children Act 1975

102. Section 105 of the Children Act 1975 (which among other things provides that every five years there shall be laid before Parliament by the Secretary of State a report on the operation of such sections of that Act as are for the time being in force) shall cease to have effect.

Interpretation, rules, regulations and Parliamentary control

103.—(1) Any reference in this Act, or in any enactment amended by this Act, to a person having, or to there being vested in him, parental responsibilities or parental rights shall, unless the context otherwise requires, be construed as a reference to his having, or to there being so vested, any of those rights or as the case may be responsibilities.

(2) Any reference in this Act to something being "prescribed" is, unless the context otherwise requires, a reference to its being prescribed by regulations; and any power conferred by this Act on the Secretary of State or the Lord Advocate to make rules or regulations shall be exercisable by statutory instrument which shall be subject to annulment in pursuance of a resolution of either House of Parliament.

(3) Rules or regulations made under this Act—

(*a*) may make different provision for different cases or classes of case; and

(*b*) may exclude certain cases or classes of case.

Financial provision

104. There shall be paid out of money provided by Parliament—

(*a*) any expenses of the Secretary of State incurred in consequence of the provisions of this Act; and

(*b*) any increase attributable to this Act in the sums payable out of money so provided under any other enactment.

Extent, short title, minor and consequential amendments, repeals and commencement

105.—(1) This Act, which subject to subsections (8) to (10) below extends to Scotland only—

(*a*) may be cited as the Children (Scotland) Act 1995; and

(*b*) except for subsections (1), (2) and (6) to (10) of this section, shall come into force on such day as the Secretary of State may by order made by statutory instrument appoint;

and different days may be appointed under paragraph (*b*) above for different purposes.

(2) An order under subsection (1)(*b*) above may contain such transitional and consequential provisions and savings as appear to the Secretary of State to be necessary or expedient in connection with the provisions brought into force.

(3) The transitional provisions and savings contained in Schedule 3 to this Act shall have effect but are without prejudice to sections 16 and 17 of the Interpretation Act 1978 (effect of repeals).

(4) Schedule 4 to this Act, which contains minor amendments and amendments consequential upon the provisions of this Act, shall have effect.

(5) The enactments mentioned in Schedule 5 to this Act (which include spent provisions) are hereby repealed to the extent specified in the third column of that Schedule.

(6) The Secretary of State may by order made by statutory instrument make such further amendments or repeals, in such enactments as may be specified in the order, as appear to him to be necessary or expedient in consequence of any provision of this Act.

(7) A statutory instrument containing an order under subsection (6) above shall be subject to annulment in pursuance of a resolution of either House of Parliament.

(8) Sections 18, 26(2), 33, 44, 70(4), 74, 82, 83, 93 and 104 of this Act and this section extend to England and Wales, and those sections and this section (except section 70(4)) also extend to Northern Ireland; but—

(*a*) subsection (4) of this section so extends—

(i) to England and Wales, only in so far as it relates to paragraphs 8, 10, 19, 31, 37, 41(1), (2) and (7) to (9), 48 to 52, 54 and 55 of Schedule 4; and

(ii) to Northern Ireland, only in so far as it relates to paragraphs 31, 37, 41(1), (2) and (7) to (9), 54, 55 and 58 of that Schedule; and

(*b*) subsection (5) of this section so extends—

(i) to England and Wales, only in so far as it relates to the entries in Schedule 5 in respect of Part V of the Social Work (Scotland) Act 1968, the Maintenance Orders (Reciprocal Enforcement) Act 1972, section 35(4)(*c*) of the Family Law Act 1986, the Children Act 1989, the Child Support Act 1991 and the Education Act 1993; and

(ii) to Northern Ireland, only in so far as it relates to the entries in that Schedule in respect of Part V of the Social Work (Scotland) Act 1968, the Maintenance Orders (Reciprocal Enforcement) Act 1972 and section 35(4)(*c*) of the Family Law Act 1986.

(9) This section, so far as it relates to the repeal of Part V of the Social Work (Scotland) Act 1968, also extends to the Channel Islands.

(10) Her Majesty may by Order in Council direct that any of the relevant provisions specified in the Order shall extend, with such exceptions, adaptations and modifications (if any) as may be specified in the Order, to any of the Channel Islands; and in this subsection "the relevant provisions" means sections 74, 82, 83 and 93 of this Act and any regulations made under section 74 of this Act.

SCHEDULES

Section 39(2)

SCHEDULE 1

CHILDREN'S PANELS

Appointment

1. The Secretary of State shall, for each local government area, appoint such number of members of children's panels as he considers appropriate and from among that number appoint a chairman and a deputy chairman.

2. A member of a children's panel shall hold office for such period as is specified by the Secretary of State, but may be removed from office by the Secretary of State at any time.

Children's Panel Advisory Committees

3. Subject to paragraph 8 below, each local authority shall form a body (to be known as a "Children's Panel Advisory Committee") consisting of two members nominated by the local authority and three members nominated by the Secretary of State.

4. The Secretary of State may at the request of the local authority provide for an increase in the membership of the Children's Panel Advisory Committee appointed under paragraph 3 above by such number, not exceeding five, of additional members as the authority specify in relation to their request, the additional members to be nominated as follows—

(*a*) the first, and any second or fourth additional member, by the Secretary of State;

(*b*) any third or fifth additional member, by the local authority.

5. The chairman of the Children's Panel Advisory Committee shall be appointed by the Secretary of State from among such of the members he has nominated as are resident in the local government area for which the panel is appointed.

6. It shall be the duty of the Children's Panel Advisory Committee—

(*a*) to submit names of possible panel members to the Secretary of State;

(*b*) to advise the Secretary of State, in so far as he requires advice, on the suitability of persons referred to him as potential panel members; and

(*c*) to advise the Secretary of State on such matters relating to the general administration of the panels as he may refer to them.

7. The Children's Panel Advisory Committee shall have power—

(*a*) to appoint sub-committees;

(*b*) to appoint to any such sub-committee a person who is not a member of the Children's Panel Advisory Committee; and

(*c*) to refer all or any of the duties set out in paragraph 6 above to any such sub-committee for their advice.

Joint Advisory Committees

8.—(1) Two or more local authorities may, instead of each acting under paragraph 3 above, make arrangements to form a Children's Panel Advisory Committee for their areas (a "joint advisory committee").

(2) A joint advisory committee shall not be formed in pursuance of arrangements made under sub-paragraph (1) above unless the authorities concerned have obtained the consent in writing of the Secretary of State.

(3) The Secretary of State may give a direction, in any case where a joint advisory committee has not been formed, to two or more local authorities requiring them to form a joint advisory committee; and they shall comply with any such direction.

(4) Paragraphs 3 to 7, 10(*a*) and 11(*b*) of this Schedule shall apply to a joint advisory committee as they apply in respect of a Children's Panel Advisory Committee and, for the purposes of those paragraphs the local authorities acting under sub-paragraph (1) above shall be regarded as a single local authority.

Recruitment and training of panel members

9. The Secretary of State may make such arrangements as he considers appropriate to recruit and train members, or possible members, of the children's panels.

10. Each local authority shall make such arrangements as they consider appropriate—

(*a*) to enable the Children's Panel Advisory Committee to obtain names for submission to the Secretary of State as potential panel members; and

(*b*) to train panel members or potential panel members.

Expenses of panel members

11. A local authority may pay—

(*a*) to a member or a potential member of a children's panel,

(*b*) to a member of the Children's Panel Advisory Committee,

(*c*) to any person appointed under paragraph 7 above,

such allowances as may be determined by the Secretary of State; and he may determine differently in relation to different cases or different classes of case.

Publication of list of members of children's panel

12. Each local authority shall publish a list of names and addresses of members of the children's panel for their area, and that list shall be open for public inspection at the principal offices of the local authority, and at any place where an electors list for the local government area is available for inspection.

Section 98(1) SCHEDULE 2

AMENDMENTS OF THE ADOPTION (SCOTLAND) ACT 1978

1. The Adoption (Scotland) Act 1978 shall be amended in accordance with this Schedule.

2. In section 1(2) (facilities to be provided as part of adoption service)—

(*a*) paragraph (*a*) shall cease to have effect; and

(*b*) for paragraph (*c*) substitute—

"(*bb*) counselling and assistance (but, without prejudice to sections 51 to 51B, not assistance in cash) to children who have been adopted and to persons who have adopted a child; and

(*c*) counselling for other persons if they have problems relating to adoption.".

3. In section 3(3) (factors to be considered by Secretary of State in considering application for approval of adoption society), after paragraph (*a*) insert—

"(*aa*) the procedures in accordance with which the applicant deals with, or as the case may be proposes to deal with, complaints arising in relation to its exercise of its functions and, where the applicant is already an approved adoption society, the manner in which it deals with particular complaints,".

4. Section 8 (direction where adoption society inactive or defunct) shall cease to have effect.

5. In section 9 (regulations relating to an adoption agency's exercise of its functions)—

(*a*) in subsection (2), at the end add—

"including, without prejudice to the generality of this subsection, regulations as to procedures for dealing with complaints arising in relation to such exercise."; and

(*b*) after subsection (3) insert—

"(3A) Regulations under this section may make provision—

(*a*) as to the determination by an adoption agency of whether, as regards a child for whose adoption it proposes to make arrangements, any such agreement as is mentioned in sections 16(1)(*b*)(i) and 18(1)(*a*) is likely to be forthcoming and as to a period by the end of which, if they have determined that the agreement is unlikely to be forthcoming and if no application has been made for an adoption order in relation to the child, application for an order under section 18(1) shall require to be made in relation to him; and

(*b*) where the case of a child for whose adoption an adoption agency proposes to make arrangements is referred under section 73(4)(*c*)(ii) or (iii) of the Children (Scotland) Act 1995 to the Principal Reporter (within the meaning of Part II of that Act), as to circumstances in which and, on the occurrence of such circumstances, a period by the end of which, if no application has been made for an adoption order in relation to the child, application for an order under section 18(1) shall require to be made in relation to him.".

6. In section 11(3) (offence of receiving child illegally placed for adoption), for paragraph (*c*) substitute—

"(*c*) both receives a child placed with him in contravention of subsection (1) and knows that the placement is with a view to his adopting the child,".

7. In section 12 (adoption orders)—

(*a*) in subsection (1)—

(i) for the words "rights and duties relating" substitute "responsibilities and parental rights in relation"; and

(ii) at the end add—

"; except that an adoption order may be made in relation to a person who has attained the age of 18 years if the application for it was made before such attainment.";

(*b*) in subsection (2), for the words "rights and duties" substitute "responsibilities and parental rights";

(*c*) in subsection (3)—

(i) in paragraph (*a*), for the words "right or duty" substitute "responsibility or parental right"; and

(ii) in paragraph (*b*)(ii), for the words "rights and duties" substitute "responsibilities and parental rights"; and

(*d*) at the end add—

"(9) Where a court making an adoption order in relation to a child who is subject to a supervision requirement is satisfied that, in consequence of its doing so, compulsory measures of supervision in respect of the child are no longer necessary, it may determine that the child shall forthwith cease to be subject to that requirement.".

8. In section 14 (adoption by married couple)—

(*a*) in subsection (1), the words from "Subject" to "certain cases)" shall cease to have effect; and

(*b*) in subsection (2), after paragraph (*b*) add—

", or

(*c*) both of them were habitually resident in any of the places mentioned in paragraph (*a*) above throughout the period of one year which ends with the date of their application".

9. In section 15 (adoption by one person)—

(*a*) in subsection (1), the words from "Subject" to "certain cases)" shall cease to have effect; and

(*b*) in subsection (2), after paragraph (*b*) add

", or

(*c*) he was habitually resident in any of the places mentioned in paragraph (*a*) above throughout the period of one year which ends with the date of his application".

10. In section 16 (provision for parental agreement to adoption order)—

(*a*) for subsection (2) substitute—

"(2) The grounds mentioned in subsection (1)(*b*)(ii) are, that the parent or guardian—

(*a*) is not known, cannot be found or is incapable of giving agreement;

(*b*) is withholding agreement unreasonably;

(*c*) has persistently failed, without reasonable cause, to fulfil one or other of the following parental responsibilities in relation to the child—

(i) the responsibility to safeguard and promote the child's health, development and welfare; or

(ii) if the child is not living with him, the responsibility to maintain personal relations and direct contact with the child on a regular basis;

(*d*) has seriously ill-treated the child, whose reintegration into the same household as the parent or guardian is, because of the serious ill-treatment or for other reasons, unlikely."; and

(*b*) subsection (5) shall cease to have effect.

11. In section 18 (making and effect of orders freeing for adoption)—

(*a*) in subsection (1), after the word "agency" insert "which is a local authority";

(*b*) for subsection (5) substitute—

"(5) On the making of an order under this section, the parental responsibilities and parental rights in relation to the child are transferred to the adoption agency.";

(*c*) for subsection (7) substitute—

"(7) Before making an order under this section in the case of a child whose father is not, and has not been, married to the mother and does not have any parental responsibilities or parental rights in relation to the child, the court shall satisfy itself in relation to any person claiming to be the father that—

(*a*) he has no intention of applying for, or, if he did so apply, it is likely that he would be refused, an order under section 11 of the Children (Scotland) Act 1995 (orders in relation to parental responsibilities and parental rights); and

(*b*) he has no intention of entering into an agreement with the mother under section 4(1) of that Act (acquisition by natural father by agreement of such responsibilities and rights), or, if he has such an intention, that no agreement under that subsection is likely to be made."; and

(*d*) at the end add—

"(9) Where a court making an order under this section in relation to a child who is subject to a supervision requirement is satisfied that, in consequence of its doing so, compulsory measures of supervision in respect of the child are no longer necessary, it may determine that the child shall forthwith cease to be subject to that requirement.".

12. In section 19 (progress reports)—

(*a*) in subsection (1)—

(i) for the words "("the former parent")" substitute "(in this section and in section 20 referred to as the "relevant parent")"; and

(ii) for the words "did not do so" substitute—

"either—

(*a*) did not do so; or

(*b*) having done so, subsequently by written notice under this subsection to the adoption agency to which the parental responsibilities and parental rights have been transferred, has withdrawn such declaration.";

(*b*) in subsection (2)—

(i) for the words "in which the parental rights and duties were vested" substitute "to which the parental responsibilities and parental rights were transferred"; and

(ii) for the word "former", in both places where it occurs, substitute "relevant";

(*c*) in subsection (3)—

(i) for the word "former", wherever it occurs, substitute "relevant"; and

(ii) for the words "have his home with a person with whom he has been placed for adoption" substitute "be placed with a person with a view to his being adopted by that person"; and

(*d*) in subsection (4)—

(i) for the words "the former" substitute "the relevant";

(ii) after paragraph (*b*) add—

"but a declaration under this subsection may be withdrawn in the same way as may a declaration under subsection (6) of section 18, in which event the agency shall no longer be so released"; and

(iii) for the words "that former" substitute "that relevant".

13. In section 20 (revocation of order under section 18)—

(*a*) in subsection (1)—

(i) for the word "former" substitute "relevant"; and

(ii) for the words "rights and duties" substitute "responsibilities and parental rights";

(*b*) after subsection (1) insert—

"(1A) The adoption agency, at any time after the making of the order under section 18 when the conditions mentioned in paragraphs (*a*) and (*b*) of subsection (1) above are satisfied, may apply to the court which made the order for a further order revoking it.";

(*c*) in subsection (2)—

(i) for the words "the application" substitute "an application under subsection (1) or (1A)"; and

(ii) for the words "rights and duties" substitute "responsibilities and parental rights";

(*d*) for subsection (3) substitute—

"(3) Where an order freeing a child for adoption is revoked under this section, the court shall, by an order under section 11 of the Children (Scotland) Act 1995 determine on whom are to be imposed the parental responsibilities, and to whom are to be given the parental rights, in relation to the child.";

(*e*) in subsection (4)—

(i) for the words "if the application" substitute "if an application under subsection (1)"; and

(ii) in paragraph (*a*), for the word "former" substitute "relevant"; and

(*f*) in subsection (5), for the word "former" substitute "relevant".

14. In section 21 (variation of order under section 18 so as to substitute one adoption agency for another)—

" Deputy Principal Clerk " means the Deputy Principal Clerk in charge of the Petition Department of the Court of Session;

" Sheriff Clerk " includes Sheriff Clerk Depute.

(3) Other expressions used in this Act of Sederunt to which meanings have been assigned by the Act shall, unless the context otherwise requires, have the same meanings in this Act of Sederunt as in the Act.

(4) The Interpretation Act 1889 shall apply for the interpretation of this Act of Sederunt as it applies for the interpretation of an Act of Parliament.

2. The provisions of Part II of this Act of Sederunt shall apply for the purposes of the Act to orders made by the Court of Session, and the provisions of Part III of this Act of Sederunt shall apply for the purposes of the Act to orders made by or registered in any Sheriff Court.

[1] **3.**—(1) For the purpose of this Act of Sederunt and of Parts I and II of the Act the Deputy Principal Clerk shall be the " prescribed officer " for the Court of Session and the Sheriff Clerk shall be the " prescribed officer " for the Sheriff Court.

[2] (1A) For the purpose of Part II of the Act as applied to a specified State under the Recovery of Maintenance (United States of America) Order 1979, the prescribed officer shall be the sheriff clerk.

(2) All communications which the prescribed officer is required by the Act to send in a prescribed manner to:

(*a*) an addressee in the United Kingdom shall be sent by recorded delivery post and

(*b*) an addressee outwith the United Kingdom shall be sent by air mail post.

NOTES

[1] As amended by S.I. 1975 No. 474.

[2] Added by S.I. 1980 No. 423.

Part II

Court of Session

Provisions in relation to transmission of maintenance orders made by the Court of Session for enforcement in a reciprocating country

4.—(1) All applications to the Court of Session for the transmission of any maintenance order for enforcement in a reciprocating country shall be made by letter addressed to the Deputy Principal Clerk, and the following documents shall be lodged with the application—

(*a*) a certified copy of the relevant order;

(*b*) a statement signed by the applicant or his solicitor of any arrears outstanding in respect of the order;

(*c*) a statement signed by the applicant or his solicitor giving such information as to the whereabouts of the payer as he possesses;

(*d*) a statement signed by the applicant or his solicitor giving such information as the applicant possesses for facilitating the identification of the payer;

(*e*) where available, a photograph of the payer.

(2) On receipt of such application and documents the Deputy Principal Clerk shall send to the Secretary of State the documents specified in section 2 (4) of the Act.

5.—(1) If a maintenance order such as is referred to in the preceding paragraph is varied or revoked by a subsequent order of the Court of Session it shall be the duty of the applicant to inform the Deputy Principal Clerk of any such variation or revocation and to provide the Deputy Principal Clerk with a certified copy of the new order, together with a copy of the extended notes of evidence certified by the Lord Ordinary before whom the evidence was given, if such order was varied after proof, or a copy of the judgment containing the reasons for any such variation in all other cases.

(2) On receipt of such information and documents, the Deputy Principal Clerk shall send the certified copy of the said order and said notes of evidence or extended notes to the relevant Court in the reciprocating country.

Provisions in relation to orders made by Courts in reciprocating countries.

6. On receipt of a certified copy of a provisional order in terms of section 5 (5) of the Act the Deputy Principal Clerk shall write by recorded delivery letter to the payee or payer under the order as the case may be enclosing a copy of said provisional order, advising him that said provisional order has been received and that said order will be confirmed by the Court of Session unless the payee or payer within fourteen days of posting of said letter takes the following steps—viz. in respect of a provisional order to which section 5 (5) of the Act applies the payee shall lodge with the Deputy Principal Clerk an application narrating the reasons why the provisional order should be refused or the maintenance order should not be varied as the case may be, and shall serve a copy of said application on the payer on an *induciae* of fourteen days.

7. After the payee has lodged the application referred to in Rule 6 hereof, answers may be lodged by the payer within fourteen days of service. In the event of said period expiring without answers or after answers have been received, the cause shall be placed before a Lord Ordinary for determination by him of whether said provisional order should be confirmed, refused or altered in terms of section 5 (5) of the Act as may be appropriate.

8. Any decree pronounced under this part of these Rules shall be extractable and any extract of such decree shall, for the purpose of diligence or otherwise, have the same force and effect as an extract decree of the Court of Session.

[1] **9.** Where any request is made to the Court of Session by or on behalf of a Court in a reciprocating country for the evidence of a person to be taken in terms of section 14 of the Act, such evidence shall be taken before the Sheriff of the Sheriffdom in which the witness resides. The prescribed officer shall on receipt of such request forward it to the Sheriff Clerk of the Sheriffdom in which the witness resides.

NOTE

[1] As amended by S.I. 1974 No. 1981.

PART III—SHERIFF COURT

Provisions in relation to transmission of maintenance orders made by the Sheriff Court for enforcement in a reciprocating country.

10.—(1) All applications to the Sheriff Court for the transmission of any maintenance orders for enforcement in a reciprocating country shall be made by letter addressed to the Sheriff Clerk and the following documents shall be lodged with the application—

(*a*) a certified copy of the relevant order;

(*b*) a statement signed by the applicant or his solicitor of any arrears outstanding in respect of the order;

(*a*) in subsection (1)—
  (i) for the words "rights and duties" substitute "responsibilities and parental rights"; and
  (ii) for the words "in which they are vested under" substitute "to which they are transferred by virtue of"; and
(*b*) in subsection (3)—
  (i) for the words "rights and duties" substitute "responsibilities and parental rights"; and
  (ii) for the words "vested in" substitute "been transferred to".

15. After section 22 insert—

"**Children subject to supervision requirements**

22A.—(1) An approved adoption society shall refer the case of a child who is subject to a supervision requirement to the Principal Reporter where it is satisfied that the best interests of the child would be served by its placing the child for adoption and it intends so to place him.

(2) On a case being referred to him under subsection (1), the Principal Reporter shall arrange for a children's hearing to review the supervision requirement in question and shall make any arrangements incidental to that review.

(3) Subsections (9), (13) and (14) of section 73 of the Children (Scotland) Act 1995 (which provide, respectively, for acting on the review of a supervision requirement, a report by a children's hearing and consideration of that report) shall apply in relation to a children's hearing arranged under this section as those subsections apply in relation to one arranged by virtue of subsection (4)(*c*)(iii) of that section.

(4) In this section "Principal Reporter" has the same meaning as in Part II of the Children (Scotland) Act 1995.".

16. In section 24 (restrictions on making adoption orders), for subsection (2) substitute—

"(2) The court may make an adoption order in relation to a child even where it is found that the applicants have, as respects the child, contravened section 51.

(3) In considering whether to make an adoption order or an order under section 18(1), the court shall regard the welfare of the child concerned as its paramount consideration and shall not make the order in question unless it considers that it would be better for the child that it should do so than that it should not.".

17. In section 25(1) (making of interim order and preconditions for so doing)—
(*a*) for the words "of sections 16(1) and 22(1) are complied with" substitute—
  "—
  (*a*) of section 16(1); and
  (*b*) in a case where the child was not placed with the applicant by an adoption agency, of section 22(1),
  are complied with"; and
(*b*) for the words "vesting the custody of the child in" substitute "giving parental responsibilities and parental rights to".

18. After section 25 insert—

"**Timetable for resolving question as to whether agreement to adoption order etc. should be dispensed with**

25A. In proceedings in which the question arises as to whether the court is satisfied as is mentioned in section 16(1)(*b*)(ii) or 18(1)(*b*), the court shall, with a view to determining the question without delay—
  (*a*) draw up a timetable specifying periods within which certain steps must be taken in relation to those proceedings; and
  (*b*) give such directions as it considers appropriate for the purpose of ensuring, so far as is reasonably practicable, that the timetable is adhered to.".

19. In section 27 (restrictions on removal of a child by a parent or guardian who has agreed to an adoption order or to an order freeing the child for adoption)—
(*a*) for subsections (1) and (2), substitute—
  "(1) Where—
  (*a*) an adoption agency has placed a child with a person with a view to his being adopted by the person; and
  (*b*) the consent of each parent or guardian of the child has been duly obtained to that placement (whether or not in knowledge of the identity of the person),
  any such parent or guardian shall not be entitled to remove the child from the care and possession of the person without the leave either of the adoption agency or of the court.
  (2) The reference in subsection (1) to consent having been duly obtained is to its having been obtained in accordance with such regulations as may be made by the Secretary of State for the purposes of this section."; and

(*b*) in subsection (3), for the words "contravenes subsection (1) or (2)" substitute "removes a child in contravention of subsection (1)".

20. In section 28 (restriction on removal of child from care and possession of applicant for adoption order etc.)—

(*a*) in subsection (4), for the words from ", in terms of" to the end substitute "under or by virtue of Chapter 2 or 3 of Part II of the Children (Scotland) Act 1995"; and

(*b*) in subsection (5), the words "or of a voluntary organisation" and "or the organisation" shall cease to have effect.

21. Sections 32 to 37 (protected children) shall cease to have effect.

22. In section 45(5) (restrictions as to persons to whom information contained in the Adopted Children Register or in certain other registers or books may be provided, including a restriction as to the minimum age which an adopted person must be for it to be provided to him), for the word "17" substitute "16".

23. In section 49(1) (adoption of children abroad), for the words "vesting in him the parental rights and duties relating" substitute "transferring to him the parental responsibilities and parental rights in relation".

24. In section 51 (prohibition on certain payments)—

(*a*) in subsection (1), after the word "section" insert "and of section 51A(3)";

(*b*) in subsection (2), for the words "the court may order any child in respect of whom the offence was committed" substitute "without prejudice to any power which the court has to make any other order in relation to the child as respects whom the offence was committed, it may order him";

(*c*) in subsection (5)—

(i) at the beginning insert "Subject to section 51B,"; and

(ii) at the end add "(including any such payment made by virtue of section 51B)"; and

(*d*) subsections (6)(*a*) and (7) to (11) shall cease to have effect.

25. After section 51 insert—

"**Adoption allowances schemes**

51A.—(1) Subject to subsection (2), an adoption agency which is—

(*a*) a local authority shall, within such period after the coming into force of this section as the Secretary of State may by order direct;

(*b*) an approved adoption society may,

prepare a scheme (in this section and in section 51B referred to as an "adoption allowances scheme") for the payment by the agency of allowances to any person who has adopted, or intends to adopt, a child in any case where arrangements for the adoption were made, or as the case may be are to be made, by the agency.

(2) The Secretary of State may make regulations as respects adoption allowances schemes; and without prejudice to the generality of this subsection such regulations may in particular make provision as to—

(*a*) the procedure to be followed by an agency in determining whether a person should be paid an allowance;

(*b*) the circumstances in which an allowance may be paid;

(*c*) the factors to be taken into account in determining the amount of an allowance;

(*d*) the procedure for review, variation and termination of allowances;

(*e*) the information about allowances which is to be supplied by an agency to a person who intends to adopt a child; and

(*f*) the procedure to be followed by an agency in drawing up, in making alterations to, or in revoking and replacing, an adoption allowances scheme.

(3) Section 51(1) shall not apply to any payment made in accordance with an adoption allowances scheme (including any such payment made by virtue of section 51B).

Transitional provisions as respects adoption allowances

51B. After the coming into force of section 51A—

(*a*) no scheme for the payment of allowances shall be submissible under subsection (5) of section 51; and

(*b*) a scheme which has been approved under that subsection of that section shall forthwith be revoked under subsection (6)(*b*) of that section, so however that where a person was before its revocation receiving payments made in accordance with that scheme he may continue to receive payments so made which, had there been no revocation, would have fallen to be made to him or he may agree to receive, instead of the continued payments, payments made in accordance with an adoption allowances scheme.".

26. In section 58 (curators *ad litem* and reporting officers), in subsection (2)(*c*), for the words "rights and duties relating" substitute "responsibilities and parental rights in relation".

27. In section 59(4) (disapplication of provisions regarding rules), for the words ", 11 and 32 to 37" substitute "and 11".

28. In section 60(3) (affirmative procedure for certain orders), the words "or 51(9)" shall cease to have effect.

29. In section 65 (interpretation)—

(*a*) in subsection (1)—

(i) in the definition of "adoption order", in each of paragraphs (*b*) and (*c*), for the words "and 30 to 32" substitute "30 and 31";

(ii) after the definition of "child" insert—

"compulsory measures of supervision has the same meaning as in Part II of the Children (Scotland) Act 1995;";

(iii) in the definition of "guardian", paragraph (*b*) shall cease to have effect;

(iv) in the definition of "local authority", the words ", 35(1)" shall cease to have effect;

(v) after the definition of "overseas adoption" insert—

"parent means, irrespective of whether or not they are, or have been, married to each other—

(*a*) the mother of the child, where she has parental responsibilities or parental rights in relation to him;

(*b*) the father of the child where he has such responsibilities or rights; and

(*c*) both of his parents, where both have such responsibilities or rights;

"parental responsibilities" and "parental rights" have the meanings respectively given by sections 1(3) and 2(4) of the Children (Scotland) Act 1995 (analogous expressions being construed accordingly);";

(vi) in the definition of "relative" for the words from "and any person" to the end substitute "where he is not a parent within the meaning of this Act, and any person who would be a relative within the meaning of this definition if the father were such a parent; " and

(vii) after the definition of "specified order" insert—

"supervision requirement" has the same meaning as in Part II of the Children (Scotland) Act 1995; ";

(*b*) in subsection (3), for the words "44 of the Social Work (Scotland) Act 1968" substitute "70 of the Children (Scotland) Act 1995"; and

(*c*) after subsection (5) add—

"(6) Any reference in this Act to a child being in, received into or kept in, care (whether or not such care is expressed as being the care of a local authority and except where the context otherwise requires) shall be taken to be a reference to his being looked after by a local authority and shall be construed in accordance with section 17(6) of the Children (Scotland) Act 1995; and any reference to the authority in whose care a child is, shall be construed accordingly.".

Section 105(3)

SCHEDULE 3

Transitional Provisions and Savings

1. Where, immediately before the day appointed for the coming into force of section 25 of this Act, a child is by virtue of section 15 of the 1968 Act (duty of local authority to provide for orphans, deserted children etc.) in the care of a local authority, the child shall on and after that day be treated as if he had been provided with accommodation under (and within the meaning of) subsection (1) of the said section 25.

2. Sections 29 and 30 of this Act shall apply in respect of a person who, at the time when he ceased to be of school age (as defined in section 31 of the Education (Scotland) Act 1980) or at any subsequent time, was—

(*a*) in the care of a local authority by virtue of the said section 15 or of section 16 of the 1968 Act (assumption of parental rights and powers); or

(*b*) subject to a supervision requirement (within the meaning of section 44(1) of the 1968 Act),

as they apply in respect of a person who at such time was looked after (within the meaning of Part II of this Act) by a local authority.

3. Where the parental rights in respect of a child have, by a resolution under the said section 16 or under section 16A of the 1968 Act (duty of local authority in cases of necessity to assume parental rights and powers vested in a voluntary organisation), vested in a local authority and immediately before the day appointed for the coming into force of section 86 of this Act those rights remain so vested, the resolution shall on and after that day have effect as if it were a

parental responsibilities order transferring the appropriate parental rights and responsibilities (as defined in subsection (3) of the said section 86) relating to the child to the authority; and any access order made under section 17B of the 1968 Act in relation to the child (with any order made under section 17C of that Act as respects the access order) being (in either case) an order which immediately before that day remains undischarged, shall on and after that day have effect as if it were an order made under section 88(3) of this Act as respects the child.

4. Where the parental rights in respect of a child have, by a resolution under the said section 16, vested in a voluntary organisation (as defined in section 93 of this Act) and immediately before the day mentioned in paragraph 3 above those rights remain so vested, the resolution shall, notwithstanding the repeal by this Act of the said section 16, continue to have effect until one of the following occurs—

(*a*) the child attains the age of eighteen years;

(*b*) the resolution is rescinded by the local authority because it appears to them that their doing so would promote the child's welfare;

(*c*) the period of six months commencing with that day expires;

(*d*) an order is made by virtue of section 11(2)(*b*), or under section 86(1), of this Act in relation to the child;

(*e*) an order is made under section 12 (adoption order) or 18 (order freeing for adoption) of the Adoption (Scotland) Act 1978 in relation to the child.

5. Where the circumstance by virtue of which a resolution under the said section 16 ceases to have effect is that mentioned in sub-paragraph (*c*) of paragraph 4 above, the appropriate parental rights and responsibilities (defined as mentioned in paragraph 3 above) in relation to the child shall transfer forthwith to the local authority in whose area he resides; and for the purposes of sections 86(6) and 87 to 89 of this Act the transfer shall be deemed effected by a parental responsibilities order applied for by that authority.

6. While a resolution continues to have effect by virtue of paragraph 4 above, sections 17(3A) and (6) to (10), 17A, 17B, 17D, 17E and 20(3) of the 1968 Act (together with the code of practice last published under subsection (5) of the said section 17E) shall continue to have effect in relation to the child in question notwithstanding the repeal by this Act of those sections.

7. Where an order made under—

(*a*) section 10 (power of court in actions of divorce etc. to commit care of child to local authority) or 12 (power of court to provide for supervision of child) of the Matrimonial Proceedings (Children) Act 1958;

(*b*) section 11 of the Guardianship Act 1973 (orders relating to care and custody of children); or

(*c*) section 26 of the Adoption (Scotland) Act 1978 (provision for supervision or care where adoption order refused),

committed the care of the child to, or as the case may be placed the child under the supervision of, a local authority and immediately before the repeal by this Act of the section in question (the "relevant repeal") that order remained undischarged, the order shall continue to have effect notwithstanding the relevant repeal until one of the following occurs—

(i) the period of six months commencing with the date of the relevant repeal expires;

(ii) the Court of Session direct, or the sheriff directs, that the order be discharged; or

(iii) there is an event in consequence of which, but for the provisions (apart from this paragraph) of this Act, the order would have fallen to be discharged.

8.—(1) Where relevant proceedings in relation to a child have been commenced and on the relevant date have not been concluded, the provisions of Part III of the 1968 Act shall continue to apply to those proceedings until the proceedings are concluded, notwithstanding the repeal of any of those provisions by this Act.

(2) For the purposes of this paragraph, "relevant proceedings" means any proceedings at a children's hearing under Part III of the 1968 Act, any application to the sheriff under that Part for a warrant or under section 42(2)(*c*) of that Act to establish any ground of referral, and any appeal under section 49 or 50 of that Act; and a reference to the commencement, or to the conclusion, of such proceedings shall be construed in accordance with sub-paragraph (3) or, as the case may be, (4) below.

(3) Relevant proceedings are commenced when one of the following occurs—

(*a*) a children's hearing is arranged under section 37(4) or section 39(3) of the 1968 Act;

(*b*) an application under section 42(2)(*c*) of that Act is lodged;

(*c*) an appeal to the sheriff under section 49 of that Act is lodged;

(*d*) an application under section 50(2) of that Act is made.

(4) Relevant proceedings are concluded when one of the following occurs—

(*a*) the sheriff discharges the referral under section 42(5) of the 1968 Act;

(*b*) a children's hearing discharge the referral under section 43(2) of that Act;

(*c*) the period of three weeks after a children's hearing make a supervision requirement under section 44 of that Act or on remission to them under section 49(5) of that Act, expires provided that no appeal has been lodged within that period against that decision under section 49 of that Act;

(*d*) subject, as respects a decision under section 49(5)(*b*) of that Act, to head (*c*) above, the period of twenty eight days after the sheriff has disposed of an appeal under section 49(4), (5) or (6) of that Act expires provided that no application has been made within that period to him to state a case under section 50(2) of that Act;

(*e*) the period of twenty eight days after the sheriff has disposed of a case remitted to him under section 50(3) expires provided that no further application under the said section 50(2) has been made.

9. Where a child has been taken to a place of safety, or is being detained in such a place, in accordance with section 37(2) of the 1968 Act before the relevant date, and the first lawful day for the purposes of subsection (4) of that section is on or after that date, the child's case shall be proceeded with as if that day had been before the relevant date.

10.—(1) Where on the relevant date a child is subject to a supervision requirement imposed under section 44 of the 1968 Act, he shall be treated as if the requirement had been imposed under section 70 of this Act; and in calculating any period of time for the purposes of section 73 of this Act, that requirement shall be deemed to have been imposed on the day on which the requirement was imposed under the said section 44 or, as the case may be, was last reviewed or varied under the said Act of 1968.

(2) Where any relevant proceedings are concluded as mentioned in paragraph 8(4)(*c*) above, a supervision requirement imposed under section 44 of the 1968 Act shall have effect as if it were made under section 70 of this Act.

(3) Where before the relevant date, or in any relevant proceedings, the sheriff has in relation to a supervision requirement made an order under section 49(6) of the 1968 Act, that order shall have effect in relation to the supervision requirement deemed to have been made under section 70 of this Act as it would have had effect in relation to the supervision requirement made under section 44 of the 1968 Act.

11. In this Schedule—

"the 1968 Act" means the Social Work (Scotland) Act 1968;

"the relevant date" means the date on which the repeal of Part III of the 1968 Act by this Act takes effect; and

"relevant proceedings" shall be construed in accordance with paragraph 8(2) above.

Section 105(4)

SCHEDULE 4

Minor and Consequential Amendments

Lands Clauses Consolidation (Scotland) Act 1845 (c. 19)

1.—(1) The Lands Clauses Consolidation (Scotland) Act 1845 shall be amended in accordance with this paragraph.

(2) In section 7 (which makes provision for certain persons to have full power to sell and convey land)—

(*a*) after the word "husbands," insert "persons who, within the meaning of Part I of the Children (Scotland) Act 1995, are entitled to act as the legal representatives of a child,";

(*b*) after the words "guardians for" the words "persons under a legal disability by reason of nonage" shall cease to have effect; and

(*c*) after the word "whether", the words "persons under legal disability by reason of nonage" shall cease to have effect;

(*d*) after the word "such" where it appears for the sixth time, insert "legal representatives,"; and

(*e*) after the word "such" where it appears for the seventh time, the words "persons under legal disability by reason of nonage" shall cease to have effect.

(3) In section 67 (certain payments to persons under a disability to be deposited with the Bank)—

(*a*) after the word "husband," insert "a person who, within the meaning of Part I of the Children (Scotland) Act 1995, is entitled to act as a legal representative of a child"; and

(*b*) the words "persons under legal disability by reason of nonage" shall cease to have effect.

(4) In section 69 (nomination of trustees to whom certain payments of under £200 may be paid)—

(*a*) the words "legal disability by reason of nonage" shall cease to have effect; and
(*b*) after the word "husbands," insert "legal representatives of a child (within the meaning of Part I of the Children (Scotland) Act 1995),".

(5) In section 70 (sums of under £20 to be paid to certain persons), after the word "husbands," insert "legal representatives of a child (within the meaning of Part I of the Children (Scotland) Act 1995),".

Judicial Factors (Scotland) Act 1849 (c. 51)

2.—(1) The Judicial Factors (Scotland) Act 1849 shall be amended in accordance with this paragraph.

(2) In section 1 (interpretation), the words from "the word "Guardian" to "years;" shall cease to have effect.

(3) In section 10 (duty of accountant to supervise judicial factors and others), for the words "guardians and tutors" substitute ", tutors".

(4) Section 25(2) (guardians to be subject to the provisions of the Act), shall cease to have effect.

(5) In section 27 (limitation by court of amount of caution), the words "guardians and" shall cease to have effect.

(6) In section 31 (power of court to remove tutors etc.), the word "guardian" shall cease to have effect.

(7) In section 32 (provisions of the Act not to alter existing powers, rights and duties of offices), the word "guardian," shall cease to have effect.

(8) In section 33 (power of accountant to obtain information from banks), the words "guardians or" shall cease to have effect.

(9) In section 34 (petitions for discharge of office), in both places where it occurs, the word "guardian," shall cease to have effect.

(10) In section 34A (act of sederunt to provide for other forms of discharge), for the words ", death or coming of age" substitute "or death".

(11) In section 36 (records held by accountant to be open to inspection), the word "guardianships," shall cease to have effect.

(12) In section 37 (accumulation of interest on accounts), the word "guardian," shall cease to have effect.

(13) In section 40 (act of sederunt to regulate *inter alia* application of the Act to offices other than judicial factors), in both places where it occurs, the word "guardians," shall cease to have effect.

Improvement of Land Act 1864 (c.114)

3. In section 24 of the Improvement of Land Act 1864 (representation of persons under disability in certain applications etc.), for the words from the beginning to "feoffee" where it last occurs substitute "Any person entitled to act as the legal representative of a person under legal disability by reason of non age or mental incapacity shall be entitled to act on behalf of that person for the purposes of this Act; and any trustee, judicial factor, executor or administrator shall, subject to any other enactment, have the same rights and powers for the purposes of this Act as if the property vested in or administered by him had been vested in him in his own right; but no such legal representative".

Judicial Factors (Scotland) Act 1880 (c. 4)

4. In section 3 of the Judicial Factors (Scotland) Act 1880 (interpretation), in the definition of "judicial factor"—
(*a*) for the word "*absentis*," substitute "*absentis* and"; and
(*b*) the words from "and" to "required," shall cease to have effect.

Heritable Securities (Scotland) Act 1894 (c. 44)

5. In section 13 of the Heritable Securities (Scotland) Act 1894 (persons to have powers conferred by Act where person subject to legal disability), for the words "and trustees" substitute "and—
(*a*) any person entitled, within the meaning of Part I of the Children (Scotland) Act 1995, to act as the legal representative of a child; and
(*b*) trustees".

Trusts (Scotland) Act 1921 (c. 58)

6. In section 2 of the Trusts (Scotland) Act 1921 (interpretation)—

(*a*) in the definition of "trustee", the words "(including a father or mother acting as guardian of a child under the age of 16 years)" shall cease to have effect; and

(*b*) after the definition of "trustee" insert—

" "curator" and "tutor" shall have respectively the meanings assigned to these expressions by section 1 of the Judicial Factors Act 1849;

"guardian" shall not include any person who, within the meaning of Part I of the Children (Scotland) Act 1995, is entitled to act as the legal representative of a child;".

Children and Young Persons (Scotland) Act 1937 (c. 37)

7.—(1) The Children and Young Persons (Scotland) Act 1937 shall be amended in accordance with this paragraph.

(2) In section 12 (cruelty to persons under sixteen)—

(*a*) in subsection (1), for the words from "has the custody" to "that age" substitute "who has parental responsibilities in relation to a child or to a young person under that age or has charge or care of a child or such a young person,";

(*b*) in subsection (2)(*a*), after the words "young person" insert "or the legal guardian of a child or young person"; and

(*c*) in subsection (4), for the words from "of whom" to "or care" substitute "and he had parental responsibilities in relation to, or charge or care of, that child or young person".

(3) In section 15 (causing or allowing persons under sixteen to be used for begging), in each of subsections (1) and (2), for the words "the custody" substitute "parental responsibilities in relation to, or having".

(4) In section 22 (exposing children under seven to risk of burning), for the words from "having the custody" to "seven years" substitute "and who has parental responsibilities in relation to a child under the age of seven years or charge or care of such a child".

(5) In section 27 (interpretation)—

(*a*) the first paragraph shall cease to have effect; and

(*b*) in the second paragraph, for the words "the custody of" substitute "parental responsibilities in relation to".

(6) In section 110(1) (interpretation)—

(*a*) after the definition of "local authority" insert—

" "parental responsibilities" has the same meaning as in section 1(3) of the Children (Scotland) Act 1995 and includes the responsibilities which a father would have as a parent but for the operation of section 3(1)(*b*) of that Act;";

(*b*) for the definition of "place of safety", substitute ""place of safety" has the meaning give by section 93(1) of the Children (Scotland) Act 1995;"; and

(*c*) for the definition of "residential establishment" substitute """residential establishment" has the meaning given by the said section 93(1);".

Mines and Quarries Act 1954 (c. 70)

8. In section 182(1) of the Mines and Quarries Act 1954 (interpretation), in the definition of "parent", for the words from "means" to "and includes" substitute "means a parent of a young person or any person who is not a parent of his but who has parental responsibility for him (within the meaning of the Children Act 1989) or who has parental responsibilities in relation to him (within the meaning of section 1(3) of the Children (Scotland) Act 1995), and includes".

Matrimonial Proceedings (Children) Act 1958 (c. 40)

9. In section 11(1) of the Matrimonial Proceedings (Children) Act 1958 (reports as to arrangements for future care and upbringing of children), for the words from the beginning to "the court may" substitute "Where the court is considering any question relating to the care and upbringing of a child, it may".

Factories Act 1961 (c. 34)

10. In section 176(1) of the Factories Act 1961 (interpretation)—

(*a*) for the definition of "child" substitute—

" "child" means any person who is not over—

(*a*) compulsory school age (construed in accordance with section 277 of the Education Act 1993); or

(*b*) school age (construed in accordance with section 31 of the Education (Scotland) Act 1980);"

(*b*) in the definition of "parent", for the words from "means" to "and includes" substitute "means a parent of a child or young person or any person who is not a parent of his but who has parental responsibility for him (within the meaning of the Children Act 1989) or who has parental responsibilities in relation to him (within the meaning of section 1(3) of the Children (Scotland) Act 1995), and includes".

Education (Scotland) Act 1962 (c. 47)

11. In section 145(33) of the Education (Scotland) Act 1962 (interpretation), for the words "the actual custody of" substitute "parental responsibilities (within the meaning of section 1(3) of the Children (Scotland) Act 1995) in relation to, or has the care of,".

Registration of Births, Deaths and Marriages (Scotland) Act 1965 (c. 49)

12.—(1) The Registration of Births, Deaths and Marriages (Scotland) Act 1965 shall be amended in accordance with this paragraph.

(2) In section 20(3)(*a*) (re-registration of birth of person under sixteen), for sub-paragraphs (i) and (ii) substitute ", by any person (whether or not he has himself attained the age of sixteen years) having parental responsibilities in relation to that person;".

(3) In section 43 (recording of baptismal name or change of name or surname)—

(*a*) in subsection (3), the words from "In this" to the end shall cease to have effect;

(*b*) in subsections (6)(*a*) and (7), for the words "the parent or guardian" substitute "the qualified applicant";

(*c*) after subsection (9) insert—

"(9A) In this section "qualified applicant" means—

(*a*) where only one parent has parental responsibilities in relation to the child, that parent;

(*b*) where both parents have such responsibilities in relation to the child, both parents; and

(*c*) where neither parent has such responsibilities, any other person who has such responsibilities.

(9B) A person may be a qualified applicant for the purposes of this section whether or not he has attained the age of sixteen years"; and

(*d*) subsection (10) shall cease to have effect.

(4) In section 53(3)(*c*) (offence of failure by parent to give information concerning birth), after the word "fails" insert "without reasonable excuse".

(5) In section 56(1) (interpretation), after the definition of "parentage" insert—

" "parental responsibilities" has the meaning given in section 1(3) of the Children (Scotland) Act 1995;".

13. Where, at any time after the coming into force of the Age of Legal Capacity (Scotland) Act 1991 but before the coming into force of—

(*a*) sub-paragraph (2) of paragraph 12 of this Schedule, a person's mother or father, who had not at that time attained the age of sixteen years, purported to apply under section 20(3)(*a*) of that Act to re-register the person's birth, the mother, or as the case may be the father, shall be presumed to have had legal capacity to make the application; or

(*b*) sub-paragraph (3)(*c*) of that paragraph, a person who had not at that time attained the age of sixteen years purported to make an application under any provision of section 43 of that Act ("making an application" including for the purposes of this sub-paragraph, without prejudice to the generality of that expression, signing and delivering a certificate in accordance with subsection (3) of that section) the person shall be presumed to have had legal capacity to make the application.

Law Reform (Miscellaneous Provisions)(Scotland) Act 1966 (c. 19)

14. In section 8 of the Law Reform (Miscellaneous Provisions) (Scotland) Act 1966 (variation and recall of certain orders in respect of maintenance, custody etc.)—

(*a*) in subsection (1), after paragraph (*c*) insert—

"(*cc*) an order under section 11 of the Children (Scotland) Act 1995 (orders in respect of parental responsibilities etc.) or under any earlier enactment relating to the custody, care or supervision of a child, or access to a child;"; and

(*b*) in subsection (6), in the definition of "sheriff", in paragraph (*a*), for the words "or (*c*)" substitute ", (*c*) or (*cc*)".

Social Work (Scotland) Act 1968 (c. 49)

15.—(1) The Social Work (Scotland) Act 1968 shall be amended in accordance with this paragraph.

(2) In section 1(1) (duty of local authority to implement statutory duties not falling on other authorities), after the word "Act" insert "or Part II of the Children (Scotland) Act 1995".

(3) In section 4 (arrangements for provision of assistance to local authorities by other bodies), after "1984" insert "or Part II of the Children (Scotland) Act 1995".

(4) In section 5 (powers of the Secretary of State in relation to certain functions of local authorities)—

(*a*) in subsection (1) after the word "Act" insert "and Part II of the Children (Scotland) Act 1995";

(*b*) in subsection (1B)—

(i) before paragraph (*o*), the word "and" shall cease to have effect; and

(ii) at the end add "; and

(*p*) Part II of the Children (Scotland) Act 1995.";

(*c*) in subsection (2), in paragraph (*c*) for the words "and (*o*)" substitute ", (*o*) and (*p*)"; and

(*d*) for subsection (3) substitute—

"(3) Without prejudice to the generality of subsection (2) above, regulations under this section may make such provision as is mentioned in subsection (4) of this section as regards—

(*a*) the boarding out of persons other than children by local authorities and voluntary organisations, whether under any enactment or otherwise; and

(*b*) the placing of children under paragraph (*a*), or the making of arrangements in respect of children under paragraph (*c*), of section 26(1) of the Children (Scotland) Act 1995, by local authorities.

(4) The provision referred to in subsection (3) of this section is—

(*a*) for the recording—

(i) by local authorities and voluntary organisations, of information relating to those with whom persons are so boarded out, or who are willing to have persons so boarded out with them; and

(ii) by local authorities, of information relating to those with whom children are so placed or with whom such arrangements are made or who are willing to have children so placed with them or to enter into such arrangements;

(*b*) for securing that—

(i) persons are not so boarded out in any household unless it is for the time being approved by such local authority or voluntary organisation as may be prescribed by the regulations; and

(ii) children are not so placed or, in accordance with such arrangements, provided with accommodation, in any household unless it is for the time being approved by the local authority placing the child or as the case may be making the arrangements;

(*c*) for securing that, where possible, the person with whom a child is so placed or with whom such arrangements are made is either of the same religious persuasion as the child or gives an undertaking that the child shall be brought up in that persuasion;

(*d*) for securing—

(i) that a person who is, and the place in which he is, so boarded out by a local authority or voluntary organisation is supervised and inspected by that authority or organisation; and

(ii) that a child who is, and the place in which he is, so placed or, in accordance with such arrangements, provided with accommodation, by a local authority is supervised and inspected by that authority,

and that he shall be removed from the place in question if his welfare appears to require it.

(5) In subsections (3) and (4) of this section, "child" has the same meaning as in Chapters 2 and 3 of Part II of the Children (Scotland) Act 1995."

(5) In section 5B (requirement to establish complaints procedures)—

(*a*) in subsection (4), in paragraph (*b*), for the words "rights in respect of" substitute "responsibilities and parental rights (within the meaning of section 1(3) and section 2(4) respectively of the Children (Scotland) Act 1995) in relation to"; and

(*b*) in subsection (5), at the end of the definition of "child", the words from "and" to the end of the subsection shall cease to have effect.

(6) In section 6 (power to enter certain establishments to conduct examination)—

(*a*) in subsection (1)—

(i) in paragraph (*a*), after the word "1984" insert "or Part II of the Children (Scotland) Act 1995";

(ii) in paragraph (*b*), sub-paragraph (ii) shall cease to have effect;
(iii) in paragraph (*c*), after the word "person" insert ", other than a child,"; and
(iv) after paragraph (*c*) add—
"(*cc*) any place where a child is for the time being accommodated under paragraph (*a*) of, or by virtue of paragraph (*c*) of, section 26(1) of the Children (Scotland) Act 1995."; and

(*b*) in subsection (2), after the words "1984" insert "or Part II of the Children (Scotland) Act 1995".

(7) For subsection (1) of section 6A (power of the Secretary of State to hold inquiries), substitute—

"(1) Without prejudice to section 6B(1) of this Act, the Secretary of State may cause an inquiry to be held into—
(*a*) the functions of a local authority under this Act or any of the enactments mentioned in section 5(1B) of this Act;
(*b*) the functions of an adoption society, within the meaning of section 65 of the Adoption (Scotland) Act 1978;
(*c*) the functions of a voluntary organisation in so far as those functions relate to establishments to which sections 61 to 68 of this Act apply;
(*d*) the detention of a child under—
(i) section 57 of the Children and Young Persons (Scotland) Act 1937; or
(ii) section 206 or 413 of the Criminal Procedure (Scotland) Act 1975; or
(*e*) the functions of the Principal Reporter under Part III of the Local Government (Scotland) Act 1994, the Children (Scotland) Act 1995 or any other enactment."

(8) In section 9 (powers of the Secretary of State with regard to training etc.), in subsections (1) and (2), after the word "Act" insert "or Part II of the Children (Scotland) Act 1995".

(9) In section 10(1) (making of grants and loans for social work), for the words "and (*l*)" substitute ", (*l*) and (*p*)".

(10) In section 11(1) (local authority authorised by Secretary of State to purchase compulsorily land), in subsection (1), after the word "Act" insert "or Part II of the Children (Scotland) Act 1995".

(11) In section 12 (general social welfare services of local authorities), for the words from "be given" in subsection (1) to "a person" in subsection (2)(*b*) substitute—

", subject to subsections (3) to (5) of this section, be given in kind or in cash to, or in respect of, any relevant person.

(2) A person is a relevant person for the purposes of this section if, not being less than eighteen years of age, he is".

(12) In section 28 (burial or cremation)—
(*a*) in subsection (1), after the word "from," insert "or was a child being looked after by,"; and
(*b*) after subsection (2) add—

"(3) In subsection (1) of this section, the reference to a child being looked after by a local authority shall be construed in accordance with section 17(6) of the Children (Scotland) Act 1995.".

(13) In section 29 (power of local authority to defray expenses of parents etc. visiting persons accommodated by a local authority or attending certain funerals)—
(*a*) in subsection (1)—
(i) for the words from "a person" to "respect" substitute—
"—
(*a*) a person, other than a child, in the care of the authority or receiving assistance from the authority; or
(*b*) a child who is being looked after by the authority,
in respect";
(ii) after the words "visiting the person" insert "or child"; and
(iii) for the words "the person", where they occur for the second time, substitute "him";
(*b*) in subsection (2), for the words from "a person" to "for" substitute—
"—
(*a*) a person, other than a child, who had been in the care of the authority or receiving assistance from the authority; for
(*b*) a child who had been looked after by the authority, for"; and
(*c*) after subsection (2), add—

"(3) In subsections (1) and (2) above, references to a child looked after by a local authority shall be construed as is mentioned in subsection (3) of section 28 of this Act.".

(14) Part III (children in need of compulsory measures of care) shall cease to have effect, with the exception of subsections (1) and (3) of section 31 and the amendments provided for by the said subsection (3) and contained in Schedule 2 to that Act.

(15) In section 59(1) (provision and maintenance of residential and other establishments) after the word "Act,", where it occurs for the second time insert "or under Part II of the Children (Scotland) Act 1995,".

(16) In section 68 (visiting of persons in establishments)—

(*a*) in subsection (2), for the words "in the care or under the supervision of the authority under Part II or Part III of this Act" substitute "being looked after by the authority"; and

(*b*) after subsection (3) add—

"(4) In subsection (2) of this section, the reference to children being looked after by a local authority shall be construed in accordance with section 17(6) of the Children (Scotland) Act 1995.".

(17) In section 78 (duty to make contributions in respect of children in care etc.)—

(*a*) in subsection (1)—

(i) for the words "has been received into care under Part II of this Act" substitute "is being looked after by a local authority"; and

(ii) in paragraph (*a*), for the words "his father and mother" substitute "any natural person who has parental responsibilities (within the meaning of section 1(3) of the Children (Scotland) Act 1995) in relation to him"; and

(*b*) for subsection (2) substitute—

"(2) This Part of this Act applies to any supervision requirement which, under paragraph (*a*) of section 70(3) of the Children (Scotland) Act 1995, requires the child concerned to reside in a place or places other than his own home.".

(18) In section 78A (recovery of contributions), in subsection (2)(*a*), for the words "in their care or under their supervision" substitute "looked after by them".

(19) In section 79 (recipients of contributions)—

(*a*) in subsection (1), for the words "in the care or under the supervision of" substitute "looked after by"; and

(*b*) in subsection (2), for the words "having the care or supervision of" substitute "looking after".

(20) In section 80 (enforcement of duty to make contributions)—

(*a*) in subsection (1), for the words from "received" to "requirement" substitute "looked after by a local authority";

(*b*) in subsection (4), for paragraphs (*a*) and (*b*) substitute "throughout the period during which he is looked after by a local authority";

(*c*) in subsection (5), for the words "is the maintainable child's father or mother" substitute ", being a natural person, has parental responsibilities (within the meaning of section 1(3) of the Children (Scotland) Act 1995) in relation to the maintainable child"; and

(*d*) in subsection (7), for the words "having the care or supervision of" substitute "looking after".

(21) In section 82(1) (recovery of arrears of contributions), for the words "having the care or supervision of" substitute "looking after".

(22) In section 83(2) (variation of trusts where person in whose care a child has been residing is for the time being residing in England, Wales or Northern Ireland), for the words "having the care or supervision of" substitute "looking after".

(23) After section 83 insert—

"**References in this Part of this Act to child being looked after**

83A. In this Part of this Act, references to a child being looked after by a local authority shall be construed in accordance with section 17(6) of the Children (Scotland) Act 1995".

(24) In section 86 (adjustments between local authorities as regards certain expenditure)—

(*a*) in subsection (1)—

(i) in paragraph (*a*), after the word "Act" insert ", or under section 25 of the Children (Scotland) Act 1995,"; and

(ii) in paragraph (*b*), for the words from "of services" to "Act" where it occurs for the second time, substitute ", or under or by virtue of Part II of the said Act of 1995, of services and facilities for a person ordinarily so resident (including, in the case of a child, any expenses incurred after he has ceased to be a child, and, in the event of another local authority taking over, under section 25(4) of that Act, the provision of accommodation for him,"; and

(*b*) in subsection (3), after the words "1989" insert "or provided with accommodation under paragraph (*a*) of, or by virtue of paragraph (*c*) of, section 26(1) of the Children (Scotland) Act 1995".

(25) In section 87 (charges which may be made for services and accommodation), in each of subsections (1) and (1A), after the words "1984" there shall be inserted "or under or by virtue of Part II of the Children (Scotland) Act 1995".

(26) Section 88 (duty of parents to notify change of address) shall cease to have effect.

(27) In section 90(1) (power to make regulations, orders or rules), the words "(other than orders under section 52 and 58 and Part V of this Act)" shall cease to have effect.

(28) In section 94(1) (interpretation)—

(*a*) the definition of "children's panel" and of "children's hearing" shall cease to have effect;

(*b*) the definition of "compulsory measures of care" shall cease to have effect;

(*c*) in the definition of "establishment", after the word "Act," insert "or of Part II of the Children (Scotland) Act 1995,";

(*d*) the definition of "guardian" shall cease to have effect;

(*e*) for the definition of "parent" substitute—

" "parent" means either parent or both parents, except that where the child was born out of wedlock and the parents have not subsequently married each other it means the natural mother but not the natural father;";

(*f*) the definition of "place of safety" shall cease to have effect;

(*g*) in the definition of "prescribed"—

(i) in paragraph (*a*), for the words "sections 3 and 36" substitute "section 3"; and

(ii) paragraph (*b*) shall cease to have effect;

(*h*) in the definition of "residential establishment", after the word "Act" insert "or of Part II of the Children (Scotland) Act 1995";

(*i*) the definition of "school age" shall cease to have effect;

(*j*) in the definition of "supervision requirement", for the words "section 44(1) of this Act" substitute "section 70(1) of the Children (Scotland) Act 1995"; and

(*k*) for the definition of "training school" substitute—

" "training school" has the meaning assigned to it by section 180(1) of the Children and Young Persons Act (Northern Ireland) 1968;".

(29) In section 97 (provisions of the Act which extend to England and Wales)—

(*a*) in subsection (1), the words "section 44(1) (except head (*b*)) and (1A)", "section 58" and "Part V" shall cease to have effect; and

(*b*) subsections (2) and (3) shall cease to have effect.

(30) In Schedule 2 (general adaptations of Part IV of Children and Young Persons (Scotland) Act 1937), for paragraph 1 substitute—

"1. Any reference to a child or to a young person shall be construed as a reference to a child as defined in section 93(2)(*b*) of the Children (Scotland) Act 1995.".

Children and Young Persons Act 1969 (c. 54)

16. In Schedule 5 to the Children and Young Persons Act 1969, paragraphs 57 and 65(1) (which relate to the provision of accommodation for children outside Scotland) shall cease to have effect.

Chronically Sick and Disabled Persons Act 1970 (c. 44)

17.—(1) The Chronically Sick and Disabled Persons Act 1970 shall be amended in accordance with this paragraph.

(2) In section 18(2) (information as to accommodation of younger with older persons), for the words "having functions under the Social Work (Scotland) Act 1968" substitute ", in respect of their functions both under the Social Work (Scotland) Act 1968 and under the Children (Scotland) Act 1995,".

(3) In section 29(2) (modifications of provisions of the Act in their application to Scotland)—

(*a*) in paragraph (*a*), at the end add "except that in the case of persons under eighteen years of age such references shall instead be construed as references to duties to disabled children (within the meaning of Chapter I of Part II of the Children (Scotland) Act 1995)"; and

(*b*) for paragraph (*b*) substitute—

"(*b*) any references to services provided under arrangements made by a local authority under the said section 29 shall be construed as references to services for—

(i) such chronically sick or disabled, or such mentally disordered, persons provided by virtue of the said section 12; or

(ii) such disabled children provided under section 23(1) of the said Act of 1995,

by a local authority;".

Sheriff Courts (Scotland) Act 1971 (c. 58)

18.—(1) The Sheriff Courts (Scotland) Act 1971 shall be amended in accordance with this paragraph.

(2) In section 32(1) (power of Court of Session to regulate civil procedure in the sheriff court), after paragraph (*i*) insert—

"(*j*) permitting a person who is not an advocate or solicitor and is not represented by an advocate or solicitor to transmit, whether orally or in writing, the views of a child to the sheriff for the purposes of any enactment which makes provision (however expressed) for the sheriff to have regard to those views;".

(3) In section 37(2A) (remit to Court of Session), for the words "the custody" substitute "parental responsibilities or parental rights (within the meaning of sections 1(3) and 2(4) respectively of the Children (Scotland) Act 1995) in relation to a child or the".

Employment of Children Act 1973 (c. 24)

19. In section 2(2A) of the Employment of Children Act 1973 (supervision by education authorities), for paragraph (*b*) substitute—

"(*b*) in Scotland, if he has parental responsibilities (within the meaning of section 1(3) of the Children (Scotland) Act 1995) in relation to the child or care of him.".

Domicile and Matrimonial Proceedings Act 1973 (c. 45)

20.—(1) The Domicile and Matrimonial Proceedings Act 1973 shall be amended in accordance with this paragraph.

(2) In section 10 (ancillary and collateral orders)—

(*a*) in subsection (1)—

(i) for the words from the beginning to "in connection with" substitute "Where after the commencement of this Act an application is competently made to the Court of Session or to a sheriff court for the making, or the variation or recall, of an order which is ancillary or collateral to";

(ii) the words "as respects the person or property in question" shall cease to have effect; and

(*b*) after subsection (1) insert—

"(1A) For the purposes of subsection (1) above, references to an application for the making, or the variation or recall, of an order are references to the making, or the variation or recall, of an order relating to children, aliment, financial provision on divorce, judicial separation, nullity of marriage or expenses.".

(3) In paragraph 11 of Schedule 3 (sisting of consistorial action)—

(*a*) in sub-paragraph (1), in the definition of "the relevant order", for the words from "made" to the end substitute "relating to aliment or children"; and

(*b*) in sub-paragraph (3), for the words "custody of a child, and the education of a child" substitute "arrangements to be made as to with whom a child is to live, contact with a child, and any other matter relating to parental responsibilities within the meaning of section 1(3) of the Children (Scotland) Act 1995 or parental rights within the meaning of section 2(4) of that Act".

Land Compensation (Scotland) Act 1973 (c. 56)

21.—(1) The Land Compensation (Scotland) Act 1973 shall be amended in accordance with this paragraph.

(2) In section 35(3) (disturbance payments where modification of dwelling required for disabled person), in paragraph (*a*), after "1968" insert "or section 23 of the Children (Scotland) Act 1995".

(3) In section 80(1) (interpretation), in the definition of "disabled person"—

(*a*) after "means" insert "—

(*a*) "; and

(*b*) after "1972" insert "; and

(*b*) a child in need within the meaning of section 93(4)(*a*)(iii) of the Children (Scotland) Act 1995".

Local Government (Scotland) Act 1973 (c. 65)

22.—(1) The Local Government (Scotland) Act 1973 shall be amended in accordance with this paragraph.

(2) In section 56(9) (enactments exempted from repeal by virtue of that section), for paragraph (*d*) substitute—

"(*d*) paragraphs 3 and 8 of Schedule 1 to the Children (Scotland) Act 1995 (Children's Panel Advisory Committees and joint advisory committees);".

(3) In Schedule 25, paragraph 41 shall cease to have effect.

(4) In Schedule 27, paragraphs 185 and 187 shall cease to have effect.

Rehabilitation of Offenders Act 1974 (c. 53)

23.—(1) The Rehabilitation of Offenders Act 1974 shall be amended in accordance with this paragraph.

(2) In section 3 (special provision with respect to certain disposals by children's hearings)—

(*a*) for the words "Social Work (Scotland) Act 1968 is that mentioned in section 32(2)(*g*)" substitute "Children (Scotland) Act 1995 is that mentioned in section 52(2)(i)"; and

(*b*) for the words "to the satisfaction of the sheriff under section 42 of that Act, the acceptance or establishment" substitute "(or deemed established) to the satisfaction of the sheriff under section 68 or 85 of that Act, the acceptance, establishment (or deemed establishment)".

(3) In section 5 (rehabilitation periods for particular sentences)—

(*a*) in subsection (3)(*b*), for the words "43(2) of the Social Work (Scotland) Act 1968" substitute "69(1)(*b*) and (12) of the Children (Scotland) Act 1995";

(*b*) in subsection (5)(*f*), for the words "Social Work (Scotland) Act 1968" substitute "Children (Scotland) Act 1995";

(*c*) in subsection (10), for the words "Social Work (Scotland) Act 1968" substitute "Children (Scotland) Act 1995"; and

(*d*) subsection (10A) shall cease to have effect.

(4) In section 7(2) (limitations on rehabilitation)—

(*a*) for paragraph (*c*) substitute—

"(*c*) in any proceedings relating to parental responsibilities or parental rights (within the meaning of section 1(3) and section 2(4) respectively of the Children (Scotland) Act 1995), guardianship, adoption or the provision by any person of accommodation, care or schooling for children under the age of 18 years;

(*cc*) in any proceedings under Part II of the Children (Scotland) Act 1995;";

(*b*) paragraph (*e*) shall cease to have effect; and

(*c*) the words from "In the application" to the end shall cease to have effect.

Criminal Procedure (Scotland) Act 1975 (c. 21)

24.—(1) The Criminal Procedure (Scotland) Act 1975 shall be amended in accordance with this paragraph.

(2) Section 14 shall cease to have effect.

(3) In section 23 (which, as amended by the Criminal Justice (Scotland) Act 1995, provides for remand of persons under twenty-one in secure accommodation)—

(*a*) in sub-paragraph (i) of paragraph (*a*) of subsection (1), for the words "the Social Work (Scotland) Act 1968" substitute "Part II of the Children (Scotland) Act 1995"; and

(*b*) in paragraph (*a*) of subsection (4), for the words "the Social Work (Scotland) Act 1968" substitute "Part II of the Children (Scotland) Act 1995".

(4) In section 37 (power to order parent to give security for child's good behaviour) after subsection (3) add—

"(4) In this section "parent" means either of the child's parents, if that parent has parental responsibilities or parental rights (within the meaning of sections 1(3) and 2(4) respectively of the Children (Scotland) Act 1995) in relation to him.".

(5) In section 39 (attendance at court of parent of child charged with an offence: solemn procedure)—

(*a*) for subsection (4) substitute—

"(4) The parent or guardian whose attendance shall be required under this section shall be—

(*a*) any parent who has parental responsibilities or parental rights (within the meaning of sections 1(3) and 2(4) respectively of the Children (Scotland) Act 1995) in relation to the child; or

(*b*) the guardian having actual possession and control of him."; and

(*b*) in subsection (5), for the word "custody" substitute "care".

(6) In section 168 (power of court to refer child to reporter where accused convicted of certain offences: solemn proceedings)—

(*a*) in paragraph (*c*), the word "female" shall cease to have effect;

(*b*) in paragraph (ii), after the word "above" insert "or the person in respect of whom the offence so mentioned was committed"; and

(*c*) for the words "Part III of the Social Work (Scotland) Act 1968" substitute "Chapter 3 of Part II of the Children (Scotland) Act 1995".

(7) In section 171(2) (regard to be had to certain provisions in presumption of age of child: solemn proceedings)—

(*a*) for the words "application of the provisions of section 30(1) of the Social Work (Scotland) Act 1968" substitute "definition of a child for the purposes of Chapters 2 and 3 of Part II of the Children (Scotland) Act 1995"; and

(*b*) for the words "under Part V of that Act" substitute "by virtue of regulations made under that Act for the purpose of giving effect to orders made in different parts of the United Kingdom".

(8) In section 177 (directions by court in solemn proceedings as to conveyance of person to residential establishment), the words "provided by a local authority under Part IV of the Social Work (Scotland) Act 1968" shall cease to have effect".

(9) In section 296 (powers of police in relation to children apprehended)—

(*a*) in subsection (3), the words from "and the child" to the end shall cease to have effect; and

(*b*) subsection (4) shall cease to have effect.

(10) In section 304 (power to require parent to give security for child's good behaviour), after subsection (3) add—

"(4) In this section "parent" means either of the child's parents, if that parent has parental responsibilities or parental rights (within the meaning of sections 1(3) and 2(4) respectively of the Children (Scotland) Act 1995) in relation to him.".

(11) In section 307 (attendance at court of parent of child charged with an offence: summary procedure)—

(*a*) for subsection (4) substitute—

"(4) The parent or guardian whose attendance shall be required under this section shall be—

(*a*) any parent who has parental responsibilities or parental rights (within the meaning of sections 1(3) and 2(4) respectively of the Children (Scotland) Act 1995) in relation to the child; or

(*b*) the guardian having actual possession and control of him."; and

(*b*) in subsection (5), for the word "custody" substitute "care".

(12) Section 323 shall cease to have effect.

(13) In section 329 (which, as amended by the Criminal Justice (Scotland) Act 1995, provides for remand of persons under twenty-one in secure accommodation)—

(*a*) in sub-paragraph (i) of paragraph (*a*) of subsection (1), for the words "the Social Work (Scotland) Act 1968" substitute "Part II of the Children (Scotland) Act 1995"; and

(*b*) in paragraph (*a*) of subsection (4), for the words "the Social Work (Scotland) Act 1968" substitute "Part II of the Children (Scotland) Act 1995".

(14) In section 364 (power of court to refer child to reporter where accused convicted of certain offences: summary proceedings)—

(*a*) in paragraph (*c*), the word "female" shall cease to have effect;

(*b*) in paragraph (ii), after the word "above" insert "or the person in respect of whom the offence so mentioned was committed"; and

(*c*) for the words "Part III of the Social Work (Scotland) Act 1968" substitute "Chapter 3 of Part II of the Children (Scotland) Act 1995".

(15) In section 368(2) (regard to be had to certain provisions in presumption of age of child: summary proceedings)—

(*a*) for the words "application of the provisions of section 30(1) of the Social Work (Scotland) Act 1968" substitute "definition of a child for the purposes of Chapters 2 and 3 of Part II of the Children (Scotland) Act 1995"; and

(*b*) for the words "under Part V of that Act" substitute "by virtue of regulations made under that Act for the purpose of giving effect to orders made in different parts of the United Kingdom".

(16) In section 378 (directions by court in summary proceedings as to conveyance of person to residential establishment), the words "provided by a local authority under Part IV of the Social Work (Scotland) Act 1968" shall cease to have effect.

(17) In section 413 (detention of children found guilty in summary proceedings)—

(*a*) in subsection (1), for the words "residential care" substitute "residential accommodation provided under Part II of the Children (Scotland) Act 1995";

(*b*) in subsection (3)—

(i) the definitions of "care" and of "the 1968 Act" shall cease to have effect; and

(ii) after the definition of "the appropriate local authority" insert—
"secure accommodation" has the meaning assigned to it in Part II of the Children (Scotland) Act 1995";

(*c*) after subsection (3) insert the following subsection—
"(3A) Where a child in respect of whom an order is made under this section is detained by the appropriate local authority, that authority shall have the same powers and duties in respect of the child as they would have if he were subject to a supervision requirement.";

(*d*) in subsection (4), the words "within the meaning of the 1968 Act" shall cease to have effect;

(*e*) in subsection (5), the words "(within the meaning of the 1968 Act)" shall cease to have effect;

(*f*) in subsection (6), for the word "care" substitute "accommodation";

(*g*) in subsection (6A), the words "within the meaning of the 1968 Act" shall cease to have effect;

(*h*) in subsection (6B)—
(i) for the words "care of" substitute "accommodation provided by"; and
(ii) for the words "their care" substitute "that accommodation or any other such accommodation provided by that authority"; and

(*i*) in subsection (6C)—
(i) for the word "care", 'where it first occurs', substitute "accommodation provided by the appropriate local authority";
(ii) in paragraph (*a*), for the word "care" substitute "accommodation"; and
(iii) in paragraph (*b*), for the words "residential care" where they first occur substitute "detention in residential accommodation" and for those words where they secondly occur substitute "such detention".

(18) In section 462 (interpretation) in the definition of—

(*a*) "child", for the words "by section 30 of the Social Work (Scotland) Act 1968" substitute "for the purposes of Chapters 2 and 3 of Part II of the Children (Scotland) Act 1995";

(*b*) "children's hearing", for the words "by section 34(1) of the Social Work (Scotland) Act 1968" substitute "in Part II of the Children (Scotland) Act 1995";

(*c*) "place of safety", for the words "section 94(1) of the Social Work (Scotland) Act 1968" substitute "Part II of the Children (Scotland) Act 1995";

(*d*) "residential establishment", for the words from "has" to the end substitute "means an establishment within the meaning of that expression for the purposes of the Social Work (Scotland) Act 1968 or, as the case may be, of Part II of the Children (Scotland) Act 1995"; and

(*e*) "supervision requirement", for the words "by section 44(1) of the Social Work (Scotland) Act 1968" substitute "in Part II of the Children (Scotland) Act 1995".

Local Government (Scotland) Act 1975 (c. 30)

25. In section 23(2) of the Local Government (Scotland) Act 1975 (bodies subject to investigation by Commissioner for Local Administration in Scotland), for paragraph (*d*) substitute—

"(*d*) any Children's Panel Advisory Committee formed under paragraph 3, or joint advisory committee formed under paragraph 8, of Schedule 1 to the Children (Scotland) Act 1995;".

Children Act 1975 (c. 72)

26.—(1) The Children Act 1975 shall be amended in accordance with this paragraph.

(2) Sections 47 to 49 shall cease to have effect.

(3) In section 50 (payments towards maintenance for children), for the words from "custody" to "authority" substitute "a child under the age of sixteen is residing with and being cared for (other than as a foster child) by a person other than a parent of the child, a council constituted under section 2 of the Local Government (Scotland) Act 1994".

(4) In section 51 (restriction on removal of child where applicant has provided home for three years)—

(*a*) in subsection (1), for the words "custody of" substitute "a residence order in relation to";

(*b*) for subsection (2) substitute—

"(2) In any case where subsection (1) applies, and the child—

(*a*) was being looked after by a council constituted under section 2 of the Local Government etc. (Scotland) Act 1994 before he began to have his home with the applicant, and

(*b*) continues to be looked after by such a council,

the council by whom the child is being looked after shall not remove him from the applicant's care and possession except—

(i) with the applicant's consent;

(ii) with the leave of the court; or

(iii) in accordance with an order made, or authority or warrant granted, under Chapter 2 or 3 of Part II of the Children (Scotland) Act 1995."; and

(*c*) at the end add—

"(5) In this section "looked after" and "residence order" have the meanings given respectively by section 17(6) and section 11(2)(*c*) of the Children (Scotland) Act 1995; and "residence order" shall have the same meaning in sections 52 and 53 of this Act.".

(5) In section 52 (return of child taken away in breach of section 51), for the words "custody of" substitute "a residence order in relation to".

(6) Section 53 (custody order on application for adoption in Scotland) shall cease to have effect.

(7) In section 55 (interpretation and extent), for the words "sections 47 to 54", in both places where they occur, substitute "sections 50 to 53".

(8) Sections 73 to 84, 89, 99, 100, 102 and 103 shall cease to have effect.

(9) Section 107 (interpretation), except in so far as subsection (1) defines "adoption society", "child" and "voluntary organisation", shall cease to have effect.

(10) In Schedule 3 (minor and consequential amendments), paragraphs 52 to 57 shall cease to have effect.

Sexual Offences (Scotland) Act 1976 (c. 67)

27.—(1) The Sexual Offences (Scotland) Act 1976 shall be amended in accordance with this paragraph.

(2) In section 11(1) (causing or encouraging seduction, prostitution etc. of girls under sixteen), for the words "the custody" substitute "parental responsibilities (within the meaning of section 1(3) of the Children (Scotland) Act 1995), in relation to, or having".

(3) In section 14(1) (allowing child to be in brothel), for the words "the custody" substitute "parental responsibilities (within the meaning of section 1(3) of the Children (Scotland) Act 1995), in relation to, or having".

Education (Scotland) Act 1980 (c. 44)

28.—(1) The Education (Scotland) Act 1980 shall be amended in accordance with this paragraph.

(2) In section 36(3) (referral to reporter of case of irregular school attendance), for the words from "may" to the end substitute ", where no requirement arises under section 53(1) of the Children (Scotland) Act 1995 to give information about the child to the Principal Reporter, may under this subsection provide the Principal Reporter with such information.".

(3) In section 44—

(*a*) subsection (1) (referral by court to Principal Reporter of case involving offence against section 35) shall cease to have effect; and

(*b*) in subsection (2) (powers of court where no referral to Principal Reporter), for the words "subsection (1) above, make a direction" substitute "section 54(1) of the Children (Scotland) Act 1995, refer the matter to the Principal Reporter".

(4) In section 65B(6) (sending of report in relation to recorded child)—

(*a*) paragraph (*a*) shall cease to have effect; and

(*b*) at the end add—

"and the local authority as education authority shall also ensure that the local authority for the purposes of Part II of the Children (Scotland) Act 1995 receive such a copy.".

(5) In section 135(1) (interpretation)—

(*a*) in the definition of "parent", for the words "the actual custody of" substitute "parental responsibilities (within the meaning of section 1(3) of the Children (Scotland) Act 1995) in relation to, or has care of";

(*b*) the definition of "reporter of the appropriate local authority" shall cease to have effect;

(*c*) for the definition of "residential establishment" substitute—

" "residential establishment" has the meaning given by paragraph (*a*) of the definition of that expression in section 93(1) of the Children (Scotland) Act 1995;"; and

(*d*) for the definition of "supervision requirement" substitute—

" "supervision requirement" has the meaning given by section 70(1) of the said Act of 1995;".

Criminal Justice (Scotland) Act 1980 (c. 62)

29.—(1) The Criminal Justice (Scotland) Act 1980 shall be amended in accordance with this paragraph.

(2) In section 3 (right to have someone informed when arrested or detained), in subsection (5)(*b*), for the words "actual custody" substitute "care".

(3) In Schedule 7, paragraph 21 (which confers jurisdiction on a sheriff for the purposes of certain applications under section 42 of the Social Work (Scotland) Act 1968) shall cease to have effect.

Matrimonial Homes (Family Protection) (Scotland) Act 1981 (c. 59)

30. In section 22 of the Matrimonial Homes (Family Protection) (Scotland) Act 1981 (interpretation), in the definition of "child", for the word "accepted" substitute "treated".

Civil Jurisdiction and Judgments Act 1982 (c. 27)

31. In Schedule 9 to the Civil Jurisdiction and Judgments Act 1982 (excluded proceedings), after paragraph 2 insert—

"2A. Proceedings relating to parental responsibilities within the meaning of section 1(3) of the Children (Scotland) Act 1995 or parental rights within the meaning of section 2(4) of that Act.".

Health and Social Services and Social Security Adjudications Act 1983 (c. 41)

32. In Schedule 2 to the Health and Social Services and Social Security Adjudications Act 1983, paragraphs 4 to 6 and 8 (which amend provisions of the Social Work (Scotland) Act 1968 repealed by this Act) shall cease to have effect.

Mental Health (Scotland) Act 1984 (c. 36)

33.—(1) The Mental Health (Scotland) Act 1984 shall be amended in accordance with this paragraph.

(2) In section 10(1) (application of provisions relating to certain patients suffering from mental disorder)—

(*a*) in paragraph (*a*), sub-paragraph (i), and the word "or" immediately following that sub-paragraph, shall cease to have effect; and

(*b*) after paragraph (*a*) insert—

"(*aa*) a child or young person in relation to whom parental rights and responsibilities have been transferred to a local authority by virtue of section 86(1) of the Children (Scotland) Act 1995;".

(3) In section 54 (local authority to be deemed nearest relative of certain children and young persons), for paragraph (*a*) substitute—

"(*a*) the parental rights and responsibilities in relation to a patient who is a child or young person have been transferred to a local authority by virtue of section 86(1) of the Children (Scotland) Act 1995;".

(4) In section 55 (nearest relative of child under guardianship etc.)—

(*a*) for subsection (1) substitute—

"(1) Where—

(*a*) a guardian has been appointed for a child who has not attained the age of eighteen years; or

(*b*) there is in force a residence order, or a custody order, granted by a court in the United Kingdom, or an analogous order granted by a court outwith the United Kingdom (being an order which is entitled to recognition in Scotland), identifying a person as the person with whom a child under the age of sixteen years is to live,

that guardian or person shall, to the exclusion of any other person, be deemed to be the child's nearest relative.";

(*b*) for subsection (3) substitute—

"(3) In this section "guardian" does not include a guardian under this Part of this Act or, in relation to a child, a guardian whose appointment takes effect under section 7, or on an order under section 11(1), of the Children (Scotland) Act 1995 where there is a parent who has parental responsibilities and parental rights in relation to the child."; and

(*c*) subsection (4) shall cease to have effect.

Child Abduction Act 1984 (c. 37)

34. In section 6 of the Child Abduction Act 1984 (offence in Scotland of person connected with a child taking or sending that child out of United Kingdom)—

(*a*) in subsection (1)(*a*)(i), after the word "person" insert "or naming any person as the person with whom the child is to live";

(*b*) in subsection (2)(*b*), after the words "to him" insert "or naming him as the person with whom the child is to live"; and

(*c*) in subsection (3)(*a*)(i)(*b*), for the word "(whether" substitute "or who is named as the person with whom the child is to live (whether the award is made, or the person so named is named".

Foster Children (Scotland) Act 1984 (c. 56)

35.—(1) The Foster Children (Scotland) Act 1984 shall be amended in accordance with this paragraph.

(2) In section 2 (exceptions to definition of "foster child')—

(*a*) in subsection (1), for the words "in the care of a local authority or a voluntary organisation" substitute "being looked after by a local authority";

(*b*) in subsection (3), the words "within the meaning of the Social Work (Scotland) Act 1968" shall cease to have effect;

(*c*) in subsection (5), the words "; or (*b*) while he is a protected child within the meaning of section 32 of the said Act of 1978" shall cease to have effect; and

(*d*) after subsection (5) add—

"(6) The reference in subsection (1) above to a child being looked after by a local authority shall be construed as if it were a reference to which section 17(6) of the Children (Scotland) Act 1995 applies.".

(3) In section 3(4) (saving for Social Work (Scotland) Act 1968), for the words "the Social Work (Scotland) Act 1968" substitute "Part II of the Children (Scotland) Act 1995".

(4) In section 7(1) (persons disqualified from keeping foster children)—

(*a*) in paragraph (*b*), after the word "1968" insert "or under section 70 of the Children (Scotland) Act 1995"; and

(*b*) after paragraph (*d*) insert—

"(*dd*) his parental rights and parental responsibilities (within the meaning of the Children (Scotland) Act 1995) have been transferred, by an order under section 86(1) of that Act, to a local authority;".

(5) In section 12 (removal of foster children on complaint of local authority), for subsection (5) substitute—

"(5) For the purposes of section 25 of the Children (Scotland) Act 1995 (and for the reason mentioned in subsection (1)(*c*) of that section) a child removed under this section shall be regarded as requiring accommodation.".

(6) In section 13 (which makes provision as to the effect of a refusal to allow a visit to a foster child or to allow premises to be inspected), for the words from "sections" to the end substitute "section 55 of the Children (Scotland) Act 1995 (child assessment orders) as giving the local authority reasonable cause for the suspicion mentioned in subsection (1)(*a*) of that section).

(7) In section 21(1) (interpretation)—

(*a*) in the definition of "residential establishment", after the word "1968" insert "or of Part II of the Children (Scotland) Act 1995"; and

(*b*) for the definition of "supervision requirement", substitute—

" "supervision requirement" has the meaning given by section 70(1) of the Children (Scotland) Act 1995;".

Family Law (Scotland) Act 1985 (c. 37)

36. In section 2 of the Family Law (Scotland) Act 1985 (actions for aliment)—

(*a*) in subsection (2), for paragraph (*c*) substitute—

"(*c*) concerning parental responsibilities or parental rights (within the meaning of sections 1(3) and 2(4) respectively of the Children (Scotland) Act 1995) or guardianship in relation to children;"; and

(*b*) in subsection (4)(*c*), for sub-paragraph (iii) substitute—

"(iii) a person with whom the child lives or who is seeking a residence order (within the meaning of section 11(2)(*c*) of the Children (Scotland) Act 1995) in respect of the child.".

Child Abduction and Custody Act 1985 (c. 60)

37.—(1) The Child Abduction and Custody Act 1985 shall be amended in accordance with this paragraph.

(2) In section 9 (suspension of court's powers in cases of wrongful removal), for paragraph (*d*) substitute—

"(*d*) making, varying or discharging an order under section 86 of the Children (Scotland) Act 1995;".

(3) In section 20 (further provision as regards suspension of court's powers)—

(*a*) for paragraph (*d*) substitute—

"(*d*) in the case of proceedings for, or for the variation or discharge of, a parental responsibilities order under section 86 of the Children (Scotland) Act 1995, make, vary or discharge any such order;"; and

(*b*) in subsection (5), for the words "within the meaning of Part III of the Social Work (Scotland) Act 1968" substitute "(as defined in section 93(1) of the Children (Scotland) Act 1995)".

(4) In section 25 (termination of existing custody orders etc.), subsection (6) shall cease to have effect.

(5) In section 27(4) (interpretation), after the word "Wales" insert "or Scotland".

(6) In Schedule 3 (custody orders)—

(*a*) in paragraph 5—

(i) for the words "custody, care or control of a child or" substitute "residence, custody, care or control of a child or contact with, or";

(ii) in sub-paragraph (iii), for the words "tutory or curatory" substitute "guardianship";

(iii) in sub-paragraph (iv), for the words "16(8), 16A(3) or 18(3) of the Social Work (Scotland) Act 1968" substitute "86 of the Children (Scotland) Act 1995"; and

(iv) for sub-paragraph (v), substitute—

"(v) an order made, or warrant or authorisation granted, under or by virtue of Chapter 2 or 3 of Part II of the Children (Scotland) Act 1995 to remove the child to a place of safety or to secure accommodation, to keep him at such a place or in such accommodation, or to prevent his removal from a place where he is being accommodated (or an order varying or discharging any order, warrant or authorisation so made or granted);";

(*b*) for paragraph 6 substitute—

"6. A supervision requirement made by a children's hearing under section 70 of the Children (Scotland) Act 1995 (whether or not continued under section 73 of that Act) or made by the sheriff under section 51(5)(*c*)(iii) of that Act and any order made by a court in England and Wales or in Northern Ireland if it is an order which, by virtue of section 33(1) of that Act, has effect as if it were such a supervision requirement."; and

(*c*) paragraph 7 shall cease to have effect.

Law Reform (Parent and Child) (Scotland) Act 1986 (c. 9)

38.—(1) The Law Reform (Parent and Child) (Scotland) Act 1986 shall be amend in accordance with this paragraph.

(2) In section 1 (legal equality of children), for subsection (3) substitute—

"(3) Subsection (1) above is subject to subsection (4) below, to section 9(1) of this Act and to section 3(1)(*b*) of the Children (Scotland) Act 1995 (parental responsibilities and parental rights of natural father).".

(3) In section 6(2) (consent to taking of sample of blood), for the words from "guardian" to "custody or" substitute "any person having parental responsibilities (within the meaning of section 1(3) of the Children (Scotland) Act 1995) in relation to him or having".

Disabled Persons (Services, Consultation and Representation) Act 1986 (c. 33)

39.—(1) The Disabled Persons (Services, Consultation and Representation) Act 1986 shall be amended in accordance with this paragraph.

(2) In section 1(3) (regulations with respect to appointment of authorised representatives of disabled persons)—

(*a*) in paragraph (*a*), for the words from the beginning to "appoint" substitute—

"may provide for—

(i) any person who has parental responsibilities in relation to a disabled person under the age of sixteen ("parental responsibilities" having the meaning given by section 1(3) of the Children (Scotland) Act 1995); or

(ii) any other person who is entitled to act as the disabled person's legal representative (as defined in section 15(5) of the Children (Scotland) Act 1995),

to appoint"; and

(*b*) in paragraph (*b*), for the words "in the care of" substitute "looked after by".

(3) In section 2 (rights of certain authorised representatives of disabled persons)—

(*a*) in subsection (3)(*a*), for the words "the words "the parent or guardian of" shall be inserted after the words "if so requested by";" substitute "for the words "by the disabled person" there shall be substituted the words "by any person appointed by virtue of regulations made under section 1(3)(*a*)(i) or (ii) of this Act";"; and

(*b*) in subsection (5), after paragraph (*bb*) insert—

"(*bc*) in Scotland, in accommodation provided by or on behalf of a local authority under Chapter 1 of Part II of the Children (Scotland) Act 1995, or".

(4) In section 13(8)(*b*) (limitation on requirement for assessment of needs)—

(*a*) for the words "his parent" substitute "any person having parental responsibilities in relation to him"; and

(*b*) after the word "request" insert "("parental responsibilities" having the meaning given in section 1 (3) of the Children (Scotland) Act 1995)".

(5) In section 16 (interpretation)—

(*a*) in the definition of "disabled person", for paragraph (*b*) substitute—

"(*b*) in relation to Scotland, means—

(i) in the case of a person aged eighteen or over, one chronically sick or disabled or one suffering from mental disorder (being, in either case, a relevant person for the purposes of section 12 of the Social Work (Scotland) Act 1968); and

(ii) in any other case, a disabled child ("disabled child" being construed in accordance with Chapter 1 of Part II of the Children (Scotland) Act 1995);";

(*b*) in the definition of "guardian", paragraph (*b*) shall cease to have effect;

(*c*) in the definition of "the welfare enactments", in paragraph (*b*), for the words "and sections 7 and 8 of the 1984 Act", substitute ", sections 7 and 8 of the 1984 Act and Chapter 1 of Part II of the Children (Scotland) Act 1995"; and

(*d*) the existing provisions as so amended shall be subsection (1) of the section and at the end of the section there shall be added—

"(2A) In this Act as it applies in relation to Scotland, any reference to a child who is looked after by a local authority shall be construed in accordance with section 17(6) of the Children (Scotland) Act 1995.".

Legal Aid (Scotland) Act 1986 (c. 47)

40. In section 41 of the Legal Aid (Scotland) Act 1986 (interpretation)—

(*a*) in the definition of "legal aid", for the words "Part III of the Social Work (Scotland Act 1968" substitute "Chapter 2 or Chapter 3 of Part II of the Children (Scotland) Act 1995; and

(*b*) in the definition of "person", the existing words from "does" to the end shall be paragraph (*a*) and after that paragraph there shall be added—

"; and

(*b*) includes a person under the age of sixteen years.".

Family Law Act 1986 (c. 55)

41.—(1) The Family Law Act 1986 shall be amended in accordance with this paragraph.

(2) In section 1(1)(*b*) (meaning of "custody order")—

(*a*) for the words "custody, care or control of a child" substitute "residence, custody, care or control of a child, contact with or"; and

(*b*) in sub-paragraph (iv), for the words "for the custody of" substitute "giving parental responsibilities and parental rights in relation to".

(3) In section 13 (jurisdiction ancillary to matrimonial proceedings)—

(*a*) in subsection (2), for the words "under section 9(1) of the Matrimonial Proceedings (Children) Act 1958" substitute "in those proceedings"; and

(*b*) in subsection (4), for the words "under section 9(1) of the Matrimonial Proceedings (Children) Act 1958" substitute "in matrimonial proceedings where the court has refused to grant the principal remedy sought in the proceedings".

(4) In section 15 (duration, variation and recall of orders)—

(*a*) in subsection (1)(*b*), for the words "for the custody of" substitute "relating to the parental responsibilities or parental rights in relation to"; and (*b*) in subsection (4), for the words from the beginning to "above" substitute "Where, by virtue of subsection (1) above, a child is to live with a different person".

(5) In section 17 (orders for delivery of child)—

(*a*) in subsection (3), for the words from "is the child" to "other party" substitute ", although not a child of both parties to the marriage, is a child of the family of those parties"; and

(*b*) at the end of the section add—

"(4) In subsection (3) above, "child of the family" means any child who has been treated by both parties as a child of their family, except a child who has been placed with those parties as foster parents by a local authority or a voluntary organisation.".

(6) For section 26 (recognition: special Scottish rule), substitute—

"**Recognition: special Scottish rule**

26. An order relating to parental responsibilities or parental rights in relation to a child which is made outside the United Kingdom shall be recognised in Scotland if the order was made in the country where the child was habitually resident.".

(7) In section 33(3) (power to order disclosure of child's whereabouts), for the words "for the custody of" substitute "relating to parental responsibilities or parental rights in relation to".

(8) In section 35(3) (power to restrict removal of child from jurisdiction), for the words "whose custody" substitute "whose care".

(9) In section 42 (interpretation)—

(*a*) in subsection (1), before the definition of "part of the United Kingdom" insert—

" "parental responsibilities" and "parental rights" have the meanings respectively given by sections 1(3) and 2(4) of the Children (Scotland) Act 1995;"; and

(*b*) in subsection (4)(*b*), for the words from "of one of the parties" to the end substitute "who has been treated by both parties as a child of their family, except a child who has been with those parties as foster parents by a local authority or a voluntary organisation;".

Housing (Scotland) Act 1987 (c. 26)

42. In section 61 of the Housing (Scotland) Act 1987 (exemption from secure tenant's right to purchase)—

(*a*) in subsection (4)(*f*)(iii) for the words "have left the care of" substitute "as children have been looked after by"; and

(*b*) after subsection (4) add—

"(4A) The reference in subsection (4)(*f*)(iii) above to children looked after by a local authority shall be construed in accordance with section 17(6) of the Children (Scotland) Act 1995.".

Criminal Justice (Scotland) Act 1987 (c. 41)

43. In section 49(4)(*b*) of the Criminal Justice (Scotland) Act 1987 (right to have someone informed when detained), for the words "actual custody" substitute "care".

Civil Evidence (Scotland) Act 1988 (c. 32)

44. In paragraph (*a*) of the definition of "civil proceedings" in section 9 of the Civil Evidence (Scotland) Act 1998 (interpretation)—

(*a*) the words "under section 42 of the Social Work (Scotland) Act 1968" shall cease to have effect;

(*b*) after the word "application" where it first occurs insert "under section 65(7) or (9) of the Children (Scotland) Act 1995";

(*c*) after the word "established," insert "or of an application for a review of such a finding under section 85 of that Act";

(*d*) after the word "application" where it occurs for the second time insert "or, as the case may be, the review"; and

(*e*) for the words "32(2)(*g*)" substitute "52(2)(*i*)".

Court of Session Act 1988 (c. 36)

45. In section 5 of the Court of Session Act 1988 (power to regulate procedure etc. by act of sederunt), after paragraph (*e*) insert—

"(*ee*) to permit a person who is not an advocate or solicitor and is not represented by an advocate or solicitor to transmit, whether orally or in writing, the views of a child to the Court for the purposes of any enactment which makes provision (however expressed) for the Court to have regard to those views;".

School Boards (Scotland) Act 1988 (c. 47)

46. In section 22(2) of the School Boards (Scotland) Act 1988 (interpretation), in the definition of "parent", for the word "custody" substitute "parental responsibilities (within the meaning of section 1(3) of the Children (Scotland) Act 1995) in relation to him or who has care".

Self-Governing Schools etc. (Scotland) Act 1989 (c. 39)

47. In section 80(1) of the Self-Governing Schools etc. (Scotland) Act 1989 (interpretation), in the definition of "parent", for the words "the actual custody" substitute "parental responsibilities (within the meaning of section 1(3) of the Children (Scotland) Act 1995) in relation to him or has care".

Children Act 1989 (c. 41)

48.—(1) The Children Act 1989 shall be amended in accordance with this paragraph.

(2) In section 31(7)(*b*)(iii) (restriction on applications for care and supervision orders), for the words "the Social Work (Scotland) Act 1968" substitute "Part II of the Children (Scotland) Act 1995".

(3) In section 51(7) (enactments which do not apply where a child is granted refuge), for paragraph (*b*) substitute—

"(*b*) sections 82 (recovery of certain fugitive children) and 83 (harbouring) of the Children (Scotland) Act 1995, so far as they apply in relation to anything done in England and Wales;".

(4) In section 79(*e*) (application of Part X to Scotland), for the words from "in whom" to "vested" substitute "having parental responsibilities (within the meaning of section 1(3) of the Children (Scotland) Act 1995) relating to the child".

(5) In Schedule 8 (privately fostered children), in paragraph 3(*b*), for the words "the Social Work (Scotland) Act 1968" substitute "Part II of the Children (Scotland) Act 1995".

Local Government and Housing Act 1989 (c. 42)

49.—(1) The Local Government and Housing Act 1989 shall be amended in accordance with this paragraph.

(2) In section 14(5) (restriction of effect of provisions of that section in relation to certain committees), for paragraph (*d*) substitute—

"(*d*) a Children's Panel Advisory Committee formed under paragraph 3, or a joint advisory committee formed under paragraph 8, of Schedule 1 to the Children (Scotland) Act 1995;".

Access to Health Records Act 1990 (c. 23)

50.—(1) The Access to Health Records Act 1990 shall be amended in accordance with this paragraph.

(2) In section 3(1) (right of access to health records), for paragraphs (*c*) and (*d*) substitute—

"(*cc*) where the patient is a child, a person having parental responsibility for him;".

(3) In section 4 (cases where right of access may be wholly excluded)—

(*a*) in subsection (1), for paragraphs (*a*) and (*b*) substitute "the patient is a child"; and

(*b*) in subsection (2), for the words "(1)(*c*) or (*d*)" substitute "(1)(*cc*)".

(4) In section 5(3) (access to records not to be given where record compiled on basis that access would not be available to particular applicant), for the words "(1)(*c*), (*d*), (*e*) or (*f*)" substitute "(1)(*cc*), (*e*) or (*f*)".

(5) In section 11 (interpretation), for the definition of "parental responsibility" substitute—

" "parental responsibility", in the application of this Act—

(*a*) to England and Wales, has the same meaning as in the Children Act 1989; and

(*b*) to Scotland, shall be construed as a reference to "parental responsibilities" within the meaning given by section 1(3) of the Children (Scotland) Act 1995.".

Horses (Protective Headgear for Young Riders) Act 1990 (c. 25)

51. In section 1(2)(*a*)(ii) (application), of the Horses (Protective Headgear for Young Riders) Act 1990, for the word "custody" substitute "parental responsibilities (within the meaning given by section 1(3) of the Children (Scotland) Act 1995) in relation to, or has".

Child Support Act 1991 (c. 48)

52.—(1) The Child Support Act 1991 shall be amended in accordance with this paragraph.

(2) In section 3(4)(*d*) (interpretation), for the words from "having" to the end substitute "with whom a child is to live by virtue of a residence order under section 11 of the Children (Scotland) Act 1995.".

(3) In section 5(1) (supplemental provisions as respects child support maintenance), the words "(or, in Scotland, parental rights over)", in both places where they occur, shall cease to have effect.

(4) In section 54 (interpretation)—

(*a*) for the definition of "parental responsibility" substitute—

" "parental responsibility", in the application of this Act—

(*a*) to England and Wales, has the same meaning as in the Children Act 1989; and

(*b*) to Scotland, shall be construed as a reference to "parental responsibilities" within the meaning given by section 1(3) of the Children (Scotland) Act 1995;"; and

(*b*) the definition of "parental rights" shall cease to have effect.

Age of Legal Capacity (Scotland) Act 1991 (c. 50)

53.—(1) The Age of Legal Capacity (Scotland) Act 1991 shall be amended in accordance with this paragraph.

(2) In section 1(3) (age of legal capacity)—

(*a*) in sub-paragraph (i) of paragraph (*f*), for the words "who has no guardian or whose guardian" substitute "in relation to whom there is no person entitled to act as his legal representative (within the meaning of Part I of the Children (Scotland) Act 1995), or where there is such a person"; and

(*b*) in paragraph (*g*), for sub-paragraphs (i) and (ii) substitute "exercising parental responsibilities and parental rights (within the meaning of sections 1(3) and 2(4) respectively of the Children (Scotland) Act 1995) in relation to any child of his.".

(3) In section 2 (exceptions to the general rule), after subsection (4) insert—

"(4A) A person under the age of sixteen years shall have legal capacity to instruct a solicitor, in connection with any civil matter, where that person has a general understanding of what it means to do so; and without prejudice to the generality of this subsection a person twelve years of age or more shall be presumed to be of sufficient age and maturity to have such understanding.

(4B) A person who by virtue of subsection (4A) above has legal capacity to instruct a solicitor shall also have legal capacity to sue, or to defend, in any civil proceedings.

(4C) Subsections (4A) and (4B) above are without prejudice to any question of legal capacity arising in connection with any criminal matter.".

(4) In section 5(1) (construction of references to "tutor")—

(*a*) the words "or tutory" shall cease to have effect; and

(*b*) for the words from "the guardian", where they first appear, to the end substitute "a person entitled to act as a child's legal representative (within the meaning of Part I of the Children (Scotland) Act 1995), and any reference to the tutory of such a child shall be construed as a reference to the entitlement to act as a child's legal representative enjoyed by a person by, under or by virtue of the said Part I.".

(5) In section 5(2) (restriction on appointment of guardian to person under sixteen), for the words from "section 3" to the end substitute "section 7 of the Children (Scotland) Act 1995.".

Armed Forces Act 1991 (c. 62)

54.—(1) The Armed Forces Act 1991 shall be amended in accordance with this paragraph.

(2) In paragraph (*f*) of section 17(4) (persons to whom notice of an application for an assessment order must be given)—

(*a*) after the word "order" insert "—

(i) "; and

(*b*) at the end insert "; or

(ii) under section 88 of the Children (Scotland) Act 1995".

(3) In paragraph (*f*) of section 18(7) (persons who may apply for variation etc. of assessment order)—

(*a*) after the word "order" insert "—

(i) "; and

(*b*) at the end insert "; or

(ii) under section 88 of the Children (Scotland) Act 1995".

(4) In section 21(4) (which makes provision in relation to a child returned to the United

Kingdom under a protection order under that Act) for the words "Social Work (Scotland) Act 1968" substitute "Children (Scotland) Act 1995".

(5) In section 23(1) (interpretation)—

(*a*) in the definition of "contact order"—

(i) after the word "meaning" insert "—

(*a*) except in relation to an order made in Scotland,"; and

(ii) at the end, add "; and

(*b*) in relation to an order there made, given by section 11(2)(*d*) of the Children (Scotland) Act 1995."; and

(*b*) in the definition of "parental responsibility"—

(i) after the word "responsibility" " insert "—

(*a*) except in relation to Scotland,"; and

(ii) at the end add "; and

(*b*) in relation to Scotland, shall be construed as a reference to "parental responsibilities" within the meaning given by section 1(3) of the Children (Scotland) Act 1995;".

Tribunals and Inquiries Act 1992 (c. 53)

55. In paragraph 61 in column 2 of Schedule 1 to the Tribunals and Inquiries Act 1992 (which specifies certain tribunals in relation to social work in Scotland)—

(*a*) in sub-paragraph (*a*), for the words "Social Work (Scotland) Act 1968 (c. 49)" substitute "Children (Scotland) Act 1995 (c. 36)"; and

(*b*) in sub-paragraph (*b*), for the words "that Act" substitute "the Social Work (Scotland) Act 1968 (c. 49)".

Prisoners and Criminal Proceedings (Scotland) Act 1993 (c. 9)

56.—(1) The Prisoners and Criminal Proceedings (Scotland) Act 1993 shall be amended in accordance with this paragraph.

(2) In paragraph 8 of Schedule 3 (which provides for the definition of certain expressions in relation to the admission of documentary evidence in criminal proceedings), in the definition of "criminal proceedings"—

(*a*) the words "under section 42 of the Social Work (Scotland) Act 1968" shall cease to have effect;

(*b*) after the word "application" where it appears for the first time insert "under section 65(7)for (9) of the Children (Scotland) Act 1995";

(*c*) after the word "established" insert "or for a review of such a finding under section 85 of that Act"; and

(*d*) after the word "application", where it appears for the second time, insert "or, as the case may be, the review".

(3) In paragraph 1 of Schedule 6 (which provides for the definition of certain expressions in relation to transitional provisions), in the definition of "existing child detainee", for the words "section 30 of the Social Work (Scotland) Act 1968" substitute "section 93(2)(*b*) of the Children (Scotland) Act 1995".

Local Government etc. (Scotland) Act 1994 (c. 39)

57.—(1) The Local Government etc. (Scotland) Act 1994 shall be amended in accordance with this paragraph.

(2) In section 128 (establishment of Scottish Children's Reporter Administration)—

(*a*) in subsection (3), for the words from "the 1968 Act" to the end substitute "the Children (Scotland) Act 1995 and any other enactment conferring functions upon him"; and

(*b*) in subsection (8), for the words from "the 1968 Act" to the end substitute "the Children (Scotland) Act 1995 and any other enactment conferring functions upon him".

(3) In section 130 (annual reports by Principal Reporter) in sub-paragraph (i) of paragraph (*a*) of subsection (1), for the words "the 1968 Act and the Criminal Procedure (Scotland) Act 1975" substitute "the Children (Scotland) Act 1995 and any other enactment (except this Act) conferring functions upon him".

(4) In section 132 (duty of Administration to provide accommodation for children's hearings), for the words "section 34 of the 1968 Act" substitute "section 39 of the Children (Scotland) Act 1995".

Children (Northern Ireland) Order 1995 (SI 1995/755 (N.I. 2))

58. In Article 70(7) of the Children (Northern Ireland) Order 1995 (enactments not to apply where child given refuge), in sub-paragraph (*c*), for the words "section 71 of the Social Work (Scotland) Act 1968" substitute "section 83 of the Children (Scotland) Act 1995".

Civil Evidence (Family Mediation) (Scotland) Act 1995 (c. 6)

59. In section 2 of the Civil Evidence (Family Mediation) (Scotland) Act 1995 (which provides for exceptions to the general inadmissibility of evidence concerning family mediation), in paragraph (*d*)(ii)—

(*a*) for the words "Part III of the Social Work (Scotland) Act 1968" substitute "Chapter 2 or 3 of Part II of the Children (Scotland) Act 1995"; and

(*b*) after the word "hearing" insert—

", before a sheriff or before a justice of the peace;

(iia) on any appeal arising from such proceedings as are mentioned in sub-paragraph (ii) above".

Criminal Justice (Scotland) Act 1995 (c. 20)

60. In section 20 of the Criminal Justice (Scotland) Act 1995 (construction of sections relating to the admissibility of certain evidence)—

(*a*) in subsection (3), in the definition of "criminal proceedings"—

(i) for the words from "under" to "application", where it appears for the first time, substitute "of an application made under Chapter 3 of Part II of the Children (Scotland) Act 1995"; and

(ii) after the word "child" insert "or for a review of such a finding"; and

(*b*) in subsection (5), after the words "1968" insert "or by virtue of Chapter 3 of Part II of the Children (Scotland) Act 1995".

Section 105(5)

SCHEDULE 5

REPEALS

Chapter	Short title	Extent of repeal
8 & 9 Vict. c. 19.	Lands Clauses Consolidation (Scotland) Act 1845.	In section 7, the words "persons under legal disability by reason of nonage" in each place where they occur. In section 67, the words "persons under legal disability by reason of nonage". In section 69, the words "persons under legal disability by reason of nonage".
12 & 13 Vict. c. 51.	Judicial Factors Act 1849.	In section 1, the words from "the word "Guardian" " to "years;". Section 25(2) In section 27, the words "guardians and". In section 31, the word "guadian,". In section 32, the word "guardian,". In section 33, the words "guardians or". In section 34, in both places where it occurs, the word "guardian,". In section 36, the word "guardianships,". In section 37, the word "guardian," In section 40, the word "guardians," in both places where it occurs.
27 & 28 Vict. c. 114.	Improvement of Land Act 1864.	In section 18, the words from "nor shall they" to the end. In section 21, the words from "or if the land-owner" to "minors"; and the words "or circumstance" in both places where they occur.

Chapter	Short title	Extent of repeal
43 & 44 Vict. c. 4.	Judicial Factors (Scotland) Act 1880.	In section 3, in the definition of "judicial factor", the words from "and" to "required".
7 Edw. 7 c. 51.	Sheriff Courts (Scotland) Act 1907.	Section 5(2C). Section 38C.
11 & 12 Geo. 5 c. 58.	Trusts (Scotland) Act 1921.	In section 2, in the definition of "trustee", the words from "guardian" to "years)".
1 Edw. 8 & 1 Geo 6 c. 37.	Children and Young Persons (Scotland) Act 1937.	In section 27, the first paragraph.
1 & 2 Geo. 6 c. 73.	Nursing Homes Registration (Scotland) Act 1938.	In section 4(1)(b)(iii), the words "custody or".
14 & 15 Geo. 6 c. 65.	Reserve and Auxiliary Forces (Protection of Civil Interests) Act 1951.	In section 8(1)(d), the words from "or any order" to the end.
6 & 7 Eliz. 2 c. 40.	Matrimonial Proceedings (Children) Act 1958.	Sections 8 to 10. Section 12.
1965 c. 49.	Registration of Births, Deaths and Marriages (Scotland) Act 1965.	In section 43, in subsection (3) the words from "In this" to the end; and subsection (10)
1968 c. 49.	Social Work (Scotland) Act 1968.	In section 5(1B), before paragraph (o), the word "and". In section 5B(5), the words from "and" at the end of the definition of child to the end of the subsection. Section 6(1)(b)(ii). Sections 15 to 26. Part III, except section 31(1) and (3). Part V. Section 88. In section 90(1), the words "(other than orders under sections 52 and 58 and part V of this Act)". In section 94(1), the definition of "children's panel" and of "children's hearing"; the definitions of "compulsory measures of care", "guardian" and "place of safety"; in the definition of "prescribed", paragraph (b); and the definition of "school age". In section 97, in subsection (1), the words "section 44(1) (except head (b)) and (1A)", "section 58" and "Part V"; and subsections (2) and (3).
1969 c. 54.	Children and Young Persons Act 1969.	In Schedule 5, paragraphs 57 and 65(1).
1972 c. 18.	Maintenance Orders (Reciprocal Enforcement) Act 1972.	Section 4(3).
1972 c. 24.	Social Work (Scotland) Act 1972.	The whole Act.
1973 c. 29	Guardianship Act 1973.	The whole Act.
1973 c. 65.	Local Government (Scotland) Act 1973.	In Schedule 25, paragraph 41. In Schedule 27, paragraphs 185 and 187.
1974 c. 53.	Rehabilitation of Offenders Act 1974.	Section 5(10A). In section 7(2), paragraph (e); and the words from "in the application" to the end.

Chapter	Short title	Extent of repeal
1975 c. 21.	Criminal Procedure (Scotland) Act 1975.	Section 14. In section 168(c), the word "female". In section 177, the words "provided by a local authority under Part IV of the Social Work (Scotland) Act 1968". In section 296, in subsection (3), the words from "and the child" to the end; and subsection (4). Section 323. In section 364(c), the word "female". In section 378, the words "provided by a local authority under Part IV of the Social Work (Scotland) Act 1968". In section 413, in subsection (3), the definitions of "care" and of "the 1968 Act"; in subsection (4), the words "within the meaning of the 1968 Act"; in subsection (5), the words "(within the meaning of the 1968 Act)"; and in subsection (6A), the words "within the meaning of the 1968 Act". In Schedule 9, paragraphs 43 and 44.
1975 c. 72.	Children Act 1975.	Sections 47 to 49. Section 53. Sections 73 to 84. Sections 99 and 100. Section 102. Section 103. Section 105. Section 107, except the definitions, in subsection (1) of "adoption society", "child" and "voluntary organisation". In Schedule 3, paragraphs 52 to 57.
1978 c. 28.	Adoption (Scotland) Act 1978.	In section 1(2), paragraph (a). In section 2, paragraph (d). In section 3(3)(a), the words "including in particular its ability to make provision for children who are free for adoption". Section 8. In section 12, in subsection (3)(b), the words "or by"; and in subsection (4) the word "—(a)" and paragraph (b). In section 14(1), the words from "Subject" to "certain cases)". In section 15, in subsection (1), the words from "Subject" to "certain cases)"; and in subsection (3), the word "natural" wherever it occurs. In section 16, subsection (5). Section 26. In section 28(5), the words "or of a voluntary organisation" and "or the organisation". Sections 32 to 37. In section 51, subsections 6(a) and (7) to (11). In section 60(3), the words "or 51(9)". In section 65(1), in the definition of "guardian", paragraph (b); and in the definition of "local authority", the words ", 35(1)".

Chapter	Short title	Extent of repeal
		In Schedule 3, paragraphs 13, 14 and 15.
1980 c. 44.	Education (Scotland) Act 1980.	Section 44(1). In section 65B(6), paragraph (a). In section 135(1), the definition of "reporter of the appropriate local authority".
1980 c. 62.	Criminal Justice (Scotland) Act 1980.	In Schedule 7, paragraph 21.
1983 c. 33.	Solvent Abuse (Scotland) Act 1983.	The whole Act.
1983 c. 41.	Health and Social Services and Social Security Adjudications Act 1983.	Section 7. Section 8(1) and (4). In Schedule 2, paragraphs 4 to 6 and 8.
1984 c. 15.	Law Reform (Husband and Wife) (Scotland) Act 1984.	Section 3(2).
1984 c. 36.	Mental Health (Scotland) Act 1984.	In section 10(1)(a), sub-pargraph (i); and the word "or" immediately following that sub-paragraph. Section 55(4).
1984 c. 56.	Foster Children (Scotland) Act 1984.	In section 2, in subsection (3), the words "within the meaning of the Social Work (Scotland) Act 1968"; and in subsection (5), the words "; or (b) while he is a protected child within the meaning of section 32 of the said Act of 1978.".
1985 c. 37.	Family Law (Scotland) Act 1985.	In section 21, the words from "or an order" to "child".
1985 c. 60.	Child Abduction and Custody Act 1985.	In section 25, subsection (6). In Schedule 3, paragraph 7.
1986 c. 9.	Law Reform (Parent and Child) (Scotland) Act 1986.	Sections 2 to 4. In section 8, the definitions of "child" and "parental rights". In Schedule 1, paragraph 3.
1986 c. 33.	Disabled Persons (Services, Consultation and Representation) Act 1986.	In section 16, in the definition of "guardian", paragraph (b).
1986 c. 55.	Family Law Act 1986	In section 15(4), the words from "under section" to "1973". In section 17, in subsection (1), the words "Subject to subsection (2) below"; and subsection (2). In section 35(4)(c), the words "custody or".
1988 c. 32.	Civil Evidence (Scotland) Act 1988.	In section 9, in the definition of "civil proceedings", in paragraph (a), the words "under section 42 of the Social Work (Scotland) Act 1968".
1988 c. 36.	Court of Session Act 1988.	Section 20.
1989 c. 41.	Children Act 1989.	In Schedule 13, paragraph 13.
1989 c. 42.	Local Government and Housing Act 1989.	In Schedule 11, paragraph 15.
1991 c. 48.	Child Support Act 1991.	In section 5(1), the words "(or, in Scotland, parental rights over)" in both places where they occur. In section 54, the definition of "parental rights".
1991 c. 50.	Age of Legal Capacity (Scotland) Act 1991.	In section 5(1), the words "or tutory". In section 9, the definition of "parental rights". In Schedule 1, paragaphs 3 to 5 and 7 to 15.

Chapter	Short title	Extent of repeal
1993 c. 9.	Prisoners and Criminal Proceedings (Scotland) Act 1993.	In paragraph 8 of Schedule 3, in the definition of "criminal proceedings", the words "under section 42 of the Social Work (Scotland) Act 1968".
1993 c. 35.	Education Act 1993.	In Schedule 19, paragraph 36.
1994 c. 39.	Local Government etc. (Scotland) Act 1994.	Section 139. In Schedule 13, paragraphs 76(6) and (10) to (25); 92(14)(b)(iii); 100(6)(b)(iv); 103; and 161(7)(c).

[THE NEXT PAGE IS K 401]

Acts of Sederunt

Maintenance Orders Act 1950 (Courts of Summary Jurisdiction) Rules 1951

(S.I. 1951 No. 552)

[28th March 1951]

The Lords of Council and Session, under and by virtue of the powers conferred on them by sections 17, 20, 22, 23, 24, 28 and 29 of the Maintenance Orders Act 1950 and of all other powers competent to them in that behalf, do hereby enact and declare as follows:

1.—(1) This Act of Sederunt may be cited as the Act of Sederunt (Maintenance Orders Act 1950, Courts of Summary Jurisdiction, Rules) 1951, and shall come into operation on the 31st day of March 1951.

(2) In this Act of Sederunt the following expressions shall, unless the context otherwise requires, have the meanings hereby respectively assigned to them:

" The Act " means the Maintenance Orders Act 1950;

" the court of summary jurisdiction in Scotland " means any two or more justices of the peace or any magistrate or magistrates, by whatever name called, officiating in Scotland under the provisions of any general or local police Act and having jurisdiction to make a maintenance order, but does not include the sheriff;

" maintenance order " means a contribution order under section 91 of the Children and Young Persons (Scotland) Act 1937.

(3) The Interpretation Act 1889, shall apply to the interpretation of this Act of Sederunt as it applies to the interpretation of an Act of Parliament.

2.—(1) An application for the registration in a court of summary jurisdiction in England or Northern Ireland under the Act of a maintenance order made by a court of summary jurisdiction in Scotland shall be made to the clerk of the court which made the order by lodging at his office a statutory declaration or affidavit by the applicant (with a copy thereof) setting forth:

(*a*) the name and address of the person liable to make payments under the order;

(*b*) the reason why it is convenient that the order should be enforceable in England or Northern Ireland, as the case may be;

(*c*) the amount of any arrears due under the order; and

(*d*) that the order is not already registered under the Act

(2) If it appears to the clerk that the person liable to make payments under the order resides in England or Northern Ireland and that it is convenient that the order should be enforceable there, he shall send a certified copy of the order and the applicant's declaration or affidavit to the clerk of the court of summary jurisdiction in England or Northern Ireland having jurisdiction where the person liable to make payments under the order appears to be.

(3) Particulars of the order and of the proceedings taken under the last foregoing paragraph for its registration in a court in England or Northern Ireland shall be entered in a book to be kept by the clerk of the court (in this Act of Sederunt referred to as " the Maintenance Orders Register "). The clerk of the court which made the order shall be the prescribed officer to whom notice under subsection (4) of section 17 of the Act of the registration

of the order shall be sent, and on receipt of such notice he shall note in the Maintenance Orders Register that the order has been so registered.

3.—(1) An application to a court of summary jurisdiction in Scotland under subsection (5) of section 22 of the Act to adduce evidence in connection with a maintenance order made by that court and registered in a court in England or Northern Ireland shall be made in writing by or on behalf of the applicant to the clerk of the court.

The provisions of Rule 65 of the First Schedule to the Sheriff Courts (Scotland) Act 1907 shall apply in relation to the taking and recording of any evidence adduced in pursuance of such an application, with the substitution, however, for references to the sheriff of references to the court; and the transcript or summary of the evidence so adduced shall be sent to the clerk of the court in which the order is registered.

(2) The clerk of the court of summary jurisdiction in Scotland by which a maintenance order registered in a court in England or Northern Ireland was made shall be the prescribed officer to whom any transcript or summary of evidence adduced in a court in England or Northern Ireland under subsection (5) of section 22 of the Act in connection with that order shall be sent.

4.—(1) Where a maintenance order made by a court of summary jurisdiction in Scotland and registered in a court in England or Northern Ireland is varied under subsection (1) of section 22 of the Act by the court in which it is registered, the clerk of the court which made the order shall be the prescribed officer to whom under subsection (1) of section 23 of the Act notice of the variation shall be given; and on receipt of such notice he shall enter particulars of the variation in the Maintenance Orders Register.

(2) Where a maintenance order made by a court of summary jurisdiction in Scotland and registered in a court in England or Northern Ireland is discharged or varied by the court which made it, the clerk of that court shall enter particulars of the discharge or variation in the Maintenance Orders Register and shall give notice to the clerk of the court in which the order is registered by sending him a certified copy of the order discharging or varying the maintenance order.

5. An application under subsection (2) of section 24 of the Act in connection with a maintenance order made by a court of summary jurisdiction in Scotland and registered in a court in England or Northern Ireland shall be made to the clerk of the court which made the order by lodging at his office a statutory declaration or affidavit by the person liable to make payments under the order stating the facts on which the application is founded; and if it appears to the clerk that that person has ceased to reside in England or Northern Ireland, as the case may be, the clerk shall send notice to that effect to the clerk of the court in which the order is registered.

6. Where the registration of a maintenance order made by a court of summary jurisdiction in Scotland and registered in a court in England or Northern Ireland is cancelled under subsection (1) or subsection (2) of section 24 of the Act, the clerk of the court which made the order shall be the prescribed officer to whom notice under subsection (3) of that section shall be sent; and on receipt of such notice he shall note in the Maintenance Orders Register that the registration of the order has been so cancelled.

7.—(1) The Maintenance Orders Register required by paragraph (3) of Rule 2 of this Act of Sederunt to be kept by the clerk of a court of summary jurisdiction in Scotland shall be in, or as nearly as may be in, the form set out in the Schedule to this Act of Sederunt.

(2) Any person who satisfies the clerk of a court of summary jurisdiction in Scotland that he is entitled to, or liable to make, payments under a maintenance order made by that court, or a solicitor acting on behalf of any such person or, with the leave of the clerk, any other person, may inspect the Maintenance Orders Register concerned, and any transcript or summary of evidence relating to the order and sent under section 22 of the Act to the clerk of that court, and may take copies of any entry relating to any order registered therein or of any such transcript or summary.

. . . .

Social Work (Sheriff Court Procedure Rules) 1971

(S.I. 1971 No. 92)

[15th January 1971]

The Lords of Council and Session, under and by virtue of the powers conferred on them by section 34 of the Administration of Justice (Scotland) Act 1933 and of all other powers enabling them in that behalf, do by this Act of Sederunt enact and declare the following Rules:—

Part I

General

Citation and commencement

1. These Rules may be cited as the Act of Sederunt (Social Work) (Sheriff Court Procedure Rules) 1971 and shall come into operation on 15th February 1971.

Interpretation

2. (1) In these Rules, unless the context otherwise requires—

"the Act" means the Social Work (Scotland) Act 1968;

"appeal" means an appeal under section 49 of the Act;

"application" means an application under section 42 of the Act;

[1] "child" has the meaning assigned to that term by section 30 (1) of the Act as read with section 30 (3) of the Act;

"parent" has the meaning assigned to that term by section 94 (1) as read with section 30 (2), of the Act;

"reporter" includes deputy reporter;

[2] "safeguarder" means a person appointed under section 34A of the Act for the purposes of safeguarding the interests of a child;

"sheriff clerk" includes sheriff clerk depute.

(2) Unless the context otherwise requires, words and expressions used in these Rules and in Part III of the Act shall have the same meanings in these Rules as they have in the said Part III.

(3) In these Rules any reference, however expressed, to disputed grounds of referral shall be construed as a reference to grounds of referral which form the subject of an application under subsection (2) (*c*) or subsection (7) of section 42 of the Act.

(4) In these Rules any reference to any enactment shall be construed as a reference to that enactment as amended or extended, and as including a reference thereto as applied, by or under any other enactment.

(5) The Interpretation Act 1889 shall apply for the interpretation of these Rules as it applies for the interpretation of an Act of Parliament.

NOTE

[1] As amended by S.I. 1972 No. 1671.
[2] Inserted by S.I. 1985 No. 781.

Schedule of forms

3. The Forms in Schedule 1 to these Rules, or forms to the like effect, shall be used with such variations as circumstances may require and any reference to these Rules to a numbered Form shall, unless the context otherwise requires, be construed as a reference to the Form bearing that number set out in that Schedule.

Part II

Procedure in Application under Section 42 of the Act

Procedure prior to hearing before sheriff

Lodging of application, etc.

4.—(1) Within a period of seven days beginning with the date on which the reporter was directed to make the application, the reporter shall lodge it with the sheriff clerk.

(2) An application by the reporter to the sheriff shall be made in the form as nearly as may be of Form 1.

[1] (3) Where a safeguarder has been appointed by the chairman at the children's hearing, the reporter shall intimate such appointment to the sheriff clerk and shall lodge any report made by the safeguarder, along with the application.

NOTE

[1] Added by S.I. 1985 No. 781.

Appointment of Safeguarder

4A.—(1) The sheriff—

(*a*) shall, as soon as reasonably practicable, consider whether it is necessary to appoint a safeguarder in the proceedings; and

(*b*) may, at any later stage of the proceedings, if he thinks fit, appoint a safeguarder.

(2) A safeguarder appointed by the sheriff under paragraph (1) shall be selected from a panel of persons appointed under the Social Work (Panels of Persons to Safeguard the Interests of Children) (Scotland) Regulations 1984 and may be the same person appointed as safeguarder by the chairman at the children's hearing.

(3) A safeguarder appointed under paragraph (1)—

(*a*) shall be entitled to receive from the reporter, copies of the application, all of the productions in the proceedings and any papers which were before the children's hearing; and

(*b*) may make such enquiries with regard to the proceedings as he considers appropriate.

(4) Without delay and, if practicable, before the hearing on the application, a safeguarder appointed under paragraph (1) shall intimate in writing to the sheriff clerk whether or not he intends to become a party to the proceedings.

(5) Where a safeguarder intimates that he does not intend to become a party to the proceedings he shall, at the same time, report in writing to the sheriff on the extent of his enquiries and his conclusions as to the interests of the child in the proceedings.

(6) The sheriff clerk shall intimate to a safeguarder appointed by the sheriff all subsequent interlocutors in the proceedings whether or not the safeguarder has become a party to those proceedings.

(7) Where a safeguarder becomes a party to the proceedings he shall have all of the powers and duties at common law of a curator *ad litem* in respect of the child and may appear personally in the proceedings or instruct an advocate or a solicitor to appear on his behalf.

(8) Where an advocate or a solicitor is appointed to act as a safeguarder, he shall not act also as an advocate or a solicitor for the child in the proceedings.

NOTE

[1] Inserted by S.I. 1985 No. 781.

Form of warrant for diet in applications

5. As soon as practicable after the lodging of the application, the sheriff clerk shall assign a diet for the hearing of the application and shall issue a warrant in the form as nearly as may be of Form 2.

Citation of child and intimation to parent in applications

6.—(1) After the issue of the first warrant, the reporter shall forthwith cite the child by serving on him a copy of the application and the warrant, together with a citation in the form as nearly as may be of Form 3.

[1] (2) At the same time or as soon as possible thereafter, the reporter shall intimate the hearing of the application to any parent whose whereabouts are known to him by serving on him and to any safeguarder appointed by the sheriff copies of the said application and warrant together with a citation in the form as nearly as may be of Form 4.

(3) An execution of citation or of intimation under this Rule shall be made in the form as nearly as may be of Form 5.

NOTE

[1] As amended by S.I. 1985 No. 781.

Provisions applicable to all stages prior to determination of application

Abandonment of application

[1] **7.** At any stage of the proceedings before the application is determined the reporter may abandon the application, either in whole or insofar as it relates to any ground of referral in dispute, by lodging a minute to that effect or by motion at the hearing and by intimating the abandonment to the child and his parent and to any safeguarder appointed by the sheriff and in that event the sheriff shall dismiss the application and discharge the referral in whole or, as the case may be, in respect of that ground.

NOTE

[1] As amended by S.I. 1985 No. 781.

Conduct of hearing

Hearing of evidence

[1] **8.**—(1) In the case of any condition mentioned in section 32 (2) of the Act, the sheriff shall, in relation to the grounds of referral which are in dispute, hear evidence tendered by or on behalf of the reporter.

(2) At the close of the case for the reporter the sheriff shall, unless he considers that a *prima facie* case has not been made out, tell the child and his parent or representative and any safeguarder appointed that they may give evidence or make a statement and call witnesses.

(3) Where the nature of the case or the evidence to be given is such that in the opinion of the sheriff it is in the interests of the child that the

evidence should not be given in his presence, the sheriff may hear any such evidence in the absence of the child and in that event any safeguarder appointed and the parent or representative of the child shall be permitted to remain in court during the absence of the child.

(4) The sheriff may exclude the parent while the child is giving evidence or making a statement if the sheriff is satisfied that in the special circumstances it is proper so to do:

Provided that the sheriff shall inform the parent of the substance of any allegation made by the child and shall give the parent an opportunity of meeting the allegation by leading evidence or otherwise.

(5) Where evidence in a referral has been heard in part and a safeguarder thereafter intimates under paragraph (4) of rule 4A that he intends to become a party to such proceedings, the sheriff may order the hearing of evidence to be commenced of new.

NOTE

[1] As amended by S.I. 1985 No. 781.

Adjournment for inquiry, etc.

9. Subject to the provisions of section 42(4) of the Act (applications to be heard within twenty-eight days of lodging), in order to allow time for further inquiry into any case or for any other necessary cause, the sheriff on the motion of any party or on his own motion may continue the case for such reasonable time as he may in the circumstances consider necessary.

Miscellaneous

Power of sheriff in making findings as to offences

10. Where the grounds of referral are alleged to constitute an offence or offences or any attempt thereat the sheriff may find on the facts that any offence established by the facts has been committed.

Decision of sheriff

[1] **11.** The sheriff shall give his decision orally at the conclusion of the hearing, and a copy of the interlocutor embodying his decision shall be transmitted by the sheriff clerk to the child and his parents, any safeguarder appointed by the sheriff and, with any productions lodged, to the reporter.

NOTE

[1] As amended by S.I. 1985 No. 781.

Part III

Procedure in Appeals under Section 49 of the Act

Form, etc., of appeals under section 49 of the Act

12.—(1) An appeal to the sheriff under section 49 of the Act shall be made in the form as nearly as may be of Form 6A, 6B or 6C whichever is appropriate.

[1] (2) The appeal shall be signed by the child or his parent or any safeguarder appointed by the chairman at the children's hearing on behalf of the child.

[1] (3) The reporter may lodge answers to the appeal and in that event shall serve a copy thereof on the child or his parent or any safeguarder appointed by the chairman at the children's hearing.

(4) The sheriff clerk shall endorse on the appeal and on any answers thereto the date on which they were lodged.

NOTE
[1] As amended by S.I. 1985 No. 781.

Appointment of safeguarder

[1] **12A.**—(1) The sheriff—

(*a*) shall, as soon as reasonably practicable, consider whether it is necessary to appoint a safeguarder in the appeal; and

(*b*) may, at any later stage of the appeal, if he thinks fit, appoint a safeguarder in the appeal.

(2) Where the appeal has been signed by a safeguarder appointed by the chairman of a children's hearing, the sheriff shall appoint him to act as a safeguarder in the appeal.

(3) A safeguarder appointed by the sheriff under paragraphs (1) or (2) shall be appointed in the same manner, and shall have the same powers and duties, as a safeguarder appointed under rule 4A.

(4) The sheriff clerk shall intimate to a safeguarder appointed by the sheriff all subsequent interlocutors in the appeal whether or not the safeguarder has become a party to the appeal.

(5) Where an advocate or a solicitor is appointed to act as a safeguarder, he shall not act also as an advocate or a solicitor for the child in the appeal.

NOTE
[1] Inserted by S.I. 1985 No. 781.

Warrant for first diet in appeals: intimation to reporter

13. As soon as practicable after the lodging of the appeal, the sheriff clerk shall—

(*a*) assign a diet for the hearing of the appeal;

(*b*) issue a warrant in the form as nearly as may be of Form 7; and

[1] (*c*) send the reporter, and any person other than the appellant who was concerned in the original proceedings, a copy of the appeal and that warrant.

NOTE
[1] As amended by S.I. 1985 No. 781.

Procedure at hearing of appeal

[1] **14.**—(1) Before proceeding in accordance with section 49 (3) of the Act to examine the reporter and the authors or compilers of any reports or statements, the sheriff shall hear the appellant or his representative including any safeguarder appointed.

(2) Where a ground of appeal is an alleged irregularity in the conduct of a case, the sheriff shall, except insofar as the facts stated in the appeal may be admitted by the reporter, hear evidence as to the irregularity tendered by or on behalf of the appellant and any evidence of the reporter relating to it and of any witnesses called by the parties.

(3) Where the nature of the appeal is such that in the opinion of the sheriff the child should not be present during the examination of an author or compiler of any report or at any other stage of the proceedings, the sheriff may exclude the child from the court during that stage; and in that event his parent and any representative of the child including a safeguarder shall be permitted to remain in court during the absence of the child.

(4) Paragraph (4) of Rule 8 above shall apply with any necessary modifications to the hearing of an appeal as it applies to the hearing of evidence in an application.

(5) Where evidence in an appeal has been heard in part and a safeguarder thereafter intimates that he intends to become a party to the appeal, the sheriff may order the hearing of evidence to be commenced of new.

NOTE

[1] As amended by S.I. 1985 No. 781.

Adjournments in appeals

15.—(1) Subject to paragraph (2) below, the sheriff in order to allow time for the lodging of any further report which he may have called for under section 49 (3) of the Act or for any other necessary cause, may on the motion of either party or on his own motion adjourn the hearing of the appeal for such reasonable time as may in the circumstances be necessary.

[1] (2) If the child or his parent or a representative including a safeguarder desires to lead evidence with regard to information disclosed to them in the course of an appeal, the sheriff may adjourn the diet to enable further evidence to be produced.

(3) The adjournment shall be made in the form as nearly as may be of Form 8.

NOTE

[1] As amended by S.I. 1985 No. 781.

Form and transmission of sheriff's decision in appeals

16.—(1) The sheriff shall give his decision orally either at the conclusion of the appeal or on such day as he shall appoint and where he has decided under section 49(5)(*b*) of the Act to remit the case to the children's hearing for reconsideration of their decision, he shall also issue a note of the reasons for his decision.

(2) The interlocutor containing the decision of the sheriff shall be in the form as nearly as may be of Form 9A, 9B or 9C whichever is appropriate.

[1] (3) The sheriff clerk shall transmit a copy of the said interlocutor together with the said note to the reporter and to the appellant and to any safeguarder appointed by the sheriff, and shall also return to the reporter any documents lodged by virtue of section 49(2) or (3) of the Act.

NOTE

[1] As amended by S.I. 1985 No. 781.

PART IV

CITATION AND INTIMATION IN PROCEEDINGS UNDER SECTIONS 42 AND 49 OF THE ACT

Period of notice in giving citation or intimation

17. Citation or intimation authorised or required by these Rules shall be made not later than forty-eight hours, or in the case of postal citation seventy-two hours, before the date of the diet to which the citation or intimation relates: Provided that this Rule shall not apply to the intimation of an appeal against a decision to issue a warrant for the detention of a child.

Warrants and form of citation of witnesses and havers

18.—(1) The following shall be warrants for citation of witnesses and havers, namely:—

(*a*) the warrant for the first diet in an application;

(*b*) a warrant fixing a diet for the continued hearing of an application;

(*c*) any interlocutor certified by the sheriff clerk allowing a proof or for examination of witnesses in an appeal under section 49 of the Act concerned with an irregularity.

(2) In an application or an appeal under section 49 of the Act, witnesses or havers may be cited in the form as nearly as may be of Form 10.

(3) The execution of citation of witnesses and havers shall be in the form as nearly as may be of Form 11.

Modes of citation and intimation

19.—(1) Where a warrant in that behalf has been issued under these Rules, it shall be competent—

(*a*) to cite a child to any diet in an application or an appeal under section 49 of the Act;

(*b*) to cite witnesses to any diet in such an application or in an appeal under the said section 49 concerned with an irregularity in the conduct of a case;

[1] (*c*) to give intimation to a parent and any safeguarder to any diet in an application,

by any mode specified in paragraph (2) below.

(2) It shall be deemed a legal citation of, or intimation to, a person mentioned in paragraph (1) above if the citation or, as the case may be, the intimation is—

(*a*) delivered to him personally; or

(*b*) left for him at his dwelling-house or place of business with some person resident or employed therein; or

(*c*) where it cannot be delivered to him personally and he has no known dwelling-house or place of business, left for him at any other place at which he may at the time be resident; or

(*d*) where he is the master of, or a seaman or person employed in, a vessel, left with a person on board thereof or connected therewith; or

(*e*) sent by post in a registered or recorded delivery letter, to his dwelling-house or place of business, or if he has no known dwelling-house or place of business to any other place in which he may at the time be resident:

Provided that in an application a copy of the application and warrant required to be sent under Rule 6 above shall be sent along with the citation to the child and, along with the intimation (if any) to the parent.

NOTE

[1] As amended by S.I. 1985 No. 781, reading "substitute" as "insert".

Persons who may execute citation and intimation under these Rules

[1] **20.**—(1) Subject to paragraph 3 of this Rule, citation and intimation shall be executed either—

(*a*) by a sheriff officer of the jurisdiction in which the warrant was issued or of the jurisdiction in which the warrant is to be executed; or

(*b*) in the case of postal citation and intimation, by a solicitor or a reporter.

(2) In relation to the citation of witnesses and havers, "reporter" in paragraph (1)(*b*) above means any officer appointed under section 36 of the Act as reporter or as deputy reporter who has held such an appointment for any period or periods amounting to not less than one year, in accordance with the provisions of Regulation 4 of the Reporters (Conduct of Proceedings before the Sheriff) (Scotland) Regulations 1975.

(3) The sheriff clerk shall cite the reporter and the authors or compilers of any reports or statements whom the sheriff may wish to examine under section 49(2) of the Act.

NOTE

[1] Substituted by S.I. 1980 No. 1443.

Production of executions of citation and intimation

21.—(1) The production before the sheriff of—

(*a*) an execution of citation or intimation duly completed in the appropriate form prescribed by these Rules; and

(*b*) additionally, in the case of postal citation, the post office receipt of the registered or recorded delivery letter, shall be sufficient evidence that such citation or intimation, as the case may be, was duly given.

(2) It shall not be necessary to lodge with the sheriff clerk any execution of citation or intimation before a diet for the hearing of an application or appeal.

Endorsation of warrants of citation unnecessary

22. Any warrant of citation, intimation, or service under these Rules may be executed within the jurisdiction of any sheriff without endorsation by the sheriff clerk of that jurisdiction.

PART V

MISCELLANEOUS AND SUPPLEMENTAL

Signature of warrants

23. Warrants, other than warrants under section 42(3) of the Act, may be signed by the sheriff clerk but any warrant may, and a warrant under the said section 42(3) shall, be signed by the sheriff.

Expenses not exigible

24. No expenses shall be awarded in any proceedings to which these Rules apply.

25. [Revoked by S.I. 1985 No. 1976.]

Record of proceedings

26. Proceedings under sections 42 and 49 of the Act shall be conducted summarily.

Exclusion, modification and amendment of certain enactments: Schedule 2

27.—(1) The enactments specified in column (1) of Part I of Schedule 2 to these Rules (being enactments relating to matters with respect to which these Rules are made) shall not, to the extent specified in column (3) of that Part, apply in relation to proceedings in the sheriff court under section 42 or section 49 of the Act.

(2) The provisions of the enactments specified in column (1) of Part II of the said Schedule 2 (being enactments which are specified in column (1) of Part I of that Schedule but which are not excluded from proceedings in the sheriff court under section 42 or section 49 of the Act by virtue of column (3) of that Part) shall have effect in relation to those proceedings subject to the amendments and modifications specified in relation thereto in column (3) of the said Part II.

And the Lords appoint this Act of Sederunt to be inserted in the Books of Sederunt.

Rule 3

SCHEDULE 1

Rule 4(2)

[1] FORM 1

FORM OF APPLICATION TO SHERIFF UNDER SECTION 42 OF THE ACT

Sheriff Court at ( )

Application
under
Section [42(2)(*c*)] [42(7)] of the Social Work (Scotland) Act 1968
by
XY (address), Reporter of (local authority)
in the case of
AB (address)

1. On (date) a children's hearing for (local authority area) gave a direction to the reporter of (local authority) under section [42(2)(*c*)] [42(7)] of the Social Work (Scotland) Act 1968 in respect of AB.

2. A copy of the statement by the reporter of the grounds for the referral of the case of the said AB to the children's hearing is appended hereto together with any report of the safeguarder appointed for the purpose of safeguarding the interests of the child in the proceedings.

3. The said [(AB or BB (address) the [father] [mother] [guardian] of the said AB)] did not accept the grounds of referral so far as relating to conditions to of the statement appended hereto.

OR

The children's hearing were satisfied that the said AB did not understand the explanation of the grounds of referral given under section 42 (1) of the said statement of grounds of referral. The reporter therefore craves the court to find whether or not the grounds of referral not accepted by the child or his parent (or not understood by the child) are established.

....
[Reporter]

NOTE
[1] As amended by S.I. 1985 No. 781.

Rule 5

[1] FORM 2

FORM OF WARRANT FOR DIET IN APPLICATION UNDER SECTION 42 OF THE ACT

(Place and date) The court assigns (date) at (hour) within the (name court) in chambers at (place) for the hearing of the application; appoints the reporter forthwith to cite (name of child), and to intimate to his/her [parents] [guardian] whose whereabouts are known and to (AB) (name and design) the safeguarder appointed by the sheriff, by serving a copy of the application and relative statement of grounds of referral; and grants warrant to cite witnesses and havers.

....
Sheriff Clerk (depute)

NOTE
[1] As amended by S.I. 1985 No. 781.

Rule 6(1)

FORM 3

FORM OF SCHEDULE OF CITATION OF CHILD IN APPLICATION UNDER SECTION 42 OF THE ACT

Under the Social Work (Scotland) Act 1968
(Place, date)

You are hereby served with the foregoing application and warrant. You are required to attend the hearing by the sheriff of the application [within (name court) at (street address) on (date) at (hour)] or [at the time and place specified in the warrant].

....

NOTES

1. If you fail to attend the hearing by the court of the application you may be detained in a place of safety to ensure your attendance at a subsequent hearing.

2. You may ask witnesses to attend the hearing or arrange for their citation by a solicitor or sheriff officer.

Rule 6(2)

[1] FORM 4

FORM OF INTIMATION TO PARENT OR SAFEGUARDER IN APPLICATION UNDER SECTION 42 OF THE ACT

Under the Social Work (Scotland) Act 1968
(Place, date)
(Name of parent or safeguarder) Take notice that the reporter of (local authority) has lodged an application in the Sheriff Court at ( ) for a finding as to [a ground] [grounds] for the referral of the case of (name of child as in application) to a children's hearing. You are hereby served with a copy of the application and warrant. You may attend the hearing [within the said court at (street address) on (date) at (hour)] or [at the time and place specified in the warrant].

....
Reporter*

On behalf of Reporter*

NOTE

You may ask witnesses to attend the hearing or arrange for their citation by a solicitor or sheriff officer.

*delete as appropriate

NOTE

[1] As amended by S.I. 1985 No. 781.

Rule 6(3)

[1] FORM 5

FORM OF EXECUTION OF CITATION OF CHILD AND INTIMATION TO PARENT OR SAFEGUARDER

I reporter* / on behalf of the reporter* of (local authority lawfully cited / gave intimation to* (name of child as in citation* / parent or safeguarder as in intimation*) by [delivering a copy of the foregoing application, warrant and citation* / intimation* to him in person at (place) on (date)].* [leaving a copy of the foregoing application, warrant and citation* / intimation* for him at his dwellinghouse* / place of business at (address) on (date)]*.
[leaving a copy of the foregoing application, warrant and citation* / intimation* for him on board (name of vessel) at (place) on (date)].*
[posting on (date) between the hours of ( ) and ( ) at the (place)
Post Office a copy of the foregoing application, warrant and citation* / intimation* to him in a recorded delivery* / registered* first class service letter and the post office receipt for the said letter accompanies this certificate].*

....

* delete as appropriate

NOTE
[1] As amended by S.I. 1985 No. 781.

Rule 12(1) [1] FORM 6A

FORM OF APPEAL TO SHERIFF UNDER SECTION 49 OF THE ACT AGAINST DECISION OF CHILDREN'S HEARING

Sheriff Court at ( )

Appeal
under
section 49 of the Social Work (Scotland) Act 1968
by
AB (or/and CB, parent of the said AB)
both residing at ( )
against
a decision of the children's hearing for (local authority area) at ( )

1. On (date) the said AB [along with the said CB, his parent] appeared before the children's hearing of (local authority area) at ( ).

[1] 2. DE (design) was appointed to act as safeguarder [*or* No safeguarder was appointed].

3. The grounds for the referral of the case stated by the reporter [were accepted by the appellant(s)] [were established to the satisfaction of the sheriff] at (place) on (date). A copy of the statement of the grounds of referral is attached hereto, or [A supervision requirement, made on (date) in respect of the said AB, was under review by the children's hearing. The supervision requirement was to the effect that (state terms of requirement).]

4. The children's hearing decided that the said AB was in (continuing) need of compulsory measures of care and ordered (state the terms of the decision in the report of the proceedings of the children's hearing).

5. The measures prescribed by the supervision requirement are not appropriate in all the circumstances in respect that (state shortly the reasons for this view) (or if appeal is on a point of law or on grounds of irregularity state briefly that point or the facts which constitute the irregularity).

6. The said AB and/or CB appeals to the sheriff against the said decision.

(signed by appellant(s) or solicitor)

NOTE
[1] As amended by S.I. 1985 No. 781.

Rule 12(1) [1] FORM 6B

FORM OF APPEAL TO SHERIFF UNDER SECTION 49 OF THE ACT AGAINST ISSUE OF WARRANT BY CHILDREN'S HEARING

Sheriff Court at ( )

Appeal
under
section 49 of the Social Work (Scotland) Act 1968
by
AB (or/and CB, parent of the said AB)
both residing at ( )
against

a decision by a children's hearing for (local authority area) at ( ) to issue a warrant for the detention of the said AB.

1. On (date) the said AB was apprehended and detained at (place) on a warrant issued by the children's hearing at ( ) [under section [ ] of the Social Work (Scotland) Act 1968].

[1] 2. DE (design) was appointed to act as safeguarder [or No safeguarder was appointed.]

3. The said warrant is unnecessary because (state reasons).

4. The said AB (or/and CB) appeals to the sheriff to recall the said warrant.

(signed by appellant(s) or solicitor)

NOTE

[1] As amended by S.I. 1985 No. 781.

Rule 12(1)

[1] FORM 6C

FORM OF APPEAL TO SHERIFF UNDER SECTION 49 OF THE ACT AGAINST ISSUE OF WARRANT BY CHILDREN'S HEARING

SHERIFF COURT AT ( )

APPEAL
UNDER
SECTION 49 OF THE SOCIAL WORK (SCOTLAND) ACT 1968
by
AB (or/and CB, parent of the said AB)
both residing at ( )
against
a decision by a children's hearing for (local authority area) at ( ) to issue a warrant for the detention of the said AB.

1. On (date) a children's hearing for (local authority area) made a requirement under section 43(4) of the Social Work (Scotland) Act 1968. [A copy of] the said requirement is appended hereto.

2. DE (design) was appointed to act as safeguarder [or No safeguarder was appointed].

3. The said requirement is unnecessary because (state reasons).

4. The said AB (or/and CB) appeals to the sheriff to [state remedy].

(signed by appellant(s) or solicitor).

NOTE

[1] As amended by S.I. 1985 No. 781.

Rule 13

[1] FORM 7

FORM OF WARRANT (ASSIGNMENT OF FIRST DIET AND WARRANT OF INTIMATION) IN APPEAL UNDER SECTION 49 OF THE ACT

(Place and date) The court assigns (date) at (hour) within the (name court) in chambers at (place) for the hearing of the appeal: appoints the appellant(s) forthwith to intimate the appeal and the diet to the reporter and to (name and design) the safeguarder appointed by the sheriff.

Sheriff Clerk (Depute)

NOTE

[1] As amended by S.I. 1985 No. 781.

Rule 15(3)

FORM 8

FORM OF INTERLOCUTOR CONTINUING HEARING OF APPEAL

(Place and date) The Sheriff Substitute, having heard the appellant(s)' (solicitor) and the reporter on the appeal, and having considered the documents produced, adjourns the diet to (date) at (hour) to enable (e.g. the parties to enable further reports to be obtained or the parties to lead (further) evidence).

....

Sheriff Clerk

Rule 16(2)

FORMS 9A, 9B AND 9C

FORMS OF INTERLOCUTORS CONTAINING DECISIONS OF SHERIFF IN APPEALS UNDER SECTION 49 OF THE ACT

FORM 9A

DECISION UNDER SECTION 49(4) AND (6)

(Place, date) The Sheriff Substitute, being satisfied that the appeal has failed, confirms the decision of the children's hearing; [where necessary, add, being further satisfied that the appeal is frivolous, orders that no appeal against a decision by a children's hearing, to continue the supervision requirement, made on a subsequent review shall lie until the expiration of a period of twelve months beginning with this date].

(Signed by sheriff)

....

FORM 9B

DECISION UNDER SECTION 49(5)(*a*)

(Place, date) The Sheriff Substitute, being satisfied that the decision of the children's hearing to issue the warrant is not justified in all the circumstances of the case, allows the appeal and recalls the warrant.

(Signed by sheriff)

....

FORM 9C

DECISION UNDER SECTION 49(5)(*b*)

(Place, date) The Sheriff Substitute, being satisfied that the decision of the children's hearing is not justified in all the circumstances of the case [for the reasons given in the attached Note, remits the case to the children's hearing for reconsideration of their decision] or [discharges the child from any further hearing or other proceedings in relation to the grounds for the referral of the case.]

(Signed by sheriff)

....

Rule 18(2)

[1] FORM 10

FORM OF SCHEDULE OF CITATION OF WITNESS OR HAVER

Under the Social Work (Scotland) Act 1968
(Place, date, add if necessary hour)
(Name of witness), you are hereby required to attend at the Sheriff Court House at (street address) in chambers on ( ), the ( ) day of ( ) at o'clock noon, to give evidence in the hearing of [an application by the reporter of (local authority) to the sheriff for a finding as to grounds for the referral of the case of (name of child) to a children's hearing] OR [an appeal to the sheriff against a decision of a children's hearing in a case of (name of child)].
[if necessary, add—You are required to bring with you (specify documents.)]

....
Sheriff Officer*
Solicitor*
Reporter*

*delete as appropriate

NOTE
[1] As amended by S.I. 1980 No. 1443.

Rule 18(3)

[1] FORM 11

FORM OF EXECUTION OF CITATION OF WITNESSES AND HAVERS

reporter of (local authority)*
on behalf of reporter of (local authority)*

(name of person who executed citation)
sheriff officer*
solicitor*

lawfully cited (name of witness) by—
[delivering a copy of the foregoing citation to him in person at (place) on (date)].*

[leaving a copy of the foregoing citation for him at his dwelling-house* / place of business* at (address on (date)].*

[leaving a copy of the foregoing citation for him on board (name of vessel) at (place) on (date)].*

[Sending a copy of the foregoing citation to him in a recorded delivery* / registered* letter and the post office receipt for the said letter accompanies this certificate].*

(to be signed by person who executed the citation)
Sheriff Officer*
Solicitor*
Reporter*

*delete as appropriate

NOTE
[1] Substituted by S.I. 1980 No. 1443.

FORM 12

[Revoked by S.I. 1985 No. 1976.]

Rule 27(1)

SCHEDULE 2

PART 1

(Exclusion of enactments relating to matters with respect to which these Rules are made)

Column (1) Enactment Excluded	Column (2) References	Column (3) Extent and exclusion
The Citation Act 1540	1540 c. 10	The whole Act
The Citation Act 1592	1592 c. 59	The whole Act
The Citation Act 1686	1686 c. 5	The whole Act
The Citation Act 1693	1693 c. 21	The whole Act
The Debtors (Scotland) Act 1838, section 32 (as explained by the Citation (Scotland) Act 1846)	1838 c. 114	The words "and that, excepting in the case of poindings, more than one witness shall not be required for service or execution thereof."
The Citation Amendment (Scotland) Act 1882 as amended	1882 c. 77	The whole Act except paragraph (4) of section 4.
The Sheriff Courts (Scotland) Act 1907, section 39 and Schedule I	1907 c. 51	The whole section; the whole schedule except Rule 73[1] (second diligence against witness failing to attend).

Rule 27(2)

PART II

(Modification and amendment of enactments in their application to proceedings under section 42 or section 49 of the Act)

Column (1) Enactment modified or amended	Column (2) References	Column (3) Modifications and Amendments
The Citation Amendment (Scotland) Act 1882, section 4, paragraph (4) (which makes provision for letters containing citations, etc., to be returned to the court by the post office and for connected purposes)	1882 c. 77	For the words "such registered letter" there shall be substituted the words "a letter containing a citation or intimation from a sheriff court in proceedings under section 42 or section 49 of the Social Work (Scotland) Act 1968"; [and for the words "in the case of a party" there shall be substituted the words "in the case of a child within the meaning of Part III of the said Act of 1968."]

Column (1) Enactment modified or amended	Column (2) References	Column (3) Modifications and Amendments
The Sheriff Courts (Scotland) Act 1907, Schedule 1, Rule 73,[1] (second diligence against witness failing to attend)	1907 c. 51	The word "further" shall be omitted; and for the words "said witness or haver" there shall be substituted the words "or witness or haver cited under the Act of Sederunt (Social Work) (Sheriff Court Procedure Rules) 1971".

NOTE

[1] The relevant rule since Schedule 1 was substituted by S.I. 1983 No. 747 is rule 76, but the wording is not identical.

Reporter's Duties and Transmission of Information, etc. (Scotland) Rules 1971

(S.I. 1971 No. 525)

[24th March 1971]

In exercise of the powers conferred on me by sections 36(8) and 45 of the Social Work (Scotland) Act 1968, and of all other powers enabling me in that behalf, I hereby make the following rules:—

Part I

General

Citation and commencement

1. These rules may be cited as the Reporter's Duties and Transmission of Information, etc. (Scotland) Rules 1971 and shall come into operation on 15th April 1971.

Interpretation

2.—(1) In these rules, unless the context otherwise requires—

"the Act" means the Social Work (Scotland) Act 1968;

"the Act of 1937" means the Children and Young Persons (Scotland) Act 1937;

"child" except in rule 9 has the meaning assigned to that term by section 30(1) of the Act;

"enactment" includes any order, regulation or other instrument made under the Act;

"parent" has the meaning assigned to that term by section 30(2) of the Act;

"reporter" includes "deputy reporter".

(2) Any reference in these rules to any enactment shall be construed as a reference to that enactment as amended or extended, and as including a reference thereto as applied, by or under any other enactment.

(3) In these rules, unless the context otherwise requires, any reference in relation to a reporter—

(*a*) to the local authority shall be construed as a reference to the local authority which appointed the reporter;

(*b*) to a children's hearing shall be construed as a reference to a children's hearing for the area of that local authority.

(4) The Interpretation Act 1889 shall apply for the interpretation of these rules as it applies for the interpretation of an Act of Parliament.

Part II

Reporter's Duties

Recording and transmission of information at beginning of case

3.—(1) Where a reporter receives information from any source of a case which may require a children's hearing to be arranged, he shall keep or cause to be kept a record of the name and address of the person from whom the information was received.

(2) Where the reporter decides that no further action on the case is required as mentioned in subsection (1) of section 39 of the Act, or refers the case to the local authority under subsection (2) of that section, or arranges a children's hearing under subsection (3) of that section, he shall—

(*a*) keep or cause to be kept a record of that decision or, as the case may be, that course of action; and

(*b*) if the said information was received from a local authority or an officer of a police force, notify that local authority or as the case may be the chief constable of that police force accordingly.

Liberation by reporter of child in interim detention

4.—(1) Where a reporter—

(*a*) has been informed in accordance with section 37(2) of the Act that a child is detained in a place of safety under either—

(i) section 40 of the Act of 1937 (interim detention of child under arrest) and the reporter has been informed in accordance with subsection (3) of that section that it has been decided not to proceed with the charge against the child; or

(ii) section 47(1) of the Act of 1937 (interim detention of child assaulted etc. or in respect of whom certain offences committed); or

(iii) section 37(2) of the Act (interim detention of child prevented by vagrant from receiving education or who has taken refuge in a place of safety etc.); and

(*b*) is satisfied that the further detention of the child is unnecessary in his interest and has no reason to believe that the child will run away during the investigation of his case,

the reporter may authorise the person in charge of the place of safety to liberate the child.

(2) Where the reporter so authorises he shall give notification—

(*a*) to the person in charge of the place of safety and such notification shall be as nearly as may be in the form set out in the schedule to these rules and

(*b*) to the parent of the child.

Notification of children's hearing to director of social work

5. Where the reporter arranges any children's hearing he shall notify the director of social work for the local authority area in which the children's hearing is sitting of the date, time and place of the hearing, and of the names, date of birth and address so far as is known of the child whose case is to be considered.

Transmission of information etc., on disposal of case by children's hearing

6.—(1) Where a children's hearing have made a decision disposing of the case of a child on referral or at a review of a supervision requirement, the reporter shall as soon as reasonably practicable give notice of the said decision—

(*a*) to the local authority; and

(*b*) where the information leading to the investigation of the case of the child was given by an officer of a police force, to the chief constable of that police force.

(2) Where the said decision was to make, to continue or to vary a supervision requirement, the reporter shall send a copy of that requirement as so made, continued or varied to—

(*a*) the local authority; and

(*b*) any person, not being the local authority, responsible for the child under the requirement as so made, continued or varied.

(3) Where the said decision was to terminate or to vary a supervision requirement and by virtue of such termination or variation a person ceases to be responsible for the child under that requirement, the reporter shall as soon as reasonably practicable give notice of the said decision to the said person.

(4) Where the said decision was—

(*a*) to make a supervision requirement in relation to a child who has attained the age of 16 years; or

(*b*) to terminate a supervision requirement relating to such a child.

the reporter shall as soon as reasonably practicable give notice of the said decision to the chief constable of the police area in which the local authority area is situated and if the child resides outwith the said police area, to the chief constable of the police area in which the child resides.

(5) In this rule any reference, however expressed, to a person responsible for a child under a supervision requirement shall be construed as a reference—

(*a*) in the case of a requirement under section 44(1)(*a*) of the Act, to any person under whose supervision the requirement places the child and, where a condition as to the place where a child is to reside is imposed, any person in charge of the child by virtue of that condition;

(*b*) in the case of a supervision requirement under section 44(1)(*b*) of the Act, to the person in charge of the residential establishment named in the supervision requirement.

Transmission of information and returns

7. The reporter shall make such reports and returns and give such information as the Secretary of State may direct.

Notification of 16th birthday of child subject to supervision requirement

8. When a child subject to a supervision requirement attains the age of 16 years, the reporter shall as soon as reasonably practicable give notice of that fact to the chief constable of the police area in which the local authority area is situated and, if the child resides outwith the said police area, to the chief constable of the police area in which the child resides.

Reporter to arrange hearings in transitional cases

9. [Spent.]

Reporter to arrange periodic reviews of supervision requirements

10. When a supervision requirement has not been reviewed by a children's hearing before the expiry of the period of nine months commencing on the date of the making of the requirement or the date of the last review of the requirement whichever date last occurred (in this rule called "the relevant date"), the reporter shall arrange for a children's hearing to sit before the expiry of the period of one year commencing on the relevant date to review that requirement.

PART III

TRANSMISSION OF INFORMATION ABOUT AND CONVEYANCE OF CHILD SUBJECT TO A SUPERVISION REQUIREMENT

Transmission by local authority of information on child subject to supervision requirement

11.—(1) Where—

(*a*) in any case a children's hearing have made, continued or varied a supervision requirement; and

(*b*) a person not being the local authority is responsible for a child under that requirement; and

(*c*) it appears to the local authority that the report on the child and his social background used by the children's hearing in their consideration of the case would assist the said person in the care and supervision of the child,

the local authority shall, as soon as reasonably practicable after they receive notice under rule 6 above of the making, continuation or variation of the requirement, send a copy of the said report to the said person.

(2) Where at any time while the said supervision requirement is in force it appears to the local authority that any information in their possession would assist the said person as aforesaid, they shall make that information available to him.

(3) In this rule any reference, however expressed, to a person responsible for a child under a supervision requirement has the same meaning as in rule 6(5) above.

Temporary accommodation of child subject to supervision requirement

12.—(1) Where—

(*a*) a children's hearing have made or varied a supervision requirement; and

(*b*) a child is required to reside in a residential establishment or other place specified in the requirement; but

(*c*) the local authority are unable forthwith to make arrangements for his reception in that establishment or place,

the local authority may arrange for the child to be temporarily accommodated in some suitable place, other than the establishment or place specified as aforesaid, for any period not exceeding the period of 21 days commencing on the date of the making or variation of the requirement.

(2) If it appears to the local authority that they will be unable to make such arrangements as are mentioned in paragraph (1)(*c*) above before the expiry of the said period of 21 days, they shall, before that period has expired, recommend to the reporter that a children's hearing review the supervision requirement and where the authority so recommend—

(*a*) the reporter shall arrange a children's hearing to sit to review the said requirement as soon as may be and in any event before the expiry of the period of seven days commencing on the date on which he received the recommendation; and

(*b*) where the date of the sitting of the children's hearing arranged under head (*a*) of this paragraph occurs after the expiry of the period of 21 days mentioned in paragraph (1) above, that period shall be deemed to extend until that date for the purpose of that paragraph.

Conveyance by local authority of child to residential establishment etc.

13.—(1) Whenever it is necessary to convey a child to a residential establishment or other place in which he is required to reside by virtue of a supervision requirement, it shall be the duty of the local authority to ensure that the child is conveyed to that residential establishment or place and for that purpose the authority may place the child under the control of any person authorised by them.

(2) Any person having control over the said child under this rule shall have all the powers, protection and privileges of a constable, so far as these are necessary for the control of the child, while he is conveying the said child to the said residential establishment or other place.

Rule 4 SCHEDULE

Form of Notice by Reporter Authorising Liberaton of Child from Interim Detention

I, (*full name of reporter*) reporter of (*local authority*) being satisfed that the further detention of (*name of child*) in (*name and address of place of safety*), a place of safety, is unnecessary in his interest and having no reason to believe that the said child will run away during the investigation of his case, hereby authorised the person in charge of the place of safety in which the child is detained to liberate him.

Dated the day of

....
(Reporter)

Maintenance Orders (Reciprocal Enforcement) Act 1972 Rules 1974

(S.I. 1974 No. 939)

[29th May 1974]

Part I

General

1.—(1) This Act of Sederunt may be cited as the Act of Sederunt (Maintenance Orders (Reciprocal Enforcement) Act 1972 Rules) 1974, and shall come into operation on the first day of July 1974.

(2) In this Act of Sederunt the following expressions shall, unless the context otherwise requires, have the meanings hereby respectively assigned to them:–

"the Act" means the Maintenance Orders (Reciprocal Enforcement) Act 1972;

[THE NEXT PAGE IS K 413]

(c) a statement signed by the applicant or his solicitor giving such information as to the whereabouts of the payer as he possesses;

(d) a statement signed by the applicant or his solicitor giving such information as the applicant possesses for facilitating the identificaion of the payer;

(e) where available, a photograph of the payer.

(2) On receipt of such application and documents the Sheriff Clerk shall send to the Secretary of State the documents specified in section 2(4) of the Act.

Provision in relation to transmission of provisional maintenance orders made by Sheriff Court for enforcement in a reciprocating country.

11. A certificate signed by the Sheriff Clerk in terms of section 3(5)(*c*) of the Act as read with section 4(6) thereof shall also be signed by the Sheriff.

Provision in relation to revocation of provisional maintenance order made by Sheriff.

12. Where before a provisional order is confirmed the Sheriff Court which made that order has considered evidence under section 5(9) of the Act and if, having done so, it appears to it that the order ought not to have been made, the Sheriff Clerk shall write by recorded delivery letter to the person on whose application the order was made, advising him that he may consider that evidence, make representations with respect to it and adduce further evidence. If he wishes to make representations he shall lodge within fourteen days of the date of posting of the letter from the Sheriff Clerk a minute narrating the representations and the further evidence which he intends to adduce. On the expiry of the said period of fourteen days the cause shall be enrolled before the Sheriff.

Provision in relation to registration of orders

13.—[1] (1) The Sheriff Clerk shall keep a register called "The Maintenance Orders (Reciprocal Enforcement) Act 1972 Register" for the purpose of registering such orders as the Act or any other enactment directs the prescribed officer to register. Every entry registering an order shall specify the section of the Act or any other enactment under which the order in question is registered. When a registered order is varied, revoked or cancelled, the Sheriff Clerk shall make an appropriate entry against the entry registering the order.

(2) Any person who satisfies the Sheriff Clerk that he is entitled to or liable to make payments under any order which has been registered or any solicitor acting on behalf of such person or any other person with leave of the Sheriff Clerk may inspect the Maintenance Orders (Reciprocal Enforcement) Act 1972 Register.

NOTE

[1] As amended by S.I. 1986 No. 1947.

Provisions in relation to entering appearance

14.—(1) Where the Act provides that on intimation to a payer or payee of the receipt by the Court of an order or a provisional order the payer or payee is to enter appearance within a prescribed period, the said period shall be a period of fourteen days from the date of the posting of the said intimation.

(2) To enter appearance in terms of section 5(6) of the Act, as substituted for Scotland by section 5(10)(*b*) thereof, in respect of a provisional order received by the Court in terms of section 5(5) thereof, the payee shall lodge an application in such a form as to enable the Court to proceed as if an application under section 5 thereof for the variation or revocation of the maintenance order in question had been made to it.

(3) To enter appearance in terms of section 7(4) of the Act, as substituted for Scotland by section 7(7)(*a*) thereof, in respect of a provisional order received by the Court in terms of section 7(2) thereof, the payer shall lodge an application in such a form as to enable the Court to proceed as if an application for a maintenance order against the payer under the provisional order had been made to it in accordance with the procedure and practice in civil proceedings in the Sheriff Court.

(4) To enter appearance in terms of section 9(7) of the Act, as substituted for Scotland by section 9(11)(*b*) thereof, in respect of a provisional order received by the Court in terms of section 9(6) thereof, the payer shall lodge an application in such a form as to enable the Court to proceed as if an application under section 9 thereof for the variation of the registered order had been made to it.

Provision in relation to revocation of registered order

15. Where a registered order is revoked in the circumstances set out in section 10(1) of the Act the payee or his solicitor shall provide the Sheriff Clerk so far as is possible with the certificate and statements referred to in section 10(7) of the Act.

Authentication of documents

16. Where the Act provides that a document is to be authenticated in a prescribed manner it shall be authenticated by a certificate signed by the Sheriff Clerk declaring that the document is authentic.

Evidence

17.—[1] (1) Where any request is made by or on behalf of the Court in a reciprocating country in terms of section 14 of the Act or by the Secretary of State in terms of section 38 thereof such evidence shall be taken before the Sheriff of the Sheriffdom in which the witness resides and shall be taken down by the Sheriff or by the Sheriff Clerk or shorthand writer nominated by the Sheriff to whom the oath *de fideli administratione* shall be administered, and evidence may be recorded in narrative form or by question and answer as the Sheriff shall direct, and the extended notes of evidence certified by such Sheriff Clerk or shorthand writer shall be the notes of the oral evidence taken.

(2) In the event of a provisional order being made under sections 4, 5 or 9 of the Act the applicant or his solicitor shall provide the Sheriff Clerk with a copy of the extended notes of evidence where evidence has been taken by a shorthand writer.

NOTE
[1] As amended by S.I. 1975 No. 475.

Application under sections 4, 5, 9 and 20 of the Act

18. Subject to the provisions of the Act—

(*a*) an application for a provisional order under section 4 of the Act and an application under sections 5 and 9 of the Act for variation or revocation of the maintenance order referred to in section 5(1) thereof shall be made by bringing a new action in accordance with the procedure and practice in civil proceedings in the Sheriff Court.

(*b*) an application under section 20 of the Act for leave to enforce the payment of any arrears due under a maintenance order registered in Scotland shall be made by lodging a minute in the process.

Reciprocal Enforcement of Maintenance Orders (Republic of Ireland) Order 1974 Rules 1975

(S.I. 1975 No. 475)

[19th March 1975]

Part I

General

1.—(1) This Act of Sederunt may be cited as the Act of Sederunt (Reciprocal Enforcement of Maintenance Orders (Republic of Ireland) Order 1974 Rules) 1975 and shall come into operation on the 2nd day of April 1975.

(2) In this Act of Sederunt the following expressions shall, unless the context otherwise requires, have the meanings hereby respectively assigned to them—" the Act " means the Maintenance Orders (Reciprocal Enforcement) Act 1972 as amended by the Reciprocal Enforcement of Maintenance Orders (Republic of Ireland) Order 1974; " Deputy Principal Clerk " means the Deputy Principal Clerk of the Court of Session; " the Maintenance Orders (Reciprocal Enforcement) Act 1972 Register " means the Register referred to in Rule 13 (1) of the Act of Sederunt (Maintenance Orders (Reciprocal Enforcement) Act 1972 Rules) 1974; " Sheriff Clerk " includes Sheriff Clerk Depute.

(3) Other expressions used in this Act of Sederunt to which meanings have been assigned by the Act shall, unless the context otherwise requires, have the same meanings in this Act of Sederunt as in the Act.

(4) The Interpretation Act 1889 shall apply for the interpretation of this Act of Sederunt as it applies for the interpretation of an Act of Parliament.

2. The provisions of Part II of this Act of Sederunt shall apply for the purposes of the Act to orders made by the Court of Session and the provisions of Part III of this Act of Sederunt shall apply for the purposes of the Act to orders made by or registered in the Sheriff Court.

3.—(1) For the purpose of this Act of Sederunt and of Part I of the Act the Deputy Principal Clerk shall be the " prescribed officer " for the Court of Session and the Sheriff Clerk shall be the " prescribed officer " for the Sheriff Court.

(2) All communications which the prescribed officer is required by the Act to send in a prescribed manner to:

(*a*) an addressee in the United Kingdom or the Republic of Ireland shall be sent by recorded delivery post and

(*b*) an addressee outwith the United Kingdom and the Republic of Ireland shall be sent by Air Mail post.

Part II

Court of Session

Provisions in relation to transmission of Maintenance Orders made by the Court of Session for enforcement in the Republic of Ireland

4.—(1) All applications to the Court of Session for the transmission of any maintenance order for enforcement in the Republic of Ireland shall be made by letter addressed to the Deputy Principal Clerk and the following documents shall be lodged with the application—

(*a*) a certified copy of the relevant order;
(*b*) a statement signed by the applicant or his solicitor of any arrears outstanding in respect of the order;
(*c*) a statement signed by the applicant or his solicitor giving such information as to the whereabouts of the payer as he possesses;
(*d*) a statement signed by the applicant or his solicitor giving such information as the applicant possesses for facilitating the identification of the payer;
(*e*) where available, a photograph of the payer;
(*f*) a document signed by the applicant or his solicitor which establishes that notice of the order was sent to the payer;
(*g*) if the payee received legal aid in the proceedings a document to that effect; and
(*h*) if the payer did not appear in the proceedings in which the maintenance order was made the original or a certified true copy of a document which establishes that notice of the institution of the proceedings was served on the payer;

(2) On receipt of such application and documents the Deputy Principal Clerk shall send to the Secretary of State for Scotland the documents specified in section 2 (4) of the Act.

5.—(1) If a Maintenance Order such as is referred to in the preceding paragraph is varied or revoked by a subsequent order of the Court of Session it shall be the duty of the applicant to inform the Deputy Principal Clerk of any such variation or revocation and to provide the Deputy Principal Clerk with a certified copy of the new order, together with a copy of the extended Notes of Evidence certified by the Lord Ordinary before whom the evidence was given, if such order was varied after Proof, or a copy of the Judgment containing the reasons for any such variation in all other cases.

(2) On receipt of such information and documents, the Deputy Principal Clerk shall send the certified copy of the said order and said Notes of Evidence or extended Notes to the said Secretary of State.

6. Where any request is made to the Court of Session by or on behalf of a Court in the Republic of Ireland for the evidence of a person to be taken in terms of section 14 of the Act, such evidence shall be taken before the Sheriff of the Sheriffdom in which the witness resides. The prescribed officer shall on receipt of such request forward it to the sheriff clerk of the Sheriff Court District in which the witness resides.

Part III

Sheriff Court

Provisions in relation to transmission of maintenance orders made by the Sheriff Court for enforcement in the Republic of Ireland

7.—(1) All applications to the Sheriff Court for the transmission of any maintenance orders for enforcement in the Republic of Ireland shall be made by letter addressed to the Sheriff Clerk and the following documents shall be lodged with the application—

(*a*) a certified copy of the relevant order;
(*b*) a statement signed by the applicant or his solicitor of any arrears outstanding in respect of the order;
(*c*) a statement signed by the applicant or his solicitor giving such information as to the whereabouts of the payer as he possesses;

(*d*) a statement signed by the applicant or his solicitor giving such information as the applicant possesses for facilitating the identification of the payer;

(*e*) where available, a photograph of the payer;

(*f*) a document signed by the applicant or his solicitor which establishes that notice of the order was sent to the payer;

(*g*) if the payee received legal aid in the proceedings a document to that effect; and

(*h*) if the payer did not appear in the proceedings in which the maintenance order was made the original or a certified true copy of a document which establishes that notice of the institution of the proceedings was served on the payer;

(2) On receipt of such application and documents the Sheriff Clerk shall send to the Secretary of State the documents specified in section 2 (4) of the Act.

Provision in relation to registration of orders

8.—(1) The Sheriff Clerk shall register in " the Maintenance Orders (Reciprocal Enforcement) Act 1972 Register " such orders as the Act directs the prescribed officer to register. Every entry registering an order shall specify the section of the Act under which the order in question is registered. When a registered order is varied, revoked or cancelled the Sheriff Clerk shall make an appropriate entry against the entry registering the order.

(2) Where the payer wishes to make application to the court under section 6 (7) of the Act he shall do so by lodging a minute in which is set out the grounds of his application.

(3) When a Minute under paragraph (2) hereof or an application under section 6 (11) of the Act is lodged the cause shall be enrolled before the court.

Provision in relation to revocation of registered order

9. Where a registered order is revoked in the circumstances set out in section 10 (1) of the Act the payee or solicitor shall provide the Sheriff Clerk so far as is possible with the certificate and statements referred to in section 10 (7) of the Act.

Evidence

10. Where any request is made by or on behalf of a court in the Republic of Ireland in terms of section 14 of the Act such evidence shall be taken before the Sheriff of the Sheriffdom in which the witness resides and shall be taken down by the Sheriff or by the Sheriff Clerk or shorthand writer nominated by the Sheriff to whom the oath *de fideli administratione* shall be administered and evidence may be recorded in narrative form or by question and answer as the Sheriff shall direct, and the extended notes of evidence certified by such Sheriff Clerk or shorthand writer shall be the notes of the oral evidence taken.

Reciprocal Enforcement of Maintenance Orders (Hague Convention Countries) 1980

(S.I. 1980 No. 291)

[29th February 1980]

PART I

GENERAL

Citation and commencement

1.—(1) This Act of Sederunt may be cited as the Act of Sederunt (Reciprocal Enforcement of Maintenance Orders) (Hague Convention Countries) 1980 and shall come into operation on 24th March 1980.

(2) This Act of Sederunt shall be inserted in the Books of Sederunt.

Interpretation

2.—(1) In this Act of Sederunt, unless the context otherwise requires—

" Act " means the Maintenance Orders (Reciprocal Enforcement) Act 1972 as amended by the Reciprocal Enforcement of Maintenance Orders (Hague Convention Countries) Order 1979;

" Court in a Hague Convention Country " includes any judicial or administrative authority in a Hague Convention Country;

" Deputy Principal Clerk " means the Deputy Principal Clerk of the Court of Session;

" Hague Convention " means the convention on the Recognition and Enforcement of Decisions relating to maintenance obligations concluded at the Hague on 2nd October 1973;

" Hague Convention Country " means the country or territory specified in Schedule 1 to the Reciprocal Enforcement of Maintenance Orders (Hague Convention Countries) Order 1979 being a country or territory (other than the United Kingdom) in which the Hague Convention is in force;

" Register " means the Register referred to in rule 13 (1) of the Act of Sederunt (Maintenance Orders (Reciprocal Enforcement) Act 1972 Rules) 1974;

" Sheriff Clerk " includes the Sheriff Clerk Depute.

(2) This Act of Sederunt and the Act shall be read as one.

Application

3.—(1) The provisions of Part II of this Act of Sederunt shall apply for the purposes of the Act to orders made by the Court of Session.

(2) The provisions of Part III of this Act of Sederunt shall apply for the purposes of the Act to orders made by or registered in the Sheriff Court.

Prescribed officer

4.—(1) For the purposes of Part I of the Act, the prescribed officer shall be—

(*a*) in relation to the Court of Session, the Deputy Principal Clerk;

(*b*) in relation to the Sheriff Court, the Sheriff Clerk.

(2) For the purposes of the Act, the prescribed manner of communication by the Deputy Principal Clerk and the Sheriff Clerk shall be—

(*a*) to an address within the United Kingdom, by recorded delivery letter;

(*b*) to any other address, by air mail letter.

Part II

Court of Session

Transmission of order to convention country

5.—(1) All applications to the Court of Session for the transmission of a maintenance order to which this Part applies to a Court in a Hague Convention Country for registration and enforcement shall be made by letter to that effect addressed to the Deputy Principal Clerk.

(2) There shall be sent together with any such application—

(*a*) a certified copy of the maintenance order;

(*b*) a statement signed by the applicant or his solicitor—

(i) giving such information as to the whereabouts of the payer as he possesses;

(ii) giving such information as the applicant possesses for facilitating the identification of the payer including a photograph, if available;

(iii) of any arrears outstanding under the order;

(*c*) a document signed by the applicant or his solicitor which establishes that notice of the order was sent to the payer;

(*d*) if the payee received legal aid in the proceedings relating to the maintenance order, a document to that effect;

(*e*) if the payee did not appear in those proceedings, the original or a certified true copy of a document establishing that notice of these proceedings was served on the payer.

(3) The Deputy Principal Clerk, on receiving the application and documents specified in paragraph (2), shall send the documents specified in section 2 (4) of the Act to the Secretary of State.

Transmission of order varying or revoking maintenance order

6.—(1)Where a maintenance order transmitted under rule 5 is varied or revoked by a subsequent order of the Court of Session, the applicant in respect of the order so transmitted shall inform the Deputy Principal Clerk that such an order of variation or revocation has been made and send him—

(*a*) a certified copy of that order;

(*b*) a statement signed by the applicant or his solicitor—

(i) as to whether or not the defender appeared in the proceedings for the variation or revocation of the order;

(ii) as to whether or not the payer or payee received legal aid in these proceedings;

(*c*) where the defender did not appear in the proceedings, the original or a certified copy of a document which establishes that notice of the institution of the proceedings has been served on the defender;

(*d*) a document which establishes that notice of the order of variation or revocation was sent to the defender.

(2) The Deputy Principal Clerk, on being informed of the order of variation or revocation and receiving the documents referred to in paragraph (1), shall send the documents specified in section 5 (4) of the Act to the Secretary of State.

Request to take evidence

7. Where any request is made to the Court of Session by or on behalf of a Court in a Hague Convention Country for the evidence of a person to be taken under section 14 of the Act, such evidence shall be taken by the Sheriff of the Sheriffdom in which that person resides, and the Deputy Principal Clerk shall accordingly send any such request to the Sheriff Clerk of the Sheriff Court district in which that person resides and such request shall be treated for the purposes of taking that person's evidence as a request to the Sheriff by or on behalf of that Court.

PART III

SHERIFF COURT

Service on defender in convention country

8. Rule 15B of the First Schedule to the Sheriff Courts (Scotland) Act 1907 shall apply to service of a copy of an initial writ on a defender residing in a Hague Convention Country in an action in which the Sheriff has jurisdiction by virtue of section 4 (1) of the Act, as it applies to service of an initial writ on a defender in an action to which that rule applies.

Transmission of order to convention country

9.—(1) All applications to the Sheriff Court for the transmission of a maintenance order to which this Part applies to a Court in a Hague Convention Country for registration and enforcement shall be made by letter to that effect addressed to the Sheriff Clerk.

(2) Paragraphs (2) and (3) of rule 5 shall apply to an application made under this rule as they apply to an application made under that rule with the substitution in paragraph (3) of the words " Sheriff Clerk " for the words " Deputy Principal Clerk ".

Registration of incoming orders

10.—(1) The Sheriff Clerk—

(*a*) on receiving a maintenance order made in a Court of a Hague Convention Country for registration in the Sheriff Court under the Act;

(*b*) on receiving a subsequent order so made varying or revoking or cancelling that order,

shall enter the details relating to that order in the Register.

(2) An application to the Sheriff under subsections (9) or (12) of section 6 of the Act shall be made by way of minute setting out the grounds on which the application is made, and on any such minute being lodged it shall be brought before him.

Request to take evidence

11. Where any request is made to a Sheriff by or on behalf of a Court in a Hague Convention Country for the evidence of a person residing within his sheriffdom to be taken under section 14 of the Act, that evidence shall be taken in such manner as the Sheriff may direct.

Maintenance Orders Acts, Rules 1980

(S.I. 1980 No. 1727)

[11th November 1980]

The Lords of Council and Session under and by virtue of the powers conferred upon them by section 16 of the Administration of Justice (Scotland) Act 1933, Part II of the Maintenance Orders Act 1950, and Part I of the Maintenance Orders Act 1958 as amended by Schedule 3 to the Administration of Justice Act 1977, and of all other powers enabling them in that behalf, do hereby enact and declare—

PART I

GENERAL

Citation, commencement, interpretation and revocation

1.—(1) This Act of Sederunt may be cited as the Act of Sederunt (Maintenance Orders Acts, Rules) 1980 and shall come into operation on 1st January 1981.

(2) In this Act of Sederunt, unless the context otherwise requires—

" the 1950 Act " means the said Act of 1950;

" the 1958 Act " means the said Act of 1958;

" affidavit " includes statutory declaration;

" decree " includes extract decree;

" Deputy Principal Clerk " means the Deputy Principal Clerk of Session;

" the Registrar " in relation to the High Court in England means the Senior Registrar of the principal registry of the Family Division of the High Court in England and in relation to the High Court in Northern Ireland means the Chief Registrar of the Queens Bench Division (Matrimonial) of the High Court in Northern Ireland.

(3) Except as expressly provided in paragraph (2), expressions used in this Act of Sederunt and in the 1950 and 1958 Acts have, unless the context otherwise requires, the meaning given to them by those Acts.

(4) This Act of Sederunt shall be inserted in the Books of Sederunt.

(5) Part II of the Act of Sederunt (Maintenance Orders Act, 1950, Rules) 1950 and Part I of that Act in so far as it relates to Part II, and the Act of Sederunt (Amendment to Maintenance Order Rules) 1978 are revoked.

Application

2.—(1) Part II of this Act of Sederunt shall have effect in relation to the registration in other parts of the United Kingdom of decrees granted by the Court of Session to which the 1950 and 1958 Acts apply, and such decrees are referred to in this Act of Sederunt as " outgoing orders ".

(2) Part III of this Act of Sederunt shall have effect in relation to the registration in the Court of Session of orders made by courts in other parts of the United Kingdom to which those Acts apply, and such orders are referred to in this Act of Sederunt as " incoming orders ".

Maintenance Orders Register

3.—(1) The Deputy Principal Clerk shall maintain a Register called " the Maintenance Orders Register " for the purposes of the 1950 and 1958 Acts Part I of which shall relate to outgoing orders and Part II to incoming orders.

(2) The Deputy Principal Clerk shall make appropriate entries in the Maintenance Orders Register in respect of any action taken by him or notified to him in accordance with the provisions of those Acts, and shall keep in such manner as he considers appropriate any documents sent to him in connection with any such action.

Inspection of Register

4.—(1) The Deputy Principal Clerk shall, on an application in that behalf by—

(*a*) any person entitled to, or liable to make, payments under an order in respect of which any entry has been made in the Maintenance Orders Register; or

(*b*) a solicitor acting on behalf of that person,

permit that person or his solicitor, as the case may be, to inspect any such entry and any document in his possession relating to that entry and to take copies of any such entry or document.

(2) The Deputy Principal Clerk may, on an application in that behalf by any person, and on being satisfied of that person's interest, grant that person permission to inspect or take copies of any such entry or document.

Transcript of evidence

5.—(1) For the purposes of section 21 of the 1950 Act (evidence adduced in other parts of the United Kingdom) the Deputy Principal Clerk is the officer of the Court of Session to whom any transcript or summary of evidence should be sent.

(2) On receiving any such transcript or summary, the Deputy Principal Clerk shall cause it to be lodged in the appropriate process, and shall give notice to the parties to the action or the solicitors acting on their behalf that he has done so.

Part II

Outgoing Orders

Applications for registration

6.—(1) An application for the registration in the High Court in England or Northern Ireland of a decree granted by the Court of Session shall be made by sending to the Deputy Principal Clerk—

(*a*) a letter of application in that behalf;
(*b*) an affidavit by the applicant;
(*c*) a copy of that affidavit; and
(*d*) a certified copy of the decree.

(2) An affidavit under this rule shall include—

(*a*) the name and address of the person liable to make payments under the decree;
(*b*) the arrears due under the decree, if any, and the date to which they are calculated;
(*c*) the reason for the application; and
(*d*) a statement that the decree is not already registered under the 1950 Act.

Transmission

7.—(1) If it appears that the person liable to make payments under the decree resides in another part of the United Kingdom and that it is convenient that the decree should be enforceable there the Deputy Principal Clerk shall send to the Registrar—

(*a*) the affidavit of the applicant;
(*b*) a certified copy of the decree;
(*c*) a letter stating that the application has been granted and requesting registration of the decree, and notification of registration.

(2) On so acting, the Deputy Principal Clerk shall enter in Part I of the Maintenance Orders Register—

(*a*) particulars of the decree; and
(*b*) details of those actings.

Notice of registration

8.—(1) For the purposes of section 17 (4) of the 1950 Act (notice of registration), the Deputy Principal Clerk is the officer of the Court to whom notice of registration of the decree should be sent by the Registrar.

(2) On receiving such notice, the Deputy Principal Clerk shall make an entry to that effect in Part I of the Maintenance Orders Register.

Re-registration in magistrates' court

9.—(1) When a decree has been registered in the High Court in England or Northern Ireland, an application to the Court of Session for the registration of that decree in the magistrates' court under the 1958 Act, shall be made by sending to the Deputy Principal Clerk—

(*a*) a letter of application in that behalf specifying the magistrates' court in which registration is sought;

(*b*) an affidavit by the applicant;

(*c*) a copy of that affidavit; and

(*d*) a certified copy of the decree.

(2) An affidavit under this rule shall include—

(*a*) the matters mentioned in sub-paragraphs (*a*), (*b*) and (*c*) of paragraph (2) of rule 6;

(*b*) the date and place of the original registration;

(*c*) where the order has been re-registered, the date and place of the last re-registration and whether or not that has been cancelled or where any of these facts is not known a statement to that effect; and

(*d*) the steps, if any, taken to enforce the registered order.

Transmission for re-registration

10.—(1) The prescribed period for the purpose of section 2 (2) of the 1958 Act shall be 14 days.

(2) If the application under rule 9 is granted, the Deputy Principal Clerk shall send to the clerk of the magistrates' court in which re-registration is sought—

(*a*) the affidavit of the applicant;

(*b*) a certified copy of the decree;

(*c*) a letter stating that the application has been granted and requesting him to take steps to register the order, and to notify him accordingly.

(3) On receiving notice that the order has been so registered, the Deputy Principal Clerk shall enter the name of the magistrates' court and the date of registration of the order in that Court in Part I of the Maintenance Orders Register.

Registration and re-registration

11. Application may be made for registration under rule 6 and for re-registration under rule 9 in one letter of application made to the Deputy Principal Clerk and accompanied by—

(*a*) an affidavit by the applicant, which shall include the matters mentioned in rule 6 (2);

(*b*) two copies of that affidavit;

(*c*) two certified copies of the decree referred to in rule 6 (1).

Transmission for registration and re-registration

12. If the application under rule 11 is granted the Deputy Principal Clerk shall act in accordance with the requirements of rules 7 and 8 and on complying with rule 8 (2) shall act in accordance with the requirements of rule 10 (2).

Discharge and variation

13.—(1) If the Court of Session makes an order varying or discharging a decree registered under the 1950 or 1958 Acts, the party on whose application the order is made shall so inform the Deputy Principal Clerk and he shall on being so informed send to the Registrar, and where the order is registered in a magistrates' court, to the Clerk of that court—

(*a*) a certified copy of the interlocutor;

(*b*) a letter requesting the Registrar and, as the case may be, the clerk of the magistrates' court, to take the appropriate action under those Acts, in accordance with the interlocutor, and to notify him of the result.

(2) The Deputy Principal Clerk shall enter in Part I of the Maintenance Orders Register—

(*a*) the date and nature of the interlocutor;

(*b*) the date of its transmission under paragraph (1); and

(*c*) on receiving notice under sub-paragraph (*b*) of that paragraph, the particulars contained in that notice.

Cancellation

14.—(1) Where the registration of a decree is cancelled under section 24 (1) of the 1950 Act, the Deputy Principal Clerk is the officer of the Court to whom notice of the cancellation should be sent.

(2) On receiving such notice, he shall make an entry to that effect in Part I of the Maintenance Orders Register.

Part III

Incoming Orders

.Registration

15.—(1) For the purposes of section 17 (2) of the 1950 Act, the Deputy Principal Clerk is the officer of the Court to whom an order of the High Court in England or Northern Ireland should be sent for registration in the Court of Session.

(2) On receiving a certified copy of such an order for registration, he shall—

(*a*) make an entry in respect of the order in Part II of the Maintenance Orders Register;

(*b*) if the certified copy of the order is accompanied by an affidavit or certificate of arrears due under the order, make an entry in respect of those arrears in Part II of the Maintenance Orders Register;

(*c*) on receipt of the dues of extract, endorse on the certified copy of the order a warrant for registration in the Books of Council and Session and send the copy so endorsed to the Keeper of the Registers of Scotland, who shall cause registration to be made in accordance with the warrant, and an extract of the registered order may then be issued with a warrant for diligence in common form to the Deputy Principal Clerk, for transmission by him to the applicant;

(*d*) notify the Registrar that the order has been registered.

Discharge and variation

16.—(1) For the purposes of section 23 of the 1950 Act, the Deputy Principal Clerk is the officer of the Court to whom notice of an order varying or discharging a registered order should be given by the Registrar.

(2) On receiving a certified copy of such an order, the Deputy Principal Clerk shall—

(*a*) make an entry in respect of the order in Part II of the Maintenance Orders Register;

(*b*) notify the Registrar that he has done so.

(3) In the case of an order varying the registered order, sub-paragraphs (*b*) and (*c*) of rule 15 (2) shall apply in relation to that order, as they apply in relation to an order under that rule.

Cancellation

17.—(1) An application for the cancellation of an order registered under this Part shall be made by sending to the Deputy Principal Clerk—

(*a*) a letter of application in that behalf;

(*b*) an affidavit by the applicant.

(2) An affidavit under this rule shall include—

(*a*) the date of the registration of the order;

(*b*) the reason for the application;

(*c*) the arrears, if any, that are due under the order.

(3) If the registration is cancelled, the Deputy Principal Clerk shall—

(*a*) notify the Registrar;

(*b*) notify the person liable under the order;

(*c*) make an entry in respect of the cancellation in the Maintenance Orders Register.

Maintenance Orders Acts, Rules 1980

(S.I. 1980 No. 1732)

[11th November 1980]

The Lords of Council and Session under and by virtue of the powers conferred on them by section 32 of the Sheriff Courts (Scotland) Act 1971 and by virtue of the provisions of Part II of the Maintenance Orders Act 1950 and Part I of the Maintenance Orders Act 1958 as amended by Schedule 3 to the Administration of Justice Act 1977, and of all other powers enabling them in that behalf, do hereby enact and declare:—

Part I

General

Citation, commencement, interpretation and revocation

1.—(1) This Act of Sederunt may be cited as the Act of Sederunt (Maintenance Orders Act, Rules) 1980 and shall come into operation on 1st January 1981.

(2) In this Act of Sederunt unless the context otherwise requires—

" the 1950 Act " means the Maintenance Orders Act 1950;

" the 1958 Act " means the Maintenance Orders Act 1958;

" affidavit " includes statutory declaration;

" clerk of the court " means the clerk to the magistrates' court in England or Northern Ireland and in relation to a county court in England or Northern Ireland means the registrar of that court;

" clerk of the magistrates' court " means the clerk to the magistrates' court in England or Northern Ireland as the case may be;

" decree " includes extract decree;

" sheriff clerk " includes sheriff clerk depute;

" the Registrar " in relation to the High Court in England means the Senior Registrar of the principal registry of the Family Division of the High Court in England.

(3) Except as expressly provided in paragraph (2), expressions used in this Act of Sederunt and in the 1950 and 1958 Acts have, unless the context otherwise requires, the meaning given to them by those Acts.

(4) Part III of the Act of Sederunt (Maintenance Orders Act, 1950, Rules) 1950 and Part I of that Act in so far as it relates to Part III, is revoked.

Application

2.—(1) Part II of this Act of Sederunt shall have effect in relation to the registration in other parts of the United Kingdom of decrees granted by the Sheriff to which the 1950 and 1958 Acts apply, and such decrees are referred to in this Act of Sederunt as " outgoing orders ".

(2) Part III of this Act of Sederunt shall have effect in relation to the registration in the Sheriff Court of orders made by courts in other parts of the United Kingdom to which those Acts apply, and such orders are referred to in this Act of Sederunt as " incoming orders ".

Prescribed Officer

3. The sheriff clerk shall be the prescribed officer for the purpose of the 1950 Act and the 1958 Act.

Maintenance Orders Register

4.—(1) The sheriff clerk shall maintain a Register called " the Maintenance Orders Register " for the purpose of the 1950 and 1958 Acts, Part I of which shall relate to outgoing orders and Part II to incoming orders.

(2) The sheriff clerk shall make appropriate entries in the Maintenance Orders Register in respect of any action taken by him or notified to him in accordance with the provisions of those Acts, and shall keep in such manner as he considers appropriate any documents sent to him in connection with any such action.

Inspection

5.—(1) The sheriff clerk shall, on an application in that behalf by—

(*a*) any person entitled to, or liable to make, payments under an order in respect of which any entry has been made in the Maintenance Orders Register; or

(*b*) a solicitor acting on behalf of that person,

permit that person or his solicitor, as the case may be, to inspect any such entry and any document in his possession relating to that entry and to take copies of any such entry or document.

(2) The sheriff clerk may, on an application in that behalf by any person, and on being satisfied of that person's interest, grant that person permission to inspect or take copies of any such entry or document.

Part II

Outgoing Orders

Commencement of proceedings

6.—(1) Every initial writ by which proceedings are begun in a sheriff court having jurisdiction under or by virtue of Part I of the 1950 Act against a person residing in another part of the United Kingdom, and all minutes and writs (other than productions) lodged in any proceedings taken in a sheriff court under or by virtue of the 1950 Act or the 1958 Act shall be headed " Maintenance Orders Act 1950 " or as the case may be " Maintenance Orders Act 1958 ".

(2) The warrant of citation granted upon any writ which by virtue of those Acts is to be served upon a person residing in another part of the United Kingdom shall be in ordinary form and shall proceed upon fourteen days' *induciae*, to be reckoned from the date of service, and such warrant of citation may be signed by the sheriff clerk. In connection with the service under section 15 of the 1950 Act of an initial writ from a sheriff court the expression " initial writ " in the said section and in the forms contained in the Second Schedule to that Act shall include the warrant of citation relative to the said writ.

(3) The provisions of Rule 15 of the First Schedule to the Sheriff Courts (Scotland) Act 1907 (which relate to edictal citation) shall not apply to service made in terms of section 15 of the 1950 Act.

Application for registration

7.—(1) An application for registration in a magistrates' court in England or Northern Ireland of a decree granted by a sheriff court to which the 1950 Act applies shall be made by lodging with the sheriff clerk—

(*a*) a letter of application in that behalf;
(*b*) an affidavit by the applicant;
(*c*) a copy of that affidavit; and
(*d*) a certified copy of the decree.

(2) An affidavit under this rule shall include—

(*a*) the name and address of the person liable to make payments under the decree;
(*b*) the arrears due under the decree, if any, and the date to which they are calculated;
(*c*) the reason for the application; and
(*d*) a statement that the decree is not already registered under the 1950 Act.

Transmission

8.—(1) If it appears that the person liable to make payments under the decree resides in another part of the United kingdom and that it is convenient that the decree should be enforceable there, the sheriff clerk shall send to the clerk of the magistrates' court—

(*a*) the affidavit of the applicant;
(*b*) the certified copy of the decree; and
(*c*) a letter stating that the application has been granted and requesting registration of the decree.

(2) On so acting the sheriff clerk shall enter in Part I of the Maintenance Orders Register—

(*a*) particulars of the decree; and
(*b*) details of those actings.

(3) On receiving notice from the clerk of the magistrates' court that the decree has been registered, the sheriff clerk shall make an entry to that effect in Part I of the Maintenance Orders Register.

Application to adduce evidence

9.—(1) An application to a sheriff court under section 22 (5) of the 1950 Act to adduce evidence in connection with a decree granted by that court and registered in a court in England or Northern Ireland shall be made by initial writ. Any evidence adduced in pursuance of such an application shall be taken and recorded in the manner prescribed by Rule 65 of the First Schedule to the Sheriff Courts (Scotland) Act 1907 and the transcript or summary of the evidence so adduced shall be sent to the clerk of the magistrates' court in which the decree is registered.

(2) The sheriff clerk of the court by which a decree registered in a magistrates' court in England or Northern Ireland was granted shall on receipt of any transcript or summary of evidence adduced in a court in England or Northern Ireland under section 22 (5) of the 1950 Act in connection with that decree lodge such transcript or summary in the process of the cause in which the decree was granted.

Re-registration in the High Court

10.—(1) When a decree has been registered in the magistrates' court, an application to the sheriff court for the re-registration of that decree in the

High Court in England under the 1958 Act shall be made by lodging with the sheriff clerk—

(*a*) a letter of application in that behalf;
(*b*) an affidavit by the applicant; and
(*c*) a copy of that affidavit;

(2) An affidavit under this rule shall include—

(*a*) the matters mentioned in sub-paragraphs (*a*), (*b*) and (*c*) of paragraph (2) of rule 7;
(*b*) the date and place of the original registration;
(*c*) where the decree has been re-registered, the date and place of the last re-registration and whether or not that has been cancelled or where any of these facts is not known a statement to that effect; and
(*d*) the steps, if any, taken to enforce the registered order.

Transmission for re-registration

11.—(1) If the application under Rule 10 is granted, the sheriff clerk shall send to the Registrar—

(*a*) the affidavit of the applicant; and
(*b*) a letter stating that the application has been granted and requesting him to take steps to have the order registered in the High Court.

(2) On receiving notice that the order has been so registered, the sheriff clerk shall enter the details of the registration of the order in Part I of the Maintenance Orders Register.

Discharge and variation

12.—(1) Where a decree granted by a sheriff court and registered under the 1950 Act or the 1958 Act in a court in England or Northern Ireland is varied by the court in which it is registered, the sheriff clerk shall, on receipt of a notice of variation enter particulars of that variation in Part I of the Maintenance Orders Register.

(2) If the sheriff court makes an order varying or discharging a decree registered under the 1950 Act or the 1958 Act—

(*a*) the sheriff clerk shall send to the clerk of the magistrates' court, and, where the order is registered in the High Court, to the Registrar—
   (i) a certified copy of the interlocutor; and
   (ii) a letter requesting the clerk of the magistrates' court and, as the case may be, the Registrar, to take the appropriate action under those Acts, in accordance with the interlocutor, and to notify him of the result;
(*b*) the sheriff clerk shall enter in Part I of the Maintenance Orders Register—
   (i) the date and nature of the interlocutor;
   (ii) the date of its transmission under sub-paragraph (*a*); and
   (iii) on receiving notice under sub-paragraph (*a*) (ii), the particulars contained in that notice.

Cancellation

13.—(1) An application under section 24 (2) of the 1950 Act in connection with a decree granted by a sheriff court and registered in a court in England or Northern Ireland shall be made by lodging with the sheriff clerk an affidavit by the person liable to make payments under the decree stating the facts on which the application is founded; and if it appears to the sheriff clerk that that person has ceased to reside in England or Northern Ireland, as the case may be, the sheriff clerk shall send notice to that effect to the clerk of the magistrates' court and the Registrar, as the case may be, of any court in which the decree is registered.

(2) Where the registration of a decree made by a sheriff court and registered in a court in England or Northern Ireland is cancelled under section 24(1) or (2) of the 1950 Act the sheriff clerk, on receipt of notice of the cancellation, shall make an entry to that effect in Part I of the Maintenance Orders Register.

Part III

Incoming Orders

Registration

14.—(1) On receiving a certified copy of a maintenance order made by a court in England or Northern Ireland the sheriff clerk shall—

(a) make an entry in respect of the order in Part II of the Maintenance Orders Register;

(b) retain in the office of the sheriff clerk any certificate or affidavit sent with the certified copy of the order as to the amount of any arrears due under the order;

(c) endorse thereon an attestation, signed by himself, of the registration thereof in the form set out in the Schedule to this Act of Sederunt and retain such certified copy of the order and attestation in the office of the sheriff clerk; and

(d) notify the clerk of the court which made the order that it has been registered.

(2) The sheriff clerk may make an extract certified by himself of the certified copy of the order with the attestation thereon, and such certified extract shall be of the like force and effect and may be enforced in all respect as if it were an extract decree of the sheriff court in which the certified copy is registered with a warrant for diligence in common form.

Variation of rate payment

15. An application to a sheriff court for variation under section 22(1) of the 1950 Act of the rate of payments under a maintenance order made by a court in England or Northern Ireland and registered in that sheriff court shall be made by initial writ.

Application to adduce evidence

16.—(1) An application to a sheriff court under section 22(5) of the 1950 Act to adduce evidence in connection with a maintenance order made by a court in England or Northern Ireland and registered in that sheriff court shall be made by initial writ. Any evidence adduced in pursuance of such an application shall be taken and recorded in the manner prescribed by Rule 65 of the First Schedule to the Sheriff Courts (Scotland) Act 1907 and the transcript or summary of the evidence so adduced shall be sent to the clerk of the court by which the order was made.

(2) The sheriff clerk of the court in which a maintenance order was made by a court in England or Northern Ireland is registered shall, on receipt of any transcript or summary of evidence adduced in England or Northern Ireland under section 22(5) of the 1950 Act in connection with that order, lodge such transcript or summary in the process of any proceedings before that sheriff court for the variation of the order.

Discharge and variation

17.—(1) Where a maintenance order made by a court in England or Northern Ireland and registered under the 1950 Act in a sheriff court is varied by that sheriff court, the sheriff clerk shall—

(a) enter particulars of the variation in Part II of the Maintenance Orders Register; and

(b) shall give notice of the variation to the clerk of the court by which the order was made by sending him a certified copy of the order or interlocutor varying the order.

(2) Where a maintenance order made by a court in England or Northern Ireland and registered in a sheriff court is discharged or varied by any court other than that sheriff court, the sheriff clerk shall on receipt of a certified copy of an order discharging or varying the registered order—

(a) make an entry in respect of the order in Part II of the Maintenance Orders Register; and

(b) notify the clerk of the court that he has done so.

(3) In the case of an order varying a registered order, sub-paragraphs (*b*) and (*c*) of rule 14(1) and paragraph (2) of rule 14 shall apply in relation to that order as they apply in relation to an order under that rule.

Cancellation

18.—(1) An application for the cancellation under section 24(1) of the 1950 Act or section 5(1) of the 1958 Act of the registration of a maintenance order made by a court in England or Northern Ireland and registered in a sheriff court shall be made by lodging with the sheriff clerk—

(a) an application for the purpose (which shall state the date of the registration of the order and which shall be signed by or on behalf of the applicant); and

(b) a copy of the order the registration of which is sought to be cancelled.

(2) Where under section 24(1) or (2) of the 1950 Act or section 5(1) of the 1958 Act the sheriff clerk cancels the registration of a maintenance order, he shall—

(a) make an entry in respect of the cancellation in Part II of the Maintenance Orders Register;

(b) notify the clerk of the court by which the order was made; and

(c) notify the person liable to make payments under the order.

SCHEDULE

Rule 14(2)

FORM OF ATTESTATION

I hereby declare that the foregoing certified copy of a maintenance order has been duly registered by me in Part II of the Maintenance Orders Register kept in this court in terms of the Maintenance Orders Act 1950 and the Maintenance Orders Act 1958, as amended, and rule 14(2) of the Act of Sederunt (Maintenance Orders Act, Rules) 1978.

[*Signed*] A. B.
Sheriff Clerk Depute

Adoption of Children 1984

(S.I. 1984 No. 1013)

[13th July 1984]

The Lords of Council and Session, under and by virtue of the powers conferred on them by section 32 of the Sheriff Courts (Scotland) Act 1971, section 59 of the Adoption (Scotland) Act 1978 and of all other powers competent to them in that behalf, after consultation with the Sheriff Court Rules Council, do hereby enact and declare:—

Citation and commencement

1.—(1) This Act of Sederunt may be cited as the Act of Sederunt (Adoption of Children) 1984 and shall come into operation on 1st September 1984.

(2) This Act of Sederunt shall be inserted in the Books of Sederunt.

(3) In this Act of Sederunt—

"the 1978 Act" means the Adoption (Scotland) Act 1978;

"adoption agency" means a local authority or an approved adoption society;

"Her Majesty's Forces" means the Royal Navy, the regular armed forces as defined by section 225 of the Army Act 1955, the regular air force as defined by section 223 of the Air Force Act 1955, the Queen Alexandra's Royal Naval Nursing Service and the Women's Royal Naval Service; and

"Registrar General" means the Registrar General of Births, Deaths and Marriages for Scotland.

(4) Expressions used in this Act of Sederunt which are used in the 1978 Act have the same meaning as in the 1978 Act.

(5) In this Act of Sederunt a form referred to by number means the form so numbered in the Schedule to this Act of Sederunt or a form substantially to the like effect, with such variation as circumstances may require.

Revocation

2. The Act of Sederunt (Adoption of Children) 1959 is revoked.

PART I

APPLICATION FOR AN ORDER DECLARING A CHILD FREE FOR ADOPTION

Petition

3.—(1) An application under section 18(1) of the 1978 Act for an order declaring a child free for adoption shall be made by petition in form 1.

(2) There shall be lodged in process at the same time as the lodging of a petition under sub-paragraph (1)—

(*a*) an extract of the entry in the Register of Births relating to the child who is the subject of the application;

(*b*) a report of the adoption agency on the proposed adoption proceedings and the prospects for adoption, if such report is available;

(*c*) the consent of a parent or guardian of the child to the petition (unless application for dispensation of consent is sought by the petitioner); and

(*d*) any other document founded upon by the petitioner in support of the terms of the petition.

Consents and agreements to order freeing child for adoption

4.—(1) An agreement to an order under paragraph 3(1) required by section 18(1)(*a*), or a consent required by section 18(8), of the 1978 Act shall be in form 2 or 9 as appropriate and such form duly executed shall be sufficient evidence of such agreement or consent whether the document is executed before or after the commencement of proceedings.

(2) A form of consent or agreement under sub-paragraph (1) shall, if not available at the time of lodging the petition, be lodged so soon as is practicable thereafter.

(3) A form of consent or agreement executed outwith the United Kingdom shall be sufficient evidence of consent if it is executed—

(*a*) if the person by whom the document is executed is serving in Her Majesty's forces, by an officer holding a commission in any of those forces; or

(*b*) in any other case, by a British consular official, or by any person for the time being authorised by the law of the country in which the form is executed to administer an oath for any judicial or legal purpose.

Appointment of curator ad litem *and reporting officer*

5.—(1) The sheriff shall, after the lodging of a petition under paragraph 3, appoint a curator *ad litem* and reporting officer or reporting officers and, where reasonably practicable, shall appoint the same person as curator *ad litem* and reporting officer in the same petition.

(2) The sheriff may appoint a person who is not a member of a panel established under the Curators *Ad Litem* and Reporting Officers (Panels) (Scotland) Regulations 1984 to be a curator *ad litem* or a reporting officer.

(3) The sheriff may, on cause shown, appoint a reporting officer prior to the lodging of a petition.

(4) An application for an appointment under sub-paragraph (3) shall be made by letter addressed to the sheriff clerk specifying the reasons for the appointment, and shall not require to be intimated to any other person.

Duties of reporting officer and curator ad litem

6.—(1) A reporting officer appointed under this part of this Act of Sederunt shall—

(*a*) witness any agreement executed within the United Kingdom by a parent or guardian to the making of an adoption order in respect of his child and shall lodge the agreement in process;

(*b*) investigate the giving by a parent or guardian of his consent to the lodging of the petition;

(*c*) ascertain that each parent or guardian who can be found understands that the effect of an adoption order would be to deprive him permanently of his parental rights;

(*d*) ascertain whether there is any person other than those mentioned in the petition upon whom notice of the petition should be served;

(*e*) where a parent or guardian can be found, ascertain whether alternatives to adoption have been discussed with him;

(*f*) confirm that each parent or guardian who can be found understands the implications of an order freeing the child for adoption;

(*g*) confirm that each parent or guardian who can be found understands that he may withdraw his agreement at any time before an order under paragraph 3 is made;

(*h*) confirm that each parent or guardian who can be found is aware that he may in certain circumstances apply to the court for revocation of the order freeing the child for adoption and the appropriate procedure for such an application;

(*i*) confirm that each parent or guardian who can be found has been given an opportunity to make a declaration in terms of section 18(6) of the 1978 Act (declaration of preference not to be involved in future questions concerning the adoption of the child); and

(*j*) in the case of an illegitimate child, consider the likelihood of any person reputed to be the father of the child successfully raising proceedings for custody of, or access to, the child,

and shall report to the sheriff thereon.

(2) A curator *ad litem* appointed under this part of this Act of Sederunt shall—

(*a*) generally safeguard the interests of the child who is the subject of the petition and ensure that consideration has been given to the interests of the child required by section 6 of the 1978 Act (duty to promote welfare of child);

(*b*) ascertain whether the facts stated in the petition are correct except where investigation of such facts falls within the duties of the reporting officer;

(*c*) confirm that the child, if he is a minor, consented to the application;

(*d*) ascertain whether an order freeing the child for adoption would promote the child's well-being; and

(*e*) report on the current circumstances and care of the child,

and shall report to the sheriff thereon.

Declaration made under section 18(6) of the 1978 Act

7.—(1) A declaration made under section 18(6) of the 1978 Act shall be in form 3, be signed by each parent or guardian of the child and shall be witnessed by the reporting officer.

(2) The reporting officer shall provide a copy of the form of declaration to each parent or guardian of the child for signature and shall explain to him the consequences of signing the declaration and of the terms of section 19 of the 1978 Act (progress reports to former parents).

(3) The reporting officer shall submit the executed declaration to the sheriff clerk who shall thereafter record the declaration in the manner prescribed in paragraph 10.

Hearing

8.—(1) When the reports of the reporting officer and the curator *ad litem* have been received by the court, the sheriff shall order a diet of hearing to be fixed.

(2) Intimation of the diet of hearing shall be made in form 11 by the petitioner to every person who can be found and whose agreement or consent to the making of the order freeing the child for adoption is required to be given or dispensed with.

(3) If no person entitled to appear at such a hearing appears to be heard, the sheriff may make an order freeing the child for adoption on the motion of the petitioner.

(4) If a person, entitled to appear, appears and wishes to be heard, the sheriff may hear him or may order a further diet to be fixed at which he may be heard and evidence given at any such diet shall be given in the presence of the petitioner or his solicitor.

Confidentiality

9.—(1) All documents lodged in process, including the reports of the reporting officer and curator *ad litem* shall, unless the sheriff otherwise directs, be available only to the court, the reporting officer, the curator *ad litem* and the parties. Such documents shall be treated as confidential by any persons involved in, or a party to, the proceedings and by the sheriff clerk.

(2) The reporting officer or curator *ad litem* shall treat all information obtained by him in the exercise of his duties as confidential and shall not disclose any such information to any person unless disclosure of such information is necessary for the proper discharge of his duties.

Register of Adoptions

10.—(1) The sheriff clerk shall maintain a register known as the "Adoption Register".

(2) The sheriff clerk shall enter any declaration made under section 18(6) of the 1978 Act submitted to him by the reporting officer in the Adoption Register.

(3) A declaration under section 19(4) of the 1978 Act (declaration by former parent not to be involved in future questions concerning the adoption) shall be made in form 3 and the adoption agency shall submit the declaration to the sheriff clerk who shall enter it in the Adoption Register.

PART II

REVOCATION ORDERS, ETC.

Application for revocation

11.—(1) An application for revocation, under section 20(1) of the 1978 Act, of an order freeing a child for adoption shall be made by minute in the process of the original application in form 4 and shall specify detailed proposals for the future well-being of the child.

(2) On the lodging of a minute under sub-paragraph (1), the sheriff shall make an order requiring the applicant to intimate the minute to the petitioner in the original application and to such other person as shall to the sheriff seem appropriate.

(3) Any person to whom intimation has been made under sub-paragraph (2) may, within 14 days after the date on which intimation is made, lodge answers to the minute.

Appointment of curator ad litem

12. On the lodging of a minute under paragraph 11(1) the sheriff may appoint a curator *ad litem* who shall—

(*a*) investigate the facts contained in the minute, and

(*b*) investigate the circumstances and care of the child with regard to the promotion of his welfare throughout his childhood and, so far as practicable, ascertain his wishes and feelings regarding the minute, having regard to his age and understanding.

and shall report to the sheriff thereon.

Hearing

13.—(1) Where answers to the minute have been lodged, the sheriff shall order a diet of hearing to be fixed.

(2) Where no answers to the minute have been lodged, the sheriff may either—

(*a*) order a diet of hearing to be fixed, or

(*b*) order the relevant adoption agency to submit a report to him.

Application to place a child

14.—(1) An application by an adoption agency under section 20(2) of the 1978 Act (leave of court to place a child) shall be made by minute in the original process in form 5.

(2) A minute under sub-paragraph (1) shall be intimated by the applicant to such persons as shall to the sheriff seem appropriate.

Further applications with leave of the court

15. Any further application made with leave of the sheriff in terms of section 20(5) of the 1978 Act (further application by former parent with leave of the court) shall be made by minute in the original process and such minute shall be in form 6, and the provisions of paragraphs 11(2) and (3), 12 and 13 shall apply to an application under this paragraph as they apply to an application under paragraph 11(1).

PART III

ADOPTION ORDERS

Application for adoption order

16.—(1) An application for an adoption order, or for an order vesting parental rights and duties relating to a child under section 49(1) of the 1978 Act (adoption of children abroad), shall be made by petition in form 7 or 8 as appropriate.

(2) A petition under sub-paragraph (1) shall specify—

(*a*) the date upon which the child was received into the care and possession of the petitioner;

(*b*) whether the child has since that date been continously in the care and possession of the petitioner;

(*c*) the date upon which the petitioner notified the local authority for the area in which he was then resident of this intention to apply for an adoption order in respect of the child;

(*d*) whether the petitioner has received or given any reward or payment for or in consideration of the adoption of the child or for the giving of agreement or consent to the making of an adoption order;

(*e*) What persons have taken part in the arrangement for placing the child in his care; and

(*f*) particulars of any order freeing the child for adoption.

(3) There shall be lodged in process along with the petition—

(*a*) an extract of the entry in the Register of Births relating to the child who is the subject of the application;

(*b*) in the case of a joint peitition by a married couple, an extract of the entry in the Register of Marriages relating to their marriage;

(*c*) a medical certificate of the health of the petitioner or each of the joint petitioners except where the petitioner or one of the joint petitioners is a parent of the child;

(*d*) any report by the adoption agency required by section 23 of the 1978 Act (report on the suitability of the applicants);

(*e*) any report by the local authority required by section 22(2) of the 1978 Act (investigation by local authority on receipt of notice of intention to apply for adoption order);

(*f*) subject to the terms of paragraph 18(2), any consent required by section 12(8) (consent of minor), or any agreement required by section 16(1) (parental agreement), of the 1978 Act; and

(*g*) any other document founded upon by the petitioner in support of the terms of his petition.

(4) If no report by the adoption agency under sub-paragraph (3)(*d*) is available to be lodged along with the petition, the petitioner shall intimate the petition to the adoption agency concerned with a request that such a report be produced.

Additional requirements where child to be adopted abroad

17.—(1) In a petition for an order under section 49(1) of the 1978 Act, the petitioner shall, in addition to complying with paragraph 16, adduce evidence of the law of adoption in the country in which he is domiciled.

(2) The evidence of the law of adoption required under sub-paragraph (1) may be in the form of an affidavit by a person who is conversant with the law of adoption of that country and who practises or has practised law in that country or is a duly accredited representative of the government of that country in the United Kingdom.

Consents and agreement to adoption orders

18.—(1) A consent to an order under paragraph 16 required by section 12(8) or an agreement required by section 16(1), of the 1978 Act shall be in form 9 or 10 as appropriate and such form duly executed shall be sufficient evidence of such consent or agreement whether the document is executed before or after the commencement of proceedings.

(2) A form of consent or agreement under sub-paragraph (1) shall, if not available at the time of lodging the petition, be lodged so soon as is practicable thereafter.

(3) A form of consent or agreement executed outwith the United Kingdom shall be sufficient evidence of consent if it is executed—

(*a*) if the person by whom the document is executed is serving in Her Majesty's forces, by an officer holding a commission in any of those forces; or

(*b*) in any other case, by a British consular official, or by any person for the time being authorised by the law of the country in which the form is executed to administer an oath for any judicial or legal purpose.

Protection of identity of petitioner

19.—(1) When any person who proposes to apply for an order under paragraph 16 wishes to prevent his identity being disclosed to any person whose agreement to the order is required, he may, before presenting his petition, apply to the sheriff clerk for a serial number to be assigned to him for all purposes connected with the petition.

(2) On receipt of an application for a serial number, the sheriff clerk shall assign such a number to the applicant and shall enter a note of it opposite the name of the applicant in a register of such serial numbers.

(3) The contents of the register of serial numbers and the names of the persons to whom each number relates shall be treated as confidential by the sheriff clerk and shall not be disclosed to any person other than the sheriff.

(4) Where a serial number has been assigned to an applicant in terms of sub-paragraph (2), any form of agreement to an adoption order which is required shall not contain the name or designation of the petitioner but shall refer to him by means of the serial number assigned to him and shall specify the year in which, and by which court, such serial number has been assigned.

Appointment of reporting officer and curator ad litem

20.—(1) The sheriff shall, after the lodging of a petition under paragraph 16, appoint a curator *ad litem* and a reporting officer or reporting officers, and, where reasonably practicable, appoint the same person as curator *ad litem* and reporting officer in the same petition.

(2) The sheriff may appoint a person who is not a member of a panel established under the Curators *Ad Litem* and Reporting Officers (Panels) (Scotland) Regulations 1984 to be curator *ad litem* or a reporting officer.

Duties of reporting officer and curator ad litem

21.—(1) A reporting officer appointed under this part of this Act of Sederunt shall—

(*a*) witness any agreement executed within the United Kingdom by a parent or guardian to the making of an adoption order in respect of his child and shall lodge the agreement in process;

(*b*) ascertain that each parent or guardian whose agreement is required or may be dispensed with understands that the effect of the adoption order would be to deprive him permanently of his parental rights;

(*c*) ascertain whether there is any person other than those mentioned in the petition upon whom notice of the petition should be served;

(*d*) where a parent or guardian whose agreement is required or may be dispensed with can be found, ascertain whether alternatives to adoption have been discussed with him; and

(*e*) confirm that each parent or guardian whose agreement is required understands that he may withdraw his agreement at any time before an order under paragraph 16 is made,

and shall report to the sheriff thereon.

(2) A curator *ad litem* under this part of this Act of Sederunt shall—

(*a*) generally safeguard the interests of the child whose adoption is the subject of the petition;

(*b*) ascertain whether the facts stated in the petition are correct and if they are not establish the true facts;

(*c*) obtain particulars of the accommodation in the home of the petitioner and the condition of the home;

(*d*) obtain particulars of all members of the household of the petitioner and their relationship to the petitioner;

(*e*) in the case of a petition by one of two spouses, the reasons of the other spouse for not joining in the application;

(*f*) ascertain whether the means and status of the petitioner are sufficient to enable him to maintain and bring up the child suitably;

(*g*) ascertain what rights or interests in property the child has;

(*h*) establish that the petitioner understands the nature and effect of an adoption order and in particular that the making of the order will render him responsible for the maintenance and upbringing of the child;

(*i*) ascertain when the mother of the child ceased to have the care and possession of the child and to whom care and possession was then transferred;

(*j*) ascertain whether any payment or other reward in consideration of the adoption has been given or agreed upon;

(*k*) establish whether the adoption is likely to safeguard and promote the welfare of the child throughout his childhood;

(*l*) ascertain whether the life of the child has been insured and for what sum;

(*m*) ascertain whether it is in the interests of the welfare of the child that the sheriff should make any interim order or make the adoption order subject to particular terms and conditions or require the petitioner to make special provision for the child and if so what provision;

(*n*) where the petitioner is not ordinarily resident in the United Kingdom, establish whether a report has been obtained on the home and living conditions of the petitioner from a suitable agency in the country in which he is ordinarily resident;

(*o*) establish the reasons of the petitioner for wishing to adopt the child;

(*p*) establish to which religion, if any, the petitioner subscribes;

(*q*) assess the considerations which might arise where the difference in ages as between the petitioner and the child is greater or less than the normal difference in age as between parents and their children;

(*r*) consider such other matters, including the personality of the petitioner and, where appropriate, that of the child, which might affect the suitability of the petitioner and the child for the relationship created by adoption and affect the ability of the petitioner to bring up the child; and

(*s*) ascertain, so far as practicable, the wishes and feelings of the child regarding the proposed adoption,

and shall report to the sheriff thereon.

Hearing

[1] **22.**—(1) When the reports of the reporting officer and the curator *ad litem* in respect of a child who is not free for adoption have been received by the court, the sheriff shall order a diet of hearing to be fixed.

(1A) When the report of the curator *ad litem*, in respect of a child who is free for adoption, has been received by the court, the sheriff may order a diet of hearing to be fixed.

(2) Intimation of the diet of hearing referred to in sub-paragraphs (1) and (1A) shall be made in form 11 by the petitioner to the following persons—

(*a*) in a petition for an adoption order, every person who can be found and whose agreement or consent to the making of such an order is required to be given or dispensed with, or

(*b*) in a petition for an order under section 49(1) of the 1978 Act, every person who can be found and whose agreement to the making of such an order would be required if the application were for an adoption order.

(3) The sheriff may, if he considers it appropriate, ordain the petitioner to serve notice of the date of the hearing in form 11, on the following persons—

(*a*) any person or body having the rights and powers of a parent of the child or having the custody or care of the child or a local authority having the child committed to its care by virtue of section 5 of the Guardianship of Infants Act 1886, section 10 of the Matrimonial Proceedings (Children) Act 1958, sections 16 and 17 of the Social Work (Scotland) Act 1968, section 9 of the Guardianship of Minors Act 1971, section 43 of the Matrimonial Causes Act 1973, or sections 2(2)(*b*) and (11)(1)(*a*) of the Guardianship Act 1973;

(*b*) any person liable by virtue of any order or agreement to contribute to the maintenance of the child;

(*c*) the local authority to whom the petitioner has given notice of his intention to apply for an adoption order;

(*d*) any other person or body who in the opinion of the sheriff ought to be served with notice of the hearing.

(4) If no person entitled to appear at such a hearing appears to be heard, the sheriff may grant an adoption order on the motion of the petitioner.

(5) If a person, entitled to appear, appears and wishes to be heard, the sheriff may hear him or may order a further diet to be fixed at which he may be heard. Evidence given at such diets shall be given in the presence of the petitioner or his solicitor.

NOTE

[1] As amended by S.I. 1992 No. 1076 (effective 21st May 1992).

Insufficient evidence

23. If the sheriff is not satisfied that the facts stated in the petition are supported by the documents lodged along with the petition or by the reports of the curator *ad litem* and reporting officer, or if for any reason he considers it appropriate, he may refuse to grant any adoption order or interim order without production of further documents or hearing oral evidence and may order that such productions be lodged or evidence led.

Confidentiality

24.—(1) Unless the sheriff otherwise directs, all documents lodged in process including the reports by the curator *ad litem* and the reporting officer shall be available only to the sheriff, the curator *ad litem*, the reporting officer and the parties. Such documents shall be treated as confidential by all persons involved in, or a party to, the proceedings and by the sheriff clerk.

(2) The reporting officer or curator *ad litem* shall treat all information obtained by him in the exercise of his duties as confidential and shall not disclose any such information to any person unless disclosure of such information is necessary for the proper discharge of his duties.

Adoption by married couples

25. A married couple may petition for an adoption order in respect of a child who has already been adopted by one of them.

Communications to the Registrar General

26. The communication to the Registrar General of an adoption order or order for the revocation of an adoption order required to be made by the sheriff clerk shall be made by sending a certified copy of the order to the Registrar General either by recorded delivery post in an envelope marked "Confidential" or by personal delivery by the sheriff clerk in a sealed envelope marked "Confidential".

Adoption orders

27.—(1) An adoption order granted by the sheriff shall specify the name and address of the adoption agency, if any, which has taken part in the arrangements for placing the child in the care of the petitioner.

(2) No extract of an adoption order shall be issued except with the authority of the sheriff who made the order.

(3) The authority required by sub-paragraph (2) shall be obtained by lodging a petition setting forth the reasons for which the extract is required.

Final procedure

28.—(1) After the granting of an order under this part of this Act of Sederunt the court process shall, immediately upon the communication under paragraph 26 being made or, in the event of an extract of the order being issued under paragraph 27, immediately upon the issue of such extract, be sealed by the sheriff clerk in an envelope marked "Confidential".

(2) The envelope referred to in sub-paragraph (1) shall not be unsealed by the sheriff clerk or any other person having control of the records of that or any court, and the process shall not be made accessible to any person, for 100 years after the date of the granting of the adoption order except—

(*a*) to an adopted child who has attained the age of 17 years and to whose adoption the process refers;

(*b*) to the sheriff clerk, on an application made to him by an adoption agency and with the consent of the adopted person for the purpose only of ascertaining the name of the agency, if any, responsible for the placement of that person and informing the applicant of that name;

(*c*) to a court, public authority or administrative board (whether in the United Kingdom or not) having power to authorise an adoption, on petition by it to the court which granted the original order requesting that information be made available from the process for the purpose of discharging its duties in considering an application for adoption and specifying the precise reasons for which access to the process is required; or

(*d*) to a person who is authorised by the Secretary of State to obtain information from the process for the purposes of such research as is intended to improve the working of adoption law and practice.

Amendment of adoption order

29—(1) An application under paragraph 4(1) of Schedule 1 to (amendment of orders and rectification of Registers), or section 46(1) of (revocation where adoptive parent marries other parent), the 1978 Act shall be by petition to the court which pronounced the adoption order.

(2) The sheriff may order the petitioner to intimate the petition to such persons as to the sheriff may seem appropriate.

(3) In an application for revocation of an adoption order the sheriff shall not grant a petition unless he is satisfied that the petition has been served upon every parent of the child whose whereabouts can be ascertained.

Application for removal of child pending adoption

30.—(1) An application under section 27(1) (restrictions on removal where adoption agreed or application made under section 18(1)), section 28 (restrictions on removal where applicant has provided home for five years), section 29 (return of child taken away in breach of section 27 or 28), or section 30(2) (return of children placed for adoption), of the 1978 Act shall be made by minute lodged in the process of the original adoption petition.

(2) A minute under paragraph (1) shall set forth the relevant facts and the crave which the minuter wishes to make.

(3) On receipt of the minute the sheriff shall order a diet of hearing to be fixed and shall ordain the minuter to send a notice of such hearing in form 12 together with a copy of the minute by registered post or by recorded delivery letter to the petitioner or petitioners in the original petition, to the curator *ad litem* in the original petition, to any person who may have care and possession of the child and to such other persons as the sheriff may deem appropriate.

PART IV

EXPENSES

Expenses

31. The sheriff may make such order with regard to the expenses of an application under this Act of Sederunt as he thinks fit and may modify such expenses or direct them to be taxed on such scale as he may determine.

SCHEDULE

Paragraph 3(1) Form 1

APPLICATION FOR AN ORDER DECLARING A CHILD FREE FOR ADOPTION UNDER THE ADOPTION (SCOTLAND) ACT 1978 SECTION 18

PETITION OF

A.B. (address), Petitioner

For an order in relation to the child, C.D.

(*Full Name*)
(*Date of Birth*)

Presently residing at

(*Address*)

The Petitioner craves the court [(1)] to make an order declaring the child, C.D., free for adoption [; and (2) to dispense with the agreement [or consent] of
on the ground that
].

The following documents are produced herewith:

a. An extract of the entry in the Register of Births relating to the child;

b. *Consent of (*name and address*) to the making of this application;

c. *Consent by the child dated

d. *Adoption agency report dated

Signed ....
and designation

Date ....

*Delete as appropriate.

Paragraph 4(1) Form 2

FORM OF PARENTAL AGREEMENT UNDER THE ADOPTION (SCOTLAND) ACT 1978 SECTION 18

In the petition by (*adoption agency, name and address*)

for an order declaring the child—
—(*full name of child*)

free for adoption,

I, (*name, address*)

confirm that I am the mother/father/guardian of the child. I fully understand that on the making of an order under section 18 of the Adoption (Scotland) Act 1978 any parental right or duty which I have at present relating to the child vests in the petitioners and that the effect of an adoption order will be permanently to deprive me of these parental rights or duties. I freely agree generally and unconditionally to the making of an adoption order in relation to the child.

I have signed this agreement at (*place of signing*)

on the day of Nineteen hundred and years.

(*Signature*) ....

This agreement was signed in the presence of:—

(*Signature of reporting officer*) ....

Full name

Address

Paragraph 7(1) or 10(3) Form 3

DECLARATION UNDER SECTION 18(6) OR SECTION 19(4) OF THE ADOPTION (SCOTLAND) ACT 1978

In the petition by (*adoption agency, name and address*)

for an order declaring the child (*full name*)

free for adoption,

I/We,

being the

of the child, hereby declare that I/we prefer not to be involved in future questions concerning the adoption of the child.

In witness whereof I/we have signed this declaration on the day of , Nineteen hundred and

Signature ....
Signature ....

Signed in presence of

(*Signature*) ....
Full name

Designation and Reporting Officer

Address

FOR OFFICIAL USE ONLY

The foregoing declaration was received at the Sheriff Clerk's Office,

on 19 , and has been duly entered in the adopted register of that court.

Signature ....

Sheriff Clerk Depute

Paragraph 11(1) Form 4

APPLICATION TO REVOKE AN ORDER FREEING A CHILD FOR ADOPTION UNDER THE ADOPTION (SCOTLAND) ACT 1978 SECTION 20(1)

MINUTE

by

(full name, address)

in relation to the child

(full name and date of birth)

The minuter craves the court to revoke the order declaring the child free for adoption on the ground that he/she wishes to resume parental rights and duties and condescends as follows:

1. An order freeing the child for adoption was made on
2. More than 12 months have elapsed since the child was freed for adoption
3. No adoption order has been made in respect of the child
4. The child at present resides at
   and does not have his home with a person with whom he had been placed for adoption
5. The minuter makes the following proposals for the future well-being of the child:—

Signed ....
and designation

Date ....

Paragraph 14(1) Form 5

APPLICATION (FOR LEAVE OF COURT) TO PLACE CHILD FOR ADOPTION UNDER THE ADOPTION (SCOTLAND) ACT 1978 SECTION 20(2)

MINUTE BY

(full name, address)

in relation to the child

(full name and address and date of birth)

presently residing at

The minuters crave leave of the court to place the child for adoption and condescend as follows:

a. An order in terms of section 18 of the Adoption (Scotland) Act 1978 declaring the child free for adoption was made by the court on 19 , in a petition by the minuters.

b. An application to revoke the aforesaid order was lodged on 19 , by and application for revocation has not yet been determined by the court.

c. *(Set out here the circumstances justifying the placing of the child)*

Date .... Signature ....
and designation

Paragraph 15 Form 6

FURTHER APPLICATION BY FORMER PARENT TO REVOKE AN ORDER FREEING A CHILD FOR ADOPTION UNDER THE ADOPTION (SCOTLAND) ACT 1978 SECTION 20(5)

MINUTE BY

(*full name and address*)

in relation to the child

(*full name and address*) born on (*date of birth*)

The minuter craves leave of the court to make this further application on the ground that:—
(*narrate the change in circumstances or other proper reason for application*)

The minuter craves the court to revoke the order declaring the child free for adoption on the ground that he wishes to resume parental rights and duties and condescends as follows:

a. An order freeing the child for adoption was made on

b. An application to the court to revoke the order was made on , but was refused on

c. More than 12 months have elapsed since the child was freed for adoption.

d. No adoption order has been made in respect of the child.

e. The child at present resides at and does not have his home with a person with whom he has been placed for adoption.

f. The minuter makes the following proposals for the future well-being of the child:—

Signature ....
and designation

Date ....

Paragraph 16(1) Form 7

PETITION FOR ADOPTION ORDER UNDER THE ADOPTION (SCOTLAND) ACT 1978 SECTION 12

Petition of

A.B. (*full name*)

[and (*full name of spouse*)

Maiden surname

Any previous married surname]

(*Address*)

For authority to adopt the child

(*Full name of child as shown on birth certificate*), born on

(*Child's date of birth*)

(*Child's present address*)

1. The petitioner(s) crave(s) the court [(1)] to make an adoption order in his/her/their favour under section 12 of the Adoption (Scotland) Act 1978, in relation to the child [; and to dispense with the agreement [*or* consent] of on the ground that] and condescends as follows:

a. The petitioner(s) is/are domiciled in
and reside(s) at
[*or* the male/female petitioner is domiciled in
and both petitioners reside at].

b. The occupation(s) of the petitioner(s) is/are

c. The petitioner(s) is/are married [*or* unmarried *or* widow *or* widower]. (*If married, state whether spouse resides with, or apart, from, the petitioner.*)

d. The petitioner(s) is/are [respectively] [and]
years of age.

e. The petitioner(s) has/have resident with him/her/them the following persons, namely

f. The child was received into the care and possession of the petitioners on (*date*)

g. The child has been continuously in the care and possession of the petitioner(s) since the date shown above.

h. The petitioner(s) notified (*give name of local authority notified*) of his/her/their intention to apply for an adoption order in relation to the child on (*date*)

i. *Arrangements for placing the child in the care of the petitioner(s) were made by (*give full name and address of agency or authority or person making such arrangements*)

(*Delete this statement if it does not apply)

j. An order freeing the child for adoption was made at
Sheriff Court on (*date*)
[*or* An order declaring the child free for adoption has not been made.]

k. No reward or payment has been given or received by the petitioner(s) for or in consideration of the adoption of the child or the giving of consent to the making of an adoption order.

2. a. The child is years of age, having been born on the day of
19 , at
in the County of

b. The child is not and never has been married and is male/female.

c. The child's natural mother is
(*full name and address*)

d.* The child's natural father is
(*full name and address*)

e.* Paternity of the child has not been admitted or established by decree of any court.

(*Delete either d. or e. as appropriate)

f. The child is of British/or nationality.

g. The child is entitled to the following property, namely

h. The child has the following tutors, curators or guardians. (*Either give full names and addresses or delete the paragraph if it does not apply*).

3. is/are liable to contribute to the support of the child.

4. The child has not been the subject of an adoption order or of a petition for an adoption order save that

5. The petitioner(s) is/are prepared to undertake, if any order is made on this petition, to make for the said child the following provisions, namely:—

6. There is lodged along with this application the following documents

(i) extract birth certificate relating to the child

(ii) extract marriage certificate relating to the petitioner(s)
(*Note: this need be lodged only in the case of a joint application by spouses*)

(iii) medical certificate relating to the health of the male petitioner

(iv) medical certificate relating to the health of the female petitioner
(*Note: medical certificate need not be produced where either the petitioner or one of the joint petitioners is a parent of the child*)

(v)* agreement to the adoption by the child's natural mother

(vi)* agreement to the adoption by the child's natural father

(vii)* consent to the adoption by the child

(viii)* consent to the adoption by the tutor or curator

(ix)* acknowledgement by local authority of letter by petitioner(s) intimating intention to apply for adoption order

(x)* report by local authority in terms of section 22(2) of the Adoption (Scotland) Act 1978

(xi)* report by the adoption agency in terms of section 23 of the Adoption (Scotland) Act 1978

(xii)* any other document not referred to above.

(*Delete as appropriate)

7. have taken part in the arrangements for placing the child in the care of the petitioner(s)

The petitioner(s) humbly crave(s) the court to dispense with intimation and to order notice of this petition to be served on such persons, if any, as the court may think proper, and thereafter, on resuming consideration hereon, to make

an adoption order in favour of the petitioner(s) under the Adoption (Scotland) Act 1978 section 12 on such terms and conditions (if any) as the court may think fit, and to direct the Registrar General for Scotland to make an entry regarding the adoption in the Adopted Children Register in the form prescribed by him, giving
as the forename(s), and the surname of the adopter(s) as the surname, of in the form; and further, upon proof to the satisfaction of the court in the course of the proceedings to follow hereon, that (*name of child*)
was born on the day of
in the year nineteen hundred and
and is identical with the
to whom any entry numbered and made on the day of
in the year 19 , in the Register of Births for the Registration District of in the relates, to direct the said Registrar General to cause such birth entry to be marked with the word "adopted" and to include the above-mentioned date of birth in the entry recording the adoption in the manner indicated in the Schedule to the and to pronounce such other or further orders or directions upon such matters, including the expenses of this petition, as the court may think fit.

....
Signature of male petitioner

....
Signature of female petitioner

or

....
Signature of solicitor with designation and address
....

....

Paragraph 16(1) Form 8

PETITION FOR AN ORDER UNDER THE ADOPTION (SCOTLAND) ACT 1978 SECTION 49

Petition of

A.B. (*full name*)

[and (*full name of spouse*)

Maiden surname

Any previous married surname]

(*Address*)

For an order vesting in him/her/them the parental rights and duties relating to the child.

(*Full name of child as shown on birth certificate*), born on

(*Child's date of birth*)

(*Child's present address*)

1. The petitioner(s) crave(s) the court [(1)] to make an order under section 49 of the Adoption (Scotland) Act 1978 vesting in him/her/them the parental rights and duties relating to the child [; and to dispense with the agreement [*or* consent] of on the ground that] and condescends as follows:

a. The petitioner(s) is/are domiciled in and reside(s) at

b. The occupation(s) of the petitioner(s) is/are

c. The petitioner(s) is/are married [*or* unmarried *or* widow *or* widower]. (*If married, state whether spouse resides with, or apart from, the petitioner.*)

d. The petitioner(s) is/are [respectively] [and] years of age.

e. The petitioner(s) has/have resident with him/her/them the following persons, namely

f. The child was received into the care and possession of the petitioners on (*date*)

g. The child has been continuously in the care and possession of the petitioner(s) since the date shown above.

h. The petitioner(s) notified (*give name of local authority notified*) of his/her/their intention to apply for an adoption order in relation to the child on (*date*)

i. *Arrangements for placing the child in the care of the petitioner(s) were made by (*give full name and address of agency or authority or person making such arrangements*)

(*Delete this statement if it does not apply)

j. An order freeing the child for adoption was made at Sheriff Court on (*date*)

[*or* an order declaring the child free for adoption has not been made.]

k. No reward or payment has been given or received by the petitioner(s) for or in consideration of the adoption of the child or the giving of consent to the making of an adoption order.

2. a. The child is years of age, having been born on the day of 19 , at in the County of

b. The child is not and has never been married and is male/female.

c. The child's natural mother is (*full name and address*)

d.* The child's natural father is (*full name and address*)

OR

e.* Paternity of the child has not been admitted or established by decree of any court.

(*Delete either d. or e. as appropriate)

f. The child is of British/or nationality.

g. The child is entitled to the following property, namely

h. The child has the following tutors, curators or guardians. (*Either give full names and addresses or delete the paragraph if it does not apply*).

3. is/are liable to contribute to the support of the child.

4. The child has not been the subject of an adoption order or of a petition for an adoption order save that

5. The petitioner(s) is/are prepared to undertake, if any order is made on this petition, to make for the said child the following provision, namely:—

6. There is lodged along with this application the following documents

(i) extract birth certificate relating to the child

(ii) extract marriage certificate relating to the petitioner(s)
(*Note: this need be lodged only in the case of a joint application by spouses*)

(iii) medical certificate relating to the health of the male petitioner

(iv) medical certificate relating to the health of the female petitioner
(*Note: medical certificates need not be produced where either the petitioner or one of the joint petitioners is a parent of the child*)

(v)* agreement to the adoption by the child's natural mother

(vi)* agreement to the adoption by the child's natural father

(vii)* consent to the adoption by the child

(viii)* consent to the adoption by the tutor or curator

(ix)* acknowledgement by local authority of letter by petitioner(s) intimating intention to apply for adoption order

(x)* report by local authority in terms of section 22(2) of the Adoption (Scotland) Act 1978

(xi)* report by the adoption agency in terms of section 23 of the Adoption (Scotland) Act 1978

(xii)* an affidavit by who is conversant with the law of adoption of and has practised law as a [*or* represents that country as (*state capacity*) in the United Kingdom].

(*Delete where appropriate)

7. have taken part in the arrangement for placing the child in the care of the petitioner(s).

The petitioner(s) humbly crave(s) the court to dispense with intimation and to order notice of this petition to be served on such persons, if any, as the court may think proper, and thereafter, on resuming consideration hereof, to make

an order under the Adoption (Scotland) Act 1978 section 49, vesting in the petitioners the parental rights and duties relating to (*name of child*) on such terms and conditions (if any) as the court may think fit; to authorise removal of the child for the purpose of adoption under the laws of ; to find the petitioners entitled to the custody of the child pending such adoptions and to direct the Registrar General for Scotland to make an entry regarding the order in the Adopted Children Register in the form prescribed by him, giving
as the forename(s), and the surname of the proposed adopters as the surname, of in the form; and further, upon proof to the satisfaction of the court in the course of the proceedings to follow hereon, that the child
was born on the day of
in the year Nineteen hundred and
and is identical with the
to whom any entry numbered and made on the
day of in the year 19 , in the Register of Births for the Registration District of in the relates, to direct the said Registrar General to cause such birth entry to be marked with the words "proposed foreign adoption" and to include the above-mentioned date of birth in the entry recording the order in the manner indicated in the Schedule to the said Act; and to pronounce such other or further orders or directions upon such matters, including the expenses of this petition, as the court may think fit.

....
Signature of male petitioner or agent

....
Signature of female petitioner or agent

or

....
Signature of solicitor with designation and address
....

....

Paragraph 4(1) or 18(1) Form 9

FORM OF CONSENT UNDER THE ADOPTION (SCOTLAND) ACT 1978 SECTION 12(8) OR SECTION 18(8)

in the

Petition

by

(*Name and address*) Petitioner

I, (*full name of child*) confirm that I understand the nature and effect of any order declaring me free for adoption/adoption order for which application is made. I hereby consent to the making of such an order in the petitioners' favour in respect of myself.

I have signed this consent at (*place of signing*)

on the day of Nineteen

hundred and years.

(*Signature*)

This consent was signed in the presence of:—

1st Witness	2nd Witness
Signature	Signature
Full Name	Full Name
Designation	Designation
Address	Address

Paragraph 18(1) Form 10

FORM OF PARENTAL AGREEMENT UNDER THE ADOPTION (SCOTLAND) ACT 1978 SECTION 16(1)

In the petition relating to the adoption of

(*Insert the full name of the child as it is given in the birth certificate*)

to which petition the court has assigned the serial number

I, (*name and address*)

confirm that I am the mother/father/guardian of the child. I fully understand that the effect of the adoption order for which application has been made will be permanently to deprive me of any parental right or duty which I have at present over the child. I freely agree generally and unconditionally to the making of an adoption order in relation to the child.

I have signed this agreement at (*place of signing*)

on the day of Nineteen

hundred and years.

(*Signature*)

This agreement was signed in the presence of:—

(*Signature of reporting officer*)

Full name

Address

Paragraph 8(2) or 22 Form 11

FORM OF INTIMATION OF DIET OF HEARING UNDER THE ADOPTION (SCOTLAND) ACT 1978 SECTION 12 OR SECTION 18

To:—

(*Full name and address of person to whom this intimation is to be sent*)

Notice is given that a hearing will take place at

Sheriff Court

(*Name of sheriff court*)

(*Full address of court*)

on at

(*date*) (*time*)

in relation to the child (*full name of child as given in the birth certificate*)

when the court will consider an application for an order declaring the child free for adoption [*or* an application for adoption of the child].

You do not need to attend this hearing if you do not wish to be heard by the court.

If you do not attend this hearing the court may make an order as noted above.

Signature
and designation ....
Date

Paragraph 30(3) Form 12

FORM OF INTIMATION OF DIET OF HEARING UNDER THE ADOPTION (SCOTLAND) ACT 1978 SECTION 27, 28, 29 OR 30

Notice of hearing of minute in petition for authority to adopt:

(*Full name of child as given in the birth certificate*)

To:—

(*Full name and address of person to whom this intimation is to be sent*)

Notice is hereby given that a hearing in the petition for authority to adopt the child, which hearing will be restricted to matters bearing upon the crave of the minute, a copy of which is attached hereto, will take place at (*name of sheriff court*)

Sheriff Court (*address*)
on
(*date*) at (*time*) when, if so advised, you may appear and be heard personally or by solicitor or counsel.

Signature
....
Designation

Date

Social Work (Scotland) Act 1968 (Safeguarders) 1985

(S.I. 1985 No. 780)

[17th May 1985]

The Lords of Council and Session, under and by virtue of the powers conferred on them by section 18A(2) of the Social Work (Scotland) Act 1968, section 32 of the Sheriff Courts (Scotland) Act 1971 and of all other powers competent to them in that behalf, do hereby enact and declare:—

Citation and commencement

1.—(1) This Act of Sederunt may be cited as the Act of Sederunt (Social Work (Scotland) Act 1968) (Safeguarders) 1985 and shall come into operation on 30th June 1985.

(2) This Act of Sederunt shall be inserted in the Books of Sederunt.

(3) In this Act of Sederunt—

"safeguarder" means a person appointed under section 18A(1) of the Social Work (Scotland) Act 1968 for the purpose of safeguarding the interests of a child.

Rules for safeguarders

2.—(1) Where, in proceedings to which section 18A of the Social Work (Scotland) Act 1968 applies, the sheriff considers it necessary to appoint a person for the purpose of safeguarding the interests of the child in the proceedings, he may, if he thinks fit, appoint a safeguarder for that purpose selected from a panel of persons appointed under the Social Work (Panels of Persons to Safeguard the Interests of Children) (Scotland) Regulations 1984.

(2) The sheriff—

(*a*) shall consider whether it is necessary to appoint a safeguarder as soon as reasonably practicable after the lodging of defences in the proceedings; and

(*b*) may, at any later stage of the proceedings, if he thinks fit, appoint a safeguarder.

3.—(1) A safeguarder appointed under paragraph 2—

(*a*) shall be entitled to have copies of the pleadings and productions in the proceedings in respect of which he is appointed provided to him by the sheriff clerk; and

(*b*) may make such enquiries with regard to the proceedings as he considers appropriate.

(2) Within 21 days after his appointment, a safeguarder shall lodge a minute with the sheriff clerk stating whether he intends to enter the process and become a party to the proceedings.

4.—(1) If a safeguarder does not intend to enter the process, he shall append to the minute to be lodged under paragraph 3(2) a report specifying the extent of his enquiries and his conclusion as to the interests of the child in the proceedings.

(2) A safeguarder who has not entered the process shall have intimated to him by the sheriff clerk all subsequent interlocutors in the proceedings and may, on cause shown, seek leave to enter the process at any time or where competent to appeal against any interlocutor or decree.

5.—(1) If a safeguarder intends to enter the process, he shall lodge defences in the proceedings within 14 days of lodging the minute under paragraph 3(2).

(2) On entering the process, a safeguarder shall have all of the powers and duties at common law of a curator *ad litem* in respect of the child.

6.—(1) A safeguarder may appear personally in the proceedings or may instruct an advocate or a solicitor to appear on his behalf.

(2) Where an advocate or a solicitor is appointed to act as a safeguarder, he shall not act also as advocate or solicitor for the child in the proceedings.

Children's Hearings (Scotland) Rules 1986

(S.I. 1986 No. 2291)

[17th December 1986]

ARRANGEMENT OF RULES

PART I

INTERPRETATION, ETC.

Rule

PART II

CONSTITUTION AND ARRANGEMENT OF CHILDREN'S HEARINGS

PART III

GENERAL PROVISIONS AS TO CHILDREN'S HEARINGS

Part IV

Children's Hearings on Referral and at Review of Supervision Requirements, etc.

Part V

References for Advice and Suspension of Supervision Requirements

Part VI

Miscellaneous and Supplemental

Schedule

Arrangement of Forms in Schedule

The Secretary of State, in exercise of the powers conferred on him by sections 34A(2), 35(4) and (5), 36(8) and 44(8) of the Social Work (Scotland) Act 1968 and of all other powers enabling him in that behalf, and after consultation with the Council on Tribunals, hereby makes the following Rules:—

PART I

INTERPRETATION, ETC.

Citation and commencement

1. These rules may be cited as the Children's Hearings (Scotland) Rules 1986 and shall come into operation on 2nd February 1987.

Interpretation

2.—(1) In these rules, –

"the Act" means the Social Work (Scotland) Act 1968;

"the 1975 Act" means the Criminal Procedure (Scotland) Act 1975;

"the 1983 Regulations" means the Secure Accommodation (Scotland) Regulations 1983;

"chairman" means the chairman of a children's hearing;

"child" has the meaning assigned to that term by section 30(1) of the Act;

"day" means a period of 24 hours commencing at midnight;

"enactment" includes any order, regulation or other instrument made under the Act;

"parent" has the meaning assigned to that term by section 94(1), as read with section 30(2) of the Act;

"reporter" means an officer of a local authority appointed under section 36(1) of the Act;

"representative" has the meaning assigned to that term by rule 11(4) below;

"safeguarder" means a person appointed under section 34A of the Act for the purpose of safeguarding the interests of a child;

"secure accommodation" means accommodation provided in a residential establishment in accordance with the 1983 regulations for the purpose of restricting the liberty of children.

(2) In these rules, unless the context otherwise requires, any reference in relation to a children's hearing—

(*a*) to the local authority shall be construed as a reference to the local authority for the area of the children's hearing;

(*b*) to the reporter shall be construed as a reference to the reporter of the said local authority.

(3) In these rules any reference to a numbered rule or form shall be construed as a reference to the rule or form bearing that number in these rules.

Schedule of Forms

3. In these rules any requirement that a writing shall be in the form of a numbered Form shall be construed as a requirement that the writing shall be in a form to the like effect as the Form bearing that number set out in the Schedule to these rules, but with such variations as circumstances may require.

Application of rules to certain young persons

4. Where under section 373 of the 1975 Act a court has either—

(*a*) requested the reporter to arrange a children's hearing for the purpose of obtaining their advice as to the treatment of a person; or

(*b*) remitted the case of a person for disposal by a children's hearing,

the provisions of these rules shall apply in relation to that person as if he were a child.

Part II

Constitution and Arrangement of Children's Hearings

Constitution of children's hearings

5.—(1) The selection of the chairman and the members of any children's hearing from among the members of the children's panel for a local authority area shall be made either directly by the chairman of the children's panel, or in his absence by the deputy chairman, or by the operation of standing arrangements in that behalf made by the chairman of the children's panel after consulting the reporter and such members of the panel as he may think fit. Such standing arrangements may provide for the selection of the chairman and members of any hearing to be made by members of the panel appointed for that purpose by the chairman of the panel.

(2) The chairman of the children's panel shall keep under review any standing arrangements which he has made under paragraph (1) above and

shall from time to time consult the reporter and such members of the panel as he may think fit as to the operation of those arrangements.

Notification of children's hearing to chairman and members; provisions about relevant documents

6.—(1) Subject to the 1983 regulations, where the reporter arranges any children's hearing, he shall, wherever practicable at least seven days before the date of the hearing, notify the chairman and members of the time and place of the hearing and, subject as aforesaid, as soon as possible, but not later than three clear days before the date of the hearing, he shall give to each of them any of the following documents if it is relevant to the case of a child to be considered at the hearing:—

(*a*) a copy of a report of a local authority on the child and his social background;

(*b*) a copy of the statement of the grounds for the referral of the case to the children's hearing given to the child under rule 16 below;

(*c*) a copy of any judicial remit or reference or of any reference by a local authority;

(*d*) where the child is subject to a supervision requirement, a copy of that requirement;

(*e*) where a safeguarder has been appointed, a copy of any report which the safeguarder may have prepared.

(2) If the reporter has obtained any information or any document, other than a document mentioned in paragraph (1) above, which is material to the consideration of the case of a child at any children's hearing, he shall make that information or, as the case may be, that document or copies thereof available to the chairman and members of the children's hearing before the hearing.

(3) Subject to paragraph (5) below, the chairman and members of children's hearings shall keep securely in their custody any documents made available to them under this rule and, except as otherwise provided in rules 19(3) and 21(4) below, they shall not cause or permit any information contained in the said documents or otherwise disclosed during the hearing to be made known to any person.

(4) Any information or document which the reporter makes available in compliance with the foregoing (under exception of rule 6(1) or otherwise to the chairman and members of any children's hearing shall also be made available to any safeguarder who is appointed under the Act by a chairman of a hearing regardless of the date of his appointment.

(5) Any safeguarder appointed under the Act shall keep securely in his custody any documents made available to him under this rule, shall not cause or permit any information contained in the said documents or otherwise disclosed during the hearing to be made known to any person, other than may be necessary for the performance of his own duties, and shall return to the reporter any document which has been made available to him by the reporter when he has completed performance of all the duties associated with his appointment.

(6) Immediately after the conclusion of a children's hearing the chairman and members shall return to the reporter any documents which have been made available to them under this rule.

(7) Any information or document which the reporter makes available in compliance with the foregoing or otherwise to the chairman and members of any children's hearing shall also be made available, if requested, to any member of the Council on Tribunals who is attending that hearing.

(8) Any information or document which the reporter makes available in compliance with the foregoing or otherwise to the chairman and members of any children's hearing shall also be made available, if requested, to any member of the Children's Panel Advisory Committee or to any member of

a sub-committee of the Advisory Committee who has given notice of his intention to attend that hearing as an observer. Any persons provided with papers under this rule shall not cause or permit any information contained in the said documents or otherwise disclosed during the hearing to be made known to any person and shall return to the reporter at the end of the hearing any document which has been made available to him.

Notification of children's hearings to children

7.—(1) Where the reporter arranges a children's hearing—

(*a*) to consider under section 37(4) or section 40(6) of the Act the case of a child detained in a place of safety; or

(*b*) to consider and determine under Part III of the Act in pursuance of a referral, the case of a child placed in secure accommodation under regulation 7 or 9 of the 1983 regulations; or

(*c*) to consider the case of a child detained in a place of safety where a warrant for detention involving secure accommodation has been granted under section 58E(1) of the Act; or

(*d*) to review in terms of section 44(7) the case of a child transferred from a place under section 44(6) of the Act or placed in secure accommodation under regulation 6 of the 1983 regulations; or

(*e*) to consider an application under section 49(8) of the Act for the suspension of a supervision requirement; or

(*f*) to review a condition imposed under section 58A(3) of the Act with respect to residence in secure accommodation, being a review required to a child under regulation 12 of the 1983 regulations; or

(*g*) to consider under section 69(3) of the Act the case of a child where the occupier of the place of safety or the person under whose control he has been placed is unwilling or unable to receive him,

he shall as soon as possible before the hearing give to the child notification of the hearing in the form of Form 1:

Provided that if the notification cannot be given in writing, the reporter may notify the child orally that he is required to attend the hearing and inform him of the date, time and place of the hearing.

(2) Where the reporter arranges a children's hearing—

(*a*) to consider and determine under Part III of the Act the case of a child in pursuance of a referral; or

(*b*) to review a supervision requirement; or

(*c*) to consider the giving of advice on a remit by a court under sections 173(1), 372(1) and 373 of the 1975 Act; or

(*d*) for any purpose not mentioned in the foregoing provisions of this rule and where a previous children's hearing have determined that the attendance of the child will be necessary or expedient,

the reporter shall, subject to the 1983 regulations, not less than seven clear days before the hearing give to the child notification of the hearing in the form of Form 1.

Notification of children's hearings to parents

8.—(1) Where the parent of a child whose case is to be considered at a children's hearing has a duty under section 41(2) of the Act, to attend that hearing, the reporter shall give notification to the said parent, if his whereabouts are known, of his said duty and of the time and place of the said hearing and such notification shall, subject to paragraph (4) below, be in writing in the form of Form 2.

(2) Where under section 41(2) of the Act a children's hearing are satisfied either that it would be unreasonable to require the attendance of a parent of a child at any children's hearing who are considering the case of the child or that the attendance of the parent would be unnecessary to the consideration of the case, the reporter shall give notification to the said parent, if his whereabouts are known, of his right under section 41(1) of

the Act to attend the said hearing and of the time and place of the said hearing and such notification shall, subject to paragraph (4) below, be in writing in the form of Form 3.

(3) Any notification under this rule, except a notification to a parent of a children's hearing mentioned in rule 7(1) above, shall be given not later than seven clear days before the date of the children's hearing to which it relates.

(4) In the case of such a children's hearing as is mentioned in rule 7(1) above, the notification to the parent under paragraph (1) above may be given orally and, subject to the 1983 regulations, shall be given as soon as practicable.

Part III

General Provisions as to Children's Hearings

Functions of chairman of children's hearing

9.—(1) Except as otherwise provided by these rules and any other enactment, the procedure at any children's hearing shall be such as the chairman shall in his discretion determine.

(2) Without prejudice to the generality of paragraph (1) above and to the power of a children's hearing under the Act to continue a hearing for the further investigation of a case, the chairman of a children's hearing may at any time during the hearing adjourn the hearing provided that any adjournment under this rule shall be such as to enable the children's hearing to sit again on the same day as the adjournment was made.

(3) As soon as may be after a children's hearing make—

(*a*) a decision disposing of the case of a child on a referral or at a review of a supervision requirement or a condition imposed under section 58A(3) of the Act with respect to residence in secure accommodation;

(*b*) a decision to issue a warrant for the apprehension or the detention of a child or to renew a warrant for the detention of a child;

(*c*) a decision to appoint a person to act as a safeguarder in accordance with section 34A of the Act; or

(*d*) a requirement in terms of section 43(4) of the Act,

the chairman shall make or cause to be made a report of the said decision and a statement in writing of the reasons for the said decision and shall sign the said report and statement.

Continuation of cases before children's hearings

10. At any time during a children's hearing, the children's hearing may continue the hearing for the further investigation of the case which is before them to a subsequent children's hearing.

Representation of children and parents at children's hearing

11.—(1) Any child whose case comes before a children's hearing whether for consideration and determination under Part III of the Act or for some other reason and the parent of such a child, being a child or a parent who attends that hearing, may each be accompanied at that hearing by one person for the purpose of representing the child or, as the case may be, the parent at that hearing:

Provided that a child and his parent attending the hearing may be represented as aforesaid by the same person.

(2) Any person attending any children's hearing for the purpose of representing a child or his parent or both a child and his parent, as the case may be, shall assist the person whom he represents in the discussion of the case of the child with the children's hearing.

(3) Notwithstanding anything in these rules, the chairman of a children's hearing may exclude a representative from the hearing if the children's hearing are satisfied, either of their own accord or on the motion of the child or his parent or the reporter, that the representative is persisting in behaviour which disrupts the proceedings at the hearing or which is otherwise likely to be detrimental to the interests of the child.

(4) In these rules any reference to a representative is a reference to a person who under this rule represents a child or a parent or both a child and a parent and includes, unless the context otherwise requires, a reference both to any representative of a child and any representative of his parent.

Safeguarder's attendance at children's hearings

12. Any safeguarder appointed under the Act by the chairman of a children's hearing shall be entitled to be present throughout the duration of any children's hearing until the disposal of the child's case.

Attendance at hearings of constable, prison officer or other person duly authorised

13. A constable, prison officer, or other person duly authorised who has in his lawful custody a person who has to attend a children's hearing shall be entitled to be present at the hearing for the purposes of escorting that person.

Persons who may attend children's hearings at chairman's discretion

14. Without prejudice to the right of a child and of a parent under rule 11 above to be accompanied at a children's hearing by a representative, and subject to subsections (1) to (3) of section 35 of the Act (provisions as to privacy of children's hearings), the persons whose presence at a children's hearing may be permitted by the chairman under the said subsection (1) shall be—

(*a*) the chairman and members of the Children's Panel Advisory Committee for the local authority area of the children's hearing and the clerk of the local authority;

(*b*) any members or possible members of children's panels whose attendance is required at children's hearings for the purpose of their training as members of children's hearings, and their instructors;

(*c*) any student engaged in formal education or training in social work or any person engaged in research relating to children who may be in need of compulsory measures of care;

(*d*) any other person whose presence at the sitting may in the opinion of the chairman be justified by special circumstances; and

(*e*) any clerk, interpreter, janitor, messenger or other person whose attendance in a like executive capacity is required or expedient for the proper conduct of the proceedings of the children's hearing.

PART IV

CHILDREN'S HEARINGS ON REFERRAL AND AT REVIEW OF SUPERVISION REQUIREMENTS, ETC.

Application of Part IV

15.—(1) This Part shall, subject to the provisions thereof, apply to any children's hearing, arranged either for the purposes of considering and determining on referral the case of any child or for the review of a supervision requirement or a condition imposed under section 58A(3) of the Act with respect to residence in secure accommodation, being—

(*a*) a hearing arranged by virtue of any enactment specified in paragraph (2) below; or

(*b*) unless the contrary intention appears, a hearing arranged by virtue of any enactment passed or made after the date of the making of these rules which provides that the case of a child shall be referred to a children's hearing for consideration and determination under Part III of the Act.

(2) The enactments referred to in paragraph (1)(*a*) above are as follows—

Initial referral

section 39(3) of the Act (referral of case to children's hearing on initial investigation by reporter);

section 42(6) of the Act (remit by sheriff after grounds of referral established);

section 51(1) of the Act (remit by court for reconsideration of case by children's hearing following appeal) insofar as that provision relates to a remit following an appeal under section 49 or section 50 of the Act against a decision disposing of a case by a children's hearing arranged under any of the other provisions of the Act mentioned in this rule;

section 54(2) of the Act (transfer of case to another children's hearing), subsections (1)(*a*), (2) or (3) of section 173 or 372, or section 373, of the 1975 Act (cases of children or young persons convicted of offence) insofar as those provisions relate to a referral in pursuance of a remit by the court of a case of a child, whether or not subject to a supervision requirement, or of a young person;

section 73(1)(ii) of the Act (referral in pursuance of notification to reporter of order of court in England or Wales or Northern Ireland where child moving to Scotland);

subsections (1) or (2) of section 75 of the Act (referral of the cases of children subject to certain orders in England or Wales or Northern Ireland, where parent moving to Scotland);

section 44(1) of the Education (Scotland) Act 1980 (powers of the court in relation to the child):

Review of a supervision requirement

section 44(7) of the Act (review of a supervision requirement on transfer of child under section 44(6) of the Act);

section 47 of the Act (duration of supervision requirements and their variation) and section 48 (review of requirement of children's hearing);

section 72(1) of the Act (review of supervision requirement where parent of a child in residential establishment moving to England or Wales or Northern Ireland).

Notification of statement of grounds of referral

16.—(1) Where the reporter arranges a children's hearing which will proceed in relation to the case of a child in accordance with section 42 of the Act, he shall—

(*a*) prepare a statement of the grounds for the referral of the case to the children's hearing in the form of Form 4A or Form 4B, whichever is appropriate; and

(*b*) not less than seven clear days before the date of the said hearing give a copy of the said statement to the child and, if the whereabouts of his parent are known, to his parent.

Provided that where before the said hearing the child is detained in a place of safety, or by virtue of the 1983 regulations, sub-paragraph (*b*) above shall have effect as if for the words "not less than seven clear days" there were substituted the words "as soon as practicable".

(2) Notwithstanding that a children's hearing proceed in accordance with section 42 of the Act at more than one hearing, nothing in this rule shall require a copy of the said statement to be given to any person more than once.

Form, etc. of statement of grounds of referral

17.—(1) A statement by a reporter of the grounds for the referral of a case to a children's hearing shall be in the form as nearly as may be of Form 4A in the case of any condition mentioned in paragraphs (*a*) to (*gg*) or (*i*) of section 32(2) of the Act and in the form of Form 4B in the case of a condition mentioned in section 32(2)(*h*) of the Act.

(2) The statement shall be signed by the reporter and shall specify which one or more of the conditions mentioned in section 32(2) of the Act is or are considered by the reporter to be satisfied with respect to the child.

(3) In the case of any condition mentioned in paragraph (*a*) to (*gg*) or (*i*) of section 32(2) of the Act, the said statement shall state the facts on the basis of which it is sought to show that the condition is satisfied.

(4) In the case of a condition mentioned in section 32(2)(*g*) of the Act, the statement of the facts constituting the offence shall have the same degree of specification as is required by section 312 of the 1975 Act in a charge in a complaint and the statement shall also specify the nature of the offence in question.

Notification of application to sheriff for finding as to grounds of referral

18. Where a children's hearing have given a direction to the reporter to apply to the sheriff for a finding as to whether or not any grounds for the referral of any case to them are established, being a direction under subsection (2)(*c*) (grounds of referral not accepted by child or parent) or subsection (7) (child not capable of understanding explanation of grounds of referral or explanation of grounds of referral not understood by child) of section 42 of the Act, the reporter shall give notification in the form of Form 5 to the child and in the form of Form 6 to the parent.

Conduct of children's hearing considering case on referral or at review of supervision requirement

19.—(1) Unless a children's hearing consider the case of a child in the absence of the child, his parent, and any representative, the chairman shall, before the children's hearing proceed to consider the case, explain the purpose of the hearing to such of the said persons as are present.

(2) Thereafter the children's hearing shall consider the case of the child and during such consideration shall—

(*a*) consider a report of a local authority on the child and his social background, and any judicial remit or other relevant document and any relevant information available to them;

(*b*) consider any report the submission of which has been requested by the manager of the residential establishment in which the child is required to reside;

(*c*) discuss the case with the child, parent, any safeguarder appointed under the Act and representative if attending the hearing;

(*d*) endeavour to obtain the views of the said child, his parent, and any safeguarder appointed under the Act, if attending the hearing, on what arrangements with respect to the child would be in the best interests of the child.

(3) The chairman shall inform the child and his parent of the substance of any reports, documents and information mentioned in paragraph (2)(*a*)

if it appears to him that this is material to the manner in which the case of the child should be disposed of and that its disclosure would not be detrimental to the interests of the child.

(4) After the children's hearing have completed their consideration of the case of the child and made a decision disposing of the case, but before the conclusion of the hearing at which the decision was made, the chairman shall inform the child, his parent, any safeguarder appointed under the Act, and any representative, if attending the hearing, of—

(*a*) the decision of the hearing;
(*b*) the reasons for the decision;
(*c*) the right of the child and of the parent under section 49(1) of the Act to appeal to the sheriff against the decision; and
(*d*) the right of the child and of the parent under rule 20 below to receive a statement in writing of the reasons for the decision.

(5) The children's hearing shall not dispose of the case by making a supervision requirement under section 44(1)(*a*) of the Act imposing a condition that the child is to reside in a place (which for the purposes of this rule is a household where he is to be under the care of a person who is not his parent or guardian) unless—

(*a*) they have received and considered a report for the purposes of paragraph (2)(*a*) above from the local authority, together with the local authority's recommendations, on the child's needs and the suitability to meet these needs of—
  (i) the place in which the child is to reside by virtue of the supervision requirement, and
  (ii) the person who is to have care of the child, and
(*b*) the local authority have confirmed that in compiling the report they have carried out the procedures and gathered the information described in Regulation 20 of the Boarding-Out and Fostering of Children (Scotland) Regulations 1985.

Notification of decisions, etc. on referral or at review of supervision requirement

20.—(1) Where a children's hearing have made a decision disposing of the case of a child, the child's parent and any safeguarder appointed under the Act may ask the reporter for a copy of the statement of the reasons for the said decision made under rule 9(3) above and the reporter shall as soon as reasonably practicable comply with any such request.

(2) Where the child or his parent or any safeguarder appointed under the Act did not attend the said hearing at which the said decision was made, the reporter shall notify the child or, as the case may be, the parent of—

(*a*) the decision;
(*b*) the right of the child or, as the case may be, the parent or any safeguarder appointed under the Act, under this rule to receive a copy of the said statement of the reasons for the decision;
(*c*) except in the case of a review which continued a supervision requirement, being a review in relation to which an order under section 49(6) of the Act is in force, the right of the child or, as the case may be, the parent under section 49(1) of the Act to appeal to the sheriff against the decision;

and such notification shall be given in writing in the form of Form 7, 8A, 8B, or 8C whichever is appropriate.

Part V

References for Advice and Suspension of Supervision Requirements

Conduct of children's hearing on reference for advice by court or local authority

21.—(1) This rule shall apply to any children's hearing arranged in order to consider the case of a child for the purpose of giving advice to the court or the local authority under section 47(2) of the Act (reference by local authority for advice in case of child subject to supervision requirement) or any of the following provisions of the 1975 Act:—

sections 173(1)(*b*) or 372(1)(*b*) (reference by court for advice in case of child not subject to supervision requirement);

sections 173(3) and 372(3) (case of child subject to supervision requirement) insofar as those provisions relate to a reference by the court for advice;

section 373 (case of young person not subject to supervision requirement) insofar as that provision relates to a reference by the court for advice.

(2) Unless the children's hearing consider the case of a child in the absence of the child, his parent and any representative, the chairman shall, before the children's hearing proceed to consider the case, explain the purpose of the hearing to such of the said persons as are present.

(3) The children's hearing shall consider the case of the child and during such consideration shall—

(*a*) consider the reference by the local authority or the court, any supervision requirement to which the child is subject, a report of a local authority on the child and his social background, and any other relevant document or any relevant information available to them;

(*b*) discuss the case of the child and afford to the said child, parent and representative, if attending the hearing, an opportunity of participating in the discussion and of being heard on the case;

(*c*) endeavour to obtain the views of the said child and his parent, if attending the hearing, on what arrangements with respect to the child would be in the best interests of the child; and

(*d*) accord to any safeguarder appointed under the Act the same opportunity to discuss the case of the child and of being heard on the case and on what arrangements with respect to the child would be in the best interests of the child as are accorded to the parties mentioned in sub-paragraphs (3)(*b*) and (*c*) above,

and the children's hearing shall thereafter determine what advice they will give to the court or, as the case may be, the local authority.

(4) The chairman shall inform the child and his parent of the substance of any reports, documents and information mentioned in paragraph (3)(*a*) if it appears to him that this is material to the advice that will be given and that its disclosure would not be detrimental to the interests of the child.

Application for suspension of supervision requirements pending hearing of appeals

22.—(1) An application to a children's hearing by a child or parent under section 49(8) of the Act for the suspension of a supervision requirement pending an appeal under section 49(1) of the Act shall be made in writing to the reporter.

(2) The reporter shall give notification in writing separately to the child and parents of the date, time and place of the children's hearing at which the application will be considered, and such notification shall be in the form of Form 9.

(3) The children's hearing shall afford the applicant, or his representative, and any safeguarder appointed under the Act, if attending the hearing, and the reporter an opportunity of being heard.

(4) The chairman of the children's hearing shall inform the applicant at the conclusion of the hearing of the decision of the hearing and the reasons therefor.

(5) If the applicant fails to attend the hearing, the application shall be treated as abandoned.

(6) An application shall not be valid unless an appeal under section 49(1) of the Act has already been lodged.

Part VI

Miscellaneous and Supplemental

Social background report where child in interim detention

23. Subject to the 1983 regulations, where a children's hearing is arranged under section 37(4) of the Act, the children's hearing shall not proceed in relation to the case of the child in accordance with section 44 of the Act unless the reporter has made available to them a report of a local authority on the child and his social background.

Form of supervision requirement

24.—(1) Subject to paragraph (2) below, a supervision requirement under section 44(1) of the Act shall be in the form of Form 10A.

(2) A supervision requirement under section 44(1) of the Act with a condition under section 58A(3) of the Act (residence in secure accommodation) shall be in the form of Form 10B.

(3) Subject to paragraph (4) below, a supervision requirement under section 44(1), as applied by section 47(1), of the Act (variation of supervision requirements) shall be in the form of Form 11A.

(4) A supervision requirement under section 44(1) of the Act, as so applied, and with a condition under section 58A(3) of the Act, shall be in the form of Form 11B.

(5) A supervision requirement shall be continued by an instrument in the form of Form 12 and terminated by an instrument in the form of Form 13.

(6) A supervision requirement varying, and an instrument continuing or terminating, a supervision requirement shall be endorsed thereon or attached thereto and, if so attached, the second mentioned supervision requirement shall be docqueted with reference thereto.

Procedure relating to warrants, and to requirements under section 43(4) of the Act

25.—(1) Where a children's hearing consider in relation to a child the question whether they should issue a warrant under any of the following provisions of the Act:—

section 37(4) (warrant for detention);
section 37(5) (warrant renewing warrant under section 37(4));
section 40(7) (warrant for detention);
section 40(8) (warrant renewing warrant under section 40(7)),

or a warrant under regulation 11 of the 1983 regulations (authorisation of detention in secure accommodation under section 58B(3) of the Act), or a requirement under section 43(4) of the Act (*interim* requirement to reside at clinic, etc.), the children's hearing shall, before they make a decision to issue that warrant or as the case may be that requirement, afford to the child, his parent, and any representative, if attending the hearing, an opportunity of being heard on that question.

(2) Where a children's hearing have issued such a warrant or such a requirement as is mentioned in paragraph (1) above, the child or his parent or both the child and his parent may ask the reporter for a copy of the said warrant or requirement, and the reporter shall as soon as reasonably practicable comply with any such request.

(3) A safeguarder appointed under the Act shall be afforded the same opportunities of being heard and of receiving copies of the said warrant as are to be afforded to the parties mentioned in paragraphs (1) and (2) above.

Form of requirement under section 43(4) of the Act

26. A requirement under section 43(4) of the Act shall be in the form of Form 14.

Forms of warrants for apprehension and detention

27.—(1) Subject to paragraph (2) below, a warrant for detention under section 37(4) of the Act and a warrant under section 37(5) renewing a warrant under the said section 37(4) shall be in the form of Forms 15A and 16A respectively.

(2) A warrant issued under the said section 37(4) and section 58E(1) of the Act and the renewal of a warrant under section 37(5), ordering that a child be detained in a named residential establishment, and that said detention shall be in secure accommodation there at such times as the person in charge of the establishment with the agreement of the director of social work for the area of the children's hearing considers necessary, shall be in the form of Forms 15B and 16B respectively.

(3) Subject to paragraph (4) below, a warrant for apprehension under section 40(4) of the Act shall be in the form of Form 17A.

(4) A warrant issued under the said section 40(4) and the said section 58E(1) ordering that a child be apprehended and detained in a named residential establishment, and that said detention shall be in secure accommodation there at such times as the person in charge of the establishment with the agreement of the direction of social work for the area of the children's hearing considers necessary, shall be in the form of Form 17B.

(5) Subject to paragraph (6) below, a warrant for detention under section 40(7) of the Act and a warrant under section 40(8) renewing a warrant under the said section 40(7) shall be in the form of Forms 18A and 19A respectively.

(6) A warrant issued under the said section 40(7) and the said section 58E(1), and the renewal of such a warrant under section 40(8), ordering that a child be detained in a named residential establishment, and that said detention shall be in secure accommodation there at such times as the person in charge of the establishment with the approval of the director of social work for the area of the children's hearing considers necessary, shall be in the form of Forms 18B and 19B respectively.

(7) A warrant issued under regulation 11 of the 1983 regulations and section 58B(3) of the Act ordering that a child be detained in a named residential establishment, and that said detention shall be in secure accommodation there at such times as the person in charge of the establishment with the agreement of the director of social work for the area of the children's hearing considers necessary, shall be in the form of Form 19C.

Authentication of documents

28.—(1) A report of any decision, a statement of reasons for a decision or of advice, a warrant for apprehension and detention, or any other writing, authorised or required by Part III of the Act or these rules to be made, given, issued or granted by a children's hearing or by the chairman of a children's hearing shall be sufficiently authenticated if it is signed by the chairman, or, if he is unavailable, by a member of that hearing.

(2) Any document authorised or required by these rules to be made or executed by a reporter shall be sufficiently authenticated if it is signed by the reporter or by a person duly authorised by him.

(3) Any copy of any document authorised or required by these rules to be given or issued by a reporter may be certified as a true copy by the reporter or by a person duly authorised by him.

Service of notification and other documents

29.—(1) Any notification in writing or other document and any oral notification authorised or required under these rules to be given or issued by a reporter may be given or issued by the reporter or by a person duly authorised by the reporter or by any police officer.

(2) Any notification in writing or other document authorised or required by these rules to be given or issued to a child or to a parent may be—

(*a*) delivered to him in person; or

(*b*) left for him at his dwelling-house or place of business or where he has no known dwelling-house or place of business, at any other place in which he may at the time be resident; or

(*c*) where he is the master of, or a seaman or other person employed in, a vessel, left with a person on board thereof and connected therewith; or

(*d*) sent by post in a registered or first class service recorded delivery letter to his dwelling-house or place of business.

(3) Where the reporter or a person duly authorised by him gives to any parent a notification in writing under paragraph (1) of rule 8 above, or an oral notification under that paragraph as read with paragraph (4) of that rule, he shall execute a certificate of notification in the form of Form 20.

(4) Where a notification under rule 7 or rule 8 above or a copy of such a statement as is mentioned in rule 16 above is sent by post in accordance with paragraph (2)(*d*) of this rule, the notification or copy shall be deemed, for the purpose of the said rule 7, 8 or 16, as the case may be, to have been given the day following the date of posting.

Reports of proceedings of children's hearings

30.—(1) In relation to the case of any child which comes before a children's hearing, it shall be the duty of the reporter to keep or cause to be kept a report of the proceedings of that hearing and the said report—

(*a*) shall include the information specified in paragraph (2) below; and

(*b*) may include such other information about the proceedings as the reporter thinks appropriate.

(2) The information referred to in paragraph (1)(*a*) above is as follows:—

(*a*) particulars of the place and date of the hearing;

(*b*) the full name and address of the child and his or her sex and date of birth;

(*c*) the full name and address (so far as these can be obtained) of the father, the mother and the guardian (if any) of the child;

(*d*) a record as to which (if any) of the persons mentioned in heads (*b*) and (*c*) above was present;

(*e*) the full name and address of any representative attending the hearing;

(*f*) the full name and address of any safeguarder appointed under the Act;

(*g*) the terms of any decision disposing of the case of the child, or of any decision to issue a warrant, made by the children's hearing or any other course of action taken by them with respect to the child; and

(*h*) in any case where the children's hearing proceed in accordance with section 42 of the Act—

(i) particulars of which of the grounds of referral are accepted or, as the case may be, not accepted, and by whom;

(ii) a record of any direction under subsection (2)(*c*) or (7) of the said section 42 to make application to the sheriff for a finding under that section; and

(iii) a record of whether the children's hearing proceeded to consider the case at that hearing.

Travelling and subsistence expenses

31.—(1) Subject to paragraph (2) below, the local authority for the area of a children's hearing shall, if a claim therefor is made to them, pay to or in respect of any child, or to any parent, or to any one representative of either attending any children's hearing a sum equal to such travelling expenses and such expenses on subsistence as have, in the opinion of the local authority, been reasonably incurred by or in respect of the child or, as the case may be, by the parent or by any representative of either for the purpose of enabling the said child, parent or representative to attend that hearing.

(2) A claim under this rule shall be in writing and shall be made before the expiry of the period of one month commencing with the date of the children's hearing to which the claim relates.

Revocation of previous rules and amendments

32. . . .

Rule 3 SCHEDULE

Rule 7 Form 1

SOCIAL WORK (SCOTLAND) ACT 1968

NOTIFICATION OF CHILDREN'S HEARING TO CHILD REQUIRED TO ATTEND HEARING

To (*name and address of child*)
You have been referred to a children's hearing (*state shortly the purpose of the hearing, for example* "and the grounds of referral are described in the attached statement" *or* "for the purpose of reviewing the supervision requirement made on (*date*)").
You are required in terms of section 40(1) of the Social Work (Scotland) Act 1968 to attend the hearing on (*date*). (*time*). (*place*).
Please read the Notes set out below.

(*Address of Reporter*)

....

(*Date*)

(Reporter)* (On behalf of the Reporter)*

*Delete as appropriate

NOTES

(To be incorporated in the notification and any copies thereof.)

A children's hearing is formed by members of the children's panel for [ ] Region. They have been selected from many walks of life especially for their interest and concern in understanding and helping children with problems. The panel members will discuss with you and your parents difficulties which have arisen and will try to reach a decision which will be in your best interests.

During the discussion the panel will want to hear your views. You may, if you wish, bring with you to the hearing someone to help you in discussing your difficulties and what might be done. The personal expenses of this representative (but not any fees) may be refunded.

You must attend the hearing unless you have been told by me that the hearing have decided that your attendance is not necessary. If you do not attend, steps may be taken, including possibly your detention, to make sure that you do appear before a hearing. If there is a very good reason, such as illness, why you will be unable to attend the hearing, you should contact the Reporter immediately (*insert address and telephone number*).

Further information on the hearing is set out in the leaflet entitled "To Tell You about the Children's Hearing", a copy of which accompanies this notification.

Rule 8 Form 2

SOCIAL WORK (SCOTLAND) ACT 1968

NOTIFICATION OF CHILDREN'S HEARING TO PARENT HAVING A DUTY TO ATTEND HEARING

To (*name and address of parent*)
Your child (*name and address*) has been referred to a children's hearing (*specify the reason, eg.* "on the basis of the attached grounds for referral" *or* "for the purpose of reviewing the supervision requirement made on (*date*)"). It is important that [you]*/[both you and your wife/husband*]* should be there to take part in the discussion about the child. The hearing is on (*date*), (*time*), (*place*), and [you]/[both you and your wife/husband*]* are required in terms of section 41(2) of the Social Work (Scotland) Act 1968 to attend.
Please read the Notes set out below.

(*Address of Reporter*)

....

(*Date*)

(Reporter)* (On behalf of the Reporter)*

*Delete as appropriate

NOTES

(To be incorporated in the notification and any copies thereof.)

A children's hearing is formed by members of the children's panel for [ ] Region. They have been selected from many walks of life especially for their interest and concern in understanding and helping children with problems. The panel members will discuss with you and your child difficulties which have arisen and will try to reach a decision which will be in your child's best interests.

During the discussion the panel will want to hear your views. You may, if you wish, bring with you to the hearing someone to help you in discussing your difficulties and what might be done. The personal expenses of this representative (but not any fees) may be refunded.

You must attend the hearing unless you have been told by me that the hearing have decided that your attendance is not necessary. If there is a very good reason, such as illness, why you will be unable to attend the hearing, you should contact the Reporter immediately at (*insert address and telephone number*).

Further information on the hearing is set out in the leaflet entitled "To Tell You about the Children's Hearing", a copy of which accompanies this notification.

Rule 8 Form 3

SOCIAL WORK (SCOTLAND) ACT 1968

NOTIFICATION OF CHILDREN'S HEARING TO PARENT NOT REQUIRED TO ATTEND HEARING

To (*name and address of parent*)
Your child (*name and address*) has been referred to a children's hearing (*specify reason*). The children's hearing to which your child has been referred are satisfied that it would be unreasonable to require you to attend or that your attendance is not essential.
However, if you wish, you have the right to attend the hearing on (*date*), (*time*), (*place*).

Please read the Notes set out below.

(*Address of Reporter*)

....

(*Date*)

(Reporter)* (On behalf of the Reporter)*

*Delete as appropriate

NOTES

(To be incorporated in the notification and any copies thereof.)

A children's hearing is formed by members of the children's panel for [ ] Region. They have been selected from many walks of life especially for their interest and concern in understanding and helping children with problems. The panel members will discuss with you and your child difficulties which have arisen and will try to reach a decision which will be in your best interests.

If you do attend the hearing you may, if you wish, bring with you someone to help you during the discussion of what is best for your child. The personal expenses of this representative (but not any fees) may be refunded.

Further information on the hearing is set out in the leaflet which has been written for your child entitled "To Tell You about the Children's Hearing", a copy of which accompanies this notification.

Rules 16 and 17 Form 4A

SOCIAL WORK (SCOTLAND) ACT 1968

FORM OF STATEMENT BY REPORTER OF GROUNDS FOR THE REFERRAL OF A CASE TO A CHILDREN'S HEARING

(Conditions in section 32(2)(*a*) to (*gg*) or (*i*) of the Act.)

(*Name and address of child*) is being referred to a children's hearing for (*local authority area*) on the grounds of the following conditions:—
(Here specify which one or more of the conditions mentioned in section 32(2) of the Act is or are considered by the reporter to be satisfied with respect of the child, for example:—
"(*a*) that he is beyond the control of his parents;
(*b*) that he has failed to attend school regularly without reasonable excuse; and
(*c*) that he has committed the two offences specified at paragraphs (3) and (4) below".)

STATEMENT OF FACTS

(*Here state the facts on the basis of which it is sought to show that the condition or, as the case may be, the conditions specified as aforesaid is or are satisfied, for example:*—

1. In support of condition (*a*) above it is stated:—

that the said (*name of child*) resides in family with his father (*name*) and mother (*name*) at (*address*);

that on several occasions and in particular on (*dates*) he has been absent from home overnight without the consent of his parents;

that he is habitually absent from home until a late hour of the night;

that on one weekend (*date*) he absented himself from home without the knowledge or permission of his parents and was discovered in a house at (*address*) which was frequented by persons of doubtful character;

that he defies all his parents' efforts to guide and control him.

2. In support of condition (*b*) above, it is stated:—

that as mentioned above (*name of child*) was born (*so far as has been ascertained*) on (*date*) and is and was at all material times a child of school age;

that he is and was at all material times a pupil enrolled in ( ) school under the management of ( ) education authority;

that he failed to attend the school on various occasions between (*state date*) or thereby and (*state date*) or thereby;

that during that period his absences from school amounted to (*number*) of half days out of a total (*number*) of half days, within that period, during which he was required to attend the school;

that he had no reasonable excuse for those absences.

3. In support of condition (*c*) above, it is stated:—

that on (*date*) between the hours of ( ) and ( ) (*state time*) at (*place*) he (*hereby specify the facts constituting the offence*) contrary to section ( ) of the Civic Government (Scotland) Act 1982.

4. In support of condition (*c*) above, it is further stated:—

that on (*date*) between the hours of ( ) and ( ) (*state time*) at (*place*) he stole (*specify the facts constituting the further offence*) being an offence of theft.)

(*Address of Reporter*)

....

(*Date*)

(Reporter)* (On behalf of the Reporter)*

*Delete as appropriate

NOTES

(To be incorporated in the notification and any copies thereof.)

At the children's hearing the child or his parents may or may not accept the grounds for bringing the child before the hearing. If the grounds are accepted by the child, and his parents, if present, the children's hearing will discuss and consider with the child and his parents what is best for the child. If any of the grounds are not accepted, the hearing may either discharge the referral or direct the reporter to apply to the sheriff for a decision as to whether or not any of the grounds exist. If this happens the child will have to appear before the sheriff at a later date. If the sheriff decides that any of the grounds do exist, the children's hearing will then discuss and consider what is best for the child, as if these grounds had been accepted. If the sheriff decides that no grounds exist, the referral will be discharged.

Rules 16 and 17 Form 4B

SOCIAL WORK (SCOTLAND) ACT 1968

FORM OF STATEMENT BY REPORTER OF GROUNDS FOR THE REFERRAL OF A CASE TO A CHILDREN'S HEARING

(Condition in section 32(2)(*h*) of the Act.)

(*Name and address of child*) is being referred to a children's hearing for (*local authority area*) under section [73(1)(ii)]* [75(1)]* [75(2)]* in Part V of the Social Work (Scotland) Act 1968 as being a child subject to an order made by a court in England or Wales or Northern Ireland.

In support of this condition it is stated that on (*date*) the said child appeared before (*insertion description of English, Welsh or Irish court*) and that that court made a (*insert description of order, eg. supervision order, care order*).

(*Address of Reporter*)

....

(*Date*)

(Reporter)* (On behalf of the Reporter)*

*Delete as appropriate

Rule 18 Form 5

SOCIAL WORK (SCOTLAND) ACT 1968

NOTIFICATION TO CHILD OF APPLICATION TO SHERIFF FOR A FINDING AS TO WHETHER GROUNDS OF REFERRAL ARE ESTABLISHED

To (*name and address of child*)

[[You]* [Your parent (*name and address of parent*)]* did not accept]*

[The children's hearing were satisfied that you did not understand the explanation of]*

[The children's hearing were satisfied that you were not able to understand an explanation of]*

the grounds of referral set out in the attached statement, and accordingly the children's hearing directed me to apply to the sheriff who will decide whether any of these grounds are established. You will have to attend the hearing of this application by the sheriff. You will be told later of the time and place.

(*Address of Reporter*)

....

(*Date*)

(Reporter)* (On behalf of the Reporter)*

*Delete as appropriate

Rule 18 Form 6

SOCIAL WORK (SCOTLAND) ACT 1968

NOTIFICATION TO PARENT OF APPLICATION TO SHERIFF FOR A FINDING AS TO WHETHER GROUNDS OF REFERRAL ARE ESTABLISHED

To (*name and address of parent*)

[[You]* [Your husband*/wife*]* [Your child (*name of child*)]* did not accept]*

[The children's hearing were satisfied that your child did not understand the explanation of]*

[The children's hearing were satisfied that your child was not able to understand an explanation of]*

the grounds of referral set out in the attached statement, and accordingly the children's hearing directed me to apply to the sheriff who will decide whether any of these grounds are established. You will be told later of the time and place of the hearing by the sheriff of this application.

(*Address of Reporter*)

....

(*Date*)

(Reporter)* (On behalf of the Reporter)*

*Delete as appropriate

Rule 20 Form 7

SOCIAL WORK (SCOTLAND) ACT 1968

NOTIFICATION TO CHILD OR PARENT OF DECISION OF CHILDREN'S HEARING TO MAKE OR NOT TO MAKE A SUPERVISION REQUIREMENT

To (*name and address of child/parent*)

On (*date*) a children's hearing for (*local authority area*) decided, after considering [your case]* [the case of (*name of child*)]*, that compulsory measures of care were [not]* necessary, and [made]* [did not make]* a supervision requirement [of which a copy is enclosed]*.

You or your parent/child* may appeal to the sheriff against the decision with a period of three weeks from the date of the decision.

You may ask me for a statement of the reasons for the decision of the children's hearing.

(*Address of Reporter*)

....

(*Date*)

(Reporter)* (On behalf of the Reporter)*

*Delete as appropriate

NOTES

(To be incorporated in the notification and any copies thereof.)

Section 88 of the Social Work (Scotland) Act 1968 requires the parents of a child placed under a supervision requirement to inform the local authority of any change of address.

Rule 20 Form 8A

SOCIAL WORK (SCOTLAND) ACT 1968

NOTIFICATION TO CHILD OR PARENT OF DECISION OF CHILDREN'S HEARING AT A REVIEW OF A SUPERVISION REQUIREMENT

To (*name and address of child/parent*)

On (*date*) a children's hearing for (*local authority area*), after reviewing the supervision requirement dated ( ) relating to [you]* [name of child]*, decided (*here specify the decision in question*).

You or your parent/child* may appeal to the sheriff against the decision within a period of three weeks from the date of the decision.

You may ask me for a statement of the reasons for the decision of the children's hearing.

(*Address of Reporter*)

....

(*Date*)

(Reporter)* (On behalf of the Reporter)*

*Delete as appropriate

Rule 22 Form 8B

SOCIAL WORK (SCOTLAND) ACT 1968

NOTIFICATION TO CHILD OR PARENT OF DECISION OF CHILDREN'S HEARING AT A REVIEW OF A SUPERVISION REQUIREMENT INVOLVING THE IMPOSITION, VARIATION OR CONTINUATION OF A CONDITION AUTHORISING PLACEMENT IN SECURE ACCOMMODATION

To (*name and address of child/parent*)

On (*date*) a children's hearing for (*local authority area*), after reviewing the supervision requirement dated ( ) relating to [you]* [name of child]* and being satisfied [that [you have]* [your child has]* a history of absconding and are/is* likely to abscond unless kept in secure accommodation and that if [you abscond]* [your child absconds]* it is likely that you/your child's physical, mental or moral welfare will be at risk]*

[that [you are]* [your child is]* likely to injure [yourself]* [himself]* [herself]* or other persons unless kept in secure accommodation]*,

decided (*here specify the decision in question to include the decision with respect to the condition about secure accommodation*).

You or your parent/child* may appeal to the sheriff against the decision within a period of three weeks from the date of the decision.

You may ask me for a statement of the reasons for the decision of the children's hearing.

(*Address of Reporter*)

(*Date*) ....

(Reporter)* (On behalf of the Reporter)*

*Delete as appropriate

Rule 20 Form 8C

SOCIAL WORK (SCOTLAND) ACT 1968

NOTIFICATION TO CHILD OR PARENT OF DECISION OF CHILDREN'S HEARING AT A REVIEW OF SECURE ACCOMMODATION CONDITION SEPARATE FROM A REVIEW OF A SUPERVISION REQUIREMENT

To (*name and address of child/parent*)

On (*date*) a children's hearing for (*local authority area*), after reviewing the condition about residence in secure accommodation contained in the supervision requirement dated (   ) relating to [you]* [name of child]* and [not]* being satisfied

[that [you have]* [your child has]* a history of absconding and are/is* likely to abscond unless kept in secure accommodation and that if [you abscond]* [your child absconds]* it is likely that you/your child's physical, mental or moral welfare will be at risk]*

[that [you are]* [your child is]* likely to injure [yourself]* [himself]* [herself]* or other persons unless kept in secure accommodation]*,

decided (*here specify the decision in question with respect to the condition about secure accommodation*).

You or your parent/child* may appeal to the sheriff against the decision within a period of three weeks from the date of the decision.

You may ask me for a statement of the reasons for the decision of the children's hearing.

(*Address of Reporter*)

(*Date*) ....

(Reporter)* (On behalf of the Reporter)*

*Delete as appropriate

Rule 22 Form 9

SOCIAL WORK (SCOTLAND) ACT 1968

NOTIFICATION TO CHILD AND PARENTS OF CHILDREN'S HEARING TO CONSIDER APPLICATION UNDER SECTION 49(8) OF THE ACT

To (*name and address of child/parents*)

On (*insert date*) (*name or names of applicant*) under section 49(8) of the Social Work (Scotland) Act 1968 applied to the children's hearing for the suspension of a supervision requirement made on (*date*).

The application for the suspension of the said supervision requirement will be considered by the hearing on (*date*), (*time*), (*place*).

(*Address of Reporter*)

(*Date*) ....

(Reporter)* (On behalf of the Reporter)*

*Delete as appropriate

NOTES

In accordance with Rule 22(5) of The Children's Hearings (Scotland) Rules 1986 failure of the applicant to attend the hearing called to consider his application will mean that he will be held to have abandoned the application.

Rule 24

Form 10A

SOCIAL WORK (SCOTLAND) ACT 1968

SUPERVISION REQUIREMENT

(*Place and date*)

A children's hearing for (*local authority area*), in exercise of the powers conferred by section 44(1) of the Social Work (Scotland) Act 1968, being satisfied that (*child's name and address*) is in need of compulsory measures of care require him/her* [to reside in (*name of residential establishment)* //*[to be under the supervision of (name of local authority or other supervisor*)]* subject to the conditions noted below.

[The operation of this supervision requirement is postponed until (*specify date*)]*.

....
Chairman of the Children's Hearing

CONDITIONS REFERRED TO IN THE FOREGOING SUPERVISION REQUIREMENT

†1. The child is required to observe the rules of conduct of the residential establishment.

†2. The requirement to reside is subject to the discretion of the managers of the residential establishment to grant leave of absence from time to time.

3. etc.

....
Chairman of the Children's Hearing

*Delete as appropriate
†Where a supervision requirement requires a child to reside in a residential establishment, conditions 1 and 2 shall be inserted in the supervision requirement.

Rule 24

Form 10B

SOCIAL WORK (SCOTLAND) ACT 1968

SUPERVISION REQUIREMENT AUTHORISING PLACEMENT IN SECURE ACCOMMODATION

(*Place and date*)

A children's hearing for (*local authority area*) in exercise of the powers conferred by section 44(1)(*b*) and 58A(3) of the Social Work (Scotland) Act 1968 being satisfied (firstly) that (*child's name and address*) is in need of compulsory measures of care, and (secondly)

[that he/she* has a history of absconding and is likely to abscond unless he/she* is kept in secure accommodation and that if he/she* absconds it is likely that his/her* physical, mental or moral welfare will be at risk]*

[that he/she* is likely to injure himself/herself* or other persons unless he/she* is kept in secure accommodation]*,

require him/her* to reside in (*name of residential establishment providing secure accommodation*) subject to the conditions noted below.

[The operation of this supervision requirement is postponed until (*specify date*).]*

....
Chairman of the Children's Hearing

CONDITIONS REFERRED TO IN THE FOREGOING SUPERVISION REQUIREMENT

1. The child is liable to be placed and kept in secure accommodation in (*name of residential establishment*) at such times as the person in charge of the residential establishment, with the

agreement of the director of social work of (*name of local authority*), considers it necessary that the child do so.

2. The child is required to observe the rules of conduct of the residential establishment.

3. Subject to condition 1 above, the requirement to reside is subject to the discretion of the managers of the residential establishment to grant leave of absence from time to time.

4. etc.

....
Chairman of the Children's Hearing

*Delete as appropriate

Rule 24 Form 11A

SOCIAL WORK (SCOTLAND) ACT 1968

SUPERVISION REQUIREMENT VARYING EXISTING SUPERVISION REQUIREMENT

(*Place and date*)

A children's hearing for (*local authority area*), by way of variation of [and in substitution for]* the supervision requirement dated (*date of previous supervision requirement*) to which (*name of child*) is subject, hereby require him/her* [to reside in (*name of residential establishment*)]* /[to be under the supervision of (*name of local authority or other supervisor*)]* subject to the conditions noted below and the said requirement dated is hereby revoked.

....
Chairman of the Children's Hearing

CONDITIONS REFERRED TO IN THE FOREGOING SUPERVISION REQUIREMENT

†1. The child is required to observe the rules of conduct of the residential establishment.

†2. The requirement to reside is subject to the discretion of the managers of the residential establishment to grant leave of absence from time to time.

3. etc.

....
Chairman of the Children's Hearing

*Delete as appropriate
†Where a supervision requirement requires a child to reside in a residential establishment, conditions 1 and 2 shall be inserted in the supervision requirement.

Rule 24 Form 11B

SOCIAL WORK (SCOTLAND) ACT 1968

VARIATION OF SUPERVISION REQUIREMENT TO AUTHORISE PLACEMENT IN SECURE ACCOMMODATION

(*Place and date*)

A children's hearing for (*local authority area*) by way of variation of [and in substitution for]* the supervision requirement dated (*date of previous supervision requirement*) to which (*name and address of child*) is subject, being satisfied that

[that he/she* has a history of absconding and is likely to abscond unless he/she* is kept in secure accommodation, and that if he/she* absconds it is likely that his/her* physical, mental or moral welfare will be at risk]*

[that he/she* is likely to injure himself/herself* or other persons unless he/she* is kept in secure accommodation]*.

hereby require him/her* to reside in (*name of residential establishment providing secure accommodation*) subject to the conditions noted below and the said requirement dated is hereby revoked.

....
Chairman of the Children's Hearing

CONDITIONS REFERRED TO IN THE FOREGOING SUPERVISION REQUIREMENT

1. The child is liable to be placed and kept in secure accommodation in (*name of residential establishment*) at such times as the person in charge of the residential establishment, with the agreement of the director of social work of (*name of local authority*), considers it necessary that the child do so.

2. The child is required to observe the rules of conduct of the residential establishment.

3. Subject to condition 1 above, the requirement to reside is subject to the discretion of the managers of the residential establishment to grant leave of absence from time to time.

4. etc.

....
Chairman of the Children's Hearing

*Delete as appropriate

Rule 24 Form 12

SOCIAL WORK (SCOTLAND) ACT 1968

INSTRUMENT CONTINUING SUPERVISION REQUIREMENT

(*Place and date*)

A children's hearing for (*local authority area*), considering that the supervision requirement attached and docqueted with reference hereto is due to expire on (*insert date being one year from the making or last review of the requirement whichever last occurred*), and being satisfied that it is proper so to do, hereby continue the said requirement in force.

....
Chairman of the Children's Hearing

Rule 24 Form 13

SOCIAL WORK (SCOTLAND) ACT 1968

INSTRUMENT TERMINATING SUPERVISION REQUIREMENT

(*Place and date*)

A children's hearing for (*local authority area*) hereby terminate the supervision requirement attached and docqueted with reference hereto as from (*date on which termination to take effect*).

....
Chairman of the Children's Hearing

Rule 26 Form 14

SOCIAL WORK (SCOTLAND) ACT 1968

REQUIREMENT UNDER SECTION 43(4) OF THE ACT

(*Place and date*)

A children's hearing for (*local authority area*), in exercise of the powers conferred on them by section 43(4) of the Social Work (Scotland) Act 1968, require (*name and address*) to [attend]* [reside at]* (*insert name of clinic, hospital or establishment*) during (*insert time or period not exceeding 21 days*) for the purpose of further investigation in relation to him/her* and his/her* history.

....
Chairman of the Children's Hearing

*Delete as appropriate

Rule 27 Form 15A

SOCIAL WORK (SCOTLAND) ACT 1968

WARRANT FOR DETENTION UNDER SECTION 37(4) OF THE ACT

(*Place and date*)

A children's hearing for (*local authority area*), in exercise of the powers conferred on them by section 37(4) of the Social Work (Scotland) Act 1968, [being satisfied that the further detention of (*name and address*) is necessary in his/her* own interest]* [having reason to believe that (*name and address*) will run away during the investigation of his/her* case]* grant warrant for the detention of the said (*name*) in a place of safety [chosen by (*local authority*)]* [(*or insert name of a place of safety*)]* for a period from (*date*) to (*date*) both days inclusive (*insert period not exceeding 21 days*).

....
Chairman of the Children's Hearing

*Delete as appropriate

Rule 27 Form 15B

SOCIAL WORK (SCOTLAND) ACT 1968

WARRANT FOR DETENTION IN NAMED RESIDENTIAL ESTABLISHMENT PROVIDING SECURE ACCOMMODATION UNDER SECTIONS 37(4) AND 58E(1) OF THE ACT

(*Place and date*)

A children's hearing for (*local authority area*), in exercise of the powers conferred on them by sections 37(4) and 58E(1) of the Social Work (Scotland) Act 1968.

(firstly) [being satisfied that the further detention of (*child's name and address*) is necessary in his/her* own interests]* [having reason to believe that (*child's name and address*) will run away during the investigation of his/her* case]* and

(secondly) being satisfied [that he/she* has a history of absconding and is likely to abscond unless he/she* is kept in secure accommodation, and that if he/she* absconds it is likely that his/her* physical, mental or moral welfare will be at risk]* [that he/she* is likely to injure himself/herself* or other persons unless he/she* is kept in secure accommodation]*,

grant warrant ordering the detention of the said (*name*) in (*name of residential establishment providing the secure accommodation*) for the period from (*date*) to (*date*) (*insert period not exceeding 21 days*) both days inclusive and said detention there shall be in secure accommodation at such times as the person in charge of the residential establishment, with the agreement of the director of social work of (*name of local authority*), considers necessary.

....
Chairman of the Children's Hearing

*Delete as appropriate

Rule 27 Form 16A

SOCIAL WORK (SCOTLAND) ACT 1968

WARRANT UNDER SECTION 37(5) OF THE ACT RENEWING WARRANT FOR DETENTION UNDER SECTION 37(4) OF THE ACT

(*Place and date*)

A children's hearing for (*local authority area*), in exercise of the powers conferred on them by section 37(4) of the Social Work (Scotland) Act 1968, [being satisfied that the further detention of (*name and address*) is necessary in his/her* own interest]* [having reason to believe that (*name and address*) will run away during the investigation of his/her* case]*, grant warrant for the renewal from .... (*day*) to .... (*day*) of the warrant for detention of the said (*name*) granted by a children's hearing on (*insert date of previous warrant*).

....
Chairman of the Children's Hearing

*Delete as appropriate

Rule 27 Form 16B

SOCIAL WORK (SCOTLAND) ACT 1968

WARRANT UNDER SECTIONS 37(5) AND 58E(1) OF THE ACT RENEWING WARRANT FOR DETENTION IN NAMED RESIDENTIAL ESTABLISHMENT PROVIDING SECURE ACCOMMODATION UNDER SECTIONS 37(4) AND 58E(1) OF THE ACT

(*Place and date*)

A children's hearing for (*local authority area*), in exercise of the powers conferred on them by sections 37(4) and 58E(1) of the Social Work (Scotland) Act 1968, having heard the reporter of the local authority, and being satisfied

[that (*the child's name and address*) has a history of absconding and is likely to abscond unless he/she* is kept in secure accommodation, and that if he/she* absconds it is likely that his/her* physical, mental or moral welfare will be at risk]*

[that (*child's name and address*) is likely to injure himself/herself* or other persons unless he/she is kept in secure accommodation]*,

grant warrant for the renewal from (*date*) to (*date*) (*insert period not exceeding 21 days*) both days inclusive, of the warrant granted by a children's hearing on (*insert date of previous warrant*) ordering his/her* detention in (*name of residential establishment providing the secure accommodation*) at such times as the person in charge of the residential establishment, with the agreement of the director of social work of (*name of local authority*), considers necessary.

....
Chairman of the Children's Hearing

*Delete as appropriate

Rule 27 Form 17A

SOCIAL WORK (SCOTLAND) ACT 1968

WARRANT FOR APPREHENSION UNDER SECTION 40(4) OF THE ACT

(*Place and date*)

A children's hearing for (*local authority area*) in exercise of the powers conferred on them by section 40(4) of the Social Work (Scotland) Act 1968, being satisfied that the grant of this warrant is necessary, grant warrant to officers of law to apprehend (*name and address*) for the purpose of securing his/her* attendance at a children's hearing.

....
Chairman of the Children's Hearing

*Delete as appropriate

Rule 27

Form 17B

SOCIAL WORK (SCOTLAND) ACT 1968

WARRANT FOR APPREHENSION AND DETENTION IN NAMED RESIDENTIAL ESTABLISHMENT PROVIDING SECURE ACCOMMODATION UNDER SECTIONS 40(4) AND 58E(1) OF THE ACT

(*Place and date*)

A children's hearing for (*local authority area*), in exercise of the powers conferred on them by sections 40(4) and 58E(1) of the Social Work (Scotland) Act 1968, being satisfied (firstly)

[that (*the child's name and address*) has a history of absconding and is likely to abscond unless he/she* is kept in secure accommodation, and that if he/she* absconds it is likely that his/her* physical, mental or moral welfare will be at risk]*

[that (*child's name and address*) is likely to injure himself/herself* or other persons unless he/she is kept in secure accommodation]*,

and (*secondly*) of the necessity for the grant of this warrant, grant warrant to officers of law to apprehend the said (*name*) for the purpose of securing his/her* attendance at a children's hearing, and ordering his/her* detention in (*name of residential establishment providing the secure accommodation*) at such times as the person in charge of the residential establishment, with the agreement of the director of social work of (*name of local authority*), considers necessary.

....
Chairman of the Children's Hearing

*Delete as appropriate

Rule 27

Form 18A

SOCIAL WORK (SCOTLAND) ACT 1968

WARRANT FOR DETENTION UNDER SECTION 40(7) OF THE ACT

(*Place and date*)

A children's hearing for (*local authority area*), in exercise of the powers conferred on them by section 40(7) of the Social Work (Scotland) Act 1968, having reason to believe that (*child's name and address*) may [not attend at a further hearing of his/her* case]* [not attend at proceedings arising from his/her* case]* [fail to comply with a requirement under section 43(4) of that Act]* and being satisfied that detention of (*child's name and address*) is necessary in his/her* interest, grant warrant for the said (*name*) to be detained in a suitable place of safety chosen by the local authority for a period not exceeding 21 days from this date.

....
Chairman of the Children's Hearing

*Delete as appropriate

Rule 27 Form 18B

SOCIAL WORK (SCOTLAND) ACT 1968

WARRANT FOR DETENTION IN NAMED RESIDENTIAL ESTABLISHMENT PROVIDING SECURE ACCOMMODATION UNDER SECTIONS 40(7) AND 58E(1) OF THE ACT

(*Place and date*)

A children's hearing for (*local authority area*), in exercise of the powers conferred on them by sections 40(7) and 58E(1) of the Social Work (Scotland) Act 1968.

(firstly) [having reason to believe that (*child's name and address*) may [not attend a further hearing of his/her* case]* [not attend at proceedings arising from his/her* case]* [fail to comply with a requirement under section 43(4) of that Act]*]* [being satisfied that detention of (*child's name and address*) is necessary in his/her* own interest]* and

(secondly) being satisfied [that he/she* has a history of absconding and is likely to abscond unless he/she* is kept in secure accommodation, and that if he/she* absconds it is likely that his/her* physical, mental or moral welfare will be at risk]* [that he/she* is likely to injure himself/herself* or other persons unless he/she* is kept in secure accommodation]*,

grant warrant ordering the said (*name*) to be detained in (*name of residential establishment providing the secure accommodation*) from (*date*) to (*date*) (*insert period not exceeding 21 days*) both days inclusive and said detention there shall be in secure accommodation at such times as the person in charge of the residential establishment, with the agreement of the director of social work of (*name of local authority*), considers necessary.

....
Chairman of the Children's Hearing

*Delete as appropriate

Rule 27 Form 19A

SOCIAL WORK (SCOTLAND) ACT 1968

WARRANT UNDER SECTION 40(8) OF THE ACT RENEWING WARRANT FOR DETENTION UNDER SECTION 40(7) OF THE ACT

(*Place and date*)

A children's hearing for (*local authority area*), in exercise of the powers conferred on them by section 40(8) of the Social Work (Scotland) Act 1968, having heard the reporter of the local authority, grant warrant for the renewal from .... (*day*) to .... (*day*) (*insert period not exceeding 21 days*) of the warrant for the detention of (*name and address*) granted by a children's hearing on (*insert date of previous warrant*).

....
Chairman of the Children's Hearing

Rule 27 Form 19B

SOCIAL WORK (SCOTLAND) ACT 1968

WARRANT UNDER SECTIONS 40(8) AND 58E(1) OF THE ACT RENEWING WARRANT FOR DETENTION IN NAMED RESIDENTIAL ESTABLISHMENT PROVIDING SECURE ACCOMMODATION UNDER SECTIONS 40(7) AND 58E(1) OF THE ACT

(*Place and date*)

A children's hearing for (*local authority area*), in exercise of the powers conferred on them by sections 40(8) and 58E(1) of the Social Work (Scotland) Act 1968, having heard the reporter of the local authority, and being satisfied [that (*child's name and address*) has a history of absconding and is likely to abscond unless he/she* is kept in secure accommodation, and that if he/she* absconds it is likely that his/her* physical, mental or moral welfare will be at risk]*

[that (*child's name and address*) is likely to injure himself/herself* or other persons unless he/she is kept in secure accommodation]*,

grant warrant for the renewal from (*date*) to (*date*) (*insert period not exceeding 21 days*) both days inclusive, of the warrant granted by a children's hearing on (*insert date of previous warrant*) ordering the detention of the said (*name*) in (*name of residential establishment providing the secure accommodation*) and said detention there shall be in secure accommodation at such times as the person in charge of the residential establishment, with the agreement of the director of social work of (*name of local authority*), considers necessary.

....
Chairman of the Children's Hearing

*Delete as appropriate

Rule 27 Form 19C

SOCIAL WORK (SCOTLAND) ACT 1968

WARRANT UNDER REGULATION 11 OF SECURE ACCOMMODATION (SCOTLAND) REGULATIONS 1983 FOR DETENTION IN NAMED RESIDENTIAL ESTABLISHMENT PROVIDING SECURE ACCOMMODATION UNDER SECTION 58B(3) OF THE ACT

(*Place and date*)

A children's hearing for (*local authority area*), in exercise of the powers conferred on them by section 58B(3) of the Social Work (Scotland) Act 1968, and by virtue of regulation 11 of the Secure Accommodation (Scotland) Regulations 1983, having directed that an application be made to the sheriff for a finding under section 42(2)(*c*) of that Act and being satisfied

[that (*child's name and address*) has a history of absconding and is likely to abscond unless he/she* is kept in secure accommodation, and that if he/she* absconds it is likely that his/her* physical, mental or moral welfare will be at risk]*

[that (*child's name and address*) is likely to injure himself/herself* or other persons unless he/she is kept in secure accommodation]*,

grant warrant ordering the said (*name*) to be [detained]* [further detained]* in (*name of residential establishment providing secure accommodation*) from (*date*) to (*date*) (*insert period not exceeding 21 days*) both days inclusive and said detention there shall be in secure accommodation at such times as the person in charge of the residential establishment, with the agreement of the director of social work of (*name of local authority*), considers it necessary that the child be so detained, pending determination of his/her* case in accordance with section 42(5) or (6) of that Act.

....
Chairman of the Children's Hearing

*Delete as appropriate

Rule 29 Form 20

SOCIAL WORK (SCOTLAND) ACT 1968

CERTIFICATE OF NOTIFICATION OF CHILDREN'S HEARING TO PARENT

(to be subjoined to copy of notification)*

I, ... [Reporter/on behalf of the Reporter]* of (*local authority*) notified the within-named person by

[speaking to him in person on (*date*), (*time*), (*place*)]*

[delivering a copy of the notification to him in person on (*date*), (*time*), (*place*)]* [leaving a copy of the notification for him at his [dwellinghouse/place of business*] at (*address*) on (*date*)]*

[leaving a copy of the notification for him on board (*name of vessel*) at (*place*) on (*date*)]*

[sending it to him in a [recorded delivery/registered*] letter and the post office receipt for the said letter accompanies this certificate]*

....

Reporter to the Children's Hearing

*Delete as appropriate

Rules for the Registration of Custody Orders of the Sheriff Court 1988

(S.I. 1988 No. 613)

[4th April 1988]

The Lords of Council and Session, under and by virtue of the powers conferred on them by section 32 of the Sheriff Courts (Scotland) Act 1971, sections 27(2) and 28(1) of the Family Law Act 1986 and of all other powers enabling them in that behalf, after consultation with the Sheriff Court Rules Council, do hereby enact and declare:—

Citation and commencement

1.—(1) This Act of Sederunt may be cited as the Act of Sederunt (Rules for the Registration of Custody Orders of the Sheriff Court) 1988 and shall come into force on 4th April 1988.

(2) This Act of Sederunt shall be inserted in the Books of Sederunt.

Interpretation

[1] **2.** In this Act of Sederunt—

"the Act of 1986" means the Family Law Act 1986;

"appropriate court" means the High Court in England and Wales or the High Court in Northern Ireland or, in relation to a specified dependent territory, the corresponding court in that territory, as the case may be;

"appropriate register" means the court book in which there is registered the action in which the custody order was originally sought;

"corresponding court" in relation to a specified dependent territory means the corresponding court specified in relation to that territory in Schedule 3 to the Family Law Act 1986 (Dependent Territories) Order 1991;

"custody order" has the meaning assigned to it by sections 1, 32, 40, 42(5) and 42(6) of the Act of 1986;

"proper officer" means the Secretary of the Principal Registry of the Family Division of the High Court in England and Wales or the Master (Care and Protection) of the High Court in Northern Ireland or, in relation to a specified dependent territory, the corresponding officer of the appropriate court in that territory, as the case may be; and

"specified dependent territory" means a dependent territory specified in column 1 of Schedule 1 to the Family Law Act 1986 (Dependent Territories) Order 1991.

NOTE

[1] As amended by S.I. 1991 No. 2205.

Applications for registration of custody orders in another court

3.—[1] (1) An application under section 27 of the Act of 1986 to register a custody order made by a sheriff court in an appropriate court in England and Wales or Northern Ireland or a specified dependent territory shall be made by letter to the sheriff clerk of the court in which the order was made.

(2) An application under paragraph (1) of this rule shall be accompanied by—

(*a*) a copy of the letter of application;

(*b*) an affidavit by the applicant;

(*c*) a copy of that affidavit;

(*d*) a certified copy interlocutor of the custody order;

(*e*) a certified copy interlocutor of any variation which is in force of the custody order; and

(*f*) any other document relevant to the application together with a copy of it.

(3) An affidavit required under this rule should set out—

(*a*) the name and address of the applicant and his right under the custody order;

(*b*) the name and date of birth of the child in respect of whom the custody order was made, the present whereabouts or suspected whereabouts of the child and the name of any person with whom he is alleged to be;

(*c*) the name and address of any other person who has an interest in the custody order;

(*d*) whether the custody order is to be registered in England and Wales, Northern Ireland or a specified dependent territory and the court in which it is to be registered;

(*e*) whether the custody order is in force;

(*f*) whether the custody order is already registered and, if so, where it is registered; and

(*g*) details of any order known to the applicant which affects the child and is in force in the jurisdiction in which the custody order is to be registered.

(4) Where the court refuses to send an application under this rule to the appropriate court on the ground that the custody order is no longer in force, the sheriff clerk shall notify the applicant in writing of the court's decision.

(5) The sheriff clerk shall retain the letter of application under this rule together with any documents which accompanied it and which are not transmitted to the appropriate court under section 27(3) of the Act of 1986.

NOTES

[1] As amended by S.I. 1991 No. 2205.

[2] As substituted by S.I. 1991 No. 2205.

Transmission of application for registration

4.—(1) Unless it appears to the court that the custody order is no longer in force, the sheriff clerk shall send the documents mentioned in section 27(3) of the Act of 1986 to the proper officer of the court in which the custody order is to be registered.

(2) For the purposes of section 27(3)(*b*) of the Act of 1986 the prescribed particulars of any variation which is in force of a custody order shall be a certified copy interlocutor of any such variation.

(3) On sending an application under paragraph (1) of this rule, the sheriff clerk shall record the date and particulars of the application and the custody order in the appropriate register.

(4) On receiving notification from the proper officer of an appropriate court that the custody order has been registered in that court under section 27(4) of the Act of 1986, the sheriff clerk shall record the date of registration in the appropriate register.

Cancellation or variation of registered custody order

5.—(1) Where the court revokes, recalls or varies a custody order which it has made, the sheriff clerk shall—

(*a*) send a certified copy interlocutor of the revocation, recall or variation to the proper officer of the court in which the custody order is registered;

(*b*) record the transmission of the certified copy in the appropriate register; and

(*c*) record the revocation, recall or variation in the appropriate register.

(2) On receiving notification from the proper officer of the court in which the custody order is registered that he has amended his record, the sheriff clerk shall record the fact that the amendment has been made in the appropriate register.

Evidence in Divorce Actions (Scotland) Order 1989

(S.I. 1989 No. 582)

[23rd March 1989]

The Lord Advocate, in exercise of the powers conferred on him by section 8(4) of the Civil Evidence (Scotland) Act 1988, and of all other powers enabling him in that behalf, hereby makes the following Order, a draft of which has been laid before and approved by resolution of each House of Parliament:

1. This Order may be cited as the Evidence in Divorce Actions (Scotland) Order 1989 and shall come into force on 3rd April 1989.

2.—(1) The provisions of this Order shall have effect in relation to the following class of actions, namely actions for divorce in which—

(*a*) the action is undefended;

(*b*) the action is brought in reliance on the facts set out in section 1(2)(*d*) (two years' non-cohabitation and the defender's consent to decree) or in section 1(2)(*e*) (five years' non-cohabitation) of the Divorce (Scotland) Act 1976;

(*c*) no other proceedings are pending in any court which could have the effect of bringing the marriage to an end;

(*d*) there are no children of the marriage under the age of 16 years;

(*e*) neither party applies for an order for financial provision on divorce; and

(*f*) neither party suffers from mental disorder within the meaning of section 1(2) of the Mental Health (Scotland) Act 1984.

(2) For the purpose of this Order an action shall be treated as undefended when the defender has not entered appearance or, having entered appearance, has not lodged defences or has withdrawn them.

3. Section 8(3) of the Civil Evidence (Scotland) Act 1988 shall not apply in respect of the class of action specified in article 2 above.

Family Law Act 1986 (Dependent Territories) Order 1991

(S.I. 1991 No. 1723)

[24th July 1991]

Her Majesty, in exercise of the powers conferred upon Her by section 43 of the Family Law Act 1986 is pleased, by and with the advice of Her Privy Council, to order, and it is hereby ordered, as follows:

1. This Order may be cited as the Family Law Act 1986 (Dependent Territories) Order 1991 and shall come into force on 14th October 1991.

2. In this Order—
"the Act" means the Family Law Act 1986;
"specified dependent territory" means a dependent territory specified in column 1 of Schedule 1 to this Order;
"Part I order" has the meaning given by section 1(1) of the Act;
"part of the United Kingdom" has the meaning given by section 42(1) of the Act.

3.—(1) This Order applies in relation to a specified dependent territory from the date specified opposite the name of that territory in column 2 of Schedule 1 to this Order.

(2) Part I of the Act shall apply, for the purpose of regulating, as between any specified dependent territory and any part of the United Kingdom, the jurisdiction of courts to make Part I orders, and the recognition and enforcement of orders corresponding to such orders, with the modifications specified in Schedule 2 to this Order.

(3) Each Part of Schedule 3 to this Order shall have effect for the construction of Part I of the Act as modified by this Order in relation to the specified dependent territory named in the heading to that Part of that Schedule.

4. This Order does not extend to any territory outside the United Kingdom.

Article 2

SCHEDULE 1

SPECIFIED DEPENDENT TERRITORIES

Dependent Territory	*Date from which this Order applies*
The Isle of Man	14th October 1991

Article 3(2)

SCHEDULE 2

MODIFICATIONS OF PART I OF THE FAMILY LAW ACT 1986

Chapter I—Preliminary

1.—(1) In section 1(1) after paragraph (*e*) insert—
"(*f*) an order made by a court in a specified dependent territory corresponding to an order within paragraphs (*a*) to (*e*) above."

(2) In section 1(2)—
(*a*) in paragraph (*a*), after "subsection (1)(*c*)" insert "or (*f*)";
(*b*) in paragraph (*c*), after "paragraph (*e*)" insert "or (*f*)."

(3) In section 1(3) after paragraph (*b*) insert—
"and
(*c*) excludes any order falling within subsection (1)(*f*) above made before the date specified opposite the name of the territory concerned in Column 2 of Schedule 1 to the Family Law Act 1986 (Dependent Territories) Order 1991, as from time to time in force."

Chapter II—Jurisdiction of courts in England and Wales

2.—(1) In section 2A(2), for "Scotland or Northern Ireland" substitute "Scotland, Northern Ireland or a specified dependent territory."

(2) In section 2A(3)—

(*a*) in paragraph (*a*), after "section 13(6)(*a*)(i)), or" insert "a corresponding dependent territory order, or";

(*b*) in paragraph (*b*), after "this Act" insert ", or a corresponding dependent territory order,".

3.—(1) In section 3(1)(*b*), after "United Kingdom" insert "or a specified dependent territory."

(2) In section 3(2), for "Scotland or Northern Ireland" substitute "Scotland, Northern Ireland or a specified dependent territory."

(3) In section 3(3)—

(*a*) in paragraph (*a*), after "section 13(6)(*a*)(i)), or" insert "a corresponding dependent territory order, or";

(*b*) in paragraph (*b*), after "this Act" insert ", or a corresponding dependent territory order,".

4.—(1) In section 6(1), for "Scotland or Northern Ireland"—

(*a*) (in the first place) substitute "Scotland, Northern Ireland or a specified dependent territory"; and

(*b*) (in the second place) substitute "Scotland, Northern Ireland or the territory."

(2) In section 6(3), for "Scotland or Northern Ireland" substitute "Scotland, Northern Ireland or a specified dependent territory."

(3) In section 6(4)—

(*a*) in paragraph (*a*), after "section 13(6)(*a*)(i)), or" insert "a corresponding dependent territory order, or";

(*b*) in paragraph (*b*), after "this Act" insert ", or a corresponding dependent territory order,".

Chapter III—Jurisdiction of courts in Scotland

5. In section 10(*a*)(ii) and (*b*)(ii), after "United Kingdom" insert "or a specified dependent territory".

6.—(1) In section 11(1), after "United Kingdom" insert "or a specified dependent territory."

(2) In section 11(2)—

(*a*) in paragraph (*a*), after the words "section 13(6)(*a*)(ii))" insert "or a corresponding dependent territory order";

(*b*) in paragraph (*b*), after "this Act" insert ", or a corresponding dependent territory order,".

7.—(1) In section 13(3) and (4), after "United Kingdom" insert "or a specified dependent territory."

(2) In section 13(5)—

(*a*) in paragraph (*a*), after "paragraph (*a*)(ii) of that subsection), or" insert "a corresponding dependent territory order, or";

(*b*) in paragraph (*b*), after "this Act" insert ", or a corresponding dependent territory order,".

(3) In section 13(6)(*a*)(ii)—

(*a*) after "this Act" insert "or a corresponding dependent territory provision";

(*b*) after "United Kingdom" insert "or a specified dependent territory."

8. In section 15(1)—

(*a*) in paragraph (*a*), after "United Kingdom" insert "or in a specified dependent territory";

(*b*) in paragraph (*b*), after "United Kingdom" insert "and any specified dependent territory";

(*c*) after "the other court in the United Kingdom" insert "or in the specified dependent territory."

Chapter IV—Jurisdiction of courts in Northern Ireland

9.—(1) In section 20(1)(*b*), after "United Kingdom" insert "or in a specified dependent territory."

(2) In section 20(2), for "England and Wales or Scotland" substitute "England and Wales, Scotland or a specified dependent territory."

(3) In section 20(3)—

- (*a*) in paragraph (*a*), after "section 13(6)(*a*)(i)), or" insert "a corresponding dependent territory order, or";
- (*b*) in paragraph (*b*), after "this Act" insert ", or a corresponding dependent territory order,".

10.—(1) In section 21(3), for "England and Wales or Scotland" substitute "England and Wales, Scotland or a specified dependent territory."

(2) In section 21(4)—

- (*a*) in paragraph (*a*), for "section 13(6)(*a*)(i), or" substitute "section 13 (6)(*a*)(i)), or a corresponding dependent territory order, or";
- (*b*) in paragraph (*b*), after "this Act" insert ", or a corresponding dependent territory order,".

11.—(1) In section 23(1), for "England and Wales or Scotland"—

- (*a*) (in the first place) substitute "England and Wales, Scotland or a specified dependent territory"; and
- (*b*) (in the second place) substitute "England and Wales, Scotland or the territory."

(2) In section 23(3), for "England and Wales or Scotland" substitute "England and Wales, Scotland or a specified dependent territory."

(3) In section 23(4)—

- (*a*) in paragraph (*a*), after "section 13(6)(*a*)(i)), or" insert "a corresponding dependent territory order, or";
- (*b*) in paragraph (*b*) after "this Act" insert ", or a corresponding dependent territory order,".

Chapter V—Recognition and Enforcement

12. In section 25(1)—

- (*a*) after the words "a court in any part of the United Kingdom" insert "or in a specified dependent territory";
- (*b*) after the words "shall be recognised in any other part" insert "or, in the case of a dependent territory order, any part";
- (*c*) for the words "in that other part," in both places where they occur, substitute "in that part."

13. In section 26, after "United Kingdom" insert "and a specified dependent territory."

14.—(1) In section 27(1), after "under this section" insert ", or in a specified dependent territory under a corresponding provision."

(2) In section 27(3), after "part of the United Kingdom" insert "or dependent territory."

(3) In section 27(4)—

- (*a*) after "the appropriate court" insert "in any part of the United Kingdom"; and
- (*b*) after "subsection (3) above" insert "or under a corresponding dependent territory provision,".

15. In section 28(2)—

- (*a*) in paragraph (*a*), after "United Kingdom" insert "or in a specified dependent territory"; and
- (*b*) in paragraph (*b*), after "United Kingdom" insert "and any specified dependent territory."

16.—(1) In section 31(1), after "United Kingdom" insert "or specified dependent territory."

(2) In section 31(2), after "outside the United Kingdom" insert "and any specified dependent territory."

17.—(1) In section 32(1)—

(*a*) in the definition of "the appropriate court," after "the Court of Session" insert "and, in relation to a specified dependent territory, means the corresponding court in that territory";

(*b*) in the definition of "Part I order," in paragraph (*a*), after "this Part" insert "or the corresponding dependent territory provisions."

(2) In section 32(3)(*a*), after "this Part" insert "or the corresponding dependent territory provisions, as the case may be,".

Chapter VI—Miscellaneous and supplemental

18. In section 33(3), after "United Kingdom" insert "and any specified dependent territory."

19.—(1) In section 35(2), after "specified in the order," insert "or out of any specified dependent territory specified in the order,".

(2) In section 35(3), after "any part of the United Kingdom" insert "or any specified dependent territory."

20.—(1) In section 36(1)—

(*a*) after "in the United Kingdom" insert "or any specified dependent territory"; and

(*b*) after "specified part of it" insert "or from any such territory."

(2) In section 36(2)—

(*a*) after "this section applies," ", made by a court in one part of the United Kingdom or in a specified dependent territory,";

(*b*) after "shall have effect in each" insert "other part, or, in the case of an order made in a dependent territory, each";

(*c*) the words "other than the part in which it was made" shall be omitted;

(*d*) in paragraphs (*a*) and (*b*), the word "other" shall be omitted.

21. In section 37(1), after "part of it" insert "or from a specified dependent territory."

22.—(1) In section 38(2)—

(*a*) in paragraph (*a*), after "of which he is a ward), or" insert "in a specified dependent territory, or"; and

(*b*) in paragraph (*b*), after "United Kingdom" insert "or in a specified dependent territory."

(2) In section 38(3)(*a*) and (*b*), after "United Kingdom" insert "or the specified dependent territory."

23.—(1) In section 41(1)—

(*a*) in paragraph (*b*) after "United Kingdom" insert "or in a specified dependent territory";

(*b*) after "that part of the United Kingdom," in both places, insert "or that territory."

(2) In section 41(2)—

(*a*) after "the part of the United Kingdom" insert "or the territory";

(*b*) in paragraph (*a*), after "that part of the United Kingdom" insert "or that territory";

(*c*) in paragraph (*b*), after "the United Kingdom" insert "or in a specified dependent territory."

(3) In section 41(3)—

(*a*) after "a Part of the United Kingdom" insert "or a specified dependent territory";

(*b*) in paragraph (*b*)—

(i) after "outside that part of the United Kingdom" insert "or that territory";

(ii) after "a court in any part of the United Kingdom" insert "or in any specified dependent territory."

24.—(1) In section 42(1)—

(*a*) after the definition of "certified copy" insert—

" 'corresponding dependent territory order,' 'corresponding dependent territory provision' and similar expressions, in relation to a specified dependent territory, shall be construed in accordance with Schedule 3 to the Family Law Act 1986 (Dependent Territories) Order 1991 as from time to time in force;

'dependent territory' has the meaning given by section 43(2) of this Act;' ";

(*b*) after the definition of "prescribed" insert—
" 'specified dependent territory' means a dependent territory for the time being specified in Schedule 1 to the said Order of 1991.' ".

(2) In section 42(2), for "England and Wales or in Northern Ireland" substitute "England and Wales, Northern Ireland or a specified dependent territory."

(3) In section 42(4), after paragraph (*c*) insert—
"(*d*) if the proceedings are in a specified dependent territory, means any child who has been treated by both parties as a child of their family, except a child who has been placed with those parties as foster parents by a public authority in that territory.".

(4) In section 42(6), after paragraph (*d*) insert—
"and
(*e*) an order under a corresponding dependent territory provision."

(5) In section 42(7)(*a*), after "United Kingdom" insert "and any specified dependent territory."

Article 3(3)

SCHEDULE 3

INTERPRETATION OF CERTAIN EXPRESSIONS IN PART I OF THE FAMILY LAW ACT 1986 AS MODIFIED BY SCHEDULE 2 TO THIS ORDER

PART I

The Isle of Man

1. In section 1(1)(*f*) "an order made by the court in a specified dependent territory corresponding to an order within paragraphs (a) to (e) above" means—
(*a*) an order under section 9 of the Family Law Act 1991 (an Act of Tynwald) or any of the following enactments (being enactments repealed by that Act)—
(i) section 3(5) of the Guardianship of Infants Act 1953 (an Act of Tynwald), so far as it relates to the custody of infants;
(ii) section 4(1) of that Act, except so far as it relates to costs, but including that section as applied by section 3(1) of the Legitimacy Act 1962 (an Act of Tynwald);
(iii) section 42(1) or (2) of the Judicature (Matrimonial Causes) Act 1976 (an Act of Tynwald);
(iv) section 8(2) or 18(1)(ii) of the Domestic Proceedings Act 1983 (an Act of Tynwald);
(v) section 34(1) of that Act;
(vi) section 49(1) of that Act, so far as it relates to the custody of or access to a child;
(*b*) an order made by the High Court of Justice of the Isle of Man in the exercise of its jurisdiction relating to wardship or its inherent jurisdiction with respect to children—
(i) so far as it gives care of a child to any person or provides for contact with or access to, or the education of, a child but
(ii) excluding an order varying or revoking such an order, or an order relating to a child of whom care or control is (immediately after the making of the order) vested in a public authority in the Isle of Man.

2. In each of sections 2A(3), 3(3), 6(4), 11(2), 13(5), 20(3), 21(4) and 23(4)—
(*a*) in paragraph (*a*) "corresponding dependent territory order" means an order under section 3(3) of the Child Custody Act 1987 (an Act of Tynwald);
(*b*) in paragraph (*b*) "corresponding dependent territory order" means an order under section 4(2) of that Act.

3. In section 13(6)(*a*)(ii), "corresponding dependent territory provision" means section 2(2) or 5(3) of the Child Custody Act 1987 (an Act of Tynwald).

4.—(1) In section 27(1) "corresponding provision" means section 7 of the Child Custody Act 1987 (an Act of Tynwald).

(2) In section 27(4) "corresponding dependent territory provision" means section 12(3) of that Act.

5.—(1) In section 32(1) "the corresponding court" means the High Court of Justice of the Isle of Man.

(2) In section 32(1) and (3)(*a*) "the corresponding dependent territory provisions" means Part I of the Child Custody Act 1987 (an Act of Tynwald).

6. In section 42(6)(*e*) "corresponding dependent territory provision" means—
(*a*) section 42(6) or (7) of the Judicature (Matrimonial Causes) Act 1976 (an Act of Tynwald);
(*b*) section 18(6) of the Domestic Proceedings Act 1983 (an Act of Tynwald).

Child Support Act 1991 (Commencement No. 3 and Transitional Provisions) Order 1992

(S.I. 1992 No. 2644)

[26th October 1992]

The Secretary of State for Social Security, in exercise of the powers conferred upon him by section 58(2) to (6) of the Child Support Act 1991, hereby makes the following Order:

Citation

1. This Order may be cited as the Child Support Act 1991 (Commencement No. 3 and Transitional Provisions) Order 1992.

Date appointed for the coming into force of certain provisions of the Child Support Act 1991

2. Subject to the following provisions of this Order, the date appointed for the coming into force of all the provisions of the Child Support Act 1991, in so far as they are not already in force, except sections 19(3), 30(2), 34(2), 37(2) and (3) and 58(12), is 5th April 1993.

Transitional provisions

3. The transitional provisions set out in the Schedule to this Order shall have effect.

Article 3 SCHEDULE

[1] PART I

PHASED TAKE-ON OF CASES

NOTE

[1] Substituted by S.I. 1993 No. 966.

---

1. In this Part of this Schedule—

"The Act" means the Child Support Act 1991;

"benefit" means income support, family credit, or disability working allowance under Part VII of the Social Security Contributions and Benefits Act 1992, or any other benefit prescribed under section 6(1) of the Act (applications by parents receiving benefit);

"parent with care" means a person who, in respect of the same child or children, is both a parent and a person with care; and

"transitional period" means the period beginning with 5th April 1993 and ending with 6th April 1997.

(2) For the purposes of paragraph 5 below, in England and Wales, an application for a maintenance order is pending before a court if—

(i) notice of the application has been filed, in accordance with rules of court, before 5th April 1993;

(ii) in the case of an application contained in a petition for divorce, nullity or judicial separation, or the answer to it, notice of intention to proceed with it was given, in the form required by rules of court, before 5th April 1993.

2. Subject to paragraph 4 below, during the transitional period no application under section 4 of the Act (applications for child support maintenance) in relation to a qualifying child or any qualifying children may be made at any time when—

(*a*) there is in force a maintenance order or written maintenance agreement (being an agreement made before 5th April 1993) in respect of that qualifying child or those qualifying children and the absent parent; or

(*b*) benefit is being paid to a parent with care of that child or those children.

3. Subject to paragraph 4 below, during the transitional period no application under section 7 of the Act (right of child in Scotland to apply for assessment) may be made by a qualifying child at any time when there is in force a maintenance order or written maintenance agreement (being an agreement made before 5th April 1993) in resepct of that child and the absent parent.

4. Paragraphs 2 and 3 above do not apply to an application made—

(*a*) in that part of the transitional period beginning with 8th April 1996, if the surname of the person with care begins with any of the letters A to D inclusive;

(*b*) in that part of the transitional period beginning with 1st July 1996, if the surname of the person with care begins with any of the letters E to K inclusive;

(*c*) in that part of the transitional period beginning with 7th October 1996, if the surname of the person with care begins with any of the letters L to R inclusive; and

(*d*) in that part of the transitional period beginning with 6th January 1997, if the surname of the person with care begins with any of the letters S to Z inclusive.

5.—(1) For so long as either—

(*a*) paragraph 2 or 3 above operates in a case so as to prevent an application being made under section 4 of the Act or, as the case may be, section 7 of the Act, and no application has been made under section 6 of the Act; or

(*b*) an application has been made under section 6 of the Act but no maintenance assessment has yet been made pursuant to that application,

then in relation to that case—

(i) section 8(3) of the Act (role of the courts with respect to maintenance orders) shall be modified so as to have effect as if the word "vary" were omitted;

(ii) in a case falling within sub-paragraph (*a*) above, section 9(3) of the Act shall not apply; and

(iii) section 9(5) of the Act shall be modified so as to have effect as if paragraph (*b*) were omitted.

(2) In a case where there is, at any time during the transitional period, pending before a court an application for a maintenance order or an application for an order varying a written maintenance agreement, section 8(3) or, as the case may be, section 9(5)(*b*) of the Act, shall not apply in relation to that case.

PART II

MODIFICATION OF MAINTENANCE ASSESSMENT IN CERTAIN CASES

6. In this Part of this Schedule—

"the Act"' means the Child Support Act 1991;

"formula amount" means the amount of child support maintenance that would, but for the provisions of this Part of this Schedule, be payable under an original assessment, or any fresh assessment made during the period specified in paragraph 8 consequent on a review under section 17, 18 or 19 of the Act;

"the Maintenance Assessment Procedure Regulations" means the Child Support (Maintenance Assessment Procedure) Regulations 1992;

"modified amount" means an amount which is £20 greater than the aggregate weekly amount which was payable under the orders, agreements or arrangements mentioned in paragraph 7(1)(*a*) below; and

"original assessment" means a maintenance assessment made in respect of a qualifying child where no previous such assessment has been made or, where the assessment is made in respect of more than one child, where no previous such assessment has been made in respect of any of those children.

[1] 7.—(1) Subject to sub-paragraph (2), the provisions of this Part of this Schedule apply to cases where—

(*a*) on 4th April 1993, and at all times thereafter until the date when a maintenance assessment is made under the Act, there is in force, in respect of all the qualifying children in respect of whom an application for a maintenance assessment is made under the Act and the absent parent concerned, one or more—

(i) maintenance orders;
(ii) orders under section 151 of the Army Act 1955 (deductions from pay for maintenance of wife or child) or section 151 of the Air Force Act 1955 (deductions from pay for maintenance of wife or child) or arrangements corresponding to such an order and made under Article 1(*b*) or 3 of the Naval and Marine Pay and Pensions (Deductions for Maintenance) Order 1959; or
(iii) maintenance agreements (being agreements which are made or evidenced in writing); and

(*b*) the absent parent is responsible for maintaining a child or children residing with him other than the child or children in respect of whom the application is made; and
(*c*) the formula amount is not more than £60; and
(*d*) the formula amount exceeds the aggregate weekly amount which was payable under the orders, agreements or arrangements mentioned in sub-paragraph (*a*) above by more than £20 a week.

(2) Nothing in this Part of this Schedule applies to a category A interim maintenance assessment within the meaning of regulation 8(1B) of the Child Support (Maintenance Assessment Procedure) Regulations 1992 made under section 12 of the Act.

NOTE
[1] As amended by S.I. 1993 No. 966.

---

8. In a case to which this Part of this Schedule applies, the amount payable under an original assessment, or any fresh assessment made consequent on a review under section 17, 18 or 19 of the Act, during the period of one year beginning with the date on which the original assessment takes effect or, if shorter, until any of the conditions specified in paragraph 7(1) is no longer satisfied, shall, instead of being the formula amount, be the modified amount.

[THE NEXT PAGE IS K 495]

9. For the purpose of determining the aggregate weekly amount payable under the orders, agreements or arrangements mentioned in paragraph 7(1)(*a*) above any payments in kind and any payments made to a third party on behalf of or for the benefit of the qualifying child or qualifying children or the person with care shall be disregarded.

10. If, in making a maintenance assessment, a child support officer has applied the provisions of this Part of this Schedule, regulation 10(2) of the Maintenance Assessment Procedure Regulations shall have effect as if there was added at the end—

"(*g*) the aggregate weekly amount which was payable under the orders, agreements or arrangements specified in paragraph 7(1)(*a*) of the Schedule to the Child Support Act 1991 (Commencement No. 3 and Transitional Provisions) Order 1992 (modification of maintenance assessment in certain cases).".

11. The first review of an original assessment under section 16 of the Act (periodical reviews) shall be conducted on the basis that the amount payable under the assessment immediately before the review takes place was the formula amount.

12.—(1) The provisions of the following sub-paragraphs shall apply where there is a review of a previous assessment under section 17 of the Act (reviews on change of circumstances) at any time when the amount payable under that assessment is the modified amount.

(2) Where the child support officer determines that, were a fresh assessment to be made as a result of the review, the amount payable under it (disregarding the provisions of this Part of this Schedule) (in this paragraph called "the reviewed formula amount") would be—

(*a*) more than the formula amount, the amount of child support maintenance payable shall be the modified amount plus the difference between the formula amount and the reviewed formula amount;

(*b*) less than the formula amount but more than the modified amount, the amount of child support maintenance payable shall be the modified amount;

(*c*) less than the modified amount, the amount of child support maintenance payable shall be the reviewed formula amount.

(3) The child support officer shall, in determining the reviewed formula amount, apply the provisions of regulations 20 to 22 of the Maintenance Assessment Procedure Regulations.

Child Support (Maintenance Arrangements and Jurisdiction) Regulations 1992

(S.I. 1992 No. 2645)

[26th October 1992]

The Secretary of State for Social Security, in exercise of the powers conferred upon him by sections 8(11), 10(1), (2) and (4), 44(3), 51, 52(4) and 54 of, and paragraph 11 of Schedule 1 to, the Child Support Act 1991 and of all other powers enabling him in that behalf hereby makes the following Regulations:

Citation, commencement and interpretation

1.—(1) These Regulations may be cited as the Child Support (Maintenance Arrangements and Jurisdiction) Regulations 1992 and shall come into force on 5th April 1993.

(2) In these Regulations—

"the Act" means the Child Support Act 1991;

"Maintenance Assessments and Special Cases Regulations" means the Child Support (Maintenance Assessments and Special Cases) Regulations 1992;

"effective date" means the date on which a maintenance assessment takes effect for the purposes of the Act;

"maintenance order" has the meaning given in section 8(11) of the Act.

(3) In these Regulations, unless the context otherwise requires, a reference—

(*a*) to a numbered regulation is to the regulation in these Regulations bearing that number;

(*b*) in a regulation to a numbered paragraph is to the paragraph in that regulation bearing that number;

(*c*) in a paragraph to a lettered or numbered sub-paragraph is to the sub-paragraph in that paragraph bearing that letter or number.

Prescription of enactment for the purposes of section 8(11) of the Act

2. The Affiliation Proceedings Act 1957 is prescribed for the purposes of section 8(11) of the Act.

Relationship between maintenance assessments and certain court orders

3.—(1) Orders made under the following enactments are of a kind prescribed for the purposes of section 10(1) of the Act—

(*a*) the Affiliation Proceedings Act 1957;
(*b*) Part II of the Matrimonial Causes Act 1973;
(*c*) the Domestic Proceedings and Magistrates' Courts Act 1978;
(*d*) Part III of the Matrimonial and Family Proceedings Act 1984;
(*e*) the Family Law (Scotland) Act 1985;
(*f*) Schedule 1 to the Children Act 1989.

(2) Subject to paragraphs (3) and (4), where a maintenance assessment is made with respect to—

(*a*) all of the children with respect to whom an order falling within paragraph (1) is in force; or
(*b*) one or more but not all of the children with respect to whom an order falling within paragraph (1) is in force and where the amount payable under the order to or for the benefit of each child is separately specified,

that order shall, so far as it relates to the making or securing of periodical payments to or for the benefit of the children with respect to whom the maintenance assessment has been made, cease to have effect.

(3) The provisions of paragraph (2) shall not apply where a maintenance order has been made in accordance with section 8(7) or (8) of the Act.

(4) In Scotland, where—

(*a*) an order has ceased to have effect by virtue of the provisions of paragraph (2) to the extent specified in that paragraph; and
(*b*) a child support officer no longer has jurisdiction to make a maintenance assessment with respect to a child with respect to whom the order ceased to have effect,

that order shall, so far as it relates to that child, again have effect from the date a child support officer no longer has jurisdiction to make a maintenance assessment with respect to that child.

(5) Where a maintenance assessment is made with respect to children with respect to whom an order falling within paragraph (1) is in force, the effective date of that assessment shall be two days after the assessment is made.

(6) Where the provisions of paragraph (2) apply to an order, that part of the order to which those provisions apply shall cease to have effect from the effective date of the maintenance assessment.

Relationship between maintenance assessments and certain agreements

4.—(1) Maintenance agreements within the meaning of section 9(1) of the Act are agreements of a kind prescribed for the purposes of section 10(2) of the Act.

(2) Where a maintenance assessment is made with respect to—

(*a*) all of the children with respect to whom an agreement falling within paragraph (1) is in force; or
(*b*) one or more but not all of the children with respect to whom an agreement falling within paragraph (1) is in force and where the amount payable under the agreement to or for the benefit of each child is separately specified,

that agreement shall, so far as it relates to the making or securing of periodical payments to or for the benefit of the children with respect to whom the maintenance assessment has been made, become unenforceable from the effective date of the assessment.

(3) Where an agreement becomes unenforceable under the provisions of paragraph (2) to the extent specified in that paragraph, it shall remain unenforceable in relation to a particular child until such date as a child support officer no longer has jurisdiction to make a maintenance assessment with respect to that child.

Notifications by child support officers

5.—(1) Where a child support officer is aware that an order of a kind prescribed in paragraph (2) is in force and considers that the making of a maintenance assessment has affected, or is likely to affect, that order, he shall notify the persons prescribed in paragraph (3) in respect of whom that maintenance assessment is in force, and the persons prescribed in paragraph (4) holding office in the court where the order in question was made or subsequently registered, of the assessment and its effective date.

(2) The prescribed orders are those made under an enactment mentioned in regulation 3(1).

(3) The prescribed persons in respect of whom the maintenance assessment is in force are—

(*a*) a person with care;

(*b*) an absent parent;

(*c*) a person who is treated as an absent parent under regulation 20 of the Maintenance Assessments and Special Cases Regulations;

(*d*) a child who has made an application for a maintenance assessment under section 7 of the Act.

(4) The prescribed person holding office in the court where the order in question was made or subsequently registered is—

(*a*) in England and Wales—

(i) in relation to the High Court, the senior district judge of the principal registry of the Family Division or, where proceedings were instituted in a district registry, the district judge;

(ii) in relation to a county court, the proper officer of that court within the meaning of Order 1, Rule 3 of the County Court Rules 1981;

(iii) in relation to a magistrates' court, the clerk to the justices of that court;

(*b*) in Scotland—

(i) in relation to the Court of Session, the Deputy Principal Clerk of Session;

(ii) in relation to a sheriff court, the sheriff clerk.

Notification by the court

6.—(1) Where a court is aware that a maintenance assessment is in force and makes an order mentioned in regulation 3(1) which it considers has affected, or is likely to affect, that assessment, the person prescribed in paragraph (2) shall notify the Secretary of State to that effect.

(2) The prescribed person is the person holding the office specified below in the court where the order in question was made or subsequently registered—

(*a*) in England and Wales—

(i) in relation to the High Court, the senior district judge of the principal registry of the Family Division or, where proceedings were instituted in a district registry, the district judge;

(ii) in relation to a county court, the proper officer of that court within the meaning of Order 1, Rule 3 of the County Court Rules 1981;

(iii) in relation to a magistrates' court, the clerk to the justices of that court;

(*b*) in Scotland—
  (i) in relation to the Court of Session, the Deputy Principal Clerk of Session;
  (ii) in relation to a sheriff court, the sheriff clerk.

Cancellation of a maintenance assessment on grounds of lack of jurisdiction

7.—(1) Where—
(*a*) a person with care;
(*b*) an absent parent; or
(*c*) a qualifying child
with respect to whom a maintenance assessment is in force ceases to be habitually resident in the United Kingdom, a child support officer shall cancel that assessment.

(2) Where the person with care is not an individual, paragraph (1) shall apply as if sub-paragraph (*a*) were omitted.

(3) Where a child support officer cancels a maintenance assessment under paragraph (1) or by virtue of paragraph (2), the assessment shall cease to have effect from the date that the child support officer determines is the date on which—
(*a*) where paragraph (1) applies, the person with care, absent parent or qualifying child; or
(*b*) where paragraph (2) applies, the absent parent or qualifying child
with respect to whom the assessment was made ceases to be habitually resident in the United Kingdom.

Maintenance assessments and maintenance orders made in error

8.—(1) Where—
(*a*) at the time that a maintenance assessment with respect to a qualifying child was made a maintenance order was in force with respect to that child;
(*b*) the absent parent has made payments of child support maintenance due under that assessment; and
(*c*) the child support officer cancels that assessment on the grounds that it was made in error,
the payments of child support maintenance shall be treated as payments under the maintenance order and that order shall be treated as having continued in force.

(2) Where—
(*a*) at the time that a maintenance order with respect to a qualifying child was made a maintenance assessment was in force with respect to that child;
(*b*) the absent parent has made payments of maintenance due under that order; and
(*c*) the maintenance order is revoked by the court on the grounds that it was made in error,
the payments under the maintenance order shall be treated as payments of child support maintenance and the maintenance assessment shall be treated as not having been cancelled.

Recovery of Maintenance (United States of America) Order 1993

(S.I. 1993 No. 591)

[10th March 1993]

Whereas Her Majesty is satisfied that arrangements have been made in the States of the United States of America specified in the Schedule to this Order to ensure that applications by persons in the United Kingdom for the recovery of maintenance from persons in those States can be entertained by courts in those States:

And whereas Her Majesty is satisfied that in the interest of reciprocity it is desirable to ensure that applications by persons in those States for the recovery of maintenance from persons in the United Kingdom can be entertained by courts in the United Kingdom:

Now, therefore, Her Majesty, in exercise of the powers conferred upon Her by sections 40 and 45(1) of the Maintenance Orders (Reciprocal Enforcement) Act 1972, is pleased, by and with the advice of Her Privy Council, to order, and it is hereby ordered, as follows:—

1.—(1) This Order may be cited as the Recovery of Maintenance (United States of America) Order 1993.

(2) This Order shall come into force on 5th April 1993.

2. In this Order, unless the context otherwise requires—

"the Act" means the Maintenance Orders (Reciprocal Enforcement) Act 1972;

"specified State" means a State specified in the Schedule to this Order.

3.—(1) The provisions of Part II of the Act shall apply in relation to a specified State as they apply in relation to a convention country, subject to the modification set out in paragraph (2) below.

(2) After section 26(3) of the Act there shall be inserted:—

"(3A) An application under subsection (1) or (2) above, for the purpose of recovering maintenance from a person in a specified State within the meaning of the Recovery of Maintenance (United States of America) Order 1993, and a certificate signed by a justice of the peace or, where the applicant is residing in Scotland, the sheriff, to the effect that the application sets forth facts from which it may be determined that the respondent owes a duty to maintain the applicant and any other person named in the application and that a court in the specified State may obtain jurisdiction of the respondent or his property, shall be registered in the court in the prescribed manner by the appropriate officer or, in Scotland, by the sheriff clerk in the Maintenance Orders (Reciprocal Enforcement) Act 1972 register.".

4. The following orders are hereby revoked:

(*a*) the Recovery of Maintenance (United States of America) Order 1979;

(*b*) the Recovery Abroad of Maintenance (United States of America) Order 1981; and

(*c*) the Recovery of Maintenance (United States of America) (Variation) Order 1984.

Article 2

SCHEDULE

Specified States

Alaska	Kentucky
Arizona	Louisiana
Arkansas	Maine
California	Maryland
Colorado	Massachusetts
Connecticut	Michigan
Delaware	Minnesota
Florida	Missouri
Georgia	Montana
Hawaii	Nebraska
Idaho	Nevada
Illinois	New Hampshire
Indiana	New Jersey
Iowa	New Mexico
Kansas	New York

Specified States	
North Carolina	Tennessee
North Dakota	Texas
Ohio	Utah
Oklahoma	Vermont
Oregon	Virginia
Pennsylvania	Washington
Rhode Island	Wisconsin
South Dakota	Wyoming

Reciprocal Enforcement of Maintenance Orders (Hague Convention Countries) Order 1993

(S.I. 1993 No. 593)

[5th April 1993]

Whereas Her Majesty is satisfied that arrangements have been made in the countries and territories specified in Schedule 1 to this Order to ensure that maintenance orders made by courts in the United Kingdom against persons in those countries and territories can be enforced there:

And whereas Her Majesty is satisfied that in the interest of reciprocity it is desirable to ensure that maintenance orders made by courts in the countries and territories specified in Schedule 1 to this Order against persons in the United Kingdom can be enforced in the United Kingdom:

Now, therefore, Her Majesty, in exercise of the powers conferred by sections 40 and 45(1) of the Maintenance Orders (Reciprocal Enforcement) Act 1972 is pleased, by and with the advice of Her Privy Council, to order, and it is hereby ordered, as follows:

1. This Order may be cited as the Reciprocal Enforcement of Maintenance Orders (Hague Convention Countries) Order 1993 and shall come into force on 5th April 1993.

2. In this Order, unless the context otherwise requires—

"Act" means the Maintenance Orders (Reciprocal Enforcement) Act 1972;

"court in a Hague Convention country" includes any judicial or administrative authority in a Hague Convention country;

"Hague Convention" means the Convention on the Recognition and Enforcement of Decisions Relating to Maintenance Obligations concluded at The Hague on 2nd October 1973; and

"Hague Convention country" means a country or territory specified in Schedule 1 to this Order, being a country or territory (other than the United Kingdom) in which the Hague Convention is in force.

3.—(1) The provisions of Part I of the Act shall apply in relation to a Hague Convention country as they apply in relation to a reciprocating country, subject to the exceptions, adaptations and modifications set out in Schedule 2 to this Order.

(2) Accordingly, Part I of the Act shall, in relation to—

(*a*) maintenance orders made by courts in the United Kingdom against persons in a Hague Convention country, and

(*b*) maintenance orders made by courts in a Hague Convention country against persons in the United Kingdom,

have effect as set out in Schedule 3 to this Order.

4. The Orders specified in Schedule 4 to this Order are hereby revoked.

Article 2

SCHEDULE 1

Hague Convention Countries

[1] Denmark
Federal Republic of Germany
Finland
France
Italy
Luxembourg
Netherlands (Kingdom in Europe and Netherlands Antilles)
Norway
Portugal
Slovakia
Sweden
Switzerland
The Czech Republic
Turkey

NOTE
[1] Inserted by S.I. 1994 No. 1902 (effective 1st September 1994).

Article 3(1)

SCHEDULE 2

Modifications to Part I of the Act

[For the effect of the modifications see Part I as set out in Sched. 3.]

Article 3(2)

SCHEDULE 3

[1] Part I of the Act as Modified by Schedule 2

NOTE
[1] Sections and subsections not printed are disapplied by Sched. 2.

Orders made by courts in the United Kingdom

Transmission of maintenance order made in United Kingdom for recognition and enforcement in Hague Convention country

2.—(1) Subject to subsection (2) below, where the payer under a maintenance order made, whether before, on or after 5th April 1993, by a court in the United Kingdom is residing in a Hague Convention country, the payee under the order may apply for the order to be sent to that country for recognition and enforcement.

(2) Subsection (1) above shall not have effect in relation to a maintenance order made under section 3 of this Act or to an order by virtue of a provision of Part II of this Act.

(3) Every application under this section shall be made in the prescribed manner to the prescribed officer of the court which made the maintenance order to which the application relates.

(4) If, on an application duly made under this section to the prescribed officer of a court in the United Kingdom, that officer is satisfied that the payer under the maintenance order to which the application relates is residing in a Hague Convention country, the following documents, that is to say—

(*a*) a certified copy of the maintenance order;
(*b*) a certificate signed by that officer certifying that the order is enforceable and that it is no longer subject to the ordinary forms of review;
(*c*) a certificate of arrears so signed;
(*d*) a statement giving such information as the officer possesses as to the whereabouts of the payer;
(*e*) a statement giving such information as the officer possesses for facilitating the identification of the payer;

(*f*) where available, a photograph of the payer;

(*g*) a written statement signed by that officer as to whether or not the payer appeared in the proceedings in which the maintenance order was made and, if he did not appear, the original or a certified copy of a document which establishes that notice of the institution of the proceedings, including notice of the substance of the claim, was served on the payer;

(*h*) a document which establishes that notice of the order was sent to the payer; and

(*i*) a written statement signed by that officer as to whether or not the payee received legal aid either in the said proceedings or in connection with the said application,

shall be sent by that officer, in the case of a court in England and Wales or Northern Ireland, to the Lord Chancellor, or, in the case of a court in Scotland, to the Secretary of State, with a view to their being transmitted by the Lord Chancellor, or, as the case may be, the Secretary of State, to the appropriate authority in the Hague Convention country if he is satisfied that the statement relating to the whereabouts of the payer gives sufficient information to justify that being done.

(5) Nothing in this section shall be taken as affecting any jurisdiction of a court in the United Kingdom with respect to a maintenance order to which this section applies, and subject to section 5 any such order may be enforced, varied or revoked accordingly.

Power of magistrates' court to make maintenance order against person residing in Hague Convention country

3.—(1) Where an application is made to a magistrates' court for a maintenance order by a person who is habitually resident in England and Wales against a person residing in a Hague Convention country and the court would have jurisdiction to determine the application under the Domestic Proceedings and Magistrates' Courts Act 1978 or the Children Act 1989 if at any time when the proceedings were instituted that person—

(*a*) were residing in England and Wales, and

(*b*) received reasonable notice of the date of the hearing of the application,

the court shall subject to the following provisions of this section have jurisdiction to determine the application.

(4) No enactment (or provision made under an enactment) requiring or enabling—

(*a*) a court to transfer proceedings from a magistrates' court to a county court or the High Court, or

(*b*) a magistrates' court to refuse to make an order on an application on the ground that any matter in question is one that would be more conveniently dealt with by the High Court,

shall apply in relation to an application to which subsection (1) above applies.

(5) On the making of an application to which subsection (1) above applies, the following documents, that is to say—

(*a*) notice of the institution of the proceedings, including notice of the substance of the application;

(*b*) a statement signed by the prescribed officer of the court giving such information as he possesses as to the whereabouts of the respondent;

(*c*) a statement giving such information as the officer possesses for facilitating the identification of the respondent; and

(*d*) where available, a photograph of the respondent,

shall be sent by that officer to the Lord Chancellor with a view to their being transmitted by the Lord Chancellor to the appropriate authority in the Hague Convention country in which the respondent is residing for service on him of the document mentioned in paragraph (*a*) above if the Lord Chancellor is satisfied that the statement relating to the whereabouts of the respondent gives sufficient information to justify that being done.

(6) In considering whether or not to make a maintenance order pursuant to an application to which subsection (1) above applies the court shall take into account any representations made and any evidence adduced by or on behalf of the respondent.

(6A) Where the respondent makes any representations or adduces any evidence, a copy of the representations or evidence shall be served on the applicant by the prescribed officer of the court before the hearing.

(6B) The prescribed officer of the court shall give the respondent notice in writing of the date fixed for the hearing by sending the notice by post addressed to his last known or usual place of abode.

(6C) A maintenance order pursuant to an application to which subsection (1) above applies shall not be made unless the document mentioned in paragraph (*a*) of subsection (5) above has been served on the respondent in accordance with the law for the service of such documents in the Hague Convention country in which he is residing or in such other manner as may be authorised by the Lord Chancellor not less than six weeks previously.

(6D) Where a maintenance order has been made under this section, the prescribed officer of the court shall send the following documents, that is to say—

(*a*) a certified copy of the order;

(*b*) a certificate signed by that officer certifying that the order is enforceable and that it is no longer subject to the ordinary forms of review;

(*c*) a written statement, signed by that officer as to whether or not the respondent appeared in the proceedings in which the order was made, and, if he did not appear, the original or a certified copy of a document which establishes that the document mentioned in paragraph (*a*) of subsection (5) above has been served on the payer in accordance with subsection (6C) above;

(*d*) a document which establishes that notice of the order was sent to the respondent; and

(*e*) a written statement signed by that officer as to whether or not the applicant received legal aid in the proceedings,

to the Lord Chancellor with a view to their being transmitted by him to the appropriate authority in the Hague Convention country in which the respondent resides for recognition and enforcement of the order.

(6E) A maintenance order made under this section may, subject to section 5 of this Act, be enforced, varied or revoked in like manner as any other maintenance order made by a magistrates' court.

(7) In the application of this section to Northern Ireland—

(*a*) for subsection (1) there shall be substituted—

"(1) Where a complaint is made to a magistrates' court by a person who is habitually resident in Northern Ireland against a person residing in a Hague Convention country and the complaint is one on which the court would have jurisdiction by virtue of any enactment to make a maintenance order if—

(*a*) that person were residing in Northern Ireland, and

(*b*) a summons to appear before the court to answer the complaint had been duly served on him,

the court shall have jurisdiction to hear the complaint and may make a maintenance order on the complaint.", and

(*b*) for subsection (4) there shall be substituted—

"(4) No enactment empowering a magistrates' court to refuse to make an order on a complaint on the ground that any matter in question is one which would be more conveniently dealt with by the High Court of Justice in Northern Ireland shall apply in relation to a complaint to which subsection (1) above applies.".

Power of sheriff to make maintenance order against person residing in Hague Convention country

4.—(1) The sheriff shall have jurisdiction in any action to which this section applies if at the time when the proceedings were instituted—

(*a*) the pursuer is habitually resident in Scotland and resides within the jurisdiction of the sheriff; and

(*b*) the sheriff is satisfied that, to the best of the information or belief of the pursuer, the defender is residing in a Hague Convention country; and

(*c*) the sheriff would not, apart from this subsection, have jurisdiction in that action.

(2) This section applies to any action for the payment, variation or revocation of aliment which is competent in the sheriff court, and includes an action of affiliation and aliment, but does not include an action of separation and aliment or adherence and aliment, or any action containing a crave for the custody of a child.

(3) Where in any action in which the payment of aliment in respect of a child is claimed, being an action in which the sheriff has jurisdiction by virtue of subsection (1) above, the sheriff is satisfied—

(*a*) that there are grounds on which a maintenance order containing a provision requiring the payment of aliment in respect of that child may be made in that action, but

(*b*) that he has no power to make that order unless he also makes an order providing for the custody of the child,

then, for the purpose of enabling the sheriff to make the maintenance order, the pursuer shall be deemed to be a person to whom the custody of the child has been committed by a decree of the sheriff which is for the time being in force.

(4) In any action in which the sheriff has jurisdiction by virtue of subsection (1) above, no decree shall be granted in favour of the pursuer unless a copy of the initial writ or summons has been served on the defender in the prescribed manner and in sufficient time to enable him to arrange for his defence.

Variation and revocation of maintenance order made in United Kingdom

5.—(1) This section applies to a maintenance order a certified copy of which has been sent to a Hague Convention country for recognition and enforcement of the order.

(2) The jurisdiction of a magistrates' court to revoke or vary a maintenance order shall be exercisable notwithstanding that the proceedings for the revocation or variation, as the case may be, of the order are brought by or against a person residing in a Hague Convention country.

(3) Where subsection (1) of section 60 of the Magistrates' Courts Act 1980 (revocation, variation etc. of orders for periodical payment) applies in relation to a maintenance order to which this section applies, that subsection shall have effect as if for the words "by order on complaint," there were substituted "on an application being made, by order".

(4) Where an application is made by the payee to a court in England and Wales or Northern Ireland for the variation or revocation of an order to which this section applies, and the payer is residing in a Hague Convention country, the prescribed officer of the court shall send to the Lord Chancellor notice of the institution of the proceedings, including notice of the substance of the application, with a view to its being transmitted by him to the appropriate authority in the Hague Convention country for service on the payer.

(5) Where an application is made by the payee to a court in England and Wales or Northern Ireland for the variation or revocation of an order to which this section applies, and the payer is residing in a Hague Convention country—

(*a*) the court, in considering whether or not to vary or revoke the order, shall take into account any representations made and any evidence adduced by or on behalf of the payer;

(*b*) a copy of any such representations or evidence shall be served on the payee in the prescribed manner before the hearing;

(*c*) the prescribed officer of the court shall give the payer notice in writing of the date fixed for the hearing by sending the notice by post addressed to his last known or usual place of abode.

(6) Where an application is made by the payee to a court in England and Wales or Northern Ireland for the variation or revocation of an order to which this section applies, and the payer is residing in a Hague Convention country, the order shall not be varied or revoked unless the document mentioned in subsection (4) above has been served on the payer in accordance with the law for the service of such a document in the Hague Convention country not less than six weeks previously.

(7) Where an application is made by the payer to a court in England and Wales or Northern Ireland for the variation or revocation of an order to which this section applies, the prescribed officer of the court shall arrange for the service of the document mentioned in subsection (4) above on the payee.

(8) Where an order to which this section applies has been varied or revoked by a court in the United Kingdom the prescribed officer of the court shall send the following documents, that is to say—

(*a*) a certified copy of the order of variation or revocation;

(*b*) a certificate signed by that officer certifying that the order of variation or revocation is enforceable and that it is no longer subject to the ordinary forms of review;

(*c*) a written statement, signed by that officer as to whether or not the respondent or, in Scotland the defender, appeared in the proceedings for the variation or revocation of the order, and, if he did not appear, the original or a certified copy of a document which establishes that notice of the institution of the proceedings has been served on the respondent, or, as the case may be, the defender; and

(*d*) a document which establishes that notice of the order of variation or revocation was sent to the respondent; and

(*e*) a written statement signed by that officer as to whether or not the payer or the payee received legal aid in the proceedings,

in the case of a court in England and Wales or Northern Ireland, to the Lord Chancellor, or, in the case of a court in Scotland, to the Secretary of State, with a view to their being transmitted by him to the appropriate authority in the Hague Convention country for recognition and enforcement of the order of variation or revocation.

(9) Where a maintenance order to which this section applies has been varied by an order made by a court in the United Kingdom or by a competent court in a Hague Convention country the maintenance order shall, as from the date on which the order of variation took effect, have effect as varied by that order.

(10) Where a maintenance order to which this section applies has been revoked by an order made by a court in the United Kingdom or by a competent court in a Hague Convention country the maintenance order shall, as from the date on which the order of revocation took effect, be deemed to have ceased to have effect except as respects any arrears due under the maintenance order at that date.

(11) Where a maintenance order to which this section applies has been varied or revoked by an order made by a competent court in a Hague Convention country, the prescribed officer of the court shall register the order of variation or revocation in the prescribed manner.

(12) In the application of this section to Northern Ireland, in subsection (8), for the word "respondent" in each place where it occurs, there shall be substituted "defendant".

Orders made by courts in Hague Convention countries

Registration in United Kingdom court of maintenance order made in Hague Convention country

6.—(1) This section applies to a maintenance order made whether before, on or after 5th April 1993 by a competent court in a Hague Convention country.

(2) Where a certified copy of an order to which this section applies is received by the Lord Chancellor or the Secretary of State from a Hague Convention country, and it appears to him that the payer under the order is residing in the United Kingdom, he shall send the copy of the order and the accompanying documents to the prescribed officer of the appropriate court.

(3) Where the prescribed officer of the appropriate court receives from the Lord Chancellor or the Secretary of State a certified copy of an order to which this section applies, he shall, subject to the following subsections, register the order in the prescribed manner in that court.

(4) Before registering an order under this section an officer of a court shall take such steps as he thinks fit for the purpose of ascertaining whether the payer under the order is residing within the jurisdiction of the court, and if after taking those steps he is satisfied that the payer is not so residing he shall return the certified copy of the order and the accompanying documents to the Lord Chancellor or the Secretary of State, as the case may be, with a statement giving such information as he possesses as to the whereabouts of the payer.

(5)(*a*) The prescribed officer of the appropriate court may refuse to authorise the registration of the order if the court in the Hague Convention country by or before which the order was made did not have jurisdiction to make the order; and for these purposes a court in a Hague Convention country shall be considered to have jurisdiction if—

(i) either the payer or the payee had his habitual residence in the Hague Convention country at the time when the proceedings were instituted; or

(ii) the payer and the payee were nationals of that country at that time; or

(iii) the respondent in those proceedings had submitted to the jurisdiction of the court, either expressly or by defending on the merits of the case without objecting to the jurisdiction; or

(iv) in the case of an order made by reason of a divorce or a legal separation or a declaration that a marriage is void or annulled, the court is recognised by the law of the part of the United Kingdom in which enforcement is sought as having jurisdiction to make the order.

(*b*) In deciding whether a court in a Hague Convention country had jurisdiction to make an order the prescribed officer shall be bound by any finding of fact on which the court based its jurisdiction.

(6) The prescribed officer of the appropriate court may refuse to authorise the registration of the order—

(*a*) if such registration is manifestly contrary to public policy;

(*b*) if the order was obtained by fraud in connection with a matter of procedure;

(*c*) if proceedings between the same parties and having the same purpose are pending before a court in the same part of the United Kingdom and those proceedings were the first to be instituted; or

(*d*) if the order is incompatible with an order made in proceedings between the same parties and having the same purpose, either in the United Kingdom or in another country, provided that the latter order itself fulfils the conditions necessary for its registration and enforcement under this Part of this Act.

(7) Without prejudice to subsection (6) above, if the payer did not appear in the proceedings in the Hague Convention country in which the order was made, the prescribed officer of the appropriate court shall refuse to authorise the registration of the order unless notice of the institution of the proceedings, including notice of the substance of the claim, was served on the payer in accordance with the law of that Hague Convention country and if, having regard to the circumstances, the payer had sufficient time to enable him to defend the proceedings.

(8) If the order is registered under subsection (3) above, the prescribed officer of the appropriate court shall serve notice in a prescribed form on the payer and give notice to the payee that the order has been registered.

(9) The payer may, before the end of the period of one calendar month beginning with the date of service of the said notice, appeal to the court in which the order is registered to set aside the registration of the order on one of the grounds set out in paragraphs (5), (6) and (7) above.

(10) If the payer appeals to the court in which the order is registered to set aside the registration of the order, the prescribed officer of the court shall give notice to the payee of the appeal and of the date of the hearing of the appeal.

(11) If the prescribed officer refuses to register the order, he shall give notice to the payee in a prescribed form that registration has been refused.

(12) A payee to whom notice has been given by the prescribed officer of any court under subsection (11) above may, before the end of the period of one calendar month beginning with the date when notice was given, appeal to that court against the refusal to register the order.

(13) If the payee appeals to the court against the refusal to register the order, the prescribed officer of the court shall give notice to the payer of the appeal and of the date of the hearing of the appeal.

(14) In the application of this section to Scotland—

(*a*) in subsection (8), for the words "serve notice in a prescribed form on" there shall be substituted the words "intimate to in the prescribed manner";

(*b*) in subsection (9), for the words "service of the said notice" there shall be substituted the words "the said intimation";

(*c*) in subsections (9), (10), (12) and (13) for any reference to an appeal there shall be substituted a reference to an application and cognate expressions shall be construed accordingly; and

(*d*) in subsection (11), for the words "in a prescribed form" there shall be substituted the words "in the prescribed manner".

(15) In the application of this section to Northern Ireland, in subsection (5), for the word "respondent" there shall be substituted "defendant".

Enforcement of maintenance order registered in United Kingdom court

8.—(1) Subject to subsections (2), (2A) and (2B) below, a registered order may be enforced in the United Kingdom as if it had been made by the registering court and as if that court had had jurisdiction to make it; and proceedings for or with respect to the enforcement of any such order may be taken accordingly.

(2) Subsection (1) above does not apply to an order which is for the time being registered in the High Court under Part I of the Maintenance Orders Act 1958 or to an order which is for time being registered in the High Court of Justice in Northern Ireland under Part II of the Maintenance and Affiliation Orders Act (Northern Ireland) 1966.

(2A) Where in a maintenance order made in a Hague Convention country there are provisions which are not enforceable under this Part of this Act, this section shall apply only to the remaining provisions of the order.

(2B) The payee under a registered order may request the partial enforcement of that order.

(3) Any person for the time being under an obligation to make payments in pursuance of a registered order shall give notice of any change of address to the clerk of the registering court, and any person failing without reasonable excuse to give such a notice shall be liable on summary conviction to a fine not exceeding level 2 on the standard scale.

(4) An order which by virtue of this section is enforceable by a magistrates' court in England and Wales shall, subject to the modifications of sections 76 and 93 of the Magistrates' Court Act 1980 specified in subsections (4A) and (4B) below, be enforceable as if it were a magistrates' court maintenance order made by that court.

In this subsection, "magistrates' court maintenance order" has the same meaning as in section 150(1) of the Magistrates' Courts Act 1980.

(4A) Section 76 (enforcement of sums adjudged to be paid) shall have effect as if for subsections (4) to (6) there were substituted the following subsections—

"(4) Where proceedings are brought for the enforcement of a magistrates' court maintenance order under this section, the court may vary the order by exercising one of its powers under subsection (5) below.

(5) The powers of the court are—

(*a*) the power to order that payments under the order be made directly to the clerk of the court or the clerk of any other magistrates' court;

(*b*) the power to order that payments under the order be made to the clerk of the court, or to the clerk of any other magistrates' court, by such method of payment falling within section 59(6) above (standing order, etc.) as may be specified;

(*c*) the power to make an attachment of earnings order under the Attachment of Earnings Act 1971 to secure payments under the order.

(6) In deciding which of the powers under subsection (5) above it is to exercise, the court shall have regard to any representations made by the debtor (within the meaning of section 59 above).

(7) Subsection (4) of section 59 above (power of court to require debtor to open account) shall apply for the purposes of subsection (5) above as it applies for the purposes of that section but as if for paragraph (*a*) there were substituted—

"(*a*) the court proposes to exercise its power under paragraph (*b*) of section 76(5) below, and"."

(4B) In section 93 (complaint for arrears), subsection (6) (court not to impose imprisonment in certain circumstances) shall have effect as if for paragraph (*b*) there were substituted—

"(*b*) if the court is of the opinion that it is appropriate—

(i) to make an attachment of earnings order; or

(ii) to exercise its power under paragraph (*b*) of section 76(5) above.".

(5) The magistrates' court by which an order is enforceable by virtue of this section, and the officers thereof, shall take all such steps for enforcing the order as may be prescribed.

(6) In any proceedings for or with respect to the enforcement of an order which is for the time being registered in any court under this Part of this Act a certificate of arrears sent to the prescribed officer of the court shall be evidence of the facts stated therein.

(7) Subject to subsection (8) below, a sum of money payable under a registered order shall be payable in accordance with the order, or such part thereof as the payee may have requested should be enforced, as from the date on which the order took effect.

(8) Where a registered order was made by a court in a Hague Convention country before the date of the entry into force of the Hague Convention between the United Kingdom and that country, no sum of money falling due before that date shall be payable in accordance with the order.

(9) In the application of this section to Scotland—

(*a*) subsections (2) to (5) shall be omitted; and

(*b*) in subsection (6), for the word "evidence" there shall be substituted the words "sufficient evidence".

Variation of maintenance order registered in United Kingdom court

9.—(1) Subject to the provisions of this section—

(*a*) the registering court shall have the like power, on an application made by the payer or payee under a registered order, to vary the order as if it had been made by the registering court and as if that court had had jurisdiction to make it;

(*b*) the jurisdiction of a magistrates' court to vary a registered order shall be exercisable notwithstanding that the proceedings for the variation of the order are brought by or against a person residing in a Hague Convention country.

(1ZA) Where the registering court is a magistrates' court in England and Wales, section 60 of the Magistrates' Courts Act 1980 (revocation, variation etc. of orders for periodical payment) shall have effect in relation to the registered order—

(*za*) as if in subsection (1) for the words "by order on complaint" there were substituted "on an application being made, by order";

(*a*) as if in subsection (3) for the words "paragraphs (*a*) to (*d*) of section 59(3) above" there were substituted "subsection (3A) below" and after that subsection there were inserted—

"(3A) The powers of the court are—

(*a*) the power to order that payments under the order be made directly to the clerk of the court or the clerk of any other magistrates' court;

(*b*) the power to order that payments under the order be made to the clerk of the court, or to the clerk of any other magistrates' court, by such method of payment falling within section 59(6) above (standing order, etc.) as may be specified;

(*c*) the power to make an attachment of earnings order under the Attachment of Earnings Act 1971 to secure payments under the order.";

(*b*) as if in subsection (4) for paragraph (*b*) there were substituted—

"(*b*) payments under the order are required to be made to the clerk of the court, or to the clerk of any other magistrates' court, by any method of payment falling within section 59(6) above (standing order, etc.)",

and as if after the words "the court" there were inserted "which made the order";

(*c*) as if in subsection (5) for the words "to the clerk" there were substituted "in accordance with paragraph (*a*) of subsection (3A) above";

(*d*) as if in subsection (7), paragraph (*c*) and the word "and" immediately preceding it were omitted;

(*e*) as if in subsection (8) for the words "paragraphs (*a*) to (*d*) of section 59(3) above" there were substituted "subsection (3A) above";

(*f*) as if for subsections (9) and (10) there were substituted the following subsections—

"(9) In deciding, for the purposes of subsections (3) and (8) above, which of the powers under subsection (3A) above it is to exercise, the court shall have regard to any representations made by the debtor.

(10) Subsection (4) of section 59 above (power of court to require debtor to open account) shall apply for the purposes of subsection (3A) above as it applies for the purposes of that section but as if for paragraph (*a*) there were substituted—

"(*a*) the court proposes to exercise its power under paragraph (*b*) of section 60(3A) below, and".".

(2) The registering court shall not vary a registered order unless—

(*a*) the payer under the order had his habitual residence in the United Kingdom at the time when the proceedings to vary the order were instituted; or

(*b*) the respondent in those proceedings had submitted to the jurisdiction of the registering court, either expressly or by defending on the merits of the case without objecting to the jurisdiction.

(3) Where an application is made to a registering court in England and Wales or Northern Ireland by the payer for the variation of a registered order, and the payee is residing in a Hague Convention country, the prescribed officer of the court shall send to the Lord Chancellor notice of the institution of the proceedings, including notice of the substance of the application, with a view to its being transmitted by him to the appropriate authority in the Hague Convention country for service on the payee.

(4) Where an application is made by the payer to a registering court in England and Wales or Northern Ireland for the variation of a registered order—

(*a*) the court, in considering whether or not to vary the order, shall take into account any representations made and any evidence adduced by or on behalf of the payee;

(*b*) a copy of any such representations and evidence shall be served on the payer by the prescribed officer of the court before the hearing;

(*c*) the prescribed officer of the court shall give the payee notice in writing of the date fixed for the hearing by sending the notice by post addressed to his last known or usual place of abode.

(5) Where an application is made by the payer to a registering court in England and Wales or Northern Ireland for the variation of a registered order and the payee is residing in a Hague Convention country, the order shall not be varied unless the document mentioned in subsection (3) above has been served on the payee in accordance with the law for the service of such a document in the Hague Convention country not less than six weeks previously.

(6) Where an application is made by the payee to a registering court in England and Wales or Northern Ireland for the variation of a registered order, the prescribed officer of the court shall serve the document mentioned in subsection (3) above on the payer.

(7) Where a registered order is varied by a registered court in the United Kingdom the prescribed officer of the court shall send the following documents, that is to say—

(*a*) a certified copy of the order of variation;

(*b*) a certificate signed by that officer certifying that the order of variation is enforceable and that it is no longer subject to the ordinary forms of review;

(*c*) a written statement signed by that officer as to whether or not the respondent or, in Scotland, the defender appeared in the proceedings for the variation of the order, and, if he did not appear, the original or a certified copy of a document which establishes that notice of the institution of the proceedings has been served on the respondent or, as the case may be, the defender; and

(*d*) a written statement signed by that officer as to whether or not the payer or the payee received legal aid in the proceedings,

in the case of a court in England and Wales or Northern Ireland, to the Lord Chancellor, or, in the case of a court in Scotland, to the Secretary of State, with a view to their being transmitted by the Lord Chancellor, or, as the case may be, the Secretary of State, to the appropriate authority in the Hague Convention country for recognition and enforcement of the order of variation.

(8) Where a registered order has been varied by the registering court or by a court in a Hague Convention country, the prescribed officer of the registering court shall register the variation order in the prescribed manner.

(9) Where a registered order has been varied by the registering court or by a court in a Hague Convention country, the registered order shall, as from the date on which the variation order took effect, have effect as so varied.

(10) In the application of this section to Northern Ireland, in subsections (2) and (7), for the word "respondent" in each place where it occurs, there shall be substituted "defendant".

Cancellation of registration and transfer of order

10.—(1) Where a registered order is revoked by an order made by a court in a Hague Convention country and notice of the revocation is received by the registering court, the prescribed officer of the registering court shall cancel the registration; but any arrears due under the registered order at the date on which the order of revocation took effect, other than, in the case of a registered order made by a court in a Hague Convention country before the date of the entry into force of the Hague Convention between the United Kingdom and that country, arrears due before that date, shall continue to be recoverable as if the registration had not been cancelled.

(2) Where the prescribed officer of the registering court is of opinion that the payer under a registered order has ceased to reside within the jurisdiction of that court, he shall cancel the

registration of the order and, subject to subsection (3) below, shall send the certified copy of the order to the Lord Chancellor.

(3) Where the prescribed officer of the registering court, being a magistrates' court, is of opinion that the payer is residing within the jurisdiction of another magistrates' court in that part of the United Kingdom in which the registering court is, he shall transfer the order to that other court by sending the certified copy of the order to the prescribed officer of that other court.

(4) On the transfer of an order under subsection (3) above the prescribed officer of the court to which it is transferred shall, subject to subsection (6) below, register the order in the prescribed manner in that court.

(5) Where the certified copy of an order is received by the Lord Chancellor under this section and it appears to him that the payer under the order is still residing in the United Kingdom, he shall transfer the order to the appropriate court by sending the certified copy of the order together with the related documents to the prescribed officer of the appropriate court and, subject to subsection (6) below, that officer shall register the order in the prescribed manner in that court.

(6) Before registering an order in pursuance of subsection (4) or (5) above an officer of a court shall take such steps as he thinks fit for the purpose of ascertaining whether the payer is so residing, and if after taking those steps he is satisfied that the payer is not residing within the jurisdiction of the court he shall send the certified copy of the order to the Lord Chancellor.

(7) The officer of a court who is required by any of the foregoing provisions of this section to send to the Lord Chancellor or to the prescribed officer of another court the certified copy of an order shall send with that copy—

(*a*) a certificate of arrears signed by him;

(*b*) a statement giving such information as he possesses as to the whereabouts of the payer; and

(*c*) any relevant documents in his possession relating to the case.

(8) In the application of this section to Scotland—

(*a*) in subsection (2), for the words "within the jurisdiction of that court" there shall be substituted the words "in Scotland";

(*b*) subsections (3) and (4) shall be omitted; and

(*c*) for the words "Lord Chancellor", in each place where they occur, there shall be substituted the words "Secretary of State".

Steps to be taken by Lord Chancellor or Secretary of State where payer under certain orders is not residing in the United Kingdom

11.—(1) If it appears to the Lord Chancellor or the Secretary of State that the payer under a maintenance order, a certified copy of which has been received by him from a Hague Convention country, is not residing in the United Kingdom or, in the case of an order which subsequently became a registered order, has ceased to reside therein, he shall send to the appropriate authority in that country—

(*a*) the certified copy of the order in question and a certified copy of any order varying that order;

(*b*) if the order has at any time been a registered order, a certificate of arrears signed by the prescribed officer;

(*c*) a statement giving such information as the Lord Chancellor or the Secretary of State possesses as to the whereabouts of the payer; and

(*d*) any other relevant documents in his possession relating to the case.

Appeals

Appeals

12. Where in pursuance of section 9 above a registering court makes or refuses to make an order varying a registered order, the payer or the payee under the registered order shall have the like right of appeal (if any) from the order of variation or from the refusal to make it as he would have if the registered order had been made by the registering court.

Evidence

Admissibility of evidence given in Hague Convention country

13.—(1) A statement contained in—

(*a*) a document, duly authenticated, which purports to set out or summarise evidence given in proceedings in a court in a Hague Convention country; or

(*b*) a document, duly authenticated, which purports to set out or summarise evidence taken in that country for the purpose of proceedings in a court in the United

Kingdom under this Part of this Act, whether in response to a request made by such a court or otherwise; or

(*c*) a document, duly authenticated, which purports to have been received in evidence in proceedings in a court in that country or to be a copy of a document so received; or

(*d*) a document purporting to be signed by a judicial officer, official or other competent person in a Hague Convention country which establishes that certain documents were served on a person,

shall in any proceedings in a court in the United Kingdom relating to a maintenance order to which this Part of this Act applies be admissible as evidence of any fact stated therein to the same extent as oral evidence of that fact is admissible in those proceedings.

(2) A document purporting to set out or summarise evidence given as mentioned in subsection (1)(*a*) above, or taken as mentioned in subsection (1)(*b*) above, shall be deemed to be duly authenticated for the purposes of that subsection if the document purports to be certified by the judicial officer or other person before whom the evidence was given, or, as the case may be, by whom it was taken, to be the original document containing or recording, or, as the case may be, summarising, that evidence or a true copy of that document.

(3) A document purporting to have been received in evidence as mentioned in subsection (1)(*c*) above, or to be a copy of a document so received, shall be deemed to be duly authenticated for the purposes of that subsection if the document purports to be certified by a judge or officer of the court in question to have been, or to be a true copy of a document which has been, so received.

(4) It shall not be necessary in any such proceedings to prove the signature or official position of the person appearing to have given such a certificate.

(5) Nothing in this section shall prejudice the admission in evidence of any document which is admissible in evidence apart from this section.

Obtaining of evidence needed for purpose of certain proceedings

14.—(1) Where for the purpose of any proceedings in a court in a Hague Convention country relating to a maintenance order to which this Part of this Act applies a request is made by or on behalf of that court for the taking in the United Kingdom of the evidence of a person residing therein relating to matters specified in the request, such court in the United Kingdom as may be prescribed shall have power to take that evidence and, after giving notice of the time and place at which the evidence is to be taken to such persons and in such manner as it thinks fit, shall take the evidence in such manner as may be prescribed.

Evidence taken in compliance with such a request shall be sent by the prescribed officer of the court—

(*a*) in England and Wales or Northern Ireland, to the Lord Chancellor, or

(*b*) in Scotland, to the Secretary of State,

for transmission to the appropriate authority in the Hague Convention country.

(2) Where any person, not being the payer or the payee under the maintenance order to which the proceedings in question relate, is required by virtue of this section to give evidence before a court in the United Kingdom, the court may order that there shall be paid out of moneys provided by Parliament such sums as appear to the court reasonably sufficient to compensate that person for the expense, trouble or loss of time properly incurred in or incidental to his attendance.

(3) Section 97(1), (3) and (4) of the Magistrates' Courts Act 1980 (which provide for compelling the attendance of witnesses, etc.) shall apply in relation to a magistrates' court having power under subsection (1) above to take the evidence of any person as if the proceedings in the court in a Hague Convention country for the purpose of which a request for the taking of the evidence has been made were proceedings in the magistrates' court and had been begun by complaint.

(4) Paragraphs 71 and 73 of Schedule 1 to the Sheriff Courts (Scotland) Act 1907 (which provide for the citation of witnesses, etc.) shall apply in relation to a sheriff having power under subsection (1) above to take the evidence of any person as if the proceedings in the court in a Hague Convention country for the purpose of which a request for the taking of the evidence has been made were proceedings in the sheriff court.

(5) A court in—

(*a*) England and Wales or Northern Ireland may for the purpose of any proceedings in that court under this Part of this Act relating to a maintenance order to which this Part of this Act applies send to the Lord Chancellor, or

(*b*) Scotland may for the purpose of such proceedings in that court relating to such an action, send to the Secretary of State,

for transmission to the appropriate authority in a Hague Convention country a request for a court in a Hague Convention country to take or provide evidence relating to such matters as may be specified in the request.

(6) In the application of this section to Northern Ireland, in subsection (3), for the reference to section 97(1), (3) and (4) of the Magistrates' Courts Act 1980 there shall be substituted a reference to Articles 118(1), (3) and (4), 119 and 120 of the Magistrates' Courts (Northern Ireland) Order 1981.

Order, etc. made in Hague Convention country need not be proved

15. For the purposes of this Part of this Act, unless the contrary is shown—

(*a*) any order made by a court in a Hague Convention country purporting to bear the seal of that court or to be signed by any person in his capacity as a judge or officer of the court, shall be deemed without further proof to have been duly sealed or, as the case may be, to have been signed by that person;

(*b*) the person by whom the order was signed shall be deemed without further proof to have been a judge or officer, as the case may be, of that court when he signed it and, in the case of an officer, to have been authorised to sign it; and

(*c*) a document purporting to be a certified copy of an order made by a court in a Hague Convention country shall be deemed without further proof to be such a copy.

Supplemental

Payment of sums under orders made in Hague Convention countries: conversion of currency

16.—(1) Payment of sums due under a registered order shall, while the order is registered in a court in England, Wales or Northern Ireland, be made in such manner and to such person as may be prescribed.

(2) Where the sums required to be paid under a registered order are expressed in a currency other than the currency of the United Kingdom, then, as from the relevant date, the order shall be treated as if it were an order requiring the payment of such sums in the currency of the United Kingdom as, on the basis of the rate of exchange prevailing at that date, are equivalent to the sums so required to be paid.

(3) Where the sum specified in any statement, being a statement of the amount of any arrears due under a maintenance order made by a court in a Hague Convention country, is expressed in a currency other than the currency of the United Kingdom, that sum shall be deemed to be such sum in the currency of the United Kingdom as, on the basis of the rate of exchange prevailing at the relevant date, is equivalent to the sum so specified.

(4) For the purposes of this section a written certificate purporting to be signed by an officer of any bank in the United Kingdom certifying that a specified rate of exchange prevailed between currencies at a specified date and that at such a rate a specified sum in the currency of the United Kingdom is equivalent to a specified sum in another specified currency shall be evidence of the rate of exchange so prevailing on that date and of the equivalent sums in terms of the respective currencies.

(5) In this section "the relevant date" means—

(*a*) in relation to a registered order or to a statement of arrears due under a maintenance order made by a court in a Hague Convention country, the date on which the order first becomes a registered order;

(*b*) in relation to a registered order which has been varied, the date on which the last order varying that order is registered in the registering court.

(6) In the application of this section to Scotland—

(*a*) subsection (1) shall not apply;

(*b*) in subsection (4), for the word "evidence" there shall be substituted the words "sufficient evidence".

Proceedings in magistrates' courts

17.—(4) Anything authorised or required by this Part of this Act to be done by, to or before the magistrates' court by, to or before which any other thing was done may be done by, to or before any magistrates' court acting for the same petty sessions area (or, in Northern Ireland, petty sessions district) as that court.

(5) Any application which by virtue of a provision of this Part of this Act is made to a magistrates' court in Northern Ireland shall be made by complaint.

(5A) Where the respondent to an application for the variation or revocation of—

(*a*) a maintenance order made by a magistrates' court in England and Wales, being an order to which section 5 of this Act applies; or

(*b*) a registered order which is registered in such a court,

is residing in a Hague Convention country, a magistrates' court in England and Wales shall have jurisdiction to hear the application (where it would not have such jurisdiction apart from this subsection) if it would have had jurisdiction to hear it had the respondent been residing in England and Wales.

(6) A magistrates' court in Northern Ireland shall have jurisdiction to hear a complaint for the variation or revocation—

(*a*) of a maintenance order made by such a court, and to which section 5 of this Act applies; or

(*b*) to hear a complaint for the variation of a registered order which is registered in that court.

if the defendant to the complaint is residing in a Hague Convention country and if the court would have had jurisdiction to hear the complaint had the defendant been residing in Northern Ireland and been served with a summons to appear before the court to answer the complaint.

(7) Where the respondent to an application—

(*a*) for the variation or revocation of a maintenance order made by a magistrates' court, and to which section 5 of this Act applies; or

(*b*) for the variation of a registered order registered in a magistrates' court,

does not appear at the time and place appointed for the hearing of the application, but the court is satisfied that the respondent is residing in a Hague Convention country, and that the requirements of section 5(4), (6) or (7) or section 9(3), as the case may be, have been complied with, the court may proceed to hear and determine the application at the time and place appointed for the hearing or for any adjourned hearing as if the respondent had appeared at that time and place.

(7A) In the application of this section to Northern Ireland, in subsection (7)—

(*a*) for the word "respondent", in each place where it occurs, there shall be substituted "defendant"; and

(*b*) for the words "an application" and "the application", in each place where they occur, there shall be substituted "a complaint" and "the complaint" respectively.

Magistrates' courts rules

18.—(1) Without prejudice to the generality of the power to make rules under section 144 of the Magistrates' Courts Act 1980 (magistrates' courts rules) provision may be made by such rules with respect to any of the following matters, namely—

(*a*) the circumstances in which anything authorised or required by this Part of this Act to be done by, to or before a magistrates' court acting for a particular petty sessions area or by, to or before an officer of that court may be done by, to or before a magistrates' court acting for such other petty sessions area as the rules may provide or by, to or before an officer of that court;

(*b*) the orders made, or other things done, by a magistrates' court, or an officer of such a court, under this Part of this Act, or by a court in a Hague Convention country, notice of which is to be given to such persons as the rules may provide and the manner in which such notice shall be given;

(*c*) the cases and manner in which courts in Hague Convention countries are to be informed of orders made, or other things done, by a magistrates' court under this Part of this Act;

(*d*) the cases and manner in which a justices' clerk may take evidence needed for the purpose of proceedings in court in a Hague Convention country relating to a maintenance order to which this Part of this Act applies;

(*f*) the circumstances and manner in which magistrates' courts may for the purposes of this Part of this Act communicate with courts in Hague Convention countries.

(1A) For the purpose of giving effect to this Part of this Act, rules made under section 144 of the Magistrates' Courts Act 1980 may make, in relation to any proceedings brought under or by virtue of this Part of this Act, any provision not covered by subsection (1) above which—

(*a*) falls within subsection (2) of section 93 of the Children Act 1989, and

(*b*) may be made in relation to relevant proceedings under that section.

(2) Rules with respect to the matters mentioned in subsection (1) above may be made in accordance with Article 13 of the Magistrates' Courts (Northern Ireland) Order 1981 in relation to proceedings or matters in magistrates' courts in Northern Ireland under this Part of this Act.

Rules for sheriff court

19. Without prejudice to the generality of the powers conferred on the Court of Session by section 32 of the Sheriff Courts (Scotland) Act 1971 to regulate by act of sederunt the procedure of the sheriff court, the said powers shall include power—

(*a*) to prescribe the decrees granted, or other things done, by the sheriff, or an officer of the sheriff court, under this Part of this Act, or by a court in a Hague Convention country, notice of which is to be given to such persons as the act of sederunt may provide and the manner in which such notice shall be given;

(*b*) to provide that evidence needed for the purpose of proceedings in a court in a Hague Convention country relating to a maintenance order to which this Part of this Act applies may, in such cases and manner as the act of sederunt may provide, be taken by a sheriff clerk or sheriff clerk depute;

(*c*) to prescribe the cases and manner in which courts in a Hague Convention country are to be informed of decrees granted, or other things done, by the sheriff under this Part of this Act;

(*d*) to prescribe the circumstances and manner in which the sheriff may for the purposes of this Part of this Act communicate with courts in a Hague Convention country.

Interpretation of Part I

21.—(1) In this Part of this Act unless the context otherwise requires—

"affiliation order" means an order (however described) adjudging, finding or declaring a person to be the father of a child, whether or not it also provides for the maintenance of the child;

"the appropriate court", in relation to a person residing in England and Wales or in Northern Ireland means a magistrates' court, and in relation to a person residing in Scotland means the sheriff court, within the jurisdiction of which that person is residing;

"certificate of arrears", in relation to a maintenance order, means a certificate certifying that the sum specified in the certificate is to the best of the information or belief of the officer giving the certificate the amount of the arrears due under the order at the date of the certificate except any arrears that accrued before the date of the entry into force of the Hague Convention between the United Kingdom and the Hague Convention country in which the payer is residing, or, as the case may be, that to the best of his information or belief there are no arrears due thereunder at the date of the certificate;

"certified copy", in relation to an order of a court, means a copy of the order certified by the proper officer of the court to be a true copy;

"court" includes any tribunal or person having power to make, confirm, enforce, vary or revoke a maintenance order and "competent court in a Hague Convention country" means a court having jurisdiction on one of the grounds specified in section 6(5)(*a*) above;

"maintenance order" means an order (however described), including any settlement made by or before a competent court in a Hague Convention country, of any of the following descriptions, and in the case of an order which is not limited to the following descriptions, the part of the order which is so limited, that is to say—

(*a*) an order (including an affiliation order or order consequent upon an affiliation order) which provides for the periodical payment of sums of money towards the maintenance of any person, being a person whom the person liable to make payments under the order is, according to the law applied in the place where the order was made, liable to maintain;

(*aa*) an order which has been made in Scotland, on or after the granting of a decree of divorce, for the payment of a periodical allowance by one party to the marriage to the other party;

(*b*) an affiliation order or order consequent upon an affiliation order, being an order which provides for the payment by a person adjudged, found or declared to be a child's father of expenses incidental to the child's birth or, where the child has died, of his funeral expenses; and

(*c*) an order within the foregoing provisions of this definition made against a payer on the application of a public body which claims reimbursement of sums of money payable under the order with respect to the payee if the reimbursement can be obtained by the public body under the law to which it is subject,

and in the case of a maintenance order which has been varied (including a maintenance order which has been varied either by a court in the United Kingdom or by a competent court in a Hague Convention country whether or not the original order was made by such a court), means that order as varied:

Provided that the expression "maintenance order" shall not include an order made in a Hague Convention country of a description which that country or the United Kingdom has reserved the right under Article 26 of the Hague Convention not to recognise or enforce;

"order" means an order however described giving effect to a decision rendered by a court and, as respects Scotland, includes any interlocutor, and any decree or provision contained in an interlocutor;

"payee", in relation to a maintenance order, means the person entitled to the payments for which the order provides and includes a public body which has provided benefits for the payee and which is entitled *ipso jure* under the law to which it is subject to claim enforcement of the said order to the extent of the benefits so provided in place of the said person;

"payer", in relation to a maintenance order, means the person liable to make payments under the order;

"prescribed", in relation to a magistrates' court in England and Wales or in Northern Ireland, means prescribed by rules made under section 144 of the Magistrates' Court Act 1980 or by rules made in accordance with Article 13 of the Magistrates' Courts (Northern Ireland) Order 1981, as the case may be, and in relation to any other court means prescribed by rules of court;

"registered order" means a maintenance order which is for the time being registered in a court in the United Kingdom under this Part of this Act and "registered" and "registration" shall be construed accordingly;

"registering court", in relation to a registered order, means the court in which that order is for the time being registered under this Part of this Act;

"revoke" and "revocation" include discharge.

(3) Any reference in this Part of this Act to the payment of money for the maintenance of a child shall be construed as including a reference to the payment of money for the child's education.

Article 4 SCHEDULE 4

REVOCATIONS

Title	*Reference*
The Reciprocal Enforcement of Maintenance Orders (Hague Convention Countries) Order 1979	S.I. No. 1979/1317
The Reciprocal Enforcement of Maintenance Orders (Hague Convention Countries) (Variation) Order 1981	S.I. No. 1981/837
The Reciprocal Enforcement of Maintenance Orders (Hague Convention Countries) (Variation) (No. 2) Order 1981	S.I. No. 1981/1545
The Reciprocal Enforcement of Maintenance Orders (Hague Convention Countries) (Variation) (No. 3) Order 1981	S.I. No. 1981/1674
The Reciprocal Enforcement of Maintenance Orders (Hague Convention Countries) (Variation) Order 1983	S.I. No. 1983/885
The Reciprocal Enforcement of Maintenance Orders (Hague Convention Countries) (Variation) (No. 2) Order 1983	S.I. No. 1983/1523
The Reciprocal Enforcement of Maintenance Orders (Hague Convention Countries) (Variation) Order 1987	S.I. No. 1987/1282

Reciprocal Enforcement of Maintenance Orders (Republic of Ireland) Order 1993

(S.I. 1993 No. 594)

[10th March 1993]

Whereas Her Majesty is satisfied that arrangements have been made in the Republic of Ireland to ensure that maintenance orders made by courts in the United Kingdom against persons in the Republic of Ireland can be enforced there:

And whereas Her Majesty is satisfied that in the interest of reciprocity it is desirable to ensure that maintenance orders made by courts in the

Republic of Ireland against persons in the United Kingdom can be enforced in the United Kingdom:

Now, therefore, Her Majesty, in exercise of the powers conferred by sections 40 and 45(1) of the Maintenance Orders (Reciprocal Enforcement) Act 1972 is pleased, by and with the advice of Her Privy Council, to order, and it is hereby ordered, as follows:

1. This Order may be cited as the Reciprocal Enforcement of Maintenance Orders (Republic of Ireland) Order 1993 and shall come into force on 5th April 1993.

2.—(1) The provisions of Part I of the Maintenance Orders (Reciprocal Enforcement) Act 1972 (in this Order referred to as "the Act") shall apply in relation to the Republic of Ireland as they apply in relation to a reciprocating country, subject to the exceptions, adaptations and modifications set out in Schedule 1 to this Order.

(2) Accordingly, Part I of the Act shall, in relation to—

(*a*) maintenance orders made by courts in the United Kingdom against persons in the Republic of Ireland, and

(*b*) maintenance orders made by courts in the Republic of Ireland against persons in the United Kingdom,

have effect as set out in Schedule 2 to this Order.

3. The Reciprocal Enforcement of Maintenance Orders (Republic of Ireland) Order 1974 is hereby revoked.

Article 2(1)

SCHEDULE

MODIFICATIONS TO PART I OF THE ACT

[For the effect of the modifications see Part I as set out in Sched. 2.]

Article 2(2)

SCHEDULE 2

[1] PART I OF THE ACT AS MODIFIED BY SCHEDULE 1

NOTE

[1] Sections and subsections not printed are disapplied by Sched. 1.

Orders made by courts in the United Kingdom

Transmission of maintenance order made in United Kingdom for enforcement in the Republic of Ireland

2.—(1) Subject to subsection (2) below, where the payer under a maintenance order made, whether before, on or after 5th April 1993, by a court in the United Kingdom is residing in the Republic of Ireland, the payee under the order may apply for the order to be sent to that country for enforcement.

(2) Subsection (1) above shall not have effect in relation to a provisional order or to an order made by virtue of a provision of Part II of this Act.

(3) Every application under this section shall be made in the prescribed manner to the prescribed officer of the court which made the maintenance order to which the application relates.

(4) If, on an application duly made under this section to the prescribed officer of a court in the United Kingdom, that officer is satisfied that the payer under the maintenance order to which the application relates is residing in the Republic of Ireland, the following documents, that is to say—

(*a*) a certified copy of the maintenance order;

(*b*) a certificate signed by that officer certifying that the order is enforceable in the United Kingdom;

(*c*) a certificate of arrears so signed;
(*d*) a statement giving such information as the officer possesses as to the whereabouts of the payer;
(*e*) a statement giving such information as the officer possesses for facilitating the identification of the payer;
(*f*) where available, a photograph of the payer;
(*g*) if the payer did not appear in the proceedings in which the maintenance order was made, the original or a certified copy of a document which establishes that notice of the institution of the proceedings was served on the payer;
(*h*) a document which establishes that notice of the order was sent to the payer; and
(*i*) if the payee received legal aid in the proceedings, a written statement to that effect signed by that officer,

shall be sent by that officer, in the case of a court in England and Wales or Northern Ireland, to the Lord Chancellor, or, in the case of a court in Scotland, to the Secretary of State, with a view to their being transmitted by the Lord Chancellor, or, as the case may be, the Secretary of State, to the responsible authority in the Republic of Ireland if he is satisfied that the statement relating to the whereabouts of the payer gives sufficient information to justify that being done.

(5) Nothing in this section shall be taken as affecting any jurisdiction of a court in the United Kingdom with respect to a maintenance order to which this section applies, and any such order may be enforced, varied or revoked accordingly.

Power of magistrates' court to make and confirm provisional maintenance order against person residing in the Republic of Ireland

3.—(1) Where an application is made to a magistrates' court for a maintenance order against a person residing in the Republic of Ireland and the court would have jurisdiction to determine the application under the Domestic Proceedings and Magistrates' Courts Act 1978 or the Children Act 1989 if that person—
(*a*) were residing in England and Wales, and
(*b*) received reasonable notice of the date of the hearing of the application,

the court shall (subject to subsection (2) below) have jurisdiction to determine the application.

(2) A maintenance order made by virtue of this section shall be a provisional order.

(4) No enactment (or provision made under an enactment) requiring or enabling—
(*a*) a court to transfer proceedings from a magistrates' court to a county court or the High Court, or
(*b*) a magistrates' court to refuse to make an order on an application on the ground that any matter in question is one that would be more conveniently dealt with by the High Court,

shall apply in relation to an application to which subsection (1) above applies.

(5) Where a court makes a maintenance order which is by virtue of this section a provisional order, the following documents, that is to say—
(*a*) a certified copy of the maintenance order;
(*b*) a document, authenticated in the prescribed manner, setting out or summarising the evidence given in the proceedings;
(*c*) a certificate signed by the prescribed officer of the court certifying that the grounds stated in the certificate are the grounds on which the making of the order might have been opposed by the payer under the order;
(*ca*) a notice addressed to the payer stating that a provisional order has been made, that it has no effect unless and until confirmed with or without alteration by the court making the order, and that in considering whether or not to confirm the provisional order the court will take into account any representations made or any evidence adduced by or on behalf of the payer within three weeks from the date of service of the notice;
(*d*) a statement giving such information as was available to the court as to the whereabouts of the payer;
(*e*) a statement giving such information as the officer possesses for facilitating the identification of the payer; and
(*f*) where available, a photograph of the payer,

shall be sent by that officer to the Lord Chancellor with a view to their being transmitted by the Lord Chancellor to the responsible authority in the Republic of Ireland if he is satisfied that the statement relating to the whereabouts of the payer gives sufficient information to justify that being done.

(6) The court which made a provisional order by virtue of this section shall not earlier than three weeks after the date of service of the notice referred to in paragraph (*ca*) of subsection

(5) above consider whether or not to confirm the order and with or without alteration and shall take into account any representations made and any evidence adduced by or on behalf of the payer.

(6A) Where the payer makes any representations or adduces any evidence, a copy of the representations or evidence shall be served on the person on whose application the provisional order was made before the date of the hearing at which confirmation of the provisional order will be considered and that person shall be notified in the prescribed manner of the date fixed for the hearing.

(6B) The court shall not confirm such an order unless the documents mentioned in paragraphs (*a*), (*b*), (*c*) and (*ca*) of subsection (5) above have been served on the payer in accordance with the law for the service of such documents in the Republic of Ireland and in sufficient time to enable him to arrange for his defence.

(6C) Where an order has been confirmed under this section, the prescribed officer of the court shall—

(*a*) send to the payer by registered post notice of the confirmation of the order; and

(*b*) send the following documents, that is to say—

(i) a certified copy of the maintenance order as confirmed;

(ii) a certificate signed by that officer certifying that the order is enforceable in the United Kingdom;

(iii) if the payer did not appear in the proceedings in which the order was confirmed, the original or a certified copy of a document which establishes that the documents mentioned in paragraphs (*a*), (*b*), (*c*) and (*ca*) of subsection (5) above have been served on the payer;

(iv) a document which establishes that notice of the confirmation of the order has been sent to the payer by registered post;

(v) if the payee received legal aid in the proceedings, a written statement to that effect signed by that officer,

to the Lord Chancellor with a view to their being transmitted by him to the responsible authority in the Republic of Ireland.

(6D) Where the court decides not to confirm a provisional order, it shall revoke the order.

(7) In the application of this section to Northern Ireland—

(*a*) for subsection (1) there shall be substituted—

"(1) Where a complaint is made to a magistrates' court against a person residing in the Republic of Ireland and the complaint is one on which the court would have jurisdiction by virtue of any enactment to make a maintenance order if—

(*a*) that person was residing in Northern Ireland, and

(*b*) a summons to appear before the court to answer the complaint had been duly served on him,

the court shall have jurisdiction to hear the complaint and may (subject to subsection (2) below) make a maintenance order on the complaint.", and

(*b*) for subsection (4) there shall be substituted—

"(4) No enactment empowering a magistrates' court to refuse to make an order on a complaint on the ground that any matter in question is one which would be more conveniently dealt with by the High Court of Justice in Northern Ireland shall apply in relation to a complaint to which subsection (1) above applies.".

Power of sheriff to make maintenance order against person residing in the Republic of Ireland

4.—(1) The sheriff shall have jurisdiction in any action to which this section applies if—

(*a*) the pursuer resides within the jurisdiction of the sheriff;

(*b*) the sheriff is satisfied that, to the best of the information or belief of the pursuer, the defender is residing in the Republic of Ireland; and

(*c*) the sheriff would not, apart from this subsection, have jurisdiction in that action.

(2) This section applies to any action for the payment, variation or revocation of aliment which is competent in the sheriff court, and includes an action of affiliation and aliment, but does not include an action of separation and aliment or adherence and aliment, or any action containing a crave for the custody of a child.

(3) Where in any action in which the payment of aliment in respect of a child is claimed, being an action in which the sheriff has jurisdiction by virtue of subsection (1) above, the sheriff is satisfied—

(*a*) that there are grounds on which a maintenance order containing a provision requiring the payment of aliment in respect of that child may be made in that action, but

(*b*) that he has no power to make that order unless he also makes an order providing for the custody of the child,

then, for the purpose of enabling the sheriff to make the maintenance order, the pursuer shall be deemed to be a person to whom the custody of the child has been committed by a decree of the sheriff which is for the time being in force.

(4) In any action in which the sheriff has jurisdiction by virtue of subsection (1) above, no decree shall be granted in favour of the pursuer unless—

(*a*) a copy of the initial writ or summons together with a copy of the warrant for citation has been sent to the responsible authority in the Republic of Ireland for service on the defender; and

(*b*) a copy of the initial writ or summons has been served on the defender in accordance with the law for the service of such documents in the Republic of Ireland and in sufficient time to enable him to arrange for his defence; and

(*c*) the grounds of action have been substantiated by sufficient evidence, and section 36(3) of the Sheriff Courts (Scotland) Act 1971 shall not apply in relation to any such action which is a summary cause.

Variation and revocation of maintenance order made in United Kingdom

5.—(1) This section applies to a maintenance order a certified copy of which has been sent to the Republic of Ireland in pursuance of section 2 of this Act and to a provisional order made in pursuance of section 3 of this Act which has been confirmed by a court in England and Wales or Northern Ireland under that section.

(2) Where subsection (1) of section 60 of the Magistrates' Courts Act 1980 (revocation, variation etc. of orders for periodical payment) applies in relation to a maintenance order to which this section applies, that subsection shall have effect as if for the words "by order on complaint," there were substituted "on an application being made, by order".

(3) Where an application is made to a court in England and Wales or Northern Ireland by the payee for the variation or revocation of an order to which this section applies, and the payer is residing in the Republic of Ireland, the prescribed officer of the court shall send to the Lord Chancellor a certified copy of the application, together with a document, authenticated in the prescribed manner, setting out or summarising the evidence in support of the application, with a view to their being transmitted by him to the responsible authority in the Republic of Ireland for service on the payer.

(4) A court in England and Wales or Northern Ireland shall not vary or revoke such an order before the expiry of three weeks from the date of service of the documents mentioned in subsection (3) above and before varying or revoking the order shall take into account any representations made and any evidence adduced by or on behalf of the payer.

(5) Where such an order is varied or revoked by a court in England and Wales or Northern Ireland a certified copy of the order of the court and a statement as to the service of the documents mentioned in subsection (3) above on the payer shall be sent to the court in the Republic of Ireland by which the order is being enforced.

(6) Where a maintenance order to which this section applies has been varied by an order made by a court in the United Kingdom, the maintenance order shall, as from the date on which the order of variation was made, have effect as varied by that order.

(7) Where a maintenance order to which this section applies has been revoked by an order made by a court in the United Kingdom, the maintenance order shall, as from the date on which the order of revocation was made, be deemed to have ceased to have effect except as respects any arrears due under the maintenance order at that date.

Orders made by courts in the Republic of Ireland

Registration in United Kingdom court of maintenance order made in the Republic of Ireland

6.—(1) This section applies to a maintenance order made whether before, on or after 5th April 1993 by a court in the Republic of Ireland.

(2) Where a certified copy of an order to which this section applies is received by the Lord Chancellor or the Secretary of State from the responsible authority in the Republic of Ireland, and it appears to him that the payer under the order is residing in the United Kingdom, he shall send the copy of the order and the accompanying documents to the prescribed officer of the appropriate court.

(3) Where the prescribed officer of the appropriate court receives from the Lord Chancellor or the Secretary of State a certified copy of an order to which this section applies, he shall, subject to the following subsections, register the order in the prescribed manner in that court.

(4) Before registering an order under this section an officer of a court shall take such steps as he thinks fit for the purpose of ascertaining whether the payer under the order is residing within the jurisdiction of the court, and if after taking those steps he is satisfied that the payer is not so residing he shall return the certified copy of the order and the accompanying documents to the Lord Chancellor or, as the case may be, the Secretary of State with a statement giving such information as he possesses as to the whereabouts of the payer.

(5) The order shall not be registered—

(*a*) if such registration is contrary to public policy;

(*b*) if the payer did not appear in the proceedings in the Republic of Ireland and he was not served in accordance with the law of the place where he was residing with the summons or other notice of the institution of the proceedings in sufficient time to enable him to arrange for his defence;

(*c*) if the order is irreconcilable with a judgment given in the United Kingdom in proceedings between the same parties.

(6) If the order is registered under this section, the prescribed officer of the appropriate court shall serve notice in a prescribed form on the payer and give notice to the payee that the order has been registered.

(7) The payer may within one calendar month from the date of service of the said notice appeal to the court in which the order is registered to set aside the registration of the order on one of the grounds set out in subsection (5) above.

(8) If the payer appeals to the appropriate court to set aside the registration of the order, the prescribed officer of the court shall give notice to the payee of the appeal and of the date of the hearing of the appeal.

(9) If the payer appeals to the appropriate court to set aside the registration of the order, the court may, on the application of the payer, stay, or in Scotland sist, the proceedings if either—

(*a*) enforcement of the maintenance order has been suspended in the Republic of Ireland pending the determination of any form of appeal; or

(*b*) the time for an appeal has not yet expired and enforcement has been suspended pending the making of an appeal,

and in the latter case the court may lay down the time within which the proceedings will be stayed or sisted.

(10) If the order is not registered by virtue of subsection (5) above, the prescribed officer shall give notice to the payee in a prescribed form that the order has not been registered.

(11) A payee to whom notice has been given by the officer of any court under subsection (10) above may within one calendar month of the date of the notice appeal to that court to set aside the decision not to register the order.

(12) In the application of this section to Scotland—

(*a*) in subsection (6), for the words "serve notice on" there shall be substituted the words "intimate to";

(*b*) in subsection (7), for the words "service of the said notice" there shall be substituted the words "the said intimation"; and

(*c*) in subsections (7) to (11), for any reference to an appeal there shall be substituted a reference to an application and cognate expressions shall be construed accordingly.

Enforcement of maintenance order registered in United Kingdom court

8.—(1) Subject to subsections (1A), (2), (2A) and (2B) below, a registered order may be enforced in the United Kingdom as if it had been made by the registering court and as if that court had had jurisdiction to make it; and proceedings for or with respect to the enforcement of any such order may be taken accordingly.

(1A) During the period within which an appeal to set aside the registration of a registered order may be made under section 6(7) and until any such appeal has been determined, no measures of enforcement may be taken against the property of the payer other than those designed to protect the interests of the payee:

Provided that nothing in this subsection shall be construed as preventing a registered order from being registered as mentioned in subsection (2) below.

(2) Subsection (1) above does not apply to an order which is for the time being registered in the High Court under Part I of the Maintenance Orders Act 1958 or to an order which is for the time being registered in the High Court of Justice in Northern Ireland under Part II of the Maintenance and Affiliation Orders Act (Northern Ireland) 1966.

(2A) Where in a maintenance order made in the Republic of Ireland there are provisions which are not enforceable, this section shall apply only to the remaining provisions of the order.

(2B) The payee under a registered order may request the partial enforcement of that order.

(3) Any person for the time being under an obligation to make payments in pursuance of a registered order shall give notice of any change of address to the clerk of the registering court, and any person failing without reasonable excuse to give such a notice shall be liable on summary conviction to a fine not exceeding level 2 on the standard scale.

(4) An order which by virtue of this section is enforceable by a magistrates' court in England and Wales shall subject to the modifications of sections 76 and 93 of the Magistrates' Courts Act 1980 specified in subsections (4A) and (4B) below be enforceable as if it were a magistrates' court maintenance order made by that court.

In this subsection, "magistrates' court maintenance order" has the same meaning as in section 150(1) of the Magistrates' Courts Act 1980.

(4A) Section 76 (enforcement of sums adjudged to be paid) shall have effect as if for subsections (4) to (6) there were substituted the following subsections—

"(4) Where proceedings are brought for the enforcement of a magistrates' court maintenance order under this section, the court may vary the order by exercising one of its powers under subsection (5) below.

(5) The powers of the court are—

(*a*) the power to order that payments under the order be made directly to the clerk of the court or the clerk of any other magistrates' court;

(*b*) the power to order that payments under the order be made to the clerk of the court, or to the clerk of any other magistrates' court, by such method of payment falling within section 59(6) above (standing order, etc.) as may be specified;

(*c*) the power to make an attachment of earnings order under the Attachment of Earnings Act 1971 to secure payments under the order.

(6) In deciding which of the powers under subsection (5) above it is to exercise, the court shall have regard to any representations made by the debtor (within the meaning of section 59 above).

(7) Subsection (4) of section 59 above (power of court to require debtor to open account) shall apply for the purposes of subsection (5) above as it applies for the purposes of that section but as if for paragraph (*a*) there were substituted—

"(*a*) the court proposes to exercise its power under paragraph (*b*) of section 76(5) below, and"."

(4B) In section 93 (complaint for arrears), subsection (6) (court not to impose imprisonment in certain circumstances) shall have effect as if for paragraph (*b*) there were substituted—

"(*b*) if the court is of the opinion that it is appropriate—

(i) to make an attachment of earnings order; or

(ii) to exercise its power under paragraph (*b*) of section 76(5) above."

(5) The magistrates' court by which an order is enforceable by virtue of this section, and the officers thereof, shall take all such steps for enforcing the order as may be prescribed.

(6) In any proceedings for or with respect to the enforcement of an order which is for the time being registered in any court under this Part of this Act a certificate of arrears sent to the prescribed officer of the court shall be evidence of the facts stated therein.

(7) Subject to subsection (8) below, sums of money payable under a registered order shall be payable in accordance with the order, or such part thereof as the payee may have requested should be enforced, as from the date on which the order took effect.

(8) No sums of money accruing before 1st April 1975 under a registered order shall be payable in accordance with the order.

(9) In the application of this section to Scotland—

(*a*) in subsection (1A), for any reference to an appeal there shall be substituted a reference to an application;

(*b*) subsections (2) to (5) shall be omitted; and

(*c*) in subsection (6), for the word "evidence" there shall be substituted the words "sufficient evidence".

Variation and revocation of maintenance order registered in United Kingdom court

9.—(1) Where a registered order has been varied by a court in the Republic of Ireland, the registered order shall, as from the date on which the order of variation took effect or 1st April 1975, whichever is the later, have effect as varied by that order.

(2) Where a registered order has been revoked by a court in the Republic of Ireland, the registered order shall, as from the date on which the order of revocation took effect or 1st April 1975, whichever is the later, be deemed to have ceased to have effect except as respects any arrears due under the registered order at that date.

(3) The prescribed officer of the registering court shall register in the prescribed manner any order varying a registered order.

Cancellation of registration and transfer of order

10.—(1) Where a registered order is revoked by an order made by a court in the Republic of Ireland and notice of the revocation is received by the registering court, the prescribed officer of the registering court shall cancel the registration; but any arrears due under the registered order at the date on which the order of revocation took effect or 1st April 1975, whichever is the later, shall continue to be recoverable as if the registration had not been cancelled.

(2) Where the prescribed officer of the registering court is of opinion that the payer under a registered order has ceased to reside within the jurisdiction of that court, he shall cancel the registration of the order and, subject to subsection (3) below, shall send the certified copy of the order to the Lord Chancellor.

(3) Where the prescribed officer of the registering court, being a magistrates' court, is of opinion that the payer is residing within the jurisdiction of another magistrates' court in that part of the United Kingdom in which the registering court is, he shall transfer the order to that other court by sending the certified copy of the order to the prescribed officer of that other court.

(4) On the transfer of an order under subsection (3) above the prescribed officer of the court to which it is transferred shall, subject to subsection (6) below, register the order in the prescribed manner in that court.

(5) Where the certified copy of an order is received by the Lord Chancellor under this section and it appears to him that the payer under the order is still residing in the United Kingdom, he shall transfer the order to the appropriate court by sending the certified copy of the order together with the related documents to the prescribed officer of the appropriate court and, subject to subsection (6) below, that officer shall register the order in the prescribed manner in that court.

(6) Before registering an order in pursuance of subsection (4) or (5) above an officer of a court shall take such steps as he thinks fit for the purpose of ascertaining whether the payer is so residing, and if after taking those steps he is satisfied that the payer is not residing within the jurisdiction of the court he shall send the certified copy of the order to the Lord Chancellor.

(7) The officer of a court who is required by any of the foregoing provisions of this section to send to the Lord Chancellor or to the prescribed officer of another court the certified copy of an order shall send with that copy—

(*a*) a certificate of arrears signed by him;

(*b*) a statement giving such information as he possesses as to the whereabouts of the payer; and

(*c*) any relevant documents in his possession relating to the case.

(8) In the application of this section to Scotland—

(*a*) in subsection (2), for the words "within the jurisdiction of that court" there shall be substituted the words "in Scotland";

(*b*) subsections (3) and (4) shall be omitted; and

(*c*) for the words "Lord Chancellor" in each place where they occur, there shall be substituted the words "Secretary of State".

Steps to be taken by Lord Chancellor or Secretary of State where payer under certain orders is not residing in the United Kingdom

11.—(1) If it appears to the Lord Chancellor or the Secretary of State that the payer under a maintenance order, a certified copy of which has been received by him from the Republic of Ireland, is not residing in the United Kingdom, he shall send to the responsible authority in that country—

(*a*) the certified copy of the order in question;

(*b*) if the order has at any time been a registered order, a certificate of arrears signed by the prescribed officer;

(*c*) a statement giving such information as the Lord Chancellor or the Secretary of State possesses as to the whereabouts of the payer; and

(*d*) any other relevant documents in his possession relating to the case.

Appeals

Appeals

12.—(1) No appeal shall lie from a provisional order made in pursuance of section 3 of this Act by a court in England and Wales or Northern Ireland.

(2) Where in pursuance of that section any such court confirms or refuses to confirm such a provisional order, the payer or payee under the order shall have the like right of appeal (if any) from the confirmation of, or refusal to confirm, the provisional order as he would have if that order were not a provisional order and the court had made or, as the case may be, refused to make the order on the occasion on which it confirmed or, as the case may be, refused to confirm the order.

(3) Nothing in subsection (2) shall be construed as affecting any right of appeal conferred by any other enactment.

Evidence

Admissibility of evidence given in the Republic of Ireland

13.—(1) A statement contained in—

(*a*) a document, duly authenticated, which purports to set out or summarise evidence given in proceedings in a court in the Republic of Ireland; or

(*b*) a document, duly authenticated, which purports to set out or summarise evidence taken in that country for the purpose of proceedings in a court in the United Kingdom under this Part of this Act, whether in response to a request made by such a court or otherwise; or
(*c*) a document, duly authenticated, which purports to have been received in evidence in proceedings in a court in that country or to be a copy of a document so received; or
(*d*) a document purporting to be signed by a judge or officer of a court in the Republic of Ireland which establishes that certain documents were served on a person,

shall in any proceedings in a court in the United Kingdom relating to a maintenance order to which this Part of this Act applies be admissible as evidence of any facts stated therein to the same extent as oral evidence of that fact is admissible in those proceedings.

(2) A document purporting to set out or summarise evidence given as mentioned in subsection (1)(*a*) above, or taken as mentioned in subsection (1)(*b*) above, shall be deemed to be duly authenticated for the purposes of that subsection if the document purports to be certified by the judge or other person before whom the evidence was given or, as the case may be, by whom it was taken, to be the original document containing or recording, or, as the case may be, summarising, that evidence or a true copy of that document.

(3) A document purporting to have been received in evidence as mentioned in subsection (1)(*c*) above, or to be a copy of a document so received, shall be deemed to be duly authenticated for the purposes of that subsection if the document purports to be certified by a judge or officer of the court in question to have been, or to be a true copy of a document which has been, so received.

(4) It shall not be necessary in any such proceedings to prove the signature or official position of the person appearing to have given such a certificate.

(5) Nothing in this section shall prejudice the admission in evidence of any document which is admissible in evidence apart from this section.

Obtaining of evidence needed for purpose of certain proceedings

14.—(1) Where for the purpose of any proceedings in a court in the Republic of Ireland relating to a maintenance order to which this Part of this Act applies a request is made by or on behalf of that court for the taking in the United Kingdom of the evidence of a person residing therein relating to matters specified in the request, such court in the United Kingdom as may be prescribed shall have power to take that evidence and, after giving notice of the time and place at which the evidence is to be taken to such persons and in such manner as it thinks fit, shall take the evidence in such manner as may be prescribed.

Evidence taken in compliance with such a request shall be sent by the prescribed officer of the court—

(*a*) in England and Wales or Northern Ireland, to the Lord Chancellor, or
(*b*) in Scotland, to the Secretary of State,

for transmission to the responsible authority in the Republic of Ireland.

(2) Where any person, not being the payer or the payee under the maintenance order to which the proceedings in question relate, is required by virtue of this section to give evidence before a court in the United Kingdom, the court may order that there shall be paid—

(*a*) if the court is a court in England, Wales or Scotland, out of moneys provided by Parliament; and
(*b*) if the court is a court in Northern Ireland, out of moneys provided by Parliament,

such sums as appear to the court reasonably sufficient to compensate that person for the expense, trouble or loss of time properly incurred in or incidental to his attendance.

(3) Section 97(1), (3) and (4) of the Magistrates' Courts Act 1980 (which provide for compelling the attendance of witnesses, etc.) shall apply in relation to a magistrates' court having power under subsection (1) above to take the evidence of any person as if the proceedings in the court in the Republic of Ireland for the purpose of which a request for the taking of the evidence has been made were proceedings in the magistrates' court and had been begun by complaint.

(4) Paragraphs 71 and 73 of Schedule 1 to the Sheriff Courts (Scotland) Act 1907 (which provide for the citation of witnesses, etc.) shall apply in relation to a sheriff having power under subsection (1) above to take the evidence of any person as if the proceedings in the court in the Republic of Ireland for the purpose of which a request for the taking of the evidence has been made were proceedings in the sheriff court.

(5) A court in—

(*a*) England and Wales or Northern Ireland may for the purpose of any proceedings in that court under this Part of this Act relating to a maintenance order to which this Part of this Act applies, send to the Lord Chancellor, or
(*b*) Scotland may for the purpose of such proceedings in that court relating to such an action, send to the Secretary of State,

for transmission to the responsible authority in the Republic of Ireland a request for a court in the Republic of Ireland to take or provide evidence relating to such matters as may be specified in the request.

(6) In the application of this section to Northern Ireland, in subsection (3), for the reference to section 97(1), (3) and (4) of the Magistrates' Courts Act 1980 there shall be substituted a reference to Articles 118(1), (3) and (4), 119 and 120 of the Magistrates' Courts (Northern Ireland) Order 1981.

Order, etc. made in the Republic of Ireland need not be proved

15. For the purposes of this Part of this Act, unless the contrary is shown—

(*a*) any order made by a court in the Republic of Ireland purporting to bear the seal of that court or to be signed by any person in his capacity as a judge or officer of the court, shall be deemed without further proof to have been duly sealed or, as the case may be, to have been signed by that person;

(*b*) the person by whom the order was signed shall be deemed without further proof to have been a judge or officer, as the case may be, of that court when he signed it and, in the case of an officer, to have been authorised to sign it; and

(*c*) a document purporting to be a certified copy of an order made by a court in the Republic of Ireland shall be deemed without further proof to be such a copy.

Supplemental

Payment of sums under orders made in the Republic of Ireland

16. Payment of sums due under a registered order shall, while the order is registered in a court in England, Wales or Northern Ireland, be made in such manner and to such person as may be prescribed.

Proceedings in magistrates' courts

17.—(4) Anything authorised or required by this Part of this Act to be done by, to or before the magistrates' court by, to or before which any other thing was done may be done by, to or before any magistrates' court acting for the same petty sessions area (or, in Northern Ireland, petty sessions district) as that court.

(5) Any application which by virtue of a provision of this Part of this Act is made to a magistrates' court in Northern Ireland shall be made by complaint.

(5A) Where the respondent to an application for the variation or revocation of—

(*a*) a maintenance order made by a magistrates' court in England and Wales, being an order to which section 5 of this Act applies; or

(*b*) a registered order which is registered in such a court,

is residing in the Republic of Ireland, a magistrates' court in England and Wales shall have jurisdiction to hear the application (where it would not have such jurisdiction apart from this subsection) if it would have had jurisdiction to hear it had the respondent been residing in England and Wales.

(6) A magistrates' court in Northern Ireland shall have jurisdiction to hear a complaint for the variation or revocation of a maintenance order made by such a court, being an order to which section 5 of this Act applies, if the defendant to the complaint is residing in the Republic of Ireland and the court would have jurisdiction to hear the complaint had the defendant been residing in Northern Ireland.

(7) Where the respondent to an application for the variation or revocation of a maintenance order made by a magistrates' court, being an order to which section 5 of this Act applies, does not appear at the time and place appointed for the hearing of the application, but the court is satisfied that the respondent is residing in the Republic of Ireland, the court may proceed to hear and determine the application at the time and place appointed for the hearing or for any adjourned hearing in like manner as if the respondent had appeared at that time and place.

(7A) In the application of this section to Northern Ireland, in subsection (7)—

(*a*) for the word "respondent", in each place where it occurs, there shall be substituted "defendant"; and

(*b*) for the words "an application" and "the application", in each place where they occur, there shall be substituted "a complaint" and "the complaint" respectively.

Magistrates' courts rules

18.—(1) Without prejudice to the generality of the power to make rules under section 144 of the Magistrates' Courts Act 1980 (magistrates' courts rules), provision may be made by such rules with respect to any of the following matters, namely—

(*a*) the circumstances in which anything authorised or required by this Part of this Act to be done by, to or before a magistrates' court acting for a particular petty sessions area or by, to or before an officer of that court may be done by, to or before a magistrates' court acting for such other petty sessions area as the rules may provide or by, to or before an officer of that court;

(*b*) the orders made, or other things done, by a magistrates' court, or an officer of such a court, under this Part of this Act, or by a court in the Republic of Ireland, notice of which is to be given to such persons as the rules may provide and the manner in which such notice shall be given;

(*c*) the cases and manner in which courts in the Republic of Ireland are to be informed of orders made, or other things done, by a magistrates' court under this Part of this Act;

(*d*) the cases and manner in which a justices' clerk may take evidence needed for the purpose of proceedings in a court in the Republic of Ireland relating to a maintenance order to which this Part of this Act applies;

(*e*) the circumstances and manner in which cases may be remitted by magistrates' courts to courts in the Republic of Ireland;

(*f*) the circumstances and manner in which magistrates' courts may for the purposes of this Part of this Act communicate with courts in the Republic of Ireland.

(1A) For the purpose of giving effect to this Part of this Act, rules made under section 144 of the Magistrates' Courts Act 1980 may make, in relation to any proceedings brought under or by virtue of this Part of this Act, any provision not covered by subsection (1) above which—

(*a*) falls within subsection (2) of section 93 of the Children Act 1989, and

(*b*) may be made in relation to relevant proceedings under that section.

(2) Rules with respect to the matters mentioned in subsection (1) above may be made in accordance with Article 13 of the Magistrates' Courts (Northern Ireland) Order 1981 in relation to proceedings or matters in magistrates' courts in Northern Ireland under this Part of this Act.

Rules for sheriff court

19. Without prejudice to the generality of the powers conferred on the Court of Session by section 32 of the Sheriff Courts (Scotland) Act 1981 to regulate by act of sederunt the procedure of the sheriff court, the said powers shall include power—

(*a*) to prescribe the decrees granted, or other things done, by the sheriff, or an officer of the sheriff court, under this Part of this Act, or by a court in the Republic of Ireland, notice of which is to be given to such persons as the act of sederunt may provide and the manner in which such notice shall be given;

(*b*) to provide that evidence needed for the purpose of proceedings in a court in the Republic of Ireland relating to a maintenance order to which this Part of this Act applies may, in such cases and manner as the act of sederunt may provide, be taken by a sheriff clerk or sheriff clerk depute;

(*c*) to prescribe the cases and manner in which courts in the Republic of Ireland are to be informed of decrees granted, or other things done, by the sheriff under this Part of this Act;

(*d*) to prescribe the circumstances and manner in which cases may be remitted by the sheriff to courts in the Republic of Ireland;

(*e*) to prescribe the circumstances and manner in which the sheriff may for the purposes of this Part of this Act communicate with courts in the Republic of Ireland.

Interpretation of Part I

21.—(1) In this Part of this Act—

"affiliation order" means an order (however described) adjudging, finding or declaring a person to be the father of a child, whether or not it also provides for the maintenance of the child;

"the appropriate court", in relation to a person residing in England and Wales or in Northern Ireland means a magistrates' court, and in relation to a person residing in Scotland means the sheriff court, within the jurisdiction of which that person is residing;

"certificate of arrears", in relation to a maintenance order, means a certificate certifying that the sum specified in the certificate is to the best of the information or belief of the officer giving the certificate the amount of the arrears due under the order at the date of the certificate except any arrears due under the order in respect of a period ending before 1st April 1975 or, as the case may be, that to the best of his information or belief there are no arrears due thereunder at the date of the certificate;

"certified copy", in relation to an order of a court, means a copy of the order certified by the proper officer of the court to be a true copy;

"court" includes any tribunal or person having power to make, confirm, enforce, vary or revoke a maintenance order;

"maintenance order" means an order (however described) of any of the following descriptions, that is to say—

(*a*) an order (including an affiliation order or order consequent upon an affiliation order) which provides for the periodical payment of sums of money towards the maintenance of any person, being a person whom the person liable to make payments under the order is, according to the law applied in the place where the order was made, liable to maintain;

(*aa*) an order which has been made in Scotland, on or after the granting of a decree of divorce, for the payment of a periodical allowance by one party to the marriage to the other party; and

(*b*) an affiliation order or order consequent upon an affiliation order, being an order which provides for the payment by a person adjudged, found or declared to be a child's father of expenses incidental to the child's birth or, where the child has died, of his funeral expenses,

and, in the case of a maintenance order which has been varied, means that order as varied;

"order", as respects Scotland, includes any interlocutor, and any decree or provision contained in an interlocutor;

"payee", in relation to a maintenance order, means the person entitled to the payments for which the order provides;

"payer", in relation to a maintenance order, means the person liable to make payments under the order;

"prescribed", in relation to a magistrates' court in England and Wales or in Northern Ireland, means prescribed by rules made under section 144 of the Magistrates' Courts Act 1980 or by rules made in accordance with Article 13 of the Magistrates' Courts (Northern Ireland) Order 1981, as the case may be, and in relation to any other court means prescribed by rules of court;

"provisional order" means an order made by a court in England and Wales or Northern Ireland which is provisional only and has no effect unless and until confirmed, with or without alteration, by that court;

"registered order" means a maintenance order which is for the time being registered in a court in the United Kingdom under this Part of this Act;

"registering court", in relation to a registered order, means the court in which that order is for the time being registered under this Part of this Act;

"the responsible authority", in relation to the Republic of Ireland, means any person who in that country has functions similar to those of the Lord Chancellor or the Secretary of State under this Part of this Act; and

"revoke" and "revocation" include discharge.

(2) For the purposes of this Part of this Act an order shall be taken to be a maintenance order so far (but only so far) as it relates to the periodical payment of sums of money as mentioned in paragraph (*a*) of the definition of "maintenance order" in subsection (1) above, to the payment of a periodical allowance as mentioned in paragraph (*aa*) of that definition, or to the payment by a person adjudged, found or declared to be a child's father of any such expenses as are mentioned in paragraph (*b*) of that definition.

(3) Any reference in this Part of this Act to the payment of money for the maintenance of a child shall be construed as including a reference to the payment of money for the child's education.

Act of Sederunt (Child Support Rules) 1993

(S.I. 1993 No. 920)

[26th March 1993]

The Lords of Council and Session, under and by virtue of the powers conferred on them by section 32 of the Sheriff Courts (Scotland) Act 1971 and of all other powers enabling them in that behalf, having approved, with modifications, draft rules submitted to them by the Sheriff Court Rules Council in accordance with section 34 of that Act, do hereby enact and declare:

Citation and commencement

1.—(1) This Act of Sederunt may be cited as the Act of Sederunt (Child Support Rules) 1993 and shall come into force on 5th April 1993.

(2) This Act of Sederunt shall be inserted in the Books of Sederunt.

(3) In this Act of Sederunt—

"the Act of 1991" means the Child Support Act 1991;

"deduction from earnings order" means an order under section 31(2) of the Act of 1991;

"liability order" means an order under section 33(2) of the Act of 1991; and

"liable person" means a person liable to make payments of child support maintenance.

(4) A reference in rules 1 to 6 of this Act of Sederunt to a numbered form is a reference to the form so numbered in the Schedule to this Act of Sederunt or a form substantially to the same effect, with such modifications as circumstances may require.

Application for a liability order

2.—(1) An application by the Secretary of State for a liability order under section 33(2) of the Act of 1991 shall be by summary application in Form 1, and rule 3 and Form A of the Ordinary Cause Rules of the sheriff court shall not apply to such an application.

(2) The sheriff clerk shall, on receiving an application under paragraph (1) above, order the application to be served on the liable person with a notice in Form 2; and service of the application and notice shall be by a solicitor or officer of court, who shall complete an execution of service.

(3) Where the liable person wishes to object to the grant of the application he shall do so by completing Form 2 and returning it to the sheriff clerk within 21 days after the date of service of the application.

(4) The sheriff clerk, on receipt of an objection which is in accordance with paragraph (3) above, shall—

(*a*) put out the cause for hearing; and

(*b*) intimate the hearing to the parties.

(5) The sheriff may consider the application, and any objection which has been received, on the date fixed for hearing, or at any continuation of it, whether or not any of the parties appear.

(6) Where no objection to the grant of the application in accordance with paragraph (3) above has been received within 21 days after the date of service, the applicant may return the application, together with a duly completed execution of service, to the sheriff clerk requesting the sheriff to make a liability order.

(7) A liability order shall be in Form 3.

(8) An extract of the liability order, or other order of the sheriff, may be issued on the expiry of 14 days from the date of making of the order.

(9) An extract of the liability order shall be in Form 4.

Enforcement of non-Scottish liability orders within Scotland

3. Where a liability order made by a court in England and Wales or any corresponding order made by a court in Northern Ireland is, by virtue of regulations made under section 39(1) of the Act of 1991, to be enforced in Scotland, the liability order or corresponding order shall be registered for enforcement by the sheriff clerk appending to it a docquet in the following terms:–

"(*Insert name of sheriff court and date of registration*)

This order is registered for enforcement in accordance with the Child Support Act 1991.

signed (*signature of sheriff clerk*).".

Service of charge following the making of a liability order

4.—(1) Where a liability order has been made, a charge for payment under section 38 of the Act of 1991 shall be in Form 5.

(2) The period for payment specified in any charge under this rule shall be—

(*a*) 14 days where the person on whom it is served is within the United Kingdom; and

(*b*) 28 days where the person on whom it is served is outwith the United Kingdom or his whereabouts are unknown.

Appeal against a deduction from earnings order

5.—(1) An appeal against a deduction from earnings order as provided for in regulations made under section 32(5) of the Act of 1991 shall be by summary application in Form 6, and rule 3 and Form A of the Ordinary Cause Rules of the sheriff court shall not apply to such an appeal.

(2) The sheriff clerk, on receiving an application under paragraph (1) above, shall—

(*a*) fix a date for the hearing of the appeal; and

(*b*) order service of the application on the Secretary of State.

Representation

6.—(1) A party to an application for a liability order or to an appeal against a deduction from earnings order may be represented by—

(*a*) an advocate;

(*b*) a solicitor; or

(*c*) subject to the following paragraphs of this rule, any other person (hereinafter referred to as an "authorised lay representative"), where the sheriff is satisfied that such person is a suitable representative and is duly authorised to represent the party.

(2) An authorised lay representative shall not represent a party at any diet appointed for the leading of evidence or for debate but may do all other things in the preparation and conduct of a claim as may be done by an individual who conducts his own claim.

(3) A party who is, or has been, represented by an authorised lay representative, and who would have been found entitled to expenses and outlays if he had been represented by an advocate or a solicitor, may be allowed the expenses and outlays to which a party litigant may be found entitled by virtue of the Litigants in Person (Costs and Expenses) Act 1975 or any enactment made under that Act.

Amendment

7.—(1) The forms in the Schedule to the Act of Sederunt (Proceedings in the Sheriff Court under the Debtors (Scotland) Act 1987) 1988 shall be amended in accordance with the following paragraphs.

(2) In Form 37 omit the words "to three instalments" and substitute "one instalment".

(3) In—

(*a*) paragraph (2) of the Notes in Form 30;

(*b*) paragraph (1) of the Notes for Employer in Form 34; and

(*c*) paragraph (1) of the Notes in Form 45,

after the words "section 73 of the Act" insert the words "as amended by the Child Support Act 1991".

SCHEDULE

Rule 2(1)

FORM 1

Form of summary application for a liability order under section 33 of the Child Support Act 1991

SUMMARY APPLICATION
for a liability order under section 33
of the Child Support Act 1991

by

SECRETARY OF STATE
(*insert address*)

Applicant

against

[A.B.]
(*insert full name and address of liable person*)

Respondent

1. The applicant is the Secretary of State.

2. The respondent is a "liable person" within the meaning of the Act.

The court has jurisdiction to deal with this application by virtue of (*state ground of jurisdiction*).

3. In terms of an assessment made by the Child Support Officer (*insert address*) on (*insert date of assessment*), the respondent is obliged to pay to the Secretary of State the sum of £ per

4. The respondent has failed to make payment(s) under the assessment and the applicant served notice(s) of arrears on the respondent on (*insert date(s)*). At the date of this application there remains a total of £ of maintenance unpaid. *Additionally, there remains due by the respondent interest at the rate of % per annum for the period from (*insert date*) to (*insert date*), as detailed in the notice of arrears lodged with this application, amounting in total to £

5. It appears to the applicant that—

*(*a*) it is inappropriate to make a deduction from earnings order against the respondent because (*state reason*),

or

*(*b*) a deduction from earnings order was made against the respondent on (*insert date*) but has proved ineffective as a means of securing payment because (*state reason*).

6. The applicant craves the court to make a liability order against the respondent in the sum of £ , *(including interest of £). In addition the applicant asks the court to award expenses to him.

Date (*insert date*) signed (*signature of applicant*)

*(*delete as appropriate*)

Rule 2(2)

FORM 2

Form of notice to liable person in an application for a liability order under the Child Support Act 1991

PART A
(to be completed by applicant before service)

Sheriff Court: Court Ref. No.:

1. (*Insert place and date*)
To: (*insert name and address of liable person*).
The application which accompanies this notice is served on you on (*insert date of service*).

signed (*signature and designation of solicitor/officer of court*)

2. If you wish to object to the grant of the application you must complete PART B below stating the grounds(s) upon which you object. Please note that in terms of section 33 of the Child Support Act 1991 the sheriff may not question the maintenance assessment and he must make the liability order if he is satisfied that the payments in question have become payable but have not been paid.

3. If you decide to object to the application you must return this form to the court with PART B completed within 21 days of the date of service of this notice, together with the court fee of £

The address of the court is (*insert name and address of court*).

4. You will be advised by the sheriff clerk of the date which has been fixed for the hearing of the application. On that date you should attend or be represented at court.

5. If you fail either to return this form to the court as directed or, having returned it, fail to attend or be represented at the hearing, the application may be granted in your absence.

IF YOU REQUIRE ANY FURTHER ADVICE, CONTACT ANY SOLICITOR, CITIZENS ADVICE BUREAU OR OTHER ADVICE CENTRE.

PART B
(to be completed by
liable person)

I object to the grant of the application on the following grounds (*state grounds of objection, and provide relevant supporting information, e.g. if you claim that payments are not due, provide details of payments made*).

Date (*insert date*) signed (*signature of liable person*)

If space is insufficient continue on a separate paper
and attach to this form.

Rule 2(7)

FORM 3

Form of liability order under the Child Support Act 1991

(*insert place and date*)

The sheriff makes a liability order against the liable person named in the application for payment of the undernoted sum of the Secretray of State.

Amount of maintenance unpaid	£
Amount of interest on maintenance unpaid	£
Expenses	£
Aggregate amount of liability order	£

Signed (*signature of sheriff*)
Sheriff.

Rule 2(9)

FORM 4

Form of extract of liability order under the Child Support Act 1991

Sheriff Court: Court Ref. No.:

Date of order

Full name and address of liable person

The sheriff has made a liability order against the above named liable person for payment of the undernoted sum to the Secretary of State.

Amount of maintenance unpaid	£
Amount of interest on maintenance unpaid	£
Expenses	£
Aggregate amount of liability order	£

This liability order is authority for enforcement of the amount due by the means specified by the Child Support Act 1991.

Date of extract:

signed (*signature of sheriff clerk*)

Rule 4(1) FORM 5

Form of charge for payment following the making of a liability order under the Child Support Act 1991

CHARGE FOR PAYMENT ON A LIABILITY ORDER UNDER SECTION 33 OF THE CHILD SUPPORT ACT 1991

in causa

SECRETARY OF STATE
(*insert address*)
against

[A.B.]
(*insert full name and address of liable person*)
LIABLE PERSON

To: (*insert full name and address of liable person*)

On (*insert date*) a liability order against you was made in the sheriff court at (*insert place*) for payment of a sum of money in terms of a maintenance assessment made by the Child Support Agency on (*insert date of assessment*).

I, (*insert name and address*), sheriff officer, by virtue of an extract order of court in Her Majesty's name and authority and in the name and authority of the sheriff, charge you to pay the total sum due as set out below *(together with any further interest due) within *(14/28) days from the date of this charge. Payment should be made to (*insert details as to whom payment is to be made*).

If you do not pay this sum within *(14/28) days you are liable to have further action taken against you, including the poinding and sale of articles belonging to you.

This charge is served on you today by (*state method of service*) and is witnessed by (*insert name and address of witness*).

Date (*insert date*)

Signed (*signature of witness*) signed (*signature of sheriff officer*)

**delete as appropriate*

The sum now due by you is:—	
Unpaid maintenance	£
Interest on unpaid maintenance	£
Expenses	£
Aggregate amount of liability order	£
Less paid to account	£
Net aggregate amount outstanding	£

Agents fee	£
Expenses of sheriff officer	£
Charge fee	£
Travelling	£
Witness fee	£
Other outlays in connection with service of charge (*specify*)	£
TOTAL SUM DUE	$

IF YOU ARE UNSURE AS TO WHAT YOU SHOULD DO ON RECEIPT OF THIS CHARGE YOU SHOULD CONSULT A SOLICITOR, CITIZENS ADVICE BUREAU OR OTHER ADVICE CENTRE IMMEDIATELY. A LEAFLET EXPLAINING DEBT COLLECTION PROCEDURES IS AVAILABLE FROM ALL ADVICE AGENCIES AND SHERIFF COURTS.

Rule 5(1) FORM 6

Form of application for appeal against a deduction from earnings order

APPEAL AGAINST A DEDUCTION FROM EARNINGS ORDER

by

[A.B.]

(*insert full name and address of appellant*)

Appellant

against

SECRETARY OF STATE FOR SOCIAL SECURITY

(*insert address*)

Respondent

1. The appellant is (*insert full name and address of appellant*).

2. The respondent is the Secretary of State for Social Security.

3. The appellant is a liable person within the meaning of section 31 of the Child Support Act 1991.

4. On (*insert date*) a deduction from earnings order was made against the appellant by the Secretary of State for Social Security. The making of the deduction from earnings order was intimated to the appellant on (*insert date*).

5. *(*a*) The appellant states that the deduction from earnings order is defective on the ground(s) that (*state reason*),
or
*(*b*) The appellant disputes that the following payments, which were taken into account by the Secretary of State for Social Security in making the deduction from earnings order, are earnings on the ground(s) that (*give details of payments and nature of dispute*)
and accordingly appeals to the sheriff.

6. The appellant asks the court to award expenses to him.

Date (*insert date*) signed (*signature of appellant*)

*(*delete as appropriate*)

Parental Orders (Human Fertilisation and Embryology) (Scotland) Regulations 1994

(S.I. 1994 No. 2804)

[31st October 1994]

The Secretary of State in exercise of the powers conferred upon him by sections 30(9) and 45 of the Human Fertilisation and Embryology Act 1990 (c.

37) and of all other powers enabling him in that behalf hereby makes the following Regulations a draft of which has been laid before and approved by resolution of each House of Parliament:

Citation, commencement and interpretation

1.—(1) These Regulations may be cited as the Parental Orders (Human Fertilisation and Embryology) (Scotland) Regulations 1994 and shall come into force on 1st November 1994.

(2) In these Regulations unless the context otherwise requires—

"the 1990 Act" means the Human Fertilisation and Embryology Act 1990;

"the 1978 Act" means the Adoption (Scotland) Act 1978;

"husband" and "wife" have the same meaning respectively as in section 30 of the 1990 Act;

"parental order" means an order under section 30 of the 1990 Act.

Application of the Adoption (Scotland) Act 1978

2. The provisions of the 1978 Act set out in Schedule 1 to these Regulations shall have effect, with such modifications (if any) as are specified in that Schedule, in relation to parental orders and to applications for such orders.

References in other enactments

3. The references to expressions in connection with adoption, in the enactments mentioned in Schedule 2 to these Regulations are to be read, in relation to parental orders and to applications for such orders, in accordance with that Schedule.

Regulation 2

SCHEDULE 1

APPLICATION OF THE ADOPTION (SCOTLAND) ACT 1978 IN RELATION TO PARENTAL ORDERS AND APPLICATIONS FOR SUCH ORDERS

General

1.—(1) The following paragraphs set out the provisions of the 1978 Act which have effect, with such modifications (if any) as are specified in those paragraphs, in relation to parental orders and applications for such orders.

(2) Of the modifications referred to in sub-paragraph (1) above, those in paragraphs 2, 3, 5 to 15, 17(2) and 18 are specified by being incorporated in the text of the respective provisions of the 1978 Act set out in those paragraphs.

(3) Any reference in this Schedule to a numbered section or Schedule is, unless otherwise expressly provided, a reference to the section or Schedule bearing that number in the 1978 Act.

Section 6

2. Section 6 shall have effect as follows:—

"**Duty to promote welfare of child**

6. In reaching any decision relating to an application for a parental order, a court shall have regard to all the circumstances, first consideration being given to the need to safeguard and promote the welfare of the child throughout his childhood; and shall so far as practicable ascertain the wishes and feelings of the child regarding the decision and give due consideration to them, having regard to his age and understanding.".

Section 12

3. Section 12 shall have effect as follows:—

"**Parental orders**

12.—(1) Without prejudice to section 30(1) of the 1990 Act (which empowers the court to make an order providing for a child to be treated in law as the child of the parties to a marriage), a parental order vests the parental rights and duties relating to the child in the parties to the marriage, namely the husband and the wife.

(2) The parental order does not affect the parental rights and duties so far as they relate to any period before the making of the order.

(3) The making of a parental order operates to extinguish—

(*a*) any parental right or duty relating to the child which, immediately before the making of the order, was vested in a person (not being either the husband or the wife) who was—

(i) the mother or father of the child by virtue of section 27 or 28 of the 1990 Act, or otherwise; or

(ii) a guardian of the child appointed by a deed or by the order of a court;

(*b*) any duty owed to or by the child—

(i) to pay or provide aliment in respect of any period occurring after the making of the order;

(ii) to make payment arising out of parental rights and duties in respect of such a period.

(4) Nothing in subsection (3) shall—

(*a*) extinguish any duty arising under a deed or agreement which constitutes a trust or which expressly provides that the duty is not to be extinguished by the making of a parental order;

(*b*) of itself terminate the appointment or functions of any judicial factor loco tutoris or curator bonis appointed to administer the whole or any part of the child's estate.

(5) A parental order may contain such terms and conditions as the court thinks fit.".

Section 24

4. Section 24(1) shall have effect with the following substitutions:—

(*a*) for the words "an adoption order", there shall be substituted the words "a parental order"; and

(*b*) for the words "a British adoption order" there shall be substituted the words "such an order".

Section 26

5. Section 26 shall have effect as follows:—

"**Care of child on refusal of parental order**

26.—(1) Where on an application for a parental order the court refuses to make an order then—

(*a*) if it appears to the court that there are exceptional circumstances making it desirable that the child should be under the supervision of an independent person, the court may order that the child shall be under the supervision of a specified local authority;

(*b*) if it appears to the court that there are exceptional circumstances making it impracticable or undesirable for the child to be entrusted either to the person who is the mother or the father of the child by virtue of section 27 or 28 of the 1990 Act, or otherwise, or to any other individual, the court may by order commit the child to the care of a specified local authority.

(2) Where the court makes an order under subsection (1)(*b*) the order may require the person who is either the mother or the father of the child by virtue of section 27 or 28 of the 1990 Act, or otherwise, to pay to the local authority, while it has the care of the child, such weekly or other periodical sum towards the aliment of the child as the court thinks reasonable.

(3) Subsections (2), (4) and (5) of section 11 of the Guardianship Act 1973 (jurisdiction and orders relating to care and custody of children) apply in relation to an order under this section as they apply in relation to an order under that section.".

Section 27

6. Section 27(1) shall have effect as follows:—

"**Restrictions on removal where application pending**

27.—(1) Where an application for a parental order is pending, the person who is either the mother or the father of the child by virtue of section 27 or 28 of the 1990 Act, or otherwise, or any guardian of the child, is not entitled, against the will of the person with whom the child has his home, to remove the child from the care and possession of that person except with the leave of the court.".

Section 29

7. Section 29 shall have effect as follows:—

"**Return of child taken away in breach of section 27**

29.—(1) An authorised court may on the application of a person from whose care and possession a child has been removed in breach of any of the provisions specified in subsection (3) of this section order the person who has so removed the child to return the child to the applicant.

(2) An authorised court may, on the application of a person who has reasonable grounds for believing that another person is intending to remove the child from the care and possession of the applicant in breach of any of the provisions specified in subsection (3) of this section by order direct that other person not to remove the child from the care and possession of that applicant in breach of those provisions.

(3) The provisions specified in this subsection are—

(*a*) section 27;

(*b*) section 27 of the Adoption Act 1976 as modified by the Parental Orders (Human Fertilisation and Embryology) Regulations 1994; and

(*c*) Article 28 of the Adoption (Northern Ireland) Order 1987, as modified by the Parental Orders (Human Fertilisation and Embryology) Regulations 1994.".

Section 39

8. Section 39 shall have effect as follows:—

"**Status conferred by parental order**

39.—(1) Without prejudice to section 30(1) of the 1990 Act (which empowers the court to make an order providing for a child to be treated in law as the child of the parties to a marriage), the child who is the subject of the parental order shall be treated in law—

(*a*) as if he had been born as the child of the parties to that marriage; and

(*b*) as if he were not the child of any person other than the parties to that marriage, namely the husband and wife.

(2) This section has effect from the date on which the court makes the parental order.

(3) Subject to the provisions of this Part, this section applies for the construction of enactments or instruments passed or made before or after the date of coming into force of the 1994 Regulations unless the context otherwise requires.".

Section 41

9. Section 41(1) and (2) shall have effect with the substitution for subsection (1) of the following:—

"**Miscellaneous**

(1) Notwithstanding the effect of the making of a parental order but without prejudice to section 39(1)(*a*), the child who is the subject of that parental order shall be treated for the purposes of determining the forbidden degrees of consanguinity and affinity in respect of the law relating to marriage and in respect of the crime of incest, as if—

(*a*) he were the child of the parties to the marriage who applied for the parental order; and

(*b*) he were also the child of any other person who, prior to the making of the parental order, was the mother or father by virtue of section 27 or 28 of the 1990 Act, or otherwise.".

Section 45

10. Section 45 shall have effect as follows:—

"**Parental Order Register**

45.—(1) The Registrar General for Scotland shall maintain at the General Register Office a register, to be called the Parental Order Register, in which shall be made such entries as may be directed to be made therein by parental orders, but no other entries.

(2) An extract of any entry in the Parental Order Register maintained under this section, if purporting to be sealed or stamped with the seal of the General Register Office, shall, without any further or other proof of that entry, be received as evidence of the parental order to which it relates and, where the entry contains a record of the date of the birth or the country of the birth of the person who is the subject of the said parental order, shall also be received as aforesaid as evidence of that date or country.

(3) The Registrar General for Scotland shall cause an index of the Parental Order Register maintained under this section to be made and kept in the General Register Office; and the Registrar General for Scotland shall—

(*a*) cause a search to be made of that index on behalf of any person or permit that person to search the index himself, and

(*b*) issue to any person an extract of any entry in that register which that person may require,

in all respects upon and subject to the same terms, conditions and regulations as to payment of fees and otherwise as are applicable under the Registration of Births, Deaths and Marriages (Scotland) Act 1965 in respect of searches in other indexes kept in the General Register Office and in respect of the supply from that office of extracts of entries in the registers of births, deaths and marriages.

(4) The Registrar General for Scotland shall, in addition to the Parental Order Register and the index thereto, keep such other registers and books, and make such entries therein, as may be necessary to record and make traceable the connection between any entry in the register of births which has been marked "Parental Order" pursuant to paragraph 1 of Schedule 1 or any enactment at the time in force and any corresponding entry in the Parental Order Register maintained under this section.

(5) The registers and books kept under subsection (4) shall not be, nor shall any index thereof be, open to public inspection or search, nor, except under an order of the Court of Session or a sheriff, shall the Registrar General for Scotland furnish any information contained in or any copy or extract from any such registers or books to any person other than a person who is the subject of a parental order and who has attained the age of 17 years and to whom that information, copy or extract relates or a local authority or Board falling within subsection (6) or adoption society falling within paragraph (*b*) of subsection (6B), which is providing counselling for that person.

(6) Where the Registrar General for Scotland furnishes a person, who is the subject of a parental order, with information under subsection (5), he shall advise that person that counselling services are available—

(*a*) if the person is in Scotland—

(i) from the local authority in whose area he is living;

(ii) where the parental order relating to him was made in Scotland, from the local authority in whose area the court which made the order sat; or

(iii) from any other local authority in Scotland;

(*b*) if the person is in England and Wales—

(i) from the local authority in whose area he is living;

(ii) where the parental order relating to him was made in England and Wales, from the local authority in whose area the court which made the order sat; or

(iii) from any other local authority in England and Wales;

(*c*) if the person is in Northern Ireland—

(i) from the Board in whose area he is living;

(ii) where the parental order relating to him was made in Northern Ireland, from the Board in whose area the court which made the order sat; or

(iii) from any other Board.

(6A) Where a person, who is the subject of a parental order and who is in Scotland, is furnished with information under subsection (5), any body mentioned in subsection (6B) to which that person applies for counselling shall have a duty to provide counselling for him.

(6B) The bodies referred to in subsection (6A) are—

(*a*) any local authority falling within subsection (6)(*a*); and

(*b*) any adoption society approved under section 3 of the Adoption (Scotland) Act 1978 so far as it is acting in Scotland for the purposes of providing counselling in relation to parental orders.

(7) Where a person who is the subject of a parental order has arranged to receive counselling from a local authority or Board falling within subsection (6) or an adoption society falling within paragraph (*b*) of subsection (6B), the Registrar General for Scotland shall, on receipt of a request from the local authority, Board or adoption society, and on payment of the appropriate fee, send to the local authority, Board or adoption society, an extract of the entry relating to that person in the register of births.

(8) The provisions of the Registration of Births, Deaths and Marriages (Scotland) Act 1965 with regard to the correction of errors in entries shall apply to the Parental Order Register maintained by the Registrar General for Scotland and to registration therein in like manner as they apply to any register of births and to registration therein.

(9) Schedule 1 to this Act which, among other things, provides for the registration of parental orders and the amendment of such orders, shall have effect.

(10) In this section—

"'Board" means a Health and Social Services Board established under Article 16 of the Health and Personal Social Services (Northern Ireland) Order 1972 and "local authority", in relation to England and Wales, means the council of a county (other than a metropolitan county), a metropolitan district, a London borough or the Common Council of the City of London.".

Section 55

11. Section 55 shall have effect as follows:—

"**Evidence of agreement or consent**

55.—(1) Any agreement or consent which is required by section 30 of the 1990 Act to be given to the making of a parental order or application for an order may be given in writing and, if the document signifying the agreement or consent is witnessed in accordance with rules, it shall be sufficient evidence without further proof of the signature of the person by whom it was executed.

(2) A document signifying such agreement or consent which purports to be witnessed in accordance with rules, shall be presumed to be so witnessed, and to have been executed and witnessed on the date and at the place specified in the document, unless the contrary is proved.".

Section 56

12. Section 56 shall have effect as follows:—

"**Courts**

56.—(1) In this Act, 'authorised court', as respects an application for a parental order has the same meaning as 'the court' has, in relation to Scotland, for the purposes of section 30 of the 1990 Act, namely—

(*a*) the Court of Session;

(*b*) the sheriff court of the sheriffdom within which the child is.

(2) Subsection (1) does not apply in the case of an application under section 29 but for the purposes of such an application the following are authorised courts:—

(*a*) if there is pending in respect of the child an application for a parental order, the court in which that application is pending;

(*b*) in any other case—

(i) the Court of Session;

(ii) the sheriff court of the sheriffdom within which the applicant resides.".

Section 57

13. Section 57 shall have effect as follows:—

"**Proceedings to be in private**

57. All proceedings before the court in relation to a parental order or under section 29 shall be heard and determined in private unless the court otherwise directs.".

Section 58

14. Section 58 shall have effect as follows:—

"**Curator ad litem and reporting officers**

58.—(1) For the purpose of any application for a parental order, rules shall provide for the appointment, in such cases as are prescribed—

(*a*) of a person to act as curator *ad litem* of the child upon the hearing of the application, with the duty of safeguarding the interests of the child in the prescribed manner; and

(*b*) of a person to act as reporting officer for the purpose of witnessing agreements to the parental order and performing such other duties as the rules may prescribe.

(2) A person appointed as reporting officer may be the same person as is appointed as curator *ad litem* but shall not be any person or employee of any person holding a licence granted under section 11 of the 1990 Act.

(3) Rules may provide for the reporting officer to be appointed before the application is made.".

Section 59

15. Section 59 shall have effect as follows:—

"**Rules of procedure**

59. Provision shall be made by act of sederunt with regard to any matter to be prescribed under this Act and generally with regard to all matters of procedure and incidental matters arising out of an application under section 30 of the 1990 Act and out of this Act and for carrying this Act into effect.".

Section 60 **Sched. 1**

16.—(1) Section 60, except subsection (3), shall have effect with the following modifications.

(2) For subsection (1), there shall be substituted—

"(1) Any power to make regulations conferred by this Act on the Registrar General for Scotland shall be exercisable by statutory instrument.".

(3) In subsection (2) the words "except section 3(1)" shall be omitted.

Section 65

17.—(1) Section 65, except subsections (2) and (3), shall have effect with the following modifications.

(2) For subsection (1), there shall be substituted—

"(1) In this Act, unless the context otherwise requires—

'the 1990 Act' means the Human Fertilisation and Embryology Act 1990;

'the 1994 Regulations' means the Parental Orders (Human Fertilisation and Embryology) (Scotland) Regulations 1994;

'authorised court' shall be construed in accordance with section 56;

'body of persons' means any body of persons, whether incorporated or unincorporated;

'guardian' means a person appointed by deed or will or by a court of competent jurisdiction to be the guardian of the child;

'husband' and 'wife' have the same meaning respectively as in section 30 of the 1990 Act;

'local authority' means a regional or islands council;

'parental order' means an order under section 30 of the 1990 Act;

'prescribed' means prescribed by act of sederunt;

'Registrar General for Scotland' means the Registrar General of Births, Deaths and Marriages for Scotland;

'rules' means rules made by act of sederunt;

and any reference to this Act or to any provision of this Act shall be construed as a reference to this Act or to that provision as it has effect, with such modifications (if any) as are specified in Schedule 1 to the 1994 Regulations, in relation to parental orders and applications for such orders.".

Schedule 1

18. Schedule 1 shall have effect as follows:—

Section 45 "SCHEDULE 1

REGISTRATION

Registration of orders

1.—[1] (1) Every parental order shall contain a direction to the Registrar General for Scotland to make in the Parental Order Register maintained by him an entry recording the order in such form as the Registrar General for Scotland may by regulations specify.

(2) For the purposes of compliance with the requirements of sub-paragraph (1)—

(*a*) where the precise date of the child's birth is not proved to the satisfaction of the court, the court shall determine the probable date of his birth and the date so determined shall be specified in the order as the date of his birth;

(*b*) where the country of birth of the child is not proved to the satisfaction of the court, then, if it appears probable that the child was born within the United Kingdom, the Channel Islands or the Isle of Man, he shall be treated as having been born in Scotland, and in any other case the particulars of the country of birth may be omitted from the order and from the entry in the Parental Order Register;

and the names to be specified in the order as the name and surname of the child shall be the name or names and surname stated in that behalf in the application for the order, or, if no name or surname is so stated, the original name or names of the child and the surname of the husband and wife who applied for the order.

(3) There shall be produced with every application for a parental order in respect of a child whose birth has been registered under the Registration of Births, Deaths and Marriages (Scotland) Act 1965 or under any enactment repealed by that Act an extract of the entry of the birth.

(4) Where on an application to a court for a parental order there is proved to the satisfaction of the court the identity of the child with a child to whom an entry in the register of births relates, any order made in pursuance of the application shall contain a direc-

Sched. 1

tion to the Registrar General for Scotland to cause the entry in that register to be marked with the words 'Parental Order'.

(5) Where a parental order is made, the clerk of the court which made the order shall cause the order to be communicated to the Registrar General for Scotland and upon receipt of the communication the Registrar General for Scotland shall cause compliance to be made with the directions contained in the order.

NOTE

[1] See S.I. 1994 No. 3147.

Registration of orders made in England, Northern Ireland, the Isle of Man and the Channel Islands

2.—(1) Where the Registrar General for Scotland is notified by the Registrar General that a parental order has been made by a court in England in respect of a child to whom an entry in the register of births or the Parental Order Register relates, the Registrar General for Scotland shall cause the entry to be marked 'Parental Order (England)', or as the case may be, 'Parental Order (Wales)'.

(2) Where the Registrar General for Scotland is notified by the authority maintaining a register of parental orders in Northern Ireland, the Isle of Man or any of the Channel Islands that an order has been made in that country authorising the parental order in respect of a child to whom an entry in the register of births or the Parental Order Register relates, he shall cause the entry to be marked 'Parental Order', followed by the name in brackets of the country in which the order was made.

(3) Where, after an entry has been marked under the foregoing provisions of this paragraph, the Registrar General for Scotland is notified as aforesaid that the order has been quashed, that an appeal against the order has been allowed or that the order has been revoked, he shall cause the marking to be cancelled; and an extract of an entry in any register being an entry the marking of which is cancelled under this sub-paragraph, shall be deemed to be accurate if and only if both the marking and the cancellation are omitted therefrom.

Amendment of orders and rectification of registers

3.—(1) The court by which a parental order has been made may, on the application of the husband and wife who applied for that order or the person who is the subject of that order, amend the order by the correction of any error in the particulars contained therein, and may—

(*a*) if satisfied on such an application that within one year beginning with the date of the order any new name has been given to that person (whether in baptism or otherwise), or taken by him, either in lieu of or in addition to a name specified in the particulars required to be entered in the Parental Order Register in pursuance of the order, amend the order by substituting or adding that name in those particulars, as the case may require;

(*b*) if satisfied on the application of any person concerned that a direction for the marking of an entry in the register of births or the Parental Order Register included in the order in pursuance of sub-paragraph (4) of paragraph 1 above was wrongly so included, revoke that direction.

(2) Where a parental order is amended or a direction revoked under sub-paragraph (1) above, the clerk of the court shall cause the amendment to be communicated in the prescribed manner to the Registrar General for Scotland who shall as the case may require—

(*a*) cause the entry in the Parental Order Register to be amended accordingly; or

(*b*) cause the marking of the entry in the register of births or the Parental Order Register to be cancelled.

(3) Where a parental order is quashed or an appeal against such an order allowed by any court, the court shall give directions to the Registrar General for Scotland to cancel any entry in the Parental Order Register, and any marking of an entry in that Register, or the register of births as the case may be, which was effected in pursuance of the order.

Marking of entries on re-registration of birth

4. Without prejudice to any other provision of this Act where, after an entry in the register of births has been marked in accordance with paragraph 2 or 3 above, the birth is re-registered under section 20(1) of the Registration of Births, Deaths and Marriages (Scotland) Act 1965 (re-registration of birth in certain cases), the entry made on re-registration shall be marked in like manner.

5. In this Schedule 'Registrar General' means the Registrar General for England and Wales.".

Regulation 3

SCHEDULE 2

REFERENCES IN CONNECTION WITH ADOPTION IN ENACTMENTS

Succession (Scotland) Act 1964

1. In section 37(1) of the Succession (Scotland) Act 1964, the reference to "the Adoption (Scotland) Act 1978" shall be read, in relation to parental orders and to applications for such orders, as a reference to—

(*a*) the Adoption (Scotland) Act 1978, as modified by the Parental Orders (Human Fertilisation and Embryology) (Scotland) Regulations 1994; and

(*b*) section 30 of the Human Fertilisation and Embryology Act 1990.

Registration of Births, Deaths and Marriages (Scotland) Act 1965 (c. 49)

2.—(1) In section 40(2) of the Registration of Births, Deaths and Marriages (Scotland) Act 1965 the reference to—

(*a*) "the Adopted Children Register maintained under section 22(1) of the Adoption Act 1958" shall be read, in relation to parental orders and to applications for such orders, as a reference to the Parental Order Register maintained under section 45(1) of the Adoption (Scotland) Act 1978 as modified by the Parental Orders (Human Fertilisation and Embryology) (Scotland) Regulations 1994;

(*b*) "adoption" shall be read, in relation to parental orders and to applications for such orders, as the effect of a parental order made under section 30 of the Human Fertilisation and Embryology Act 1990.

(2) In section 43(1) of that Act, the reference to "the Adopted Children Register maintained by the Registrar General under section 22 of that Act", shall be read, in relation to parental orders and to applications for such orders, as a reference to the Parental Order Register maintained by the Registrar General under section 45(1) of the Adoption (Scotland) Act 1978 as modified by the Parental Orders (Human Fertilisation and Embryology) (Scotland) Regulations 1994.

Foster Children (Scotland) Act 1984

3. In section 2(5)(*a*) of the Foster Children (Scotland) Act 1984 the reference to adopting a child "under arrangements made by an adoption agency within the meaning of section 1 of the Adoption Act 1976 or section 1 of the Adoption (Scotland) Act 1978" shall be read, in relation to parental orders and to applications for such orders, as a reference to making an application for a parental order in respect of a child under section 30 of the Human Fertilisation and Embryology Act 1990.

Child Abduction and Custody Act 1985

4. In paragraph 5(ii) of Schedule 3 to the Children Abduction and Custody Act 1985, the reference to "an adoption order under section 12(1) of the Adoption (Scotland) Act 1978" shall be read, in relation to parental orders, as a reference to a parental order under section 30 of the Human Fertilisation and Embryology Act 1990.

Family Law Act 1986

5. In section 1(1)(*b*)(ii) of the Family Law Act 1986, the reference to "an adoption order as defined in section 12(1) of the Adoption (Scotland) Act 1978" shall be read, in relation to parental orders, as a reference to a parental order under section 30 of the Human Fertilisation and Embryology Act 1990.

Human Fertilisation and Embryology Act 1990

6. In relation to Scotland in section 27(2) and section 28(5)(*c*) of the Human Fertilisation and Embryology Act 1990 the reference to the child being "treated by virtue of adoption as not being the child of any person other than the adopter or adopters" shall be read, in relation to parental orders, as a reference to the child being treated by virtue of a parental order as not being the child of any person other than the husband and wife within the meaning of section 30 of that Act.

Act of Sederunt (Sheriff Court Parental Orders (Human Fertilisation and Embryology) Rules) 1994

(S.I. 1994 No. 2805)

[21st October 1994]

The Lords of Council and Session, under and by virtue of the powers conferred on them by section 32 of the Sheriff Courts (Scotland) Act 1971 (c. 58), section 59 of the Adoption (Scotland) Act 1978 (c. 28) as modified and applied in relation to parental orders under section 30 of the Human Fertilisation and Embryology Act 1990 (c. 37) and applications for such orders by paragraph 15 of Schedule 1 to the Parental Orders (Human Fertilisation and Embryology) (Scotland) Regulations 1994 (S.I. 1994 No. 2804), and of all other powers enabling them in that behalf, having approved, with modifications, draft rules submitted to them by the Sheriff Court Rules Council in accordance with section 34 of the said Act of 1971, do hereby enact and declare:

Citation and commencement

1.—(1) This Act of Sederunt may be cited as the Act of Sederunt (Sheriff Court Parental Orders (Human Fertilisation and Embryology) Rules) 1994 and shall come into force on the date of coming into force of the Parental Orders (Human Fertilisation and Embryology) (Scotland) Regulations 1994.

(2) This Act of Sederunt shall be inserted in the Books of Sederunt.

Sheriff court parental orders rules

2. The provisions of the Schedule to this Act of Sederunt shall have effect for the purpose of providing rules in relation to parental orders under section 30 of the Human Fertilisation and Embryology Act 1990 and applications for such orders.

Paragraph 2

SCHEDULE

SHERIFF COURT PARENTAL ORDERS (HUMAN FERTILISATION AND EMBRYOLOGY) RULES

Arrangement of Rules

Citation and application

1.—(1) These Rules may be cited as the Sheriff Court Parental Orders (Human Fertilisation and Embryology) Rules 1994.

(2) These Rules apply in relation to parental orders under section 30 of the Human Fertilisation and Embryology Act 1990 and applications for such orders.

Interpretation

2.—(1) In these Rules, unless the context otherwise requires—

"the Act of 1978" means the Adoption (Scotland) Act 1978;

"the Act of 1990" means the Human Fertilisation and Embryology Act 1990;

"Her Majesty's Forces" means the Royal Navy, the regular armed forces as defined in section 225 of the Army Act 1955, the regular air force as defined in section 223 of the Air Force Act 1955 and the Queen Alexandra's Royal Naval Nursing Services;

"the Regulations" means the Parental Orders (Human Fertilisation and Embryology) (Scotland) Regulations 1994.

(2) Unless the context otherwise requires, a reference to a specified rule or form is a reference to the rule or form in the Appendix so specified in these Rules; and a reference to a specified paragraph, sub-paragraph or head is a reference to that paragraph of the rule or form, that sub-paragraph of that paragraph or that head of that sub-paragraph, in which the reference occurs.

(3) Where there is a reference in these Rules to the use of a form, that form in the Appendix to these Rules, or a form substantially to the same effect, shall be used with such variation as circumstances may require.

Applications for parental order

3.—(1) An application for a parental order shall be made by petition in Form 1.

(2) On presentation of the petition, there shall be lodged in process as productions—

(*a*) an extract of any entry in the register of births relating to the birth of the child;

(*b*) extracts of any entries in the register of births relating to the birth of each of the petitioners;

(*c*) an extract of any entry in the register of marriages relating to the marriage of the petitioners; and

(*d*) any other document founded on by the petitioners in support of the terms of the petition.

Confidentiality of documents in process

4. Unless the sheriff otherwise directs—

(*a*) any document lodged in process, including a report by a reporting officer or a curator *ad litem*, shall be treated as confidential and open only to the sheriff, the parties, the reporting officer and the curator *ad litem*; and

(*b*) a reporting officer or curator *ad litem* shall treat any information obtained by him in relation to the cause as confidential, and shall not disclose any such information to any person unless it is necessary for the proper execution of his duties.

Agreements to parental order

5.—(1) An agreement for the purposes of section 30(5) of the Act of 1990 (agreement to parental order by a father who is not the husband of the female petitioner or by the woman who carried the child) shall, if given in writing, be in Form 2.

(2) An agreement referred to in this rule which is executed furth of Scotland shall be witnessed—

(*a*) where it is executed in England, Wales or Northern Ireland, by a justice of the peace or commissioner for oaths; or

(*b*) where it is executed furth of the United Kingdom—

(i) in the case of a person who is serving in Her Majesty's Forces, by an officer holding a commission in those forces; or

(ii) by a British consular official or any person authorised, by the law of the country where the agreement is executed, to administer an oath for any legal purpose.

Orders for evidence

6.—(1) The sheriff may, before determining the cause, order—

(*a*) production of further documents (including affidavits); or

(*b*) parole evidence.

(2) A party may apply by motion for the evidence of a person to be received in evidence by affidavit; and the sheriff may make such order as he thinks fit.

Expenses

7. The sheriff may make such order as to expenses, including the expenses of a reporting officer, a curator *ad litem*, or any other person who attended a hearing, as he thinks fit.

Protection of identity of petitioners

8.—(1) Where a married couple, who seek to apply for a parental order, wish to prevent their identity being disclosed to any person whose agreement is required under section 30(5) of the Act of 1990 (agreement to parental order by a father who is not the husband of the female petitioner or by the woman who carried the child), they may, before presenting a petition, apply to the sheriff clerk for a serial number to be assigned to them.

(2) On receipt of an application for a serial number, the sheriff clerk shall assign a serial number to the applicants and shall enter a note of it opposite the names of the applicants in a register of serial numbers.

(3) Where a serial number has been assigned under paragraph (2)—

(*a*) the record of the serial number and the persons to whom it applies shall be treated as confidential and disclosed only to the sheriff;

(*b*) any agreement under section 30(5) of the Act of 1990 shall not name or design the petitioners but shall refer to them by means of the serial number; and

(*c*) it shall be used to name or design the petitioners for all purposes connected with the petition.

Appointment of reporting officer and curator ad litem

9.—(1) On the presentation of the petition, the sheriff shall appoint—

(*a*) a reporting officer; and

(*b*) a curator *ad litem*.

(2) The sheriff shall, where it is practicable to do so, appoint the same person to be the curator *ad litem* and the reporting officer.

(3) Where the curator *ad litem* is not also the reporting officer, the sheriff may order the reporting officer to make available to the curator *ad litem* any report or information in relation to the child.

(4) A married couple may, before presenting the petition, apply to the sheriff for the appointment of a reporting officer.

(5) An application under paragraph (4) shall—

(*a*) be made by letter setting out the reasons for which the appointment is sought; and

(*b*) not require to be intimated to any person.

Selection of reporting officer and curator ad litem

10. The reporting officer and curator *ad litem* appointed by the sheriff shall be selected from a panel established under the Curators ad Litem and Reporting Officers (Panels) (Scotland) Regulations 1984 unless the sheriff considers that it would be appropriate to appoint a person who is not on the panel.

Duties of reporting officer and curator ad litem

11.—(1) A reporting officer appointed under rule 9(1)(*a*) shall, where appropriate—

(*a*) inquire into the facts and circumstances averred in the petition;

(*b*) ascertain whether the conditions in subsections (2) to (7) of section 30 of the Act of 1990 have been satisfied;

(*c*) witness any execution in Scotland of any agreement in Form 2 under section 30(5) of the Act of 1990 (agreement to parental order by a father who is not the husband of the female petitioner or by the woman who carried the child), and investigate whether the agreement is given freely, unconditionally and with full understanding of what is involved;

(*d*) where a person whose agreement is required is furth of Scotland, confirm his views in writing, ensure that any agreement under section 30(5) of the Act of 1990 is witnessed in accordance with rule 5(2) and investigate whether the agreement is given freely, unconditionally and with full understanding of what is involved;

(*e*) ensure that each person whose agreement is required understands that in agreeing to the parental order he is giving up all future claims to the child and that all parental rights and duties will vest in the petitioners;

(*f*) investigate whether there are any other persons with a relevant interest and whether they should be informed of the petition;
(*g*) ascertain from any person whose agreement is required and who can be found whether alternatives to a parental order have been discussed with him;
(*h*) ensure that any person whose agreement is required is aware of the date (if known) of the hearing to determine the application if he wishes to appear, and confirm that any such person understands that he may withdraw his agreement at any time before a parental order is made;
(*i*) draw to the attention of the court any matter which may be of assistance; and
(*j*) prepare a report in relation to the exercise of his duties within such period as the sheriff may specify.

(2) A curator *ad litem* appointed under rule 9(1)(*b*) shall—
(*a*) safeguard generally the interests of the child;
(*b*) inquire, so far as he considers necessary, into the facts and circumstances averred in the petition;
(*c*) ascertain whether any money or other benefit has been received or agreed upon which is prohibited by section 30(7) of the Act of 1990 (prohibition on gift or receipt of money or other benefit);
(*d*) establish that the petitioners understand that the nature and effect of a parental order is to transfer the parental rights and duties in relation to the child to the petitioners and make them responsible for the maintenance and upbringing of the child;
(*e*) ascertain whether the proposed parental order is likely to safeguard and promote the welfare of the child throughout his childhood;
(*f*) ascertain whether it may be in the interests of the child that the court should make a parental order subject to particular conditions including the making of special provision for the child;
(*g*) perform such other duties as appear to him to be necessary or as the court may require; and
(*h*) prepare a report in relation to the exercise of his duties within such period as the sheriff may specify.

(3) The reporting officer shall, on completion of his report, send to the sheriff clerk—
(*a*) the report and a copy of it for each party; and
(*b*) any agreement for the purposes of section 30(5) of the Act of 1990.

(4) The curator *ad litem* shall, on completion of his report, send the report and a copy of it for each party, to the sheriff clerk.

Hearing

12.—(1) On receipt of the reports referred to in rule 11, the sheriff shall fix a hearing.

(2) The sheriff may—
(*a*) order any person whose agreement is required to be given to attend the hearing;
(*b*) order intimation of the date of the hearing to any person not mentioned in paragraph (3)(*a*), (*b*) or (*c*); and
(*c*) order the reporting officer or curator *ad litem* to perform additional duties to assist him in determining the petition.

(3) The petitioners shall intimate the date of the hearing in Form 3 by registered post or recorded delivery letter to—
(*a*) every person whose whereabouts are known to them and whose agreement is required to be given;
(*b*) the reporting officer appointed under rule 9(1)(*a*);
(*c*) the curator *ad litem* appointed under rule 9(1)(*b*); and
(*d*) any person on whom intimation has been ordered under paragraph (2)(*b*).

(4) At the hearing—
(*a*) the petitioners, the reporting officer and the curator *ad litem* shall, if required by the sheriff, appear and may be represented;
(*b*) any person required by the sheriff to attend the hearing shall appear and may be represented;
(*c*) any other person to whom intimation was made under paragraph (3)(*a*) or (*d*) may appear or be represented.

Supervision by or committal to care of local authority

13.—(1) Where the sheriff refuses to make a parental order and considers—
(*a*) that the child should be placed under the supervision of a specified local authority, or
(*b*) that the child should be committed to the care of a specified local authority,

the sheriff shall order intimation of the terms of the proposed order to be made to the local authority and give the local authority an opportunity to make representations.

(2) Any representations of the local authority shall be made by minute in the process of the petition for a parental order to which it relates.

(3) A minute under paragraph (2) shall include an appropriate crave and statement of facts.

(4) On receipt of the minute the sheriff shall order a hearing to be fixed and ordain the minuter to send a notice of such hearing in Form 4 and a copy of the minute by registered post or recorded delivery letter to the petitioners, the reporting officer and the curator *ad litem* and to such other persons as the sheriff thinks fit.

Applications for return, removal or prohibition of removal of child

14.—(1) An application under section 29 of the Act of 1978, as modified and applied in relation to applications for parental orders by Schedule 1 to the Regulations (order to return a child to, or not to remove a child from, the care of the applicants), in relation to a breach of section 27(1) of that Act as so modified and applied (restriction on removal of child where application for parental order pending), or under section 27(1) of that Act as so modified and applied for leave to remove a child, shall be made by minute in the process of the petition for a parental order to which it relates.

(2) A minute under paragraph (1) shall include an appropriate crave and statement of facts.

(3) On receipt of the minute, the sheriff shall order a hearing to be fixed and ordain the minuter to send a notice of such hearing in Form 5 and a copy of the minute by registered post or recorded delivery letter to the reporting officer and the curator *ad litem* and to such other persons as the sheriff thinks fit.

Applications to amend, or revoke a direction in, a parental order

15.—(1) An application under paragraph 3(1) of Schedule 1 to the Act of 1978, as modified and applied in relation to parental orders by Schedule 1 to the Regulations (amendment, or revocation of a direction in, a parental order), shall be made by petition to the court which pronounced the order.

(2) The sheriff may order the petitioners to intimate the petition to such persons as the sheriff thinks fit.

Registration of certified copy interlocutor

16. On the sheriff pronouncing an interlocutor making—

(*a*) a parental order,

(*b*) an amendment to, or revocation of a direction in, a parental order, or

(*c*) a revocation of a parental order,

the sheriff clerk shall send a certified copy of that interlocutor to the Registrar General for Scotland in a sealed envelope marked "confidential".

Extract of order

17. An extract of a parental order shall not be issued except by order of the court on an application to it—

(*a*) where there is a petition for the parental order depending before the court, by motion in that process; or

(*b*) where there is no such petition depending before the court, by petition.

Final procedure

18.—(1) After a certified copy of an interlocutor mentioned in rule 16 has been sent to the Registrar General for Scotland, the sheriff clerk shall forthwith—

(*a*) place the whole process in an envelope bearing only—

(i) the name of the petitioners;

(ii) the full name of the child to whom the process relates; and

(iii) the date of the order; and

(*b*) seal the envelope and mark it "confidential".

(2) No person shall open a process referred to in paragraph (1) or inspect its contents within 100 years after the date of the parental order, except—

(*a*) the person in respect of whom the parental order was made after he has reached the age of 17 years;

(*b*) any other person or body entitled under section 45(5) of the Act of 1978, as modified and applied in relation to parental orders and applications for such orders by Schedule 1 to the Regulations, to access to the registers and books kept under section 45(4) of that Act, as so modified and applied, with the written authority of the person in respect of whom the parental order was made;

(*c*) by order of the court on an application made by petition presented by another court or authority (whether within the United Kingdom or not) having the power to make a parental order for the purpose of obtaining information in connection with an application to it for such an order;

(*d*) by order of the court on an application made by petition presented by any person; and

(*e*) a person who is authorised in writing by the Secretary of State to obtain information from the process for the purpose of research designed to improve the working of human fertilisation and embryology law and practice.

APPENDIX

Rule 3(1)

FORM 1

Form of petition for parental order under section 30 of the Human Fertilisation and Embryology Act 1990

SHERIFFDOM OF (*insert name of sheriffdom*)

AT (*insert place of sheriff court*)

PETITION

of

[A.B.] (*designation and address*)

and

[C.D.] (*designation and address*)
[*or serial number where one has been assigned*]

Petitioners

for

A parental order under section 30 of the
Human Fertilisation and Embryology Act 1990

in respect of

[E.F.] (*name as in birth certificate*)

The petitioners condescend as follows—

1. The petitioners are married to each other, are domiciled in Scotland and reside at (*state full address*).

2. The petitioners are respectively   and   years of age.

3. (*State name of child, the subject of the petition*) is made [*or* female] and is   months old having been born on   at

4. The child was received into the home of the petitioners on

5. The child was carried by a woman other than the female petitioner as the result of the placing in her of an embryo [*or* the placing in her of sperm and eggs] [*or* her artificial insemination].

6. The gametes of (*state which petitioner or if both state both petitioners*) were used to bring about the creation of the embryo of the child.

7. The child is not the subject of any other pending or completed court proceedings (*if the child is so subject give full details*).

[8. (*State full name and address of the father of the child*), who is not the male petitioner, is the father of the child by virtue of section 28 of the Human Fertilisation and Embryology Act 1990 [*or otherwise*] and has freely and with full understanding of what is involved, agreed unconditionally to the making of the order sought.]

[[9.] (*State full name and address of the woman who carried the child*), is the woman who carried the child and has freely and with full understanding of what is involved, agreed unconditionally to the making of the order sought.]

[10.] No money or benefit, other than for expenses reasonably incurred, has been given or received by the petitioners for or in consideration of—
(*a*) the making of the order sought,
(*b*) any agreement required for the making of the order sought,
(*c*) the handing over of the child to the petitioners, or
(*d*) the making of any arrangements with a view to the making of the order,
[other than (*state any money or other benefit given or received by authority of the court and specify such authority*)].

[[11.] The father of the child [and] [*or*] [the woman who carried the child] cannot be found (*state the efforts which have been made to find the person(s) concerned*) [*or* is [*or* are] incapable of giving agreement by reason of (*state reasons*)].]

The petitioners crave the court—

1. To order notice of the petition to be intimated to such person or persons as the court thinks fit.

2. To appoint a reporting officer and a curator *ad litem* to the child and direct them to report.

[3. To dispense with the agreement of the father of the child [and] [*or*] [the woman who carried the child] who cannot be found [*or* who is [*or* are] incapable of giving agreement].]

[4.] On resuming consideration of this petition and the report by the reporting officer and the curator *ad litem*, to make a parental order in their favour under section 30 of the Human Fertilisation and Embryology Act 1990 in respect of the child.

[5.] To direct the Registrar General for Scotland to make an entry regarding the parental order in the Parental Order Register in the form prescribed by him giving   as the forename(s) and   as the surname of the child; and upon proof to the satisfaction of the court in the course of the proceedings to follow hereon, to find that the child was born on the   day of   in the year   and is identical with the child to whom an entry numbered   and made on the   day of   in the year   , in the register of births for the registration district of   relates; and to direct the Registrar General for Scotland to cause such birth entry to be marked with the words "Parental Order" and to include the abovementioned date of birth in the entry recording the parental order in the manner indicated in that form.

[6.] To pronounce such other or further orders or directions upon such matters, including the expenses of this petition, as the court thinks fit.

(*Signed*)

Male petitioner

(*Signed*)

Female petitioner

[*or* (*Signed*)

Solicitor for petitioners
(*Address*)]

Rule 5(1)

FORM 2

Form of agreement for parental order under section 30(5) of the Human Fertilisation and Embryology Act 1990

in the

Petition

of

[A.B.] (*designation and address*)

and

[C.D.] (*designation and address*)
[*or serial number where one has been assigned*]

for

A Parental Order under the Human Fertilisation and Embryology Act 1990

in respect of

[E.F.] (*name as in birth certificate*)

I, (*name and address*), being the father of the child by virtue of section 28 of the Human Fertilisation and Embryology Act 1990 [*or otherwise*] [*or* the woman who carried the child] hereby state—

(1) That I understand that the effect of the parental order for which application has been made will be to deprive me permanently of parental rights and duties relating to the child and to vest them in the petitioners; and, in particular, I understand that, if an order is made, I shall have no right to see or get in touch with the child or to have him [*or* her] returned to me.

(2) That I understand that the court cannot make a parental order in relation to the child without my agreement and the agreement of the woman who carried the child [*or* the father of the child, where he is not one of the petitioners] unless the court dispenses with an agreement on the ground that the person concerned cannot be found or is incapable of giving agreement.

(3) That I understand that when the hearing of the petition to determine the application for a parental order in relation to the child is heard, this document may be used as evidence of my agreement to the making of the order unless I inform the court that I no longer agree.

(4) That I freely, and with full understanding of what is involved, agree unconditionally to the making of a parental order in relation to the child.

(5) That I have not received or given any money or benefit, other than for expenses reasonably incurred, for or in consideration of—

(*a*) the making of a parental order,
(*b*) the execution of this agreement,
(*c*) the handing over of the child to the petitioners, or
(*d*) the making of any arrangements with a view to the making of a parental order,

[other than (*state any money or other benefit given or received by authority of the court and specify such authority*)].

I have signed this agreement at (*place of signing*) on the day of

(*Signed by father of the child or woman who carried the child*)

This agreement was signed by before me at on the day of

(*Signed*)

Reporting Officer
[*or* Witness
(*full name and address*)]

Rule 12(3)

FORM 3

Form of intimation of diet of hearing of application for a parental order under section 30 of the Human Fertilisation and Embryology Act 1990

To: (*full name and address of person to whom this intimation is to be sent*)

You are given NOTICE that a hearing will take place at (*name of sheriff court*) Sheriff Court (*full address of court*) on (*date*) at (*time*) in relation to the child (*full name of child as given in the birth certificate*)

when the court will consider an application for a parental order under section 30 of the Human Fertilisation and Embryology Act 1990 in respect of the child.

You are [not] obliged to attend the hearing [unless you wish to do so].

If you do not attend this hearing the court may make an order as noted above.

[While the petition is pending you must not, except with the leave of the court, remove the child from the custody of the petitioners.]

[The court has been requested to dispense with your agreement to the making of an order on the ground[s] that (*specify ground(s)*).]

Date (*insert date*)

(*Signed*)

Male petitioner

(*Signed*)

Female petitioner

[*or* (*Signed*)

Solicitor for petitioners
(*Address*)]

Rule 13(4)

FORM 4

Form of intimation of diet of hearing of minute by local authority

To: (*full name and address of person to whom this intimation is to be sent*)

You are given NOTICE that a hearing will take place at (*name of sheriff court*) Sheriff Court (*full address of court*) on (*date*) at (*time*) in relation to the child (*full name of child as given in the birth certificate*)

when the court will consider representations made by minute under rule 13 of the Act of Sederunt (Sheriff Court Parental Orders (Human Fertilisation and Embryology) Rules) 1994 in respect of the child. A copy of the minute is attached.

You do not need to attend this hearing if you do not wish to be heard by the court.

Date (*insert date*)

(*Signed*)

Local Authority

[*or* (*Signed*)

Solicitor for Local Authority
(*Address*)]

Rule 14(3) FORM 5

Form of intimation of diet of hearing of application under section 27(1) or 29 of the Act of 1978 as modified and applied in relation to parental orders

To: (*full name and address of person to whom this intimation is to be sent*)

You are given NOTICE that a hearing will take place at (*name of sheriff court*) Sheriff Court (*full address of court*) on (*date*) at (*time*) in relation to the child (*full name of child as given in the birth certificate*)

when the court will consider a minute of application under rule 14 of the Act of Sederunt (Sheriff Court Parental Orders (Human Fertilisation and Embryology) Rules) 1994 in respect of the child. A copy of the application is attached.

You do not need to attend this hearing if you do not wish to be heard by the court.

Date (*insert date*)

(*Signed*)

Minuter

[*or* (*Signed*)

Solicitor for Minuter
(*Address*)]

[THE NEXT PAGE IS K701]

Notes

Disclosure of Addresses from Official Records: Assistance in Tracing Maintenance Defaulters

Note:—Whilst every effort has been made to ensure that the information in this guidance leaflet is correct, it should be noted that the details concerning the government departments can be subject to alteration.

This guidance has been prepared by the Scottish Courts Administration for the purpose of providing information about the government offices to which application may be made for assistance in tracing maintenance defaulters.

Arrangements for the disclosure of addresses apply to any proceedings, either initial or for enforcement which include a claim for the payment of maintenance. An up-to-date address will not always be available, but departments will give such assistance as they can on the understanding that the information disclosed will be used solely for the purpose for which it was supplied and will not be made known to the complainant or anyone else except as may be required in the normal course of proceedings. *A written assurance in these terms should therefore accompany the request for information.*

1. Department of Social Security

If the complainant is receiving income support [and/or family credit?] it will be advisable to refer in the first place to the local DSS office which is dealing with the claim for income support [and/or family credit?], in order to avoid a possible duplication of enquiries.

In other cases where difficulty is experienced in tracing maintenance defaulters, application for assistance should be addressed to the [Records Branch of the DSS at Newcastle]; if the application does not produce an address, resort should then be made to the National Health Service Central Register.

Applications to the Department of Social Security should be addressed to Department of Social Security, Special Section A, Contributions Agency Central Operations, Newcastle-Upon-Tyne, NE98 1YX, and should include as much of the following information as possible:—

(*a*) the defaulter's name, in full;
(*b*) the exact date of birth or, if this is not known, his/her approximate age;
(*c*) his/her national insurance number (if known);
(*d*) the exact date of the marriage and the spouse's forenames;
(*e*) the defaulter's last known address with the date when he/she was living there;
(*f*) any other known address with dates; and
(*g*) if the defaulter is a war pensioner, his/her war pension number and service particulars (if known).

2. National Health Service Central Register

Applications for disclosure of an address from Health Service records should be made to the National Health Service Central Register, Ladywell House, Ladywell Road, Edinburgh EH12 7TF, tel. 031–334 0380; fax 031–334 7027). All requests should, if possible, be accompanied by the following information:—

(*a*) the defaulter's name, in full;
(*b*) the exact date of his/her birth or, if that is not known, his/her approximate age;
(*c*) his/her National Health Service number (if known);
(*d*) his home address as it was in 1939: (if applicable) and
(*e*) any subsequent known address with dates.

The following details should always be given on any application or correspondence:— File Reference NHB/5/4

3. United Kingdom Passport Agency

If the records of the DSS and the National Health Service Central Register have failed to provide an address or there are grounds for believing that the defaulter may have made a recent application for a passport, the Passport Agency may be able to assist. In these circumstances applications should be addressed to the Special Files Section, United Kingdom Passport Agency, Headquarters, Clive House, Petty France, London SW1H 9HD (tel. 071–271 8633; fax 071–271 8645).

If possible, the following information should be given in any application to the Passport Agency:—

(*a*) the defaulter's name, in full;
(*b*) the exact date of his/her birth or, if this is not known, his/her approximate age;
(*c*) his/her place of birth;
(*d*) whether he/she is known to have travelled abroad, and if so, the destination and dates;
(*e*) his/her last known address with the date he/she was living there; and
(*f*) any other known address with dates.

4. Ministry of Defence

Where it is known or there are grounds for believing that the defaulter is serving in HM Forces, application for the disclosure of his/her address may be made, by a solicitor, to the Ministry of Defence as follows:—

(*a*) *Royal Air Force Officers*—to: PM (AR1b(RAF)), Ministry of Defence, Personal Management Centre, RAF Innsworth, Gloucester GL3 1EZ (tel. 0452 712612, ext. 7900; fax 0452 712612, ext. 7431).
(*b*) *Airmen or ex-Airmen*—to: P. Man 3d(2)a(RAF), Ministry of Defence, RAF Personnel Management Centre, RAF Innsworth, Gloucester GL3 1EZ (tel. 0452 712612, ext. 7615/7622; fax 0452 712612, ext. 7431).
(*c*) *Naval Officers*—to: Ministry of Defence, Naval pay, Pensions and conditions of Service (NPC 1b), Room 322, Old Admiralty Building, Archway South, Spring Gardens, London SW1A 2BE (tel. 071–218 6982; fax 071–218 3443).
(*d*) *Naval Ratings*—to: Naval Pay and Pensions (Accounts), (NPP(Acs) 2B(i)), HMS Centurion, Grange Road, Gosport, Hants PO13 9XA (tel. 0705 822351, ext. 2376; fax 0705 528424).
(*e*) *Ex-Naval Ratings*—to: Naval pay and Pensions (Accounts) (NPP(Acs)1c) HMS Centurion, Grange Road, Gosport, Hants PO13 9XA (tel. 0705 822351, ext. 2606 A-K; ext. 2247 L-Z; fax 0705 528424).
(*f*) *Members or former members of the Regular Army*—
  (i) *in the case of commissioned officers*—Ministry of Defence (MS(A0D0)) Government Buildings, Stanmore, Middlesex, HA7 4PZ.
  (ii) *Warrant Officers, Non-Commissioned Officers and Soldiers*—If the person's regiment or corps is known—application should be to the appropriate Manning and Record Office (see below).
  —If the person's regiment or corps is *not* known—application should be to: The Officer in Charge, Central Manning Support Office, Higher Barracks, Exeter EX4 4HD.

Note:—Applications to any of the addresses given in paragraphs 4 (*a*) to (*e*) inclusive, should include the service person's full name, date of birth and service number, rank and regiment/corps, if known. Applications *must* be accompanied by an undertaking by the solicitor that the information is needed in connection with maintenance proceedings, and that, so far as is possible, the serviceperson's address will not be disclosed by the solicitor to their client or any other person other than a court for the purposes of serving process in the proceedings.

Regiment or Corps	*Abbreviated Title*	*Address of Manning and Record Office*
The Household Cavalry	H CAV	Officer in Charge—Household Cavalry & Royal Armoured Corps
The Life Guards	LG	Manning & Records Office
The Blues & Royals (Royal Horse Guards and 1st Dragoons)	RHG/D	Queen's Park Avenue Chester CH4 7AW
Royal Armoured Corps	RAC	
1st The Queen's Dragoon Guards	QDG	
The Royal Scots Dragoon Guards	SCOTS DG	
4th/7th Royal Dragoon Guards	4/7 DG	
5th Royal Inniskilling Dragoon Guards	5 INNIS DG	
The Queen's Own Hussars	QOH	
The Queen's Own Royal Irish Hussars	QRIH	
9th/12th Royal Lancers	9/12L	
The Royal Hussars	RH	
13th/18th Royal Hussars	13/18H	
14th/20th Royal Hussars	14/20H	
15th/19th The King's Royal Hussars	15/19H	
16th/5th The Queen's Royal Lancers	16/5L	
17th/21st Lancers	17/21L	
Royal Tank Regiment	RTR	
Royal Regiment of Artillery	RA	Officer in Charge RA Manning & Record Office
Royal Horse Artillery	RHA	Imphal Barracks Fulford Road York YO1 4HD
Corps of Royal Engineers	RE	Officer in Charge RE Manning & Record Office or
Royal Corps of Signals	R SIGNALS	R SIGNALS Manning & Record Office Kentigern House 65 Brown Street Glasgow G2 8EX
Infantry		
The Guards Division		
Grenadier Guards	GREN GDS	Officer in Charge
Coldstream Guards	COLDM GDS	Foot Guards & Infantry
Scots Guards	SG	Manning & Record Office
Irish Guards	IG	(North)
Welsh Guards	WG	
The Scottish Division		
The Royal Scots	RS	
The Royal Highland Fusiliers	RHF	
The King's Own Scottish Borderers	KOSB	
The Black Watch	BW	
Queen's Own Highlanders	QO HLDRS	
The Gordon Highlanders	GORDONS	

Regiment or Corps	*Abbreviated Title*	*Address of Manning and Record Office*
The Argyll and Sutherland Highlanders	A and SH	
The King's Division		
The King's Own Royal Border Regiment	KINGS OWN BORDER	Officer in Charge Foots Guards & Infantry Manning & Record Office Imphal Barracks Fulford Road York YO1 4HD
The King's Regiment	KINGS	
The Prince of Wales' Own Regiment of Yorkshire	PWO	
The Green Howards	GREEN HOWARD	
The Royal Irish Rangers	R IRISH	
The Queen's Lancashire Regiment	QLR	
The Duke of Wellington's Regiment	DWR	
The Prince of Wales' Division		
The Devonshire and Dorset Regiment	D an D	
The Cheshire Regiment	CHESHIRE	
The Royal Welsh Fusiliers	RWF	
The Royal Regiment of Wales	RRW	
The Gloucestershire Regiment	GLOSTERS	
The Worcestershire and Sherwood Foresters Regiment	WFR	
The Royal Hampshire Regiment	R HAMPS	
The Staffordshire Regiment	STAFFORDS	
The Duke of Edinburgh's Royal Regiment	DERR	
The Queen's Division		
The Queen's Regiment	QUEENS	Officer in Charge Infantry Manning and Record Office (South) The Higher Barracks Exeter EX4 4HD
The Royal Regiment of Fusiliers	RRF	
Royal Anglian Regiment	R ANGLIAN	
The Light Division		
The Light Infantry	LI	Officer in Charge Infantry Manning and Record Office (South) Higher Barracks Exeter EX4 4ND
The Royal Green Jackets	RGJ	
The Parachute Regiment	PARA	
Special Air Service Regiment	SAS	
Small Arms School Corps	SASC	
Royal Corps of Transport	RCT	Officer in Charge RCT Manning & Record Office Kentigern House 65 Brown Street Glasgow G2 8EX
Royal Army Medical Corps	RAMC	Officer in Charge Medical & Women's Services Manning and Record Office Queen's Park Avenue Chester CH4 7AW
Royal Army Dental Corps	RADC	
Queen Alexandra's Royal Army Nursing Corps	QARANC	
Women's Royal Army Corps	WRAC	
Royal Army Ordnance Corps	RAOC	Officer in Charge RAOC (or) REME Manning and Record Office 51 Saffron Road Wigston Leicester LE8 2US
Corps of Royal Electrical and Mechanical Engineers	REME	

Regiment or Corps	*Abbreviated Title*	*Address of Manning and Record Office*
Army Air Corps Corps of Royal Military Police Royal Army Pay Corps Royal Pioneer Corps Intelligence Corps	AAR RMP RAPC RPC INT CORPS	Officer in Charge Combined Manning and Record Office Higher Barracks Exeter EX4 4HD
Army Physical Training Corps Army Catering Corps Royal Army Veterinary Corps Military Provost Staff Corps	APTC ACC RAVC MPSC	Officer in Charge Combined Manning and Record Office Higher Barracks Exeter EX4 4HD
Ulster Defence Regiment General Service Corps	UDR GSC	Officer in Charge Foot Guards and Infantry Manning and Record Office (North) Imphal Barracks Fulford Road York YO1 4HD

Notes:—

1. There are no soldiers in the following Corps:
(*a*) Royal Army Chaplins Department (RAChD)
(*b*) Royal Army Education Corps (RAEC)
(*c*) Army Legal Corps (ALC)

2. Enquiries concerning the address of officers should be addressed to:
Ministry of Defence (AODO)
Government Buildings
Stanmore
Middlesex HA7 4PZ

3. Court orders in respect of officers of any regiment or corps should be sent to:
Ministry of Defence (PS4d(A))
Room 1001
Empress State Building
London SW6 1TR

4. Where a soldier's regiment or corps is not known enquiries should be addressed to:
Officer in Charge
Central Manning Support Office
Higher Barracks
Exeter EX4 4ND

It should be appreciated that the records available may not always show the present address of a maintenance defaulter but it is hoped that solicitors will make the fullest use of these sources of information where it is possible they could be of assistance.

August 1991

DIVISION M

Succession, Trusts, Liferents and Judicial Factors

Statutes

Acts of Sederunt

Notes

Statutes

Judicial Factors Act 1849

(12 & 13 Vict. c. 51)

An Act for the better protection of the property of pupils, absent persons, and persons under mental incapacity in Scotland.

[28th July 1849]

[1] **1.** The following words and expressions in this Act shall have the meanings hereby assigned to them, unless there be something in the subject or context repugnant to such construction: (that is to say,) the expression "Judicial Factor" or "Factor" shall mean factor *loco absentis*, and *curator bonis*: the word "Guardian" shall mean any person appointed to be the guardian of a person who is under the age of 16 years: the word "Tutor" shall mean any person who after the passing of this Act shall be served tutor of law or be appointed tutor-dative to any person suffering from mental disorder within the meaning of the Mental Health (Scotland) Act 1960; the word "Curator" shall mean any person who after the passing of this Act shall be served as curator to any person suffering from mental disorder within the meaning of the Mental Health (Scotland) Act 1960; the word "Accountant" shall mean the accountant of the Court of Session, to be appointed under the authority of this Act; the expression "Lord Ordinary" shall mean the Lord Ordinary of the Court of Session discharging the duties of junior Lord Ordinary in time of session, and the Lord Ordinary on the Bills in the time of vacation; the expression "Court of Session" or "Court" shall, excepting as to the power of passing acts of sederunt, mean either division of the Court of Session; the word "Estate" shall include all property and funds, and all rights heritable and moveable; the word "Lands" shall include all heritable subjects; words used in the singular number shall be held to include several persons or things, and words importing the masculine gender shall extend and be applied to females as well as males.

NOTE

[1] As amended by the Mental Health (Scotland) Act 1960, Sched. 4 and the Age of Legal Capacity (Scotland) Act 1991, Sched. 1, para. 7 and Sched. 2. See now the Mental Health (Scotland) Act 1984.

Judicial factor to find caution for duly performing his duties

[1] **2.** Every judicial factor shall, within such time after his appointment as the Court shall direct, find caution for his duly accounting for his intromissions and management, and observing and performing every duty incumbent upon him as factor, in terms of the rules prescribed or to be prescribed for the discharge of his office, and in case of his failure to do so his appointment shall fall: and no factor shall enter upon the duties of his office, nor shall a certified copy interlocutor of his appointment be issued, until after such caution is found and received as sufficient; and the factor shall obtain a certified copy interlocutor of his appointment without delay.

NOTE

[1] As amended by S.I. 1967 No. 487.

Judicial factor to lodge with the accountant a distinct rental of lands committed to his management, a list of funds, and an inventory of moveables, etc.

[1] **3.** Every judicial factor shall, as soon as may be after obtaining an official certified copy interlocutor of his appointment and within six months at least from the date on which his bond of caution shall have been received,

lodge with the accountant a distinct rental of all lands committed to his management, specifying the rents, revenues, and profits of such lands, the existing leases and other rights affecting the lands, and the public burdens and other burdens thereon, and a list of all monies and funds belonging and debts due to the estate, specifying the particulars of each item, and the interest or revenue arising from the same, the document by which the same is vouched, and the nature and value of any security held for the same, and also an inventory of any household furniture, farm stocking, goods, or moveables, including rights moveable, forming part of the estate; and he shall, without delay after obtaining an official certified copy interlocutor of his appointment, recover all writs and documents of importance belonging to the estate, and collect all monies due to the same not securely invested, and use all reasonable diligence in ascertaining the exact nature and amount of the estate placed under his charge; and he shall produce all such writs and documents, and information so obtained by him, along with the said rental, list of funds, and inventory, to the accountant, which rental, list, and inventory, when adjusted and approved of by the accountant, shall be signed by him and the factor, and shall form a ground of charge against the factor; and if at any time thereafter any new claims on property belonging to the estate shall be discovered the factor shall report the same in his next account of charge and discharge to the accountant, who shall make such alteration on the rental, list, and inventory as may be thereby rendered necessary.

NOTE

[1] As amended by S.I. 1967 No. 487.

Factor to close his accounts once a year, and lodge the same with Accountant

4. The factor shall close his account of charge and discharge once in every year, on a day to be fixed by the accountant, and within one month thereafter shall lodge such account in the office of the accountant, with the vouchers numbered, and referred to in the account by number: Provided always, that it shall be competent for the accountant, on cause shewn, to prorogate the time for lodging such accounts and vouchers, but in no case shall such prorogation extend beyond three months from the day fixed for the closing of the accounts.

Factor to lodge monies in one of the Banks of Scotland

5.—[1] (1) The factor shall lodge the money in his hands in some one of the following institutions, that is to say—

(*a*) an institution authorised under the Banking Act 1987;

(*b*) the National Savings Bank; or

(*c*) a building society incorporated (or deemed to be incorporated) under the Building Societies Act 1986,

in a separate account or on deposit, such account or deposit being in his own name as judicial factor on the estate; and if the factor shall keep in his hands more than £500 of money belonging to the estate for more than ten days, he shall be charged with a sum to the estate at the rate of £20 per centum per annum on the excess of the said sum of £500, for such time as it shall be in his hands beyond the said ten days; and, unless the money has been so kept from innocent causes, the factor shall be dismissed from his office, and shall have no claim for commission.

[2] (2) The Secretary of State may by order made by regulations amend subsection (1) above by substituting for any sum for the time being specified in that subsection such other sum as appears to him to be justified by a change in the value of money.

[2] (3) The power to make regulations under subsection (2) above shall be exercisable by statutory instrument; and no such regulations shall be made unless a draft of them has been approved by resolution of each House of Parliament.

[3] (4) In lodging money under subsection (1) above the judicial factor shall not require to have regard to any provision of the Trustee Investments Act 1961 which would, apart from the provisions of this subsection, require him to seek advice before depositing money in any of the institutions mentioned in that subsection.

NOTES

[1] As amended by the Law Reform (Miscellaneous Provisions) (Scotland) Act 1980, s.7, and the Law Reform (Miscellaneous Provisions) (Scotland) Act 1990, Sched. 8, para. 21(1)(*a*) with effect from 1st January 1991.

[2] Added by the Law Reform (Miscellaneous Provisions) (Scotland) Act 1980, s.7.

[3] Added by the Law Reform (Miscellaneous Provisions) (Scotland) Act 1990, Sched. 8, para. 21(1)(*b*), with effect from 1st January 1991.

Penalties on Factor for misconduct

6. If the factor shall misconduct himself, or fail in the discharge of his duty, he shall be liable to such fine, and to the forfeiture of the whole or any part of his commission, and to suspension or removal from his office as factor, and to payment of expenses, or to any one or more of such penalties, as the Court in its discretion shall decide; and that over and above such further liability as he may be subject to, as accords of law, in reparation of any loss or damage sustained by the estate in consequence of such misconduct or failure.

Factor may apply for special powers

[1] **7.** If at any time it shall appear to the factor that there is a strong expediency for granting abatement of rent, either temporarily or permanently, or for renewing or granting a lease for a period of years, or for draining, or for erecting buildings or fences, or for otherwise improving the estate in a manner not coming within the ordinary course of factorial management, he shall report the same to the accountant, who may order any necessary inquiry, and shall state his opinion thereon in writing; and such report and opinion may be submitted by the factor to the Lord Ordinary, with a note praying for the sanction of the Court to the measure proposed; and the Lord Ordinary shall, with or without further inquiry, report the matter to the Court, who, if they consider it expedient and consistent with due regard to the amount of the estate at the time, may sanction the measure, and the decision of the Court shall be final, and not subject to appeal; and if the estate be held under entail, it shall be lawful to the Court to authorise the factor to take proceedings for constituting as a charge against the future heirs of entail, or otherwise recovering, the money expended in making any improvements upon the estate, under and in terms of the Entail Improvement Act 1770, and under and in terms of the Entail Amendment Act 1848; but nothing herein contained shall be held as conferring power on the Court to authorise the factor to build or enlarge a mansion-house upon the estate, or to charge the estate and future heirs of entail to a greater extent than one-half the amount with which the heir in possession, if under no incapacity to act, could have charged the estate under the said Acts, or either of them; and if any factor having charge of the estate of any person suffering from mental disorder within the meaning of the Mental Health (Scotland) Act 1960, or other person incapable of managing his own affairs shall deem it proper for the comfort or welfare of such person that the whole or a part of such estate should be sunk on annuity, he shall report the matter to the accountant, who shall state his opinion thereon in writing, and such report and opinion shall be submitted by the factor, with a note as aforesaid, to the Lord Ordinary, who shall report the matter to the Court, and it shall be in the power of the Court to sanction the measure, and the decision of the Court shall be final, and not subject to appeal; and in all other matters in which special powers are, according to the existing practice, in use to be granted by the Court, the Court shall

have power to grant the same in like manner and form as is above provided.

NOTE

[1] As amended by the Mental Health (Scotland) Act 1960, Sched. 4.

Before special powers, etc., granted, Court to order such intimation to be made as may be deemed proper

8. In all cases in which application shall be made to the Lord Ordinary or the Court by any factor, or other person having right to make the same, for special powers, or for the extraordinary application of money or funds or property belonging to any estate, the Lord Ordinary or Court shall order such intimation to be made as may be deemed proper.

9. [Repealed by the Judicial Factors (Scotland) Act 1889, s.1.]

General nature of Accountant's duty

[1] **10.** The accountant shall superintend generally the conduct of all judicial factors guardians and tutors and curators coming under the provisions of this Act already appointed or to be hereafter appointed, and shall see that they duly observe all rules and regulations affecting them for the time.

NOTE

[1] As amended by the Age of Legal Capacity (Scotland) Act 1991, Sched. 1, para. 8.

To assign a day for closing first account

11. On the factor's bond of caution being received as sufficient, it shall be transmitted by the clerk to the process to the accountant, who shall forthwith give a written intimation, dated and signed, to the factor or his agent, stating that the bond has been received, and assigning the day on which the factor is to close his first account, being not less than six nor more than eighteen months from the date of such intimation; and on the death or insolvency of the cautioner of any factor such factor shall forthwith give notice in writing to the accountant of such death or insolvency, and the accountant shall, as soon as the fact shall come to his knowledge, by means of such notice or otherwise, require new caution to be found.

To adjust the Rental, List, and Inventory

12. The accountant shall see that the factor lodges a rental, list, and inventory in terms of this Act, and shall, along with the factor or his agent, examine, verify, and adjust, and with the factor sign the same, and shall ascertain the circumstances of the estate, and call for all necessary documents, so as to form a clear rule of charge against the factor at the commencement of his office, and the accountant shall retain such rental, list, and inventory.

And to audit the accounts

13. The accountant shall see that the factor's accounts of charge and discharge, with the vouchers thereof, are duly lodged, and shall thereafter examine the same without undue delay, and audit the account on the general principles of good ordinary management for the real benefit of the estate and of those interested therein, and he shall consider the investments of the estate and the sufficiency thereof, and he shall be entitled to require from the factor all necessary information and evidence, and he shall fix the amount of the factor's commission for the period embraced by the audit, according to his opinion of what is just in each particular case, and he shall strike the balance, and shall state the result of his audit in the form of a short report; and if he has made any corrections on the account, he shall, if required by the factor, explain such corrections and his reasons for making them.

Rules of exact diligence may be dispensed with

14. The accountant shall have power, upon report to and with the approval of the Lord Ordinary, where the sum involved exceeds £20, and without such report and approval where the sum involved is less than £20, to dispense with the rules of exact diligence in any matter of factorial management.

Accountant's report conclusive against Factor if not objected to, and if objections, how to be disposed of

15. The accountant's audit and report shall be conclusive against the factor and his cautioner if written objections shall not be lodged by the factor with the accountant within twenty days from the date of such audit and report being communicated to the factor; but if objections be lodged, the accountant shall consider the same, and may alter his report if he sees cause; and unless the objections are allowed or departed from, the account and report and whole proceedings shall be transmitted by the accountant to the Lord Ordinary, who shall call the factor or his agent, and if necessary the accountant, before him at chambers in reference thereto, and the Lord Ordinary or the Court, if the matter shall be reported or brought under review, may affirm, vary or reverse the audit and report of the accountant, and may reserve any question or questions which are raised in the objections for the factor till the final audit of his accounts, directing the account to be balanced for the present, as the Lord Ordinary or the Court may think expedient and just; and no judgment of the Lord Ordinary, pronounced as aforesaid, shall be subject to review at the instance of the accountant, nor, in case the Lord Ordinary shall reserve any question as aforesaid, shall it be competent to the factor to reclaim against such reservation; but in case the Lord Ordinary shall decide against the factor, he may bring the interlocutor under review of the Court, by a short note of appeal from the Lord Ordinary's judgment, and the judgment of the Court shall not be subject to appeal at this stage nor till the termination of the factory, without the leave of the Court: Provided always, with reference to such discussion between the accountant and the factor, that at the audit of the factor's accounts, at the termination of his factory, it shall be competent to the factor and his representatives, or to any succeeding factor, or to any parties beneficially interested in the estate, to enter upon such matter of objection, if the same has been reserved, but if the same has been decided by the Lord Ordinary or the Court, the decision shall not be opened up except upon cause shewn; and the factor shall not be entitled to charge the expense of any such proceedings against the estate without the special authority of the Lord Ordinary or the Court.

Cautioner may be heard before the Accountant

16. It shall be lawful for the cautioner to appear and be heard before the accountant during the course of the audit, or to state objections to the audit within twenty days from the date of the report being intimated to the factor as aforesaid, unless the accountant shall grant further time, not exceeding six weeks, and for the purpose of stating such objections the accountant shall, if required, furnish to the cautioner a copy of his report, and the expense of such copy, and of any discussion that shall take place during or after the audit at the instance of the cautioner, shall be borne by the cautioner, and not by the estate: Provided always, that no objection stated on the part of the cautioner shall be any ground for delaying any consignation of any balance ordered by the accountant or otherwise giving immediate effect to the audit.

Parties interested may, upon cause shewn, open up audit of accounts

17. Either at the termination of the factory or during its subsistence, it shall be competent for any party beneficially interested in the estate, or for any succeeding factor, to make appearance, and upon cause shewn to open up the audit of all accounts which have been audited by the accountant in absence of such party or succeeding factor, and also all questions in the accounting which have either not been submitted to the decision of the Lord Ordinary or the Court, or been reserved, and also all questions which have been decided merely as between the accountant and the factor, or between the factor and some other beneficiary, reserving always to the factor and his representatives their answers and defences as accords of law; but if such party or succeeding factor shall so appear, and such questions shall be opened up and decided, the judgment, if pronounced between the factor and a party beneficially interested, shall be final and conclusive as between them and their representatives, and if pronounced between the factor and succeeding factor, shall be final and conclusive against the factor and the estate.

Accountant to make an annual report of all Judicial Factories, which shall be printed

18. The accountant shall make an annual report to the Court of Session, containing such particulars as he may think fit, or as the Court may by act of sederunt or otherwise require, of all judicial factories, whether granted before or after the passing of this Act, then subsisting or remaining unsettled, and of his own proceedings in reference to the same, and such annual report shall be printed at the cost of the fee-fund established by this Act.

Accountant to make requisitions and orders on the Factor

[1] **19.** The accountant shall make all such requisitions or orders on the factor as he may consider necessary; and if such requisition or order shall be disobeyed or neglected, he shall report the same to the Lord Ordinary giving previous notice to the factor or his agent, who shall lodge objections in writing, if he has any, within seven days after such notice; and the Lord Ordinary is hereby empowered, on considering such requisition or order, with the objections thereto, if any, to recall or vary, confirm or repeat such requisition or order; and the interlocutor of the Lord Ordinary shall be final and conclusive against the accountant, and also against the factor, unless he shall, at the time of pronouncing judgment, give notice of his intention to bring the judgment under review, in which case the Lord Ordinary shall dispose of the matter of expenses, and give any interim order that may be necessary, which interim order shall not be subject to review.

NOTE

[1] As amended by the Law Reform (Miscellaneous Provisions) (Scotland) Act 1980, s.7.

And to report to the Lord Ordinary or the Court the Factor's failure in duty

20. The accountant shall, at all times when requisite, report to the Lord Ordinary or the Court any disobedience of any requisition or order, and any misconduct or failure in duty on the part of a factor, or any claims arising against a dismissed factor or a factor's cautioner, or against the representatives of a factor or cautioner deceased; and it shall be competent for the Lord Ordinary or the Court, on the accountant's report, to deal immediately with the matter as accords of law.

When malversation reasonably suspected, a case to be submitted to Her Majesty's Advocate

21. If the accountant shall possess information that shall lead him on reasonable grounds to suspect malversation or misconduct on the part of the factor, such as may infer removal or punishment, he shall be entitled to lay a case before Her Majesty's Advocate, who shall have power to direct such inquiry, and to take such proceedings by petition and complaint, or otherwise, as he shall think proper.

22. [Repealed by the Statute Law Revision Act 1892.]

Provision as to past Factories informally settled or desperate

[1] **23.** In regard to all factories constituted before the passing of this Act, any settlement made of any such factory, though informal, shall be held as a *prima facie* discharge to the factor, and the accountant shall not report the same as a subsisting factory, or require further proceedings therein, but reserving the right of all parties interested in the estate to shew cause to the accountant or the Court why such settlement should not be held as a discharge to the factor, in which case, if the cause shewn shall be satisfactory to the accountant or the Court, the factory shall be held as subsisting and be proceeded with; and in any such factory in which, though there has been no settlement, it shall appear that no benefit is likely to be derived by the parties interested in the estate from further proceedings therein, and no party interested shall make appearance and require such proceedings, the accountant shall place amongst the papers connected with the estate a memorandum of the circumstances, and shall state in his report that further proceedings are for the present unadvisable.

NOTE

[1] Applied by the Judicial Factors (Scotland) Act 1889, s.20.

24. [Repealed by the Statute Law Revision Act 1892.]

Provisions of the Act made applicable to Tutors of Law, Tutors-dative, and Curators to Insane Persons

[1] **25.**—(1) Except as to the mode of appointment and caution, the provisions of this Act relating to judicial factors or relating to the office, powers, and duties of the accountant appointed by this Act shall be applicable, in so far as the same admit of application, to every person who, after the passing of this Act, shall be served tutor of law, or appointed tutor-dative to any person suffering from mental disorder within the meaning of the Mental Health (Scotland) Act 1960, or served curator to any person suffering from mental disorder within the meaning of the Mental Health (Scotland) Act 1960.

[2] (2) Any guardian who shall, by virtue of his office, administer the estate of any person under the age of 16 years shall be subject to the provisions of this Act, but shall not be bound to find caution in terms of sections 26 and 27 of this Act unless the court, on the application of any party having an interest, shall so direct.

NOTES

[1] As amended by the Mental Health (Scotland) Act 1960, Sched. 4 and the Age of Legal Capacity (Scotland) Act 1991, Sched. 1, para. 9 and Sched. 2. See now the Mental Health (Scotland) Act 1984.

[2] Added by the Law Reform (Parent and Child) (Scotland) Act 1986, Sched. 1, para. 1.

Bonds of Caution for Tutors and Curators

[1] **26.** From and after the passing of this Act, in every service of a person as tutor of law, or as a curator to a person suffering from mental disorder within the meaning of the Mental Health (Scotland) Act 1960, there shall, besides the obligations usually inserted therein, be inserted in the bond of caution taken by the clerk in such service an obligation to observe and perform every duty incumbent on such person, in terms of the rules prescribed or to be prescribed for the discharge of his office in all respects, together with a consent to registration in the books of Council and Session for execution; and such bond of caution shall be transmitted, with the other steps of procedure, to the Director of Chancery, who shall forthwith transmit the same to the accountant; and no extract of the retour in such service shall be given out, nor any letters of tutory or curatory be issued thereon, until such bond of caution shall have been received by the Director of Chancery; and in bonds of caution to be taken in the Court of Exchequer from tutors-dative to persons suffering from mental disorder within the

meaning of the Mental Health (Scotland) Act 1960, there shall, besides the usual obligations, be inserted an obligation to the effect aforesaid; and such bonds of caution shall remain in the Court of Exchequer, according to the rules of that Court.

NOTE

[1] As amended by the Mental Health (Scotland) Act 1960, Sched. 4, and the Age of Legal Capacity (Scotland) Act 1991, Sched. 2. See now the Mental Health (Scotland) Act 1984. Functions of Director of Chancery now exercisable by the Keeper of the Registers of Scotland: see the Reorganisation of Offices (Scotland) Act 1928, s.7, S.R. & O. 1932 No. 148, the Public Records (Scotland) Act 1937, s.13 and the Public Registers and Records (Scotland) Act 1948, s.1(2).

Amount of caution for Factors, etc., may be limited, and bonds of caution by Guarantee Associations, etc., taken

[1] **27.** It shall be lawful for the Court of Session or Court of Exchequer, as the case may be, to limit, upon cause shewn, the caution to be found by factors, guardians and tutors and curators to a specified amount, and also to authorise, if they shall deem it expedient, bonds or policies of the British Guarantee Association, or other public company incorporated by Act of Parliament or Royal Charter carrying on guarantee business within Scotland, to be accepted and taken instead of bonds of caution by private individuals.

NOTE

[1] As amended by the Age of Legal Capacity (Scotland) Act 1991, Sched. 1, para. 10. See Rules of Court, r. 200(*e*).

Certified copy of Letters of Tutory or Curatory to form the basis of a summary process

[1] **28.** Whenever the Director of Chancery shall issue letters of tutory or curatory, proceeding on any service or gift dated after the passing of this Act, he shall transmit a certified copy of such letters to the accountant, who, after making an entry thereof in his books, shall transmit the same to one of the principal clerks of Session in order of seniority and by rotation; and such certified copy, when so transmitted, shall be held as establishing a summary process in regard to the estate to which such letters relate, before that Division of the Court to which such clerk shall belong, to the same effect as if the tutor or curator to whom such letters are issued had been appointed judicial factor by the Court on a petition in ordinary form; and such certified copy shall be held for the purposes of this Act as equivalent to such appointment.

NOTE

[1] See note to s.26, *supra*, as to functions of Director of Chancery.

29. [Repealed by the Statute Law Revision Act 1892.]

30. [Repealed by the Age of Legal Capacity (Scotland) Act 1991, Sched. 2.]

Resignation and removal of Tutors and Curators

[1] **31.** The Court shall have power, on cause shewn, to remove or accept the resignation of any guardian, tutor or curator coming under the provisions of this Act, and to appoint a factor or *curator bonis* in his room.

NOTE

[1] As amended by the Age of Legal Capacity (Scotland) Act 1991, Sched. 1, para. 11 and Sched. 2.

Remuneration and responsibility of Factors and Curators not altered

[1] **32.** Nothing herein contained shall be held to confer on any such guardian, tutor or curator a right not now existing in law to remuneration for the discharge of the duties attached to his office, or to limit his powers or alter

the rules of his responsibility as by law now existing, excepting in so far as is herein expressly provided.

NOTE

[1] As amended by the Age of Legal Capacity (Scotland) Act 1991 (c. 50), Sched. 1, para. 11.

Power to Accountant to require information from banks

[1] **33.** The accountant shall have power to require the officers of any institution such as is mentioned in paragraphs (*a*) to (*c*) of section 5(1) of this Act with which any factor guardian or tutor or curator shall have opened an account for the estate under his care, to exhibit all entries in the books of such institution connected with such estate, and the officers of such institution are hereby required to exhibit the same accordingly, and to allow the accountant to take such copies thereof as he may require.

NOTE

[1] As amended by the Law Reform (Miscellaneous Provisions) (Scotland) Act 1990 (c. 40), Sched. 8, para. 21(2) and by the Age of Legal Capacity (Scotland) Act 1991 (c. 50), Sched. 1, para. 12.

Discharge of Factors, Tutors, and Curators

[1] **34.** Subject to section 34A of this Act, it shall be competent for any factor, guardian, tutor, or curator at the termination of his office, to present a petition to the Court for his discharge, calling all persons interested in the estate, so far as known to him, as parties to such petition, and the Court shall order such intimation and service as they may think fit, and it shall be competent to any person so called, or to any other person shewing right and interest, to appear as parties, and upon cause shewn to open up the audit of the factor's accounts, and thereafter, and after receiving the report of the accountant, and making any further inquiry which may be necessary, the Court shall pronounce judgment thereon; and such judgment, if it shall discharge such factor, guardian, tutor, or curator, shall be final and conclusive against all parties concerned, though pronounced in absence, provided the same shall not be opened up as a decree in absence in the Court of Session within the time limited for appealing to the House of Lords, or shall not be appealed from within that time.

NOTE

[1] As amended by the Law Reform (Miscellaneous Provisions) (Scotland) Act 1990 (c. 40), Sched. 8, para. 21(3), and the Age of Legal Capacity (Scotland) Act 1991 (c. 50), Sched. 1, para. 12.

[1] **34A.** The Court may by act of sederunt make provision for the discharge of factors, tutors and curators by means other than the presentation of a petition under section 34 of this Act where the factory, tutory or curatory is terminated by reason of the recovery, death or coming of age of the ward, or by reason of the exhaustion of the estate.

NOTE

[1] Inserted by the Law Reform (Miscellaneous Provisions) (Scotland) Act 1990 (c. 40), s. 67.

Accountant to be custodier of bank receipts

[1] **35.** The accountant shall be custodier of all bank deposit receipts and other vouchers for sums of money already placed or to be hereafter placed in bank under authority of the Court, and of all judicial bonds of caution and other judicial bonds granted or to be granted under the authority of the Court, or any of the judges thereof, or in reference to the business thereof, and all other documents of a like nature, which, according to the present law or practice, are entrusted to the keeping of the senior principal clerk of Session, who, after the commencement of this Act, shall cease to discharge his present duty as custodier of such documents, and shall transfer all such documents as are in his possession to the accountant; and thereafter the clerk in each process in which consignation is made shall

lodge all such bank receipts and bonds or vouchers in the hands of the accountant, whose acknowledgment therefor shall be an acquittance of such clerk.

NOTE

[1] The Court of Session Consignations (Scotland) Act 1895 (c. 19), s. 3, as amended by S.I. 1994 No. 1443 (effective 5th September 1994), provides: "The provisions of section 35 of the Judicial Factors Act 1849, and of ss. 5 and 6 of the Bill Chamber Procedure Act 1857, so far as relating to consignations, are hereby repealed, and in lieu thereof it is hereby provided that the Accountant shall be the sole custodier of all consignations under this Act.

"No fees shall be payable to the Accountant in cases of consignations other than those which are or may be prescribed by the Lords of Council and Session with the sanction of the Treasury".

See also the Rules of the Court of Session 1994, r. 35.11(2).

Records in the Accountant's office to be open for inspection

[1] **36.** The whole records and papers relating to factories, guardianships, tutories, and curatories retained in the accountant's office shall be open to inspection on payment of such fees as may be fixed by the Court; but shall remain in the office, and not be lent out unless under authority of the Court or of the Lord Ordinary, and copies therefrom, attested by the accountant, shall have the same authority as the originals themselves, and shall be furnished to any party requiring the same, on payment therefor of such fees as may be fixed by the Court; and such fees for inspection and attested copies shall be paid weekly by the accountant into the fund hereinafter established.

NOTE

[1] As amended by the Age of Legal Capacity (Scotland) Act 1991 (c. 50), Sched. 1, para. 13.

Banks to accumulate principal and interest on accounts and deposits

[1] **37.** From and after the passing of this Act, every institution such as is mentioned in paragraphs (*a*) to (*c*) of section 5(1) of this Act with which any money shall have been or shall be deposited or lodged by any judicial factor, guardian, tutor, or curator, or under authority of any Court in Scotland, or with reference to any suit in any Court in Scotland, whether on deposit receipt or on account current, or otherwise, shall once at least in every year accumulate the interest with the principal sum, so that both shall thereafter bear interest together as principal; and any such institution failing so to do shall be liable to account as if such money had been so accumulated.

NOTE

[1] As amended by the Law Reform (Miscellaneous Provisions) (Scotland) Act 1990 (c. 40), Sched. 8, para. 21(4), and the Age of Legal Capacity (Scotland) Act 1991 (c. 50), Sched. 1, para. 14.

Provision for Accountant's illness or temporary absence

38. In case of the illness or temporary absence of the accountant, the Lord President of the Court of Session, or other judge acting as President for the time, may authorise any one of the accountant's clerks or other qualified person to discharge the duties of the accountant for the time.

39. [Repealed by the Statute Law Revision Act 1891 (c. 67).]

Power to pass Acts of Sederunt

[1] **40.** It shall be competent to the Court of Session, and they are hereby authorised and required, from time to time to pass such Acts of Sederunt as shall be necessary or proper for the further regulation of the manner of appointing judicial factors, and the manner of discharging their duty, and the manner of discharging the duties of the accountant, and the manner of applying the provisions of this Act to the case of guardians, tutors and curators, and the forms of process to be used in pursuance of this Act, and the manner of verifying by affidavit, declaration, certificate, or otherwise, the sufficiency of the caution offered for factors, guardians, tutors, and curators, and all other matters requisite for more effectually carrying out the purposes of this Act.

NOTE
[1] As amended by the Age of Legal Capacity (Scotland) Act 1991, Sched. 1, para. 15.

41. [Repealed by the Statute Law Revision Act 1875.]

[1] Judicial Factors (Scotland) Act 1880

(43 & 44 Vict. c. 4)

NOTE
[1] Amended by the Judicial Factors (Scotland) Act 1889, s. 6 (all judicial factors to be under the supervision of the accountant).

An Act to provide for the appointment of judicial factors in sheriff courts in Scotland. [9th July 1880]

Short title

1. This Act may be cited for all purposes as the Judicial Factors (Scotland) Act 1880.

2. [Repealed by the Statute Law Revision Act 1894.]

Interpretation of terms

[1] **3.** In this Act the following words and expressions shall have the meanings hereinafter assigned to them, unless there be something in the subject or context repugnant to such construction; that is to say—

The expression "judicial factor" shall include a *curator bonis*, a factor *loco absentis*, a factor on trust or other estates, and a guardian where caution is required, but does not include a judicial factor appointed under section 11A of the Judicial Factors (Scotland) Act 1889:

The expressions "accountant of the Court of Session" or "accountant", shall mean the accountant of the Court of Session appointed under the recited Act:

The expression "prescribed" means prescribed by the regulations which the Court of Session are by this Act authorised to make from time to time by act of sederunt:

The expression "Lord Ordinary" shall mean the Lord Ordinary in the Court of Session discharging the duties of junior Lord Ordinary in time of session, and the Lord Ordinary on the Bills in the time of vacation:

"Estate" shall include all property and funds, and all rights heritable and moveable.

NOTE
[1] As amended by the Law Reform (Miscellaneous Provisions) (Scotland) Act 1980, s. 14(*a*), the Bankruptcy (Scotland) Act 1985, Sched. 7, para. 1, and the Age of Legal Capacity (Scotland) Act 1991, Sched. 2.

Sheriff empowered to appoint judicial factors in small estates

[1] **4.** The sheriff shall have the same powers to appoint judicial factors as have the Court of Session and he shall have and may exercise over and with regard to judicial factors appointed in the sheriff court the same powers and authorities that under the recited Act either division of the Court of Session or the Lord Ordinary respectively have and may exercise under the recited Act over and with regard to judicial factors appointed in the Court of Session; and for the purposes of this enactment the following provisions shall have effect; that is to say—

[2] (1) Proceedings for appointment of judicial factors in the sheriff court shall commence by petition to be presented in an appropriate sheriff court as nearly as may be in the form in use in ordinary actions in that court:

[3] (1A) In paragraph 1 above, the expression "appropriate sheriff court"—

(*a*) in the case of a petition for the appointment of a judicial factor on a trust estate, shall have the same meaning as in sections 22 to 24 of the Trusts (Scotland) Act 1921; and

(*b*) in any other case shall mean—

(i) where the petition is for the appointment of a judicial factor (other than a factor *loco absentis*) to an individual, a sheriff court of the sheriffdom in which the individual is resident;

(ii) where the petition is for the appointment of a factor *loco absentis* to an individual, a sheriff court of the sheriffdom in which the individual was last known to the petitioner to be resident; or

(iii) where the petition is not as mentioned in either of the foregoing provisions of this sub-paragraph, the sheriff court at Edinburgh:

(2) (3). [Repealed by the Law Reform (Miscellaneous Provisions) (Scotland) Act 1980, Sched. 3.]

(4) Subject to such rules as may from time to time be made by act of sederunt as hereinafter provided, the whole provisions of the recited Act, and any Acts amending the same, and any acts of sederunt made in terms thereof applicable to judicial factors appointed in the Court of Session, shall apply as nearly as may be to judicial factors appointed in the sheriff court:

(5) In all cases of any appeal or reclaiming note being competent from a determination of the Lord Ordinary in the Court of Session to a division of the Inner House of that court an appeal shall be competent in the like cases from a determination by a sheriff to the sheriff principal, and in all cases of the Accountant of the Court of Session being bound to make any report to the Lord Ordinary in the Court of Session he shall be bound in the like case to make his report to a sheriff principal or sheriff:

(6) Until otherwise prescribed, proceedings in the fixing of caution, in applying for special powers, in the auditing of accounts, in the exoneration and discharge or removal of judicial factors, and all other proceedings necessary for the management of the estates dealt with under this Act, shall be taken in the sheriff court in as nearly as may be the same form and manner in which the like proceedings are taken before the Lord Ordinary:

(7) It shall be the duty of the accountant, when it appears to him that there is a diversity of judgment or practice in proceedings in judicial factories in the sheriff courts which it would be important to put an end to, to report the same to the First Division of the Court of Session, specifying the proceedings in which such diversity appeared, and asking for a rule to be laid down to secure uniformity of judgment or practice in such proceedings, and the court shall consider such report, and if they shall see fit shall lay down such a rule accordingly, which rule the several sheriffs and their substitutes shall be bound to observe:

(8) Decrees in absence shall not be opened up after the elapse of twelve months:

(9) It shall be competent for the sheriff principal or for the Court of Session, upon the application of any person interested, to recall any appointment made under this Act:

(10) The decision of the sheriff principal in all cases under this Act shall be final, and the decision of the Court of Session in all applications for recall of appointments under this Act shall be final.

NOTES

[1] As amended by the Mental Health (Scotland) Act 1960, Sched. 4, the Sheriff Courts (Scotland) Act 1971, Sched. 4 and the Law Reform (Miscellaneous Provisions) (Scotland) Act 1980, s. 14(*b*).

[2] As substituted by the Law Reform (Miscellaneous Provisions) (Scotland) Act 1980, s. 14(*b*)(ii).

[3] Inserted by the Law Reform (Miscellaneous Provisions) (Scotland) Act 1980, s. 14(*b*)(ii).

Power to pass acts of sederunt

5. It shall be competent to the Court of Session, and they are hereby authorised and required, from time to time to pass such acts of sederunt as shall be necessary or proper for regulating or prescribing the manner of appointing judicial factors in the sheriff courts, and of finding caution by such judicial factors, and the manner in which such judicial factors shall discharge their duties, and the manner in which the accountant shall discharge his duties, and the forms of process to be used in pursuance of this Act, and the manner of verifying by affidavit, declaration, certificate, or otherwise the sufficiency of the caution offered for judicial factors in the sheriff courts, and all other matters requisite for more effectually carrying out the purposes of this Act.

Fees payable by estates deriving benefit from Act

[1] **6.** There shall be payable by each estate under charge of a judicial factor appointed under this Act, such fees as shall from time to time be authorised by the Court of Session, having due regard to the sums required for the purposes of this Act and to the interests of the estates to be benefited thereby; and it shall be lawful for the Lords Commissioners of Her Majesty's Treasury to make such additions as they shall think fit to the salaries of the Accountant and clerks appointed and acting under the recited Act, and to grant such salary or salaries as shall seem proper to any other clerk or clerks who the said Commissioners shall think fit to appoint for the purposes of this Act.

NOTE

[1] As amended by the Statute Law Revision Act 1894.

Judicial Factors (Scotland) Act 1889

(52 & 53 Vict. c. 39)

An Act to amend and extend the law relating to judicial factors and others in Scotland and to unite the Offices of the Accountant of the Court of Session and the Accountant in Bankruptcy in Scotland. [12th August 1889]

Appointment of accountant

[1] **1.** It shall be lawful for Her Majesty to appoint a person versant in law and accounts, to be called the accountant of court (hereinafter referred to as the accountant), with such yearly salary as may from time to time be fixed by the Treasury, payable out of any moneys to be voted by Parliament for that purpose, and the accountant shall, subject to the approval of the Secretary for Scotland, appoint such number of clerks as may from time to time be necessary, and with such salaries as may be fixed by the Treasury, which salaries shall be paid out of any moneys to be voted by Parliament for that purpose.

The principal civil service pensions scheme within the meaning of section 2 of the Superannuation Act 1972 and for the time being in force shall apply in relation to the accountant and the said clerks as it applies in relation to persons to whom section 1 of that Act applies.

NOTE

[1] As amended by the Statute Law Revision Acts 1908 and 1963 and the Superannuation Act 1972 (c. 11), Sched. 6, para. 2.

Accountant to hold no other office

[1] **2.** The accountant to be appointed under this Act, and his successors in office, shall hold no other office, and shall not directly or indirectly, by

himself or any partner, be engaged in or transact any business for profit other than the business devolving upon him as accountant of court.

NOTE

[1] As amended by the Bankruptcy (Scotland) Act 1985 (c. 66), Sched. 7, para. 3, and the Bankruptcy (Scotland) Act 1993 (c. 6), Sched. 2 (effective 1st April 1993: S.I. 1993 No. 438).

3, 4. [Repealed by the Statute Law Revision Act 1963.]

Judicial Factors and Bankruptcy Acts to apply to accountant

[1] **5.** The provisions of the Judicial Factors Act 1849 relating to the accountant of the Court of Session shall, so far as not altered by this Act, apply to the accountant to be appointed in terms of this Act and his successors in office.

NOTE

[1] As amended by the Bankruptcy (Scotland) Act 1985 (c. 66), Sched. 8.

All judicial factors to be under supervision of accountant

[1] **6.** In addition to the factors specified in the recited Act of 1849, the accountant shall superintend the conduct of all other factors and persons already appointed or to be appointed by the Court of Session or any of the Lords Ordinary in the said court, or by any of the sheriffs principal or sheriffs in the several sheriff courts in Scotland, to hold, administer, or protect any property or funds belonging to persons or estates in Scotland; and all such factors and others, subject to such rules as may from time to time be made by Acts of sederunt as hereinafter provided, shall be and hereby are made subject to the provisions affecting judicial factors of the said recited Act of 1849, and of any Acts amending the same, or in terms of the Judicial Factors (Scotland) Act 1880, and of any Acts of sederunt made in terms of said Acts, and the accountant shall see that they duly observe all rules and regulations affecting them for the time: Provided that nothing in this section contained shall be held to apply to executors dative or to trustees appointed by the court under the Trusts (Scotland) Acts, the Entail (Scotland) Act 1882, or in virtue of any other power; but nothing in this section contained shall prevent trustees appointed by the court from availing themselves of the powers contained in section 18 of this Act.

NOTE

[1] Excluded by the Criminal Justice (Scotland) Act 1987 (c. 41), s. 13(8).

Penalties for misconduct

7. Any person who in virtue of his office is subject to the provisions of this Act, and who fails to comply therewith, or who misconducts himself or fails in the discharge of his duties, shall be liable to the penalties imposed by section 6 of the Judicial Factors Act 1849, or to any one or more of them as the court in its discretion shall decide.

8, 9. [Repealed by the Statute Law Revision Act 1963.]

Accountant in certain cases to apply for appointment of successor to factor deceased

10. In the event of its being found that any factor or other person referred to in section 6 hereof has died undischarged or has ceased to discharge the duties of his office without anyone having been appointed in succession to him, unless the purposes of his appointment have, in the opinion of the accountant, been exhausted, it shall be the duty of the accountant, unless the persons interested in such factory or any of them shall make the application on his requisition, to apply to the court for the appointment of a factor in place of such factor or other person, and it shall be the duty of the factor so appointed to investigate the accounts of the former factor or other person aforesaid, and to receive any balance due from his representatives or his cautioner or cautioners.

11. [Repealed by the Age of Legal Capacity (Scotland) Act 1991, Sched. 2.]

Application for judicial factor on estate of person deceased

[1] **11A.**—(1) It shall be competent to one or more creditors of parties deceased, or to persons having an interest in the succession of such parties, in the event of the deceased having left no settlement appointing trustees or other parties having power to manage his estate or part thereof, or in the event of such parties not accepting or acting, to apply by summary petition to the Court of Session or to the sheriff of the sheriffdom within which the deceased resided or carried on business during the year immediately preceding the date of the petition, or within which heritage belonging to the deceased at the time of his death is situated, for the appointment of a judicial factor.

(2) After such intimation of the petition to the creditors of the deceased, and other persons interested, as may be considered necessary, and after hearing parties, the court or sheriff may appoint such factor, who shall administer the estate subject to the supervision of the accountant in accordance with this Act and the Judicial Factors (Scotland) Act 1880 and relative acts of sederunt[2]; and, if the deceased's estate is absolutely insolvent within the meaning of section 73(2) of the Bankruptcy (Scotland) Act 1985, section 51 of, and Schedule 1 to, that Act shall apply as if for references to—

(*a*) the interim trustee or permanent trustee there were substituted references to the judicial factor; and

(*b*) the date of sequestration there were substituted references to the date of the judicial factor's appointment.

NOTES

[1] Inserted by the Bankruptcy (Scotland) Act 1985, Sched. 7, para. 4. See the Third Parties (Rights Against Insurers) Act 1930, s. 4(*b*), the Conveyancing and Feudal Reform (Scotland) Act 1970, Sched. 3, para. 9(2)(*b*), the Road Traffic Act 1972, s. 150(2), the Employment Protection (Consolidation) Act 1978, ss. 106(6) and 125(2), and the Value Added Tax Act 1983, s. 22(4)(*a*)(ii), all as amended by the said Sched. 7. See also the said 1985 Act, ss. 34(2), 36(1) and (6), and 37(7) and (9).

[2] See Rule of Court 201, reprinted in Division C.

Judicial factor's duties to be regulated by act of sederunt

[1] **11B.** The Court of Session shall have full power to regulate by act of sederunt—

(*a*) the caution to be found by a factor appointed under section 11A above;

(*b*) the mode in which he shall proceed in realising and dividing the funds, and otherwise in the discharge of his duties; and

(*c*) any other matter which they may deem necessary.

NOTE

[1] Inserted by the Bankruptcy (Scotland) Act 1985, Sched. 7, para. 4.

Audit of accounts

12. In all cases coming for the first time under the supervision of the accountant he shall be required to audit the accounts from their commencement, and if for this purpose it shall appear to him to be necessary, he shall have power to remit such cases or any of them to such duly qualified persons as he may with the approval of the Lord Advocate select to audit, but all such audits shall be supervised by him, and he shall be responsible for the correctness thereof, and such persons shall be paid such remuneration for their services in such audit as the Lord Advocate with the approval of the Treasury shall determine, out of moneys to be provided by Parliament.

Provided always, that the accountant may, if he thinks fit, on the production of reports of a professional or official auditor in any case, accept such report as sufficient for the period up to the date thereof, and shall not be required to audit the said accounts for that period.

As to funds, etc., furth of Scotland

[1] **13.** An official certified copy interlocutor of the appointment of any judicial factor, trustee, tutor, curator, or other person judicially appointed and subject to the provisions of the recited Acts or of this Act, shall have throughout the British dominions, as well out of Scotland as in Scotland, the full force and effect of an assignment or transfer, executed in legal and appropriate form, of all funds, property, and effects situated or invested in any part of the British dominions, and belonging to or forming part of the estate under his charge; and all debtors and others holding any such funds, property, or effects, shall be bound, on production of such official certified copy interlocutor, to pay over, assign, or transfer the same to such judicial factor, trustee, tutor, curator, or other person.

NOTE

[1] As amended by S.I. 1967 No. 487.

Procedure

[1] **14.** All applications under this Act or any of the recited Acts shall, except as after mentioned, and notwithstanding any provision in any of the recited Acts to the contrary, be dealt with in the manner directed by sections 4, 5, 6, and 10 of the Court of Session Act 1857.

NOTE

[1] As amended by the Bankruptcy (Scotland) Act 1985, Sched. 8.

15, 16. [Repealed by the Bankruptcy (Scotland) Act 1985, Sched. 8.]

17. [Repealed by the Bankruptcy (Scotland) Act 1913, Sched. 1.]

18, 19. [Repealed by the Trusts (Scotland) Act 1921, Sched. C.]

Application of section 23 of Judicial Factors Act

20. Section 23 of the Judicial Factors Act 1849 (as to factories informally settled), shall be held to apply to all factories brought under the supervision of the accountant by virtue of this Act.

Acts of Sederunt

21. It shall be competent to the Court of Session, and they are hereby authorised and required, from time to time to pass such Acts of Sederunt as shall be necessary or proper relating to all matters requisite for effectually carrying out the purposes of this Act.

22. [Repealed by the Bankruptcy (Scotland) Act 1985, Sched. 8.]

Short title

23. This Act may be cited as the Judicial Factors (Scotland) Act 1889.

[1] Trusts (Scotland) Act 1921

(11 & 12 Geo. 5, c. 58)

NOTE

[1] The Trustee Investments Act 1961, Sched. 4, para. 1 provides:—"References in the Trusts (Scotland) Act 1921, to section 10 or 11 of that Act, or to provisions which include either of those sections, shall be construed respectively as references to section 1 of this Act and as including references to that section".

An Act to consolidate and amend the law relating to trusts in Scotland. [19th August 1921]

Citation

1. This Act may be cited as the Trusts (Scotland) Act 1921.

Definitions

[1] **2.** In the construction of this Act unless the context otherwise requires—

[2] "Trust" shall mean and include—

(*a*) any trust constituted by any deed or other writing, or by private or local Act of Parliament, or by Royal Charter, or by resolution of any corporation or public or ecclesiastical body, and

(*b*) the appointment of any tutor, curator, guardian or judicial factor by deed, decree, or otherwise;

"Trust deed" shall mean and include—

(*a*) any deed or other writing, private or local Act of Parliament, Royal Charter, or resolution of any corporation or ecclesiastical body, constituting any trust, and

(*b*) any decree, deed, or other writing appointing a tutor, curator, guardian or judicial factor;

[3] "Trustee" shall mean and include any trustee under any trust whether nominated, appointed, judicially or otherwise, or assumed, whether sole or joint, and whether entitled or not to receive any benefit under the trust or any remuneration as trustee for his services, and shall include any trustee *ex officio*, executor nominate, tutor, curator, guardian (including a father or mother acting as guardian of a child under the age of 16 years) and judicial factor;

[4] "Judicial factor" shall mean any person holding a judicial appointment as a factor or curator on another person's estate;

"Local authority" and "rate" shall have respectively the meanings assigned to these expressions by the Local Authorities Loans (Scotland) Act 1891;

"The court" shall mean the Court of Session;

NOTES

[1] As repealed in part by the Statute Law (Repeals) Act 1976 and amended by the Age of Legal Capacity (Scotland) Act 1991, Sched. 1, para. 25.

[2] Applied: see the Children Act 1975, s.74.

[3] As amended by the Law Reform (Parent and Child) (Scotland) Act 1986, Sched. 1, para. 4. Now also includes an executor-dative—see the Succession (Scotland) Act 1964, s.20.

[4] As substituted by the Trusts (Scotland) Act 1961, s.3.

[THE NEXT PAGE IS M 19]

What trusts shall be held to include

3. All trusts shall be held to include the following powers and provisions unless the contrary be expressed (that is to say):—

(*a*) Power to any trustee to resign the office of trustee;

(*b*) Power to the trustee, if there be only one, or to the trustees, if there be more than one, or to a quorum of the trustees, if there be more than two, to assume new trustees;

(*c*) A provision that a majority of the trustees accepting and surviving shall be a quorum;

(*d*) A provision that each trustee shall be liable only for his own acts and intromissions and shall not be liable for the acts and intromissions of co-trustees and shall not be liable for omissions:

Provided that—

(1) A sole trustee shall not be entitled to resign his office by virtue of this Act unless either (1) he has assumed new trustees and they have declared their acceptance of office, or (2) the court shall have appointed new trustees or a judicial factor as hereinafter in this Act provided; and

(2) A trustee who has accepted any legacy or bequest or annuity expressly given on condition of the recipient thereof accepting the office of trustee under the trust shall not be entitled to resign the office of trustee by virtue of this Act, unless otherwise expressly declared in the trust deed, nor shall any trustee appointed to the office of trustee on the footing of receiving remuneration for his services be entitled so to resign that office in the absence of an express power to resign; but it shall be competent to the court, on the petition of any trustee to whom the foregoing provisions of this proviso apply, to grant authority to such trustee to resign the office of trustee on such conditions (if any) with respect to repayment or otherwise of his legacy as the court may think just; and

(3) A judicial factor shall not, by virtue of this Act, have the power of assumption, nor shall he have the power by virtue of this Act to resign his office without judicial authority.

Nothing in this section shall affect any liability incurred by any trustee prior to the date of any resignation or assumption under the provisions of this Act or of any Act repealed by this Act.

General powers of trustees

[1] **4.**—(1) In all trusts the trustees shall have power to do the following acts, where such acts are not at variance with the terms or purposes of the trust, and such acts when done shall be as effectual as if such powers had been contained in the trust deed, *viz.*:—

(*a*) To sell the trust estate or any part thereof, heritable as well as moveable.

(*b*) To grant feus of the heritable estate or any part thereof.

(*c*) To grant leases of any duration (including mineral leases) of the heritable estate or any part thereof and to remove tenants.

(*d*) To borrow money on the security of the trust estate or any part thereof, heritable as well as moveable.

(*e*) To excamb any part ot the trust estate which is heritable.

[2] (*ee*) To acquire with funds of the trust estate any interest in residential accommodation (whether in Scotland or elsewhere) reasonably required to enable the trustees to provide a suitable residence for occupation by any of the beneficiaries.

(*f*) To appoint factors and law agents and to pay them suitable remuneration.

(*g*) To discharge trustees who have resigned and the representatives of trustees who have died.

(*h*) To uplift, discharge, or assign debts due to the trust estate.

(*i*) To compromise or to submit and refer all claims connected with the trust estate.

(*j*) To refrain from doing diligence for the recovery of any debt due to the truster which the trustees may reasonably deem irrecoverable.

(*k*) To grant all deeds necessary for carrying into effect the powers vested in the trustees.

(*l*) To pay debts due by the truster or by the trust estate without requiring the creditors to constitute such debts where the trustees are satisfied that the debts are proper debts of the trust.

(*m*) To make abatement or reduction, either temporary or permanent, of the rent, lordship, royalty, or other consideration stipulated in any lease of land, houses, tenements, minerals, metals, or other subjects, and to accept renunciations of leases of any such subjects.

(*n*) To apply the whole or any part of trust funds which the trustees are empowered or directed by the trust deed to invest in the purchase of heritable property in the payment or redemption of any debt or burden affecting heritable property which may be destined to the same series of heirs and subject to the same conditions as are by the trust deed made applicable to heritable property directed to be purchased.

[3] (*o*) To concur, in respect of any securities of a company (being securities comprised in the trust estate), in any scheme or arrangement—

(i) for the reconstruction of the company,

(ii) for the sale of all or any part of the property and undertaking of the company to another company,

(iii) for the acquisition of the securities of the company, or of control thereof, by another company,

(iv) for the amalgamation of the company with another company, or

(v) for the release, modification, or variation of any rights, privileges or liabilities attached to the securities or any of them,

in like manner as if the trustees were entitled to such securities beneficially; to accept any securities of any denomination or description of the reconstructed or purchasing or new company in lieu of, or in exchange for, all or any of the first mentioned securities; and to retain any securities so accepted as aforesaid for any period for which the trustees could have properly retained the original securities.

[3] (*p*) To exercise, to such extent as the trustees think fit, any conditional or preferential right to subscribe for any securities in a company (being a right offered to them in respect of any holding in the company), to apply capital money of the trust estate in payment of the consideration, and to retain any such securities for which they have subscribed for any period for which they have power to retain the holding in respect of which the right to subscribe for the securities was offered (but subject to any conditions subject to which they have that power); to renounce, to such extent as they think fit, any such right; or to assign, to such extent as they think fit and for the best consideration that can reasonably be obtained, the benefit of such right or the title thereto to any person, including any beneficiary under the trust.

(2) This section shall apply to acts done before as well as after the passing of this Act, but shall not apply so as to affect any question relating to an act enumerated in head (*a*), (*b*), (*c*), (*d*), or (*e*) of this section which may, at the passing of this Act, be the subject of a depending action.

NOTES

[1] Extended: see the National Parks, etc., Act 1949, s. 16(5)(*b*); the Forestry Act 1967, Sched. 2; the Countryside (Scotland) Act 1967, s. 13(5); the Agriculture Act 1970, s. 33; the Ancient Monuments and Archaeological Areas Act 1979, s. 18(5); and the Field Monuments Act 1972, s. 1(4) and Sched., para. 2(2).

[2] Added by the Trusts (Scotland) Act 1961, s. 4.

[3] Added by the Trustee Investments Act 1961, s. 10.

Powers which may be granted to trustees by the court

5. It shall be competent to the court, on the petition of the trustees under any trust, to grant authority to the trustees to do any of the acts mentioned in the section of this Act relating to general powers of trustees, notwithstanding that such act is at variance with the terms or purposes of the trust, on being satisfied that such act is in all the circumstances expedient for the execution of the trust.

In this section the expression "trust" shall not include any trust constituted by private or local Act of Parliament, and the expression "trustees" shall be construed accordingly.

Method of sale by trustees

6. All powers of sale conferred on trustees by the trust deed or by virtue of this Act may be exercised either by public roup or private bargain unless otherwise directed in the trust deed or in the authority given by the court, and when the estate is heritable it shall be lawful in the exercise of such powers to sell subject to or under reservations of a feu-duty or ground annual at such rate and on such conditions as may be agreed upon, and in such sales and feus it shall be lawful to reserve the mines and minerals.

Deeds granted by trustees

7. Any deed bearing to be granted by the trustees under any trust, and in fact executed by a quorum of such trustees in favour of any person other than a beneficiary or a co-trustee under the trust where such person has dealt onerously and in good faith shall not be void or challengeable on the ground that any trustee or trustees under the trust was or were not consulted in the matter, or was or were not present at any meeting of trustees where the same was considered, or did not consent to or concur in the granting of the deed, or on the ground of any other omission or irregularity of procedure on the part of the trustees or any of them in relation to the granting of the deed.

Nothing in this section shall affect any question of liability or otherwise between any trustee under any trust on the one hand and any co-trustee or beneficiary under such trust on the other hand. This section shall apply to deeds granted before as well as after the passing of this Act, but shall not apply so as to affect any question which may, at the passing of this Act, be the subject of a depending action.

In this section the expression "quorum" means a quorum of the trustees under any trust entitled to act in terms of the trust deed or in virtue of this Act, or of any Act repealed by this Act, as the case may be.

Conveyances to non-existing or unidentifiable persons

8.—(1) Where in any deed, whether *inter vivos* or *mortis causa*, heritable or moveable property is conveyed to any person in liferent, and in fee to persons who, when such conveyance comes into operation, are unborn or incapable of ascertainment, the person to whom the property is conveyed in liferent shall not be deemed to be beneficially entitled to the property in fee by reason only that the liferent is not expressed in the deed to be a liferent allenarly; and all such conveyances as aforesaid shall, unless a contrary intention appears in the deed, take effect in the same manner and in all respects as if the liferent were declared to be a liferent allenarly; provided always that this subsection shall not apply to any conveyance which has come into operation before the passing of this Act.

For the purposes of this subsection, the date at which any conveyance in liferent and fee as aforesaid comes into operation shall be deemed to be the date at which the person to whom the liferent is conveyed first becomes entitled to receive the rents or income of the property.

(2) Where under any conveyance, whether coming into operation before or after the passing of this Act, any property is conveyed to one person in liferent and in fee to persons who, when such conveyance comes into operation, are unborn or incapable of ascertainment, it shall be competent to the court, on the application of the liferenter, whether or not he would, according to the existing law, be deemed to be fiduciary fiar, or of any person to whom the fee or any part thereof bears to be presumptively destined, or who may have an interest under such conveyance notwithstanding that such interest is prospective or contingent, or of the accountant of court:—

(*a*) To grant authority to the fiduciary fiar to exercise all or such of the powers, or to do all or such of the acts, competent to a trustee at common law or under this Act, as to the court may seem fit:

(*b*) To appoint a trustee or trustees (of whom the liferenter or fiduciary fiar may be one) with all the powers of trustees at common law and under this Act, or a judicial factor, to hold the said property in trust in place of the liferenter or fiduciary fiar; and to authorise and ordain the fiduciary fiar to execute and deliver all such deeds as may be necessary for the completion of title to the said property by such trustee or trustees or judicial factor; or otherwise, to grant warrant to such trustee or trustees or judicial factor to complete a title to the said property in the same manner and to the same effect as under a warrant in favour of a trustee or trustees granted in terms of the section of this Act relating to the appointment of new trustees by the court, or a warrant in favour of a judicial factor granted in terms of section 24 of the Titles to Land Consolidation (Scotland) Act 1868 or section 44 of the Conveyancing (Scotland) Act 1874, as the case may be. The expense of completing the title as aforesaid shall, unless the court otherwise directs, be a charge against the capital of the estate.

(3) For the purposes of this section, all references to a trust deed in this Act contained shall be read and construed as a reference to the conveyance of the property in liferent and fee as aforesaid.

Liferents of personal estate beyond certain limits prohibited

[1] **9.** It shall be competent to constitute or reserve by means of a trust or otherwise a liferent interest in moveable and personal estate in Scotland in favour only of a person in life at the date of the deed constituting or reserving such liferent, and, where any moveable or personal estate in Scotland shall, by virtue of any deed dated after the 31st day of July 1868 (the date of any testamentary or *mortis causa* deed being taken to be the date of the death of the granter, and the date of any contract of marriage being taken to be the date of the dissolution of the marriage) be held in liferent by or for behoof of a person of full age born after the date of such deed, such moveable or personal estate shall belong absolutely to such person, and, where such estate stands invested in the name of any trustees, such trustees shall be bound to deliver, make over, or convey such estate to such person:

Provided always that, where more persons than one are interested in the moveable or personal estate held by trustees as hereinbefore mentioned, all the expenses connected with the transference of a portion of such estate to any of the beneficiaries in terms of this section shall be borne by the beneficiary in whose favour the transference is made.

NOTE

[1] As amended by the Conveyancing (Scotland) Act 1924, s. 45 (termination of perpetual trusts of moveables): excluded by the Law Reform (Miscellaneous Provisions) (Scotland) Act 1968, s. 18 (4) which provides: "... section 9 of the Trusts (Scotland) Act 1921 shall not have effect in relation to any deed executed after the commencement of this Act".

10, 11. [Repealed by the Trustee Investments Act 1961, Sched. 5.]

Investment on charges under Improvement of Land Acts, etc.

[1] **12.**—(1) A trustee having power to invest in real securities, unless expressly forbidden by the trust deed, may invest, and shall be deemed to have always had power to invest, on any charge or on any mortgage on such charge made under the Improvement of Land Acts 1864 and 1899, or on any charge created for payment of estate or other Government duty under the Finance Act 1894, or the Finance (1909–10) Act 1910.

(2) A trustee having power to invest in the mortgages or bonds of any railway company or of any other description of company may, unless the contrary is expressed in the trust deed, invest in the debenture stock of a railway company or such other company as aforesaid.

(3), (4) [Repealed by the Trustee Investments Act 1961, Sched. 5.]

NOTE

[1] As amended by the Trustee Investments Act 1961, Sched. 5.

Power to invest notwithstanding drainage charges

[1] **13.** A trustee having power to invest in the purchase of land or on heritable security may invest in the purchase of or on heritable security over any land notwithstanding that the same is charged by an absolute order made under the Improvement of Land Act 1864, unless the terms of the trust expressly provide that the land to be purchased or taken in security shall not be subject to any such prior charge.

NOTE

[1] As amended by the Statute Law (Repeals) Act 1977.

Powers of investment in trust deeds not to be restricted

14.—(1) The powers of investment conferred upon trustees by the four immediately preceding sections of this Act shall not be held or construed as restricting or controlling any powers of investment of trust funds expressly contained in any trust deed.

(2) In the aforesaid sections and in this section the expression "trustee" includes any person holding funds in a fiduciary capacity, and the expressions "trust" and "trust deed" shall be construed accordingly.

Trustees not to hold certificates or bonds payable to bearer

15.—(1) A trustee, unless authorised by the terms of his trust, shall not apply for purchase, acquire, or hold beyond a reasonable time for realisation or conversion into registered or inscribed stock any certificate to bearer or debenture or other bond or document payable to bearer.

(2) Nothing in this section shall impose on the Bank of England or the Bank of Ireland or on any person authorised by or under any Act of Parliament to issue any such certificate, bond, or document any obligation to inquire whether a person applying for such a certificate, bond, or document is or is not a trustee, or subject them to any liability in the event of their

granting any such certificate, bond or document to a trustee, nor invalidate any such certificate, bond or document if granted.

The court may authorise the advance of part of the capital of a trust fund

16. The court may, from time to time under such conditions as they see fit, authorise trustees to advance any part of the capital of a fund destined either absolutely or contingently to beneficiaries who at the date of the application to the court are not of full age, if it shall appear that the income of the fund is insufficient or not applicable to, and that such advance is necessary for, the maintenance or education of such beneficiaries or any of them, and that it is not expressly prohibited by the trust deed, and that the rights of such beneficiaries, if contingent, are contingent only on their survivance.

Trustees may apply to court for superintendence order as to investment and distribution of estate

17. It shall be competent for the trustees under any trust deed or one or more of them to apply to the court for an order on the accountant of court to superintend their administration of the trust insofar as it relates to the investment of the trust funds and the distribution thereof among the creditors interested and the beneficiaries under the trust, and the court may grant such order accordingly, and if such order be granted the accountant of court shall annually examine and audit the accounts of such trustees, and at any time, if he thinks fit, he may report to the court upon any question that may arise in the administration of the trust with regard to any of the foresaid matters and obtain the directions of the court thereupon.

Discharge of trustees resigning and heirs of trustees dying during the subsistence of the trust

18. When a trustee who resigns or the representatives of a trustee who has died or resigned cannot obtain a discharge of his acts and intromissions from the remaining trustees, and when the beneficiaries of the trust refuse or are unable from absence, incapacity or otherwise to grant a discharge, the court may on petition to that effect at the instance of such trustee or representative and after such intimation and inquiry as may be thought necessary, grant such discharge.

Form of resignation of trustees

19.—(1) Subject to the provisions of subsection (2) of this section, any trustee entitled to resign his office may do so by minute of the trust entered in the sederunt book of the trust and signed in such sederunt book by such trustee and by the other trustee or trustees acting at the time, or he may do so by signing a minute of resignation in the form of Schedule A to this Act annexed or to the like effect, and may register the same in the books of council and session, and in such case he shall be bound to intimate the same to his co-trustee or trustees, and the resignation shall be held to take effect from and after the date of the receipt of such intimation, or the last date thereof if more than one, and in case after inquiry the residence of any trustee to whom intimation should be given under this provision cannot be found, such intimation shall be sent by post in a registered letter [1] addressed to the Keeper of the Register of Edictal Citations [2].

(2) A sole trustee desiring to resign his office may apply to the court stating such desire and praying for the appointment of new trustees or of a judicial factor to administer the trust, and the court, after intimation to the beneficiaries under the trust, or such of them as the court may direct, may thereafter appoint either a judicial factor or new trustees, and if the court appoint new trustees the court may grant warrant to complete title as

provided in the section of this Act relating to appointment of new trustees by the court.

NOTES

[1] Now also recorded delivery service: see the Recorded Delivery Service Act 1962.

[2] Functions of Keeper of Edictal Citations now exercisable by clerks and officers of the Court of Session: see the Reorganisation of Offices (Scotland) Act 1928, s.8, S.R. & O. 1929 No. 588 and the Public Records (Scotland) Act 1937, s.13.

Effect of resignation

20. Where a trustee entitled to resign his office shall have resigned in either of the modes provided by the immediately preceding section or otherwise, and his resignation shall have been duly completed, such trustee shall be thereby divested of the whole property and estate of the trust, which shall accrue to or devolve upon the continuing trustees or trustee without the necessity of any conveyance or other transfer by the resigning trustee, but without prejudice to the right of the continuing trustee or trustees to require the resigning trustee to execute and deliver to the continuing trustees or trustee at the expense of the trust a conveyance or transfer (or conveyances or transfers) of the property or estate belonging to the trust, or any part thereof if the continuing trustees or trustee shall consider this expedient, and the resigning trustee when so required shall be bound at the expense of the trust to execute and deliver such conveyance or conveyances, transfer or transfers accordingly.

Appointment of new or additional trustees by deed of assumption

21. When trustees have the power of assuming new trustees, such new trustees may be assumed by deed of assumption executed by the trustee or trustees acting under the trust deed or by a quorum of such trustees, if more than two, in the form of Schedule B to this Act annexed or to the like effect, and a deed of assumption so executed, in addition to a general conveyance of the trust estate, may contain a special conveyance of heritable property belonging to the trust estate, and in such case shall be effectual as a conveyance of such heritable property in favour of the existing trustees and the trustees so to be assumed, and such deed of assumption shall also be effectual as an assignation in favour of such existing and assumed trustees of the whole personal property belonging to the trust estate, and in the event of any trustee acting under any trust deed being insane or incapable of acting by reason of physical or mental disability or by continuous absence from the United Kingdom for a period of six months or upwards, such deed of assumption may be executed by the remaining trustee or trustees acting under such trust deed: Provided that, when the signatures of a quorum of trustees cannot be obtained, it shall be necessary to obtain the consent of the court to such deed of assumption on application either by the acting trustee or trustees or by any one or more of the beneficiaries under the trust deed.

Appointment of new trustees by the court

[1] **22.** When trustees cannot be assumed under any trust deed, or when any person who is the sole trustee appointed in or acting under any trust deed is or has become insane or is or has become incapable of acting by reason of physical or mental disability, or by being absent continuously from the United Kingdom for a period of at least six months, or by having disappeared for a like period, the Court of Session or an appropriate sheriff court may, upon the application of any party having interest in the trust estate, after such intimation and inquiry as may be thought necessary, appoint a trustee or trustees under such trust deed with all the powers incident to that office, and, on such appointment being made in the case of any person becoming insane or incapable of acting as aforesaid, such person shall cease to be a trustee under such trust deed, and the court to which

application is made may, on such application, grant a warrant[2] to complete a title to any heritable property forming part of the trust estate in favour of the trustee or trustees so appointed, which warrant shall specify and describe the heritable property to which it is applicable, or refer in terms of law to a recorded deed containing a description thereof, and shall also specify the moveable or personal property, or bear reference to an inventory appended to the petition to the court in which such moveable or personal property is specified, and such warrant shall be effectual as a conveyance of such heritable property in favour of the trustee or trustees so appointed in like manner and to the same effect as a warrant in favour of a judicial factor granted under the authority of section 24 of the Titles to Land Consolidation (Scotland) Act 1868, or section 44 of the Conveyancing (Scotland) Act 1874, and shall also be effectual as an assignation of such moveable or personal property in favour of the trustee or trustees so appointed.

NOTES

[1] As amended by the Law Reform (Miscellaneous Provisions) (Scotland) Act 1980, s.13(*a*). Applied by the Law Reform (Miscellaneous Provisions) (Scotland) Act 1990, s.7(4)(*f*).

[2] A warrant to complete title is no longer necessary in the case of a trustee appointed by the court: see the Conveyancing Amendment (Scotland) Act 1938, s.1.

Court may remove trustees in certain cases

[1] **23.** In the event of any trustee being or becoming insane or incapable of acting by reason of physical or mental disability or being absent from the United Kingdom continuously for a period of at least six months, or having disappeared for a like period, such trustee, in the case of insanity or incapacity of acting by reason of physical or mental disability, shall, and in the case of continuous absence from the United Kingdom or disappearance for a period of six months or upwards, may, on application in manner in this section provided by any co-trustee or any beneficiary or other person interested in the trust estate, be removed from office upon such evidence as shall satisfy the court to which the application is made of the insanity, incapacity, or continuous absence or disappearance of such trustee. Such application may be made either to the Court of Session or to an appropriate sheriff court.

NOTE

[1] As amended by the Law Reform (Miscellaneous Provisions) (Scotland) Act 1980, s.13.

Completion of title by the beneficiary of a lapsed trust

[1] **24.** Any person who shall be entitled to the possession for his own absolute use of any heritable property or moveable or personal property the title to which has been taken in the name of any trustee who has died or become incapable of acting without having executed a conveyance of such property, or any other person deriving right whether immediately or otherwise from the person entitled as aforesaid, may apply by petition to the Court of Session of an appropriate sheriff court for authority to complete a title to such property is his own name, and such petition shall specify and describe the heritable property, or refer to a description thereof in terms of law, and refer to an inventory in which the moveable or personal property is specified to which such title is to be completed and after such intimation and inquiry as may be thought necessary it shall be lawful for the court to which application is made to grant a warrant for completing such title as aforesaid, which warrant shall specify and describe the heritable property to which it is applicable, or refer in terms of law to a description thereof, and shall also specify the moveable or personal property or shall bear reference to an inventory appended to the petition in which such moveable or personal property is specified, and such warrant shall be effectual as a conveyance of such heritable property in favour of the petitioner in like manner and to the

same effect as a warrant in favour of a judicial factor granted under the authority of section 24 of the Titles to Land Consolidation (Scotland) Act 1868, or section 44 of the Conveyancing (Scotland) Act 1874, and shall also be effectual as an assignation of such moveable or personal property in favour of the petitioner.

NOTE

[1] As amended by the Law Reform (Miscellaneous Provisions) (Scotland) Act 1980, s. 13.

Interpretation of sections 22–24

[1] **24A.** In sections 22 to 24 of this Act the expression "appropriate sheriff court" means—

(*a*) in the case of a trust other than a marriage contract—

(i) where the truster, or any of the trusters, was at the date of the coming into operation of the trust domiciled in a sheriffdom, a sheriff court of that sheriffdom; or

(ii) where sub-paragraph (i) of this paragraph does not apply, or where the applicant does not possess sufficient information to enable him to determine which sheriff court, if any, would by virtue of that sub-paragraph be an appropriate sheriff court, the sheriff court at Edinburgh;

(*b*) in the case of a marriage contract—

(i) where either spouse is, or was when he died, domiciled in a sheriffdom, a sheriff court of that sheriffdom; or

(ii) where sub-paragraph (i) of this paragraph does not apply, or where the applicant does not possess sufficient information to enable him to determine which sheriff court, if any, would by virtue of that sub-paragraph be an appropriate sheriff court, the sheriff court at Edinburgh.

NOTE

[1] Inserted by the Law Reform (Miscellaneous Provisions) (Scotland) Act 1980, s. 13 (*d*).

Completion of title of judicial factors

25. Application for authority to complete the title of a judicial factor to any trust property or estate may be contained in the petition for the appointment of such factor, and such application may include moveable or personal property.

Powers of court under this Act to be exercised by Lord Ordinary

26. Applications to the court under the authority of this Act shall be by petition addressed to the court, and shall be brought in the first instance before one of the Lords Ordinary officiating in the Outer House, who may direct such intimation and service thereof and such investigation or inquiry as he may think fit, and the power of the Lord Ordinary before whom the petition is enrolled may be exercised by the Lord Ordinary on the Bills during vacation, and all such petitions shall, as respects procedure, disposal and review, be subject to the same rules and regulations as are enacted with respect to petitions coming before the Junior Lord Ordinary in virtue of the Court of Session Act 1857: Provided that, when in the exercise of the powers pertaining to the court of appointing trustees and regulating trusts, it shall be necessary to settle a scheme for the administration of any charitable or other permanent endowment, the Lord Ordinary shall, after preparing such scheme, report to one of the divisions of the court, by whom the same shall be finally adjusted and settled, and in all cases where it shall be necessary to settle any such scheme, intimation shall be made to His Majesty's Advocate, who shall be entitled to appear and intervene for the interests of the charity or any object of the trust or the public interest.

Court may pass Acts of Sederunt

[1] **27.** The court shall be and is hereby empowered from time to time to make such regulations by Act or Acts of Sederunt as may be requisite for carrying into effect the purposes of this Act.

NOTE

[1] As amended by the Trustee Investments Act 1961, Sched. 5.

Resignation of trustee who is also executor to infer resignation as executor

28. In all cases where a trust deed appoints the trustees to be also executors the resignation of any such trustee shall infer, unless where otherwise expressly declared, his resignation also as an executor under such trust deed.

Extent of liability of trustee

29. Where a trustee shall have improperly advanced trust money on a heritable security which would, at the time of the investment, have been a proper investment in all respects for a less sum than was actually advanced thereon, the security shall be deemed an authorised investment for such less sum, and the trustee shall only be liable to make good the sum advanced in excess thereof with interest.

Trustee not to be chargeable with breach of trust for lending money on security of any property on certain conditions

[1] **30.**—(1) Any trustee lending money on the security of any property shall not be chargeable with breach of trust by reason only of the proportion borne by the amount of the loan to the value of such property at the time when the loan was made, provided that it shall appear to the court that in making such loan the trustee was acting upon a report as to the value of the property made by a person whom the trustee reasonably believed to be an able practical valuator instructed and employed independently of any owner of the property, whether such valuator carried on business in the locality where the property is situated or elsewhere, and that the amount of the loan by itself or in combination with any other loan or loans upon the property ranking prior to or *pari passu* with the loan in question does not exceed two equal third parts of the value of the property as stated in such report, and this section shall apply to a loan upon any property on which the trustees can lawfully lend.

(2) This section shall apply to transfers of existing securities as well as to new securities, and in its application to a partial transfer of an existing security the expression " the amount of the loan " shall include the amount of any other loan or loans upon the property ranking prior to or *pari passu* with the loan in question.

NOTE

[1] See also the Trustee Investments Act 1961, s. 6 (7).

Power of court to make orders in case of breach of trust

31. Where a trustee shall have committed a breach of trust at the instigation or request or with the consent in writing of a beneficiary, the court may, if it shall think fit, make such order as to the court shall seem just for applying all or any part of the interest of the beneficiary in the trust estate by way of indemnity to the trustee or person claiming through him.

Court may relieve trustee from personal liability

32.—(1) If it appears to the court that a trustee is or may be personally liable for any breach of trust, whether the transaction alleged to be a breach of trust occurred before or after the passing of this Act, but has acted honestly and reasonably, and ought fairly to be excused for the breach of trust, then the court may relieve the trustee either wholly or partly from personal liability for the same.

(2) In this section and in the two immediately preceding sections the expression "the court" shall mean any court of competent jurisdiction in which a question relative to the actings, liability, or removal of a trustee comes to be tried.

Investment ceasing to be an authorised investment

[1] **33.** A trustee shall not be liable for breach of trust by reason only of his continuing to hold an investment which has ceased to be an investment authorised by the trust deed or by or under this Act.

NOTE

[1] See also the Trustee Investments Act 1961 (c. 62), s. 3(4) and Sched. 3, para. 2, *infra*.

Expenses of applications under this Act

34.—(1) The court shall determine all questions of expenses in relation to any application made under this Act, and may direct that any such expenses shall be paid out of the trust estate where the court considers this reasonable.

(2) In this section the expression "the court" shall include any court to which an application may be made under this Act.

Application of Act

35. Save as in this Act expressly otherwise provided—

(1) This Act shall apply to trusts which have come into operation before as well as to trusts coming into operation after the passing of this Act.

(2) Nothing in this Act contained shall be held to extend the liability of trustees.

36. [Repealed by the Statute Law Revision Act 1950 (c. 6).]

SCHEDULES

Section 19

[1] SCHEDULE A

FORM OF MINUTE OF RESIGNATION

NOTE

[1] As amended by the Requirements of Writing (Scotland) Act 1995 (c. 7), Sched. 4, para. 29 (effective 1st August 1995: s. 15(2)).

I, *A.B.*, do hereby resign the office of trustee under the trust disposition and settlement (*or other deed*) granted by *C.D.* dated the day of ,* (*If the trustee was assumed add,* and to which office of trustee I was assumed by deed of assumption granted by *E.F.* and *G.H.*, dated day of .*). Testing clause †

*If recorded specify register and date of recording.

†Note—Subscription of the document by the granter of it will be sufficient for the document to be formally valid, but witnessing of it may be necessary or desirable for other purposes (see the Requirements of Writing (Scotland) Act 1995).

Section 21

[1] SCHEDULE B

FORM OF DEED OF ASSUMPTION

NOTE

[1] As amended by the Requirements of Writing (Scotland) Act 1995 (c. 7), Sched. 4, para. 30 (effective 1st August 1995: s. 15(2)).

I, *A.B.* (*or* we, *A.B.* and *C.D.*), the accepting and surviving (*or* remaining) trustee (*or* trustees, *or* a majority and quorum of the accepting and surviving trustees), acting under a trust disposition and settlement (*or other deed*) granted by *E.F.*, dated the day of (*if recorded, specify register and date of recording*), do hereby assume *G.H.* (*or* *G.H.* and *I.K.*) as a trustee (*or* trustees) under the said trust disposition and settlement (*or other deed*); and I (*or* we) dispone and convey to myself (*or* ourselves) and the said *G.H.* (*or* *G.H.* and *I.K.*) as trustees under the said trust disposition and settlement (*or other deed*), and the survivors or survivor, and the heir of the last survivor, the majority, while more than two are acting, being a quorum (*or otherwise in accordance with the terms of the trust deed*), all and sundry the whole trust, estate and effects, heritable and moveable, real and personal, of every description and wherever situated, at present belonging to me (*or* us) or under my (*or* our) control as trustee (*or* surviving trustees, *or otherwise as the case may be*), under the said trust disposition and settlement (*or other deed*), together with the whole vouchers, titles, and instructions thereof. (*Then may follow, if wished, special conveyances of heritable or personal property, with the usual clauses of a conveyance applicable to such property, and as the case may require.*) Testing clause †

†Note—Subscription of the document by the granter or granters of it will be sufficient for the document to be formally valid, but witnessing of it may be necessary or desirable for other purposes (see the Requirements of Writing (Scotland) Act 1995).

SCHEDULE C

[Repealed by the Statute Law Revision Act 1950.]

Consular Conventions Act 1949

(12, 13 & 14 Geo. 6, c. 29)

An Act to confer upon the consular officers of foreign states with which consular conventions are concluded by His Majesty certain powers relating to the administration of the estates and properties of deceased persons; . . . [26th April 1949]

. . . . . .

Powers of consular officers in relation to property in Scotland of deceased persons

2.—(1) Where any person who is a national of a State to which this section applies is named as executor in the will of a deceased person disposing of property in Scotland, or is otherwise a person who may be appointed or confirmed as executor on the estate in Scotland of a deceased person, a consular officer of the said State, if satisfied that the said national is not resident in Scotland, and that he is not represented by a person duly authorised by power of attorney to act for him in that behalf, may make application to the court for the said national to be appointed or confirmed as executor on the estate of the deceased as if the said officer were so authorised as aforesaid.

(2) Where the court has granted an application for appointment or confirmation as executor on the estate of a deceased person made by a consular officer by virtue of this section that officer or his successors in office shall be entitled to receive and administer the said estate and to do all things necessary in that behalf as if duly authorised so to act by power of attorney granted by the executor.

(3) Where any person who is a national of a State to which this section applies—

(*a*) is entitled to payment or delivery of any money or property in respect of any interest in the estate of a deceased person or is entitled to payment or delivery of any money or property becoming due on the death of any person; or

(*b*) is a person to whom any money or property comprised in the estate of a deceased person may be paid or delivered in pursuance of any enactment, rule or regulation, whether passed or made before or after the commencement of this Act, authorising the payment or delivery of such money or property without production of confirmation;

then if the said national is not resident in Scotland a consular officer of that State shall have the like right and power to give a valid discharge for any such money or property in Scotland, to take all such steps as may be necessary for completing the title of the said national to such property and to administer or dispose of that property as if he were duly authorised by power of attorney to act for him in that behalf:

[THE NEXT PAGE IS M 31]

Provided that no person shall be authorised or required by this subsection to pay or deliver any money or property to a consular officer if it is within his knowledge that any other person in Scotland has been expressly authorised to receive that money or property on behalf of the said national.

Supplementary provisions as to sections 1 and 2

3. Notwithstanding any rule of law conferring immunity or privilege in respect of the official acts and documents of consular officers, a consular officer shall not be entitled to any immunity or privilege in respect of any act done by virtue of powers conferred on him by or under section one or section two of this Act, or in respect of any document for the time being in his possession relating thereto.

. . . . . .

Short title

9. This Act may be cited as the Consular Conventions Act 1949.

Trusts (Scotland) Act 1961

(9 & 10 Eliz. 2, c. 57)

An Act to amend the law of Scotland relating to trusts.

[27th July 1961]

Jurisdiction of court in relation to variation of trust purposes

[1] **1.**—(1) In relation to any trust taking effect, whether before or after the commencement of this Act, under any will, settlement or other disposition, the court may if it thinks fit, on the petition of the trustees or any of the beneficiaries, approve on behalf of—

[1a](*a*) any of the beneficiaries who because of any legal disability by reason of nonage or other incapacity is incapable of assenting, or

(*b*) any person (whether ascertained or not) who may become one of the beneficiaries as being at a future date or on the happening of a future event a person of any specified description or a member of any specified class of persons, so however that this paragraph shall not include any person who is capable of assenting and would be of that description, or a member of that class, as the case may be, if the said date had fallen or the said event had happened at the date of the presentation of the petition to the court, or

(*c*) any person unborn,

any arrangement (by whomsoever proposed, and whether or not there is any other person beneficially interested who is capable of assenting thereto) varying or revoking all or any of the trust purposes or enlarging the powers of the trustees of managing or administering the trust estate:

Provided that the court shall not approve an arrangement under this subsection on behalf of any person unless it is of the opinion that the carrying out thereof would not be prejudicial to that person.

[2] (2) For the purposes of the foregoing subsection a person who is of or over the age of 16 years but has not attained the age of 18 years shall be deemed to be incapable of assenting; but before approving an arrangement under that subsection on behalf of any such person the court shall take such account as it thinks appropriate of his attitude to the arrangement.

(3) [Repealed by the Age of Legal Capacity (Scotland) Act 1991, Sched. 2.]

(4) Where under any trust such as is mentioned in subsection (1) of this section a trust purpose entitles any of the beneficiaries (in this subsection referred to as "the alimentary beneficiary") to an alimentary liferent of, or any alimentary income from, the trust estate or any part thereof, the court may if it thinks fit, on the petition of the trustees or any of the beneficiaries, authorise any arrangement varying or revoking that trust purpose and making new provisions in lieu thereof, including, if the court thinks fit, new provision for the disposal of the fee or capital of the trust estate or, as the case may be, of such part thereof as was burdened with the liferent or the payment of the income:

Provided that the court shall not authorise an arrangement under this subsection unless—

(*a*) it considers that the carrying out of the arrangement would be reasonable, having regard to the income of the alimentary beneficiary from all sources, and to such other factors, if any, as the court considers material, and

(*b*) the arrangement is approved by the alimentary beneficiary, or, where the alimentary beneficiary is a person on whose behalf the court is empowered by subsection (1) of this section or that subsection as extended by subsection (2) of this section to approve the arrangement, the arrangement is so approved by the court under that subsection.

(5) Nothing in the foregoing provisions of this section shall be taken to limit or restrict any power possessed by the court apart from this section under any Act of Parliament or rule of law.

(6) In this section the expression "beneficiary" in relation to a trust includes any person having, directly or indirectly, an interest, whether vested or contingent, under the trust.

NOTES

[1] Extended by the Married Women's Policies of Assurance Act 1980, s.4. Saved by the Age of Legal Capacity (Scotland) Act 1991, s. 1(3)(*f*).

[1a] As amended by the Age of Legal Capacity (Scotland) Act 1991, Sched. 1, para. 27.

[2] As amended by the Age of Majority (Scotland) Act 1969, Sched. 1, and the Age of Legal Capacity (Scotland) Act 1991, Sched. 1, para. 27 and Sched. 2.

Validity of certain transactions by trustees

2.—(1) Where, after the commencement of this Act, the trustees under any trust enter into a transaction with any person (in this section referred to as "the second party"), being a transaction under which the trustees purport to do in relation to the trust estate or any part thereof an act of any of the descriptions specified in paragraphs (*a*) to (*ee*) of subsection (1) of section 4 of the Act of 1921 (which empowers trustees to do certain acts where such acts are not at variance with the terms or purposes of the trust) the validity of the transaction and of any title acquired by the second party under the transaction shall not be challengeable by the second party or any other person on the ground that the act in question is at variance with the terms or purposes of the trust:

Provided that in relation to a transaction entered into by trustees who are acting under the supervision of the accountant of court this section shall have effect only if the said accountant consents to the transaction.

[1] (2) Nothing in subsection (1) of this section shall affect any question of liability between any of the trustees on the one hand and any co-trustee or any of the beneficiaries on the other hand.

[1] (3) Without prejudice to the operation of subsection (1) of this section, where in relation to the trust estate or any part thereof a judicial factor thinks it expedient to do any of the acts mentioned in that subsection but the act in question might be at variance with the terms or purposes of the trust,

he may, subject to the following provisions of this section, apply to the accountant of court for his consent to the doing of the act.

[1] (4) Where an application is made under subsection (3) of this section to the accountant of court for his consent to the doing of an act to which that subsection applies, he may grant the application subject to such conditions (including conditions as to price) as he thinks fit if—

(*a*) he considers that the doing of the act is in the best interests of the owner of the trust estate to which the judicial factor's appointment relates or of any person to whom the owner owes a duty of support; and

(*b*) he is satisfied—

(i) that the judicial factor is not expressly prohibited by the terms of his appointment from doing the act; and

(ii) that there has been compliance with the provisions of subsection (5) of this section and of any rules made thereunder; and

(*c*) no objection is made to the doing of the act under subsection (5) of this section.

[1,2] (5) A judicial factor proposing to make an application under subsection (3) of this section to the accountant of court shall notify such persons or such class or classes of persons as may be specified in rules of court in such manner as may be so specified of the proposed application, the act to which it relates, and of their right to object to him doing that act within such time and in such manner as the rules may specify; and the rules may make different provision in respect of different classes of judicial factors, and may make provision exempting a judicial factor or a class of judicial factors from giving notification under this subsection in such circumstances as the rules may specify.

[1] (6) Where a judicial factor does any act in accordance with the consent of the accountant of court granted under subsection (4) of this section and in compliance with the provisions of this section and of any rules made thereunder, it shall be treated as being not at variance with the terms or purposes of the trust.

NOTES

[1] New subss. (2)–(6) substituted for former subs. (2) by the Law Reform (Miscellaneous Provisions) (Scotland) Act 1980, s. 8.

[2] See S.I. 1980 No. 1803, *infra*.

. . . . . .

Accumulations of income

[1] **5.**—(1) The following provisions of this section shall have effect in substitution for the provisions of the Accumulations Act 1800, and that Act is hereby repealed.

(2) No person may by any will, settlement or other disposition dispose of any property in such manner that the income thereof shall be wholly or partially accumulated for any longer period than one of the following, that is to say—

(*a*) the life of the grantor; or

(*b*) a term of twenty-one years from the death of the grantor; or

(*c*) the duration of the minority or respective minorities of any person or persons living or *in utero* at the death of the grantor; or

(*d*) the duration of the minority or respective minorities of any person or persons who, under the terms of the will, settlement or other disposition directing the accumulation, would for the time being, if of full age, be entitled to the income directed to be accumulated.

(3) In every case where any accumulation is directed otherwise than as aforesaid, the direction shall, save as hereinafter provided, be void, and the income directed to be accumulated shall, so long as the same is directed to be

accumulated contrary to this section, go to and be received by the person or persons who would have been entitled thereto if such accumulation had not been directed.

(4) For avoidance of doubt it is hereby declared that, in the case of a settlement or other disposition *inter vivos*, a direction to accumulate income during a period specified in paragraph (*d*) of subsection (2) of this section shall not be void, nor shall the accumulation of the income be contrary to this section, solely by reason of the fact that the period begins during the life of the grantor and ends after his death.

(5) The restrictions imposed by this section apply to wills, settlements and other dispositions made on or after the 28th day of July, 1800, but, in the case of wills, only where the testator was living and of testamentary capacity after the end of one year from that date.

(6) In this section " minority " in relation to any person means the period beginning with the birth of the person and ending with his attainment of the age of twenty-one years, and " grantor " includes settlor and, in relation to a will, the testator.

NOTE

[1] Amended by the Law Reform (Miscellaneous Provisions) (Scotland) Act 1966, s. 6, *infra*.

Interpretation

6.—(1) In this Act, unless the context otherwise requires,—

" Act of 1921 " means the Trusts (Scotland) Act 1921;

" the court " means the Court of Session; and

" trust " and " trustee " [1] have the same meanings respectively as in the Act of 1921.

(2) Unless the context otherwise requires references in this Act to any other Act are references to that Act as amended, modified or extended by any Act including this Act.

NOTE

[1] Now also includes an executor-dative: see the Succession (Scotland) Act 1964, s. 20.

Short title, citation, application and commencement

7.—(1)This Act may be cited as the Trusts (Scotland) Act 1961, and this Act and the Act of 1921 may be cited together as the Trusts (Scotland) Acts 1921 and 1961.

(2) This Act shall apply to trusts which have come into operation before, as well as to trusts coming into operation after, the commencement of this Act.

(3) This Act shall come into operation on the expiration of the period of one month beginning with the date of the passing thereof.

Trustee Investments Act 1961

(9 & 10 Eliz. 2, c. 62)

An Act to make fresh provision with respect to investment by trustees and persons having the investment powers of trustees, and by local authorites, and for purposes connected therewith.

[3rd August 1961]

New powers of investment of trustees

1.—[1] (1) A trustee may invest any property in his hands, whether at the time in a state of investment or not, in any manner specified in Part I or II of

Schedule 1 to this Act or, subject to the next following section, in any manner specified in Part III of that Schedule, and may also from time to time vary any such investments.

(2) The supplemental provisions contained in Part IV of that Schedule shall have effect for the interpretation and for restricting the operation of the said Parts I to III.

(3) No provision relating to the powers of the trustee contained in any instrument (not being an enactment or an instrument made under an enactment) made before the passing of this Act shall limit the powers conferred by this section, but those powers are exercisable only in so far as a contrary intention is not expressed in any Act or instrument made under an enactment, whenever passed or made, and so relating or in any other instrument so relating which is made after the passing of this Act.

For the purposes of this subsection any rule of the law of Scotland whereby a testamentary writing may be deemed to be made on a date other than that on which it was actually executed shall be disregarded.

(4) In this Act "narrower-range investment" means an investment falling within Part I or II of Schedule 1 to this Act and "wider-range investment" means an investment falling within Part III of that Schedule.

NOTE

[1] Section extended by S.I. 1991 No. 1999.

Restrictions on wider-range investment

[1] **2.**—(1) A trustee shall not have power by virtue of the foregoing section to make or retain any wider-range investment unless the trust fund has been divided into two parts (hereinafter referred to as the narrower-range part and the wider-range part), the parts being, subject to the provisions of this Act, equal in value at the time of the division; and where such a division has been made no subsequent division of the same fund shall be made for the purposes of this section, and no property shall be transferred from one part of the fund to the other unless either—

(*a*) the transfer is authorised or required by the following provisions of this Act, or

(*b*) a compensating transfer is made at the same time.

In this section "compensating transfer," in relation to any transferred property, means a transfer in the opposite direction of property of equal value.

(2) Property belonging to the narrower-range part of a trust fund shall not by virtue of the foregoing section be invested except in narrower-range investments, and any property invested in any other manner which is or becomes comprised in that part of the trust fund shall either be transferred to the wider-range part of the fund, with a compensating transfer, or be reinvested in narrower-range investments as soon as may be.

(3) Where any property accrues to a trust fund after the fund has been divided in pursuance of subsection (1) of this section, then—

(*a*) if the property accrues to the trustee as owner or former owner of property comprised in either part of the fund, it shall be treated as belonging to that part of the fund;

[2] (*b*) in any other case, the trustee shall secure, by apportionment of the accruing property or the transfer of property from one part of the fund to the other, or both, that the value of each part of the fund is increased by the same amount.

Where a trustee acquires property in consideration of a money payment the acquisition of the property shall be treated for the purposes of this section as investment and not as the accrual of property to the trust fund, notwithstanding that the amount of the consideration is less than the value of the property acquired; and paragraph (*a*) of this subsection shall not include the case of a dividend or interest becoming part of a trust fund.

(4) Where in the exercise of any power or duty of a trustee property falls to be taken out of the trust fund, nothing in this section shall restrict his discretion as to the choice of property to be taken out.

NOTES

[1] Modified in relation to charities by the Charities Act 1992 (c. 41), s. 38 (effective 1st September 1992: S.I. 1992 No. 1900).

[2] Modified in relation to charities by S.I. 1995 No. 1092, *infra*.

Relationship between Act and other powers of investment

3.—(1) The powers conferred by section 1 of this Act are in addition to and not in derogation from any power conferred otherwise than by this Act of investment or postponing conversion exerciseable by a trustee (hereinafter referred to as a "special power").

[1] (2) Any special power (however expressed) to invest property in any investment for the time being authorised by law for the investment of trust property, being a power conferred on a trustee before the passing of this Act or conferred on him under any enactment passed before the passing of this Act, shall have effect as a power to invest property in like manner and subject to the like provisions as under the foregoing provisions of this Act.

[1] (3) In relation to property, including wider-range but not including narrower-range investments,—

(*a*) which a trustee is authorised to hold apart from—

(i) the provisions of section 1 of this Act or any of the provisions of Part I of the Trustee Act 1925, or any of the provisions of the Trusts (Scotland) Act 1921, or

(ii) any such power to invest in authorised investments as is mentioned in the foregoing subsection, or

(*b*) which became part of a trust fund in consequence of the exercise by the trustee, as owner of property falling within this subsection, of any power conferred by subsection (3) or (4) of section 10 of the Trustee Act 1925, or paragraph (*o*) or (*p*) of subsection (1) of section 4 of the Trusts (Scotland) Act 1921,

the foregoing section shall have effect subject to the modifications set out in Schedule 2 to this Act.

[1] (4) The foregoing subsection shall not apply where the powers of the trustee to invest or postpone conversion have been conferred or varied—

(*a*) by an order of any court made within the period of ten years ending with the passing of this Act, or

(*b*) by any enactment passed, or instrument having effect under an enactment made, within that period, being an enactment or instrument relating specifically to the trusts in question; or

(*c*) by an enactment contained in a local Act of the present Session;

but the provisions of Schedule 3 to this Act shall have effect in a case falling within this subsection.

NOTE

[1] Excluded by the House of Commons Members' Fund Act 1962 (c. 53), s. 1(5).

Interpretation of references to trust property and trust funds

4.—[1] (1) In this Act "property" includes property of any description (whether heritable or moveable, corporeal or incorporeal) which is presently enjoyable, but does not include a future interest whether vested or contingent.

(2) So much of the property in the hands of a trustee shall for the purposes of this Act constitute one trust fund as is held on trusts which (as respects the beneficiaries or their respective interests or the purposes of the trust or as respects the powers of the trustee) are not identical with those on which any other property in his hands is held.

[2] (3) Where property is taken out of a trust fund by way of appropriation so as to form a separate fund, and at the time of the appropriation the trust

fund had (as to the whole or a part thereof) been divided in pursuance of subsection (1) of section 2 of this Act, or that subsection as modified by Schedule 2 to this Act, then if the separate fund is so divided the narrower-range and wider-range parts of the separate fund may be constituted so as either to be equal, or to bear to each other the same proportion as the two corresponding parts of the fund out of which it was so appropriated (the values of those parts of those funds being ascertained as at the time of appropriation), or some intermediate proportion.

NOTES

[1] As applied to Scotland by subs. (4).

[2] Modified in relation to charities by S.I. 1995 No. 1092, *infra*.

Certain valuations to be conclusive for purposes of division of trust fund

5.—(1) If for the purposes of section 2 or 4 of this Act or Schedule 2 thereto a trustee obtains, from a person reasonably believed by the trustee to be qualified to make it, a valuation in writing of any property, the valuation shall be conclusive in determining whether the division of the trust fund in pursuance of subsection (1) of the said section 2, or any transfer or apportionment of property under that section or the said Schedule 2 has been duly made.

(2) The foregoing subsection applies to any such valuation notwithstanding that it is made by a person in the course of his employment as an officer or servant.

Duty of trustees in choosing investments

6.—(1) In the exercise of his powers of investment a trustee shall have regard—

(*a*) to the need for diversification of investments of the trust, in so far as is appropriate to the circumstances of the trust;

(*b*) to the suitability to the trust of investments of the description of investment proposed and of the investment proposed as an investment of that description.

(2) Before exercising any power conferred by section 1 of this Act to invest in a manner specified in Part II or III of Schedule 1 to this Act, or before investing in any such manner in the exercise of a power falling within subsection (2) of section 3 of this Act, a trustee shall obtain and consider proper advice on the question whether the investment is satisfactory having regard to the matters mentioned in paragraphs (*a*) and (*b*) of the foregoing subsection.

(3) A trustee retaining any investment made in the exercise of such a power and in such a manner as aforesaid shall determine at what intervals the circumstances, and in particular the nature of the investment, make it desirable to obtain such advice as aforesaid, and shall obtain and consider such advice accordingly.

(4) For the purposes of the two foregoing subsections, proper advice is the advice of a person who is reasonably believed by the trustee to be qualified by his ability in and practical experience of financial matters; and such advice may be given by a person notwithstanding that he gives it in the course of his employment as an officer or servant.

(5) A trustee shall not be treated as having complied with subsection (2) or (3) of this section unless the advice was given or has been subsequently confirmed in writing.

(6) Subsections (2) and (3) of this section shall not apply to one of two or more trustees where he is the person giving the advice required by this section to his co-trustee or co-trustees, and shall not apply where powers of a trustee are lawfully exercised by an officer or servant competent under subsection (4) of this section to give proper advice.

(7) Without prejudice to section 8 of the Trustee Act 1925, or section 30 of the Trusts (Scotland) Act 1921 (which relate to valuation, and the pro-

portion of the value to be lent, where a trustee lends on the security of property) the advice required by this section shall not include, in the case of a loan on the security of freehold or leasehold property in England and Wales or Northern Ireland or on heritable security in Scotland, advice on the suitability of the particular loan.

Application of sections 1–6 to persons, other than trustees, having trustee investment powers

7.—(1) Where any persons, not being trustees, have a statutory power of making investments which is or includes power—

(*a*) to make the like investments as are authorised by section 1 of the Trustee Act 1925, or section 10 of the Trusts (Scotland) Act 1921, or

(*b*) to make the like investments as trustees are for the time being by law authorised to make,

however the power is expressed, the foregoing provisions of this Act shall with the necessary modifications apply in relation to them as if they were trustees:

Provided that property belonging to a Consolidated Loans Fund or any other fund applicable wholly or partly for the redemption of debt shall not by virtue of the foregoing provisions of this Act be invested or held invested in any manner specified in paragraph 6 of Part II of Schedule 1 to this Act or in wider-range investments.

(2) Where, in the exercise of powers conferred by any enactment, an authority to which paragraph 9 of Part II of Schedule 1 to this Act applies uses money belonging to any fund for a purpose for which the authority has power to borrow, the foregoing provisions of this Act, as applied by the foregoing subsection, shall apply as if there were comprised in the fund (in addition to the actual content thereof) property, being narrower-range investments, having a value equal to so much of the said money as for the time being has not been repaid to the fund, and accordingly any repayment of such money to the fund shall not be treated for the said purposes as the accrual of property to the fund:

Provided that nothing in this subsection shall be taken to require compliance with any of the provisions of section 6 of this Act in relation to the exercise of such powers as aforesaid.

[1] (3) In this section "Consolidated Loans Fund" means a fund established under section 55 of the Local Government Act 1958, and includes a loans fund established under Schedule 3 to the Local Government (Scotland) Act 1975, and "statutory power" means a power conferred by an enactment passed before the passing of this Act or by any instrument made under any such enactment.

NOTE

[1] As amended by the Local Government and Planning (Scotland) Act 1982 (c. 43), Sched. 3, para. 4.

Application of sections 1–6 in special cases

8.—(1) In relation to persons to whom this section applies—

(*a*) notwithstanding anything in subsection (3) of section 1 of this Act, no provision of any enactment passed, or instrument having effect under an enactment and made, before the passing of this Act shall limit the powers conferred by the said section 1;

(*b*) subsection (1) of the foregoing section shall apply where the power of making investments therein mentioned is or includes a power to make some only of the investments mentioned in paragraph (*a*) or (*b*) of that subsection.

(2) This section applies to—

(*a*) the persons for the time being authorised to invest funds of the Duchy of Lancaster;

(*b*) any persons specified in an order made by the Treasury by statutory instrument, being persons (whether trustees or not) whose power to make investments is conferred by or under any enactment contained in a local or private Act.

(3) An order of the Treasury made under the foregoing subsection may

[THE NEXT PAGE IS M 39]

provide that the provisions of sections 1 to 6 of this Act (other than the provisions of subsection (3) of section 1) shall, in their application to any persons specified therein, have effect subject to such exceptions and modifications as may be specified.

Supplementary provisions as to investments

9.—(1) In subsection (3) of section 10 of the Trustee Act 1925, before paragraph (*c*) (which enables trustees to concur in any scheme or arrangement for the amalgamation of a company in which they hold securities with another company, with power to accept securities in the second company) there shall be inserted the following paragraph:—

"(*bb*) for the acquisition of the securities of the company, or of control thereof, by another company".

(2) It is hereby declared that the power to subscribe for securities conferred by subsection (4) of the said section 10 includes power to retain them for any period for which the trustee has power to retain the holding in respect of which the right to subscribe for the securities was offered, but subject to any conditions subject to which the trustee has that power.

10. [See print of the Trusts (Scotland) Act 1921 (c. 58), s. 4, *supra*.]

Local authority investment schemes

[1] **11.**—[2] (1) Without prejudice to powers conferred by or under any other enactment, any authority to which this section applies may invest property held by the authority in accordance with a scheme submitted to the Treasury by any association of local authorities and approved by the Treasury as enabling investments to be made collectively without in substance extending the scope of powers of investment.

(2) A scheme under this section may apply to a specified authority or to a specified class of authorities, may make different provisions as respects different authorities or different classes of authorities or as respects different descriptions of property or property held for different purposes, and may impose restrictions on the extent to which the power conferred by the foregoing subsection shall be exercisable.

[3] (3) In approving a scheme under this section, the Treasury may direct that the Financial Services Act 1986, shall not apply to dealings undertaken or documents issued for the purposes of the scheme, or to such dealings or documents of such descriptions as may be specified in the direction.

(4) The authorities to which this section applies are—

[4] (*a*) in England and Wales, the council of a county, a borough a district or a parish, a river authority, the Common Council of the City of London, the Broads Authority, a police authority established under section 3 of the Police Act 1964, a joint authority established by Part IV of the Local Government Act 1985 and the Council of the Isles of Scilly;

[5] (*b*) in Scotland, a local authority within the meaning of the Local Government (Scotland) Act 1947;

(*c*) in any part of Great Britain, a joint board or joint committee constituted to discharge or advise on the discharge of the functions of any two or more of the authorities mentioned in the foregoing paragraphs (including a joint committee established by those authorities acting in combination in accordance with regulations made under section 7 of the Superannuation Act 1972;

(*d*) in Northern Ireland, the council of a county, a county or borough, or an urban or rural district, and the Northern Ireland Local Government Officers' Superannuation Committee established under the Local Government (Superannuation) Act (Northern Ireland) 1950.

NOTES

[1] See also the Local Authorities Mutual Investment Trust Act 1968 (c. 25), s. 1. Excluded by the Financial Services Act 1986 (c. 60), s. 45 (1)(*j*).

[2] As amended by the London Government Act 1963 (c. 33), Sched. 18, Pt. II, and the Local Government Act 1985 (c. 51), Sched. 17.

[3] As amended by the Financial Services Act 1986 (c. 60), Sched. 16, para. 2.

[4] As amended by the London Government Act 1963 (c. 33), Sched. 18, Pt. II, the Water Resources Act 1963 (c. 38), Sched. 13, para. 16, the Superannuation Act 1972 (c. 11), Sched. 6, para. 40, the Local Government Act 1972 (c. 70), Sched. 30, the Local Government Act 1985 (c. 51), Sched. 14, para. 38 and Sched. 17, the Norfolk and Suffolk Broads Act 1988 (c. 4), Sched. 6, para. 3, the Education Reform Act 1988 (c. 40), Sched. 13 and the Police and Magistrates' Courts Act 1994 (c. 29), Sched. 4, para. 46 (effective 1st October 1994 for certain purposes: S.I. 1994 No. 2025). Prospective amendment in the Local Government (Wales) Act 1994 (c. 19), Sched. 16, para. 19, inserts "a county borough" after "county".

[5] See the Local Government (Scotland) Act 1973 (c. 65), Sched. 27, Pt. I, para. 1(2).

Power to confer additional powers of investment

12.—(1) Her Majesty may by Order in Council extend the powers of investment conferred by section 1 of this Act by adding to Part I, Part II or Part III of Schedule 1 to this Act any manner of investment specified in the Order.

(2) Any Order under this section shall be subject to annulment in pursuance of a resolution of either House of Parliament.

Power to modify provisions as to division of trust fund

13.—(1) The Treasury may by order made by statutory instrument direct that, subject to subsection (3) of section 4 of this Act, any division of a trust fund made in pursuance of subsection (1) of section 2 of this Act during the continuance in force of the order shall be made so that the value of the wider-range part at the time of the division bears to the then value of the narrower-range part such proportion, greater than one but not greater than three to one, as may be prescribed by the order; and in this Act "the prescribed proportion" means the proportion for the time being prescribed under this subsection.

(2) A fund which has been divided in pursuance of subsection (1) of section 2 of this Act before the coming into operation of an order under the foregoing subsection may notwithstanding anything in that subsection be again divided (once only) in pursuance of the said subsection (1) during the continuance in force of the order.

(3) If an order is made under subsection (1) of this section, then as from the coming into operation of the order—

(*a*) paragraph (*b*) of subsection (3) of section 2 of this Act and sub-paragraph (*b*) of paragraph 3 of Schedule 2 thereto shall have effect with the substitution, for the words from "each" to the end, of the words "the wider-range part of the fund is increased by an amount which bears the prescribed proportion to the amount by which the value of the narrower-range part of the fund is increased";

(*b*) subsection (3) of section 4 of this Act shall have effect as if for the words "so as either" to "each other" there were substituted the words "so as to bear to each other either the prescribed proportion or".

(4) An order under this section may be revoked by a subsequent order thereunder prescribing a greater proportion.

(5) An order under this section shall not have effect unless approved by a resolution of each House of Parliament.

Amendment of section 27 of Trusts (Scotland) Act 1921

14. So much of section 27 of the Trusts (Scotland) Act 1921, as empowers the Court of Session to approve as investments for trust funds any stocks, funds or securities in addition to those in which trustees are by that Act authorised to invest trust funds shall cease to have effect.

Saving for powers of court

15. The enlargement of the investment powers of trustees by this Act shall not lessen any power of a court to confer wider powers of investment on trustees, or affect the extent to which any such power is to be exercised.

Minor and consequential amendments and repeals

16.—(1) The provisions of Schedule 4 to this Act (which contain minor amendments and amendments consequential on the foregoing provisions of this Act) shall have effect.

(2) [Repealed by the Statute Law (Repeals) Act 1974 (c. 22).]

Short title, extent and construction

[1] **17.**—(1) This Act may be cited as the Trustee Investments Act 1961.

(2) Sections 11 and 16 of this Act shall extend to Northern Ireland, but except as aforesaid and except so far as any other provisions of the Act apply by virtue of subsection (1) of section 1 of the Trustee Act (Northern Ireland) 1958, or any other enactment of the Parliament of Northern Ireland, to trusts the execution of which is governed by the law in force in Northern Ireland, this Act does not apply to such trusts.

[2] (3) So much of section 16 of this Act as relates to the National Savings Bank shall extend to the Isle of Man and the Channel Islands.

(4) Except where the context otherwise requires, in this Act, in its application to trusts the execution of which is governed by the law in force in England and Wales, expressions have the same meaning as in the Trustee Act 1925.

(5) Except where the context otherwise requires, in this Act, in its application to trusts the execution of which is governed by the law in force in Scotland, expressions have the same meaning as in the Trusts (Scotland) Act 1921.

NOTES

[1] Modified in relation to charities by S.I. 1995 No. 1092, *infra*.

[2] As amended by the Post Office Act 1969 (c. 48), Sched. 6, the Trustee Savings Banks Act 1976 (c. 4), Sched. 6, and the Trustee Savings Banks Act 1985 (c. 58), Sched. 4.

SCHEDULES

Section 1

[1] SCHEDULE 1

MANNER OF INVESTMENT

NOTE

[1] See the Finance Act 1986 (c. 41), s. 31 and Sched. 7, and the Charities Act 1992 (c. 41), s. 39.

PART I

NARROWER-RANGE INVESTMENTS NOT REQUIRING ADVICE

[1] 1. In Defence Bonds, National Savings Income Bonds, National Savings Certificates and Ulster Savings Certificates, National Savings Deposit Bonds, National Savings Capital Bonds, National Savings FIRST Option Bonds and National Savings Pensioners Guaranteed Income Bonds.

NOTE

[1] As extended by S.I. 1962 No. 2611, S.I. 1964 No. 703, S.I. 1968 No. 470, S.I. 1982 No. 1086, S.I. 1983 No. 1525, S.I. 1988 No. 2254, S.I. 1992 No. 1738 and S.I. 1994 No. 265.

[1] 2. In deposits in the National Savings Bank, and deposits in a bank or department thereof certified under subsection (3) of section 9 of the Finance Act 1956.

NOTE

[1] As extended by the Post Office Act 1969 (c. 48), Sched. 6, and the Trustee Savings Banks Act 1976 (c. 4), Sched. 6.

PART II

NARROWER-RANGE INVESTMENTS REQUIRING ADVICE

[1] 1. In securities issued by Her Majesty's Government in the United Kingdom, the Government of Northern Ireland or the Government of the Isle of Man not being securities falling within Part I of this Schedule and being fixed-interest securities registered in the United Kingdom or the Isle of Man, Treasury Bills or Tax Reserve Certificates or any variable interest securities issued by Her Majesty's Government in the United Kingdom and registered in the United Kingdom.

NOTE

[1] As extended by S.I. 1977 No. 831.

2. In any securities the payment of interest on which is guaranteed by Her Majesty's Government in the United Kingdom or the Government of Northern Ireland.

3. In fixed-interest securities issued in the United Kingdom by any public authority or nationalised industry or undertaking in the United Kingdom.

4. In fixed-interest securities issued in the United Kingdom by the government of any overseas territory within the Commonwealth or by any public or local authority within such a territory, being securities registered in the United Kingdom.

References in this paragraph to an overseas territory or to the government of such a territory shall be construed as if they occurred in the Overseas Service Act 1958.

[1] 4A. In securities issued in the United Kingdom by the government of an overseas territory within the Commonwealth or by any public or local authority within such a territory, being securities registered in the United Kingdom and in respect of which the rate of interest is variable by reference to one or more of the following:—

(*a*) the Bank of England's minimum lending rate;
(*b*) the average rate of discount on allotment on ninety-one-day Treasury bills;
(*c*) a yield on ninety-one-day Treasury bills;
(*d*) a London sterling inter-bank offered rate;
(*e*) a London sterling certificate of deposit rate.

References in this paragraph to an overseas territory or to the government of such a territory shall be construed as if they occurred in the Overseas Service Act 1958.

NOTE

[1] Extension made by S.I. 1977 No. 1878.

[1] 5. In fixed-interest securities issued in the United Kingdom by the African Development Bank, the Asian Development Bank, the Caribbean Development Bank, the European Bank for Reconstruction and Development, the International Finance Corporation, the International Monetary Fund or by the International Bank for Reconstruction and Development, being securities registered in the United Kingdom. In fixed-interest securities issued in the United Kingdom by the inter-American Development Bank. In fixed-interest securities issued in the United Kingdom by the European Atomic Energy Community, the European Economic Community, the European Investment Bank or by the European Coal and Steel Community, being securities registered in the United Kingdom.

NOTE
[1] As extended by S.I. 1964 No. 1404, S.I. 1972 No. 1818, S.I. 1983 No. 772, and S.I. 1991 No. 999.

[1] 5A. In securities issued in the United Kingdom by
(i) the International Bank for Reconstruction and Development or by the European Investment Bank or by the European Coal and Steel Community, being securities registered in the United Kingdom, or
(ii) the Inter-American Development Bank,

being securities in respect of which the rate of interest is variable by reference to one or more of the following:—
(*a*) the Bank of England's minimum lending rate;
(*b*) the average rate of discount on allotment on ninety-one-day Treasury bills;
(*c*) a yield on ninety-one-day Treasury bills;
(*d*) a London sterling inter-bank offered rate;
(*e*) a London sterling certificate of deposit rate.

NOTE
[1] Extension made by S.I. 1977 No. 1878.

[1] 5B. In securities issued in the United Kingdom by the African Development Bank, the Asian Development Bank, the Caribbean Development Bank, the European Atomic Energy Community, the European Bank for Reconstruction and Development, the European Economic Community, the International Finance Corporation or by the International Monetary Fund, being securities registered in the United Kingdom and in respect of which the rate of interest is variable by reference to one or more of the following:—
(*a*) the average rate of discount on allotment on 91-day Treasury bills;
(*b*) a yield on 91-day Treasury bills;
(*c*) a London sterling inter-bank offered rate;
(*d*) a London sterling certificate of deposit rate.

NOTE
[1] Extension made by S.I. 1983 No. 772, as extended by S.I. 1991 No. 999.

6. In debentures issued in the United Kingdom by a company incorporated in the United Kingdom, being debentures registered in the United Kingdom.

[1] 7. In stock of the Bank of Ireland. In Bank of Ireland 7 per cent. Loan Stock 1986/91.

NOTE
[1] As extended by S.I. 1966 No. 401.

8. In debentures issued by the Agricultural Mortgage Corporation Limited or the Scottish Agricultural Securities Corporation Limited.

[1] 9. In loans to any authority to which this paragraph applies charged on all or any of the revenues of the authority or on a fund into which all or any of those revenues are payable, in any fixed-interest securities issued in the United Kingdom by any such authority for the purpose of borrowing money so charged, and in deposits with any such authority by way of temporary loan made on the giving of a receipt for the loan by the treasurer or other similar officer of the authority and on the giving of an undertaking by the authority that, if requested to charge the loan as aforesaid, it will either comply with the request or repay the loan.

This paragraph applies to the following authorities, that is to say—

(*a*) any local authority in the United Kingdom;
(*b*) any authority all the members of which are appointed or elected by one or more local authorities in the United Kingdom;
(*c*) any authority the majority of the members of which are appointed or elected by one or more local authorities in the United Kingdom, being an authority which by virtue of any enactment has power to issue a precept to a local authority in England and Wales, or a requisition to a local authority in Scotland, or to the expenses of which by virtue of any enactment, a local authority in the United Kingdom is or can be required to contribute;
[1a] (*d*) the Receiver for the Metropolitan Police District or a police authority established under section 3 of the Police Act 1964;
(*e*) the Belfast City and District Water Commissioners;
[2] (*f*) Great Ouse Water Authority;
[3] (*g*) any district council in Northern Ireland;
[4] (*h*) the Inner London Education Authority;
(*i*) [Added by S.I. 1986 No. 601 but repealed with effect from 1st April 1990 by the Education Reform Act 1988 (c. 40), Sched. 13.]

NOTES
[1] Extension made by the Post Office Act 1969 (c. 48), Sched. 2, paras. 4 and 15.
[1a] As amended by the Police and Magistrates' Courts Act 1994 (c. 24), Sched. 4, para. 47 (effective 1st October 1994 for certain purposes: S.I. 1994 No. 2025).
[2] Extension made by S.I. 1962 No. 658.
[3] Extension made by S.I. 1973 No. 1332.
[4] Extension made by S.I. 1986 No. 601.

[1] 9A. In any securities issued in the United Kingdom by any authority to which paragraph 9 applies for the purpose of borrowing money charged on all or any of the revenues of the authority or on a fund into which all or any of these revenues are payable and being securities in respect of which the rate of interest is variable by reference to one or more of the following:—

(*a*) the Bank of England's minimum lending rate;
(*b*) the average rate of discount on allotment on ninety-one-day Treasury bills;
(*c*) a yield on ninety-one-day Treasury bills;
(*d*) a London sterling inter-bank offered rate;
(*e*) a London sterling certificate of deposit rate.

NOTE
[1] Extension made by S.I. 1977 No. 1878.

[1] 10. In debentures or in the guaranteed or preference stock of any incorporated company, being statutory water undertakers within the meaning of the Water Act 1945, or any corre-

sponding enactment in force in Northern Ireland, and having during each of the ten years immediately preceding the calendar year in which the investment was made paid a dividend of not less than 3½ per cent. on its ordinary shares.

NOTE
[1] As extended by S.I. 1973 No. 1393.

---

[1] 10A. In any units of a gilt unit trust scheme.

References in this Schedule to a gilt unit trust scheme are references to a collective investment scheme—

(*a*) which is an authorised unit trust scheme within the meaning of the Financial Services Act 1986, a recognised scheme within the meaning of that Act or a UCITS; and

(*b*) whose objective is to invest not less than 90 per cent of the property of the scheme in loan stock, bonds and other instruments creating or acknowledging indebtedness which are transferable and which are issued or guaranteed by—

(i) the government of the United Kingdom or of any other country or territory,

(ii) by a local authority in the United Kingdom or in a relevant state, or

(iii) by an international organisation the members of which include the United Kingdom or a relevant state;

and, in respect of the remainder of the property of the scheme, whose objective is to invest in any instrument falling within any of paragraphs 1 to 3, 5 or 6 of Schedule 1 to the Financial Services Act 1986.

NOTE
[1] Added by the Finance Act 1982 (c. 39), s. 150. As amended by the Income and Corporation Taxes Act 1988 (c. 1), Sched. 29, p. 1000. Substituted by S.I. 1994 No. 1908 (effective 22nd August 1994) and as amended by S.I. 1995 No. 768 (effective 18th April 1995).

---

11. [Repealed by the Trustee Savings Banks Act 1976 (c. 4), Sched. 6.]

[1] 12. In deposits with a building society within the meaning of the Building Societies Act 1986.

NOTE
[1] As amended by the Housing (Consequential Provisions) Act 1985 (c. 71), Sched. 2, para. 5(2), and the Building Societies Act 1986 (c. 53), Sched. 18, para. 4(2).

---

13. In mortgages of freehold property in England and Wales or Northern Ireland and of leasehold property in those countries of which the unexpired term at the time of investment is not less than sixty years, and in loans on heritable security in Scotland.

14. In perpetual rent-charges on land in England and Wales or Northern Ireland and free-farm rents (not being rent-charges) issuing out of such land, and in feu-duties or ground annuals in Scotland.

[1] 15. In Certificates of Tax Deposit.

NOTE
[1] Added by S.I. 1975 No. 1710.

---

[1] 16. In fixed-interest or variable interest securities issued by the government of a relevant state.

NOTE
[1] Added by S.I. 1995 No. 1908 (effective 22nd August 1994).

[1] 17. In any securities the payment of interest on which is guaranteed by the government of a relevant state.

NOTE
[1] Added by S.I. 1995 No. 1908 (effective 22nd August 1994).

[1] 18. In fixed-interest securities issued in any relevant state by any public authority or nationalised industry or undertaking in that state.

NOTE
[1] Added by S.I. 1995 No. 1908 (effective 22nd August 1994).

[1] 19. In fixed-interest or variable interest securities issued in a relevant state by the government of any overseas territory within the Commonwealth or by any public or local authority within such a territory.

References in this paragraph to an overseas territory or to the government of such a territory shall be construed as if they occurred in the Overseas Development and Co-operation Act 1980.

NOTE
[1] Added by S.I. 1995 No. 1908 (effective 22nd August 1994).

[1] 20. In fixed-interest or variable interest securities issued in a relevant state by—
(*a*) the African Development Bank;
(*b*) the Asian Development Bank;
(*c*) the Caribbean Development Bank;
(*d*) the International Finance Corporation;
(*e*) the International Monetary Fund;
(*f*) the International Bank for Reconstruction and Development;
(*g*) the Inter-American Development Bank;
(*h*) the European Atomic Energy Community;
(*i*) the European Bank for Reconstruction and Development;
(*j*) the European Economic Community;
(*k*) the European Investment Bank; or
(*l*) the European Coal and Steel Community.

NOTE
[1] Added by S.I. 1995 No. 1908 (effective 22nd August 1994).

[1] 21. In debentures issued in any relevant state by a company incorporated in that state.

NOTE
[1] Added by S.I. 1995 No. 1908 (effective 22nd August 1994).

[1] 22. In loans to any authority to which this paragraph applies secured on all or any of the revenues of the authority or on a fund into which all or any of those revenues are payable, in fixed-interest or variable interest securities issued in a relevant state by any such authority in that state for the purpose of borrowing money so secured, and in deposits with any authority to which this paragraph applies by way of temporary loan made on the giving of a receipt for the loan by the treasurer or other similar officer of the authority and on the giving of an undertaking by the authority that, if requested to charge the loan as aforesaid, it will either comply with the request or repay the loan.

This paragraph applies to the following authorities, that is to say—

(*a*) any local authority in a relevant state; or

(*b*) any authority all the members of which are appointed or elected by one or more local authorities in any such state.

NOTE
[1] Added by S.I. 1995 No. 1908 (effective 22nd August 1994).

[1] 23. In deposits with a mutual investment society whose head office is located in a relevant state.

NOTE
[1] Added by S.I. 1995 No. 1908 (effective 22nd August 1994).

[1] 24. In loans secured on any interest in property in a relevant state which corresponds to an interest in property falling within paragraph 13 of this Part of this Schedule.

NOTE
[1] Added by S.I. 1995 No. 1908 (effective 22nd August 1994).

Part III

Wider-Range Investments

1. In any securities issued in the United Kingdom by a company incorporated in the United Kingdom, being securities registered in the United Kingdom and not being securities falling within Part II of this Schedule.

[1] 2. In shares in a building society within the meaning of the Building Societies Act 1986.

NOTE
[1] As amended by the Housing (Consequential Provisions) Act 1985 (c. 71), Sched. 2, para. 5(2), and the Building Societies Act 1986 (c. 53), Sched. 18, para. 4(3).

[1] 3. In any units of an authorised unit trust scheme within the meaning of the Financial Services Act 1986.

NOTE
[1] Substituted by the Financial Services Act 1986 (c. 60), Sched. 16, para. 2.

[1] 4. In any securities issued in any relevant state by a company incorporated in that state or by any unincorporated body constituted under the law of that state, not being (in either case) securities falling within Part II of this Schedule or paragraph 6 of this Part of this Schedule.

NOTE
[1] Inserted by S.I. 1994 No. 1908 (effective 22nd August 1994).

[1] 5. In shares in a mutual investment society whose head office is located in a relevant state.

NOTE
[1] Inserted by S.I. 1994 No. 1908 (effective 22nd August 1994).

[1] 6. In any units of a collective investment scheme which is—

(*a*) a recognised scheme within the meaning of the Financial Services Act 1986 which is constituted in a relevant state; or

(*b*) a UCITS;

and which does not fall within Part II of this Schedule.

NOTE
[1] Inserted by S.I. 1994 No. 1908 (effective 22nd August 1994).

Part IV

Supplemental

[1] 1. The securities mentioned in Parts I to III of this Schedule do not include any securities where the holder can be required to accept repayment of the principal, or the payment of any interest, otherwise than in sterling, in the currency of a relevant state or in the european currency unit (as defined in article 1 of Council Regulation No. 3180/78/EEC.

NOTE
[1] As amended by S.I. 1994 No. 1908 (effective 22nd August 1994).

[1] 2. The securities mentioned in paragraphs 1 to 8 of Part II, other than Treasury Bills or Tax Reserve Certificates, securities issued before the passing of this Act by the Government of the Isle of Man, securities falling within paragraph 4 of the said Part II issued before the passing of this Act or securities falling within paragraph 9 of that Part, and the securities mentioned in paragraph 1 of Part III of this Schedule, do not include—

(*a*) securities the price of which is not quoted on a recognised investment exchange within the meaning of the Financial Services Act 1986 or on an investment exchange which constitutes the principal or only market established in a relevant state on which securities admitted to official listing are dealt in or traded;

(*b*) shares or debenture stock not fully paid up (except shares or debenture stock which by the terms of issue are required to be fully paid up within nine months of the date of issue).

NOTE

[1] As amended by the Financial Services Act 1986 (c. 60), Sched. 16, para. 2 and S.I. 1994 No. 1908 (effective 22nd August 1994).

---

[1] 2A. The securities mentioned in paragraphs 16 to 21 of Part II of this Schedule, other than securities traded on a relevant money market or securities falling within paragraph 22 of Part II of this Schedule, and the securities mentioned in paragraph 4 of Part III of this Schedule do not include—

(*a*) securities the price for which is not quoted on a recognised investment exchange within the meaning of the Financial Services Act 1986 or on an investment exchange which constitutes the principal or only market established in a relevant state on which securities admitted to official listing are dealt in or traded;

(*b*) shares or debenture stock not fully paid up (except shares or debenture stock which by the terms of issue are required to be fully paid up within nine months of the date of issue or shares issued with no nominal value).

NOTE

[1] Inserted by S.I. 1994 No. 1908 (effective 22nd August 1994).

---

[1] 3. The securities mentioned in paragraphs 6 and 21 of Part II and paragraph 1 or 4 of Part III of this Schedule do not include—

(*a*) shares or debentures of an incorporated company of which the total issued and paid up share capital is less than one million pounds;

[2] (*ab*) shares or debentures of an incorporated company of which the total issued and paid up share capital at any time on the business day before the investment is made is less than the equivalent of one million pounds in the currency of a relevant state (at the exchange rate prevailing in the United Kingdom at the close of business on the day before the investment is made);

(*b*) shares or debentures of an incorporated company which has not in each of the five years immediately preceding the calendar year in which the investment is made paid a dividend on all the shares issued by the company, excluding any shares issued after the dividend was declared and any shares which by their terms of issue did not rank for the dividend for that year.

For the purposes of sub-paragraph (*b*) of this paragraph a company formed—

(i) to take over the business of another company or other companies, or

(ii) to acquire the securities of, or control of, another company or other companies,

or for either of those purposes and for other purposes shall be deemed to have paid a dividend as mentioned in that sub-paragraph in any year in which such a dividend has been paid by the other company or all the other companies, as the case may be.

NOTES

[1] Modified by the British Aerospace Act 1980 (c. 26), s. 11, the Civil Aviation Act 1980 (c. 60), s. 9, the Oil and Gas (Enterprise) Act 1982 (c. 23), s. 34, the Telecommunications Act 1984 (c. 12), s. 71, the Ordnance Factories and Military Services Act 1984 (c. 59), s. 9, the Trustee Savings Banks Act 1985 (c. 58), Sched. 1, para. 10, the Airports Act 1986 (c. 31), s. 11(1), the Gas Act 1986 (c. 44), s. 59, the British Steel Act 1988 (c. 35), s. 12, the British

Technology Group Act 1991 (c. 66), s. 13(1), the Agriculture Act 1993 (c. 39), Sched. 2, para. 34, and the Railways Act 1993 (c. 43), s. 108 (effective 6th January 1994: S.I. 1993 No. 3237).

[2] Inserted by S.I. 1994 No. 1908 (effective 22nd August 1994).

3A. [Inserted by the Housing (Consequential Provisions) Act 1985 (c. 71), Sched. 2, para. 5(3). Repealed by the Building Societies Act 1986 (c. 53), Sched. 19, Pt. I.]

[1] 4. In this Schedule, unless the context otherwise requires, the following expressions have the meanings hereby respectively assigned to them, that is to say—

"debenture" includes debenture stock and bonds, whether constituting a charge on assets or not, and loan stock or notes;

"enactment" includes an enactment of the Parliament of Northern Ireland;

"fixed-interest securities" means securities which under their terms of issue bear a fixed rate of interest;

"local authority" in relation to the United Kingdom, means any of the following authorities—

[2] (*a*) in England and Wales, the council of a county, a borough an urban or rural district or a parish, the Common Council of the City of London, the Greater London Council and the Council of the Isles of Scilly;

(*b*) in Scotland, a local authority within the meaning of the Local Government (Scotland) Act 1947;

[3] "mutual investment society" means a credit institution which operates on mutual principles and which is authorised by the appropriate supervisory authority of a relevant state;

[3] "relevant money market" means a money market which is supervised by the central bank, or a government agency, of a relevant state;

[3,4] "relevant state" means Austria, Finland, Iceland, Liechtenstein, Norway, Sweden or a member state other than the United Kingdom;

[5] "securities" includes shares, debentures, units within paragraph 3 or 6 of Part III of this Schedule, Treasury Bills and Tax Reserve Certificates;

"share" includes stock;

"Treasury Bills" includes bills issued by Her Majesty's Government in the United Kingdom and Northern Ireland Treasury Bills.

NOTES

[1] As amended by the London Government Act 1963 (c. 33), Scheds. 17 and 18, the National Loans Act 1968 (c. 13), Sched. 6, Pt. I, the Local Government Act 1972 (c. 51), Sched. 30, the Trustee Savings Banks Act 1976 (c. 4), Sched. 6, the Statute Law (Repeals) Act 1981 (c. 19), Sched. 1, Pt. IV, and the Financial Services Act 1986 (c. 60), Sched. 16, para. 2.

[2] Prospective amendment in the Local Government (Wales) Act 1994 (c. 19), Sched. 16, para. 19, inserts "a county borough" after "county".

[3] Inserted by S.I. 1994 No. 1908 (effective 22nd August 1994).

[4] As amended by S.I. 1995 No. 768 (effective 18th April 1995).

[5] As amended by S.I. 1995 No. 1908 (effective 22nd August 1994).

---

5. It is hereby declared that in this Schedule "mortgage," in relation to freehold or leasehold property in Northern Ireland, includes a registered charge which, by virtue of subsection (4) of section 40 of the Local Registration of Title (Ireland) Act 1891, or any other enactment, operates as a mortgage by deed.

[1] 6. In relation to the United Kingdom references in this Schedule to an incorporated company are references to a company incorporated by or under any enactment and include references to a body of persons established for the purpose of trading for profit and incorporated by Royal Charter.

NOTE
[1] As amended by S.I. 1994 No. 1908 (effective 22nd August 1994).

[1] 6A. References in this Schedule to a UCITS are references to a collective investment scheme which is constituted in a relevant state and which complies with the conditions necessary for it to enjoy the rights conferred by Council Directive 85/611/EEC co-ordinating the laws, regulations and administrative provisions relating to undertakings for collective investment in transferable securities; and section 86(8) of the Financial Services Act 1986 (meaning of "constituted in a member state") shall apply for the purposes of this paragraph as it applies for the purposes of that section but as if for references in that section to a member state there were substituted references to a relevant state.

NOTE
[1] Inserted by S.I. 1994 No. 1908 (effective 22nd August 1994).

7. [Repealed by the Building Societies Act 1986 (c. 53), Sched. 19, Pt. I.]

Section 3

[1] SCHEDULE 2

MODIFICATION OF SECTION 2 IN RELATION TO PROPERTY FALLING WITHIN S. 3(3)

NOTE
[1] Excluded by the House of Commons Members' Fund Act 1962 (c. 53), s. 1 (5).

1. In this Schedule "special-range property" means property falling within subsection (3) of section 3 of this Act.

2.—(1) Where a trust fund includes special-range property, subsection (1) of section 2 of this Act shall have effect as if references to the trust fund were references to so much thereof as does not consist of special-range property, and the special-range property shall be carried to a separate part of the fund.

(2) Any property which—

(*a*) being property belonging to the narrower-range or wider-range part of a trust fund, is converted into special-range property, or

(*b*) being special-range property, accrues to a trust fund after the division of the fund or part thereof in pursuance of subsection (1) of section 2 of this Act or of that subsection as modified by sub-paragraph (1) of this paragraph,

shall be carried to such a separate part of the fund as aforesaid; and subsections (2) and (3) of the said section 2 shall have effect subject to this sub-paragraph.

3. Where property carried to such a separate part as aforesaid is converted into property other than special-range property,—

(*a*) it shall be transferred to the narrower-range part of the fund or the wider-range part of the fund or apportioned between them, and

[1] (*b*) any transfer of property from one of those parts to the other shall be made which is necessary to secure that the value of each of those parts of the fund is increased by the same amount.

NOTE
[1] Modified in relation to charities by S.I. 1995 No. 1092, *infra*.

Section 3

[1] SCHEDULE 3

PROVISIONS SUPPLEMENTARY TO S. 3 (4)

NOTE

[1] Excluded by the House of Commons Members' Fund Act 1962 (c. 53), s. 1 (5).

1. Where in a case falling within subsection (4) of section 3 of this Act, property belonging to the narrower-range part of a trust fund—

(*a*) is invested otherwise than in a narrower-range investment, or

(*b*) being so invested, is retained and not transferred or as soon as may be reinvested as mentioned in subsection (2) of section 2 of this Act,

then, so long as the property continues so invested and comprised in the narrower-range part of the fund, section one of this Act shall not authorise the making or retention of any wider-range investment.

2. Section 4 of the Trustee Act 1925, or section 33 of the Trusts (Scotland) Act 1921 (which relieve a trustee from liability for retaining an investment which has ceased to be authorised), shall not apply where an investment ceases to be authorised in consequence of the foregoing paragraph.

[THE NEXT PAGE IS M 47]

Section 16

SCHEDULE 4

MINOR AND CONSEQUENTIAL AMENDMENTS

1.—(1) References in the Trustee Act 1925, except in subsection (2) of section 69 of that Act, to section 1 of that Act or to provisions which include that section shall be construed respectively as references to section 1 of this Act and as including references to section 1 of this Act.

(2) References in the Trusts (Scotland) Act 1921, to section 10 or 11 of that Act, or to provisions which include either of those sections, shall be construed respectively as references to section one of this Act and as including references to that section.

2. [Repealed by the Building Societies Act 1962, Sched. 10, Pt. I.]

3. The following enactments and instruments, that is to say—
- (*a*) subsection (3) of section 74 of Schedule 3 to the Water Act 1945, and any order made under that Act applying the provisions of that subsection;
- (*b*) any local and personal Act which, or any order or other instrument in the nature of any such Act, which, modifies paragraph (*l*) of subsection (1) of section 1 of the Trustee Act 1925,

shall have effect as if for any reference to the said paragraph (*l*) there were substituted a reference to paragraph 10 of Part II of Schedule 1 to this Act.

4, 5. [Repealed by the National Savings Bank Act 1971, Sched. 2.]

6. For the reference in subsection (2) of section 1 of the House Purchase and Housing Act 1959, to paragraph (*a*) of subsection (1) of that section there shall be substituted a reference to paragraph 12 of Part II and paragraph 2 of Part III of Schedule 1 to this Act.

Succession (Scotland) Act 1964

(1964 c. 41)

An Act to assimilate and amend the law of Scotland with respect to the succession to the heritable and moveable property of deceased persons; to amend the law in relation to the legal and other prior rights exigible out of such property, to the administration of deceased persons' estates and other property passing on death, to the capacity of minors to test, and to the presumption of survivorship; to provide for certain testamentary dispositions to be probative; to provide for adopted persons to be treated for certain purposes as children of their adopters; to make new provision as to the financial rights and obligations of the parties on the dissolution of a marriage; and for purposes connected with the matters aforesaid. [10th June 1964]

PART I

INTESTATE SUCCESSION

Assimilation of heritage to moveables for purpose of devolution on intestacy

1.—(1) The whole of the intestate estate of any person dying after the commencement of this Act (so far as it is estate the succession to which falls to be regulated by the law of Scotland) shall devolve, without distinction as between heritable and moveable property, in accordance with—
- (*a*) the provisions of this Part in this Act; and
- (*b*) any enactment or rule of law in force immediately before the commencement of this Act which is not inconsistent with those pro-

visions and which, apart from this section, would apply to that person's moveable intestate estate, if any;

and, subject to section 37 of this Act, any enactment or rule of law in force immediately before the commencement of this Act with respect to the succession to intestate estates shall, in so far as it is inconsistent with the provisions of this Part of this Act, cease to have effect.

(2) Nothing in this Part of this Act shall affect legal rights or the prior rights of a surviving spouse; and accordingly any reference in this Part of this Act to an intestate estate shall be construed as a reference to so much of the net intestate estate as remains after the satisfaction of those rights, or the proportion thereof properly attributable to the intestate estate.

Rights of succession to intestate estate

2.—(1) Subject to the following provisions of this Part of this Act—

(*a*) where an intestate is survived by children, they shall have right to the whole of the intestate estate;

(*b*) where an intestate is survived by either of, or both, his parents and is also survived by brothers or sisters, but is not survived by any prior relative, the surviving parent or parents shall have right to one half of the intestate estate and the surviving brothers and sisters to the other half thereof;

(*c*) where an intestate is survived by brothers or sisters, but is not survived by any prior relative, the surviving brothers and sisters shall have right to the whole of the intestate estate;

(*d*) where an intestate is survived by either of, or both, his parents, but is not survived by any prior relative, the surviving parent or parents shall have right to the whole of the intestate estate;

(*e*) where an intestate is survived by a husband or a wife, but is not survived by any prior relative, the surviving spouse shall have right to the whole of the intestate estate;

(*f*) where an intestate is survived by uncles or aunts (being brothers or sisters of either parent of the intestate), but is not survived by any prior relative, the surviving uncles and aunts shall have right to the whole of the intestate estate;

(*g*) where an intestate is survived by a grandparent or grandparents (being a parent or parents of either parent of the intestate), but is not survived by any prior relative, the surviving grandparent or grandparents shall have right to the whole of the intestate estate;

(*h*) where an intestate is survived by brothers or sisters of any of his grandparents (being a parent or parents of either parent of the intestate), but is not survived by any prior relative, those surviving brothers and sisters shall have right to the whole of the intestate estate;

(*i*) where an intestate is not survived by any prior relative, the ancestors of the intestate (being remoter than grandparents) generation by generation successively, without distinction between the paternal and maternal lines, shall have right to the whole of the intestate estate; so however that, failing ancestors of any generation, the brothers and sisters of any of those ancestors shall have right thereto before ancestors of the next more remote generation.

(2) References in the foregoing subsection to brothers or sisters include respectively brothers and sisters of the half blood as well as of the whole blood; and in the said subsection " prior relative ", in relation to any class of person mentioned in any paragraph of that subsection, means a person of any other class who, if he had survived the intestate, would have had right to the intestate estate or any of it by virtue of an earlier paragraph of that subsection or by virtue of any such paragraph and section 5 of this Act.

Succession of collaterals

3. Subject to section 5 of this Act, where brothers and sisters of an intestate or of an ancestor of an intestate (in this section referred to as "collaterals") have right to the whole, or, in a case to which subsection (1)(*b*) of the last foregoing section applies, to a half, of the intestate estate, the collaterals of the whole blood shall be entitled to succeed thereto in preference to the collaterals of the half blood; but where the collaterals of the half blood have right as aforesaid they shall rank without distinction as between those related to the intestate, or, as the case may be, the ancestor, through their father and those so related through their mother.

4. [Repealed by the Law Reform (Parent and Child) (Scotland) Act 1986 (c. 9), Sched. 2.]

Representation

5.—(1) Subject to section 6 of this Act, where a person who, if he had survived an intestate, would, by virtue of any of the foregoing provisions of this Part of this Act, have had right (otherwise than as a parent or spouse of the intestate) to the whole or to any part of the intestate estate has predeceased the intestate, but has left issue who survive the intestate, such issue shall have the like right to the whole or to that part of the intestate estate as the said person would have had if he had survived the intestate.

(2) The right of any issue entitled to share in an intestate estate by virtue of the foregoing subsection to be appointed to the office of executor on the intestate estate shall be postponed to the right thereto of any person who succeeds to the whole or part of the intestate estate by virtue of the foregoing provisions of this Act apart from this section and who applies for appointment to that office.

Division of intestate estate among those having right thereto

6. If, by virtue of the foregoing provisions of this Part of this Act, there are two or more persons having right among them to the whole, or, in a case to which section 2(1)(*b*) of this Act relates, to a half, of an intestate estate, then the said estate, or, as the case may be, that half thereof, shall—

(*a*) if all of those persons are in the same degree of relationship to the intestate, be divided among them equally; and

(*b*) in any other case, be divided equally into a number of parts equal to the aggregate of—

(i) those of the said persons who are nearest in degree of relationship to the intestate (in this section referred to as "the nearest surviving relatives"), and

(ii) any other persons who were related to the intestate in that degree, but who have predeceased him leaving issue who survive him;

and, of those parts, one shall be taken by each of the nearest surviving relatives, and one shall be taken *per stirpes* by the issue of each of the said predeceased persons.[1]

NOTE

[1] Further sentence added by the Law Reform (Miscellaneous Provisions) (Scotland) Act 1968 (c. 70), Sched. 1 (estate of any person dying after the commencement of that Act), and repealed by the Law Reform (Parent and Child) (Scotland) Act 1986 (c. 9), Sched. 2.

Saving of right of Crown as ultimus haeres

7. Nothing in this Part of this Act shall be held to affect the right of the Crown as *ultimus haeres* to any estate to which no person is entitled by virtue of this Act to succeed.

PART II

[1] LEGAL AND OTHER PRIOR RIGHTS IN ESTATES OF DECEASED PERSONS

NOTE

[1] See the Finance Act 1985 (c. 54), s.84(5) and (6).

Prior rights of surviving spouse, on intestacy, in dwelling house and furniture

[1] **8.**—(1) Where a person dies intestate leaving a spouse, and the intestate estate includes a relevant interest in a dwelling house to which this section applies, the surviving spouse shall be entitled to receive out of the intestate estate—

(*a*) where the value of the relevant interest does not exceed £110,000[2] or such larger amount as may from time to time be fixed by order of the Secretary of State—

(i) if subsection (2) of this section does not apply, the relevant interest;

(ii) if the said subsection (2) applies, a sum equal to the value of the relevant interest;

(*b*) in any other case, the sum of £110,000[2] or such larger amount as may from time to time be fixed by order of the Secretary of State:

Provided that, if the intestate estate comprises a relevant interest in two or more dwelling houses to which this section applies, this subsection shall have effect only in relation to such one of them as the surviving spouse may elect for the purposes of this subsection within six months of the date of death of the intestate.

(2) This subsection shall apply for the purposes of paragraph (*a*) of the foregoing subsection if—

(*a*) the dwelling house forms part only of the subjects comprised in one tenancy or lease under which the intestate was the tenant; or

(*b*) the dwelling house forms the whole or part of subjects an interest in which is comprised in the intestate estate and which were used by the intestate for carrying on a trade, profession or occupation, and the value of the estate as a whole would be likely to be substantially diminished if the dwelling house were disposed of otherwise than with the assets of the trade, profession or occupation.

(3) Where a person dies intestate leaving a spouse, and the intestate estate includes the furniture and plenishings of a dwelling house to which this section applies (whether or not the dwelling house is comprised in the intestate estate), the surviving spouse shall be entitled to receive out of the intestate estate—

(*a*) where the value of the furniture and plenishings does not exceed £20,000[3] or such larger amount as may from time to time be fixed by order of the Secretary of State, the whole thereof;

(*b*) in any other case, such part of the furniture and plenishings, to a value not exceeding £20,000[3] or such larger amount as may from time to time be fixed by order of the Secretary of State, as may be chosen by the surviving spouse:

Provided that, if the intestate estate comprises the furniture and plenishings of two or more such dwelling houses, this subsection shall have effect only in relation to the furniture and plenishings of such one of them as the surviving spouse may elect for the purposes of this subsection within six months of the date of death of the intestate.

(4) This section applies, in the case of any intestate, to any dwelling house in which the surviving spouse of the intestate was ordinarily resident at the date of death of the intestate.

[4] (5) Where any question arises as to the value of any furniture or plenishings, or of any interest in a dwelling house, for the purposes of any provision of this section the question shall be determined by arbitration by a single arbiter appointed, in default of agreement, by the sheriff of the sheriffdom in which the intestate was domiciled at the date of his death or, if that sheriffdom is uncertain or the intestate was domiciled furth of Scotland, the sheriff of Lothian and Peebles at Edinburgh.

(6) In this section—

(*a*) "dwelling house" includes a part of a building occupied (at the date of death of the intestate) as a separate dwelling; and any reference to a dwelling house shall be construed as including any garden or portion of ground attached to, and usually occupied with, the dwelling house or otherwise required for the amenity or convenience of the dwelling house;

(*b*) "furniture and plenishings" includes garden effects, domestic animals, plate, plated articles, linen, china, glass, books, pictures, prints, articles of household use and consumable stores; but does not include any article or animal used at the date of death of the intestate for business purposes, or money or securities for money, or any heirloom;

(*c*) "heirloom", in relation to an intestate estate, means any article which has associations with the intestate's family of such nature and extent that it ought to pass to some member of that family other than the surviving spouse of the intestate;

(*d*) "relevant interest", in relation to a dwelling house, means the interest therein of an owner, or the interest therein of a tenant, subject in either case to any heritable debt secured over the interest; and for the purposes of this definition "tenant" means a tenant under a tenancy or lease (whether of the dwelling house alone or of the dwelling house together with other subjects) which is not a tenancy to which the Rent Acts 1971–74 apply.

NOTES

[1] As amended by S.I. 1993 No. 2690, in the case of a person dying on or after 26th November 1993. Saved by the Prescription and Limitation (Scotland) Act 1973 (c. 52), Sched. 1, para. 2(*f*).

[2] Earlier values: 10th September 1964 to 22nd May 1973—£15,000: 22nd May 1973 to 31st July 1981—£30,000; 1st August 1981 to 30th April 1988—£50,000; 1st May 1988 to 25th November 1993—£60,000 (S.I. 1988 No. 633).

[3] Earlier values: 10th September 1964 to 22nd May 1973—£5,000; 22nd May 1973 to 31st July 1981—£8,000; 1st August 1981 to 30th April 1988—£10,000; 1st May 1988 to 25th November 1993—£12,000 (S.I. 1988 No. 633).

[4] Amended by the Sheriff Courts (Scotland) Act 1971, Sched. 1, para. 1. For interpretation of the term "sheriff," see *ibid.* s.4(2) and the Interpretation Act 1978, Sched. 1.

Prior right of surviving spouse to financial provision on intestacy

[1] **9.**—[2] (1) Where a person dies intestate and is survived by a husband or wife, the surviving spouse shall be entitled to receive out of the intestate estate—

(*a*) if the intestate is survived by issue, the sum of £30,000[3] or such larger amount as may from time to time be fixed by order of the Secretary of State, or

(*b*) if the intestate is not survived by issue, the sum of £50,000[4] or such larger amount as may from time to time be fixed by order of the Secretary of State,

together with, in either case, interest at the rate of 7 per cent[5] per annum or at such rate as may from time to time be fixed by order of the Secretary of State on such sum from the date of the intestate's death until payment:

Provided that where the surviving spouse is entitled to receive a legacy out of the estate of the intestate (other than a legacy of any dwelling house to which the last foregoing section applies or of any furniture and plenishings of any such dwelling house), he or she shall, unless he or she renounces the legacy, be entitled under this subsection to receive only such sum, if any, as remains after deducting from the sum fixed by virtue of paragraph (*a*) of this subsection or the sum fixed by virtue of paragraph (*b*) of this subsection, as the case may be, the amount or value of the legacy.

(2) Where the intestate estate is less than the amount which the surviving spouse is entitled to receive by virtue of subsection (1) of this section the right conferred by the said subsection on the surviving spouse shall be satisfied by the transfer to him or her of the whole of the intestate estate.

(3) The amount which the surviving spouse is entitled to receive by virtue of subsection (1) of this section shall be borne by, and paid out of, the parts of the intestate estate consisting of heritable and moveable property respectively in proportion to the respective amounts of those parts.

(4) Where by virtue of subsection (2) of this section a surviving spouse has right to the whole of the intestate estate, he or she shall have the right to be appointed executor.

(5) The rights conferred by the Intestate Husband's Estate (Scotland) Acts 1911 to 1959 on a surviving spouse in his or her deceased spouse's estate shall not be exigible out of the estate of any person dying after the commencement of this Act.

(6) For the purposes of this section—

(*a*) the expression "intestate estate" means so much of the net intestate estate as remains after the satisfaction of any claims under the last foregoing section; and

(*b*) the expression "legacy" includes any payment or benefit to which a surviving spouse becomes entitled by virtue of any testamentary disposition; and the amount or value of any legacy shall be ascertained as at the date of the intestate's death.

NOTES

[1] Saved by the Prescription and Limitation (Scotland) Act 1973, s.6(2), Sched. 1, para. 2(*f*).

[2] As amended by the Law Reform (Miscellaneous Provisions) (Scotland) Act 1968 (c. 70), Sched. 1 (estate of any person dying on or after 25th November 1968); the Succession (Scotland) Act 1973 (c. 25), s.1(1)(*b*), the Law Reform (Miscellaneous Provisions) (Scotland) Act 1980 (c. 55), s.4, the Law Reform (Parent and Child) (Scotland) Act 1986 (c. 9), Sched. 2 and S.I. 1993 No. 2690 (persons dying on or after 26th November 1993).

[3] Earlier values: 10th September 1964 to 22nd May 1973—£2,500; 23rd May 1973 to 30th December 1977—£4,000; 31st December 1977 to 31st July 1981—£8,000 (S.I. 1977 No. 2110); 1st August 1981 to 30th April 1988—£15,000 (S.I. 1981 No. 806); 1st May 1988 to 25th November 1993—£21,000 (S.I. 1988 No. 633).

[4] Earlier values: 10th September 1964 to 22nd May 1973—£5,000; 23rd May 1973 to 30th December 1977—£8,000; 31st December 1977 to 31st July 1981—£16,000 (S.I. 1977 No. 2110); 1st August 1981 to 30th April 1988—£25,000 (S.I. 1981 No. 806); 1st May 1988 to 25th November 1993—£35,000 (S.I. 1988 No. 633).

[5] As from 1st August 1981 the rate of interest is fixed at 7 per cent.: see S.I. 1981 No. 805. (Earlier rate (1964–81) 4 per cent.).

Provisions supplementary to sections 8 and 9

[1] **9A.** Any order of the Secretary of State, under section 8 or 9 of this Act, fixing an amount or rate—

(*a*) shall be made by statutory instrument which shall be subject to annulment in pursuance of a resolution of either House of Parliament; and

(*b*) shall have effect in relation to the estate of any person dying after the coming into force of the order.

NOTE

[1] Added by the Law Reform (Miscellaneous Provisions) (Scotland) Act 1980 (c. 55), s.4.

Abolition of terce and courtesy, and calculation of legal rights

10.—(1) The right of courtesy of a surviving husband in his deceased wife's estate and the right of terce of a surviving wife in her deceased husband's estate shall not be exigible out of the estate of a person dying after the commencement of this Act.

(2) The amount of any claim to *jus relicti, jus relictae* or legitim out of an estate shall be calculated by reference to so much of the net moveable estate as remains after the satisfaction of any claims thereon under the two last foregoing sections.

10A. [Added by the Law Reform (Miscellaneous Provisions) (Scotland) Act 1968 (c. 70), s.2, in respect of estates of persons dying on or after 25th November 1968, and repealed by the Law Reform (Parent and Child) (Scotland) Act 1986 (c. 9), Sched. 2.]

Representation in, and division of, legitim

[1] **11.**—(1) Subject to the next following subsection, where a person (hereinafter in this section referred to as "the deceased") dies predeceased by a child who has left issue who survive the deceased, and the child would, if he had survived the deceased, have been entitled to legitim out of the deceased's estate, such issue shall have the like right to legitim as the child would have had if he had survived the deceased.

(2) If, by virtue of the foregoing subsection or otherwise, there are two or more persons having right among them to legitim, then the legitim shall—

(*a*) if all of those persons are in the same degree of relationship to the deceased, be divided among them equally, and

(*b*) in any other case, be divided equally into a number of parts equal to the aggregate of—

(i) those of the said persons who are nearest in degree of relationship to the deceased (in this paragraph referred to as "the nearest surviving relatives") and

(ii) any other persons who were related to the deceased in that degree and who (if they had survived him) would have been entitled to legitim out of his estate, but who have predeceased him leaving issue who survive him and are entitled to legitim out of his estate;

and, of those parts, one shall be taken by each of the nearest surviving relatives, and one shall be taken *per stirpes* by the issue of each of the said predeceased persons, being issue who are entitled as aforesaid.

(3) Nothing in the last foregoing subsection shall be construed as altering any rule of law as to collation of advances; and where any person is entitled to claim legitim out of the estate of a deceased person by virtue of subsection (1) of this section he shall be under the like duty to collate any advances made by the deceased to him, and the proportion appropriate to him of any advances so made to any person through whom he derives such entitlement, as if he had been entitled to claim such legitim otherwise than by virtue of the said subsection (1).

(4) For the avoidance of doubt it is hereby declared that where any person is entitled by virtue of subsection (1) of this section to legitim out of the estate of the deceased, and the deceased is not survived by any child, the proportion of the estate due to any surviving spouse in respect of *jus relicti* or *jus relictae* shall be ascertained as if the deceased had been survived by a child.

NOTE

[1] As amended by the Law Reform (Miscellaneous Provisions) (Scotland) Act 1968 (c. 70), Sched. 1, in respect of estate of any person dying on or after 25th November 1968, and by the Law Reform (Parent and Child) (Scotland) Act 1986 (c. 9), Sched. 2.

Legitim not to be discharged by ante-nuptial marriage contract

12. Nothing in any ante-nuptial contract of marriage executed after the commencement of this Act shall operate so as to exclude, on the occurrence of the death of either party to the marriage, the right of any child of the marriage (or of any issue of his coming in his place by virtue of the last foregoing section) to legitim out of the estate of that party unless such child or issue shall elect to accept in lieu of legitim the provision made in his favour under the contract.

Equitable compensation

[1] **13.** Every testamentary disposition executed after the commencement of this Act by which provision is made in favour of the spouse or of any issue of the testator and which does not contain a declaration that the provision so made is in full and final satisfaction of the right to any share in the testator's estate to which the spouse or the issue, as the case may be, is entitled by virtue of *jus relicti, jus relictae* or legitim, shall (unless the disposition contains an express provision to the contrary) have effect as if it contained such a declaration.

NOTE

[1] As amended by the Law Reform (Miscellaneous Provisions) (Scotland) Act 1968 (c. 70), Sched. 1, in respect of estate of any person dying on or after 25th November 1968, and by the Law Reform (Parent and Child) (Scotland) Act 1986 (c. 9), Sched. 2.

PART III

ADMINISTRATION AND WINDING UP OF ESTATES

Assimilation for purposes of administration, etc., of heritage to moveables

14.—(1) Subject to subsection (3) of this section the enactments and rules of law in force immediately before the commencement of this Act with respect to the administration and winding up of the estate of a deceased person so far as consisting of moveable property shall have effect (as

[THE NEXT PAGE IS M 55]

modified by the provisions of this Act) in relation to the whole of the estate without distinction between moveable property and heritable property: and accordingly on the death of any person (whether testate or intestate) every part of his estate (whether consisting of moveable property or heritable property) falling to be administered under the law of Scotland shall, by virtue of confirmation thereto, vest for the purposes of administration in the executor thereby confirmed and shall be administered and disposed of according to law by such executor.

[1] (2) Provision shall be made by the Court of Session by act of sederunt made under the enactments mentioned in section 22 of this Act (as extended by that section) for the inclusion in the confirmation of an executor, by reference to an appended inventory or otherwise, of a description, in such form as may be so provided, of any heritable property forming part of the estate.

(3) Nothing in this section shall be taken to alter any rule of law whereby any particular debt of a deceased person falls to be paid out of any particular part of his estate.

NOTE

[1] The Administration of Estates Act 1971, s. 6, provides: "6.—(1) It shall be competent to include in the inventory of the estate of any person who dies domiciled in Scotland any real estate of the deceased situated in England and Wales or Northern Ireland, and accordingly in section 9 of the Confirmation of Executors (Scotland) Act 1858 the word 'personal' wherever it occurs is hereby repealed.

(2) Section 14(2) of the Succession (Scotland) Act 1964 (act of sederunt to provide for description of heritable property) shall apply in relation to such real estate as aforesaid as it applies in relation to heritable property in Scotland".

Provisions as to transfer of heritage

15.—(1) Section 5(2) of the Conveyancing (Scotland) Act 1924 (which provides that a confirmation which includes a heritable security shall be a valid title to the debt thereby secured) shall have effect as if any reference therein to a heritable security, or to a debt secured by a heritable security, included a reference to any interest in heritable property which has vested in an executor in pursuance of the last foregoing section by virtue of a confirmation:

[1] Provided that a confirmation (other than an implied confirmation within the meaning of the said section 5(2)) shall not be deemed for the purposes of the said section 5(2) to include any such interest unless a description of the property, in accordance with any act of sederunt such as is mentioned in subsection (2) of the last foregoing section, is included or referred to in the confirmation.

(2) Where in pursuance of the last foregoing section any heritable property has vested in an executor by virtue of a confirmation, and it is necessary for him in distributing the estate to transfer that property—

(*a*) to any person in satisfaction of a claim to legal rights or the prior rights of a surviving spouse out of the estate, or

(*b*) to any person entitled to share in the estate by virtue of this Act, or

(*c*) to any person entitled to take the said property under any testamentary disposition of the deceased,

the executor may effect such transfer by endorsing on the confirmation (or where a certificate of confirmation relating to the property has been issued in pursuance of any act of sederunt, on the certificate) a docket in favour of that person in the form set out in Schedule 1 to this Act, or in a form as nearly as may be to the like effect, and any such docket may be specified as a midcouple or link in title in any deduction of title; but this section shall not be construed as prejudicing the competence of any other mode of transfer.

NOTE

[1] As amended by the Law Reform (Miscellaneous Provisions) (Scotland) Act 1968, s. 19.

Provisions relating to leases

[1] **16.**—(1) This section applies to any interest, being the interest of a tenant under a lease, which is comprised in the estate of a deceased person and has accordingly vested in the deceased's executor by virtue of section 14 of this Act; and in the following provisions of this section "interest" means an interest to which this section applies.

(2) Where an interest—

(*a*) is not the subject of a valid bequest by the deceased, or

(*b*) is the subject of such a bequest, but the bequest is not accepted by the legatee, or

[2] (*c*) being an interest under an agricultural lease, is the subject of such a bequest, but the bequest is declared null and void in pursuance of section 16 of the Act of 1886 or section 11 of the 1991 Act, or becomes null and void under section 10 of the Act of 1955,

and there is among the conditions of the lease (whether expressly or by implication) a condition prohibiting assignation of the interest, the executor shall be entitled, notwithstanding that condition, to transfer the interest to any one of the persons entitled to succeed to the deceased's intestate estate, or to claim legal rights or the prior rights of a surviving spouse out of the estate, in or towards satisfaction of that person's entitlement or claim; but shall not be entitled to transfer the interest to any other person without the consent—

(i) in the case of an interest under an agricultural lease, being a lease of a croft within the meaning of section 3(1) of the Act of 1955, of the Crofters Commission;

(ii) in any other case, of the landlord.

(3) If in the case of any interest—

(*a*) at any time the executor is satisfied that the interest cannot be disposed of according to law and so informs the landlord, or

(*b*) the interest is not so disposed of within a period of one year or such longer period as may be fixed by agreement between the landlord and the executor or, failing agreement, by the sheriff on summary application by the executor—

[2] (i) in the case of an interest under an agricultural lease which is the subject of a petition to the Land Court under section 16 of the Act of 1886 or an application to that court under section 11 of the 1991 Act, from the date of the determination or withdrawal of the petition or, as the case may be, the application.

(ia) in the case of an interest under an agricultural lease which is the subject of an application by the legatee to the Crofters Commission under section 10(1) of the Act of 1955, from the date of any refusal by the Commission to determine that the bequest shall not be null and void,

(ib) in the case of an interest under an agricultural lease which is the subject of an intimation of objection by the landlord to the legatee and the Crofters Commission under section 10(3) of the Act of 1955, from the date of any decision of the Commission upholding the objection.

(ii) in any other case, from the date of death of the deceased,

either the landlord or the executor may, on giving notice in accordance with the next following subsection to the other, terminate the lease (in so far as it relates to the interest) notwithstanding any provision therein, or any enactment or rule of law, to the contrary effect.

(4) The period of notice given under the last foregoing subsection shall be—

(*a*) in the case of an agricultural lease, such period as may be agreed, or, failing agreement, a period of not less than one year and not more than two years ending with such term of Whitsunday or Martinmas as may be specified in the notice; and

(*b*) in the case of any other lease, a period of six months:

Provided that paragraph (*b*) of this subsection shall be without prejudice to any enactment prescribing a shorter period of notice in relation to the lease in question.

(5) Subsection (3) of this section shall not prejudice any claim by any party to the lease for compensation or damages in respect of the termination of the lease (or any rights under it) in pursuance of that subsection; but any award of compensation or damages in respect of such termination at the instance of the executor shall be enforceable only against the estate of the deceased and not against the executor personally.

(6) Where an interest is an interest under an agricultural lease, and—

(*a*) an application is made under section 3 of the Act of 1931 or section 13 of the Act of 1955 to the Land Court for an order for removal, or

[2](*b*) a reference is made under section 23(2) and (3) of the 1991 Act to an arbiter to determine any question which has arisen under section 22(2)(*e*) of that Act in connection with a notice to quit,

the Land Court shall not make the order, or, as the case may be, the arbiter shall not make an award in favour of the landlord, unless the court or the arbiter is satisfied that it is reasonable having regard to the fact that the interest is vested in the executor in his capacity as executor, that it should be made.

(7) Where an interest is not an interest under an agricultural lease, and the landlord brings an action of removing against the executor in respect of a breach of a condition of the lease, the court shall not grant decree in the action unless it is satisfied that the condition alleged to have been breached is one which it is reasonable to expect the executor to have observed, having regard to the fact that the interest is vested in him in his capacity as an executor.

[2] (8) Where an interest is an interest under an agricultural lease and is the subject of a valid bequest by the deceased, the fact that the interest is vested in the executor under the said section 14 shall not prevent the operation, in relation to the legatee, of paragraphs (*a*) to (*h*) of section 16 of the Act of 1886, or, as the case may be, section 11(2) to (8) of the 1991 Act, or, as the case may be, subsections (2) to (7) of section 10 of the Act of 1955.

[2] (9) In this section—

"agricultural lease" means a lease of a holding within the meaning of the Small Landholders (Scotland) Acts 1886 to 1931 or of the 1991 Act or a lease of a croft within the meaning of section 3(1) of the Act of 1955;

"the Act of 1886" means the Crofters Holdings (Scotland) Act 1886;

"the Act of 1931" means the Small Landholders and Agricultural Holdings (Scotland) Act 1931;

"the 1991 Act" means the Agricultural Holdings (Scotland) Act 1991;

"the Act of 1955" means the Crofters (Scotland) Act 1955;

"lease" includes tenancy.

NOTES

[1] As amended by the Law Reform (Miscellaneous Provisions) (Scotland) Act 1968 (c. 70), Sched. 2 (estates of any person dying on or after 25th November 1968). See the Agriculture Act 1986 (c. 49), Sched. 2, para. 3. As regards notices to quit, see the Agricultural Holdings (Scotland) Act 1991 (c. 55), s. 25, *supra*, Div. L.

[2] As amended by the Agricultural Holdings (Scotland) Act 1991 (c. 55), Sched. 11, para. 24.

Protection of persons acquiring title

[1] **17.** Where any person has in good faith and for value acquired title to any interest in or security over heritable property which has vested in an executor as aforesaid directly or indirectly from—

(*a*) the executor, or

(*b*) a person deriving title directly from the executor,

the title so acquired shall not be challengeable on the ground that the confirmation was reducible or has in fact been reduced, or, in a case falling under paragraph (*b*) above, that the title should not have been transferred to the person mentioned in that paragraph.

NOTE

[1] Saved by the Law Reform (Miscellaneous Provisions) (Scotland) Act 1968 (c. 70), s. 7.

Provisions as to entails and special destinations

18.—[1] (1) On the death of the heir of entail in possession of any property subject to an entail, the entailed property shall, if the executor of the deceased is confirmed thereto, vest in the executor for the purpose of enabling it to be conveyed to the heir of entail next entitled thereto under the entail (if such conveyance is necessary) and for that purpose only.

[1] (2) On the death of a person entitled to any heritable property subject to a special destination in favour of some other person, being a destination which the deceased could not competently have, or in fact has not, evacuated by testamentary disposition or otherwise, the property shall, if the executor of the deceased is confirmed thereto, vest in the executor for the purpose of enabling it to be conveyed to the person next entitled thereto under the destination (if such conveyance is necessary) and for that purpose only.

(3) Section 14(2) of this Act shall apply in relation to property to which this section refers as it applies to property to which the said section 14(2) refers.

(4) Sections 15 and 17 of this Act shall apply to property which has vested in an executor by virtue of this section as they apply to property which has vested in an executor by virtue of section 14 of this Act, as if the person next entitled to the first mentioned property were a person entitled to share in the estate of the deceased.

NOTE

[1] See the Inheritance Tax Act 1984 (c. 51), s. 209(1).

19. [Repealed by the Finance Act 1975 (c. 7), Sched. 13.]

Executor dative to have powers of a trustee

20. An executor dative appointed to administer the estate of a deceased person shall have in his administration of such estate the whole powers, privileges and immunities, and be subject to the same obligations, limitations and restrictions, which gratuitous trustees have, or are subject to, under any enactment or under common law, and the Trusts (Scotland) Acts 1921 and 1961 shall have effect as if any reference therein to a trustee included a reference to such an executor dative:

Provided that nothing in this section shall exempt an executor dative from finding caution for his intromissions or confer upon him any power to resign or to assume new trustees.

Evidence as to holograph wills in commissary proceedings

[1] **21.**—(1) Notwithstanding any rule of law or practice to the contrary, confirmation of an executor to property disposed of in a holograph testamentary disposition shall not be granted unless the court is satisfied by evidence consisting at least of an affidavit by each of two persons that the writing and signature of the disposition are in the handwriting of the testator.

(2) This section shall not apply to a testamentary document executed after the commencement of the Requirements of Writing (Scotland) Act 1995.

NOTE

[1] As amended by the Requirements of Writing (Scotland) Act 1995 (c. 7), Sched. 4, para. 38 (effective 1st August 1995: s. 15(2)).

Evidence as to testamentary documents in commissary proceedings

[1] **21A.** Confirmation of an executor to property disposed of in a testamentary document executed after the commencement of the Requirements of Writing (Scotland) Act 1995 shall not be granted unless the formal validity of the document is governed—

(*a*) by Scots law and the document is presumed under section 3 or 4 of that Act to have been subscribed by the granter so disposing of that property; or

(*b*) by a law other than Scots law and the court is satisfied that the document is formally valid according to the law governing such validity.

NOTE

[1] Inserted by the Requirements of Writing (Scotland) Act 1995 (c. 7), Sched. 4, para. 39 (effective 1st August 1995: s. 15(2)).

Court of Session may regulate procedure in commissary proceedings

[1] **22.**—(1) The powers exercisable by the Court of Session by act of sederunt under section 18 of the Confirmation of Executors (Scotland) Act 1858, section 16 of the Sheriff Courts and Legal Officers (Scotland) Act 1927 and section 34 of the Administration of Justice (Scotland) Act 1933 (which empower the court to regulate *inter alia* procedure in proceedings in the sheriff court and in proceedings for the confirmation of executors) shall include power to regulate the procedure to be followed, and to prescribe the form and content of any petition, writ or other document to be used, in connection with the confirmation of executors in cases where, by virtue of this Act, heritable property devolves upon the executor.

(2) Without prejudice to the generality of the powers conferred on the court by the said sections and by this section, the power conferred by the said section 34 to modify, amend or repeal by act of sederunt enactments relating to certain matters shall include power so to modify, amend or repeal any enactment relating to the procedure to be followed in proceedings for the confirmation of executors in such cases as aforesaid.

(3) [Repealed by the Law Reform (Miscellaneous Provisions) (Scotland) Act 1966 (c. 19), Sched., Part I.]

(4) [Repealed by the Finance Act 1975 (c. 7), Sched. 13.]

NOTE

[1] See S.I. 1964 No. 1143 and S.I. 1971 No. 1165.

PART IV

ADOPTED PERSONS

Adopted person to be treated for purposes of succession, etc., as child of adopter

[1] **23.**—(1) For all purposes relating to—

(*a*) the succession to a deceased person (whether testate or intestate), and

(*b*) the disposal of property by virtue of any *inter vivos* deed,

an adopted person shall be treated as the child of the adopter and not as the child of any other person.

In this subsection and in the following provisions of this Part of this Act any reference to succession to a deceased person shall be construed as including a reference to the distribution of any property in consequence of the death of the deceased person and any claim to legal rights or the prior rights of a surviving spouse out of his estate.

(2) In any deed whereby property is conveyed or under which a succession arises, being a deed executed after the making of an adoption order, unless the contrary intention appears, any reference (whether express or implied)—

(*a*) to the child or children of the adopter shall be construed as, or as including, a reference to the adopted person;

(*b*) to the child or children of the adopted person's natural parents or either of them shall be construed as not being, or as not including, a reference to the adopted person; and

(*c*) to a person related to the adopted person in any particular degree shall be construed as a reference to the person who would be related to him in that degree if he were the child of the adopter and were not the child of any other person:

Provided that for the purposes of this subsection a deed containing a provision taking effect on the death of any person shall be deemed to have been executed on the date of death of that person.

[2] (3) Where the terms of any deed provide that any property or interest in property shall devolve along with a title, honour or dignity, nothing in this section or in the Children Act 1975 or in the Adoption (Scotland) Act 1978 shall prevent that property or interest from so devolving.

(4) Nothing in this section shall affect any deed executed, or the devolution of any property on, or in consequence of, the death of a person who dies, before the commencement of this Act.

(5) In this Part of this Act the expression "adoption order" has the same meaning as in section 38 of the Adoption (Scotland) Act 1978 (whether the order took effect before or after the commencement of this Act); and "adopted" means adopted in pursuance of an adoption order.

NOTE

[1] As amended by the Adoption (Scotland) Act 1978 (c. 28), Sched. 3, para. 4. See also the Legitimation (Scotland) Act 1968 (c. 22), ss. 2(6), 6(2). Excluded by the Law Reform (Miscellaneous Provisions) (Scotland) Act 1966 (c. 19), s. 5.

Provisions supplementary to section 23

[1] **24.**—(1) For the purposes of the law regulating the succession to any property and for the purposes of the construction of any such deed as is mentioned in the last foregoing section, an adopted person shall be deemed to be related to any other person, being the child or the adopted child of the adopter or (in the case of a joint adoption) of either of the adopters,

(*a*) where he or she was adopted by two spouses jointly and that other person is the child or adopted child of both of them, as a brother or sister of the whole blood;

(*b*) in any other case, as a brother or sister of the half blood.

[2] (1A) Where, in relation to any purpose specified in section 23(1) of this Act, any right is conferred or any obligation is imposed, whether by operation of law or under any deed coming into operation after the commencement of the Children Act 1975, by reference to the relative seniority of the members of a class of persons, then, without prejudice to any entitlement under Part I of the Law Reform (Miscellaneous Provisions) (Scotland) Act 1968 of an illegitimate child who is adopted by one of his parents,

(*a*) any member of that class who is an adopted person shall rank as if he had been born on the date of his adoption, and

(*b*) if two or more members of the class are adopted persons whose dates of adoption are the same, they shall rank as between themselves in accordance with their respective times of birth.

[3] (2) Notwithstanding anything in the last foregoing section, a trustee or an executor may distribute any property for the distribution of which he is responsible without having ascertained that no adoption order has been made by virtue of which any person is or may be entitled to any interest therein, and shall not be liable to any such person of whose claim he has not had notice at the time of the distribution; but (without prejudice to section 17 of this Act) nothing in this subsection shall affect any right of any such person to recover the property, or any property representing it, from any person who may have received it.

(3) Where an adoption order is made in respect of a person who has been previously adopted, the previous adoption shall be disregarded for the purposes of the last foregoing section in relation to the devolution of any property on the death of any person dying after the date of the subsequent adoption order, and in relation to any deed executed after that date whereby property is conveyed or under which a succession arises.

(4) [Repealed by the Adoption (Scotland) Act 1978 (c. 28), Sched. 4.]

NOTES

[1] Saved by the Legitimation (Scotland) Act 1968 (c. 22), ss. 2(6), 6(2).

[2] Added by the Children Act 1975 (c. 72), Sched. 2, para. 5.

[3] As amended by the Adoption Act 1964 (c. 57), s. 1(1).

Part V

Financial Provisions on Divorce

25–27. [Repealed by the Divorce (Scotland) Act 1976 (c. 39), Sched. 2.]

Part VI

Miscellaneous and Supplementary

28. [Repealed by the Age of Legal Capacity (Scotland) Act 1991 (c. 50), Sched. 2.]

Right of tenant to bequeath interest under lease

29.—(1) A bequest by a tenant of his interest under a tenancy or lease to any one of the persons who, if the tenant had died intestate, would be, or would in any circumstances have been, entitled to succeed to his intestate estate by virtue of this Act shall not be treated as invalid by reason only that there is among the conditions of the tenancy or lease an implied condition prohibiting assignation.

[1] (2) This section shall not prejudice the operation of section 16 of the Crofters Holdings (Scotland) Act 1886, or section 11 of the Agricultural Holdings (Scotland) Act 1991 (which relate to bequests in the case of agricultural leases), or of section 10 of the Crofters (Scotland) Act 1955 (which makes similar provision in relation to crofts).

NOTE

[1] As amended by the Law Reform (Miscellaneous Provisions) (Scotland) Act 1968 (c. 70), Sched. 2 (estate of persons dying after the commencement of that Act), and the Agricultural Holdings (Scotland) Act 1991 (c. 55), Sched. 11, para. 25.

Effect of testamentary dispositions on special destinations

30. A testamentary disposition executed after the commencement of this Act shall not have effect so as to evacuate a special destination (being a destination which could competently be evacuated by the testamentary disposition) unless it contains a specific reference to the destination and a declared intention on the part of the testator to evacuate it.

Presumption of survivorship in respect of claims to property

31.—(1) Where two persons have died in circumstances indicating that they died simultaneously or rendering it uncertain which, if either, of them survived the other, then, for all purposes affecting title or succession to property or claims to legal rights or the prior rights of a surviving spouse,

(*a*) where the persons were husband and wife, it shall be presumed that neither survived the other; and

(*b*) in any other case, it shall be presumed that the younger person survived the elder unless the next following subsection applies.

(2) If, in a case to which paragraph (*b*) of the foregoing subsection would (apart from this subsection) apply, the elder person has left a testamentary disposition containing a provision, however expressed, in favour of the younger if he survives the elder and, failing the younger, in favour of a third person, and the younger person has died intestate, then it shall be presumed for the purposes of that provision that the elder person survived the younger.

Certain testamentary dispositions to be formally valid

[1] **32.**—(1) For the purpose of any question arising as to entitlement, by virtue of a testamentary disposition, to any relevant property or to any interest therein, the disposition shall be treated as valid in respect of the formalities of execution.

(2) Subsection (1) above is without prejudice to any right to challenge the validity of the testamentary disposition on the ground of forgery or on any other ground of essential invalidity.

(3) In this section "relevant property" means property disposed of in the testamentary disposition in respect of which—

(*a*) confirmation has been granted; or

(*b*) probate, letters of administration or other grant of representation—

(i) has been issued, and has noted the domicile of the deceased to be, in England and Wales or in Northern Ireland; or

(ii) has been issued outwith the United Kingdom and had been sealed in Scotland under section 2 of the Colonial Probates Act 1892.

NOTE

[1] Substituted by the Requirements of Writing (Scotland) Act 1995 (c. 7), Sched. 4, para. 40.

Construction of existing deeds

[1] **33.**—[1a] (1) Subject to subsection (2) of this section, any reference in any deed taking effect after the commencement of this Act to *jus relicti, jus relictae* or legitim shall be construed as a reference to the right to *jus relicti, jus relictae* or legitim, as the case may be, as modified by Part II of this Act; and any reference in any such deed to courtesy or terce shall be of no effect.

[2] (2) Any reference to legal rights in a marriage contract made before the commencement of this Act and taking effect in consequence of a decree of divorce granted in an action commenced after the commencement of this Act shall be construed as a reference to any right which the husband or the wife, as the case may be, might obtain by virtue of the provisions of section 26 of this Act or section 5 of the Divorce (Scotland) Act 1976 or section 29 of the Matrimonial and Family Proceedings Act 1984 or section 8 of the Family Law (Scotland) Act 1985.

NOTES

[1] As amended by the Law Reform (Miscellaneous Provisions) (Scotland) Act 1968 (c. 70), Sched. 1, in respect of estate of any person dying on or after 25th November 1968.

[1a] As amended by the Law Reform (Parent and Child) (Scotland) Act 1986 (c. 9), Sched. 1, para. 7(1) and Sched. 2, with effect from 8th December 1986.

[2] As amended by the Divorce (Scotland) Act 1976 (c. 39), Sched. 1, para. 2, the Matrimonial and Family Proceedings Act 1984 (c. 42), Sched. 1, para. 6, and the Family Law (Scotland) Act 1985 (c. 37), Sched. 1, para. 4.

Modification of enactments and repeals

34.—(1) Subject to the provisions of section 37 of this Act, the enactment mentioned in Schedule 2 to this Act shall have effect subject to the modifications specified in that Schedule, being modifications consequential on the provisions of this Act.

(2) [Repealed by the Statute Law (Repeals) Act 1974 (c. 22).]

Transfer of certain jurisdiction to Sheriff of Chancery

35.—(1) If at any time it appears to the Secretary of State expedient to do so he may by order transfer to the Sheriff of Chancery the jurisdiction of any other sheriff in relation to the service of heirs.

(2) An order made under this section may contain such consequential provisions as appears to the Secretary of State to be necessary, including provisions for the consequential repeal or consequential modification of any enactment relating to the matters dealt with in the order.

(3) Any order made under this section shall be made by statutory instrument.

Interpretation

36.—(1) In this Act the following expressions shall, unless the context otherwise requires, have the meanings hereby respectively assigned to them, that is to say—

"deed" includes any disposition, contract, instrument or writing, whether *inter vivos* or *mortis causa*;

"an intestate" means a person who has died leaving undisposed of by testamentary disposition the whole or any part of his estate, and "intestate" shall be construed accordingly;

"intestate estate", in relation to an intestate, means (subject to sections 1(2) and 9(6)(*a*) of this Act) so much of his estate as is undisposed of by testamentary disposition;

[0] "issue" means issue however remote;

"Land Court" means the Scottish Land Court;

"lease" and "tenancy" include sub-lease and sub-tenancy, and tenant shall be construed accordingly;

"legal rights" means *jus relicti, jus relictae*, and legitim;

"net estate" and "net intestate estate" means respectively so much of an estate or an intestate estate as remains after provision for the satisfaction of [1]estate duty and other liabilities of the estate having priority over legal rights, the prior rights of a surviving spouse and rights of succession, or, as the case may be, the proportion thereof properly attributable to the intestate estate;

"owner" in relation to any heritable property means the person entitled to receive the rents thereof (other than rents under a sub-lease or sub-tenancy);

"prior rights", in relation to a surviving spouse, means the rights conferred by sections 8 and 9 of this Act;

"testamentary disposition" in relation to a deceased, includes any deed taking effect on his death whereby any part of his estate is disposed of or under which a succession thereto arises.

(2) Any reference in this Act to the estate of a deceased person shall, unless the context otherwise requires, be construed as a reference to the whole estate, whether heritable or moveable, or partly heritable and partly moveable, belonging to the deceased at the time of his death or over which the deceased had a power of appointment and, where the deceased immediately before his death held the interest of a tenant under a tenancy or lease which was not expressed to expire on his death, includes that interest:

Provided that—

(*a*) where any heritable property belonging to a deceased person at the date of his death is subject to a special destination in favour of any person, the property shall not be treated for the purposes of this Act as part of the estate of the deceased unless the destination is one which could competently be, and has in fact been, evacuated by the deceased by testamentary disposition or otherwise; and in that case the property shall be treated for the purposes of this Act as if it were part of the deceased's estate on which he has tested; and

(*b*) where any heritable property over which a deceased person had a power of appointment has not been disposed of in exercise of that power and is in those circumstances subject to a power of appointment by some other person, that property shall not be treated for the purposes of this Act as part of the estate of the deceased.

(3) Without prejudice to the proviso to section 23(2) of this Act, references in this Act to the date of execution of a testamentary disposition shall be construed as references to the date on which the disposition was actually executed and not to the date of death of the testator.

(4) References in this Act to any enactment shall, except where the context otherwise requires, be construed as references to that enactment as amended by or under any other enactment, including this Act.

[2] (5) Section 1(1) (legal equality of children) of the Law Reform (Parent and Child) (Scotland) Act 1986 shall apply to this Act; and any reference (however expressed) in this Act to a relative shall be construed accordingly.

NOTES

[0] As amended by the Law Reform (Parent and Child) (Scotland) Act 1986 (c. 9), Sched. 2.

[1] Includes inheritance tax: see the Inheritance Tax Act 1984 (c. 51), Sched. 6, para. 1.

[2] Added by the Law Reform (Parent and Child) (Scotland) Act 1986 (c. 9), Sched. 1, para. 7(2), with effect from 8th December 1986.

Exclusion of certain matters from operation of Act

37.—[1] (1) Save as otherwise expressly provided, nothing in this Act or (as respects paragraph (*a*) of this subsection) in the Children Act 1975 or the Adoption (Scotland) Act 1978 shall—

(*a*) apply to any title, coat of arms, honour or dignity transmissible on the death of the holder thereof or affect the succession thereto or the devolution thereof;

(*b*) [Repealed by the Law Reform (Miscellaneous Provisions) (Scotland) Act 1968, Sched. 3 (estate of any person dying after the commencement of that Act)];

(*c*) affect any right on the part of a surviving spouse to claim from the representatives of his or her deceased spouse payment of aliment out of the estate of that spouse;

[2] (*d*) affect the administration, winding up or distribution of or the making up of title to any part of the estate of any person who died before the commencement of this Act or the rights of succession to such an estate or any claim for legal rights or terce or courtesy or any rights arising under the Intestate Husband's Estate (Scotland) Acts 1911 to 1959, out of such an estate or the right to take any legal proceedings with respect to any such matters;

(*e*) affect any claim for legal rights arising out of an action of divorce commenced before the commencement of this Act;

and in relation to the matters aforesaid the law in force immediately before the commencement of this Act shall continue to have effect as if this Act had not passed.

(2) Nothing in this Act shall be construed as affecting the operation of any rule of law applicable immediately before the commencement of this Act to the choice of the system of law governing the administration, winding up or distribution of the estate, or any part of the estate, of any deceased person.

NOTES

[1] As amended by the Children Act 1975 (c. 72), Sched. 2, para. 5, and the Adoption (Scotland) Act 1978 (c. 28), Sched. 3, para. 5.

[2] Saved by the Law Reform (Miscellaneous Provisions) (Scotland) Act 1980 (c. 55), s. 6.

Citation, extent and commencement

38.—(1) This Act may be cited as the Succession (Scotland) Act 1964.

(2) This Act shall extend to Scotland only.

(3) This Act shall come into operation on the expiration of the period of three months beginning with the date on which it is passed.

SCHEDULES

Section 15

[1] SCHEDULE 1

FORM OF DOCKET

NOTE

[1] As amended by the Requirements of Writing (Scotland) Act 1995 (c. 7), Sched. 4, para. 41 (effective 1st August 1995: s. 15(2)).

I, AB, being by virtue of the within confirmation [*or certificate of confirmation*] the executor on the estate of the deceased CD so far as specified in the confirmation [*or certificate or inventory attached hereto*] hereby nominate EF [*designed*] as the person entitled—

(*a*) in [part] satisfaction of his claim to prior rights, as a surviving spouse, on the death of the deceased,

(*b*) in [part] satisfaction of his claim to legal rights on the death of the deceased,

(*c*) in [part] satisfaction of his share in the said estate,

(*d*) in [part] implement of a trust disposition and settlement, [*or will, or as the case may be*] of the deceased dated   and registered in the Books of Council and Session   ,

to the following item of estate, that it to say, [*short description*] being number   of the items of the estate specified in the said confirmation [*or certificate or inventory*].

Testing clause †

†Note—Subscription of the document by the granter of it will be sufficient for the document to be formally valid, but witnessing of it may be necessary or desirable for other purposes (see the Requirements of Writing (Scotland) Act 1995).

Section 34

SCHEDULE 2

MODIFICATION OF ENACTMENTS

General modifications

[1] 1. Subject to the specific modifications made by the following provisions of this Schedule, references in any enactment to the heir-at-law of a deceased person in relation to any heritable property shall be construed as references to the persons who by virtue of this Act are entitled to succeed to such property on intestacy.

NOTE

[1] As amended by the Law Reform (Miscellaneous Provisions) (Scotland) Act 1968 (c. 70), Sched. 3 (estate of any person dying after the commencement of that Act).

---

2. Subject as aforesaid references in general terms in any enactment to the heirs of a deceased person shall include—

(*a*) the persons entitled by virtue of this Act to succeed on intestacy to any part of the estate of the deceased; and

(*b*) so far as is necessary for the purposes of Part III of this Act, the executor of the deceased.

3. References in any enactment relating to the confirmation of executors or the administration of the moveable estates of deceased persons to the moveable or personal property or estate of a deceased person shall, except where the context otherwise requires, be construed as references to the whole estate of the deceased person.

4. References in any enactment (other than in this Act) to courtesy or terce shall be of no effect.

Specific modifications

See
Registration of Leases (Scotland) Act 1857, ss. 8, 9 and Scheds. (C), (F).
Titles to Land Consolidation (Scotland) Act 1868, s. 20.
Conveyancing (Scotland) Act 1924, ss. 32, 33.

Law Reform (Miscellaneous Provisions) (Scotland) Act 1966

(1966 c. 19)

An Act . . . to provide in Scotland for the succession of an adopted person to the estate of his natural parent in certain circumstances; to amend section 5 of the Trusts (Scotland) Act 1961; . . . [3rd August 1966]

1–4. [See Division D.]

Adopted person to be treated as child of natural parents for purposes of succession in certain circumstances

5.—(1) Notwithstanding section 23(1) of the Succession (Scotland) Act 1964 (adopted person to be treated for purposes of succession as the child of the adopter), where the adopter of an adopted person has died before 10th September 1964, the adopted person shall be treated for the purposes of succession to the estate of a natural parent, who dies after the commencement of this Act, as the child of that parent.

(2) In the foregoing subsection, in relation to a person adopted jointly by spouses any references, however worded, to the death of an adopter shall be construed as a reference to the death of both spouses; and other expressions shall have the same meaning as in Part IV of the Succession (Scotland) Act 1964.

Amendment of section 5 of the Trusts (Scotland) Act 1961

6.—(1) The periods for which accumulations of income under a settlement or other disposition are permitted by section 5 of the Trusts (Scotland) Act 1961 shall include—

(*a*) a term of 21 years from the date of the making of the settlement or other disposition, and

(*b*) the duration of the minority or respective minorities of any person or persons living or *in utero* at that date,

and a direction to accumulate income during a period specified in paragraph (*a*) or paragraph (*b*) of this subsection shall not be void, nor shall the accumulation of the income be contrary to the said section 5, solely by reason of the fact that the period begins during the life of the grantor and ends after his death.

(2) The restrictions imposed by the said section 5 shall apply in relation to a power to accumulate income whether or not there is a duty to exercise that power, and they shall apply whether or not the power to accumulate extends to income produced by the investment of income previously accumulated.

(3) This section shall apply only in relation to instruments taking effect after the passing of this Act, and in the case of an instrument made in the exercise of a special power of appointment shall apply only where the instrument creating the power takes effect after the passing of this Act.

7–10. [See Division D.]

Interpretation, repeals, citation and extent

11.—(1) Any reference in this Act to an enactment shall be construed as a reference to that enactment as amended by any other enactment including this Act.

. . . .

(3) This Act may be cited as the Law Reform (Miscellaneous Provisions) (Scotland) Act 1966, and shall extend to Scotland only.

[THE NEXT PAGE IS M 67]

Law Reform (Miscellaneous Provisions) (Scotland) Act 1968

(1968 c. 70)

An Act to amend the law of Scotland relating to succession to the property of deceased persons in cases of illegitimacy; to confer on illegitimate persons in Scotland the right to legitim out of their deceased parents' estates; to amend the law of Scotland with respect to the construction of certain provisions made by deed or otherwise; to extend the provisions of the Succession (Scotland) Act 1964 to tenancies of crofts; to amend the law of evidence in civil proceedings in Scotland; to re-enact, with amendments, the provisions of certain enactments relating to the duration of liferents in Scotland; to amend section 15(1) of the Succession (Scotland) Act 1964; further to amend the law of Scotland relating to prorogation of the jurisdiction of the sheriff court; to remove a restriction on the extent of land in Scotland which a trade union may purchase or take upon lease and otherwise deal with; and for purposes connected with the matters aforesaid. [25th October 1968]

PART I

SUCCESSION, CONSTRUCTION OF DEEDS, ETC., IN CASES OF ILLEGITIMACY

Rights in estates of deceased persons in cases of illegitimacy

1–6. [Repealed by the Law Reform (Parent and Child) (Scotland) Act 1986, Sched. 2, with effect from 8th December 1986.]

Protection of trustees and executors

Protection of trustees and executors

[1] **7.** A trustee or an executor may distribute any property vested in him as such trustee or executor, or may make any payment out of any such property, without having ascertained—

(*a*) that no illegitimate person exists who is or may be entitled to an interest in that property or payment in consequence of any of the said provisions, and

(*b*) that no illegitimate person exists or has existed, the fact of whose existence is, in consequence of any of the said provisions, relevant to the ascertainment of the persons entitled to an interest in that property or payment, and

(*c*) that no paternal relative of an illegitimate person exists who is or may be entitled to an interest in that property or payment,

and such trustee or executor shall not be personally liable to any person so entitled of whose claim he has not had notice at the time of the distribution or payment; but (without prejudice to section 17 of the Act of 1964) nothing in this section shall affect any right of any person so entitled to recover the property, or any property representing it, or the payment, from any person who may have received that property or payment.

NOTE

[1] As amended by the Law Reform (Parent and Child) (Scotland) Act 1986, Sched. 1, para. 10 and Sched. 2, with effect from 8th December 1986.

Part II

Application of Succession (Scotland) Act 1964 to Tenancies of Crofts

. . . .

Part III
[See Division B.]

Part IV

Miscellaneous Amendments of the Law

Restriction on duration of liferents

18.—(1) Where by any deed executed after the commendement of this Act there is created a liferent interest in any property and a person who was not living or *in utero* at the date of the coming into operation of the said deed becomes entitled to that interest, then—

(*a*) if that person is of full age at the date on which he becomes entitled to the liferent interest, as from that date, or

(*b*) if that person is not of full age at that date, as from the date on which, being still entitled to the liferent interest he becomes of full age,

the said property shall, subject to subsection (2) of this section, belong absolutely to that person, and, if the property is vested in trustees, those trustees shall, subject as aforesaid, be bound to convey, deliver or make over the property to that person.

(2) The fact that, by virtue of subsection (1) of this section any property has come to belong absolutely to any person shall not affect—

(*a*) the rights in the property of any person holding a security over the property;

(*b*) any rights in the property created independently of the deed by which the liferent in question was created;

(*c*) in the case of heritable property, the rights therein of the superior of the property.

(3) The expenses of the conveyance, delivery or making over of any property to any person in pursuance of subsection (1) of this section shall be borne by that person.

(4) Section 48 of the Entail Amendment Act 1848 and section 9 of the Trusts (Scotland) Act 1921 shall not have effect in relation to any deed executed after the commencement of this Act.

(5) For the purposes of this section—

(*a*) the date of the coming into operation of any testamentary or other *mortis causa* deed shall, subject to paragraph (*c*) below, be taken to be the date of the death of the granter thereof;

(*b*) the date of the coming into operation of any marriage contract shall, subject as aforesaid, be taken to be the date of the dissolution of the marriage;

(*c*) the date of the execution, or of the coming into operation, of any deed made in the exercise of a special power of appointment shall be taken to be the date of the execution, or as the case may be of the coming into operation, of the deed creating that power.

Amendment of section 15(1) of the Succession (Scotland) Act 1964

19. [See the Succession (Scotland) Act 1964, s.15(1).]

Agreement to prorogate jurisdiction of particular sheriff court in certain moneylenders' contracts to be void

20. Section 4 of the Law Reform (Miscellaneous Provisions) (Scotland) Act 1940 (which makes void any provision or agreement in or in relation to a contract to which that section applies, whereby any party to such contract prorogates the jurisdiction of a particular sheriff court) shall have effect as if at the end of subsection (2) thereof (wherein are specified the contracts to which the section applies) there were added the following words:—

"and

(*c*) any contract entered into by a moneylender within the meaning of the Moneylenders Acts 1900 to 1927 in the course of his business as a moneylender, being a contract which contains an agreement with respect to the advance or repayment of money, or in respect of money lent, or as to the taking or release of any security in respect of money lent.".

Removal of restriction on purchase, etc., of land by trade unions

21. Section 7 of the Trade Union Act 1871 (which empowers trade

[THE NEXT PAGE IS M 71]

unions to purchase or take upon lease, and to deal otherwise with, land not exceeding one acre in extent) shall have effect as if the words " not exceeding one acre " were omitted.

PART V

SUPPLEMENTARY

Short title, interpretation, repeals, extent and commencement

22.—(1) This Act may be cited as the Law Reform (Miscellaneous Provisions) (Scotland) Act 1968.

(2) In this Act—

(*a*) " enactment " includes any instrument having effect by virtue of an Act;

(*b*) any reference to any enactment shall be construed as a reference to that enactment as amended, and as including a reference thereto as extended or applied, by or under any other enactment including, unless the context otherwise requires, this Act.

(3) The enactments mentioned in Schedule 3 to this Act are hereby repealed to the extent specified in relation thereto in column 3 of that Schedule:

Provided that no repeal effected by this subsection in any of the provisions of the Crofters (Scotland) Act 1955 or the Succession (Scotland) Act 1964 shall have effect in relation to the estate of any person dying before the commencement of this Act.

(4) This Act shall extend to Scotland only.

(5) This Act (except sections 10 to 15 thereof) shall come into operation on the expiry of a period of one month beginning with the date on which it is passed; and sections 10 to 15 of this Act shall come into operation on such date as the Secretary of State may appoint by an order made by statutory instrument and different days may be appointed under this section for different purposes.

Any reference in this Act or in any other enactment to the commencement of this Act shall be construed as a reference to the date on which this Act (except sections 10 to 15 thereof) comes into operation.

Succession (Scotland) Act 1973

(1973 c. 25)

An Act to increase the amounts of the sums payable to a surviving spouse under sections 8 and 9 of the Succession (Scotland) Act 1964 and to empower the Secretary of State by order further to increase such amounts. [23rd May 1973]

Amendment of sections 8 and 9 of Succession (Scotland) Act 1964

1.—(1) In the case of a person dying after the commencement of this Act—

(*a*) section 8 of the Succession (Scotland) Act 1964 (prior rights of surviving spouse, on intestacy, in dwelling house and furniture) shall apply as if—

(i) for the words " £15,000 " in subsection (1) (*a*) and (*b*) there were substituted the words " £30,000 or such larger amount as may from time to time be fixed by order of the Secretary of State ";

(ii) for the words " £5,000 " in subsection (3) (*a*) and (*b*) there were substituted the words " £8,000 or such larger amount as may from time to time be fixed by order of the Secretary of State ";

(*b*) section 9 of the said Act of 1964 (prior right of surviving spouse to financial provision on intestacy) shall apply as if—

(i) for the words " £2,500, or " in subsection (1) (*a*) there were substituted the words " £4,000 or such larger amount as may from time to time be fixed by order of the Secretary of State, or ";

(ii) for the words " £5,000 " in subsection (1) (*b*) there were substituted the words " £8,000 or such larger amount as may from time to time be fixed by order of the Secretary of State ";

(iii) in the proviso to the said subsection (1) for the words from " of £2,500 " to " £5,000 " there were substituted the words " fixed by virtue of paragraph (*a*) of this subsection or the sum fixed by virtue of paragraph (*b*) of this subsection ".

(2), (3) [Repealed by the Law Reform (Miscellaneous Provisions) (Scotland) Act 1980, Sched. 3.]

Short title

2. This Act may be cited as the Succession (Scotland) Act 1973.

Presumption of Death (Scotland) Act 1977

(1977 c. 27)

An Act to make fresh provision in the law of Scotland in relation to the presumed death of missing persons; and for connected purposes. [22nd July 1977]

Action of declarator

1.—(1) Where a person who is missing is thought to have died or has not been known to be alive for a period of at least seven years, any person having an interest may raise an action of declarator of the death of that person (hereafter in this Act referred to as the " missing person ") in the Court of Session or the sheriff court in accordance with the provisions of this section.

(2) An action such as is mentioned in subsection (1) above is, in this Act, referred to as an " action of declarator ".

(3) The Court of Session shall have jurisdiction to entertain an action of declarator if and only if—

(*a*) the missing person was domiciled in Scotland on the date on which he was last known to be alive or had been habitually resident there throughout the period of one year ending with that date; or

(*b*) the pursuer in the action—

(i) is the spouse of the missing person, and

(ii) is domiciled in Scotland at the date of raising the action or was habitually resident there throughout the period of one year ending with that date.

(4) The sheriff court shall have jurisdiction to entertain an action of declarator if and only if—

(*a*) the provisions of subsection (3) (*a*) above are satisfied and the missing person's last known place of residence in Scotland was in the sheriffdom; or

(*b*) the provisions of subsection (3) (*b*) above are satisfied and the pursuer was resident in the sheriffdom for a period of not less than forty days ending with the date of raising the action.

(5) Any person having an interest may, in an action of declarator, lodge a minute seeking the making by the court under section 2 of this Act of any determination or appointment not sought by the pursuer.

(6) At any stage of the proceedings the sheriff may, of his own accord or on the application of any party to the action, and shall, if so directed by the Court of Session (which direction may be given on the application of any party to the action), remit to the Court of Session an action of declarator raised in the sheriff court where he or, as the case may be, the Court of Session considers such remit desirable because of the importance or complexity of the matters at issue.

Decree in action of declarator and determination of incidental questions in other proceedings

2.—(1) In an action of declarator, the court, having heard proof and being satisfied on a balance of probabilities that the missing person—

(*a*) has died, shall grant decree accordingly and shall include in the decree a finding as to the date and time of death:

Provided that where it is uncertain when, within any period of time, the missing person died, the court shall find that he died at the end of that period;

(*b*) has not been known to be alive for a period of at least seven years, shall find that the missing person died at the end of the day occurring seven years after the date on which he was last known to be alive and shall grant decree accordingly.

(2) The court, in granting decree under subsection (1) above, shall have power to—

(*a*) determine the domicile of the missing person at the date of his death;

(*b*) determine any question relating to any interest in property which arises as a consequence of the death of the missing person;

(*c*) appoint a judicial factor on the estate of the missing person notwithstanding (in relation to such an appointment by the sheriff) what the value of the estate may be.

(3) Where, for the purpose of deciding any issue before it, a court or statutory tribunal has to determine any incidental question as to the death of a person, the court or tribunal may, if it thinks fit, determine that question (but for the purpose only of deciding that issue); and in the determination of that question the court or tribunal shall apply the criteria set out in subsection (1) above.

Effect of decree

3.—(1) Subject to the provisions of this section and sections 4 and 5 of this Act, where no appeal is made against decree in an action of declarator within the time allowed for appeal, or where an appeal against such a decree has been made and refused or withdrawn, the decree shall be conclusive of the matters contained in the decree and shall, without any special form of words, be effective against any person and for all purposes including the dissolution of a marriage to which the missing person is a party and the acquisition of rights to or in property belonging to any person.

(2) A decree under section 2(1)(*b*) of this Act or a determination as mentioned in section 2(3) of this Act shall not determine a substantive question which is properly referable to a foreign law otherwise than in accordance with that law.

(3) Where a marriage to which the missing person is a party has been dissolved by virtue of decree in an action of declarator, the dissolution of the marriage shall not be invalidated by the circumstance that the missing person was in fact alive at the date specified in the decree as the date of death.

(4) Where the missing person or any other person has committed any crime or offence, the responsibility of that person therefor shall not be affected by the circumstance that decree in an action of declarator has been

granted if the missing person was in fact alive at the date specified in the decree as the date of death.

Recall or variation of decree

4.—(1) Decree in an action of declarator may, on application made at any time by any person having an interest, be varied or recalled by an order of the court which granted the decree or, in a case to which subsection (4) below applies, by an order of the Court of Session.

An order of the court pronounced under this subsection is hereafter in this Act referred to as a "variation order".

(2) By a variation order the court may make any determination or appointment referred to in section 2 of this Act.

[1] (3) Any person having an interest may, in an application for a variation order, make an application to the court seeking the making by the court of any determination or appointment referred to in section 2 of this Act, which has not been sought by the person making the application for the variation order.

(4) At any stage of the proceedings the sheriff may, of his own accord or on the application of any party to the proceedings, and shall, if so directed by the Court of Session (which direction may be given on the application of any party to the proceedings), remit to the Court of Session an application made in the sheriff court for a variation order where he or, as the case may be, the Court of Session considers such remit desirable because of the importance or complexity of the matters at issue.

(5) Nothing in this section shall operate so as to revive a marriage of the missing person dissolved by virtue of decree in an action of declarator.

NOTE

[1] As amended by S.I. 1994 No. 1443 (effective 5th September 1994).

Effect on property rights of recall or variation of decree

5.—(1) Subject to the following provisions of this section, a variation order shall have no effect on rights to or in any property acquired as a result of a decree under section 2 of this Act.

(2) Notwithstanding the generality of subsection (1) above, where a decree under section 2 of this Act has been varied or recalled by a variation order, the court shall make such further order, if any, in relation to any rights to or in any property acquired as a result of that decree as it considers fair and reasonable in all the circumstances of the case; but no such further order shall affect any income accruing between the date of that decree and the date of the variation order.

(3) In considering what order shall be made under subsection (2) above, the court shall, so far as practicable in the circumstances, have regard to the following considerations, namely:—

(*a*) that, in the case of any property which is being or has been administered under a trust, any person who on account of the variation order would, apart from subsection (1) above, have been entitled to rights to or in any such property, or any person deriving right from him, shall be entitled to have made over to him by the trustee in full satisfaction of these rights only—

(i) the said rights to or in any such property or other property for the time being representing it which is still in the hands of the trustee at the date of the variation order, and

(ii) the value, as at the date of distribution, of the said rights to or in any such property which has been distributed;

(*b*) that any capital sum paid by an insurer as a result of the said decree (other than a capital sum which has been distributed by way of an annuity or other periodical payment) or any part of such sum should be repaid to the insurer if the facts in respect of which the variation order was pronounced justify such repayment.

(4) The court shall not make an order under subsection (2) above unless

application for the variation order has been made to the court within the period of five years beginning with the date of the decree under section 2 of this Act.

(5) Where any person who has acquired rights to or in any property as a result of a decree under section 2 of this Act, or any person deriving right from him, enters into a transaction with another person whereby that other person acquires in good faith and for value any right to or in that property or any part of it, the transaction and any title acquired under it by that other person shall not be challengeable on the ground that an order under subsection (2) above has been made in relation to that property.

(6) A trustee shall be liable to any person having entitlement by virtue of an order under subsection (2) above for any loss suffered by that person on account of any breach of trust by the trustee in the administration or distribution of the whole or any part of the property, except in so far as the liability of the trustee may be restricted under any enactment or by any provision in any deed regulating the administration of the trust.

(7) Nothing in this section shall apply to estate duty or capital transfer tax which falls to be repaid as a result of a variation order having been pronounced.

Insurance against claims

6.—(1) Where decree has been granted under section 2 of this Act then, unless the court otherwise directs, the trustee, if any, shall as soon as may be effect a policy of insurance in respect of any claim which may arise by virtue of an order under section 5 (2) of this Act.

(2) Any premium payable by the trustee in respect of a policy of insurance effected under subsection (1) above shall be a proper charge on the estate being administered by the trustee.

(3) Where decree has been granted under section 2 of this Act, an insurer may, before making payment of any capital sum (other than in respect of an annuity or other periodical payment) to any person as a result of that decree, require that person to effect in his own name for the benefit of that insurer a policy of insurance to satisfy any claim which that insurer may establish in the event of a variation order being pronounced.

Value of certain rights may be declared irrecoverable

7. Where decree has been granted under section 2 of the Act, the court may—

(*a*) on the application of—

(i) any person whom the missing person would, at the time of the making of the said application (apart from the said decree), have had a duty (other than a contractual duty) to aliment, or

(ii) the trustee, and

(*b*) subject to such conditions, if any, as it thinks fit,

then or at any time thereafter, make an order directing that the value of any rights to or in any property acquired as a result of the said decree shall not be recoverable by virtue of an order under section 5 (2) of this Act.

Repayment of estate duty

8. Where estate duty or capital transfer tax falls to be repaid as a result of a variation order having been pronounced—

(*a*) the court which pronounced the variation order may order the duty or tax to be repaid to the person entitled to receive repayment;

(*b*) nothing in this Act shall affect the obligation of any person to whom the duty or tax is repaid to account for the amount of the duty or tax to any other person.

Disclosure of information

9.—(1) Any person (including the Secretary of State for Social Services) who possesses information relating to the survival or death of the missing person, and who is aware that an action of declarator has been raised or an application for a variation order has been made, shall have a duty to disclose that information—

(*a*) by means of written communication to the Principal Clerk of Session or, as the case may be, the appropriate sheriff clerk; or

(*b*) in such other manner as may be prescribed by act of sederunt.

(2) Nothing in this section shall impose any duty to disclose information where the person possessing the information would, if cited as a witness or haver, have been entitled to refuse to disclose such information under any rule of law or practice relating to the privilege of witnesses and havers, confidentiality of communications and withholding or non-disclosure of information on the grounds of public interest.

(3) A statement purporting to be an instrument made or issued by or on behalf of any Minister of the Crown and disclosing to the court facts relating to an action of declarator which has been raised or an application for a variation order which has been made in that court shall be sufficient evidence of those facts.

Decree of court furth of Scotland to be sufficient evidence

10. Where a court in any country furth of Scotland in which a person was domiciled or habitually resident on the date on which he was last known to be alive issues a decree or judgment declaring that that person has died or is presumed to have died, or has died or is presumed to have died on a specified date or within a specified period, that decree or judgment shall, in any proceedings in Scotland, be sufficient evidence of the facts so declared.

Appointment or confirmation of executor

11.—(1) Where, in proceedings for the appointment or confirmation of an executor of any person, a document to which subsection (2) below refers is produced, an oath or affirmation that to the best of the deponent's knowledge and belief that person is dead shall, for the purposes of those proceedings, be equivalent to an oath or affirmation that that person has died or died at any place or on any date appearing in such document as the place or date at or on which he died or was presumed to have died or was lost or missing.

(2) This subsection refers to the following documents, that is to say—

(*a*) a duly certified copy of a decree or judgment such as is referred to in section 10 of this Act;

(*b*) a certificate or intimation issued by or on behalf of a competent authority within the United Kingdom that the person—

(i) has died,

(ii) is presumed to have died, or

(iii) is lost or missing in circumstances affording reasonable ground for the belief that he has died as a result of an incident in or in connection with a ship, aircraft, hovercraft or off-shore installation.

(3) Notwithstanding any provision in or under any enactment, it shall not be necessary, in any petition for appointment as executor of any person in regard to whom a duly certified copy of such a decree or judgment as aforesaid or such a certificate or intimation as aforesaid is produced with the petition, to aver that the person died at any specified place or on any specified date, but it shall be sufficient to aver that the duly certified copy of the decree or judgment or (as the case may be) the certificate or intimation is

produced and that to the best of the petitioner's knowledge and belief the person is dead.

Particulars of decree or variation order to be intimated to Registrar General

[1] **12.**—(1) Where a decree under section 2 of this Act or a variation order has been granted by any court, the clerk of court shall, where no appeal has been made against such decree or order, on the expiration of the time within which such an appeal may be made, or where an appeal has been made against such a decree or order, on the conclusion of any appellate proceedings, notify the prescribed particulars in connection with such decree or order to the Registrar General of Births, Deaths and Marriages for Scotland, who shall thereupon cause to be made such entry, if any, as appears to him to be appropriate, in a register kept for that purpose.

(2) In this section, " prescribed " means prescribed by regulations made under section 54 of the Registration of Births, Deaths and Marriages (Scotland) Act 1965.

NOTE

[1] See S.I. 1978 No. 160.

Defence to charge of bigamy

13. It shall be a defence against a charge of bigamy for the accused to prove that at no time within the period of seven years immediately preceding the date of the purported marriage forming the substance of the charge had he any reason to believe that his spouse was alive.

Report of proceedings

14. For the avoidance of doubt, it is hereby declared that section 1 (1) (*b*) of the Judicial Proceedings (Regulation of Reports) Act 1926 does not apply to an action of declarator.

Rules of procedure

[1] **15.**—(1) Without prejudice to the generality of the powers conferred on the Court of Session by section 16 of the Administration of Justice (Scotland) Act 1933 and section 32 of the Sheriff Courts (Scotland) Act 1971 to regulate procedure by act of sederunt, the said powers shall include power to make rules of procedure for the purpose of giving effect to the provisions of this Act.

(2) Such rules of procedure shall include provisions—

(*a*) specifying the persons (including the Lord Advocate) upon or to whom service or intimation of the summons or initial writ in an action of declarator or of an application for a variation order is to be made; and

(*b*) relating to the advertisement of the raising of the said action or the making of the said application.

NOTE

[1] See S.I. 1978 Nos. 161 and 162.

Entailed estates

16.—(1) The following provisions of this section shall apply where decree has been granted under section 2 of this Act declaring the death of the missing person who is the heir in possession of an entailed estate.

(2) In the circumstances set out in subsection (1) above, the next heir may apply to the court for authority to disentail the estate and the court may make it a condition of granting such authority that the next heir gives security of such amount and in such manner as the court may direct to meet any contingent interest of the heir if he shall reappear and, within the period

of five years beginning with the date of the said decree, application for the relative variation order shall be made.

(3) Where, in the circumstances set out in subsection (1) above—

(*a*) the estate has not been disentailed,

(*b*) the absent heir reappears,

(*c*) application for the relative variation order is made within the period of five years beginning with the date of the said decree, and

(*d*) the relative variation order is pronounced,

then, notwithstanding section 5 of this Act, the absent heir who reappears shall be entitled to resume possession of the estate but shall not be entitled to recover the fruits or income of the estate from any following heir in respect of the period of that heir's possession.

(4) In this section, " the court " means the Court of Session.

Interpretation

17. In this Act, unless the context otherwise requires,

" action of declarator " has the meaning assigned to it by section 1 of this Act;

" any person having an interest " includes the Lord Advocate for the public interest;

" the court " means the Court of Session or the sheriff;

" insurer " includes a society registered under the Acts relating to friendly and industrial and provident societies and any person or body which provides for the payment of benefits on the death of another person;

" missing person " has the meaning assigned to it by section 1 (1) of this Act;

" statutory tribunal " means a tribunal established by or under any enactment;

" trust " means—

(*a*) any trust or executry for the administration of property which comes into operation as a result of a decree under section 2 of this Act, or

(*b*) any trust under which property devolves upon or is transmitted to any person by reason of the death of the missing person;

and " trustee " means the trustee, executor, judicial factor or other person administering any such property;

" variation order " has the meaning assigned to it by section 4 (1) of this Act.

Amendment of other enactments

18. The enactments specified in Schedule 1 to this Act shall have effect subject to the amendments specified in that Schedule.

Repeals

19. The enactments specified in Schedule 2 to this Act are hereby repealed to the extent specified in column 3 of that Schedule.

Short title, commencement and extent

20.—(1) This Act may be cited as the Presumption of Death (Scotland) Act 1977.

[1] (2) This Act, except this section, shall come into force on such date as the Lord Advocate may by order made by statutory instrument appoint.

(3) This Act shall extend to Scotland only.

NOTE

[1] The Act came into force on 1st March 1978: see S.I. 1978 No. 159.

[1] SCHEDULES 1, 2

NOTE

[1] The amendments and repeals contained in these Schedules have been given effect to in so far as they affect material contained in *The Parliament House Book*.

Forfeiture Act 1982

(1982 c. 34)

An Act to provide for relief for persons guilty of unlawful killing from forfeiture of inheritance and other rights; to enable such persons to apply for financial provision out of the deceased's estate; . . . and for connected purposes. [13th July 1982]

The "forfeiture rule"

1.—(1) In this Act, the "forfeiture rule" means the rule of public policy which in certain circumstances precludes a person who has unlawfully killed another from acquiring a benefit in consequence of the killing.

(2) References in this Act to a person who has unlawfully killed another include a reference to a person who has unlawfully aided, abetted, counselled or procured the death of that other and references in this Act to unlawful killing shall be interpreted accordingly.

Power to modify the rule

2.—(1) Where a court determines that the forfeiture rule has precluded a person (in this section referred to as "the offender") who has unlawfully killed another from acquiring any interest in property mentioned in subsection (4) below, the court may make an order under this section modifying the effect of that rule.

(2) The court shall not make an order under this section modifying the effect of the forfeiture rule in any case unless it is satisfied that, having regard to the conduct of the offender and of the deceased and to such other circumstances as appear to the court to be material, the justice of the case requires the effect of the rule to be so modified in that case.

(3) In any case where a person stands convicted of an offence of which unlawful killing is an element, the court shall not make an order under this section modifying the effect of the forfeiture rule in that case unless proceedings for the purpose are brought before the expiry of the period of three months beginning with his conviction.

(4) The interests in property referred to in subsection (1) above are—

(*a*) any beneficial interest in property which (apart from the forfeiture rule) the offender would have acquired—

(i) under the deceased's will (including, as respects Scotland, any writing having testamentary effect) or the law relating to intestacy or by way of *jus relicti, jus relictae* or legitim;

(ii) on the nomination of the deceased in accordance with the provisions of any enactment;

(iii) as a *donatio mortis causa* made by the deceased,; or

(iv) under a special destination (whether relating to heritable or moveable property); or

(*b*) any beneficial interest in property which (apart from the forfeiture rule) the offender would have acquired in consequence of the death of the deceased, being property which, before the death, was held on trust for any person.

(5) An order under this section may modify the effect of the forfeiture rule in respect of any interest in property to which the determination referred to in subsection (1) above relates and may do so in either or both of the following ways, that is—

(*a*) where there is more than one such interest, by excluding the application of the rule in respect of any (but not all) of those interests; and

(*b*) in the case of any such interest in property, by excluding the application of the rule in respect of part of the property.

(6) On the making of an order under this section, the forfeiture rule shall have effect for all purposes (including purposes relating to anything done before the order is made) subject to the modifications made by the order.

(7) The court shall not make an order under this section modifying the effect of the forfeiture rule in respect of any interest in property which, in consequence of the rule, has been acquired before the coming into force of this section by a person other than the offender or a person claiming through him.

(8) In this section—

"property" includes any chose in action or incorporeal moveable property; and

"will" includes codicil.

Application for financial provision not affected by the rule

3.—(1) The forfeiture rule shall not be taken to preclude any person from making any application under a provision mentioned in subsection (2) below or the making of any order on the application.

(2) The provisions referred to in subsection (1) above are—

(*a*) any provision of the Inheritance (Provision for Family and Dependants) Act 1975; and

(*b*) sections 31(6) (variation etc. of periodical payments orders) and 36(1) (variation of maintenance agreements) of the Matrimonial Causes Act 1973 and section 5(4) of the Divorce (Scotland) Act 1976 (variation etc. of periodical allowances).

. . . .

Exclusion of murderers

[1] **5.** Nothing in this Act or in any order made under section 2 or referred to in section 3(1) of this Act or in any decision made under section 4 (1A) of this Act shall affect the application of the forfeiture rule in the case of a person who stands convicted of murder.

NOTE

[1] As amended by the Social Security Act 1986, s.76(4).

. . . .

Short title, etc.

7.—(1) This Act may be cited as the Forfeiture Act 1982.

(2) Section 4 of this Act shall come into force on such day as the Secretary of State may appoint by order made by statutory instrument; and sections 1 to 3 and 5 of this Act shall come into force on the expiry of the period of three months beginning with the day on which it is passed.

(3) This Act, except section 6, does not extend to Northern Ireland.

(4) Subject to section 2(7) of this Act, an order under section 2 of this Act or an order referred to in section 3(1) of this Act and made in respect of a person who has unlawfully killed another may be made whether the unlawful killing occurred before or after the coming into force of those sections.

[1] Recognition of Trusts Act 1987

(1987 c. 14)

NOTE
[1] This Act came into force on 1st August 1987: S.I. 1987 No. 1177.

An Act to enable the United Kingdom to ratify the Convention on the law applicable to trusts and on their recognition which was signed on behalf of the United Kingdom on 10th January 1986.
[9th April 1987]

Applicable law and recognition of trusts

1.—(1) The provisions of the Convention set out in the Schedule to this Act shall have the force of law in the United Kingdom.

(2) Those provisions shall, so far as applicable, have effect not only in relation to the trusts described in Articles 2 and 3 of the Convention but also in relation to any other trusts of property arising under the law of any part of the United Kingdom or by virtue of a judicial decision whether in the United Kingdom or elsewhere.

(3) In accordance with Articles 15 and 16 such provisions of the law as are there mentioned shall, to the extent there specified, apply to the exclusion of the other provisions of the Convention.

(4) In Article 17 the reference to a State includes a reference to any country or territory (whether or not a party to the Convention and whether or not forming part of the United Kingdom) which has its own system of law.

(5) Article 22 shall not be construed as affecting the law to be applied in relation to anything done or omitted before the coming into force of this Act.

Extent

2.—(1) This Act extends to Northern Ireland.

(2) Her Majesty may by Order in Council direct that this Act shall also form part of the law of the Isle of Man, any of the Channel Islands or any colony.

(3) An Order in Council under subsection (2) above may modify this Act in its application to any of the territories there mentioned and may contain such supplementary provisions as Her Majesty considers appropriate.

(4) An Order in Council under subsection (2) above shall be subject to annulment in pursuance of a resolution of either House of Parliament.

Short title, commencement and application to the Crown

3.—(1) This Act may be cited as the Recognition of Trusts Act 1987.

(2) This Act shall come into force on such date as the Lord Chancellor and the Lord Advocate may appoint by an order made by statutory instrument.

(3) This Act binds the Crown.

Section 1

SCHEDULE

Convention on the Law Applicable to Trusts and on Their Recognition

Chapter I—Scope

Article 1

This Convention specifies the law applicable to trusts and governs their recognition.

Article 2

For the purposes of this Convention, the term "trust" refers to the legal relationship created—inter vivos or on death—by a person, the settlor, when assets have been placed under the control of a trustee for the benefit of a beneficiary or for a specified purpose.

A trust has the following characteristics—

(*a*) the assets constitute a separate fund and are not a part of the trustee's own estate;

(*b*) title to the trust assets stands in the name of the trustee or in the name of another person on behalf of the trustee;

(*c*) the trustee has the power and the duty, in respect of which he is accountable, to manage, employ or dispose of the assets in accordance with the terms of the trust and the special duties imposed upon him by law.

The reservation by the settlor of certain rights and powers, and the fact that the trustee may himself have rights as a beneficiary, are not necessarily inconsistent with the existence of a trust.

Article 3

The Convention applies only to trusts created voluntarily and evidenced in writing.

Article 4

The Convention does not apply to preliminary issues relating to the validity of wills or of other acts by virtue of which assets are transferred to the trustee.

Article 5

The Convention does not apply to the extent that the law specified by Chapter II does not provide for trusts or the category of trusts involved.

CHAPTER II—APPLICABLE LAW

Article 6

A trust shall be governed by the law chosen by the settlor. The choice must be express or be implied in the terms of the instrument creating or the writing evidencing the trust, interpreted, if necessary, in the light of the circumstances of the case.

Where the law chosen under the previous paragraph does not provide for trusts or the category of trust involved, the choice shall not be effective and the law specified in Article 7 shall apply.

Article 7

Where no applicable law has been chosen, a trust shall be governed by the law with which it is most closely connected.

In ascertaining the law with which a trust is most closely connected reference shall be made in particular to—

(*a*) the place of administration of the trust designated by the settlor;

(*b*) the situs of the assets of the trust;

(*c*) the place of residence or business of the trustee;

(*d*) the objects of the trust and the places where they are to be fulfilled.

Article 8

The law specified by Article 6 or 7 shall govern the validity of the trust, its construction, its effects and the administration of the trust.

In particular that law shall govern—

(*a*) the appointment, resignation and removal of trustees, the capacity to act as a trustee, and the devolution of the office of trustee;

(*b*) the rights and duties of trustees among themselves;

(*c*) the right of trustees to delegate in whole or in part the discharge of their duties or the exercise of their powers;

(*d*) the power of trustees to administer or to dispose of trust assets, to create security interests in the trust assets, or to acquire new assets;

(*e*) the powers of investment of trustees;

(*f*) restrictions upon the duration of the trust, and upon the power to accumulate the income of the trust;

(*g*) the relationships between the trustees and the beneficiaries including the personal liability of the trustees to the beneficiaries;
(*h*) the variation or termination of the trust;
(*i*) the distribution of the trust assets;
(*j*) the duty of trustees to account for their administration.

Article 9

In applying this Chapter a severable aspect of the trust, particularly matters of administration, may be governed by a different law.

Article 10

The law applicable to the validity of the trust shall determine whether that law or the law governing a severable aspect of the trust may be replaced by another law.

CHAPTER III—RECOGNITION

Article 11

A trust created in accordance with the law specified by the preceding Chapter shall be recognised as a trust.

Such recognition shall imply, as a minimum, that the trust property constitutes a separate fund, that the trustee may sue and be sued in his capacity as trustee, and that he may appear or act in this capacity before a notary or any person acting in an official capacity.

In so far as the law applicable to the trust requires or provides, such recognition shall imply in particular—

(*a*) that personal creditors of the trustee shall have no recourse against the trust assets;
(*b*) that the trust assets shall not form part of the trustee's estate upon his insolvency or bankruptcy;
(*c*) that the trust assets shall not form part of the matrimonial property of the trustee or his spouse nor part of the trustee's estate upon his death;
(*d*) that the trust assets may be recovered when the trustee, in breach of trust, has mingled trust assets with his own property or has alienated trust assets. However, the rights and obligations of any third party holder of the assets shall remain subject to the law determined by the choice of law rules of the forum.

Article 12

Where the trustee desires to register assets, movable or immovable, or documents of title to them, he shall be entitled, in so far as this is not prohibited by or inconsistent with the law of the State where registration is sought, to do so in his capacity as trustee or in such other way that the existence of the trust is disclosed.

Article 14

The Convention shall not prevent the application of rules of law more favourable to the recognition of trusts.

CHAPTER IV—GENERAL CLAUSES

Article 15

The Convention does not prevent the application of provisions of the law designated by the conflicts rules of the forum, in so far as those provisions cannot be derogated from by voluntary act, relating in particular to the following matters—

(*a*) the protection of minors and incapable parties;
(*b*) the personal and proprietary effects of marriage;
(*c*) succession rights, testate and intestate, especially the indefeasible shares of spouses and relatives;
(*d*) the transfer of title to property and security interests in property;
(*e*) the protection of creditors in matters of insolvency;
(*f*) the protection, in other respects, of third parties acting in good faith.

If recognition of a trust is prevented by application of the preceding paragraph, the court shall try to give effect to the objects of the trust by other means.

Article 16

The Convention does not prevent the application of those provisions of the law of the forum which must be applied even to international situations, irrespective of rules of conflict of laws.

Article 17

In the Convention the word "law" means the rules of law in force in a State other than its rules of conflict of laws.

Article 18

The provisions of the Convention may be disregarded when their application would be manifestly incompatible with public policy.

Article 22

The Convention applies to trusts regardless of the date on which they were created.

Law Reform (Miscellaneous Provisions) (Scotland) Act 1990

(1990 c. 40)

An Act, as respects Scotland, to make new provision for the regulation of charities . . . ; and to make certain other miscellaneous reforms of the law. [1st November 1990]

[1] PART I

CHARITIES

NOTE

[1] Of the provisions in Pt. I, ss. 1–3, 6–9 and 13–15 were brought into force on 27th July 1992, and ss. 4 and 5 on 30th September 1992, by S.I. 1992 No. 1599, and ss. 10–12 were brought into force on 15th September 1993 by S.I. 1993 No. 2253.

Recognition of charities

Information as to recognised charities

1.—(1) No obligation as to secrecy or other restriction upon the disclosure of information imposed by statute or otherwise shall prevent the Commissioners of Inland Revenue (in this section referred to as "the Commissioners") from disclosing—

(*a*) to the Lord Advocate, information as regards any recognised body such as is mentioned in subsection (2) below,

(*b*) to any person who requests it, the name of any recognised body and the address last used by the Commissioners for any communication with the body and the year when such communication occurred.

(2) A recognised body referred to in subsection (1)(*a*) above is a body—

(*a*) which appears to the Commissioners to be or to have been carrying on activities which are not charitable or to be or to have been applying any of its funds for purposes which are not charitable;

(*b*) which is certified by the Lord Advocate as being a body in respect of which information has been provided to the Scottish charities nominee by a relevant institution in pursuance of section 12 of this Act.

(3) Where any information is made available to any person as mentioned in subsection (1)(*b*) above, the Commissioners shall include in such information any matter noted by them in respect of the body in pursuance of a requirement made by the Lord Advocate under this Part of this Act.

(4) A recognised body shall provide to any person who requests it, on payment of such reasonable charge in respect of copying and postage as the body may stipulate, a copy of its explanatory document.

(5) Where any recognised body, within one month of its being requested to do so by any person, fails to provide to that person a copy of its explanatory document as mentioned in subsection (4) above, the Lord Advocate, on a complaint being made to him by such person, may direct that the fact of such failure shall be noted for the purposes of subsection (3) above.

(6) Where there has been a failure such as is mentioned in subsection (5) above, the court may, on an application being made by the Lord Advocate, interdict the body and any person concerned in its management or control from engaging in any activity specified in the application until the Lord Advocate intimates to the court that he is satisfied that the explanatory document has been provided.

(7) In this Part of this Act "recognised body" means any body to which the Commissioners have given intimation, which has not subsequently been withdrawn, that relief will be due under section 505 of the Income and Corporation Taxes Act 1988 in respect of income of the body which is applicable and applied to charitable purposes only, being a body—

(*a*) which is established under the law of Scotland; or

(*b*) which is managed or controlled wholly or mainly in or from Scotland,

and a recognised body shall be entitled to describe itself as "a Scottish charity."

(8) For the purposes of any proceedings under or by virtue of this Part of this Act, a certificate purporting to be signed by a person authorised to do so by the Commissioners and certifying that a body is a recognised body shall be sufficient evidence of that fact and of the authority of that person.

(9) In this section "explanatory document" means—

(*a*) the trust deed of a body or other document constituting the body; or

(*b*) such other document as the Lord Advocate may approve,

being a document which describes the nature of the body and of its charitable purposes.

Non-recognised bodies

2.—(1) A non-recognised body shall not be entitled to represent itself or hold itself out as a charity.

(2) For the purposes of this Part of this Act, any body which is not—

(*a*) a recognised body; or

(*b*) a body which is—

(i) registered as a charity in England and Wales under section 4 of the Charities Act 1960; or

(ii) a charity which is not required to register by virtue of subsection (4) of that section,

is a non-recognised body.

(3) Where a non-recognised body represents itself or holds itself out as a charity, the court may, on an application made by the Lord Advocate, interdict the body from so representing itself or holding itself out until it becomes a body such as is mentioned in paragraph (*a*) or (*b*) of subsection (2) above.

Designated religious bodies

3.—(1) The Secretary of State may from time to time, by order, designate for the purposes of this section such recognised bodies as appear to him—

(*a*) to have as their principal purpose the promotion of a religious objective;

(*b*) to have as their principal activity the regular holding of acts of public worship; and (*c*) to be bodies which satisfy each of the conditions mentioned in subsection (2) below.

(2) The conditions referred to in subsection (1)(*c*) above are—

(*a*) subject to subsection (4) below, that the body has been established in Scotland for not less than 10 years;

(*b*) that the body can demonstrate to the satisfaction of the Secretary of State that it has a membership of not less than 3,000 persons resident in Scotland who are 16 years of age or more; and

(*c*) that the internal organisation of the body is such that one or more authorities in Scotland exercise supervisory and disciplinary functions in respect of the component elements of the body and, in particular, that there are imposed on such component elements requirements as to the keeping of accounting records and the auditing of accounts which appear to the Secretary of State to correspond to those required by sections 4 and 5 of this Act.

(3) Where a body is, for the time being, designated under subsection (1) above the following provisions of this Part of this Act shall not apply to the body nor to any component or structural element of the body which is, itself, a recognised body—

section 1(6);
section 4;
section 5, other than subsections (6) to (8) and subsection (12);
section 6(2) and (6);
section 7; and
section 8.

(4) The Secretary of State may determine that the condition mentioned in subsection (2)(*a*) above shall not be required to be satisfied in the case of a body—

(*a*) which has been created by the amalgamation of two or more bodies each of which, immediately before the amalgamation, either was designated under this section or appears to the Secretary of State to have been eligible for such designation; or

(*b*) which has been constituted by persons who have removed themselves from membership of a body which, immediately before such removal, was so designated or appears to the Secretary of State to have been eligible for such designation.

Charities' accounts

Duty to keep accounting records

4.—(1) The persons concerned in the management or control of every recognised body shall ensure that there are kept in respect of the body, accounting records which are sufficient to show and explain the body's transactions and which are such as to—

(*a*) disclose with reasonable accuracy, at any time, the financial position of the body at that time; and

(*b*) enable them to ensure that any statement of accounts prepared under section 5 of this Act complies with the requirements of that section.

(2) The accounting records shall in particular contain—

(*a*) entries showing from day to day all sums of money received and expended by the body, and the matters in respect of which the receipt and expenditure takes place; and

(*b*) a record of the assets and liabilities of the body.

(3) The accounting records which are required by this section to be kept in respect of a recognised body shall be preserved, without prejudice to any requirement of any other enactment or rule of law, for six years from the date on which they are made.

(4) The Secretary of State may, by regulations—

(*a*) prescribe requirements as to the places where and the persons by whom the accounting records of recognised bodies, including bodies which have been wound up or have ceased to be active, are to be kept; and

(*b*) provide that such class or classes of recognised body as may be prescribed shall be exempt from such requirements of this section and section 5 of this Act as may be prescribed.

Annual accounts and report

5.—(1) The persons concerned in the management or control of every recognised body shall ensure that, in respect of each financial year of the body, there is prepared a statement of accounts.

(2) Subject to subsection (3) below, the statement of accounts of every recognised body shall comprise—

(*a*) a balance sheet as at the last day of the year;

(*b*) an income and expenditure account; and

(*c*) a report as to the activities of the body, having regard to its charitable purposes.

(3) As regards such class or classes of recognised body as the Secretary of State may, by regulations, prescribe a recognised body may elect that in respect of any financial year its statement of accounts shall, instead of the requirements of subsection (2) above, comprise—

(*a*) a statement of balances as at the last day of the year;

(*b*) a receipts and payments account; and

(*c*) a report as to the activities of the body, having regard to its charitable purposes.

(4) The balance sheet shall give a true and fair view of the state of affairs of the body as at the end of the financial year; and the income and expenditure account shall give a true and fair view of the surplus or deficit of the body for the financial year.

(5) The Secretary of State may, by regulations, prescribe—

(*a*) the form and content of the statement of accounts;

(*b*) any additional information to be provided by way of notes to the accounts; and

(*c*) such requirements as to auditing of the balance sheet, statement of balances, income and expenditure account and receipts and payments account and any notes thereon and as to the consideration of the report as he considers appropriate,

and different provision may be prescribed for different bodies or classes of bodies.

(6) The Lord Advocate may require any recognised body to furnish him, without payment therefor, with a copy of its statement of accounts.

(7) Every such body shall—

(*a*) make available to any person who requests it, on payment of such reasonable charge in respect of copying and postage as the body may stipulate, a copy of its most recent statement of accounts;

(*b*) inform any person who requests it of its accounting reference date.

(8) Where any recognised body fails, within 10 months, or such longer period as the Lord Advocate may allow, after the end of a financial year, to have prepared a statement of accounts, the Lord Advocate may require that such fact shall be noted for the purposes of section 1(3) of this Act.

(9) Where a body has failed to have prepared a statement of accounts as mentioned in subsection (8) above, the Lord Advocate may require the persons concerned in the management or control of the body to have prepared a statement of accounts, by such date as he may require.

(10) In any case where the statement of accounts has not been prepared by the date specified under subsection (9) above, the Lord Advocate may appoint a suitably qualified person to prepare a balance sheet and income

and expenditure account or, in the case of a body which belongs to a class to which subsection (3) above applies if it appears to such person more appropriate to do so, a statement of balances and receipts and payments account; and a person so appointed shall be entitled, for that purpose—

(*a*) on giving prior notice in writing, to enter, at all reasonable times, the premises of the body;

(*b*) to take possession of any document appearing to him to relate to the financial affairs of the body;

(*c*) to require any person concerned in the management or control of the body to give him such information as he may reasonably require relating to the activities of the body,

and the persons concerned in the management or control of the body shall be personally liable jointly and severally for the expenses incurred in the performance of his functions under this section by any person so appointed.

(11) A person appointed under subsection (10) above shall make a report to the Lord Advocate as to the affairs and accounting records of the body and shall send a copy of the report to any person appearing to him to be concerned in the management and control of the body.

(12) Where any such body, within one month of its being requested to do so by any person—

(*a*) fails to provide to that person a copy of its most recent statement of accounts as mentioned in subsection (7) above; or

(*b*) fails to inform that person of its accounting reference date,

the Lord Advocate, on a complaint being made to him by such person, may direct that the fact of such failure shall be noted for the purposes of section 1(3) of this Act.

(13) Where in the case of any recognised body, there has been a failure such as is mentioned in subsection (9) or (12) above the court may, on an application being made by the Lord Advocate, interdict the body and any person concerned in its management or control from engaging in any activity specified in the application until the Lord Advocate intimates to the court that he is satisfied that the failure has been rectified.

(14) Section 4 of this Act and subsections (1), (2), (3), (4), (5), (8), (9), (10) and (11) and, so far as it relates to a failure such as is mentioned in the said subsection (9), subsection (13) of this section shall not apply to any recognised body which is—

(*a*) a company within the meaning of section 735 of the Companies Act 1985; or

(*b*) an unregistered company to which Part VII of that Act (accounts and audit) applies by virtue of section 718 of that Act,

and, in the application of the remainder of this section to such a body, references to its income and expenditure account and its report shall be construed as references to its profit and loss account and its directors' report.

Supervision of charities

Powers of Lord Advocate to investigate charities and to suspend trustees

6.—(1) The Lord Advocate may at any time make inquiries, either generally or for particular purposes, with regard to—

(*a*) a recognised body;

(*b*) a registered, or non-registered, charity operating as such in Scotland; or

(*c*) a non-registered body which appears to him to represent itself or hold itself out as a charity and

(i) is established under the law of Scotland;

(ii) is managed or controlled wholly or mainly in or from Scotland; or

(iii) has any moveable or immoveable property situated in Scotland, or with regard to any class of any such bodies.

(2) Where it appears to the Lord Advocate—

(*a*) in the case of a body referred to in paragraph (*a*) or (*b*) of subsection (1) above—

(i) that there is or has been any misconduct or mismanagement in its administration; or

(ii) that it is necessary or desirable to act for the purpose of protecting its property or securing a proper application of such property for its purposes; or

(*b*) in any other case, that a body is a non-recognised body which appears to him to represent itself or hold itself out as a charity,

he may, if the body is managed or controlled wholly or mainly in or from Scotland, suspend any person concerned in its management or control from the exercise of his functions (but not for a period longer than 28 days), and may make provision as respects the period of the suspension for matters arising out of it.

(3) The Lord Advocate may from time to time nominate officers for the purpose of making inquiries such as are mentioned in subsection (1) above.

(4) A nominated officer may by notice in writing require any person who he has reason to believe has relevant information to answer questions or otherwise furnish information with respect to any matter relevant to inquiries being made under this section at a specified place and either at a specified time or forthwith.

(5) A nominated officer may, for the purpose of making inquiries under this section—

(*a*) require any person having in his possession or control any records relating to a body which is the subject of inquiries under this section to furnish him with copies of or extracts from any such records; or

(*b*) unless it forms part of the records of a court or of a public body or local authority, require such a person to transmit the record itself to him for inspection,

either by a specified time or forthwith.

(6) If any person fails or refuses to comply with a requirement made under subsection (4) or (5) above, the nominated officer may apply by summary application to the sheriff for an order requiring that person to—

(*a*) attend and to answer such questions or to furnish such information at a time and place specified in the order;

(*b*) furnish the nominated officer with copies or extracts of such records as are specified in the order and by such time as is specified in the order;

(*c*) transmit to the nominated officer such records as are specified in the order by such time as is specified in the order,

and the sheriff shall, if he considers it expedient to do so, make such an order.

(7) A person shall not be excused from answering such questions as he may be required to answer by virtue of subsection (6) above on the ground that the answer may incriminate or tend to incriminate him, but a statement made by him in answer to any such question shall not be admissible in evidence in any subsequent criminal proceedings against him, except in a prosecution for an offence under section 2 of the False Oaths (Scotland) Act 1933.

(8) A person who fails to comply with an order under subsection (6) above shall be guilty of an offence and liable on summary conviction to a fine not exceeding level 5 on the standard scale.

(9) Any person who wilfully alters, suppresses, conceals or destroys any record which he may be required to furnish or transmit under this section shall be guilty of an offence and liable on summary conviction to a fine not exceeding level 5 on the standard scale or to imprisonment for a term not exceeding 6 months or to both.

(10) Subject to subsections (11) and (12) below, there shall be paid to any person who complies with a requirement under subsection (4) or (5) above such expenses as he has reasonably incurred in so complying.

(11) A nominated officer shall, for the purpose of making inquiries under this section, be entitled without payment to inspect and take copies of or extracts from records in respect of which no requirement can be made under paragraph (*b*) of subsection (5) above.

(12) A nominated officer shall, for the purpose of making inquiries under this section, be entitled without payment to keep any copy or extract furnished to him under this section; and where a record transmitted to him for his inspection relates only to one or more recognised body and is not held by any person entitled as trustee or otherwise of such a body to the custody of it, the nominated officer may keep it or may deliver it to the trustees of such a body or to any other person who may be so entitled.

(13) In this section, "record" means a record held in any medium and includes books, documents, deeds or papers; and, in this Part of this Act—

"registered charity" means a body which is registered as a charity in England and Wales under section 4 of the Charities Act 1960; and

"non-registered charity" means a charity which, by virtue of sub-section (4) of section 4 of that Act, is not required to register under that section.

Powers of Court of Session to deal with management of charities

7.—(1) Where it appears to the court, in the case of a recognised body or a registered, or non-registered, charity which is managed or controlled wholly or mainly in or from Scotland, that—

(*a*) there is or has been any misconduct or mismanagement in its administration; or

(*b*) it is necessary or desirable to act for the purpose of protecting its property or securing a proper application of such property for its purposes,

it may, on the application of the Lord Advocate, exercise any of the powers specified in paragraphs (*a*) to (*f*) of subsection (4) below.

(2) Where the court is satisfied, in the case of such a body as is mentioned in subsection (1) above, that—

(*a*) there is or has been any misconduct or mismanagement in its administration; and

(*b*) it is necessary or desirable to act for the purpose of protecting its property or securing a proper application of such property for its purposes,

it may, on the application of the Lord Advocate, exercise any of the powers specified in paragraphs (*f*) to (*j*) of subsection (4) below.

(3) Where the court is satisfied that a non-recognised body—

(*a*) represents itself or holds itself out as a charity; and

(*b*) is established under the law of Scotland or is managed or controlled wholly or mainly in or from Scotland or has moveable or immoveable property situated in Scotland,

it may, on the application of the Lord Advocate, exercise any of the powers specified in subsection (4) below.

(4) The powers which may be exercised under this subsection by the court are—

(*a*) to interdict *ad interim* the body from representing itself or holding itself out as a charity or from such other action as the court, on the application of the Lord Advocate, thinks fit;

(*b*) to suspend any person concerned in the management or control of the body;

(*c*) to appoint *ad interim* a judicial factor to manage the affairs of the body;

(*d*) to make an order requiring any bank or other person holding money or securities on behalf of the body or of any person concerned in its control and management not to part with the money or securities without the court's approval;

(*e*) to make an order, notwithstanding anything in the trust deed or other document constituting the body, restricting the transactions which may be entered into, or the nature or amount of the payments which may be made, in the administration of the body without the approval of the court;

(*f*) to appoint a trustee, and section 22 of the Trusts (Scotland) Act 1921 shall apply to such a trustee as if he had been appointed under that section;

(*g*) to interdict the body from representing itself or holding itself out as a charity or from such other action as the court, on the application of the Lord Advocate, thinks fit;

(*h*) to remove any person concerned in the management or control of the body;

(*j*) to appoint a judicial factor to manage the affairs of the body.

(5) Where the court is satisfied, in the case of such a body as is mentioned in subsection (1) above, that—

(*a*) there has been in its administration any misconduct or mismanagement;

(*b*) it is necessary or desirable to act for the purpose of protecting its property or securing a proper application of such property for its purposes;

(*c*) it is not practicable nor in the best interests of the body to retain its existing administrative structure and, if appropriate, trustee body; and

(*d*) in its opinion, the body's purpose would be achieved better by transferring its assets to another such body,

or where the court is satisfied as mentioned in subsection (3) above in the case of a non-recognised body, it may approve a scheme, presented to it by the Lord Advocate and prepared by him in accordance with regulations made by the Secretary of State, for the transfer of any assets of the body to such body as the Lord Advocate specifies in the scheme, being a recognised body or a registered, or non-registered, charity which is managed or controlled wholly or mainly in or from Scotland.

(6) In the case of a registered, or non-registered, charity which is managed or controlled wholly or mainly outside Scotland but on behalf of which a bank or other person in Scotland holds moveable property, the court may, on the application of the Lord Advocate acting on information received from the Charity Commissioners for England and Wales, make an order requiring the bank or person not to part with that property without the court's approval and such an order shall be subject to such conditions as the court thinks fit.

(7) Where the court has made an order under subsection (6) above and it is satisfied, in the case of such a charity, that—

(*a*) there has been in its administration any misconduct or mismanagement; and

(*b*) it is necessary or desirable to act for the purpose of protecting its property or securing a proper application of such property for its purposes,

it may, on the further application of the Lord Advocate, make an order confirming the order made under subsection (6) above and such an order shall be subject to such conditions as the court thinks fit.

(8) Where the court has made an order under subsection (6) above and it is satisfied as to the matters specified in subsection (7) above in respect of such a charity, if in its opinion the moveable property would not be applied for the purposes of the charity, it may, on the further application of the

Lord Advocate, transfer that property to such body as the Lord Advocate specifies in the application, being a body—

(*a*) which is a recognised body or registered, or non-registered, charity the purposes of which closely resemble the purpose of the charity whose moveable property is transferred; and

(*b*) which has intimated that it will receive that property.

(9) The court shall have power—

(*a*) to vary or recall an order made under paragraph (*d*) or (*e*) of subsection (4) above or under subsection (6) or (7) above;

(*b*) to recall the suspension of a person under paragraph (*b*) of subsection (4) above;

(*c*) to approve a scheme under subsection (5) above subject to such modifications as it thinks fit;

(*d*) subject to subsection (10) below, to award expenses as it thinks fit in any proceedings before it under this section.

(10) In a case where, but for the provisions of this subsection, the court would have awarded expenses against the body which is the subject of the proceedings, the court—

(*a*) shall have regard to the desirability of applying the property of the body for the charitable purposes of that body, or the charitable purposes which are purported to be the purposes of that body, and

(*b*) may award expenses against a person concerned in the control or management of the body, or against any such persons jointly and severally.

(11) Where the court exercises in respect of a recognised body any power specified in subsection (4) or (5) above, the Lord Advocate may require that exercise to be noted for the purposes of section 1(3) of this Act.

(12) In this section "the court" means the Court of Session.

Disqualification of persons concerned in the management or control of recognised bodies

8.—(1) A person who—

(*a*) has been convicted of an offence involving dishonesty;

(*b*) is an undischarged bankrupt;

(*c*) has been removed, under section 7 of this Act, from being concerned in the management or control of any body; or

(*d*) is subject to a disqualification order under the Company Directors Disqualification Act 1986,

shall, subject to the provisions of this section, be disqualified from being concerned with the management or control of a recognised body.

(2) A person shall not be disqualified under subsection (1) above if—

(*a*) the conviction mentioned in that subsection is spent by virtue of the Rehabilitation of Offenders Act 1974; or

(*b*) the Lord Advocate has thought fit to grant in writing a waiver of that disqualification in respect of that person,

but the Lord Advocate shall not grant a waiver where to do so would prejudice the operation of the Company Directors Disqualification Act 1986.

(3) A person who is concerned with the management or control of a recognised body whilst disqualified by virtue of this section shall be guilty of an offence and liable—

(*a*) on summary conviction, to imprisonment for a term not exceeding six months or to a fine not exceeding the statutory maximum or to both; and

(*b*) on conviction on indictment, to imprisonment for a term not exceeding two years or to a fine or to both.

(4) The acts, in relation to the management or control of such a body, of such a person as is mentioned in subsection (1) above shall not be invalid only by reason of his disqualification under that subsection.

(5) Proceedings for an offence under subsection (3) above shall not be commenced after the end of the period of three years beginning with the

day on which the offence was committed but, subject to that, may be commenced at any time within six months from the date on which evidence sufficient in the opinion of the procurator fiscal to warrant proceedings came to his knowledge; and a certificate of the procurator fiscal as to the date on which such evidence came to his knowledge shall be conclusive evidence of that fact.

(6) In this section, "undischarged bankrupt" means a person who has had his estate sequestrated, been adjudged bankrupt or has granted a trust deed for or entered into an arrangement with his creditors and has not been discharged under or by virtue of—

(*a*) section 54 or section 75(4) of the Bankruptcy (Scotland) Act 1985;
(*b*) an order under paragraph 11 of Schedule 4 to that Act of 1985;
(*c*) section 279 or section 280 of the Insolvency Act 1986; or
(*d*) any other enactment or rule of law subsisting at the time of his discharge.

Reorganisation of public trusts

Reorganisation of public trusts by the court

9.—(1) Where, in the case of any public trust, the court is satisfied—

(*a*) that the purposes of the trust, whether in whole or in part—
   (i) have been fulfilled as far as it is possible to do so; or
   (ii) can no longer be given effect to, whether in accordance with the directions or spirit of the trust deed or other document constituting the trust or otherwise;
(*b*) that the purposes of the trust provide a use for only part of the property available under the trust;
(*c*) that the purposes of the trust were expressed by reference to—
   (i) an area which has, since the trust was constituted, ceased to have effect for the purpose described expressly or by implication in the trust deed or other document constituting the trust; or
   (ii) a class of persons or area which has ceased to be suitable or appropriate, having regard to the spirit of the trust deed or other document constituting the trust, or as regards which it has ceased to be practicable to administer the property available under the trust; or
(*d*) that the purposes of the trust, whether in whole or in part, have, since the trust was constituted—
   (i) been adequately provided for by other means; or
   (ii) ceased to be such as would enable the trust to become a recognised body; or
   (iii) ceased in any other way to provide a suitable and effective method of using the property available under the trust, having regard to the spirit of the trust deed or other document constituting the trust,

the court, on the application of the trustees, may, subject to subsection (2) below, approve a scheme for the variation or reorganisation of the trust purposes.

(2) The court shall not approve a scheme as mentioned in subsection (1) above unless it is satisfied that the trust purposes proposed in the scheme will enable the resources of the trust to be applied to better effect consistently with the spirit of the trust deed or other document constituting the trust, having regard to changes in social and economic conditions since the time when the trust was constituted.

(3) Where any of paragraphs (*a*) to (*d*) of subsection (1) above applies to a public trust, an application may be made under this section for the approval of a scheme—

(*a*) for the transfer of the assets of the trust to another public trust, whether involving a change to the trust purposes of such other trust or not; or

(*b*) for the amalgamation of the trust with one or more public trusts,

and the court, if it is satisfied that the conditions specified in subsection (2) above are met, may approve such a scheme.

(4) Subject to subsection (5) below, an application for approval of a scheme under this section shall be made to the Court of Session.

(5) From such day as the Lord Advocate may, by order, appoint, an application for approval of a scheme under this section may be made by a public trust having an annual income not exceeding such amount as the Secretary of State may, by order, prescribe—

(*a*) to the sheriff for the place with which the trust has its closest and most real connection;

(*b*) where there is no such place as is mentioned in paragraph (*a*) above, to the sheriff for the place where any of the trustees resides;

(*c*) where neither paragraph (*a*) nor (*b*) above applies, to the sheriff of Lothian and Borders at Edinburgh.

(6) Every application under this section shall be intimated to the Lord Advocate who shall be entitled to enter appearance as a party in any proceedings on such application, and he may lead such proof and enter such pleas as he thinks fit; and no expenses shall be claimable by or against the Lord Advocate in any proceedings in which he has entered appearance under this subsection.

(7) This section shall be without prejudice to the power of the Court of Session to approve a cy-près scheme in relation to any public trust.

Small trusts

10.—(1) Where a majority of the trustees of any public trust having an annual income not exceeding £5,000 are of the opinion—

(*a*) that the purposes of the trust, whether in whole or in part—

(i) have been fulfilled as far as it is possible to do so; or

(ii) can no longer be given effect to, whether in accordance with the directions or spirit of the trust deed or other document constituting the trust or otherwise;

(*b*) that the purposes of the trust provide a use for only part of the property available under the trust;

(*c*) that the purposes of the trust were expressed by reference to—

(i) an area which has, since the trust was constituted, ceased to have effect for the purpose described expressly or by implication in the trust deed or other document constituting the trust; or

(ii) a class of persons or area which has ceased to be suitable or appropriate, having regard to the spirit of the trust deed or other document constituting the trust, or as regards which it has ceased to be practicable to administer the property available under the trust; or

(*d*) that the purposes of the trust, whether in whole or in part, have, since the trust was constituted—

(i) been adequately provided for by other means; or

(ii) ceased to be such as would enable the trust to become a recognised body; or

(iii) ceased in any other way to provide a suitable and effective method of using the property available under the trust, having regard to the spirit of the trust deed or other document constituting the trust,

subsection (2) below shall apply in respect of the trust.

(2) Where this subsection applies in respect of a trust, the trustees may determine that, to enable the resources of the trust to be applied to better

effect consistently with the spirit of the trust deed or other document constituting the trust—

(*a*) a modification of the trust's purposes should be made;

(*b*) the whole assets of the trust should be transferred to another public trust; or

(*c*) that the trust should be amalgamated with one or more public trusts.

(3) Where the trustees of a trust determine as mentioned in subsection (2)(*a*) above, they may, subject to subsections (4) to (6) below, pass a resolution that the trust deed be modified by replacing the trust purposes by other purposes specified in the resolution.

(4) The trustees shall ensure that, so far as is practicable in the circumstances, the purposes so specified are not so far dissimilar in character to those of the purposes set out in the original trust deed or other document constituting the trust that such modification of the trust deed would constitute an unreasonable departure from the spirit of such trust deed or other document.

(5) Before passing a resolution under subsection (3) above the trustees shall have regard—

(*a*) where the trust purposes relate to a particular locality, to the circumstances of the locality; and

(*b*) to the extent to which it may be desirable to achieve economy by amalgamating two or more trusts.

(6) As regards a trust which is a recognised body, the trustees shall ensure that the purposes specified as mentioned in subsection (3) above are such as will enable the trust to continue to be granted an exemption from tax by the Commissioners of Inland Revenue under section 505(1) of the Income and Corporation Taxes Act 1988 (exemption from tax for charities).

(7) Subject to subsection (14) below, a modification of trust purposes under this section shall not have effect before the expiry of a period of two months commencing with the date on which any advertisement in pursuance of regulations made under subsection (13) below is first published.

(8) Where the trustees determine as mentioned in subsection (2)(*b*) above they may pass a resolution that the trust be wound up and that the assets of the trust be transferred to another trust or trusts the purposes of which are not so dissimilar in character to those of the trust to be wound up as to constitute an unreasonable departure from the spirit of the trust deed or other document constituting the trust to be wound up.

(9) Before passing a resolution under subsection (8) above, the trustees shall—

(*a*) where the trust purposes relate to a particular locality, have regard to the circumstances of the locality;

(*b*) where the trust is a recognised body, ensure that the purposes of the trust to which it is proposed that the assets be transferred are such as will enable the trust to be granted an exemption from tax by the Commissioners of Inland Revenue under section 505(1) of the Income and Corporation Taxes Act 1988 (exemption from tax for charities); and

(*c*) ascertain that the trustees of the trust to which it is proposed to transfer the assets will consent to the transfer of the assets.

(10) Where the trustees determine as mentioned in subsection (2)(*c*) above, they may pass a resolution that the trust be amalgamated with one or more other trusts so that the purposes of the trust constituted by such amalgamation will not be so dissimilar in character to those of the trust to which the resolution relates as to constitute an unreasonable departure from the spirit of the trust deed or other document constituting the last mentioned trust.

(11) Before passing a resolution under subsection (10) above, the trustees shall—

(*a*) where the trust purposes relate to a particular locality, have regard to the circumstances of the locality;

(*b*) where any of the trusts to be amalgamated is a recognised body, ensure that the trust purposes of the trust to be constituted by such amalgamation will be such as to enable it to be granted an exemption from tax by the Commissioners of Inland Revenue under section 505(1) of the Income and Corporation Taxes Act 1988 (exemption from tax for charities); and

(*c*) ascertain that the trustees of any other trust with which it is proposed that the trust will be amalgamated will agree to such amalgamation.

(12) Subject to subsection (14) below, a transfer of trust assets or an amalgamation of two or more trusts under this section shall not be effected before the expiry of a period of two months commencing with the date on which any advertisement in pursuance of regulations made under subsection (13) below is first published.

(13) The Secretary of State may, by regulations, prescribe the procedure to be followed by trustees following upon a resolution passed under subsection (3), (8) or (10) above, and such regulations may, without prejudice to the generality, include provision as to advertisement of the proposed modification or winding up, the making of objections by persons with an interest in the purposes of the trust, notification to the Lord Advocate of the terms of the resolution and the time within which anything requires to be done.

(14) If it appears to the Lord Advocate, whether in consideration of any objections made in pursuance of regulations made under subsection (13) above or otherwise—

(*a*) that the trust deed should not be modified as mentioned in subsection (3) above;

(*b*) that the trust should not be wound up as mentioned in subsection (8) above; or

(*c*) that the trust should not be amalgamated as mentioned in subsection (10) above,

he may direct the trust not to proceed with the modification or, as the case may be winding up and transfer of funds or amalgamation.

(15) The Secretary of State may, by order, amend subsection (1) above by substituting a different figure for the figure, for the time being, mentioned in that subsection.

(16) This section shall apply to any trust to which section 223 of the Local Government (Scotland) Act 1973 (property held on trust by local authorities) applies.

Expenditure of capital

11.—(1) This section applies to any public trust which has an annual income not exceeding £1,000 where the trust deed or other document constituting the trust prohibits the expenditure of any of the trust capital.

(2) In the case of any trust to which this section applies where the trustees—

(*a*) have resolved unanimously that, having regard to the purposes of the trust, the income of the trust is too small to enable the purposes of the trust to be achieved; and

(*b*) are satisfied that either there is no reasonable prospect of effecting a transfer of the trust's assets under section 10 of this Act or that the expenditure of capital is more likely to achieve the purposes of the trust,

they may, subject to subsection (3) below, proceed with the expenditure of capital.

(3) Not less than two months before proceeding to expend capital, the trustees shall advertise their intention to do so in accordance with regula-

tions made by the Secretary of State and shall notify the Lord Advocate of such intention.

(4) If it appears to the Lord Advocate that there are insufficient grounds for the expenditure of capital he may apply to the court for an order prohibiting such expenditure, and if the court is satisfied that there are such insufficient grounds it may grant the order.

(5) The Secretary of State may, by order, amend subsection (1) above by substituting a different figure for the figure, for the time being mentioned in that subsection.

Dormant charities

Dormant accounts of charities in banks, etc.

12.—(1) The Secretary of State may appoint a person to be the Scottish charities nominee (in this section referred to as "the nominee") who shall have the functions conferred by this section.

(2) Where the nominee receives from a relevant institution the following information—

(*a*) that every account held by the institution in the name of or on behalf of a named body is dormant; and

(*b*) the amount of the balance standing to the credit of the body in each such account,

and he is satisfied that the body is a recognised body, subsection (3) or, as the case may be, subsection (5) below shall apply as regards the body and such accounts.

(3) Where the aggregate amount standing to the credit of the body in such accounts as are mentioned in subsection (2) above does not exceed £5,000, unless it appears to the nominee—

(*a*) that a person is concerned in the management or control of the body; or

(*b*) that there are circumstances relating to the body which would make it inappropriate to do so,

he shall transfer the balance standing to the credit of the body in such accounts to such other recognised body as he may determine, having regard to the purposes of the body in whose name or on whose behalf the accounts are held and those of the body to which it is proposed to transfer the funds; and the body to which the funds are transferred under this subsection or subsection (4) below shall be entitled to apply such funds for its purposes as it thinks fit.

(4) Where, in the case of a body to which subsection (3) above applies, the nominee is unable to ascertain the purposes of the body in whose name or on whose behalf such accounts are held, he shall transfer the balance standing in the name of the body concerned to such other recognised body as appears to him expedient.

(5) Where the aggregate amount standing to the credit of the body in such accounts as are mentioned in subsection (2) above exceeds £5,000 or in any case to which paragraph (*a*) or (*b*) of subsection (3) above applies, the nominee shall advise the Lord Advocate of the information received by him in respect of the body and of any other matter which appears to him to be relevant in the circumstances.

(6) Where the Lord Advocate receives information in pursuance of subsection (5) above he shall inform the nominee—

(*a*) in the case of a body which is a trust, whether he intends to exercise his power under section 13(2) of this Act to appoint new trustees to the body; or

(*b*) in any case, if he intends to apply to the Court of Session for the appointment of an interim judicial factor under section 7(4)(*c*) of this Act, but if the Lord Advocate informs the nominee that he does not intend to proceed under either paragraph (*a*) or (*b*) above, subsection (3) above shall apply as regards the body and such accounts as are mentioned in subsection (2) above as if the aggregate amount of the balance referred to in subsection (3) did not exceed £5,000 and neither paragraph (*a*) nor (*b*) of that subsection applied.

(7) Notwithstanding anything in any enactment or rule of law to the contrary, the nominee shall, by virtue of this subsection, have the right to effect any transaction (including a transaction closing the account) in relation to any account to which subsection (3) above applies; and the receipt of the nominee in respect of any funds withdrawn or transferred from an account by virtue of this subsection shall, as regards the interest of the nominee in respect of such funds, be a full and valid discharge to the relevant institution holding the account.

(8) No liability (other than liability for a criminal offence) shall attach to the nominee in consequence of any act or omission of his in the performance of his functions under this section.

(9) The power of the nominee to effect transactions in relation to the accounts of a body shall cease to have effect—

(*a*) when the Lord Advocate notifies him of his intention to proceed under subsection (6) above;

(*b*) if the relevant institution by which the accounts are held notifies the nominee that the accounts held by or on behalf of the body are no longer dormant; or

(*c*) where the nominee becomes aware of the identity of a person concerned in the management or control of the body, when he informs the institution of that fact,

and in any case to which paragraph (*c*) above applies, the nominee shall also inform the Lord Advocate of that fact.

(10) The Secretary of State may, by regulations made under this section—

(*a*) make provision as to the procedure to be followed by the nominee in exercising his powers under this section;

(*b*) require the nominee to make to the Secretary of State an annual report as regards the exercise of his functions and such regulations may specify the form and content of such report; and the Secretary of State shall lay a copy of such report before each House of Parliament;

(*c*) prescribe the circumstances in which and the extent to which the nominee may apply any interest accruing to any account as regards which subsection (3) above applies during any period for which he is entitled to effect transactions in respect of the account for the purpose of defraying his expenses in connection with the exercise of his functions under this section;

(*d*) require the nominee to keep accounts as regards his outlays and expenses in connection with the exercise of his functions under this section; and

(*e*) amend subsections (3) and (5) above by substituting a different figure for the figure for the time being mentioned in those subsections.

(11) Where every account held by or on behalf of a body which appears to a relevant institution to be a recognised body is a dormant account, no obligation of confidentiality or requirement of secrecy (whether imposed by any enactment or rule of law or otherwise) shall prevent the institution from supplying to the nominee information such as is mentioned in subsection (12) below.

(12) Information referred to in subsection (11) above is information relating to any account such as is mentioned in that subsection which consists of any of the following—

(*a*) the amount of the balance of the account as at the date the information is supplied;
(*b*) the last date on which a transaction (other than a transaction consisting only of the accrual of interest to the account) was effected in relation to the account;
(*c*) so far as is known to the institution, the terms of the trust deed or other document constituting the body or any information as to the nature of the purposes of the body.

(13) For the purpose of this section—
(*a*) a "relevant institution" is—
(i) an institution which is authorised by the Bank of England to operate a deposit-taking business under Part I of the Banking Act 1987;
(ii) a building society which is authorised by the Building Societies Commission under section 9 of the Building Societies Act 1986 to raise money from its members;
(iii) such other institution mentioned in Schedule 2 to the Banking Act 1987 as the Secretary of State may, by regulations made under this section, prescribe;
(*b*) an account is dormant if—
(i) in the period of 10 years preceding the date on which the institution reviews the account, no transaction (other than a transaction consisting only of the accrual of interest to the account) has taken place in respect of the account; and
(ii) the institution has no knowledge of the identity of any person concerned in the management or control of the body in whose name or on whose behalf the account is held.

Miscellaneous

Appointment of trustees

13.—(1) Where a recognised body is a trust, notwithstanding anything to the contrary in the trust deed or other document constituting the trust, the trustees shall have power to appoint such number of additional trustees as will secure that, at any time, the number of trustees shall be not less than three.

(2) Where in the case of any trust which is a recognised body—
(*a*) the number of trustees is less than three; and
(*b*) it appears to the Lord Advocate that the trustees will not, or are unable to, exercise their power under subsection (1) above,

if it appears to the Lord Advocate expedient to do so, he may exercise the power in place of the trustees.

Alteration of purposes and winding-up of charitable companies

14.—(1) This section applies to a recognised body which may be wound up by the Court of Session under or by virtue of Part IV or V of the Insolvency Act 1986.

(2) Where a body to which this section applies has power to alter the instruments establishing or regulating it, it shall not alter any charitable purposes in those instruments except in such a way as will enable the body to continue to be granted an exemption from tax by the Commissioners of Inland Revenue under section 505(1) of the Income and Corporation Taxes Act 1988 (exemption from tax of charities).

(3) Notwithstanding section 124 of the Insolvency Act 1986, a petition for the winding-up under section 122 of that Act of a body to which this section applies may be presented by the Lord Advocate to any court in Scotland having jurisdiction.

Interpretation of Part I, regulations and orders

15.—(1) In this Part of this Act—

"annual income" in relation to a recognised body means the income of the body for the financial year to which its most recent statement of accounts relates;

"accounting reference period," "accounting reference date" and "financial year" shall be construed in accordance with subsections (2) to (7) below;

"body" includes the sole trustee of any trust and, as regards any reference in this Part of this Act to the institution of proceedings in any court or to any order of a court in relation to an unincorporated body, shall be construed—

(*a*) in the case of a trust, as a reference to the trustees acting in their capacity as such;

(*b*) in any other case, as a reference to the persons concerned in the management or control of the body;

"court," for the purposes of establishing jurisdiction to hear or determine any matter other than under sections 7 and 9 of this Act, means the Court of Session or the sheriff court;

"non-recognised body" shall be construed in accordance with section 2 of this Act;

"non-registered charity" has the meaning given by section 6 of this Act;

"recognised body" has the meaning given by section 1 of this Act; and

"registered charity" has the meaning given by section 6 of this Act.

(2) For the purposes of this Part of this Act, a recognised body's first financial year begins with the first day of its first accounting reference period and ends with the last day of that period or such other date, not more than seven days before or after the end of that period, as the persons concerned with the management or control of the body may determine.

(3) Subject to subsection (4) below, subsequent financial years begin with the day immediately following the end of the body's previous financial year and end with the last day of its next accounting reference period or such other date, not more than seven days before or after the end of that period as the persons responsible for its management or control may determine.

(4) A recognised body's accounting reference periods are determined according to its accounting reference date.

(5) A recognised body's accounting reference date is the date upon which its accounting reference period ends in each calendar year and it shall be ascertained as follows—

(*a*) in the case of a body which is recognised at the commencement of this section and in respect of which accounts have been prepared up to a date not more than 12 months before such commencement, its accounting reference date shall be that date;

(*b*) in the case of a body which is recognised at the commencement of this section and in respect of which no such accounts have been prepared, its accounting reference date shall be March 31, or such other date as the Secretary of State may, by order, prescribe;

(*c*) in the case of a body which is not recognised at the commencement of this section and in respect of which accounts have been prepared up to a date not more than 12 months before its recognition, its accounting reference date shall be that date; and

(*d*) a body which is not recognised at the commencement of this section and in respect of which no accounts have been prepared up to a date not more than 12 months before such commencement, unless it determines that its accounting reference date shall be March 31, or such other date as the Secretary of State may, by order, prescribe, shall by notice given to the Lord Advocate specify its accounting reference date;

(6) A recognised body's first accounting reference period is—

(*a*) in the case of a body which is recognised at the commencement of this section and in respect of which any accounts have been prepared for a period up to a date not more than 12 months before such commencement, the period beginning with that date;

(*b*) in the case of a body which is recognised at such commencement and in respect of which no such accounts have been prepared, the period beginning with such commencement;

(*c*) in the case of any other body, the period of more than six months but not more than 18 months, beginning with the date from which its recognition takes effect and ending with its accounting reference date.

(7) Its subsequent accounting reference periods are successive periods of 12 months beginning immediately after the end of the previous accounting reference period and ending with its accounting reference date.

(8) A recognised body may, on giving not less than one month's notice of its intention to do so to the Lord Advocate, unless the Lord Advocate notifies the body that he objects to the proposal, specify a new accounting reference date having effect in relation to the body's current accounting reference period and subsequent periods.

(9) Nothing in this Part of this Act, except section 1, shall affect any educational endowment within the meaning of section 122(1) of the Education (Scotland) Act 1980.

(10) The War Charities Act 1940 shall cease to have effect as regards Scotland; but nothing in this subsection shall affect any prosecution for an offence under that Act which has been instituted before the commencement of this section.

(11) Any power in this Part of this Act of the Secretary of State to make regulations or orders shall be exercisable by statutory instrument subject to annulment in pursuance of a resolution of either House of Parliament.

. . . .

Part IV

Miscellaneous Reforms

Powers of attorney

Effect of mental incapacity on powers of attorney etc.

[1] **71.**—(1) Any rule of law by which a factory and commission or power of attorney ceases to have effect in the event of the mental incapacity of the granter shall not apply to a factory and commission or power of attorney granted on or after the date on which this section comes into force.

(2) In subsection (1) above, "mental incapacity" means, in relation to a person, that he is incapable of managing his property and affairs by reason of mental disorder within the meaning of section 1 of the Mental Health (Scotland) Act 1984.

NOTE

[1] Section 71 came into force on 1st January 1991: s.75(3).

. . . .

[THE NEXT PAGE IS M 201]

Acts of Sederunt

Procedure in Actions in the Sheriff Court for Declarator that a Testamentary Writing of a Deceased Person is Holograph of Such Person

(S.R. & O. 1935 No. 756)

[19th July 1935]

The Lords of Council and Session, in virtue of the powers conferred on them by section 34 of the Administration of Justice (Scotland) Act 1933 do hereby enact and declare as follows:

1. In any action in the sheriff court for declarator that a testamentary writing of a deceased person is holograph of such person—

(1) The writ shall be served on the heir-at-law of the deceased person and on such other persons interested as the sheriff may direct;

(2) The sheriff may accept as evidence that the writing and signature of the testamentary writing are in the proper handwriting of the deceased person, affidavits, being two or more in number, by persons who depone that they are well acquainted with the handwriting and signature of the deceased person. Persons may so depone notwithstanding that they may have a patrimonial interest in the estate of the deceased person, and affidavits by such persons will be duly considered by the sheriff. Where in the opinion of the sheriff the affidavits produced are insufficient to enable the question at issue to be disposed of, or further evidence is required, the party lodging the same shall lodge such further affidavit or affidavits as the sheriff may direct, or, if the sheriff so appoint, prove the relevant facts by the ordinary rules of evidence;

(3) Such affidavits may either be endorsed on the testamentary writing, or on an extract thereof, or may be contained in separate documents which shall refer *in gremio* to such testamentary writing or extract. Such affidavits may be taken before a magistrate, commissioner for oaths, justice of the peace, or notary public, not being the solicitor of the pursuer or a partner or servant of such solicitor. or before any commissioner whom the sheriff may appoint;

(4) Subject to the provisions hereof, the action shall proceed as an ordinary action in the sheriff court.

2. Nothing herein contained shall affect any practice of the commissary court or of the sheriff court in the exercise of commissary jurisdiction, which allows affidavits to be received as to the holograph nature of testamentary writings in proceedings for confirmation of an executor-nominate.

3. This Act of Sederunt shall come into operation on the first day of August 1935.

Unopposed Executry Petitions 1948

(S.I. 1948 No. 621)

[19th March 1948]

The Lords of Council and Session, by virtue of the powers conferred on them by section 34 of the Administration of Justice (Scotland) Act 1933, and of all other powers competent to them in that behalf, do hereby enact and declare that in all petitions for the appointment of an executor or executors to a deceased person where intimation and publication have been duly made and a certificate of intimation and publication has been duly endorsed upon the petition by the sheriff clerk or commissary clerk, and nine clear days have expired from the date of such certification without any answers to the petition, and no competing petition or caveat has been lodged, and in unopposed applications for the recall of appointment of an executor or executors to a deceased person, it shall not be necessary for the petition or application to be called in court or for the petitioner or applicant or his solicitor to attend (or for a formal motion for decree or recall to be made), but the petition or application may be laid by the sheriff clerk or commissary clerk before the sheriff in chambers, who, if satisfied that the petition or application is in proper form and that the proceedings have been regular, may, without hearing any party, decern the petitioner or petitioners executor or executors or recall the appointment as craved, or may, in his discretion, direct the petition or application to be called and heard in court *quam primum*.

This Act may be cited as the Act of Sederunt (Unopposed Executry Petitions) 1948.

Judicial Factors Rules 1992

(S.I. 1992 No. 272)

[12th February 1992]

The Lords of Council and Session, under and by virtue of the powers conferred on them by section 34A of the Judicial Factors Act 1849, section 5 of the Judicial Factors (Scotland) Act 1880, sections 11B and 21 of the Judicial Factors (Scotland) Act 1889, section 32 of the Sheriff Courts (Scotland) Act 1971 and of all other powers enabling them in that behalf, having approved with modifications, draft rules submitted to them by the Sheriff Court Rules Council in accordance with section 34 of the Sheriff Courts (Scotland) Act 1971, do hereby enact and declare:

Part I

General

Citation, commencement and revocation

1.—(1) This Act of Sederunt may be cited as the Act of Sederunt (Judicial Factors Rules) 1992 and shall come into force on 9th March 1992.

(2) This Act of Sederunt shall be inserted in the Books of Sederunt.

(3) Chapter VIII of Book L of the Codifying Act of Sederunt and the Act of Sederunt (Judicial Factors) 1980 are revoked.

Interpretation

2.—(1) In these Rules unless the context otherwise requires—

"the 1849 Act" means the Judicial Factors Act 1849;

"the 1880 Act" means the Judicial Factors (Scotland) Act 1880;

"the 1889 Act" means the Judicial Factors (Scotland) Act 1889;

"Accountant" means the Accountant of Court;

"factor" includes a curator bonis, a factor *loco absentis*, a factor on trust or other estates and a guardian where caution is required.

(2) Any reference in these Rules to a numbered form shall, unless the context otherwise requires, be construed as a reference to the form so

numbered in the Schedule to these Rules or a form substantially to the same effect, with such variation as circumstances may require.

Application

3.—(1) The provisions of Part I of these Rules shall have effect in relation to—

(*a*) factors appointed under section 4 of the 1880 Act;

(*b*) guardians appointed under the Law Reform Parent and Child (Scotland) Act 1986; and

(*c*) except as provided in Part II of these Rules, factors appointed under section 11A of the 1889 Act.

(2) The provisions of Part II of these Rules shall have effect only in relation to factors appointed under section 11A of the 1889 Act.

Applications to be summary

4. An application for the appointment of a factor shall be made by summary application.

Incidental application

5.—(1) Except as otherwise provided in these rules, all incidental applications to the court shall be made by note in the proceedings.

(2) Unless included in the application for appointment of a factor an application for special powers shall be made by note in the proceedings.

Intimation and service

6.—(1) Subject to rule 15(2), 23 and 36, the first order in an application shall provide for—

(*a*) intimation of a copy of the application by display on the walls of court;

(*b*) intimation to the Accountant by first class recorded delivery post of the application together with copies of any schedules or productions lodged with the application;

(*c*) such service on those having an interest as may be deemed proper by the sheriff; and

(*d*) the lodging of answers.

(2) The sheriff may also direct notice by advertisement of the applications to be made in Form 1.

Paper to be copied to the Accountant

7.—(1) A person who has lodged answers, a note, or any other principal paper (other than an application for appointment of a factor) shall serve forthwith such answers, note or other paper on the Accountant by any competent method of service.

(2) Copies of all interlocutors issued in the process of an application for appointment of a factor shall be supplied to the Accountant forthwith by the sheriff clerk.

Accountant to send information on any prior application

8. The Accountant, on receiving intimation of an application for the appointment of a factor, shall, in the event of an application for a similar appointment to the same ward or estate having been previously intimated to him—

(*a*) forthwith report to the sheriff clerk; and

(*b*) communicate any information he may possess which may be of use to the sheriff in disposing of the application.

Procedure in fixing caution

9.—(1) The Accountant shall forthwith, on receiving intimation of an application for the appointment of a factor, fix the caution to be found in the event of appointment being made and shall notify the amount to the sheriff clerk and the applicant.

(2) During the subsistence of a judicial factory, the Accountant may, at any time—

(*a*) require the factor to increase the amount of or find new or additional caution; or

(*b*) authorise the factor to decrease the amount of existing caution.

Time for finding caution

10.—(1) Where the time within which caution is to be found is not stipulated in the interlocutor appointing a factor, the time allowed for finding caution shall be, subject to paragraph (2) of this rule, limited to one calendar month from the date of the interlocutor.

(2) The sheriff may, on application made before the expiry of the period for finding caution, and on cause shown, allow further time for finding caution.

Procedure on finding caution

11.—(1) All bonds of caution offered by a factor shall be delivered to the Accountant.

(2) Except in relation to rule 9(2), where caution has been found to the satisfaction of the Accountant, he shall notify the sheriff clerk.

Issue of certified copy interlocutor

12. A certified copy interlocutor of appointment shall not be issued by the sheriff clerk until he receives notification from the Accountant in accordance with rule 11(2).

Factor's title to act

13. A factor shall not be entitled to act until he has obtained a certified copy interlocutor of his appointment.

Requisition of process by Accountant

14. The sheriff clerk shall transmit to the Accountant the whole or any part of the process as the Accountant may request unless such part of the process is not at the time of request required by the court.

Application to encroach on capital

15.—(1) Where the income from the estate of a ward is insufficient for the maintenance of the ward, the factor may apply to the Accountant for his consent to encroach on the capital of the estate for the purpose of maintaining the ward.

(2) An application under paragraph (1) of this rule shall be made by letter and shall be supported by such information as the Accountant may require.

(3) (*a*) On receipt of such an application, the Accountant shall—

(i) appoint the factor to intimate the making of the application in accordance with paragraphs (4) and (5) of this rule; or

(ii) require him to apply by note to the sheriff for special powers.

(*b*) Any person to whom intimation is appointed to be given in accordance with paragraphs (4) and (5) of this rule shall have the right to object to the application by lodging any objection in writing with the Accountant, and intimating a copy thereof to the factor within 28 days of the date on which the intimation was given.

(4) The persons to whom intimation under paragraph (3)(*a*)(i) of this rule is to be given are—

(*a*) the cautioner of the factor;
(*b*) the applicant for the appointment of the factor;
(*c*) the ward, unless the circumstances of the ward are such as would warrant dispensing with service on him of an application for the appointment of his factor;
(*d*) the persons upon whom the application for appointment of the factor was served and whose whereabouts are known to the factor; and
(*e*) all other persons who have an interest in the estate and whose identity and whereabouts are known to the factor.

(5) Intimation under paragraph (3)(*a*)(i) of this rule shall be given by posting by registered or recorded delivery post or the nearest equivalent which the available postal service permits—
(*a*) a copy of the letter of application; and
(*b*) a notice setting out—
(i) the right of the person receiving the notice to object to the application in the manner provided in paragraph (3)(*b*) of this rule; and
(ii) that, in the absence of any such objection, the Accountant may consent to the application.

(6) The factor shall, on giving intimation under paragraph (3)(*a*)(i) of this rule, send to the Accountant a certificate of execution of service with a copy of the notice sent attached to it.

(7) Where no objections have been lodged, the Accountant may, on the expiry of the period for lodging objections, consent to the application (subject to such conditions as he thinks fit) or require the factor to apply to the sheriff for special powers.

(8) Where objections have been lodged, the factor shall, on expiry of the period for lodging objections, apply to the sheriff for special powers.

Applications under section 2(3) of the Trusts (Scotland) Act 1961

16.—(1) An application under section 2(3) of the Trusts (Scotland) Act 1961 to the Accountant for his consent to the doing of an act to which that section applies shall be made by letter and shall be supported by such information as the Accountant may require.

(2) Any person to whom intimation requires to be given in accordance with paragraphs (3) and (4) of this rule shall have the right to object to the application by lodging any objections with the Accountant, and intimating a copy thereof to the factor, within 28 days of the date on which the intimation was given.

(3) On the day on which he makes application or as soon as possible thereafter, the factor shall give intimation thereof to—
(*a*) the cautioner of the factor;
(*b*) the applicant for the appointment of the factor;
(*c*) the ward, unless the circumstances of the ward are such that would warrant dispensing with service on him of a petition for the appointment of his factor;
(*d*) the persons upon whom the application for appointment of the factor was served and whose whereabouts are known to the factor; and
(*e*) all other persons who have an interest in the estate and whose identity and whereabouts are known to the factor.

(4) Intimation under paragraph (3) of this rule shall be given by posting by registered or recorded delivery post or the nearest equivalent which the available postal service permits—
(*a*) a copy of the letter of application; and
(*b*) a notice setting out—
(i) the right of the person receiving the notice to object to the application in the manner provided in paragraph (2) of this rule; and

(ii) that, in the absence of any such objection, the Accountant may consent to the application.

(5) The factor shall, on giving intimation under paragraph (3) of this rule, send to the Accountant a duly completed execution of service with a copy of the notice sent attached to it.

Special powers

17.—(1) Except as provided for in rules 5, 15 and 16, where the factor desires special powers, he shall submit an application to the Accountant, who, after making such enquiries as may appear to him proper, shall transmit the application together with a written opinion on the application to the factor who shall submit the application and the Accountant's opinion to the court in accordance with rule 5.

(2) Upon receipt of the application and opinion, the sheriff shall, after ordering such intimation and service in terms of rule 6 as may seem to him appropriate and such procedure as he may think necessary, deal with and dispose of the application.

(3) The factor shall provide the Accountant with a copy of the interlocutor disposing of the application within two days of the disposal.

(4) An application for special powers under this rule shall not be made by the factor until the factor has obtained a certified copy interlocutor of his appointment.

Outlays of Accountant, sheriff clerk etc.

18. All outlays incurred by the Accountant and sheriff clerk, and office fees in the factory, shall form a charge against the estate, and shall be satisfied and paid by the factor therefrom, unless the sheriff shall see cause to find the factor personally liable to any extent, in which case the factor shall be bound to relieve the estate of such outlay.

Applications for discharge to the Accountant

19.—(1) This rule shall apply only to a judicial factor appointed as a—

(*a*) curator bonis;
(*b*) guardian;
(*c*) factor *loco absentis*; or
(*e*) [*sic*] commissary factor.

(2) Where a factory is terminated by reason of the recovery, death or coming of age of the ward, or by reason of the exhaustion of the estate, the factor, or where he died, his representative, may apply to the Accountant for a certificate of discharge.

(3) The factor shall send a notice in Form 2 by first class recorded delivery post of an application under paragraph (2) to—

(*a*) the cautioner; and
(*b*) any person with an interest in the estate of the ward.

(4) Any person to whom notice has been given under paragraph (3) of this rule may make written representations relating to the application to the Accountant within 21 days from the date of such notice.

(5) On the expiry of the period specified in paragraph (4) of this rule, the Accountant shall—

(*a*) consider the application and representations made; and
(*b*) intimate to the factor, to the sheriff clerk and to any party who has made representations, a copy of his determination to issue or refuse to issue a certificate of discharge together with a note of his reasons for making such determination.

(6) The Accountant—

(*a*) shall not sign a certificate of discharge until the time for lodging an appeal under rule 20 has expired; and
(*b*) shall, on issuing a certificate of discharge, give notice of such issue to the sheriff clerk.

(7) The issue of a certificate of discharge shall be sufficient authority for the factor to uplift his bond of caution.

Appeals against Accountant's determination of application for discharge

20.—(1) The factor, or any person who has made representations under rule 19(4), may within 14 days of intimation under rule 19(5)(*b*), appeal to the sheriff against the determination of the Accountant.

(2) An appeal under paragraph (1) of this rule shall be by letter to the sheriff clerk containing a statement of the grounds of appeal, and intimated to the Accountant.

(3) On receipt of an appeal under paragraph (1) of this rule, the sheriff clerk shall place the papers before the sheriff in chambers for determination of the appeal.

(4) On disposing of such appeal, the sheriff may—

(*a*) direct the Accountant to sign the certificate of discharge;

(*b*) appoint the factor to lodge an application for his discharge; or

(*c*) make such further order as he considers appropriate.

Applications for discharge to the sheriff

21.—(1) Where the discharge is desired of a factor, to whom the provisions of rule 19 do not apply, the factor, or where he has died, his representative, shall lodge an application in process.

(2) On receipt of such application the sheriff shall order intimation and service in terms of rule 6 and, where applicable, rule 36.

(3) The Accountant shall issue his written opinion to the sheriff on the application.

PART II

ADDITIONAL RULES APPLYING TO FACTORS APPOINTED UNDER SECTION 11A OF THE JUDICIAL FACTORS (SCOTLAND) ACT 1889 ON ESTATES OF DECEASED PERSONS

Form of application

22. An application for the appointment of a factor under section 11A of the 1889 Act shall include the following matters—

(*a*) the grounds of jurisdiction;

(*b*) the name, last address and date of death of the deceased person;

(*c*) the reasons for the appointment being necessary;

(*d*) the interest of the person(s) making the application, *i.e.* if a creditor or creditors, the nature and amount of the debt(s), how constituted, vouched or established, if a person or persons having an interest in the succession to the estate, the nature of that interest;

(*e*) details of the deceased person's estate so far as known to the applicant(s) including heritable and moveable property, any stock in trade, any interests in any business or partnership, debts owed to or by the deceased and any other relevant facts;

(*f*) the names and addresses of all persons known to the applicant(s) as having an interest in the estate either as creditors or as having an interest in the succession to the estate and the nature of the interest in each case; and

(*g*) the name, designation and address of the person nominated to be the judicial factor.

Intimation and service

23. The first order in an application under rule 22 shall, in addition to the requirements of rule 6 provide for—

(*a*) advertisement of the application in the *Edinburgh Gazette* in Form 3; and

(*b*) service of the application on such persons named therein as personal representatives of the deceased who are not parties to the application.

Interim appointment

24. The sheriff may make an interim appointment of a factor when the application is presented or at any time thereafter.

Notice calling for claims

25.—(1) In order to ascertain the claims upon the estate, the factor shall, within 14 days of the issue to him of the first certified copy interlocutor of his appointment, insert in the *Edinburgh Gazette* and in such other appropriate newspaper, a notice in Form 4.

(2) The factor shall lodge in process—

(*a*) a copy of each newspaper containing the notice under paragraph (1) of this rule; or

(*b*) a certificate of publication by the publisher of each such newspaper stating the date of publication and text of the notice.

(3) The period of notice for creditors to intimate their claims to the factor on the estate shall be four months from the latest date of advertisement in accordance with paragraph (1) of this rule.

Claims

26.—(1) The factor shall examine the claims of the creditors in order to ascertain whether the debts are properly due from the estate of the deceased, and may—

(*a*) call for further evidence in support of the claims;

(*b*) if he sees fit, require a creditor to constitute such claim by decree in a competent court in an action in which the factor shall be called as a defender.

(2) For the purpose of ranking and payment of creditors, the date of the factor's appointment shall be equivalent to the date of sequestration.

Inventory of estate and report of state of debts

27. The inventory of estate, when adjusted and approved by the Accountant and signed by him and the factor together with a report on the state of debts and all subsequent accounts submitted by the factor shall remain in the possession of the Accountant and shall be open to inspection, within his office, by any creditor or person interested in the succession of the deceased.

Administration, deathbed and funeral expenses

28.—(1) Out of the first funds realised by him, the factor shall reserve sufficient to defray the estimated costs of his administration including the legal expenses of the factory.

(2) Thereafter on the expiry of the period for lodging claims, the factor shall be entitled to pay out of such funds, with the prior approval of the Accountant, those claims given a preference by section 51(1) and (2) of, and Schedule 3 to, the Bankruptcy (Scotland) Act 1985.

Procedure where there are creditors

29.—(1) Where claims are lodged, the factor shall—

(*a*) where funds remain available for division after payment of the debts specified in rule 28, prepare a state of funds and scheme of division amongst the creditors; or (*b*) where no such funds remain after payment of those specified debts, prepare a state of funds only.

(2) The factor shall lodge with the Accountant the state of funds and scheme of division, or state of funds, as the case may be, together with all writings and documents relevant thereto, and shall provide the Accountant with such explanations as he shall require.

(3) The Accountant shall prepare a written report on the state of funds and scheme of division, or state of funds, as the case may be, containing such observations thereon as he considers appropriate for consideration by the sheriff.

(4) The Accountant shall issue the report under paragraph (3) of this rule to the factor.

Notice to creditors

30.—(1) As soon as the Accountant's report under rule 29 has been issued, the factor shall—

(*a*) lodge it together with the state of funds and scheme of division or state of funds, as the case may be, in process;

(*b*) send to each person who has lodged with him a claim on the estate of the deceased a notice by first class post, or if that person is abroad by air mail, stating—

(i) that the state of funds and scheme of division or state of funds only, as the case may be, and a report thereon have been lodged in court; and

(ii) the amount for which the creditor has been ranked and whether his claim is to be paid in full or by a dividend and the amount thereof; or

(iii) that his claim has been rejected; or

(iv) that no funds are available for division;

(*c*) insert in the *Edinburgh Gazette* a notice in Form 5; and

(*d*) if any person, other than those who have lodged claims with him are stated in the application or in the books, deed of settlement, or other papers of the deceased, to be a creditor of the estate or interested therein, or if he otherwise has reason to believe that any other person is either a creditor of the estate or interested therein, give notice to such person by first class post or if that person is abroad by air mail, that no dividend is allotted to him in the scheme of division.

(2) Any creditor or person interested in the succession to the deceased's estate shall be entitled to examine—

(*a*) the state of funds and scheme of division or state of funds, as the case may be, lodged in process; and

(*b*) the claims and the supporting vouchers or evidence lodged with the factor.

Approval of state of funds or scheme of division with or without objections

31.—(1) Any creditor or person interested in the succession to the deceased's estate who is dissatisfied with either the state of funds and scheme of division or state of funds may lodge with the sheriff clerk a notice of objections within 28 days of the last date of the notices given under rule 30(1)(*b*) and, until the lapse of said period, the court shall not approve the state of funds and scheme of division or state of funds.

(2) Where a notice of objections under paragraph (1) of this rule is lodged, the sheriff shall dispose of such notice after hearing any objector and the factor and making such investigations as he considers necessary.

(3) If the objections are sustained to any extent, the necessary alterations shall be made to the state of funds and scheme of division or state of funds, and shall be approved by the sheriff.

(4) Where no notice of objections is lodged, the sheriff shall approve the state of funds and scheme of division or state of funds.

Payment following approval of scheme of division

32. After the sheriff has approved a scheme of division, the factor shall pay, deliver or convey to the parties the sums or other property to which they are entitled under the scheme.

Partial division on first scheme of division

33.—(1) Where, in the opinion of the factor, a partial division of funds among the creditors who have claimed may be made with safety to the interests of all concerned, the factor may, with the approval of the Accountant, prepare a state of funds and first scheme of division as soon as may be after the time for lodging claims has expired.

(2) The provisions of rules 29(2) and (3), 30 and, subject to paragraph (3) of this rule, 31, shall apply to a state of funds and first scheme of division prepared under paragraph (1) above as they apply to a state of funds and scheme of division prepared under rule 29(1)(*a*).

(3) The sheriff may, not earlier than six months after the death of the deceased, approve the first scheme of division and, where he so approves, the factor shall pay, deliver or convey accordingly provided always that there shall be retained and deposited in an appropriate bank or institution a sufficient sum to meet—

(*a*) the amount of the claims of creditors whose debts have not at that period been admitted by the factor, or whose debts are future or contingent; and

(*b*) the full amount of such debts as are claimed as preferable but the priority of which is not admitted by the factor.

Procedure where no creditors

34. Where, on the expiry of the period for lodging claims, no creditor has lodged a claim, the factor shall not lodge a state of funds but shall prepare forthwith a report with regard to the disposal of the surplus estate in accordance with rule 35.

Disposal of surplus estate

35.—(1) Where after payment of the creditors, there is a surplus, the factor shall lodge with the Accountant a statement of the amount of the surplus, of the parties claiming that surplus and their respective grounds of claim, and of those parties who, in the opinion of the factor, are entitled to the surplus and the reasons therefor.

(2) The Accountant shall prepare a written opinion on the factor's statement lodged under paragraph (1) of this rule and issue that opinion to the factor.

(3) On receipt of the Accountant's opinion under paragraph (2) of this rule, the factor shall—

(*a*) lodge it in process together with the statement prepared under paragraph (1) of this rule;

(*b*) give notice by first class post or, if abroad, by air mail to each party claiming an interest or apparently entitled to any part of the estate, that—

(i) the factor's statement and the Accountant's opinion have been lodged in process;

(ii) should any such party desire to lodge objections to the statement he shall lodge with the sheriff clerk a notice of such objections within 28 days of the date of the posting of the notice by the factor.

(4) On expiry of the time for lodging objections, the sheriff shall consider the statement, opinion, and any objections and, after such procedure as he considers appropriate, shall—

(*a*) determine the party or parties entitled to the surplus estate and direct the factor to make payment accordingly; or

(*b*) if he considers that it is desirable that the factor should continue to administer the surplus estate, direct accordingly.

(5) Where the sheriff makes an order under paragraph (4)(*a*) of this rule, the factor shall pay over the surplus accordingly.

Discharge of factor appointed under of section 11A of the 1889 Act

36. Every application for discharge of a factor on the estate of a deceased person shall be intimated and served as required under rule 6 and shall also be served on the cautioner and on the personal representatives of the deceased and notice of the application shall be inserted in the *Edinburgh Gazette* in Form 6.

SCHEDULE

Rule 2(2) Rule 6(2)

FORM 1

FORM OF ADVERTISEMENT (GENERAL)

Notice is hereby given to all having interest, that application has been made to the Sheriff of   for the appointment of A.B. [*address*] as curator bonis [*or other type of factor*] to C.D. [*address*].

or

by A.B. [*address*] as curator bonis [*or other type of factor*] to C.D. [*address*] for discharge of his office [*or otherwise as the case may be*].

Answers must be lodged with the Sheriff Clerk [*address of court*] on or before [*date of expiry of period of notice*]

[A.B.] [Judicial Factor to C.D.]
or [Solicitor for applicant(s)]
[*Address*]

Rule 19(3)

FORM 2

FORM OF NOTICE WHERE APPLICATION FOR DISCHARGE IS MADE TO ACCOUNTANT OF COURT

[*Place, date*]

To: [*Name and address of cautioner or person with interest*] Notice is hereby given that A.B. [*address*] curator bonis [*or other type of factor*] to [*or on the estate of*] C.D. [*address*] has made application to the Accountant of Court for a certificate of discharge.

The audited accounts of the judicial factory are available for inspection at the office of the Accountant of Court, [*address*] tel. no. [*number*].

Representations relating to the application must be made in writing and lodged with the Accountant of Court on or before [*date of expiry of period of notice*].

[*Signed*]
Curator Bonis to C.D.
[or Solicitor for A.B.
Curator Bonis to C.D.]

IF YOU ARE UNCERTAIN ABOUT THE EFFECT OF THIS NOTICE PLEASE CONSULT A SOLICITOR IMMEDIATELY.

Rule 23 FORM 3

FORM OF INTIMATION OF APPLICATION TO BE INSERTED IN THE *EDINBURGH GAZETTE*

To the creditors of and persons interested in the succession of the deceased [*name and address*].

An application under section 11A of the Judicial Factors (Scotland) Act 1889 has been lodged at [*name and address of sheriff court*] by a creditor [*or* creditors] of the deceased [*or* by [*name*] having an interest in the succession of the deceased, the deceased having left no settlement appointing trustees, or other parties having power to manage his estate or the trustees under the deceased's settlement, having refused to act], for the appointment of a judicial factor to the estate of the deceased, [*name*].

A copy of the application is available for inspection at the Sheriff Clerk's office at [*name and address of court*]. Answers to the application should be lodged with the Sheriff Clerk at that address within days from the date of this notice [or *otherwise in terms of the first order*].

[*name*], [Applicant] *or* [Solicitor for Applicant(s)]

[*address*]

Rule 25 FORM 4

FORM OF INTIMATION TO BE INSERTED IN THE *EDINBURGH GAZETTE* AND OTHER APPROPRIATE NEWSPAPER CALLING FOR CLAIMS

To the creditors and other persons interested in the succession of the deceased [*name and address*].

A.B. [*address*], having been appointed by the Sheriff of [*Sheriffdom*] at [*place of court*] on [*date of appointment*] judicial factor on the estate of the said deceased under section 11A of the Judicial Factors (Scotland) Act 1889, requires all the lawful creditors of the deceased [*name*] and other persons interested in this estate, to lodge with the judicial factor, within four months after the date of this notice, a statement of their claims as creditors of the deceased, or as otherwise interested in his estate, with such vouchers or other written evidence as they may have to found upon in support of their claims: in order to enable the claims to be considered and reported by the judicial factor.

[*name*], [Judicial Factor] *or* [Solicitor for Judicial Factor]

[*address*]

Rule 30(1)(*c*), 31 and 33 FORM 5

FORM OF INTIMATION TO BE INSERTED IN THE *EDINBURGH GAZETTE* ON LODGING STATEMENT OF FUNDS AND SCHEME OF DIVISION

To the creditors of and persons interested in the succession to the estate of the deceased [*name and address*].

A.B. [*address*], judicial factor on the estate of the said deceased [*name*], hereby intimates that he has prepared and lodged with the Sheriff Clerk, [*name and address of court*] a state of funds and [first] scheme of division of the said estate, to be considered and approved by the Sheriff of [*Sheriffdom*] at [*place of court*].

[*name*], [Judicial Factor] *or* [Solicitor for Judicial Factor]

[*address*]

Rule 36 FORM 6

FORM OF INTIMATION TO BE INSERTED IN THE *EDINBURGH GAZETTE* OF APPLICATION FOR DISCHARGE

To the creditors of and other persons interested in the succession to the estate of the deceased [*name and address*].

Notice is hereby given that A.B. [*address*], judicial factor on the estate of the said deceased [*name*], has lodged with the Sheriff Clerk, [*name and address of sheriff court*] an application for discharge from the office of judicial factor, and that any person wishing to lodge answers to the application should do so with the Sheriff Clerk within days from the date of this notice [*or otherwise in terms of the first order in the application for discharge*]

[*name*], [Judicial Factor] *or* [Solicitor for Judicial Factor]
[*address*]

Commissary Court Books 1992

(S.I. 1992 No. 3256)

[17th December 1992]

The Lords of Council and Session, under and by virtue of the powers conferred on them by section 32 of the Sheriff Courts (Scotland) Act 1971, and of all other powers enabling them in that behalf, having approved, with modifications, draft rules submitted to them by the Sheriff Court Rules Council under section 34 of that Act, do hereby enact and declare:

Citation and Commencement

1.—(1) This Act of Sederunt may be cited as the Act of Sederunt (Commissary Court Books) 1992 and shall come into force on 11th January 1993.

(2) This Act of Sederunt shall be inserted in the Books of Sederunt.

Interpretation

2. In this Act of Sederunt—

"the commissary clerk" means the commissary clerk in Edinburgh.

The Commissary Court Books

3.—(1) The Commissary Court Books, together with any machinery or equipment incidental to their keeping, shall be kept by the commissary clerk at his office.

(2) Subject to sub-paragraph (3) of this paragraph the Commissary Court Books kept by the commissary clerk shall comprise—

(*a*) a microfilm record of every writ received by the commissary clerk for recording; and

(*b*) an index, recorded on computer disk, of every writ which has been recorded on microfilm.

(3) Any person may—

(*a*) inspect any writ recorded in the Commissary Court Books; or

(*b*) obtain a copy of any such writ.

(4) In relation to writs recorded in the Commissary Court Books of the commissary clerk or the sheriff clerk prior to the commencement of this Act of Sederunt, such writs may be kept in the form in which they were recorded prior to the commencement of this Act of Sederunt, until the commissary clerk records them in the Commissary Court Books kept under sub-paragraph (2) of this paragraph.

Transmission for recording

4.—(1) The sheriff principal may authorise the sheriff clerk to send to the commissary clerk any part of the Commissary Court Books kept by the sheriff clerk prior to the commencement of this Act of Sederunt.

(2) The sheriff clerk shall, upon receipt of an authorisation under sub-paragraph (1) of this paragraph and with the consent of the commissary clerk, send to the commissary clerk any part of the Commissary Court Books kept by the sheriff clerk prior to the commencement of this Act of Sederunt.

(3) In relation to any writ which is to be recorded in the Commissary Court Books after the commencement of this Act of Sederunt, the sheriff clerk shall, upon issue of confirmation, send such writ to the commissary clerk.

Recording

5. The commissary clerk shall, upon receipt of a writ under paragraph 4 of this Act of Sederunt, record the writ in the Commissary Court Books kept by him under and in accordance with paragraph 3 of this Act of Sederunt.

Disposal of writs

6. The sheriff principal may authorise the commissary clerk to dispose of by destruction or otherwise, any writ which has been recorded by the commissary clerk under paragraph 5 of this Act of Sederunt.

Revocation

7. The Act of Sederunt (Introduction of a Photographic Process for Copying Deeds and other Writings presented for registration in the Sheriff Court Books and Commissary Court Books) 1944 is revoked.

Charities (Exemption from Accounting Requirements) (Scotland) Regulations 1993

(S.I. 1993 No. 1624)

[28th July 1993]

The Secretary of State, in exercise of the powers conferred on him by section 4(4)(*b*) of the Law Reform (Miscellaneous Provisions) (Scotland) Act 1990, and of all other powers enabling him in that behalf, hereby makes the following Regulations:

Citation and commencement

1. These Regulations may be cited as the Charities (Exemption from Accounting Requirements) (Scotland) Regulations 1993 and shall come into force on 28th July 1993.

Interpretation

2. In these Regulations—

"the 1990 Act" means the Law Reform (Miscellaneous Provisions) (Scotland) Act 1990;

[1] "Scottish charitable corporation" means any recognised body which is a body corporate established by statute or Royal Charter and whose accounts are required by statute or otherwise to be examined and certified by the Comptroller and Auditor General;

"local authority trust" means any recognised body which is a trust for any charity, foundation, mortification or other purpose where a local authority or some members of such an authority are its sole trustees as mentioned in section 106(1)(*b*) of the Local Government (Scotland) Act 1973;

"registered housing association" means any recognised body which is a housing association as defined in section 1 of the Housing Associations Act 1985 which is registered with Scottish Homes under section 5 of that Act,

and, unless the context otherwise requires, any other expression which is used in these Regulations and which is also used in Part I of the 1990 Act, shall have the same meaning in these Regulations as in that Part.

NOTE

[1] As amended by S.I. 1995 No. 645 (effective 31st March 1995).

Exemption from accounting requirements

3. Any class of recognised body, which is prescribed in an entry in column 1 of the Schedule to these Regulations, shall be exempt from such of the requirements of sections 4 and 5 of the 1990 Act (relating to accounting matters) as are prescribed opposite to that entry in column 2 of that Schedule.

Regulation 3

SCHEDULE

Exemption from accounting requirements

Column 1 *Class of Recognised Body*	*Column 2* *Exempt requirements of sections 4 and 5 of the 1990 Act*
[1]Scottish charitable corporation	Section 4 and subsections (1), (2), (3), (4), (5), (8), (9), (10), (11) and (13) of Section 5.
local authority trust	Section 4 and subsections (2), (3), (4), (5) and (13) of Section 5.
registered housing association	Section 4 and subsections (2), (3), (4), (5) and (13) of Section 5.

NOTE

[1] As amended by S.I. 1995 No. 645 (effective 31st March 1995).

Charities (Trustee Investments Act 1961) Order 1995

(S.I. 1995 No. 1092)

[11th April 1995]

Whereas a draft of this Order has been approved by both Houses of Parliament:

Now, therefore, the Secretary of State, in exercise of his powers under section 70 of the Charities Act 1993 and with the consent of the Treasury, hereby makes the following Order:

1. This Order may be cited as the Charities (Trustee Investments Act 1961) Order 1995 and shall come into force on the fourteenth day after the day on which it is made.

2. It is hereby directed that, in the case of a trust fund consisting of property held by or in trust for a charity, any division of the fund in pursuance of section 2(1) of the Trustee Investments Act 1961 shall be made so that the value of the wider-range part at the time of the division bears to the then value of the narrower-range part the proportion of three to one.

3.—(1) The Trustee Investments Act 1961 shall, in its application in relation to a trust fund consisting of property held by or in trust for a charity, have effect subject to the modifications specified in the following paragraphs of this article, being modifications which the Secretary of State considers appropriate in consequence of, or in connection with, the direction contained in article 2 of this Order.

(2) Paragraph (*b*) of section 2(3) and sub-paragraph (*b*) of paragraph 3 of the Second Schedule shall have effect as if for the words from "each" to the end there were substituted the words "the wider-range part of the fund is increased by an amount which bears the specified proportion to the amount by which the value of the narrower-range part of the fund is increased".

(3) Section 4(3) shall have effect as if for the words "so as either to be equal, or to bear to each other" there were substituted the words "so as to bear to each other either the specified proportion or".

(4) Section 17 shall have effect as if at the end there were added the following subsection—

"(6) In this Act, "the specified proportion" means the proportion specified in article 2 of the Charities (Trustee Investments Act 1961) Order 1995.".

[THE NEXT PAGE IS M 301]

Notes

[1] Notes for the Guidance of Judicial Factors issued by the Accountant of Court

NOTE

Under the Judicial Factors (Scotland) Acts 1849, 1880 and 1889, the Guardianship of Infants Acts 1886 and 1925, the Trusts (Scotland) Acts 1921 and 1961, the Bankruptcy (Scotland) Act 1913, s. 163; the Solicitors (Scotland) Act 1980, s. 41, and the Rules of Court of Session, 1965.

All communications must be addressed
THE ACCOUNTANT OF COURT,
Supreme Courts,
2 Parliament Square,
Edinburgh, EH1 1RQ
(Tel. 031–225 2595: Fax 031–225 7198)
Rutland Exchange Box No. ED325.

(All letters addressed to the Accountant should be sufficiently stamped. Those containing annual accounts, vouchers and securities should be registered or sent by recorded delivery. The name and number of the factory should always be given.)

MATTERS OF PARTICULAR NOTE

(*a*) In terms of section 2(1) of the Trusts (Scotland) Act 1961, a factor must obtain the Accountant's approval prior to carrying out any of the acts detailed in sections 4(1)(*a*) to (*ee*) of the Trusts (Scotland) Act 1921. Such acts include the sale of heritable subjects—see paragraphs 25 and 26. It should be noted that the Accountant cannot give his approval to the sale of heritage *ex post facto*.

(*b*) All legal business accounts against the factorial estate must be submitted to the Accountant prior to taxation—see paragraph 14. The Accountant will not feel bound to pass as a proper charge against the estate any taxed account which has not been seen by him prior to taxation.

(*c*) Where a ward is entitled to succeed to an estate and the factor is appointed executor *qua* factor on said estate, the whole of the factor's intromissions with the executry estate fall under the Accountant's supervision and should be incorporated or included in an account attached to the factorial account. The business account of the legal agents (where the factor is not a solicitor) should be strictly limited to the legal work relative to having the factor appointed executor and obtaining confirmation. The work relative to the realisation of the estate and cash intromissions is considered factorial in nature and will be remunerated by way of commission fixed by the Accountant at the audit of the factorial account.

(*d*) Where a factor dies or his appointment is recalled and a new factor is appointed in his place, the case should be treated as a continuing trust. In such cases the inventory of the new factor should show the estate exactly as detailed at the close of the previous factor's final account, whether to date of death of previous factor or date of recall of his appointment, and the value of investments in the previous factor's accounts should be retained.

(*e*) The Accountant's prior approval should be obtained to the rate of maintenance allowances to be paid and to extra-ordinary expenditure, including major repairs to heritable subjects.

(*f*) Where a factor intends to take advantage of the wider powers of investment conferred by the Trustee Investments Act 1961, the Accountant's prior approval to his scheme of investment should be obtained (see paragraph 23(*b*)).

Caution

1. In respect of company guarantee bonds of caution, the Accountant will allow a charge, at the rate of 10p per £100 of caution, to be made in the

factor's accounts, subject currently to a minimum first premium of £15 and a minimum subsequent renewal premium of £10. Where caution is increased or decreased during the subsistence of the factory, this should be done by means of a formal memorandum of agreement (forms are obtainable from the guarantee companies) prepared with reference to the original bond. A new bond is not required.

Stamp Duty

2. The official certified copy interlocutor of appointment of a curator, factor *loco tutoris* or *absentis* appointed in the Court of Session, and the act and decree of a curator, factor *loco tutoris* or commissary factor appointed in the sheriff courts, are exempt from stamp duty. All other factors, within thirty days of receiving their official certified copy interlocutor—or extracting their original act and decree, must present the certified copy interlocutor or the decree at the Inland Revenue to be stamped with a 50p stamp.

Mental Welfare

3. The Mental Welfare Commission for Scotland (22 Melville Street, Edinburgh, EH3 7NS) was established under the Mental Health (Scotland) Act 1960, with the general duty of exercising protective functions in respect of persons who suffer from mental disorder, whether or not they are liable to be detained in hospital or subject to guardianship under the Act. The ward will be visited by a medical officer of the Commission. Before the first visit is made, the factor will be given an opportunity to make any comment he wishes to the Commission. [See now the Mental Health (Scotland) Act 1984, Pt. II.—Editor.]

Driving and Medical Fitness

4. There is a statutory duty on all licence holders to notify the licensing authority as soon as they become aware that they are suffering from any disability which is, or which may become, likely to affect their ability to drive. Mental disorder is such a disability: and where a motor car forms part of the estate coming under his charge, or the factor for an incapax ward has other reason to believe that the ward is a licence holder or intends to apply for a licence, the Licensing Authority (Department of the Environment, Driving and Vehicle Licensing Centre, Swansea, SA99 1AB) must be notified of the facts and of the factor's appointment.

Social Security Benefits

5. It is the factor's duty immediately on appointment to establish and claim from the Department of Health and Social Security all benefits to which a ward may be entitled. These may include retirement pension, very elderly persons pension, widow's pension, invalidity benefit, non-contributory invalidity pension, supplementary benefit, attendance allowance, mobility allowance, etc. Where benefits are being collected by the hospital authorities the factor will normally require to take payment into his own hands as the hospital authorities are precluded from dealing with a ward's funds where a factor has been appointed (section 94(6), Mental Health (Scotland) Act 1984). A factor should also establish and state in his inventory benefits not in issue to the ward, but in issue to others for looking after the ward, such as guardian's allowance, child benefit and invalid care allowance.

Inventory

(To be engrossed on the printed form supplied by the accountant)

6. The inventory should be lodged as soon as possible, at latest within six

months from the date on which the bond of caution is lodged. The Act allows the Accountant no discretion to extend this period. *The inventory must show the estate as at the date of the factor's appointment*, before he has had any intromissions with it or has realised any of the securities (except in the case of previous appointments—see "Matters of Particular Note" (*d*)). It must be signed by the factor on each page before lodgment. The age or date of birth and the address of ward, the name of the cautionary company, the amount of caution and the yearly premium should all be entered. It is of the utmost importance that all the funds, subjects for rental, trust interests, pensions, etc., be stated fully. When the inventory is lodged with the Accountant for adjustment, all the documents required to vouch it must be produced. All sums in bank or building society must be instructed by deposit receipts (or certificates of encashment in lieu), passbooks, or (with regard to accounts in respect of which there are no passbooks) bank sheets or certified statement by the bank or building society showing the balance at date of appointment and covering a period approximately three months prior to appointment. Cash balances in hands of law agents should be instructed by a certified copy of their cash account: and pension rates by a certificate from the paying authority.

Any funds held outwith Scotland, but within the British Commonwealth are recoverable by a judicial factor (section 13 of the Judicial Factors (Scotland) Act 1889), on production of an official certified Interlocutor or extract of his appointment. It is quite unnecessary normally for a factor, other than a commissary factor, to take out confirmation or other grant of administration.

Certified Copy Interlocutor or Extract Decree of Appointment

7. By virtue of section 66 of the Finance Act 1916, as amended, the official certified copy interlocutor is sufficient authority to the Bank of England, the National Debt Commissioners, the Postmaster-General and any savings bank authority to transfer to the factor any "Government stock" forming part of the estate, if the stock is specified in the appendix to the said interlocutor or is certified by the Accountant of Court as forming part of the estate under the factor's charge. When a certificate by the Accountant is required, it is appended to the certified copy interlocutor which should be forwarded to him for that purpose along with the relative stock certificates. It is preferable that the factor's inventory should be lodged with the Accountant before he grants such certificate. In appointments in the sheriff courts the factor's extract decree takes the place of the certified copy interlocutor.

Accounts

(*Accounts should be submitted in the form of charge and discharge—The Judicial Factors (Scotland) Act* 1849, *s.* 4. *The form of account in the Appendix may be taken as a style—but see para.* 16.)

8. Body of the Account and its Appendices

(1) Charge Side of the Account.

(*a*) Estate at Start.—The factor should commence his/her account with the estate exactly as detailed at the close of the previous audited account or in the case of a first account with the estate as given up in the factorial inventory.

The estate should be fully detailed at the start and close of every account and all heritable subjects, life policies, annuities, pensions and benefits should also be listed. Where section 2(1) of the Trustee Investments Act 1961 has been complied with, the estate including cash should be shown divided between the narrower, wider and special ranges (see paragraph 23 (*b*)).

(*b*) REVENUE.—

(i) *Stocks and shares*—a description of each stock or share, together with the dates of dividends paid, tax deducted and the net dividend received should be shown.

(ii) *Bank interest*—the description of the account together with the dates of interest payments and sum received should be shown.

(iii) *Annuities, pensions and benefits*—full details of the period covered (where appropriate income tax deducted) and with regard to Department of Health and Social Security benefits the rates in issue should be shown against each payment.

(iv) *Income tax received*—any recovery should state the period covered thereby.

(v) *Rental*—rents should be shown gross with the property expenses shown on the discharge side of the account. (All should be more fully detailed in an appendix to the account—see paragraph 18).

(*c*) ESTATE REALISED.—all estate realised should be fully detailed but only the gain or loss over the value at start of the account should be extended.

(2) DISCHARGE SIDE OF THE ACCOUNT.—Payments should be shown under the headings Administrative Expenses and Maintenance of Ward (or Payment of Beneficiaries) and where appropriate under the headings Debts Paid, Property Expenses etc. Estate invested should be shown in full but should not be extended and the expenses of purchase (brokerage, etc.) should not be shown as an administrative expense but included as part of the purchase price of the holding. The account should conclude by fully detailing the estate at close in similar manner to the estate at commencement of the account.

Where there is more than one beneficial interest in the estate (*e.g.* several minor wards) a statement should be appended to the account showing the amount of each interest in the estate at close of the account.

9. ACCOUNT-CURRENT OR STATE OF DAILY BALANCES.—The factor must annex to his account of charge and discharge an account-current, or state of the daily balances arising on said account, which should include the bank transactions. This requirement, however, may be waived by the Accountant in cases where the circumstances seem to him to justify its waiver: in such cases the factor should certify in his account that the balances of cash in hand during the period have been kept within the statutory limits.

10. ADDITIONAL ESTATE or interests ascertained after the inventory or account has been lodged, should be *specially* reported by letter and explained in the annual account next following their ascertainment and included in the charge, and, if not realised, in the last branch of the account.

11. DATES.—(1) The annual closing date must be rigidly adhered to, unless in the event of the death of the factor or ward, or of a minor reaching majority, or other event terminating the factory, when the account must be closed and balanced, and the exact amount of the estate ascertained as at the date of termination. (2) In all accounts, whenever the nature of entries admits of it, the dates must be given. (3) Intromissions of a date subsequent to the closing date of the account, cannot be admitted.

12. SIGNATURES.—Accounts must be signed by the factor, as also the states or accounts of property sub-factors: also all separate explanations, though the latter will very *rarely be necessary if accounts have been accurately kept and are properly stated.*

13. VOUCHERS.—(1) The vouchers must be properly arranged, and numbered, and referred to by number in the account of charge and discharge, and *not* according to account-current. (2) They must be accompanied by the detailed accounts (if any) which they vouch, particularly so, where the only other available evidence of a payment made is the paid cheque. (3) The entry or narrative in the account must express the transaction in simple accordance with fact and with the vouchers, and fully. (4) Special attention is called to the necessity, in the payment of board, of stating the name and address of the mental hospital or the party with whom the pupil or incapax is boarded. (5) States unsigned, or a bank account uncertified, cannot be taken as evidence. (6) Receipts by agents acting for beneficiaries of factorial funds are not acceptable unless accompanied by documentary evidence that the agents are authorised by the beneficiaries to take payment on their behalf. (7) A separate inventory of vouchers is not necessary. (8) Security writs are normally returned as soon as possible after receipt. (9) Paid cheques drawn on clients' account or photocopies of documents are in general insufficient for the Accountant's purpose.

14. LAW ACCOUNTS (*see also para.* 28 *hereof*).—(*a*) All law business accounts must be taxed by the Auditor of the Court of Session, except in sheriff court procedure, when they are taxed by the auditors of the sheriff courts. By arrangement with the auditors, all business accounts are examined by the Accountant before taxation, and for this purpose should be submitted to him, and he will transmit them to the auditor. If the factor is a partner in a law firm, his firm cannot charge for any law business in connection with the Factory (*Mitchell and Others* v. *Burness* (1878) 5 R. 1124). Where, however, such factor, or his firm, carries through the petition for his discharge, or does other necessary legal work, an additional commission, in lieu of law business charges, may be allowed by the Accountant, provided due notice is given.

(*b*) The Accountant does not procure processes for the purpose of verifying the taxed amounts of agents' accounts of expenses. The factor must arrange for exhibition of these accounts to the Accountant as a voucher of his own account.

15. BACKING ACCOUNTS.—THE BACK OF THE ACCOUNT should bear (1) The *name* of the factor and ward or factory. (2) The exact *period* covered by the account. (3) At the *bottom*, the *reference number* of the appointment. The factor or agent is requested, in all cases, to give his *precise* address, in order to secure the safe transmission of documents.

16. LODGING THE ACCOUNT.—The annual account with its appendices—that is, all that has to be retained and preserved when lodged at the Accountant's office—*should be stitched together* as ONE PAPER, and thus be so complete as to give full information to anyone having occasion to examine it *without* the vouchers, when neither the factor nor the Accountant can be present to explain. Securities should not be sent until called for. Accounts must be lodged as prescribed by the Judicial Factors (Scotland) Act 1849, ss. 4 and 11, within one month of their annual closing date (see 1947 S.L.T. (News) 55).

17. FACTORS APPOINTED UNDER SECTION 163 OF THE BANKRUPTCY (SCOTLAND) ACT, 1913, are referred to Rule of Court 201 for particulars of the additional duties devolving on them. Factors' duties in appointments under this section in the sheriff court are the same as in Court of Session cases, the sheriff taking the place of the Lord Ordinary. Factors should particularly ensure that all the prescribed intimations in the *Edinburgh Gazette* and other statutory notices are made timeously. It should be specially noted that the factor must advertise for claims within 14 days of extracting his appointment (rule 201(*d*)), must reserve out of the first funds realised sufficient to defray the estimated cost of his administration (rule 201(*n*)) and must not proceed to pay other than the prescribed preferable debts without first lodging a scheme of division with the Accountant (rule 201(*g*)).

Rental

(*For form of rental, see Appendix*)

18. Rentals.—In cases where the factorial estate includes heritable properties let to tenants, a rental must be included as an appendix to the account. In such cases the columns normally requisite are—(1) Possessions. (2) Names of tenants. (3) Arrears taken (without alteration) from last rental. (4) Rents due within period of the account. (5) Amounts received. (6) Arrears as on the date on which the account closes. (7) Fire insurance. (8) Remarks, *e.g.* note of burdens.

Each subject in the rental must be accounted for annually. If any subject, therefore, has been unoccupied or taken possession of by a creditor, the circumstances must be so explained. The amounts of columns 3 and 4 of the rental are carried to the factor's account, Charge side (normally in branches I and II respectively). The amount in column 6—Arrears (if any)—should be included in last branch of discharge. Where the rental differs from that of the preceding year, the cause of difference should be explained in column 8.

The factor should particularly see that each subject is insured against loss by fire, and the relative column in the rental should be carefully filled in.

Audit

19. Commission.—The amount of commission deemed due may be indicated, with a note showing how it is arrived at: but must not be included in the account. The amount fixed by the Accountant will form an item of discharge in the next annual account. When additional commission for special work is considered due, a detailed note of the *distinctly special* work should be supplied, with an evaluation of each item. Normal factorial work should be carefully excluded from this note.

VAT may be chargeable on factorial commissions where the factor is both registered for VAT and carries out the duties of factor as an extension of his business activities.

If no commission is desired, this should be stated at the end of the account.

20. Interest.—(1) A certificate by the bank with which money is lodged, showing the dates of the deposit receipts, when uplifted, and the amount of interest paid thereon, must be produced. (2) In other cases, the tax counterfoils of dividend warrants should be produced. (3) Progressive interest states must be furnished, as an appendix, when interest is charged on the account: the rate of interest, and the period to which it applies *must always be stated.* (4) If a factor has at his command an easily realisable asset and advances cash to an estate, interest on such advances will only be allowed at the lowest rate being earned by the realisable estate.

21. Penal Interest.—Factors will be liable for penal interest at the rate of Twenty per cent. on any balance exceeding £500 remaining in their own or their agents' hands or on any non-interest-bearing account for more than 10 days. Sums held in a firm's general clients' bank account, since this does not meet the requirements of the Act (see paragraph 22) are, for this purpose, deemed to be balances in hand. It is expected that no more will be retained in hand than is necessary for the normal administration of the factory over short periods. It is entirely within the discretion of the Accountant to remit or modify the penal interest but only if he is satisfied that such action is justified in the circumstances.

22. Bank Accounts.—See sections 5 and 37 of the Judicial Factors (Scotland) Act 1849. (1) Moneys in bank must be held in a separate account or on deposit in name of the factor as such. The choice of bank is restricted to some one of the banks in Scotland established by Act of

Parliament or Royal Charter. (2) Compound interest must be paid by the bank on encashment of deposit receipts more than one year old.

23. INVESTMENTS.—(*a*) Government and other stocks and shares in limited companies, forming part of an estate taken over by a factor at the inception of a case may remain in the name of the ward or deceased person but any new investments made by a factor should be registered in his name as such (thus, A.B. Curator Bonis to C.D.). Where, however, a factor invests in the shares of an English company the holding can only be registered in his name as an individual. In such circumstances the certificate must be endorsed by the factor to the effect that the stock or share is held by him for his ward or factorial estate. In the case of investments in bonds over heritable property, the valuations and rentals of property (certified by the assessor) on which the money has been advanced must be produced, with certificates from the factor's law agent stating the ranking of the bonds and the amount of feuduty and ground annual. The loans must not exceed two-thirds of the valuations, and in practice the Accountant meantime prefers that they should not exceed one-half thereof. The factor must append a docquet at the end of each annual account, stating that he is satisfied that the heritable properties over which the funds of the estate are lent are properly insured, and that he has seen the receipts for (1) premium of insurance: (2) feu-duty: and (3) ground annual for the current year. Loans over shop properties are not approved of. In each case full evidence must be submitted to the Accountant, to enable him to judge the validity and sufficiency of the security, and it is competent to him to object to any bond or mortgage if it appears to be in any respect objectionable, even though within the two-thirds value. With Scottish heritable loans, where there is a ward, the dispositions in security should be taken in his favour: where there is no ward, in the name of the factor as such. Generally speaking the Accountant does not regard heritable loans as suitable investments for factors to make.

(*b*) Trustee Investments Act 1961:—

When the estate taken over by a factor contains investments designated wider range in terms of the Trustee Investments Act 1961, the Factor must either comply with section 2 (1) of the above Act or realise the wider-range type investments and invest them in suitable narrower range investments. In this connection it is pointed out that a building society share account is designated a wider-range type investment. Whenever a factor wishes to take advantage of the wider powers of investment conferred by the Act he/she must have the estate revalued, take advice and thereafter divide it in terms of the Act. In all such cases the factor must produce to the Accountant for his prior consideration a stockbroker's scheme of investment.

The factor should please note that:

(a) the narrower and wider ranges should be in equilibrium at the date of division.

(b) additional estate falls to be divided equally between the ranges.

(c) the surplus of revenue over expenditure in the accounting year falls to be treated in a similar manner to additional estate.

(d) heritable property, household furniture, life policies, annuities, pensions and benefits, unrealisable non-trust investments and other estate which does not fall within the scope of the narrower and wider ranges should be shown under special range.

24. REPORT.—When the account has been audited a draft report will be issued, which the factor is requested to revise and return with answers to notes (if any) within 21 days at latest, stating any objections he may have, which will be dealt with in accordance with the provisions of section 15 of the Judicial Factors Act 1849. The factor should endeavour to clear up all difficulties in HIS ANNUAL ACCOUNT, and to embody there all that he wishes to record for his future exoneration at the Accountant's office. It is only *once a year*, in ordinary circumstances, that the position of each estate can be fully gone into and reported.

When the Accountant issues his *Report and Notes*, at the annual audit, the factor's answers should be written on the blank page opposite the notes, which is provided for the purpose. Whether or not there are notes, this page should always be signed. Care in preparing and vouching the accounts greatly reduces the work of audit, obviates the need for notes, and, in some cases, saves expense which may fall upon the factor personally.

Special Powers

25. (*a*) Power to sell Heritage.—

Section 4 (1) of the Trusts (Scotland) Act 1921, authorises trustees, factors etc., to sell heritable estate where the sale is "not at variance with the terms or purposes of the trust". When a sale conforms to this condition, it can be made without the grant of special authority. Thus when a factor is appointed to realise and distribute an estate, or when a sale is necessary in order to pay debts or to maintain a ward, special authority to sell is unnecessary. Also, where heritable property is held as an investment it has been decided that special powers of sale are not required, vide *Cunningham's Tutrix, Petitioner*, 1949 S.L.T. 357. When a proposed sale is not necessary but seems to be expedient, or otherwise may be at variance with the terms or purposes of the factor's appointment, application must be made either for special powers of sale from the court in terms of section 7 of the Judicial Factors Act 1849, or for the Accountant's formal consent, in terms of section 2 (3) and (4) of the Trusts (Scotland) Act 1961. Consequently, before offering property for sale without obtaining special authority, a factor should firstly satisfy the Accountant and decide whether or not he could, if required to do so, satisfy a purchaser that the sale is not at variance with the purposes of the appointment. If the sale involves the ward's dwellinghouse or a property which is liferented by the ward, the Accountant requires a formal professional valuation of the subjects, along with evidence—normally an up-to-date medical report—that the ward's recovery is improbable or that, in any event, it is considered inadvisable he (or she) should resume occupation of the house or property. In all circumstances the factor must in addition satisfy the Accountant as to the terms and conditions of any sale he would propose to effect. No voluntary action by a factor can alter the succession to his ward's estate. Therefore the net proceeds of a sale remain and must be noted in the factor's accounts as heritable.

(*b*) Completion of Title to Heritage:—

Special powers are not required. A judicial factor on a lapsed trust or similar estate completes title in his own name. A curator bonis, or factor *loco tutoris*, completes title in name of his ward, normally by way of Service or deduction of title. It should be stated in any application for special powers to sell heritage whether or not the title is already complete in the ward's name.

26. (*a*) When a factor wishes to apply for special powers, he should make a report to the Accountant, mentioning the circumstances and his own views (as in a petition to the court), and concluding (as in the prayer of a petition) by stating briefly *the exact powers he wishes the court to grant him*. The Accountant's opinion will follow thereon. The factor then by means of a note brings his report, with the Accountant's opinion, before the court. Under Rule of Court 200 (*a*), *a copy of the interlocutor, granting or refusing the powers craved, should at once be forwarded to the Accountant along with a copy of the note*.

(*b*) When a factor wishes to apply in terms of section 2 (3) of the Trusts (Scotland) Act 1961 for the Accountant's consent to the doing of an act which may be at variance with the terms and purposes of the appointment, he must proceed as directed by Rule of Court 200 (*a*).

MISCELLANEOUS

27. INTERVIEWS.—In order to obviate the risk of misunderstanding, factors and agents should confirm by letter to the Accountant the purport of interviews with him or his staff at which sanction is given to a proposed course of action (*e.g.* the sale of property, taking opinion of counsel, or entering into legal proceedings).

28. LAW BUSINESS, LEGAL PROCEEDINGS, AND OPINION OF COUNSEL:—

(*a*) A judicial factor is only entitled to employ a solicitor for distinctively legal work or the preparation of legal documents. It is the factor's duty to do the administrative work, and the factory estate is not liable for the remuneration of solicitors for work which should have been done by the factor and is covered by his commission.

(*b*) Factors should not enter into legal proceedings or take opinion of counsel without first obtaining the Accountant's approval of the necessary expenditure, if it is proposed to charge this against the factory estate, as such expenditure will be disallowed by the Accountant if, in his opinion, it was neither necessary nor expedient.

29. NECESSARY INTIMATIONS.—The death of a factor; change in a ward's residence; the date of recall of the factor's appointment and/or the factory and the death of a ward or liferenter with the date thereof, should be promptly intimated to the Accountant, with the necessary certificate in the case of death. It should also be stated whether the ward died testate or intestate.

30. THE WARD:—(*a*) The age of the ward, with the name and address of the cautionary company and the amount of caution and annual premium payable, should be stated on each annual account. (*b*) Where the ward is already a patient in a mental or other hospital, or is removed to such hospital, the curator bonis should, without delay, intimate his appointment to the hospital superintendent.

31. FEES.—For fees payable in the Accountant's department see Rules of Court 346,1. These fees are payable by Cheque or Cash. Cash remittances sent through the post should be registered.

32. SPECIAL COMMISSION.—Commission received by the factor (or anyone instructed by him to sell or purchase stock, etc.) from stockbrokers, corporations, building societies, etc., falls to be credited to the estate. (See cases of *A B and C D Curatories*, 1927 S.C. 902; 1927 S.L.T. 430.)

33. INCOME TAX:

REPAYMENT CLAIMS.—Where income tax is recoverable, a yearly application should be made by the factor to the Inland Revenue authorities for return of tax, and a note should be appended to each annual account stating the last date to which the tax has been recovered. *Factors will be debited with any income tax that becomes irrecoverable through their failure to lodge repayment claims timeously.*

PETITIONS FOR DISCHARGE—PRACTICE TO BE OBSERVED

34. The Accountant is required to report on all applications for discharge. It is, however, the duty of the agent in all cases to transmit the process to the Accountant, who will issue a draft of his proposed report for the favour of observations. The case should be in all respects complete when laid before the Accountant for report. When the report is signed, intimation, generally in the form of a fee notice, will be given to the agent, who, in Court of Session cases, will transmit the process to the Petition Department of the court, and enrol the case. In sheriff court cases, after the report has been signed, the Accountant will forward it, with the process, to the sheriff clerk and inform the local agent in the case that this has

been done. The bond of caution can only be delivered by the Accountant on production of an extract decree authorising its upliftment.

Should the factor be willing to dispense with judicial discharge, the Accountant, on being satisfied that the estate has been fully accounted for, will report the facts to the court with a view to writing the case off, and the bond of caution will not be delivered up but will be lodged in the court process for preservation.

35. When a ward recovers, either he or his curator may petition for the curatory's recall, producing medical certificates of the ward's recovery. When recall is granted, a remit should at the same time be obtained from the court to the Accountant to report on the curator's accounts and administration. The curator's final account will close as at date of recall. When the curatory has been recalled, the ward can grant a valid receipt in the terms mentioned in paragraph 37 (1) hereof.

36. When a factor in a continuing factory dies or resigns, a new factor is appointed by the court. (Also, in the case of resignation, the appointment is recalled.) The factor or his representatives must divest themselves of the estate before discharge can be granted, procuring and producing to the Accountant a receipt by the new factor. It is usual to embrace in one petition the application for recall and discharge, and for a new appointment.

37. Documents to be produced to the Accountant by the Factor, according to the ground of the petition for Discharge, *viz.*:—

(1) When a minor Ward attains majority or an incapax becomes capax

Evidence that the ward has attained majority or become capax, as the case may be.

A receipt by the ward, acknowledging that the detailed funds and the effects under the curatory, as reported on by the Accountant at the audit of the factor's final account of intromissions, have been paid over or accounted for to the ward; and, if there is heritage, that he has received the title-deeds. A convenient form is to append to the receipt, as relative thereto, a detailed state of these funds, etc., as shown at the close of the curator's final account.

(2) When a Ward dies

(*a*) *When ward dies testate.*

Confirmation of the executors.

Receipt by the executors, in detail as in (1) above. If heritage is sold during the currency of the factory the receipt should be annotated to the effect that the executors are aware that the proceeds of sale remain heritable *quoad* succession

(*b*) *When ward dies intestate*

Confirmation of the executor-dative.

Receipt by him or his properly constituted factor or attorney for the estate, in detail, as in (1) above. If heritage is sold during the currency of the factory and the ward is survived by a spouse, the receipt should be annotated to the effect that the executor is aware that the proceeds of sale remain heritable *quoad* succession.

(3) When the Absens dies or returns (Factor *loco absentis*)

Evidence of the identity or death, as the case may be.

Receipt by the absens or his executors together with confirmation in favour of the executor.

(4) When lapsed Trust, intestate Estate, etc., due for division

According to the circumstances of the case, the factor should produce:—

Proof of death of liferenter.

Receipts by fiars, or other beneficiaries.

Inland Revenue certificates that all death and income taxes exigible have been paid. (See Rule of Court 36.) As regards death tax, the certificate should be obtained from the Accountant General

(Capital Transfer Tax and Estate Duty), 16 Piccardy Place, Edinburgh, EH1 3NB, and as regards income tax, from H.M. Controller of Taxes, 80 Lauriston Place, Edinburgh, EH3 9SL.

N.B.—All Receipts by Wards, Beneficiaries, Executors, etc., should be signed by Principals and not by Agents on their behalf.

(5) WHEN THE UNEXPENDED BALANCE OF DAMAGES ADMINISTERED BY A FACTOR APPOINTED UNDER RULES OF COURT 131–134 BECOMES AVAILABLE FOR PAYMENT TO PARTIES CONCERNED.

(NOTE.—In this type of case there is no formal petition for discharge, but an application by letter to the Deputy Principal Clerk of Session in terms of Rule of Court 134 should be made. Here delivery of the factor's bond of caution is given on production of a certified copy interlocutor discharging the factor and ordering delivery of the bond)

(*a*) *Where the ward attains majority*
As in (1) above.

(*b*) *Where the ward dies before attaining majority*
As in (2) above.

NOTE.—All of the above-noted receipts and productions should be so backed as to ensure ready identification in the process.

EDINBURGH.
August, 1984.

G. LESLIE KERR,
Accountant of Court.

[THE NEXT PAGE IS M311]

APPENDIX

FORM OF ACCOUNT FOR THE GUIDANCE OF JUDICIAL FACTORS

In order to afford assistance to those Factors who have not been used to the preparation of Accounts of Charge and Discharge, the following form has been prepared. The example is purposely of a simple character, and, although the entries are too briefly expressed, it illustrates the *principle* on which such an account should be stated. It assumes that a correct CASH BOOK and RENTAL have been kept by the Factor. The Factor must not *mix any of these branches,* and he must especially separate and distinguish Revenue from Capital. All vouchers must be lodged with the Account, duly arranged and numbered.

EXAMPLE

No. 8165.—ACCOUNT of CHARGE and DISCHARGE of the INTROMISSIONS of residing at as *Curator Bonis* (or, as the case may be) to presently residing at , from 31st December 19— to 31st December 19—.

The Cautioner is the Company.
Caution £3,000. (See Rule of Court No. 200 (*e*).)
Premium £4·00 paid up to ...., 19—.
Note.—Date of birth or age of Ward to be given.

CHARGE

I.—ESTATE AS AT CLOSE OF LAST ACCOUNT.			
Narrower Range			
£1,000, 12¾% Treasury Loan 1995			£842·50
£1,000, 10·4% Hepworth Ceramic Deb. Stock 1992/97			680·00
Sum in Bank of Scotland—			
On Deposit Account		£285·36	
On Current Account		50·23	
		£335·59	
Add: Balance in Factor's hands		3·11	
		£338·70	
Deduct: Cash balance due to Wider Range		158·10	180·60
			£1,703·10
Wider Range			
1,300, Ord. Shares, Babcock & Wilcox Ltd.		£845·00	
£700, 7% British Savings Bonds (2nd Issue)		700·00	
Cash balance due from Narrower Range		158·10	1,703·10
Special Range			
Heritable Property, *viz.*: (value not to be extended)			—
Household Furniture as valued		£350·00	
Arrears of Rent		40·00	
Annuity of £100, payable by "E.F."		—	
Department of Health & Social Security Retirement Pension £2·30 per week		—	390·00
			£3,796·20
II.—REVENUE.			
1. *Rents*			
Current Rents, as per Rental in Appendix to this Account		£480·00	
2. *Interests and Dividends*			
(*a*) £700, 7% British Savings Bonds			
19—. May 1. Interest for half year to this date	£24·50		
Carried forward		£480·00	£3,796·20

II.—REVENUE—*cont.* *Brought forward*			£480·00	£3,796·20
19—. Nov. 1. Interest for half year to this date		24·50		
		£49·00		
(*b*) 1,300, Ord. Shares Babcock & Wilcox Ltd.				
19—. May 1. Interim dividend, less tax, £6·72	£12·48			
19—. Oct. 1. Final dividend, less tax, £12·20	22·67			
		£35·15		
(*c*) £1,000, 12¾% Treasury Loan 1995				
19—. May 15. Interest for half year to this date, less tax £22·31	£41·44			
19—. Nov. 15. Interest for half year to this date, less tax £22·31	41·44			
		£82·88		
(*d*) £1,000, 10·4% Hepworth Ceramic Deb. Stock 1992/97				
19—. Jun. 1. Interest for half year to this date, less tax, £18·20	£33·80			
19—. Dec. 1. Interest for half year to this date, less tax, £18·20	33·80			
		£67·60		
(*e*) Bank Interest				
19—. Feb. 1. Deposit Account interest		20·35		
			254·98	
3. *Annuities*				
Annuity of £100 payable by "E.F."				
19—. Jun. 1. Half year due this date, less tax, £17·50		£32·50		
19—. Dec. 1. Half year due this date, less tax, £17·50		32·50		
			65·00	
4. *Pensions*				
D.H.S.S. Retirement Pension				
19—. Feb. 2. Quarter's pension to (date)—13 weeks @ £2·30		£29·90		
19—. May 3 Quarter's pension to (date)—13 weeks @ £2·30		29·90		
19—. Aug. 3 Quarter's pension to (date)—13 weeks @ £2·30		29·90		

19—. Nov. 3. Quarter's pension to (date)—12 weeks @ £2·30, 1 week @ £2·60	30·20	119·90	
5. *Income Tax recovered* 19—. Nov. 12. Year to 5th April 19—		29·94	949·82
III.—NEW CAPITAL ACQUIRED DURING YEAR OF ACCOUNT.			
19—. Nov. 1. Premium received on maturity of holding of £700, 7% British Savings Bonds			14·00
IV.—CAPITAL REALISED.			
19—. Nov. 1. £700, 7% British Savings Bonds on maturity		£700·00	
V.—BANK TRANSACTIONS			
Current Account			
Sums drawn during year (give details)	£937·62		
Deposit Account			
Sums drawn during year (give details)	£200·00	£1,137·62	

NOTE. Bank and Capital transactions should be recorded in an inner column only and not extended. Interest and profit or loss on Capital realisations, however, are extended under their appropriate headings. Where an Account Current is produced incorporating the Bank transactions, these need not be given in detail in the Account of Charge and Discharge.

SUM OF CHARGE £4,760·02

DISCHARGE

I.—BURDENS AND REPAIRS.		
Burdens		
19—. Feb. 28. Premium on House Policy (£10,000)		£10·00
" " " " " Contents (£2,000)		4·00
" Sept. 30. Rates for year 19—/19—		109·36
" Nov. 11. Feu-duty for year to date.		5·00
		£128·36
Repairs		
19—. Mar. 15. Henry Smith & Co., Slaters	£58·28	
" Sept. 12. James Brown & Co., Plumbers	26·36	84·64
		£213·00
II.—MAINTENANCE OF WARD OR PAYMENT TO BENEFICIARY (as case may be)		
19—. Mar. 15. Quarter's Expenses in Hospital to (date)	£26·00	
" June. 15. Do do do	26·00	
" Sept. 15 Do do do	26·00	
" Dec. 15. Do do do	26·00	
	£104·00	
Clothes, etc., furnished Ward during year (give dates and details)	76·00	180·00
III.—MANAGEMENT.		
Law Expenses		
19—. Jan. 25. W. S. & Co. Account for appointment of Curator Bonis as taxed	£85·60	

Commission to Factor			
19—. Feb. 28. Amount allowed by Accountant of Court at last audit		150·00	
Miscellaneous Expenses			
19—. Feb. 28. Accountant's Fee for Audit of last Account		24·00	
19—. Mar. 3. X, Y. Insurance Co., premium on Bond of Caution		4·00	
19—. Dec. 31. Posts and incidents		8·36	
			271·96
IV.—CAPITAL INVESTED.			
19—. Nov. 5. L. M. & Co., price of 825 Ord. Shares B.I.C.C., plus brokerage and stamp		£1,000·60	
V.—BANK TRANSACTIONS.			
Current Account			
Sums lodged during year (give details)	£929·47		
Deposit Account			
Sums lodged during year (give details)	217·88		
		£1.147·35	
VI.—ESTATE AS AT CLOSE OF THIS ACCOUNT.			
Narrower Range			
£1,000, 13¾% Treasury Loan 1995		£842·50	
£1,000, 10·4% Hepworth Ceramic Deb. Stock 1992/97		680·00	
Sum in Bank of Scotland			
On Deposit Account	£303·24		
On Current Account	42·08		
	£345·32		
Less: Balance due to Factor	8·36		
	£336·96		
Deduct: Cash balance due to Wider Range	13·93		
		323·03	
		£1,845·53	
Wider Range			
1,300 Ord. Shares, Babcock & Wilcox Ltd.	£845·00		
825, Ord. Shares, B.I.C.C.	1,000·60		
Cash balance due from Narrower Range	13·93		
		1,859·53	
		£3,705·06	
Special Range			
Heritable Property, *viz.* (value not to be extended)	—		
Household Furniture as valued	350·00		
Arrears of Rent	40·00		
Annuity of £100, payable by "E.F."	—		
D.H.S.S. Retirement Pension, £2·60 per week	—		
		390·00	
			4,095·06
SUM OF DISCHARGE			£4,760·02

Equal to the Charge.

NOTES BY FACTOR. The Factor is satisfied that the Loan over heritable property is sufficiently covered by insurance. The receipts for (1) premium of insurance, (2) feu-duty, and (3) ground annual for the current year have been exhibited to him.

Signature of the Factor

Date

NOTE. It is the special interest of each Factor thus to RECORD, *once a year*, by one State of Accounts (which is carefully preserved in the Accountant's office), a full and clear view of his management. This will avert the need of all other loose papers or correspondence, and the questions likely to arise from complicated corrections and explanations.

FORM OF RENTAL

RENTAL of Properties belonging to......... for the year ending 31st December 19—

NOTE.—(1) The Columns should be summed, and Numbers 3 and 4 added together, the total of which should agree in amount with the total of Numbers 5 and 6.

(2) Lands and Tenements unoccupied, or in possession of a Bondholder, or natural possession of the Proprietor, to be included, and the Rents stated though *not* carried into the Money Columns.

POSSESSIONS	NAME OF TENANTS	Arrears of Rent at close of *last* Account	Current Year's Rental	Received by Factor of Columns 3 and 4	Remains in Arrears at close of *this* Account	Fire Insurance effected	REMARKS, *e.g.* BURDENS, *etc.*
1	2	3	4	5	6	7	8
		£	£	£	£	£	
No. 5 George Street	Mrs. Joan Baxter	40.00	240.00	260.00	20.00	£10,000.00	
No. 6 Do	William Simpson	Nil	240.00	220.00	20.00		
both situated in		40.00	480.00 40.00	480.00	40.00 480.00		
			520.00		520.00	£10,000.00	

Signature of the Factor

NOTE. It is suggested that the Factor should note in the space following any decisions or practice, not covered by the above notes, which may be intimated to him from time to time.

[1] Rules of Division, according to the Law of Scotland, of the Estate of a Person who had Died Intestate on or after 10th September 1964

NOTE

[1] Figures applicable to person dying on or after 26th November 1993. For earlier figures see notes to ss. 8 and 9 of the 1964 Act.

References to a section are to that section of the Succession (Scotland) Act 1964. There being three different sets of rules, any or all of which may be called into play in a given succession, those applied are indicated against each entry by the following abbreviations:

PR—Prior rights to a house, furniture and a monetary provision under sections 8 and 9.

LR—Legal rights of *jus relicti, jus relictae* and legitim under common law as amended by the 1964 Act and other statutes.

FE—Succession to the free estate, heritable and moveable, under Part I of the 1964 Act.

I. SUCCESSION BY A SURVIVING SPOUSE

If the person dies, leaving	*Rules Applicable*	*The estate is divided thus*
1. Spouse only.	PR LR FE	Whole to spouse. Comprising (1) prior right under section 8 to deceased's interest in the house in which surviving spouse was ordinarily resident (maximum £110,000), and to the deceased's interest in the furniture and plenishings of that house (maximum £20,000); (2) prior right under section 9 to £50,000; (3) *jus relicti* or *jus relictae* (½) from balance of moveables, and (4) whole free estate under section 2 (1) (*e*). (See note 8.)
2. Spouse and the deceased's child whether by marriage to the surviving spouse or not, and whether legitimate or not.	PR LR FE	Spouse has (1) prior right under section 8 to deceased's interest in the house in which the surviving spouse was ordinarily resident (maximum £110,000) and to the deceased's interest in the furniture and plenishings of that house (maximum £20,000); (2) if net balance of the estate is less than £30,000, prior right under section 9 to whole balance; if balance is over £30,000, prior right to £30,000 therefrom, taken rateably from heritage and moveables; and (3) legal right of *jus relicti* or *jus relictae* to one-third of the moveable estate remaining after the prior rights under sections 8 and 9 have been met. Child (or children equally among them) receive the whole remainder of the estate, comprising (a) legitim—a further one-third of the moveable estate remaining after the spouse's prior rights under sections 8 and 9, and (b) free estate—the remaining one-third of the moveables plus the heritage not required for prior rights. (See note 5 and note 8.)
3. Spouse and that spouse's children by marriage to deceased and prior marriages.	PR LR FE	Spouse entitled to rights as in No. 2 Remainder (legitim and free estate as above) to deceased's children equally.
4. Spouse and children and issue of predeceasing children.	PR LR FE	Spouse entitled to rights as in No. 2. Remainder (legitim and free estate) to surviving children *per capita* and issue of predeceasing children *per stirpes*. (See note 5 for issue of predeceasing illegitimate children.)

I. SUCCESSION BY A SURVIVING SPOUSE—*cont.*

If the person dies, leaving	*Rules Applicable*	*The estate is divided thus*
5. Spouse and grandchild or grandchildren.	PR LR FE	Spouse entitled to rights as in No. 2. Remainder (legitim and free estate) to grandchild or among grandchildren equally. (See note 5.)
6. Spouse and remoter issue.	PR LR FE	Spouse entitled to rights as in No. 2. Remainder (legitim and free estate) to members of the nearest class of issue of which there are survivors, *per capita*, and to issue of predeceasing members of that class, *per stirpes*. (See note 5.)
7. Spouse and brothers and sisters. (See note 3 at end).	PR LR FE	Spouse has (1) prior right under section 8 to deceased's interest in the house in which the surviving spouse was ordinarily resident (maximum £110,000) and to the deceased's interest in the furniture and plenishing of that house (maximum £20,000); (2) If the net balance of the estate is less than £50,000, prior right under section 9 to the whole balance: if the balance is over £50,000, prior right to £50,000 therefrom, rateably from heritage and moveables, and (3) legal right of *jus relicti* or *jus relictae* to one-half of the moveable estate remaining after the prior rights under sections 8 and 9 have been met. Brothers and sisters share the whole remainder of the estate equally between them as free estate. (See note 8.)
8. Spouse and brothers and sisters and/or issue of predeceasing brothers and sisters.	PR LR FE	Spouse entitled to rights as in No. 7. Remainder to surviving brothers and sisters *per capita* and issue of predeceasing brothers and sisters *per stirpes*. If all brothers and sisters have predeceased, and there is issue of some or all of them, the remainder to members of the nearest class of issue of which there are survivors, *per capita*, and to issue of predeceasing members of that class, *per stirpes*.
9. Spouse and parent or parents, and brothers and sisters and/or issue of predeceasing brothers and sisters.	PR LR FE	Spouse entitled to rights as in No. 7. Remainder, one-half to surviving parent or to both parents equally between them, and one-half to brothers and sisters equally (or to their issue on principles noted in No. 8).
10. Spouse and parent or parents.	PR LR FE	Spouse entitled to rights as in No. 7. Remainder to surviving parent or to both parents equally between them.
11. Spouse and uncles and aunts (or issue thereof) and/or grandparents or remoter ancestors.	PR LR FE	Whole to spouse (as in No. 1).

II. SUCCESSION BY DESCENDANTS
(Illegitimate Person—see Note 5).

12. Children only.	LR FE	Whole estate to children equally. (One-half of moveable estate as legitim, whole balance of estate as free estate.)
13. Children and issue of predeceasing children.	LR FE	Whole estate to surviving children *per capita* and issue of predeceasing children *per stirpes*. (Legitim and free estate as in No. 12.)

II. SUCCESSION BY DESCENDANTS—*cont.*

If the person dies, leaving	*Rules Applicable*	*The estate is divided thus*
14. Grandchildren.	LR FE	Whole estate (being legitim and free estate as in No. 12) to grandchildren equally.
15. Remoter issue.	LR FE	Whole estate (being legitim and free estate as in No. 12) to members of the nearest class of issue of which there are survivors, *per capita*, and to issue of predeceasing members of that class, *per stirpes*.
16. Issue and spouse	PR LR FE	See Nos. 2 to 6.
17. Issue and collaterals.	LR FE	Whole to issue as in Nos. 12 to 15.
18. Issue and ascendants.	LR FE	Whole to issue as in Nos. 12 to 15.

III. SUCCESSION BY COLLATERALS

19. Brothers and sisters.	FE	Whole estate equally among them.
20. Brothers and sisters and nephews and nieces, being issue of predeceasing brothers and sisters.	FE	Whole estate to brothers and sisters *per capita* and nephews and nieces *per stirpes*.
21. Nephews and nieces.	FE	Whole estate equally among them.
22. Remoter issue of brothers and sisters.	FE	Whole estate to members of the nearest class of issue of which there are survivors, *per capita*, and to issue of predeceasing members of that class, *per stirpes*.
23. Brothers and sisters (or their issue) and issue of the intestate.	LR FE	Brothers and sisters (or their issue) are excluded: whole to issue. (See No. 17 and Nos. 12–15.)
24. Brothers and sisters (or their issue) and spouse.	PR LR FE	See Nos. 7 and 8.
25. Brothers and sisters (or their issue), spouse and parent or parents.	PR LR FE	See No. 9.
26. Brothers and sisters and parent or parents	FE	One-half of the estate to brothers and sisters equally; one-half to surviving parent or to both parents equally.
27. Brothers and sisters, nephews and nieces, and parent or parents.	FE	One-half of the estate to brothers and sisters *per capita* and nephews and nieces *per stirpes*; one-half to surviving parent or to both parents equally.
28. Remoter issue of brother and sisters, and parent or parents.	FE	One-half of the estate to members of the nearest class of issue of brothers and sisters of which there are survivors, *per capita*, and to issue of predeceasing members of that class, *per stirpes*; one-half to surviving parent or to both parents equally.

III. SUCCESSION BY COLLATERALS—*cont.*

If the person dies, leaving	*Rules Applicable*	*The estate is divided thus*
29. Brothers and sisters, (or their issue), and uncles and aunts or remoter ascendants.	FE	Whole estate to brothers and sisters or their issue, the division being to members of the class nearest to the intestate of which there are survivors, *per capita*, and to issue of predeceasing members of that class, *per stirpes*.
30. Brothers and sisters, full blood, and brothers and sisters of half blood (consanguinean and uterine).	FE	Whole estate to brothers and sisters of full blood equally among them.
31. Brothers and sisters of half blood (consanguinean and uterine).	FE	Whole estate equally among them, with no distinction between consanguinean and uterine.
32. Brothers and sisters of half blood (consanguinean or uterine) and/or issue of same.	FE	As for full blood. See Nos. 19 to 22.
33. Brothers and sisters of half blood (consanguinean or uterine), spouse and other relations of intestate.	PR LR FE	As for full blood. See Nos. 23 to 29.

IV. SUCCESSION BY ASCENDANTS

34. Father only.	FE	Whole estate to father.
35. Mother only.	FE	Whole estate to mother.
36. Father and mother.	FE	Whole estate equally between father and mother.
37. Parent or parents, uncles and aunts (paternal and maternal) and their descendants.	FE	Whole estate to the surviving parent or to both parents equally as in Nos. 34 to 36.
38. Parent or parents and grandparents (paternal and maternal) or remoter ancestors.	FE	Whole estate to the surviving parent or to both parents equally as in Nos. 34 to 36.
39. Paternal and maternal uncles and aunts, and issue of predeceasing uncles and aunts.	FE	Whole estate to uncles and aunts (paternal and maternal) *per capita* and to cousins *per stirpes*.
40. Cousins only (on paternal or maternal sides), or their issue.	FE	Whole estate to cousins (paternal and maternal) or their issue, the division being to members of the class nearest to the intestate of which there are survivors, *per capita*, and to issue of predeceasing members of that class, *per stirpes*.
41. Paternal and maternal uncles and aunts, or their issue and paternal and maternal grandparents or remoter ancestors.	FE	Whole estate to uncles and aunts (paternal and maternal) *per capita* and to cousins *per stirpes*.
42. Paternal and maternal grandparents, great uncles and great aunts.	FE	Whole estate to grandparents (paternal and maternal) equally among them.

IV. SUCCESSION BY ASCENDANTS—*cont.*

If the person dies, leaving	*Rules Applicable*	*The estate is divided thus*
43. Paternal and maternal great uncles and great aunts (or issue of such) and great grandparents or remoter ancestors (or issue of collaterals of such).	FE	Whole estate to great uncles and great aunts (paternal and maternal) or their issue, the division being to members of the class nearest to the intestate of which there are survivors, *per capita*, and to issue of predeceasing members of that class, *per stirpes*.
44. Great grandparents or remoter ancestors and issue of collaterals of such.	FE	Infinite search, with division on the principles illustrated in Nos. 34 to 43; lineal ancestors on paternal or maternal sides succeeding before their collaterals and division among such collaterals and their issue being to members of the class nearest to the intestate of which there are survivors, *per capita*, and to issue of predeceasing members of that class, *per stirpes*.
45. Parent or parents and spouse.	PR LR FE	See No. 10.
46. Remoter ascendants and spouse.	PR LR FE	See No. 11.
47. Ascendants and issue of intestate.	LR FE	See No. 18 and Nos. 12 to 15.
48. Parent or parents and collaterals.	FE	See Nos. 26 to 28.
49. Remoter ascendants and collaterals.	FE	See No. 29.
		V. CROWN
50. No other successor.	FE	Whole to Crown as *ultimus haeres*.

Notes

1. *Estate affected*

This table applies to the whole of the intestate estate, both heritable and moveable, of a deceased person so far as it is estate the succession to which falls to be regulated by the law of Scotland. There are, however, certain specialties.

(a) *Tenancies of crofts.* Crofting tenancies were originally excluded from the operation of the Succession Act, but in respect of the estates of persons dying on or after 25th November, 1968, they now fall to be dealt with under the Act (Law Reform (Miscellaneous Provisions) (Scotland) Act 1968, s. 22 (3)).

(b) *Titles, coats of arms, etc.* The 1964 Act does not apply to the succession to any title, coat of arms, honour or dignity transmissible on the death of the holder thereof. Accordingly these items fall to be regulated by the pre-existing law (section 37 (1) (*a*)).

2. *Private international law*

Briefly, this table applies to the devolution of the moveable estate of persons who die domiciled in Scotland and to the devolution of all immoveable property in Scotland, whatever the domicile of the deceased. The pre-existing rules for choice of law are preserved by section 37 (2).

3. *Collaterals of the half blood*

The previous differentiation between collaterals of the half blood consanguinean and those of the half blood uterine has been removed by the 1964 Act. Accordingly, where brothers and sisters of an intestate, or of a parent or other ancestor of an intestate, have right to the whole, or one-half as the case may be, of the free intestate estate, collaterals of the whole blood are entitled to succeed thereto in preference to collaterals of the half blood, but where collaterals of the half blood are entitled to succeed they rank without distinction as between the half blood consanguinean and the half blood uterine (section 3).

4. *Representation*

Prior to the 1964 Act, representation was unlimited in intestate heritable succession but was severely limited in moveable succession. The effect of the Act is to apply a modified version of the previous rules of intestate moveable succession to the total free estate, heritable and moveable, of an intestate. One of the modifications is the removal of the anomalies in representation.

Accordingly, infinite representation has been introduced in legitim (section 11) and also in the distribution of the free estate (sections 5 and 6). There is no representative in a surviving spouse's prior rights, nor in *jus relicti* and *jus relictae*. A class (e.g. children) through which representation would otherwise apply is ignored if all members have predeceased (sections 6 and 11).

5. *Illegitimate children*

Substantial changes in the succession rights of illegitimate children were effected by the Law Reform (Miscellaneous Provisions) (Scotland) Act 1968 in respect of the estates of persons dying on or after 25th November 1968 and the Law Reform (Parent and Child) (Scotland) Act 1986 in respect of persons dying on or after 8th December 1986.

Briefly, from 1968 to 1986 illegitimate children were on a basis of formal equality with legitimate children in the succession to both parents, but could not represent a predeceasing parent and had no collaterals.

From 8th December 1986 the status of illegitimacy is abolished in succession and all rights of succession are determined by biological blood relationship rather than by marriage of the parents. The child formerly classed as illegitimate now has complete rights of succession, including representation, and has collaterals like any other child.

6. *Adopted children*

While the previous position was that an adopted child had no rights on the intestacy of the adopting parents and retained any rights which it had in the estates of its natural parents, the 1964 Act sets out to ensure that for the purposes of succession, or of the disposal of property by deed *inter vivos*, any adopted person is to be treated as the lawful child of the adopter and that rights in the estates of its natural parents are cut off. The detailed provisions for achieving this appear in Part IV of the Act.

7. *Interest*

Interest is payable on the ascertained amounts of the legal rights of *jus relicti, jus relictae* and legitim from the date of death until paid, usually at the rate earned by the estate. No interest is payable on the value of a surviving spouse's prior right to the deceased's dwelling-house and its furniture and plenishings under section 8 of the 1964 Act. Interest is, however, payable on the £30,000 or £50,000 available to a surviving spouse as a prior right under section 9 at a rate which was fixed at 4 per cent. for deaths before 1st August 1981 but is now variable and is 7 per cent. (S.I. 1981 No. 805). This interest runs for the period from the date of death until payment. There is, of course, no interest on the value of the rights of succession to the free estate.

8. *Prior rights to a house and its furniture and plenishings*

A house to which section 8 applies is any one dwelling-house in which the surviving spouse of the intestate was ordinarily resident at the date of death of the intestate (section 8(4)). The deceased's "relevant interest" therein which may pass to the surviving spouse is the interest of an owner or of a tenant, other than one whose tenancy is subject to the Rent Acts, and is subject to any heritable debt secured over the interest. The right is applicable to only one house even if the survivor was ordinarily resident in more than one, and the maximum benefit which the surviving spouse may receive under this head is £110,000. If the value of the deceased's interest in the house is greater, the survivor receives that sum and not the house itself (section 8(1)(*b*)). Even if the value does not exceed the limit, in the cases specified in section 8(2) the survivor receives not the house itself, but the substituted value thereof.

The survivor is also entitled to the deceased's interest in the furniture and plenishings (excluding heirlooms—section 8(6)(*b*) and (*c*)) of any one house in which the survivor was ordinarily resident. A maximum limit of £20,000 is placed on the value of the furniture and plenishings to be transferred under this head. Should the value be greater, the surviving spouse may choose items to a value not exceeding that sum.